NEW

WITHDRAWN

ENCYCLOPEDIA OF WORLD BIOGRAPHY

15

ENCYCLOPEDIA OF WORLD BIOGRAPHY

SECOND EDITION

Studi
/
Visser

15

GALE

DETROIT · NEW YORK · TORONTO · LONDON

Staff

Senior Editor: Paula K. Byers
Project Editor: Suzanne M. Bourgoin
Managing Editor: Neil E. Walker

Editorial Staff: Luann Brennan, Frank V. Castronova, Laura S. Hightower, Karen E. Lemerand, Stacy A. McConnell, Jennifer Mossman, Maria L. Munoz, Katherine H. Nemeh, Terrie M. Rooney, Geri Speace

Permissions Manager: Susan M. Tosky
Permissions Specialist: Maria L. Franklin
Permissions Associate: Michele M. Lonoconus
Image Cataloger: Mary K. Grimes

Production Director: Mary Beth Trimper
Production Manager: Evi Seoud
Production Associate: Shanna Heilveil
Product Design Manager: Cynthia Baldwin
Senior Art Director: Mary Claire Krzewinski

Research Manager: Victoria B. Cariappa
Research Specialists: Michele P. LaMeau, Andrew Guy Malonis, Barbara McNeil, Gary J. Oudersluys
Research Associates: Julia C. Daniel, Tamara C. Nott, Norma Sawaya, Cheryl L. Warnock
Research Assistant: Talitha A. Jean

Graphic Services Supervisor: Barbara Yarrow
Image Database Supervisor: Randy Bassett
Imaging Specialist: Mike Lugosz

Manager of Data Entry Services: Eleanor M. Allison
Data Entry Coordinator: Kenneth D. Benson

Manager of Technology Support Services: Theresa A. Rocklin
Programmers/Analysts: Mira Bossowska, Jeffrey Muhr, Christopher Ward

Copyright © 1998
Gale Research
835 Penobscot Bldg.
Detroit, MI 48226-4094

ISBN 0-7876-2221-4 (Set)
ISBN 0-7876-2555-8 (Volume 15)

Library of Congress Cataloging-in-Publication Data

Encyclopedia of world biography / [edited by Suzanne Michele Bourgoin
    and Paula Kay Byers].
        p. cm.
        Includes bibliographical references and index.
        Summary: Presents brief biographical sketches which provide vital
    statistics as well as information on the importance of the person
    listed.
        ISBN 0-7876-2221-4 (set : alk. paper)
        1. Biography—Dictionaries—Juvenile literature. [1. Biography.]
    I. Bourgoin, Suzanne Michele, 1968-   . II. Byers, Paula K. (Paula
    Kay), 1954-   .
    CT 103.E56   1997
    920′ .003—dc21   97-42327
                                                        CIP
                                                        AC

Printed in the United States of America
10 9 8 7 6 5 4 3 2

ENCYCLOPEDIA OF
WORLD BIOGRAPHY

15

S

Wes Studi

Wes Studi (born c. 1944) got a relatively late start as a film star—he was about 44 when he landed his first movie—but prior to that career move the Native American performer had compiled a list of real-life credits that included soldier, reporter and activist.

Born Wesley Studie—a full-blooded Cherokee—in rural Oklahoma, the eldest son of a ranch hand and a housekeeper, he was educated at an American Indian boarding school and got an early taste of how Native Americans were often treated off the reservation. As a boy, Studi and his friends would venture to nearby towns, where "all the shopkeepers got very careful when we walked in," as he recalled to Mark Goodman in a *People* interview.

Served in Vietnam

Undaunted, Studi became a soldier in 1967, and eventually served in Vietnam. "At one point," Goodman wrote, "his company was pinned down in the Mekong Delta—and nearly killed—by friendly fire." Not every Army memory was traumatic, though. As Studi related to Goodman, one day he and a fellow Native American recruit were "told we didn't have duty that particular day. The rest of the company went out on a two-day operation. When they came back, we learned they had relocated entire villages. I don't know that it had anything to do with the fact that many of our own people had been relocated, but it sort of struck me as funny."

An unfocused young man on his return stateside, Studi enrolled at Tulsa Junior College, which led to his participa-

tion in the Trail of Broken Treaties protest march in 1972, according to *People.* "He was one of the protesters who briefly occupied the Bureau of Indian Affairs," Goodman noted. "The next year he joined the celebrated protest at Wounded Knee, [South Dakota], and was among those arrested on federal charges of insurrection." Studi was jailed on that charge, but earned a waiver after only a few days.

Soon afterward, Studi landed a job as reporter for the Tulsa *Indian News,* writing on Native American issues. For several years, Studi worked and ran a horse ranch in Tulsa. Then, in 1982, after divorcing his second wife, Studi felt a need to "build another life," as he said in the *People* piece. He joined the American Indian Theater Company and by 1986 had moved to Los Angeles to pursue his craft. "At first Hollywood treated me like I wasn't there," he remarked to Dana Kennedy in an *Entertainment Weekly* profile. "Then they treated me like I was marginally there, and now they treat me much better."

Lands Big Hollywood Roles

In 1988 Studi got his big break—a role in the acclaimed independent feature *Powwow Highway.* That role led to a small but intense part in the blockbuster *Dances With Wolves.* In the Kevin Costner-directed film, Studi was an "angry Pawnee warrior who scalps actor Robert Pastorelli," Goodman wrote.

Next came another big role, in the popular remake of *The Last of the Mohicans.* Though the film itself received mixed reviews, many critics took special note of Studi's performance—*New York* magazine's David Denby went so far as to say that "only vicious Magua, played by the striking Cherokee actor Wes Studi, seems like a flesh-and-blood man."

1

New Yorker, January 10, 1994.
People, December 20, 1993. □

In 1993 Studi landed his most important acting role to date—the title role in *Geronimo.* As the legendary Chiricahua Apache leader who waged a determined—and, ultimately, ill-fated—campaign against the U.S. Army, Studi crafted a layered performance. "Photographs of Geronimo in his prime show a man with a fierce, implacable demeanor and the stocky physique of a defensive lineman," stated *New Yorker* critic Terrence Rafferty. "Wes Studi . . . has a lean, wiry frame, but he nonetheless manages to convey, superbly, the essential quality of those photographs, which is the gravity of Geronimo's idea of himself." While *Geronimo* didn't pack in the audiences the way *Dances With Wolves* and *Mohicans* had, Studi earned virtually unanimous praise.

While Studi's roles have leaned toward the grimly dramatic, those close to the actor know another side. "All you see is the stoic guy onscreen," fellow Native American actor Rodney Grant told Goodman. "People don't realize how humorous he is." And how versatile; according to the article, Studi has "written two children's books in Cherokee and even translated the Pulitzer Prize-winning play *The Kentucky Cycle* into that language." "I'm a Cherokee first and an American later," explained Studi in *Entertainment Weekly.* "While I may forgive, I will never forget—and I will pass that feeling on to my own kids."

Further Reading

Entertainment Weekly, December 24, 1993; November 10, 1995.
New York, September 28, 1992

Charles Sturt

Charles Sturt (1795-1869), British officer, explorer, and colonial public servant, led three major expeditions into the interior of eastern Australia.

Charles Sturt, the eldest son of an East India Company judge, was born in India on April 28, 1795, educated at Harrow, and became an ensign in 1813. After serving in the Peninsular War and the American War of 1812, he performed garrison duties in France and Ireland before acting as an escort in 1826 for convicts being transported to New South Wales.

The discovery of inland rivers west of the Great Dividing Range in New South Wales had excited speculation about the existence of an inland sea which Capt. Sturt, now military secretary to Governor Sir Ralph Darling, was determined to find. In 1828, under conditions of considerable hardship, he led an expedition which discovered the Darling River, 500 miles inland, and he unraveled the main features of the northern river system in New South Wales.

Sturt led a second expedition, in November 1829, to track the source of the Lachlan and Murrumbidgee rivers. In an epic return journey of some 2,000 miles in 7 months, much of it in a 27-foot whaleboat, Sturt reached Lake Alexandrina at Encounter Bay on the southern coast, having outlined the huge internal river system which drains a vast area west of the Great Dividing Range and having found extensive pastures suitable for pastoral farming.

His health impaired and sight failing, Sturt went on leave to England in 1830 and published *Two Expeditions into the Interior of South Australia* (1833). After resigning from the army, he married and returned to New South Wales as a settler with a 5,000-acre land grant from the Colonial Office. Financial difficulties led him to become surveyor general in the new colony of South Australia in 1839. But his income and status as a public servant waned to such an extent that in order to restore his fortunes he sought permission from the Colonial Office to find an inland sea in the center of the continent.

Sturt's third expedition, which left Adelaide in August 1844, lasted for 17 months. Trapped by drought, the party was marooned in temperatures above 100 degrees from January to July 1845 at an isolated water hole 400 miles inland. Subsequently Sturt made a 450-mile journey toward the center but failed to reach the Tropic of Capricorn or to cross the Simpson Desert. When he returned to Adelaide, almost blind and broken in health, Sturt had abandoned his belief in the existence of a great inland sea. Like so many early explorers, he was disappointed by the hot, dry interior, which offered no prospects for farmers. But much of the area he crossed subsequently became a paradise for mineral prospectors.

On his return Sturt became colonial treasurer, received the Royal Geographical Society's Gold Medal, and published *Narrative of an Expedition into Central Australia* (1849). In 1853 he retired to Cheltenham in England, where he died on June 16, 1869.

Further Reading

The short biography by John Howard Lidgett Cumpston, *Charles Sturt: His Life and Journeys of Exploration* (1951), is detailed and well illustrated. It was the standard work until Michael Langley's perceptive account, *Sturt of the Murray: Father of Australian Exploration* (1969), which incorporates fresh material. A briskly written, popular book is George Farmwell, *Riders to an Unknown Sea: The Story of Charles Sturt, Explorer* (1963).

Additional Sources

Beale, Edgar, *Sturt, the chipped idol: a study of Charles Sturt, explorer,* Sydney: Sydney University Press, 1979.

Swan, Keith John, *In step with Sturt,* Armadale, Australia: Graphic Books, 1979. ☐

A. H. Sturtevant

Alfred Henry Sturtevant (1891–1970) was a geneticist and National Medal of Science winner whose principles of gene mapping greatly affected the field of genetics.

A. H. Sturtevant, an influential geneticist and winner of the National Medal of Science in 1968, is best known for his demonstrations of the principles of gene mapping. This discovery had a profound effect on the field of genetics and led to projects to map both animal and human chromosomes. He is the unacknowledged father of the Human Genome Project, which is attempting to map all of man's 100,000 chromosomes by the year 2000. Sturtevant's later work in the field of genetics led to discovery of the first reparable gene defect as well as the position effect, which showed that the effect of a gene is dependent on its position relative to other genes. He was a member of Columbia University's "Drosophila Group," whose studies of the genetics of fruit flies advanced new theories of genetics and evolution.

Alfred Henry Sturtevant, the youngest of six children, was born in Jacksonville, Illinois, on November 21, 1891, to Alfred and Harriet (Morse) Sturtevant. Five of his early ancestors had come to America aboard the Mayflower. Julian M. Sturtevant, his grandfather, a Yale Divinity School graduate, was the founder and former president of Illinois College. Sturtevant's father taught at Illinois College briefly but later chose farming as a profession. When Alfred Sturtevant was seven, his family moved to a farm in southern Alabama. He attended high school in Mobile, which was 14 miles from his home and accessible only by train.

Sturtevant enrolled in Columbia University in New York City in 1908, boarding with his older brother, Edgar, who taught linguistics at Columbia's Barnard College. Edgar and his wife played a significant role in young Sturtevant's life. They sent him Columbia's entrance examination, pulled strings to get him a scholarship, and welcomed him into their home in Edgewater, New Jersey, for four years. Edgar was also responsible for steering his brother toward a career in the sciences. The young Sturtevant had discovered genetic theory at an early age and often drew pedigrees of his family and of his father's horses. Edgar encouraged him to write a paper on the subject of color heredity in horses and to submit the draft to Columbia University's Thomas Hunt Morgan, the future Nobel Laureate geneticist. The paper used the recently rediscovered theories of Gregor Mendel, the 19th-century Austrian monk and founder of genetics, to explain certain coat-color inheritance patterns in horses. Sturtevant somehow mastered this subject in spite of his color-blindness.

Student Work Leads to Major Genetic Breakthrough

As a result of his paper on horses, which was published in 1910, Sturtevant was given a desk in Morgan's famous "fly room," a small laboratory dedicated to genetic research using *Drosophila* (fruit flies) as subjects. Fruit flies are ideal subjects for genetic research. They mature in ten days, are less than one-eighth inch long, can live by the hundreds in small vials, require nothing more substantial than yeast for food, and have only four pairs of chromosomes.

Morgan's early work focused on the phenomenon of "crossing-over" in the fruit fly. By 1910, he had already described the sex-limited inheritance of white eye. From this observation, he postulated the idea that genes were linked because they were carried by the same chromosome and that genes in close proximity to one another would be linked more frequently than those that were farther apart. Sometimes, dominant linked traits, such as eye color and wing size, became "unlinked" in offspring. Sturtevant studied the process of crossing-over of sex-linked traits, which are carried on the X chromosome. Female fruit flies have two X chromosomes. In addition to one X chromosome, males have a Y chromosome, which carries very few genes. Sturtevant correctly hypothesized that the exchange between X chromosomes probably occurred early on in the process of egg formation, when the paired chromosomes lie parallel to each other.

Morgan believed that the relative distance between genes could be measured if the crossing-over frequencies could be determined. From this lead, Sturtevant developed a practical method for determining this frequency rate. He began by studying six sex-linked traits and measured the occurrence of this related trait. The more frequently the traits occurred, Sturtevant reasoned, the closer the genes must be. He then calculated the percentages of crossing-over between the various traits. From these percentages, he determined the relative distance between the genes on the chromosome, the first instance of gene mapping. This major discovery, which Sturtevant published in 1913 at the age of 22, eventually enabled scientists to map human and animal genes. It is often considered to be the starting point of modern genetics.

In 1914, Sturtevant received his Ph.D. from Columbia and stayed on in Morgan's lab as an investigator for the Carnegie Institution of Washington, D.C. Along with C. B. Bridges, Hermann Joseph Muller, and Morgan, he formed part of an influential research team that made significant contributions to the fields of genetics and entomology. He later described the lab as highly democratic and occasionally argumentative, with ideas being heatedly debated. The 16 x 24-foot lab had no desks, no separate offices, one general telephone, and very few graduate assistants. Sturtevant thrived in this environment. He worked seven days a week, reserving his mornings for *Drosophila* research and his afternoons for reading the scientific literature and consulting with colleagues. He possessed a near photographic memory and wide-ranging interests. His only shortcoming as a researcher was his incessant pipe-smoking, which often left flakes of tobacco ash mixed in with the samples of fruit flies. In spite of this minor flaw, the fly-room group raised research standards and elevated research writing to an art form. They also perfected the practice of chromosome mapping, using Sturtevant's methods to develop a chromosome map of *Drosophila,* detailing the relative positions of fifty genes.

Sturtevant published a paper in 1914 that documented cases of double crossing-over, in which chromosomes that had already crossed-over broke with one another and recrossed again. His next major paper, published in 1915, concerned the sexual behavior of fruit flies and concentrated on six specific mutant genes that altered eye or body color, two factors that played important roles in sexual

selection. He then showed that specific genes were responsible for selective intersexuality. In later years, he discovered a gene that caused an almost complete sex change in fruit flies, miraculously transforming females into near males. In subsequent years, researchers identified other sex genes in many animals, as well as in humans. These discoveries led to the development of the uniquely twentieth-century view of sex as a gene-controlled trait which is subject to variability.

During the 1920s, Sturtevant and Morgan examined the unstable bar-eye trait in *Drosophila* Drosophila. Most geneticists at that time believed that bar eye did not follow the rules of Mendelian heredity. In 1925, Sturtevant showed that bar eye involved a recombination of genes rather than a mutation and that the position of the gene on the chromosome had an effect on its action. This discovery, known as the position effect, contributed greatly to the understanding of the action of the gene.

In 1928, Morgan received an offer from the California Institute of Technology to develop a new Division of Biological Sciences. Sturtevant followed his mentor to California, where he became Caltech's first professor of genetics. The new genetics group set up shop in Caltech's Kerckhoff Laboratory. Sturtevant continued working with fruit flies and conducted genetic investigations of other animals and plants, including snails, rabbits, moths, rats, and the evening primrose, *Oenothera.*

In 1929, Sturtevant discovered a "sex ratio" gene that caused male flies to produce X sperm almost exclusively, instead of X and Y sperm. As a result, these flies' offspring were almost always females. In the early 1930s, giant chromosomes were discovered in the salivary glands of fruit flies. Under magnification, these chromosomes revealed cross patterns which were correlated to specific genes. The so-called "physical" map derived from these giant chromosomes did not exactly match Sturtevant's "relative" location maps. In the physical map, some of the genes tended to cluster toward one end of the chromosome and the distances between genes was not uniform. But the linear order of the genes on the chromosome matched Sturtevant's relative maps gene for gene. This discovery confirmed that Sturtevant had been correct in his assumptions about chromosomal linearity.

In 1932, Sturtevant took a sabbatical leave and spent the year in England and Germany as a visiting professor of the Carnegie Endowment for International Peace. When he returned to America, he collaborated with his Caltech colleague Theodosius Dobzhansky, a Russian-born geneticist, on a study of inversions in the third chromosome of *Drosophila pseudoobscura*. In the 1940s, Sturtevant studied all of the known gene mutations in *Drosophila* and their various effects on the development of the species. From 1947 to 1962, he served as the Thomas Hunt Morgan Professor of Biology at Caltech. His most significant scientific contribution during that time occurred in 1951, when he unveiled his chromosome map of the indescribably small fourth chromosome of the fruit fly, a genetic problem that had puzzled scientists for decades.

During the 1950s and 1960s, Sturtevant turned his attention to the iris and authored numerous papers on the subject of evolution. He became concerned with the potential dangers of genetics research and wrote several papers on the social significance of human genetics. In a 1954 speech to the Pacific Division of the American Association for the Advancement of Science, he described the possible genetic consequences of nuclear war and argued that the public should be made aware of these possible cataclysmic hazards before any further bomb testing was performed. One of his last published journal articles, written in 1956, described a mutation in fruit flies that, by itself, was harmless but which proved lethal in combination with another specific mutant gene.

Sturtevant married Phoebe Curtis Reed in 1923, and the couple honeymooned in Europe, touring England, Norway, Sweden, and Holland. The Sturtevants had three children. Sturtevant was named professor emeritus at Caltech in 1962. He spent the better part of the early 1960s writing his major work, *A History of Genetics,* which was published in 1965. In 1968, he received the prestigious National Medal of Science for his achievements in genetics. He died on April 5, 1970, at the age of 78. ☐

Peter Stuyvesant

Peter Stuyvesant (ca. 1610-1672), Dutch director general of the New Netherland colony in America, was compelled to surrender his colony to England.

The last and most efficient of Dutch proconsuls in the European struggle for control of North America, Peter Stuyvesant is remembered as the stubborn, somewhat choleric governor of the Dutch West India Company's base on the mainland. A zealous Calvinist, he brought a relatively effective government to the colony, absorbed the nearby rival Swedish settlements, and attempted to remold New Netherland in his own and the company's image. His efforts at reform were cut short with the seizure of New Amsterdam (later, New York) by a British force in 1664.

Born at Scherpenzeel, Friesland, Stuyvesant was the son of a Calvinist Dutch Reformed minister. He attended school in Friesland, where he heard much about New Netherland and about Holland's war with Spain. He became a student at the University of Franeker but was apparently expelled, for reasons unknown, about 1629.

Patriotic, and desiring adventure, Stuyvesant entered the service of the Dutch West India Company—first as a clerk and then, in 1635, as a supercargo to Brazil. By 1638 he had become chief commercial officer for Curaçao; in 1643 he returned there as governor. The following year he led an unsuccessful attack against the Portuguese colony of St. Martin in the Leeward Islands. During the siege he was wounded in the right leg, and the crude amputation required resulted in a lengthy convalescence and a trip to Holland to obtain an artificial limb. (Because of its adorn-

ments, he was thereafter often nicknamed "Silver Leg.") In Breda he married Judith Bayard, the sister of his brother-in-law.

On Oct. 5, 1645, Stuyvesant came before the chamber of the nearly bankrupt West India Company and volunteered his services for New Netherland. The next July he was appointed director general of that colony. On Christmas Day he sailed for America with four vessels carrying soldiers, servants, traders, and a new set of officials. Also on board were his widowed sister and her children, together with his wife. The ships, proceeding by way of Curaçao, arrived at New Amsterdam on May 11, 1647, to be greeted by cheering settlers.

The inhabitants soon learned, however, that their new governor was not so liberal as themselves. Stuyvesant's first domestic order restricted sale of intoxicants and compelled observance of the Sabbath. He became a church warden of the Reformed congregation and commenced rebuilding its edifice. Clerics and councilmen easily persuaded him (in a move aimed at Lutherans and Quakers) to forbid meetings not conforming to the Synod of Dort. Though Amsterdam reproved him on this point and counseled tolerance, under the narrowly religious Stuyvesant dissent was always frowned upon.

Though harsh and dictatorial, Stuyvesant introduced a number of needed reforms, particularly directed toward improving New Amsterdam's living conditions. He appointed fire wardens and ordered chimney inspections, instituted a weekly market and annual cattle fair, required bakers to use standard weights, somewhat controlled traffic and sanitation, repaired the fort, and licensed taverns. Stuyvesant concerned himself about all aspects of town life. He organized a night watch, had streets paved, encouraged local bakeries and breweries, and promoted the colony's commerce whenever possible.

Stuyvesant expected the people to obey his will and opposed the New Amsterdam citizen's desire for a separate municipal government for the city, but he early established the Board of Nine Men to advise him in promoting the public welfare. Citizens found onerous his diligent attempts to enforce Dutch trading restrictions and to collect taxes and tolls—though when their "Remonstrance" to Holland finally procured a distinct government for New Amsterdam (1653), they continued their delinquency about such obligations.

One of Stuyvesant's first official acts was to organize a naval expedition against the Spaniards operating within the limits of the West India Company's charter. A force sent against Ft. Christina in 1655 conquered Sweden's province on the Delaware River and absorbed the settlements into New Netherland. Peace was made with marauding Native Americans, and captive Dutch colonists were ransomed. Stuyvesant promoted trading relations with New England and succeeded in achieving a modus vivendi respecting the troublesome boundary with Connecticut. In 1657 he granted a system of "burgher rights," providing (at a price) eligibility for trading and office holding; at first limited to New Amsterdam, this came to apply throughout the province.

The governor's salary plus allowances (approximately $1,600, all told) enabled Stuyvesant to purchase a bouwerie, or farm, of 300 acres north of the city wall and a town lot for a house with gardens beside the fort. He lived comfortably in these, and his two sons were both born in New Amsterdam.

In 1664, while England and Holland were still at peace, Charles II decided to seize New Netherland for his brother James, Duke of York. When four British warships under Col. Richard Nicolls reached New Amsterdam, the colony was completely unprepared. Stuyvesant wanted to resist this aggression, but word of Nicolls's lenient terms eroded his already scanty support, and after lengthy negotiations he capitulated on September 7. He obtained provisional trading rights for the West India Company in the province and, to defend his official conduct, went to Amsterdam in 1665—though his evidence as to the company's neglect of colonial defense did not endear him to its directors. Returning to New York in 1668, Stuyvesant retired to his farm until his death in February 1672.

Further Reading

Henry Kessler and Eugene Rachlis, *Peter Stuyvesant and His New York* (1959), is the most scholarly and readable study of Stuyvesant. Informative is John Franklin Jameson, *Narratives of New Netherland* (1909; new ed. 1952). Bayard Tuckerman, *Peter Stuyvesant* (1893), although outdated, is valuable. Hendrick Willem Van Loon, *Life and Times of Pieter Stuyvesant* (1918), provides a provocative character interpretation.

Additional Sources

Picard, Hymen Willem Johannes, *Peter Stuyvesant, builder of New York*, Cape Town: Hollandsch Afrikaansche Uitgevers Maatschappij, 1975. ☐

William Styron

William Styron (born 1925) was a Southern writer of novels and articles. His major works were *Lie Down in Darkness, The Long March, The Confessions of Nat Turner,* and *Sophie's Choice.* His major theme was the response of basically decent people to such cruelties of life as war, slavery, and madness.

William Styron was born January 11, 1925, in Newport News, Virginia, to a family whose roots in the South go back to the 17th century. After attending Christchurch, a small Episcopal high school in Middlesex County, Virginia, he entered Davidson College in 1942. In 1943 he transferred to Duke University but left school for service with the Marines. His experiences first as a trainee at Parris Island and then as an officer are the bases for the preoccupation with war, the military mind, and authority in his novels.

Discharged in 1945, Styron returned to Duke. There, under the guidance of William Blackburn, he became seriously interested in literature and began writing short stories. After he graduated in 1947 and took a job in New York, it was Blackburn who influenced him to enroll in a creative writing class taught by Hiram Haydn at the New School for Social Research. But Styron found that his job writing copy and reading manuscripts for McGraw Hill sapped his energy and creativity. Within six months he was fired "for slovenly appearance, not wearing a hat, and reading the *New York Post.*" The loss of his job turned out to be beneficial, since, with financial support from his father and encouragement from Haydn, he could write full-time, and in 1952 he published *Lie Down in Darkness.*

This novel is about the disintegration of a southern family, the Loftises. The immediate setting is the funeral of one of the daughters, Peyton, a suicide. But the conflicts between the narcissistic, alcoholic father and the emotionally disturbed mother, the hate between mother and daughter, and the near incestuous love of the father for Peyton—all contributors to the characters' disillusionment and the suicide itself—are unfolded in flashbacks. Though the story is told in third person, the final section is a remarkable monologue recited by Peyton before she jumps out of a window. *Lie Down in Darkness* was an impressive first novel, and in 1952 Styron won the Prix de Rome of the Academy of Arts and Letters for his achievement.

During the Korean conflict, in 1951, just before *Lie Down in Darkness* appeared, Styron was recalled briefly to the Marines. Two incidents—the accidental killing of soldiers by a stray shell and a forced march—which occurred

the novelist to "meditate" on history and augment facts with imagination.

Reactions to *Sophie's Choice* (1979) were also mixed. Stingo, the narrator, is a young Southerner, who, like Styron himself, comes to New York hoping to become a writer. In a Brooklyn rooming house he meets Sophie and her Jewish lover, Nathan, who alternates between brilliance, warmth, and charm and psychopathic fury. Most of the story centers on Sophie, a Polish Catholic refugee who was interned in a concentration camp during World War II. Tormented by her memories, particularly the loss of her children, she submits to Nathan's love and abuse up until the tragic conclusion, a double suicide. The book was a best seller, then a motion picture. But some critics claimed Styron had misrepresented the Holocaust, linking its horrors with eroticism and ignoring the plight of its major victims, the Jews. In 1982, the film version of *Sophie's Choice,* starring Meryl Streep, received several Academy Award nominations.

More recently, Styron's novels include, *Darkness Visible: A Memoir of Madness* (1990), which covers his own bouts with depression; and a trilogy of short stories, *A Tidewater Morning: Three Tales from Youth* (1993). Styron also co-authored, *The Face of Mercy: A Photographic History of Medicine at War* (1995) with Mathew Naythons, Sherwin B. Nuland, and Stanley B. Burns.

Aside from novels and articles, Styron also wrote a play, *In the Clap Shack* (1972), which was performed at Yale. A military novel, *The Way of the Warrior,* was in progress in the 1980s.

Styron is highly regarded as a Southern writer. The injustices of the old South and the materialism of the new are two themes which figure prominently in his novels. But he was more than a regional writer. His major characters generally are decent people thrust among the cruelties of the world: slavery, war, individual madness, and violence. Though he was not particularly optimistic, most of his protagonists achieve illumination or regeneration by observing or struggling with these forces. There are critics, in fact, who see his works as religious. In addition to religious imagery, the novels suggest that when one gets in touch with his humanity he finds some sort of salvation.

Further Reading

Studies entitled *William Styron*—by Robert Fossum (1968), Melvin Friedman (1974), Cooper Mackin (1969), Richard Pearce (1971), and Mark Ratner (1972)—include biography and criticism. More studies are Arthur Casciato/James West, *Critical Essays on William Styron* (1982) and Robert Morris, *The Achievement of William Styron* (revised edition, 1981), which contains a bibliography of numerous articles and books about and by Styron. In the mid-1990s, Styron was working on a semi-autobiographical novel about the Marine Corps.
In January of 1997, William Styron was the focus of a public television biographical series/documentary film, *American Masters,* during which he discussed the fact that his recent works often contain a theme of coping to understand the African American experience, which is autobiographical in nature. He has also written a commentary for the *New York Times Magazine* (1995), entitled, *A Horrid Little Racist,* discussing a boyhood incident where he was punished for mak-

at the camp where he was assigned were the sources for the plot of a novella, *The Long March.* It was written during a tour Styron took of Europe directly after his discharge and was published in 1956.

The two-year stay in Europe had other results. Styron met and married Rose Burgunder, a native of Baltimore, and helped a group of young writers establish *The Paris Review.*

Styron's next novel, *Set This House on Fire* (1960), is a long book with rape and two murders at its center. Two friends, Peter Leveritt and Cass Kinsolving, visiting together in Charleston, recall the events which took place three years earlier when they were guests at a villa in Sambucco, Italy. Though Peter is the narrator, many critics consider Cass, who kills the man he wrongly suspects of raping and murdering a peasant girl, the protagonist because he progresses from weakness and despair to self-knowledge and faith. For many readers *Set This House on Fire* was a disappointment, the narrative disjointed, the characters incompletely realized. But the book received acclaim in France and marked an important step in Styron's development.

The Confessions of Nat Turner (1967) is based on a true story, the 1831 rebellion of a group of slaves against their white oppressors. Nat Turner, the leader, in jail awaiting execution, dictates his "confessions" to his attorney. The book was a success; in 1968 it received the Pulitzer Prize. But it aroused controversy, particularly among African Americans, who felt that Nat represented a white man's condescending vision of them and that the story distorted history, a charge Styron answered by claiming the right of ing a racist remark. This and other experiences ultimately piqued his interest in trying to understand the African American experience. □

Francisco Suárez

The Spanish philosopher and theologian Francisco Suárez (1548-1617) taught an eclectic form of scholasticism and laid the first foundations for a theory of international law.

Francisco Suárez was born in Granada on Jan. 5, 1548, and studied canon law at the University of Salamanca. In 1564 he entered the Society of Jesus; he later taught philosophy and theology in Segovia, Ávila, Valladolid, Rome, Alcalá, Salamanca, and Coimbra. He died in Lisbon on Sept. 25, 1617, after a prolific writing career.

Suárez's two main works are *Disputationes metaphysicae* (1597) and *De legibus* (1612). The former is the first scholastic treatise on metaphysics that followed an order of its own rather than Aristotle's exposition. In philosophy Suárez remains primarily loyal to St. Thomas Aquinas, but at the same time he attempts to combine Thomas's ideas with doctrines found in John Duns Scotus and William of Ockham. The distinction between essence and existence, so important in Thomas's metaphysics, is all but abrogated. Suárez's metaphysical theory had an enormous influence during the 17th and 18th centuries, especially in the German Protestant universities, which largely adopted his *Disputationes* as a textbook.

Equally important and more deserved was Suárez's impact on philosophy of law and on the theory of international relations. In *De legibus* he proved to be a true and bold innovator who did not always receive the credit to which he was entitled. With his scholastic predecessors, the Spanish philosopher held that all human law participates in the eternal law which governs the entire creation. Yet what constitutes the binding force of civil law is, according to him, not its divine foundation but its human promulgation. Thus all the emphasis comes to be placed upon the positive element of law rather than upon its universal aspect. Although Suárez's philosophy of law is still founded on an ethical basis, it nevertheless provides the distinction needed to give legal theory an independence of its own. The power to legislate resides in the community as a whole, and no individual can claim to have received it directly from God (as King James I had done in his theory of divine right). Nor does the need for legality bind man to any particular form of government, even though Suárez personally considered monarchy the most expedient form.

Suárez had his greatest impact as author of those principles upon which international law came to be based. The notion of a *jus gentium,* "a law of nations," was not his invention; it had existed for centuries. But his interpretation is entirely new. Such a law, he claims, is based upon, but is

not deducible from, natural law. He considers it to be a law consisting "not in something written, but in customs, not of one or two cities or provinces, but of all or almost all nations."

Further Reading

Studies of Suárez in English are Joseph H. Fichter, *Man of Spain: Francis Suárez* (1940), and Bernice Hamilton, *Political Thought in 16th Century Spain: A Study of the Political Ideas of Vitoria, De Soto, Suárez and Molina* (1963). For Suárez's social theories see A. L. Lilley's article, "Francisco Suárez," in F. J. C. Hearnshaw, ed., *Social and Political Ideas of Some Great Thinkers of the XVI and XVII Centuries* (1926). Considerable attention is given to Suárez in Frederick Copleston, *A History of Philosophy,* vol. 3 (1953). Also useful is James Brown Scott, *The Catholic Conception of International Law* (1934). □

Roberto Suazo Córdova

Roberto Suazo Córdova (born 1927) was a small-town physician who gained international attention when he became president of Honduras in 1982 after its military rulers agreed to restore civilian government to the country. He promoted the democratic process and moderate economic reform, while at the same time cooperating with a U.S. military build-up in Honduras.

Roberto Suazo Córdova was born in La Paz, Honduras, on March 17, 1927. After receiving his M.D. at the University of San Carlos in Guatemala in 1949 and working in the Guatemala General Hospital until 1953, he returned to his native La Paz and practiced medicine for 25 years. His career as a small-town doctor put him closely in touch with the common people and folk culture of his country. He was an active, if conservative, member of the Liberal Party, serving often in the Honduran Congress and as a delegate to constitutional conventions in 1957 and 1965. He emerged as a major figure in Honduran politics in 1979 when he succeeded Modesto Rodas Alvarado as general coordinator of the Liberal Party and leader of its conservative, or *Rodista,* wing. Suazo began a rapprochement between the Liberal Party and the military, working especially with the national security chief, Colonel Gustavo Alvarez Martinez.

In 1980 Suazo won election as president of yet another constitutional convention after the military rulers agreed to restore civilian government under a new constitution. Subsequently he became the Liberal presidential nominee for the November 1981 election and convincingly defeated the National Party candidate, Ricardo Zúñiga Agustinus, winning nearly 53 percent of the vote. The Liberals also won control of Congress.

In an atmosphere of high expectations, but facing serious economic problems, Suazo took office for a four-year term on January 27, 1982, promising "a revolution of work and honesty" and to strive for peace in Central America, but his real power was limited. He named Colonel Alvarez,

soon promoted to general, as head of the Armed Forces. In accordance with an agreement a month before the election between Suazo, Zúñga, and the military, the Armed Forces retained a veto power over cabinet appointments and would have full authority over "national security" matters. Moreover, the agreement precluded any investigation into alleged corruption in the military or in the outgoing government.

Concerned over the rise of the Sandinistas of Nicaragua and the guerrillas in El Salvador, Suazo was strongly anti-Communist and cooperated with U.S. efforts to aid Nicaraguan counterrevolutionaries who operated from Honduras. Suazo joined with the governments of El Salvador and Costa Rica in forming the Central American Democratic Community, with support from Venezuela and the United States. The United States held large-scale military and naval maneuvers in Honduras designed to intimidate Nicaragua and the Salvadoran guerrillas. U.S. military and economic aid to Honduras rose dramatically after Ronald Reagan visited Suazo in Tegucigalpa in December 1982.

Within Honduras, despite civilian rule, there was an increase in the presence of the military. Salvadoran and Nicaraguan refugee camps within Honduras were one source of security problems. The turmoil and terrorism in Central America touched Suazo directly in December 1982 when a revolutionary organization kidnapped his Guatemalan daughter, Dr. Judith Xiomara Suazo Estrada, not releasing her until several Central American newspapers published the organization's declarations. Although guerrilla activity was not significant within Honduras, the military instituted more security measures and increased the army's size.

Constitutional amendments in late 1982 added to the military's power, most notably transferring the title of commander-in-chief of the armed forces from Suazo to Alvarez. The impression was widespread by early 1983 that Alvarez was the real ruler of the country in collaboration with U.S. Ambassador John Negroponte. Suazo was under increased criticism even from within his own party, and there were manifestations of a rising anti-Americanism in opposition to the military build-up and Honduran involvement in the Salvadoran and Nicaraguan civil wars. Relations with Nicaragua deteriorated steadily. Assassinations and mysterious disappearances became a part of Honduran political life, leading moderate and leftist groups to accuse the government of applying the "Argentine solution" to Honduras. Human rights violations contributed to a rift between Suazo and some Catholic clergy.

When heart and stomach illness forced Suazo into the hospital in July 1983, first in Honduras and later in the United States for 12 days in September, Alvarez appeared even stronger. There were rumors of a coup throughout 1983, but as Suazo recuperated he appeared to recover control of the situation. In March 1984 he dismissed General Alvarez. Resignations of several more high-ranking military officers followed. Suazo quickly named the leader of what had amounted to a coup within the military, Air Force Brigadier General Walter López Reyes (a nephew of former President Oswaldo López Arellano), as the new commander-in-chief. In November 1984 the FBI arrested Alvarez and seven others in Miami for plotting Suazo's assassination.

While improving Suazo's prestige and confirming civilian authority over the military, the military shake-up did not signal any significant change in Honduras' close relationship with the United States or its support of the Nicaraguan *contras*. A major cabinet shakeup in August 1984 reflected the continued turmoil within the Suazo government and his inability to reverse a severe economic decline. Government deficits soared as military expenditures rose. Suazo supported a modest agrarian reform program, but he lost much of his earlier popularity, especially among teachers and labor. Promises of democratic rule with social and economic reform had borne little fruit by mid-1985.

Suazo had served U.S. policy goals in Central America, but American support of "democratization" in Honduras under Suazo appeared to many to be simply a cover for "militarization." Border incidents involving Nicaraguan forces and the *contras* concerned the Suazo government, which expressed growing annoyance at the use of its territory for the anti-Sandinista campaign. Ineligible for reelection, Suazo faced considerable opposition from within his own party as he tried to secure the nomination of his choice, Carlos Flores Facussé, as successor. The effort failed, however, as Jose Azcona Hoyo won the election. There were continuing rumors of a possible military coup by General Reyes.

In 1989, Honduras and Suazo became embroiled in the Iran-Contra affair (involving the trial of White House aide Oliver North). During that trial, evidence was introduced that implicated Presidents Ronald Reagan and George Bush as circumventing the Congressional ban on aide to Nicaraguan rebels. This was premised on allegations that President Bush had met with Suazo to offer increased aid to Honduras in return for its assistance to Nicaraguan contras (rebels). (Such allegations were later dispelled by additional documentary evidence provided by the White House.) Although the Nicaraguan conflict was ultimately resolved, the Honduran election of 1989 took its toll on the Liberal party. Rafael Leonardo Callejas became the first opposition candidate to win an election in Honduras since 1932. However, during the 1990s, the established democracy in Honduras remained intact.

Further Reading

Detailed information on the first two years of the Suazo administration may be found in James D. Rudolph, editor, *Honduras, A Country Study* (1984). Also informative are James A. Morris, *Honduras, Caudillo Politics and Military Rulers* (1984) and Morris' chapter on Honduras in Steve C. Ropp and James A. Morris, editors, *Central America: Crisis and Adaptation* (1984). For additional coverage see *Keesing's Contemporary Archives*. A good source of information about contemporary Honduras and its government may be found in, Merrill, Tim L., ed., *Honduras: A Country Study* (Federal Reserve Division, Library of Congress, 1995). □

Sir John Suckling

The English poet and playwright Sir John Suckling (1609-1642) was one of the Cavalier poets of the reign of Charles I.

B orn into an old Norfolk family early in February 1609, John Suckling was the son of the secretary of state to King James I. He studied at Cambridge and Gray's Inn, London, the latter one of the chief English institutions for the training of lawyers. Then Suckling traveled on the Continent. After his knighting in 1630 he served in the volunteer forces that aided King Gustavus II of Sweden in 1631.

From the time of his return to London in 1632 until his life ended a decade later, Suckling devoted his energies to living the life of a courtier. He achieved a reputation as a gallant and gamester, as a brilliant wit and prolific lover. He is credited with having invented the game of cribbage.

Suckling wrote four plays, including the tragedy *Aglaura* (1637) and the comedy *The Goblins* (1638). A number of his lyric poems were first published posthumously in *Fragmenta aurea* (1646). Some of Suckling's letters survive and are notable for their witty, colloquial prose style.

Toward the end of his life Suckling became involved in political events. In 1639 he accompanied Charles I on an expedition against the Scots, which ended in a humiliating defeat. Suckling was said to be more fit for the boudoir than the battlefield. In 1641 he participated in an abortive plot to free the 1st Earl of Strafford from the Tower of London. Suckling fled to Paris, where, according to a biography published later in the century, he committed suicide in 1642 because he was unable to face poverty.

Suckling was one of the Cavalier poets, a group of sophisticated courtiers whose political allegiances lay with the Crown and whose intellectual interests were largely amatory. Suckling's poetry is marked by common sense, precision, grace, and a light touch. He modeled his style on the secular lyrics of John Donne, imitating their light conversational tone, abrupt metrical patterns, humor, and once in a while their cosmological imagery. Donne's influence is frequently palpable: "Out upon it, I have lov'd/ Three whole days together;/ And am like to love three more,/ If it prove fair weather." However, unlike Donne's, Suckling's spirit was cynical, rational, and social, and his intellect was slight. The irony that informs his poetry is far from simple, though, and Suckling wrote a number of fine lyrics, including "Ballad upon a Wedding" and the song "Why so pale and wan, fond lover?"

Further Reading

Suckling's plays are discussed in Kathleen M. Lynch, *The Social Mode of Restoration Comedy* (1926), and Alfred Harbage, *Cavalier Drama* (1936). There is no work devoted to his poetry, but he is adequately treated in discussions of Cavalier poetry in such works as Douglas Bush, *English Literature in the Earlier Seventeenth Century* (1948; 2d ed. 1962). A sym-

pathetic treatment of Suckling's work can be found in Hugh M. Richmond, *The School of Love: The Evolution of the Stuart Love Lyric* (1964), which argues that 17th-century lyric poetry manifests an increasing and remarkable sophistication in its attitudes toward romantic love. □

Antonio José de Sucre

Antonio José de Sucre (1795-1830) was a Venezuelan general and first constitutional president of Bolivia. He was one of the ablest military commanders in the war for independence against Spain and an intimate collaborator of Simón Bolívar.

Antonio José de Sucre was born on Feb. 3, 1795, at Cumaná in eastern Venezuela. When he was 13, his family, which belonged to the local aristocracy, sent him away to study in Caracas. Two years later, at the outbreak of the revolution against Spain, he joined the patriot army, and he shared in both the successes and the reverses of the Venezuelan First and Second Republics. After the collapse of the latter in 1814, he took refuge in the Antilles, fought at Cartagena in New Granada, and fled again, to Haiti, toward the end of 1815.

In 1816 Sucre was once more in Venezuela. He served with distinction under Gen. Santiago Mariño against the royalists but refused to follow Mariño when he sought to challenge Bolívar's authority. For these and other reasons the young Sucre—slight of build, sensitive, intensely self-reliant—became a special favorite of Bolívar, and Sucre reciprocated with an unquestioned loyalty to his chief.

In 1821 Sucre undertook his most important assignment to date, which was to invade the Ecuadorian highlands from the Pacific coast. He met with success at the battle of Pichincha (May 24, 1822), which delivered Quito into patriot hands and paved the way for its incorporation into the unified republic of Gran Colombia. Subsequently Sucre went with a Colombian advance guard to continue the struggle in Peru. Though Bolívar ultimately came to Peru himself, it was Sucre who commanded the patriot army at the decisive victory of Ayacucho (Dec. 9, 1824), the last major engagement of the war.

After Ayacucho, Sucre moved into Upper Peru (modern Bolivia), where Spanish resistance rapidly crumbled. He remained to help organize the region and in 1826 was inaugurated as president of the new republic of Bolivia. But his presidency was not wholly successful. Many Bolivians resented him as a foreigner; and he was saddled with an inordinately complicated constitution which Bolívar had drafted. Amid mounting unrest, Sucre resigned in August 1828 and returned to Gran Colombia.

Sucre's intention was to settle down at Quito, where he had married a member of the local aristocracy. But the coming of war between Gran Colombia and Peru brought him back into active service; he defeated a Peruvian invasion force at the battle of Tarqui on Feb. 27, 1829. Early in

1830 he served as president of a constitutional convention, meeting at Bogotá, which proved unable to halt the disintegration of Gran Colombia. On his way back to Quito, he was assassinated at Berruecos near Pasto on June 4, 1830. Suspicion fell on Bolívar's liberal opponents, who regarded Sucre as his political heir; but the origins of the crime are still hotly debated.

Further Reading

A brief account of Sucre's life is Guillermo Antonio Sherwell, *Antonio José de Sucre* (*Gran Mariscal de Ayacucho*), *Hero and Martyr of American Independence* (1924), and a section is devoted to him in William S. Robertson, *The Rise of the Spanish-American Republics, as Told in the Lives of Their Liberators* (1918). For historical background see Charles W. Arnade, *The Emergence of the Republic of Bolivia* (1957).

Additional Sources

Hoover, John P, *Admirable warrior: Marshal Sucre, fighter for South American independence = Guerrero admirable: El mariscal Sucre, luchador por la independencia sudamericana,* Detroit: B. Ethridge, Books, 1977. □

Hermann Sudermann

The works of the German dramatist and novelist Hermann Sudermann (1857-1928) reflect both the scope and the limitations of naturalism.

Hermann Sudermann was born in Matziken, East Prussia, on Sept. 30, 1857. He described his youthful poverty in *Das Bilderbuch meiner Jugend* (1922). He found initial success in Berlin with his novel *Frau Sorge* (1887), in which an East Prussian farmer triumphs over poverty and other vicissitudes through dedication to hard work, self-reliance, and self-sacrifice.

More directly in the stream of naturalism was Sudermann's four-act drama, *Die Ehre,* produced in November 1889. It treats of class conflict and the relativity of the concept of honor, contrasting the rich, dwelling in the "front of the house," with the humble occupants of the "rear of the house." Without glorifying the latter, Sudermann defends the viability of bourgeois principles and a persistent idealistic sense.

The structural symmetry of *Die Ehre*—not a characteristically naturalistic technique—is present also in *Sodoms Ende* (1890), a drama depicting the society of Sudermann's artistic colleagues as an amoral morass fraught with tragedy and death. In *Heimat* (1893) Sudermann defends the cause of women in their struggle against the pressures of tradition and parental authority. *Das Glück im Winkel* (1896) echoes in a country setting the moral bankruptcy of *Sodoms Ende,* but the victimized woman is preserved from tragedy by her understanding and forgiving husband.

The one-act play *Fritzchen* (1897) effectively develops the familial complications for the young officer who transgresses the traditional code, while *Johannisfeuer*

(1900) opposes the natural and passionate affinity of two young people to the requirements of material expediency, regretfully resolving the dilemma in favor of the latter. *Stein unter Steinen* (1905) is authentically naturalistic in presenting the problem of social rehabilitation faced by the released convict and the unmarried mother.

Sudermann's novel *Das hohe Lied* (1908) is notable for its ruthless exposure of depravity in Berlin society as well as for its analysis of the capital's artist colony. In the narrative collection *Litauische Geschichten* (1917) Sudermann realistically portrays scenes and characters of his East Prussian homeland. He died in Berlin on Nov. 21, 1928.

Notable in Sudermann's work is the occasional gleam of optimism amid the encircling gloom of naturalism. Even the most sorely oppressed may win out through an unusual effort of will. In treating the newer sociological themes, Sudermann as a dramatist retains certain effective traditional techniques: a combination which makes for more effective theater than strict naturalism would provide, and assures for the plays a degree of continuing interest. A number of works, *Heimat* among them, have been successful as films.

Further Reading

Still useful are the discussions of Sudermann in Otto Heller, *Studies in Modern German Literature: Sudermann, Hauptmann, Women Writers of the Nineteenth Century* (1905), and Georg Witkowski, *The German Drama of the Nineteenth Century* (1909). For a balanced appraisal see

Jethro Bithell, *Modern German Literature, 1880-1950* (1939; 3d ed. 1959). ☐

Gaius Suetonius Tranquillus

Gaius Suetonius Tranquillus (ca. 70-ca. 135) was a Roman administrator and writer. In a life which covered the reigns of five emperors, he held various public offices and in his spare time wrote biographies of literary men and emperors.

Born probably at Hippo Regius (Bone) in North Africa, Suetonius belonged to a wealthy family of Italian origin and equestrian status. At an early age he went to Rome, where he received most of his education, and as a young man he started a career as a barrister, though before long he changed to teaching. By 98 he had become friendly with the younger Pliny, who encouraged him to publish some of his early writings.

In 102 or 103 Pliny obtained for him a commission as a military tribune in one of the legions stationed in Britain, but Suetonius declined the offer. When Pliny was sent to Bithynia as governor (109-111), Suetonius probably went with him. After Pliny's death he was helped by another friend, Septicius Clarus, who obtained various posts for him from the emperor Trajan, including appointments as *a studiis,* which put Suetonius in charge of the Emperor's personal library, and as *a bibliothecis,* which involved control of the public libraries of Rome.

In 119 Septicius became praetorian prefect, and at about the same time Suetonius was promoted by Hadrian to the important post of *ab epistulis,* which headed the secretariat that dealt with most of the Emperor's official correspondence. But he did not hold the post long: in 122 he and Septicius were both dismissed from their posts by Hadrian. Thereafter Suetonius lived quietly either at Rome or possibly at Hippo Regius until he died.

His Writings

A considerable number of short works, mostly on literary subjects, are ascribed to Suetonius, but these have all been lost. His first major work was the *De viris illustribus,* published between 106 and 113, which was a series of biographies of literary men. The original text has not survived, but the section on grammarians and several of the lives of the poets are extant in abridged editions.

This work was followed by the extant *De vita Caesarum,* of which the first six books, covering the Julio-Claudian emperors from Julius Caesar to Nero, were published between 119 and 122. Later, perhaps as late as 130, Suetonius added two further books, which dealt, much more briefly, with the three short-lived emperors of 69 and the Flavian dynasty.

These imperial biographies are not very profound works. Suetonius made some use, though certainly not enough, of the opportunities for access to the imperial archives which his official appointments gave him, but most of his material came from earlier writers, and he showed little critical sense in his assessment of their reliability.

Suetonius's *Lives* are collections of facts mixed with gossip, scandal, and sheer fiction, strung loosely together on a rough chronological thread. They provide the modern historian with much information and are particularly valuable for the details they record of the physical appearance of the emperors, together with some of their *obiter dicta* and other minor matters which at that time were regarded as beneath the dignity of regular history.

Further Reading

There is a complete translation of Suetonius's works, including what remains of *De viris illustribus,* by J. C. Rolfe in the Loeb Classical Library (2 vols., 1914). A good version of the imperial biographies is Robert Graves, *The Twelve Caesars* (1957). The best account of Suetonius and his work is G. B. Townend and T. A. Dorey, eds., *Latin Biography* (1967). There are brief accounts in most books on Latin literature, such as John Wight Duff, *A Literary History of Rome in the Silver Age* (1935; 3d ed. by A. M. Duff, 1964), and Moses Hadas, *A History of Latin Literature* (1952). The history of the emperors whose lives Suetonius recorded and of the period in which he himself lived is covered in Edward T. Salmon, *A History of the Roman World from 30 B.C. to A.D. 138* (1944; 6th ed. 1968). The best account of the period of Julius Caesar and the Julio-Claudian emperors is in Howard H. Scullard, *From the Gracchi to Nero* (1959). ☐

Suharto

The second president after Indonesia's independence, Suharto (born 1921) was a strong anti-Communist who drew Indonesia closer to the West and presided during a period of economic improvement in the country. Notwithstanding, his tenure was plagued with negative publicity regarding suppression of opposition and serious human rights violations, particularly in East Timor, a former Portuguese colony that Indonesia forcibly occupied starting in 1975.

Suharto was born in the village of Kemusu near Jogjakarta, Central Java, on June 8, 1921. His father was a low-ranking agricultural technician, and Suharto's early home environment was quite poor. It also was unstable, alternating between the separate homes of his mother and his father who, having divorced when he was quite young, each had remarried and had additional children. At times Suharto also lived with other family friends and relatives in homes which were typically Javanese.

As Suharto completed high school and took his first job, in a small bank, the Dutch colonial government in Indonesia was hastily trying to build a defense force. Suharto was among the large number of Indonesian recruits to the Royal Netherlands Indies Army. By March 1942 Suharto had spent a year and a half in training and active duty under Dutch commanders and had been promoted to the rank of sergeant; but when the Netherlands, already occupied in Europe by Germany, surrendered the colony to Japan later in 1942 after mounting only minimal resistance, Suharto returned to his village.

A Professional Soldier

Shortly thereafter Suharto volunteered for service in a Japanese police organization in Jogjakarta. He then joined the PETA, the Japanese-sponsored Volunteer Army of Defenders of the Homeland, and, after receiving additional formal military training at Bogor, became a company commander. When the Japanese surrendered and the Netherlands sought to reestablish control over the Dutch East Indies, PETA units and officers provided the framework for a People's Security Corps which was forerunner to the Indonesian National Army. Among these officers Suharto acquired a reputation for able leadership and sound strategy in opposing not only the Dutch military forces but also various Indonesian factions—including Communists and Islamic extremists—which were challenging the political leadership of the embryonic Republic of Indonesia.

Indonesian independence was proclaimed in August 1945, and the Dutch finally abandoned their effort to retain sovereignty four years later. The new nation was so geographically far-flung, culturally diverse, and economically disadvantaged that the government under the presidency of the forceful nationalist leader Sukarno had difficulty maintaining constitutional norms and procedures. The army inevitably came to be viewed as a key political actor, all the more so as Sukarno declared martial law in 1957 and a struggle for succession accelerated in the early 1960s.

During this period Suharto was advancing through the ranks of the Indonesian National Army. As a lieutenant colonel he participated in 1950 in an expedition which succeeded in suppressing an incipient rebellion in South Sulawesi. Most of his infrequent command assignments were in Central Java, somewhat removed from the more dynamic center of national politics and administration in the capital, Jakarta. In 1957 Suharto was promoted to the rank of colonel; in 1960 he became a brigadier general; and in 1963, as major general, he assumed command of the Army Strategic Command.

Providing Leadership in a "New Order"

Although he was not highly visible among the military elite, Suharto had developed close associations throughout the army and was especially supportive and protective of his staff. In addition, he cultivated an unyielding anti-Communism along with vigorous economic enterprise by army units under his command. These qualities were especially characteristic of the Indonesian army in the years leading up to 1965, and they became increasingly associated with the state under Suharto's presidency.

Ironically, Suharto would not have been in a position of such influence if the organizers of the "30th of September Movement"—a dramatic if politically confused coup attempt—had deemed him important enough to include in their list of generals targeted for execution. As it was six generals were abducted and, either immediately or soon thereafter, killed on the night of September 30, 1965. In the ensuing hours and days Suharto gained control of the military in Jakarta and successfully portrayed the generals' assassination as an operation of the Communist Party of Indonesia. President Sukarno, whose role in the so-called coup was not clear, sought to protect the Communists from the military's retaliation, but Suharto was relentless. In March 1966 President Sukarno was maneuvered into a transfer of executive powers to Suharto. A further series of official acts, culminating in the March 27, 1968, decree of the People's Consultative Congress, formalized Suharto's assumption of the presidency. Sukarno, under close surveillance at his Bogor palace, died in June 1970.

Meanwhile, the Communist Party of Indonesia had been banned and large numbers of Communists and alleged Communist sympathizers were killed or imprisoned throughout Indonesia. Suharto, as president, reversed some of the previous regime's foreign policies, such as confrontation with Malaysia and general hostility to the West, and displayed a sober, problem-solving style in his approach to domestic problems. The "New Order" regime, as it came to be called, also drew legitimacy from leading roles assigned to the Sultan of Jogjakarta, Hamengku Buwono IX, and Adam Malik, an "Old Order" politician. In addition, Suharto augmented his trusted personal staff with a corps of "technocrats," highly-placed economists trained in the United States.

Partly because of a surge in oil revenues during the 1970s, Indonesia's economic situation improved substantially during Suharto's presidency. Beginning in 1968 he was re-appointed to the presidency every five years with virtually no opposition. Yet his tenure was not free of controversy. Allegations of favoritism and greed were directed at the palace and, among other relatives, involved especially his aristocratic Javanese wife, Tien Suharto. In the 1980s government corruption and repression combined with international trends to fuel Islamic political activity. In 1990, Suharto created the Indonesian Association of Muslim Intellectuals (ICMI) to accommodate growing concern over the potentially strong political force of the Muslim groups. President Suharto and his military supporters were able to contain these and all other political rivals, and he began to give more attention to preparation of a successor regime.

In the 1990s, continued corruption and oppression of opposition presented a growing obstacle to sustained economic growth. Nonetheless, Suharto was elected to his sixth five-year term in 1993.

Further Reading

Some of Suharto's speeches and proclamations are reprinted in *Focus on Indonesia,* a quarterly publication of the Embassy of Indonesia in Washington, D.C. A full length and semi-official biography is available: O. G. Roeder, *The Smiling General* (1969). The "New Order" is the subject of Hamish McDonald's highly readable *Suharto's Indonesia* (1980); and David Jenkins focuses more narrowly on the role of the military in *Suharto and His Generals: Indonesian Military Politics, 1975-1983* (1984). See also, Schwarz, Adam, *A Nation of Waiting: Indonesia in the 1990s* (Westview, 1994).

Several surveys place Suharto's presidency in a more historical and cultural perspective, ranging from the relatively introductory work by J. D. Legge, *Indonesia* (1980), to Benedict Anderson and Audrey Kahin (editors), *Interpreting Indonesian Politics: Thirteen Contributions to the Debate* (1982). Several periodicals have also published articles on Suharto's handling of East Timor, e.g., Eyal Press's article, *The Suharto Lobby* in *The Progressive* (May, 1997). □

Empress Suiko

Empress Suiko (554-628) was the thirty-third ruler of Japan. She was the first empress regnant, and during her 35-year reign the 12 grades in court ranking—in the cap ranks—and the Seventeen-article Constitution were proclaimed.

Suiko was the second daughter of Emperor Kimmei and was known as Toyo-mike Kashiki-ya-hime. In her childhood she was called princess Nukada-be. According to *Nihongi,* her appearance was beautiful and her conduct was marked by propriety. At the age of 18 she was appointed empress-consort of Emperor Bidatsu (reigned 572-585).

When Emperor Sujun (reigned 588-593) was murdered by the great imperial chieftain Mumako no Sukune, ministers besought Nukada-be, the widow of Emperor Bidatsu, to ascend the throne. She refused, but the public functionaries urged her in memorials three times until she consented.

Actually, it was Soga no Umako who made Nukada-be, his own niece, empress of Japan after the powerful Soga chieftain caused Emperor Sujun to be assassinated. This was a sharp departure from precedent, as there had been no reigning empress since legendary matriarchal times. It is clear from the genealogical table of the imperial clan at this time that the imperial family had numerous male members who could be made to ascend the throne. Soga no Umako, however, was following the policy of his father, Iname, by putting on the throne the child of a Soga mother.

Choice of a Coruler

Once Empress Suiko was on the throne, Umako nominated as heir apparent and regent not one of Suiko's seven sons but the second son of Yomei, the Prince Umayado (Shotoku Taishi). *Nihongi* makes it clear that the prince regent had "general control of the government, and was entrusted with all the details of administration."

In 594, in the second year of her reign, Suiko instructed Shotoku Taishi to promote Buddhism in the country. In the following year a priest of the Koryŏ kingdom in Korea, named Hye-cha, emigrated to Japan and became the teacher for Prince Shotoku. In the same year, another Korean priest, named Hye-chong, arrived from the kingdom of Paekche. These two priests began to preach Buddhist religion widely under the official support of the imperial court. By 596, the construction of the Hokoji was completed, and the two Korean priests took up their residence in that temple.

In the winter of 602, another Korean priest, Kwal-leuk, arrived from Paekche with books on calendar making, astronomy, and geography. Almost immediately, a number of students were selected to study these new sciences.

Reforms of the Bureaucracy

The 12 grades of cap ranks were first instituted in 603. The system was modeled after the Chinese one of distinguishing ranks of court officials by the form and materials of the official caps. *Nihongi* recorded that the prince regent also prepared in person the first written "constitution" of Japan, which was promulgated in 604. It is evident, however, that the document was rather of the nature of moral maxims and some political principles, which the prince regent was said to have regarded as essential conditions for political reforms in Japan.

The Seventeen-article Constitution is an important document and one of considerable historical interest, as it reveals the conditions of Japanese government and politics at the time. According to some historians of Japan, including George Sansom, the document is not accepted today as Shotoku Taishi's own work. Sansom believes that the document was probably written as a tribute to his memory a generation or more after his death, when some of the reforms which he desired had at last been introduced. This was a not unnatural act of piety, since the prince regent did beyond doubt play a leading part in the importation of new ideas and practices from China and Korea.

The Constitution

Many aspects of Japan at about the time of Empress Suiko, who outlived the prince regent, were revealed in the constitution. According to *Nihongi,* the first article declared that "harmony is to be valued, and an avoidance of wanton opposition to be honored." The nation was told to sincerely revere the three treasures of Buddhism as "the supreme objects of worship" in the second article. The third article provided, "When you receive the imperial commands, fail not scrupulously to obey them." The functionaries of the state should make "decorous behavior" (*li* in Chinese) their leading principle, according to the next article.

"Ceasing from gluttony and abandoning covetous desires," state officials were enjoined by the document to "deal impartially with the suits which are submitted to you," and also to "chastise that which is evil and encourage that which is good." The seventh and eighth clauses declared that the "spheres of duty" should not be confused and the ministers and functionaries should attend the court early in the morning and retire late. The constitution then held that "good faith is the foundation of right," and the tenth article stated, "Let us cease from wrath, and refrain from angry looks."

The eleventh article commanded the state officials to "give clear appreciation to merit and demerit, and deal out to each its sure reward or punishment." Indicating that local authorities were at this time giving way to the central government, the twelfth article provided that provincial authorities should not levy exactions on the people. "Let all persons entrusted with office attend equally to their functions" was the thirteenth command, and the fourteenth prescribed that the ministers and functionaries should not be envious of one another. To turn away from that which is private, and to set the faces toward that which is public— this was declared to be the right path of a minister. Again revealing what must have been a widespread practice at the time, the sixteenth article directed, "Let the people be employed [in forced labor] at seasonable times." The last clause stipulated that decisions on important matters should not be made by one person alone.

During the reign of Empress Suiko, expeditionary troops were sent to the kingdom of Silla on the Korean peninsula. The most notable development, however, was that Buddhism thrived in Suiko's reign, and the Shitennoji, the Horyuji, and many other temples were built at the order of the Empress.

Further Reading

There are 36 pages on the major events of the reign of Suiko in William G. Aston, trans., *Nihongi: Chronicles of Japan From the Earliest Times to A.D. 697* (1956). See also the incisive analyses and interpretations on major developments during the reign of the first empress of Japan in George Sansom, *A History of Japan* (3 vols., 1958-1963). □

Sui Wen-ti

Sui Wen-ti (541-604) is the formal posthumous name of the Chinese emperor Yang Chien, founder of the Sui dynasty. He brought about the unification of China after more than 3 centuries of political division.

The ancestry of Sui Wen-ti, born Yang Chien, is not certain, but it is likely that his antecedents served as officials under several of the non-Chinese states in North China. His father, Yang Chung, was a soldier and was given a title of nobility and a fief by the last ruler of the Northern Wei and again earned a noble title and fief by his distinguished military service to Yü-wen T'ai, the founder of the Western Wei dynasty. Yü-wen T'ai gave him the title of Duke of Sui, a title which Yang Chien inherited.

Yang Chien was born in a Buddhist monastery in North China and grew up in the care of a nun. When he was 13 he entered the imperial college in the capital, a school dedicated to teaching the Confucian classics to the children of officials and nobles. At the school he was said to have been reserved and distant in manner.

Civil Service

The classical curriculum of the imperial college held little appeal for Yang Chien, and a year after entering the college he withdrew. He was given a military appointment, for which he was well qualified, having been trained in the martial arts when he was young. He rose in the military under the Northern Chou and also held several civil posts, both in the capital and in the provinces. He held a high military command in the successful war against the state of Northern Ch'i (550-577), a war in which the Northern Chou united North China.

Yang Chien married into the Tu-ku family, one of the most powerful non-Chinese families in the state. His wife, a very able person, became his lifelong adviser and confidante. His marriage brought him closer to the inner circles of power. His connections were further strengthened when their daughter married the Northern Chou crown prince in 573.

After the Northern Chou reunited North China in 578, there was every indication that they would go on to conquer the rest of China. All that stood in their way was the weak Chinese state of Ch'en in the South. Yang Chien presumably looked forward to a promising career under the Northern Chou, but unexpected events placed him in a far more fateful and consequential position.

In 578 Yü-wen Yung, the emperor of the Northern Chou, died. The crown prince, Yang Chien's son-in-law, succeeded to the throne. This man, who was clearly pathological, proceeded to destroy in a short time the dynasty built by his father. Although he formally abdicated the throne to his young son in 579, he continued to dominate the government from behind the scenes. The fact that Yang Chien's daughter was his consort momentarily posed a great threat to the Yang family when the capricious tyrant, planning to elevate someone else to her place, decided to execute her and her family. But he fell ill and died before he could carry out his intentions.

Before the mad ruler died, Yang Chien had received from friends a forged order instructing him to appear at the bedside of the dying man. The friends wanted him to seize the opportunity that would be offered by the father's death to become regent for the child emperor. Yang Chien was reluctant to make any dramatic move, but his friends finally persuaded him that he could succeed. He soon found himself, as the apt proverb had it, "riding a tiger," with no way to get off.

After taking over the regency, Yang Chien moved swiftly and ruthlessly against the princes of the royal family and all others who might confound his bid for power. Yang Chien was fortunate to have able adherents, and by spring of the following year, helped along by a variety of ruses and several military campaigns, he had eliminated all his important enemies.

Consolidation of Power

In 581, when Yang Chien came to the throne, he must have realized that his dynasty might be just one more short-lived effort to establish a viable and lasting regime. His generally cautious temperament—which permitted bold action when necessary—was well suited to the tasks before him, tasks that would require patience and perseverance. It

was one thing to proclaim a dynasty; it was quite another to make it endure.

Wen-ti's personality deeply influenced the court and the government during his reign. He was cautious and parsimonious, never fully confident of his power, and reluctant to indulge in conspicuous display and extravagance. He was fearful and suspicious, afraid that he had offended the gods with his sudden rise to power and worried that those around him, including his own sons, might turn against him. The insecurity that always hounded him sometimes provoked him to violent and uncontrollable rage. He never got over these deep-rooted emotions and engaged in extensive efforts to build up ideological sanctions which would buttress his legitimacy.

The creation of an aura of legitimacy is, of course, important for any regime. What was significant about Emperor Wen's measures was the effective way he utilized all the major religions and ideologies of China—Taoism, Buddhism, and Confucianism—to support his regime. He was rather perfunctory in his patronage of the popular native Taoist tradition. Buddhism received his more active and enthusiastic support, which was probably inspired, if not prompted, by his genuine devotion to the religion. Finally, he followed and affirmed basic Confucian ritual and doctrines; this, we might assume, was particularly directed at the official class, whose support was essential.

Wen-ti established a uniform system of state-supported Buddhist and Taoist temples that were put under the general direction of the great, imperially controlled head temples in the capital. He allied himself with the major faiths in order to get the support of their faithful, but at the same time he was determined to control the size, strength, and autonomy of the religious establishments.

The measures of Emperor Wen to establish a wide base of support from the people did not, however, provide the means for running the state. He had to forge a united state responsive to imperial direction. This required that the state not be dependent on the innumerable pockets of local hereditary power that had been permitted to exist during the period of disunion. Emperor Wen enforced the "rule of avoidance," by which officials were not permitted to serve in their home provinces. This policy was intended to prevent local elite from maintaining political and financial independence. This rule set the tone for the centralizing efforts of the Sui regime. It must be noted that Sui achievements in political and economic institutions and administration did not come to an end when the dynasty fell in 618, but they were adopted and preserved by the T'ang dynasty (618-907), which followed and, in a very real sense, grew out of the Sui.

Unification of China

Beginning in 317, when they were driven from their homeland, six Chinese regimes, all with their capital in the area of modern Nanking, had successfully withstood conquest from the North. When Emperor Wen came to the throne, the "legitimate" Chinese state of Ch'en (557-589) was reigning in the South. Emperor Wen gave his most trusted and able minister the task of preparing the strategy for conquest of the South.

An important part of the Sui plan was an extensive program of propaganda designed to undermine the Southerners' support of their government and prepare the people psychologically for assimilation into a united empire with its capital in the North. In 588 Emperor Wen issued an edict which explained and justified the imminent conquest of the South and ordered 300,000 copies of the edict to be distributed throughout the area below the Yangtze River. We cannot estimate the effectiveness of this strategy, but when Sui armies swept south in 588-589, they met only limited resistance.

The Ch'en dynasty was overthrown in 589, but the work of fully pacifying the South and of bringing the area into the Sui regime remained. During the 590s Emperor Wen devoted himself to this task of political unification. His success in finally bringing the South into the institutional structure of the Sui dynasty was the most important achievement of his career and was certainly a feat of great consequence. When it was accomplished, Sui Wen-ti was ruler of the largest and most populous empire in the world.

Last Years

In 601 Emperor Wen celebrated his sixtieth birthday, an event of great significance in China as it marked the end of a 60-year cycle. He was old for a man of that time and had not expected to live so long.

Emperor Wen remained active during the last years of his life, but he became less concerned with the administration of the government and more concerned with the cultural and spiritual unification of China. He undertook an elaborate effort to build a united society based on the tenets of Buddhism; he simultaneously proscribed the teaching of Confucian values. He had already assumed the roles of the Cakravartin king, the ruler who governs well through his devotion to Buddhism, and the Mahadanapati, the munificent patron of Buddhism whose pious acts transform him into a kind of living bodhisattva. In these acts of his last years we can perhaps also detect his final efforts to overcome his lifelong insecurity.

Like every successful ruler, Wen-ti had to confront the problems of succession. He had four sons and was always fearful that they had usurpative designs on the throne. One of his sons was poisoned in 600, and Wen-ti managed to displace his eldest son, the crown prince, later that year. Wen-ti probably felt little sorrow that these two were gone, and Yang Kuang, his second son and the Empress's favorite, became crown prince.

Sui Wen-ti fell ill in the summer of 604. He died shortly thereafter, in circumstances which suggested that the new crown prince may have been at least partly responsible for his death. Yang Kuang ascended the throne in August 604 as Sui Yang-ti. His extravagant and ambitious undertakings brought the empire that his father had worked so hard to build to a dramatic collapse in 618.

Further Reading

For a fine essay on Sui Wen-ti see Arthur F. Wright's "The Formation of Sui Ideology" in John K. Fairbank, ed., *Chinese Thought and Institutions* (1957). See also Wright's "Sui Yang-ti: Personality and Stereotype" in Arthur F. Wright, ed., *The Confucian Persuasion* (1960), for an excellent study of the second, and last, Sui emperor. □

Sukarno

Sukarno (1901-1970) was the first president of Indonesia, a nationalist leader, and a demagogue. He was the founder of the Republic of Indonesia and a dominant figure throughout its history until his death.

Sukarno was born on June 6, 1901, in Surabaya, East Java, of a Javanese father and Balinese mother. At an early age the family moved to Modjokerto, where his father taught school. Sukarno's adequate knowledge of Dutch made it possible for him to enter the European elementary school. In 1916 he enrolled at a high school in Surabaya. During this period he lived with H. O. S. Tjokroaminoto a prominent Islamic leader and head of Sarekat Islam. The 5 years (1916-1921) Sukarno spent in Surabaya were most important in his future intellectual and political development, for here he came in contact with prominent Indonesian nationalists and with Dutch socialists.

In 1920 the left wing of the Sarekat Islam split away and formed the Indonesian Communist party (PKI). The following year Sukarno entered the Institute of Technology in Bandung, from which he graduated in 1926 as an engineer. He embarked on a political career, publishing a series of articles in which he endeavored to reconcile the two contending factions by trying to show that Islam and communism (socialism) were not incompatible.

The rallying force for Indonesian independence was to be nationalism, aggressively pursued. The enemies common to all groups in Indonesia were, in his judgment, imperialism and capitalism, both exemplified in the Dutch. Sukarno's belief that a misunderstanding had brought about the conflict between Islam and communism was first presented in 1926 and continued into the sixties.

Revolutionary and Independence Leader

In 1927 Sukarno became chairman of the Nationalist Study Club in Bandung. With the founding of the Indonesian Nationalist party (PNI) in 1927 and the earlier banning of the PKI as a result of the Madiun revolt in 1926, Sukarno's task of unifying the various nationalist groups was made much easier. His spellbinding oratory and his ability to phrase his political goals in a language the masses could understand soon made him a national hero. His influence and fame were greatly enhanced by his trial in 1930. As a result of anticolonialist utterances, he had been accused by the government of the Dutch Indies of treason and sen-

tenced to 4 years in prison, only 2 of which he had to serve. It was on the occasion of this trial that he delivered his famed defense speech, *Indonesia Menggugat* (Indonesia Accuses), which is considered one of the most important statements of his credo.

Shortly after his release Sukarno was arrested again, and was exiled to Ende on the island of Flores in February 1934. Four years later he was moved to Bencoolen in Sumatra. Sukarno was released when the Japanese occupied Indonesia in March 1942. The Japanese, familiar with Sukarno's strong anticolonialist views, made him a leader in their various organizations, and in June 1945 he headed the very important preparatory Committee for Indonesian Independence.

Sukarno indicated clearly that his goal had always been, and still was, Indonesia's independence. On this occasion he set forth in eloquent terms the Pantjasila, or Five Pillars: nationalism, internationalism, democracy, social justice, and belief in God. On Aug. 17, 1945, Sukarno, at the strong urging of youth groups and colleagues, proclaimed his country's independence in Djakarta, and he became the first president of the new Republic of Indonesia, a position he retained for almost 21 years.

Internal Strife

After the transfer of sovereignty on December 27, 1949, the unity which Sukarno succeeded in maintaining during the revolution fell apart, and the three ideological groups began attacking each other. In this feuding, Sukarno found allies in the Indonesian Communist party and in the Nahdatul Ulama, a conservative Islamic party. He could also continue to count on the support of his PNI.

In 1959 Sukarno reintroduced the Constitution of 1945, which gave the president full powers, responsible only to a very weak Congress. He dissolved Congress, banned the Masjumi (liberal Moslem) party and the Socialist party (PSI), and ruled by decree. He then introduced the concept of "guided democracy" and called for the extermination of neoimperialism and neocolonialism and the establishment of a socialist society.

To achieve these goals, Sukarno united three groups whose philosophies were respectively nationalism (*nasionalisme*), religion (*agama*), and communism (*komunisme*) into an ideological front to which he gave the acronym Nasakom. This union was not successful, however, because the first two groups became unhappy at the extraordinarily rapid rise of the PKI and at Sukarno's strong praise of this party.

Upheaval and Death

The army and the PKI had been enemies from the earliest days of the republic, and with the abortive coup on Oct. 1, 1965, led by alleged Communist sympathizers, Sukarno's days as president were numbered. Thousands of people were killed in the purge that followed. The army, under Gen. Suharto, assisted in the pogrom and supported the Indonesian students in their move to bring down Sukarno.

Under this pressure Sukarno, on March 11, 1966, transferred his presidential powers to Gen. Suharto, who was reluctant to remove Sukarno completely from the scene. The latter refused to go along with the new developments, and a year later he was deposed and placed under house confinement in Bogor, where he remained, a physically ill man, until a few days before his death in a Djakarta hospital on June 21, 1970, of complications from kidney trouble and high blood pressure. Sukarno was not accorded a place in the Heroes' Cemetery in Djakarta but was buried beside his mother in Blitar, East Java.

Sukarno's significance in the establishment of the Republic of Indonesia is tremendous. His devotion to his principles, first enunciated in 1926, was unswerving. A brilliant orator, a charismatic leader, and an idealist, he achieved his original goal but failed as a "man of facts" and readily admitted that he was not an economist. His rule has been called the era of slogans rather than performance.

Further Reading

Important insights into Sukarno's political thinking are in the English translations of his *Marhaen and Proletarian* (1960) and *Nationalism, Islam and Marxism* (1970). Useful and interesting is *Sukarno: An Autobiography as Told to Cindy Adams* (1965). Somewhat less useful and journalistic in style is Cindy Adams, *My Friend the Dictator* (1967). There is as yet no full-length biography of Sukarno. Bernhard Dahm, *Sukarno and the Struggle for Indonesian Independence* (1969), is an important political biography. A less detailed but useful work on Sukarno's ideology is Donald E. Weatherbee, *Ideology in Indonesia: Sukarno's Indonesian Revolution* (1966). Very brief but informative is Hal Kosut, ed., *Indonesia; The Sukarno Years* (1967), which serves as an introduction to the study of those turbulent years in Southeast Asian history. ☐

Suleiman I

Suleiman I (1494-1566) was the tenth ottoman sultan, known to the Turks as Kunani, or lawgiver, and to the Western historians as "the Magnificent," he ruled the Osmanli empire with undisputed strength and brilliance.

The only son of Selim I, Suleiman attended the palace school and served his apprenticeship as a governor, first at Bolu, where he was assigned when about 15, later at Kaffa, the homeland of his mother, daughter of a Crimean Tatar khan. He also supervised the state when his father was campaigning. In education and experience Suleiman surpassed every European ruler of his day.

Campaigns of Expansion

Suleiman continued Selim's expansionist activites, personally participating in 13 campaigns. This military activity was in part due to the nature of the state, since, without raiding, as the Sultan is said to have realized, the Janissaries lacked income and apolitical outlets for their energies. This was certainly a crucial cause of later Ottoman decline. The first of Suleiman's military moves was against Belgrade, captured on Aug. 29, 1521, in retaliation for the harsh treatment accorded a Turkish embassy seeking tribute of the king of Hungary. Thus the way into the heartland of central Europe was opened.

Rhodes, only 6 miles off the Turkish coast, was the Sultan's second military objective. The resident Knights of St. John had long protected Christian pirates harassing the sealanes to Egypt. The island capitulated in December 1522 after a bloody 6-month siege. Inhabitants not choosing to leave were given their full civil rights and a 5-year remission of taxes, an indication of Suleiman's just—and shrewd—nature.

Suleiman enjoyed the succeeding 3 years at leisure in or near the capital. However, the groundwork was laid at this time for two situations—harem influence and the elevation of favorites—which were to become disastrous for the empire in later centuries. A slave girl, Roxelana ("the Russian"), so attracted the sultan that he made her his legal wife. Khurrem Sultan, as she was formally called, had three children, his successor Selim II (born 1524), Prince Bayezid, and Princess Mihrimah.

Favoritism also appeared, undermining the morale of a government service in which promotions had resulted from meritorious service. The Sultan's favorite, Ibrahim, was a Greek, sold into slavery by pirates. His mistress educated him, and he became attached to Suleiman while the latter was still a prince. On June 27, 1524, Ibrahim was made grand vizier. He was remarkably capable, but those sup-

planted in service were disaffected. One of Ibrahim Pasha's first duties was to reorganize Ottoman affairs in Egypt in response to uprisings there. The new arrangements successfully combined a degree of local autonomy with overall ottoman supervision. Egypt's laws were later codified on the basis of Ibrahim's changes.

In the summer of 1526 Suleiman broke the power of Hungary. The Turks advanced into and temporarily occupied the capital in a major raid necessitated in part by Janissary restlessness over several years' inactivity. May 1529 saw Suleiman again in the Danubian area, now in support of the Transylvanian duke, John Zapolya, in opposition to the Austrians who had occupied Buda. Ousting them, Suleiman installed Zapolya as his vassal in Hungary and launched the famous siege of Vienna, Sept. 27-Oct. 15, 1529. On the very eve of the city's surrender, the Janissaries withdrew, perhaps because Turkish forces were limited in their military operations by climatic factors. No winter campaigns were undertaken because the rains made movement of artillery, men, and supplies too difficult.

Eastern Campaigns

The Sultan's fifth campaign was a minor one against the emperor Charles V in 1532. Then the wars moved East. In July 1534, the grand vizier, Ibrahim, took Tabriz and, in November, Baghdad. There the Sultan spent 18 months, settling the administration and visiting Kufa, Kerbala, and other holy places. Meanwhile his foe, Shah Tahmasp, reoccupied many of his conquered territories, thus necessitating Suleiman's return and leading to the sack of Tabriz in 1536.

That same year Ibrahim fell from favor. Favorite, confidant, adviser, policy maker, and even brother-in-law of Suleiman, Ibrahim was found outside the palace strangled the morning of March 15, 1536. He had apparently overstepped the bounds of his position, frequently assuming titles beyond his rank. Since he was still Suleiman's slave, his extensive property reverted to his master.

Corfu and Moldavia occupied Ottoman attention between 1537 and the reconquest and then annexation of Hungary in 1541. Austria's opposition to the latter act resulted only in further Ottoman annexations and an annual tribute payment established by peace treaty in 1547. Austrian treaty violations, however, led to Turkish acquisition of Temesvar in 1552, but Suleiman did not participate in that expedition—he was again in pursuit of Shah Tahmasp.

Court Intrigues

When, in 1553, full-scale operations against Persia resumed, Roxelana's politicking appeared. Rustem Pasha, the grand vizier and husband of princess Mihrimah, led the Ottoman forces but reported the Janissaries were talking of replacing an aging sultan with his more vigorous eldest son, Mustafa. At Roxelana's urging, the Sultan joined the army. He met and executed Mustafa at Eregli on October 16. Prince Jahangir, Mustafa's deformed brother, committed suicide when he heard the news. Since Mehmed, Suleiman's favorite, had died in 1543, only Roxelana's sons now remained alive.

After Mustafa's death, the Sultan continued the war with Tahmasp, finally settling the border in 1555 after prolonged treaty negotiations. The Ottomans retained Baghdad and the Persian Gulf port of Basrah.

The last years of Suleiman's life were marred by the death of Roxelana in April 1558 and the war, beginning the following year, between her sons, the sly, intriguing, alcoholic Selim and the younger Bayezid. Selim was aided by Rustem Pasha and Mihrimah, whose influence over the Sultan was considerable. Defeated in battle, Bayezid fled to Iran, vainly asking parental forgiveness; apparently his request was never received. He was surrendered to the Sultan's agent, in exchange for gold, and was executed.

Suleiman's last campaign, carried out when he was past 70, was again into Hungary. His forces besieged and took the last non-Turkish fortress, Sziget, in 1566. The Sultan died during the night of Sept. 5-6, his death kept secret over 3 weeks until Selim's succession.

Suleiman's Role

Suleiman's military exploits and interest in the hunt indicate an indefatigable nature. He was also active as a legislator, bringing to its peak the administrative system of the burgeoning empire. The laws for which he is famed were necessitated by the rapid expansion of the state and the governing system. Predominating were such matters as inheritance rights, ceremony within the government, criminal punishments, and, in 1530, regulations to reorganize feudal grants in an effort to end corruption. Although the income of the state was extensive, the sumptuous nature of

the court and the subcourts of the princes and slave viziers created problems which later led to widespread corruption.

Internationally, the expansion of the empire rearranged European politics. In 1536 the French king, Francis I, concluded an alliance with the Turks, raising France's position to that of Venice and others. Ottoman sea power was long established in the eastern Mediterranean; now, under Khair al-Din Barbarossa, Ottoman suzereignty over North Africa was firmed up. Barbarossa and his successors roamed the Mediterranean, raiding Spanish coastal areas at will. After the French alliance they often cooperated with French ships. The only setback occurred in 1565, when an attack on Malta failed. Ottoman sea power dominated the area long after Suleiman's death.

Other naval ventures in the Red Sea and Indian Ocean brought Yemen and Aden into the Ottoman Empire and even led to a siege of the Portuguese-held Indian city of Diu in 1538. Turkey produced several famous naval commanders during this period, including Piri Reis, noted for his cartographic work but executed for his failure to break Portugal's hold on Ormuz at the mouth of the Persian Gulf.

Cultural progress was also made during Suleiman's reign. Foreign concepts receded as Ottoman civilization found its own footing. The Sultan himself, using the name Muhibbi, was quite a poet and beyond that a patron of poets and inspiration of historians. His diary is an invaluable record of his reign. He seems also to have been a humble religious man, composing prayers and eight times copying the Koran. His religious nature further is evidenced in the large number of mosques he commissioned.

Architecture was a major achievement of Suleiman's time, most of the domes and minarets of Istanbul dating from then. Works ordered by the Sultan include mosques for his father, Roxelana, Mehmed, Jahangir, Mihrimah, and himself; the aqueducts at Mecca and Istanbul; and a tomb for the Ottoman-favored Islamic legalist Abu Hanifa.

Further Reading

Full-length biographical studies of the Sultan are Roger B. Merriman, *Suleiman the Magnificent* (1944), and Harold Lamb, *Suleiman the Magnificent, Sultan of the East* (1951). An early but exhaustive examination of 16th-century Osmanli administration appears in Albert H. Lybyer, *The Government of the Ottoman Empire in the Time of Suleiman the Magnificent* (1913; repr. 1966). □

Lucius Cornelius Sulla I

The Roman general and dictator Lucius Cornelius Sulla (138-78 B.C.) was the first man to use the army to establish a personal autocracy at Rome.

Sulla first came into prominence when he served as quaestor (107-106 B.C.) under Gaius Marius in the wars against the Numidian rebel Jugurtha. Sulla raised important cavalry forces for Marius and was responsible for the capture of Jugurtha. He also participated in the defeat of the German tribe, the Cimbri, by Marius and Catullus in 101 B.C. Sulla was praetor in 97 B.C. and had a command in Cilicia in Asia Minor.

In the wars against Rome's allies (the Social Wars) Sulla continued his military successes with several victories over the Samnites (89 B.C.). Elected consul for 88 B.C., he was selected to campaign against Mithridates, the king of Pontus who was threatening Rome's position in the East. However, no sooner had he departed from Rome than the popular tribune and supporter of Marius, P. Sulpicius Rufus, as part of a general program directed against the senatorial oligarchy, had Sulla's command revoked. Sulla marched on Rome with his troops, evicted Sulpicius and the Marians, reestablished a caretaker government, and departed for the East.

Sulla defeated the army of Mithridates in Greece and besieged and sacked Athens, which had been supporting the cause of Mithridates. Meanwhile, events in Rome had turned against him. Marius, supported by the consul Cinna, returned to power and massacred the followers of Sulla. Sulla was declared an outlaw, and a replacement was sent to take over his army. Sulla made a hurried peace with Mithridates, extracted all he could from Asia, and in 83 B.C. landed at Brindisi. A number of young adventurers flocked to him, including Pompey and M. Licinius Crassus. Sulla marched on Rome and by 82 B.C., having defeated the Marians and their Samnite allies, was in command at the capital.

Sulla was determined to ruthlessly eliminate both communities and individuals who had opposed him. Etruria and Samnium suffered tremendously. At Rome 40 senators and 1,600 knights (equites-members of the financial class) were executed. Sulla settled his veterans in colonies scattered at key points around Italy.

Dictatorship and Reform

In Rome, Sulla based his political power in the revival of the old Roman office of dictator and then proceeded to reform Roman law to ensure the power of the senatorial oligarchy. The tribunate, which had been the focus of popular agitation against the Senate, was stripped of most political power by a prohibition against its introducing legislation and the office holders' being made ineligible for other offices (thus removing the most ambitious from trying for the office).

The Senate, which had been depleted by war and proscription, was filled with men selected by Sulla. The power of the Senate was increased by turning over to it the control of the law courts. To prevent the too rapid rise of popular young men, Sulla rigidly established the age and order at which magistracies could be held.

Sulla did not limit himself to political reform. He started a number of building projects, including a new public-records office, and rebuilt temples. In this construction activity to enhance his image, as in his political reforms, he set the pattern for later potentates, like Pompey and Caesar, and for the Roman emperors.

In 79 B.C. Sulla felt that his aims of establishing Senate control had been accomplished, so he retired. Even though popular leaders like Lepidus began agitating almost immediately against Sulla's constitution, the old dictator did not leave retirement in Campania, where he died the following year. His use of the army to seize the state and his term as dictator provided an example for Julius Caesar.

Further Reading

The ancient biography of Sulla written by Plutarch is useful. Sulla's career is recounted in detail in Howard Hayes Scullard, *From the Gracchi to Nero: A History of Rome from 133 B.C. to A.D. 68* (1959; 2d ed. 1963), and Stewart Perowne, *Death of the Roman Republic: From 146 B.C. to the Birth of the Roman Empire* (1969). Also useful for understanding Sulla's career are the article by E. Baddian in Robin Seager, ed., *The Crisis of the Roman Republic: Studies in Political and Social History* (1969), and David Stockton, *Cicero: A Political Biography* (1971).

Additional Sources

Keaveney, Arthur, *Sulla, the last republican,* London: Croom Helm, 1982.

Vives, Juan Luis, *Declamationes Sullanae,* Leiden; New York: E.J. Brill, 1989. □

church music, including such old-time favorite hymns as "Lead, Kindly Light," "Rock of Ages," and "Onward, Christian Soldiers," many songs, incidental music to plays, a few tidbits for piano, a violoncello concerto (1886), an *Irish Symphony* (1866), six overtures, two ballets, several large choral works commissioned for festival performance, and one grand opera, *Ivanhoe* (1891).

What keeps Sullivan's name alive are his operettas. The list begins with *Cox and Box* (1867) and ends with *The Rose of Persia* (1899). In between are 19 others, 14 with texts by Sir William Gilbert, of which the most successful are *Trial by Jury* (1875), *H. M. S. Pinafore* (1878), *The Pirates of Penzance* (1879), *Patience* (1881), *Iolanthe* (1882), *The Mikado* (1885), *The Yeoman of the Guard* (1888), and *The Gondoliers* (1889). Similar to the French *opéra comique* and the German Singspiel in their mixture of song and spoken dialogue, these works offer a brisk, light-handed satire on social customs of the time. Musically, they are memorable not only for earcatching tunes but for the clever variations on poetic meters that Sullivan brought to his settings of the verses. No composer since Henry Purcell had treated the English language so skillfully. Sullivan's orchestrations, too, are models of their kind, disposing a small pit orchestra to support the singers firmly yet lightly and with many subtle touches of instrumental color.

Further Reading

A detailed analysis of Sullivan's musical style is in Gervase Hughes, *The Music of Arthur Sullivan* (1960). Sullivan's place in the history of the operetta is defined in Gervase Hughes, *Composers of Operetta* (1962). Frank Howes, *The English Musical Renaissance* (1966), shows Sullivan as one of the targets for the 20th-century reaction against Victorian music.

Additional Sources

Baily, Leslie, *Gilbert and Sullivan, their lives and times*, Harmondsworth, Eng.; New York: Penguin Books, 1979, 1973.

Findon, Benjamin William, *Sir Arthur Sullivan, his life and music*, New York: AMS Press, 1976.

Jacobs, Arthur, *Arthur Sullivan: a Victorian musician*, Aldershot, England: Scolar Press; Brookfield, Vt.: Ashgate Pub. Co., 1992.

James, Alan, *Gilbert & Sullivan*, London; New York: Omnibus Press, 1989.

Lawrence, Arthur, *Sir Arthur Sullivan: life story, letters, and reminiscences*, New York: Da Capo Press, 1980.

Wolfson, John, *Sullivan and the Scott Russells: a Victorian love affair told through the letters of Rachel and Louise Scott Russell to Arthur Sullivan, 1864-1870*, Chichester: Packard, 1984. □

Sir Arthur Seymour Sullivan

The English composer Sir Arthur Seymour Sullivan (1842-1900) collaborated with the librettist Sir William Gilbert to produce operettas that are the finest examples of light, satirical comedy in the English musical theater.

Arthur Sullivan had a thorough schooling in music, beginning early with instruction from his father, who was then bandmaster at the Royal Military College in London. His studies continued at the Chapel Royal, where he was enrolled as a chorister at the age of 12, then at the Royal Academy of Music, and at the Leipzig Conservatory (1858-1861). It was a musical education in the conservative German mode of the time, which was as strongly entrenched in England as in Germany itself.

Sullivan then entered on a career marked by versatility and enormous popular success. At first he earned his way as an organist. Later he turned to conducting and held a variety of posts, notably as conductor of the Philharmonic Society of London (1885-1887) and of the Leeds Festival (1880-1899). He also taught composition at the Royal Academy of Music and was the first director of the Royal College of Music.

All the while Sullivan kept at his primary vocation of composing. His first published piece was an anthem written when he was 13. Thereafter he composed a quantity of

Harry Stack Sullivan

The American psychiatrist Harry Stack Sullivan (1892-1949) based his approach to mental illness primarily upon interpersonal theory.

Harry Stack Sullivan, born on Feb. 21, 1892, in the farming community of Norwich, N.Y., was the only surviving child of a poor Irish farmer. His childhood was apparently a lonely one, his friends and playmates consisting largely of the farm animals. His mother, who was sickly, was unhappy with the family's poor situation, and is reported to have shown her son little affection. These personal experiences seem to have had a marked effect on Sullivan's professional views in later life.

Sullivan took his medical degree in 1917 at the Chicago College of Medicine and Surgery. In 1919 he began working at St. Elizabeth's Hospital in Washington, D.C., with William Alanson White, an early American psychoanalyst. Clinical research at Sheppard and Enoch Pratt Hospital occupied a portion of Sullivan's life, as did an appointment in the University of Maryland's School of Medicine. In 1936 he helped establish the Washington School of Psychiatry. In later life he served as professor and head of the department of psychiatry in Georgetown University Medical School, president of the William Alanson White Psychiatric Foundation, editor of *Psychiatry,* and chairman of the Council of Fellows of the Washington School of Psychiatry.

Sullivan's approach to psychiatry emphasized the social factors which contribute to the development of personality. He differed from Sigmund Freud in viewing the significance of the early parent-child relationship as being not primarily sexual but, rather, as an early quest for security by the child. It is here that one can see Sullivan's own

childhood experiences determining the direction of his professional thought.

Characteristic of Sullivan's work was his attempt to integrate multiple disciplines and ideas borrowed from those disciplines. His interests ranged from evolution to communication, from learning to social organization. He emphasized interpersonal relations. He objected to studying mental illness in people isolated from society. Personality characteristics were, he felt, determined by the relationship between each individual and the people in his environment. He avoided thinking of personality as a unique, individual, fixed unchanging entity and preferred to define it as a manifestation of the interaction between people.

On Jan. 14, 1949, while returning from a meeting of the executive board of the World Federation for Mental Health, Sullivan died in Paris. He was buried in Arlington National Cemetery.

Further Reading

Two quite different works relating to Sullivan's contributions to psychiatric thought and to his place in its history are Patrick Mullahy, ed., *The Contributions of Harry Stack Sullivan: A Symposium on Interpersonal Theory in Psychiatry and Social Science* (1952), and Martin Birnbach, *Neo-Freudian Social Philosophy* (1961). Sullivan and his work are discussed in Henri F. Ellenberger, *The Discovery of the Unconscious: The History and Evolution of Dynamic Psychiatry* (1970).

Additional Sources

Chapman, A. H. (Arthur Harry), *Harry Stack Sullivan: his life and his work,* New York: Putnam, 1976.

Chatelaine, Kenneth L., *Good me, bad me, not me: Harry Stack Sullivan: an introduction to his thought,* Dubuque, Ia.: Kendall/Hunt Pub. Co., 1992.

Chatelaine, Kenneth L., *Harry Stack Sullivan, the formative years,* Washington, DC: University Press of America, 1981.

Perry, Helen Swick, *Psychiatrist of America, the life of Harry Stack Sullivan,* Cambridge, Mass.: Belknap Press, 1982. □

John Lawrence Sullivan

John Lawrence Sullivan (1858-1918), American boxer, who claimed he could "lick any man on earth," was the last bare-knuckles heavyweight champion.

John L. Sullivan was born in Roxbury, Mass., on Oct. 15, 1858. His father was a pugnacious hod carrier, 5 feet 3 inches tall and weighing 125 pounds. His mother stood 5 feet 10 inches tall and weighed 180 pounds. John inherited his father's temperament and his mother's physique. Though his mother wanted John to become a priest, he left school in his middle teens and spent over a year as an apprentice tinsmith. He then joined his father "in the masonry trade," while earning extra money as a talented baseball player. He always insisted he could have been a professional in that sport.

In 1877 Sullivan had his first important boxing encounter at Boston's Dudley Street Opera House. Accepting Tom Scannel's challenge to fight anyone present, Sullivan knocked Scannel off the stage in the first round. Two years later Sullivan was champion of Massachusetts and seeking to develop a national reputation that would provide him a chance at the American title. Because boxing matches were illegal in most cities, various ruses were employed to circumvent the law. When Sullivan was arrested in Cincinnati after having knocked out a challenger, he was found innocent on the grounds that he had participated in a foot race which his opponent lost.

Called the Boston Strong Boy, Sullivan met Patty Ryan, the titleholder, in Mississippi City, Miss., in 1882; Ryan lasted through nine knockdowns before giving up. Now known as the Great John L., he became the most popular and flamboyant champion in boxing history. He fought under the London Prize Ring rules with bare knuckles, defending his title innumerable times, notably against Charlie Mitchell in Europe; Herbert Slade, the Maori Giant; and, in 1889, Jake Kilrain in the last fight under the London rules. Henceforth, under the Marquis of Queensberry rules, all fighters wore gloves and fought 3-minute rounds instead of "coming to scratch" after each knockdown.

Sullivan was not a giant: just 5 feet 10 inches tall and about 190 pounds. His skill consisted in "hitting as straight and almost as rapidly as light" and in overwhelming his opponent. This technique made him vulnerable to the scientific fighter, who could manage to stay away and rest every 3 minutes under the new rules. In 1892, after 21 rounds, Sullivan, soft and wasted from drinking and an undisciplined life that left no time for training, was defeated by James J. Corbett.

Wisely, Sullivan never staged a comeback but sustained his popularity on the vaudeville stage and, after reforming in 1905, as a temperance lecturer. He died in Abingdon, Mass., on Feb. 2, 1918.

Further Reading

Sullivan's own *Life and Reminiscences of a 19th Century Gladiator* (1892) is rare and almost certainly ghost written. Donald Barr Chidsey, *John the Great* (1942), is an excellent portrait placing Sullivan in the panorama of his time, as does Nat Fleischer, *John L. Sullivan: Champion of Champions* (1952). For a good short history see Fleischer's *The Heavyweight Championship* (1949; rev. ed. 1961).

Additional Sources

Isenberg, Michael T., *John L. Sullivan and his America,* Urbana: University of Illinois Press, 1988. □

Leon Howard Sullivan

As pastor of the Zion Baptist Church in Philadelphia, much of the ministry of Leon H. Sullivan (born 1922) was directed toward improving employment prospects of African Americans. This led to his founding the Opportunities Industrialization Center (O.I.C.) in 1964 in order to impart employment skills to inner city youths.

American civil rights leader Reverend Leon H. Sullivan's revelation to *Fortune* magazine that he was undertaking "a bold new venture" to assist the continent of Africa during the 1990s was no startling proposal from this pastor, who has been a life-long social activist. Sullivan, who early in his career accepted the ministry of Zion Baptist Church, which was located In a poor section of north Philadelphia, pioneered the protest concept of economic boycott of stores and companies that do not employ blacks. He created the job-training agency Opportunities Industrialization Center of America Inc., which spawned 75 similar centers throughout the country and trained nearly two million people.

Long an advocate of black entrepreneurship, Sullivan led the members of his church to form Zion Investment Associates, Inc., which in turn developed Progress Aerospace Enterprises, Inc., a company that manufactured aerospace parts and actively created jobs for the unemployed. But he is most famous, perhaps, for devising the Sullivan Principles, a business code by which companies worldwide operating in South Africa enacted equal treatment of black

workers—prior to sanctions imposed by the United States in 1987. Upon his retirement from Zion Baptist Church, Sullivan told *Fortune* that he would shift his focus to the needs of Africa since his "work at the [Zion Baptist] church is done. We finally paid off the mortgage."

Born October 16, 1922, in Charleston, West Virginia, Sullivan's parents were divorced when he was a child. Growing up in the alleys of a poor neighborhood, he demonstrated unusual intellectual and athletic gifts. During his childhood and adolescence, he avidly pursued religion and sports. At 17, Sullivan became an ordained Baptist minister. After earning an athletic scholarship to play football and basketball, he entered West Virginia State University. When Sullivan lost his scholarship following a knee injury, he worked evenings in a steel mill in order to continue his studies. Furthering his education in New York City, Sullivan obtained a degree in theology from Union Theological Seminary and a degree in sociology from Columbia University during the mid-1940s. Upon graduation, he served as an assistant to Adam Clayton Powell, pastor of the Abyssinia Baptist Church in New York's Harlem and later congressman from the State of New York. Sullivan served his initial pastorate at First Baptist Church in South Orange, New Jersey, and was voted president of the South Orange Council of Churches.

Early Works Close to Home

Sullivan became the pastor of the Zion Baptist Church in 1950. The Philadelphia neighborhood surrounding the church was overrun with juvenile crime, so Sullivan insti-

tuted youth programs to counter the rampant adolescent delinquency and gang warfare. In 1955, as a result of his efforts, he was named an "outstanding young man" by the U.S. Junior Chamber of Commerce. That year he was also chosen as one of ten outstanding young men in the United States by the same organization.

In the late 1950s Sullivan observed that unemployment was a major cause of crime in his area. In response, Sullivan organized an economic boycott that opened 3,000 jobs to blacks in Philadelphia in 1961. Job training programs followed the opening of Opportunities Industrialization Centers in 1964. In 1962 Sullivan organized his church congregation into shareholders of a company he helped them form, Zion Investment Associates, Inc. Progress Aerospace Enterprises, Inc., founded in 1968, was one of several economic-improvement projects Sullivan formed after the establishment of Zion Investment Associates. Many organizations and companies, including the Ford Foundation and General Electric Corporation, have contributed funds to Sullivan's enterprises.

Sullivan devised his now well-known principles of fair business practices in 1977. And though the Sullivan Principles were widely implemented, discrimination against black employees working in South Africa for American companies continued to consume him. Disillusioned over the disregard of his Principles there, he urged the U.S. government to institute sanctions against South Africa in the late 1980s, which would pressure that country's government—in which the black majority at that time had no voice—to revise its racist employment practices.

Retired to Pursue Global Concerns

In 1982 Sullivan established the Phoenix-based International Foundation for Education and Self-Help, through which he examined methods of achieving social and political equity for blacks around the world. He envisioned a series of conferences where African and African-American leaders, working in unison, would take steps toward African self-reliance. In 1988, after 38 years at his pulpit—his congregation having grown from 500 to 6,000—Sullivan retired to Phoenix, Arizona. Though he continued to preach occasionally at Zion, he focused most of his energies on more global concerns.

One of these was his organization of the first African and African-American Summit, which in April of 1991 addressed the lack of black American involvement in African affairs. Sullivan told Kenneth B. Noble in the *New York Times,* "Psychologically, we've been brainwashed to believe that Africa was the dark continent, a place of crocodiles, trees and Tarzan," and as such, not worthy of mutual discourse.

African/African-American Summit

At the African and African-American Summit at Abidjan, Ivory Coast, Sullivan predicted that Africa was the economic future of the world. His plan to realize that projection included debt relief for African nations as well as aid from American blacks for the development of education, food production, and industrialization. Of his design to generate hundreds of African support committees similar to the Peace Corps, Sullivan disclosed to *New York Times* contributor Noble, "I envision the best and the brightest professionals giving a year . . . to work with Africa."

Sullivan remains undaunted by obstacles to the future of his African ministry. "The economic progress we've seen in Asia in recent years is also possible in Africa," Sullivan told Carolene Langie in *Black Enterprise.* "If in just 40 years, Asians and others can build factories, electronic devices and automobiles, with the proper tools, Africans can do the same."

Further Reading

Black Enterprise, October 1988; April 1991.
Fortune, July 9, 1984; July 6, 1987; August 1, 1988.
Jet, January 28, 1991; July 29, 1991; December 9, 1991.
New Republic, November 14, 1988.
New York Times, April 18, 1991.
Time, November 3, 1986; June 15, 1987. □

Louis Henri Sullivan

Louis Henri Sullivan (1856-1924), American architect, was the link between Henry Hobson Richardson and Frank Lloyd Wright in the development of modern American architecture.

Louis Sullivan was born in Boston on Sept. 3, 1856. Always impatient with classroom education, he spent only a year at the Massachusetts Institute of Technology, where he studied with William Ware, the well-known High Victorian Gothic architect. At the end of 1873, Sullivan went to Philadelphia and spent a short time in the office of architect Frank Furness. He soon set out for Chicago, where his parents and brother were living. In Chicago he was employed by William Le Baron Jenney. In 1874 he went to Paris and was admitted to the École des Beaux-Arts. He stayed about 6 months, returning to Chicago in March 1875. His training had introduced him to High Victorian Gothic, an extension of which had been boldly and imaginatively expressed in American architecture by Furness.

Sullivan's early work in Chicago suggests a continuation of modified High Victorian Gothic developments, especially the Rothschild Store (1880-1881) and the Ryerson Building (1884). Many of Chicago's buildings of the 1870s reflected High Victorian Gothic, particularly after the completion of Richardson's impressive and trendsetting American Merchants' Union Express Company Building (1872). In 1881 Sullivan formed a partnership with Dankmar Adler, and the firm contributed to the sprawling, burgeoning city of Chicago some of its finest buildings.

Partnership with Adler, 1881-1895

Adler's earlier architectural contributions date from the mid-1860s, when he entered into partnership with Ashley Kinney. From 1871 to 1879 he associated with Edward Burling, and in 1879 he opened his own firm, D. Adler and Co. During these years Adler's designs developed from structures ornamented with classical or Italianate detailing to a more utilitarian style. Sullivan met Adler in 1879, joined Adler's firm in 1880, and became a partner the following year. In their collaboration Sullivan provided the designs while Adler provided the clients and solved the engineering and acoustical problems.

One of their most brilliant efforts was the Auditorium Building in Chicago (1886-1889). Sullivan's designs for this complex structure—which combined theater, hotel, and office building—passed through three stages: first, a block with pitched roof and squat towers; second, a raised tower with a pyramidal cap; and third, a massive, unornamented block with a tower rising seven stories above the larger structure. The third design was influenced by Richardson's Marshall Field Wholesale Store in Chicago (1885-1887). The acoustical perfection of the theater, which Frank Lloyd Wright described as "the greatest room for music and opera in the world bar none," was only part of Adler's contribution. Since the building was being constructed on a moving bed of mud, with basements 7 feet below the water level of Lake Michigan, Adler paid particular attention to the foundation design. By using artificial loading, he prevented uneven subsidence between the tower, which weighed 15,000 tons, and the lighter and lower remainder of the block.

The Auditorium Building was the showplace of Chicago until the Great Depression, when it lay idle and only the exorbitant cost of demolition prevented it from being razed. Roosevelt University moved into the building in 1947, and an Auditorium Theater Council was established to restore the theater. On Oct. 31, 1967, after the theater had been closed for a quarter century, the New York City Ballet performed for an audience that was as enthusiastic about the architecture as they were about the ballet.

The Schiller Building in Chicago (1891-1892; demolished), a 17-story, towerlike structure with nine-story wings by Adler and Sullivan, also housed a theater. Because the theater was relatively narrow, cantilever construction was employed, providing a total space uninterrupted by intermediate columns.

Adler and Sullivan's practice expanded outside Chicago in the 1890s. Sullivan designed two of his most famous skyscrapers—the Wainwright Building in St. Louis, Mo. (1890-1891), and the Guaranty Building in Buffalo, N. Y. (1894-1895). In these buildings, as on the Getty Tomb in Chicago (1890) and the Wainwright Tomb in St. Louis (1892), Sullivan's ornamentation, which had become an integral part of his designs, developed from the geometric to the naturalistic. So organic is the work on the Guaranty Building that the foliage appears to be sprouting from the terra-cotta facing. The most famous example of Sullivan's ornamentation was on the Transportation Building (1893) for the World's Columbian Exposition, held in 1893 in Chicago. Amid a series of classical structures, Sullivan's building stood for rational architecture, and its "Golden Door," a brightly decorated, massive arch, was the exposition's most unique motif.

The Adler and Sullivan partnership dissolved in 1895, when Adler wanted to introduce his two sons into the firm. Sullivan rejected Adler's overtures to restablish their partnership the following year.

Sullivan's Architecture, 1895-1924

Sullivan's last big commercial building was the Schlesinger and Meyer Department Store (now the Carson Pirie Scott and Company Building) in Chicago (1899-1904). It has an abundance of cast-iron Art Nouveau decoration, especially around the entrances in the curved corner pavilion. His last years were mainly spent designing a series of small but architecturally outstanding banks for towns of the midwest.

Carl Bennett, vice president of the National Farmers' Bank at Owatonna, Minn., had been impressed by an article in a trade journal written by Sullivan in 1906 entitled "What is Architecture: A Study of the American People of Today." Bennett commissioned him to design new premises for his bank (1907-1908). In this bank Sullivan produced what has been considered one of his major works. Other similar commissions came from bankers at Newark, Ohio (1914), Algona and Grinnell, Iowa (both 1914), Sidney, Ohio (1917), and Columbus, Wis. (1919).

Sullivan's last commission was for the Krause Music Store in Chicago (1922). He died on April 14, 1924, in Chicago.

Writings and Philosophy

Sullivan's writings incorporate philosophy, music, and biological evolutionary theories. Frank Lloyd Wright in his *Autobiography* says of Sullivan, "He adored [Walt] Whitman as I did, and explain it as you can was deep in Herbert Spencer. Spencer's *Synthetic Philosophy* he gave me to take home to read. . . ." Sullivan's philosophy was expounded in the autobiographical *Kindergarten Chats* (1901-1902), reprinted from the *Interstate Architect and Builder,* and in his *The Autobiography of an Idea* (1926). In these two books Sullivan's hero is the architect with a "poetic imagination . . . broad sympathy, human character, common sense and a thoroughly disciplined mind . . . a perfect technique and . . . a gracious gift of expression." His unpublished manuscript of 1905, "Natural Thinking: A Study in Democracy," upheld the meaning and dignity of the individual man. "It is my profound conviction that every infant born in what is generally called normal health, is gifted by Nature with normal receptivity . . . too much importance is attached to heredity and too little to environment. . . . In a human and democratic philosophy there is no room for such a thing as an unfit human being."

Frank Lloyd Wright, who worked for Adler and Sullivan from 1887 to 1893, had called Sullivan *lieber Meister.* The historian Henry Steele Commager described Sullivan as "the most philosophical of American architects . . . a disciple of Walt Whitman . . . [who] sought to make architecture a vehicle for democracy as Whitman had made for poetry."

Further Reading

Although not definitive, Hugh Morrison, *Louis Sullivan: Prophet of Modern Architecture* (1935), is the best and most comprehensive study. Sherman Paul, *Louis Sullivan: An Architect in American Thought* (1962), analyzes Sullivan's writings and philosophy and contains a complete Sullivan bibliography of 37 works. Other studies include Charles H. Caffin, *Louis H. Sullivan: Artist among Architects* (1899); Chicago Art Institute, *Louis Sullivan: The Architecture of Free Enterprise,* edited by Edgar Kaufmann, Jr. (1956); John Szarkowski, *The Idea of Louis Sullivan* (1956); Albert Bush-Brown, *Louis Sullivan* (1960); and Willard Connely, *Louis Sullivan as He Lived* (1960). See also Frank Lloyd Wright, *Genius and the Mobocracy* (1949), and Hugh D. Duncan, *Culture and Democracy* (1965).

Additional Sources

Twombly, Robert C., *Louis Sullivan: his life and work,* Chicago: University of Chicago Press, 1987, 1986. □

Arthur Ochs Sulzberger

Arthur Ochs Sulzberger (born 1926), long-time publisher of the *New York Times,* was involved in the transformation of this newspaper from a New York City enterprise into one of broad national influence.

Arthur Ochs Sulzberger was born February 5, 1926, in the city of New York. He was the son of Arthur Hays Sulzberger, chairman of the board of the New York Times Company, and of Iphigene Bertha, née Ochs, through whom he was a descendant of Adolph Ochs, the founder of the *New York Times.* He was the youngest of four children and was affectionately called "Punch" by family and friends, having arrived after his sister Judy. His preparatory education took place in several schools because he suffered from hereditary dyslexia. He finally earned a diploma from the Loomis School in Windsor, Connecticut.

When only 17, in 1944 he joined the United States Marine Corps. The war in the Pacific was still raging, and as a corporal he was stationed first at Lehu and then at Luzon in the Philippines. His duties were those of a naval intercept radio operator. Shortly before the Japanese surrender he was attached to the staff of General Douglas MacArthur, the supreme commander of Allied Forces in the Southwest Pacific, and accompanied the general to Japan for the surrender. He told his mother about his experiences in the corps: "Before I entered the Marines I was a lazy good-for-nothing; the Marines woke me up."

His war experiences did not end with World War II. When in 1951 the North Koreans, under Communist rule, invaded the non-Communist territory of South Korea, the United Nations came to the aid of South Korea and Sulzberger was called back into the Marine Corps. He had just graduated with a Bachelor of Arts degree from Columbia University. Commissioned a second lieutenant, he was sent to Korea as an officer in the First Marine Division at

Panmunjom, where he remained until a truce ended active combat and redrew the line dividing north and south. By the time his service came to an end in 1953 he had risen to the rank of captain, a rank that he held in the Marine Corps Reserve until 1963, the date of his resignation.

The year 1963 was an extremely important one in his life. Since his resumption of civilian status ten years earlier he had become a reporter for the *New York Times,* owned by his family. To broaden his experience he briefly joined the *Milwaukee Journal* as a cub reporter and served also at its news desk until he returned to the *New York Times* in 1954. He worked at the foreign news desk for three months and was subsequently sent to the London, Paris, and Rome offices of the *Times* as a correspondent. This was a brief experience, however, and in 1955 he returned to New York to become assistant to the publisher and in 1958 the assistant treasurer of the New York Times Company. Arthur Sulzberger had turned from news gathering to administration and financial responsibilities. This was evident in 1963 when he succeeded his brother-in-law, Orvil E. Dryfoos, who had just died of a heart attack, as president of the company. Although he was only 37 years old, his parents chose him over others because his forthright personality invited communication with the editors who helped make policy. He was now the publisher of the *Times,* and he became fully in charge after his father's death in December 1968.

As heir to a family business—one that subsequently became a public corporation—he assumed responsibility for management and sat as one of three trustees who collectively oversaw the interests of the company and of the stock holders and who supported the several editors in their policies to preserve the paper's traditions of objective reporting and freedom of editorial policy. Beginning in the late 1960s, however, the several great newspapers of New York City faced serious financial problems. As more and more readers moved from the city to the suburbs, the retail merchants who advertised in the *Times* moved out with them and took their advertising to smaller suburban papers. Both readership and advertising fell off. The suburban press enjoyed lower costs of production. In order to compete the major city papers sought to reduce their work forces and to introduce more efficient printing technology. This led to a city-wide strike of the work force in 1978. Some of the weaker journals went out of business; others, like the *Times,* survived and carried out policies to increase productivity. The *Times* remained one of the great newspapers of the world into the 1990s, also available on the World Wide Web at http://www.nytimes.com.

The New York Times Company, with Arthur Sulzberger at its head, also owned dozens of other enterprises, including 17 trade and consumer magazines, 32 regional newspapers, three publishing companies, five television stations and the Interstate Broadcasting Company, which is a wholly-owned subsidiary operating a 17-station network in the Northeast. In 1992, the company started up its new facility in Edison, New Jersey. That same year, Sulzberger turned over his publishing responsibilities to his son, Arthur, Jr., but remained active as the company's chairman and chief executive officer. During Sulzberger's tenure as publisher, *Times* associates had won a total of 31 Pulitzer Prizes.

Apart from his business activities, Sulzberger was a public-minded citizen who was directly involved in civic activities. At Columbia University, his alma mater, he was the senior trustee and one of two remaining life trustees in 1985. He served on the board of the Metropolitan Museum of Art and was also a visiting trustee for the Department of Arms and Armor, for which he served as fund raiser. He was chairman of the board of the Fresh Air Fund, an organization devoted to sending underprivileged children to the country during the summer to enjoy the fun of camping. This organization was "under the wing" of the *New York Times,* which gave it editorial support. At various times Sulzberger was also active as director or board member of the American Arbitration Association, the New York Convention and Visitors Bureau, the Greater New York Safety Council, the Greater New York Council of the Boy Scouts, the New York University Center for Safety Education, and the New York World's Fair of 1964-1965. He received an honorary LL.D. degree from Dartmouth College in 1964. In connection with his journalism he belonged to the New York City Newspaper Reporter Association, the Overseas Press Club, and Sigma Delta Chi, the newspapermen's fraternity.

In his private life Sulzberger was married twice, first on July 2, 1948, to Barbara Grant. They had two children: Arthur Ochs, Jr., and Karen Alden. After his divorce in 1956 he married Carol Furman, née Fox, former wife of Seymour Furman. He formally adopted her daughter by the previous marriage, Cathy Jean, and in 1964 they produced another daughter, Cynthia. Sulzberger was a member of Temple Emanu-El in New York City. One of his hobbies was golf, and he belonged to the Century Country Club of White Plains, New York. However, his favorite hobby was fishing. To him, nothing was more exciting and fun than a few days on a salmon river.

Further Reading

There are no books on Arthur O. Sulzberger. There is pertinent information in the memoirs of his mother, *Iphigene: Memoirs of Iphigene Ochs Sulzberger* (1979). Useful data about the *New York Times* and the Times Company can be found in Martin Walker, *Powers of the Press* (1982), and Anthony Smith, *Goodbye Gutenberg, the Newspaper Revolution of the 1980's* (1980).

For more recent profiles of Sulzberger and his family, see Joseph Nocera's article, *Family Plot* in *GQ: Gentlemens Quarterly* (1994). □

Charles Sumner

American senator Charles Sumner (1811-1874), an uncompromising opponent of slavery, worked to arouse the nation against it. He was a staunch supporter of African American rights legislation and stringent Reconstruction in the South.

harles Sumner was born on Jan. 6, 1811, in Boston, Mass. His father was a lawyer and, briefly, a sheriff. Sumner attended the Boston Latin School and graduated from Harvard University in 1830. He obtained a law degree in 1833 from the Harvard Law School, where he was greatly influenced by the legal scholar Joseph Story. Although a brilliant student of the law and a frequent contributor to legal journals, Sumner disliked the routine of actual practice, preferring the life of Boston's intellectual community.

Through his Boston friends, particularly Samuel Gridley Howe and William Ellery Channing, Sumner became involved in the humanitarian reform movements currently blossoming in New England, especially movements to improve education and prisons and for universal peace and the abolition of slavery. The reformers were influenced by evangelical Protestantism as well as by secular commitments to change. They believed that mankind's progress was inevitable if men lived by true and inflexible moral principles and worked assiduously, without hesitation or considerations of expediency, to destroy corrupting influences still present in society. Sumner shared their ideals and became noted for his particularly inflexible principles and idealistic oratory against the evils of war.

Antislavery Politics

Sumner had always viewed slavery as one of the basic moral evils in the United States. When the annexation of Texas revealed to him the unscrupulous greed and expansionism of the slaveholders, he joined the Conscience Whig

faction in its efforts to challenge slavery by political means. The Massachusetts Whig party was controlled by the Cotton Whigs, who opposed antislavery agitation as divisive and pointless; many Conscience Whigs left their party, therefore, to form the Free Soil party in 1848. Sumner unsuccessfully ran for Congress as a Free Soiler that year. In 1851 when the Free Soilers gained the balance of power in the Massachusetts Legislature, they joined with the Democrats to elect Sumner to the Senate.

Sumner arrived in Congress at an inopportune moment for an antislavery agitator, for both parties had accepted the Compromise of 1850 as the final solution of the slavery question. As a representative of a party that was fast losing support, Sumner seemed headed for political oblivion. But the Kansas-Nebraska Act in 1854 reintroduced slavery into politics, and slavery and other issues soon led to the formation of the Republican party, committed to halt further expansion of slavery. Sumner quickly became a leading Republican. In the renewed debates over slavery the uncompromising absolutism of his sppeeches brought much attention. Ignoring the fact that his views were more radical than those of most Republicans, Southerners used his speeches to demonstrate to their constituents the fanaticism of the new party and its violent hostility to Southern interests.

In 1856 Sumner delivered his "Crime against Kansas" speech, vehemently attacking the introduction of slavery into that territory and bitterly assailing three involved Democratic leaders, Senators Stephen A. Douglas, Andrew Pickens Butler, and James Murray Mason. Two days later, at his Senate desk Sumner was beaten unconscious with a cane by Butler's nephew, Representative Preston Brooks of South Carolina. The brutal assault helped fire up Northern opinion against the South as few other things had, especially since many Southerners praised Brooks's action. Sumner was unable to return to the Senate for almost 4 years because of persistent problems with his injuries. His empty chair became a noted symbol of Southern viciousness against their opponents.

Civil War

Returning to the Senate on the eve of the 1860 election, Sumner renewed his assaults on the South. His inflexibility worried and alienated conservative Republicans and kept Sumner out of key party policy-making positions. He opposed any compromise with slavery in the secession crisis of 1860-1861. On the outbreak of war he became a vigorous advocate of a strong military policy to force the South into submission. He also was among the first to accept the war's revolutionary potential, calling for military emancipation, the use of black troops, and all measures promising equal rights for African Americans, including suffrage. Fearing the consequences if the South was restored to power before the rights of emancipated slaves had been guaranteed, Sumner argued that the Southern states, by seceding, had deprived themselves of their status under the Constitution. Before they could reenter the Union, therefore, Congress must restore and ensure their "republican form of government," in which Sumner wanted political rights for freedmen included.

Sumner was also active in foreign affairs during the war. As chairman of the Senate Committee on Foreign Relations, he strove to maintain friendly relations with Europe, which were vital to Northern success. Realizing that European intervention would immeasurably aid the South, he helped kill offensive resolutions directed against France and England.

Reconstruction Period

After the war Sumner led in opposing President Andrew Johnson's conservative Reconstruction policies. He supported the various Radical Republican legislative proposals: establishment of the Freedmen's Bureau, the 14th Amendment, and the various civil rights and Reconstruction acts, although he thought most of them overly conservative. Sumner wanted more extensive aid to the freedmen, land distribution to ensure economic survival, and free schools, for example; but the nationwide antipathy toward African Americans, and Republican fears of a white political backlash, ultimately prevented such radical action. Sumner himself was denied a seat on the potent Joint Committee on Reconstruction, where less intransigent members were favored.

Sumner enthusiastically supported Johnson's impeachment in 1868 but was no happier under President Ulysses S. Grant. He strongly opposed Grant's pet project for annexing Santo Domingo in 1870. He also opposed administration plans for settling, on moderate terms, disputes with England stemming from the Civil War. In retaliation, he was deprived of his Foreign Relations Committee chairmanship by the administration. From then on Sumner carried on a fierce war against the administration. "No wild bull," Secretary of State Hamilton Fish wrote of Sumner in 1871, "ever dashed more violently at a red rag than he goes at anything that he thinks the President is interested in."

Sumner joined the Liberal Republicans in 1872 in order to continue his opposition to Grant. Unlike many of the Republicans in the movement, however, he did not give up his interest in the Southern freedmen. At the time of his death of a heart attack in Washington on March 11, 1874, he was trying to secure the passage of a civil rights bill. (It passed the following year.) With his death passed much of the idealism of Radical Reconstruction.

Further Reading

Sumner's *Works* (15 vols., 1870-1883) contains what he considered to be his most important writings. Edward L. Pierce, *Memoir and Letters of Charles Sumner* (4 vols., 1877-1893), is a sympathetic biography by a friend. An excellent biography in two volumes is by David Donald: volume 1: *Charles Sumner and the Coming of the Civil War* (1960), was awarded the Pulitzer Prize for biography in 1961; and volume 2: *Charles Sumner and the Rights of Man* (1970), deals with the remainder of Sumner's life. □

William Graham Sumner

The American sociologist and educator William Graham Sumner (1840-1910) was one of the earliest proponents of sociology in the United States and was especially notable for his advocacy of the evolutionary viewpoints of Herbert Spencer in academic and public circles.

William Graham Sumner was born on Oct. 30, 1840, in Paterson, N. J. His parents were both of English ancestry and of modest social background. The family moved to Connecticut, where Sumner attended the public schools and Yale College. After graduation, he studied ancient languages and history at Göttingen (1864) and theology and philosophy at Oxford (1866). The following year he was appointed tutor at Yale and then was ordained in the Protestant Episcopal Church. In 1869 he left Yale to be rector of churches in New York City and Morristown, N. J. In 1872 he became the first professor of political and social science at Yale—a position he long held.

Sumner had been greatly influenced by Herbert Spencer's essays on the structure of human society, and he used them as the basis for the first course in sociology ever given in a university in the United States (1875). As his teaching evolved, he planned a massive treatise on a comparative institutional analysis of societies, but he interrupted this task to produce the work that gave him worldwide renown—*Folkways* (1907). *Folkways* was notable in several respects. It contributed terms that have become widely used—such as folkways, mores, the wegroup, and ethnocentrism. In addition, Sumner established the notion of different degrees of social pressure for conformity in his analyses of folkways, mores, and institutions. A crucial and fundamental idea in this book was the observation that social life is mainly concerned with creating, sustaining, and changing values. But Sumner insisted that the values in folkways and mores are inherently nonrational and yet powerful in influencing thought and behavior. Consequently, he regarded conflict and struggle as inseparable components of human society in any age. "Nothing but might has ever made right . . . nothing but might makes right now" is a much cited and fairly representative statement of Sumner's approach to the essentials of society.

Sumner brought a forceful and undeviating conservatism to numerous discussions, though he was one of the earliest defenders of academic freedom while at Yale. He was a tireless exponent of laissez-faire (which he defined as "mind your own business") and a sharp critic of the imperialism of the United States. Many articles emphasized the validity of economic rather than political considerations. A favorite theme was the futility of trying to obtain "progress" by governmental policy. Perhaps the most persistent argument by Sumner concerned the plight of the "forgotten man," the middle class taxed against its will for programs designed to serve other groups.

On April 12, 1910, Sumner died in Englewood, N.J. His disciple, A. G. Keller, prepared Sumner's long, unfinished manuscript for publication in four volumes as *The Science of Society* (1927). In subsequent years many of Sumner's articles were collected in book form.

Further Reading

Short biographical studies of Sumner are Harris E. Starr, *William Graham Sumner* (1925), and Maurice R. Davie, *William Graham Sumner* (1963). See also Harry Elmer Barnes, ed., *An Introduction to the History of Sociology* (1948), and Robert G. McCloskey, *American Conservatism in the Age of Enterprise* (1951).

Additional Sources

Curtis, Bruce, *William Graham Sumner,* Boston: Twayne, 1981.
□

William Ashley Sunday

The fame of American evangelist William Ashley Sunday (1862-1935) rests on his reputation as an immensely popular revivalist preacher. His fiery platform style differed dramatically from the dignified manner of his predecessors.

illy Sunday was born in Ames, Iowa, on Nov. 18, 1862. His father, a Civil War soldier, died a month later. Poverty, hard work, and orphans' homes all figured in Sunday's early life. By the age of 14 he was on his own, drifting from job to job, even serving as janitor in a high school so that he could attend classes. While clerking in Marshalltown, Iowa, Sunday began to play baseball on the local team; this led ultimately to his employment with the Chicago White Sox (1883) and later the Pittsburgh and Philadelphia teams. During these years Sunday married and embraced Christianity. Before his departure from baseball in 1891, he was widely known as a Christian ballplayer in a game not then noted for the high moral character of all its participants.

Sunday next worked for the Young Men's Christian Association in Chicago, later assisted the well-known evangelist J. Wilbur Chapman, and in 1896 embarked on his own ministerial career. He was licensed to preach in 1898 and ordained by the Chicago Presbytery in 1903. Combining musical spectacle with harsh rebukes to sinners and backsliders, Sunday rapidly became famous as he induced tens of thousands to "hit the sawdust trail" (walk down the sawdust-strewn aisles of his tabernacle, publicly declaring themselves for Christ). He especially captivated his audiences with his baseball allusions, such as throwing an imaginary baseball at the congregation while exhorting them to "put it over the plate for Jesus."

Fundamentalist in outlook, Sunday viewed Sabbath-breaking and alcohol as the gravest social problems besetting modern society. Among his other achievements, he was significant in bringing about prohibition. The peak of his career came between 1910 and 1920 as he staged massive rallies in cities across the nation, spread his message in such works as *Burning Truths from Billy's Bat* (1914) and *Great Love Stories of the Bible and Their Lessons for Today* (1917), and reportedly amassed a fortune.

Less idolized in the 1920s, he lived out his declining years in Winona Lake, Ind. On Nov. 6, 1935, he died of a heart attack. He had stirred the religious enthusiasm of thousands of Americans and had buttressed the conservative religious and social attitudes of many fundamentalists.

Further Reading

William C. McLoughlin, *Billy Sunday Was His Real Name* (1955), is the most scholarly and dispassionate biography. Others include Lee Thomas, *The Billy Sunday Story* (1961). A contemporary account is William T. Ellis, *Billy Sunday: The Man and His Message, with His Own Words* (1914). Also revealing is the work of one of Sunday's associates and an heir to his evangelistic tradition, Homer Alvan Rodeheaver, *Twenty Years with Billy Sunday* (1936).

Additional Sources

Bruns, Roger, *Preacher: Billy Sunday and big-time American evangelism,* New York: W.W. Norton, 1992.
Dorsett, Lyle W., *Billy Sunday and the redemption of urban America,* Grand Rapids, Mich.: W.B. Eerdmans Pub. Co., 1991. □

Sundiata Keita

Sundiata Keita (ca. 1210-ca. 1260) was the founder of the Mali empire in West Africa. He is now regarded as a great magician-king and the national hero of the Malinke-speaking people.

undiata, or Sun Djata, was also known in the *Tarikhs* (Moslem chronicles) as Mari Djata. Keita is a widely used family name. He is to West African history what King Arthur is to English history, in that both are popular figures about whom very little is known with certainty. Most knowledge about both has come to us orally from traditions passed down through the centuries. Moslem chroniclers wrote very little about Sundiata because he was not a devout Moslem. Much of what was written can be regarded with some skepticism because it is very difficult to separate fact from legend in such old oral traditions. We can, however, be sure that he was a real historical personage.

Sundiata was the son of Maghan Kon Fatta, ruler of the small Malinke kingdom of Kangaba, situated on the Niger River a short distance to the southwest of Bamako, the capital of modern Mali. Sundiata was handicapped from birth, and his life story follows the universal theme of a culture hero's overcoming of extreme adversity to attain greatness.

About 1224 the Susu people to the north conquered Kangaba in a wave of expansion under their magician-king,

Sumanguru Kante. There are several different traditions concerning Sundiata's experiences at this time. According to a contemporary version, he and his mother went into voluntary exile from Kangaba about 1220 to avoid the risk of assassination by his jealous half brother, Kankaran Tuman, who had become king about 1218. Kankaran then meekly submitted to Susu rule, and later Sundiata was recalled by his people to free them from this foreign tyranny.

A version written into the *Tarikh al-Sudan* in the 16th century has Sumanguru Kante first conquering Sundiata's father and then killing 11 of the King's 12 sons, sparing only the handicapped Sundiata. Sundiata then went into exile, later to return as a liberator.

In either case, about 1230 Sundiata put together a rabble force in the far north and slowly advanced to the south, increasing his troop strength with successive victories over Susu provinces. By 1234 he was ready to take on the main Susu army, which he met and defeated in the epic battle of Kirina northeast of Kangaba. This victory is clearly the major event in his life, and it marks the beginning of the Mali empire. Before he retired from active leadership of his armies about 1240, Sundiata and his generals expanded the new empire in all directions, even incorporating the formerly great Ghana empire and the previously unconquered gold fields of the Senegal River valley.

We know that Sundiata ruled for about 25 years, but little is known about his later life. He died about 1260, apparently the victim of an accident in his capital.

Further Reading

An exciting and colorful full-length account of Sundiata's life in English is D. T. Niane, *Sundiata: An Epic of Old Mali* (1965). Otherwise, there is almost no literature dealing mainly with Sundiata. Several general works that touch on him and his times are A. Adu Boahen, *Topics in West African History* (1966), and Basil Davidson, *A History of West Africa to the Nineteenth Century* (rev. ed. 1967; 1965 edition entitled *The Growth of African Civilisation*). □

Sung T'ai-tsu

Sung T'ai-tsu (927-976) was a Chinese emperor and the founder of the Sung dynasty, one of the great Chinese dynasties and a major period of transition in Chinese history.

In 755 the T'ang dynasty was dealt a stunning blow when An Lu-shan, a frontier general in command of a great army on the northeastern border of China, turned his forces against the dynasty. The rebel armies swept over the rich and heavily-populated North China Plain (modern Hopei, Honan, and Shantung provinces) and captured both T'ang capitals, Lo-yang and Ch'ang-an. The rebellion was finally quelled in 763, but its impact on the social and political fabric of China was felt long afterward. The old aristocracy of North China had fled before the rebel armies, abandoning their lands—the basis of their personal power.

A great part of the territory previously controlled by this regional aristocracy and by the T'ang central government came under the control of hardened military men, many of them former generals of An Lu-shan who continued to occupy conquered territory. The loyalty of these newly risen soldiers was doubtful at best. The T'ang still held their capital of Ch'ang-an in northwest China and tried gradually to reextend their power over the northeast. They had some successes but were never really able to reestablish a firm hold over that part of their former empire.

The court itself was filled with corruption, and imperial power fell into the hands of eunuchs. After the rebellion of Huang Ch'ao, China was even further militarized and politically fragmented. The once powerful T'ang dynasty existed in name only until its extinction in 907. The fall of the T'ang was followed by a period of political division known as the Five Dynasties (907-960), named for the five successive and short-lived regimes which ruled in North China during this period; in this same half century, South China was divided into a number of small states.

The ancestors of Sung T'ai-tsu ("Great Ancestor of the Sung," a formal posthumous name for Chao K'uang-yin) lived in the chaotic age just described and served as officials in northeast China, the area hardest hit by the An Lu-shan rebellion and the region of greatest political and social instability. Chao K'uang-yin, who grew up during this troubled time, was the man who finally brought the era to an end.

Early Life

Chao K'uang-yin was born in Chia-ma-ying, a military camp near Lo-yang, 20 years after the fall of the T'ang dynasty. His father, Chao Hung-yin, was a man of exceptional military ability who had attracted the attention of the Emperor of the Later T'ang dynasty (923-937) and had become a commander of the Emperor's private guard. He must have been an adroit and tenacious man, for he held this same trusted and privileged position under the rulers of several of the short-lived dynasties which followed the Later T'ang.

Chao K'uang-yin was the second son of Chao Hung-yin. He grew up in Lo-yang, which was the capital of the Later Chin (937-947), the second dynasty his father served. His father, who wanted to provide him with the kind of background which would qualify him later to hold civil office, hired a tutor to train the boy in the classical curriculum. But Chao had little taste for such studies. One story has it that when Chao and his fellow students left school at the end of the day, they would take crude weapons and play-act at fighting. They walked home in military formation, with Chao K'uang-yin playing the commander, and travelers on the road would have to step aside and let them pass. Another story indicates Chao's determination to make himself into a fighting man. Once, when he was still a boy, he decided to try to ride a fierce and untrained horse. The wild horse jumped onto a ramp of the city wall, bucked, and threw his young rider. The onlookers thought Chao was badly hurt, but the boy slowly picked himself up, caught the horse, and undaunted, climbed back on.

When he was 21 years old, Chao K'uang-yin made the decision to leave his family and set off on his own. His father was still commander of the palace troops, at that time under the Emperor of the Later Han dynasty (947-951), and it probably seemed that he would never have enough power to help his son get more than a minor military post. So Chao left his family, looking for a position under one of the numerous regimes in power elsewhere in China. For several years he traveled, first to the far northwest, then toward the south, but he had no success and his situation became desperate. Finally, it is said, he met a Buddhist monk who somehow recognized that he was an extraordinary man, gave him money, and told him to go back north, where he would surely find success.

Career as a Soldier

Chao did return to North China, which was then in an extremely chaotic state, rife with danger and with opportunity. In the year he returned, 950, the ruling dynasty had to confront attacks in northeast China from one of China's foreign enemies, the Khitan. The Emperor sent one of his generals, Kuo Wei, to fight the Khitan. Chao K'uang-yin, returning north just at this time, responded to Kuo's call for support and joined his army.

After a brief campaign against the Khitan, Kuo turned his forces against the Emperor and soon overthrew the dynasty, replacing it in 951 with his own dynasty, the Later Chou. Chao K'uang-yin had distinguished himself in the fighting and was given an officer's position in the new emperor's private guard. Two years later, when he was about to be sent to a post some distance from the capital, Chao attracted the attention of the heir apparent, and, when the heir apparent became emperor the following year, Chao K'uang-yin was appointed commander of the palace army. Fighting continued throughout the 950s, and Chao was in much of it. He became increasingly powerful as he gained the loyalty of the troops under his personal command.

The second emperor of the Later Chou died in 959 and was succeeded by his 7-year-old son. In such difficult and unstable times, in which one regime followed another with great rapidity, there was little chance that the authority of this boy-emperor would be respected. In 959, two of the dynasty's enemies, the Khitan and a small state in the northeast called Northern Han, made an alliance against the Later Chou. Chao K'uang-yin was sent with an army to deal with this threat, but, like Kuo Wei before him, he soon turned his army against his own dynasty. It is said that it was only upon the urging of his own troops that he took this step. To those living at the time, this probably seemed no more than one more futile effort to establish peace and unity out of the prevailing chaos. But peace and unity were achieved, and the dynasty Chao K'uang-yin brought to power endured for more than 3 centuries.

Career as Emperor

The dynasty Chao K'uang-yin established was called the Sung, named, as was usual in China, after the personal fief held by the ruling family before they came to power. His capital was the great commercial city of K'ai-feng, which had become the economic hub of North China and eastern capital for several of the minor military regimes which followed the T'ang, but which only now became the principal capital of a major dynasty. Chao K'uang-yin reigned as emperor from 960 to 976. During those years the last areas outside central control were brought firmly within the imperial sway; Chao personally led several of the major campaigns of pacification. More importantly, in those early years of the dynasty the basic institutions—military, financial, legal—necessary for the administration of a great empire took shape.

During the Sung dynasty fundamental changes occurred in many aspects of Chinese life. Economically, China became increasingly urbanized, trade prospered, and the population grew rapidly, especially after the introduction in 1012 of a strain of early-ripening rice, which made possible two or three rice crops in a year. Culturally there were important developments in all of the arts, particularly in poetry, painting, and popular literature, the last greatly stimulated by the widespread use of printing and the rapid increase in literacy which date from Sung times. A change with the greatest social and political consequences was the great broadening of the group from which officials were selected: the old entrenched aristocracy, already quite literally on the run in the days when Chao K'uang-yin's ancestors were officials of the T'ang, was completely eclipsed, and it was succeeded by a new elite and a significantly strengthened monarchy.

The new elite was chosen by merit. Aspirants were required to go through a lengthy and exhaustive education which required a thorough exposure to the traditionalistic, conservative, and rigidly interpreted set of personal, social, and political norms embedded in the classical curriculum. It is a historical irony that the dynasty which established as the ruling elite of China a class of thoroughly educated, profoundly conservative, and austerely moralistic scholar-officials, a group typically hostile toward military men and their values, was established by a slightly educated army officer named Chao K'uang-yin, known to history as Sung T'ai-tsu.

Further Reading

There is very little information about Sung T'ai-tsu in English. A valuable but very detailed study of the complex events of the early 10th century in China is Wang Gungwu, *The Structure of Power in North China during the Five Dynasties* (1963). For a fine general account of the early Sung government the reader should consult E. A. Kracke, Jr., *Civil Service in Early Sung China, 960-1067* (1953). □

Sun Yat-sen

Sun Yat-sen (1866-1925) was the preeminent leader of China's republican revolution. He did much to inspire and organize the movement that overthrew the Manchu dynasty in 1911 and through the

Kuomintang party paved the way for the eventual reunification of the country.

Sun Yat-sen was born on Nov. 12, 1866, into a peasant household in Choyhung in Kwangtung near the Portuguese colony of Macao. His early education, like his birthplace, established him as a man of two worlds, China and the West. After a rudimentary training in the Chinese classics in his village school, he was sent to Hawaii in 1879 to join his émigré elder brother. There he enrolled at an Anglican college where he studied Western science and religion. Upon graduation in 1882, he returned to his native village, but he soon was banished for defacing the village idols.

Though he returned home briefly to undergo an arranged marriage, Sun spent the formative years of his late teens and early 20s studying in Hong Kong. He began his medical training in Canton but in 1887 returned to Hong Kong and enrolled in the school of medicine attached to Alice Memorial Hospital under Dr. James Cantlie, dean of the school. After graduation in June 1892, he went to Macao, where Portuguese authorities refused to give him a license to practice.

By the time Sun returned to Hong Kong in the spring of 1893, he had become more interested in politics than in medicine. Appalled by the Manchu government's corruption, inefficiency, and inability to defend China against foreign aggressors, he wrote a letter to Li Hung Chang, one of

China's most important reform leaders, advocating a program of reform. Ignored, Sun returned to Hawaii to organize the Hsing-chung hui (Revive China Society). When the Sino-Japanese War appeared to present possibilities for the overthrow of the Manchus, Sun returned to Hong Kong and reorganized the Hsing-chung hui as a revolutionary secret society. An uprising was planned in Canton in 1895 but was discovered, and several of Sun's comrades were executed. Having become a marked man, Sun fled and found refuge in Japan.

Peripatetic Revolutionist

The pattern for Sun's career was established: hastily organized plots, failures, execution of co-conspirators, overseas wanderings in search of sanctuary and financial backing for further coups. Sun grew a moustache, donned Western-style clothes, and, posing as a Japanese, set out once again, first to hawaii, then to San Francisco, and finally to England to visit Cantlie. There he was kidnaped by the Chinese legation and held captive pending deportation back to China. Rescued at the last minute through the efforts of Cantlie, he emerged from captivity with an international reputation enhanced by his own account of the event, *Kidnapped in London* (1897). Before leaving England, he frequented the reading room of the British Museum, where he became acquainted with the writings of Karl Marx and of the American single-tax advocate Henry George.

In July 1897 Sun returned to Japan, where he adopted the pseudonym Nakayama (Chinese, Chung-shan). He also attracted the support of prominent Japanese Sinophiles, liberals, and adventurers who hoped that Japan, by promoting political change in China, could build an Asian bloc against the West. On the other hand, Sun failed to consummate an alliance with the followers of the radical monarchial loyalist K'ang Yu-wei, who also found asylum in Japan after the failure of his Hundred Days Reform. After the failure of the Waichow uprising in October 1900, Sun spent 3 years in Yokohama, establishing a relationship with the growing number of Chinese students who flocked to Japan for a modern education. From 1903 to 1905 he renewed his travels, recruiting adherents among overseas Chinese in Southeast Asia, Hawaii, the United States, and Europe.

Sun returned to Japan in July 1905 to find the Chinese student community stirred to a pitch of patriotic excitement. In league with other revolutionary refugees such as Huang Hsing and Sung Chiao-jen, Sun organized, and was elected director of, the T'ung-meng hui (Revolutionary Alliance). Though based upon a merger of the Hsing-chung hui and other existing organizations, the T'ung-meng hui was a centralized body, meticulously organized, with a sophisticated and highly educated membership core drawn from all over China.

By this time Sun's ideas had crystallized into the "Three People's Principles"—nationalism, democracy, and people's livelihood. These became the ideological basis for the T'ung-meng hui. When Sun returned from another fundraising trip in the fall of 1906, his student following in Japan numbered in the thousands. However, under pressure from Peking, the Japanese government expelled him. From

March 1907 to March 1908 Sun staged several uprisings from Hanoi, where the sympathetic French had given him a base, but once again Manchu pressure prevailed, and he was compelled to flee to Singapore.

Sun's fortunes had reached a low point. The failure of a series of poorly planned and armed coups relying upon the scattered forces of secret societies and rebel bands had undermined the prestige of the T'ung-meng hui in Southeast Asia, and in August 1908 Japanese authorities banned the highly successful party organ, the *Min Pao*. Receiving scant encouragement upon revisiting Europe, Sun found that Chinese opinion in the United States was turning against his promonarchial rivals. After a triumphal tour through New York, Chicago, and San Francisco, he returned to Japan via Honolulu. Ten days later he was expelled once again. He went on to Singapore, then to Penang, from which he was ousted for an inflammatory speech. Sun returned to the United States and was en route from Denver to Kansas City on a successful fundraising tour when he read in a newspaper that a successful revolt had occurred in the central Yangtze Valley city of Wuchang.

President of the Chinese Republic

The revolution had occurred in Sun's absence. The instigators were low-ranking army officers in units sympathetic to the T'ung-meng hui. Sun continued to travel eastward across the Atlantic and through Europe to solicit diplomatic and financial support for the revolutionary regime. By the time he arrived back in China on Christmas Day, rebellion had spread through the Yangtze Valley. A tumultuous welcome greeted Sun, and in Nanking, revolutionary delegates from 14 provinces elected him president of a provisional government. On Jan. 1, 1912, Sun Yat-sen proclaimed the establishment of the Republic of China.

However, the revolutionists lacked the power to dethrone the Manchu ruler in Peking. Only Yüan Shih-kai, strongman of North China, could accomplish this. Sun, therefore, agreed to relinquish the presidency in exchange for the abdication of the Manchus and Yüan's acceptance of a republican form of government. Yüan gave his assent and was duly elected by the National Assembly in Nanking and inaugurated in Peking on March 12. Yüan thereupon maneuvered the provisional government into moving to Peking instead of transferring the capital to Nanking. Sung Chiao-jen, parliamentary leader of the T'ung-meng hui, attempted to check Yüan's power through the National Assembly. He brought leaders of the T'ung-meng hui and four smaller parties into a federated organization called the Kuomintang (National People's party). Sun Yat-sen, however, having little taste for such parliamentary maneuvers, set about to promote his program of people's livelihood. As newly appointed director of railroad development, he spent the autumn and winter of 1912 touring the rail lines of China and Japan and developing grandiose plans for the future.

Meanwhile a bitter power struggle was under way in Peking. In the national elections of February 1913, the Kuomintang won control of the Assembly. On March 20, Yüan's agents assassinated Sung Chiao-jen at the Shanghai railroad station. Sun hurried back and demanded that

the culprits be brought to justice. Yüan, backed by a "reorganization loan" from a foreign consortium, took political and military steps against the Kuomintang. This precipitated scattered but ineffectual resistance, the so-called second revolution. Sun denounced Yüan; Yüan removed Sun from office and on September 15 ordered his arrest. By early December, Sun was once again a political refugee in Japan.

Preparations for a Comeback

Sun now began to work for the overthrow of Yüan. On June 23, 1914, he replaced the Kuomintang with a new party, the Chung-hua ko-ming tang (China Revolutionary party), based upon a personal oath of allegiance to himself. However, Yüan was undone by his own miscalculations rather than by Sun's plots. His attempt to replace the republic with a monarchy touched off revolts in southwestern China followed by uprisings of Sun's followers in several other provinces. Sun hopefully returned to Shanghai in April 1916, 2 months before Yüan's death.

The disintegration of centralized authority opened the gates to warlordism. Power first fell into the hands of Tuan Ch'i-jui, who dissolved the Parliament and convened his own provisional assembly in its place. Sun responded by forming a military government in Canton in league with naval chief Ch'en Pi-kuang, Kwangtung warlord Ch'en Chiung-ming, and other southern military leaders. A rump parliament was convened. However, failing to secure independent military power, Sun was forced to withdraw from the Canton government in May 1918. This need to rely upon warlord support continued to plague him.

Following a fruitless quest for Japanese assistance, Sun established residence in the French concession in Shanghai. There he wrote two of the three treatises later incorporated into his *Chien-kuo fang-lueh* (*Principles of National Reconstruction*). In the first part (*Social Reconstruction*), completed in February 1917, Sun had attributed the failure of democracy in China to the people's lack of practice in its implementation. The second treatise, *Psychological Reconstruction*, argued that popular acceptance of his program had been obstructed by acceptance of the old adage "Knowledge is easy, action is difficult." Sun proposed the transposition of this to read "Knowledge is difficult, action is easy." Once the knowledge, provided by himself, had been made available, the people should have no difficulty putting it into practice. The third part (*Material Reconstruction*) constituted a master plan for the industrialization of China to be financed by lavish investments from abroad.

Sun's preoccupation with literary endeavors did not exclude him from political schemes. Once again he reorganized his party, this time as the Chinese Kuomintang. He also kept a hand in the political intrigues of Canton. When the city was occupied on Oct. 26, 1920, by Ch'en Chiung-ming and other supporters, Sun named Ch'en governor of Kwangtung. Sun returned to Canton in November and laid plans to counter the Peking government with a rival regime that would attract foreign support and serve as a military base for an eventual campaign of national reunification. In

April 1921 the Canton Parliament established a new government and elected Sun president.

Having brought the neighboring province of Kwangsi under control, Sun now took sides in the altercations of the northern warlords by forming an alliance with Chang Tso-lin and Tuan Ch'i-jui against Ts'ao K'un and Wu P'ei-fu and preparing to send troops into Hunan and Kiangsi. However, Ch'en Chiung-ming opposed Sun's grandiose nationwide goals, preferring to wield regional power in a decentralized federation. Sun responded by assuming direct command of his troops in Kweilin, but Ch'en undermined his efforts from Canton. After driving Ch'en from the city, Sun resumed preparation for the northern expedition, but Ch'en recaptured Canton and forced Sun to flee to a gunboat in the Pearl River. There, in the company of a young military aide named Chiang Kai-shek, Sun tried unsuccessfully to engineer a comeback.

Communist Alliance

Never one to be discouraged by failure, Sun returned to Shanghai and continued his plans to retake Canton via alliances with northern warlords and the exertions of his forces in Fukien and Kwangsi. He undertook, moreover, to breathe new life into the faltering Kuomintang and to set in motion a thoroughgoing reorganization of the party. Of equal consequence was Sun's decision to accept support from the Soviet Union, a mark of his disappointment with the Western powers and Japan and his need for political, military, and financial aid. Part of the agreement provided for the admission of individual Chinese Communists into the Kuomintang. On Jan. 26, 1923, in a joint manifesto with Sun, Soviet envoy Adolph Joffe guaranteed Russian support for the reunification of China.

Meanwhile Sun's military allies were paving the way for a return to Canton. By the middle of February 1923 Sun was back again as head of a military government. On October 6 Michael Borodin arrived in Canton, having been sent by the Comintern in response to Sun's request for an adviser on party organization. In January 1924 the first National Congress of the Kuomintang approved a new constitution which remodeled the party along Soviet lines. At the top of a tightly disciplined pyramidal structure was to be a Central Executive Committee with bureaus in charge of propaganda, workers, peasants, youth, women, investigation, and military affairs. Sun's Three People's Principles were restated to emphasize anti-imperialism and the leading role of the party.

One significant departure from the Soviet model was the creation of the position of *Tsung-li* (party director), to which Sun was given a lifetime appointment. The most controversial development was the election of three Chinese Communists to the Central Executive Committee and to leadership in the organization and peasants bureaus. Party conservatives were shocked. To prevent further polarization, Sun placed ultimate authority in his own hands via the establishment of the Central Political Council.

Even the most disciplined party, Sun realized, would be ineffectual without a military arm. To replace the unreliable warlord armies, Sun chose the Soviet model of a party army.

The Soviets agreed to help establish a military academy, and a mission headed by Chiang kai-shek was sent to the U.S.S.R. to secure assistance. The new school was located on Whampoa Island 10 miles downriver from Canton. Sun appointed Chiang commandant, Liao Chung-kai party representative, and other close followers as political instructors.

Final Days in Peking

However, the lure of warlord alliances remained strong. In response to an invitation from Chang Tso-lin and Tuan Ch'i-jui, Sun set out for Peking to deliberate upon the future of China. After a journey via Shanghai, Japan, and Tientsin, Sun and his party reached Peking at the end of December 1924. However, negotiations with Tuan Ch'i-jui soon collapsed. This proved to be the last time that Sun would be disappointed by his allies. Following several months of deteriorating health, he found that he had incurable cancer.

Sun passed his final days at the home of Wellington Koo. There he signed the pithy "political testament" drafted by Wang Ching-wei, urging his followers to hold true to his ideals in carrying the revolution through to victory. He also signed a highly controversial valedictory to the Soviet Union reconsecrating the alliance against Western imperialism. The following day, March 12, 1925, Sun died. He was given a state funeral under orders of Tuan Ch'i-jui.

Sun's Legacy

Though the guiding spirit of the Chinese revolution, Sun was widely criticized during his lifetime. His involvement in warlord politics combined with frequent pronunciamentos heralding new ventures had won him the derisive epithet of "Big Gun Sun." After his death, however, he became the object of a cult that elevated him to a sacrosanct position. His title of *Tsung-li* was enshrined, never to be used by another leader (although Chiang Kai-shek came close in 1938, when he dubbed himself *Tsung-tsai,* or party leader).

During the years of Kuomintang rule (1928-1949), Sun's face looked out from portraits in homes and government offices and appeared on bank notes. His name, Chung-shan, was attached to every variety of public place. His writings became a national bible. This was anything but an unmixed blessing, since Sun was neither a systematic ideologist nor a practical political planner. His Three People's Principles had undergone many changes over the years. The target of his "nationalism" had changed from the Manchus to the imperialist powers. His "people's livelihood" had been loosely identified with socialism and with communism. His "democracy" had been hedged about by more and more qualifications, including the requirement of a period of party tutelage before it could become effective. His manuscripts, left behind when he fled from Ch'en Chiung-ming in 1922, were destroyed by fire. The published work that we know as the *Three People's Principles,* or *Three Principles of the People,* was transcribed from lectures delivered between January and August 1924. In practice, this provided neither a viable program for national construction nor a viable alternative to the more rigorous Marxist ideologies.

Sun Yat-sen has also been honored by the Chinese Communists, who stress the last period of his life and speak of his "Three Great Policies" of relying upon the Soviet Union, the Chinese Communists, and the working and peasant masses. The radical interpretation of Sun was carried forth by his widow, Soong Ch'ing-ling, who fearlessly accused Chiang Kai-shek of subverting her husband's teachings and, after 1949, was a prominent figure in the Communist government. His son, Sun Fo, though often at odds with the Kuomintang leadership, pursued a career in Nationalist politics and held a succession of administrative posts in the Nationalist government.

Further Reading

Sun Yat-Sen's *Three Principles of the People* is available in many Western-language editions; *San min chu-i: Three Principles of the People* (1964) contains a biographical sketch of Sun. The second and third parts of Sun's *Chien-kuo fang-lueh* (*Principles of National Reconstruction*) are translated respectively in his *Memoirs of a Chinese Revolutionary* (1927) and in his *The International Development of China* (1922).

The standard biography of Sun is Lyon Sharman, *Sun Yat-sen: His Life and Its Meaning* (1934). This is superseded in part by Harold Z. Schiffrin, *Sun Yat-sen and the Origins of the Chinese Revolution* (1968), which carries Sun's story to the founding of the T'ung-meng hui in 1905. Sun's Three Principles are elucidated in Paul M. A. Linebarger, *The Political Doctrines of Sun Yat-sen: An Exposition of the San Min Chu I* (1937). His political and ideological relationship with the Russian and Chinese Communists is examined in Shao Chuan Leng and Norman D. Palmer, *Sun Yat-sen and Communism* (1960). Sun's early career is placed in perspective in Mary Calbaugh Wright, ed., *China in Revolution: The First Phase, 1900-1913* (1968), which contains an essay on Sun by Harold Z. Schiffrin. Also useful for understanding Sun in the context of his times is Michael Gasster, *Chinese Intellectuals and the Revolution of 1911* (1969). Additional perspective can be gained from the biographies of two contemporaries: Jerome Ch'ên, *Yüan Shih-kai, 1859-1916* (1961), and Chün-tu Hsüeh, *Huang Hsing and the Chinese Revolution* (1961). □

Su Shih

Su Shih (1037-1101), also known as Su Tung-p'o, was a Chinese author and artist. He was the most versatile genius in the history of Chinese literature. He excelled in every form of verse and prose he attempted and further distinguished himself as a calligrapher and painter.

Su Shih was born in Meishan, in present-day Szechwan, to a most remarkable family of rather obscure origins. His father, Su Hsün (1009-1066), and younger brother, Su Ch'e (1039-1112), also attained literary fame, and all three are listed among the eight prose masters of T'ang and Sung. The Su brothers studied under the personal guidance of their father and mother, an educated woman and devout Buddhist. In 1056, accompanied by their father, the brothers went to the capital, Kaifeng, to take the civil service examination, and the next year they both earned the *Chin-shih* degree with high honors.

The chief examiner, Ou-yang Hsiu, highly impressed by the literary talent of the three Sus, took them under his wing and spread their fame in the capital. However, upon the death of their mother in the same year, the brothers left with their father for Szechwan to observe the customary mourning period, and it was not until 1060 that they journeyed back to the capital to receive official appointments. In 1066 Su Hsün died, and the brothers returned home for the last time to observe the mourning period.

Official Career

Su Shih served the government from 1061 until the year of his death in a series of capital and provincial posts. One had to be a high-ranking minister to be in a position to achieve deeds of statesmanship, but, unfortunately, during his official career Su Shih stood in opposition to the powerful Wang An-shih and his "New Laws" party and served in the capital only during the brief periods when the New Laws party was out of favor.

Though his memorials to the throne regarding the policies of the New Laws party show his responsible statesmanship in the Confucian fashion, Su never played a leading role in national politics as did his great fellow writers Ou-yang Hsiu, Wang An-shih, and the historian Ssu-ma Kuang. After each brief stay in the capital Su would be maligned and exiled to local posts. However, as a humane and capable magistrate, he was much loved by the people of every district or prefecture where he served.

After serving in a series of provincial posts from 1071 to 1079, Su was arrested on charges of slandering the Emperor, imprisoned in the capital, and then banished to Huang-chou in a minor official capacity. In 1085, following the death of Emperor Shen-tsung, the New Laws party temporarily lost power, and Su was recalled to court, serving in the Imperial Hanlin Academy and filling other high offices. After he had contracted enmity with his blunt criticism, he repeatedly requested a provincial post. In 1089 he was appointed prefect of Hangchow, where he built a dike on the West Lake which is still named after him.

Su was back at court in 1091, and for the next 3 years he served alternately at the capital and as prefect of important cities. When the New Laws party returned to power in 1094, Su was banished to Hui-chou in Kwangtung and then ordered further south to Hainan Island off the coast of Kwangtung. Now in his 60s, Su bore his existence there cheerfully, partly because of his faith in Buddhism and partly because of his strong, irrepressible sense of humor, which inclined him to take things philosophically. With the accession of Emperor Hui-tsung in 1100, he was pardoned and restored to favor. The next year he died at Ch'ang-chou.

Literary Achievement

As a writer Su's achievement is so manifold that only a brief description of his contributions can be attempted here. He is one of the greatest prose writers in the "Ancient style," equally adept in governmental criticism, reassessment of historical personages, and personal essays descriptive of his excursions. Like Ou-yang Hsiu, Su is a master of the lyrical *fu*. His two *fu* on the Red Cliff are a perennial delight to Chinese readers. He is the greatest poet in the *shih* style of the Sung period, at once descriptive and philosophic, combining an effortless use of metaphor and conceit with an expression of self that has imbibed the best in Confucianism, Buddhism, and Taoism.

Su was a great innovator in *tz'u* poetry. He and his follower in the Southern Sung dynasty, Hsin Ch'i-chi, rank as the two greatest *tz'u* poets in the heroic mode. Until Su's time, the *tz'u* had retained its connections with the kind of popular song sung by courtesans, and most *tz'u* poets wrote about sentimental and mildly erotic themes suggestive of the feminine voice. Su turned the *tz'u* into a man's song, capable of philosophic meditation on events of the past. But he also wrote some of the best love poems in the *tz'u* style.

From all his writings one gathers the impression of Su as a most lovable person, affectionate, humorous, and capable of philosophic detachment. A great number of his *shih* poems were addressed to his younger brother, Su Ch'e, showing his great attachment to him. Su Shih wrote a most touching *tz'u* poem in memory of his first wife, who died at the age of 26. He had a second wife and a concubine named Chao-yün, whom he loved dearly. Upon her death in 1096, he wrote some of his most moving poems to her memory.

One of the four great calligraphers of the Sung dynasty, Su is also famous for his paintings of bamboo. In subsequent times, Chinese men of letters took Su as their model in trying to be scholar, poet, essayist, calligrapher, and painter. The literary style of painting, scorning laborious imitation for the expression of personality through the simple depiction of spare natural objects, may be said to have started with Su Shih.

Further Reading

A good introduction to Su's *shih* and *tz'u* poetry is *Su Tung-p'o: Selections from a Sung Dynasty Poet,* edited and translated by Burton Watson (1965), which also contains a succinct biography of Su. His works in the *fu* style are available, with copious notes, in *The Prose-poetry of Su Tung-p'o,* edited and translated by Cyril Drummond Le Gros Clark (1935; repr. 1964), which contains an excellent foreword by Ch'ien Chung-shu and a useful introduction by the translator. Le Gros Clark also edited and translated *Selections from the Works of Su Tung-p'o* (1931). Kenneth Rexroth, *One Hundred Poems from the Chinese* (1956), contains 25 poems of Su in a free rendering. The standard biography of Su in English is Lin Yutang, *The Gay Genius: The Life and Times of Su Tungpo* (1947), a highly readable book that contains ample information on Sung culture and politics and many extracts from Su's writings; it is written from a point of view characterized by abhorrence of Wang An-shih and his policies. □

Graham Sutherland

Graham Sutherland (1903-1980), the leading painter of the English neoromantic movement, was noted for his imaginative pictures based on landscape and plant forms and for his portraits.

Graham Sutherland was born in London on Aug. 24, 1903. He studied at Goldsmiths' College of Art, London, specializing in engraving, and worked until 1930 as an engraver of landscape subjects in the tradition of Samuel Palmer. In 1935-1936 Sutherland found himself as a painter, partly under the influence of the landscape of Pembrokeshire. This was also the period when surrealism made a big impact in England, and he combined surrealist elements with the romantic landscape tradition. Objects such as the roots of an uprooted tree seen in violent foreshortening were given a mysterious, ominous, monster-like character, the impact being enhanced by strong, unrealistic colors.

During part of World War II Sutherland was an official war artist. He made a series of remarkable paintings of bombed buildings which vividly captured the drama and tragedy of the devastation, as well as studies of iron foundries and coal mines. Most of these works were predominantly black. However, by 1944 he began to use bright colors again in a series of imaginary landscapes, including a very distinctive range of orange, mustard, and pink. Many of these were executed in watercolor and gouache, which he used extensively for his smaller works and studies for oil paintings.

Sutherland's work began to take a new turn when he received a commission in 1944 to paint a Crucifixion for St. Matthew's Church, Northampton, a picture he executed two years later. In this work Christ's body, suspended in torment against a purple background, becomes a powerful image of physical and spiritual suffering. While planning this picture, Sutherland became fascinated by thorn-bushes, whose thorns reminded him of the crucifixion of Christ, and he painted a series of "Thorn Trees" and "Thorn Heads" which paraphrased the crucifixion. This procedure of evoking the presence of a human figure through a kind of substitution became characteristic of a great deal of his subsequent work.

From 1947 Sutherland spent much of his time in the south of France and often painted motifs characteristic of that region, such as vine pergolas and palm palisades. The motifs are usually isolated and set against a strongly colored background in a shallow picture space; they tend to be amalgamations of plant and animal forms, of a definitely organic character.

By 1949 Sutherland had begun to feel the need to narrow the gap between his series of "Standing Forms" and the human figure, and this led him to paint his first portrait, that of the novelist Somerset Maugham (1949), shown seated like an Oriental sage. Some of his other portraits included Edward Sackville-West, Helena Rubinstein, and Lord Clark. When Winston Churchill was in his eighties, Sutherland painted his portrait, which had the look of a befuddled bulldog. Churchill openly reviled the work, and the portrait was destroyed. *ARTnews Magazine* stated, "that act has guaranteed Sutherland a place in any history of art vandalism." Although Sutherland received a number of portrait commissions, the greater part of his output was still based on landscape and plant themes. He also painted a series of animals and of machine forms.

Sutherland's most ambitious work of the 1950s was his design for a vast tapestry, *Christ in Glory in the Tetramorph,* for the new Coventry Cathedral, a project that occupied him from 1952 to 1958 and for which he made a large number of studies.

Sutherland's work slowed considerably during the last 20 years of his life. During the 1960s and 1970s, he continued working, occasionally doing exhibits, but not producing the grand tapestries on the scale of the new Coventry Cathedral. His 1950s style never changed. His outdoors depictions continued to be overcast and gloomy, with eerie trees, nasty expressions, tortured landscapes, and angry plants.

Sutherland's last exhibition occurred in London just a few months before his death. Art critic William Feaver wrote, "although fashion inevitably passed him by, this had no effect on his way of seeing. Style-bound maybe, he did at least have style, a capacity to turn things into his mechanized idiom." Sutherland died on Feb. 17, 1980 in London.

Further Reading

The most comprehensive monograph on Sutherland is Douglas Cooper, *The Work of Graham Sutherland* (1961). Other studies include Edward Sackville-West, *Graham Sutherland* (1943; 2d ed. 1955), and Robert Melville, *Graham Sutherland* (1950). ☐

John Augustus Sutter

John Augustus Sutter (1803-1880), German-born American adventurer and colonizer, is generally regarded as one of the founding fathers of California.

Born in Kandern, Baden, on Feb. 15, 1803, Johann August Sutter (as he spelled the name before he Anglicized it) grew to manhood at Rünenberg, Switzerland. He possibly attended a military academy there, and he served in the army. He married in 1826, but after failing in business he emigrated to the United States in 1834.

Sutter settled at St. Charles, Mo., where he became a trader. Twice he made unsuccessful trading trips to New Mexico. He left Missouri in 1838, one jump ahead of his creditors. From Oregon he sailed to Honolulu and to Alaska, arriving in San Francisco in July 1839. He received a land grant from the Mexican governor of California of approximately 50,000 acres, which he decided to locate at the junction of two rivers in northern California. Employing former mission Native Americans, he cleared land, dug irrigation ditches, planted crops, and erected a fortified post. Soon he was growing wheat, ranching, milling, mining, fur trading, salmon fishing, and shipping. He predicted that California's greatness lay in agriculture and commerce.

Sutter became a Mexican citizen in 1841, and his wife and child joined him at what came to be known as Sutter's Fort. Short, heavy, and bald, except for a fringe of gray hair, he proved a genial, expansive host to Americans arriving in Mexican California. His fort became the focal point of the Bear Flag Revolution, which quickly merged into the Mexican War and ended with California in the hands of the United States. Sutter was a delegate at the constitutional convention of 1849 and a candidate for governor in the first election following statehood.

In January 1848 one of Sutter's employees discovered gold on Sutter's property. This triggered the famous gold rush of 1849, during which Sutter's employees deserted him, his herds disappeared, his fields fell into ruin, and his lands were overrun by squatters searching for gold. He began drinking heavily and by 1852 was bankrupt. Even when the Federal courts upheld his Mexican land grant, he could not afford the court costs to recover it and was left almost penniless. The state of California paid him a pension of $250 per month from 1864 to 1878. He moved to Lititz, Pa., in 1873 but spent his winters in Washington, D.C., pushing a petition in Congress for his relief. He died in Washington on June 18, 1880, still awaiting passage of his bill.

Further Reading

The Diary of Johann August Sutter (1932) contains good autobiographical detail. An early and somewhat derogatory biography is Thomas J. Schoonover, *The Life and Times of Gen. John A. Sutter* (1895), while Julian Dana, *Sutter of California* (1936), is eulogistic. A balanced treatment is Richard Dillon, *Fool's Gold: The Decline and Fall of Captain John Sutter of California* (1967). See also Oscar Lewis, *Sutter's Fort: Gateway to the Gold Fields* (1966).

Additional Sources

Dana, Julian, *Sutter of California; a biography,* Westport, Conn.: Greenwood Press, 1974.

Dillon, Richard H., *Fool's gold: the decline and fall of Captain John Sutter of California,* Santa Cruz: Western Tanager, 1981.

John A. Sutter's last days: the Bidwell letters, Sacramento: Sacramento Book Collectors Club, 1986.

John Sutter and a wider West, Lincoln: University of Nebraska Press, 1994. □

Bertha von Suttner

Austrian writer and activist Bertha von Suttner (1843-1914) became a leading figure in peace activism at the turn of the twentieth century with the publication of her anti-war novel, *Lay Down Your Arms*. She continued her efforts as a public speaker and played a key role in the formation of the first Hague Peace Conference and the Nobel Peace Prize. For her efforts in the peace movement, she received the Nobel Peace Prize in 1905.

Bertha von Suttner was a leading figure in the growing peace movement at the end of the nineteenth century in Europe. Suttner used her literary talents to produce the 1889 political novel *Die Waffen nieder,* or *Lay Down Your Arms;* a call for disarmament, the book became a best-seller and was translated into a number of languages. The activist also promoted world peace by helping to organize the first Hague Peace Conference and encouraging her friend, Alfred Nobel, to create the internationally respected Nobel Peace Prize. Her many activities helped to remove the labels of "utopians" and unrealistic "idealists" from those involved in peace activism by gaining the support of respected world leaders and intellectuals for the movement.

Suttner was born as the Countess Bertha Kinsky on June 9, 1843. An only child, she came from a noble military family of Prague in what was then the Austro-Hungarian Empire. Her father, Count Joseph Kinsky, was a field marshal who died before her birth. Her mother, a relative of the poet Joseph von Korner, was left with a modest income after the death of her husband, and the limited funds were strained even further by her compulsive gambling at the fashionable casinos of Europe. She did find money, however, to provide her daughter with governesses, who instructed her in French and English, as well as singing lessons. As a teenager, Suttner had dreams of becoming an

opera singer, but after a while, she realized that her voice was not adequate for such a career. She instead turned to academics, reading the works of the ancient Greek philosopher Plato and the German scientist Alexander von Humbolt by the time she was 16. She also taught herself Italian. She enjoyed a reputation as a great beauty, and supposedly her hand was sought in marriage by a prince when she was only 13. But she remained fairly isolated, with few companions other than her mother, well into her adult years.

Because of her mother's financial situation, Suttner was finally obliged to seek employment to support herself. At the age of 30 she became a governess in the home of the Baron and Baroness von Suttner. Their 23-year-old son, Arthur, was soon attracted to the older woman, and the two fell in love. Although the young man's sisters were very pleased by the romance, his mother was not. Upon discovering her son's attachment to Suttner, she found a new position for the governess in the distant city of Paris. There Suttner became the secretary and housekeeper for Alfred Nobel, the Swedish scientist who had invented dynamite. Only a week after she arrived in Paris, Nobel left for a trip to Sweden at the request of the king of that country; Suttner was also called out of town. During this time she received a telegram from Arthur von Suttner asking her to marry him. They met in Vienna and were secretly married before departing for a honeymoon in the Caucasus region of Russia.

Estranged from her husband's family, the couple stayed for nine years in the Caucasus, remaining as guests and employees of a friend who was a prince of the region. Suttner served as an instructor in music and languages, while her husband worked as an architect. They both were also welcomed as peers at the prince's social events, where they fraternized with the local aristocracy. Her husband eventually began to write articles that were successfully published in Austrian newspapers. Inspired by his success, Suttner also began to write and was encouraged when she published her first essay under a pseudonym. She soon attempted a longer work, and in 1883 published her first novel, *Inventarium einer Seele,* or *Inventory of a Soul,* which drew notice in literary circles. The couple decided that they would be able to make a living as writers and returned to Austria in May of 1885. There they joined the von Suttner family, who had forgiven them for their marriage.

Suttner continued to produce acclaimed works, including *Daniela Dormes* in 1886 and *Das Maschinenzeitalter: Zukunftsvorlesungen uber unsere Zeit* in 1889. Her books were distinguished by both moral views and an interest in scientific and philosophical ideas. In fact, sensing that the scientific themes of *Das Maschinenzeitalter* would not be taken seriously if published under a woman's name at that time, Suttner released the book under the pseudonym "Jemand," or "anyone." The book did sell well and provided Suttner and her husband with enough money to move to Paris.

In Paris, Suttner was reintroduced to Nobel, who in turn brought her and her husband in contact with members of leading social and intellectual circles. It was shortly after arriving in Paris that the couple learned about the London-based International Peace and Arbitration Society. Suttner was immediately drawn to the goals of the organization and decided to devote all her energies to this cause. She realized that she could use her literary talents to spread the message of peace to many people through a work of fiction and began writing her best-known work, *Lay Down Your Arms.* The anti-war themes of the book were considered controversial by publishers, and many refused to handle it. When it finally was accepted by a publisher, a number of changes were requested to make the work more socially acceptable. Suttner allowed a number of cuts and rewrites to be made to her manuscript, but she refused to change the title. Upon the book's debut in 1892, it exceeded its publisher's expectations by becoming a best-seller. Suttner received generous praise from a number of luminaries, including Russian novelist Leo Tolstoy, who compared the work's influence on the peace movement to the impact of American author Harriet Beecher Stowe's *Uncle Tom's Cabin* on the anti-slavery movement.

The book's success brought Suttner into the forefront of the anti-war movement. She was named president of the Austrian Peace Society and with the journalist Alfred Hermann Fried began a popular monthly journal, entitled *Lay Down Your Arms,* that detailed developments and activities in the peace movement for eight years. She participated in the first Hague Peace Conference, an event that marked a major victory for peace activists. The event was attended by high-ranking officials from countries such as the United States, Britain, and France and gave credibility to the peace efforts that had often been dismissed as unrealistic and naive by critics. Suttner herself was a featured speaker at the conference and was well-received by her admiring audience.

After the death of her husband in 1902, Suttner attempted to overcome her loss by working even harder to spread the message of peace. She continued writing and attended numerous conferences and meetings on the subject. She launched a speaking tour of the United States in 1904, during which she met President Theodore Roosevelt and visited Quaker communities that offered an inspiring example of life devoted to non-violence. She also saw hope for world peace in international developments of the time, such as the British movement to give former colonies Commonwealth status and the changes that seemed likely to follow the death of the aging Austrian emperor. For her efforts to promote the ideals of a peaceful world society, Suttner was awarded the Nobel Peace Prize in 1905.

Suttner died of stomach cancer on June 21, 1914. Only weeks after her death, the assassination of the heir to the Austrian empire launched World War I, an event that no doubt would have brought great sorrow to the advocate of peace. Despite such a turn of events, Suttner's contributions to the peace movement were not in vain. Her writings and organizational efforts led to a number of success in the struggle for peace, particularly by gaining support for non-violent ideals among the general public as well as political and intellectual figures. The Hague Peace Conferences and the Nobel Peace Prize have become annual traditions that sustain the hope of peace to which Suttner devoted her life.

Further Reading

Kemp, Beatrix, *Woman for Peace: The Life of Bertha von Suttner,* translated by R. W. Last, Oswald Wolff, 1972.

Playne, Caroline E., *Bertha von Suttner and the Struggle to Avert the World War,* Allen & Unwin, 1936.

Suttner, Bertha von, *Memoirs of Bertha von Suttner: The Records of an Eventful Life,* Ginn, 1910. □

Aleksandr Vasilievich Suvorov

The Russian general Aleksandr Vasilievich Suvorov (1730-1800) was never defeated in battle. Although he demanded discipline and sacrifice, he understood the needs and feelings of his soldiers better than any other commander of his time.

The descendant of an ancient Russian family of Novgorod, Aleksandr Suvorov was born in Moscow. His grandfather had a great influence in the molding of his moral character. Aleksandr's father paid little attention to the boy's education, and only his natural gifts and insatiable thirst for study prevented him from growing into an uneducated man. He acquired a greater store of knowledge than was usual among young gentlemen of his day. He began to master foreign languages and mathematics, but his first love was the study of military subjects. With characteristic stubbornness and persistence Aleksandr prepared himself for a military career.

Suvorov lived and worked in a feudal society. Catherine the Great's military policy was based chiefly on the interests of the great feudal landowners, whose control of the Russian masses was complete. But Suvorov's most characteristic trait, next to his military skills, was the absence in him of the universal contempt felt by the Russian gentleman-officer for the soldier. He protested against senseless cruelties inflicted upon the population in conquered countries, against the Prussification of the Russian army, and against the social, economic, and political exploitation of the Russian masses. "I have shed rivers of blood," he said, "and this horrifies me, but I love my neighbor; I have brought misfortune to no one. I have never signed a death sentence, I have never crushed a beetle."

Suvorov took part in the Russo-Turkish War of 1768-1774 and helped put down the rebellion of Pugachev in 1775. He was created a count for his victories in the Russo-Turkish War of 1787-1792. In 1794 he crushed Polish resistance by winning the battle of Praga and capturing Warsaw. Perhaps his greatest achievement was in the War of the Second Coalition, one of the French Revolutionary Wars. Leading the Austro-Russian forces, he succeeded in driving the French from northern Italy.

Assessment of His Career

Suvorov's brilliant military skills, his daring disregard of current military theories, and the original methods of waging war peculiar to him seldom found proper appreciation among the military experts of his time. His resolute and independent character did not permit him to engage in court intrigues, thus he could not hope for recognition at home. Abroad, contradictory judgments on Suvorov were the order of the day. Some regarded him as "a general without a science," a mere rough-and-ready bruiser who rushed headlong into battle with an utter disregard of all rules of warfare; others saw him as a sort of wizard who could conjure up victories as if by magic. Karl Clausewitz described him as a "crude, practical soldier." Napoleon I said that "Suvorov had the soul of a great general, but not the headpiece." But Lord Nelson wrote to Suvorov: "I am being overwhelmed with honors, but I was to-day found worthy of the greatest of them all: I was told that I was like you. I am proud that, with so little to my credit, I resemble so a great man."

In the Franco-Russian War of 1812, the disciples of Suvorov used his military strategy for the destruction of the enemy's main power. As a result, Napoleon was forced to retreat with hardly a hundredth of his original army.

Further Reading

The best source on Suvorov available in English is K. Osipov, *Alexander Suvorov,* translated by Edith Bone (1944). See also Walter Lyon Blease, *Suvarov* (1920), and Philip Longworth,

The Art of Victory: The Life and Achievements of Field Marshall Suvorov (1965). Nikolaus Basseches, The Unknown Army, translated by Marion Saerchinger (1943), is a perceptive interpretation of the nature of the Russian army under imperial Russia and the Soviet regime until World War II. A well-written account of Russian military history is Albert Parry, Russian Cavalcade: A Military Record (1944); the first half of the book deals with the army prior to 1917 and the remainder with the period 1917 to 1943. □

Helen Suzman

A member of the South African House of Assembly for the Progressive Federal Party for over three decades, Helen Suzman (born 1917) was known internationally for her forthright opposition to *apartheid* and uncompromising advocacy of the interests of millions of nonwhite and liberally-minded South Africans.

Helen Suzman was born on November 7, 1917, at Germiston in the Transvaal province of South Africa, the daughter of Samuel and Freda Gavronsky. Her father, a Jewish immigrant to South Africa from Lithuania, worked initially as a hides dealer but in time made a fortune in real estate. Suzman was educated in Johannesburg at the Parktown Convent and later at the University of Witwatersrand, where in 1940 she obtained a Bachelor of Commerce degree in economics and economic history. In 1937 she married physician Moses B. Suzman, a member of a prominent Johannesburg family.

In 1944 Suzman was appointed as a part-time lecturer in the Department of Economics and Economic History at the University of the Witwatersrand following three years work as a statistician for the South African War Supplies Board. Her later research into the economic conditions of the country instilled in her a deep concern for the depressed economic circumstances afflicting most nonwhite South Africans, especially those in the cities. This awareness drew her ever more into national political life. When in May 1948 the governing and relatively liberal United Party was narrowly defeated by the conservative National Party, Suzman organized a branch of the United Party at her own university and became its first chairperson. Five years later, unable to recruit a suitable United Party candidate for her own highly affluent Houghton parliamentary constituency, Suzman ran herself and won the seat in the House of Assembly that she held for over three decades.

Founding of the Progressive Party

By 1959 the experience of being in parliamentary opposition to the National Party government had sapped the United Party of much of its one-time optimism, coherence, and vigor, causing it to drift gradually to the right politically. This alienated Suzman who, together with 11 other members of Parliament (MPs) sharing her liberal beliefs, finally resigned from the United Party to found the new Progressive Party under the leadership of Jan van A. Steytler.

The Progressive Party at first advocated a "qualified" franchise for all South African citizens regardless of race or color and a central government of carefully defined and limited powers. By the mid-1980s Progressive Party policy embraced the idea of a nonracial and universal franchise, but within a federated South African state. However, in the 1960s the Progressives had little influence on government policy and limited popular following. Thus in 1961 Suzman was the only Progressive MP to secure reelection—by a margin of just 564 votes—at a general election the government called especially in hopes of crushing the new party. For the next 13 years she would be her party's sole representative in Parliament—a courageous, overworked, and often lonely voice defending liberal values in a context that became steadily less hospitable to liberalism.

The Valiant Fight

Though politically alone in the House of Assembly after 1961, Suzman continued her advocacy of a multiracial and democratic society for South Africa against overwhelming parliamentary odds. Her personal dynamism and quick wit led to lively but also sometimes bitter exchanges between her and her Assembly colleagues. Invariably outvoted, Suzman nevertheless got her frequent dissents onto the record and thereby to some degree succeeded in keeping liberal perspectives continuously before the South African public. The eloquence and intelligence of her positions, the doggedness of her efforts, and the very isolation of her position in the House of Assembly gained for her a special political notoriety both at home and abroad, as well as an admiring personal following.

In 1963 Suzman registered the only vote in the House against Minister of Justice (later Prime Minister) B. J. Vorster's infamous security legislation, which rendered all South Africans liable to arrest without charge for periods of up to 90 days at a time. Later she was the only member of Parliament to condemn the Rhodesian government's seizure of independence (so-called "UDI") in November 1965. Though not always so alone, through the 1960s and early 1970s Suzman registered a long series of powerful dissents at various government apartheid and security proposals—the so-called Sabotage Bill of 1962, press controls, "independent" African "homelands," labor policy, and influx control, to mention only a few. In a legislative sense she lost all these fights, but she gained immense personal respect outside the House of Assembly as seemingly the only true parliamentary opponent of the apartheid state. Her own electoral majorities in Houghton steadily grew, but her party's fortunes at first languished.

Then in the general election of 1974 Suzman's party succeeded in returning six additional MPs to the House of Assembly, reducing her previous heavy burden—carried for more than a decade—of individually opposing government spokesmen from more than 20 different departments. In 1985 she shared this duty with her party's 26 other MPs, within which group she was the highly respected senior member. Suzman's political views, which often adopted an economic perspective, were frequently considered radical by her fellow white South Africans, though they would be considered conservative in most Western countries. She advocated a multiracial society for South Africa in which equality of opportunity rather than absolute economic equality should be the standard to be achieved. Her views, among others, finally prevailed with the free, democratic elections in the early 1990s and the ultimate election of Nelson Mandela as president. Suzman decided not to run for Parliament in the 1989 elections, thus ending her 36 years of public service. She visited Parliament in February, 1991, as honoree to accept a recently-commissioned portrait of herself destined to hang in the halls of Parliament.

Helen Suzman ranked among the best known South Africans overseas and among the most widely respected. Together with other senior leaders of her party she traveled widely in nonwhite Africa and was received by many of Africa's principal leaders. In 1972 she was invited to give the first Moshoeshoe 1 lecture in Lesotho. She was awarded honorary degrees by Oxford, Harvard, and Columbia universities, among several others, and in 1978 was granted the United Nations' Human Rights Award. She also received the Moses Mendelssohn Prize, Berlin Senate, in 1988; the B'Nai B'Rith Dor L'Dor Award in 1992; and a Notre Dame University, Indiana (USA) award in 1995.

Moses and Helen Suzman had two daughters. The family was affiliated with the Great Synagogue in Johannesburg and resided in the Hyde Park district of that city. From 1990-1993, Suzman served as president of the South African Institute of Race Relations in Johannesburg.

Further Reading

Suzman's own autobiographical book, *In No Uncertain Terms* (Knopf, 1993), with a forward by Nelson Mandela, has been generally well-received. Another principal biography is entitled *A Cricket in the Thorntree: Helen Suzman and the Progressive Party*, by Joanna Strangewayes-Booth (Johannesburg, 1976). On the fate of liberalism and liberals in South Africa in general one might consult Margaret Ballinger's *From Union to Apartheid: A Trek to Isolation* (Cape Town, 1969); Paul B. Rich's *White Power and the Liberal Conscience: Racial Segregation and South African Liberalism, 1921-1960* (Manchester University Press, 1984); or particularly Janet Robertson's *Liberalism in South Africa, 1948-1963* (Oxford University Press, 1971). Alan Paton's *South African Tragedy: The Life and Times of Jan Hofmeyer* (1965) treats much the same problem in the context of a different figure and an earlier time. □

Daisetz Teitaro Suzuki

Daisetz Teitaro Suzuki (1870-1966) was a Japanese translator, teacher, and constructive interpreter of Zen Buddhist thought to the West.

Teitaro Suzuki was born in Kanazawa in western Japan on October 18, 1870. His ancestors as well as his father, grandfather, and great grandfather were physicians of the samurai class. Suzuki was expected to follow in their footsteps, but with the death of his father while he was six his family was unable to bear the expense of a medical education. At about 17, he said, he began to contemplate the misfortunes of his family as manifested in the early deaths of his father, grandfather, and great grandfather. He turned to the Rinzai temple where his family was registered. Upon graduation from secondary school he became an English teacher in Takojima, a fishing village on the Noto peninsula, and later at Mikawa, a town near Kanazawa. From 1888 to 1889 he studied at Ishikawa College. Relocating in Tokyo, he occasionally studied at Imperial University (1891-1892) but gradually grew more interested in undergoing the discipline of a novitiate at the Engakuji Rinzai Zen monastery in Kamakura (1892-1897) where his master gave him his Buddhist name, Daisetz, meaning "great humility."

Suzuki exhibited a strong linguistic ability and as early as 1893 translated into English the speech of Shaku Soyen, the successor of his first Zen master, Imagita Kosen, entitled "The Law of Cause and Effect, as Taught by Buddha" for the World's Parliament of Religions in Chicago. In Chicago Shaku Soyen met Paul Carus and recommended Suzuki as a translator in Carus' firm, Open Court Publishing Company of La Salle, Illinois. From 1897 to 1909 Suzuki lived in the United States and translated Sanskrit, Pali, Chinese, and Japanese texts for Open Court. In 1907 he published *Outlines of Mahayana Buddhism*, which began his interpretation of the variety of Buddhist traditions as if they were one and essentially Rinzai Zen. In 1911 he married a college teacher interested in Oriental religion, Beatrice Lane, who died in 1938. During his stay in the United States he trav-

elled to Europe and there translated the writings of the Swedish thinker Emanuel Swedenborg into Japanese.

Suzuki returned to Japan in 1909 as lecturer of English at Imperial University and professor of English at Gakushu-in (Peers' School). In 1921 he left these posts to become professor of English and Buddhist philosophy at Otani University, Kyoto, where he received an honorary D.Litt. In the same year he founded the journal *The Eastern Buddhist.* While at Otani University he became known in the West through a variety of publications, including the three volume *Essays in Zen Buddhism* (1927-1934) and *The Training of the Zen Buddhist Monk* (1934), but especially his translation of the *Lankavatara Sutra* (1932) and his book *Zen Buddhism and Its Influence on Japanese Culture* (1938).

He remained at Otani University until he began an active retirement in 1940. During World War II he was under suspicion of the Japanese government for his opposition to militarism, but in 1949 he was made a member of the Japanese Academy and decorated by the emperor with the Cultural Medal. Following the war 20 of his works on Zen and Buddhism were published in England and the United States, consisting of monographs and collections of essays. He travelled and lectured at universities in the United States and Europe during the 1950s and died in Kamakura on July 12, 1966, leaving numerous unpublished manuscripts.

Suzuki's writings were not descriptive studies of Buddhism or Zen. He was a constructive thinker who wrote out of his own experience and who treated Buddhism as if it had an unchanging essence which was mystical and irrational or transrational. He intended to introduce Zen to the West as a nonhistorical paradox beyond all categories of rational thought. Though his writings often include metaphysical discussions, Suzuki denied all theoretical moorings. Since Zen has historically emphasized technique more than philosophy (*zen* means "meditation"), Suzuki's emphasis was not unfounded. He spoke of his own enlightenment, *satori,* as the end of the separateness of the self and objects of thought. It was precipitated by breaking through the well-known Zen problem without rational solution, or *koan,* his master had given him, *Mu.* But enlightenment, he continually emphasized, did not end with a meditational breaking through the limitations of thought. It required a return to the world with a radically new understanding of it: "When I came out of that state . . . I said, 'I see. This is it.'"

To make Zen comprehensible, Suzuki adopted categories of American psychology of religion. He borrowed the four characteristics of mystical experience of William James and then set forth eight characteristics of *satori:* irrationality, intuitive insight, authoritativeness, affirmation, a sense of the beyond, a feeling of exaltation, momentariness, and an impersonal tone. Attaching primary importance to the last, he spoke of it as that characteristic which distinguishes *satori* from Christian mysticism, whose mystics emphasize "the personal and frequently sexual feelings." Using the term "unconscious" to describe the potential enlightenment within all beings, called the "Buddha-nature," Suzuki opened the door for the use of Zen by modern depth psychology. On the basis of Suzuki's interpretation Carl Jung presented the experience of Zen as the liberation of the unconscious.

Further Reading

For a historical treatment of Zen which includes discussion of Suzuki's place see Heinrich Dumoulin, *A History of Zen Buddhism* (1963). Suzuki's many writings are available in numerous popular paperback editions, any of them a good place to begin: for example, *Essays in Zen Buddhism* (1961), *Introduction to Zen Buddhism* (1964), *Manual of Zen Buddhism* (1960), and *Zen and Japanese Culture* (1959), a revised version of his *Zen Buddhism and Its Influence on Japanese Culture* (1938).

Additional Sources

Switzer, A. Irwin, *D.T. Suzuki: a biography,* London: The Buddhist Society, 1985.

A Zen life: D.T. Suzuki remembered, New York: Weatherhill, 1986. □

Italo Svevo

Italo Svevo (1861-1928) was one of the first Italian novelists to consequentially apply psychoanalytical discoveries to literature.

Italo Svevo was born Ettore Schmitz on Dec. 19, 1861, in Trieste, one of eight children of a businessman. The pseudonym he later chose reflects his mixed origins: his paternal ancestors had come from the German Rhineland, whereas his mother was of Italian descent. At 12 Svevo was sent to Germany to complete his secondary education in Segnitz, Franconia. At this time he became acquainted with the German classics, developing later special predilection for Arthur Schopenhauer.

After Svevo's return to Trieste at the age of 17, he studied economics for 2 years at a local institute. In 1880 the failure of his father's business forced him to take a job at the Triestine branch of the Viennese Unionsbank, which he held until he began working full time for his father-in-law's business in 1902. From the time of his return to Trieste he contributed for some 10 years to the local Italian paper *L'Indipendente*. His first two novels, *Una vita* and *Senilità*, were published in 1892 and 1898 but received scant attention. In 1896 he married Livia Veneziani, the daughter of a well-to-do industrialist. After his second novel Svevo seemingly devoted all his time to business and published nothing for 25 years until *La coscienza di Zeno* (*The Confessions of Zeno*) appeared in 1923.

Svevo's friendship with James Joyce goes back to the early years of the century when he took English lessons from Joyce, who then taught English in Trieste for a living. The friendship continued after Joyce had moved to Zurich and then Paris, where he was instrumental in making the Italian known. Svevo died in an automobile accident at Motta di Livenza on Sept. 13, 1928.

His Works

For a long time Svevo had doubts of his own talent, yet he turned out to be one of the best Italian novelists of the century. In a loose form and a low-keyed style imbued with irony, he adopted forms of narration and a treatment of the time element that definitely ranked him among the avant-garde and proved him to be one of the early representatives of the psychoanalytical novel. Svevo, who could equally well have written in German, detested rhetoric and was not interested in artistic prose and a refined style. What some critics referred to as "Pidgin-Italian" indicates only a use of language in conformity with the psychological situation it represents: as there are no consequential heroes, there is no consequential style.

To Svevo, writing, in a sense, represented a therapeutic catharsis for all sorts of "diseases," real or imaginary, from cigarette smoking to senility. Lending itself by definition to—retroactive—introspective analysis, senility indeed became one of the dominant motives of Svevo's narrative: old age and youth, "the old man and the pretty girl."

Svevo's first novel, as most of his writing, is to a large degree autobiographical. *Una vita* (1892), published at his own expense, bore the original title *Un inetto*—the story of a young man "incapable" of mastering life. The analytical and introspective modes already visible in this first novel become more prominent in the second: *Senilità* (1898). Again, the perennial indecision and incapacity to face the facts of life characterize the actions of the central character.

His feelings are being analyzed with supreme irony, and in true Schopenhauerian fashion life's realities are being dissolved before the all-important reality of the hero's mind and imagination.

The corrosive play of contrapuntal irony is brought to perfection in *La coscienza di Zeno* (1923), the "story of a disease." In a series of loosely knit episodes—concerning his cigarette-smoking habit of which he wants to be cured, his father's death, his marriage—Zeno Cosini writes down his case history for his psychoanalyst. Svevo's relationship to Freud, whose ideas he deliberately applied, was not very different from those of his characters to their "diseases" which they both hate and love. Svevo always ended up reading Freud again after having laid the books aside out of true antipathy.

The theme of senility—and the implication of a possible distant review of things—is also predominant in a volume of short stories that was published posthumously: *La novella del buon vecchio e della bella fanciulla* (1929). It contains the fragment of what was to be Svevo's mature masterpiece: *Il vecchione*. *Corto viaggio sentimentale* (1949) is a collection of short stories and fragments of stories left unfinished. *Saggi e pagine sparse* (1954) presents various articles and essays. Svevo's dramatic production was collected in *Commedie* (1960).

Further Reading

Most works on Svevo are in Italian. In English, P. N. Furbank, *Italo Svevo: The Man and the Writer* (1967), gives an account of Svevo's life and an intelligent analysis of his work. Recommended for general historical background is Sergio Pacifici, *The Modern Italian Novel: From Manzoni to Svevo* (1967).

Additional Sources

Gatt-Rutter, John, *Italo Svevo: a double life,* Oxford: Clarendon Press; New York: Oxford University Press, 1988.
Veneziani Svevo, Livia, *Memoir of Italo Svevo,* Marlboro, Vt.: Marlboro Press, 1990. □

Jan Swammerdam

The Dutch natural scientist Jan Swammerdam (1637-1680) was a founder of comparative anatomy and entomology and was very skillful in the art of microdissection.

Jan Swammerdam was born on Feb. 12, 1637, in Amsterdam. His father, a prosperous apothecary, had collected a museum of curiosities. Jan soon developed a passion for natural history, in particular for the study of insects. His collection of insects, begun in his youth, eventually included some 3,000 species. At the age of 24 he went to Leiden to study medicine, where he graduated in 1667. His graduation thesis included the observation that the lung of a newborn mammal sinks in water but floats once the animal has breathed. Much to his father's displeasure, Swammerdam did not practice medicine but continued his microdissections of insects.

Swammerdam designed a simple dissecting microscope that had two arms: one for holding the object and the other for the lens; the arms had coarse and fine adjustments. He used very fine scissors for dissection and capillary tubes of glass for inflating or injecting blood vessels. He was one of the first to dissect under water and to remove fat by organic solvents. In 1669 he published his "General account of bloodless animalculae," a history of insects which dealt with their modes of transformation and development.

His interest in religion led Swammerdam to meet the Flemish mystic Antoinette Bourignon in 1673, who had a profound influence on his life. At this time he was engaged in a study of the life history of the mayfly which was, to Antoinette Bourignon, a "little beast which lives for only a single day, and throughout that time endures many miseries." She reluctantly allowed Swammerdam to publish his studies in 1675 (*Emphemerae vita*) on condition that he would study religion in the future. The book contains many remarkable pieces of minute anatomy, but these were diluted by allusions to the Bible and the development of an ethical system. During the remainder of his life he sufferred from periods of depression, during which he destroyed much of his work. He died on Feb. 17, 1680.

Swammerdam left many manuscripts which Hermann Boerhaave published in 1737 in two volumes called *Biblia naturae* (*Bible of Nature*). This book, which contained work done mainly between 1668 and 1675, is the finest collection of microscopical observations ever produced by one worker, and some of the figures have never been excelled. The book is the foundation of our modern knowledge of the structure, metamorphosis, and classification of insects. It also includes detailed observations on the Crustacea and Mollusca and on the life history of the frog.

Perhaps the most complete study is that on the honeybee, which is illustrated by beautiful drawings. In his studies on the frog, Swammerdam used a nerve-muscle preparation and invented a form of plethysmograph. He established that when the nerve was mechanically stimulated the muscle contracted, and he contradicted the idea, accepted in his time, that when a muscle contracted it increased in volume due to the passage of liquid from nerve to muscle.

Further Reading

Abraham Schierbeek, *Jan Swammerdam* (trans. 1967), is the only modern biography. For Swammerdam's place in the history of biology, the student can consult Charles Singer, *A History of Biology to about the Year 1900* (1931; 3d ed. 1959); F. J. Cole, *A History of Comparative Anatomy from Aristotle to the Eighteenth Century* (1944); and M. J. Sirks and Conway Zirkle, *The Evolution of Biology* (1964). □

Emanuel Swedenborg

The Swedish scientist, theologian, and mystic Emanuel Swedenborg (1688-1772) founded a religious system known as Swedenborgianism, ideas of which were incorporated in the Church of the New Jerusalem.

Emanuel Swedenborg was born Emanuel Swedberg on Jan. 29, 1688, in Uppsala. His father, Bishop Jesper Swedberg, was a professor at the University of Uppsala. The family name was changed in 1719 to Swedenborg when the family was ennobled. After studies at the University of Uppsala, where he concentrated on mathematics and astronomy, Swedenborg traveled for 5 years throughout Europe (1710-1714). After a 2-year period in which he engaged in scientific journalism, Swedenborg became assessor at the Royal College of Mines in 1716. For the next 30 years, Swedenborg's main work was concentrated in the Swedish metal-mining industry. His engineering skill earned him a wide reputation. From 1747 onward, he devoted most of his time to the acquisition of knowledge through traveling and observation and to the elaboration and publication of scientific and theological theories.

Throughout his career in mining, Swedenborg studied and wrote. In 1718 Swedenborg published the first Swedish work on algebra. In 1721 he issued a voluminous work in which he attempted to demonstrate the geometrical character of physics and chemistry. Swedenborg spent the next 13 years researching and writing a three-volume work on the nature of physics, *Opera philosophica et mineralia,* published at Leipzig in 1734. He conceived of the atom as a particle vortex, each particle being composed of its own inner motions. This theory approximated the electron-nucleus framework of the atom in modern physics. Swedenborg reasoned from a general principle of matter, in which he thought of the infinite as pure motion. He conceived of pure motion as a tendency to create, and any subsequent molding of creation became a complex of pure motion.

After the publication of his work on physics, Swedenborg's studies and researches focused on man as a physiological and anatomical whole and on man in his relationship to God. His new studies led to the publication of two works: *Oeconomia regni animalis* (1740-1741) and *Regnum animale* (1744-1745). Some of Swedenborg's physiological discoveries were important. He was among the first to discover the nature of cerebrospinal fluid. He identified the correspondence between particular parts of the body and certain motor regions of the cerebral cortex. His studies of the physiology of the blood, brain, lung, and heart led him to characterize correctly the relationship between these organs. He also attempted to describe the physiological basis for human perception and thus to find a way to define and describe man's soul.

After these studies Swedenborg devoted his energies to the philosophy of theology. Although not a theologian in the strict sense, he was an outstanding philosopher or theological speculator. Utilizing some basic Christian truths, Swedenborg elaborated—partly on a scientific basis, partly on a philosophical basis—a theory of God, of man, and of divine revelation and redemption. On the basis of these theorizings, the Church of the New Jerusalem was founded in 1784.

Swedenborg did not himself found any church or sect. Although his reputation has been established on his theological theories, his greatness as a scientist and philosopher of nature probably exceeds his greatness as a theological speculator. The basis of Swedenborg's speculations was his assumption that the infinite was an indivisible power, a personal god indivisible in essence or power or person. He rejected the traditional Christian teaching of the Trinity.

A systematic presentation of Swedenborg's theology appeared in 1771 entitled *Vera Christiana religio.* He viewed all things as created by divine love and according to divine wisdom. Each material thing corresponded to a "spiritual form." Swedenborg thus achieved a modified Neoplatonism: all effects in the material world have spiritual causes and therefore a divine purpose.

Swedenborg analyzed the biblical books of Genesis and Exodus in his *Arcana coelestia* (1749-1756), and Revelation in his *Apocalypsis explicata* (1785-1789), the latter published posthumously. He elaborated the purely philosophical aspect of his reasoning in three major works: *De coelo et ejus mirabilibus, et de inferno* (1758), *Sapientia angelica de divino amore et de divina sapientia* (1763), and *Sapientia angelica de divina providentia* (1764).

Swedenborg's theory of redemption rejected any notion that Jesus Christ was in himself a divine person, but it held that the inmost soul of Jesus was divine. This divine soul had taken on a human form from Mary, and Jesus' human nature had been glorified by his exemplary life. By resisting all the temptations and ills of the powers of darkness, Jesus had opened a way for divine life to flow into all mankind. Man had become free to know truth and to be able to obey its dictates. Human salvation lay in this knowledge and obedience.

Swedenborg defended his theological speculation by claiming it resulted from a divine call. He maintained that he had received special light from God. He also maintained that all of his exegetical and philosophical treatises constituted a new revelation from God. Mankind must live according to this revelation in order to usher in a new age of reason and truth.

Swedenborg died in London on March 29, 1772. In 1908 the Swedish government requested that his remains be transferred to Uppsala Cathedral.

Further Reading

Primary material is in Rudolph L. Tafel, ed., *Documents concerning the Life and Character of Emanuel Swedenborg* (3 vols., 1875-1877). Other studies include Signe Toksvig, *Emanuel Swedenborg: Scientist and Mystic* (1949); Cyriel S. Sigstedt, *The Swedenborg Epic* (1953); John H. Spalding, *Introduction to Swedenborg's Religious Thought* (1956); and George Trobridge, *Swedenborg: Life and Teaching* (4th ed. 1968).

Additional Sources

Dole, George F., *A scientist explores spirit: a compact biography of Emanuel Swedenborg with key concepts of Swedenborg's theology,* New York; West Chester, Pa.: Swendenborg Foundation, 1992.

Keller, Helen, *Light in my darkness,* West Chester, Pa.: Chrysalis Books, 1994.

Suzuki, Daisetz Teitaro, *Swedenborg: buddha of the North,* West Chester, Pa.: Swedenborg Foundation, 1996.

Toksvig, Signe, *Emanuel Swedenborg, scientist and mystic,* New York, N.Y.: Swedenborg Foundation, 1983. □

Jan Pieterszoon Sweelinck

Jan Pieterszoon Sweelinck (1562-1621) was a Dutch composer, organist, and teacher. His vocal works are in the outgoing late Renaissance tradition; his keyboard works synthesize various traditions into the first great formulation of the baroque keyboard style.

Jan Pieterszoon Sweelinck was born in Deventer. He received some musical training from his father, Pieter Swybertszoon (Sweelinck adopted his mother's surname), who was the organist of the Oude Kerk (Old Church) in Amsterdam. Sweelinck's brilliance as a performer is attested by the likely possibility that he followed his father in the position at the age of 15. He is definitely known to have been employed at the church by 1580, and he remained in the post for the rest of his life.

Sweelinck played twice daily for the burghers, who were connoisseurs of organ performance. He probably did not leave Amsterdam for more than a few days at a time. His knowledge of the theory of music must have been derived from reading the works of Gioseffo Zarlino, the important Italian theorist, for Sweelinck's own *Rules for Composition* are based on Zarlino's principles.

In 1590 Sweelinck married Claesgen Puyner. They had six children; the eldest son, Dirck, succeeded his father as organist at the Oude Kerk. Sweelinck died in Amsterdam on Oct. 16, 1621.

Only a portion of Sweelinck's music was published during his lifetime. The *Chansons a 5* (1594) stand very much within the tradition of the late-16th-century chanson in their emphasis on counterpoint and frequent madrigalisms. The *Rimes françaises et italiennes* (1619) are for a reduced number of parts. Highly vocal, they emphasize canonic techniques. Five of the 15 Italian pieces in the collection were based on pieces in four to six parts by Italian composers. The *Cantiones sacrae* (1619) are motets with Latin texts, fairly traditional in their somewhat northern counterpoint, with less emphasis on linear beauty than the work of the Roman school of the late 16th century. Sweelinck's feeling for major-minor tonality was quite modern, as was his use of basso continuo.

Sweelinck's organ music established a new style, and, because of his eminence as a teacher, it spread throughout northern Germany. None of his organ works were published during his lifetime; most exist only in copies, and there are, therefore, problems of correct attribution. Undoubtedly many works have been lost.

In his keyboard music Sweelinck turned from the melodic ornamentation that dominated the current Germanic style. He fused the contrapuntal facility of Netherlandish vocal writing, the formal clarity of Italian organ music, and the idiomatic patterned figuration of English keyboard composers of the Jacobean period, some of whom he knew personally because they were religious exiles in northern Europe.

Sweelinck's most significant advances probably were in the variation form. The techniques he used in variations on sacred melodies were different from the ones he employed on secular melodies, probably reflecting his growing feeling for idiomatic distinction between the organ and the harpsichord. In his secular variations Sweelinck tended to use the patterned figures of the English virginalists, although his individual movements are tighter formally than the English compositions. In his variations on Lutheran chorale melodies Sweelinck employed a more contrapuntal style, often retaining the chorale melody intact, in longer note values, in one part. His pupils, especially Samuel Scheidt, preserved this manner and transmitted it to Germany, where its influence lasted until the time of Johann Sebastian Bach.

Further Reading

Sweelinck is studied as a composer for the organ in Robert L. Tusler, *The Organ Music of Jan Pieterszoon Sweelinck* (1958). His vocal music is discussed in Gustave Reese, *Music in the Renaissance* (1954; rev. ed. 1959). For his keyboard music and its significance see Manfred F. Bukofzer, *Music in the Baroque Era: From Monteverdi to Bach* (1947). □

Jonathan Swift

The Anglo-Irish poet, political writer, and clergyman Jonathan Swift (1667-1745) ranks as the foremost prose satirist in the English language and as one of the greatest satirists in world literature.

Jonathan Swift was born in Dublin, Ireland, on Nov. 30, 1667. His father, Jonathan Swift (1640-1667), an Englishman who had settled in Ireland, died a few months before Swift's birth. He had married Abigaile Erick, the daughter of an old Leicestershire family, about 1664. Swift's uncle, Godwin Swift, a Tipperary official, supported the young Jonathan. With his help he entered Kilkenny School, where William Congreve was a fellow student, at the age of 6. In 1682 Swift matriculated at Trinity College, Dublin, where his record was undistinguished. He received his bachelor of arts degree in 1686. Swift continued his education at Trinity, having almost obtained a master of arts degree when his uncle's death and political violence in

Ireland combined in 1688 to make him leave Ireland and to seek his mother's counsel in Leicester.

Swift began his first employment toward the end of 1689 by becoming secretary to Sir William Temple, a retired diplomat and distant relative of his mother's, at Moor Park near London. Here Swift first met Esther Johnson (1680-1728), the "Stella" of his famous *Journal to Stella,* who was 8 years old at the time. She was the daughter of a servant at Moor Park, and Swift—who was 22 years old— taught her how to write and formed a lifelong friendship with her. Swift's position at Moor Park was frequently disagreeable to him because of his uncertain status and prospects. In 1692, after a short residence at Oxford, he obtained a master of arts degree from that institution. Returning to Temple's employ, he remained at Moor Park until 1694, when he left in anger at Temple's delay in obtaining him preferment. That year Swift was ordained in the Church of Ireland (Anglican). In January 1695 Swift obtained the small prebend of Kilroot near Belfast.

First Works

Temple proposed that Swift return to Moor Park in 1696 as a literary executor to help him prepare his papers for publication. Tired of Irish life, Swift gladly accepted, living at Moor Park until Temple's death in 1699. During this 3-year period Swift read and wrote extensively. His *Pindaric Odes,* written in the manner of Abraham Cowley, date from this period, as does his first essay in satiric prose, *The Battle of the Books,* written in 1697 in defense of

Temple's *Essay upon Ancient and Modern Learning* but not published until 1704.

After Temple's death Swift, after several delays, obtained the rectory of Agher in Meath with the united vicarages of Laracor and Rathbeggan, to which was added the prebend of Dunlavin in St. Patrick's, Dublin. He also became chaplain to the 2d Earl of Berkeley, a lord justice of Ireland. In 1701 Swift received a doctor of divinity degree from Trinity College, Dublin, but his hopes for higher Church office were disappointed. Unhappy with life in Ireland, he paid frequent visits to Leicester and London. With the advent of a new Tory government in England and the pending impeachment of Whig leaders responsible for William III's second Partition Treaty, Swift decided to put his pen to political use. In 1701 he published *A Discourse of the Contests and Dissensions between the Nobles and Commons in Athens and Rome* in an attempt to dissuade the impeachment of John Somers and Lords Orford, Halifax, and Portland.

Swift lived in England between 1701 and 1704, and he became friends with Alexander Pope, Joseph Addison, and Richard Steele. In 1704 he published in one volume his first great satires, *A Tale of a Tub, The Battle of the Books,* and *The Mechanical Operation of the Spirit.* Full of brilliant parody and extravagant wit, these satires exhibit Swift at his most dazzling.

Meantime, in 1701 Swift had invited Esther Johnson and her companion, Rebecca Dingley, a poor relative of Temple's, to Laracor. They soon permanently established themselves in Dublin. Swift's friendship with Johnson lasted through her lifetime, and contemporary rumor reported he married her in 1716. No marriage was ever acknowledged. Swift's letters to Johnson from London between 1710 and 1713 make up his *Journal to Stella,* first published in 1768.

In November 1707 Swift wrote his most distinguished narrative poem, *Baucis and Philemon,* and a few months later he produced one of the finest examples of his irony, the *Argument to Prove That the Abolishing of Christianity in England May, as Things Now Stand, Be Attended with Some Inconveniences* (1708). In the early months of 1708 Swift also wrote an amusing piece decrying the quackery of astrologers, *Vindication of Isaac Bickerstaff, Esq.*

Political Activities

From February 1708 to April 1709 Swift was domiciled in London, attempting to obtain for the Irish clergy the financial benefits of Queen Anne's Bounty, in which he failed. By November 1710 he was again in London and produced a series of brilliant pamphlets, including *A Letter concerning the Sacramental Test,* the *Sentiments of a Church of England Man,* and a *Project for the Advancement of Religion.*

Finally convinced that the Whigs would not aid his Church cause, Swift turned to the ministers of the new Tory government in 1710 and became for the next 4 years the chief journalist and principal pamphleteer for Robert Harley, Earl of Oxford, and Henry St. John, Viscount Bolingbroke. Swift wrote for the Tory paper, the *Examiner,* from Nov. 2, 1710, to June 7, 1711, and in his weekly contributions he lampooned the reputation of Whig leaders and their popular hero, the Duke of Marlborough. His most influential work of this period of his greatest political power in England was *The Conduct of the Allies* (1711), which helped to prepare public opinion for the end of the war with France and the Peace of Utrecht.

In 1713 Queen Anne appointed Swift to the deanery of St. Patrick's, Dublin, and in June 1713 he left London to take possession of it, disappointed he had not received as a reward for his political writings an English deanery or bishopric. Dissensions between Oxford and Bolingbroke speedily forced his return to London. Unable to smooth over the differences between them and probably sensing Oxford's impending fall, Swift retired for several weeks to Upper Letcombe, Berkshire, where he wrote *Some Free Thoughts on the Present State of Affairs,* a pamphlet detailing Swift's conversion to Bolingbroke's policies. Queen Anne died on Aug. 1, 1714, and with the accession of George I, the Tories were a ruined party. Swift's career in England was over.

But his past 4 years of London life had been important ones for Swift. In addition to his political activities and writings, he had become treasurer and a leading member of the Brothers, a society of wits; he had contributed to the *Tatler,* the *Spectator,* and the *Intelligence;* he had promoted the subscription for Pope's *Homer;* and he had joined with Pope, John Arbuthnot, John Gay, and others to found the celebrated Scriblerus Club, contributing to *Martin Scriblerus.* To this busy era also belong several miscellanies, including *A Meditation upon a Broomstick,* and the poems "Sid Hamet's Rod," "The City Shower," "The Windsor Prophecy," "The Prediction of Merlin," and "The History of Vanbrugh's House." His *Proposal for Correcting, Improving and Ascertaining the English Tongue* (1712) also dates from these London years.

During his various stays in London, Swift had become friendly with the Vanhomrighs, the family of a Dublin merchant of Dutch origins. Their daughter Esther—Swift called her Vanessa—had fallen passionately in love with Swift, and she followed him to Ireland, hoping that Swift would marry her.

Return to Ireland meant for Swift a sudden fall from great political power to absolute insignificance. Coldly received by the Irish as the dean of St. Patrick's, he was also denied all share in the administration of Irish affairs. Johnson and Dingley continued to reside near him, and Esther Vanhomrigh (1690-1723) lived at Cellbridge, about 10 miles distant. Perhaps Swift wished to marry Johnson, but he could not do so without destroying Vanhomrigh. He seemed psychologically incapable of deserting either beauty, although his feeling for each was devoid of passion. He was capable of friendship and even tender regard but not of love. He probably preferred Johnson, but his attempts were directed toward soothing Vanhomrigh. He had earlier addressed one of the best examples of his serious poetry, "Cadenus and Vanessa," to her in 1713. Finally, Vanhomrigh, exhausted by Swift's evasions, demanded to know the nature of his relations with Johnson in a letter, in

1723. After a final confrontation with Swift, Vanhomrigh died a few weeks later. Johnson died on Jan. 28, 1728.

In 1720 Swift published anonymously his *Proposal for the Universal Use of Irish Manufactures,* in which he urged the Irish to discontinue using English goods. Political events once again made Swift a national hero in 1724-1725. His six famous letters, signed M. B. Drapier, written between April and December 1724, were a protest against English debasement of Irish coinage and the inflation that would ensue. *The Drapier's Letters* inflamed all Ireland, caused the cancellation of the coinage scheme, and made Swift into an Irish hero. The fourth of the six letters, *A Letter to the Whole People of Ireland,* which rose to a pitch of defiance, was labeled seditious, but no one charged Swift, who was known to be the author.

Gulliver's Travels

As early as 1720 Swift had started the composition of his great satirical masterpiece, *Gulliver's Travels.* It was published anonymously in 1726 as *Travels into Several Remote Nations of the World,* in four parts, by Lemuel Gulliver. Immediate acclaim greeted it, many people choosing to read as childish fantasy its mordant satire on courts, parties, and statesmen. The work purported to be the travels of Captain Lemuel Gulliver, and Swift told his story in the first person, with simplicity and directness. The *Travels* constitute a subtle commentary on political and social conditions in 18th-century England. Gulliver first visits Lilliput, a land of pygmies. Their court factions and petty intrigues seem ridiculous on so miniature a scale. He next visits Brobdingnag, a land of giants. When he relates the glories of England, the inhabitants are as disdainfully and scornfully amused as he had been in the land of the Lilliputians. Gulliver's third voyage carries him to the flying island of Laputa, the Island of the Sorcerers, and the land of the Struldbrugs. Their inhabitants exhibit the extremities of literary and scientific pedantry, the deceptiveness of written history, and the curse of the desire for immortal life. Gulliver's final visit, to the land of the Houyhnhnms, a country governed by noble and rational horses who are served by bestial creatures in debased human form, shows the depths to which mankind may sink when it allows passions to overcome reason.

Swift next displayed his powers in his *Modest Proposal for Preventing the Children of Poor People from Being a Burden to Their Parents or Their Country* in 1729. This ironic pamphlet proposed to cure Ireland's imbalance of people and exports by fattening poor people's children and selling them as delicacies for gentlemen's tables. A satire on domestics, *Directions to Servants* (first published in 1745), followed, and it was succeeded by *Polite Conversation,* written in 1731 and published in 1738. Occasional verse—often indecent—rolled from Swift's pen, but the 1730s were also marked by three important poems: the delightful *Hamilton's Bawn,* the verses on his own death (1731), and the fierce satire *The Legion Club* (1736).

Swift's popularity remained at a high pitch, and he performed his ecclesiastical duties with strictness and regularity. But his melancholy and his attacks of giddiness increased with his sense of growing isolation and of failing powers. At first a cousin, Martha Whiteway, cared for him, and in March 1742 both his person and his estate were entrusted to guardians. In September his illness reached a crisis, and he emerged paralyzed. Swift died in Dublin on Oct. 19, 1745, and he was buried in St. Patrick's. He left his great fortune to build a hospital for the mentally challenged.

Further Reading

Standard editions of Swift's works are *The Prose Works of Jonathan Swift,* edited by Herbert Davis (14 vols., 1939-1968); *Poems,* edited by Harold Williams (3 vols., 1937; 2d ed. 1958); and *Correspondence,* edited by Harold Williams (5 vols., 1963-1965). Irvin Ehrenpreis's *Mr. Swift and His Contempories* (vol. 1, 1962; 1983); *Doctor Swift* (vol. 2, 1967; 1983); and *Swift The Man, His Works, and the Age* (vol. 3, 1983) is a standard biographical study. John Middleton Murry, *Jonathan Swift: A Critical Biography* (1954), remains useful.

Other critical and biographical studies of value include Leslie Stephen, *Swift* (1882); Carl Van Doren, *Swift* (1930); Ricardo Quintana, *The Mind and Art of Jonathan Swift* (1936); John M. Bullitt, *Jonathan Swift and the Anatomy of Satire: A Study of Satiric Techniques* (1953); Martin Price, *Swift's Rhetorical Art: A Study in Structure and Meaning* (1953); William B. Ewald, *The Masks of Jonathan Swift* (1954); Louis A. Landa, *Swift and the Church of Ireland* (1954); Ricardo Quintana, *Swift: An Introduction* (1955); Irvin Ehrenpreis, *The Personality of Jonathan Swift* (1958); Kathleen Williams, *Jonathan Swift and the Age of Compromise* (1958); Bertrand A. Goldgar, *The Curse of Party: Swift's Relations with Addison and Steele* (1961); William A. Eddy, *Gulliver's Travels: A Critical Study* (1963); Edward W. Rosenheim, *Swift and the Satirist's Art* (1963); Herbert John Davis, *Jonathan Swift: Essays on His Satire and Other Studies* (1964); Nigel Dennis, *Jonathan Swift* (1964); Ernest Lee Tuveson, ed., *Swift: A Collection of Critical Essays* (1964); Milton Voigt, *Swift and the Twentieth Century* (1964); Richard I. Cook, *Jonathan Swift as a Tory Pamphleteer* (1967); Robert Hunting, *Jonathan Swift* (1967); and Denis Donoghue, *Jonathan Swift: A Critical Introduction* (1969). □

Algernon Charles Swinburne

The English poet, dramatist, and critic Algernon Charles Swinburne (1837-1909) was famous in Victorian England for the innovative versification of his poetry and infamous for his violent attacks on Victorian morality.

Algernon Charles Swinburne was born in London on April 5, 1837. He was nervous and frail from birth, but he was also fired with nervous energy and fearlessness to the point of being reckless. Much of his childhood was spent on the Isle of Wight, a circumstance that fostered his deep love of the sea. He also made frequent visits to his grandfather's estate in Northumberland, where he was fascinated by the medieval border ballads that the servants sang to him. Swinburne attended Eton from 1849 to 1853. At school he became an avid reader and won first prizes in French and Italian. The corporal punishment that was traditional at Eton may have developed the abnormal pleasure in the experience of pain that characterized his adult behavior.

Years at Oxford

Swinburne entered Balliol College, Oxford, in January 1856, and he studied there intermittently for almost 4 years. Though he continued to read widely, he chafed at academic discipline and neglected his studies. His appearance was strikingly unusual. He was abnormally short with narrow, sloping shoulders and tiny hands and feet. His eyes were green, and his disproportionately large head was topped by a great aureole of bright red hair. His appearance, plus his habit of fluttering his hands and hopping about as he excitedly talked, provoked Henry Adams to compare him to "a crimson macaw." Swinburne supplemented his astounding physique with equally bizarre behavior. He became known for his violent attacks on Christianity and on conventional morality as well as for his late hours and heavy drinking. Swinburne replaced the religious faith of his youth with political fervor, declaiming verses to a portrait of the Italian patriot Giuseppe Mazzini that he hung in his room at Oxford.

At the university Swinburne formed lasting friendships with two of Oxford's most famous scholars, Walter Pater and Benjamin Jowett. In 1857 Swinburne became intimate with the Pre-Raphaelites Dante Gabriel Rossetti, William Morris, and Edward Burne-Jones. By 1860 Swinburne's Balliol colleagues considered him "dangerous," but his decision to leave Oxford without a degree was apparently

his own. His father, greatly disturbed by his son's withdrawal, nevertheless provided him with a permanent allowance. Swinburne moved to London and devoted his life to writing.

His Works

In 1861 Swinburne began his long association with Rossetti, who exerted a steadying influence and thus enabled him to write some of his finest lyric poetry. Swinburne published two plays in 1860, *The Queen Mother* and *Rosamond,* but they received no critical notice. However, in 1865, his powerful imitation of Greek tragedy, *Atlanta in Calydon,* was an instant success. Most critics were entranced by the metrical virtuosity displayed in the constantly shifting rhythms of the play's choruses, and few noticed its darkly amoral theme. But *Poems and Ballads, First Series,* published in April 1866, made Swinburne's sensuality and anti-Christianity unmistakable. This volume contains his finest poetry—beautiful in supple and unusual rhythms, in melodious sound combinations, and in intricately extended images. The most notable poems in it were clearly intended to shock the Victorian public. The "Hymn to Proserpine" denounces Christ as the "pale Galilean," and "Faustine," "Laus Veneris," "Anactoria," and "Dolores" boldly flaunt Swinburne's sadomasochistic sexuality. The book was savagely attacked by the press, and a controversy raged. Swinburne answered in "Notes on Poems and Reviews."

In 1867 Swinburne met Mazzini, who told him to turn from "love frenzy" to the utilization of his poetic gift in the "service of the republic." The result was *Songs before Sunrise* (1871), a volume of poems dedicated to the cause of freedom and democracy and championing the Italian struggle for independence. In 1878 Swinburne published *Poems and Ballads, Second Series,* but this volume contained few poems as beautiful and none so shocking as those of the *First Series.* It marked the end of Swinburne's greatest poetic achievement.

Throughout this period of literary activity, Swinburne had also been living a dissolute life of heavy drinking and masochistic sexual practices. His dissipation had brought on a number of attacks similar to epileptic fits, but his amazing energy had enabled him to return each time to his frenzied style of life.

In September 1879, however, Swinburne collapsed so completely that a friend, Walter Theodore Watts-Dunton, took him to his home in Putney, a suburb of London. There Watts-Dunton imposed a regimen that probably saved Swinburne's life. The poet spent the remaining 30 years of his life with Watts-Dunton in a manner as subdued as his youth had been wild. The sober discipline imposed on him enabled Swinburne to write and to publish 23 volumes of poetry, prose, and drama during these years. But *A Century of Roundels* (1883) clearly showed that Swinburne's rhythmic virtuosity had degenerated into excessive fluency of meter and that the fiery radical of Oxford was no more. In spite of continued avid reading and writing, Swinburne did not develop intellectually or artistically beyond his university days. He died of pneumonia on April 10, 1909, at Putney.

Further Reading

Swinburne's essays in defense of his work were collected by Clyde Kenneth Hyder in *Swinburne Replies* (1966). A wealth of fascinating detail is in Cecil Y. Lang's edition of *The Swinburne Letters* (6 vols., 1959-1962). The best biography is Georges Lafourcade, *Swinburne: A Literary Biography* (1932). The best critical appraisal is T.S. Eliot, "Swinburne as Poet," in *The Sacred Wood* (1920). Major studies include Thomas Earle Welby, *A Study of Swinburne* (1926), and Samuel C. Chew, *Swinburne* (1929).

Additional Sources

Henderson, Philip, *Swinburne; portrait of a poet,* New York: Macmillan, 1974.

Kernahan, Coulson, *Swinburne as I knew him: with some unpublished letters from the poet to his cousin the Hon. Lady Henniker Heaton,* Philadelphia: R. West, 1978.

Mayfield, John S., *Swinburneiana: a gallimaufry of bits and pieces about Algernon Charles Swinburne,* s.l.: s.n., 1974 (Gaithersburg, Md.: Waring Press).

Thomas, Donald Serrell, *Swinburne, the poet in his world,* New York: Oxford University Press, 1979. □

Mary E. Switzer

Serving the public for 48 years, Mary E. Switzer (1900-1971) dedicated her life to advancing the cause of rehabilitation. She was involved in establishing the World Health Organization, was director of the Office of Vocational Rehabilitation, and was administrator of the Social and Rehabilitation Service at the Department of Health, Education and Welfare.

Mary Elizabeth Switzer was born on February 16, 1900, in Newton Upper Falls, Massachusetts, the oldest of three children. Her mother, Margaret Moore Switzer, died when Mary was 11 years old. Since Mary's father, Julius F. Switzer, had deserted the family some years before, Mary and her sister made their home with relatives. The most influential of these, her Uncle "Mike" Moore, was an Irish patriot and socialist. He made a great impression on Mary, encouraging her to adopt a useful life's work.

Switzer was raised a Roman Catholic and attended Newton Classical High. After she graduated in 1917 she enrolled in Radcliffe College, where she majored in international law, the first undergraduate to do so. She received an A.B. degree in 1921. While at Radcliffe, Switzer helped establish the Inter-Collegiate Liberal League, a group dedicated to reform.

Moving to Washington, D.C., she found employment with the Minimum Wage Board. In the nation's capital she shared a home with Isabelle Stevenson Diamond, later a librarian in the Treasury Department. In 1922 Switzer entered the civil service and obtained a position as junior economist in the Treasury Department. Between 1928 and

1933 she had responsibility for press intelligence for the secretary of the treasury. In 1934 she began working as assistant to Josephine Roche, assistant secretary of the treasury. There Switzer was assigned to the U.S. Public Health Service, where she worked toward development of the Federal Security Agency. This agency became the Department of Health, Education and Welfare (HEW) in 1953 (now two separate departments—Education, and Health and Human Services).

By 1939 Switzer was assistant to the administrator of the Federal Security Agency (FSA), Paul McNutt, and after the attack on Pearl Harbor she did confidential work with the War Research Service and was the FSA representative on the War Manpower Commission. Her dedication brought her the Presidential Certificate of Merit, given in recognition of her contribution to the war effort. This certificate was the highest award going to a regular civil service worker.

Mary E. Switzer helped establish the World Health Organization, and on November 9, 1950, was named director of the Office of Vocational Rehabilitation (OVR), succeeding Michael J. Shortley. In her capacity as director she concentrated on bringing vocational training to all physically and mentally handicapped persons. The OVR had been established in 1920 and during its first two decades had rehabilitated only about 10,000 persons annually. Due to Switzer's efforts, the number of people returning to work annually rose from 56,000 in 1950 to 240,000 in 1970. Her commitment was well-known, and she was instrumental in the unanimous passage of the Vocational Rehabilitation Act

of 1954. This legislation was critical in funding research and training and in establishing rehabilitation centers nationwide. Further, Switzer was responsible for adding, in 1960, an international research program for the handicapped.

Her adroitness in working with federal and state-level officials was a skill she worked hard to develop. She was also able to maintain an excellent relationship with Congress throughout her years of service, despite changing administrations with often conflicting goals. Colleagues respected her energy, and she was admired for her optimism and concern for handicapped workers. In 1955 she received the President's Award from the National Rehabilitation Association.

On August 23, 1960, Mary E. Switzer was the first female recipient of the prestigious Albert Lasker Award. This award was given in recognition of her position as the "prime architect of a workable rehabilitation service for the nation's physically handicapped." Switzer was also awarded honorary doctorates from Tufts University, Gallaudet College, Western College for Women, Adelphi University, Boston University, and Women's Medical College. She was also on the board of Brandeis University and was a trustee of Radcliffe College.

She retired in 1970 as administrator of the Social and Rehabilitation Service of HEW at a banquet attended by over 1,000 people. Still committed to public service, however, Switzer's retirement merely enabled her to assume a position as vice president of the World Rehabilitation Fund, with offices in the nation's capital. Mary E. Switzer died of cancer in Washington, D.C., on October 16, 1971.

Further Reading

The Department of Health, Education and Welfare compiled a list of Switzer's publications entitled "Articles by Miss Mary E. Switzer." Also, her friend and life-long companion Isabelle Stevenson Diamond wrote a booklet, "Mary Elizabeth Switzer, 'The Dedicated Bureaucrat.'" And *Rehabilitation Record,* January-February 1972, carried a piece, "Mary Elizabeth Switzer: A Tribute." She is included in Jonathan R. T. Hughes, *The Vital Few* (several editions).

Additional Sources

Walker, Martha Lentz, *Beyond bureaucracy: Mary Elizabeth Switzer and rehabilitation,* Lanham: University Press of America, 1985. □

Gerard Swope

Gerard Swope (1872-1957) was an engineer who became president of General Electric during a period of exponential growth. He was also a public servant who was influential in the early New Deal.

Gerard Swope was born in St. Louis, Missouri, on December 1, 1872, the son of Isaac and Ida (Cohn) Swope. Isaac Swope was a Jewish immigrant to the New World in 1857 who lived for a time in Cincinnati before settling in St. Louis to open a watch-assembly factory. He returned to Germany in 1865 to marry Ida Cohn, the daughter of the chief rabbi in Thuringia, and to bring her to the United States. Two of their sons became famous, Gerard as an industrialist and Herbert Bayard as a Pulitzer-Prize winning journalist for the *New York World*.

Gerard, who was the older brother, became interested in how things operated at an early age and decided, even before going to Central High School in St. Louis, to become an engineer. His parents sent him to Massachusetts Institute of Technology (MIT), from which he graduated in 1895 with a B.S. in electrical engineering.

His first job, however, was in the summer of his sophomore year in college (1893). He had gone to Chicago to the World's Fair and had managed to find a job with General Electric. When he graduated, he went to work for Western Electric, a General Electric subsidiary in Chicago. He was hired not because of his engineering skill, but because of a letter from an old friend of his father.

While in Chicago, Swope became involved in the settlement house movement, which kindled an interest in social reform that lasted all his life. He lived at Hull House for several years and taught algebra and electricity to workers in the night school. He also met his future wife, May Dayton

Hill, there. She had come to Chicago to study with John Dewey.

Swope returned to St. Louis in 1899 to help open a subsidiary of Western Electric, Mercantile Electric. By this time he had shown great talent for sales and had moved out of engineering. In two years he had become the manager of the branch. At that time he also married May Hill. The marriage was a happy one, and the Swopes had five children—Henrietta H., Isaac G., Gerard, David, and John.

The Swopes became involved in charitable activities in St. Louis. Although there was no settlement house, Gerard became a founding member of the first playground committee in the city in 1901 and chairman of the first public bath committee in 1903. His energy was not diverted from his business efforts, however, and in 1906 Western Electric called him back to Chicago to become assistant supervisor of all branch houses and sales manager. Two years later he was promoted to general sales manager and moved to New York City. By 1913, when he was 41, he had become vice-president and director of the company.

When World War I involved the United States, Swope entered public service as assistant director of purchase, storage, and traffic for the army, a position which won him the Distinguished Service Medal. He also associated with two men—Bernard Baruch and Hugh S. Johnson—who were to become public servants again a few years later.

In 1919 Swope became president of International General Electric, a new division which Swope organized. His work, which entailed much travel to Japan and England, was highly successful. As a result, he became president of General Electric in 1922, a position he held until his retirement in 1939. He presided over the tremendous growth of the electric company in the 1920s.

Swope continued his interest in public affairs, serving as chairman of the Eighth American Red Cross Roll Call in 1924. As a result of the Depression, Swope wrote the book *Stabilization of Industry* (1931), in which he proposed that industry control itself by associations and suggested an expanded pension plan. Because of the "Swope Plan," as it was called, Franklin D. Roosevelt called upon Swope to serve in a variety of roles in the New Deal: member, Industrial Advisory Board of the National Recovery Administration (NRA) (1933), an agency run by Hugh Johnson; member, Bureau of Advertising and Planning of the Department of Commerce (1933); chairman, Coal Arbitration Board (1933); member, National Labor Board (1933); member, President's Advisory Council on Economic Security (1934); and member, Advisory Council on Social Security (1937-1938). His service did not end with his retirement from General Electric: he continued to be honorary president of the company from 1940 to 1942 and president from 1942 to 1944, as well as serving in the government's war effort. He was an assistant to the secretary of the treasury in 1942. At the same time he was chairman of the Committee to Study Budgets of Relief Appeals for Foreign Countries, a service which won him the 1942 Hoover Medal.

Before he died on November 10, 1957, Swope had won many honors. He was a chevalier of the Legion of Honor (France) and a member of the Order of the Rising Sun

(Japan). He had honorary doctorates from Rutgers (1923), Union (1924), Colgate (1927), Stevens Institute of Technology (1929), and Washington University in St. Louis (1932). He had also influenced American society by both his business and his public service.

Further Reading

The only biography of Swope is David Goldsmith Loth's *Swope of G.E.: The Story of Gerard Swope and G.E. in American Business* (1955). The biography is popularly written and focuses on Swope's later career. Ely Jacques Kahn's biography of Herbert Bayard Swope, *The World of Swope* (1965), sheds more light on Gerard's personal life, particularly his relationship with his brother.

Additional Sources

Loth, David Goldsmith, *Swope of G.E.,* New York: Arno Press, 1976, 1958. □

Baron Sydenham

Charles Edward Poulett Thomson, Baron Sydenham (1799-1841), was an English merchant turned politician. As governor general of British North America, he attempted to implement the recommendations of the Durham Report.

Charles Thomson (the father did not add his mother's family name, Poulett, to his own until 1820) was born on Sept. 13, 1799, the youngest child of a prosperous merchant with extensive Russian trade connections. He was privately educated, never attending a public school or university, and at 16 went to Russia in the employ of his father's firm. After extensive travels, during which he became fluent in several languages, he made several unsuccessful attempts to obtain a diplomatic post and after further experiences in Russia returned to England in 1824. In 1826, much against his family's wishes, Poulett Thomson was elected member of Parliament for Dover and in 1832 for both Dover and Manchester; although he had not sought the second seat, he chose thereafter to sit for it.

Poulett Thomson in politics was an ardent reformer whose friends included John Stuart Mill, Jeremy Bentham, and Joseph Hume. An able student of the relatively new subject of political economy, he was a strong exponent of free trade, and his first speeches in Parliament quickly attracted the attention of his Liberal colleagues. In 1830 he was appointed vice president of the Board of Trade and treasurer of the navy and, in 1834, president of the Board of Trade. In 1839, offered a choice between becoming chancellor of the Exchequer or governor general of British North America, Poulett Thomson chose the second, happy by now to escape the heavy grind of Cabinet and parliamentary sessions.

Poulett Thomson had used his ministerial positions to institute many enlightened reforms, not only in the steady reduction of customs duties but in the general improvement of Britain's trade relations. He had helped found the School of Design to enhance the marketability of British products and had worked hard for the recognition of international copyright; he had also reformed the parliamentary procedure for private bills, most of which concerned the incorporation of companies. His greatest achievements, however, came in Canada, where he arrived as governor on Oct. 19, 1839.

What is now central Canada was then racked by bitter disputes, not only between French-speaking and English-speaking Canadians but, in both Lower and Upper Canada, between oligarchical executives and more popular elements; abortive revolutions had occurred in 1837-1838.

Lord Durham, Poulett Thomson's predecessor, had in 1838, in a report which assumed the ultimate assimilation of the French Canadians, advocated the union of the two colonies and proposed making the executive responsible to the elected branch of the legislature. Poulett Thomson's assignment was to accomplish both these tasks, and in the face of enormous difficulties he completed the establishment of the Province of Canada and laid the groundwork fundamental to responsible government. He did the same for a system of municipal government, resolved the complex problem of the Clergy Reserves (tracts of land for the support of religious institutions), and contributed to the settlement of the Maine boundary dispute. He was elevated to the peerage in 1840 and died in Kingston, Ontario, on Sept. 19, 1841.

Further Reading

Two sound biographies of Sydenham are George Poulett Scrope, ed., *Memoir of the Life of the Right Honourable Charles Lord Sydenham* (1843), and Adam Shortt, *Lord Sydenham* (1926). Scrope was Sydenham's admiring brother, and most of his book is a narrative of Sydenham's Canadian career by his secretary, T. W. C. Murdock.

Additional Sources

Meynell, G. G. (Geoffrey, Guy), *A bibliography of Dr. Thomas Sydenham (1624-1689)*, Folkestone: Winterdown Books, 1990.

Meynell, G. G. (Geoffrey Guy), *Materials for a biography of Dr. Thomas Sydenham (1624-1689): a new survey of public and private archives,* Folkestone: Winterdown Books, 1988. □

Thomas Sydenham

The English physician Thomas Sydenham (1624-1689) emphasized, in practicing medicine, careful observation and experience and earned the title "English Hippocrates."

Born in Winford Eagle, Dorset, the fifth son of a wealthy country gentleman, Thomas Sydenham entered Magdalen College, Oxford, in 1642. His studies were interrupted by the outbreak of the civil war, during which the Sydenhams fought for the parliamentarians. He returned to Oxford in 1647, receiving his bachelor degree the following year. In 1651 he rejoined the army, after which he stayed at Oxford until 1663, when he was married and opened his London practice.

With only 18 months of formal medical education, consisting of a mixture of classics, anatomical dissections, and formal disputations, Sydenham found little use in theoretical learning, and experimental science seemed just as useless to him. He was convinced that only the careful observation of diseases at the bedside could lead to medical progress, and he spent all his efforts on detailed clinical observations. Despite his objection to theory and his insistence on a purely empirical medicine, he accepted the traditional concept that diseases resulted from disturbances of the bodily humors. He revived the Hippocratic notion that the seasons and atmospheric conditions played an equally important role, but he differed from Hippocrates in the emphasis he placed on the recognition of specific diseases. He believed that the detailed study of the natural history of any disease would eventually indicate what specific medication should be used for its treatment. Recognizing that Peruvian bark (crude quinine) was the only specific he knew, he prescribed it for malaria, which was the most prevalent fever in the London of his time.

At a time when most physicians were deeply concerned with theoretical questions, with systematization and attempts to relate medicine to experimental physics or chemistry, Sydenham's empiricism and emphasis on clinical description did not make him popular among his medical colleagues.

Some of Sydenham's writings became classics, like his description of gout (1683), which he suffered from for years and which ultimately led to his death. He differentiated scarlet fever from measles. His description of hysteria, which is frequently mentioned for its accuracy, included other conditions as well. The prevalence of smallpox led him to the conclusion that it was a physiological process which everyone had to go through. Because of his accurate portrayal of St. Vitus's dance, this disease became known as Sydenham's chorea. In therapy he insisted on simple prescriptions and measures, a fact which may have contributed to his great success as a practitioner.

His personal friend and fellow physician John Locke applied Sydenham's empiric medical ideas to philosophy. Succeeding generations of physicians found Sydenham's emphasis on bedside observation most useful and proclaimed him the "English Hippocrates." His emphasis on the study of the natural history of diseases and of all the factors surrounding their occurrence gave great impetus to the subsequent development of epidemiology.

Further Reading

A detailed biography, which also contains some of Sydenham's works in translation, is Kenneth Dewhurst, *Dr. Thomas Sydenham, 1624-1689* (1966). Other studies are Joseph F. Payne, *Thomas Sydenham* (1900), and David Riesman, *Thomas Sydenham, Clinician* (1926). For background see

Fielding H. Garrison, *An Introduction to the History of Medicine* (4th ed. repr. 1967). □

Syed Ahmed Khan

Syed Ahmed Khan (1817-1898) was a Moslem religious leader, educationalist, and politician. He contributed to the intellectual and institutional foundation of Moslem modernization in southern Asia.

Born on Oct. 17, 1817, Syed Ahmed trained himself in Moslem law and religion and was employed by the British government. He served in several Indian administrative posts, gave assistance during the 1857 mutiny, and retired with honor 20 years later to devote himself to social and religious reform.

Throughout his life Syed Ahmed showed concern with how Indian Moslems could adapt to intellectual and political change accompanying Western rule. His first mission became reinterpretation of Moslem ideology so as to reconcile tradition with Western education and science. He argued in several books on Islam that the Koran rested on a deep appreciation of reason and natural law and therefore did not preclude Moslem involvement in scientific methodology. These themes, mixed with a call for Moslem education, continually appeared in his journals, the *Mohammedan Social Reformer* and the *Aligarh Institute Gazette.*

Syed Ahmed's ideas became institutionalized despite criticism from theologians. In 1862 he formed a scientific society, and 13 years later he assisted in establishing the Muhammadan Anglo-Oriental College, which prospered and became the key intellectual center for Indian Moslems, Aligarh University. The success of the college was largely due to his leadership and a curriculum embodying both Western and Oriental studies.

At the same time Syed Ahmed's views on Islam in India fostered his political interest. First, he tried to assure the British of Moslem loyalty by countering the dual charge that Moslems had instigated the mutiny and that they were compelled by religious injunction to rebel against a Christian government. He also urged Moslems to avoid "seditious" political activity. These tactics reflected his belief that if the British were convinced of Moslem support, the resulting official patronage would help Moslems overcome their relative backwardness in education and employment. Two factors were judged necessary for Moslem advance, special British assistance and a reorientation of attitudes among Moslems.

Syed Ahmed increasingly opposed Hindu and nationalist leaders after the creation of the Indian National Congress in 1885. Although sympathetic to criticism of British injustice, he saw Congress as a potentially dangerous organization. If enacted, Congress proposals favoring open competition for jobs and elected legislative councils would further hamper the growth of the Moslem minority. Too, association with anti-British politicians might undercut Syed Ahmed's attempt to strengthen Moslem-British ties. He accordingly formed in 1888 an anti-Congress organization, the United Patriotic Association, and called on coreligionists to withdraw from Congress. The massive Moslem response left the Congress without significant Moslem cooperation for 3 decades.

By his death on March 27, 1898, Syed Ahmed had indelibly stamped the ideology and life-style of Indian Moslems. His institutions such as the college and the Moslem Educational Conference continued to influence intellectuals, while his political stance remained a basic determinant of Moslem attitudes toward agitation and nationalism.

Further Reading

English biographies of Syed Ahmed include G.F.I. Graham, *The Life and Work of Sir Syed Ahmed Khan* (1885), and Shan Muhammad, *Sir Syed Ahmed Kahn: A Political Biography* (1969). Aziz Ahmed, *Islamic Modernism in India and Pakistan, 1857-1964* (1967), and a recent study on Aligarh by S.K. Bhatnagar, *History of the M.A.O. College, Aligarh,* provide background on Syed Ahmed's life and milieu.

Additional Sources

Graham, George Farquhar Irving, *The life and work of Sir Syed Ahmed Khan,* Karachi: Oxford University Press, 1974. □

William Sylvis

American labor leader William Sylvis (1828-1869) pioneered many trade union methods and was the guiding spirit behind the first attempt to form a united trade union movement.

William Sylvis was born in Armagh, Pa., on Nov. 26, 1828, of hopelessly poor parents. He had 3 months of formal schooling; it has been said that he learned to write only after becoming secretary of a local union, obligated to correspond with other locals. He was an iron molder by trade and as a young man held part ownership in a foundry. In 1852 he married and moved to Philadelphia. He became secretary of the iron molders' union in Philadelphia in 1857 and, 2 years later, helped organize the Iron Molders International Union.

Sylvis led a movement of workingmen opposed to war, but when the Civil War began, he helped to recruit for the army. However, his chief interest remained unionism. "I love this Union cause," he wrote, "I hold it more dear than I do my family or my life. I am willing to devote to it all that I am or have or hope for in this world." In 1863, elected president of the Molders Union, Sylvis almost single-handedly built it into the most significant labor organization of its time. In 1862 he undertook the first nationwide organizational drive, personally traveling over 10,000 miles. He built the union from 2,000 members in 15 locals with a treasury of $1,600 to 6,000 members, 54 locals, and $25,000.

Sylvis was an excellent administrator. He insisted on centralized structure so that locals could not strike without national agreement, introduced a per capita tax to build up strike funds, issued union cards, and urged a closed shop where possible. Sylvis disliked strikes as representing too great a sacrifice but sanctioned them as a last resort. He also encouraged workers' cooperatives.

In 1866 Sylvis assisted in founding the first united trade union, the National Labor Union (NLU). He became its president in 1868. Although the father of practical business unionism in the United States, he advocated numerous reform measures and independent political action. He also advocated international labor cooperation and tried unsuccessfully to send a delegate to the Lausanne conference of the First International in 1867. In 1869 the NLU was represented at the annual meeting. At the time of his death at the age of 41, he was urging the formation of a national Labor Reform party.

Further Reading

There is a short but valuable account of Sylvis's life in James C. Sylvis, *The Life, Speeches, Labor and Essays of William H. Sylvis* (1872). Also informative are Norman J. Ware, *The Labor Movement in the United States, 1860-1895* (1929); Charlotte Todes, *William H. Sylvis and the National Labor Union* (1942); and Jonathan Grossman, *William Sylvis: Pioneer of American Labor* (1945). □

Edmund John Millington Synge

The Irish dramatist Edmund John Millington Synge (1871-1909), one of the greatest playwrights of Dublin's Abbey Theatre, made the folklore and dialect of the Irish peasantry the subject of his plays.

John Millington Synge was born on April 16, 1871, in Rathfarnham, a suburb of Dublin. He was the youngest of the eight children of John Hatch Synge, a lawyer who died when John Millington was an infant, and Kathleen Traill Synge, the daughter of a Protestant clergyman. As a child, Synge showed signs of the tubercular condition that claimed his life at the age of 38.

Synge attended private schools in Dublin and was awarded a bachelor of arts degree by Trinity College in 1892. He then traveled to Germany, intending to study the violin; but after a year of wandering, he joined the diversified group of Irish expatriates then studying in Paris. There Synge lived an almost ascetic life in the midst of bohemian surroundings, a pattern his later life also followed.

Synge's career took an unexpected turn in 1896, when he was introduced to William Butler Yeats in Paris. The older Irish poet urged Synge to abandon his French studies and to devote himself to a study of his own people and their culture, for which his knowledge of Gaelic had well prepared him. Synge took Yeats's advice. After intensive research in the remote Aran Islands and in County Wicklow, he presented his first play, *The Shadow of the Glen* (1903), to the Irish National Theatre. Irish newspapers greeted it as "an insult to every decent woman in Ireland."

In 1904 Synge became codirector of the Abbey Theatre with Yeats and Lady Augusta Gregory. The Abbey produced his classic tragedy of the Aran Islands, *Riders to the Sea,* in 1904. Synge's plays met with continued hostility because of their seeming slight to Irish country people. Audiences walked out of *The Well of the Saints* (1905); *The Tinker's Wedding* (1907) has never been produced professionally in Ireland.

Synge's comic masterpiece, *The Playboy of the Western World* (1907), caused riots upon its presentation both in Dublin and in the United States. The author once commented mildly on the furor caused by his work, "We shall have to establish a Society for the Preservation of Irish Humor." His last play, *Deirdre of the Sorrows* (1909), was produced posthumously; it was found nearly completed in the Dublin nursing home where Synge died on March 24, 1909. He had been nursed in his final illness by Marie O'Neill, a leading actress of the Abbey Theatre, whom he had hoped to marry.

Further Reading

An early and still useful biography of Synge is Maurice Bourgeois, *John Millington Synge and the Irish Theatre* (1913). Several later studies bring to light information not available to his first

biographer: David H. Greene and Edward M. Stephens, *John Millington Synge, 1871-1909* (1959); Daniel Corkery, *Synge and Anglo-Irish Literature* (1965); and Donna L. Gerstenberger, *John Millington Synge* (1965).

On Synge's work with the Abbey Theatre, Alan Price, *Synge and Anglo-Irish Drama* (1961), and Elizabeth Coxhead, *John Millington Synge and Lady Gregory* (1962), provide the necessary background, while Adelaide D. Estill, *The Sources of Synge* (1939), discusses the materials Synge used in his plays. The best short study of Synge is Denis Johnston's pamphlet, *John Millington Synge* (1965). Important references to Synge are in William Butler Yeats, *Autobiographies* (1914; repr. 1961), and valuable essays on him are in Robin Skelton and David R. Clark, eds., *Irish Renaissance; A Gathering of Essays, Memoirs and Letters from the Massachusetts Review* (1965), and Robin Skelton and Ann Saddlemyer, eds., *The World of W. B. Yeats: Essays in Perspective* (1965).

Additional Sources

Bickley, Francis Lawrance, *J. M. Synge and the Irish dramatic movement,* Norwood, Pa.: Norwood Editions, 1975.

J.M. Synge, 1871-1909, New York: New York University Press, 1989.

J. M. Synge: interviews and recollections, New York: Barnes & Noble, 1977.

Kiely, David M., *John Millington Synge: a biography,* New York: St. Martin's Press, 1995.

Masefield, John, *John M. Synge: a few personal recollections with biographical note,* Norwood, Pa.: Norwood Editions, 1978.

Stephens, Edward M., *My uncle John; Edward Stephens's life of J. M. Syng,* London, Oxford University Press, 1974. □

Albert von Szent-Györgyi

The Hungarian-American biochemist Albert von Szent-Györgyi (1893-1986) was awarded the Nobel Prize in Physiology or Medicine for his discoveries relating to cell respiration and to the composition of vitamin C. He also did important work on the chemistry of muscle contraction.

The son of a landed proprietor, Albert von Szent-Györgyi was born in Budapest on Sept. 16, 1893. He became a medical student at the University of Budapest in 1911. His studies were interrupted by World War I, when he joined the military and was wounded in battle. Upon discharge from the army he resumed his studies and graduated in 1917 as a doctor of medicine. After further study at Prague, Berlin, and Hamburg and a post in pharmacology at Leiden, he worked from 1922 to 1926 as an assistant in the Institute of Physiology of the University of Groningen.

Biological Oxidation

By 1920 there was great interest in the method whereby the energy of the foodstuff molecule was released and utilized by the living cell. It was realized that the process could not be one of "slow combustion" with molecular oxygen, as the heat produced in such a process would have destroyed the living cell. Otto Warburg held that the liberation of the foodstuff's energy was the result of oxidation of the foodstuff molecule by activated oxygen. Heinrich Wieland argued that the release of energy was due to loss of hydrogen by the foodstuff molecule. Chemically, the two processes are equivalent. In 1924 Warburg isolated his "respiratory enzyme," which activated oxygen and allowed it to be taken up by the foodstuff molecule. This discovery strongly favored Warburg's theory.

At Groningen, Szent-Györgyi studied biological oxidation in the animal cell. Warburg had studied the inhibition of cell respiration—that is, oxidation by activated oxygen—by cyanide. It was known that methylene blue acts as an artificial hydrogen acceptor (H-acceptor). In minced tissue Szent-Györgyi now inhibited oxygen activation by cyanide and then added methylene blue. The dye lost its blue color, showing that it had acted as an H-acceptor and that respiration had been restored. He thus clearly demonstrated that in cell respiration the two processes of oxygen activation and hydrogen activation were both active.

Ascorbic Acid

While at Groningen, Szent-Györgyi became interested in the bronze pigmentation of the skin in Addison's disease, the cause of which was unknown. He decided to study the brown discoloration produced by injury in the catechol group of plants, and he clarified the method of its production. Nothing was known of the oxidative system of the peroxidase group of plants, which do not show this discoloration, except that they contain an active peroxidase

which activates peroxide and that they can oxidize various pigments. He found that if peroxide was added to a mixture of peroxidase and benzidine an intense blue color appeared immediately. But if he repeated this reaction, using juice squeezed from a peroxidase plant instead of purified peroxidase, the blue color appeared only after a second or so. He concluded that the plant juice must also have contained a powerful reducing agent which reduced the oxidized benzidine until it had itself been used up. Arguing on these lines, he found that the adrenal cortex contained a similar reducing substance. The adrenal was a very rich source, but he later found that it was merely a storehouse for the substance.

At the invitation of Sir F. Gowland Hopkins, Szent-Györgyi spent the year 1927 at Cambridge University, where he isolated the reducing substance from adrenal glands, orange juice, and cabbage. With a thesis on this work he graduated as a doctor of philosophy. He found that the reducing agent had the empirical composition $C_6H_8O_6$, and he called it provisionally hexuronic acid. As the enormous quantities of adrenals required for his further analysis were not available in Great Britain, he spent the year 1928 at the Mayo Clinic in Rochester, Minn., where supplies of adrenal were available from the St. Paul slaughterhouses. In 1929 he returned to Cambridge with 25 grams of hexuronic acid. Most of this he gave to (Sir) Norman Haworth of the University of Birmingham and to other specialists in carbohydrate analysis.

In 1930 Szent-Györgyi became professor of medical chemistry at the University of Szeged in Hungary. He had long thought that hexuronic acid was vitamin C, and he was now joined by J. Svirbely, who was experienced in the necessary animal tests. In April 1932 they announced that they had, by the administration of one milligram of hexuronic acid daily, protected guinea pigs from scurvy for 56 days. Three weeks later they claimed the identity of hexuronic acid and vitamin C. Simultaneously Charles G. King and W. A. Waugh announced their isolation of crystalline vitamin C and its apparent identity with hexuronic acid. On the basis of these results Szent-Györgyi and Haworth changed the name hexuronic acid to ascorbic acid.

Szent-Györgyi's supply of ascorbic acid was now exhausted, but Szeged was the center of the paprika industry. He now, for the first time, tested paprika for the presence of ascorbic acid and found that it was a very rich source. He soon prepared several hundred grams for distribution to chemists. The structural formula of ascorbic acid was determined by Haworth in 1932, and by Paul Karrer in 1933. It was synthesized by Haworth, and independently by Tadeus Reichstein in 1933. Synthetic ascorbic acid was soon available commercially.

Intermediate Stages in Cell Respiration

In 1925 David Keilin of Cambridge University rediscovered an intracellular pigment, which he called "cytochrome." In living cells it showed a reversible oxidoreduction. It was fundamentally important in the final reaction of cell respiration, by which activated oxygen combined with activated hydrogen. It was later realized that Warburg's respiratory enzyme oxidized cytochrome, and the enzyme is now called cytochrome oxidase.

About 1926 Szent-Györgyi was intrigued by the peculiarities of succino-dehydrogenase. It was already known that this dehydrogenase could be inhibited by malonic acid, and he now showed that when he added malonic acid to minced tissue, respiration ceased. He concluded that succinic acid was not an ordinary metabolite but that it had to have some catalytic function. Following this observation Szent-Györgyi elucidated in succeeding years the role of the C_4-dicarboxylic acids—oxaloacetic, malic, fumaric, and succinic, in that order—in transmitting hydrogen molecules along the chain from the foodstuff molecule to cytochrome, resulting in its final oxidation to water. At each link in the chain a portion of the energy of the foodstuff was released.

In the early stages of these researches Szent-Györgyi was interested in a fluorescent yellow pigment which showed reversible oxidation. He called it provisionally "cytoflav." It was inactive when added to a test system. In 1932 Warburg described his "yellow enzyme" and showed that it consisted of two components—a specific protein and this yellow pigment; neither by itself had any catalytic action. This flavoprotein was later shown to be vitamin B_2 (riboflavin). In 1937 Szent-Györgyi attempted to suggest its position in the cell respiratory system. For these researches he was awarded the Nobel Prize in 1937.

Biochemistry of Muscular Contraction

About 1860 Willi Kühne extracted from muscle a protein that he called "myosin." Little further was done until 1939, when it was found that purified myosin showed the properties of adenosine triphosphatase, an enzyme that splits off the terminal phosphate group of adenosine triphosphate (ATP), thus releasing energy. In 1939, at Szeged, Szent-Györgyi repeated Kühne's work, and in 1941, with L. Banga, he showed that two types of protein could be extracted from muscle, depending on the length of the extraction period. Extraction for 20 minutes yielded a protein of low viscosity, further lowered on addition of ATP. They called this protein "myosin." Extraction overnight yielded a second protein which formed a loose complex with myosin, and it was this complex that constituted the "myosin" of Kühne. Banga and Szent-Györgyi called this second protein "actin," and they showed that, if solutions of myosin and actin are mixed, the result is a solution of the loose complex which they called "actomyosin." In 1941 Szent-Györgyi made threads of actomyosin by squirting a solution of this complex through a fine extruder into water. He then added ATP to the water and found that the threads contracted to about ten percent of their original length. In 1942 actin was isolated and characterized by Szent-Györgyi's pupil F. B. Straub, and in 1943 Szent-Györgyi prepared crystalline myosin and worked out a method for its purification.

In 1949 Szent-Györgyi introduced the glycerinated fiber bundle; a strip of muscle treated with glycerol can be kept to study the effects of ATP. In 1952-1953 he studied the "staircase effect" in heart muscle and the action of drugs on it.

Later Life

During World War II Hungarian leaders asked Szent-Görgyi to try to rescue Hungary from the Nazi stranglehold. He made an adventurous journey to Istanbul to consult with British and American diplomats. On his return he found that Hitler had personally demanded his delivery. Smuggled by friends out of Budapest, he hid near the Soviet lines. Rescued on Molotov's personal order, he was taken to Moscow and treated as a distinguished scientist. After the war Szent-Györgyi accepted the chair of medical chemistry at Budapest, and he tried to help Hungary through political activity. But it was impossible to counteract communist influence. In 1947 he emigrated to the United States, where he founded the Institute for Muscle Research at Woods Hole Marine Laboratory, Mass.

Szent-Györgyi received many honors, including the Cameron Prize of Edinburgh University (1946) and the Lasker Award (1954), and he was a member of many scientific societies in several countries. Among his most important books are *On Oxidation, Fermentation, Vitamins, Health and Disease* (1939), *Chemistry of Muscular Contraction* (1947), *Chemical Physiology of Contraction in Body and Heart Muscle* (1953), and *Bioenergetics* (1957).

Szent-Györgyi died on October 22, 1986 of kidney failure at his home in Woods Hole, Mass. He was in his eighties when he founded the National Foundation for Cancer Research. Through this organization, his work continues to help individuals throughout the world.

Further Reading

There is a biography of Szent-Györgyi in *Nobel Lectures, Physiology or Medicine, 1922-1941* (1965), which also includes his Nobel Lecture. For the history of ascorbic acid see F. Bicknell and F. Prescott, *The Vitamins in Medicine* (1953). For biological oxidation see C. W. Carter, R. V. Coxon, D. S. Parsons, and R. H. S. Thompson, *Biochemistry in Relation to Medicine* (1959). For muscle biochemistry see G. H. Bourne, ed., *The Structure and Function of Muscle,* vol. 2 (1960), and Dorothy M. Needham, *Machina Carnis* (1971). □

Leo Szilard

The Hungarian-American physicist—and later molecular biologist—Leo Szilard (1898-1964) helped initiate the atomic age and later worked for nuclear disarmament and world peace.

Leo Szilard was born in Budapest, Hungary, on February 11, 1898, the oldest of three children. His father was an engineer. "As far as I can see," he wrote, "I was born a scientist." He received most of his instruction at home until the age of ten, learning German and French with governesses. From the age of ten to 18 he went to a public school. His attraction to physics began when he was 13.

In 1916, one year before his draft into the army, he entered the Hungarian Institute of Technology to study electrical engineering. He had returned there by the summer of 1919. At the end of 1919 he went to Berlin and registered at the Technische Hochschule, which he left in mid-1920 to complete his studies at the University of Berlin. He gave up engineering for physics. At the University of Berlin physics was thriving with Albert Einstein, Max Planck, Max von Laue, and Walter Nernst. Fritz Haber was director of one of the Kaiser Wilhelm institutes. Szilard was awarded a Doctor's degree in physics under von Laue in 1922. He served as *Privatdozent* (lecturer) at the University of Berlin, 1926 to 1933.

After the February 1933 Reichstag fire, Szilard left Germany. In 1934, in London, he joined the physics staff of the medical college of St. Bartholomew's Hospital. He also worked at the Clarendon Laboratory, Oxford University. Together with T. A. Chalmers, Szilard developed in 1934 the first method of separating isotopes of artificial radioactive elements.

In 1931 Szilard came to America on an immigrant visa. He stayed about four months. He immigrated to the United States on January 2, 1938, and became a naturalized citizen in 1943.

Launching the Atomic Age

The Albert Einstein letter to President F. D. Roosevelt in 1939 initiated the atomic project. Szilard was the "ghost writer" [Julius Tabin]. Later Einstein acknowledged: "I made one great mistake in my life—when I signed the letter to President Roosevelt recommending that atom bombs be

Leo Szilard (left)

made," he said in old age to Linus Pauling, "but there was some justification—the danger that the Germans would make them" [Donald Clark].

Between early 1939 and November 1940 Szilard had no formal affiliation. When Columbia University got a contract to develop the Enrico Fermi-Szilard system, Szilard was put on its payroll, on November 1, 1940.

From 1942 until the end of the war, Szilard conducted nuclear research at the University of Chicago. As recalled by Bernard Feld, Szilard had been "an indispensable factor in the successful achievement of the first man-made nuclear chain reaction and in the vast wartime enterprise known as the Manhattan Project, which culminated in the first man-made nuclear explosion." For Szilard, the "Father of the Bomb" [Donald Fleming], success was also a tragedy: "And on December 2, 1942, the chain reaction was actually started at Stagg Field on the campus of the University [of Chicago]. There was a crowd there and then Fermi and I stayed there alone. I shook hands with Fermi and I said I thought this day would go down as a black day in the history of mankind."

In October 1946 Szilard became professor of biophysics—with a joint appointment in social sciences—at the University of Chicago. He was seldom in residence. At the age of 65, in 1963, he became professor emeritus.

Two themes guided Szilard's life, as he noted in a letter to Niels Bohr on November 7, 1950: "Theoretically I am supposed to divide my time between finding what life is and trying to preserve it by saving the world." The man who "initiated the atomic age" [in the words of Edward Teller] was also the man who helped found the Pugwash conferences and pleaded for nuclear disarmament and world peace.

Although Szilard "always was a biologist at heart" [Jacques Monod], he made what he called "the switch to biology" in 1946. Together with Aaron Novick, he got his training in biology by attending summer courses given by Max Delbrück at Cold Spring Harbor on bacterial viruses and by C. B. Van Niel at Pacific Grove on bacterial biochemistry. Szilard and Novick developed the chemostat, a device used in growing bacterial populations in a stationary state. Szilard described himself as a "theoretical biologist."

Between 1923 and 1931, Szilard filed his earliest patent applications, several with Einstein as a joint inventor. The graphite-moderated nuclear reactor, listing Fermi and Szilard as co-inventors, received a patent in 1955.

On Szilard's influence, Teller said: "He was the most stimulating of all the people I have known. In a world in which conformity is almost a duty, Szilard remained a dedicated nonconformist." And further: "He [Szilard] played a unique role in American history. His ideas about atomic energy were ridiculed by Ernest Rutherford and doubted by Niels Bohr and Enrico Fermi, but accepted and acted upon by Albert Einstein and President Roosevelt." Monod remarked: "I have also recorded, in my Nobel lecture, how it was Szilard who decisively reconciled me with the idea (repulsive to me, until then) that enzyme induction reflected an antirepressive effect, rather than the reverse, as I tried, unduly, to stick to it."

A Man of Many, Many Interests

Szilard lived in a world of ideas. For Monod, "Indeed, he [Szilard] loved ideas, especially his own. But he felt that these lovely objects only revealed all their virtues and charms by being tossed around, circulated, shared, and played with." As noted by Teller: "Szilard was the originator of many ideas, ranging from information theory to the sexual life of bacteria, from how to release atomic energy to a proposal that people who inform about violations of disarmament treaties ought to receive international awards."

A paper he wrote in 1929 in which he showed a relationship between information and entropy, "to which for over 35 years nobody paid any attention," claims Szilard, "is a cornerstone of modern information theory." He also stated: "I hit upon the idea of the cyclotron, may be a few years before Ernest Lawrence."

For Szilard "in science the greatest thoughts are the simplest thoughts" and "if you want to succeed in this world you don't have to be much cleverer than other people, you just have to be one day earlier than most people." He mentions his long walks or spending several months with the sole activity of dreaming about experiments.

Between 1957 and 1963 Szilard helped create the EMBO (European Molecular Biology Organization). He was visiting professor at the University of Colorado Medical Center and at Brandeis University. He was consultant to the National Institute of Mental Health, the World Health Organization, and the West German government. He helped create the Salk Institute, which he joined as non-resident fellow in July 1963 and as resident fellow on April 1, 1964.

Szilard was honored as fellow, American Academy of Arts and Sciences, 1954; as Humanist of the Year, American Humanist Association, 1960; as recipient of the Einstein Gold Medal of the Lewis and Rosa Strauss Memorial Fund, 1960, and of the Atoms for Peace Award, 1960; by election to membership in the National Academy of Sciences, 1961; and as recipient of an Honorary Doctor of Humane Letters from Brandeis University, 1961.

He was hospitalized for about a year in 1959-1960 and died in La Jolla, California, on May 30, 1964.

"To his friends," wrote Monod, "his memory will remain as a unique image of a man to whom science was more than a profession, or even an avocation: a mode of being."

In 1970, a crater on the far side of the moon (34°N; 106°E) was named "Szilard" by the International Astronomical Union.

Further Reading

In over 40 years of scientific research, Szilard published only 29 articles in scientific journals; the last paper appeared posthumously. His only book of fiction, *The Voice of the Dolphins* (1961), is a collection of short stories of political satire. Szilard also wrote some autobiographical fragments. The collected works of Szilard were published by the MIT Press in 3 volumes: *The Collected Works of Leo Szilard: Scientific Papers,* Bernard T. Feld and Gertrud Weiss Szilard, editors, with Kathleen R. Winsor, with a foreword by Jacques Monod and introductory essays by Carl Eckart, Bernard T. Feld, Maurice Goldhaber, Aaron Novick, and Julius Tabin (1972); *Leo Szilard: His Version of the Facts. Selected Recollections and Correspondence,* Spencer R. Weart and Gertrud Weiss Szilard, editors (1978); and *Toward a Livable World: Leo Szilard and the Crusade for Nuclear Arms Control,* G. Allen Greb, Gertrud Weiss Szilard, and Helen S. Hawkins, editors, foreword by Norman Cousins, introduction by Barton J. Bernstein (1987).

On Szilard see William Lanouette, *Genius in the Shadows: A biography of Leo Szilard, the man behind the bomb;* Edward Teller, *Better A Shield Than A Sword. Perspectives on Defense and Technology* (1987); Richard Rhodes, *The Making of the Atomic Bomb* (1986); Emilio Segrè, "Historical Perspective. Refugee Scientists and Nuclear Energy," in: *Sixth International Conference on Collective Phenomena: Reports from the Moscow Refusnik Seminar,* Inga Fischer-Hjalmars and Joel L. Lebowitz, editors, *Annals of the New York Academy of Sciences, 452* (1985); Edward Teller, *Energy. From Heaven and Earth* (1979) (chapter 8); Ronald W. Clark, *Einstein. The Life and Times* (1971); Donald Fleming, "Émigré Physicists and the Biological Revolution," and Leo Szilard, *Reminiscences* (edited by Gertrud Weiss Szilard and Kathleen R. Winsor) in: *The Intellectual Migration. Europe and America, 1930-1960,* Donald Fleming and Bernard Bailyn, editors. See also "Patent Is Issued On First Reactor. Fermi-Szilard Invention Gets Recognition—A.E.C. Holds Ownership," *The New York Times,* May 19, 1955. □

Henrietta Szold

The American Jewish leader Henrietta Szold (1860-1945) founded Hadassah and organized the first Youth Aliyah projects, which were directed at rescuing Jewish youth from Nazi Europe.

Henrietta Szold was born in Baltimore, Md., on Dec. 21, 1860. Her father, Benjamin Szold, was a rabbi and an active leader in the movement for African American emancipation. During the wave of immigration to the United States by European Jews, the Szold household was well known as a place where guidance, advice, and assistance could be found.

Szold taught school in Baltimore, also directing an evening school for newly arrived Jewish immigrants. Between 1892 and 1916 she served as secretary of the Jewish Publication Society. Beginning in 1895, she edited the *American Jewish Yearbook* with Cyrus Adler. She first visited Palestine in 1909, writing from there that she was confident that Jewish redemption would come only through Zionism. To that end she dedicated the rest of her life. She emphasized the significance of Zionism as a solution to the problems of Jewish immigration and the cultural and spiritual development of Judaism. In 1912 she founded Hadassah, a women's Zionist organization, and guided its efforts to improve health conditions in Palestine.

In 1914 Szold was appointed by Justice Louis D. Brandeis to head the American Zionist Medical Unit for Palestine. Her party of 44 doctors, nurses, and administrative and medical engineers left for Palestine in 1918, along with supplies for a 50-bed hospital. In 1919 she founded a school of nursing in Palestine. In 1926 she was elected to the presidency of Hadassah and in the following year to the Zionist Executive as health and education minister. In 1930 she was elected to the National Council of Jews in Palestine and served as head of social welfare.

With the Nazi rise to power in 1933, Szold was designated to deal with the emigration of children from Germany to Palestine. She directed this work of the Youth Aliyah, as well as supervising accommodation of the children in Palestine. As a token of the high esteem in which she was held for these efforts, German immigrants in Palestine founded the settlement Kfar-Szold. In 1940 she was appointed to the Hadassah Emergency Committee, which was organized to deal with problems arising from the war. In 1941 she conducted a study of the occupational needs of young women and on this basis founded the Alice Seligsberg Trade School for Girls in Jerusalem.

Henrietta Szold was deeply concerned with Arab-Jewish relations and joined Ihud, a movement devoted to achieving mutual understanding between Arab and Jew. Her life and work in behalf of both Zionist and humanitarian

causes are the very embodiment of selfless and dedicated creativity. She died in Jerusalem on Feb. 13, 1945.

Further Reading

Marvin Lowenthal, *Henrietta Szold: Life and Letters* (1942), is a serious and penetrating study. An enthusiastic and admiring portrait is in Elma Ehrlich Levinger, *Fighting Angel: The Story of Henrietta Szold* (1946). An interesting literary treatment of the Szold family is in Alexandra L. Levin, *The Szolds of Lombard Street: A Baltimore Family, 1859-1909* (1960).

Additional Sources

Dash, Joan, *Summoned to Jerusalem: the life of Henrietta Szold,* New York: Harper & Row, 1979.
Lowenthal, Marvin, *Henrietta Szold, life and letter,* Westport, Conn.: Greenwood Press, 1975, 1942. ☐

Karol Szymanowski

The Polish composer Karol Szymanowski (1882-1937) treated national subjects in an original and highly effective manner.

On Oct. 6, 1882, Karol Szymanowski was born at Timoshovka in the Ukraine to a wealthy, highly cultured Polish family that encouraged his obvious musical talent. While still in his teens he wrote elegant

pieces for the piano obviously inspired by Frédéric Chopin. In 1901 he entered the Warsaw Conservatory, and after graduation he went to Berlin in 1905. There he and three other young Polish composers founded a society called Young Poland in Music. In 1908 Szymanowski returned to Timoshovka. He spent the years 1912-1914 in Vienna.

Compositions of this early period are numerous piano pieces—Preludes (1901, 1905), Etudes (1902), and Variations (1901, 1904)—introduced by Artur Rubinstein in his concerts; and violin pieces—a Sonata (1904), *Romance* (1909), and *Notturn e tarantella* (1914)—introduced by Paul Kochanski. The *Love Songs of Hafiz* (1910, 1914) and the opera *Hagith* (1912-1913) reflect Szymanowski's interest in Oriental mysticism and philosophy.

Szymanowski's *Mythes* (1915) is a set of three pieces for violin and piano. The second of these, the *Fountain of Arethusa,* became his best-known and most frequently performed composition. Over a shimmering, dissonant piano part the violin soars in arabesque-filled melody. The harmonies are dissonant but are treated in the impressionist manner, not for their tension but for their color.

The Szymanowski family estate was lost in the 1917 Revolution, and the composer's affluent position changed overnight. In 1920 he went to Warsaw, where he lived until 1935.

During the 1920s Szymanowski's compositions became known to a wider audience through their inclusion in the annual programs sponsored by the International Society of Contemporary Music, and he emerged as Poland's most

eminent composer. He became director of the Warsaw Conservatory in 1926. At this time Szymanowski's works began to reflect his national heritage. *Harnassie* (1926) is a ballet-opera based on Polish peasant music and traditions, similar to Igor Stravinsky's treatment of Russian folklore in *Les Noces* and Bohuslav Martinu's use of Czech themes in *Spalicek.* Szymanowski's *Stabat Mater* (1928) for solo voices, mixed chorus, and orchestra reconciles Palestrina counterpoint with Slavic melodies. A cycle of 12 songs (1930) was inspired by the folk music of the Kurpie region of Poland. Other important compositions are the Second Violin Concerto (1930) and the Symphonie Concertante for piano and orchestra (1932), both distinctly Polish in character.

Szymanowski died of tuberculosis in Lausanne, Switzerland, on March 28, 1937.

Further Reading

Stefan Jarocinski, ed., *Polish Music* (1965), contains a chapter on Szymanowski's life and music. See also Homer Ulrich and Paul A. Pisk, *A History of Music and Musical Style* (1963).

Additional Sources

Chylianska, Teresa, *Karol Szymanowski: his life and works,* Los Angeles: University of Southern California, School of Music, 1993.

Chylianska, Teresa, *Szymanowski,* Cracow: Polskie Wydawn. Muzyczne, 1981.

Karol Szymanowski: an anthology, Warszawa: Interpress, 1986.
□

T

Muhammad ibn Jarir al-Tabari

Muhammad ibn Jarir al-Tabari (839-923) was a Moslem historian and religious scholar whose annals are the most important source for the early history of Islam. He is also a renowned author of a monumental commentary on the Koran.

Al-Tabari was born in Amol in the province of Tabaristan south of the Caspian Sea. His family was probably of Persian origin. Gifted with a prodigious memory, he knew the Koran by heart at the age of 7. After receiving his early education in the religious sciences at Amol, he continued his studies in Rayy and Baghdad, which he reached about the year 855. Not later than 857 he visited Basra, Wasit, and Kufa to hear the famous scholars there. After his return to Baghdad he studied religious law according to the doctrine of al-Shafii, which he followed for some time before establishing his own doctrine.

After visiting several towns in Syria al-Tabari went to Egypt in 867, where he, already a famous scholar, was honored by a splendid reception. After revisiting Syria he returned to Egypt for a second stay in 870. In Egypt he defended his own independent legal doctrine in disputations with the prominent Shafiite scholar al-Muzani. He returned to Baghdad to stay there for the remainder of his life, though he made at least two trips to Tabaristan, the second one in 903.

Fully devoted to writing and teaching, al-Tabari refused an appointment as judge in 912. His lectures attracted large flocks of students. However, after his second trip to Tabaristan, he aroused the hostility of the Hanbalite school, which was predominant in Baghdad, by refusing to recognize its founder, Ibn Hanbal, as a scholar of the law. The Hanbalites accused him of heresy in minor doctrinal points, attacked him and his house, and, even after he apologized to them, continued to prevent students from attending his lectures. Al-Tabari died on Feb. 15, 923. His school of legal doctrine survived for only a few generations.

His Scholarship

In his numerous books on all fields of religious learning al-Tabari summed up the work of the earlier generations of Moslem scholars. His enormous commentary on the Koran, which he completed in 883/884, gathers the statements of all famous early exegetes concerning the circumstances of the promulgation of the Koranic verses and their meaning. His own comments are mostly concerned with lexical and grammatical questions. Sometimes he points out theological or juristic implications favoring traditionalist doctrine.

Al-Tabari's universal history, completed in 915, begins with the age of the prophets, patriarchs, and early kings, followed by Sassanian history, the age of Mohammed, and the era of Islam to the year 915. After the *hijra* (622) it is arranged annalistically. Al-Tabari scrupulously states his sources, most of which are lost, and reproduces them without changes. Often he quotes two or more conflicting reports on the same event. With few exceptions he shows remarkable discrimination in the choice of his sources. Particularly valuable are the sections on Sassanian and Umayyad history. Al-Tabari's other works are lost except for some fragments and minor treatises.

Further Reading

A small section of al-Tabari's history was translated into English by Elma Marin as *The Reign of al-Mutasim, 833-842* (1951). Information on al-Tabari is in Reynold A. Nicholson, *A Literary History of the Arabs* (1907; 2d ed. 1930), and H. A. R. Gibb, *Arabic Literature: An Introduction* (1926; 2d rev. ed. 1963). □

Horace Austin Warner Tabor

Horace Austin Warner Tabor (1830-1899), an American mining magnate and politician, was a great benefactor of Colorado.

Horace Tabor was born in Orleans County, Vt., on Nov. 26, 1830. He left home while still in his teens and became a stonecutter. In 1855 he migrated to Kansas. While farming there, he also served in the Free State legislature; neither endeavor proved rewarding, so he joined the Pike's Peak gold rush in 1859.

For the next 18 years Tabor's activities shifted from camp to camp, where he gained mining experience and operated a store. The merchant-miner combination produced a steady income, but his chance for wealth came with the opening of the Leadville, Colo., silver mines. A fortunate grubstake by Tabor to two prospectors in 1878 led to the discovery of the Little Pittsburg Mine and his first million dollars; then successful investments parlayed his worth to $5-7 million.

Tabor invested in mines in almost all the western states and Mexico. Once he was financially secure, he turned to politics. He served two terms as Republican lieutenant governor of Colorado (1879-1883) and hoped to become a senator, but after an expensive and bitter campaign in 1882-1883 he was chosen by the legislature only to fill an unexpired 30-day term. Later attempts for the party's gubernatorial nomination failed, but he liberally supported the Republicans despite the rebuffs.

Tabor moved to Denver in 1879 and significantly contributed to the city's growth. The first of the Colorado mining millionaires to invest his fortune at home, he built the Tabor Block and the famous Tabor Grand Opera House. He displayed his confidence in the future of the state by investing in Leadville and other towns and helping to open the San Juan, Gunnison, and Aspen areas.

This faith in western growth led Tabor into marginal investments which failed. By the late 1880s decreasing mine production and a falling silver price forced him to mortgage sound holdings to continue development. When the economic crash of 1893 came, his business-mining empire was debt-ridden. Collapse followed, and a final Mexican mining venture failed to save Tabor. Appointed Denver postmaster in 1898, he died on April 10, 1899.

The scandal of Tabor's divorce from Augusta Pierce and his remarriage to Elizabeth McCourt (Baby) Doe in 1883 made him a pariah to many contemporaries but he outlived the stigma. Douglas Moore's opera *The Ballad of Baby Doe* (1955) is based on the event.

Further Reading

Tabor has been the subject of numerous articles and several books: Lewis Gandy, *The Tabors* (1934), and David Karsner, *Silver Dollar: The Story of the Tabors* (1954), are dated and fail to do justice to the man. See also George F. Willison, *Here They Dug Gold* (1931; 3d ed. 1946).

Additional Sources

Smith, Duane A., *Horace Tabor: his life and the legend,* Boulder: University Press of Colorado, 1989. □

Tacitus

Tacitus (c. 56/57-ca. 125) was a Roman orator and historian. In a life that spanned the reigns of the Flavian emperors and of Trajan and Hadrian, he played a part in the public life of Rome and became its greatest historian.

Tacitus was born into a wealthy family of equestrian status. It is not known for certain where his home was, but he probably came from one of the towns of Gallia Narbonensis (modern Provence). His father had been an imperial official, holding the important post of procurator (chief financial agent) for Gallia Belgica, and he was clearly able to give his son an excellent education.

Official Career

In 77 the young Tacitus was betrothed to, and soon after married, the only daughter of Gnaeus Julius Agricola, an able soldier and administrator. Although not himself of aristocratic birth, Tacitus was allowed by the emperor Vespasian to start on a political career. The early stages of this career cannot be followed in detail, but Tacitus reached the praetorship in 88, by which time he had also become a member of one of the important priestly colleges which controlled the official religion of the Roman state.

For the next 4 years Tacitus was away from Rome, as he had been appointed by Domitian to a post in the imperial administration, either the command of a legion or the governorship of one of the less important provinces, but we do not know exactly what the post was or where he held it. In 97, during the brief reign of Nerva, Tacitus finally attained the highest traditional magistracy, the consulship, which at this date was a ceremonial post and a necessary qualification for most of the really important appointments in the Emperor's service. But as far as we know, none of these posts was offered to Tacitus. Instead he spent a year (112-113) as governor of the peaceful senatorial province of Asia,

and there is no evidence that he held any further public office.

Meanwhile, in the intervals of his official career Tacitus had spent much time in the study and practice of rhetoric, and by the time of his consulship he had won a reputation as one of the leading forensic orators of his generation. His most famous case came in 100, when together with his friend Pliny the Younger he successfully prosecuted Marius Priscus for misgovernment in Africa.

By this date Tacitus had also started on a career as a writer, and it seems likely that after this he gradually withdrew from legal practice to concentrate on his literary work. He continued to live and work in Rome until his death.

Tacitus's Writings

Tacitus's first published work was *Agricola,* a laudatory biography of his late father-in-law, which came out between 96 and 98. This was followed by *Germania* (98), a short monograph on the habits and customs of the independent tribes of Germany. Then came *Dialogus de oratoribus,* a discussion in dialogue form of the decay of Roman oratory. This has often been regarded as an early work, mainly on stylistic grounds, but it was probably written and published between 102 and 107.

After this Tacitus produced his first major historical work, the *Histories,* an account of Rome under the Flavian emperors (69-96) perhaps written mainly in the years 105-109. When complete, it was divided into 12 or 14 books, but only books 1-4 and a small part of book 5 have survived. These books were written on a very large scale, for between them they cover the events of only 2 years, 69 and 70, and it is probable that in the later books Tacitus reduced the scale of his narrative.

At one time Tacitus had intended to follow up the *Histories* with an account of the reigns of Nerva and Trajan (96-117), but he changed his mind and went back to the time of the Julio-Claudian emperors with the *Annals,* written probably between 118 and 123. This was a history of Rome from the death of Augustus in 14 to the suicide of Nero in 68. It was divided into 16 or 18 books, but well over a third of the text has been lost.

We do not have Tacitus's narrative for several of the later years of Tiberius, the whole of the brief reign of Caligula, the start of Claudius's reign, and the final years of Nero's reign, though the absence of this last section may be a result of a failure on Tacitus's part to complete the work before he died.

Tacitus as Historian

Tacitus's reputation as a historian rests primarily on the two major works of his maturity. In the *Histories* and *Annals* Tacitus produced a historical corpus that for all its battered condition ranks very high in the record of Greco-Roman historiography. It is admittedly open to criticism in certain respects: his understanding of military affairs was not very deep, so that his accounts of campaigns are sometimes obscure; and his vision tended to be concentrated unduly on events in Rome itself and extended to the provinces only in time of war, so that he failed to note the excellent work that was done, sometimes even by "bad" emperors, for the more efficient, honest, and peaceful administration of the Roman world.

More important are Tacitus's undoubted merits. On the whole, he showed good judgment in his handling of the material he found in earlier writers—he passed over in silence most of the more scandalous stories that enliven the pages of Suetonius—and he almost certainly did extensive research into the available documentary evidence, especially the records of meetings of the Senate. Moreover, unlike Livy, Tacitus possessed considerable insight into political life and a deep understanding of human nature, especially its darker sides; and he managed for the most part to live up to his own expressed intention to write "without anger and partiality."

Tacitus's one failure in this respect is his picture of Tiberius in the early books of the *Annals,* where he could not shake himself loose from the traditional picture of that emperor as a morose, cruel, and suspicious tyrant. Even here, however, when he found in the record some actions by Tiberius which did not fit his preconceived view, he did not willfully distort or omit them but contented himself with ascribing to Tiberius disreputable motives for apparently honorable acts.

In his technique Tacitus made no real innovations. In both major works he retained the annalistic system of chronology, though he sometimes found it awkward and had to put into a single year series of events which in fact had been spread over several. Similarly he regularly included in his narrative speeches by leading figures, some of which, like the address of a Caledonian chieftain in the *Agricola,* were certainly free compositions by Tacitus himself.

But in most cases Tacitus seems to have taken pains to reproduce in his own words the general sense of what was actually said: that was certainly the case with a speech of Claudius to the Senate reported in book 6 of the *Annals,* where the preservation of most of the original text in an inscription shows clearly that Tacitus wrote his own version with a copy of the original before him. This was probably the case with many of the other speeches.

His Writing Style

In the *Dialogus* Tacitus adopted a smooth, flowing, almost Ciceronian style so unlike that of his other writings that its authenticity has sometimes—though wrongly—been doubted. But in the *Agricola* and *Germania,* and still more in the two major works, Tacitus evolved a quite remarkable style of his own, which owed much to Sallust and the Augustan poets but still more to his own genius and his rhetorical training.

Terse, powerful, and abrupt, this approach contrives to pack a remarkable amount of meaning into a few words. It can at times become monotonous, and occasionally its weightiness seems out of scale with the content, but at its best its strength and vigor enabled Tacitus to present unforgettably vivid accounts of important events. Particularly notable is his ability to sum up the salient characteristics of

an individual in a few sharp, epigrammatic phrases, as in his description of Nero as "haudquaquam sui detractor (by no means a man to denigrate himself)" or his famous remark about Galba, "omnium consensu capax imperii nisi imperasset (all would have agreed that he was capable of ruling, if he had not actually reigned)." Even if Tacitus's qualities as a historian had been negligible—and they are far from that—the power and originality of his writing would still have placed him among the greatest writers of imperial Rome.

Further Reading

There are numerous English translations of Tacitus's works, most of which are reasonably reliable. Apart from a complete translation by various writers in the Loeb Classical Library series, *Dialogus, Agricola, Germania* (trans. 1914) and *The Histories; The Annals* (trans., 4 vols., 1925-1937), the following individual versions can be recommended: *The Annals and the Histories* by Alfred J. Church and William J. Brodribb (2 vols., 1864-1876; repr., 1 vol., 1952); *Tacitus: The Histories* by W. Hamilton Fyfe (2 vols., 1912); and *Tacitus on Britain and Germany: A New Translation of the "Agricola" and the "Germania"* by H. Mattingly (1948). Select passages in translation may be found in *The Annals of Imperial Rome* by Michael Grant (1956).

The major work in English on Tacitus himself is the massive and erudite book by Sir Ronald Syme, *Tacitus* (2 vols., 1958), which contains an immense amount of information about Tacitus himself and many other aspects of Rome in the 1st century; but it is a difficult and baffling work for the layman to use. An easier and more approachable account is that contained in part 1 of Clarence W. Mendell, *Tacitus: The Man and His Work* (1957); Donald R. Dudley, *The World of Tacitus* (1968), may also be consulted. There is a detailed and technical but very interesting account of Tacitus's historical technique in Bessie Walker, *The Annals of Tacitus: A Study in the Writing of History* (1952). A brief and not very sympathetic account of Tacitus is in Max L. W. Laistner, *The Greater Roman Historians* (1947).

The period of Roman history which Tacitus described in his major works is covered by Edward T. Salmon, *A History of the Roman World from 30 B.C. to A.D. 138* (1944; 2d rev. ed. 1950), but the best account of the period of the Julio-Claudian emperors is in Howard H. Scullard, *From the Gracchi to Nero: A History of Rome from 133 B.C. to A.D. 68* (1959). There is an excellent brief introduction to imperial Rome in Martin P. Charlesworth, *The Roman Empire* (1951). There is a good introduction to the history of the Roman occupation of Britain in I. A. Richmond, *Roman Britain* (1947; rev. ed. 1964), and the events of Agricola's governorship are well discussed in the introduction to the edition of Tacitus's *De vita Agricolae,* edited by R. M. Ogilvie and I. A. Richmond (1967). For Roman oratory see Stanley F. Bonner, *Roman Declamation* (1949), and Martin L. Clarke, *Rhetoric at Rome: A Historical Survey* (1953).

Additional Sources

Benario, Herbert W., *An introduction to Tacitus,* Athens: University of Georgia Press, 1975. □

Sophie Taeuber-Arp

The Swiss-born painter, designer, and dancer Sophie Taeuber-Arp (1889-1943) was an active member of the Zurich Dada group, a participant in the "International" Constructivist movement, and an advocate of concrete art and geometric abstraction. She believed that melding the fine and applied arts could establish a visual vocabulary for the technological age and was committed to the concept of the "total work of art."

Sophie Taeuber-Arp, nee Taeuber, was born in Davos, Switzerland, on January 19, 1889. She studied at the School of Applied Arts (St. Gallen, Switzerland) from 1908 to 1910 and at the experimental studios of Wilhelm von Debschits (Munich), a workshop of the Blaue Reiter epoch, in 1911 and 1913. In 1912 Taeuber attended the School of Arts and Crafts (Hamburg) and in 1916 the famous Leban School of Dance (Zurich). From 1915 to 1932 she belonged to the Swiss Werkbund, an organization whose members believed that the applied arts could be used to create an appropriate expression of the technological age, and in 1925 she served as a member of the jury for the Exposition Internationale des Arts Décoratifs (Paris).

Taeuber-Arp was a member of the Cercle et Carré group, an organization dedicated to non-figurative art, and of the Abstraction-Creation group which succeeded it, in 1930 and 1931-1934 respectively. In 1934 she protested the organization's policies and formally withdrew along with Jean Hélion, Otto Freundlich, Fernandez, Antoine Pevsner, Naum Gabo, Robert Delauney, Georges Valmier, and Hans (Jean) Arp. In 1937 she was a member of the Allianz group (Zurich).

Taeuber met Arp, whom she married on October 20, 1922, at the Gallery Tanner exhibition (Zurich) in 1915. This initial meeting served as a turning point for both of them, and they were to collaborate on works from that time until her death in 1943. Between 1915 and 1920 Taeuber lived a dual life. During the day she was a lecturer in embroidery and weaving at the School of Applied Arts (Zurich), a post she held until 1929, and in the evenings she participated in Dada sorées, usually in disguise to avoid recognition and the loss of her teaching job.

Arp and Taeuber were involved in many Dada events in Zurich. Taeuber's interests during this period revolved around dance, performance, puppetry, costumes, and artistic collaborations. Her concern for the total work of art was shared by many of the other Zurich Dadaists. Taeuber worked on puppet designs and set decorations for French and Swiss theater productions from 1916 to 1929, and from 1918 to 1920 she produced a series of heads constructed from hatstands, portraits in polychromed turned wood which hold their own amidst any of Dada's sophisticated objects. During her Dada period she collaborated with Käthe Wulff on the choreography for the ballet "The Merchent" (backdrops by Arp and Hans Richter) and cho-

reographed the "Noir Kukado" using the Leban system of notation. The choreographic element, her prowess as a dancer, and her background in textile design continually influenced her two dimensional work.

In 1915 Taeuber worked on a series of duo collages with Arp which he later identified as the first manifestations of "Concrete Art." From 1915 to 1920 the prevailing formal elements of her two dimensional work were horizontal/vertical sectioning, often compared to her textile designs. The period 1920-1926 marked a relatively inactive period in her career during which she produced costume designs and guaches. Taeuber-Arp travelled to Pompeii in 1926 and that same year completed a mural painting for Paul Horn, an architect in Strasbourg. The mural led to a commission for the interior of the Café de l'Aubette, a total artistic environment and the first realized Constructivist public space which integrated art and function. The project was completed in 1927, in collaboration with Arp and de Stijl (style) artist Theo van Doesburg. Taeuber-Arp coauthored a manual for the decorative arts entitled *Design and Textile Arts* with Blanche Gauchet in 1927 and ten years later founded and edited the Constructivist review, *Plastique/Plastic* (Paris).

In 1928 Taeuber-Arp and her husband moved to Meudon-Val Fleury, outside Paris. Their house and its furnishings, which have been described as a merging of art and utilitarian concerns, were designed by Taeuber-Arp, who made use of principles that ran parallel to those of the Bauhaus. In 1930 she began her "ping" picture series, works dominated by circles, a form that she believed contained all forms, and, in 1932, her "space paintings," based on a straightforward grid. During the mid to late 1930s she worked on biomorphic/geometric pieces, some of which were executed in wood relief. Taeuber-Arp and Arp fled Paris in 1940 and settled in Grasse. In 1942 they executed a series of lithographs with Sonia Delaunay and Alberto Magnelli. For Taeuber-Arp, this was the last of a long series of joint artistic ventures. She died in Zurich, on January 13, 1943 (Arp died in 1966).

Sophie Taeuber-Arp participated in a number of group exhibitions during her lifetime. Particular note should be made of her inclusion in the first Carré exhibition at the Galeries 23 (Paris) in 1930. The show involved representatives from many of the 20th century's most advanced manifestations of modernism, including Futurism, Dada, the Bauhaus, German Abstraction, Constructivism, the Polish Blok group, the French Cubists, Purists, and de Stijl. After her death numerous exhibitions, some of which included works by her husband Hans (Jean) Arp, were organized in both Europe and America. In 1981 the Museum of Modern Art (New York) mounted the one woman show "Sophie Taeuber-Arp" which travelled to the Museum of Contemporary Art (Chicago), the Museum of Fine Arts (Houston), and the Musée d'Art Contemporain (Montreal).

Based in part upon eulogies by her husband and her friends, Taeuber-Arp is best known for her work as a painter and as a forerunner of non-objective art. However, her utopian concern with the marriage of the fine and the applied arts and her experiments in dance, choreography, performance, and puppet theater should not be minimized. It was Taeuber-Arp's commitment to the total work of art that guaranteed her an important place in the history of 20th-century modernism.

Further Reading

To date, much of the literature on Taeuber-Arp has been published in French and German. *Sophie Taeuber-Arp* (1970), a catalogue/folio from an exhibition at the Albert Loeb & Krugier Gallery Inc. (New York), is available in both French and English and includes entries by Hans (Jean) Arp, Gabrielle Buffet-Picabia, and Wassily Kandinsky, among others. Carolyn Lanchner's *Sophie Taeuber-Arp* (1981), the catalogue for the Museum of Modern Art's exhibition, is of particular value to the English-speaking public and includes an informative essay, a bibliography, and a selected list of her exhibitions. □

Hŭngsŏn Taewŏn'gun

Hŭngsŏn Taewŏn'gun (1820-1898) was a Korean imperial regent and the father of king Kojong. Even after the personal rule by Kojong was inaugurated, Taewŏn'gun was one of the most powerful figures in the last decades of the Yi dynasty.

Hŭngsŏn Taewŏn'gun was born Yi Ha-ŭng and became Prince Hŭngsŏn at the age of 20. Although he was a member of the royal family, he had not become king and had spent his early years in the gay quarters of the capital's lower-class people. When King Ch'ŏljong died without an heir apparent, Hŭngsŏn Taewŏn'gun managed to place his 12-year-old son on the throne, and he became the imperial regent, or the de facto ruler under the circumstances.

Imperial Regent

Taewŏn'gun built up his own political power by balancing one faction against another in the swirling party politics of the decaying dynasty and took advantage of his position to establish a strong party of his own. He promoted the reestablishment of a strong bureaucratic state and the reconstruction of the magnificent Kyŏngbok Palace in Seoul. He suppressed his critics and opponents and abolished the *sŏwŏn,* or study centers, which had turned into focal points of factional groupings. He relentlessly persecuted foreign missionaries and native Christians (Catholics), who were said to threaten the traditional religious-moral order of the nation that was once called the Hermit Kingdom.

It was Taewŏn'gun who had turned down the requests of foreign powers to open Korea for diplomatic and commercial relations. In his antiforeignism and in his struggle with foreign nations, he emphasized the need to expel the "Western barbarians" who were then rapidly expanding into various parts of Asia—often spearheaded by their gunboats. The forcible but brief entries of the French and the Americans into Kanghwa Island and elsewhere occurred during the regency of Taewŏn'gun.

Taewŏn'gun's forceful and often eccentric handling of domestic and foreign affairs of the nation aroused strong opposition from various directions. The large expenditures needed for armaments for the outmoded Korean army to "expel the barbarians," and the heavy expenses and enormous requisitions of labor and materials needed for the renovation of the capital, increased the burdens of the peasantry. Numerous officials ousted by Taewŏn'gun, and the literati of the *sŏwŏn* whose lands had been confiscated, resisted the government of Taewŏn'gun. Faced with such opposition, Taewŏn'gun availed himself of the coming of age of his son, King Kojong, to retire from the chores of regency in 1873.

Retirement from Regency

Soon after Taewŏn'gun's retirement, political leadership passed from his party to that of the strong-willed Queen Min. Persons appointed during the Taewŏn'gun regency were gradually replaced, and members of the Min family filled most important government position. The former policies of the government were also changed. At the insistence of the literati, some *sŏwŏn* were restored, and antiforeignism was modified to a policy of conciliation. During this period of change the Japanese efforts to open Korea were finally successful.

The influx of Japanese and Japanese goods after the Treaty of Kanghwa (1876) and the introduction of Japanese-style reforms created many new problems and dislocations in Korea, leading to some bloody disturbances. During the so-called *emeute* of 1882, for instance, soldier-rioters attacked the residences of the privileged Min family, set fire to the Japanese legation, killed the Japanese military instructors, and entered the royal palace. Queen Min herself fled to a remote province, and most leaders of the Min party were eliminated. Taewŏn'gun, with the support of the Korean military, took over the royal palace and attempted to reinstate his old policies, including antiforeignism.

International Rivalries

At the invitation of the remnants of the Min party, Ch'ing China, anxious to maintain its influence over Korea, sent an army of 4,500 men. While suppressing the uprising in Seoul, they also managed to capture Taewŏn'gun, who was sent to China at the order of the Ch'ing emperor. Taewŏn'gun was well cared for in China, however, until his return to Korea 3 years later. Alarmed at these developments, Japan also sent troops to Korea, but the Chinese army already had the Korean political situation under control, and Japan did not have the strength at that time to dislodge the Chinese from Korea.

When Tonghak (Eastern Learning) rebellions broke out in Korea, and when China again sent 1,500 troops to Korea in 1894 at the request of the pro-Chinese Korean court, Japan sent a larger number of troops to Korea, ostensibly to protect Japanese nationals in Korea. Japan, which had been rapidly modernizing, had been eagerly looking for an opportunity to reenter the Korean peninsula. The Japanese army entered Seoul with great strength and by its armed presence began to dominate the political scene in Korea. Even after the Tonghak rebellions subsided, Japan showed no intention of leaving Korea. This Japanese stand brought about the outbreak of the Sino-Japanese War in August 1894.

Japan then swiftly moved to eliminate the Min family—dominated government, and pro-Japanese "progressives" were quickly placed in office. Taewŏn'gun then reemerged briefly as a leader of the progressives because both Taewŏn'gun and the progressives had been strongly opposed to the Mins and also because the progressives at this time were still politically weak and needed influential allies. As the pro-Japanese political forces became stronger and better entrenched with the support of the victorious Japanese army, there was no longer any reason to keep Taewŏn'gun in a powerful position, and he was soon removed. He died a few years later in February 1898.

Further Reading

Several sections on Taewŏn'gun and his times are in Takashi Hatada, *A History of Korea,* translated and edited by Warren W. Smith, Jr., and Benjamin Hazard (1969). A rather detailed description of his activities appears in Homer B. Hulbert, *History of Korea,* edited by Clarence N. Weems, vol. 2 (1969). Fred Harvey Harrington, *God, Mammon and the Japanese* (1944), contains brief discussions of Taewŏn'gun which depict him as a "savage foe of all outsiders." □

Sir Abubakar Tafawa Balewa

Alhaji Sir Abubakar Tafawa Balewa (1912-1966) was the first prime minister of independent Nigeria, serving from 1957 to 1966.

Abubakar Tafawa Balewa was born in Tafawa Balewa, North East State, Nigeria. Unlike the majority of Northern Nigerian political leaders, he was of humble background, his father having been a client to a district head. After attending Katsina Teacher Training College (1928-1933), he was a teacher and later headmaster of the Bauchi Middle School. He studied at the London University Institute of Education (1945-1946), where he received a teacher's certificate in history.

During World War II Tafawa Balewa had become interested in political activities. In 1943 he founded the Bauchi Discussion Circle, an organization interested in political reform. In 1948 he was elected vice president of the Northern Teacher's Association, the first trade union in Northern Nigeria. In 1949 he helped organize the Northern People's Congress (NPC), originally conceived as a cultural organization but by 1951 a political party.

In 1946 Tafawa Balewa had been selected by the Bauchi Native Authority as their representative to the Northern House of Assembly, and the House of Assembly in turn selected him to become a member of the Nigerian Legislative Council. In 1951, in the North's first elections, Tafawa Balewa won seats in the Northern House of Assembly and in the House of Representatives in Lagos, where he became a minister in the Central Council. In 1952 he became Nigerian minister of works and in 1954 minister of transport and the senior minister and leader of the NPC in the House of Representatives. In 1957 he became the first prime minister of Nigeria, a position he held until his death.

As prime minister, Tafawa Balewa developed a favorable reputation in international circles. He was considered a pro-Western leader but was very critical of South African racial policies and of French plans to test atomic devices in the Sahara. His last public act was to convene a Commonwealth Conference in Lagos to discuss action against the white supremacist unilateral declaration of independence by Rhodesia.

Throughout his career Tafawa Balewa played a leading role in national policy making. In 1950 in the Northern House of Assembly he had advocated fundamental reforms to the system of Native Authorities in the North, a proposal highly unpopular among many of the Northern leaders. Throughout the 1950s he participated with great skill in the discussions on constitutional reform which ultimately led to independence. Nevertheless, Tafawa Balewa often seemed limited in his own personal power, because as vice president of the NPC he was answerable theoretically to Sir Ahmadu Bello, premier of the Northern Region and president of the NPC. Some observers have concluded that this relationship with Bello hindered Tafawa Balewa in handling the major crises which arose in the first years of Nigeria's independence. It was one of these crises, the Western Region elections of 1965, which led to chaos in the Western Region and was the immediate cause of the downfall of Tafawa Balewa's government. In January 1966 a discontented segment of the army attempted a coup d'etat in which Tafawa Balewa was kidnaped and murdered.

Further Reading

There is no biography of Tafawa Balewa, but one can read of his activities in Richard Sklar, *Nigerian Political Parties: Power in an Emergent African Nation* (1963). □

Lorado Taft

Lorado Taft (1860-1936), the first midwestern American sculptor, pioneered in large group compositions and in the use of nontraditional materials. His lectures and writing helped create a national concern for art.

Born in Elmwood, Ill., on April 29, 1860, Lorado Taft grew up in Urbana, along with the new State Industrial University (now the University of Illinois). There his preacher father, Don Carlos Taft, an Amherst graduate, taught a group of sciences, including anatomy. While working in the new art museum, 14-year-old Lorado decided to become a sculptor. After he received a master's degree in 1880, he left for Paris to study at the Ecole des Beaux-Arts. He also broadened his outlook by contacts with the impressionist painters and with the sculptor Auguste Rodin.

In 1887 Taft settled in Chicago; in 1896 he married Ada Bartlett, by whom he had three daughters. To support the family, Taft taught at the Chicago Art Institute and lectured widely. He gave the Clay Talk on the processes of sculpture 1500 times. His research led to writing. Besides many articles, he published two books, *American Sculpture* (1903, updated and reissued in 1905 and again in 1969) and *Recent Tendencies in Sculpture* (1921).

Although Taft had made two decorative panels for the World's Columbian Exposition of 1893 in Chicago, the subsequent depression delayed further commissions. On his own, and in freer style than in earlier efforts, he produced the *Solitude of the Soul* (1901), which won two medals and was bought by the Chicago Art Institute. The Fountain of the Great Lakes (1913) in Chicago was commissioned by the Ferguson Fund. In this fountain the water, falling from five great shells, repeats the flowing lines of the symbolic figures that hold the shells. For Seattle he made a giant statue of George Washington with sheathed sword and austere silhouette (1908). That year he won a competition for a commemorative fountain to Columbus for Union Station Plaza in the nation's capital. Here the architectural treatment foreshadowed that of his future fountains, including the Thatcher Memorial (1918) in Denver.

Taft continued to do important pieces on his own initiative, such as the 40-foot statue of Black Hawk (1911) on a bluff near Oregon, Ill., overlooking Rock River. This colossus, seen for miles around, represents the American Indian saying good-bye to his homeland. Here the sculptor gambled successfully on the use of cement. His most ambitious plan was for the Chicago Midway, the site of the Fountain of Time (1911). Time, a craglike figure, reviews the endless march of mankind. Once again the magnitude of the project suggested cement, this time "glorified" by quartz chips. The Fountain of Creation, planned for the other end of the Midway, was never commissioned, but a few completed figures are on the campus of the University of Illinois. For Urbana, Taft also made the *Alma Mater* (1929) and *Lincoln, the Young Lawyer* (1927). Other works include the *Pioneers* (1928) in Elmwood, the Victor Lawson Memorial (1932) in Chicago, and the Lincoln-Douglas Debate Plaque (1936) in Quincy.

For Taft art was not a surface decoration but rather the expression and transmission to future generations of man's highest standards of excellence. For this reason he lavished time and effort on young artists and on the introduction to the general public of examples of great sculpture from around the world. He died in Chicago on Oct. 30, 1936.

Further Reading

There are two biographies of Taft: Ada Bartlett Taft, *Lorado Taft: Sculptor and Citizen* (privately printed, 1946), and Lewis W. Williams, *Lorado Taft: American Sculptor and Art Missionary* (University of Chicago Dissertation, 1958).

Additional Sources

Weller, Allen Stuart, *Lorado in Paris: the letters of Lorado Taft, 1880-1885,* Urbana: University of Illinois Press, 1985. □

Robert Alphonso Taft

Robert Alphonso Taft (1889-1953) was a conservative politician who served three terms in the U.S. Senate, where he was recognized as "Mr. Republican."

Robert Alphonso Taft was born September 8, 1889, in Cincinnati, Ohio, to William Howard Taft and Helen Herron Taft. His grandfather Alphonso had been President Grant's secretary of war and attorney general and his father was to be in turn solicitor general, a federal appeals judge, civil governor of the Philippines, and ultimately the only person ever to serve as president of the United States and afterward as Chief Justice of the Supreme Court.

At the age of ten Robert left Cincinnati with his family for Manila for three years. In 1903 he was sent to Taft School in Connecticut which his uncle Horace had founded and which placed a premium on academic achievement. He then enrolled at Yale as his father and grandfather had done before him. While he was a junior at Yale, his father entered the White House, but Robert never lived there for any extended periods. Robert Taft's adult personality reflected his upbringing as the first-born son of prosperous, ambitious, talented parents who constantly demanded excellence. Although he was proud of his father's accomplishments, he wanted to have his own identity and was abrupt to those who played up his family ties. Even as a young person he was decidedly cool to all those outside his inner circle and to anyone he believed was wasting his time.

After completing his studies at Yale in 1910, he attended Harvard Law School and, as he had at both Taft School and at Yale, graduated first in his class. He declined a clerkship with Supreme Court Justice Oliver Wendell Holmes and moved in 1913 to Cincinnati where his father had arranged a place for him in a prestigious law firm. In October 1914 he married Martha Bowers, sister of a Yale classmate and the daughter of a solicitor general in President Taft's administration. They had four sons. Disqualified by nearsightedness from military service in World War I, Taft leaped at the chance to join Herbert Hoover's Food Administration in Washington as an assistant counsel. His experiences with the Food Administration helped confirm the philosophy he had absorbed from his father. "Whatever price we fixed, everybody howled," he recalled in commenting upon the futility of government regulation of the economy. With the armistice in 1918 he accompanied Hoover to Paris to work on postwar relief problems, and his stay there did much to fix his views on foreign relations. He was horrified at what he saw as the amorality of European

realpolitik and vowed to always work to keep American diplomacy untainted by cynicism and free of corrupting alliances. These years of government service seem to have developed his maturity and intellectual and personal independence from his father.

Upon his return home in 1919 he settled in Cincinnati and established a law practice with his younger brother Charles, specializing in corporate clients. Robert Taft was also a civic leader. He was active in the planning of the Union Station in Cincinnati and helped his uncle develop the Dixie Terminal Building, an interurban streetcar terminus with professional and business offices and shops, still a much-used architectural landmark in the 1980s. He participated in the protracted struggle over reform of the municipal government.

Republican Party regularity was always to be his gospel, for he was mindful of how factionalism had marred his father's administration and destroyed his chances for a second term as president. Robert Taft served six years in the lower house of the Ohio legislature, attaining the speakership in his final term in 1926. While in the legislature he worked for tax reform and opposed the Ku Klux Klan at a time when it was a significant force in Ohio politics. In 1931 he returned to Columbus, serving in the state senate for one term, but he was defeated for re-election for the only time in his career in 1932, a landslide year for Democrats.

The Senate Years

Coming to national attention in the late 1930s when he was elected to the U.S. Senate for the first of three terms, Taft earned a reputation as an opponent of the New Deal and as an isolationist in foreign affairs. He did his political homework, soon gained the respect of Senate colleagues, and from the start of his career served on such important committees as appropriations, banking and currency, and education and labor. He was superbly organized and had absolute command of statistical analyses of the problems he wanted to investigate. Although he had accepted such New Deal measures as unemployment insurance and old-age pensions during his campaign, he disliked much about the New Deal's approach, which he regarded as too often representing wasteful spending, careless administration, and excessive interference with private enterprise.

Taft was a bright man, but his interests outside politics were narrow. He played golf avidly each Sunday in nice weather but otherwise proved himself one of the hardest-working senators of any era. He was uncomfortable with such traditional political activities as working a crowd, wearing fraternal regalia, kissing babies, or flattering local worthies. A poor public speaker, he was given to dry recitations of facts. Martha Taft, on the other hand, was an excellent speaker and an important figure in the national League of Women Voters. Delighting in campaigning for her husband, she impressed crowds with her forceful and witty style. "To err is Truman" was her most famous oneliner.

As early as 1940 Taft was regarded as a serious Republican presidential contender. While the nomination that year went to Wendell Willkie, Taft was the favorite of conservative Republicans and remained so for the rest of his career. His quick rise to prominence made him a quotable figure, and at times he did the expedient—for instance, when he backed Joseph McCarthy's witch hunt for Communists in the early 1950s, hoping to gain for his presidential candidacy the endorsement of the then-powerful Wisconsin senator. But by and large he remained consistent to the best of his conservative principles. For instance, his reverence for strict construction of the Constitution even led him in 1946 to take the highly unpopular step of denouncing the Nuremberg war crimes trials. He thought that the Nazis deserved punishment but would have favored a military tribunal, rather than the civilian proceeding, which in his belief was *ex post facto.*

Taft is best remembered for co-sponsoring the Taft-Hartley Act of 1947, which modified a number of provisions in New Deal labor law. He was widely and unjustly hated for it by organized labor, but it did not stifle unionism as had been feared. On many occasions since, Taft-Hartley's "cooling-off period" has been invoked when major strikes have threatened, buying time for settlements to be arranged. Taft worked for mildly reformist measures including the Taft-Wagner-Ellender housing bill, modest federal aid to education, and a plan for federal grants to the states to improve health care. Although Taft's support seemed puzzling to conservatives and liberals alike, the bills were actually in keeping with his conservative philosophy that America's opportunity, available to all, should begin with a fair start.

Presidential Ambitions Never Fulfilled

In foreign affairs Taft could also be flexible. He backed American entry into the United Nations and was a supporter of Zionism. His attitude toward these major postwar issues revealed that Taft was not the rigid isolationist he had been reputed to be ever since his pre-Pearl Harbor opposition to Lend-Lease and other measures that had tied the United States to the support of Great Britain. Particularly with the death of Senator Arthur Vandenberg of Michigan, the GOP's (Grand Old Party's) most influential voice on international affairs, Taft became a spokesman for his party on matters of foreign policy. He voted against joining the North Atlantic Treaty Organization, but once the United States had entered it felt American commitments to the alliance should be honored. Although he was reluctant to see American ground forces stationed in Europe, he berated the Truman administration for "losing" China and advocated a stronger U.S. effort during the Korean War, endorsing many of the views of General Douglas MacArthur.

While Taft's opinions were generally logically stated and formulated, at times he did speak with an unflattering shrillness—as on Korea—for, after failing again to win the GOP's nomination in 1948, there is clear evidence that he badly wanted his party's nomination in 1952 and felt he could win the presidency. Prominent figures in his party, however, perceived him as a loser and backed Dwight Eisenhower, who handily won the nomination after a bitterly contested primary season in which the Taft forces at times overreached themselves. After some months of estrangement, Taft and Eisenhower reconciled. Aware that if the immensely popular Eisenhower were elected in 1952 he would certainly seek to succeed himself, Taft mellowed as he came to realize that he would never be president.

Taft was a tall and large-framed man who possessed exceptional physical stamina and good health until April 1953. Family and colleagues were stunned when tests revealed that soreness after a round of golf was the first symptom of a widespread and rapidly advancing cancer that would claim his life by the end of July.

Three times he had sought his party's presidential nomination; each time other leaders recognized that he would not make a viable national candidate. His failures shed light upon the nature of the American political system, which in the modern era often rewards charisma and electability more than experience and understanding. Although Taft held several positions of public responsibility, he will always be identified with the U.S. Senate where he achieved prompt recognition as "Mr. Republican." Two of his sons would also enter government service, extending the family's record as one of the most effective and prominent political dynasties in American history.

Further Reading

Studies of Taft are legion and include innumerable magazine and newspaper articles covering not only his own long career in Cincinnati and Washington but also much about his youth and family heritage. The student of Taft, however, should be directed to the large collection of his papers in the Manuscripts Division of the Library of Congress and to these studies: William S. White, *The Taft Story* (1954); Russell Kirk and James McClellan, *The Political Principles of Robert A. Taft* (1967); and particularly James T. Patterson, *Mr. Republican: A Biography of Robert A. Taft* (1972). Taft himself authored two books, *A Foreign Policy for Americans* (1951) and (with Congressman T. V. Smith of Illinois) *Foundations of Democracy: A Series of Debates* (1939), which provide insights into his thinking. □

William Howard Taft

William Howard Taft (1857-1930), as twenty-seventh president of the United States and a chief justice, failed to rise adequately to the challenges of the times, despite his many strong qualities.

William Howard Taft was born in Cincinnati, Ohio, on Sept. 15, 1857, into a family of old New England stock. Both his father and grandfather had served terms as judges, and young Taft aspired to a judicial career. A bright but unimaginative youngster, he attended high school in Cincinnati, and at Yale University he finished second in a graduating class of 121 in 1878. Two years later he graduated from the Cincinnati Law School.

An outsize, congenial young man with a tendency to procrastinate, Taft took an active interest in Republican politics. He was rewarded with appointments to various offices. Between 1880 and 1890 he served successively as assistant prosecuting attorney for Hamilton County, Ohio, collector of internal revenue for Cincinnati, and judge of the Superior Court of Ohio. Named solicitor general of the United States in 1890, he distinguished himself for his thorough preparation and won 15 of the first 18 cases he argued in the Supreme Court.

Meanwhile, in 1886, Taft had married Helen Herron of Cincinnati. Eventually they had three children. A driving, ambitious woman, she wanted her husband to follow a political rather than a legal career. When a Federal judgeship opened in 1891, she protested that his appointment would "put and end to all your opportunities . . . of being thrown with bigwigs." And she twice influenced him to reject offers of a Supreme Court seat during Theodore Roosevelt's first administration in order to maintain his availability for the presidency.

Federal Service

Disregarding his wife's admonitions, Taft accepted appointment to the Sixth Circuit Court in 1892. Though he again distinguished himself for thoroughness and technical command of the law, he was inhibited by his lack of imagination. Yet he was in no sense a reactionary and in some respects not even a conservative. He broke new ground in employers' liability cases and revitalized the Sherman Antitrust Act. He also upheld labor's right to strike. He disapproved of secondary boycotts, however, and by insisting on enforcing the injunctive power he acquired a somewhat

exaggerated reputation as an antilabor judge. His written opinions, like his oral arguments, were learned but verbose.

In 1899 Taft turned down the presidency of Yale University, partly because he believed his Unitarianism would offend traditionalists. Then, in March 1900, he reluctantly acceded to President William McKinley's request that he become president of the Philippine Commission. The 4 most creative years of his life followed. Overriding the will of the autocratic military governor, Gen. Arthur MacArthur, he instituted civil government and became in 1901 the archipelago's first civil governor.

In the Philippines, Taft established an educational system, built roads and harbors, and negotiated the purchase of 400,000 acres from the Dominican friars for resale on generous terms to the Filipinos. He also pushed limited self-government rapidly. Taft's conviction that the Philippines should be administered in the interests of its citizens, coupled with his open, conciliatory presence, won him respect and affection. And though he failed to prevent the islands from entering into an economic relationship with the United States which adversely affected their development in the long run, his tenure was probably the most enlightened colonial administration to that time.

Secretary of War

On Feb. 1, 1904, Taft succeeded Elihu Root as U.S. secretary of war. The duties again proved surprisingly congenial, largely because he became one of President Roosevelt's most intimate advisers and his principal troubleshooter. Continuing to supervise administration of the Philippines, he assumed responsibility for starting construction of the Panama Canal and represented the President on various missions. His most important mission was to Japan; it culminated in the secret recognition of Japan's suzerainty over Korea. He also helped suppress a threatened revolution in Cuba in 1906.

Although Taft still yearned to join the Supreme Court, he allowed his wife and brothers to kindle presidential aspirations. Impressed by Taft's "absolutely unflinching rectitude" and "literally dauntless courage and willingness to bear responsibility," as he phrased it, Roosevelt decided in 1907 to make Taft his successor as president. Both men believed mistakenly at the time that they agreed totally on public policy. Yet by February 1908, after several thunderous messages to Congress had revealed the real depth of Roosevelt's progressivism, his wife urged him not to "make any more speeches on the Roosevelt policies."

Nevertheless, the presidential campaign of 1908 was waged mainly on the "Roosevelt policies." Though Taft defeated William Jennings Bryan handily, his plurality dropped about 1,500,000 votes below Roosevelt's in 1904. Moreover, the election of numerous Progressive Republicans and Democrats shifted the balance in Congress.

The Presidency

Whatever Taft thought about Roosevelt's objectives, he never had approved of his freewheeling, often extralegal, procedures. This was especially true of conservation, a field in which Roosevelt and his subordinates had consistently interpreted the law loosely in order to protect the public interest. Taft decided, accordingly, that his mission was to consolidate rather than push forward—to give the Roosevelt reforms, as he privately said, "the sanction of law." To this end he surrounded himself with lawyers. At the same time, he underestimated both the temper of the times and the zeal of the Progressive Republicans in Congress. Worse still, he proved incapable of giving the nation the kind of moral, intellectual, and political leadership it had grown accustomed to under Roosevelt.

Taft's troubles started early. True at first to his campaign promises, he called a special session of Congress to revise the tariff. The resultant bill was not a bad measure by Republican standards, but it failed abysmally to meet expectations. Disguising his disappointment, Taft called it "the best bill that the party has ever passed" and signed it into law. This alienated many insurgent Republicans, most of whom were already seething over his refusal to support their effort to reduce the powers of Joseph "Uncle Joe" Cannon, the czarlike Speaker of the House.

Taft's replacement of Roosevelt's secretary of the interior contributed to the polarization of the party. The new secretary, Richard A. Ballinger, was a moderate conservationist and a strict legal constructionist in the manner of Taft himself." I do not hesitate to say," the President wrote, that the presidential power to withdraw public lands from private use "was exercised far beyond legal limitation under Secretary Garfield." With Taft's endorsement, Ballinger insisted on opening much valuable land to private entry while the Geological Survey completed surveys. Angered by this and other inhibiting policies, Roosevelt's intimate friend, Chief Forester Gifford Pinchot, finally charged Ballinger with a "giveaway" of Alaskan mineral lands to the Guggenheim-Morgan financial interests. Taft thereupon removed Pinchot from office. Although Ballinger was eventually exonerated, Taft was fatally, and somewhat unfairly, stamped as anticonservationist.

Ironically, Taft's relentless prosecution of trusts further exacerbated his relations with Roosevelt. Unlike the former president, he believed that dissolution rather than regulation was the preferred solution. He gave Attorney General George W. Wickersham free rein to institute proceedings, and by the end of 4 years almost twice as many actions had been initiated as in 7½ years under Roosevelt. Among these were proceedings against the U.S. Steel Corporation, which had absorbed the Tennessee Coal and Iron Company during the Panic of 1907 with Roosevelt's tacit approval.

In Congress, meanwhile, a coalition of Progressive Republicans and Democrats drove through half a dozen reform measures. Some were supported warmly by Taft, some halfheartedly, and others not at all. But all owed their passage to the Progressive ferment Roosevelt had done so much to create during his presidency and after his return from abroad in 1910. They included amendments for an income tax and the direct election of senators, the Mann-Elkins Act to increase the powers of the Interstate Commerce Commission, creation of the Children's Bureau, a corporation tax, safety standards for mines, Postal Savings and Parcel Post, and workmen's compensation legislation.

Foreign Affairs

Taft's conduct of foreign policy was governed by an uncritical extension of the concepts behind the Open-Door Notes of 1899 and 1900. Disregarding Roosevelt's warning that the United States should accept Japanese preeminence in eastern Asia and abandon commercial aspirations in Manchuria and North China, he pursued a policy of "active intervention to secure for our merchandise and our capitalists opportunity for profitable investment."

In the Caribbean, Taft was even more ingenious than Roosevelt in devising means to protect the Panama Canal. He put American troops into Nicaragua in 1912 to install and maintain in power a conservative, pro-United States party. And in what came to be termed "dollar diplomacy," he encouraged American capital to displace European capital elsewhere in the region. The end result was security for the canal and ultraconservative and often repressive government for the Caribbean peoples.

By 1912 Taft had so isolated himself from his party's Progressive and was under such heavy fire from Roosevelt and Senator Robert M. La Follette that the Progressives were prepared to support either Roosevelt or La Follette for the presidential nomination. Taft lost to the former president by more than 2 to 1 in the 13 state primaries that winter and spring. However, his control of Republican party machinery gave him enough delegates to win renomination in convention. Embittered further by Roosevelt's decision to run on the Progressive ticket, Taft waged an angry, defensive, and ineffectual campaign. He finished behind Woodrow Wilson and Roosevelt.

Taft's best qualities, especially his capacity for disinterested public service, again became dominant after he left the White House and accepted the Kent chair of constitutional law at Yale. His views on World War I were closer to President Wilson's than to those of interventionist Republicans like Roosevelt and Lodge, and he generously backed the President during the period of neutrality. His work as joint chairman of the War Labor Board contributed greatly to the relatively smooth course of labor-management relations during the war. He afterward gave broad support to Wilson's plan for the League of Nations Covenant.

Chief Justice

On June 30, 1921, President Warren G. Harding fulfilled Taft's "heart's desire" by appointing him chief justice. Taft brought to his new position a consuming belief in the rule of law, an unshakable conviction that the protection of property rights was crucial to orderly government, and a driving determination to perfect the administration of justice. He further brought a fierce resolve to mold the Court in his own moderately conservative image. In 1916 he had bitterly opposed Wilson's nomination of Louis D. Brandeis. Now, as chief justice, he discouraged Harding from considering men like Benjamin Cardozo, Learned Hand, and Henry Stimson because they might "herd" with the liberals, Holmes and Brandeis. Yet, he also said, it would be equally unwise to have too many men as reactionary as James McReynolds. He was largely responsible for the selection of Pierce Butler in 1922.

As chief justice, Taft compiled a mixed record. Although he succeeded in massing the Court along generally conservative lines, few of his opinions ring down through the years. One exception was his dissent in 1923 from the majority finding in the Adkins case that a minimum-wage act interfered with freedom of contract. Otherwise, as a careful student of Taft's chief justiceship writes, "Taft endorsed decisions, sometimes writing the majority opinion, that seemed to fasten both the national government and the states in a strait jacket." He wrote the majority opinion in the second child-labor case. He ruled, again for the majority, that a Kansas statute for compulsory arbitration of wage disputes was unconstitutional. And he declared, once more for the conservative majority, that an Arizona limitation on the use of injunctions against labor violated due process. He also held in the famous Coronado case that labor unions could be sued under the antitrust laws.

Conversely, Taft sanctioned the exercise of broad regulatory powers by the Federal government under the commerce clause. He also sustained the presidential power to remove executive officers.

As an administrator, Taft ranks with Melville W. Fuller and Charles Evans Hughes; he was notably successful in effecting administrative reforms. He wrote more opinions than any other member of his Court, expedited the hearing of cases, and won congressional authorization to create a conference of senior circuit judges. He also shaped and influenced passage of the Judge's Bill of 1925, which gave the Court wide discretionary power and enabled it to reduce the number of unimportant cases that came before it. In addition, Taft was preeminently responsible for the decision to construct the Supreme Court Building. However, he made little enduring impression upon constitutional law. He retired in February 1930 and died in Washington on March 30.

Taft's reputation among contemporary historians is somewhat higher as president and somewhat lower as chief justice than it was in his lifetime. More than any other major figure of his times, perhaps, he exemplified the conservative virtues and weaknesses. Yearning always "for the absolute"—for a system of law devoid of vagueness—he failed in the end to find or to fashion it. He also failed in the main to adjust creatively to the social and economic changes induced by the industrialization of the nation.

Further Reading

The standard work on Taft is Henry F. Pringle, *The Life and Times of William Howard Taft* (2 vols., 1939). A brief account of Taft's presidential years is in George E. Mowry, *The Era of Theodore Roosevelt, 1900-1912* (1958). Alpheus Thomas Mason's penetrating study *William Howard Taft: Chief Justice* (1965) offers a revealing account of Taft's chief justiceship. Taft's relations with Roosevelt are related in detail in William H. Harbaugh, *Power and Responsibility: The Life and Times of Theodore Roosevelt* (1961; new rev. ed. 1963), and William Manners, *TR and Will: A Friendship That Split the Republican Party* (1969). See also Archie Butt, *Taft and Roosevelt: The Intimate Letters of Archie Butt* (2 vols., 1930). James Penick, Jr., *Progressive Politics and Conservation: The Ballinger-Pinchot Affair* (1968), sheds new light on that episode. □

Taharqa

Taharqa (reigned ca. 688-ca. 663 B.C.) was a Nubian pharaoh of Egypt. He was the last ruler of the Twenty-fifth Dynasty, the so-called Ethiopian Dynasty, and was driven out of Lower Egypt by the Assyrians as they began to conquer Egypt.

When Shabaka conquered Lower Egypt and thus asserted Nubian rule, he was accompanied by his nephew Taharqa, who was about age 20. Later, during Shabaka's reign as pharaoh, Egypt confronted the growing might of Assyria on the battlefield. Taharqa was at the head of the Egyptian army, but it is not clear whether the two forces actually fought. Taharqa's brother Shabataka succeeded Shabaka, and he made Taharqa his coregent in order to assure his succession. About 688 B.C., approximately 23 years after Nubian rule had been imposed over Egypt, Taharqa assumed the throne in his own right.

The next few years were peaceful, and Taharqa moved his capital to Tanis in the Delta so that he could stay well informed about events in the neighboring Asian countries. By 671 B.C. Egypt and Assyria again approached a confrontation, so Taharqa prepared to fight for the continued survival of Egypt. But the Assyrian king, Esarhaddon, crossed the Sinai Desert and defeated Taharqa's army on the frontier. In 2 weeks he was besieging Memphis. The Egyptian army crumbled under the attack of the better-disciplined Assyrian army, which was armed with iron weapons.

Taharqa fled to Upper Egypt, leaving Esarhaddon to take control of Lower Egypt. Two years later Taharqa returned with a fresh army and managed to recover control of the Delta, but this success was short-lived, and Esar-haddon's successor, Ashurbanipal, drove Taharqa south again. After this final defeat he never again tried to campaign in the north. Egypt then entered into a long era of successive foreign rulers.

During his period of Egyptian rule Taharqa had encouraged many architectural projects, as had his Nubian predecessors. He erected monuments at Karnak, Thebes, and Tanis in Lower Egypt, and he built a number of important temples in Cush, as the Upper Egyptian Nubian state was then known. During the last 8 years of his life in Cush, he continued to foster his architectural interests.

In 663 B.C. Taharqa accepted as a coregent Tanutamon, whose precise relationship to him is not clear. The next year Taharqa died and was buried in a pyramid in Nuri. Tanutamon had immediately invaded Lower Egypt himself when he was named coregent, and he managed to gain control of it for almost a decade, only to be driven out by the Assyrians, as Taharqa had been. Although the Nubians had managed to rule Egypt for only about 75 years, their kingdom of Cush in the northern Sudan survived for almost a millennium.

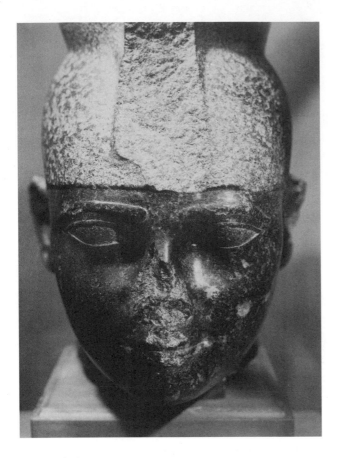

Further Reading

Some of the inscriptions pertaining to Taharqa's career are translated and commented upon in *Egyptian Literature,* edited with translation by E. A. Wallis Budge (2 vols., 1912). Since there is no biography of him, the reader must turn to the general histories of Egypt and the Sudan. Useful sources include the classic work by James Henry Breasted, *A History of Egypt* (1905; 2d rev. ed. 1909), and Anthony J. Arkell, *A History of the Sudan* (1955; 2d rev. ed. 1961). □

Hippolyte Adolphe Taine

The French critic and historian Hippolyte Adolphe Taine (1828-1893) was one of the most prominent intellectual figures of his period in France. His emphasis on scientific methods in criticism formed the basis of contemporary critical techniques.

Hippolyte Taine was born in Vouziers in the Ardennes on April 21, 1828, into a family of civil servants. His childhood was spent in an enlightened cultural atmosphere in which earnest intellectual pursuits mingled with an early exposure to the arts and to nature. By the age of 14, when he moved to Paris with his widowed mother, he had developed an intense intellectuality matched only by his profound love of nature.

Taine's passion for knowledge and especially for philosophy made him highly receptive to the multitude of intellectual and scientific trends of his time. By the time he had completed his university studies at the École Normale Supérieure, he had investigated almost every philosophical and scientific concept known. Upon leaving the university he was prepared to formulate his own critical apparatus in order to investigate bodies of knowledge.

Taine's most productive years coincided with the reign of Napoleon III. The Second Empire, beneath its social glitter and economic growth, was highly oppressive to liberal intellectuals. Taine abandoned all hopes of a professorial career at the university. He withdrew from public life and devoted his energies to research in a large variety of fields. All of his studies centered on the problem of the human condition and were underlain by his naive but honest belief in the explicability of human nature by means of scientific inquiry.

The culmination of this belief found its expression in Taine's central work, *De l'intelligence* (1870). It summed up all his previous interests in psychology and philosophy and fused the converging lines of his critical thought. His works preceding *De l'intelligence* encompass a great variety of interests and touch on almost every phase of intellectual and artistic production. His dissertation on the fables of Jean de La Fontaine, completed in 1853 and published in its final form in 1860 (*La Fontaine et ses fables*), was a presentation of Taine's concept of esthetics. It expressed in essence his doctrine of scientific determinism by attributing "racial" distinctions to climatic and geographical differences. His work on the French philosophers of the 19th century (*Les Philosophes français du XIX siècle,* 1857) was a critical evaluation of the major philosophical concepts of the century, and his essays on a wide variety of subjects represented a further elaboration of his critical system. These volumes included *Essais de critique et d'histoire* (1858), *Nouveaux essais* (1865), and *Derniers essais* (1894).

Taine formulated his critical system most clearly in the introduction to the five volumes of one of his major works, *Histoire de la littérature anglaise* (1863). He stated that every reality, psychological, esthetic, or historical, can be reduced to a distinctly definable formula by discovering in each reality a single operative principle. This basic principle is governed by a system of laws that he reduced to his famous triad of race, environment, and time ("la race, le milieu, le moment"). Taine applied this critical system in all of his works, including his analyses of the development of the arts of Greece, Italy, and the Netherlands, presented in a series of lectures spanning more than 20 years at the École des Beaux-Arts and published in two volumes, *Philosophie de l'art* (1865-1869).

The Franco-Prussian War of 1870 profoundly disturbed Taine. From then until his death, he applied himself to an analysis of French history in an attempt to uncover the causes of France's defeat and the Commune of 1871 (*Les Origines de la France contemporaine,* 1875-1893). He died in Paris on March 9, 1893.

Further Reading

There is no biography of Taine in English. Sholom J. Kahn, *Science and Aesthetic Judgement: A Study in Taine's Critical Method* (1953), analyzes Taine's esthetic theory. For an evaluation of his influence upon modern literary criticism see William K. Wimsatt, Jr., and Cleanth Brooks, *Literary Criticism: A Short History* (1957). A cogent defense of the methodology of historical criticism is in Edmund Wilson, *The Triple Thinkers* (1938). □

T'ang T'ai-tsung

T'ang T'ai-tsung (600-649), emperor of China during the seventh century, took over much of Asia and created a dynasty that was culturally as well as economically prosperous.

Chinese emperor T'ang T'ai-tsung (also known as Li Shih-min and Taizong) firmly established the Tang dynasty in imperial China and conquered much of Asia during his reign, setting the stage for one of the most celebrated eras in all of Chinese history. After helping to orchestrate the overthrow of the Sui dynasty, T'ai-tsung watched as his father assumed control of the nation. When his turn to rule arrived, T'ai-tsung consolidated Chinese territory lost to invading forces in from the north and west in previous centuries and presided over a culture flowering with poetry and art and an economy brimming with growing trade among the Western nations.

Rose to Power through Ruthless Political Maneuvering

T'ai-tsung's early years were in many respects representative of the turbulent Chinese political arena in medieval times. His father, Li Yuan, was a trusted member of the Sui government administration and served in various posts. The family had long been familiar with the reigns of power—ancestors had ruled portions of North China both before and during foreign occupations by Turkish forces. Born Li Shih-min in the year 600, T'ai-tsung was raised in a fashion fitting with the aristocratic history of his family. He received training in horsemanship and hunting along with his two brothers before academic tutors versed him in history and the thought of Confucius. T'ai-tsung also traveled extensively throughout much of the empire, accompanying his father on administrative missions and gathering first-hand knowledge of the territories he would eventually dominate.

Prior to the Tang dynasty, China was governed by the Sui dynasty that rose to power in 589 and made significant strides toward ousting the Turks and Mongols who for centuries marauded through North and West China, taking territory and blocking trade routes to the West. After successful campaigns, the emperor reclaimed significant portions of what were traditionally Chinese lands and appeared to have secured longevity for his dynasty. The Sui emperor ordered the construction of several palaces and temples both to celebrate his victories and elicit a measure of grandeur among the citizenry. With treasuries already emptied to pay for military operations, including three unsuccessful campaigns in Korea, the emperor levied additional taxes—an unpopular policy with several important noblemen. In 613, rebel armies sprung up around the nation to protest the increased taxation, and the emperor, anxious to maintain control, commissioned many of his key advisors, including Li Yuan, to the military ranks. T'ai-tsung's father sensed in the situation an opportunity to restore in full measure his family's aristocratic tradition and, rather than engage the rebels in conflict, he negotiated for their support in his designs on the throne.

Li Yuan gathered enough support to eventually depose the emperor and in his place he appointed the emperor's young son. It was customary in the Chinese political system for a ruler to be replaced if he was deemed unfit by enough of those with political connections, and with armed bands of rebels approaching from the north, the emperor saw the need to acquiesce. With an inexperienced emperor in place, Li Yuan acted almost immediately to complete his plan. He declared the beginning of the Tang dynasty, a proclamation that was fully supported by the many nobles that T'ai-tsung, as an adolescent diplomat, helped enlist to the cause. T'ai-tsung was rewarded by his father with a military commission and given control of massive armies. Li Yuan charged his young son with solidifying Tang support in China's western regions.

With heralded military skill, T'ai-tsung vanquished all rebellious armies by the year 624 and developed a sterling reputation as a leader. His political stock soaring, T'ai-tsung turned his efforts toward the throne. In Chinese dynastic structure, the eldest son was named the crown prince and first in line for his father's post; T'ai-tsung's older brother received this honor. This development did not sit well with the ambitious T'ai-tsung and he began crafting a plan by which he would become China's ruler. When his two brothers rode into the palace on July 4, 626, T'ai-tsung ambushed both of them and took their lives, establishing himself as China's eventual ruler. His father, old and intimidated by his son's daring exploits, removed himself as emperor and by August of 626, T'ai-tsung was the emperor of China.

Empire Flourished under His Reign

T'ai-tsung inherited a society on the verge of enormous cultural development. Already a culture of great technical achievement, including the magnetic compass, herbal medicines, paper, and alchemy, all achievements predating their development in the West, Chinese arts and sciences flourished as the empire was at last stable politically and freed from barbarian invaders. A student of poetry and calligraphy, T'ai-tsung consulted frequently with the scholar-cleric class that for many centuries prior to and following his rule served as the core of Chinese government administrators. The Tang dynasty under T'ai-tsung's command firmly entrenched this class as an insulated mechanism of governance. This reduced the necessity for reliance on powerful noble families who were frequently at the heart of political revolt, as T'ai-tsung, seizing power in a similar fashion, was only too well aware. He established civil service examinations to recruit the best and the brightest Chinese to serve his government at all levels and these institutions survived until the beginning of the twentieth century. In so doing, he placed significant emphasis on education and literacy and also subdued the power held by religious sects including the Confucionists and the Buddhists by subjecting their members to the same examinations and eliminating any direct link to power.

The strong government apparatus instituted by T'ai-tsung and the Tang dynasty re-established the empire as one of the three strongest in the world, the others being the Roman and Persian empires. T'ai-tsung assumed the title ''Son of Heaven,'' which reflected his divine right to govern and his inevitable position as the spiritual center of the empire. As the physical embodiment of China, T'ai-tsung was responsible for conducting diplomatic relations with this status in mind. Accordingly, visitors from neighboring nations were welcomed in great halls decorated with silk, gold, and jade, and protected by elaborately costumed palace guards and strikingly clad musicians wielding bells, lutes, drums, harps, and flutes. With the ''silk route'' again open for free and relatively unencumbered trade, Western merchants from the Middle East and Europe met with their counterparts from Burma, Thailand, Vietnam, and Korea to create the most international and cosmopolitan city the world had ever seen.

The element of trade loomed large for T'ai-tsung and later Tang emperors. To supply artisans with the materials for their luxuries and insure that quantities of Chinese goods could reach the West, the trade routes had to be maintained through either conquest or coercion. To pacify tribes and nations from the interior of China to the distant empires of Persia and Arabia, gifts of jade and silk were sent by the emperor, and female courtesans were sent to become brides to influential chieftains. T'ai-tsung effectively managed these diplomatic feats and was able to call territory ranging from the Caspian Sea to the East China Sea—several thousand miles across Asia—part of the Chinese empire.

Saw Decline in Last Years of Rule

By the year 636, T'ai-tsung had firmly established China as a major power in the medieval world. In the West, stories of Chinese grandeur and cultural advances would become legendary through accounts handed down centuries later by Marco Polo and other Westerners familiar with Chinese history. T'ai-tsung contributed to the splendor of China by commissioning many public works and even more palaces and vacation estates. Unfortunately, his architectural vision of the great city of Chang'an drained royal coffers and taxes, and tariffs were raised to pay for T'ai-tsung's projects. This same decision was in many respects responsible for the downfall of his Sui predecessors and led to a diminishing empire for T'ai-tsung. Nonetheless, during T'ai-tsung's lifetime the city of Chang'an was unlike any other in the world. It was designed on a grid pattern with avenues wider than the length of the modern football field and organized into several self-contained neighborhoods,

market areas, parks, and royal hunting grounds. Many houses were cooled in the summer by an air conditioning system run by underground ice storage pits and many also contained bathing pools, fountains, and gardens.

While the interior of the empire surrounded itself with the luxuries of profitable trade, the more remote territories experienced a resurgence in attacks by Western invaders. Unable to appease the Mongols and Turks and suffering the humiliation after Korean troops repelled his invading armies, T'ai-tsung grew more insular and suspicious of his advisors, consulting them less and less. In addition to his military setbacks, T'ai-tsung was disturbed by the line of succession to follow him. His oldest son turned away from traditional Chinese customs and adopted the life of a Turk, living in tents and garbed in Turkish gowns. The crown prince also hatched a plan with his brother against their father, though T'ai-tsung quelled their efforts and passed them both over by appointing his youngest son as the crown prince. T'ai-tsung's youngest son, though, was a sickly child and a weak ruler, and saw losses to barbarian enemies in both the Northern and Western fronts.

While the close of his rule saw the celebrated emperor lose a portion of his lustre, T'ai-tsung's reputation in Chinese history remains secure as a magnanimous leader, responsible for both broadening and glorifying the empire. Recorded dialogues between himself and his clerics survived the ages to become regularly consulted manuals of conduct for later emperors.

Further Reading

The only full-length biography of T'ai-tsung is the readable but uncritical work by Charles Patrick Fitzgerald, *Son of Heaven* (1933). For an interpretive view see Arthur F. Wright, ''T'ang T'ai-tsung and Buddhism,'' in *Perspectives on the T'ang* (1971).

Additional Sources

Schafer, Edward H., *Ancient China*, Time Inc., 1967.
Fairbank, John, *China: A New History*, Harvard University Press, 1992.
Shinn, Rinn-Sup, and Robert L. Wordon, *Countries of the World*, Electronic Library, Inc., CD-ROM. □

Korekiyo Takahashi

The Japanese statesman Korekiyo Takahashi (1854-1936) was an economically liberal finance minister who resisted military spending. For this he was assassinated in the attempted military coup of 1936.

K orekiyo Takahashi was born on July 27, 1854, in Edo (Tokyo) and temporarily given the name Wakiji by his real father, Shozaemon Kawamura, a master painter attached to the Shogun's court. But because Korekiyo was an illegitimate child, he was adopted by a low-ranking samurai of Sendai Province named Koretaka Kakuji Takahashi. Precociously bright, at 11 Korekiyo studied English with Hepburn; at 13 he was sent to study in the United States. In San Francisco he unwittingly signed a paper indenturing himself to 3 years' labor but soon extricated himself from this plight and hurriedly returned to Japan in December 1868, shortly after the Meiji restoration. Thereafter he taught and translated English and became a Christian.

Takahashi's successful career in the bureaucracy started in 1881 in the newly established Ministry of Agriculture and Commerce, where he made several important contributions to modern business practices, such as developing the registration of patents. In 1889 he was also appointed president of the Tokyo Agricultural College, where he worked out his philosophy of "self-help" for farmers, which he later implemented as finance minister.

Takahashi's successful banking career began in 1893, after a quixotic try at operating a silver mine in Peru. By 1900 he was a vice-governor of the Bank of Japan. For contributing to Japan's war effort against Russia by raising great sums through selling war bonds abroad, he was made a member of the House of Peers in 1905, at the age of 52. The next year he became president of the Shokin Bank. In 1907 he received the first of several decorations from the Emperor. Takahashi was made a baron and later a viscount, and in 1911 he became governor of the Bank of Japan, where he lowered interest rates as an anti-depression measure.

In 1913 Takahashi entered politics by becoming finance minister in Gonnohyoe (Gombei) Yamamoto's Cabinet and joining the Seiyukai. He succeeded to that party's presidency and also to the premiership in 1921 upon Kei Hara's assassination, concurrently maintaining the finance portfolio. But Takahashi's leadership was weak, and his Cabinet fell the following year, contributing to the political instability of the 1920s. He gave up his peerage, was elected to the House of Representatives, and fought for "constitutional government." In 1924 he accepted the post of agriculture minister in Takaakira Kato's coalition Cabinet. In 1927, as Premier Giichi Tanaka's finance minister, he managed the bank moratorium. Taking the finance portfolio for the fourth time in 1931, he succeeded to the premiership upon Tsuyoshi Inukai's assassination in 1932. After this, he became minister of finance two more times, in Makoto Saito's and Keisuke Okada's Cabinets, before being gunned down on Feb. 26, 1936, with many others, by radical young officers who saw him as a representative of the interests of the *zaibatsu* (industrial combines), thwarting renovation at home and expansion abroad.

Further Reading

There is no biography of Takahashi in English. Useful general histories of the period are Chitoshi Yanaga, *Japan since Perry* (1949); Hugh Borton, *Japan's Modern Century* (1955; 2d ed. 1970); W. G. Beasley, *The Modern History of Japan* (1963); and George O. Totten, ed., *Democracy in Prewar Japan: Groundwork or Facade?* (1965). Somewhat more specialized are Count Shigenobu Okuma, comp., *Fifty Years of New Japan* edited by Marcus B. Huish (2 vols., 1909; 2d ed. 1910), and A. Morgan Young *Japan in Recent Times, 1912-1926* (1929) and *Imperial Japan, 1926-1938* (1938). □

Josef Tal

Josef Tal (born 1910) Israeli composer, pianist, and professor of music, allowed Middle Eastern music to influence him, but stayed in the mainstream of contemporary European music, in which tradition he had been trained.

Josef Tal (formerly Gruenthal) was born in 1910 in Pinne, near Poznan, German Poland. He studied composition and music education with Max Trapp and Heinz Tiessen at the Berlin Hochschule für Musik. Other teachers there included Hindemith, Sachs, Kreutzer, and Saal. When the Nazis came to power in Germany, Josef Tal emigrated to Palestine. For two years he was an agricultural worker at Kibbutz Gesher.

Three years later, in 1937, Tal became a professor of piano and composition at the Academy of Music in Jerusalem. After the establishment of Israel as a sovereign nation the academy was renamed the Israel Academy of Music, and Tal became its first director, a post he held from 1948 to 1952. In 1950 Josef Tal added a professorship at the Hebrew University to his vitae and eventually became the first chairman of the Department of Musicology there. In 1961 he created the University Center for Electronic Music, an independent program.

Tal was the Israeli representative at International Society for Contemporary Music conferences and other musical events and attended a wide range of international conferences throughout the world. He received the International Society for Contemporary Music Festival Award in 1954, a UNESCO (United Nations Educational, Scientific, and Cultural Organization) research fellowship for the study of electronic music in 1957-1958, and two state prizes from his adopted country, Israel. Josef Tal belonged to the Israel Broadcasting Authority from 1965 to 1968 and was chairman of its musical committee. In 1969 he became a corresponding member of the Berlin Academy of Arts in West Germany; in 1971 he received a full membership in that organization (an ironic turn of history).

Josef Tal, unlike other contemporary eastern Mediterranean composers such as Paul Ben-Haim, did not make of Middle Eastern— in particular, Israeli—folk elements a compositional discipline. Tal was influenced by Middle Eastern elements, using the rhythms of Hebrew in his music, for example, but he maintained a contemporary European approach to composition. In addition to being the director of an electronic music institute, he was also Israel's leading composer of electronic, or electronically enhanced, music, holding a position somewhat analogous to that of Karlheinz Stockhausen in Germany. While he developed material from the Hebrew (the Christian Old Testament), Tal never cut himself off from his Central European roots nor ceased to identify himself with the ongoing tradition of European music, which music is, however, increasingly international in scope.

His early work—for example, his *First Symphony* (1952), his two string quartets, and his *Cello Concerto*—make use of the 12-tone row of the Second Viennese School of Schönberg, Berg, and Webern, but Tal avoided a strict application of serialist dictates in these compositions. However, his *Five Methodical Piano Pieces* are virtually didactic in their employment of dodecaphony, perhaps a reflection of Tal's career as a teacher more than his calling as a composer. Tal was also non-doctrinaire in his approach to electronic music, in which he was quite practical, believing there was no necessary conflict between what it is possible to perform and what a composer can envision. Tal's electronic music is especially noted for the complex sounds the composer was able to develop from a simple, limited use of electronic sources. Tal also firmly believed that all music, including electronic music, requires human participation. His approach to electronic music can be seen in his concertos for piano and tape, which are streamlined to allow a pianist to obtain concerto accompaniment at the touch of a button.

Tal's music is filled with drama and intense energy, created often by ostinato or sustained by an accretion of exciting textures. His popular *Second Symphony* and several dance compositions display complex rhythms. His musical and philosophical bent was perhaps best expressed in opera, most notably the full-scale, 12-tone *Ashmedai*, which was commissioned and first performed by the Hamburg Opera. Originally written with a Hebrew libretto, this music-drama tells a modern Jewish allegory which alludes to Nazi Germany. It is expressionistic in character and Wagnerian in its scope and its combination of artistic media. Another opera, electronic in style—*Massada 967*—was composed in honor of Israel's 25th anniversary. Tal's later works included, *Der Turm* (1987); *Der Garten* (1988); and *Josef* (1993). Through his compositions, as well as his work in theory and his teaching, Josef Tal had great influence upon the music of modern Israel. He remained for several years as department head and professor of Musicology at Hebrew University in Jerusalem.

Further Reading

Articles on Josef Tal appear in both *The New Grove Dictionary of Music and Musicians* (London, 1980) and *Baker's Biographical Dictionary,* 6th edition (1978). Tal's *Symphony no. 3* is discussed by R. Thackeray in *Musical Times,* 120 (November 1979). Tal is dealt with in *Interface,* (1980). His *Double Concerto for Two Pianos* is considered in "Uraufführungen in Israel," by P. Gradenwitz in *Neue Zeitung* (July-August 1981). □

Mary Morris Burnett Talbert

Mary Morris Burnett Talbert (1866-1923) was an African American educator, feminist, civil rights activist, and lecturer.

Born on September 18, 1866, to Cornelius and Caroline (Nicholls) Burnett of Oberlin, Ohio, Mary Morris Burnett spent her childhood in the city of her birth. At the age of 16 she was graduated from high school and, with the aid of a benefactor, enrolled in Oberlin College where she pursued a degree in the literary program. Mary Burnett was popular among her fellow students, who elected her treasurer of Aeolian, one of the school's two literary clubs for young women. When Burnett, the only African American in her graduating class, was one of six student representatives at her class day exercises, she read a poem which she had written for the occasion. After receiving her Bachelor of Arts degree in 1886, some of her biographers contend that she later enrolled in courses at the University of Buffalo where she received a doctorate degree. The university cannot confirm the awarding of the degree. (The University of Buffalo did not begin to confer doctoral degrees in arts and letters on a regular basis until 1935. She may have attended a continuing education program in which students were awarded certificates called doctorates.)

In 1886 she began her career as an educator when she accepted a teaching position at Bethel University in Little Rock, Arkansas, where she taught algebra, geometry, Latin, and history. Educators across the nation spoke highly of her accomplishments, and in January 1887 she was elected assistant principal of the Little Rock High School, the highest position held by any woman in the state and the only African American woman to accede to such a position (at the time).

On September 8, 1891, Mary Burnett married William H. Talbert, a Buffalo municipal government bookkeeper and realtor, and moved to that city. In 1892 she gave birth to a daughter, Sarah May, who later enrolled in the New England Conservatory of Music and became an accomplished pianist and composer.

An Active Life in Buffalo

In Buffalo Mary Talbert took up the pursuits of other privileged, educated, middle class women of her day. She affiliated with her husband's congregation, the Michigan Avenue Baptist Church. It was there that in 1901 she organized the Christian Culture Congress, a literary society and forum to address social issues pertaining to African Americans. Talbert served as its president until her death some 20 years later. Often nationally prominent African American spokespersons such as Nannie Helen Burroughs were invited to address the forum.

Talbert also was an active feminist and civil rights advocate. She was a member of the Phyllis Wheatley Club, founded in 1899 and the oldest organization of African American women in Buffalo that was affiliated with the National Association of Colored Women (NACW), and later served as its president. In a letter expressing the club's desire to affiliate with the national organization of African American women, Mary Talbert noted, "The organization was founded solely for the betterment of our race and the uplifting of our fallen women in Buffalo." She described the Phyllis Wheatley chapter as a working club which sought reforms and the promotion of the rights of mothers and children.

It was during her administration that the Phyllis Wheatley Club invited the National Association for the Advancement of Colored People (NAACP) to consider organizing activities in Buffalo. Once the NAACP was established in 1910, Burnett Talbert was elected to the board of directors and frequently lobbied the local news media to provide fairer coverage of African Americans.

Mary Talbert invited teenage girls to meet in her home on Friday afternoons to discuss contemporary African American political ideology; to hold sessions on dress, manners, and morals; and to use her home for social activities.

Self-help organizations had been an important vehicle in the lives of African Americans, but this was especially true during the post-Reconstruction period when African Americans found their status deteriorating. Mary Burnett Talbert was involved in many such organizations, including the Naomi Chapter of the Order of the Eastern Star in Buffalo, and was this benevolent organization's first Worthy Matron or chief administrative officer.

Reaching Out to All Women

The litany of activities enumerated above would have been enough to challenge the ability and tenacity of any individual. But Talbert's contributions did not end in Buffalo, New York. Her abhorrence of racism and sexism carried her into the national and international arenas. One of the most pressing issues that demanded Mary Burnett Talbert's time was concern over the plight of women. On the eve of World War I, Talbert noted that a woman's sphere is not limited and "she has a right to enter any sphere where she can do the most good." She believed that African American women possessed a unique quality and that it was incumbent upon them to help African American men "free themselves from the yoke of moral and political [bondage]."

Talbert's feminism took on global dimensions. She worked with the International Council of Women of the Darker Races, for she adhered to a philosophy predicated upon working with "the forward thinking women of China, Japan, Constantinople [Turkey], and Africa" to solve the problems of women of color. But much of her energy in the movement to grant women equality was devoted to the National Association of Colored Women, founded in 1896. Talbert was NACW president from 1916 to 1920.

As president she toured the nation twice, inspecting council camps, reformatories, and penitentiaries. Because of the inequities in the penal system in the South, Talbert actively sought prison reform. She especially deplored the lax administration of prisons in which African Americans were confined, the incarceration of young children in maximum security prisons with hardcore criminals, and the harsh sentences which they received for minor infractions of the law. With the aid of NACW club women, Talbert brought about sweeping penal reforms in the South.

Talbert believed that the National Association of Colored Women should collaborate with white women's groups to address their mutual grievances. She was a member of the American Association of University Women. As president of the NACW she was the first African American elected delegate to the International Council of Women in 1920. On September 16, 1920, Mary B. Talbert addressed the 660 delegates, representing 33 countries, on the discrimination which African American women experienced in the United States. Fluent in several languages, Talbert travelled to Italy, Denmark, England, and the Netherlands, where she lectured on the conditions of African American men and women in the United States and solicited international support for their cause. European newspapers gave widespread coverage to her lectures.

One of Mary Talbert's most notable achievements as president of the NACW was spearheading a project designed to purchase and restore the Anacostia, District of Columbia, home of the venerable Frederick Douglass as a national shrine to honor Douglass and the achievements of African Americans. This drive was successful. She viewed the efforts of supporters as an example of "[race] loyalty and race consciousness." Upon her death on October 15, 1923, the NACW established the $10,000 Mary B. Talbert Memorial Fund to honor one of "its most noble who left ineffaceable footprints upon the sands of time. . . ." Monies collected would be used to maintain the Douglass home.

A Ceaseless Quest for Reform

The National Association for the Advancement of Colored People also provided a forum for Talbert to implement some of her reform efforts. She was member of the board of directors, served as a vice president, and was national director of the NAACP's Anti-Lynching Crusade. This movement spearheaded a campaign to pass the Dyer Anti-Lynching Bill which had been introduced into Congress by Leonidas Dyer in 1921. The crusade also hoped to elicit international support in its efforts to raise one million dollars to fight the lynching of African American men and women in the United States, as well as other crimes perpetrated against them. Talbert alone raised over $12,000 during a nationwide lecture tour. Congress, however, failed to ratify the anti-lynching bill, and in response Talbert urged club women to withhold their support from candidates who voted against it. In 1922 the NAACP awarded Mary Burnett Talbert the coveted Spingarn Medal for her efforts in uplifting her race; she was the first woman to be honored in this manner.

The death of Booker T. Washington in 1915 provided a catalyst for African Americans and whites across the political spectrum to discuss solutions to the race problems and to resolve their differences. Under the auspices of the NAACP Joel Spingarn invited 50 African American and white leaders to meet at his New York estate in August 1916; Mary Talbert accepted his invitation. Conferees unanimously agreed upon such principles as the need to encourage education, to achieve complete political freedom for African Americans, and to open communication lines between the races. This consensus describes the work to which Talbert had devoted her life.

The U.S. entry into World War I and the use of African American men in combat provided another vehicle for Mary B. Talbert to aid her race and her country. During the war she served abroad for four months as YMCA secretary and Red Cross nurse. She lectured to African American soldiers, boosted their morale, and taught classes on religion during her tour of duty in Romagne, France, in 1919.

On the home front, Talbert travelled under the auspices of the United States government lecturing on food conservation to African American women's organizations and led the Liberty Bond Campaign among African American women's clubs. On September 28, 1921, Talbert joined other prominent African American leaders who petitioned President Warren G. Harding to grant clemency to the 24th Infantry of African American soldiers convicted of inciting the Houston, Texas, riots in 1917. Talbert noted that African Americans must continue their protests until they are recognized as American citizens and accorded full and equal rights.

Mary Talbert wrote extensively about the history and conditions of African Americans. In 1901 she published an article in a collection of essays on 20th-century African Americans in which she first turned to "our first and greatest historian—George Washington Williams" before enumerating the advances African Americans had made since slavery. She contended that education was one of their most significant accomplishments during the first generation of freedom. Talbert described this period as a new era of "self-culture and general improvement." She perceived the love of knowledge among African Americans to be "intuitive" and noted that no people ever learned more in so short a time. Historians today provide demographic evidence to substantiate her contentions. Talbert also published "The Achievements of Negro Women During the Past 50 Years" (1915) and the "Life of Harriet Tubman" (n.d.).

Further Reading

Mary B. Talbert is deserving of a major biography. Biographical sketches of Talbert appear in the following: Hallie Q. Brown, *Homespun Heroines and Other Women of Distinction;* Wilhelmina S. Robinson, *Historical Negro Biographies* (1968); Sylvia G. L. Dannett, *Profiles of Negro Womanhood;* and Rayford Logan and Michael Winston, *The Dictionary of American Negro Biography.* Articles about her were published in *The Oberlin Alumni Magazine* (April 1917), *The Buffalo Express* (July 15, 1923), *The Buffalo Enquirer* (October 16, 1923), *The National Notes* (May 1926), and *The Crisis* (February and December 1923). □

Maria Tallchief

Maria Tallchief (born 1925) is a world-renowned ballerina and one of the premiere American ballerinas of all time. She was the first American to dance at the Paris Opera and has danced with the Paris Opera Ballet, the Ballet Russe, and with the Balanchine Ballet Society (New York City Ballet).

Tallchief was born in Fairfax, Oklahoma, on January 24, 1925. She was raised in a wealthy family. Her grandfather had helped negotiate the Osage treaty, which created the Osage Reservation in Oklahoma and later yielded a bonanza in oil revenues for some Osage people. Tallchief began dance and music lessons at age four. By age eight, she and her sister had exhausted the training resources in Oklahoma, and the family moved to Beverly Hills, California. By age twelve, Tallchief was studying under Madame Nijinska (sister of the great Nijinsky) and David Lichine, a student of the renowned Russian ballerina Pavlova. At age fifteen at the Hollywood Bowl, Tallchief danced her first solo performance in a number choreographed by Nijinska. Following high school, it was apparent that ballet would be Tallchief's life. Instead of college, she joined the Ballet Russe, a highly acclaimed Russian ballet troupe. Tallchief was initially treated with skepticism—the Russian troupe was unwilling to recognize the Native American's greatness. When choreographer George Balanchine took control of the company, however, he recognized Tallchief's talent and selected her for the understudy role in *The Song of Norway.* Under Balanchine, Tallchief's reputation grew, and she was eventually given the title of ballerina. During this time, Tallchief married Balanchine, and when he moved to Paris, she went with him.

As with the Ballet Russe, Tallchief was initially treated with condescension in Paris. Her debut at the Paris Opera was the first ever for any American ballerina, and Tallchief's talent quickly won French audiences over. She later became the first American to dance with the Paris Opera Ballet at the

Bolshoi Theatre in Moscow. She quickly became the ranking soloist and, soon after, joined the Balanchine Ballet Society, now the New York City Ballet. At the New York City Ballet, Tallchief became recognized as one of the greatest dancers in the world. When she became the prima ballerina, she was the first American dancer to achieve this title. In 1949, Tallchief danced what was perhaps her greatest role in the Balanchine-choreographed version of the *Firebird*. Balanchine had choreographed the role for Tallchief, and her dazzling blend of physical control and mysticism enchanted audiences. In the late 1950s, Tallchief retired from performances and took charge of the Chicago City Ballet. □

Charles Maurice de Talleyrand

The French statesman Charles Maurice de Talleyrand, Duc de Talleyrand-Périgord (1754-1838), remains the classic case of a successful turncoat in politics. For half a century he served every French regime except that of the Revolutionary "Terror."

Charles Maurice de Talleyrand was a masterful diplomat of the old school as ambassador and foreign minister. Admired and often distrusted, sometimes even feared by those he served, he was not easily replaced as a negotiator of infinite wiles. Talleyrand has been an extraordinarily difficult figure for historians to understand and appraise. His moral corruption is beyond question: he was an unabashed liar and deceiver; he not only took but sought bribes from those with whom he was negotiating; and he lived with a niece as his mistress for decades. He repeatedly shifted political allegiance without visible compunction and possessed no political principle on which he would stand firm to the last; and he was also at least technically guilty of treason, engaging in secret negotiations with the public enemies of his country while in its service.

Yet closer scrutiny of what Talleyrand did shows an apparent steady purpose beneath the crust of arrogant contempt for the ordinary standards of mankind's judgment, expressed in the comment attributed to him on the kidnaping and execution of the Duc d'Enghien at Napoleon's command: "It was worse than a crime, it was a mistake." Talleyrand had his own vision of the interests of France, which lay in making the transition from the Old Regime to the new as painless as possible, at the same time preserving the territorial interests of the French nation. His fidelity to whichever persons happened to be at the head of the French state lasted at best only as long as their power, but this matchless cynic seems to have possessed genuine devotion for France as a country, and his apparent treasons can be seen as the products of a higher loyalty. Yet this picture of him may be false, for Talleyrand destroyed many of the records by which the truth regarding his career could have been more closely reached. It is easier to decide his guilt than to specify what he was guilty of, easier to affirm his deeper innocence than to prove it. The problem lies both in the man himself and in the eye of the beholder.

Education and Priesthood

Talleyrand was born in Paris on Feb. 13, 1754, into one of the most ancient and distinguished families of the French nobility. As the eldest son of Charles Daniel, Comte de Talleyrand, a lieutenant general in the French army, he was destined to follow his father's career until a childhood accident caused a permanent injury. His father compelled him to accept a career in the Church over Talleyrand's protests, for he had no vocation as a priest. But he took Holy Orders in 1775 after studies at the Collège d'Harcourt, a secondary school, and at the seminary in Reims. His rapid promotions came to him as an ecclesiastical administrator with powerful backing, not as a shepherd of souls. His first important post was as general agent for the assembly of the French clergy in 1780, negotiating with the government for the "voluntary" payments made by churchmen in lieu of the taxes from which they were exempt. Then, in 1788, he was appointed bishop of Autun and was consecrated the next year, as the French Revolution was about to begin.

Elected to the Estates General as a deputy of the clergy, Talleyrand quickly showed that he wished the First Estate to cooperate in the transformation of the Old Regime into a new order, even at the expense of its own privileges. Passing over into open opposition to the court, he was influential in persuading his fellow ecclesiastics to join the Third Estate in the newly proclaimed National Assembly on June 19, 1789. He proposed on October 10 that the vast properties of the Church be put at the disposal of the state in exchange for salaries to be paid by the state, and in line with this policy he accepted the Civil Constitution of the Clergy and was one of the consecrators of the new bishops established under its provisions. For these violations of Church discipline, Pope Pius VI excommunicated Talleyrand in 1791. His report on public education in September 1791 won wide praise for its principles but was never applied.

Diplomatic Missions and Exile

In 1792 Talleyrand repeatedly went to England as an unofficial envoy with the mission of keeping that country neutral in the war beginning with Austria and Prussia, but the French invasion of the Austrian Netherlands (Belgium) as well as the rise of revolutionary extremism, culminating in the execution of Louis XVI, brought England into the war in 1793. Talleyrand, condemned as an émigré by the Revolutionary authorities at home, was expelled by England in 1794, and he went to the United States for 2 years. There he visited many parts of the country and probably engaged in land speculation.

In 1796, after the formation of the Directory, Talleyrand returned to France. He was named to the Institute and became foreign minister in July 1797. He took part in the coup d'etat of 18 Fructidor (Sept. 4, 1797), which confirmed the republican regime against royalist conspiracies, and he pocketed a fortune in bribes from those who wanted his favor (although the American negotiators in the "XYZ affair" not only rebuffed his demands for money but made them public on their return home). He was forced to resign the Foreign Ministry in July 1799, when his republicanism fell under suspicion. His destiny then became intertwined with that of Gen. Napoleon Bonaparte, whose expedition to Egypt Talleyrand had sponsored and whom he helped to come to power in the coup d'etat of 18 Brumaire (Nov. 9, 1799).

Napoleon's Foreign Minister

Talleyrand served as foreign minister for Napoleon under the Consulate and the Empire until August 1807 and was rewarded in 1804 with the post of grand chamberlain and in 1806 with the title of Prince de Benevento (French, Bénévent). However, his relations with the Emperor became clouded as Napoleon's obsessive aggressiveness became clear to him. Talleyrand wanted to end the exhausting wars against the recurring European coalitions by making peace with England and Russia, the principal foes, on terms that preserved for France its major territorial gains. Remaining in the Emperor's service, he began a perilous game of intrigues designed to thwart his master's ambitions. In 1808 at Erfurt he encouraged Czar Alexander I to resist Napoleon's demands and was dismissed in 1809 by the suspicious Napoleon but allowed to reside at his country estate. However, after the invasion of Russia in 1812, Talleyrand began a secret correspondence with Louis XVIII and, as head of a

provisional government established on April 1, 1814, was a principal figure in the King's first restoration.

Congress of Vienna

Again named foreign minister, Talleyrand skillfully maneuvered to win the full support of the Allies for the Bourbons, obtained relatively favorable terms for France in the first Peace of Paris, then played upon the dissensions of the victors to gain a place for France among the negotiators at the Congress of Vienna, and finally turned the victors against each other to France's advantage. This brilliant feat of diplomacy was partly dimmed by the wrath of the Allies when France welcomed Napoleon back in the Hundred Days, but the final peace terms that emerged from the Vienna negotiations brought France back to its prerevolutionary frontiers.

Upon the second restoration of Louis XVIII, Talleyrand served as prime minister and foreign minister from July until September, but the ultraroyalists who dominated the new government were less forgiving than the king, least of all of an apostate bishop, and Talleyrand lost his office. However, he received the title of Duc de Dino in 1815, in place of the princely title of Benevento, which had been extinguished with Napoleon's departure, and in 1817 he became Duc de Talleyrand-Périgord. During the remainder of the reign of Louis XVIII, Talleyrand was a member of the Chamber of Peers, where he often voted against the government.

Final Diplomatic Achievements

After the Revolution of 1830, in which he was a minor participant but encouraged Louis Philippe to take the crown, Talleyrand was sent to London as ambassador. He negotiated an agreement with England, upon recognition of the new independent Belgian state, that was favorable to French interests. The signing of the Quadruple Alliance of 1834 (with England, Spain, and Portugal), which assured Anglo-French collaboration in support of the constitutional government in Spain against the Carlist rebels, was Talleyrand's final achievement as a diplomat. He died in Paris on May 17, 1838, soon after becoming reconciled with the Roman Catholic Church.

Further Reading

Duff Cooper, *Talleyrand* (1932), and Louis Madelin, *Talleyrand* (trans. 1948), are the best of the modern biographies concerned with Talleyrand as diplomat and politician. Crane Brinton, *The Lives of Talleyrand* (1936), a witty and provocative study, goes behind the enigmatic public figure to seek the deeper meaning of Talleyrand's life and work. Françoise de Bernardy, *Talleyrand's Last Duchess* (1965; trans. 1966), deals with the private life of his last decades. Guglielmo Ferrero, *The Reconstruction of Europe: Talleyrand and the Congress of Vienna* (trans. 1941), is important for the understanding of Talleyrand's supreme achievement. □

Thomas Tallis

The English composer and organist Thomas Tallis (ca. 1505-1585) wrote anthems, services, and other music for the Anglican rite. He is considered the father of English cathedral music.

Evidence points to Leicestershire as the birthplace of Thomas Tallis. Of his youth, education, and musical training nothing certain is known. The earliest official record of his professional activity places him as organist at Dover Priory in 1532. From his Benedictine cloister he moved first to St. Mary-at-Hill in Billingsgate about 1537 and then to the Augustinian Abbey of the Holy Cross at Waltham, where he served until its dissolution in 1540.

Under the adverse circumstances which ensued, Tallis next joined the musical establishment at Canterbury, leaving 2 years later to become a gentleman of the Chapel Royal. He stayed in that position for the rest of his life. For nearly a half century he composed, played, sang, and taught music at the English court. During that period he witnessed the stylistic transition from medieval to tonal polyphony, which culminated in his own compositions and in those of his brilliant pupil William Byrd. Tallis died in Greenwich on Nov. 23, 1585, survived by his widow, Joan.

Tallis composed mainly sacred works, and his oeuvre may most conveniently be divided into two kinds: those with Latin texts and those with English texts. Of the former

there are four Marian motets, the colossal 40-voiced *Spem in alium,* along with some two dozen other motets; several responsories, antiphons, and office hymns; two Lamentations and two Magnificats; and three Masses. His sacred compositions on English texts include a "Great" and a "Short" Service; two service movements; various preces, litanies, responses, and psalms; and, most important of all, 28 anthems, among which 10 are clearly derived from his own Latin motets. The few extant secular pieces actually do not compose a separate class, since most of these are somehow related to sacred compositions. The instrumental *In nomine* and *Felix namque* compositions were composed upon sacred *cantus firmi,* and at least one piece, "Fond youth is a bubble," is a secular *contrafactum.*

Some of Tallis's Marian motets, especially *Gaude Virgo,* reflect the hocketed, elaborate polyphony of the previous century, while the seven-part *Miserere,* with six parts in canon, and the elaborate polyphonic imitation of *Spem in alium* demonstrate the "deep learning" for which both Tallis and Byrd were famous. The same quality, but in more modern guise, is found in some of the 17 motets which make up Tallis's contribution to the *Cantiones sacrae,* a collection he and Byrd published jointly in 1575 as the first edition appearing under their new royal license.

Clarity of harmony and word setting become more pronounced in Tallis's compositions on English texts. Here too the transition from ancient to modern style may be traced, as can be seen by comparing the retrospective "Dorian" Short Service with the brighter and more tuneful anthems "Heare the voyce and prayer" and "If ye love me."

Further Reading

Studies of Tallis include Leonard Ellinwood's "Tallis' Tunes and Tudor Psalmody" in Armen Carapetyan, ed., *Musica Discipline,* vol. 2 (1948), and Paul Doe, *Tallis* (1968). Additional information can be found in Ernest Walker, *A History of Music in England* (1907; 3d rev. ed. 1952); Morrison C. Boyd, *Elizabethan Music and Musical Criticism* (1940); and Harold C. Schonberg, *The Lives of the Great Composers* (1970). □

Jean Talon

Jean Talon (1626-1694), a French intendant of New France, was responsible for implementing his country's policy of colonial development in Canada.

Born at Châlons-sur-Marne in Champagne and baptized on Jan. 8, 1626, Jean Talon entered the royal service in his late 20s, serving as army commissary in Flanders and as intendant of Turenne's army. In 1655 he was appointed intendant of Hainaut.

When, in 1663, Louis XIV placed his American colonies under royal government, the minister in charge of colonial affairs, Jean Baptiste Colbert, persuaded Talon to accept the intendancy of New France for a 2-year term. He arrived in September 1665 at Quebec, where he was responsible for civil administration, finance, and justice.

Colbert had grandiose plans for the development of Canada. He established a new administrative system, sent a regiment of regular troops which quelled the Iroquois, and then invested vast sums in economic development, establishing new industries such as lumbering and ship-building and subsidizing the immigration of skilled and unskilled labor, and marriageable girls for the superfluity of bachelors.

Talon's task was to superintend this economic expansion, and he set about it with considerable energy. Under his supervision several ships were constructed, a brewery was built, much virgin land was brought into production, crops were diversified, and surplus foodstuffs and timber were exported to the West Indies. In fact, he was perhaps too active, for some of the colony's leading merchants complained that he was concentrating all these activities under his own control for his private profit and putting them out of business.

To make the best use of the available manpower, Colbert demanded that the Canadian proclivity to voyage to the distant Indian villages to obtain furs at firsthand had to be curbed. He wanted the colonists concentrated in the central colony, working on the land or in industry. Talon, however, favored expansion into the west, and he sent out fur-trading expeditions under the guise of exploration parties. In this fashion the entire basin of the Great Lakes was claimed for France, although only a handful of itinerant French traders were in the area. The merchants in the colony, seeing Talon's exploration parties return with canoes laden with furs, were quick to follow suit. Within a very few years several hundred *coureurs de bois* were operating out of the colony. In 1672 Talon sent Louis Jolliet to discover the outlet of a river called the Mississippi, in the hope that it would provide an easy route to the Pacific.

In 1668 Talon returned to France but was persuaded by Colbert and Louis XIV to go back to the colony for a second term. While in France, he acquired the posts of first valet of the king's wardrobe and secretary in his privy chamber. En route to Quebec in 1669, he was shipwrecked and did not reach the colony until 1670.

During his first term Talon's relations with the governor general, Rémy de Courcelle, had not been good. Courcelle resented what he regarded as Talon's usurping of the governor's powers. Unfortunately, only Talon's correspondence has survived. He contrived always to exalt his own activities and to belittle his critics. He over-stepped the bounds, however, when he proposed that he should combine in his own person the powers of both intendant and governor-general. He also requested blank *letters de cachet* to send malcontents back to France.

In 1672 Talon was recalled. He subsequently sought to return to Canada as the director of an almshouse which he proposed to establish. He certainly accumulated a fortune while in Canada and likely wished to add to it. Two years before his death he sold for 253,000 livres the posts acquired in 1670. He died on Nov. 24, 1694, in Paris.

There can be no doubt that Talon was an efficient administrator, but his contribution to the colony's develop-ment has been exaggerated by historians who have accepted his accounts at face value.

Further Reading

There is no good biography of Talon in English. The general background for the period is given in W. J. Eccles, *Canada under Louis XIV, 1663-1701* (1964). □

Oliver Reginald Tambo

Oliver Reginald Tambo (1917-1993) was, as acting president of the African National Congress (ANC), a principal spokesman for the Black African opposition to apartheid in South Africa. He remained active in the ANC, ultimately living to witness the political end of apartheid in the early 1990s.

Born in poverty of peasant parents in Pondoland in 1917, Oliver Reginald Tambo's early education was at St. Peter's School in Johannesburg. He won a scholarship to Fort Hare, the only college Blacks could attend, where he studied science. He was expelled in 1939 for participating in a student strike but later studied law by correspondence and qualified as an attorney in 1952. He and another Black leader, Nelson Mandela, then began a law partnership in Johannesburg.

In the early 1940s Tambo joined the African National Congress, an organization founded in 1912 that opposed white supremacy. Dissatisfied with the ANC's moderation, Tambo, Mandela, Walter Sisulu, and Anton Lembede helped form the ANC Youth League in 1944. Its activity caused the ANC to adopt more militant tactics. The Defiance Campaign of 1952, involving mass protests and open disobedience of apartheid laws, was the first manifestation of this change. Tambo became secretary-general of the ANC in 1955.

The Gathering Storm

The South African government responded to the Defiance Campaign by "banning" Tambo and other ANC leaders in 1952. Banning is a punishment whose victims may not be quoted and are isolated from other people. In 1956 Tambo and many other anti-apartheid activists of all races were arrested. (At this time, Tambo had taken steps to become an Anglican priest, an aspiration ended by his arrest.) Their treason trial lasted almost five years and resulted in the acquittal of all defendants. Tambo was, however, banned again in 1959.

During the late 1950s several issues threatened the ANC's effectiveness. Inspired by Lembede's "Africanist" philosophy, dissidents challenged the ANC principle, expressed in its Freedom Charter, that South Africa "belongs to all who live in it," including whites. The Africanists' exclusive racial doctrine was opposed by Tambo, Mandela, and ANC president Albert Luthuli. The dissidents, led by

Robert Sobukwe, broke away from the ANC and founded the Pan-Africanist Congress (PAC) in 1959.

Another problem was the role of the South African Communist Party. After much confusion over the huge problem of uniting the white and Black working classes, the Party had come to oppose apartheid, thereby casting its lot with the Blacks. But Tambo, Mandela, and others viewed Communism as alien to Africa and initially opposed Communist membership in the ANC. After much debate, however, the ANC concluded that alliances with all anti-apartheid groups were necessary.

Tambo became deputy president of the ANC in 1958. Because of his dignified, austere, and articulate bearing, he was chosen to represent the ANC overseas. He was therefore out of the country when, after the Sharpeville and Langa shootings in 1960 in which police killed nearly a hundred Blacks, the ANC was banned and its leaders arrested.

Tambo and the ANC in Exile

By 1963 Tambo was the most important ANC leader who remained free. Luthuli was banned and confined to his village in Zululand. Mandela had gone underground and initially escaped arrest, but was captured in 1962, convicted of treason, and sentenced to life imprisonment. Sisulu suffered the same fate. When Luthuli was killed by a train in 1967, Mandela became president in his prison cell; Tambo, acting president.

As leader of the exiled ANC, Tambo had to cope with a variety of difficulties. After the Sharpeville shooting, the

ANC concluded that peaceful protest against apartheid was futile and that its policy of non-violence must be abandoned. One problem was to attack the government from bases outside the country and to keep those bases secure. Another problem was that of avoiding the "exile condition." Exiled organizations often have their attention diverted by internal squabbling and the problems of daily existence in alien environments. They often lose sight of their reason for existence: to return home and defeat their enemies.

Apparently the ANC did not completely avoid these problems. Under Tambo's leadership it participated in the South African United Front, which also included the PAC and the South African Indian Congress. Internal disputes broke this coalition in 1962. In the late 1960s the ANC helped the Zimbabwe African Peoples Union fight the white settlers of Rhodesia. This move, while it may have provided needed action for ANC guerrilla fighters, caused dissension. Many felt that the goal of liberating South Africa was compromised.

In the 1970s the ANC conducted minor raids into South Africa and occasionally sabotaged government installations or police stations. ANC policy forbade attacks on civilians but proved difficult to enforce because of communications problems. A spontaneous attack on apartheid in 1976 by students in Soweto, the huge Black township near Johannesburg, apparently caught the ANC by surprise. More than 500 Blacks were killed in this uprising.

Tambo continued as ANC acting president in the 1980s. His leadership was solid and diplomatic, and he managed to steer the organization clear of destructive divisions. The ANC maintained prestige among the Black population within South Africa, despite brutal measures by the government to suppress it. It apparently collaborated with the United Democratic Front, a multi-racial anti-apartheid coalition. The Front was banned in 1986 and its leaders arrested.

A major difficulty, which the ANC managed to survive, was the Nkomati Accord, concluded in 1984 between the South African government and Mozambique. South Africa agreed to halt its attempts to destabilize Mozambique in return for Mozambique expelling the ANC. (Mozambique kept its side of the bargain; South Africa did not.) On other occasions South Africa made direct attacks on Lesotho, Zimbabwe, Zambia, and Botswana in efforts to destroy ANC bases. According to Tambo, the loss of external bases in Mozambique helped stimulate the renewed violence inside South Africa that began in 1984.

That violence continued into 1987 and cost well over 2,000 lives, mostly Black. ANC tactics during this rebellion were to "make the townships ungovernable," in Tambo's phrase, through attacks on local government officials. The government was able to control some townships only with a massive presence of troops and the free use of firepower. Isolated sabotage of government installations continued.

The 1984 uprising was the most serious attack on apartheid in history. The stature of the ANC rose considerably. Tambo and other representatives had contacts with both a number of Western governments and South African business leaders. An important development was Tambo's meeting with U.S. Secretary of State George Shultz in early 1987. The ANC approached the status of a government-in-exile, although Tambo maintained that there were other groups that had claims of influence in a post-apartheid South Africa and that Nelson Mandela was the ANC's legitimate leader. When Mandela was released from prison in late 1989, Tambo assumed the post of Chairman of the ANC. Mandela took over the presidency. Tambo died of a stroke on April 24, 1993, at the age of 75, following his eight-hour attendance at the funeral of Chris Hani, murdered a few days earlier.

Further Reading

There is no biography of Tambo. Much information can be found in Mary Benson, *The Struggle for a Birthright* (1966) and *Nelson Mandela* (1986); Peter Walshe, *The Rise of African Nationalism in South Africa* (1970); and Tom Lodge, *Black Politics in South Africa since 1945* (1983). A moderately-comprehensive biographical entry also can be found in Brockman, Norbert C., *An African Biographical Dictionary* (ABC-CLIO, 1994). □

Tamerlane

Tamerlane (1336-1405) was a celebrated Turko-Mongol conqueror whose victories, characterized by acts of inhuman cruelty, made him the master of the greater part of western Asia. His vast empire disintegrated at his death.

T amerlane or Timur (Tamerlane is a corruption of the Persian Timur-i Lang, "Timur the Lame"), belonged to the Turkized Mongol clan of the Barlas, which had accompanied the Mongol armies westward and had settled in the Kashka Valley to the south of Samarkand, between Shakhrisyabz and Karshi. He was born near Shakhrisyabz on April 9, 1336. This whole region, the present-day Soviet Socialist Republic of Uzbekistan, was then part of the Chaghatai khanate, which received its name from its founder, the second son of Genghis Khan, and which included, besides Transoxiana—the countries between the Amu Darya (Oxus) and the Syr Darya—the whole area to the east of the Syr Darya up to the western borders of Mongolia.

In 1346/1347 the Chaghatai khan, Kazan, who had his residence at Karshi, was defeated and killed by a tribal leader called Kazaghan, and Transoxiana ceased to be part of the khanate. Kazaghan's death (1358) was followed by a period of anarchy, and Tughluk-Temür, the ruler of the territories beyond the Syr Darya (now known as Moghulistan, "land of the Moguls, or Mongols"), invaded Transoxiana in 1360 and again in 1361 in an attempt to reestablish Chaghatai rule.

Tamerlane declared himself Tughluk-Temür's vassal and was made ruler of the Shakhrisyabz-Karshi region. He soon, however, rebelled against the Moguls and formed an alliance with Husain, the grandson of Kazaghan. Together in 1363 they drove Ilyas Khoja, Tughluk-Temür's son, out of Transoxiana; he returned in the following year, having succeeded his father as khan, and inflicted a defeat upon Tamerlane and Husain, but they were able, after his withdrawal, to consolidate their power as joint rulers of the country. They were often on bad terms but with some interruptions maintained an uneasy partnership until 1370, when open war erupted. Besieged at Balkh, Husain was captured and executed, and Tamerlane, now the undisputed master of Transoxiana, took up residence at Samarkand, henceforward his capital city and the base of his operations against eastern and western Asia.

Expansion of Power

Tamerlane's first campaigns were directed against Khiva and his old enemies, the Moguls; it was not until 1381 that he turned his attention westward, leading an expedition into eastern Iran; further expeditions in subsequent years extended gradually into Iraq, Asia Minor, and Syria. The atrocities committed in the course of these campaigns are recorded even by his own court historian. At Sabzawar, in what is now Afghanistan, Tamerlane directed a tower to be constructed out of live men heaped on top of one another and cemented together with bricks and mortar. To punish a revolt in Isfahan, he ordered a general massacre of the population, and the heads of 70,000 people were built up into minarets.

In 1387 an invasion of Transoxiana by Toktamish, the ruler of the Golden Horde, obliged Tamerlane to interrupt his operations in western Asia, and the repulsion of the invader, followed by expeditions into Moghulistan, was to keep him occupied for the next 4 years. It was not until 1392 that he resumed the conquest of western Asia in what is known as the Five Years' Campaign. After suppressing the Muzaffarid dynasty in Fars (spring 1393), Tamerlane entered present-day Iraq, received the submission of Baghdad, whose Jalayirid ruler, Sultan Ahmad, had fled at his approach, continued northward into eastern Turkey and the Caucasus area, defeated Toktamish in a battle on the Terek (April 1395), and advanced up the Don to capture the Russian town of Yelets, on the border between the Russian principalities and the territory of the Golden Horde. The campaign ended, in the winter of 1395-1396, with the destruction of the two main centers of the Horde at Astrakhan and New Saray, and Tamerlane returned to Samarkand to prepare for his invasion of India.

India, Turkey, and Egypt

This, the briefest of his campaigns, lasting less than 6 months, was the occasion of Tamerlane's greatest massacre: the execution in cold blood, before the gates of Delhi, of 100,000 Hindu prisoners. There followed immediately the so-called Seven Years' Campaign (1399-1403), which brought Tamerlane into conflict with the two most powerful rulers in western Asia, the Ottoman sultan of Turkey and the Mamluk sultan of Egypt.

Syria, then part of Egypt's territory, was invaded in 1400, Aleppo falling in October of that year and Damascus in March 1401. Tamerlane now turned eastward against Baghdad, which had been reoccupied by Sultan Ahmad's forces and offered stubborn resistance to Tamerlane's attack. It was taken in June 1401, and the slaughter which followed was such that the heads of the dead were piled up into 120 towers. Tamerlane passed the winter of 1401/1402 in the eastern Caucasus before moving westward into Anatolia to deal the final blow to Sultan Bayazid (Bajazet), who was defeated and taken prisoner at the Battle of Ankara (July 20, 1402).

The Sultan died while still in captivity, but the story, familiar from Marlowe's *Tamburlaine the Great,* that he was transported in an iron cage like a wild beast, is based on a misunderstanding of a phrase in the record of the historian Arabshah. The last action of the campaign was the storming and sacking of Smyrna, then held by the Knights of St. John, who had recaptured it from the Ottoman Turks a half century before.

Tamerlane returned from the Seven Years' Campaign by slow stages, reaching Samarkand in August 1404. He set off before the end of the year upon a still more grandiose enterprise, the conquest of China, liberated only some 30 years previously form its Mongol masters. He was, however, taken ill at Otrar, on the eastern bank of the Syr Darya, and died on Feb. 18, 1405.

Further Reading

Hilda Hookham's gracefully written *Tamburlaine the Conqueror* (1964) is the most detailed and up-to-date work addressed to the general reader. Older works include a 14th-century account in Arabic by Ahmed ibn Arabshah, *Tamerlane,* translated by J. H. Sanders (1936), and Harold Lamb, *Tamerlane, the Earth Shaker* (1928). See also the relevant sections in René Grousset, *Empire of the Steppes* (1939; trans. 1970); Richard N. Frye, *Iran* (1954); Sir John Glubb, *The Lost Centuries* (1967), which contains an excellent chapter on Tamerlane; and the *Cambridge History of Iran,* vol. 6 (1971). □

Amy Tan

Amy Tan (born 1952) is known for her lyrically written tales of emotional conflict between Chinese-American mothers and daughters separated by generational and cultural differences. Together with her distinctive writing style and rich imagery, Tan's treatment of such themes as loss and reconciliation, hope and failure, friendship and familial conflict, and the healing power of storytelling have brought her popular success and critical attention.

Tan was born in Oakland, California. Her father was a Chinese-born Baptist minister; her mother was the daughter of an upper-class family in Shanghai. While still in her teens, Tan experienced the loss of both her father and her sixteen-year-old brother to brain tumors and learned that two sisters from her mother's first marriage in China were still alive (one of several autobiographical elements she would later incorporate into her fiction). Tan majored in English at San Jose State in the early 1970s rather than fulfill her mother's expectations of becoming a neurosurgeon, and after graduate work at the University of California, Berkeley, she began a career as a technical writer. After meeting her new-found sisters in China in 1987, Tan was, she has said, "finally able to say, 'I'm both Chinese and American.' . . . Suddenly some piece fit in the right place and something became whole." As a release from the demands of her technical writing career, she turned to fiction writing, having gained inspiration from her reading of Louise Erdrich's novel of Native American family life, *Love Medicine.* Tan's first novel, *The Joy Luck Club,* received the Commonwealth Club gold award for fiction and the American Library Association's best book for young adults award in 1989 and stayed on the *New York Times*'s bestseller list for nine months. In 1993, with Tan serving as a producer and coauthor of the screenplay, *The Joy Luck Club* was made into a critically acclaimed film. Tan's second novel, *The Kitchen God's Wife,* was published in 1991 followed by the children's books *The Moon Lady* (1992) and *The Chinese Siamese Cat* (1994).

The Joy Luck Club comprises sixteen stories told by four Chinese immigrant women and their four American-born daughters, linked together by the narrative of Jing-mei Woo, whose mother had founded a women's social club in China to sustain its members' spirits during the communist revolution. In the novel, the club becomes a metaphor for the reconciliation of the conflict between maternal expecta-

about the usefulness of storytelling as a way of . . . evaluating human experience.''

Further Reading

Bestsellers 89, issue 3, Gale, 1989, pp. 69-71.
Contemporary Literary Criticism, Gale, Volume 59, 1990.
Canadian Literature, summer, 1992, p. 196.
Chicago Tribune, August 6, 1989; March 17, 1991.
Chicago Tribune—Books, March 12, 1989, pp. 1, 11.
Critique, no. 3, 1993.
Detroit News, March 26, 1989, p. 2D.
New York Times, April 1, 1996, p. A10. □

Kakuei Tanaka

Tanaka Kakuei (1918-1993) was the most controversial of the post-World War II prime ministers of Japan. As the leader of the largest faction in the ruling Liberal Democratic Party (LDP) he dominated Japanese politics for many years.

Although Tanaka Kakuei served as prime minister for only two years, he was instrumental in bringing three successor prime ministers to office and ensuring that his predecessor stayed in office longer than any other prime minister. The only prime minister since World War I not to have attended a university, he served with distinction as the minister in three of the all-important economic ministries and may come to be seen as the author of the body of communication law which permitted Japan to slide so readily into the information age. He is pictured in the press as the ultimate corrupter, using money to manipulate rather than ideals to inspire Japanese politics. He was twice charged with accepting bribes, once acquitted, the second time convicted (with the sentence continually deferred, as it remained under appellate review up until his death in 1993). Nevertheless he was routinely re-elected to a Diet seat in every election after 1948, winning more votes than ever before *after* his bribery conviction.

Tanaka Kakuei was born on May 4, 1918, in the village of Futada of Niigata prefecture, known for its deep snows and utter poverty. He was the eldest son of a cattle dealer, Kakuji, and his wife, Fume. Childhood was difficult. Before reaching two years of age Tanaka had come close to death from diphtheria. Buried under snow sliding from an overburdened roof, he had been saved from suffocation by his grandmother, who discovered him when a twig in her broom caught his lip, causing it to bleed, staining the snow and revealing his whereabouts. At the age of 16, after graduating from grammar school, he went to Tokyo to work at construction during the day and to study it at night at the Central Technical High School. He graduated and started his own construction business, but at the age of 20 he was drafted and sent to Manchuria as a cavalryman. He became ill with pleurisy and was returned to the home islands. The illness deepened and was re-diagnosed as tuberculosis, and for several months Tanaka was expected to die. Eventually,

tion and tradition, and filial individuality and cultural independence. In *The Kitchen God's Wife,* Tan again focused on the mother-daughter relationship in the context of the transition from the suffering and traditions of the Chinese past to the freedom and anxiety of the Chinese-American present. In particular, Tan explored themes of secrecy and misunderstanding, physical abuse and illness, and female friendship and acceptance in the story of the reconciliation of a mother and daughter alienated from each other by the personal truths they conceal from each other. Written for children, *The Moon Lady* developed a story first told in *The Joy Luck Club:* a young girl's experience of danger, magic, and wish fulfillment at a celebration of the Moon Festival in traditional China.

Some reviewers of *The Joy Luck Club* argued that Tan's thematic development was unsuccessful and resulted in strained, ''over-significant'' scenes, while others found her use of multiple narrative voices to be ''limiting'' and ''*over*-schematic.'' However, critical reception of the novel was generally favorable. Carolyn See, for example, described Tan as a ''magician of language'' while Michael Dorris called Tan a ''writer of dazzling talent.'' Tan solidified her critical reputation with *The Kitchen God's Wife.* Reviewers found it superior in structure and execution to *The Joy Luck Club* and applauded Tan's decision to narrow the scope of the narrative to a single mother-daughter relationship. Critics generally commended Tan's storytelling ability and characters development. Josephine Humphreys wrote that *The Kitchen God's Wife* proved ''something profound . . .

though, he recovered, was discharged from the army, and returned to construction work. Business flourished. By 1943 Tanaka's company was ranked among the nation's top 50 construction firms.

Tanaka married Sakamoto Hana, the daughter of a medium size construction company owner, with whom he had two children: a son, Masanori, born in 1942, and a daughter, Makiko, born in 1944. The son died at the age of six, but the daughter lived to become a member of the Diet.

Tanaka Enters Politics—Successfully

Tanaka's business success was predicated partly on working closely with government agencies. Early on he had been encouraged to fund one of the emerging political parties. He wrote of the immense task of reconstruction the Japanese nation faced after World War II. Tanaka, then, took only a short step when he decided to stand for election as a representative of the third district of Niigata. Tanaka lost in the 1946 election. He won in the 1947 election when he was 28 years of age. He won every subsequent election, serving until 1990.

His first post of significance came in 1948, when he was appointed parliamentary vice minister for the Justice Ministry under the second Yoshida cabinet. In 1952 he became head of the board of directors as well as dean of the Central Technical School where he had studied construction when he first came to Tokyo. He was 34 years old.

At age 36 he became the chairman of the standing committee on commerce in the House of Representatives.

In 1957 he became the minister for posts and telecommunications in the first Kishi cabinet. He early recognized that the gathering and transmission of information was to be a key to future social organization. His interest in posts and telecommunications was to remain with him. He served as the finance minister under the second and third Ikeda cabinets and under the first Sato cabinet. He headed the Ministry for International Trade and Industry (MITI) under the third Sato cabinet. While MITI minister he put forward his plan for remodeling the Japanese archipelago, a far-reaching plan for raising standards of living in the rural areas, doing away with blight in the old cities, and establishing new industries in new cities and creating the transportation system to supply them. He authored, *A proposal for remodeling the Japanese Archipelago*.

The ability to command a ministry was just one of the talents Tanaka had to demonstrate. Another was to be able to persuade other politicians to accept his leadership. In 1955 the Liberal Democratic Party (LDP) became the ruling party. While it was the ruling party its Dietmen served as the ministers and vice ministers; its party president served as the prime minister. Men who wished to become prime minister created factions. The maneuvering of these faction leaders—the building up and taking over of a faction, the making and breaking of factional alliances, the bargaining over posts, the collection and disbursement of political funds—constituted the heart of Japanese politics. In all these activities Tanaka excelled. Critics claim money generated his power. Historians will add two other sources: imagination and hard work.

A Master at the Game of Politics

Initially, Tanaka had been a member of the Japan Democratic Party. In 1948 he switched parties to become a member of the Japan Liberal Party, then under the leadership of Prime Minister Yoshida Shigeru, the maker of the still-enduring American alliance and the architect of the postwar recovery strategy. When Yoshida retired, Tanaka aligned himself with Sato Eisaku, a Yoshida lieutenant, quelling anti-Sato revolts within the LDP by serving as secretary general of the LDP during four of Sato's seven cabinets, allowing Sato to serve as prime minister for seven years eight months, the longest tenure for any prime minister. Tanaka also looked out for his own interests. He took over enough of the Sato faction so that he was able to succeed Sato as prime minister, though Sato favored another man.

When Tanaka became prime minister in 1972, he received the highest rating that any prime minister has ever received in the public opinion polls: 61 percent of the respondents supported his cabinet. Within two years, however, this public enthusiasm had gone: only 12 percent of the respondents then said they supported him. Investigative reporters had set forth the jumble of companies and their activities through which Tanaka had supported his political activities. It looked corrupt. It was called corrupt, though no prosecutor chose to bring charges. Men serving in Tanaka's cabinet, one who was a long-time ally, threatened resignation. Tanaka resigned instead, though he continued to build his faction. Within four years it had become so large that no man could become party president without Tanaka's assent. No longer king, Tanaka had become king-maker.

In February 1976 A. Carl Kotchian, the president of the Lockheed Corporation, told the U.S. Senate Foreign Relations Committee that he had given $2 million to Tanaka and other sums to seven other Japanese politicians to secure their cooperation in having the Japanese government purchase 21 L-1011 Tristar airplanes for All Nippon Airways, Japan's number two airline. Kotchian's Senate testimony led to the indictment of Tanaka, who, after a lengthy trial, was convicted on October 12, 1983. Tanaka appealed his conviction, thereby prolonging the sentence such that it was never served.

Tanaka was still defended vigorously by writers from the political and intellectual communities. That money had changed hands was proved to most writers' satisfaction. Questioned, though, was the court's decision that this money was a bribe, not a legitimate political contribution; a second question was that Tanaka had the authority to issue, and did indeed issue, orders that the Tristar airplanes be purchased. Also questioned was whether a higher degree of accountability was demanded of Tanaka than was expected of other politicians.

On February 27, 1985, Tanaka suffered a cerebral hemorrhage. His daughter, Makiko, took care of him, first at the hospital, later at his home. She allowed no one to see him. How seriously had Tanaka been affected? No one knew until January 1987, when he celebrated the New Year. He met with four politicians and turned another politician—the politician who had claimed his political mantle—away from his door. He shook hands with his left hand, his speech was slurred, but he was back in political business (maintaining his seat until 1990). He died on December 16, 1993.

Why was Tanaka willing to persevere at politics? In an autobiography he wrote for children, he discussed why he first ran for office. He recalled his many illnesses, his brushes with death, the blood on the snow which saved him from suffocation. He concluded, "Hadn't I heard the voice of heaven? Perhaps the reason I had not died was that I was put on earth to do something." Corruption, then—if what Tanaka did was corrupt—had been subordinated to high purpose.

Further Reading

More information about contemporary Japan and its government may be found in Hayes, Louis D., ed., *Introduction to Japanese Politics* (1992); and Sakaiya, Taichi (translation by Steven Karpa, *What Is Japan?* (Kodansha International, 1993). Another general but insightful explanation of Japanese government and politics is Gerald L. Curtis, *The Japanese Way of Politics* (1988). A sympathetic interpretation of Tanaka and his brand of politics is Chalmers Johnson, "Tanaka Kakuei, Structural Corruption, and the Advent of Machine Politics in Japan," in *Journal of Japanese Politics* 12 (January 1986). □

Roger Brooke Taney

Roger Brooke Taney (1777-1864) was an American political leader and as chief justice of the U.S. Supreme Court greatly contributed to constitutional law.

Roger B. Taney was born in Calvert County, Md., on March 17, 1777, into a landed, slaveholding family that proudly traced its line back five generations. He received the rudiments of a classical education from a private tutor and at the age of 15 entered Dickinson College. There he found little to upset his aristocratic prejudices, but he did gain an abiding love of learning and graduated with honors in 1795.

As a younger son with no prospect of inheriting the family estate, young Taney chose the profession of law, with his eye on politics. In 1799 he was admitted to the bar and served one term as a Federalist representative in the state legislature. In private practice he quickly distinguished himself as one of Maryland's most promising young lawyers. He married Anne Key on Jan. 7, 1806, and she and their seven children were a constant solace throughout Taney's strenuous public life.

In Jackson's Cabinet

From 1816 through 1821 Taney served as state senator. When new parties emerged from the confusion of the

1820s, Taney cast his lot with the forces of Andrew Jackson. In 1831 he resigned his office as state attorney general, which he had held since 1827, in order to accept an appointment in President Jackson's Cabinet as attorney general. Among his opinions as attorney general, two revealed his stand on slavery: one supported South Carolina's law prohibiting free Blacks from entering the state, and one argued that Blacks could not be citizens. In 1833, as secretary of the Treasury, Taney ordered an end to the deposit of Federal money in the Second Bank of the United States, an act which killed the institution.

Aware of Taney's ability and certain of his political orthodoxy, President Jackson, on Dec. 28, 1835, appointed him to the office of chief justice of the United States, left vacant by the death of John Marshall. Taney was instrumental in shaping constitutional law to fit the new age. His opinion in *Charles River Bridge v. Warren Bridge* (1837) set the tone of the new Court. The Massachusetts Legislature had chartered a new, prospectively toll-free bridge across the Charles River. The old bridge company contended that its original charter implied monopoly rights. Taney's opinion refused to recognize the doctrine of implied contract, thus giving the states more latitude to legislate in the public interest. Taney also argued that the refusal to grant monopoly by implication would encourage economic progress by preventing entrenched capital from thwarting new corporate development.

Taney was a moderate, standing between old nationalists on the Court and the more extreme states'-rightists. The Chief Justice also made clear that he was a firm friend of private property. Despite his suspicion of corporate power (his opinion in *Bank of Augusta v. Earle,* 1839), he broadened the interstate operation of corporations by holding that a corporations chartered in one state had the right to do business in another unless positively prohibited by that state.

Personal and Professional Qualities

Thin, stooped, and sallow, Taney did not fit a heroic mold; but his mind was acute, his pen lucid. His patience, tact, and ability were instrumental in overcoming personal and doctrinal divisions among the justices, and though the Court was frequently divided, it continued to administer the law effectively. Under Taney's leadership the Court showed more tolerance of legislative power than it had under Marshall, but it did not surrender its hard-won powers to decide.

The issue of slavery was the downfall of the Court and detracted permanently from the image of Taney's statesmanship. In *Dred Scott v. Sanford* (1857) Taney wrote the majority opinion for a bitterly divided Court which unwisely confronted all the explosive political questions in the case. Blacks, he said in a racist vein that has since been irrevocably associated with his name, could not be a citizen of the United States because he was recognized as inherently unequal by the Constitution. Congress, moreover, could not prohibit slavery in the territories because the 5th Amendment to the Constitution protected citizens in the possession of their property, and slaves were property.

Reaction to Taney's opinion was vehement. Almost overnight the Court fell to a new low in the opinion of the majority of Americans, who were now antislavery in sentiment. The years following the Dred Scott case until Taney's death on Oct. 12, 1864, were sad ones for the Chief Justice. Only after the passions of the Civil War had receded was it apparent that, the Dred Scott case excepted, Taney in his own way had contributed almost as much to the development of constitutional government as his great predecessor.

Further Reading

The standard biography, Carl Swisher, *Roger B. Taney* (1935), relates Taney's political-economic experience to his philosophy and judicial career. Walker Lewis, *Without Fear or Favor: A Biography of Chief Justice Roger Brooke Taney* (1965), supplements Swisher by concentrating on Taney's personal qualities. Samuel Tyler, *Memoir of Roger Brooke Taney* (1872), though old, still contains useful information, as does Charles W. Smith, Jr., *Roger B. Taney: Jacksonian Jurist* (1936). Two general accounts of the Supreme Court that include much information on Taney's legal career are Charles Warren, *The Supreme Court in United States History* (3 vols., 1922; rev. ed., 2 vols., 1926), and Charles G. Haines and Foster Sherwood, *The Role of the Supreme Court in American Government and Politics* vol. 2: *1835-1864* (1957). A work in progress, Holmes Devisee, *History of the Supreme Court,* will devote one volume to the Taney Court.

Additional Sources

Siegel, Martin, *The Taney court, 1836-1864,* Millwood, N.Y.: Associated Faculty Press, 1987. □

Kenzo Tange

The Japanese architect Kenzo Tange (born 1913), a student of Le Corbusier, was one of the first modern architects in Japan and played an important design role in postwar rebuilding of Japanese cities.

K enzo Tange was born in 1913 in the town of Imabari on Shikoku, the smallest of the four principal islands in the Japanese archipelago. He received his degree in architecture from the University of Tokyo in 1938 and returned to the university to do graduate studies in urban planning and design between 1942 and 1945. The four intervening years were spent in the Tokyo architectural firm of Kunio Maekawa, who had worked in the Paris office of the great Swiss architect Le Corbusier and who was one of a small number of modern architects in Japan at the time. Thus, at the end of World War II Tange was equipped to play a major design role in the reconstruction of Japan's war-ravaged cities.

In 1949, after participating in planning studies to aid the rebuilding of numerous towns and cities, Tange won a national competition to design a Peace Park in central Hiroshima, the area that had been directly hit by the atomic bomb dropped from an American plane on August 6, 1945. The complex, comprising a memorial, a museum, a community center, and an auditorium-hotel building, was completed in 1956. The free-standing memorial monument, a dramatic saddle-like arch made of reinforced concrete, is a 20th-century statement that recalls a building type in which the tombs of prehistoric Japanese rulers were placed. The museum, a long, horizontal structure of glass and concrete raised above ground on concrete columns (called pilotis), is reminiscent of buildings by Le Corbusier and also of ancient Japanese prototypes (specifically, the Shosoin in Nara, a building that housed the Imperial Treasury and dates back more than 1,000 years). This theme of synthesizing modern architecture with traditional symbolism characterized the first phase of Tange's career.

Throughout the 1950s Tange was engaged in designing a variety of civic projects—town halls, libraries, auditoriums, sports centers. One of the more notable of these was the town hall complex he designed for his home town, Imabari, which was completed in 1959. These buildings, including an auditorium, an office center, and the town hall proper, show Tange's increasing skill at manipulating the expressive possibilities of exposed concrete. The auditorium, with just a few projecting square windows on a high concrete wall shadowed by a dramatically projecting roof, is especially powerful. These strong structures were arranged compactly around a public plaza, a spatial form not to be found in traditional Japanese cities. Tange's interest in such communal spaces dates back to his university studies of the Greek agora—the place, as Tange wrote, where the "citizen moved from the private realm to establish connections with society."

In 1960 Tange published his monumental "Plan for Tokyo," a stimulating—and widely publicized—theoretical exercise which foresaw a need to restructure the 20th-century city. Based in part upon an analogy with nature—"the various architectural works will form the leaves, and the transportation and communications facilities the trunk of a great tree," Tange wrote—the plan envisioned a vast radial overlay of buildings and roadways above and beyond traditional Tokyo. Although somewhat terrifying in scale, the buildings, structures of concrete, shown in photographs and models were physically impressive, even beautiful. None was ever built, although Tange's stupendous Yamanashi Press and Broadcasting Building (1966) in Kofu, a medium-size city in central Japan, inherits something of the plan's monumental vision. The building comprises an array of horizontal units plugged into, and supported by, 16 huge concrete columns whose hollow cores contain the needed support services (stairwells, elevators, air-conditioning plant, and rest rooms). A feature of the building, as of the Tokyo plan, is its ability to be added to without change to the fundamental structural system (this in fact was done in 1975).

Tange's best-known buildings are the two national gymnasiums erected in Tokyo for the 1964 Olympic Games (the first to be held in Asia). The roofs of these two circular buildings indelibly recall the massive forms of traditional Japanese temples, but they are, also, altogether contemporary in form and technique. These roofs, suspended by cable from massive concrete pillars (a single pillar for the smaller structure, a pair for the larger), consist of prestressed steel nets onto which are attached welded steel plates. The drama of these forms continues in the interiors—bold, elegant, welcoming open spaces illuminated by a combination of artificial with natural light.

From the mid-1960s onward Tange received widespread international attention and commissions. His firm, called the Urbanists and Architects Team (URTEC), provided the master plan (1965) for the reconstruction of Skopje, Yugoslavia, after its devastation by an earthquake and did important planning studies for cities and regions in Africa, the Middle East, and Europe as well as in Japan. Among Tange's more important later architectural works is the Akasaka Hotel (1982) in central Tokyo, a bi-winged structure whose gleaming skin of aluminum and glass demonstrated a decisive turn away from the aesthetic of exposed concrete.

In 1986 Tange again won a competition to design the New Tokyo City Hall Complex, as he had done in 1952. As all of his best work, the new design presents an impressive image: twin skyscraper towers, adorned at the top with a panoply of communications equipment, rising cathedral-like over the Shinjuku district in western Tokyo. He also began work on the Otsu Prince Hotel, the United Nations University in Tokyo, and the Place d'Italie in Paris, France (completed 1991). An American example of his work is the American Medical Association Headquarters Building in Chicago, Illinois, completed in 1990.

Tange has received numerous awards, including the Medal of Honour, Danish Royal Academy of Fine Arts,

Grand Prix, Architectural Institute of Japan (1986); the Pritzker Architecture Prize (1987); and in 1993, he received the prestigious Japanese Praemium Imperiale award for lifetime achievement in the arts.

Further Reading

The first decades of Tange's work are fully treated in *Kenzo Tange, 1946-1969,* edited by Udo Kultermann (1970). His architecture and ideas also are dealt with in books by Robin Boyd, *New Directions in Japanese Architecture* (1968), and Botond Bognar, *Contemporary Japanese Architecture: Its Development and Challenge* (1985). He wrote a short autobiographical work, *Kenzo Tange,* published in Switzerland (1987). Articles about him and his work also appear in special issues of *Space Design* (January 1980, September 1983, 1987 and 1991). □

Yves Tanguy

Yves Tanguy (1900-1955) was a French surrealist painter who specialized in strange osseous and vegetal formations placed in a barren, lunarlike landscape or an eerie underwater setting.

Born in Paris on Jan. 5, 1900, to Breton parents, Yves Tanguy spent his childhood vacations in Finistère, an area of Brittany that contained many prehistoric menhirs and dolmens. His memories of this terrain may have gone into the fashioning of his fantastic landscapes. In 1918 he shipped out on cargo boats to Africa and South America. Drafted into the French army in 1920, he served in Tunis. After 1922 he was closely associated in Paris with the surrealist writers Jacques Prévert and Marcel Duhamel.

In 1923, upon seeing a painting of the "metaphysical" Italian artist Giorgio de Chirico, Tanguy decided to become a painter. He met André Breton in 1925, and the following year, some of his work having appeared in the magazine *La Révolution surréaliste,* Tanguy officially joined the surrealist movement. His works of 1926 are marked by a certain whimsical, naive quality, sometimes showing the influence of De Chirico. In 1927 he matured abruptly. His *Mama, Papa Is Wounded!* (1927), a title taken from a psychiatric case history, contains in the foreground a great hairy stalk and in the background a green cactuslike element from which emanates a cat's cradle type of filigree binding. There is an illusion of a deep space, yet laws of geometrical perspective do not operate logically. The ambiguous organic elements—some floating, some growing out of the ground—are bathed in a cold light and are situated in an unearthly looking, barren landscape marked by a strong horizon line. In other paintings of the 1920s there is no horizon line: the bonelike and vegetal forms seem to be either airborne or floating at the bottom of the sea, as in *The Lovers* (1929).

As a result of a trip to Africa in 1930-1931, Tanguy painted a series of rocklike formations, monumentally conceived and harshly lighted. But this was a brief departure,

and he went back to his tiny osseous conglomerations, though by the mid-1930s he usually omitted the fixed horizon line and presented a continuous floating space.

In 1939 Tanguy moved to America and settled with his wife, Kay Sage, in a farmhouse in Woodbury, Conn. His colors became richer, and his objects began to loom larger, perhaps partially as the result of a trip to Arizona. Several paintings, such as *Indefinite Divisibility* (1942) and *Slowly toward the North* (1942), contain tubular, geometrical constructions (along with the organic elements) which suggest the world of machines. He had a fine collection of guns with telescopic sights, and this interest may partially have accounted for the formal changes in his paintings. His last painting, the ambitious *Multiplication of the Arcs* (1954), contains a profusion of unidentifiable, shell-like elements set in great clusters. He died in Woodbury on Jan. 15, 1955.

Further Reading

A useful work whose text is short but well illustrated is New York Museum of Modern Art, *Yves Tanguy,* exhibition and catalog by James Thrall Soby (1955). Recommended for background are Marcel Jean, *The History of Surrealist Painting* (1959; trans. 1960); Werner Haffmann, *Painting in the Twentieth Century* (trans., 2 vols., 1961; rev. ed. 1965); J. H. Matthews, *An Introduction to Surrealism* (1965); William S. Rubin, *Dada and Surrealist Art* (1968); and Sarane Alexandrian, *Surrealist Art* (1969; trans. 1970). □

Junichiro Tanizaki

Junichiro Tanizaki (1886-1965) was a Japanese novelist, essayist, and playwright known for his stylistic virtuosity and depiction of unusual psychological situations.

Junichiro Tanizaki, born in Tokyo, the son of a rice broker, received a conventional education. Entering the Imperial University in 1908, he studied Japanese classical literature but left without taking a degree. From a very young age he was interested in literary pursuits and soon achieved his ambition of devoting his life to art.

Eschewing the flourishing naturalism of the day, Tanizaki sought to create works of beauty through style and mood, inspired in part by the Japanese past and also by certain Western writers such as Edgar Allan Poe, Charles Baudelaire, and Oscar Wilde. Throughout his fiction run strains of eroticism and lyricism together with a good deal of imagery taken from the acute observation of real life. The character of a dominant or destructive woman is much in evidence in many of his novels, as are subtle contrasts of new and old, Japanese and Occidental. Tanizaki saw and depicted vividly the clash between Japan and the West, but on the esthetic plane.

Career as a Novelist

Shisei (1910; *The Tatoo*), set in the premodern era of the early 19th century, depicts a tattooer and artist who becomes enslaved to a beautiful woman after tattooing a spider on her back while she slept. The richness and beauty of the style brought Tanizaki to the immediate attention of the reading public. *Shonen* (1912; *Children*) pursues the vein of "diabolism" with the depiction of children committing unspeakable, and unspecified, horrors. *Jotaro* (1914) explores the subjects of masochism and madness on the part of a famous author. *O-Tsuya Goroshi* (1915; *The Killing of O-Tsuya*), with a picturesque setting of city life in the recent premodern past, is a tale of infidelity, lust, and murder in a vivid, dramatic, and essentially modern technique.

In *Itansha no Kanashimi* (1917; *The Sorrows of a Heretic*) the theme of masochism is again set forth. *Haha o Kouru-ki* (1919; *Pining for Mother*) depicts mother love and nostalgia for the world of the preceding generation. *Chiisana Okoku* (1918; *A Small Kingdom*) has for its theme masochism as well as subjection to inevitable tyranny. It is almost political but not quite. The play *Okuni and Gohei* (1922) is complex, historical, and violent.

With *Chijin no Ai* (1925; *A Fool's Love*) Tanizaki embarked on his first long novel. Set in the foreign quarter of Yokohama, it depicts a man's obsession with a Eurasian prostitute who bears a resemblance to Mary Pickford. It may be an ironic commentary on Japan's dilemma of Westernization. After the great earthquake of 1923 Tanizaki had left Tokyo to establish himself in the more traditional and picturesque Kyoto-Osaka area, where he was to remain. He now turned his attention to depicting the more glamorous aspects of the Japanese past and could look back on modern Tokyo with a certain disdain.

From this time on, Tanizaki's greatest works were written. *Tade Kuu Mushi* (1929; *Some Prefer Nettles*) portrays modern life in Kobe and Kyoto, the muted charms of Kyoto versus the blatant cheapness of the modern port city with its shabby cosmopolitanism. *Manji* (1930; *Whirl*), a stylistic tour de force written entirely in Osaka dialect, deals with suicide and the perverse. In *Yoshino Kudzu* (1931), a tone poem that is part essay, part fiction, the hero falls in love with a girl who reminds him of his deceased mother. *Momoku Monogatari* (1931; *A Blind Man's Tale*) is a historical tale of the 16th century in which prominent historical personages are "seen" through the eyes of a narrator who is a blind masseur and musician. Stylistically it is one of Tanizaki's greatest achievements, as is *Ashikari* (1932), a discursive evocation of passion somewhat reminiscent of a No play. *Kaoyo* (1933), a play set in the 14th century, depends on mood and strangeness for its effect.

Shunkinsho (1934; *A Portrait of Shunkin*), a most exotic tale, depicts an imperious woman named Shunkin, who is a beautiful blind musician, and her abject body servant. *Neko to Shozo to Futari no Onna* (1936; *A Cat, Shozo, and Two Women*) is a perverse and comic novel with a modern setting and humorous tone.

During the 1930s Tanizaki had been working on a modern version of the *Tale of Genji,* the great classic novel of 10th-century life by Lady Murasaki. This appears to have influenced some of the descriptive passages in his long novel *Sasameyuki* (1948; *The Makioka Sisters*), a study of a prominent old Osaka merchant family in decline. It is an

important document of contemporary social customs. Returning to the Japanese past with *Shosho Shigemoto no Haha* (1949; *The Mother of Captain Shigemoto*), Tanizaki again treated the theme of a youth burdened by the memory of his beautiful mother. *Kagi* (1956; *The Key*) and *Futen Rojin Nikki* (1962; *Diary of a Mad Old Man*) offer vivid and humorous descriptions of modern depravity in the postwar world.

Elected to the Japanese Academy of Art in 1923 and decorated with the Order of Culture in 1949, Tanizaki occupied a position of eminence in the world of letters for many years. He died in July 1965.

Further Reading

For background see Donald Keene, *Modern Japanese Literature* (1955); John W. Morrison, *Modern Japanese Fiction* (1955); and Armando M. Janeira, *Japanese and Western Literature: A Comparative Study* (1970).

Additional Sources

Tanizaki, Junichiro, *Childhood years: a memoir*, Tokyo; New York: Kodansha International, 1989. □

Henry Ossawa Tanner

Henry Ossawa Tanner (1859-1937) was a black American painter. He earned a formidable reputation at a time when it was rare for a black American to pursue a career as a professional artist.

Henry O. Tanner was born in Pittsburgh, Pa., on June 21, 1859. His father, a clergyman, writer, and educator, moved the family to Philadelphia in 1866. After Henry graduated from high school, he secured a job in a flour mill; the work was strenuous, and he soon became seriously ill. With his recovery, Bishop Tanner consented to let him study art.

In 1880 Tanner began his studies at the Philadelphia Academy of Fine Arts, where his principal teachers were Thomas Eakins and William Merritt Chase. By 1882 Tanner was painting on his own, occasionally selling a painting or a drawing. In 1888 he set up a photography studio in Atlanta, Ga. The venture failed, but he secured a teaching position at Clark University in Atlanta.

At Clark, Tanner met Bishop Joseph L. Hartzell. The bishop, impressed with Tanner's artistic ability, arranged an exhibition in Cincinnati. Not one piece was sold, but the bishop bought them all to help the young artist—morally and financially. With this money Tanner left for Europe to work in an atmosphere free of the virulent racism that permeated American life.

After 5 years of study at the Académie Julian in Paris, Tanner showed the painting *The Young Sabot-maker* at the prestigious Salon des Artistes Français. He participated continually in Salon exhibitions until 1924. In 1897 he became

internationally known when the French government purchased the *Resurrection of Lazarus.*

The young woman who posed for the figure of Mary in the *Annunciation* (1898) became Tanner's wife in 1899. They returned to the United States in 1902. After their only child was born in New York City the next year, Tanner moved his family to Paris. Except for occasional visits to America, he remained abroad for the rest of his life.

The years brought numerous awards and honors, the most significant being Tanner's election in 1923 by the French government as a chevalier of the Légion d'Honneur. Later, America honored him with full membership in its National Academy of Art and Design. He was the first black American to achieve this distinction.

After his death in Paris on May 25, 1937, interest in Tanner's works diminished considerably. The most renowned of all black artists was rediscovered, largely as a result of a major exhibit in New York, in 1967. Two years later the Smithsonian Institution presented a large retrospective that circulated extensively throughout the United States.

Tanner was an excellent draftsman. Often compared to Eakins, he can be more accurately compared to Albert P. Ryder and Ralph Blakelock. Yet his work also relates to Rembrandt in terms of technique and composition, as clearly illustrated in Tanner's *Daniel in the Lion's Den.* Dramatic lighting made Tanner's paintings between 1890 and 1905 prime examples of modern chiaroscuro. His skillful use of glazing was a unique element of his style. Al-

though his *Banjo Lesson* (1893) is considered a classic work of an ethnic subject, Tanner usually found his inspiration in landscapes and biblical themes.

Further Reading

The biography of Tanner by Marcia M. Mathews, *Henry Ossawa Tanner: American Artist* (1969), depicts the virtually enforced Europeanization of Tanner's talent and ascribes his obscurity as an American artist to changes in taste. Ralph W. Bullock, *In Spite of Handicaps: Brief Biographical Sketches* (1927), and Langston Hughes, *Famous American Negroes* (1954), both contain chapters on Tanner. Brief biographies of Tanner and discussions of his work appear in Alain Locke, *Negro Art: Past and Present* (1936); James A. Porter, *Modern Negro Art* (1943); Russell L. Adams, *Great Negroes: Past and Present* (1963); Wilhelmena S. Robinson, *Historical Negro Biographies* (1968); and Henri Ghent, *Eight Afro-American Artists* (1971), an exhibition catalog. □

Tao-an

Tao-an (312-385) was the first native Chinese Buddhist monk of major importance. He inspired his disciples to seek the word of the Buddha in the best translations of texts from India and to interpret them in a critical, almost "scientific," spirit.

Tao-an, whose family name was Wei, came from a traditionally Confucian family who lived in what is now southern Hopei Province. He was born in a period of constant bloody warfare and seems to have been orphaned at an early age. He became a Buddhist novice at the age of 11, slowly distinguishing himself by his phenomenal intelligence, although his appearance was extremely unprepossessing. As was the custom, he left his monastery after ordination to wander from place to place seeking instruction from different masters, studying sometime after 335 with Fo-t'u-teng in Yeh (northern Honan).

Tao-an soon led his own disciples in various monasteries in the North, being joined by his most famous disciple, Hui-yüan, on Mt. Heng in northern Shansi in 354. During this period (until 365) Tao-an was, since he came from a scholarly family, exposed to the prevailing theories of metaphysical Taoism (*hsüan-hsüeh*) based mainly on the commentaries by Wang Pi (226-249) upon the *Tao-te ching* and by Kuo Hsiang (died 312) upon the *Chuang-tzu.* After joining the Buddhist sangha, he read widely in early translations of texts on *dhyana* (meditation) and perhaps on Prajnaparamita philosophy. He then began his bibliographical and exegetical work, being the first Chinese to make sentence-by-sentence commentaries on Buddhist works, commentaries that attempted to understand what the text really meant.

In 365 Tao-an fled the chaos that incessant warfare among barbarian dynasties had made of North China and settled in Hsiang-yang (northern Hupei) with 400 or 500 disciples. Because the Pai-ma monastery was too small, he soon moved to the T'an-hsi monastery, a private mansion. Here Tao-an reached his maturity as philosopher, scholar, and religious leader.

Tao-an's Teachings

Tao-an's philosophy is known as the theory of *Penwu*, which may be translated as "Fundamental non-[differentiation]," and which attempts to interpret the Buddhist idea of *sunya* (emptiness) in terms reminiscent of Wang Pi. The differentiated world as we know it is based upon a substratum of *wu* (basic non-differentiation). It is only by realizing, through meditation, the basic oneness of this substratum that we can shake off the impediments of the mundane world and arrive at truth and salvation.

Tao-an's scholarship at this period is represented by his analytical bibliography of over 600 Buddhist works called *Tsung-li chung-ching mu-lu* and finished in 374, a truly revolutionary work that set the pattern for all later Buddhist bibliographies. His religious development was especially noteworthy for his devotion to the worship of Maitreya, which he seems to have originated in China, and for his unceasing study of the rules of monastic life (Vinaya). He also originated the practice of giving monks the surname "Shih," underlining the fact that they are sons of Buddha (*Sakyamuni is Shih-chia-mu-ni* in Chinese).

When, in 379, Fu P'i captured Hsiang-yang, Tao-an followed him to the Former Ch'in capital, Ch'ang-an, after having sent most of his disciples away to form their own centers. In the capital he was extremely active in secular as well as in Buddhist cultural life, and very close to Fu Chien, the reigning emperor, and to the center of political power. Tao-an devoted himself chiefly to the supervision of the translation of new materials from India and central Asia; in 382 he laid down a series of principles that were used by translators long afterward, although he himself knew no Sanskrit.

These new translations were of enormous importance for the understanding of the true meaning of Buddhist texts. Toward the very end of his life, Tao-an felt overwhelmed by the feeling that he could no longer assimilate this obviously more profound understanding of the Buddhist message. This feeling was typical of him, of his conscientiousness, his humility, and his intellectual honesty, making him the most important figure in early Chinese Buddhism, before he was overshadowed by his disciple Hui-Yüan and by Kumarajiva, who was brought to China through Tao-an's influence. Tao-an died in Ch'ang-an.

Further Reading

The once voluminous writings of Tao-an survive today mainly in relatively short citations in other works. The standard work on him is in Japanese, but Erik Zürcher, *The Buddhist Conquest of China* (2 vols., 1959), gives an excellent discussion of his life and doctrines, and Seng-chao, *The Book of Chao,* translated and edited by Walter Liebenthal (1948), gives a fuller account of the doctrines. □

T'ao Ch'ien

T'ao Ch'ien (365-427) was one of China's foremost poets in the five-word shih style, and his influence on subsequent poets was very great.

Also known as T'ao Yüan-ming, T'ao Ch'ien lived during the Eastern Chin and Liu Sung dynasties. He was born in Ch'ai-sang in present-day Kiangsi Province, the great-grandson of T'ao K'an, a famed Chin general. Both his grandfather and father had served as perfects, but by T'ao Ch'ien's time the family must have become poorer, and despite his preference for a life of seclusion he held at least four different posts during some dozen years (393-405) in order to support his family.

T'ao did not serve very long, however, in his last post as magistrate of P'eng-tse (405). According to a famous anecdote recorded in his official biographies, he voluntarily resigned when summoned to appear before a superior so that he did not have to bow in obeisance for the sake of a meager salary. In any event, upon returning home on that occasion, he wrote a sequence of fiveword poems as well as a long poem entitled *Kuei-ch'ülai tz'u* (On Returning Home) in celebration of his liberation from the shackles of official life. He was then only 40 years old. Subsequently, many eminent men sought him out for an official appointment, but he resolutely declined. He apparently enjoyed the remainder of his life as a gentleman farmer, reading his favorite books at leisure, exchanging visits with his neighbors, and watching resignedly the lack of promise of his several sons.

T'ao Ch'ien has been too often described as a Taoist nature poet with his fondness for wine and for chrysanthemums. It is true that he delights in nature and in wine, but he is far more a philosophic or meditative poet than an idyllic or bucolic one. He represents the culmination of the fiveword poetry of the Han dynasty with its obsession with life's meaning; and with his strong attraction to Confucian endeavor and knightly chivalry, his intellectual makeup is far more complex than the word "Taoist" would convey.

One of T'ao's best-known poems is a debate among "Substance, Shadow, and Spirit," who speak respectively for hedonism, Confucian fame, and a kind of Taoist stoicism which accepts life in its totality. T'ao Ch'ien is thus an existentialist: the elegies written on the supposed occasion of his own death are among the most moving poems in the Chinese language.

The simpler view of T'ao Ch'ien as a Taoist recluse is supported by some of his most celebrated works. In a brief idealized autobiography, he styles himself Mr. Five Willows and speaks of his contentment with poverty, his fondness for wine, and his joy in reading, though he makes no attempt to probe the deeper meanings of books. His prose description of the Peach Fount Colony living in happy oblivion of the outside world has been celebrated since his time as the Taoist vision of a simple, good life unrealizable on earth.

T'ao Ch'ien was not recognized as a major poet until the T'ang dynasty. By the Sung times, however, his status as one of China's greatest lyrical poets had become generally recognized, and his poetry has never ceased to fascinate the Chinese since.

Further Reading

The poems of T'ao Ch'ien were translated by William Acker as *T'ao the Hermit: Sixty Poems by T'ao Ch'ien* (1952) and by Lily Pao-hu Chang and Marjorie Sinclair as *Poems* (1953). A number of anthologies of Chinese poetry in translation contain selections from T'ao Ch'ien, including Arthur Waley, *Chinese Poems* (1946); Robert Payne, *The White Pony: An Anthology of Chinese Poetry* (1947); and J. D. Frodsham and Ch'eng Hsi, *An Anthology of Chinese Verse: Han, Wei, Chin and the Northern and Southern Dynasties* (1967). Every history of Chinese literature for Western readers discusses T'ao Ch'ien at some length, though there is no full-length study in English. James R. Hightower has done notable work on the poet in his articles ''The *Fu* of T'ao Ch'ien'' in John L. Bishop, ed., *Studies in Chinese Literature* (1965), and ''T'ao Ch'ien's 'Drinking Wine' Poems'' in Chow Tse-tsung, ed., *Wen-lin: Studies in the Chinese Humanities* (1968). □

Tao-hsüan

The Chinese Buddhist monk Tao-hsüan (596-667) was an important Buddhist scholar and the founder of the Disciplinary school, Lü-tsung, of Chinese Buddhism.

Tao-hsüan was born in southeast China 7 years after the unification of China by the Sui dynasty, an event which brought to a close nearly 4 centuries of political division. At least several generations of his ancestors had served as officials in the southern Chinese dynasties; nothing is known about his father. His family must have been well-to-do, because as a boy he received a classical education in the Confucian canon, a privilege of the wealthy and leisured class.

There is evidence that the family's fortunes slumped under the Sui regime (581-617). Perhaps despairing of secular success, Tao-hsüan turned toward Buddhism, which was widespread and well supported in China at that time. When he was 15 he began to study the Buddhist classics under the guidance of a well-known monk in the capital of Ch'ang-an. The next year he formally entered a monastery, and 4 years later he was ordained as a Buddhist monk.

Tao-hsüan studied under a Buddhist master who taught the *Vinaya in Four Parts (Ssu-fcn-lü)*, one version of the rules of monastic discipline. He began his writings on Buddhism at this time, compiling material concerning this Buddhist school. In 630 Tao-hsüan entered a temple in the Chungnan Mountains south of Ch'ang-an. In the following years he began to formulate his own ideas, which showed more independence after his principal teachers died between 635 and 637. Because he established his basic precepts during this period, his school is known as the Southern Mountain Disciplinary school (*Nan-shan Lü-hsüeh*), named after the location of the monastery where he had lived.

During the following years Tao-hsüan continued his scholarly work, eventually producing a corpus of formidable proportions. One of the best-known of his works is the *Continuation of the Lives of Eminent Monks,* which was an important source of inspiration for Chinese Buddhists and is a valuable source of information for the modern scholar.

In 645 Tao-hsüan took part in the translation of Buddhist scriptures that the famous pilgrim-traveler Hsüantsang had brought back from India after his lengthy and arduous trip. His collaboration with Hsüan-tsang continued for years, during which time his own reputation soared.

By 658 Tao-hsüan was abbot of a large monastery in Ch'ang-an. As an important cleric in the capital, he was on several occasions involved in disputes concerning the etiquette of Buddhists in the imperial court, an important matter which involved the relationship of the faith to the secular power. Although he was a vigorous and able defender of Buddhism, he preferred religious activity to political, and in 664 he returned to the temple in the Chung-nan Mountains, where years before he had begun his important thinking and writing.

In his old age Tao-hsüan was eager to practice the ideas that he had developed. He was mainly concerned with the actual practice of Buddhism, particularly with matters of monastic discipline. A special building was constructed to house an ordination platform, where his school could practice his formulas for religious discipline and ceremony.

Tao-hsüan was a mystic and visionary. Insisting that his interpretations of doctrine were simply what he had been told by the gods, he dogmatically asserted that their otherworldly provenance freed his views from error. He passed his teachings on to a small group of disciples who carried on after his death in 667.

Further Reading

There is nothing available in English on Tao-hsüan's life. For a general interpretation and discussion on Buddhism in China see Arthur F. Wright, *Buddhism in Chinese History* (1959), and Kenneth K. S. Ch'en, *Buddhism in China* (1964). □

Tappan brothers

American merchants and reformers Arthur (1786-1865) and Lewis (1788-1873) Tappan were religious moralists and abolitionists who helped create important new institutions.

Born in Northampton, Mass., Arthur and Lewis Tappan were among the 11 children of a goldsmith and merchant. Their mother kept a strict Calvinistic household. Both Arthur and Lewis early showed aptitude for business and rose rapidly as wholesale and retail merchants in Boston and Canada. Arthur, a stern man, moved to New York, where he attained wealth in selling silks and a reputation for social and religious concerns. His most notable innovation was the one-price system on sales. Lewis, a warmer and more expressive personality, was won over by the Reverend William Ellery Channing and troubled his family by becoming a Unitarian. His return to Calvinism in 1828 created a sensation in Boston and beyond.

In 1827 Lewis joined Arthur in New York. They became influential in numerous fields. They began the *Journal of Commerce* to create a business paper which also had a religious perspective. Their connection with the Magdalen Society, intended to end prostitution in the city, exposed them to antagonism and ridicule, as did their campaigns against Sunday mails. They contributed to church funds and building.

Arthur took himself and his brother into the antislavery crusade. Impelled by evangelicism, both embraced William Lloyd Garrison's radical doctrine of ''immediate'' abolition. In 1833 they helped organize the New-York Antislavery Society and the American Antislavery Society. Public dissatisfaction with their activities the next year resulted in a riot during which Lewis Tappan's home was sacked. Arthur was active in founding Lane Seminary in Cincinnati, Ohio, as a religious outpost. He also helped build Oberlin College in Ohio.

The economic crisis of 1837 ruined Arthur, and despite Lewis's loyalty and cooperation, he never regained his status as businessman or reformer. Lewis, on the other hand, continued consequential in both fields. In 1841 he founded the successful Mercantile Agency, the first commercial credit institution; it later become Dun and Bradstreet. Meanwhile he was at the center of abolitionist developments. In 1843 he visited England in a remarkable effort to persuade the British government to end slavery in Texas through a loan to the young republic.

In 1846 Lewis helped found the American Missionary Association, in opposition to groups more conservative on the slavery issue. The next year he helped found the *National Era,* which in 1852 published Harriet Beecher Stowe's *Uncle Tom's Cabin*. His pamphlet *Is It Right To Be Rich?* (1869) answered the question with a firm negative.

Further Reading

Lewis Tappan's *Life of Arthur Tappan* (1870) made his brother a major figure among later historians, at the expense of his own fame. Bertram Wyatt-Brown, *Lewis Tappan and the Evangelical War against Slavery* (1969), delineates Lewis's major significance in social and reform affairs of his era. □

Lewis Tappan

Mirza Taqi Khan Amir-e Kabir

Mirza Taqi Khan Amir-e Kabir (ca. 1806-1852) was the greatest prime minister of the Qajar dynasty. In just 3 years he accomplished more than the combined efforts of the other chief ministers of the dynasty and laid the foundations of modernization in Iran.

Karbalayi Mohammad Qorban, the father of Taqi, was a cook and later a steward in the household of Qa'em Maqam, who later became the chief minister of Mohammad Shah. It is said that when the tutor came to teach the children of Qa'em Maqam, the boy Taqi, in his eagerness to learn, would try to listen from behind the closed door of the private classroom. When Qa'em Maqam heard of this, he allowed the boy to become a regular member of the class. Later Taqi was employed as one of the secretaries, and because of his genius and capacity for work he was given positions of responsibility. He became known as Mirza (secretary) Taqi Khan Farahani (denoting his birthplace).

Travels Abroad

When the head of a Russian mission to Iran was murdered in 1829, the distraught Fath Ali Shah, fearing war, sent his grandson Khosro Mirza to St. Petersburg. Mirza Taqi Khan went as the prince's secretary and had an opportunity to observe the life and institutions of Russia. Ten years later he accompanied young Naser al-Din, the crown prince, to Russia. At this time Mirza Taqi Khan was the chief secretary and tutor of the prince, with the title of Amir-e Nezam (commander of the army). He impressed the Czar with his knowledge of Russian and arranged to see schools, factories, hospitals, and other establishments in the country.

In 1842 Taqi Khan headed the Persian delegation to the Erzerum conference for the settlement of the Irano-Turkish border dispute. His performance there was so outstanding that the British representative, Robert Curzon, wrote that Mirza Taqi Khan was "beyond all comparison the most interesting person among the commissioners of Turkey, Persia, Russia, and Great Britain who were there assembled at Erzerum." This was the period of Tanzimat reforms in the Ottoman Empire, and the significance of these reforms did not escape the discerning eyes of the young commander.

Work as Reformer

In 1848, when Naser al-Din became shah of Iran, he chose Mirza Taqi Khan Amir-e Nezam as his chief minister, with the appropriate title of Atabak-e A'zam. Mirza Taqi Khan, however, preferred to use his old and more humble title. The people gradually changed the title to Amir-e Kabir (great commander). He was now in a position to implement the reforms which he must have been planning in his mind for a long time.

This indefatigable worker began at once, and no aspect of the life of the country escaped his scrutiny. Amir-e Kabir built factories, facilitated commerce, established the first modern institution of learning, employed teachers and technicians from Europe, inaugurated a modern postal system, set up a translation bureau and a modern press, founded the first newspaper, reorganized the judicial system, did away with the sale of office, and prevented the clergy from interfering with the affairs of government.

These and many other activities aroused the anger of courtiers, landlords, and clergy, whose sources of income and power were threatened by the reforms. His greatest enemy was his own mother-in-law, the queen mother. In 1851 the Shah very reluctantly dismissed him and sent him to Kashan. A few months later the queen mother tricked her son into signing Amir-e Kabir's death warrant and hurried executioners to Kashan. They found him in the bathhouse and killed him by opening his veins.

Further Reading

There is no English-language book in print which gives the full life of Mirza Taqi Khan. Short sketches are found in Percy Sykes, *A History of Persia*, vol. 2 (1915; 3d ed. 1930); Edward G. Browne, *A Literary History of Persia*, vol. 4 (1924); and Peter Avery, *Modern Iran* (1965). □

Ida Minerva Tarbell

The crusading American journalist Ida Minerva Tarbell (1857-1944) is known as the muckraker who cracked the oil trust. She was also an outstanding biographer of Abraham Lincoln.

Ida Tarbell was born on Nov. 5, 1857, in Erie County, Pa., the daughter of a small oilman driven to the wall by the Rockefeller oil monopoly. Tarbell, unlike many famous people, spent an unusually well-adjusted childhood and had a healthy appreciation of her parents. She wrote of the log house in which she was born and of the pleasant memories it gave her. She felt loved and was perhaps even smug about it.

In Titusville High School, Tarbell led her class and decided never to marry. She took a bachelor of arts degree at Allegheny College in 1880. In 1882 she became a staff member of the *Chautauquan* newspaper and eventually became its managing editor. Driven by desire for more education, she went to Paris and studied at the Sorbonne and the University of Paris from 1891 to 1894, sustaining herself by writing magazine articles. She was with *McClure's Magazine* from 1894 to 1896, when she became associate editor of the *American Magazine;* she remained in that post until 1915.

Tarbell's fame for biography rests mainly on her two-volume *Life of Abraham Lincoln* (1900). However, in Paris she also did studies of Madame de Staël (1894), Napoleon Bonaparte (1895), Madame Roland (1896), Judge Elbert H. Gary (1925), and an "ideal businessman," Owen D. Young (1932). Eight of her books relate to Lincoln. Nevertheless, when she shifted to Lincolniana, her heart fell, and she told herself, "If you once get into American history . . . , that will finish France." It did mean the end of great attention to her other projects, her desire to determine the nature of revolutions, and any important contribution to women's rights.

Tarbell is particularly well known for her two-volume *History of the Standard Oil Company* (1904), first issued as a 19-installment series in *McClure's*. Despite her reputation as a trustbuster, she came to the defense of American business in her later years. Her book on Young, plus other writings at the time, were expressions of hope and faith in a new kind of businessman. She supported "socialized democracy" and was opposed to left-flank movements, which she said would make people "mere cogs in a machine."

Tarbell died of pneumonia in Bridgeport, Conn., on Jan. 6, 1944. The *New York Times* noted editorially that "her mind and personality never took age, they simply matured in richness and wisdom."

Further Reading

Tarbell's autobiography, *All in the Day's Work* (1939), is easily the most informative and helpful work relating to her. Harold S. Wilson, *McClure's Magazine and the Muckrakers* (1970), has extensive biographical and background material on her life and career. See also Cornelius C. Regier, *The Era of the Muckrakers* (1932), and David Mark Chalmers, *The Social and Political Ideas of the Muckrakers* (1964). □

Jean Gabriel Tarde

The French philosopher and sociologist Jean Gabriel Tarde (1843-1904) made important contributions to general social theory and to the study of collective behavior, public opinion, and personal influence.

Jean Gabriel Tarde was born in Sarlat, the son of a military officer and judge. His father died when he was 7, and Jean Gabriel was raised by his mother. He attended a Jesuit school in Sarlat, obtaining a classical training, and read law in Toulouse and then Paris. From 1869 to 1894 he held several legal posts near Sarlat. Only after Tarde's mother died did he agree to leave Sarlat, and he accepted a position as director of criminal statistics at the Ministry of Justice in Paris. After 1894 he lectured in numerous peripheral institutions outside the university, and from 1900 until his death he held the chair of modern philosophy at the Collège de France.

In the last 2 years of his life Tarde confronted personally his rival Émile Durkheim in debate in Paris, climaxing a series of published exchanges in earlier years. Durkheim was the leading representative of sociology inside the French university system. His sociology embodied the rationality and impersonal discipline characteristic of university thinkers of the Third Republic. Tarde, in contrast, maintained a more supple and individualistic approach to social theory. Nevertheless, the two men were in agreement on fundamental conceptions.

Invention, Imitation, and Opposition

These core elements of Tarde's thought constitute three interrelated processes. Tarde saw "invention" as the ulti-

mate source of all human innovation and progress. The expansion of a given sector of society—economy, science, literature—is a function of the number and quality of creative ideas developed in that sector. Invention finds its source in creative associations in the minds of gifted individuals. Tarde stressed, however, the social factors leading to invention. A necessary rigidity of class lines insulates an elite from the populace; greater communication among creative individuals leads to mutual stimulation; cultural values, such as the adventurousness of the Spanish explorers in the Golden Age, could bring about discovery.

Many inventions, however, are not immediately accepted, hence the need to analyze the process of "imitation," through which certain creative ideas are diffused throughout a society. Tarde codified his ideas in what he called the laws of imitation. For example, the inventions most easily imitated are similar to those already institutionalized, and imitation tends to descend from social superior to social inferior.

The third process, "opposition," takes place when conflicting inventions encounter one another. These oppositions may be associated with social groups—nations, states, regions, social classes—or they may remain largely inside the minds of individuals. Such oppositions can generate invention in a creative mind, beginning again the threefold processes.

Substantive Issues

Tarde was firmly convinced of the necessity for quantifying his basic concepts and processes, and he sought to measure intensities of various opinions. He thus anticipated subsequent work on attitude measurement. He also urged the collection of information on industrial production, strikes, crime rates, church attendance, voting, and similar actions in order to gauge shifts in public opinion.

Tarde held that an elite was necessary to govern society and to maintain creative innovation, basic cultural patterns, and a minimal social and political stability. Crime, mental illness, and social deviance in general were seen by Tarde as frequent results of the disintegration of traditional elites. Migration, social mobility, and contact with deviant subcultures also further the tendencies toward deviance.

In opposition to Gustave Le Bon, who analyzed modern society in terms of crowds, Tarde emphasized the importance of the public. Crowds depend on physical proximity; publics derive from shared experiences of their members, who may not be in immediate physical proximity. Trade unions, political parties, and churches all support different publics, and Tarde saw these overlapping but distinct publics as major sources of flexibility in modern industrial societies.

Such technological developments as the telegraph, the telephone, mass-produced books, and the railroad were important in effecting the emergence of modern publics, but to newspapers fell a particularly crucial and independent role. Newspapers helped create public opinions and reinforce group loyalties. Unlike most later mass-society critics, Tarde was more optimistic about these developments for the maintenance of individual autonomy. This perspective derived in part from a greater emphasis on interpersonal contacts in channeling ideas and opinions in conjunction with the mass media. In this emphasis on personal contacts, Tarde anticipated subsequent work on the effects of mass communications.

Tarde had almost no immediate followers in France, with the exception of certain criminologists. In the United States, however, he exercised considerable influence on social psychologists, anthropologists, and sociologists.

Further Reading

A recent study of Tarde's work, including new translations from many of his works and a complete bibliography, is Terry N. Clark, ed., *Gabriel Tarde on Communication and Social Influence* (1969). ☐

Newton Booth Tarkington

The prolific writings of American author Newton Booth Tarkington (1869-1946) include the novels "Penrod" and "Seventeen" and many successful Broadway plays.

Booth Tarkington was born on July 29, 1869, the second child of lawyer John S. Tarkington and Elizabeth Booth Tarkington, in Indianapolis, Ind., a city which was always his home. His childhood was as happy and secure as his doting, well-educated, church-going, and prosperous parents could make it. He showed an early interest in writing and, like his fictional Penrod, produced his plays in the family hayloft. After mediocre achievement in high school he was sent to Phillips Exeter Academy.

The family suffered financial difficulties, so Tarkington entered first a local business college and then Purdue University to study art. When family fortunes revived, his mother insisted on sending him to Princeton, from which he could not receive a degree because he lacked the requisite classics background, but where he acquired a broad education and formed many associations which served him well during his life. He left Princeton in 1893 and spent the next 5 years writing, without much success in publishing his work. After *McClure's Magazine* serialized *The Gentleman from Indiana* in 1899, his novels and short stories appeared regularly in it and other magazines. In 1902 he married Louisa Fletcher and served one term in the Indiana Legislature as a conservative Republican. In 1903 he made his first trip to Europe, to which he returned regularly. A daughter was born in 1906.

From 1907 to 1910 Tarkington spent his time writing plays, mostly comedies such as *Your Humble Servant* and *Springtime* (both 1909), many in collaboration with Harry Wilson and Julian Street. Between 1914 and 1924 he wrote some plays and a trilogy of novels chronicling the rise and fall of family fortunes in midwestern industrial society. One of these, *The Magnificent Ambersons* (1918), was awarded the Pulitzer Prize in 1919. His best novel, *Alice Adams*

(1920), also received the Pulitzer Prize. During these years he produced his famous characters modeled on his own boyhood, the title character of *Penrod* (1914) and *Penrod and Sam* (1916) and Willie Baxter of *Seventeen* (1916). During both world wars he devoted much effort to writing Allied propaganda.

In 1911 his first wife divorced him, and in 1912 he married Susanah Robinson. They had no children; his daughter, Laurel, died in 1923. Tarkington began losing his eyesight in the late 1920s, and he was blind in his later years. He learned to dictate and continued to write. On May 19, 1946, he died in Indianapolis.

Further Reading

The first full-length critical biography of Tarkington is James Woodress, *Booth Tarkington: Gentleman from Indiana* (1955). Tarkington's novels are treated in Carl Van Doren, *The American Novel, 1789-1939* (1940), and Edward Wagenknecht, *Cavalcade of the American Novel* (1952).

Additional Sources

Mayberry, Susanah, *My amiable uncle: recollections about Booth Tarkington,* West Lafayette, Ind.: Purdue University Press, 1983.

Tarkington, Booth, *The world does move,* Westport, Conn.: Greenwood Press, 1976. ☐

Sir Banastre Tarleton

The notable successes of Sir Banastre Tarleton (1754-1833), English cavalry officer during the American Revolution, earned him the sobriquet "Bloody Tarleton."

Banastre Tarleton was the son of a wealthy Liverpool merchant, a sometime mayor of the city. After attending Oxford, young Tarleton entered the King's Dragoon Guards in 1775. He volunteered for service in the American colonies and gained his first military experience in Henry Clinton's unsuccessful venture against Charleston, S.C., in June 1776. Tarleton participated in the New York, Philadelphia, and Monmouth campaigns and was a member of the small party that captured American general Charles Lee in late 1776.

Accompanying Clinton on his second expedition against Charleston in 1780, Tarleton demonstrated his ability as commander of light infantry and dragoons. In a number of engagements he sometimes annihilated the opposition at little loss to his own men. After the bloody battle at Waxhaws, S.C., in May, Tarleton was regarded by the Revolutionaries as bloodthirsty and merciless. His reputation was largely a consequence of his tactics—usually a rapid cavalry charge followed by the energetic use of sabers and bayonets—and their impact upon the often poorly trained Americans.

Tarleton helped rout Horatio Gates's army at Camden, S.C., in August 1780 and surprised and destroyed the mixed forces of Thomas Sumter at Fishing Creek. Tarleton's defeat at Cowpens, S.C., in January 1781 materially weakened British forces in the South and raised rebel morale and encouraged resistance to the British. Subsequently, he won minor engagements and led a spectacular raid deep into Virginia in July. But, as he admitted, the results of this raid did not compensate for the loss of men and horses. He served with Lord Cornwallis in the Yorktown campaign, and their forces surrendered in October.

After being paroled, Tarleton returned to England in 1782. He served (with one year's exception) as a Liverpool member of the House of Commons from 1790 to 1812. Sometimes active in the army, he advanced gradually to become full general in 1812. He received a baronetcy in 1815.

Tarleton was involved with the actress Mary Robinson, former mistress of the Prince of Wales (the future George IV), for many years. He later married an illegitimate daughter of the Duke of Ancaster. Tarleton died on Jan. 25, 1833, in Leintwardine, Shropshire.

A historian of the American Revolution wrote of Tarleton: "As a leader of cavalry, he was unmatched on either side for alertness and rapidity of movement, dash, daring and vigor of attack."

Further Reading

Tarleton wrote *A History of the Campaigns of 1780 and 1781 in the Southern Provinces of North America* (1787; repr. 1968). A colorful popular biography of Tarleton and his mistress is Robert D. Bass, *The Green Dragoon: The Lives of Banastre Tarleton and Mary Robinson* (1957). Franklin and Mary Wickwire, *Cornwallis: The American Adventure* (1970), has extensive material on Tarleton's career. Accounts from the American side are best summarized in John R. Alden, *The South in the Revolution, 1763-1780* (1957). □

Alfred Tarski

The Polish-American mathematician and logician Alfred Tarski (1902-1983) is regarded as the cofounder of metamathematics and one of the founders of the discipline of semantics.

Alfred Tarski was born in Warsaw on Jan. 14, 1902. He taught at the Polish Pedagogical Institute from 1922 to 1925, and in 1924 he received his doctorate in mathematics from the University of Warsaw. He became an adjunct professor at the University of Warsaw in 1925. He married Maria Josephine Wilowski in 1929, and they had two children.

Tarski's mathematical contributions were noteworthy. In 1924 he collaborated with S. Banach in establishing the theorem on the decomposition of the sphere. In 1938 he presented an important paper on inaccessible cardinals and wrote another paper on the same topic in 1964 with H. J. Keisler. Tarski employed algebraic tools to treat metamathematical problems, as evident in his work on cylindric algebras (1961) written with Leon Henkin.

Like most mathematicians, Tarski simply accepted the assumptions of set theory as true. Further, he employed infinitistic set concepts in his work. Such procedures set his epistemology of mathematics apart from the major rival approaches—the formalism of David Hilbert and the intuitionism of L. E. J. Brouwer. Tarski's less restrictive methodology enabled him to introduce new concepts more freely.

Metamathematics studies formal theories. Tarski began working in the field of metamathematics in the 1920s. He presented an axiomatic theory of formal systems which capably embraces all the formal theories known up to 1930, and he was able to define such metamathematical notions as consistency, completeness, and independence. By 1935 he had presented a program for the description of all systems.

Tarski's most important achievement in logic is his formulation of the semantic method. Semantics is the study of the relations between terms (words or sentences) and their objects. He stated that his aim was "to construct . . . a materially adequate and formally correct definition of the term 'true sentence.'" His early work in semantics, applying his method to logic and mathematics, centered on formalized languages, and in this context he began his pioneering work on the theory of models. His papers on logic from 1923 to 1936, collected and translated by J. H. Woodger, were published as *Logic, Semantics, Metamathematics* (1956).

In 1939 Tarski went to the United States. He was a research associate at Harvard University from 1939 to 1941 and a visiting professor at the College of the City of New York in 1941. In 1941-1942 he was a member of the Institute for Advanced Study, Princeton, and in 1942 he joined the faculty of the University of California, Berkeley.

Pursuing his researches in semantics, Tarski furnished significant definitions not only of the term "logical consequence" but even of the term "definability." His paper "The Semantic Conception of Truth and the Foundations of Semantics" (1944), had considerable impact on epistemology outside mathematics and logic, and is regarded as one of the major versions of the correspondence theory of truth.

Tarski became a naturalized American citizen in 1945. He was a professor of mathematics at Berkeley after 1946, a member of the National Academy of Sciences, and a president of the Association of Symbolic Logic.

Tarski spent the rest of his academic career at the University of California, Berkeley, serving as professor from 1946 to 1968, and being named Professor Emeritus in 1968. He helped establish the Institute of Basic Research in Science at Berkeley from 1958-60. He received the Alfred Jurzykowski Foundation Award in 1966, and honorary doctorates from the Catholic University of Chile, the University of Marseille, and the University of Calgary.

His books included *Introduction to Logic* (English version, 1941), *Undecidable Theories* (with others, 1953),

Ordinal Algebras (1956), *The Theory of Modules* (editor, with others, 1965), and *Cylindric Algebras* (with others, 1971). He contributed more than 100 articles on logic and mathematics to professional journals during his career. In 1971, the University of California sponsored an international conference to discuss Tarski's influence and ideas on math, logic and philosophy, which Tarski himself attended.

Tarski was a visiting professor to the Catholic University of Chile during 1974-75. His last major work, with contributions from others, was *Cylindric Set Algebras,* published in 1981. He died in Berkeley, CA, on Oct. 26, 1983.

Further Reading

Little has been written about Tarski. For some background on his work see I. M. Bochenski, *A History of Formal Logic* (1956; trans. 1961), and William and Martha Kneale, *The Development of Logic* (1962). □

Niccolo Tartaglia

The Italian mathematician Niccolo Tartaglia (1500-1557) was the first person to apply mathematics to the solution of artillery problems.

Niccolo Tartaglia, born Niccolo Fontana in Brescia, was raised in poverty by his mother. His father was killed in the French occupation of the town in 1512, and it was then that Niccolo received a saber cut which was supposed to have been the cause of his stammering for the rest of his life. Because of this disability, he gave himself the nickname of Tartaglia, the "stutterer." He was a self-taught engineer, surveyor, and bookkeeper and is said to have used tombstones as slates because he was too poor to buy writing materials. As he grew to manhood, he demonstrated definite mathematical abilities, and he established himself as a teacher of mathematics in Venice in 1534.

"New Science"

Tartaglia's pioneer work on ballistics and falling bodies, *Nova scientia* (1537; *New Science*) represents an original attempt to establish theories for knowledge which had previously been known empirically. Leonardo da Vinci had studied the science of ballistics earlier, but his work was not nearly so comprehensive. In his analysis of the dynamics of moving bodies, Tartaglia differentiated types of motion. Thus, a freely falling body possesses a natural motion if it is an "evenly heavy" body; by this phrase it was understood that the object was made of dense material and was of a form which would not develop much air resistance. Such bodies fall at an accelerated rate, and each has its maximum velocity at the moment of impact with the earth. The natural motion of descent varies with the distance traveled by the body.

The other case is that of the violent motion characteristic of a projectile. Tartaglia opposed the prevailing view that a projectile was subject to an initial acceleration and

NICOLO TARTALEA (V.)

and that the force of propulsion of a shot guaranteed that it would move in a straight line for part of its flight. Some mathematicians agreed, but Tartaglia insisted that under the influences of violent and natural motion not even the smallest part of a missile's trajectory could be rectilinear.

In convincing his opponents, Tartaglia was less than successful, and they would accept only the triple-phase trajectory of his earlier work. Not until Galileo gave his mathematical proofs did scientists realize that all projectile motions are parabolic and hence trace a curved path.

Later Years

Tartaglia's *Treatise on Numbers and Measurements* (3 vols., 1556-1560) was the best work on arithmetic written in Italy in his century. He also was responsible for the first translations of the works of Euclid into Italian and for the first Latin edition of Archimedes. Tartaglia died in Venice on Dec. 13, 1557.

Further Reading

The reader who wishes to learn about Tartaglia and understand the Renaissance environment of science and mathematics should consult George Sarton, *Six Wings: Men of Science in the Renaissance* (1957). In addition, two books by Morris Kline are very helpful: *Mathematics in Western Culture* (1953) and *Mathematics and the Physical World* (1959). □

claimed that a violently propelled body starts to lose velocity as soon as it is detached from the propelling force. In his diagram of an evenly heavy body in violent motion, the first phase is a straight line upward at an angle, the second a curve, and the third a straight vertical line representing the body in a state of natural motion. He claimed that the curved part of the trajectory was the result of the body's own weight, but he recognized that this was theory inconsistent with his description of the first phase of violent motion. To save his theory, Tartaglia suggested that the whole path was actually curved but that the curvature was so slight as to be imperceptible.

In his discussions of violent motion, it is obvious that Tartaglia was still in harmony with the earlier "impetus" school of physics, which held that a quantity of force was impressed into a body when it was put in motion. Motion ceased when this force was exhausted, and a body in flight had its motion changed from violent to natural at that point.

"Diverse Problems and Inventions"

In his second book on the subject, *Quesiti et inventioni diverse* (1546; *Diverse Problems and Inventions*), Tartaglia made some important modifications in the theories he had expounded in *Nova scientia*. He stated that a body could possess violent and natural motion at the same time and that the only motion which could occur as a straight line was purely vertical. Thus, in the case of a cannonball, unless the cannon was fired straight upward, the projectile was bound to have a curved path. Artillerymen, who based their conclusions on field observations, insisted that this was not so

Giuseppe Tartini

Giuseppe Tartini (1692-1770) was an Italian violinist, composer, and theorist. He laid the foundation of the modern school of bowing in a manner more "singing" than that of his contemporaries.

Giuseppe Tartini was born in Pirano, Istria, on April 8, 1692. At his father's wish he studied for the priesthood. In 1710 he entered Padua University as a law student, where he remained until 1713, when he secretly married a niece of Cardinal Cornaro, which led to accusations of abduction. Leaving his wife in Padua, Tartini took refuge in a monastery at Assisi, where he practiced the violin and studied music theory. Here he wrote the *Trillo del diavolo* (Devil's Trill), an attempt to reconstruct a sonata he said the devil had played to him in a dream. In 1714 he discovered the "resultant" tone, a means for improving intonation. While this tone cannot be heard on a modern violin, it is clearly audible on an old one with its smaller bass-bar and other fittings.

In 1715 the cardinal withdrew his objections to the marriage, and Tartini and his wife were reunited in Padua. In 1716 Tartini heard the violinist Francesco Maria Veracini in Venice and was so impressed with his playing that he sent his wife to relatives so that he could continue his studies in Ancona.

Tartini was solo violinist and director at S. Antonio in Padua (1721-1723) and chamber musician in Prague to

Count Kinsky (1723-1725). Tartini returned to Padua in 1726. Two years later he founded a school of violin playing, which became known as the School of the Nations. Among his pupils was Maddalena Lombardi-Sirmen, to whom he addressed an important letter on performance which is mistakenly called the *Art of Bowing* by some writers. That title, however, refers to a series of variations Tartini wrote on a theme by Arcangelo Corelli. In the letter Tartini provides clear evidence that even the fastest notes were separated by a silence, which is not the case today.

Although Tartini's *Treatise on Music,* which dealt mainly with acoustics, was published in Padua (1754), it had less of an impact upon performance than his unpublished *Treatise on Ornamentation* (ca. 1750), which circulated widely in manuscript. Whole sections of it were incorporated into Leopold Mozart's *Violin School* (1756) without any acknowledgment, and it was published in French as *Treatise on the Ornaments of Music* (1771).

Tartini wrote about 150 concertos and 100 violin sonatas with figured-bass accompaniment. They combined the dignity and serenity of Corelli with a passion and grace all his own. Tartini's violin works were technically more complicated and advanced than those of his predecessors. He died in Padua on Feb. 26, 1770.

Further Reading

Tartini's *Treatise on the Ornaments of Music* was translated and edited by Sol Babitz (1949; reissued in enlarged form 1970). A contemporary account of Tartini is in Charles Burney, *An Eighteenth Century Musical Tour,* edited by Percy Scholes

(1959). He is discussed or referred to in Grace O'Brien, *The Golden Age of Italian Music* (1950); Siegmund Levarie, *Musical Italy Revisited* (1963); and David D. Boyden, *The History of Violin Playing* (1965). □

Abel Janszoon Tasman

Abel Janszoon Tasman (ca. 1603-1659) was a Dutch navigator who discovered Tasmania and New Zealand's South Island and charted the northwest Australian coastline.

Abel Tasman was born at Lutjegast near Groningen. After his second marriage, to Joanna Tierex in 1633, he became a ship's captain in the Dutch East India Company and lived in Batavia, capital of the new Dutch commercial empire in the East Indies.

A southern continent had long been thought to exist, but Spanish navigators who crossed the Pacific Ocean from the Americas had failed to locate it. After 1611 Dutch vessels which were blown east by the "roaring forties" after rounding the Cape of Good Hope occasionally touched the coastline of "Terra Australis" en route to Java. The Batavian authorities soon decided to find out whether this "South Land" had any commercial potential, and in 1642, Governor General Anton Van Diemen chose Tasman to command an expedition.

Tasman left Djakarta in August 1642 with two ships, the *Heemskerk* of 60 tons and the *Zeehaen* of 100 tons, carrying 110 men and sufficient supplies for 18 months. From Mauritius he sped east on latitude 44°S, discovering Van Diemen's Land (renamed Tasmania after 1856) on November 24. After crossing the Tasman Sea, he reached the west coast of Staeten Landt (New Zealand's South Island) on December 13, and a landing party was attacked by Maoris at Golden Bay on December 18. Tasman then sailed up the west coast of New Zealand's North Island to the Tonga and Fiji islands and returned to Batavia along the northern coast of New Guinea in June 1643 after a voyage lasting 10 months.

Although Tasman circumnavigated a new continent, he seldom sailed close enough to the coastline to chart it accurately on a map. Sent to establish a base in the Tonga Islands in 1644, he failed to find a passage through Torres Strait, and instead he surveyed the northwestern coastline of New Holland (Australia) from Cape York Peninsula to Willem's River on the Tropic of Capricorn.

On his return to Batavia after a 6-months' voyage, Tasman was promoted to commander. But his superiors were disappointed. Although he had discovered more about "the remaining unknown part of the terrestrial globe" than any of his predecessors, his accounts of a barren landscape and primitive natives banished all prospects of trade and settlement. Europeans consequently displayed little interest in the colonization of New Holland for more than a century.

In 1647 Tasman led a mission to the king of Siam. His reputation subsequently suffered owing to the way in which he commanded a fleet against the Spaniards in 1648-1649. Soon afterward he left the service of the East India Company and became a merchant. He died in Batavia, a wealthy man.

Further Reading

The study by Andrew Sharp, *The Voyages of Abel Janszoon Tasman* (1968), reproduces Tasman's journals together with an excellent commentary and contains a full account of his career. The standard work on the exploration of the whole region, J. C. Beaglehole, *The Exploration of the Pacific* (1934; 3d ed. 1966), includes a good chapter on Tasman. A copy of Tasman's map of 1644, showing New Guinea, Australia, and Tasmania as one land mass, was published by the Public Library of New South Wales in 1948.

Additional Sources

Allen, Oliver E., *The Pacific navigators,* Alexandria, VA: Time-Life Books; Morristown, N.J.: School and library distribution by Silver Burdett, 1980.

Slot, B., *Abel Tasman and the discovery of New Zealand,* Amsterdam: O. Cramwinckel, 1992. □

Torquato Tasso

The Italian poet Torquato Tasso (1544-1595), author of "Gerusalemme liberata," the greatest epic poem written in Italian, was the finest poet of his time.

Torquato Tasso born on March 11, 1544, was the son of Bernardo Tasso, a member of the Bergamasque nobility and the author of *Amadigi,* a retelling of the Spanish poem *Amadis de Gaula.* Torquato received his first instruction from a priest in his native Sorrento. When he was 8 years old, he entered a Jesuit school in Naples. Within 2 years he had made great progress in Latin and Greek. In 1554 he left his mother—who died 2 years later without the boy's seeing her again—to join his father in Rome. As secretary to the prince of Salerno, Ferrante Sanseverino, the elder Tasso had followed the prince into exile and poverty.

Torquato's early religious instruction and separation from his mother left indelible marks on his personality. Another lasting influence was an early exposure to aristocratic society. In 1557 his father's favor with Duke Guidolbaldo II of Urbino secured for Torquato a position as companion, or perhaps tutor, to the duke's son Francesco Maria, as well as access to instruction in the chivalric arts. Tasso's courtly tastes and ambitions, scarcely commensurate with his family's straitened circumstances, and coupled with the humanists' exalted ideal of the worth and importance of poets, led to some rebuffs and disappointments.

In 1559 Tasso assisted his father in Venice in the revision of *Amadigi,* as Bernardo attempted to modify his chivalric poem to make it conform to Aristotelian precepts for heroic poetry. Three years later Torquato's epicchivalric poem *Rinaldo,* written in 12 cantos, won him considerable acclaim. He was forced to abandon his studies at the University of Bologna after being charged with lampooning professors and fellow students. In 1564 the patronage of Prince Scipione Gonzaga permitted Tasso to continue his studies of literature and philosophy in the prince's Accademia degli Eterei (Academy of the Ethereal).

Court Poet

In 1565 Tasso began his long service as court poet to the Este family in Ferrara under the sponsorship of Cardinal Luigi d'Este. Six years later he was employed by the cardinal's brother, Duke Alfonso II of Ferrara. Tasso was very proud of the fact that, unlike several other poets at court, his sole duty was to write verse—a circumstance perhaps occasioned not only by his excellence as a poet but also by his lack of ability in practical matters.

Tasso's pastoral verse play, *Aminta,* written in 1573, was an immediate and enduring success. As an example of its genre, it is perhaps more nearly perfect than even his epic, *Gerusalemme liberata,* which appeared in 1575. Tasso wrote *Aminta* in 2 months during a period when he felt more dominant than dominated at court. Extremely musical, the play idealizes court life, projecting its civility and refined sensibility into a world of myth where only gentle sentiments can survive. Even the satyr, ostensibly the embodiment of animal lust, is a sensitive and madrigalizing creature. The expression of love in both dialogue and plot, combined with a rare lyricism and charming simplicity, created an unsurpassed example of the idyllic and hedonistic ideal of the Renaissance.

Madness and Imprisonment

From about 1576 until his death Tasso suffered from an intermittent psychosis. Fits of restlessness and depression alternated with period of paranoia and at times hallucinations. Although he continued to write profusely, taking too literally the humanists' vaunt that a great poet can confer immortality on whomever he chooses to exalt in verse, he never again displayed the verve that characterizes his two masterpieces. Suspicious of everyone around him, he insisted on being examined for heresy by the Inquisition. In June 1577 he was confined in a convent after attacking a servant with a knife. Escaping to his sister's home in Sorrento, he came disguised in tattered clothing and told her that her brother Torquato was dead, revealing his true identity only after her fainting had reassured him of her love.

Having received permission to rejoin the Este court, Tasso arrived in Ferrara in February 1579 during the celebration of Duke Alfonso's third marriage, to Margherita Gonzaga. Tasso's violent outburst against the duke after his arrival drew scant attention but resulted in the poet's prompt confinement to a hospital, which was protracted for 7 years. Not until the publication in 1895 of Angelo Solerti's exhaustive biography of Tasso was the romantic myth (which inspired Johann Wolfgang von Goethe's play *Torquato Tasso*, 1790) laid to rest that Tasso was imprisoned for having dared to love the duke's sister, Duchess Leonora d'Este. A contributory factor to the length of his imprisonment may have been Alfonso's fear that Tasso's doubts about his own and others' religious orthodoxy might play into the hands of the Roman Curia in its designs on the duchy of Ferrara. The duke was without direct heirs, and his mother, Renée of Valois, daughter of Louis XII, had been exiled from Ferrara in 1560 after her conversion to Calvinism.

During his hospital confinement Tasso continued to write a great deal. He proved quite docile after his eventual release, at first conditional, in 1586. A letter of his in 1581 complains of "human and diabolic disorders" and of hearing "shouts ... mocking laughter and animal voices ... whistles ... bells."

Last Years

Following his liberation Tasso traveled restlessly up and down the Italian peninsula. He thanked the monks of Monte Oliveto in Naples for their hospitality with an unfinished poem in octave verse on the origins of their monastery, *Il Monte Oliveto*, published posthumously in 1605. In his declining years he unashamedly sought recognition and monetary rewards for encomiastic poems written to prospective patrons. In 1591, during a period of illness in Mantua, he wrote the *Genealogia di casa Gonzaga* in octave verse for his longtime protector Scipione Gonzaga,

now a cardinal. In 1592 Tasso penned a poem in blank verse, *Le sette giornate del mondo creato* (The Seven Days of the World's Creation), published in 1607. His coronation as poet laureate had been proposed before death overtook him on April 25, 1595, in the monastery of S. Onofrio in Rome.

Tasso's almost 2,000 *rime* constitute a rich collection of sonnets, canzoni, madrigals, and stanzas. His 26 dialogues, inadequately studied, afford eloquent testimony to his vast classical erudition, as well as to his lively prose style. His approximately 1,700 extant letters provide ample documentation of his troubled life.

"Gerusalemme liberata"

During the half century following the writing of *Orlando furioso* by Ludovico Ariosto, two events exerted a strong influence on the next great narrative poem in Italian, Tasso's *Gerusalemme liberata*. The "rediscovery" of Aristotle's *Poetics* meant that Tasso had to write for a critically oriented public that expected the Aristotelian precepts of unity to be observed. The influence of the Council of Trent can be seen in Tasso's selection of the First Crusade, led by Godfrey of Bouillon, as his epic theme; in the religious inspiration provided to other characters by Peter the Hermit; and in the religious purification undergone by the invented epic hero, Rinaldo. Virgilian and Homeric reminiscences also abound in *Gerusalemme liberata*. Yet the passages of sustained greatness occur chiefly in the amorous episodes of Olindo and Sofronia, Tancredi and Clorinda, and Rinaldo and Armida. For this reason some critics have characterized Tasso as a brilliant poet with a flawed architecture. The epic warfare and the bland Goffredo (Godfrey) are perhaps less interesting for the modern reader than for Tasso's contemporaries, who well remembered the Battle of Lepanto (1571) and the Turkish threat to Europe.

Tasso unfortunately paid great heed to the carping critics of his poem, some of whom were members of the newly founded Accademia della Crusca and who had created a famous polemic about the relative merits of Ariosto and Tasso. After the publication of pirated editions of his poem during his imprisonment, Tasso rewrote it in an emasculated version as *Gerusalemme conquistata*, which is now read only by specialists. His ultimate answer to his critics lay not in the apologetic *Allegory* (1576) of *Gerusalemme liberata* but in his six discourses *Del poema eroico* (1594). An amplification of an earlier treatise, *Dell'arte poetica* (1570), these discourses attempted a definitive restatement of classical and Aristotelian poetics. The end of heroic poetry was "to profit men with the example of human actions"; its means of achieving its end was *il diletto* (pleasure). Readers must be able to recognize themselves in the characters.

Gerusalemme liberata, translated as *Jerusalem Delivered* into English octaves by Edward Fairfax in 1600, enjoyed a long vogue in England and throughout Europe.

Further Reading

Edward Fairfax's translation of Tasso's *Jerusalem Delivered* was republished with an introduction by John Charles Nelson in

1963. A useful critical study of Tasso's work and life is C. P. Brand, *Torquato Tasso: A Study of the Poet and of His Contribution to English Literature* (1965). See also Cecil Maurice Bowra, *From Virgil to Milton* (1945). □

Allen Tate

Allen Tate (1899-1979), American poet, critic, biographer, and editor, was a founder and editor of the *Fugitive*. John Crowe Ransom, Robert Penn Warren, and Cleanth Brooks were also part of the Fugitive group, and they and Tate formulated the New Critical poetic theories that arose out of the early work of T. S. Eliot and Ezra Pound.

Tate's earliest publications included the interpretative biographies *Stonewall Jackson* (1928) and *Jefferson Davis* (1929). His first collection of verse, *Poems, 1928-31,* was published in 1932. While teaching English literature at several colleges, including Princeton, he held the chair of poetry at the Library of Congress from 1934 to 1944. He edited the *Sewanee Review* from 1944 to 1946. After 1951 he taught English literature at the University of Minnesota and lectured extensively at universities throughout the country.

Tate's creative work always echoed his preoccupations as a southerner. His penetrating and original novel, *The Fathers* (1938), which is experimental in form and style and in many ways similar to some of William Faulkner's fiction, is a tortured exploration of the guilt and moral significance of Tate's heritage as a son of the Confederacy.

In typical modernist fashion, Tate was determined in his poetry to be "unromantic." His poetic masterpiece, the "Ode to the Confederate Dead" (1928), is an elegy characterized by the density of its imagery, irony, and irresolvable ambiguity. The conclusion of the "Ode" offers no simple solution to the problems it presents but does suggest that the Confederacy, and, by implication, all of mankind, was its own victim in the Civil War. Most of his other poems are "accomplished" examples of romantic irony within a narrow range of feeling. Their images are original and exhibit a great deal of formal dexterity, but the poems cannot compare in substance with the best work of Robert Penn Warren.

Poems, 1922-47 (1948) and *Poems* (1961) include most of Tate's verse. His career was largely sustained by the perception and intelligence of such critical works as *Reactionary Essays on Poetry and Ideas* (1936), *On the Limits of Poetry* (1948), and *The Man of Letters in the Modern World* (1955). His *Collected Essays* was published in 1959 and *Essays of Four Decades* in 1969.

Tate converted to Catholicism in 1950, and some of his writing reflected this. A former student of Tate's, Richard Margolis, wrote in the *New Leader,* "Like his faith, Tate's verse carried plenty of doctrinal punch along with a load of ambiguity; often at its center lurked a mystery not to be solved. One could say the same for the man."

Tate married the writer Caroline Gordon, and they collaborated on some works, including a collection of short stories, *House of Fiction.* They were divorced, but later remarried, and finally divorced a second time. Tate then married an ex-nun, Helen Heinz.

Tate moved to Monteagle, TN, in 1966, where he remained until his death in 1979. While in Tennessee, he spent his time writing and visiting with old friends from his alma mater Vanderbilt, as well as the University of the South. He also kept in touch with the *Sewanee Review,* although not directly involved with it. During his final years, he visited various college campuses, giving lectures on literature and politics. He also corresponded regularly with many famous literary friends, creating a wealth of personal papers.

Tate died in Nashville, TN, on Feb. 9, 1979. During his lifetime, he published 20 books and received many literary honors, including the Bollingen Prize for poetry.

Further Reading

Studies of Tate and his work include Willard B. Arnold, *The Social Ideas of Allen Tate* (1955); George Hemphill, *Allen Tate* (1964); the section on him in Hyatt H. Waggoner, *American Poets, from the Puritans to the Present* (1968); Walter Sullivan, *Allen Tate: A Recollection* (1988). □

Vladimir Evgrafovich Tatlin

Vladimir Evgrafovich Tatlin (1885-1953) was a Russian avant garde artist whose model of the "Monument to the Third International" remains the main symbol of Constructivism.

In years to come, Vladimir Tatlin may be viewed as one of the greatest visionary artists of the 20th century. He was born in Moscow and grew up in Kharkov. His father was a railway engineer and his mother a poet, their professions and outlook representative of some of the new middle-class mobility found in late 19th-century Russia.

In 1902 Tatlin "ran away to sea" for a year and traveled abroad in Egypt, Turkey, Syria, and Libya. From the end of 1902 to 1904 he attended the Moscow School of Painting, Sculpture, and Architecture. He continued his art studies from 1904 to 1910 at the Penza Art School and studied under Goroshkin-Sorokopudov and the lesser-known *Peredvizhnik* ("Wanderers"-social realist) Afanasyev. Tatlin received his diploma in 1908 as a painter. In Penza, Tatlin had established a close relationship with the Rayonist painter Mikhail Larionov and his wife, the primitivist and cubo-futurist painter Natalia Goncharova. He exhibited with them in Odessa in December 1910 in the Second Izbedskii Salon exhibition and in "The Donkey's Tail" Exhibition in Moscow, April 1912. Larionov had a significant impact on Tatlin, especially in steering the young artist toward Russian themes.

Tatlin also established close ties with the painter David Burlyuk and the poet Khlebnikov. At the same time, however, he began to move in other directions. He exhibited with the St. Petersburg "Union of Youth" group in 1911 and in the Knave of Diamonds Exhibition in 1913, which also included David and Vladimir Burlyuk, Kazimir Malevich, Wassily Kandinsky, Robert Falk, Alexandra Exter, Ilya Mashkov, and others. Tatlin's early works were often primitive, loose in style, and focused on form, with little attention paid to background.

Tatlin's most famous early work was the painting *The Fishmonger* (1911), which emphasizes a great swirl of arcs and created a great deal of movement on the canvas. One of the results of the Knave of Diamonds Exhibition was an intensive debate that ensued between David Burlyuk, who was strongly supportive of Western art, and Natalia Goncharova, who favored Russian themes. The debate led to a split and the formation of "The Donkey's Tail," a rival group emphasizing Russian and folk idioms, with which Tatlin identified.

After 1910 Tatlin returned to the Moscow School of Painting to study with Korovin and Serov, Russian Post-Impressionist painters. During 1911 Tatlin organized a teaching studio in Moscow which provided him the opportunity to meet avant garde artists Alexander Vesnin and Liubov Popova. Tatlin also exhibited in "The World of Art" show in 1912-1913 and in "Contemporary Painting" from 1912 to 1914. He became a book illustrator for futurist works by Kruchenykh, Khlebnikov, and Mayakovsky.

Tatlin's works of this period include the painting *Nude* (1913), which marks a blend of Western avant garde and Russian tradition. In the realm of theatrical set design, Tatlin worked on Glinka's opera *A Life for the Tsar* and Tomahsevsky's play *Tsar Maximillian and his unruly son Adolf*. Both were strong in folk motif and abstraction.

In 1913 Tatlin went to Paris; met Picasso, Lipchitz, and Archipenko; and, upon his return to Russia, began experimenting in sculpture. Picasso's cubist reliefs had a significant impact upon him. The result was a series of three-dimensional painterly reliefs. These were displayed at the "First Exhibition of Painterly Reliefs" at his studio in 1914 and at the "Tramway V" Exhibition in Petrograd (now St. Petersburg) in 1915. From painterly reliefs, Tatlin moved into "counter-reliefs," which were exhibited at the exhibition "0.10" in 1916 in Petrograd and "The Store" in Moscow during the same year. Tatlin constantly experimented with the idea of extending space, as real forms came forward from a solid base. Composition became a process of construction, and construction itself was related to the materials employed in the creative process. This new type of "constructivist" art was viewed as oriented toward materials, and hence away from personal taste and toward an impersonal role for the artist. On the issue of form and construction, Tatlin moved from "counter-reliefs" executed on paper to "corner-reliefs," which were sculptures suspended in the corners of rooms.

After the Russian Revolution, Tatlin became the head of the Moscow branch of IZO Narkompros (Visual Arts Department of the Commissariat for People's Enlightenment). One of his charges was to develop Lenin's Plan for Monumental Propaganda. This provided the inspiration for the "Monument to the Third International." Tatlin also taught at the Moscow State Free Art Studios and from 1919 to 1921 in Petrograd at the State Free Art Studios. He opened his own studio, known as the Studio of Volume, Material, and Construction.

During November 1920 Tatlin exhibited a model of the "Monument to the Third International" in Petrograd at the former Academy of Arts. A month later the model was moved to Moscow for exhibition at the 8th Congress of the Soviets. Although the monument, designed to straddle the Neva River in Petrograd, was never built, it has remained an inspiration for monumental architecture and remains the main symbol of Constructivism. The basic idea of the structure, according to Nikolai Punin, one of Tatlin's associates, was to create a monumental construction utilizing architectural, sculptural, and painterly principles. It was dedicated to the branch of the new government designed to promote international revolution. The monument was a soaring and spiral-like skeletal steel structure, sometimes called a modern Tower of Babel. Within the steel structure were three large glass spaces held in place by a complex system of pivots and mechanisms which allowed them to move at different speeds. The lower space, a cube, was a building for the International's annual meetings and rotated once a year. The second building was a pyramid, which revolved at one revolution a month. This was designed to house the executive divisions and secretariat of the International. The upper building, a cylinder, rotated once a day and was to house means of disseminating information—newspapers, printshops, telegraph, large projectors, radio transmitters, and viewing screens. The tower itself was both sculpture and architecture.

In 1921 Tatlin attempted to design new types of workshops and was subsequently instrumental in setting up Petrograd GINKhUK (State Institute for Artistic Culture) and directed the Department of Material Culture, which was concerned with development of new materials and their application to the new social organization. Tatlin designed new workers' clothing and an oven.

In May 1923 Tatlin produced Khebnikov's play *Zangezi.* This enterprise marked a unique achievement, as Tatlin worked with the phonetician Lev Yakubinsky in an attempt to unify material constructions and word constructions in a theater environment. Tatlin wrote that "the word itself is a building unit, material a unit of organized space." The fusing of the two elements was supposed to create an architectural state on the state, a revolutionary event.

During the period 1925 to 1927 Tatlin moved to Kiev and worked at the Department of Theater, Cinema, and Photography at the Kiev Art School. In 1927 he returned to Moscow to work at VkhUTEIN (Higher State Artistic and Technical Institute) and taught construction of everyday objects. From 1930 to 1933 Tatlin worked in his Scientific and Experimental Laboratory under Narkompros. Here, he conceived his "flying machine project," *Letatlin,* which was reminiscent of Da Vinci's "Flying Machine," the name being taken partially from his own and from the Russian *letat,* "to fly." Tatlin, however, was criticized highly by new official critics and artists for this research, as it was viewed as a solo venture, opposed to the cooperative spirit of the new "official" Socialist Realism. Tatlin, however, defended his gliders as an experimental work that promoted thinking about new variations in forms, which avoided the monotony of contemporary manufactured goods. He indicated that the airplane was the consummate object for artistic composition, since it was a complicated form that would become an everyday object. During 1932 and 1933 and variants of *Letatlin* were exhibited at the Pushkin Museum in Moscow.

By the end of the 1930s Tatlin returned to figurative painting and spent most of his time in theater design. He was discredited after 1933, when Socialist Realism became the guiding philosophy for Soviet art. Unfortunately, very few of his artistic constructions survived and most that have been exhibited recently have been re-creations from original drawings. A new model of the "Monument to the Third International" was built for the Los Angeles County Museum and Smithsonian Institution's Constructivist show of 1980.

Tatlin died in 1953 from food poisoning, and his passing was unheralded. He is now being rediscovered in his native country, as *glasnost's* attempt to analyze the past has led to a close examination of the avant garde before 1933.

Further Reading

The most comprehensive works on Tatlin are John Milner, *Vladimir Tatlin and the Russian Avant Garde* (1983) and *Russian Revolutionary Art* (1979), and Larissa Alekseevna Zhadova, *Tatlin* (1989).
Works that blend Tatlin's ideas on art into the general framework of Constructivism and the avant garde include Stephen Bann (editor), *The Tradition of Constructivism* (1972); Stephanie Barron and Maurice Tuchman (editors), *The Avant Garde in Russia, 1910-1930* (1980); John Bowlt (editor), *Russian Art of the Avant Garde: Theory and Criticism* (1973); Christina Lodder, *Russian Constructivism* (1983); and Kestutis Paul Zygas, *Form Follows Form: Source Imagery of Constructive Architecture, 1917-1925* (1981).

Additional Sources

Milner, John, *Vladimir Tatlin and the Russian avant-garde,* New Haven: Yale University Press, 1983. □

Helen Brooke Taussig

Physician Helen Brooke Taussig discovered a surgical procedure for treating "blue babies." She proved that "blue babies" died of insufficient circulation rather than cardiac arrest, as had been previously thought.

Physician and cardiologist Helen Brooke Taussig spent her career as the head of the Children's Heart Clinic at Johns Hopkins University. In the course of her work with young children, she discovered that cyanotic infants—known as "blue-babies"—died of insufficient circulation to the lungs, not of cardiac arrest, as had been thought. She and colleague Dr. Alfred Blalock developed a surgical procedure, the Blalock-Taussig shunt, to correct the problem. First used in 1944, the Blalock-Taussig shunt has saved the lives of thousands of children. In 1961, after investigating reports of numerous birth defects in Germany, Taussig determined that the cause was use of the drug Thalidomide, and it was her intervention that prevented Thalidomide from being sold in the United States. She was the recipient of numerous honorary degrees and awards, including the Medal of Freedom in 1964 and the 1977 National Medal of Science.

Taussig was born on May 24, 1898, in Cambridge, Massachusetts, the youngest of four children of well-known Harvard economist Frank William Taussig. Her mother, Edith Guild Taussig, who had attended Radcliffe College and was interested in the natural sciences, died of tuberculosis when Helen was eleven years old. Like her mother, Taussig attended Radcliffe, where she played championship tennis. However, wishing to be further removed from the shadow of her well-known father, she transferred to the University of California at Berkeley, where she earned her B.A. in 1921.

Having decided on a career in medicine, Taussig's educational choices were limited by sex discrimination.

Taussig began her studies of congenital heart disease at the Pediatric Cardiac Clinic in 1930. Over the years she examined and treated hundreds of children whose hearts were damaged by rheumatic fever, as well as those with congenital heart disease. She developed new observational methods that led to a new understanding of pediatric heart problems. First Taussig became accomplished in the use of the fluoroscope, a new instrument which passed x-ray beams through the body and projected an image of the heart, lungs, and major arteries onto a florescent screen. Second, she used the electrocardiograph which makes a graphic record of the heart's movements. Third, she became expert at diagnosis through physical examination—made more complex in her case due to the fact that Taussig was somewhat deaf as a result of childhood whooping cough and unable to use a stethoscope, thereby necessitating her reliance on visual examination.

Taussig gradually realized that the blueness of cyanotic children was the result of insufficient oxygen in the blood. In the normal heart, bluish blood from the periphery of the body enters the right atrium (upper receiving chamber) of the heart and then goes to the right ventricle (the lower pumping chamber) to be pumped through a major artery to the lungs. In the lungs, the blood receives a new supply of oxygen that changes its color to bright red. Then it returns to the heart, entering the left atrium and descending to the left ventricle which pumps it to the rest of the body. The two sides of the heart are kept separate by a wall called the septum. Taussig discovered that the insufficient oxygen level of the blood of "blue-babies" was usually the result of either a leaking septum or an overly narrow artery leading from the left ventricle to the lungs. Although at that time surgeons were unable enter the heart to repair the septum surgically, Taussig believed that it might be possible either to repair the artery, or to attach a new vessel that would perform the same function.

She persuaded Dr. Alfred Blalock, the chairman of the Hopkins Department of Surgery, to work on the problem. Blalock was a vascular surgeon who had done experimental research on an artificial artery with the assistance of long-time associate Vivian Thomas. Accepting Taussig's challenge, Blalock set Thomas to work on the technical problems. During the next year and a half, Thomas developed the technical procedures, using about two hundred dogs as experimental animals. In 1944, although earlier than Thomas had planned, the technique was tried on a human infant, a desperately ill patient of Taussig's named Eileen Saxon. With Taussig as an observer and Thomas standing by to give advice concerning the correct suturing of the artery, Blalock performed the surgery successfully. A branch of the aorta that normally went to the infant's arm was connected to the lungs. In the years that followed, the procedure, known as the Blalock-Taussig shunt, saved the lives of thousands of cyanotic children.

The fame of the Pediatric Cardiac Clinic grew rapidly. As they became flooded with patients, Blalock and Taussig developed team methods for dealing with the different phases of treatment. Their management methods became the model for many cardiac centers, as well as other kinds of

Although she began her studies at Harvard University, the medical school did not admit women to its regular curriculum, and would not begin to do so until 1945. Taussig enrolled in Harvard's School of Public Health, where, like other women, she was permitted to take courses but not allowed to work toward obtaining a degree. She also was permitted to study histology as a special student in the medical school. After her studies at Harvard, Taussig took anatomy at nearby Boston University. There, her anatomy professor, Alexander Begg, suggested that she apply herself to the study of the heart, which she did. Also following Begg's advice, Taussig submitted her application to attend the medical school at Johns Hopkins University, where she was accepted.

During her four years of study at Johns Hopkins Medical School, Taussig worked at the Hopkins Heart Station. After receiving her M.D. in 1927, she spent another year there as a fellow, followed by an additional year and a half there as a pediatric intern. During this time, Taussig served as an attending physician at the recently established Pediatric Cardiac Clinic. The new chair of pediatrics, Edwards A. Park, recognized Taussig's abilities and became her mentor. Upon the completion of her pediatric internship in 1930, she was appointed physician-in-charge of the Pediatric Cardiac Clinic in the Harriet Lane Home, the children's division at Johns Hopkins. Taussig would spend her entire career at Johns Hopkins until her retirement in 1963. In 1946 she was appointed associate professor of pediatrics, and was promoted to full professor in 1959, the first woman in the history of the Medical School to hold that title.

medical care. Taussig's growing reputation also brought her numerous students. She trained a whole generation of pediatric cardiologists and wrote the standard textbook of the field, *Congenital Malformations of the Heart,* first published in 1947. In addition to her work in congenital heart disease, she carried out research on rheumatic fever, the leading cause of heart problems in children. Taussig is considered the founder of the specialty of pediatric cardiology. Neither her scientific and clinical acumen, nor her enormously demanding schedule, ever prevented Taussig from being a warm, compassionate physician to her many patients and their families. She followed her patients for years, even after her own retirement. She never found it necessary to distance herself from the critically-ill children that she treated, or from their parents. Her warmth and ability to see and treat people as individuals has been recalled by many who knew her.

In the 1950s Taussig served on numerous national and international committees. In 1962, a German graduate of her training program told her of the striking increase in his country of phocomelia, a rare congenital defect in which infants were born with severely deformed limbs. The defect was thought, but not yet proven, to be associated with a popular sedative called Contergan that was sold throughout Germany and other European countries and often taken by women to counteract nausea during early pregnancy. Taussig decided to investigate for herself and spent six weeks in Germany visiting clinics, examining babies with the abnormalities, and interviewing their doctors and mothers. She noted the absence of such birth defect in the infants of American soldiers living at U.S. military installations in Germany where the drug was banned. But there was one exception: a baby whose mother had gone off the post to obtain Contergan was born severely deformed. Taussig's testimony was instrumental in the U.S. Food and Drug Administration's rejection of the application from the William S. Merrell Company to market the drug they renamed Thalidomide in the United States.

Although Taussig formally retired in 1963, she remained deeply involved as a scientist, a clinician, and an activist in causes that affected the health of children. She fought for the right of scientists to use animals in experimental studies and advocated that women in the United States be able to choose to terminate their pregnancies through abortion. She was the author of a hundred major scientific publications, forty-one of which were written after her retirement. She occupied a home in Baltimore, often visited by guests and friends, and owned the cottage in Cape Cod where she had spent many happy childhood summers. Taussig enjoyed fishing, swimming, and gardening, as well as caring for her many pets. In the late 1970s she moved to a retirement community near Philadelphia. She became interested in the embryological causes of congenital heart defects and had begun a study of the hearts of birds when, on May 21, 1986, while driving some of her fellow retirees to vote in a primary election, she was killed in an automobile accident at the age of 87.

Further Reading

Baldwin, Joyce, *To Heal the Heart of A Child: Helen Taussig, M.D.* (juvenile), Walker, 1992.
Nuland, Sherwin B., *Doctors: The Biography of Medicine,* Knopf, 1988, pp. 422–456.
Harvey, W. Proctor, "A Conversation with Helen Taussig," in *Medical Times,* Volume 106, November, 1978, pp. 28–44. □

Richard Henry Tawney

The British economic historian and social philosopher Richard Henry Tawney (1880-1962) was an influential Fabian socialist and an adviser to governments.

Richard Tawney was born in Calcutta, India, on Nov. 30, 1880, the son of a distinguished civil servant and Sanskrit scholar. Educated at Rugby and Balliol College, Oxford, he graduated in classics in 1903 and then lived and worked at Toynbee Hall settlement in London. From 1906 to 1908 he lectured in economics at Glasgow University and then was a pioneer teacher for the Oxford University Tutorial Classes Committee until the outbreak of war in 1914. He was wounded at the Battle of the Somme in 1916.

Tawney was an ardent supporter of the Workers' Educational Association, serving as a member of its executive (1905) and president (1928-1944). His adult teaching, especially at Rochdale, is now legendary. His first seminal work of scholarship was *The Agrarian Problem in the Sixteenth Century* (1912), dedicated to his tutorial classes, in which he traced the impact of commercialism on English agriculture and society.

In 1918 Tawney became a fellow of Balliol. The following year he was appointed reader in economic history at the London School of Economics; he was professor of economic history there from 1931 to 1949. He was a founder member and later president of the Economic History Society and, for 7 years, joint editor of its *Review.* His editions of economic documents became standard sources for students, as did his two studies of economic morality and practice in Tudor and Stuart England: his edition of Thomas Wilson's *Discourse upon Usury* (1925) and his classic *Religion and the Rise of Capitalism* (1926). Like his other major works, including *The Rise of the Gentry* (1954), *Religion and the Rise of Capitalism* was substantially criticized by later scholars, and its conclusions were later modified. Nevertheless, its power and seminal influence were universally recognized, so much so that the 17th century is often described as "Tawney's century." In 1958 he published his long-awaited study *Lionel Cranfield: Business and Politics under James I,* which was generally acclaimed by scholars.

Throughout Tawney's life, scholarship and action were interconnected. His 1914 monograph on wage rates in the chain-making industry led to his presidency of the Chain-Making Trade Board (1919-1922). In 1919 he was a leading figure on the Sankey Coal Commission, and subsequently he served as adviser on educational matters to the Labour party, member of the Consultative Committee of the Board of Education and the Cotton Trade Conciliation Board, and Labour attaché at the British embassy in Washington during World War II. His ideas exerted a profound influence on the philosophy of the British left. His expanded Fabian Society pamphlet *The Acquisitive Society* (1922) and his essay "Equality" (1931) contained severe moral condemnations of the capitalist economic and social system.

Tawney possessed a rare combination of qualities: humility, personal asceticism bordering on eccentricity, exceptional literary skills, deep scholarship, and a rare capacity to inspire his fellowmen with ideals of humanity and social justice. He died in London on Jan. 16, 1962.

Further Reading

There is no book on Tawney's life and work. A chapter on him by W. H. Nelson is in Herman Ausubel, J. Bartlet Brebner, and Erling M. Hunt, eds., *Some Modern Historians of Britain* (1951). Tawney is also discussed in W. H. B. Court, *Scarcity and Choice in History* (1970).

Additional Sources

Terrill, Ross, *R. H. Tawney and his times: socialism as fellowship,* London: Deutsch, 1974.

Wright, Anthony, *R.H. Tawney,* Manchester, UK: Manchester University Press, 1987. □

Brook Taylor

The English mathematician Brook Taylor (1685-1731) is best known for the Taylor series and contributions to the theory of finite differences.

Brook Taylor was born at Edmonton on Aug. 18, 1685, the eldest son of John and Olivia Taylor. After instruction at home in classics and mathematics he entered St. John's College, Cambridge, where he graduated in law in 1709, receiving the doctorate in 1714. Two years earlier he was elected a fellow of the Royal Society; he served as first secretary from 1714 to 1718 and contributed several papers to the *Philosophical Transactions.* Taylor's first marriage, in 1721, ended when his wife died in childbirth. In 1725 he married again and 4 years later inherited his father's estate in Kent. The death of his second wife the following year in giving birth to his daughter, Elizabeth, affected him deeply. He died on Dec. 29, 1731, in London.

The famous Taylor series was printed for the first time in the *Methodus incrementorum directa et inversa* (1715), although there is evidence that Gottfried Wilhelm Leibniz and Isaac Newton had known the result earlier. The series expresses the value of a function in the neighborhood of a point in terms of the derivatives at the point. Taylor derived the series by taking the limiting case of the general finite difference formula, but he failed to consider the problem of convergence. He specifically mentioned the case x = 0,

which is often known as Maclaurin's series. Joseph Louis Lagrange was the first to recognize fully the importance of the Taylor series, and the first correct proof was given by Augustin Louis Cauchy.

Taylor's book was the first treatise on the method of finite differences. Although finite differences were widely used in interpolation in the 17th century, it was Taylor who developed the method into a new branch of mathematics, notably by applying it to the determination of the frequency and form of a vibrating string.

In 1717 Taylor applied his series to the solution of numerical equations, observing that the method could be used to solve transcendental equations. Other contributions to the calculus included consideration of change of variable, the first singular solution of a differential equation, and the derivation of the differential equation relating to atmospheric refraction. He also contributed a solution to the problem of the center of oscillation.

In 1715 Taylor published his *Linear Perspective,* followed in 1719 by *New Principles of Linear Perspective.* These works contained the first general statement of the principle of vanishing points. In his later years he became interested in philosophy, writing *Contemplatio philosophica,* which was printed and circulated privately in 1793.

Further Reading

A good biography, written by Taylor's grandson, William Young, is prefixed to Taylor's *Contemplatio philosophica* (1793). On

the Taylor series and finite differences see the chapter on data analysis in Cornelius Lanczos, *Applied Analysis* (1957). □

Edward Taylor

Edward Taylor (ca. 1642-1729), Puritan poet and minister, was one of the finest literary artists of colonial America.

Born in England, highly educated, and living a rather isolated frontier life at Westfield, Mass., Edward Taylor appears to have been outside the major developments in Puritan New England. His theology resembled that of his orthodox Boston contemporaries Michael Wigglesworth, Increase and Cotton Mather, and his lifelong friend Samuel Sewall, more than that of Solomon Stoddard, minister at nearby Northampton, whose liberal views on church membership Taylor strongly disapproved. He disliked James II and his colonial appointment Governor Andros, and he was heartened by the Revolution of 1688. As a strict Congregationalist, Taylor opposed the Plan of Union between Congregational and Presbyterian churches. His poetry recalls the somewhat older, baroque English tradition of George Herbert and Richard Crashaw.

Little is known about Taylor's early life. The date and exact place of his birth are uncertain. Born and raised in Leicestershire near Coventry, in a Nonconformist home, he left England because, as a devout Puritan, he felt unable to comply with the Act of Uniformity. He was in his mid-20s when he emigrated to America in 1668 and already embarked on a career in the ministry. His letters of introduction to Increase Mather and others, and his admission to Harvard in advanced standing, indicate that he was well educated. He was one of four speakers at his commencement in 1671.

Taylor accepted a call to be minister at Westfield, where he spent the rest of his life. In 1675 Westfield was threatened by Indian invasion. The village suffered no major attack, but not until 1679, when hostilities ceased, was a church formally organized. He had led in the preparations for the town's defense and had also become its teacher and physician. He drafted the creed for the new church and alone had responsibility for it in the early years.

Man of Letters

Taylor compiled a distinguished library. Of its approximately 200 volumes many were copied by hand from books he was too poor to buy. His grandson Ezra Stiles, later president of Yale, described him as a classical scholar, master of three ancient languages, and an able historian, and as "A man of small stature, but firm; of quick Passions, yet serious and grave." Stiles inherited Taylor's library and carried out his wish that the poetry not be published. Scarcely known in its own day, Taylor's work was bequeathed to Yale University by a descendant in 1883. Not until 1939 was a significant selection of poems published, edited by Thomas H. Johnson.

One of Taylor's poems is a moving and complex elegy for his first wife, Elizabeth Fitch, whom he married in 1674; she bore eight children and died in 1689. In 1692 he married Ruth Willys; they had six children.

Not usually autobiographical, Taylor's poems fall into four groups. The first, "God's Determinations Touching His Elect," is a long dramatic allegory written probably before 1690. Present critical attention centers on the second group, "Preparatory Meditations before My Approach to the Lord's Supper," 217 poems written between 1682 and 1725. The third group, his miscellaneous poems, includes some of the best-loved short pieces, in which familiar subjects are used to express metaphysical themes. The last category is the *Metrical History,* an unpublished poem over 430 manuscript pages long, which describes the history of the Protestant church.

Poetic Style

Although Taylor's poetical structures are traditional in their basic allegory, their intricacy and dynamics are deeply original. His lines move to a rough cadence; the verbs are strong, the imagery vigorous, the nouns often plain. In the celebrated preface to "God's determination," for example, he portrays God as a master builder who "Blew the Bellow of his Furnace Vast," constructed the world, and "in his Bowling Alley bowled the Sun."

Taylor's art glorifies Christian experience. Like a sermon, a poem for Taylor was a means of renewing one's awareness of his spiritual condition. Of course, conversion itself depended on the divine infusion of grace. But, once converted, the saint could, by means of meditation, recall and refresh that experience and prepare again to reenact his union with Christ at the Lord's Supper. Taylor never tired of celebrating that union; for him it was the central event in history as well as the central experience of an individual life. Frequently his meditations begin with the poet's feeling impotent and depressed; his words seem awkward and artificial. But focusing on a passage from Scripture, often from Psalms or the Song of Songs, unlocks the poet's powers of love and praise.

Taylor used biblical references to the fullest advantage. He depended on a traditional system of biblical analogues created by early Christian exegetes and widely used by later writers (Milton and George Herbert among them). Certain Old Testament stories were said to prefigure the life of Christ: Jonah and the whale, for example, typified Christ's death and resurrection, as did Abraham's sacrifice. Circumcision prefigured baptism; the Hebrew Passover, the Lord's Supper; and so forth. A meditation centered, for example, on the "wine from Canaans Vineyard" suggests communion and themes of suffering and grace, since the wine is Christ's blood. But it also implies Christ's second coming, since Canaan, the Promised Land, is the type of Christ's kingdom on earth described in Revelations. Thus Taylor here refers simultaneously to the community of saints joined with Christ in the millennium and the continuous communion of the individual with a redemptive Christ here and now.

A similar cluster of themes constitutes the basis of all Taylor's work, be it meditation, sermon, history, verse dialogue, or scientific treatise. *Christographia* is a collection of sermons about the human and divine natures of Christ. Like the Mathers, but with a view of Christ's coming that emphasized His love rather than His judgment, Taylor recorded divine providences and unusual natural phenomena. He investigated and compiled lore on the medicinal properties of natural things—a work of use of him as a physician.

As an elderly, physically challenged man, resisting the removal of his church to a new meeting house on a new site, Taylor left much in his verse unpolished and uncorrected. He seems not to have intended his poetry for the public. Evaluation of his work awaits scholarly clarification of the role of the Puritan poet in America and of Taylor's intentions for his work.

Further Reading

Donald E. Stanford, ed., *The Poems of Edward Taylor* (1960), contains the important poems, the complete text of the "Preparatory Meditations," and valuable introductions to the poetry by Louis L. Martz and by Stanford. The authoritative biography of Taylor is Norman S. Grabo, *Edward Taylor* (1962). Recommended for its analysis of the literature of the period is Kenneth B. Murdock, *Literature and Theology in Colonial New England* (1949).

Additional Sources

Keller, Karl, *The example of Edward Taylor,* Amherst: University of Massachusetts Press, 1975. □

Edward Plunket Taylor

Edward Plunket Taylor was a Canadian-born financier and thoroughbred horse breeder who orchestrated the powerful Argus Corporation empire.

Some may say that Edward Plunket Taylor's most notable accomplishment was the breeding of the famous racehorse Northern Dancer on his Windfields Farms, but Canadians know him best as the principal founder of Argus Corporation. E. P. Taylor's name became a caricature of Canadian capitalism for a quarter of a century after World War II. He was disparagingly referred to as "E(xcess) P(rofits) Taylor," an image reinforced by his rotund figure decked out in the finest attire regularly paraded at gala racing events.

Taylor made his career through international connections garnered as a major wartime procurer. In 1940 he was appointed by top Ottawa politician, C. D. Howe, to the executive committee of the Department of Munitions and Supply and in the next year to the presidency of War Supplies Limited in Washington, and, finally, by British Prime Minister Winston Churchill to the presidency of the British Supply Council in North America. His contacts as a "dollar-a-year man" projected Taylor from a run-of-the-mill upper-class Canadian (who had parlayed his family's financial connections and Brading Breweries—of which he was a

director at 22—into Canadian Breweries) onto the international financial stage.

Born January 29, 1901, in Ottawa, son of Lieutenant-Colonel Plunket Bourchier Taylor and Florence Gertrude (Magee), "Eddie" enjoyed a private school education at Ashbury College, then graduated from McGill University with a BS (mechanical engineering) in 1922. Following a few years with the investment house of McLeod Young and Weir, he became president of Canadian Breweries in 1930.

In putting together this company and taking over Carling Breweries, Taylor entered the domain of big business by forging the world's largest brewery. As a financier, he bought and closed down many smaller breweries. His means were ruthless: he threatened his competitors with price wars and cajoled them with lucrative buy-out schemes. Between 1930 and 1938 Canadian Breweries acquired 15 brewery plants, reducing the total number of plants to six and the number of labels from 50 to 27. To the distress of Canadian beer drinkers, by 1954 only four companies remained, marketing a mere eight labels.

To the financier Taylor companies were commodities; in 1968 he sold his controlling interest in Canadian Breweries to Rothmans of Pall Mall, a South African firm, for $28.8 million. By then he had acquired an empire around Argus Corporation with control over such giant enterprises as British Columbia Forest Products, Dominion Stores, Domtar Paper, and Massey-Ferguson. He created Argus (which in classical mythology means a giant guardian with a hundred eyes) in 1945 to hold the controlling shares of these operat-

ing companies. Later Argus acquisitions included Hollinger Mines and Standard Broadcasting. Taylor withdrew from active management of Argus in 1971 and eventually sold his shares to Paul Desmarais of Power Corporation during a take-over bid.

Throughout his career Taylor moved in the top international social circles, with private memberships in the exclusive Toronto, York, and Rideau clubs in Canada; the Metropolitan and The Jockey clubs in New York; the Buck's and Turf clubs in England; and the Lyford Cay (which he created himself) in the Bahamas. Following "retirement," Taylor built the community of Lyford Cay in the Bahamas as a residential playground for the wealthy. Bitten by the building bug, he galloped ahead to become the world's largest housing contractor, with extensive operations throughout the Third World constructing prefabricated houses. He was chairman of New Providence Development Company in Nassau and remained active in his horse-racing ventures until his death in 1989.

Further Reading

Edward Plunket Taylor is listed in *Canadian Who's Who* and figures prominently in *Debrett's Illustrated Guide to the Canadian Establishment* (1983), as does his former racehorse, Northern Dancer. Richard Rohmer, *E. P. Taylor: The Biography of Edward Plunket Taylor* (1978), is a full-length celebration. □

Elizabeth Rosemond Taylor

Elizabeth Rosemond Taylor (born 1932) is one of film's most legendary women. She starred in over 50 films, from such children's classics as *Lassie Come Home* and *National Velvet* to adult fare such as *Cat on a Hot Tin Roof, Cleopatra,* and *Who's Afraid of Virginia Woolf?*

Elizabeth Rosemond Taylor was born in London, England, on February 27, 1932 to American parents Francis and Sara Taylor. Her father was a prosperous art dealer who had his own gallery in a fashionable part of London. Her mother was an actress who has been successful prior to marriage under the stage name Sara Sothern. She has an older brother, Howard, who had been born two years earlier. In 1939 the family moved to Los Angeles, CA, where Elizabeth was encouraged and coached by her mother to seek work in the motion picture industry. Elizabeth learned well and was signed by Universal in 1941 for $200 a week.

The following year, Elizabeth Taylor signed a contract with Metro-Goldwyn-Mayer and landed the part of an English heiress in the successful film *Lassie Come Home.* MGM was the biggest and best studio of the time and employed stars such as Greta Garbo, Judy Garland, Katherine Hepburn, and Joan Crawford. In 1943 Taylor was cast opposite Mickey Rooney in *National Velvet,* the story of a young woman who wins a horse in the lottery and eventu-

ally rides it in England's Grand National Steeplechase. Taylor was so determined to play the role that she exercised and dieted for four months. During filming, she was thrown from a horse and suffered a broken back, but forced herself to finish the project. Her dedication was well rewarded and *National Velvet* became both a critical and commercial success.

Elizabeth Taylor loved her studio responsibilities, the costumes, the make-up, and the attention. Hedda Hopper, the columnist and friend of Sara Taylor, declared that at fifteen Elizabeth was the most beautiful woman in the world. Making films such as *Little Women, Father of the Bride, Cynthia,* and *A Place in the Sun* Taylor soon began to gain a reputation as a temperamental actress who demanded preferential treatment. It was a role she would often play in a widely publicized life.

Her private hours included friendship and romance with Glenn Davis, Bill Pawley, and Montgomery Clift. On May 6, 1950, she married hotel-heir Conrad N. Hilton, Jr., but the marriage lasted less than a year. After divorcing Hilton at 19, she married British actor Michael Wilding on February 21, 1952, with whom she had two sons.

Between 1952 and 1956 Elizabeth Taylor played in numerous romantic films that did not demand great acting talent. But in 1956 she played opposite James Dean in *Giant,* followed by the powerful *Raintree County* (1957), for which she received her first Academy Award nomination, and *Suddenly Last Summer* (1959)—for which she received

$500,000, the most ever earned by an actress for eight weeks of work, and her third Academy Award nomination.

In 1956 Elizabeth Taylor and Michael Wilding separated, and on February 2, 1957, she married producer Mike Todd. James Dean's death the year before, shortly after the two had finished filming *Giant,* devastated her. She had also endured the horror of her close friend Monty Clift's nearly fatal automobile accident, for which she felt responsible. Clift had left Taylor's home after a party and had driven into a utility pole. On March 24, 1958, her husband Mike Todd lost his life when his private plane crashed in New Mexico as he was en route to an awards banquet. Taylor's grief seemed bottomless over each tragedy, and for a time she sought relief in pills, hysterics, and alcohol. While struggling with personal losses and the concurrent addictions, she played the emotionally-wrenching part of Maggie in the film *Cat on a Hot Tin Roof* (1958). Her portrayal of Maggie won her a second Academy Award nomination and offered the opportunity to develop her friendship with Eddie Fisher, who had been Mike Todd's best man at their wedding. Soon after his scandal-ridden divorce from Debbie Reynolds (who had been Taylor's matron of honor at the ceremony) Elizabeth Taylor married Eddie Fisher on May 12, 1959.

In 1960 Taylor turned in one of her best screen performances as a call-girl in *Butterfield 8,* for which she won an Oscar as Best Actress. A few months later, in 1961, she signed with 20th Century-Fox for $1 million for the film *Cleopatra,* with Richard Burton as Marc Antony. The two stars were soon romancing off the set as well as on; even the Vatican spoke out in protest, castigating the "caprices of adult children" and accusing Taylor of "erotic vagrancy." In despair over her alliance with Burton, married and the father of two, Elizabeth Taylor attempted suicide in early 1962. But two years later, the two divorced their respective spouses and married on March 15, 1964.

Two films, *The VIPs* (1963) and *The Sandpiper* (1965), preceded Elizabeth Taylor's screen triumph, *Who's Afraid of Virginia Woolf?*, for which she won another Oscar. Her husband and co-star, Richard Burton, was nominated for an Academy Award but did not receive one for *The Taming of the Shrew.* Well over a dozen films followed, as did a divorce from Burton. The couple remarried on October 10, 1975. They divorced for the second, and final, time in July 1976.

Still, the public clamored for news about this beautifully outrageous star with the violet eyes and voluptuous body. The public's curiosity and interest was piqued once more when Taylor married for the seventh time—to John Warner, a Republican campaigning for the U.S. Senate in Virginia in 1978. According to one biographer, Elizabeth Taylor broke "all the rules for being a good political wife." In addition, she had gained considerable weight and the press hounded her mercilessly about it. Warner was elected, divorced Taylor, and was re-elected in 1984.

Taylor's performances were far from over, She moved to Broadway for the first time in a well-received staging of *The Little Foxes.* Elizabeth Taylor and Richard Burton then appeared on Broadway in 1983, attempting to rekindle the dramatic spark that had leapt between them, in Noel Coward's *Private Lives.* The critics were cool, however, feeling that the stage couple projected overtones of the actors' own private times together. It was a poor sequel to their devastatingly effective *Who's Afraid of Virginia Woolf?*

In 1983 Taylor signed herself into the Betty Ford Clinic in California for treatment of her alcohol addiction. On August 4, 1984, the sudden death of Richard Burton left her "extremely, extremely upset," according to a spokesperson. Chronic back pain and general ill-health led to her return to drinking and prescription pain killers. Moreover, a number of close friends, among them actor Rock Hudson, fashion designer Halston, and Malcolm Forbes, her private press secretary, became ill with AIDS. Despite her own medical and addiction battles, Taylor became the first actress of such legendary stature to speak out on behalf of AIDS research. In 1985 Taylor became the co-founder and chair of the American Foundation for AIDS research. Her "Commitment to Life" benefit of that year was the first major AIDS research fund-raising gala staged by the Hollywood community.

Tayor returned to the Betty Ford Clinic in 1988, where she met a 40-year old construction worked named Larry Fortensky. Their friendship continued outside the clinic and they married in 1991. She continued her benefit work and, in 1993, the Academy of Motion Picture Arts and Sciences honored Taylor with a special humanitarian award for her years with the American Foundation for AIDS Research. In 1994, Taylor returned to the silver screen after a 14-year absence for a cameo in *The Flintstones.* Taylor appeared in the film because some of the proceeds were to benefit AIDS research. Her marriage to Fortensky ended in divorce in 1996. Taylor revealed that she did not plan to marry again, but was quoted as saying, "I expect to fall in love again."

Putting her own health concerns aside, Taylor postponed brain surgery in February 1997 to participate in the star-studded ABC-TV special, "Happy Birthday Elizabeth—A Celebration of Life," which marked her 65th birthday and raised money for AIDS research. The following day, Dr. Martin Cooper removed a two-inch tumor from her brain. A week later, Elizabeth Taylor was released from Cedars-Sinai Medical Center to recover at home. Through all her triumphs and difficulties, she will always be remembered as a beautiful, much-beloved woman with a presence seemingly larger than life, both on and off the screen.

Further Reading

Among the most detailed and least restrained biographies of Elizabeth Taylor is Kitty Kelley's *Elizabeth Taylor, The Last Star* (1981). Other useful works include Brenda Maddox's *Who's Afraid of Elizabeth Taylor?* (1977) and *A Passion for Life: the Biography of Elizabeth Taylor* (1995) by Donald Spoto. For a discussion of her screen credits, with illustrations, *Elizabeth Taylor* by Foster Hirsch (1973) is rather complete. □

John Taylor

John Taylor (1753-1824), American politician and political theorist, was a major spokesman for southern agrarian, planter society.

John Taylor was born in Virginia in December 1753. His parents died while he was a child, and he was raised by his uncle, Edmund Pendleton. Taylor attended William and Mary College (1770-1772), read law in Pendleton's office (1772-1774), and then began to practice law.

At the outbreak of the Revolutionary War, Taylor joined the Virginia militia and then the Continental Army. He soon became a major. When the Continental Army was reduced in 1779, he resigned and returned home. In 1783 he married Lucy Penn, the daughter of a wealthy North Carolina planter. His legal practice prospered during the next 10 years, and building on his wife's properties, he acquired a number of plantations. By 1792 Taylor was able to devote all of his time to his two major interests: scientific agriculture and public office.

From 1779 to 1785 and again from 1796 to 1800, Taylor sat in the Virginia House of Delegates. He served as a U.S. senator in 1792-1794, 1803, and 1822-1824. He early allied himself with the emerging Jeffersonian Republican party. During the 1790s he strongly opposed the financial program of Alexander Hamilton. Toward the end of the decade Taylor introduced James Madison's famous resolutions condemning the Alien and Sedition Acts in the Virginia Assembly. In 1800 he worked enthusiastically for Thomas Jefferson's election.

By about 1808, however, Taylor had become disillusioned with Jefferson's administration, accusing it of abandoning its original principles of agrarianism and states' rights. During Madison's two terms as president, Taylor moved even more sharply into opposition, speaking out vigorously against the War of 1812 and its centralizing consequences—the increased national debt, tax program, and expanded armed forces.

Much of Taylor's lasting significance rests with his published writings. Unsystematic and tedious, they nonetheless offer a cogent criticism of Hamiltonian Federalist policies and a defense of the South's agrarian, states'-rights philosophy. Among his most important publications are *An Inquiry into the Principles and Policy of the Government of the United States* (1814) and *Constructions Construed and Constitutions Vindicated* (1820). Linked with these were his *Arator* essays (1803), suggesting agricultural reforms necessary for southern equality in the struggle against northern interests. He died on Aug. 21, 1824, at his plantation home, Hazelwood, in Virginia.

Further Reading

The modern biography of Taylor is by Henry Simms, *Life of John Taylor* (1932), which provides an adequate introduction to his life and thought. Eugene Mudge, *The Social Philosophy of John Taylor of Caroline* (1939), offers a more systematic treatment of Taylor's political and economic thought. A valuable discussion of Taylor's political activities, set in the context of the Old Republican movement, is in Norman Risjord, *The Old Republicans: Southern Conservatism* (1965).

Additional Sources

Shalhope, Robert E., *John Taylor of Caroline: pastoral republican*, Columbia: University of South Carolina Press, 1980.
Simms, Henry Harrison, *Life of John Taylor: the story of a brilliant leader in the early Virginia state rights school*, Littleton, Colo.: F.B. Rothman, 1992. □

Maxwell Taylor

General Maxwell Taylor (1901-1987) served the United States for half a century as a soldier-statesman-scholar in peacetime and in three wars.

Maxwell Davenport Taylor was born August 26, 1901, in Keytesville, Missouri. He attended school in Kansas City until accepting an appointment to West Point. Graduating fourth in his class in 1922, Taylor joined the Corps of Engineers (later transferring to the Field Artillery). During the 1920s and 1930s Taylor served in several posts in the United States and in France, Japan, and China.

An accomplished linguist, he returned to West Point as a language instructor, 1927 to 1932. But he was foremost a student of military science, graduating from the Army's Command and Staff School in 1935 and the Army War College in 1940. In between schools he held various command and staff assignments.

When the United States entered World War II in 1941, Taylor wore the silver leaf of a lieutenant colonel. From then on, however, increasing responsibilities brought rapid promotions. In 1942 he was sent to Camp Claiborne, Louisiana, to assist General Matthew Ridgway in forming the Army's first airborne division, the 82d. Taylor commanded the division's artillery in the invasion of Sicily in July 1943 and in the landing at Salerno, Italy, two months later. From there he slipped behind German lines to Rome, where he established contact with Italian authorities while assessing the strength of German troops in and around the city. Later General Dwight Eisenhower was to call Taylor's secret mission a risk "greater than I asked any other agent or emissary to undertake during the war."

In March 1944 Taylor, now a brigadier general, was ordered to England to command the 101st Airborne Division. He parachuted into Normandy with his men in the early morning darkness of D-Day, June 6, 1944. Later that year he led his division in another airborne assault—Operation Market-Garden—in which American and British forces sought but failed to open the Rhine River as far north as Arnheim, Holland. Taylor was back in the United States when the German army launched its massive attack against the "Bulge" in the Allied lines in the Ardennes. The 101st was surrounded at Bastogne, Belgium, where second-in-

command General Anthony McAuliffe made his celebrated reply of "Nuts!" to the German order to surrender.

Taylor hurried back to his command and led the division until the end of the war in Europe, May 8, 1945. Later that year he was appointed superintendent of West Point, moving to chief of staff of U.S. forces in Europe in 1949 and to deputy chief of staff of the Army in 1951.

During the Korean War he took command of the U.S. Eighth Army in February 1953 for five months of fighting until the armistice was signed in July. The next year he took command of all U.S. forces in the Far East and in 1955 was promoted to four-star general and assigned to lead all United Nations forces in the Far East. However, two months later he was recalled to the United States to become army chief of staff, serving in that post until his retirement in 1959.

Taylor reentered government service in 1961 to investigate the CIA role in the abortive Bay of Pigs invasion of Cuba. He then served as military representative of President John F. Kennedy, chairman of the Joint Chiefs of Staff, U.S. ambassador to South Vietnam in 1964, and from 1965 to 1969 as special consultant to President Lyndon Johnson. He retired again in 1969, spending much of his private life in writing on national and international affairs.

Slender and athletic, General Taylor looked every bit the picture of a soldier. His military decorations included the Distinguished Service Cross, Silver Star with Oak Leaf Cluster, Distinguished Service Medal with Oak Leaf Cluster, Bronze Star, and Purple Heart, as well as numerous foreign honors. In 1925 Taylor married Lydia Gardner Happer. They had two sons, John Maxwell and Thomas Happer.

Further Reading

For more information on General Taylor's role in World War II see almost any good history of the conflict, particularly Dwight Eisenhower, *Crusade in Europe* (reprinted 1977) and Cornelius Ryan, *The Longest Day: June 6, 1944* (paperback 1960) and *A Bridge Too Far* (paperback 1974). Additional information on Taylor can be found in his writings, which are direct and clear-headed. *The Uncertain Trumpet* (1959) was an attack on the Eisenhower administration's emphasis on "massive retaliation" as the chief defense of the United States. *Responsibility and Response* (1967) further argued the need for conventional as well as nuclear weapons. *Swords and Plowshares* (1972) was also a contribution to U.S. defense policies.

Additional Sources

Taylor, John M., *General Maxwell Taylor: the sword and the pen,* New York: Doubleday, 1989.

Taylor, Maxwell D. (Maxwell Davenport), 1901-1987, *Swords and plowshares,* New York, N.Y.: Da Capo Press, 1990. □

Susie King Taylor

During the Civil War, black American nurse Susie King Taylor (1848-1912) aided the Union Army. She later helped freedmen and Civil War veterans.

Susie King Taylor was born into slavery on Aug. 6, 1848, on a farm near Savannah, Ga. She learned to read and write, although slaves were prohibited from doing so. During the Civil War she and her uncle escaped from slavery by fleeing to a Union army in Georgia. She joined the all-black 1st South Carolina Volunteers (which later became the 33d U.S. Colored Infantry) as a nurse, teacher, and laundress.

In 1863 she married Sgt. Edward King, also a former slave, and served with him in the South Carolina Sea Islands. They participated in the 1865 capture of Charleston. She bravely attended to the needs of both black and white soldiers. Though King frequently encountered combat, she always remained brave, and her courage and cheerfulness were a source of inspiration to soldiers of both races. She also taught many illiterate Union soldiers to read and write.

Mustered out of the army in February 1866, King and her husband returned to Savannah. She opened a school for free blacks but closed it after her husband died at the end of 1866. She operated a school in Liberty Country, Ga., in 1867-1868 but returned to Savannah in late 1868 to open a night school. With the opening of new public schools for freedmen, King closed her school and worked for a wealthy family.

Moving to Boston, King married Russel L. Taylor, a former Union soldier, in 1879. She remained interested in the plight of Civil War veterans, both black and white, and

York: M. Wiener Pub.: Distributed by the Talman Co., 1988.

□

in 1886 helped organize Corps 67 of the Women's Relief Corps auxiliary to the Grand Army of the Republic. She served as guard, secretary, treasurer, and president (1893) of the Corps. During the Spanish-American War she furnished and packed boxes for wounded men in hospitals.

Taylor's well-written autobiography, *Reminiscences of My Life in Camp* (1902), detailed her wartime experiences and the contributions of blacks to the Union cause. It also criticized racial discrimination in the United States, particularly in the South. Taylor noted that blacks had contributed greatly to the preservation of the nation and were entitled to full equality.

Further Reading

Taylor's autobiography, *Reminiscences of My Life in Camp* (1902; repr. 1968), is the principal source on her life; two short excerpts appear in William L. Katz, *Eyewitness: The Negro in American History* (1967). Brief biographies of Mrs. Taylor are in Sylvia G. L. Dannett, *Profiles of Negro Womanhood, 1619-1900*, vol. 1 (1964), and in Charles H. Wesley and Patricia W. Romero, *Negro Americans in the Civil War: From Slavery to Citizenship* (1968). Benjamin Quarles, *The Negro in the Civil War* (1953), and James M. McPherson, *The Negro's Civil War: How American Negroes Felt and Acted during the War for the Union* (1965), briefly describe her war work and attitudes toward the race problem.

Additional Sources

Taylor, Susie King, b. 1848., *A Black woman's Civil War memoirs: reminiscences of my life in camp with the 33rd U.S. Colored Troops, late 1st South Carolina Volunteers*, New

Zachary Taylor

Zachary Taylor (1784-1850), twelfth president of the United States, was, as one of the two military heroes of the Mexican War, the last Whig president.

Living in a time when generals were politically appointed and the Army poorly trained, Zachary Taylor proved a great tactician even though he did not inspire the love of his troops. Quarrelsome with his superiors, blunt to the point of tactlessness, he nevertheless provided solid leadership as a general.

Taylor was born on Nov. 24, 1784, at Montebello, Va., the son of a lieutenant colonel who had been on George Washington's Revolutionary War staff. The family moved to Louisville, Ky., in 1785, where Zachary's father became collector of customs and an influential man. Poorly educated by private tutoring, young Taylor was intended for an agricultural life on the family plantation, but the death of an elder brother allowed him to enter the Army. In 1808 he was appointed a lieutenant by President Thomas Jefferson and assigned to Gen. James Wilkinson's command at New Orleans.

A bout with yellow fever forced Taylor into temporary retirement, but he was promoted to captain in 1810 and assigned to the command of Governor William Henry Harrison of Indiana Territory. That same year he married Margaret M. Smith of Maryland.

During the War of 1812 Taylor won prominence in his command of Ft. Harrison. His small garrison withstood an attack by 400 Indians led by Tecumseh. During the war he was promoted to brevet major, but at the war's end he reverted to captain. This so angered him that he resigned his commission and returned to Kentucky to raise "a crop of corn."

Garrison Duty

In May 1816 President James Madison restored Taylor to the rank of major and sent him to Wisconsin Territory to command the 3d Infantry. Fifteen years of garrison duty followed in Louisiana and Minnesota. In 1832 he was promoted to colonel, and during the Black Hawk War he had charge of 400 regulars, under the command of Gen. Henry Atkinson. After receiving the surrender of the Indian chief Black Hawk, he returned to Ft. Snelling as commanding officer. There, a subordinate, Jefferson Davis, sought to wed Taylor's second daughter, Sarah, but Taylor disliked Davis and forbade his entry into the Taylor home. Davis later resigned his commission and in 1835 the couple married. Three months later, at Davis's Mississippi plantation, his wife died of a fever.

In 1837 Taylor was assigned command of the Army prosecuting the Seminole Wars in Florida. On Christmas

Day he inflicted a stinging defeat on them at Lake Okeechobee, for which he was breveted a brigadier general. In May 1833 he assumed command of the department. Muscular and stocky, rarely in full uniform, he was dubbed "Old Rough and Ready" by his troops. In 1840 he returned to the Department of the Southwest as commander, and that year he purchased a house in Baton Rouge, La., which he thereafter considered home. He also purchased, in 1841, Cyprus Grove, a plantation near Rodney, Miss., thus becoming a slave owner.

Mexican War

In May 1845 Taylor was ordered to correspond with the government of the Republic of Texas, then negotiating annexation to the United States, and to repel any invasion of Mexicans. In July he moved his army of 4,000 men to the site of Corpus Christi, Tex. In January 1846 he was ordered to the mouth of the Rio Grande to support the American claim to that river as the boundary of Texas. In March he constructed Ft. Brown, opposite the Mexican town of Matamoros.

When Mexican forces attacked his troops, Taylor did not wait for Congress to declare war. On May 8, 1846, at Palo Alto he defeated a Mexican army three times the size of his own force, largely through the accuracy of his artillery. The next day he won the Battle of Resaca de la Palma and then occupied Matamoros. President James K. Polk thereupon named him commander of the Army of the Rio Grande and promoted him to brevet major general. A grateful Congress voted him thanks and two gold medals.

With 6,000 men Taylor set out in September 1846 for Monterrey, Mexico, which he captured on September 20-24, granting the Mexicans an 8-week armistice. The Polk administration criticized Taylor's leniency toward the Mexicans and would have replaced him but for his growing popularity. Because of that, and because Taylor's name was being prominently mentioned as the Whig nominee for president, the Democrat Polk reassigned half his troops to Gen. Winfield Scott, who was to invade Mexico at Veracruz. Taylor was ordered to hold at Monterrey and be on the defensive.

Taylor ignored his orders, advancing southward until he came into contact with Antonio López de Santa Ana's Mexican army of 15,000-20,000 men. On February 22-23 they fought the Battle of Buena Vista. Many of Taylor's men, mainly volunteers, broke and fled, but his artillery proved so effective that the Mexicans were forced to retreat. In gratitude for this victory, Congress voted him another gold medal, but Polk continued to hamper and demean his activities. Taylor remained in Mexico until November 1847, when he returned to campaign in his peculiar fashion for the presidency.

Whig Nomination

In June 1846 Taylor had written that he would decline the presidency even "if preferred and I could reach it without opposition." In August 1847 he stated, "I do not care a fig about the office." Yet by the late fall of 1847 he was becoming interested and writing his views on political issues. He said that the Bank of the United States was a dead issue, that he favored internal improvements, and that he would use the veto to protect the Constitution. His political backers, appalled at such statements, preferred that his views remain unknown.

The Whigs nominated Taylor on the fourth ballot, passing over Henry Clay, Daniel Webster, and Winfield Scott, even though Taylor had never even voted in a presidential election. The Democrats chose Lewis Cass. Because of a split in the Democratic party, Taylor carried New York State and thereby won the election. People voted for him in the North because he was a war hero; in the South he was admired as a slave owner.

The President

In his inaugural address Taylor advocated military and naval effectiveness; friendly relations with foreign powers; Federal encouragement of agriculture, commerce, and manufacturing; and congressional conciliation of sectional controversy. Four of his seven Cabinet members were Southerners, and the Cabinet contained no men of real ability.

Because of Taylor's political inability, he suffered in his relations with Congress. He also contributed to the ruination of the Whig party because he thought himself above partisan politics. "I am a Whig," he stated, "but not an ultra Whig." The result was discord and dissension within party ranks.

Although a slave owner, Taylor gradually came to support the Wilmot Proviso (mandating that there be no extension of slavery into the territory taken from Mexico at the end of the war). He encouraged Californians to seek admission as a free state, just as he did New Mexicans, despite the Texan claims to all land east of the Rio Grande. Southern Whigs thereupon turned against Taylor and the party. His steadfast opposition to the Texan claims heated the sectional controversy; yet when there was talk of secession, he stated forthrightly, "Disunion is treason." His strong stand discouraged secession and perhaps delayed the Civil War.

Taylor little understood foreign affairs and blundered badly on several occasions. His one major accomplishment in this area was the Clayton-Bulwer Treaty of 1850, which dealt with English-American efforts to build an Isthmian canal.

A lifelong admirer of George Washington, Taylor attended the laying of the cornerstone of the Washington Monument on July 4, 1850, sitting for hours in the hot sun. Afterward he drank quantities of ice water and then ate cherries with iced milk. That night he suffered what the doctors described as a cholera attack; he died 5 days later. He rallied at his deathbed to make a last statement: "I have tried to discharge my duties faithfully. I regret nothing." He was buried near Louisville, Ky.

Further Reading

There are three satisfactory biographies of Taylor. The best is Holman Hamilton's two-volume work, *Zachary Taylor: Soldier of the Republic* (1941) and *Zachary Taylor: Soldier in the White House* (1951). The others are Brainerd Dyer, *Zachary Taylor* (1946), and Silas B. McKinley and Silas Bent, *Old Rough and Ready* (1946). The standard history of the Mexican War is still Justin H. Smith, *The War with Mexico* (2. vols., 1919). □

Peter Ilyich Tchaikovsky

Peter Ilyich Tchaikovsky (1840-1893) is one of the most loved of Russian composers. He epitomized the ingenuous opening to the emotions of the romantic era in music, but his product was made durable through sound craftsmanship and rigorous work habits.

Eschewing the intellectual, Peter Ilyich Tchaikovsky was in no sense a technical innovator; moreover, he attracted, and still attracts, the barbed clevernesses of those less trustful of emotional statement. But his work is always hotly defended as each generation discovers him afresh—a process considerably quickened by a massive and ever-growing body of literature about his music and his interesting, often tragic life.

Born on May 7, 1840, in Votkinsk in the Vyatka district, Tchaikovsky was the son of a well-to-do engineer. Peter and his brothers and sister received a sound education from their French governesses. He apparently showed no early signs of unusual musical talent but was duly exposed to the music

lessons suffered by all young gentlemen. He later recalled growing up in a place "saturated with the miraculous beauty of Russian folk song" and the effect some music had on him as a child—that of exquisite torture so beautiful that he begged the music be stopped. He often referred to this in his letters as a mature artist.

Tchaikovsky attended a school of jurisprudence in St. Petersburg, and, while studying law and government, he also took music lessons, including some composing, from Gabriel Lomakin. Tchaikovsky graduated at the age of 19 and took a job as a bureau clerk. This was to be the first step of an official career, but he was already hopelessly enamored of music. He soon met the Rubinstein brothers, Anton and Nikolai; both were composers, and Anton was a pianist second only to Franz Liszt in technical brilliance and fame. In 1862 Anton opened Russia's first conservatory, under the sponsorship of the Imperial Russian Music Society (IRMS), in St. Petersburg, and Tchaikovsky was its first composition student.

Early Works

Tchaikovsky's early works were technically sound but not memorable. Anton Rubinstein was demanding and critical, often unjustly so, and when Tchaikovsky graduated 2 years later he was still somewhat cowed by Anton's harshness. In 1866 Nikolai Rubinstein invited Tchaikovsky to Moscow to live with him and serve as professor of composition at the Moscow Conservatory, which he had just established. Tchaikovsky's father was now in financial trouble, and the composer had to support himself on the meager

earnings from the conservatory. The symphonic poems *Fatum* and *Romeo and Juliet* that he wrote in 1869 were the first works to show the style he was thereafter to cultivate. *Romeo and Juliet* was redone with Mily Balakirev's help in 1870 and again in 1879.

During the seventies and later, there was considerable communication between Tchaikovsky and the Rubinsteins on the one hand and the members of the Mighty Five, Balakirev, Aleksandr Borodin, Modest Mussorgsky, Nicolai Rimsky-Korsakov, and César Cui, on the other. The traditional "enmity" between the two groups seems a concoction of romantic biographers. Tchaikovsky functioned as an all-around musician in the early seventies, and, as expected of an IRMS licentiate, he taught, composed, wrote critical essays, and conducted, the last not very well. In 1875 he composed what is perhaps his most universally known and loved work, the Piano Concerto No. 1. Anton Rubinstein was sarcastic in his dislike, although it became one of the most popular items in his own repertoire as a concert pianist. Vying in popularity with the concerto is Tchaikovsky's ballet *Swan Lake* (1876). It is the most successful ballet ever written if measured in terms of broad audience appeal.

A Disastrous Marriage

In 1877 Tchaikovsky married the 28-year-old Antonina Miliukova, his student at the conservatory; it has been suggested that she remained him of Tatiana, his heroine in his opera-in-process, *Eugene Onegin*. His unfortunate wife, who died insane in 1917, not only suffered violent rejection by her husband but also the vicious libel of Modeste Tchaikovsky, his brother's biographer. Modeste, like Peter a misogynist, vilified her in the biography in an attempt to shield Peter and mask his weaknesses. Subsequent biographers, uncritically and perhaps with relish, repeated and embroidered upon Modeste's assertion that Antonina was cheap, high-strung, and neurotic.

Tchaikovsky was scarcely to find out her character: within a few weeks he had fled Moscow alone for an extended stay abroad. He made arrangements through relatives never to see his wife again. In his correspondence of this period—indeed through a large part of his career—he was periodically morbid about all aspects of his life: about his wife, money, his friends, even his music and himself. He often spoke of suicide. This, too, is a favorite theme of his many biographers. Even during his life he was treated unkindly by critics who sharpened their sarcastic vocabularies on his open, vulnerable, emotionally based music. But he never sought to change his style, though he was dissatisfied, at one time or another, with most of his works; and he never stopped composing.

Arrangement with Madame von Meck

At about the same time as his abortive marriage, Tchaikovsky entered into a liaison of quite another kind. Through third parties an unusual but fruitful arrangement with the immensely wealthy Nadezhda von Meck was made: she was attracted by his music and the possibility of patronizing him, and he was frank in his interest in her money and what it could provide him. For 13 years she

supported him at a base rate of 6,000 rubles a year, with whatever "bonuses" he could manage to extract. He was free to quit the conservatory, and he began a series of travels and stays abroad.

Von Meck and Tchaikovsky purposely never met, save for one or two accidental encounters. In their voluminous correspondence the composer discusses his music thoughtfully; it is disenchanting to note that in letters to his family he complains cavalierly of her parsimony. He dedicated his Fourth Symphony (1877) to her. Tchaikovsky finished *Eugene Onegin* in 1879; it is his only opera generally performed outside the Soviet Union. Other works of this period are the Violin Concerto (1881), the Fifth Symphony (1888), and the ballet *Sleeping Beauty* (1889).

Tchaikovsky's fame and his activity now extended to all of Europe and America. To rest from his public appearances he chose a country retreat in Klin near Moscow. From this was derived the "Hermit of Klin" nickname, though hermit he never was. In 1890 he finished the opera *Queen of Spades,* based on Aleksandr Pushkin's story. As with many of his other works, Tchaikovsky was highly involved emotionally, and he was gratified when, despite the grousing "experts," the opera was enthusiastically received. In late 1890 Von Meck cut him off. He was self-sustaining by then, but the rebuff rankled. Even Modeste expressed surprise at his irritation. Tchaikovsky had an immensely successful tour in the United States in 1891.

The Sixth Symphony was first heard in October 1893, with the composer conducting. This work, named at Modeste's suggestion *Pathétique,* was poorly received, very likely because of the inadequate conducting. Tchaikovsky never knew of its eventual astonishing success, for he contracted cholera and died, muttering abuse of Von Meck, on November 6.

Tchaikovsky's gift was melody—sobbing, singing, exalting melody. Yet, one of his favorite and recurring melodic patterns was a simple five-or six-note minor scale, usually descending, which he enveloped in orchestral color or lush harmonies often electrifying in their piquancy and effectiveness.

Further Reading

Tchaikovsky's story is obscured, first, by the work by his brother Modeste, *Life of Peter Ilyich Tchaikovsky* (3 vols., 1900-1902; English abridgment by Rosa Newmarch, 1906), which, while otherwise authoritative, cloaks vital segments of the composer's life; second, by puritanical attitudes which keep archives in Klin tightly closed; and third, by the opportunistic sensationalism of many writers who perform Freudian acrobatics with the few facts they possess of the composer's life. M. D. Calvocoressi and Gerald Abraham, *Masters of Russian Music* (1936), is sound, as is Abraham's *Tchaikovsky: A Short Biography* (1944), derived from the former work. David Brook, *Six Great Russian Composers* (1946), includes a chapter on Tchaikovsky. John Gee and Elliot Selby, *The Triumph of Tchaikovsky* (1960), and Lawrence and Elizabeth Hanson, *Tchaikovsky: The Man behind the Music* (1966), are undistinguished biographies. The Tchaikovsky-Von Meck correspondence was published in Russian (3 vols., 1933-1936), and a one-volume English abridgment is available. *Beloved Friend* (1937), by Catherine Drinker Bowen and Barbara von Meck, is a fictionalized but not inaccurate account based on the aforementioned letters. □

Alexander Tcherepnin

Alexander (Nikolayevich) Tcherepnin (1899-1977) was a Russian-French and later American composer of ballets, operas, and instrumental music.

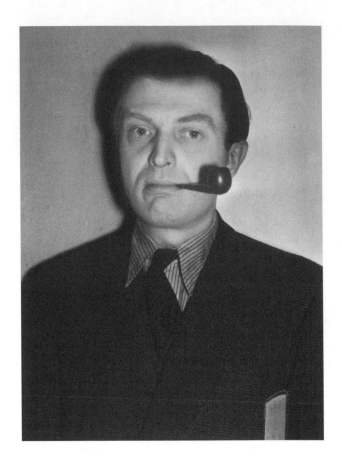

Alexander Tcherepnin was born on January 21, 1899, in St. Petersburg, Russia. Descended from a family of musicians, Alexander benefitted from the experience of his father, Nikolay Tcherepnin (1873-1945), a conductor and composer who studied with Rimsky-Korsakov. The family house in St. Petersburg was a place where many well-known musicians and artists liked to meet. In this privileged atmosphere, the gifts of Alexander Tcherepnin were confirmed at an early age. At 14 he had already written an opera, a ballet, and several pieces for piano. In 1918 the family moved to Tbilisi, where Alexander continued his studies at the music conservatory. At the same time he gave concerts as both pianist and conductor.

In 1921 the political situation forced the family to leave Russia. They settled in Paris, where Alexander completed his studies with Paul Vidal (composition) and Isidor Philipp (piano). Later he became the co-founder of L'Ecole de Paris with Bohuslav Martinů, Conrad Beck, and Marcel Mihalovici, a group of foreign composers close to the neoclassical movement, although at the same time very interested in the music of their respective homelands. He made his Western début in London (1922), and a year later his ballet *Ajanta's Frescoes,* written for Pavlova, was performed at Covent Garden.

Although he began a professional tour of America in 1926, it was in 1927 in Paris that he suddenly attained fame after the premiere of his first symphony, which was a *succès de scandale.* (An entire section of the work is performed exclusively by percussion instruments.) Between 1934 and 1937 he travelled in several Far-Eastern countries. He taught in Tokyo, where he settled down for a while and founded a music publishing corporation to promote the works of his pupils. It was in Shanghai that he met the pianist Lee Hsien Ming, whom he married a few years later. Returning to France in 1938, Alexander Tcherepnin was unfortunately forced to limit his activities during World War II.

In 1948 he returned to the United States to teach at De Paul University, Chicago, becoming an American citizen in 1958. From 1964 to his death in 1977 he divided his time between Paris and New York. An invitation from the Soviet government in 1967 allowed him to tour his native country extensively.

His Music

A highly cosmopolitan figure, Alexander Tcherepnin moved easily from St. Petersburg to Paris and New York. Even before World War II some of his compositions re-

vealed the influence of the Far East. His intense intellectual and musical curiosity found expression in compositions which can best be described as eclectic. As early as 1913 the *Pièces sans titre op. 7* for piano contain examples of bitonality. During his stay in Paris (1921-1950), his compositions show the impact of the French esthetic (simplicity of textures, clarity of melodic lines), at the time vigorously demonstrated by the members of the *Groupe des Six* (Darius Milhaud, Germaine Tailleferre, Georges Auric, Louis Durey, Arthur Honegger, and Francis Poulenc). In addition, he used the percussive rhythm that Prokofiev preferred in his music. Russian and Georgian music appear in *Rhapsodie Géorgienne* for orchestra (1922) and *Suite Géorgienne* for piano and strings (1938).

Apart from those diverse outside influences, he experimented with his own new techniques of counterpoint and of rhythm. The French composer Alexandre Tansman (born in Poland) remembered that Tcherepnin in Paris notated the rhythmic flow of the sound of people reading a newspaper. In addition to those experiments, Tcherepnin used his own melodic scale of nine notes in most of his compositions.

It was in the United States that Alexander Tcherepnin coordinated the best elements of his research. Although he avoided using serial elements, he did not hesitate to use electronic techniques (see *The Story of Ivan The Fool,* commissioned by the British Broadcasting Corporation [BBC] in 1968). His works include several ballets and operas (*Die Hochzeit der Sobeide* op. 45, story from Hofmannsthal, 1930; *The Farmer and the Nymphe* op. 72, 1952). In his chamber music, Alexander Tcherepnin often wrote for unusual instrumental combinations (see *Sonata da Chiesa* op. 101 for viola da gamba and organ, 1966, and *Caprices Diatoniques* for Celtic harp, 1973), thus revealing his particular interest in musical timbre.

This cosmopolitan composer reflected in his music the variety of cultures in which he had resided.

Further Reading

W. Reich, *Alexander Tcherepnin* (Bonn, 1959, rev. 1970) provides insights on the man and his work. □

Tecumseh

The American Indian Tecumseh (ca. 1768-1813), Shawnee chief, originated and led an Indian confederation against the encroaching white settlers in the old Northwest Territory. He was an ally of the British during the War of 1812.

According to tribal tradition, Tecumseh or Tecumtha, was born about March 1768 near what is now Springfield, Ohio. His father, Pucksinwa, was killed at the Battle of Point Pleasant in 1774, yet Tecumseh grew to manhood a distinguished warrior even without a father to guide him. He also grew to manhood angry at the encroaching whites who were forcing his tribe farther and farther west. A chief by 1808, he led the Shawnee to a site on the Wabash River near the mouth of the Tippecanoe, where they settled with permission from the Potawatomi and Kickapoo Indians.

Angry at the land hunger of the whites, Tecumseh was gradually coming to believe that no sale of land to the whites was valid unless all Indian tribes assembled and assented to such a sale. He said that the land did not belong to any one tribe, that it belonged to them all in common, and that the U.S. government had recognized this principle in 1795 at the Treaty of Greenville, when all tribes had assembled to make the agreement, after which the government had guaranteed title to all unceded land to the tribes in common. Governor William Henry Harrison of Indiana and other officials objected to this argument, realizing that such an arrangement was impractical from the government's point of view.

Tecumseh also knew that in unity there was strength, and he began to try to confederate all tribes from the Great Lakes to the Gulf of Mexico to oppose the whites. He was aided by his brother (perhaps a twin), Tenskwatawa, who was known as the Prophet. The Prophet preached with evangelical and revivalistic fervor that the Indians must return to the pure ways of their ancestors.

Tecumseh had some success in his drive to confederate the Indians. When the tribes visited his village, known as Prophet's Town, Tecumseh exhorted them not to drink alcoholic beverages, to develop their agricultural skills, and to accept nothing from whites on credit. He hoped to be left alone by the whites just long enough to consolidate his program and unify his people.

In this movement Tecumseh was aided by the British in Canada, who wanted allies against the Americans. He obtained arms, ammunition, and clothing from them. As he traveled and exhorted, he said, "Our fathers, from their tombs, reproach us as slaves and cowards." American observers noted that he was tall, straight, and lean—and a great orator. With British advice, he foretold the appearance of a comet in the heavens. When it appeared, as he had forecast, in 1812, the Creek Indians were so impressed that they arose against the whites—with disastrous results for their tribe.

In August 1810 Tecumseh met Governor Harrison at Vincennes for a conference, but he demanded the return of Indian lands so violently that the conference came to naught. The next year, at another conference, Tecumseh, overawed by militia, declared his peaceful intentions.

In 1811 Tecumseh journeyed southward to solicit more members for his confederation, warning his brother not to be drawn into battle unprepared. That summer was dry, crops were ruined, game became scarce, and the Prophet was led into a battle at Tippecanoe on Nov. 7, 1811. He was defeated, and this disaster caused many braves to desert Tecumseh. His confederation began to fall apart.

When the War of 1812 began, Tecumseh led his followers into the British camp, where he received the rank of brigadier general. He aided Sir Isaac Brock in the capture of Detroit; however, he also saved the lives of American soldiers about to be massacred there. In fact, his white enemies on the frontier always commented on his mercy and humanity, nothing that he would not torture prisoners and that his word was good.

Tecumseh and his followers fought with the British at Brownstown, Ft. Meigs, and Ft. Stephenson. His aid is often cited as the reason that the Americans failed to take Canada during this war. Yet when the British chose to retreat, following Adm. Oliver Hazard Perry's victories on Lake Erie, Tecumseh chose to cover the retreat. At the Battle of the Thames on Oct. 5, 1813, he was killed, leaving a lasting dispute as to who actually killed him.

Further Reading

Older books about Tecumseh and his movement that are of value include Benjamin Drake, *Life of Tecumseh* (1841; repr. 1969); Edward Eggleston, *Tecumseh and the Shawnee Prophet* (1878); and John M. Oskison, *Tecumseh and His Times* (1938). Recent works are Glenn Tucker, *Tecumseh: Vision of Glory* (1956); David C. Cooke, *Tecumseh: Destiny's Warrior* (1959); and a collection of documents by Carl F. Klinck, *Tecumseh: Fact and Fiction in Early Records* (1961). □

Frederick J. Teggart

Frederick J. Teggart (1870-1946) was a comparative historian, librarian, sociologist, and educator who

was responsible for initiating sociology at the University of California. He was a pioneer in advocating the fruitful interchange between history and sociology. He was one of the early modern analysts of social change, as well as a proponent of careful theoretical analysis in the study of both ancient and modern societies.

Frederick J. Teggart was born in Belfast, Ireland, in 1870, one of eleven children. First educated at Methodist College in Belfast and Trinity College in Dublin, he and his family came to the United States in 1889. Thereafter he enrolled in the then new Stanford University, where one of his classmates was Herbert Hoover. He received an A.B. degree in English in 1894. There followed a prolonged but not rewarding career as a librarian, first at Stanford and then as head librarian of a prestigious private library in San Francisco. By 1905, after several years of study and professional publishing, he became a lecturer in the extension division of Stanford, and in 1911 he was made an associate professor of history and curator of the famous Bancroft Library at the University of California, Berkeley.

After considerable academic wrangling and controversy at the University of California, he was appointed to a new department of social institutions (really sociology) in 1919, becoming a full professor in 1925. During the next decade or so his major course for undergraduates was a magisterial survey called "Progress and Civilization." Though he did not attain the doctoral degree because of fierce academic politics at Stanford, he finally was properly recognized by an honorary LL.D. degree from the University of California in 1940.

Teggart was an early, articulate critic of both overspecialized chronicling of "historical" events and grandiose philosophical abstractions in the social sciences. He vigorously championed an intellectual and practical alliance of history and sociology, with a supplementary emphasis on significant comparisons and the necessity for "world" (inter-societal) history and analysis. In all this, he constantly underscored the need to study important, deep-seated social and cultural changes, not as manifestations of evolution or progress, but as evidence of both achievement and social difficulties.

These ideas were lucidly developed in three works prepared between 1916 and 1925—*Prolegomena to History*, *Processes of History*, and *Theory of History*. The essential message of his intellectual career was that major changes could be reliably explained by locating crucial human events or processes that could be interpreted as "intrusions" on established practices and institutions. These events were conceived as "breaks" in continuity, as "transitions" between antecedent and subsequent developments, reflecting an essentially unpredictable (but nevertheless understandable) unfolding of human experience throughout recorded history. But the primary mark of such "intrusions" was, for Teggart, the evidence of mass migra-

tions due to a variety of demographic, economic, and political factors.

In a very special but controversial study, Teggart tried to explain the barbarian invasions (migrations in the Roman Empire, 58 B.C. to 107 A.D.) as cumulative responses to raids and wars in Eastern Europe and the western regions of the Chinese Empire. In studying later centuries, Teggart gave more prominence to population pressures and the accessibility afforded by intersecting travel and trade routes. However, the consequences of migrations became a major focus for Teggart. He concluded that migrations ultimately unsettled pre-existing organizations, as well as idea systems and values, since migrants carried their cultures with their bodies and belongings. While this collision creates conflicts and uncertainties, the net result was often a release from routine ways and opportunities for greater individuality and a mentality of freedom that results in new ideas and alternatives.

Teggart boldly attacked institutional sterility and complacent intellectual paralysis by pointing to previously ignored orders of facts, by criticizing undue disciplinary specialization, and by confronting the problems of conflict as normal components (not as inevitable causes or either as desirable) of the complex human record. While he was not fully appreciated by his California colleagues, he was an acknowledged influence on the thinking of such scholars as Robert Park and Arnold Toynbee.

Further Reading

Teggart's major works were *Prolegomena to History* (1916), *Processes of History* (1918), *Theory of History* (1925), and *Rome and China* (1939). In addition, there is a revealing reminiscence of Teggart in Robert A. Nisbet, *Teachers and Scholars* (1992).

Additional Sources

Dangberg, Grace, *A guide to the life and works of Frederick J. Teggart,* Reno, Nev.: Grace Dangberg Foundation, 1983. □

Marie Joseph Pierre Teilhard de Chardin

The French theologian and paleontologist Marie Joseph Pierre Teilhard de Chardin (1881-1955) synthesized scientific evolutionary theory, theological interpretation, and mystical vision into a dazzlingly creative and controversial view of man and the universe.

Pierre Teilhard de Chardin was born on May 1, 1881, at his family's ancestral estate near Auvergne. His family was a devoutly Roman Catholic one. His mother influenced Teilhard's piety, and his father awakened the boy's interest in natural history.

Formative Years, 1899-1922

Teilhard attended the Jesuit school at Villefranche, and at the age of 18, he entered the Jesuit novitiate at Aix-en-Provence. When Roman Catholic religious orders were expelled from France in 1902, his Jesuit community moved to the Isle of Jersey, where he continued his studies for 3 years. He was then sent to teach physics and natural history at the Holy Family College in Cairo, Egypt. During his 3 years there he studied geology and paleontology, and he acquired a fascination with the Eastern world.

After the Egyptian interlude Teilhard spent the last stages of his training (1908-1911) at Ore Place, Hastings, England. He began to integrate his earlier absorption in the world of matter into the world of spirit and thus to forge his characteristic world view. Taking evolution as his key idea, he saw the whole universe as an evolutionary process—what he called cosmogenesis. Everything in the universe, including man, was bound together in complete organic interconnection and unity. Matter and spirit were not two separate things but rather two dimensions of one reality. The evolution of the cosmos was the progressive spiritualization, or personalization, of matter, with God as the Omega Point, or fulfillment of the cosmic process, and Christ as the incarnation in time of this ultimate cosmic purpose. The emergence of human consciousness, the "noosphere," on this planet was the leading edge of the cosmogenesis and the clue to the direction of the whole universe. With man, cosmic evolution became self-directing; it "folds in upon itself," converging increasingly toward spirit and person.

Teilhard's two passionate loves were God and the universe, and the whole of his thought and life sought to integrate the two.

Teilhard was ordained a priest in 1911, and he completed his theological studies in 1912. He then did doctoral studies in science at the Sorbonne. When World War I broke out in 1914, he volunteered as a stretcherbearer in the French army; he served throughout the war and was twice decorated. In 1919 he returned to his studies and received a doctorate in paleontology from the Sorbonne in 1922.

Long Exile, 1923-1955

In 1922-1923 Teilhard taught as professor of geology at the Institute Catholique in Paris. His influence as a scientist began to be felt at this time. But he was eager to return to the East, and in 1923 he joined Père Licent, a fellow Jesuit and scientific pioneer in China, at Tientsin to found the French Paleontological Mission in China. Soon after Teilhard's arrival they made an expedition to Inner Mongolia and the Ordos Desert, bringing to light the first evidence that Paleolithic man had lived in North China. During this expedition Teilhard finished his mystical-philosophical "Mass on the World" (published in *Hymn of the Universe* in 1965).

In 1924 Teilhard returned to France. His superiors in the Society of Jesus had been concerned for some time over the boldness and seeming heterodoxy of some of his philosophical and theological views. They believed him to be overoptimistic about the problem of evil and heterodox in his interpretation of the Fall of Man. He was also accused of having pantheistic tendencies. As a result, Teilhard was barred from teaching in France. Thus began his lifelong ordeal with the Church, which brought him much personal suffering and prevented the publication of all his major writings until after his death. He accepted the decisions of the Church and the constant accusations of heresy with obedient submission, but the situation brought him incalculable anguish.

Teilhard returned to China, this time to Peking, a stimulating and cosmopolitan center where he enjoyed a circle of friends and professional colleagues that included scientists from all over the world. In 1926-1927 he wrote *The Divine Milieu* (1960), one of his best-known works. In 1928 he made two important paleontological expeditions into Mongolia. He later traveled in India and visited the United States several times. Teilhard returned briefly to China in 1934 and 1938, settling once again in Peking just before World War II broke out in 1939. The Japanese had occupied North China, and the Europeans and Americans in the region were isolated for the duration of the war. From 1938 to 1940 Teilhard wrote his major work, *The Phenomenon of Man* (1959).

In 1946 Teilhard returned briefly to France. He suffered a severe heart attack just before leaving on an expedition to South Africa, and he had to postpone the trip for 2 years. In 1949 he wrote *Man's Place in Nature* (1966), perhaps the best succinct introduction to the ideas more fully expressed in *The Phenomenon of Man*. In 1951 Teilhard was elected to the Académie des Sciences and went to live in New York City as a member of the Wenner Gren Foundation, where he devoted himself to anthropological studies. He returned to France only one more time in his long ecclesiastically imposed exile, in 1954. At that time new restrictions were imposed on him by his superiors. He died in New York City on Easter Sunday, 1955.

In addition to the writings mentioned, other important works by Teilhard in English include *The Future of Man* (1964), *Building of the Earth* (1965), *The Appearance of Man* (1966), *The Vision of the Past* (1966), and *Science and Christ* (1969). He ranks as one of the three or four most decisive influences in contemporary Christian theology. His thought was a significant new bridge between religion and science and between Christianity and the life and politics of modern man. His theory of cosmic evolution restored man to a central role in the universe, and his notion of human consciousness as evolving toward greater unification gave new optimism to spokesmen for social change.

His friend Père Pierre LeRoy said of Teilhard: "His own faith was in the invincible power of love: men hurt one another by not loving one another. And this was not naiveté but the goodness of the man, for he was good beyond the common measure."

Further Reading

The literature on Teilhard and his thought which has appeared in the short time since his death is enormous, and the Teilhard societies that have grown up around the world assure the appearance of much more. The most complete biographies in English are Claude Cuénot, *Teilhard de Chardin: A Biographical Study* (1965), and Robert Speaight, *Teilhard de Chardin: A Biography* (1967). Recommended studies of Teilhard's thought are Henri de Lubac, *Teilhard de Chardin: The Man and His Meaning* (1965); Christopher F. Mooney, *Teilhard de Chardin and the Mystery of Christ* (1966); and Philip J. Hefner, *The Promise of Teilhard* (1970).

Additional Sources

Carles, Jules, *Teilhard de Chardin,* Paris: Centurion, 1991.

Grim, John, *Teilhard de Chardin: a short biography,* Chambersburg, PA: Published for the American Teilhard Association for the Future of Man by ANIMA Books, 1984.

King, Ursula, *Spirit of fire: the life and vision of Teilhard de Chardin,* Maryknoll, N.Y.: Orbis Books, 1996.

Knight, Alice Valle, *The meaning of Teilhard de Chardin; a prime,* Old Greenwich Conn. Devin-Adair Co. 1974.

Lukas, Mary, *Teilhard,* New York: McGraw-Hill, 1981. □

Kiri Te Kanawa

Lyric soprano Kiri Te Kanawa (born 1944) of New Zealand rose to great popularity because of the warmth and freshness of her voice and her own physical beauty, which lent a striking stage presence.

Kiri Te Kanawa was born in Gisborne, New Zealand, on March 6, 1944, into a family that was too poor to keep her. She was adopted the following month by Tom and Nell Te Kanawa, whose respective Maori and European lineage matched that of her natural parents. (The aboriginal people of New Zealand, the Maori, are a mixture of Polynesian and Melanesian.) Although the family was not especially musical, Nell Te Kanawa encouraged her adopted daughter to sing, and at around the age of six she performed on a local radio broadcast.

In 1956 the family moved to Auckland at the insistence of Mrs. Te Kanawa, so that her daughter could be placed under the tutelage of a respected voice teacher, Sister Mary Leo, at St. Mary's College for Girls. A minimum age requirement—in the end compromised—kept her from enrolling until two years later. She admitted to being lazy in her formative years, and indeed into the beginnings of her professional career, so that she tended toward popular and lighter music, which was easier to sing. At the age of 16 she entered a business school, this practical choice being determined by her rather low academic standing at St. Mary's. Various jobs followed; first as a telephone operator, then a sales person, later an office receptionist.

Meanwhile, she continued her voice lessons with Sister Mary Leo and began singing in popular musicals, such as *Annie Get Your Gun* and *The Sound of Music,* and in cabarets. Continued successes in the popular vein, including several recordings, promised at age 16 a career as a popular singer. Such a career, however, did not suit her mother, who again took the reins, persuading those responsible for the Maori Trust Foundation to support Kiri's continued study.

Freed from the necessity of singing for a living, Te Kanawa was able to devote her efforts to more serious music and to enter singing competitions in the area. Her first triumph came as winner of the Auckland Competition in 1960. Two years later she was runner-up in the more prestigious Mobile Song Quest, and in 1965 she won this competition. In the same year she entered aria competitions of both the Sydney and Melbourne *Suns,* said to be the two most important such events in Australasia. The first awarded her second prize, but her singing of "Leise, leise" (sung in English as "Softly Singing") from Weber's *Der Freischütz* won her first place in the Melbourne *Sun* competition.

As a result of the cash prizes and scholarships awarded her by the competition, and also a special fund set up for her by the Queen Elizabeth II Arts Council of New Zealand, she began studying at the London Opera Centre in 1966. A master class with well-known conductor (and husband of Joan Sutherland) Richard Bonynge in 1966 proved beneficial, for he convinced her that she was a soprano and not a mezzo soprano, as everyone had previously assumed. But the transition from renown in her native New Zealand to the anonymity of a student—and by all accounts not a particularly good one—in London proved difficult. Her laziness persisted, and she developed a reputation for being unprepared and unreliable. This reputation followed her for years, even to Covent Garden, where she had to audition as many as nine times before she could convince its judges, not so much of her abilities, but of her sincerity and determination. In March of 1967 she met Desmond Park; her marriage to him in August of the same year had the stabilizing effect on her that made her subsequent career possible.

The period from 1969 to 1970 was a pivotal one in several respects. She left the London Opera Centre and began her new career, at first singing small *travesti* roles, as in Handel's *Alcina* at Royal Festival Hall, before her major triumph of 1969 as Ellen in Rossini's *La donna del lago* at the Camden Festival. Secondly, she began studying with Vera Rozsa, who did much to improve her intonation, diction, interpretation, and acting. Vera Rozsa also corrected the efforts of the singer's earlier teachers who had tried to make her naturally light voice much bigger. Lastly, she auditioned successfully for the Royal Opera House and was given a contract as junior principal for the 1970-1971 season.

Her Covent Garden debut took place in April 1971 as the leading flower maiden in Wagner's *Parsifal,* an unlikely opera for her, considering the lyrical repertoire she later developed. Although the role was not a large one, she did not go unnoticed; the favorable response led to wider recognition and more important roles. Her American debut was with the Santa Fe Festival in July 1971 as the Countess Almaviva in Mozart's *Marriage of Figaro.* When she repeated the role at Covent Garden in December of the same year the well-known critic of the *Financial Times,* Andrew Porter, proclaimed her "a new star."

Her debut at New York's Metropolitan Opera, as Desdemona in Verdi's *Otello,* had been scheduled for March 7, 1974, but took place, again with high acclaim, at a February 9 matinee, when she substituted for the ailing Teresa Stratas on very short notice. Other important debuts included Elvira in Mozart's *Don Giovanni* at the Paris Opera in February of 1975 and Desdemona in Verdi's *Otello* at the Vienna State Opera in October of 1980. She was accorded a special honor in April of 1981, when she was asked by Prince Charles of Wales to sing at his wedding.

Other roles, either staged or recorded, included Dido in Purcell's *Dido and Aeneas;* the title role in Donizetti's *Anna Bolena;* Micaela and the title role in Bizet's *Carmen;* Blanche in Poulenc's *Dialogue of the Carmelites;* Idamante in Mozart's *Idomeneo;* Amelia in Verdi's *Simon Boccanegra;* Marguerite in Gounod's *Faust;* Mimi in Puccini's *La Bohème;* Tatyana in Tchaikovsky's *Eugène Onegin;* Pamina in Mozart's *Magic Flute;* Fiordiligi in Mozart's *Così fan tutte;* the title role in R. Strauss' *Arabella;* Rosalinde in J. Strauss' *Die Fledermaus;* Marschallin in R. Strauss' *Der Rosenkavalier;* and Maria in Bernstein's *West Side Story.* In addition to opera, she also had a non-operatic repertoire that included Brahms' *Requiem,* Mozart's church music, R. Strauss' *Four Last Songs,* Mahler's fourth symphony, and Berlioz's *Les nuits d'été.*

She appeared as Donna Elvira in a commercial film version of *Don Giovanni* directed by Joseph Losey and released in 1979. Among her many distinctions are honorary doctorates from Dundee, Durham, Auckland, Nottingham and Oxford universities. She was made Dame Commander of the British Empire in 1982.

In the 1980s and 1990s, Te Kanawa released many recordings of both classical and popular music. Her recordings include, *Blue Skies* (1986); *Kiri Sings Gershwin* (1987): *Italian Opera Arias* (1991); *Our Christmas Songs For You* (1996); and *The Ultimate Christmas Album* (1996) with Luciano Pavarotti, Leotyne Price and Joan Sutherland. She also authored a children's book, *Land of the Long White Cloud* in 1989. She was honored in 1990 when she officially opened the Aotea Center, New Zealand's first world-class lyric theater.

Further Reading

Informed criticism of her Marschallin and Violetta by R. Jacobson appears in *Opera News* (December 24, 1983, and December 18, 1982). A revealing, if somewhat chatty, interview by the same writer appears in the same publication of February 26, 1983. Elizabeth Forbes' biographical sketch, containing some information not found here, is in the British journal *Opera* (July 1981). *Kiri Te Kanawa: A Biography,* by David Fingleton (1983) is not a well-written book, grammatically or otherwise. It omits important dates, tends toward the sentimental, and presents much irrelevant information. An objective profile of her can be found in Baker, David J., *Totally Cool: The essence of Kiri Te Kanawa* in *Opera News* (October, 1994). □

Georg Philipp Telemann

Georg Philipp Telemann (1681-1767), a German composer of the late baroque era, was one of the leaders of the Hamburg school during its preeminence in Germany.

Georg Philipp Telemann was born in Magdeburg on March 14, 1681. He was educated there and in Hildesheim. He learned the rudiments of music in school, as all German children did, but otherwise he taught himself music, mainly by studying the scores of Jean Baptiste Lully and André Campra. Telemann is said to have composed motets and other pieces of the church service when very young, and by the time he was 12 years old he had written almost the whole of an opera.

In 1701 Telemann entered Leipzig University as a law student. In 1704 he became organist at the Neukirche in Leipzig and founded a student society called the Collegium Musicum. He wrote several operas for the Leipzig theater. He was chapelmaster at the court of Eisenach (1709-1712) and in Frankfurt (1712-1721). He then became cantor of the Johanneum and music director in Hamburg, and he held these posts for the rest of his life. He was offered the position of music director at Leipzig in 1722 but declined it, and J. S. Bach received the appointment.

Telemann made a number of trips to Berlin, and in 1737 he visited Paris, where he was influenced by French musical ideas and style. He died on June 25, 1767.

Telemann composed with rare facility and fluency in a variety of styles. George Frederick Handel is reported to have said that Telemann could write a church piece of eight parts with the same ease as another would write a letter. He composed literally thousands of works, including 12 complete cantata cycles for the liturgical year, 44 Passions, oratorios, funeral and wedding services, chamber music,

about 40 operas, and over 600 overtures in the French style. Whereas J. S. Bach could maintain his individuality when he wrote in the French or Italian style, Telemann prided himself on taking on the characteristics of every national style, writing in what was then called the new *style galant*.

In his *History of Violin Playing* (1965) David Boyden translates an interesting excerpt from Telemann's autobiography: "I had an opportunity in upper Silesia as well as in Cracow of getting to know Polish music in all its barbaric beauty. One would hardly believe what wonderfully bright ideas such pipers and fiddlers are apt to get when they improvise, ideas that would suffice for an entire lifetime. There is in this music a great deal of merit provided it is treated right. I have myself written in this manner several large concertos and trios that I clad in Italian clothes with alternating Adagi and Allegri."

Opinion is divided as to whether Telemann is an unjustly neglected master or a superficial craftsman whose works lack depth and profundity because of his incredible productivity. Unquestionably he had an effortless melodic gift and wrote music of great charm. His 12 *Methodischen Sonate* (1732) provide many valuable examples of ornamentation that are particularly useful today when the art of improvised ornamentation is almost dead except in jazz.

Further Reading

Telemann's autobiography is in German. Some biographical information on him is in Romain Rolland, *A Musical Tour through the Land of the Past* (trans. 1922). His important contributions to the pedagogy of figured-bass playing are discussed by Franck T. Arnold, *The Art of Accompaniment from a Thorough-bass as Practiced in the Seventeenth and Eighteenth Centuries* (1931). His position in history is discussed by Paul Henry Lang, *Music in Western Civilization* (1941), and Manfred Bukofzer, *Music in the Baroque Era* (1947). See also Homer Ulrich and Paul A. Pisk, *A History of Music and Musical Style* (1963), and Harold C. Schonberg, *The Lives of the Great Composers* (1970).

Additional Sources

Petzoldt, Richard, *Georg Philipp Teleman*, New York, Oxford University Press, 1974. □

Bernardino Telesio

The Italian philosopher of nature Bernardino Telesio (1509-1588) was a leader in the Renaissance movement against medieval Aristotelianism.

Bernardino Telesio was born in Cosenza near Naples. He came from a noble family and received his early education in Milan under the instruction of his humanist uncle, Antonio Telesio. He completed his formal education by studying at Rome and then at Padua, where he was awarded his doctor's degree in 1535. The next few years of his life were spent in a monastery. This was only temporary, however, since he married in 1553. Beginning in 1545, he lived primarily in Naples or nearby at Cosenza. He was responsible for the establishment of an academy in Cosenza consecrated to the study of natural philosophy and based on his ideas and methods. Although Telesio did little teaching at this academy, he did have several pupils who continued the foundation after his death, which occurred in Cosenza in October 1588.

Telesio's most important work, in which his chief naturalistic ideas are advanced, is *De rerum natura iuxta propria principia*. Although the first part of this work was published in 1565, the work was not completed until 1586. In this book Telesio attacked both the method and content of Aristotelian philosophy. The Aristotelians, he felt, relied too much on reason and too little on the senses. Telesio's own emphasis on the use of the senses to reach natural truth led to the conclusion that knowledge is derived from the senses. In his attack on the content of Aristotelian philosophy, Telesio discarded the Aristotelian doctrine of matter and form. In its place, he argued that all things in nature are based on three principles: matter, which is inert and corporeal; the two natural forces of heat and cold, which are incorporeal and active; and the interaction or conflict of these forces, heat and cold, operating on corporeal, inert matter. From the fluctuating degrees of conflict arise the different types of existence. Although others pointed to contradictions in Telesio's thought, he is still an important figure in the transition from the Aristotelian emphasis on reason and the principle of authority to the modern scientists' emphasis on experiment and independent investigation and observation of nature.

Further Reading

The major studies of Telesio are in Italian. In English, an excellent chapter on him is in Paul O. Kristeller, *Eight Philosophers of the Italian Renaissance* (1964). □

Edward Teller

The Hungarian-American physicist Edward Teller (born 1908)—sometimes called the "father" or the "architect" of the hydrogen bomb—was for decades on the forefront of the nuclear question and in the 1980s was an advocate of the Strategic Defense Initiative (SDI), also known as "Star Wars."

Born in Budapest, Hungary, on January 15, 1908, Edward Teller was the second child of Ilona Deutsch and Max Teller, a lawyer from Hungarian Monrovia. When he was twelve years old, Edward was introduced to one of his father's friends, Leopold Klug, a professor of mathematics at the University of Budapest. Klug gave Edward Teller a copy of Euler's *Algebra*. Later Teller wrote: "I never shall forget him [Klug]. I knew, after meeting Professor Klug, what I wanted to do when I grew up." As he recalled: "For as long as I could remember, I had wanted to do one thing: to play with ideas and find out how the world is put together." The first 18 years of his life were spent in Budapest. Before the end of high school, Teller had befriended Eugene P. Wigner (Nobel Laureate for Physics, 1963), John von Neumann (later the celebrated mathematician), and Leo Szilard (later the "father" of the atomic bomb).

Leaving Hungary because of anti-Semitism, Teller went to Germany to study chemistry and mathematics at the Karlsruhe Institute of Technology from 1926 to 1928. A lecture he heard by Herman Mark on the new science of molecular spectroscopy made a lasting impression on him: "He [Mark] made it clear that new ideas in physics had changed chemistry into an important part of the forefront of physics." After Karlsruhe, Teller went to the University of Munich in 1928. As a result of a streetcar accident in Munich on July 14, 1928, he lost most of his right foot. Reconstructive surgery enabled him to walk without a prosthetic, but he occasionally chose to use an artificial foot. From Munich, Teller went to the University of Leipzig from 1929 to 1930. There he obtained a Ph.D. in physical chemistry under Werner Heisenberg in 1930. His dissertation was on experiments in which he used quantum mechanics to calculate energy levels in an excited hydrogen molecule. From 1929 to 1931 he was a research associate at the University of Leipzig. He held a similar position at the University of Göttingen from 1931 to 1933.

Following Heisenberg's advice, he went in 1934—as a Rockefeller Fellow—to study under Niels Bohr at the Institute of Theoretical Physics at the University of Copenhagen in Denmark. On February 26, 1934, a few weeks after starting his Copenhagen fellowship, Teller married Augusta Maria Harkanyi, having known her for many years. He then

became a lecturer at the University of London (City College of London) in 1934-1935.

Becomes an American Citizen

In 1935 Teller came to the United States. He became professor of physics at George Washington University, Washington, D.C., from 1935 to 1946. While on leave during 1941-1942, he held a similar position at Columbia University in New York. At George Washington University Teller worked with George Gamow. Together they calculated the rules for one of the major forms of radioactivity, which became known as the Gamow-Teller selection rules for beta decay. He spent the summer of 1939 at Columbia University "doing a little lecturing to graduate students but primarily as the peacemaker on the Fermi-Szilard project." He moved to Columbia University in 1941 to work on the atomic bomb project. He wrote later: "My moral decision had been made in 1941. That was the year I joined the effort to produce an atomic bomb. That was the year I became an American citizen." Indeed, he and his wife were sworn in as naturalized citizens in March 1941. Their family soon grew to include as son in 1943 and a daughter in 1946.

The Manhattan Project

As a physicist, Teller worked from 1942 to 1946 for the Manhattan Engineering District (wartime Manhattan Project). Early in 1942 he worked with Fermi on fission problems at Columbia University. In 1942-1943 he was at the Metallurgical Laboratory at the University of Chicago. In April 1943 he joined the Los Alamos Scientific Laboratory,

where he remained until 1946 when he left to teach at the University of Chicago until 1949 when he returned to Los Alamos to complete his work on the bomb. According to Teller: "In Los Alamos my metamorphosis was completed. In January 1939 I had been a pure theoretical physicist. Before the attack on Hiroshima I had started work in applied science. After the war, I tried to find my way back to the simpler life of a scientist and a teacher. I never succeeded."

Only three weeks separated the experimental explosion of the first atomic bomb at Alamogordo, in southern New Mexico (July 16, 1945), and the bombing of Hiroshima (August 6, 1945). The bomb was "The result of our wartime work at Los Alamos." And as Teller recalls: "As the oldest member of our group (I was thirty-seven), I was invited to see the test from an observation area just 20 miles away." In his book *The Legacy of Hiroshima* (1962), Teller writes: "It was necessary and right to develop the atomic bomb. It was unnecessary and wrong to bomb Hiroshima without specific warning." He adds: "Soap and water do not wash away sin. Nuclear test bans cannot erase the memory of Hiroshima."

At the University of Chicago, Teller was professor of physics from February 1946 to 1952. On leave from the university, he returned in 1949 to Los Alamos on a full-time basis. He remained there until 1952 as assistant director of what is now called Los Alamos Scientific Laboratory. Looking backward, Teller says (1987): "In 1949 I advocated work on the hydrogen bomb, a weapon of attack. . . . I am now arguing for the development of the means to defend against those weapons."

On January 31, 1950, President Harry S. Truman made a statement on the hydrogen bomb, in which he declared: ". . . I have directed the Atomic Energy Commission to continue its work on all forms of atomic weapons, including the so-called hydrogen or superbomb." J. Robert Oppenheimer and the General Advisory Committee of the Atomic Energy Commission had earlier expressed their opposition to the "Superbomb" or "Super." Apart from Teller, Ernest O. Lawrence and Luis W. Alvarez were among the principal supporters of the "Super." In fact, "Teller lobbied hard for the super in 1949, after the nation heard the news of the Soviet nuclear breakthrough."

The first full-scale thermonuclear explosion—of "Mike"—occurred on November 1, 1952. The islet of the Eniwetok chain, Elugelab, in the South Pacific, where it took place, was wiped off the face of the earth. Teller was not on hand for this first explosion. He had left Los Alamos exactly one year before, on November 1, 1951. While in California on November 1, 1952, he "attended the first hydrogen bomb explosion by watching the sensitive seismograph at the University of California in Berkeley." A bomb of ten megatons, "Mike" was about a thousand times more powerful than the bomb dropped on Hiroshima.

To whom should go the credit of the development of the H-bomb? Teller has been called its "father" or "architect." As stated by Teller himself in a 1955 issue of *Science,* "Hundreds of ideas and thousands of technical skills are required for success. The hydrogen bomb is an achievement of this kind." A capital contribution was made by Stanislaw Ulam, the Polish-born mathematician: he "formulated the original design idea that Teller adapted and made into a workable bomb" (Pringle and Spigelman). Teller also remarked in *Science,* "In the whole development [of the H-bomb] I claim credit in one respect only: I believed, and persisted in believing, in the possibility and the necessity of developing the thermonuclear bomb."

In the Matter of J. Robert Oppenheimer is the title given to the official transcript of the hearing before the Personnel Security Board in Washington, DC, April 12, 1954-May 6, 1954. After Teller's testimony at this security hearing, and the subsequent withdrawal of Oppenheimer's security clearance, "Oppenheimer was widely seen as a scientific martyr and Teller as his persecutor" (Broad). Teller was "Scorned by scientific colleagues" (Broad). As Teller remarked in 1987, "As a result of acting on my beliefs, I lost what I wished to retain: friendly fellowship with many of my fellow scientists." To this day, in spite of the passing of time, the scientific community remains divided on the Teller-Oppenheimer controversy. Later, after hearing testimony from former Prisoners of War that they were to be killed when the planned invasion of Japan began, Teller said that, "for the first time, I had a real impression which almost amounts to a moral justification for using the atomic bomb." By stopping the war with the bomb most of those POW's were saved.

Other Positions and Awards

Teller was a consultant at the Livermore Branch of the Radiation Laboratory at the University of California from 1952 to 1953. He became associate director at what is now called Lawrence Livermore Laboratory (after Ernest O. Lawrence) from 1954 to 1958; he was later director (1958-1960) and again associate director (1960-1975), and finally consultant and associate director emeritus (after 1975). At the University of California at Berkeley, he became professor of physics (1953-1960), professor of physics-at-large (1960-1970), university professor (1970-1975), and professor emeritus (after 1975). After 1975 Teller was a senior research fellow at the Hoover Institution on War, Revolution and Peace at Stanford University. Among his other positions, Teller was a member of the White House Science Council from 1982 to 1986.

After 1954 more than 20 honorary degrees were bestowed upon him. He was a recipient of numerous awards, among which were the Enrico Fermi Award for 1962 (given by President John F. Kennedy and handed over for the late president by President Lyndon B. Johnson), and the National Medal of Science for 1982 (given by President Ronald Reagan) for his research on stellar energy, fusion reaction, molecular physics, and nuclear safety. Among other awards Teller received are the Priestly Memorial Award (1957), the Einstein Award (1959), the General Donovan Memorial Award (1959), the Robins Award (1963), the Leslie R. Groves Gold Medal (1974), the Harvey Prize (1975), the Sylvanus Thayer Award (1986), the Presidential Citizen Medal (1989), and the Order of Banner with Rubies of the Republic of Hungary.

The Star Wars Project

On March 23, 1983, President Reagan announced "a long-term research and development program to begin to achieve our ultimate goal of eliminating the threat posed by strategic nuclear missiles." The Strategic Defense Initiative (SDI) became better known as "Star Wars." Teller was a strong advocate of the project—he met with the president in September 1982 to brief him on it. This controversial issue divided both the scientific and political worlds. Eventually, the plan was determined to be flawed: the satellites cost more that anticipated; the computer technology for the systems was complicated and unreliable; and the nuclear powered lasers were rejected.

Further Reading

Alone or in collaboration, Teller published more than a dozen books from 1939 to 1987. Here is a selective list: *Better A Shield Than a Sword. Perspectives on Defense and Technology* (1987); *The Pursuit of Simplicity* (1980); *Energy From Heaven and Earth* (1979); with Wilson K. Talley, Gary H. Higgins, and Gerald W. Johnson, *The Constructive Uses of Nuclear Explosives* (1968); with Allen Brown, *The Legacy of Hiroshima* (1962). Among Teller's many articles, "The Work of Many People," *Science 121* (February 1955) should be singled out.

An objective biography of Teller exists: Stanley A. Blumberg and Gwinn Owens, *Energy and Conflict: The Life and Times of Edward Teller* (1976). On the atomic bomb, the H-bomb, and Teller, read, in particular: Richard Rhodes, *The Making of the Atomic Bomb* (1986); Peter Wyden, *Day One. Before Hiroshima and After* (1985); Ferenc Morton Szasz, *The Day the Sun Rose Twice: The Story of the Trinity Site Nuclear Explosion, July 16, 1945* (1984); Robert C. Williams and Philip L. Cantelon, editors, *The American Atom: A Documentary History of Nuclear Policies From the Discovery of Fission to the Present. 1939-1984* (1984); and Herbert F. York, *The Advisors: Oppenheimer, Teller, and the Superbomb* (1976).

For the public debate on the Strategic Defense Initiative (SDI) or "Star Wars" see Franklin A. Long, Donald Hafner, and Jeffrey Boutwell, editors, *Weapons in Space* (1986), and Steven E. Miller and Stephen Van Evera, editors, *The Star Wars Controversy. An International Security Reader* (1986). □

William Temple

William Temple (1881-1944), archbishop of Canterbury, was an outstanding church and civic leader who by the time he died had achieved world status in the ecumenical movement as one who could speak with insight to statesmen as well as to religious leaders.

Born in 1881 in Exeter, Devon, where his father, Frederick, was bishop, William Temple is unique in having followed in the steps of his father, who became archbishop of Canterbury 16 years after William's birth. He had the traditional education of the English upper classes, at a public (that is, private) school—Rugby—and at an ancient university—Oxford. He was immediately recognized as a man of great gifts and became successively a fellow of Queen's College, Oxford, in 1910; headmaster of another public school—Repton—in 1910; rector of the fashionable St. James, Piccadilly, in the center of London in 1914; a canon of Westminster Abbey (which is a royal "peculiar" and outside the normal structures of the church) in 1919; bishop of Manchester, a heavily populated industrial diocese, in 1921; archbishop of York in 1929; and then archbishop of Canterbury in 1942. These rapid promotions were not due to his privileged background but to the fact that he was widely recognized as a leading figure who could not be overlooked. At his death he was recognized as such all over the world and, had he lived, he would have been the sole president of the World Council of Churches, which was officially launched in 1948.

Nor did he move primarily in privileged circles. From 1905 he was closely associated with the Workers' Educational Association, and he was its first president from 1908 to 1924. He retained a lasting commitment to educational and social causes, and in the 1930s he was active in working for the unemployed during the economic depression of that time. He was a member of the Labour Party for some years, and that before it had ousted the Liberals as the main opposition party to the Conservatives. He mixed easily with all classes, and particularly kept the confidence of those of student age. From 1907 he was associated with the Student Christian Movement, which sent him as an usher to the Edinburgh Conference of 1910, from which the modern ecumenical movement is dated. It was because of these ecumenical contacts that he was the obvious chairperson of the

first ecumenical social conference to be held in Britain, COPEC (Conference on Christian Politics, Economics and Citizenship), in Birmingham in 1924. Subsequently he was to play a leading part in both the "Faith and Order" and "Life and Work" sides of the incipient ecumenical movement.

Within the Church of England Temple was prominent in securing an enabling act from Parliament in 1919 which gave the Church a large measure of self-government instead of more direct state control and in chairing from 1925 to 1938 a commission whose report *Doctrine in the Church of England* showed how modern biblical and doctrinal criticism could legitimately be used to interpret traditional positions. His own position moved from a more liberal Protestant to a more liberal Catholic one.

In philosophy he was nurtured in the last days of Oxford idealism, and his early books—*Mens Creatrix* (1917) and *Christus Veitas* (1924)—reflect this. Idealism has difficulty with the concrete, and Temple was concerned to show the necessity and reasonableness for it to allow for a specific Incarnation. Subsequently he wrestled with A. N. Whitehead's Process philosophy and came very near to what is known as its pantheism; but he never came to terms with Logical Positivism or with Existentialism (going back to Kierkegaard), both of which became very influential philosophical movements before World War II.

His Gifford Lectures *Nature, Man and God* (1934) show his thought at its best. By this time the great economic depression from 1929 had alerted him in a general way to Marxism, and in these lectures he tried to steal its cloth by using the term "dialectical" and by his most famous sentence: "Christianity is the most avowedly materialistic of all the great religions." In his last years, as war again threatened and did break out, he took a more sombre view of irrationality in the world. Yet he never lost hope. He was a natural believer in the Christian faith who never felt serious doubt. His spirituality was reflected in his *Readings in St. John's Gospel* (1939 and 1944). His wartime *Christianity and Social Order* (1942) remained into the 1980s a classic of realistic yet hopeful social ethics, the realism being epitomized in the sentence "The art of Government in fact is the art of so ordering life that self-interest prompts what justice demands." He was unusual in being a prophet with a sense of the possible.

His spiritual leadership in wartime avoided entirely the uncritical nationalism and bellicosity which had been the dominant tone of the churches in World War I. All his life he worked at a prodigious pace over a huge range of issues and problems, and he published many books, often based on lectures and sermons. He died in the fullness of his powers in 1944.

Further Reading

By far the main source of information is the biography *William Temple, Archbishop of Canterbury* by F. A. Iremonger, even though it was published in 1948, rather soon after his death. It contains a valuable chapter by Professor Dorothy Emmet on Temple's philosophy. Two American books are *William Temple: Twentieth Century Christian* by Joseph Fletcher (1963) and *William Temple, an Archbishop for all Seasons* by Charles W. Lowry (1982). The former is more analytical and the latter more personal, but neither is exclusively so.

Additional Sources

Kent, John, *William Temple: church, state, and society in Britain, 1880-1950,* Cambridge; New York: Cambridge University Press, 1992.

Lowry, Charles Wesley, *William Temple, an archbishop for all seasons,* Washington, D.C.: University Press of America, 1982. □

Gilbert Tennent

Gilbert Tennent (1703-1764), American Presbyterian clergyman and evangelist, participated in the revival movement, the Great Awakening, in the Middle colonies and New England.

Gilbert Tennent, eldest son of William Tennent, was born on Feb. 5, 1703, in County Armagh, Ireland. The family emigrated to Pennsylvania in 1717. Educated at home by his father, a Presbyterian minister, Gilbert was excellently grounded in the classics and Hebrew and made a beginning in the study of the Bible and theology. This learning was probably regarded as a near equivalent to what a bachelor of arts degree required, because when he went to Yale, he received a master of arts in 1725.

That year Tennent was licensed to preach and began to do so at once but remained only briefly at his first charge, in Newcastle, Del. He helped his father build a log cabin to be used as a divinity school (later known as the Log College) and began the study of medicine.

In 1726 Tennent accepted a call to a congregation in New Brunswick, N.J. During his early years there he also assisted Theodorus Frelinghuysen, an evangelist among the Dutch Reformed congregations in the same area, thereby discovering his own abilities as an evangelistic preacher and also experiencing marked success. In 1738 the English evangelist George Whitefield heard Tennent preach on one occasion and wrote in his *Journal* that never before had he heard "such a searching sermon." Whitefield joined briefly in the New Jersey revival that was sweeping the colony.

As the new converts were gathered into new churches, the demand for ministers to serve them resulted in the choice of Log College graduates, who were zealous to save souls and had some training in evangelistic preaching. Several Yale graduates of similar mind joined this group, which under the leadership of Tennent organized itself into the New Brunswick Presbytery with power to license its own ministers. But the older ministers who had been trained in Scottish universities looked on in alarm. Their first move to regain control and maintain their standard of ministerial fitness was a law in their own synod requiring graduates of other than university colleges to be examined before a license to preach could be granted. This was a distinct blow to the Log College.

The Great Schism

Tennent's response to this action was his Nottingham sermon of 1739: "The Danger of an Unconverted Ministry." This was a violent denunciation of ministers who had criticized the extreme emotionalism of the revival. The all but inevitable breach in the Presbyterian ranks followed. Known as the Great Schism, it lasted for 17 years, created bitterness which lasted much longer, and destroyed much that was good.

In New England a similar rift followed, though without formal division. Tennent was in part responsible for this disunion also. When Whitefield departed after preaching in Massachusetts in 1740, leaving scores of new converts and newly awakened communities behind him, Tennent immediately followed, preaching in some 20 of the same towns before the revival fever had time to cool.

Intensely zealous as to the saving of souls, less gifted as a speaker, Tennent was in some ways more forceful than Whitefield and more disrupting to the community. Tennent was noisy rather than eloquent and lacking in the art and grace of public address. Also, in his sermons he made salvation less a better way of life and more an escape from eternal punishment. He often frightened his audience by stressing the certainty of hell for those who did not repent in time. He also offended many by his unpolished manners. Saddest of all, he widened the breach between those who believed the revival was of God and those who heard only the noise and resented the criticism against the settled ministry.

In 1743, when the revivals were no longer front-page news, Tennent left New Brunswick and accepted a call to a newly organized Presbyterian church in Philadelphia made up largely of Whitefield's friends and sympathizers. Tennent's success was moderate and his record free of any return to the excesses of his earlier ministry. After his father's death in 1746 and the consequent closing of the Log College, he was helpful in founding the College of New Jersey (now Princeton). He was one of a committee who went to England in 1753 to solicit funds for the college, and after it was founded he became one of the trustees.

In 1758 Tennent was active in bringing about the union between the Philadelphia Presbytery and the Presbytery of New York, thus ending the long division in the Presbytery in America. It is not often that a man is given a chance to heal the breach his lack of wisdom has created. He died on July 23, 1764, in Philadelphia. Tennent served high purposes, without counting the cost. His own conviction was his guide and mentor.

Further Reading

Tennent figures in general works on religion in America, among them Charles H. Maxson, *The Great Awakening in the Middle Colonies* (1920); Leonard J. Trinterud, *The Forming of an American Tradition: a Re-examination of Colonial Presbyterianism* (1949); and Edwin Scott Gaustad, *The Great Awakening in New England* (1957). Winthrop Still Hudson,

Religion in America (1965), is recommended for general historical background.

Additional Sources

Coalter, Milton J., *Gilbert Tennent, son of thunder: a case study of continental Pietism's impact on the first great awakening in the middle colonies,* New York: Greenwood Press, 1986. □

Alfred Tennyson

The English poet Alfred Tennyson, 1st Baron Tennyson (1809-1892), was regarded by his contemporaries as the greatest poet of Victorian England. A superb craftsman in verse, he wrote poetry that ranged from confident assertion to black despair.

Alfred Tennyson, who is known as Alfred, Lord Tennyson, was born on Aug. 6, 1809, in the rectory of the village of Somersby, Lincolnshire. His parents were the Reverend George Clayton Tennyson and Elizabeth Fytche Tennyson; he was one of eight sons—there were four daughters as well. Dr. Tennyson, the poet's father, was the elder of the two sons of a prosperous businessman who favored his younger son and thus left Dr. Tennyson embittered and relatively impoverished. He was an educated man, a country clergyman, and Alfred read widely in his father's library. As Dr. Tennyson grew older, he grew more passionate and melancholy: he took to drink, he suffered from lapses of memory, and he once even tried to kill his eldest son. Misfortune and madness, not surprisingly, haunted the whole Tennyson family. The year he died, Dr. Tennyson said of his children, "They are all strangely brought up."

Early Poetry and Cambridge

Tennyson began writing poetry as a child. At 12 he was writing a 6,000-line epic in imitation of Sir Walter Scott. Other youthful models were Lord Byron, whose death in 1824 he particularly mourned, and Percy Bysshe Shelley. When he was 14, Tennyson wrote a play called *The Devil and the Lady,* a dexterous imitation of Elizabethan comic verse.

In 1827 there appeared an unpretentious volume entitled *Poems by Two Brothers;* the book, despite its title, included poems by three of the Tennyson brothers, a little less than half of them probably by Alfred. That same year Alfred and Charles joined their brother Frederick at Trinity College, Cambridge University. In 1829 Tennyson joined the Apostles, an undergraduate discussion group, some of whose members would over the years continue to be his closest friends. Tennyson's undergraduate days were a time of intellectual and political turmoil in England. The institutions of church and state were being challenged, and the Apostles debated the issues which led to the passage of the Reform Bill in 1832. Among the Apostles, Tennyson's closest friend was Arthur Hallam, a wonderfully gifted young man whose early tragic death in 1833 would inspire *In Memoriam.*

In 1830 the Apostles took up the cause of a group of Spanish revolutionaries; Tennyson and Hallam went to the Pyrenees on an unsuccessful mission to aid the rebels. Also in 1830 Tennyson published his *Poems, Chiefly Lyrical;* of these poems perhaps the best-known and most characteristic is "Mariana," where melancholy is suggested by the depiction of a landscape much like that of Tennyson's native Lincolnshire. Those who knew Tennyson as a university student were impressed by his commanding physical presence and by his youthful literary achievements. In 1831 his father died, and Tennyson left the university without taking a degree.

Discovery of a Vocation

In the volume entitled *Poems,* which Tennyson published in 1832, a recurring theme is the conflict between a selfish love of beauty and the obligation to serve society. The collection includes "The Lady of Shalott," a narrative set in Arthurian England in which retired estheticism is destroyed by a dangerous "real" world, and "The Palace of Art," an allegory which finally affirms the teaching obligations of the poet. Tennyson was depressed by some of the reviews of this book, and he was cast down by Hallam's death; for the next 10 years he published nothing. In 1836 he fell in love with Emily Sellwood, whom he met at the marriage of her sister to his brother George. In 1840 he invested what money he had inherited in a scheme for woodworking machinery; by 1843 he had lost his small patrimony.

Poems, Two Volumes (1842) presaged a change in Tennyson's fortunes. Here for the first time appeared one of the several poems which would eventually make up the *Idylls of the King*. Other poems in this collection are "Ulysses," a dramatic monologue in which the aging king urges his companions to undertake a final heroic journey, and "The Two Voices," an interior debate between the death wish and the will to live. *Poems, Two Volumes* was well received, and Sir Robert Peel, the prime minister, who was particularly impressed by "Ulysses," awarded Tennyson a pension which guaranteed him £200 a year.

The Princess: A Medley (1847) is Tennyson's attempt to meet the charge that he had neglected the social responsibilities of the poet. This fable, in some 3,000 lines of blank verse, is concerned with the cause of woman's rights. The poem is a generally lighthearted work—in 1870 William S. Gilbert produced a comic stage version—and Tennyson cautiously advocates a greater appreciation of the feminine intelligence.

In Memoriam

The great year of Tennyson's life is 1850: on June 1 he published *In Memoriam,* the long elegy inspired by the death of Hallam; less than 2 weeks later he married Emily Sellwood, with whom he had fallen in love 14 years before; and in November he was appointed poet laureate to succeed William Wordsworth. Tennyson's years of uncertainty and financial insecurity were over; he became the greatly esteemed poetic spokesman of his age.

In Memoriam is in form a series of 129 lyrics of varying length, all composed in the same stanzaic form. The lyrics may be read individually, rather like the entries in a journal, but the poem has an overall organization. It begins with the death of Hallam, who was engaged to Tennyson's sister, and it ends with the marriage of another sister. Tennyson described it as a "kind of *Divina Commedia,* ending with happiness." The poem covers a period of roughly 3 years, punctuated by three celebrations of Christmas. The movement of the poem, though it is as irregular as a fever chart, is from grief through resignation to joy. The poem combines private feeling with a perplexity over the future of Christianity which was shared by many of Tennyson's contemporaries.

With his family Tennyson settled in Farringford on the Isle of Wight in a seclusion frequently interrupted by admiring tourists, many of them Americans. More welcome visitors were his friends Edward Lear, the comic poet; Charles Kingsley, the novelist; Benjamin Jowett, the master of Balliol College; and even Albert, the Prince Consort, who took away cowslips to make tea for Queen Victoria.

Although Tennyson was now settled and prosperous, his next book, *Maud and Other Poems* (1855), is notable for another study in melancholy. He called the title poem a "monodrama," a form somewhere between a dramatic monologue and a verse play. We hear only one voice, that of a hysterical young man who is sometimes close to madness. Tennyson described the poem as a "little Hamlet." It almost certainly expresses some of the author's youthful anxieties as recollected in middle age. The hero furiously rejects the materialism and callousness of 19th-century society. He is preoccupied by thoughts of his father's suicide, and his reason is endangered when he accidentally kills the brother of Maud, the girl he loves. The hero then exiles himself to France, and, when he learns of Maud's death, he enlists to fight in the Crimea in the hope that the violence of war will somehow redeem him. The poem is now much admired for its metrical virtuosity and for its dramatization of neurotic states of mind. Of the other poems in the 1855 volume, the best-known are "The Charge of the Light Brigade" and "The Ode on the Death of the Duke of Wellington," certainly the greatest of the poems written by Tennyson in his capacity as poet laureate.

The Idylls of the King

Between 1856 and 1876 Tennyson's principal concern was the composition of a series of linked narrative poems about King Arthur and the Round Table. He worked on this project for more than 20 years: one section was written as early as 1833; another part was not published until 1884. As definitively collected in 1889, *The Idylls of the King* consists of a dedication to the Prince Consort, 12 blank-verse narratives (the idylls) which deal with Arthur, Merlin, Lancelot, Guenevere, and other figures in the court, and an epilogue addressed to the Queen. The individual narratives are linked by a common theme: the destructive effect of sexual passion on an honorable society. The Round Table is brought down in ruins by the illicit love of Lancelot and Guenevere. Some of Tennyson's contemporaries regretted that he had lavished so much attention on the legendary past; it is clear, however, that this myth of a dying society expressed some of his fears for 19th-century England.

Plays and Last Years

Tennyson had a long and immensely productive literary career, and a chronology shows that he did ambitious work until late in his life. In his 60s he wrote a series of historical verse plays—*Queen Mary* (1875), *Harold* (1876), and *Becket* (1879)—on the "making of England." The plays were intended to revive a sense of national grandeur and to remind the English of their liberation from Roman Catholicism.

Tennyson's last years were crowned with many honors. The widowed Queen Victoria ranked *In Memoriam* next to the Bible as a solace in her grief. In 1883 Tennyson was awarded a peerage. He died on Oct. 6, 1892, and he was buried in Westminster Abbey after a great funeral. The choir sang a musical setting for "Crossing the Bar," the poem, written a few years earlier, which is placed at the end of all collections of his work.

Further Reading

The best edition of Tennyson's work is Christopher B. Ricks, *The Poems of Tennyson* (1969). Hallam Tennyson, *Alfred, Lord Tennyson: A Memoir* (2 vols., 1897), is the official biography. Important new materials are in Sir Charles Tennyson, *Alfred Tennyson* (1949). The most recent biography, Joanna Richardson, *The Pre-eminent Victorian: A Study of Tennyson*

(1964), is readable but shallow. Particularly valuable critical studies are J. H. Buckley, *Tennyson: The Growth of a Poet* (1960), and Valerie Pitt, *Tennyson Laureate* (1962). Important specialized studies include Edgar Finley Shannon, *Tennyson and the Reviewers* (1952); John Killham, *Tennyson and the Princess: Reflections of an Age* (1958); and R. W. Rader, *Tennyson's Maude: The Biographical Genesis* (1963). The reactions of Tennyson's first readers may be studied in John D. Jump, ed., *Tennyson: The Critical Heritage* (1967). □

Gerard Ter Borch

The Dutch painter Gerard Ter Borch (1617-1681) is noted for small portraits and genre scenes of great refinement.

Gerard Ter Borch was born in Zwolle. His first teacher was his father, Gerard Ter Borch the Elder, who in his youth had spent some years in Rome and returned with drawings he had made as well as some he had collected in Italy. The son precociously revealed his gifts as a draftsman, as shown in his drawing of a man on horseback (1625).

Ter Borch traveled widely. In 1634 he was in Haarlem, in 1635 in London, in 1640 probably in Rome. A visit to Spain is reflected in reminiscences of Diego Velázquez in the style and psychological penetration of Ter Borch's portraits. His famous portrait *Helena van der Schalke as a Child* (ca. 1644) calls to mind Velázquez's Infantas; the placement of the figure in palpable yet undefined space, without the indication of a floor line, is a masterful adoption of the Spanish master's invention.

Between 1645 and 1648 Ter Borch was in Münster, Germany, where he went to seek portrait commissions during the meetings that ended the 80 years of war between the United Provinces and Spain. His small group portrait *Swearing of the Oath of Ratification of the Treaty of Münster* is a rare example in Dutch 17th-century painting of the recording of an actual historical event. It includes more than 50 recognizable portraits. The painter asked for this work the enormous price of 6,000 guilders. Apparently no buyer was found, for the picture was in the hands of his widow after his death. From 1654 on Ter Borch lived mainly in Deventer, where he married, became a citizen, held honorary office, and died on Dec. 8, 1681.

Ter Borch's early paintings were mainly scenes of military life, painted with great subtlety of color and values. Later he showed a predilection for small, dainty interior scenes, in which he revealed his delight in the sheen of satin and the grace of charming women. The elegance of his figures has tended to obscure the fact that in many cases they are shown as participants in situations of amatory commerce. The figures and costumes are painted with care and high finish that is not matched in the settings and backgrounds, which are often not well realized. The *Music Lesson* (ca. 1675) is a characteristic late example of Ter Borch's favorite subject matter. His most able pupil, Caspar

Netscher, became a successful portraitist in the small-scale and fashionable tradition of his master.

Further Reading

The important work on Ter Borch is in Dutch. He figures in the following general studies of Dutch art: Neil Maclaren, National Gallery Catalogues, *The Dutch School* (1960), and Jakob Rosenberg, Seymour Slive, and E. H. ter Kuile, *Dutch Art and Architecture, 1600-1800* (1966). □

Terence

Terence (195-159 B.C.), or Publius Terentius Afer, was a Roman comic playwright. As a translator and adapter of the Greek New Comedy, produced about 336-250 B.C., he gave near-perfect form and expression in Latin to the comedy of manners.

Information about the life of Terence is based mainly on two sources: the prologues of Terence's plays, in which he defends himself against hostile criticism, and a life of Terence written by Suetonius (ca. A.D. 70-ca. 135) and preserved in Donatus's commentary on the plays of Terence.

The prologues provide few facts, and the brief biography is filled with contradictions. Suetonius, like other ancient biographers, gathered his information from earlier sources and undoubtedly filled out the account with inferences from Terence's plays, conventional themes, and anecdotes.

Basically accepted by most scholars is that Terence was born in Carthage and brought to Rome as a slave while quite young. Since Carthage and Rome were at peace during this period, Terence's master, Senator Terentius Lucanus, acquired him by purchase rather than as a captive in war. The youth was then educated and manumitted. Terence is described as medium in stature, graceful in person, and dark (*fuscus*) in complexion. *Fuscus* may mean that Terence was merely darker enough than the ordinary Roman to attract notice or that his complexion was that of a Moor. The second possibility would add an interesting racial dimension to the history of Latin literature.

Terence gained access to the Scipionic Circle, the foremost literary group of his day, composed of young aristocrats devoted to Greek letters and culture, but such lofty connections sparked malicious accusations that Terence either had not written his own plays or was greatly assisted in their composition.

Terence read his first play, the *Andria,* to the aged playwright Caecilius, who pronounced it a success and encouraged further works. After composing a total of six plays during the years 166-160 B.C., Terence journeyed to Greece to gather more plays to adapt into Latin and died on his way home. Terence had married but was survived by

only a daughter who inherited his small estate on the Appian way and married a Roman knight.

Chronology and Sources

The chronology of Terence's plays remains a matter of dispute, but the following enjoys the widest acceptance: *Andria* (166 B.C.), *Hecyra* (first staging, 165), *Heauton Timorumenos* (163), *Eunuchus* (161), *Phormio* (161), *Adelphoe* (160), and *Hecyra* (second staging and third staging, 160).

All six plays of Terence are adaptations (to what extent is unknown) of Greek originals no longer extant. The *Hecyra* and the *Phormio* are each based on a play by Apollodorus of Carystus (3d century B.C.). The *Heauton Timorumenos* is drawn from one play of Menander, and the *Andria* and *Eunuchus* each draw upon two plays of Menander. The *Adelphoe* borrows from a play of Menander and a play of Diphilus (ca. 340-289 B.C.).

The Plays

The *Andria,* Terence's first play, is typical. Two young men, who are friends, are in love with two girls but are prevented from marriage until the end of the play by two fathers. The plot is double and relies on devices of mistaken identity, deception, and recognition. Yet several features are atypical: attempted trickery by a father against a son and a slave; self-deception by a father when he refuses to accept the truth; and the intrigues of a slave, which, far from assisting the young man in love, only create greater difficulty for him.

The *Heauton Timorumenos* employs Terence's conventional deception and double plot of two young lovers whose affairs are closely interwoven. The treatment of the recognition of the free birth of a young girl marks an advance in technique, for it occurs in the middle of the play and complicates rather than solves a problem. The *Eunuchus* is notable for the vigor and daring of its hero, Chaerea, perhaps the most attractive of Terence's young men. After rape and impersonation, Chaerea assumes responsibility for his actions and marries the girl he both loved and offended.

The *Phormio* furnishes an amusing and clever portrait of a unique character type, a blending of sycophant, parasite, and friend, whose legal and psychological expertise secures the love affairs of his young comrades by outwitting their fathers. The *Hecyra,* Terence's least humorous play and perhaps the apex of classical high comedy, studies the dilemma of a young husband who finds that his wife is pregnant by another man. Poorly received in antiquity, the *Hecyra* now enjoys high praise and is noteworthy for a serious portrayal of married life; two exceptional female characters, a generous courtesan and a misunderstood mother-in-law; the absence of the usual double plot of two young lovers; the employment of suspense until the very end; and the diminished role of the slave.

The *Adelphoe* presents in ancient garb the problem of how to raise a son. Two methods are studied, the strict and the compliant, and both are found wanting. Demea, the play's hero and perhaps the only Terentian character to experience true growth and development, at last achieves the harmonious balance of discipline and leniency which the poet recommends.

His Prologues

The function of a Terentian prologue was neither to supply the necessary antecedents for the audience's understanding of the action of the drama nor to explain in advance the outcome of the plot, as Plautus sometimes does. An older and established playwright of whom we know little, Luscius Lanuvinus, maliciously attempted to check Terence's incipient career with three major criticisms. Terence employed the polemic prologue to defend himself. To the charge that his plays are slight compositions, Terence replies with cutting remarks about Lanuvinus's recent play. To the charge that his plays were in reality written by or greatly altered by noble friends, Terence is evasive, probably because an outright denial might have offended the distinguished men who aided his career. To the charge that he contaminated or drew from two Greek originals to create one Latin play, Terence replies that the older comic poets Naevius and Plautus set precedents for this procedure.

Plot Construction and Characterization

All Terentian plays concern youthful love, and all but one (*Hecyra*) employ the double plot. Two love affairs involve two young men, two girls, and two fathers, who are often contrasted. With the elimination of the expository prologue, Terence relies less on irony than on suspense and surprise. Impersonation, trickery, mistaken identity, and recognition (*anagnorasis*) are usual devices.

Terence himself makes us aware that his characters are human types by using telltale names rather than sharply delineated individuals. The usual cast of stock characters includes male members of the household: a young man (*adulescens*) hopelessly in love; an aged parent (*senex*), sometimes lenient and sometimes severe; and a cunning slave (*servus*). In female roles there are a young girl (*virgo*), a courtesan (*meretrix*), a wife or mother (*matrona*), and a maidservant (*ancilla*). A parasite (*parasitus*), slave dealer (*leno*), and soldier (*miles*) make up comic roles. Still, Terence varies each character within his type and occasionally invests a character with individuality that transcends typology.

His Style and Influence

The language of Terence achieves a perfection of correct expression, lightness, clarity, and elegance; and although the speech of everyday life can be detected, it is not the colloquial language of the common people but of refined society. Cicero praised the polish and refinement of Terence's style; Caesar lauded the purity. Avoiding variety or novelty which jars, Terence gave final form to many maxims: "Fortis fortuna adjuvat (Fortune favors the brave)" and "Dictum sapienti sat est (A word to the wise is sufficient)."

Terence's plays enjoyed success during his lifetime and were both read and staged with admiration by the Romans after his death. The Middle Ages valued Terence more highly than Plautus for his Latinity and moral excellence. Renaissance Italy composed comedies in Latin modeled upon Terence, staged his plays, and wrote Italian comedies in the Terentian manner.

Molière's comedy of manners owes a special debt to Terence for tone, plot, and characterization. Finally, English comedy began under the influence of Plautus and Terence from the classical revival and the composition of Neo-Latin dramas. Nicholas Udall's *Ralph Roister Doister,* the first real English comedy, draws upon the *Eunuchus,* and Terentian influence is discernible in both William Shakespeare and Ben Jonson.

Further Reading

Terence's work in translation is available in a number of editions. One with commentary is that of Sidney G. Ashmore, *The Comedies of Terence* (1908). John Sargeaunt's edition, *Terence* (2 vols., 1912), also includes the Latin text. Two more recent collections are George E. Duckworth, *The Complete Roman Drama* (2 vols., 1942), and Frank O. Copley, *The Comedies of Terence* (1967). Gilbert Norwood, *The Art of Terence* (1923), offers sensitive but occasionally overly enthusiastic criticism. For traditional and original interpretation see William Beare, *The Roman Stage* (1951), and for excellent consideration of almost every aspect of Terence see George E. Duckworth, *The Nature of Roman Comedy* (1952). □

Mother Teresa

For her work among the poor and dying of India, Mother Teresa of Calcutta (1910-1997) won the Nobel Prize for Peace in 1979.

Mother Teresa of Calcutta, a Roman Catholic nun who founded the only Catholic religious order still growing in membership, was born Agnes Gonxha Bojaxhiu in Skopje, Yugoslavia, on August 27, 1910. Her parents were Albanian grocers, and at the time of her birth Skopje lay within the Ottoman Empire. She attended public school in Skopje, and first showed religious interests as a member of a school sodality that focused on foreign missions. By the age of 12 she felt she had a calling to help the poor.

This calling took sharper focus through her teenage years, when she was especially inspired by reports of work being done in India by Yugoslav Jesuit missionaries serving in Bengal. When she was 18 Mother Teresa left home to join a community of Irish nuns, the Sisters of Loretto, who had a mission in Calcutta, India. She received training in Dublin, Ireland, and in Darjeeling, India, taking her first religious vows in 1928 and her final religious vows in 1937.

One of Mother Teresa's first assignments was to teach, and eventually to serve as principal, in a girls' high school in Calcutta. Although the school lay close to the teeming slums, the students were mainly wealthy. In 1946 Mother Teresa experienced what she called a second vocation or "call within a call." She felt an inner urging to leave the

convent life and work directly with the poor. In 1948 the Vatican gave her permission to leave the Sisters of Loretto and to start a new work under the guidance of the Archbishop of Calcutta.

Founding the Missionaries of Charity

To prepare to work with the poor, Mother Teresa took an intensive medical training with the American Medical Missionary Sisters in Patna, India. Her first venture in Calcutta was to gather unschooled children from the slums and start to teach them. She quickly attracted both financial support and volunteers, and in 1950 her group, now called the Missionaries of Charity, received official status as a religious community within the Archdiocese of Calcutta. Members took the traditional vows of poverty, chastity, and obedience, but they added a fourth vow—to give free service to the most abjectly poor. In Mother Teresa's own view, the work of her group was very different from that of secular welfare agencies. She saw her nuns ministering to Jesus, whom they encounter as suffering in the poor, especially those who are dying alone or who are abandoned children.

The Missionaries of Charity began their distinctive work of ministering to the dying in 1952, when they took over a temple in Calcutta that previously had been dedicated to the Hindu goddess Kali. The sisters working there had, as their main goal, filling with dignity and love the last days of poor people who were dying. The physical conditions of this shelter were not imposing, although they were completely clean; but the emotional atmosphere of love and concern struck most visitors as truly saintly. When the sisters

were criticized or disparaged because of the small scale of their work (in the context of India's tens of millions of desperately poor and suffering people), Mother Teresa tended to respond very simply. She considered any governmental help a benefit, but she was content to have her sisters do what they could for specific suffering people, since she regarded each individual as infinitely precious in God's sight.

The Missionaries of Charity received considerable publicity, and Mother Teresa used it rather adroitly to benefit her work. In 1957 they began to work with lepers and slowly expanded their educational work, at one point running nine elementary schools in Calcutta. They also opened a home for orphans and abandoned children. In 1959 they began to expand outside of Calcutta, starting works in other Indian cities. As in Calcutta, their focus was the poorest of the poor: orphans, the dying, and those ostracized by diseases such as leprosy. Before long they had a presence in more than 22 Indian cities, and Mother Teresa had visited such other countries as Ceylon (now Sri Lanka), Australia, Tanzania, Venezuela, and Italy to begin foundations. Although in most of these countries the problems of the poor seemed compounded by uncontrolled population growth, the Sisters held strongly negative views on both abortion and contraception. Their overriding conviction was that all lives are precious, and sometimes they seemed to imply that the more human beings there were, the better God's plan was flourishing.

In 1969 Mother Teresa allowed a group called the International Association of Co-Workers of Mother Teresa to affiliate itself with the Missionaries of Charity. This was a sort of "third order," as Catholics sometimes call basically lay groups that affiliate with religious orders both to help the orders in their work and to participate in their idealistic spirituality. These Co-Workers were drawn to Mother Teresa's work with the very poor, and their constitution specified that they wanted to help serve the poorest of the poor, without regard to caste or creed, in a spirit of prayer and sacrifice.

Dedication to the Very Poor

Mother Teresa's group continued to expand throughout the 1970s, opening works in such new countries as Jordan (Amman), England (London), and the United States (Harlem, New York City). She received both recognition and financial support through such awards as the Pope John XXIII Peace Prize and a grant from the Joseph Kennedy Jr. Foundation. Benefactors regularly would arrive to support works in progress or to stimulate the Sisters to open new ventures. Mother Teresa received increasing attention in the media, especially through a British Broadcasting Corporation special interview that Malcolm Muggeridge conducted with her in London in 1968. In 1971, on the occasion of visiting some of her sisters in London, she went to Belfast, Northern Ireland, to pray with the Irish women for peace and to meet with Ian Paisley, a militant Protestant leader. In the same year she opened a home in Bangladesh for women raped by Pakistani soldiers in the conflicts of that time. By 1979 her groups had more than 200 different operations in over 25 countries around the world, with dozens more ventures on the horizon. In 1986 she persuaded President Fidel Castro to allow a mission in Cuba. The hallmark of all of Mother Teresa's works—from shelters for the dying to orphanages and homes for the mentally ill—continued to be service to the very poor.

In 1988 Mother Teresa sent her Missionaries of Charity into Russia and also opened a home for AIDS patients in San Francisco, California. In 1991 she returned home to Albania and opened a home in Tirana, the capital. At this time, there were 168 homes operating in India. Later in 1995, plans materialized to open homes in China.

Despite the appeal of this saintly work, all commentators remarked that Mother Teresa herself was the most important reason for the growth of her order and the fame that came to it. Muggeridge was struck by her pleasant directness and by the otherworldly character of her values. He saw her as having her feet completely on the ground, yet she seemed almost unable to comprehend his suggestion (meant as an interviewer's controversial prod) that trying to save a few of India's abandoned children was almost meaningless, in the face of the hordes whom no one was helping. He realized that Mother Teresa had virtually no understanding of a cynical or godless point of view that could consider any human being less than absolutely valuable.

Another British interviewer, Polly Toynbee, was especially struck by Mother Teresa's lack of rage or indignation. Unlike many "social critics," she did not find it necessary to attack the economic or political structures of the cultures that were producing the abjectly poor people she was serving. For her the primary rule was a constant love, and when social critics or religious reformers chose to vent anger at the evils of structures underlying poverty and suffering, that was between them and God. Indeed, in later interviews Mother Teresa continued to strike an apolitical pose, refusing to take a stand on anything other than strictly religious matters. One sensed that to her mind politics, economics, and other this-worldly matters were other people's business. The business given by God to her and her group was simply serving the very poor with as much love and skill as they could muster.

In the 1980s and 1990s Mother Teresa's health problems became a concern. She suffered a heart attack while visiting Pope John Paul II in 1983. She had a near fatal heart attack in 1989 and began wearing a pacemaker.

In August 1996 the world prayed for Mother Teresa's recovery. At the age of 86, Mother Teresa was on a respirator in a hospital, suffering from heart failure and malaria. Doctors were not sure she would recover. Within days she was fully conscious, asked to receive communion, and requested that the doctors send her home. When she was sent home a few weeks later in early September, a doctor said she firmly believed, "God will take care of me."

In late November of that same year, Mother Teresa was again hospitalized. She had angioplasty surgery to clear two blocked arteries. She was also given a mild electric shock to correct an irregular heartbeat. She was released after spending almost a month in the hospital.

In March 1997, after an eight week selection process, 63-year-old Sister Nirmala was named as the new leader of the Missionaries of Charity. Although Mother Teresa had been trying to cut back on her duties for some time (because of her health problems), she stayed on in an advisory role to Sister Nirmala.

In April 1997 filming began on the movie "Mother Teresa: In the Name of God's Poor" with actress Geraldine Chaplin playing the title role. The movie aired in the fall of 1997 on "The Family Channel" even though, after viewing the movie, Mother Teresa refused to endorse it. Mother Teresa celebrated her 87th birthday in August, and died shortly thereafter of a heart attack on September 5, 1997. The world grieved her loss and one mourner noted, "It was Mother herself who poor people respected. When they bury her, we will have lost something that cannot be replaced."

In appearance Mother Teresa was both tiny (only about five feet tall) and energetic. Her face was quite wrinkled, but her dark eyes commanded attention, radiating an energy and intelligence that shone without expressing nervousness or impatience. Many of her recruits came from people attracted by her own aura of sanctity, and she seemed little changed by the worldwide attention she received. Conservatives within the Catholic Church sometimes used her as a symbol of traditional religious values that they felt lacking in their churches. By popular consensus she was a saint for the times, and a spate of almost adoring books and articles started to canonize her in the 1980s and well into the 1990s. She herself tried to deflect all attention away from what she did to either the works of her group or to the god who was her inspiration. She continued to combine energetic administrative activities with a demanding life of prayer, and if she accepted opportunities to publicize her work they had little of the cult of personality about them.

In the wake of the 1979 Nobel Prize for Peace she received many other international honors, but she sometimes disconcerted humanitarian groups by expressing her horror at abortion or her own preference for prayer rather than politics. When asked what would happen to her group and work after her death, she told people that God would surely provide a successor—a person humbler and more faithful than she. The Missionaries of Charity, who had brothers as well as sisters by the mid-1980s, are guided by the constitution she wrote for them. They have their vivid memories of the love for the poor that created the phenomenon of Mother Teresa in the first place. So the final part of her story will be the lasting impact her memory has on the next generations of missionaries, as well as in the world as a whole.

Further Reading

A good sampling of Mother Teresa's own ideas was available in her own books, *Life in the Spirit* (1983); *A Simple Path* (1995); *In My Own Words* (1996); and *No Greater Love* (1997). The books contained reflections, meditations, and prayers that provided a good basis for judging Mother Teresa's spirituality. Of the constantly growing number of biographies and studies, Malcolm Muggeridge's *Something Beautiful for God* (1984) deserved special mention, because it was one of the first and best publicized treatments. Muggeridge made no effort to conceal his admiration. Other solid, if usually almost overly admiring, treatments included Eileen Egan, *Such a Vision of the Street* (1985); Desmond Doig, *Mother Teresa: Her People and Her Work* (1976); Kathryn Spink, *The Miracle of Love* (1982); Edward Le Joly, *Mother Teresa of Calcutta* (1983); William Jay Jacobs, *Mother Teresa: Helping the Poor* (1991); Margaret Holland, *Mother Teresa* (1992); and Mildred Pond, *Mother Teresa* (1992).

See also *Maclean's* (March 24, 1997) and *People* (June 30, 1997). Information on Mother Teresa may also be accessed on the internet by doing a search of her name (August 20, 1997). □

Valentina Tereshkova

Valentina Tereshkova (born 1937) was the first woman in space, orbiting the earth 48 times in Vostok VI in 1963.

Valentina Tereshkova was the first woman in space. Tereshkova took off from the Tyuratam Space Station in the Vostok VI in 1963, and orbited the Earth for almost three days, showing women had the same resistance to space as men. She then toured the world promoting Soviet science and feminism, and served on the Soviet Women's Committee and the Supreme Soviet Presidium. Valentina Vladimirovna "Valya" Tereshkova was born on March 6, 1937, in the Volga River village of Maslennikovo. Her father, Vladimir Tereshkov, was a tractor driver; a Red Army soldier during World War II, he was killed when Valentina was two. Her mother Elena Fyodorovna Tereshkova, a worker at the Krasny Perekop cotton mill, singlehandedly raised Valentina, her brother Vladimir and her sister Ludmilla in economically trying conditions; assisting her mother, Valentina was not able to begin school until she was ten.

Tereshkova later moved to her grandmother's home in nearby Yaroslavl, where she worked as an apprentice at the tire factory in 1954. In 1955, she joined her mother and sister as a loom operator at the mill; meanwhile, she graduated by correspondence courses from the Light Industry Technical School. An ardent Communist, she joined the mill's Komsomol (Young Communist League), and soon advanced to the Communist Party.

In 1959, Tereshkova joined the Yaroslavl Air Sports Club and became a skilled amateur parachutist. Inspired by the flight of Yuri Gagarin, the first man in space, she volunteered for the Soviet space program. Although she had no experience as a pilot, her 126-jump record gained her a position as a cosmonaut in 1961. Four candidates were chosen for a one-time woman-in-space flight; Tereshkova received an Air Force commission and trained for 18 months before becoming chief pilot of the Vostok VI. Admiring fellow cosmonaut Yuri Gagarin was quoted as saying, "It was hard for her to master rocket techniques, study spaceship designs and equipment, but she tackled the job stubbornly and devoted much of her own time to study, poring over books and notes in the evening."

At 12:30 PM on June 16, 1963, Junior Lieutenant Tereshkova became the first woman to be launched into space. Using her radio callsign Chaika (Seagull), she reported, "I see the horizon. A light blue, a beautiful band. This is the Earth. How beautiful it is! All goes well." She was later seen smiling on Soviet and European TV, pencil and logbook floating weightlessly before her face. Vostok VI made 48 orbits (1,200,000 miles) in 70 hours, 50 minutes, coming within 3.1 miles of the previously launched Vostok V, piloted by cosmonaut Valery Bykovsky. Tereshkova's flight confirmed Soviet test results that women had the same resistance as men to the physical and psychological stresses of space.

Upon her return, she and Bykovsky were hailed in Moscow's Red Square. On June 22 at the Kremlin she was named a Hero of the Soviet Union and was decorated by Presidium Chairman Leonid Brezhnev with the Order of Lenin and the Gold Star Medal. A symbol of emancipated Soviet feminism, she toured the world as a goodwill ambassador promoting the equality of the sexes in the Soviet Union, receiving a standing ovation at the United Nations. With Gagarin, she travelled to Cuba in October as a guest of the Cuban Women's Federation, and then went to the International Aeronautical Federation Conference in Mexico.

On November 3, 1963, Tereshkova married Soviet cosmonaut Colonel Andrian Nikolayev, who had orbited the earth 64 times in 1962 in the Vostok III. Their daughter Yelena Adrianovna Nikolayeva was born on June 8, 1964, and was carefully studied by doctors fearful of her parents' space exposure, but no ill effects were found. After her flight, Tereshkova continued as an aerospace engineer in the space program; she also worked in Soviet politics, feminism and culture. She was a Deputy to the Supreme Soviet between 1966 and 1989, and a People's Deputy from 1989 to 1991. Meanwhile, she was a member of the Supreme Soviet Presidium from 1974 to 1989. During the years from 1968 to 1987, she also served on the Soviet Women's Committee, becoming its head in 1977. Tereshkova headed the USSR's International Cultural and Friendship Union from 1987 to 1991, and subsequently chaired the Russian Association of International Cooperation.

Tereshkova summarized her views on women and science in her 1970 "Women in Space" article in the American journal *Impact of Science on Society:* "I believe a woman should always remain a woman and nothing feminine should be alien to her. At the same time I strongly feel that no work done by a woman in the field of science or culture or whatever, however vigourous or demanding, can enter into conflict with her ancient 'wonderful mission'—to love, to be loved—and with her craving for the bliss of motherhood. On the contrary, these two aspects of her life can complement each other perfectly."

Further Reading

Drexel, John, editor, *Facts on File Encyclopedia of the 20th Century,* Facts on File, 1991, pp. 884–885.
O'Neill, Lois Decker, "Farthest Out of All: The First Woman in Space," in *Women's Book of World Records and Achievements,* Anchor Books, 1979, pp. 739–740.
Sharpe, Mitchell, *"It is I, Sea Gull": Valentina Tereshkova, First Woman in Space,* Crowell, 1975.
Uglow, Jennifer S., editor, *The International Dictionary of Women's Biography,* Continuum, 1982, p. 461.
"Soviets Orbit Woman Cosmonaut," in *New York Times,* June 17, 1963, pp. 1, 8.
"2 Russians Land in Central Asia after Space Trip," in *New York Times,* June 20, 1963, pp. 1, 3. □

Louis Terkel

The radio personality and author Louis Terkel (born 1912) was best known for his oral histories of ordinary Americans. These anthologies of interviews show how people felt about key historical events and everyday struggles and dreams.

Initially a Chicago radio personality, in mid-career Studs Terkel acquired a national reputation as a people's historian through a series of books that relied on taped interviews to document the experiences, memories, dreams, and fears of a wide cross-section of Americans. On radio he was an entertaining and opinionated speaker, but in the collections of personal accounts he demonstrated equal ability as a skilled listener.

Louis Terkel was born on May 16, 1912, in the Bronx, New York, the third son of Russian-Jewish parents, Samuel and Anna Terkel. His father was a tailor and craftsman. In

1923 the family moved to Chicago, where his mother managed a hotel for blue-collar and skilled workers.

After graduating from high school in 1928, Terkel attended college and earned a law degree from the University of Chicago in 1934. Failing the bar exam, he took a civil service job doing statistical research for the federal government, first in Nebraska and then in Washington, D.C.

Returning to Chicago in 1935, he began his career in radio, producing weekly shows for the Federal Writers Project and appearing on radio soap operas, often as a gangster. He also was involved with the Chicago Repertory Theatre. During the Great Depression he changed his name to "Studs" after the character in James T. Farrell's proletarian novels, Studs Lonnigan.

By the early 1940s he was a well-established radio voice as a news commentator, sportscaster, and disc jockey. In 1945 he created his first program for the small fine arts FM station WFMT. From 1949 to 1953 he produced a television program called "Studs' Place," which featured Terkel as the bartender-host of a barbecue restaurant. A clash with the House Un-American Activities Committee during the Joseph McCarthy era over his political involvement and beliefs led to his blacklisting and the cancellation of his show.

Throughout the 1950s he was active with the arts in several capacities. He acted in the theater, including such plays as "Of Mice and Men," and in 1959 he wrote a play, "Amazing Grace," based on his family's experience with an urban hotel in the Depression. (It didn't get performed until

1967.) He wrote a jazz column for the Chicago *Sun-Times,* which led to his first book, the *Giants of Jazz* (1957). In 1959 and 1960 he hosted the Newport Folk Festival and other festivals around Chicago. In 1958 he began his long-running daily radio program on WFMT, the Studs Terkel Show.

Terkel was 55 when he published *Division Street: America* (1967), his first book that was based on edited transcripts of oral histories. It presented a vivid and poignant view of urban life as seen by 70 people living in or near Chicago, including steelworkers, executives, window washers, and racketeers.

In his books Terkel examined history and society from the bottom up, providing an anecdotal account of events and attitudes. He viewed himself less as a historian, sociologist, or reporter than as a "guerrilla" journalist with a tape recorder. He preferred the stories of anonymous but spirited people who were not practiced at voicing their opinions.

In 1970 he published *Hard Times,* which featured interviews with a hundred Americans presenting personal memories of the Great Depression, especially the guilt and sense of failure that often accompanied the hardship. His next project, *Working: People Talk About What They Do All Day and How They Feel About What They Do* (1974), a best seller for 17 weeks, revealed the lack of satisfaction most people receive from their jobs. He gave special attention to the many aspects of the automotive industry.

Terkel then directed the tape recorder at himself, publishing a memoir, *Talking to Myself* (1977). It included impressions of many incidents and periods in his life but revealed little about him or his family.

In 1980 he published *American Dreams: Lost and Found,* presenting the familiar spectrum of people sharing their disappointments in the past and their search for a sense of purpose in the future. He returned to the same subject in 1988 with *The Great Divide.*

Terkel's personal involvement with World War II had been limited. He joined the Army, but a perforated eardrum kept him from serving. When he tried to go overseas by joining the Red Cross, he was rejected (as he later learned through the Freedom of Information Act) because of his previous political activity.

However, his best-selling oral history of the war, *"The Good War"* (1984), became his most highly-praised book, receiving the Pulitzer Prize. It wove a compelling record of experiences and memories into a powerful document that possesses the grace of literature and the authority of history.

In 1992 Terkel published *Race: How Blacks and Whites Think and Feel About the American Obsession,* which showed how race relations and attitudes became more complicated and bitter after the hopeful years of the civil rights movement. The book probes the U.S. obsession about race through the observations of a large collection of citizens from all walks of life and identity categories. The book exposed the complexity and pervasiveness of the issue and its ability to evoke opposite and conflicted feelings even within individuals.

Terkel's *Coming of Age* (1995) examined the attitudes of older Americans about growing older. The book was a tribute and platform for the generation formed by the Depression, the New Deal, and World War II. It demonstrated particularly well the often unnoticed fighting spirit and passionate personal and public committments of many of his interviewees.

Terkel's personal voice was almost missing from his books, but as a social critic on radio or as a speaker he protested what he regarded as the trivialization of public life and debate. Entering his eighties, Terkel continued to be active as the host of his hour-long, nationally-syndicated morning talk show on WFMT in which he talked, conducted interviews, read stories, or played music as his mood dictated.

He was married in 1939 to Ida Goldberg, whom he met while working at the Chicago Repertory Theatre, and they had one son, Paul.

Further Reading

Terkel's own books provide the best understanding of his style and subjects. They are all mentioned above, but the most well known are *Hard Times* (1970), *Working* (1974), *"The Good War"* (1984), *Race: How Blacks and Whites Think and Feel About the American Obsession* (1992), and *Coming of Age: The Story of Our Century by Those Who've Lived It* (1995). For a glimpse of Terkel's personal life, though not a complete autobiography, see his *Talking to Myself* (1977). Tony Parker's *Studs Terkel: A Life in Words* (1996) turns Terkel's interview method on the subject himself, offering a warm portrait of Terkel from the comments of friends and colleagues as well as from Terkel himself. Individual book reviews offer some insight into his life and personality. □

Lewis Madison Terman

Lewis Madison Terman (1877-1956) was an eminent American psychologist who is most noted for his profound and lasting impact on the measurement of intelligence and achievement in the United States and for his seminal studies of children of high intelligence.

Lewis Madison Terman was born on a farm in Johnson County, Indiana, on January 15, 1877. He was the 12th of 14 children. Though he did not dislike farming, he loved to read and had a pressing desire for education. When he was 15 he left the farm to enter Central Normal College at Danville, Illinois. Following two years of study there, he taught for one year in a one-room schoolhouse. For several years he cycled through periodic schooling followed by borrowing money or teaching to earn enough money to return to college. He acquired B.S., B. PD., and A.B. degrees from Indiana University and a doctoral degree from Clark University in Worcester, Massachusetts. He died of tuberculosis on December 21, 1956.

Terman is most well remembered for his accomplishments in intelligence and achievement testing and for his classic longitudinal research on gifted children. Early in his career as professor of psychology and of education at Stanford University Terman studied the then new Binet-Simon Scale of Intelligence and developed it for use in the United States. Published in 1916 as the Stanford-Binet, the revision of the French intelligence test was the first important and widely used individual intelligence test in the United States. It was described in his book *The Measurement of Intelligence: An Explanation of and a Complete Guide for the Use of the Stanford Revision and Extension of the Binet-Simon Intelligence Scale* (1916). The Stanford-Binet became a standard against which other intelligence tests were still measured in the mid-1980s. Working with other psychologists during World War I, Terman was largely responsible for the first notable group intelligence tests, the Army Alpha and the Army Beta. Terman also published the *Terman Group Test of Mental Ability* (1920), and he co-authored the *Stanford Achievement Test,* which was revised many times and continued to be widely used in the 1980s.

Terman defined intelligence as "the ability to carry on abstract thinking" (*Journal of Educational Psychology,* 1921) and used the label IQ or Intelligence Quotient, which had been suggested earlier by the German psychologist William Stern. The IQ obtained from the Stanford-Binet was calculated by dividing the individual's mental age (obtained from the test) by chronological age and then multiplying by 100. An average IQ is 100.

Terman's classic research on gifted children began in 1921 when he started to study the development of 1,500 California children whose IQs were over 140. Scores over 140 fall into the top 0.5 percent of the population. Terman followed the 1,500 children at later times in their childhood and in adulthood for the rest of his life, with follow-up surveys conducted in 1930, 1947, and, posthumously, in 1959 when the individuals were 17, 35, and 45. Research on the same group of individuals is still being conducted by other psychologists and may continue for many more years.

Terman's studies undoubtedly are still the most recognized and frequently quoted research on the gifted. Some say his most significant contribution to education and psychology was the multi-volume *Genetic Studies of Genius* (volumes from 1925 to 1929). His last progress report on this continuing study was *The Gifted Child Grows Up* (1947).

Among Terman's most interesting findings from his study of the development of gifted children were that they tended to be healthier and more stable emotionally than the average child and that intellect and later life achievement were not highly related—the gifted children later pursued a wide range of occupations.

Terman's interest in scientific measurement was also exemplified in his lesser known development of scales of masculinity, of femininity, and of marital happiness. He used such scales to address research issues such as the development of masculinity and femininity over time, links between the degrees of masculinity or femininity and various occupations, and factors contributing to marital happiness.

Further Reading

Biographical Memoirs (National Academy of Sciences, 1959) gives an excellent and comprehensive account of Terman's life and work. The International Encyclopedia of Social Sciences (1968) also provides a concise summary on Terman and his research. Perhaps the best account of Terman's life up to 1931 is autobiographical, found in L. M. Terman, *A History of Psychology in Autobiography* (1932). *The Encyclopedia of Educational Research* (1982) cites Terman's work and his contributions to education and psychology in the context of other related work and from an historical perspective. An appraisal of his contributions is in E. R. Hilgard, "Lewis Madison Terman: 1877-1956," *American Journal of Psychology* 70 (1957). Later results from the ongoing study of the 1,500 gifted children are presented alongside a portrayal of Terman's life and his conclusions regarding gifted people in *Psychology Today* 13 (February 1980).

Additional Sources

Minton, Henry L., *Lewis M. Terman: pioneer in psychological testing,* New York: New York University Press, 1988. □

Gabriel Terra

Gabriel Terra (1873-1942) was a Uruguayan politician. President by election, he overthrew his government by a coup d'etat in 1933 and headed a mildly authoritarian government until 1938.

Born in Montevideo, Gabriel Terra was educated at the University of Montevideo. He received a degree in law and jurisprudence in 1895, and his lifelong specialty was principally in fiscal and financial matters. He began a legal practice and also became a teacher of economics in the Escuela Superior of Montevideo. Later he served as professor of political economy in the law school of the university.

Terra entered active politics soon after receiving his degree. In 1905 he was elected to the Chamber of Deputies as a Colorado and follower of President José Batlle y Ordóñez. Terra rose rapidly in the party and, while still a deputy, announced his intention of one day becoming president of the republic. Batlle appears to have been cool to this ambition, on grounds of his doubt of Terra's judgment and good faith.

Terra served in the Chamber of Deputies until 1925 and briefly in the cabinets of several presidents as minister of industry, of labor, and of public instruction. Terra also held several diplomatic posts. In 1916 he was a delegate to the Pan-American Commercial and Financial Conference in Washington. In 1918 he was president of the Uruguayan delegation to the International Financial High Commission in Paris. Later he was Uruguayan minister to Italy.

In 1925 Terra was elected to the National Council of Administration for a 6-year term. Under the complex 1918 Constitution, this nine-member body shared the executive power with the president of the republic, who was elected

for a 4-year term. In 1930 Terra resigned to run for the presidency; he won that office for the term beginning March 1, 1931.

On March 31, 1933, after weeks of preparation, Terra overthrew the government. Congress was dissolved; six members of the council were jailed briefly, and another member, former president Baltasar Brum, shot himself. Careful preparations had assured that the event would be peaceful; one company of army infantry and the Montevideo fire department were the only uniformed units needed to support it. Terra imposed mild controls; newspapers were censored, but speakers were subjected to only mild harassment. In 1934 an elected constitutional convention elected Terra president for the term 1934-1938. In elections in 1938 he yielded power to Alfredo Baldomir.

Terra lived quietly in Uruguay until his death in Montevideo. He published many economic studies, beginning with his degree thesis of 1895, *The Public Debt of Uruguay*. Other titles included *Notes on Public Credit, The Hydroelectric Energy Potential of the Rio Negro, Cooperativism and Socialism,* and *International Politics.*

Terra's inauguration occurred at the nadir of the world depression. He felt that the council was a major cause of his country's economic collapse. As president, he had the power to subvert the government. His actions prior to the coup were well noted, but opposition proved fruitless. Economic recovery occurred after 1933, but it is not clear that the coup hastened that recovery. His image is as much that of a technocrat as of a politician. He was held in check by

Batlle until the latter's death in 1929. Terra remains a controversial figure and an exception among the proconstitution leaders of his political generation.

Further Reading

There is no work in English on Terra. Useful background material may be found in Simon G. Hanson, *Utopia in Uruguay* (1938); John J. Johnson, *Political Change in Latin America: The Emergence of the Middle Sectors* (1958); and Philip B. Taylor, Jr., *Government and Politics of Uruguay* (1962). □

Tertullian

The North African theologian and apologist Tertullian (ca. 160-ca. 220) was the founder of Latin Christian theology. The first major Christian writer to use the Latin language, he gave to Latin Christian thought a decidedly legal stamp.

Born Quintus Septimius Florens Tertullianus in Carthage, the capital city of Roman Africa, Tertullian was the son of an army officer in a family that was not Christian. He received a full liberal education and entered the practice of law, living apparently for a time in Rome. In his mid-30s he was converted to Christianity and, back in Carthage, became one of the leading figures in the Christian community of that city, though he did not enter the ordained ministry.

Tertullian quickly took up the task of the written defense of the Christian Church in a setting in which violent persecution by the state was a recurring reality. His *Apology*, addressed to the governors of the Roman provinces, is notable for its skillful legal argumentation as well as for the glimpses it affords into the life of the early Christian Church. The verve, colloquial quality, wit, and frequent sarcasm of his style make him one of the most engaging of early Christian writers.

Tertullian holds an important place among Catholic authors who sought to define and to defend the faith of the Church against those heretical interpretations and speculations that are called Gnosticism and Marcionism. In his writings against these heresies the following themes are prominent: the Bible is rightly interpreted only in the Church, where the tradition of belief coming from Christ and the Apostles is preserved; the Rule of Faith (a summary of Christian teaching similar to the later Apostles' Creed) is the proper guide to interpretation of Scripture since it is acknowledged by all the local churches founded by the Apostles, churches in which an unbroken succession of bishops from the Apostles guarantees a continuity of teaching coming from Christ; and the God of the Jewish Scriptures is identical with the God of Christian faith, Jesus being the Messiah promised by those Scriptures.

A moral rigorist at heart, Tertullian at about the age of 50 abandoned the Catholic Church for the severely moralistic Christian sect called Montanists. From this position he

coil and discovered the rotating magnetic field principle.

N ikola Tesla was born in Smiljan, Croatia on July 9, 1856. He attended the Polytechnic School at Graz for 4 years and spent a year at the University of Prague (1879-1880). His first employment was in a government telegraph engineering office in Budapest, where he made his first invention, a telephone repeater, and conceived the idea of a rotating magnetic field. He subsequently worked in Paris and Strasbourg.

In 1884 Tesla went to the United States. He was associated briefly with Thomas Edison in New Jersey, where he designed new dynamos, but the two had a salary misunderstanding and Tesla withdrew. After a difficult period, during which Tesla invented but lost his rights to an arc-lighting system, he established his own laboratory in New York City in 1887.

A controversy between alternating-current and direct-current advocates raged in the 1880s and 1890s, featuring Tesla and Edison as leaders in the rival camps. The advantages of the polyphase alternating-current system, as developed by Tesla, soon became apparent, however, particularly for long-distance power transmission. Assisted by George Westinghouse, an early convert to alternating current and Tesla's employer for a year, the system was adopted in the early 1890s for both a major power project

railed against Catholic "laxity," for example, in readmitting to Communion those who had fallen into serious sin after their baptism. While a Montanist, he wrote a work, *Against Praxeas,* that was subsequently held in high honor by Catholics and in which for the first time an explicit doctrine of the Trinity was formulated. Within Montanism, Tertullian appears to have founded his own party, the Tertullianists. The end of his life is shrouded in obscurity, the date of his death being only an intelligent guess.

Further Reading

The best general book on Tertullian is T. D. Barnes, *Tertullian: A Historical and Literary Study* (1971). A fine appreciation of smaller scope is contained in Hans von Campenhausen, *Men Who Shaped the Western Church* (1964).

Additional Sources

Barnes, Timothy David, *Tertullian: a historical and literary study,* Oxford Oxfordshire: Clarendon Press; New York: Oxford University Press, 1985, 1971. □

Nikola Tesla

The Croatian-American inventor and electrical engineer Nikola Tesla (1856-1943) invented the induction motor and the transformer known as the Tesla

(Niagara Falls) and a major lighting project (the Chicago World's Columbian Exposition).

Brilliant and eccentric, Tesla was then at the peak of his inventive powers. He produced in rapid succession the induction motor (utilizing his rotating magnetic field principle) and other electrical motors, new forms of generators and transformers, and a system for alternating-current power transmission; later he invented the Tesla coil and made basic discoveries concerning wireless communication. Tesla also invented fluorescent lights and a new type of steam turbine, and he became increasingly intrigued with the wireless transmission of power.

Tesla, a strikingly handsome, tall, slender man and a captivating public lecturer, was an unorthodox, almost mystical person; he exhibited unusual powers of perception and forecasting, but his life was increasingly that of a shy, lonely recluse. He refused to accept the 1912 Nobel Prize offered jointly to him and Edison and reluctantly accepted the Edison Medal of the American Institute of Electrical Engineers in 1917. He died in New York City on Jan. 7, 1943, the holder of more than 700 patents.

Further Reading

The outstanding biography of Tesla is John J. O'Neill, *Prodigal Genius: The Life of Nikola Tesla* (1944). O'Neill's portrait is sensitive and sympathetic, if somewhat metaphysical, but it describes Tesla's electrical contributions thoroughly. Two popular accounts are Arthur J. Beckhard, *Electrical Genius: Nikola Tesla* (1959), and Inez Hunt and Wanetta W. Draper, *Lightning in His Hand* (1964).

Additional Sources

Cheney, Margaret, *Tesla, man out of time,* Englewood Cliffs, N.J.: Prentice-Hall, 1981.

Nikola Tesla: life and work of a genius, Belgrade: Yugoslav Society for the Promotion of Scientific Knowledge Nikola Tesla, 1976.

Seifer, Marc, *Wizard: the life and times of Nikola Tesla,* Secaucus, N.J.: Carol Pub., 1996.

Tesla, Nikola, *The fantastic inventions of Nikola Tesla,* Stelle, Ill.: Adventures Unlimiteds, 1993.

Tesla, Nikola, *My inventions: the autobiography of Nikola Tesla,* Williston, Vt.: Hart Bros., 1982. □

Tewfik Pasha

The khedive of Egypt Tewfik Pasha (1852-1892) was a mild-mannered and unfortunate young ruler during a crucial period in Egyptian history, the time of the British occupation in 1882 and the important first decade of British overrule.

Tewfik Pasha was the eldest son of the khedive Ismail, whose vainglorious ambitions and economic adventures had led to Egyptian bankruptcy in 1876 and his deposition as khedive by the Ottoman sultan in 1879.

Tewfik, only 27 years old, replaced his father as Egyptian ruler. Caught immediately between the Anglo-French demands for financial conservatism and stability and the growing Egyptian nationalist movement insisting on the reduction of foreign influence in Egypt, Tewfik never secured real power. He was young, inexperienced, and indecisive; the British and French financial supervisors, in effect, ruled Egypt.

The pace of events in Egypt moved rapidly following Tewfik's accession as titular khedive in 1879 to confrontation between the Anglo-French supervisors, who refused to grant the Egyptian National Assembly full budgetary control, and the nationalist coalition, which insisted on Egyptian sovereignty. The European refusal to deal reasonably with the moderate constitutionalist group led to the dismissal of that group and the accession in early 1882 of a more rabid nationalist faction with Col. Arabi as the primary leader and minister of war. In particular, native Egyptian army officers such as Arabi resented the strict financial policies of the European debt supervisors because retrenchment directly affected them rather than higher-ranking Turks and other non-native Egyptians.

In May 1882 British and French squadrons anchored off Alexandria, and their consuls demanded the dismissal of Arabi's nationalist ministry. Tewfik first yielded and then recanted under pressure, indicating that Col. Arabi had become the most important individual in Egypt. Fearing the effect of a nationalist, antiforeign, military regime in Cairo, Britain decided on unilateral intervention in bombarding Alexandria, landing troops, and occupying Egypt. It was

preventive imperialism, the seizing of a troubled but strategic area before any other state did. Tewfik Pasha fled to British protection during the brief conflict and was restored to his position, if not power, by the British occupation troops in September 1882.

Given this background, it is easy to see why Tewfik Pasha proved to be a mild, passive, and unimaginative ruler. During this first decade of British overrule, Tewfik accepted with little question the conservative policies of Maj. Evelyn Baring (Lord Cromer), the first British consul general and thus the ranking British administrator in Egypt. Lord Cromer's main objective was to pay off the debt and its interest, and he ignored social and economic issues. Tewfik offered little opposition. He was succeeded upon his death by his son Abbas Hilmi.

Further Reading

There is no biographical study of Tewfik Pasha, but see Mary Rowlatt, *Founders of Modern Egypt* (1962), and the classic exposé by Wilfrid S. Blunt, *Secret History of the English Occupation of Egypt* (1922), for the nationalist movement and the early years of his rule. For the first decade of British overrule see Evelyn B. Cromer, *Modern Egypt* (1908). An excellent interpretation by an Egyptian is Afaf Lufti al-Sayyid, *Egypt and Cromer: A Study in Anglo-Egyptian Relations* (1968). A good recent monograph is Robert L. Tignor, *Modernization and British Colonial Rule in Egypt, 1882-1914* (1966). □

Tewodros II

Tewodros II (1820-1868), also called Theodore II, was a visionary emperor of Ethiopia who tried unsuccessfully to reconstitute and modernize traditional institutions by emulating European technological achievements.

Tewodros, or Kassa, as he was baptized, was raised by his half brother Kinfu, a reckless and ruthless warlord whose military and political struggles throughout the 1830s provided training in military skills and small-scale warfare for young Kassa. After Kinfu's death in 1839 Kassa himself became a legendary outlaw during that period of Ethiopian regionalism and disregard for centralized authority as he plundered caravans, sacked villages, and collected booty; but unlike most renegades he then redistributed this wealth to peasants.

Attracting many devoted followers, Kassa easily defeated local rivals, captured much of central Ethiopia, and made a temporary yet wise peace with the national clergy. In February 1855 he overpowered his last rivals in the north and sealed the victories by getting himself anointed and crowned emperor of Ethiopia. He chose as his throne name Tewodros, after a prophetic figure whom many Ethiopians believed one day would provide a rule of righteousness, peace, and prosperity.

Modernization of the Country

Tewodros's ambition to initiate a political reformation in order to restore Ethiopian greatness required national unification as a precondition for peace and order. Accordingly he tried to break the feudal pattern of local government by personally appointing salaried provincial governors and judges. He also ordered the integration of regional forces into a national army organized and disciplined under his command, and he called for a restoration of the Christian faith to involve a rededication of moral standards, encouragement of mission work, and an end to petty and debilitating doctrinal differences.

Furthermore Tewodros actively recruited instructors, engineers, and artisans of all kinds from Europe to provide the technical assistance deemed necessary for his active domestic and foreign policies. These expatriates constructed roads, bridges, and houses and even assisted in the local manufacture of some crude firearms and cannons.

But impressive as these efforts were, Tewodros ultimately failed to fulfill his dream because of his inability to come to terms with either the powerful landed aristocracy or the Church. For instance, for financial support the Emperor relied heavily on provincial taxation while he strived simultaneously to end the tax-exempt status of the Church and to reduce its landholds; he adamantly refused, however, even to consider any reduction in the size of his army.

Tewodros was unable to compromise or give concessions to crucial institutions of the old system; his rift with the Church eventually deteriorated into overt hostility that deprived him of the support and backing among many traditional farmers and peasants who unfailingly aligned with the Church. Increasingly dependent on an army that spent most of its time fighting rebellious leaders from traditional ruling families, Tewodros further alienated those peasants who themselves were pushed to a point of near starvation when forced to feed and quarter his 50,000-man army. Despite incessant uprisings and his escalated reprisals, Tewodros remained confident of ultimate success—provided he lived.

By the mid-1860s northern Ethiopia had once again fallen to local princes, and the national army under Tewodros was racked by desertions that reduced it to less than 5,000 men. When the monarch asked the governments of Britain and France for additional aid, assistance, or at least moral support against foreign enemies, including the Moslem states of Turkey and Egypt, the European failure to respond seemed to imply a marked indifference and diplomatic disrespect; disparaging remarks and imprudent intrigues on the part of certain Europeans within Ethiopia only served to deepen Tewodros's suspicion of all foreigners.

Conflict and Failure

When suspicion turned into anger, the incensed emperor imprisoned the consuls, artisans, and missionaries in his domain at the mountain stronghold of Magdala and retreated there with his meager military following. Alarmed but unable to effect the release of these "captives," the British government in 1867 reluctantly sent a large force to Ethiopia to free the prisoners; when the force stormed

Magdala on April 10, 1868, the proud Tewodros committed suicide rather than surrender.

The reign of Tewodros II opened a new era and closed an old one. His vigorous policies involved a commitment to break local traditions and adopt the trappings of modern technology. But an unwillingness to share responsibility and an underestimation of the social consequences of his reforms within the context of mid-19th-century Ethiopia proved his undoing.

Tewodros probably left Ethiopia as disunited as he had found it; yet, as the first emperor to conceive the idea of a united, strong, and progressive Ethiopian state equal to any in the world, he deserves the title of father of modern Ethiopia.

Further Reading

The best biography of Tewodros is Sven Rubenson, *King of Kings: Tewodros of Ethiopia* (1966). Mordechai Abir, *Ethiopia: The Era of the Princes* (1968), is a careful examination of the turbulent decades that preceded the emergence of Tewodros. Edward Ullendorff, *The Ethiopians* (2d ed. 1960), is a fine introduction to the peoples and cultures of Ethiopia, and Richard Greenfield, *Ethiopia: A New Political History* (1965), presents a useful survey of the Ethiopian past. □

William Makepeace Thackeray

The British novelist William Makepeace Thackeray (1811-1863) created unrivaled panoramas of English upper-middle-class life, crowded with memorable characters displaying realistic mixtures of virtue, vanity, and vice.

When William Makepeace Thackeray began his literary career, English prose fiction was dominated by Charles Dickens. Thackeray formed his style in conscious reaction against Dickens's programmatic indictment of social evils and against the artificial style and sentimental falsification of life and moral values of the popular historical romances. The familiar, moralizing commentaries of Thackeray's narrators, as integral a part of his novels as the characters themselves, expressed their author's detached moral disillusionment—usually touched with sentimentality. Although critical of society, Thackeray was never a radical intellectual, remaining basically conservative. He initiated a tendency toward plainer style and greater realism in the portrayal of the commonplace, a manner carried on in the English novel by Anthony Trollope.

Thackeray was born on July 18, 1811, in Calcutta, India, into a family that had made its fortunes in the East India Company for two generations. He was sent to England at the age of 5 after the death of his father. The Anglo-Indian community in which Thackeray grew up was alienated by prejudice from the English upper-class society, of which, however, it felt itself rightfully a part by reason of its achievements and wealth, and whose values it imitated. A sympathy for similar alienation manifested itself in his later attitudes.

Educated at the prestigious Charterhouse School, Thackeray acquired there the class conception of gentlemanly conduct that he later both criticized and upheld. At Trinity College, Cambridge, he was only a mediocre student, and he left the university after little more than a year in June 1830, convinced that it was not worth his while to spend more time in pursuit of a second-rate degree under an uncongenial curriculum. A 6-month stay in Weimar, Germany, where he enjoyed the intellectual life of the former home of Johann Wolfgang von Goethe and Friedrich von Schiller, gave Thackeray some cosmopolitan polish and a more objective view of English manners.

After his return to London, Thackeray drifted idly about, making a desultory gesture toward studying law at the Middle Temple. But he seemed more devoted to the expensive habits of fashionable dissipation and gambling he had acquired at Cambridge. When he came into his inheritance, debts forced him to consume part of his capital, and most of the rest was soon lost in the collapse of the Indian trading agency in which it had been invested. Financial misfortune effected a morally beneficial change in his way of life, however, and after an abortive attempt at painting he turned to journalism as a means of support.

Magazine Writing

Between 1837 and 1844 Thackeray wrote critical articles on art and literature for numerous papers and journals, but he contributed most of his fiction of this period to *Fraser's Magazine. The Memoirs of C. J. Yellowplush,* which appeared serially in 1837-1838, parodied the high-flown language of "fashnabble" novels through the Cockney malapropisms of a gentleman's gentleman. In *Catherine* (1839-1840) Thackeray began by parodying the popular criminal novel, but he soon became interested in his characters for their own sakes. "A Shabby Genteel Story" (1840) and other short compositions explored the world of rogues and fools in a spirit of extreme and bitter disillusionment. *The Irish Sketch Book* (1843) and *Notes of a Journey from Cornhill to Cario* (1845), purportedly written by the confirmed Londoner Mr. M. A. Titmarsh, were in a lighter vein. His placement of the narrator as a personality firmly in the foreground of his works has led critics to accuse him of Cockney Philistinism.

In the fall of 1840, Thackeray's wife, Isabella Shawe, whom he had married in 1836, suffered a mental breakdown from which she never recovered. This experience profoundly affected his character and work, widening his sympathies, mellowing his judgments, and bringing him to value domestic affection as life's greatest good. These new attitudes emerged clearly in the best of his early stories, "The History of Samuel Titmarsh and the Great Hoggarty Diamond" (1841), a tale of an obscure clerk who rises to sudden prosperity but finds true happiness only after ruin has brought him back to hearth and home. Adopting the mask of an aristocratic London bachelor and clubman, George Savage Fitz-Boodle, Thackeray next wrote a number of papers satirizing his way of life and a series called "Men's Wives," of which "Mr. and Mrs. Frank Berry" and "Denis Haggarty's Wife" show a maturing sense of comedy and tragedy. With *The Luck of Barry Lyndon* (1844) Thackeray arrived as a novelist. He returned to an earlier subject, the gentleman scoundrel; his central theme is the ruin of a young man's character by false ideals of conduct and worldly success.

As a regular contributor to the satiric magazine *Punch* between 1844 and 1851, Thackeray finally achieved widespread recognition. His most famous contribution was *The Snobs of England, by One of Themselves* (1846-1847). Through a series of satiric character sketches, it made a critical survey of the manners of a period in which old standards of behavior and social relationships had been shaken by the redistribution of wealth and power effected by industrialism.

Thackeray's Novels

Vanity Fair (1847-1848) established Thackeray's fame permanently. Set in the time just before and after the Battle of Waterloo, this novel departed from convention in having no hero or heroine and no plot in the conventional sense. It is a portrait of society centered on three families interrelated by acquaintance and marriage, the events of whose lives are organized by the broad movement of time rather than artificial complication and resolution. This "formlessness" helps to create an illusion of reality, given substance by an infinitude of authentic details in the description of the actions of daily life and in the differentiation of character by style of speech. In the irrepressibly resourceful, though amoral, Becky Sharp, Thackeray created one of fiction's most engaging characters.

In *Pendennis* (1849-1850) Thackeray concentrated on one character. The story of the development of a young writer, it draws in the first part on his own life at school, at college, and as a journalist. The second half, which he wrote after a severe illness, lost the novel's focus. Its ostensible theme, Pen's struggle to choose between a practical, worldly life and domestic virtue, presents only a superficial analysis of character and a doubtful moral accommodation.

The History of Henry Esmond (1852), Thackeray's most carefully planned and executed work, is a historical novel set in the 18th century. He felt a temperamental sympathy with this age of satire and urbane wit, and he had made a significant contribution to a revival of interest in it the year before in a popular series of lectures, *The English Humourists of the Eighteenth Century. Esmond* presents a vivid and convincing realization of the manners and historical background of the period and contains some of his most complex and firmly controlled characters.

The Newcomes (1854-1855) returns to the method of serial improvisation used for *Vanity Fair.* Supposedly written by the hero of *Pendennis,* it chronicles the moral history of four generations of an English family. The most massive and complex of Thackeray's social panoramas, it is also the darkest in its relentless portrayal of the defeat of humane feeling by false standards of respectability.

Feeling that he had written himself out, Thackeray returned to earlier works for subjects for his later novels, and his narrators became increasingly garrulous in their familiar moralism. *The Virginians* (1858-1859) follows the fortunes of Henry Esmond's grandsons in the United States, and *The Adventures of Philip* (1862) continues "A Shabby Genteel Story."

Thackeray's later career was varied by an unsuccessful campaign for Parliament as a reform candidate in 1857 and by two lecture trips to the United States in 1852 and 1855. A founding editor of the *Cornhill Magazine,* he served it from 1859 to 1862. A massive person, 6 feet 3 inches tall, Thackeray was a genial and modest man, fond of good food and wine. In the years of his success he candidly took great pleasure in the amenities of the society that he portrayed so critically in his novels. He died on Dec. 24, 1863, in London.

Further Reading

Gordon N. Ray edited Thackeray's *Letters and Private Papers* (4 vols., 1945-1946) and wrote the comprehensive, standard biography, in two volumes: *Thackeray: The Uses of Adversity* (1955) and *The Age of Wisdom* (1958). A reliable shorter biography with a more consecutive narrative is Lionel Stevenson, *The Showman of Vanity Fair: The Life of William Makepeace Thackeray* (1947; repr. 1968). Good critical studies are Geoffrey Tillotson, *Thackeray the Novelist* (1954), and

John Loofbourow, *Thackeray and the Form of Fiction* (1964). □

Thales

The Greek natural philosopher Thales (ca. 624-ca. 545 B.C.) founded the Ionian school of ancient Greek thinkers.

Thales was descended, according to the historian Herodotus, from Phoenicians who had settled in Miletus, a thriving Greek seaport on the west coast of Asia Minor (now Turkey). His mother, however, bore a Greek name. Thales's interest in the heavens was so well known that the philosopher Plato picked him as the example of the impractical student: while gazing upward and scanning the stars, he fell into a well.

Thales became so famous for his practical shrewdness and theoretical wisdom that in later times he began to be honored for having made important discoveries whose true origins were not known then and in some cases are still obscure. The most spectacular of these supposed achievements was his alleged prediction of a total solar eclipse (presumably that of May 28, 585 B.C.), at a time when the information needed to foresee such an event was not yet possessed by anybody. Indeed it is significant that, according to Herodotus, the time mentioned in Thales's prediction was limited only to "the year in which the eclipse occurred." Month and day were not specified, nor was there any indication of the portion of the earth's surface from which the eclipse would be visible.

Thales was also falsely credited with having found out that an eclipse of the sun is caused by the interposition of the opaque moon between the sun and the earth. However, the real nature of the moon as a dark, non-self-luminous body was first disclosed about a century after the death of Thales. In like manner he was praised for having determined the sun's apparent diameter, yet this approximately correct value was first ascertained, according to the mathematician Archimedes, some 300 years after Thales by an accomplished astronomer.

The first proof that a circle is bisected by its diameter was ascribed in antiquity to Thales. But in his lifetime the Greeks had not yet begun to enunciate geometrical theorems and to demonstrate them step by step. Hence, the ancient attribution to Thales of the earliest proof of the equality of the vertical angles formed by the intersection of two straight lines is now discarded as a misplaced anticipation of a later stage in the development of Greek geometry.

In assigning to Thales the belief that "everything is full of gods," Aristotle suggested that the Milesian perhaps derived this opinion from those who held that soul pervades the entire universe. With regard to Thales's conception of soul, Aristotle remarked that "on the basis of what people remember, Thales apparently assumed that soul causes motion, if he really said that the magnet has a soul since it attracts iron." Evidently Aristotle did not have in his hands the writings later ascribed to Thales. It is, in fact, entirely doubtful that Thales set his ideas down in written form.

In Aristotle's time the oldest traditional explanation of what held the earth up was that it rested on water. "They say that Thales the Milesian espoused this view," Aristotle states, "because the earth remains afloat like wood or some other such thing." Aristotle wryly adds: "as though the same reasoning with regard to the earth did not apply also to the water supporting the earth." Thales based his conception of water as the fundamental principle of the universe, according to Aristotle's surmise, "on the observation that the nourishment of all things was moist, and that heat itself arises from this source and is kept alive by it." As a biologist, Aristotle appended the further reason that "the seeds of all things have a moist nature," and one of his commentators contributed the remark that "dead things dry up."

The concept of the primacy of water may have been imported by Thales from the Egyptians, "who express this idea in mythical form." Whether or not Thales was familiar with the Egyptian water myths or the similar Mesopotamian stories and the corresponding notions in the Hebrew Bible, the framework of his thought was confined to the world of nature. Even though he overestimated the importance of water, its absence from the surface of the moon in part explains the nonexistence of life on this natural satellite. After the accomplishments actually due to Thales's successors have been stripped away from his previously exaggerated reputation, through the mists of early intellectual history Thales is dimly glimpsed as having turned rational thought to the demythologized understanding of the physical universe.

Further Reading

Modern discussions of Thales are necessarily limited by the fact that nothing of his has survived, and what may be gleaned from the writings of others is too little to permit the reconstruction of his thought. Nevertheless, G. S. Kirk and J. E. Raven present what is known about him in *The Presocratic Philosophers* (1964), as do John Burnet in *Early Greek Philosophy* (4th ed. 1930) and Kathleen Freeman in *The Presocratic Philosophers* (1953). Thales and his position in the development of Greek thought are also discussed in George Sarton, *The Study of the History of Science* (1936), and in Albin Lesky, *A History of Greek Literature* (1966). □

U Thant

U Thant (1909-1974) was a Burmese and the first non-European secretary general of the United Nations. Though U Thant was frustrated by his limited powers, his elevation to the highest executive position in the international organization was one of the key indicators of the new importance of Asian nations.

orn on Jan. 22, 1909, in Pantanaw in Burma (now Mynamar), U Thant was the first of four sons of U Po Hnit and his wife, Daw Nan Thaung—all of whom were to distinguish themselves in public life. Young Thant wanted to be a writer, particularly a journalist, and, although by no means an Anglophile of the sort then to be found in large numbers in still British-ruled Burma, he did enjoy writing in the English language. He published his first article in English in 1925—at the age of 16—in *Burma Boy,* an organ of the Burma Boy Scouts Association.

After leaving the National High School in his native Pantanaw, U Thant attended the University of Rangoon, graduating in 1929 at the age of 20. Returning to Pantanaw to help support his mother and permit his three brothers to continue their education, he took a job teaching in his high school alma mater, having finished first in the all-Burma teacher-certification examination. Also in 1929, young Thant published his first book, *Cities and Their Stories,* about Athens, Rome, and other great cities of history.

It was at Pantanaw National High School that U Thant became the close friend of another Rangoon University graduate (whom he had known, but not well, in college), U Nu—who was one day to become independent Burma's first premier after the termination of British colonial rule. Subsequently Thant became headmaster of the school and Nu its superintendent. At this time he also published a book on the United Nations' predecessor, the League of Nations.

When U Nu returned to Rangoon University to pursue a law degree in 1934, U Thant assumed the job of school superintendent as well as headmaster. The paths of the two young men then went off in different directions temporarily, Thant remaining in Pantanaw but increasing in stature among his fellow educators as a member of the Textbook Committee for Burma Schools, the Council of National Education, and the Burma Research Society. In 1935 he gained some limited fame as a result of a controversy—conducted by letters to newspapers—with Aung San, the emerging nationalist leader.

During World War II Thant served for a time as secretary of the Education Reorganization Committee under the occupying Japanese but, wearying of the task, returned to his teaching post in Pantanaw.

In 1945, when U Nu became vice president of the Anti-Fascist People's Freedom League (or AFPFL, Burma's main nationalist movement), he persuaded U Thant to leave his beloved Pantanaw and take charge of publicity for the AFPFL. He was subsequently asked by Nu to take charge of the press section of the Information Department, where he was so successful that he soon became secretary of the Ministry of Information under the newly independent Burmese government.

Thant emerged as one of the key figures in Burmese political life when he subsequently became secretary to the prime minister, his old friend U Nu. Thant was Nu's alter ego—without whose concurrence he rarely made a major decision. Some observers date the beginning of Nu's later political decline with the assignment of Thant in 1957 as Burma's permanent representative to the UN—a move de-signed to give the Burmese the best possible representation in the international body.

On Nov. 3, 1961, Thant was named acting UN secretary general following Dag Hammarskjöld's death and was confirmed in the post on Nov. 30, 1962. On Dec. 2, 1966, he was elected to a second 5-year term.

As leader of the world organization, Thant strove to bring peace to the Middle East and, although the June 1967 Arab-Israeli War did take place, he was successful at various times in restraining the rival combatants. He made a major effort in 1968 to end the fighting in Vietnam, and his diplomatic activity was a factor leading up to the March partial bombing halt by U.S. president Lyndon Johnson and the subsequent start of the Paris peace talks.

In December 1971 Kurt Waldheim of Austria was chosen to succeed Thant as secretary general. Thant officially retired as secretary general on Jan. 1, 1972. He moved to Harrison, NY, and died in New York City on Nov. 25, 1974.

Further Reading

U Thant's life is extremely well detailed in June Bingham, *U Thant: The Search for Peace* (1966). His long friendship with U Nu and his importance within Burma before going to the United Nations are treated in Richard Butwell, *U Nu of Burma* (1963; 2d rev. ed. 1969). Further insight into Thant's views on international relations can be obtained from William C. Johnstone, *Burma's Foreign Policy: A Study in Neutralism* (1963). For an understanding of the office of secretary general see Stephen M. Schwebel, *The Secretary-General of the United Nations* (1952). □

Marie Tharp

Geologist Marie Tharp (born 1920) is known for her maps of ocean floors. These maps are helpful in showing the structure and evolution of the sea floors.

arie Tharp is a mapmaker who charted the bottom of the ocean at a time when little was known about undersea geology. Her detailed maps showed features that helped other scientists understand the structure and evolution of the sea floor. In particular, Tharp's discovery of the valley that divides the Mid-Atlantic Ridge convinced other geologists that sea floor was being created at these ridges and spreading outward. The confirmation of "seafloor spreading" led to the eventual acceptance of the theory of continental drift, now called plate tectonics.

Tharp was born in Ypsilanti, Michigan, on July 30, 1920. Her father, William Edgar Tharp, was a soil surveyor for the United States Department of Agriculture's Bureau of Chemistry and Soils; he told his daughter to choose a job simply because she liked doing it. Marie's mother, Bertha Louise (Newton) Tharp, taught German and Latin. The family moved frequently because of William Tharp's mapping assignments across the country. Marie Tharp attended twenty-four different public schools in Iowa, Michigan, Indiana, Alabama (where she almost flunked out of the 5th grade in Selma), Washington, D.C., New York, and Ohio. In 1943 she received her bachelor's degree from Ohio University.

Since most young men were fighting in World War II at the time Tharp graduated, the University of Michigan opened the doors of its geology department to women for the first time. Tharp entered the masters program, which trained students in basic geology and then guaranteed them a job in the petroleum industry. Graduating in 1944, Tharp was hired as a junior geologist with Stanolind Oil & Gas in Tulsa, Oklahoma. Women were not permitted to search for oil in the field, so Tharp found herself organizing the maps and data for the all-male crews. While working for Stanolind, Tharp earned a B.S. in mathematics from the University of Tulsa in 1948.

The year of her second bachelor's degree, Tharp moved to Columbia University, where a group of scientists were about to revolutionize the study of oceanography. Hired as a research assistant by geologist Maurice Ewing, Tharp actually ended up helping graduate students with their data; she never told anyone that she had a graduate degree in geology. One student, Bruce Heezen, asked for help with his ocean profiles so often that after a while Tharp worked with him exclusively. Heezen and Tharp were to work closely together until his death in 1977. In 1950 the geophysical laboratory moved from Columbia University to the Lamont Geological Observatory in Palisades, New York.

Before the early 1950s, scientists knew very little about the structure of the ocean floor. It was much easier and cheaper to study geology on land. But without knowledge of the structure and evolution of the seafloor, scientists could not form a complete idea of how the entire earth worked. In the 1940s, most people believed that the earth was a shrinking globe, cooling and contracting from its initial hot birth. The work of Heezen, Tharp, and other geologists in the next decade—who gathered data on the sea floor using echo sounding equipment—helped replace that idea with the model of plate tectonics, where thin crustal "plates" shift around on the earth's mantle, colliding and grinding into each other to push up mountains and cause earthquakes.

The Mid-Atlantic Ridge, a mountainous bump that runs roughly parallel to and between the coastlines of the Americas and Africa, was one of the first topographical features on the sea floor to be identified. Initial studies were undertaken by those aboard the British ship *H.M.S. Challenger,* who discovered in the 1870s that the rise in the center of the Atlantic acted as a barrier between different water temperatures; and by those aboard the German ship *Meteor* who between 1925 and 1927 revealed the Mid-Atlantic Ridge as rugged and mountainous. The *Meteor* staff also found several "holes" in the center of the Ridge, but did not connect these holes into the continuous rift valley that they were later discovered to be. In the 1930s, the British geologists Seymour Sewell and John Wiseman suspected that a rift valley split the Ridge, but World War II prevented an expedition to confirm this.

By 1950, when Tharp and Heezen moved to Lamont, the time was right for a series of discoveries. In 1952, the pair decided to make a map of the North Atlantic floor that would show how it would look if all the water were drained away. This type of "physiographic" diagram looked very different from the usual method of drawing contour lines for ocean floor of equal depth. Heezen and Tharp chose the physiographic method because it was a more realistic, three-dimensional picture of the ocean floor, and also because contours were classified by the U.S. Navy from 1952 to 1962.

Tharp assembled her first drawing of the North Atlantic ocean floor in 1952, after rearranging Heezen's data into six seafloor profiles that spanned the Atlantic. This initial map showed a deep valley dividing the crest of the Mid-Atlantic Ridge. Tharp pointed out the valley to Heezen. "He groaned and said, 'It cannot be. It looks too much like continental drift,'" Tharp wrote later in *Natural History.* The valley represented the place where newly-formed rocks came up from inside the earth, splitting apart the mid-ocean ridge. At the time, Heezen, like most scientists, thought that continental drift was impossible.

While Tharp was working on detailing and clarifying the first map, Heezen kept another assistant busy plotting the location of the epicenters of North Atlantic earthquakes. Beno Gutenberg and Charles F. Richter had already pointed out that earthquake epicenters followed the Mid-Atlantic Ridge quite closely. But Heezen's group found that the epicenters actually fell within the suspected rift valley. The association of topography with seismicity convinced Tharp that the valley was indeed real.

It took Heezen eight months to agree. By studying rift valleys in eastern Africa, Heezen convinced himself that the land in Africa was simply a terrestrial analogy to what was going on in the middle of the Atlantic: the earth's crust was splitting apart in a huge tensional crack. Heezen then began to wonder whether the earthquake epicenters that had been recorded in the centers of other oceans might also lie in rift valleys. Perhaps, he thought, all the mid-ocean ridges could be connected into a huge 40,000 mile system.

Heezen told Maurice Ewing, director of Lamont, of the valley's discovery. For several years, only Lamont scientists knew of its existence. Heezen presented it to the scientific community in several talks during 1956. In 1959, most of the remaining skeptics were convinced by an underwater movie of the valley, made by French oceanographer Jacques Cousteau towing a camera across it. Today scientists understand how the rift valley represents the pulling apart of the seafloor as the new rock spreads outward from the ridge.

Heezen and Tharp printed their first edition of the North Atlantic map for a second time in 1959. By this time they knew that the Mid-Atlantic Ridge was cut by east-west breaks, now called transform faults. Heezen and Tharp had confirmed only one of these breaks, but they didn't know its exact length or direction. So in its place on the map they put a large legend to cover the space. In the following years,

Tharp and Heezen improved their North Atlantic map and expanded their work to cover the globe, including the South Atlantic, Indian, Arctic, Antarctic, and Pacific oceans. In 1977, three weeks before Heezen's death, they published the World Ocean Floor Panorama, based on all available geological and geophysical data, as well as more than five million miles of ocean-floor soundings. In 1978 Tharp and Heezen received the Hubbard Medal of the National Geographic Society.

After about fifteen years of work behind the scenes, Tharp finally went on research cruises herself, including trips to Africa, the Caribbean, Hawaii, Japan, New Zealand, and Australia. She retired from Lamont in 1983. Since then she has run a map distributing business in South Nyack, New York, and occasionally consults for various oceanographers. She also keeps Heezen's scientific papers and has written several articles on his life and work. Tharp enjoys gardening in her spare time.

Further Reading

Oceanus, winter, 1973–74, pp. 44–48. □

Twyla Tharp

Dancer and choreographer Twyla Tharp (born 1941) developed a unique style that merged ballet and modern dance technique with various forms of American vernacular dance.

Twyla Tharp was born in Portland, Indiana, July 1, 1941, the daughter of Lecile and William Tharp. Her grandparents on both sides were Quakers who farmed the land. She was named after Twila Thornburg, the reigning Pig Princess at the 89th Annual Muncie Fair, with the "i" changed to "y" because her mother always said it would look better on a marquee. Twyla was the eldest of her siblings: twin brothers and a sister, Twanette. Her mother, a piano teacher, began giving Twyla lessons when the child was one and one-half years old.

When Tharp was eight years old the family moved to the desert town of Rialto, California, where her parents built and operated the local drive-in movie theater. The house her father built in Rialto included a playroom with a practice section featuring a built-in tap floor, ballet barres, and closets filled with acrobatics mats, batons, ballet slippers, pointe shoes, castanets, tutus, and capes for matador routines. Her well-known tendency to consider herself a workaholic and a perfectionist began in her heavily-scheduled childhood.

Tharp began her dance lessons at the Vera Lynn School of Dance in San Bernardino, then studied with the Mraz sisters. She also studied violin, piano, and drums, plus Flamenco, castanets, and cymbals with Enrico Cansino, an uncle of Rita Hayworth, and baton twirling with Ted Otis, an ex-world champion. At age 12 she began studying ballet with Beatrice Collenette, who trained and danced with

Anna Pavlova. She attended Pacific High School and spent her summers working at the family drive-in.

Tharp entered Pomona College as a freshman, moving to Los Angeles that summer to continue her dance training with Wilson Morelli and John Butler. At mid-term of her sophomore year she transferred to Barnard College in New York. She studied ballet with Igor Schwezoff at American Ballet Theater, then Richard Thomas and his wife, Barbara Fallis. She began attending every dance concert she could and studied with Martha Graham, Merce Cunningham, and Eugene "Luigi" Lewis, the jazz teacher. In 1962 she married Peter Young, a painter whom she had met at Pomona College. Her second husband was Bob Huot, an artist. Both marriages ended in divorce. Huot and Tharp had one son, Jesse, born 1971.

Tharp graduated from Barnard in 1963 with a degree in art history. She made her professional debut that year with the Paul Taylor company, billed as Twyla Young. In the following year, at age 23, she formed her own company, which began experimenting with movement in an improvisatory manner. For the first five years Tharp and her dancers struggled, but by the early 1970s she began to be recognized for a breezy style of dance that added irreverent squiggles, shrugged shoulders, little hops, and jumps to conventional dance steps, a technique she called the "stuffing" of movement phrases. She also made dances to every kind of music and composer from Bach, Haydn, and Mozart to the early American jazz of Fats Waller and Jelly Roll Morton; American pop, including the songs of Frank Sinatra, Paul Simon, the Beach Boys, Bruce Springsteen, and David Byrne; and the experimental composers, including Philip Glass.

Among the most innovative of her early pieces is "The Fugue" (1970) for four dancers, set to the percussive beat of their own feet on a miked floor. In 1971 she choreographed "Eight Jelly Rolls" to music by Morton and The Red Hot Peppers and "The Bix Pieces" to music by Bix Beiderbecke. Tharp performed as a member of her company until the mid-1980s when she stopped dancing to concentrate on her many projects for television and film, as well as for her company. She returned to performing in 1991. Other works for her company include "Sue's Leg" (1975), "Baker's Dozen" (1979), "In The Upper Room" (1986), and "Nine Sinatra Songs" (1982).

In 1973 she created a work for the Joffrey Ballet, her first for a company other than her own and her first work for dancers on point. Tharp used the Joffrey dancers and her own company in a work entitled "Deuce Coupe," set to music by the Beach Boys. The setting was created on stage each night by teenage graffiti artists. A huge success, Tharp went on to create "As Time Goes By" (1973) for the Joffrey; five works for American Ballet Theater, including "Push Comes to Shove" (1976) and "Sinatra Suite" (1984), both with leading roles for Mikhail Baryshnikov; "Brahms-Handel" (1984) in collaboration with Jerome Robbins for New York City Ballet; and "Rules of the Game" (1989) for the Paris Opera Ballet. Tharp's dual work for her own company and for the ballet troupes made her among the first to demand a "cross-over" dancer to perform her choreography, one who would be equally at home in ballet and modern dance technique.

With the success of "Deuce Coupe," Tharp was everywhere in demand for her irreverent, funky-look choreography that had appeal to the widest array of audiences that had ever watched dance performances in the United States. She made her first television program for the PBS series Dance in America (1976), continuing in the medium with "Making Television Dance" (1980), "Scrapbook Tapes" (1982), "The Catherine Wheel" (1983) for BBC, and the television special "Baryshnikov by Tharp" (1985). Her film work began in 1978 with the Milos Forman film "Hair," followed by "Ragtime" (1980), "Amadeus" (1984), and "White Nights" (1985). Tharp directed two full-evening productions on Broadway: "The Catherine Wheel" (1981) and the stage adaptation of the film "Singing in the Rain" (1985).

By 1987 the strain of raising money to keep her dancers on salary and the attraction of the various projects that interested her forced her to disband her own company. She was invited to join American Ballet Theater (ABT) as artistic associate with Baryshnikov. When he departed ABT in 1989, she left as well, taking her ballets from the ABT repertory. After that her works were set on the Boston Ballet and the Hubbard Street Dance Company, based in Chicago.

After leaving ABT, Tharp embarked on a variety of endeavors that kept her in the forefront of American dance, including an autobiography, Push Comes to Shove, published in 1992; a series of tours with pick-up companies of dancers recruited mainly from the ballet troupes where she

had worked; and a new work for the Boston Ballet, which premiered in April 1994. She was the recipient of many awards, including a creative citation in dance from Brandeis University (1972), the MacArthur "Genius" Award (1992), and five honorary doctorates.

In 1994, Tharp continued to tour nationally and internationally in the mid-90's with her indispensable assistant, Shelley Washington Whitman, often working without a company of her own or a permanent support base. In 1996, she choreographed Born Again, a trio of new dances performed by a group of thirteen young unknowns, selected in a series of nationwide auditions and trained by Tharp and Whitman. She returned to the ABT in 1995 with a successful revisions of two recent works, "Americans We" (1995), and "How Near Heaven" (1995), and a new work, "The Elements."

Further Reading

For additional information on Twyla Tharp see her autobiography, Push Comes to Shove (1992). For interesting interviews see Elinor Rogosin, The Dance Makers: Conversations with American Choreographers (1980) and Suzanne Weil, Contemporary Dance (1978). Selected works about Tharp include Joan Acocella, "Balancing Act," in Dance Magazine (October 1990); Arlene Croce, Afterimages (1977), Going to the Dance (1982), and Sightlines (1987); Marcia Siegel, The Shapes of Change (1979); and Barbara Zuch, "Tharp Moves," Dance Magazine (January 1992). Her work has been extensively reviewed in The New York Times, Village Voice, New Yorker Magazine, and Dance Magazine. The Twyla Tharp Archives are kept at the Robert E. Lee Theater Research Institute at Ohio State University, Columbus, Ohio. □

Margaret Hilda Thatcher

Conservative Party leader for 15 years, Margaret Hilda Thatcher (born 1925) became the first female prime minister of Great Britain and served in that post from 1979 to 1990, longer than any other British prime minister in the 20th century.

Margaret Thatcher was born to grocery shop keepers in the small railroad equipment manufacturing town of Grantham. Alfred and Beatrice, her parents, were hard workers and careful savers, living over their shop and taking separate vacations so that the grocery would not be left unattended. Her father co-founded the Grantham Rotary Club, became president of the town Grocers' Association, local head of the National Savings Movement, and a member of both the boys' and girls' schools of Grantham. He served for 25 years on the Borough Council, beginning in 1927, and became chairman of its finance committee. For nine years, he was a town alderman, and became the mayor in 1943, as well as a justice of the peace at quarter sessions. He was also a Methodist lay preacher. Beatrice kept the house, sewed, baked, and helped to run the store. Thatcher's childhood family life revolved around the Methodist church, attending services three times a week, saying grace before every meal, and strictly observing the Sabbath. From age five to fifteen, Thatcher took piano lessons and sang in the church choir.

In October 1943, Thatcher was admitted to Somerville College to study chemistry at Oxford. After winning a second-class degree, Thatcher found employment as a research chemist. In 1950 and 1951, she studied to become a barrister and ran as the Conservative candidate in industrial Dartford in North Kent. During this campaign she met Denis Thatcher, who managed his family's company in North Kent. The two were married on December 13, 1951 and became the parents of twins, Mark and Carol, in August 1953.

Political Life

Thatcher became the youngest woman in the House of Commons in 1959, at the age of 34. She became known for sticking to her deeply felt, but unpopular beliefs which included quality, standards, and choice in education, for equal opportunity, and for aligning universities with industry. Thatcher ran against Ted Heath in 1975, winning the second ballot to lead the Conservatives with 146 votes. She became prime minister in May 1979, when the Conservatives won the majority of seats. In June 1987, her Conservative Party won its third consecutive general election victory. Thatcher appeared likely to continue as prime minister for many years. In the election, she had turned back a strong challenge from the Labour Party by renewing her commitment to conviction politics. She had boasted of the economic successes of her two previous governments as well as

her strong foreign and defense policies. Yet Thatcher's third term was to be her least productive. With public opinion turning decisively against her, she was forced to resign from office in November 1990 after a struggle for leadership within the Conservative Party. She was succeeded by John Major, the chancellor of the exchequer since October 1989, who was a supporter of her policies.

Thatcher's third term was marked by controversy from the outset. She pursued a radical conservative agenda, in line with her earlier policies. Her aim was to promote individualism through a further dismantling of state controls. Before 1987 several key industries and public utilities had been transferred to private ownership, including the telephone system, the ports, British Gas, and British Airways. Thatcher continued this policy of privatization, notably in two key areas: water and electricity. Legislation was passed setting up private companies and selling stock in them to the public. This had the double advantage of producing short-term financial gains for the government and helping to create what Thatcher referred to as a property-owning democracy.

Similarly, the sale of council houses to their tenants, begun in 1980, proved to be a controversial if popular measure. By 1988 nearly one million municipal properties were in private hands. The private ownership of homes in Britain was about 70 percent in 1990, one of the highest figures in the world.

Thatcher's government also initiated dramatic changes in the National Health Service, established in 1948. Thatcher favored a significant increase in private medical care and insurance to complement the state-run system. Some of her plans had to be modified, but a major reorganization of the N.H.S. was commenced in 1989 after the publication of a White Paper at the beginning of the year. Market principles were introduced into the N.H.S. Family doctors were given control over their budgets and hospitals were encouraged to opt out of local health authority administration.

Similar market provisions were introduced into state education. Schools were given the power to free themselves from local authority control and to make budgetary decisions, while a national curriculum was developed. The principle of free higher education was virtually abandoned, with universities being encouraged to seek private support. While local authorities continued to provide mandatory stipends to university students, a system of supplementary loans, based on American ideas, was adopted.

Thatcher likewise sought to reduce monopoly control of the professions. Legal reforms were initiated with the intent of lessening the traditional division of functions between solicitors and barristers. Solicitors previously had lost their exclusive power to conduct real estate transactions. Further legislation gave them the right to try cases in the higher courts along with barristers.

The reform that turned public opinion against Thatcher and ultimately led to her downfall was the introduction of the poll tax, or community charge, in 1988. This tax was levied on individuals in a particular district at the same rate, although rebates were available for the poor. It was intended to replace property taxes, hitherto the mainstay of local finance. Since local councils determined the rate of the tax, Thatcher believed that voters would repudiate the higher-spending councils dominated by the Labour Party. There were violent demonstrations against the poll tax in London and other cities, and opposition to it developed within the Conservative Party itself. Major, the new prime minister in 1990, promised to take steps to make the tax more equitable.

Thatcher's economic policies also began to fail during her third term. Her chief successes had been a significant reduction in income tax and a lessening of inflation, from more than 21 percent annually in 1980 to under 3 percent in 1986. However, inflation began to increase again, and by 1990 it had exceeded 10 percent. When combined with a persistently high level of unemployment and a severe downturn in the balance of payments, the economic gains of the Thatcher era began to be called into question. Her solution of attacking inflation by maintaining high interest rates only made matters worse for ordinary people because it increased their monthly mortgage payments.

Opposition to European Integration

The immediate issue that brought about Thatcher's resignation as prime minister was her unyielding opposition to European integration. Britain had joined the European Community in 1973 when Edward Heath was prime minister. Although Thatcher supported integration at the time, in subsequent years she turned down every proposal that seemed to bring the concept of a federal Europe closer to reality. She aligned her foreign policy with Washington rather than Europe in the belief that a special relationship existed with the United States. In economic matters, she firmly rejected proposals for a single European currency.

Thatcher's "Little England" feelings towards Europe antagonized many voters, including a large number of Conservatives. Three leading politicians in her party resigned from office over matters related to Europe: Michael Heseltine, her defense minister, in 1986; Nigel Lawson, the chancellor of the exchequer, in 1989; and Geoffrey Howe, the deputy leader of the party, in November 1990. It was Howe's resignation that produced the leadership crisis and Major's emergence as prime minister. The issue of European integration was closely related to Thatcher's other policies. Once again she championed individual sovereignty, while arguing vehemently against the encroaching bureaucratization of government.

Thatcher's 11½ years as prime minister were remarkable. She held office longer than any other prime minister in the 20th century. She impressed her vision upon Britain in a distinctive way, making the word "Thatcherism" a part of that nation's political vocabulary. By her attacks upon central government and the welfare state she undermined a political consensus that had existed since the 1950s. She helped to invigorate the economy, particularly by encouraging small businesses to develop. She challenged powerful institutions and brought about necessary reforms in industrial relations.

Yet the case against Thatcher is a strong one. She was a divisive leader, as on the issues of the poll tax and European integration. Her strident attitudes on social issues upset many people. Economic inequality increased under Thatcher, as did homelessness, and many social services deteriorated. She was accused of weakening basic civil liberties. Her foreign policy, though defined by a spectacular victory over Argentina in the Falklands War in 1982, was marked by Cold War rhetoric which seemed increasingly outdated by her third term in office. Ironically, the Soviet Union gave Thatcher the nickname she was best known by: the Iron Lady. She was proud of it, and her policies, though controversial, reflect a determination and consistency of vision that few political leaders can hope to equal.

In the month following the Thatcher resignation Queen Elizabeth II appointed the former prime minister a member of the Order of Merit, one of only 24 members (a vacancy occurred with the 1989 death of Laurence Olivier). The new Lady Thatcher's husband, Denis, received a baronetry (to become Sir Denis). A second honor came March 7, 1991, when Thatcher received the U.S. Medal of Freedom from President Bush. Although she was no longer prime minister, Thatcher remained politically active. She became president of the Bruges Group of British lawmakers opposed to a full political union with Europe, as well as of the Margaret Thatcher Foundation, designed to help bring order to the world.

On June 28, 1991, Thatcher wound up 32 years of a legislative career by announcing she would not seek to retain her seat in the House of Commons at the next election (which was called in July 1992). She had been MP for Barnet, Finchley, two suburbs northwest of London. She has remained active with lectures and appearances over the entire world, and somehow found the time to write her memoirs.

Further Reading

Margaret Thatcher wrote her memoirs in two volumes: *The Downing Street Years* (1993) and *The Path to Power* (1995). Two previous biographies of Thatcher are particularly worthwhile: Kenneth Harris, *Thatcher* (1988), and Hugo Young, *The Iron Lady: A Biography of Margaret Thatcher* 1989; (published in Britain under the title *One of Us*). Both books are by journalists who offer balanced, if critical, accounts of the Thatcher years. A number of recent studies focus on the events of the Thatcher era rather than her personality. The best of these is *Thatcherism and British Politics: The End of Consensus?*, 2nd edition (1990), by Dennis A. Kavanagh. More sympathetic to Thatcher than Kavanagh's volume is *The Thatcher Decade: How Britain Has Changed During the 1980s* by Peter Riddell (1989). Dennis Kavanagh and Anthony Seldon have edited a stimulating collection of essays titled *The Thatcher Effect* (1989), which includes contributions by leading scholars and journalists. Yet another perceptive work is *Mrs. Thatcher's Revolution: The Ending of the Socialist Era* (1987) by Peter Jenkins, who maintains that Thatcher destroyed the political order prevailing in Britain since the late 1950s. The so-called special relationship between Britain and the United States is ably covered by Geoffrey Smith in *Reagan and Thatcher* (1991). Thatcher's press secretary and long-time retainer, Bernard Ingham, gives a favorable account of Thatcher in his memoir *Kill the Messenger* (1991). □

Eli Thayer

Eli Thayer (1819-1899) was an American reformer, agitator, and promoter who used his considerable talent and generally progressive ideals to devise and support harebrained schemes.

E li Thayer was born in Mendon, Mass., on June 11, 1819, the scion of an old family of comfortable means. He was well educated but interrupted his studies several times, perhaps because of financial problems but possibly because of an erratic temperament that later became more obvious. He graduated from Brown University in 1845 and soon became president of Worcester Academy, his old school. Thayer and his wife constructed a preposterous castle-type building for Oread Collegiate Institute, a women's school under Thayer's headship. Like virtually all of Thayer's projects, Oread was a curious admixture of high idealism and canny Yankee opportunism. The school offered a far more substantial curriculum than most contemporary "female academies," while it also provided Thayer with a decent income.

By 1852 Thayer had held several public offices. But his chief work began in 1854 and 1855, when he led in organizing the New England Emigrant Aid Company. These were the days of the Kansas-Nebraska Bill, when Congress revoked the slave-free status of what became Kansas Territory and declared that the problem of slavery in the territory would be determined by popular vote within it. New England became a hotbed of opposition to this act. The Emigrant Aid Company helped finance New Englanders who wished to settle in Kansas so as to vote it free. Thayer as usual made a lucrative practice out of an ideal; he devoted most of his time between 1854 and 1856 to promoting settlement and received a percentage of all money he collected. He was perhaps the most significant figure in the proceedings. Thayer later looked back on Kansas as his chief accomplishment, writing several books about it, the most notable being *A History of the Kansas Crusade* (1889).

Thayer served in Congress between 1857 and 1861 and touted "colonization" as virtually a cure-all of the nation's (and the world's) ills. He advocated financing settlers to Utah (in order to vote out Mormon polygamy), to the border states (in order to whittle away at slavery), and to Central America (in order to guard against the introduction of slavery). By 1860, however, his political career had been hurt by his extreme individualism and his relationship with John Brown (whom Thayer may have helped subsidize). Thayer received some political patronage during the war, worked successfully as a land agent for western railroads between 1864 and 1870, and ran for Congress as a Democrat in 1874 and 1878. He died in April 1899.

Further Reading

There is probably no better insight into Thayer's personality and role in the Kansas affair than his *A History of the Kansas Crusade, Its Friends and Its Foes* (1889). A short sketch of Thayer is in Louis Filler, *The Crusade against Slavery, 1830-1860* (1960). A more complete sketch is in Lawrence Lader, *The Bold Brahmins: New England's War against Slavery, 1831-1863* (1961). □

Sylvanus Thayer

Sylvanus Thayer (1785-1872), American educator and engineer, put the U.S. Military Academy on a secure footing and promoted civil engineering as a collegiate course and profession.

S ylvanus Thayer was born on June 9, 1785, in Braintree, Mass. He entered Dartmouth College in 1803 but left in 1807 to attend the U.S. Military Academy at West Point. He graduated in 1808, was commissioned in the Corps of Engineers, and served in the War of 1812. In 1815 he was breveted a major and ordered to study European methods of educating military engineers so that he might help rescue West Point from incipient decay. The academy had a reputation for laxity in discipline and academic standards and suffered from uncertainty about whether to stress civilian or military studies.

After a year at the French École Polytechnique studying the curriculum and gathering a library, Thayer became superintendent at West Point in 1817. He accomplished sweeping reforms, setting new standards for admission, establishing minimum levels of academic proficiency, and creating a system to measure cadet progress. A commandant of cadets was appointed to regulate discipline and the military curriculum. Thayer established a board of visitors to inspect the academy annually to recommend adjustments in curriculum. He also established an academic board of faculty and administrators to develop academic policy.

Because West Point was required to provide professional officers for the Army, military subjects dominated the program. But Thayer also believed that the arts and sciences were important, as he wanted graduates to discharge the civilian offices of life with distinction. Courses in English and French, the natural and social sciences, mathematics, and ethics became staples. Refinements increased the civilian applications of West Point's curriculum. By 1831 the military engineering course was designated "civil engineering" and had lost most of its military overtones, encompassing the construction of "buildings and arches, canals, bridges, and other public works." Some graduates applied this in building the communications network to support America's developing industrial system.

Suspicion that the academy was an incubator of a military aristocracy led to tensions between Thayer and President Andrew Jackson's administration. Thayer was reassigned in 1833 as a colonel to supervise the construction of fortifications and harbor improvements in Massachusetts

and Maine. He became commander of the Corps of Engineers in 1857 but took a sick leave in the next year. Thayer retired in 1863 as a brigadier general. In 1867 he endowed the Thayer School of Engineering at Dartmouth and spent his last years arranging its curriculum. He died in Braintree on Sept. 7, 1872. His will established the Thayer Academy.

Further Reading

There is no adequate biography of Thayer. R. Ernest Dupuy, *Sylvanus Thayer: Father of Technology in the United States* (1958), concise and complete, claims more for Thayer than it proves. Sidney Forman, *West Point: A History of the United States Military Academy* (1950), describes Thayer's career in a broader context. ☐

Max Theiler

The South African-born American epidemiologist and microbiologist Max Theiler (1899-1972) received the 1951 Nobel Prize in physiology or medicine for developing a vaccine for yellow fever.

Max Theiler was born in Pretoria, South Africa, on January 30, 1899. His early schooling was in Pretoria and, because his father was Swiss, in Basel. Partly influenced by his father, who was a veterinary scientist, Max decided on a career in medicine, and in preparation he attended Rhodes University College in Grahamstown, South Africa, and the University of Capetown.

In 1911 Theiler enrolled at St. Thomas's Hospital, a well-known teaching hospital in London. In 1922 he was licensed to practice by London's Royal College of Physicians. The idea of medical practice, however, no longer appealed to him, and he enrolled in the London School of Tropical Medicine and Hygiene. Later that year he went to the United States, as he had been offered a position in the Department of Tropical Medicine at Harvard Medical School. While at Harvard he studied amebic dysentery and rat-bite fever, but his most far-reaching work was on yellow fever.

When Theiler began work on yellow fever, it was already known that a virus was responsible for the disease, that it was commonly transmitted by a mosquito, and that the disease could be controlled in populated areas by eradication of the breeding grounds of the mosquitoes. Still, an effective method of inoculation was necessary for full protection. One of Theiler's earliest contributions to the development of a yellow fever vaccine was the demonstration that laboratory white mice could be infected with the virus. When he introduced the yellow fever virus from a monkey into the brain of a white mouse and successively transferred the virus through several mice, he found that the virus underwent certain changes. It became progressively more serious in its effects on the mice, but at the same time its effects on monkeys lessened. These findings were the foundation of a mouse-derived vaccine.

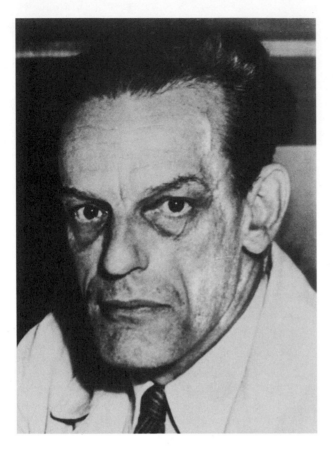

problem was in H. Harold Scott, *A History of Tropical Medicine* (2 vols., 1939). □

Themistocles

Themistocles (ca. 528-462 B.C.), an Athenian political leader, was a brilliant commander and statesman who defeated Persia at sea and made Athens a great power.

Themistocles was the son of a middle-class Athenian father and a non-Athenian mother. Ability alone made him influential. He advocated resistance to Persia when some wanted appeasement, and he urged the development of Athens's navy when most trusted in its army. When elected chief magistrate in 493 B.C., he developed Piraeus for the first time as a naval base, and 10 years later, when his rivals had been eliminated by a series of ostracisms, he persuaded Athens to build a hundred warships from the profits of state-owned mines. When Persia invaded in 480 B.C., Athens had the largest navy in Greece. Themistocles insisted on using it fully at Artemisium and at Salamis, although his naval policy meant evacuating Athens and trusting in the "wooden walls" of its ships. He saw correctly that the liberty of Greece and the future of Athens depended on first defeating Persia at sea.

As representative of Athens on the Staff Council, Themistocles urged the Spartan commander of the Greek fleet to keep his advanced position in narrow waters at Salamis. When some captains wished to withdraw, Themistocles secretly informed Xerxes, the Persian king, of this dissension and advised him to attack, promising the aid of the Athenian fleet if he did attack. Xerxes attacked, thereby preventing the dispersal of the Greek fleet, and his much larger fleet was decisively defeated in the narrow waters by the ramming tactics of the Greek squadrons. Themistocles proposed that the Greeks sail to the Dardanelles, destroy the Persian pontoon bridge there, and cut the army's lines of supply and cause it to withdraw. The proposal was defeated, but he sent information of it to Xerxes, adding that he himself was responsible for its defeat.

Themistocles worked next for the rise of Athens at the expense of Sparta. He used his popularity as victor of Salamis to lull Sparta's suspicions as Athens rebuilt its fortifications in 479-478 B.C. against Sparta's wishes, and he openly opposed Sparta's ambitions in northern Greece. His plans for making Athens supreme at sea were implemented when Athens displaced Sparta in the command of the allied fleet, and his faith in democracy was put into effect by the rule of Pericles. But Themistocles himself fell out of favor. He was ostracized, probably in 472 B.C., and then exiled and condemned to death on a charge of being in Persia's pay. He made a dramatic escape to Persia, where he was appointed governor of Magnesia in Asia Minor. The Greek historian Thucydides said that Themistocles died a natural death, though some reported suicide. Later a tomb was built at Piraeus in honor of Themistocles's achievements. The salva-

In 1928 Theiler married Lillian Graham. Two years later he joined the Rockefeller Foundation in New York City to continue his work on yellow fever. The mouse-derived vaccine was being used cautiously on humans by some researchers, but Theiler felt it was not safe enough for general use. Within a few years he succeeded in developing a vaccine called 17D, derived from a chick embryo, which proved both safe and effective and is now widely used in human immunization against yellow fever. His discovery was announced in 1937 in the *Journal of Experimental Medicine*. After that his work was concerned with other insect-borne virus infections.

In 1950 Theiler became director of the virus laboratories of the Rockefeller Foundation and the following year director of the division of medicine and public health. In 1964 he was appointed professor of epidemiology and microbiology at Yale University.

Theiler retired from Yale in 1967. Although he immigrated to the United States in 1923, and remained there until his death on August 11, 1972 at the age of 72, he never applied for U.S. citizenship.

Further Reading

Theodore L. Sourkes, *Nobel Prize Winners in Medicine and Physiology, 1902-1965* (1953; rev. ed. 1967), was a good introduction to Theiler and his work. See also Nobel Foundation, *Physiology or Medicine: Nobel Lectures, Including Presentation Speeches and Laureates' Biographies,* vol. 3 (1967). Some added insight was gained from Greer Williams, *Virus Hunters* (1959), and a detailed study of the entire yellow fever

Theocritus was a pupil of Philetas of Cos, as it is conjectured that Ptolemy Philadelphus also was. Theocritus was a friend of Callimachus, of the physician Nicias of Miletus, and of King Hiero of Syracuse. Theocritus's life has been described as falling into four divisions: the Coan, the Sicilian, the Alexandrian with a second Coan residence, and after 270 B.C.

All of Theocritus's work is not pastoral; it is as an idyllist that he is known because with great skill he established the genre and its characteristics: the use of the dactylic hexameter, the Dorian dialect, familiar forms (dialogues of herdsmen, their recitations and rivalries), and the themes of unhappy love, death, or absence of friends.

Not all of Theocritus's works have survived. The Coan period saw the production of the bucolic poems (Idylls VII, III-VI, VIII, X, XI, I). The Sicilian period saw only Idyll XVI. Possibly Idylls XXV and XXIII belong to this period. Disappointed in apparent lack of success in Sicily, Theocritus went to Egypt in 274, where he wrote Idylls XV and XVII, probably the *Berenice* (lost), Hymns XXII and XXIV, and Epyllion XIII. His works included *Daughter of Proteus, Hopes, Hymns, Heroines, Funeral Laments, Elegies, Iambics,* and *Epigrams.* Of these, 26 epigrams and 30 idylls are preserved.

Theocritus is a master of his art. His style is polished, natural, and graceful. The poems were called idylls (the Greek *eidyllia*) because they present fresh little pictures of rustic life, reflecting the simple life and conversation of the herdsman of Sicily, southern Italy, and Cos.

tion of Greece and the stature of Athens give the true measure of his greatness.

Further Reading

Ancient sources on Themistocles are Herodotus, Thucydides, and Plutarch. A modern source is Charles Hignett's *Xerxes' Invasion of Greece* (1963), which contains a useful bibliography.

Additional Sources

Lenardon, Robert J., *The saga of Themistocles,* London: Thames & Hudson, 1978. □

Theocritus

The Greek author Theocritus (ca. 310-ca. 245 B.C.) is credited with being the first and greatest pastoral poet. He expressed great delight in nature and rural life.

The best source for the biography of Theocritus is his own poems. He was a native of Syracuse who was familiar with Croton and Thurii in southern Italy, the island of Cos, Miletus, and Alexandria. He was born by at least 310 B.C., and probably earlier. His parents were Praxagoras and Philinna (who was originally from Cos).

Further Reading

Recommended books include Andrew Lang, ed. and trans., *Theocritus, Bion and Moschus* (1880); R. J. Cholmeley, ed., *The Idylls of Theocritus* (1901); R. T. Kerlin, *Theocritus in English Literature* (1910); John M. Edmonds, ed. and trans., *The Greek Bucolic Poets* (1912); James H. Hallard, trans., *The Idylls, Epigrams and Other Poems of Theocritus with the Fragments of Bion and Moschus* (1924); Gilbert Lawall, *Theocritus' Coan Pastorals: A Poetry Book* (1967); and Thomas G. Rosenmeyer, *The Green Cabinet: Theocritus and the European Pastoral Lyric* (1969). □

Theodora

Empress and wife of Justinian I, the courage and statesmanship of Theodora (ca. 500-548) complemented the genius of her husband and significantly contributed to the glories of his reign.

Theodora (center)

L ittle is know about the early life of Theodora, who rose to become one of the most famous women in Western civilization. She was born of humble origins at the beginning of the sixth century—probably in the year 500—and died on June 28, 548. Much of what is known comes from the writings of the sixth-century Byzantine historian Procopius of Caesarea (d. 565), especially his seven-volume *Anecdota* (commonly called *Secret History*). Although an important primary source for the life of Theodora and the era in which she lived, Procopius's *Secret History* must be viewed as written on the level of a modern tabloid, at least with respect to its factual accuracy. However biased, especially in the case of Theodora, it is felt that Procopius correctly portrayed the decadent lifestyle of Constantinople during the first half of the sixth century.

From Procopius and other writings of the era, including official chronicles, some outline of Theodora's early life prior to her marriage to Justinian I can be constructed. Some of the later chroniclers place her birth on the island of Cyprus, or more likely in Syria. Her father was a poor man named Acacius. Her mother's name is lost to history. Acacius was the keeper, or guardian, of the bears for the Greens at the hippodrome in Constantinople.

The hippodrome was a gigantic stadium where chariot races and other entertainments were staged, including bear-baiting. The all-important chariot races were sponsored by organizations, or factions, two of which, the Blues and the Greens, attained significant political power. These factions staged additional entertainments for the crowds, including animal contests and stage plays.

Theodora had two sisters, Comitona and Anastasia. Upon the death of her father when she was but a child, Theodora began to work on stage as a mime with her older sister Comitona, and soon became a full-fledged actress. By her late teens, she was a favorite both on the stage, where she delighted in displaying "undraped the beauty of which she was so proud," and off, where she followed in the footsteps of her sister as a prostitute and/or courtesan. In the context of the time, "actress" was synonymous with "prostitute."

Theodora was a smashing success. It is evident from all accounts that she was a stunning beauty. But she was gifted in more than her physical charms. Writes historian Charles Diehl: "She was intelligent, witty, and amusing . . . [and] . . . when she wanted to please, she knew how to put forth irresistible powers of fascination." On the stage, she was noted for what in our day would be euphemistically termed "adult" entertainment. Off the stage she was noted for her numerous lovers and her wild parties. It was said that her reputation was such that respectable people tried to avoid meeting her on the streets of Constantinople for fear of becoming contaminated. Diehl perhaps best sums up her reputation, when he writes: "Belonging to a profession of which virtue is not a necessary attribute, she amused, charmed, and scandalized Constantinople."

When she was 16, Theodora took as one of her lovers a wealthy man named Hecebolus. When Hecebolus was appointed governor of African Pentapolis, a minor province in north Africa, Theodora accompanied him to his new post. After approximately four years (in c. 521), and for reasons unknown to us, Hecebolus expelled her penniless from his house. For the next year, she traveled through the Middle East, apparently making use of her many gifts and talents as she "worked" her way back to Constantinople.

Theodora settled briefly in Alexandria, the luxurious capital of Egypt, and a favorite haunt of many famed courtesans. While there, she met leaders of the Monophysite religion—including Patriarch Timothy and Severus of Antioch—who were known to preach to women. It was apparently in Alexandria, although some sources say Antioch, that Theodora was converted to this heretical form of Christianity. Having undergone a religious conversion, she renounced her former lifestyle, returned to Constantinople in 522, settled in a house near the palace, and made a living spinning wool. It was also in 522, perhaps in Antioch, that Theodora first met Justinian.

Justinian was 40 years old when he met Theodora, then only half his age. He was the favorite nephew and heir apparent of Justin I (reigned, 518-27). Some modern scholars believe that Justinian actually ruled during his uncle's reign. In any event, the future emperor fell deeply in love with Theodora, and she with him. Justinian had his uncle confer upon Theodora the rank of patrician. Still, two obstacles stood in the way of marriage. The empress Euphemia, herself of peasant origins, firmly opposed the marriage. Also, there was an old Roman law which forbade high dignitaries to marry "women of servile condition, innkeepers' daughters, actresses, or courtesans."

Soon after Euphemia died in 523 or 524, Justin I issued an edict which decreed that "henceforth actresses who have abandoned their former life may contract a legal marriage, and those upon whom a high dignity has been conferred may marry men of the highest rank." In 525, the couple were married in the great church of Santa Sophia, built two centuries earlier by Constantine, founder of the Eastern Roman, or Byzantine, Empire. They settled down to a respectable, and by all accounts happy, married life.

Whatever she may have been in her youth, once married to Justinian, Theodora conducted herself with the nobility of character worthy of one of history's greatest female personalities. It is significant that no contemporary source, however hateful of her, ever accuses her of unfaithfulness to Justinian, and no historian since records anything that would call into question her moral conduct after her marriage. Apparently, Theodora gave birth to a daughter, either before she met Justinian, or early in their marriage, but the girl did not live. No other children were ever born to the imperial couple.

In April 527, Justin I became mortally ill. On Easter Sunday, April 4, he crowned Justinian co-emperor, granting him the title "Augustus," and Theodora "Augusta." Following the ceremony, they went to the hippodrome to receive the acclamations of the populace. One can only imagine what thoughts must have passed through Theodora's mind as she returned, now mistress of the Roman world, to that place where life's circumstances forced her into the life of a prostitute. On August 1, 527, Justin I died. It is from that date that the beginning of Justinian's reign is dated, although modern scholars believe that he actually reigned in fact as early as 518.

The imperial team of Justinian and Theodora, which lasted until the latter's death in 548, was one of history's remarkable combinations. Although they did not officially rule as joint monarchs, they in fact did. It is not correct to suggest that Theodora dominated her husband. Neither is it correct to suggest that by intrigue or otherwise she pursued goals of which he was ignorant. Rather, they complemented each other, even when, as in the case of religious issues, they pursued opposite goals. Justinian championed the cause of Christian orthodoxy, while at the same time he allowed Theodora to pursue the objective of religious tolerance for the Monophysite heretics with whom she identified.

Theodora rightly foresaw that the future of the Empire lay in the Middle East, while Justinian spent much of his reign in a futile attempt to reconquer the old Roman Empire in the West. In the area of women's rights, she achieved legislation which prohibited forced prostitution as well as alterations in the divorce laws which made them more favorable to women. Justinian allowed Theodora to share his throne, not simply because he adored her, but because he recognized in her the qualities of a true sovereign. Until her death, writes Diehl: "He never refused her anything, either the outward show or the real exercise of supreme power."

Theodora proved during the Nika Revolt of January 532 that she was a true statesman. The revolt started on Tuesday, January 13, as the chariot races were to begin in the hippodrome. The two factions, Blues and Greens, set aside their traditional rivalry and made common cause against the government. Before the day was over, many public buildings were in flames. By the evening of the next day, the crowd was proclaiming a new emperor. Failing to regain control of the situation, Justinian prepared to abandon his throne and flee.

At a meeting of the Imperial Council on Sunday, January 18, Theodora sat silently listening to the men present debating whether or not Justinian should attempt to flee. Preparations were made, and a ship sat ready in the harbor to carry the emperor and empress to safety. Then Theodora rose and—as quoted in Browning's *Justinian and Theodora*—made what must be considered one of the greatest short speeches ever recorded:

> Whether or not a woman should give an example of courage to men, is neither here nor there. At a moment of desperate danger one must do what one can. I think that flight, even if it brings us to safety, is not in our interest. Every man born to see the light of day must die. But that one who has been emperor should become an exile I cannot bear. May I never be without the purple I wear, nor live to see the day when men do not call me "Your Majesty." If you wish safety, my Lord, that is an easy matter. We are rich, and there is the sea, and yonder our ships. But consider whether if you reach safety you may not desire to exchange that safety for death. As for me, I like the old saying, that the purple is the noblest shroud.

After Theodora sat down, there were moments of nervous silence as the men present looked at one another. Any thought of fleeing fled before the courage of the empress. We are told by the chroniclers that it was two loyal generals,

Belisarius and Mundus, who first broke the silence. They began to discuss military plans.

Having assembled their German mercenaries, and joined by a third general, they proceeded to the hippodrome. After securing the exits so that none could escape, they fell upon the rebellious crowd of Blues and Greens. Soon the cries for Justinian's removal were changed to cries for mercy mingled with the screams and groaning of the dying. When the generals finally called a halt to the killing, the benches of the hippodrome were drenched with the blood of an estimated 30,000 to 40,000 rebels.

Historians agree that Theodora's timely display of courage saved Justinian his crown. She had proven herself a great statesman and a worthy partner in power. No one was more aware of that fact than Justinian. Far from arousing in him any sense of jealousy, her resolute action only deepened his respect and love for her. Throughout the remainder of her life, she was Justinian's active assistant in all matters of importance. She was not a dark power behind the throne, but shared openly in both the decision-making and the glory of her husband's reign. Her name appeared linked with his upon church walls and over the gates of citadels. Even in the mosaics that decorated the apartments of the Sacred Palace, writes Diehl, "Justinian had in like manner associated Theodora with him in connection with his military triumphs and the brightest glories of his reign." Her power was equal to, perhaps at times even greater than, Justinian's.

Following the Nika Revolt, Theodora and Justinian set about rebuilding Constantinople. They transformed it into the most splendid city in the world, so much so that Europeans during the Middle Ages referred to it as simply "The City." Constantinople, not Rome, was the center of Christian civilization from the 6th to the beginning of the 12th century. Justinian and Theodora built more that 25 churches and convents in Constantinople. The greatest of them, and indeed the greatest church in all of Christendom prior to the building of St. Peter's in Rome, was the Hegia Sophia, rebuilt by the imperial couple. With its great dome, 107 feet in diameter, and decorated in rich marbles and mosaics, it dazzled visitors for centuries. One European churchman who visited Constantinople during the high Middle Ages recorded that upon entering the Hegia Sophia he felt as if he had died and entered heaven itself.

Both Justinian and Theodora recognized the importance of religious issues. Complex theological issues dominated the lives of even the common people. They were inseparable from the important political issues of the day. Hence Justinian, who wanted to reconquer the Latin West, stoutly defended the orthodox position in such theological debates as those concerning the nature of Christ. To do so won support among the Christians in the ruins of the old Roman Empire in the West. But it also tended to alienate the Christians in the eastern provinces of the Empire who were attracted to the Monophysite heresy. Monophysitism held that Christ had but one nature, a composite divine-human one. The orthodox position, as defined by the Council of Chalcedon in 451, was that Jesus Christ was at the same time both fully human and fully divine.

While Justinian might use the carrot-and-stick approach to combat Monophysitism, Theodora championed their cause both openly and in secret. No doubt her own convictions, which went back to her conversion under Monophysite influence, were behind her efforts to secure religious tolerance for Monophysitism. But she was motivated also by her belief that the strength of the Empire was in the Middle East. Monophysitism was especially strong in the eastern provinces along the frontier with the revived Persian Empire. To grant toleration to them would be to strengthen and further the unity of the Empire where it faced a powerful enemy. But it also would undermine Justinian's dream of reuniting the old Roman Empire.

In her efforts to help the Monophysites, Theodora influenced the election of popes, provided refuge within the apartments of her palace for Monophysite leaders, and openly established a Monophysite monastery in Sycae, directly across the Golden Horn from Constantinople. In c. 542, she even influenced Justinian to appoint a Monophysite bishop for the pro-Monophysite Arab client state of the Ghassanids. By such efforts, Theodora was able to keep alive the fire of the Monophysite heresy in the eastern provinces of the Empire.

When Theodora died of cancer on June 28, 548, her body was buried in the Church of the Holy Apostles, one of the splendid churches she and Justinian had built in Constantinople. Her death was a great loss to Justinian. It is tempting to see, as some have, the decline of imperial fortunes during the latter years of Justinian's reign as the result of his loss of her counsel. But that would be unfair to Justinian's own genius. Nevertheless, he cherished her memory, as later Queen Victoria did that of her dear Prince Albert. In his latter years, Justinian was in the habit of swearing in the name of Theodora. Those who wished to win his favor learned the importance of reminding him of her virtues. How much she meant to him personally was evident in an incident which occurred on August 11, 559. Following a campaign against the Huns, Justinian was making a triumphal entry into Constantinople. The official record states that "as the procession passed before the Church of the Holy Apostles it halted while the emperor went in to offer a prayer and light candles before Theodora's tomb." Four years later at the age of 83, Justinian died. His body was taken to the Church of the Holy Apostles to lie with the one whom he was fond of calling "his sweetest delight."

Further Reading

Barker, John W. *Justinian and the Later Roman Empire.* University of Wisconsin Press, 1966.

Browning, Robert. *Justinian and Theodora.* Praeger, 1971.

Diehl, Charles. *Byzantine Portraits.* Knopf, 1906.

Lamb, Harold. *Constantinople: Birth of an Empire.* Knopf, 1966.

McCabe, Joseph. *The Empresses of Constantinople.* Gorham Press, n.d.

Bury, J. B. *A History of the Later Roman Empire from the Death of Theodosius I to the Death of Justinian (a.d. 395-565).* 2 vols. Dover Publications, 1958.

Holmes, W. G. *The Age of Justinian and Theodora.* 2 vols. G. Bell, 1905-07.

Procopius. *History of the Wars, Secret History, and Buildings.* Washington Square Press, 1967.

Ure, P. N. *Justinian and His Age.* Penguin Books, 1951.
Vandercook, John W. *Empress of the Dusk: A Life of Theodora of Byzantium.* Reynal & Hitchcock, 1940. □

Theodoric the Great

King of the Ostrogoths and conqueror of Italy, Theodoric the Great (c. 453-526) was the second barbarian to rule as king in Italy after the fall of the Roman Empire in 476.

Theodoric was the son of Theudemir, king of the Ostrogoths, a Germanic people who moved into the Roman Empire in the 5th century and who were initially retained as military allies by the Roman emperors. Theodoric was born in Pannonia. In 461, in keeping with barbarian-Roman custom, he was sent to the imperial court at Constantinople as a hostage for his people's behavior. He attracted imperial attention and received a Roman education before returning to his people in 471.

Upon his father's death in 474, Theodoric became king of the Ostrogoths. He was a vigorous and intelligent ruler, and although allied with Rome, he disliked Roman officials and possibly the terms of the treaty allying him with the Romans. On several occasions he threatened Roman settlements, and in 487 he began a march on Constantinople. The emperor Zeno convinced Theodoric that the Western part of the empire offered richer plunder than the East, and he commissioned Theodoric to go to Italy and to punish the barbarian general Odoacer, who had in 476 dismissed Zeno's coemperor and assumed his rule. Theodoric's mission was to defeat Odoacer and pacify Italy.

Theodoric marched into Italy, and by 493 he had defeated Odoacer's army, killed the usurper, and established himself with the official title of Patrician and Master of Soldiers as the actual ruler of Italy. His position, however, was not secure. He had been given his Italian commission primarily to prevent him from capturing Constantinople. His titles did not prevent Roman aristocrats in both East and West from regarding him as an uncouth barbarian invader, little better than Odoacer. Moreover, Theodoric and the Ostrogoths were Arians, their heretical version of Christianity being particularly repellent to orthodox Romans.

Theodoric's Roman education, however, offered him a means of reconciling some of the profound differences between Goths and Romans. He genuinely admired many of the Romans' social institutions, and he employed as ministers Roman aristocrats, first the philosopher Boethius and later the statesman and author Casiodorus. Theodoric retained royal title over his own subjects, but he did not claim to be king of the Romans in Italy. He depended upon his "official" status as Master of Soldiers, and his documents consistently echoed his view that the Goths were in Italy only to protect and to preserve Roman civilization by force of arms. His personal "Romanism" and the propaganda work of his subordinate officials thus made him and his people, for a time at least, acceptable to the Romans. Theodoric ruled from Ravenna, not Rome, and he beautified his capital with magnificent architectural works. He restored cities, cultivated the arts, and repeatedly announced his admiration of Roman antiquity.

After 507, however, the Arianism of the Goths and their presence in Italy began increasingly to alienate the Romans. In a fit of cruelty, Theodoric imprisoned and later executed his secretary, Boethius. The growing hostility of the Emperor at Constantinople made Theodoric distrustful of the Romans, and he persecuted Pope John I in 526 and later demanded that all churches be turned over to the Arians. During the last years of his reign, Theodoric attempted to rule within a loose framework of Roman institutions and pro-Roman propaganda. However, rebellions sprang up, his Gothic subjects grew restive under Roman rule, and the military power of the East fomented distrust and revolt among the Romans. When Theodoric died in 526, he was succeeded by his grandson Athalaric under the regency of Theodoric's daughter Amalasuntha.

Further Reading

The most extensive biography of Theodoric is by Thomas Hodgkin, *Theodoric the Great* (1891, rep. 1980). For historical background see J. B. Bury, *The Invasion of Europe by the Barbarians* (1928), and H. St. L. B. Moss, *The Birth of the Middle Ages, 395-814* (1935).

Additional Sources

Moorhead, John, *Theoderic in Italy,* Oxford: Clarendon Press; New York: Oxford University Press, 1992. □

Theodosius

The Roman emperor Theodosius (ca. 346-395) was sometimes called "the Great" because of his solution of the Gothic problem and unification of the empire and because of his championship of orthodoxy, which earned for him the extravagant praise of Catholic writers.

Theodosius was the son of a famous general of the same name who had cleared Britain of northern invaders and then had quashed a Moorish rebellion. However, the general was falsely accused at court and summarily executed in 376. Theodosius had served ably under his father in Britain, and later, in an independent command in Moesia, he had saved the province from barbarian invasion. At his father's death, however, he gained permission to retire to his family estate in Spain.

In August 378 the Eastern Roman emperor, Valens, was overwhelmed and killed at Adrianople by invading Goths. The Western emperor, Gratian, thereupon recalled Theodosius from retirement and in January 379 made him joint emperor with command over the East. Instead of fighting the Goths directly with demoralized Roman troops, by diplomacy Theodosius fostered dissensions among them, won the friendship of the Visigoths by his courteous treatment of their king, and ultimately allowed the Visigoths to remain within the empire, though they retained their own political cohesion under native chieftains. They were called allies (*foederati*) rather than subjects; and this set the legal precedent for the ultimate partition of much of the empire among immigrant barbarians.

In 383 Magnus Maximus was proclaimed emperor by British troops, and Emperor Gratian was murdered. Theodosius at first accepted his new colleague and allowed him Britain and Gaul; but when, in 387, Maximus drove from Italy Gratian's young half brother Valentinian II, Theodosius (now the husband of Galla, Valentinian's sister) marched west, destroyed Maximus, and restored Valentinian. Theodosius remained in Italy for 3 years, leaving the administration of the East to his elder son, Arcadius, whom he had declared an augustus (coruler) in 383.

In 391 Valentinian was murdered by his Frankish military commander, Arbogast, who then raised one Eugenius to the throne. Theodosius again returned to the West and defeated the usurper in the autumn of 394. The empire was then briefly reunited under one ruler; but Theodosius himself died on Jan. 17, 395, leaving the East to Arcadius and the West to a younger son, Honorius, who had been proclaimed augustus in 393. This division of the empire became permanent.

A serious illness soon after his accession prompted Theodosius's early baptism, which Christian Roman emperors usually postponed till their deathbeds. This made him very susceptible to the pressures of the Church, and he came particularly under the influence of Ambrose, the strong-willed bishop of Milan, who repeatedly placed him under heavy penance when his justice was hotheaded or severe. Theodosius was a devoted persecutor of Christian heresies, and in 391 he officially closed all the empire's temples and forbade the practice of all pagan cults.

Further Reading

Noel Q. King, *The Emperor Theodosius and the Establishing of Christianity* (1960), discusses the important role of Theodosius in the triumph of orthodox Catholicism; and A. H. M. Jones, *The Later Roman Empire* (1964), covers the secular aspects of his reign.

Additional Sources

Williams, Stephen, *Theodosius: the empire at bay,* London: Batsford,1994. □

Axel Hugo Theodor Theorell

The Swedish biochemist Axel Hugo Theodor Theorell (1903-1982) was awarded the Nobel Prize in Physiology or Medicine for his discoveries concerning the nature and mode of action of oxidation enzymes.

Hugo Theorell, the son of Ture Theorell, a medical practitioner, was born at Linköping on July 6, 1903. From 1921 he studied medicine at the Karolinska Institute at Stockholm and graduated as a bachelor of medicine in 1924. He soon became an assistant in the Institute of Medical Chemistry at Stockholm, and there he was temporary associate professor in 1928-1929. In 1930 he graduated as a doctor of medicine and was appointed lecturer in physiological chemistry at the Karolinska Institute.

In 1931, while working in Svedberg's Institute of Physical Chemistry in Uppsala, Theorell was the first to obtain crystalline myoglobin, and he determined its chemical and physical properties. In 1932 he became associate professor of medical and physiological chemistry in the University of Uppsala; but from 1933 to 1935 he worked, as a Rockefeller Fellow, in the laboratory of Otto Warburg at Berlin-Dahlem. There he began his work on oxidation enzymes.

Warburg's "Yellow Enzyme"

In 1932 Warburg and his coworker Walther Christian discovered in yeast a bright yellow enzyme. Warburg showed that it consisted of a yellow pigment and a carrier substance. When Theorell began working at Berlin, it was known that the pigment part was a flavin, called lactoflavin. It was later named riboflavin and was identified with vita-

min B_2. When separated from the carrier substance, which was itself inactive, the pigment part lost its enzymatic activity. At Berlin, Theorell, using his own electrophoretic methods, had by 1934 purified and crystallized the enzyme and had separated the pigment from the colorless protein carrier. He also showed that the pigment part—the coenzyme or prosthetic group—was a protein. He determined its constitution—a lactoflavin phosphoric ester—and named it flavin monouncleotide (FMN).

After his return to Sweden, Theorell was appointed in 1937 director of the new Biochemical Department of the Nobel Medical Institute in Stockholm. The department was transferred to a new Biochemical Institute in 1947.

Cytochrome c

Cytochrome was rediscovered independently in 1925 by David Keilin, who soon isolated cytochromes *a, b,* and *c* and showed that cytochrome c was fundamental in cell respiration. In 1938 Theorell showed that the heme nucleus of cytochrome c was linked to the protein in two different ways. This was the first occasion on which the nature of such linkages had been demonstrated in any enzyme.

In 1941 Theorell, working with Å. Åkesson, studied cytochrome *c* extensively, especially the mode of linkage of the iron to the protein and its stereochemical structure. In 1943 Theorell suggested that there were two steps in its reduction. In 1955 Theorell and Anders Ehrenberg showed that the core of the cytochrome c molecule consisted of an iron atom at the center, within a porphyrin disk bearing

histidine side chains. The core was surrounded by helical peptide chains. Theorell thought the structure was designed to protect the iron from oxidizing agents—his theory of the "embedded heme." He was able to construct a model of the core.

Peroxidases and Alcohol Dehydrogenases

In 1941 Theorell and his coworkers crystallized for the first time a peroxidase, found in horseradish, and in 1943 they isolated the lactoperoxidase in milk.

The alcohol dehydrogenases, oxidative enzymes consisting of a protein linked to diphosphopyridine nucleotide (DPN), are found especially in liver and in yeast. In 1948 the enzyme from horse liver was first crystallized in Theorell's institute, and in 1950 the velocity constant for the very rapid action of the liver dehydrogenase was determined. In succeeding years, Theorell and his coworkers elucidated the complicated action of the alcohol dehydrogenases. They found that the liver enzyme oxidized alcohol to aldehyde, whereas the yeast enzyme reduced aldehyde to alcohol. The later work of Theorell and his coworkers on these complex enzyme systems led to their development of a practically specific test for ethyl alcohol, used officially in medicolegal work.

For his discoveries on oxidation enzymes Theorell was awarded the Nobel Prize in 1955. In 1957 he was elected a Foreign Associate of the National Academy of Sciences in Washington and in 1959 a Foreign Member of the Royal Society. From 1967 to 1973, he was president of the International Union of Biochemists and in 1967-1968 president of the Swedish Academy of Sciences. A member of many foreign learned societies, he held honorary doctorates from seven universities. In 1960, he received the 150-Year Jubilee Medal of the Karolinska Institute and in 1965 the Paul Karrer Medal. In 1971, he received the Ciba Medal and the Semmelweiss Medal.

Interested in music all his life, Theorell was a member of the Swedish Royal Academy of Music and chairman of the Stockholm Symphony Society. His wife, Margit, was a professional pianist, and Theorell was a very accomplished violinist. Together, they were at the forefront of the musical life of Stockholm.

Theorell retired as director of the Nobel Medical Institute in 1970, after 33 years of service, although he continued to do research. Much of his work was done with long-time companion A. Akeson (1914-1988). Theorell died in Stockholm on Aug. 15, 1982.

Further Reading

There is a biography of Theorell in *Nobel Lectures, Physiology or Medicine, 1942-1962* (1964), which also includes his Nobel Lecture. For references to his work see C. W. Carter, R. V. Coxon, D. S. Parsons, and R. H. S. Thompson, *Biochemistry in Relation to Medicine* (1959); M. Dixon and E. C. Webb, *Enzymes* (2d ed. 1964); and Dorothy M. Needham, *Machina Carnis* (1971). □

St. Theresa

The Spanish nun St. Theresa (1515-1582) was the reformer of the Carmelite order and one of the most important mystical writers of all times.

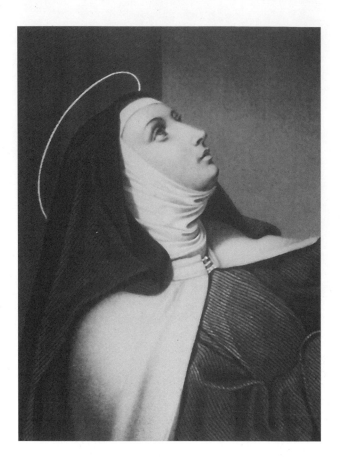

S t. Theresa, originally Teresa de Cepeda y Ahumada, was born on March 28, 1515, to a gentry family of Ávila. After some local schooling she entered the Ávila Carmelite Convent of the Incarnation in 1536. In those days the rule of Carmel was no longer the primitive one of 1248. In the Ávila convent even the mitigated version was not strictly observed, and a number of disciplinary problems existed. About 1556 Theresa was converted to a more ardent spiritual life and started making plans for the foundation of a convent under the primitive rule. After a great deal of opposition she succeeded, and in 1562 the new Ávila Convent of St. Joseph was opened.

The Reformer

The reform movement of the Discalced Carmelites expanded rapidly, and within 9 years Theresa had founded 11 new convents. Theresa herself wrote down the epic of her travels and trials in *The Book of the Foundations.* Meanwhile she had also started reforming the monasteries for men. The first friar to follow her in this venture was Juan de Yepes, later known as St. John of the Cross. When, in 1571, Theresa returned as prioress to her old Convent of the Incarnation, she brought him with her as her spiritual assistant and as confessor of the nuns.

After 3 years Theresa returned to St. Joseph's. The following period was marked by incredible hardship mainly resulting from the opposition of the unreformed, or Calced, Carmelites. Their resistance reached a climax after the appointment of Fray Gracian as apostolic visitor of the Calced in Andalusia. Gracian's tactless manner led to the closure of all Discalced houses in Andalusia. During this period John was twice abducted and imprisoned in an unreformed house. The Discalced were completely reintegrated with the Calced, and the reform was virtually abolished. Only the intervention of the King revived the movement, and finally, in 1580, Pope Gregory XIII erected the Discalced monasteries into a new province. Fray Gracian was elected provincial.

After Theresa's death at Alba on Oct. 15, 1582, her new order passed through an equally difficult period of internal trouble during which the new provincial, Doria, even attempted to abolish her constitutions. Theresa was canonized in 1622 and pronounced a Doctor of the Church in 1970.

Her Writings

In spite of this constant turmoil Theresa had steadily developed her spiritual life. The mystical graces which she had received early in her active career never left her. Her written works have a strongly autobiographical character. They are for the most part written in a nontechnical, vivid language. Although they all describe the soul's progress in the mystical life, it is not easy to obtain a coherent picture out of the various descriptions written at different periods in her life. Her first work, which is also the best to introduce a reader to her thought, is her spiritual autobiography, her *Life.* It covers only the first 50 years of her life, and the first draft of it was written while she was still at the Convent of the Incarnation in Ávila. *The Book of the Foundations* continues this biography throughout the various journeys which she made to found new monasteries.

Between the *Life* and the final chapters of the *Foundations* lie all of Theresa's other works, most important of which is *The Mansions of the Interior Castle* (1577). In this book the soul is compared to an interior castle that contains many mansions. The spiritual movement goes from the outside to the inner apartment, in which God himself lives. The mystical state begins at the fourth mansion, described as a passive recollection in which the soul abandons all mental activity in prayer. The next three mansions all describe the unitive life of prayer. Also important for the study of spiritual development are *The Way of Perfection* (1565-1566) and *Conceptions of the Love of God* (1571-1574).

Further Reading

E. Allison Peers translated *The Complete Works of St. Teresa of Jesus* (3 vols., 1946); the *Letters of St. Teresa* was translated by the Benedictines of Stanbrook (4 vols., 1919-1924). Two modern biographies stand out: E. Allison Peers, *Mother of Carmel* (1946), and, strongly psychological, Marcelle Auclair, *Teresa of Avila,* translated by Kathleen Pond (1953). For interpretations of St. Theresa's work consult E. Allison Peers, *Studies in the Spanish Mystics* (3 vols., 1927-1960), and E. W. Trueman Dicken, *The Crucible of Love* (1963). □

Paul Theroux

Paul Theroux (born 1941) was an expatriate American writer of numerous works of fiction and of the chronicles of his own travels by train throughout the world. He was a keen observer of the relationships between people and their environments.

P aul Theroux was a professional outsider. The expatriate American author of three travel books, four books of short stories, and almost a dozen novels, Theroux used his own sense of not belonging to show how others try to get along away from home. His sense of irony often revealed as much about the wayfaring author as about his subjects.

Born April 10, 1941, in Medford, Massachusetts, the third of seven children, Theroux was of French-Canadian/Italian descent. His brothers and sisters, all independent, were all encouraged to write by their father, a salesman who read aloud from Charles Dickens and Herman Melville. At an early age Theroux and two of his brothers put out competing family newspapers with stories of the day's activities.

In 1959 Theroux went to the University of Maine, but he transferred after a year to the University of Massachusetts where he studied first pre-med and then English. He received his BA in 1963 and joined the Peace Corps to avoid the draft.

Theroux's first Peace Corps assignment was in East Africa, where he lectured in English in a school in Limbe, Malawi. He was expelled in 1965, however, for his alleged involvement in a conspiracy to assassinate the president of the country. Theroux did not leave Africa. With the help of a friend he found a job teaching English and current affairs at a university in Kampala, Uganda. While there he wrote a number of freelance magazine pieces and worked on his first novel. It was also there that he was befriended by author V. S. Naipaul, who helped the young writer with his work.

Fiction Dealing With People and Environment

His first novel, *Waldo,* the picaresque story of a young man who became a success as a writer, was published in 1966. A keen manipulator of expectations versus reality, Theroux's next book, *Fong and the Indians* (1968), dealt with the complicated social changes of emerging East African countries. Theroux chose as his protagonist a bungling anti-hero, Sam Fong, a Chinese Catholic grocer. Whether in his fiction or in his travel books, Theroux's characters cut back across the grain of their expectations when confronted with a new environment.

In 1968 Theroux finally left Africa after being trapped in a street riot. Not ready to settle down, he took a position as an English literature teacher at the University of Singapore. There he wrote numerous short stories and a study of his mentor, V. S. Naipaul. He also wrote two novels set in Africa, *Girls at Play* (1969) and *Jungle Lovers* (1971). Again, his subjects were the disenfranchised.

Girls at Play deals with the psychological and social pressures exerted by a foreign environment on a group of English and American schoolteachers stationed in the bush of Kenya. *Jungle Lovers* pits two characters against their own misconceptions of Africa and ultimately against their growing disenchantment.

In 1971 Theroux left Singapore for England, where he spent most of his time into the 1980s. (His summers were usually spent on Cape Cod in the United States.) There he devoted himself to writing. In 1972 he came out with a diverse collection of short stories, *Sinning With Annie and Other Stories,* and a satirical look at the reverse culture shock he was feeling back in the West in *The Black House.* The hero of *Saint Jack* (1973) was the first of Theroux's more complicated characters, but the book explored the familiar themes. Jack Flowers, a middle-aged American expatriate in Singapore, runs a whorehouse and offers readers of *Saint Jack* a cynical narrator-philosopher. The book was later turned into a movie.

Travel Books and More Fiction

But it was as a traveler that Theroux made his greatest mark. After the publication of *The Black House* he left on a four-month train trip through Asia. The result was *The Great Railway Bazaar: By Train Through Asia*, a chronicle of his trip from London through the Middle East, Malaysia, and Siberia. In a kind of travel guide/autobiography, Theroux examined the outsider as he drew out confidences from other passengers and mixed them with personal narrative. It was his first best seller.

In *Saint Jack* Theroux wrote of fiction as a tool that offers "the second chances life denied." In *The Family Arsenal* (1976) Theroux fictionalized some of the people he had observed on his trip. This time one anti-hero is Valentine Hood, a disenchanted American who is dismissed from his diplomatic post after assaulting an official of the South Vietnamese government. In *Picture Palace* (1978) he again allowed fiction to take his characters where reality hadn't. Based on the true-life photographer Jill Krementz, Theroux's Maude Coffin Pratt explores the relationship between an artist's life and her work.

Theroux's two other travel books, *The Old Patagonian Express: By Train Through the Americas* (1979) and *The Kingdom by the Sea: A Journey Around Great Britain* (1983), continued to test the waters of strange new worlds. "What interests me," he wrote in *The Old Patagonian Express*, "is the waking in the morning, the progress from the familiar to the slightly odd, to the rather strange, to the totally foreign, and finally to the outlandish."

Prolific, Theroux also published *The Consul's File* (1977), the short novels *The Mosquito Coast* (1982) and *Half Moon Street* (1985), and *World's End and Other Stories* (1980). In 1985 *Sunrise With Seamonsters: Travels and Discoveries 1964-1984* was published. It is a series of short pieces—literary essays, travel articles, and profiles. It was followed by a long novel, *O-Zone* (1986), his first America-centered work.

More recently, Theroux wrote *Chicago Loop* (1991); *The Happy Isles of Oceania: Paddling the Pacific* (1992); *Millroy the Magician* (1994); *The Pillars of Hercules* (1995); *My Other Life* (1996); and *Kowloon Tong* (1997).

He was married to Anne Castle Theroux and was the father of two sons.

Ever the outsider, Theroux's world is populated by people who don't seem to belong in their environment. Like the author riding a train toward the outlandish, for them the mystery is what will come next.

Further Reading

In addition to his travel books as autobiography, including *My Other Life* (1996), Theroux has done numerous interviews with journalists. There is a chapter about him in *Conversations With American Writers* by Charles Ruas (1985). Two excellent magazine pieces about the author are a profile by Mel Gussow in the *New York Times* (July 28, 1976) and a retrospective review of Theroux by Hugh Hebert in *Guardian* (April 17, 1973). Susan Larner's review of *Half Moon Street* in *The New Yorker* (January 7, 1985) also discusses Theroux's earlier work. Theroux's *Five Travel Epiphanies* for *Forbes*

magazine in 1995 discusses his five most interesting experiences while traveling. □

Thibaut IV

Thibaut IV (1201-1253), Count of Champagne and Brie, and, as Thibaut I, King of Navarre, was probably the greatest trouvère.

Born in Troyes, the capital of Champagne, on May 30, 1201, shortly after the death of his father, Thibaut at birth was Count of Champagne and Brie. Troyes had a long tradition of courtly poetry. Thibaut's grandmother, Marie, the great-granddaughter of the first troubadour, had established a brilliant court there and patronized several of the most famous poets of the 1170s, among them Chrestien de Troyes, the creator of the romances about Lancelot, Parsifal, and others.

At the death of her husband, Thibaut's mother asked for royal protection, in exchange for which Thibaut was obliged to serve several years at court and later to accompany the successive French kings on their military campaigns. Among these was the Albigensian Crusade, a disastrous civil war that crushed the south of France, the home of the Provençal-speaking troubadours. Thibaut reluctantly accompanied the King in 1226, but he would not participate in the fighting and finally withdrew by night from the royal camp. The King died shortly thereafter, and Thibaut soon made his peace with the queen regent and dedicated several poems to her. However, his withdrawal antagonized certain noblemen, who invaded Champagne. In 1234, on the death of his uncle, Sancho VII, Thibaut became king of Navarre.

Although he was opposed to the Albigense war, Thibaut pursued its religious aim, the elimination of a dissident sect; and before leaving for a crusade in Palestine in 1239-1240 he had nearly 200 adherents of that sect burned at the stake. After his return he became known as a good king. He died in Pamplona, the capital of Navarre, on July 7, 1253.

As with other *trouvères*, it is difficult to determine the exact number of Thibaut's works, since several occur with different attributions in the many collections (*chansonniers*) of the period: 65 can be safely assigned to him, 5 more may be his, and 7 others are very doubtful. Almost all are preserved with melodies, a good number of them with more than one. His preserved poems are more numerous than those of any other troubadour or *trouvère*. They were highly praised by his contemporaries and quoted in France, Germany, and Italy until the 14th century.

The poems cover a wide variety of subjects, though 60 percent follow tradition and are lyrics devoted to courtly love. Fifteen poems are in the form of real or pretended debates (*jeu-parti* or tenso) on love and knightly honor. Thibaut's works in this genre were particularly appreciated; for them he sometimes used already existing melodies.

Other poems are works dealing with the Crusades, one being a letter to his lady love sent from Palestine, pastourelles and descriptions of shepherds' love, and religious songs, including several dedicated to Mary, the religious symbol of courtly love.

Further Reading

Some information on Thibaut is in Sir Steven Runciman, *A History of the Crusades* (3 vols., 1951-1954). For background see Gustave Reese, *Music in the Middle Ages* (1940), and Denis Stevens and Alec Robertson, eds., *The Pelican History of Music,* vol. 1 (1960). ☐

Louis Adolphe Thiers

The French journalist, historian, and statesman Louis Adolphe Thiers (1797-1877) was the most gifted of the literary statesmen who were an important feature of 19th-century French political life.

Born at Marseilles on April 16, 1797, Adolphe Thiers attended the local lycée and studied law at Aix. Though admitted to the bar, he forsook the legal profession to become a journalist. Moving to Paris in 1821, Thiers became a contributor to the *Constitutionnel,* a Liberal paper, and began the *History of the French Revolution* (10 vols., 1823-1827; trans., 5 vols., 1895), a sympathetic account which established his reputation as a man of letters. The work suffered from diffuseness, casuistry, bias against those with whom he disagreed, and omission of inconvenient facts, all of which evoked the protest from many participants in the described events that he had treated them and their cause unjustly.

Brilliant but arrogant, energetic but antagonistic, Thiers embarked upon a successful but controversial political career under the July Monarchy. With the financial backing of Jacques Lafitte, in 1830 Thiers joined F. A. M. Mignet and N. A. Carrel in founding the National and launching an editorial campaign to replace the Bourbon with an Orleanist dynasty. A member of the haute bourgeoisie, he played a prominent role in the July Revolution and in the ascendancy of the Duc d'Orléans to the throne. Elected deputy for Aix, he soon became the leader of the Left Center, which wanted to broaden the suffrage to include the lower bourgeoisie and thought that the King should reign but not rule.

After the fall of the Lafitte ministry (March 1831), Thiers became less liberal, and, following the suppression of the Republican insurrection of June 1832, he became minister of the interior in the Soult government. During the next 4 years Thiers advanced from one portfolio to another until he became premier (February—September 1836). The brevity of his ministry is explained by the opposition of François Guizot, leader of the Right Center, and the hostility of Louis Philippe, who resented his ambition and arrogance. In March 1840 Thiers again became premier but held the post only 6 months before his rash support of Egypt during the second Mohammed Ali crisis brought France to the brink of war with Britain and caused the King to dismiss him (Oct. 29, 1840). He continued to sit in the Chamber but seldom spoke until 1846, when he began a campaign of opposition against the Guizot ministry. When it fell on Feb. 23, 1848, the King again turned to Thiers, but this action came too late. The next day, Thiers, loyal to the end, advised Louis Philippe to leave the capital and besiege it until it could be assaulted. The King, however, rejected the plan and repaired instead to England.

Under the Second Republic, Thiers posed as a conservative republican. The "red scare" created by the June Days so intimidated him that he supported L. E. Cavaignac's bloody suppression of the workers. He backed Louis Napoleon for president, however, in the belief that, if Louis Napoleon was elected, his presumed ineptitude would pave the way for the restoration of the Orleanist dynasty. Elected to the Legislative Assembly in 1849, Thiers, Voltairean skeptic though he was, even voted for the Falloux Law (1850) because he saw the Church as an ally against the socialists. Arrested at the time of the coup of 1851, the former premier went into English exile, but within a year the Prince President granted him amnesty.

Returning to Paris in 1852, Thiers spent the next decade completing the *History of the Consulate and the Empire* (trans., 20 vols., 1845-1862), a work begun in 1840. So pro-Napoleon as to be panegyrical, it suffered, too, from the same faults which marred his first history and provoked the same criticism.

In 1863 Thiers resumed his political career as a deputy for Paris. A severe critic of Napoleon III's foreign policy, he blamed it for France's loss of prestige. After 1866 he repeatedly warned the Emperor of the Prussian menace, but few of his countrymen took his Philippics seriously. The consequences of unpreparedness were, of course, the defeat of France and the fall of Napoleon III.

On Sept. 4, 1870, the Third Republic replaced the Second Empire and opened the way for Thiers's third and greatest ascendancy. Elected provisional executive by the Assembly on Feb. 16, 1871, he at once negotiated with Bismarck the Treaty of Frankfurt (May 10) and soon thereafter (May 21-28) crushed the Paris Commune. On August 30 a grateful France elected him president, and for the next 2 years he gave the infant republic the stability and direction that it so desperately needed. A strong executive and a skillful parliamentary leader, Thiers earned the sobriquet "Adolphe I." But on May 24, 1873, a monarchist majority, which regarded him a turncoat, forced him to resign. The "grand old man" continued to sit in the Assembly until his death on Sept. 3, 1877.

Further Reading

Thiers's *Memoirs, 1870-1873* (1903; trans. 1915) was published posthumously. The best biography of Thiers in English is John M. S. Allison, *Monsieur Thiers* (1932). Allison also wrote *Thiers and the French Monarchy* (1926), a study of the statesman and the Orleanist dynasty.

Additional Sources

Albrecht-Carrie, Rene, *Adolphe Thiers: or, The triumph of the bourgeoisie,* Boston: Twayne Publishers, 1977.
Bury, J. P. T. (John Patrick Tuer), *Thiers, 1797-1877: a political life,* London; Boston: Allen & Unwin, 1986. □

Nguyen Van Thieu

Nguyen Van Thieu (born 1923) became president of South Vietnam following the 1967 election in his war-torn country. He led the Saigon government against the Communist enemy during the height of the U.S. escalation of the Vietnam War.

Born on April 5, 1923, in Ninh Tvuan in central Vietnam, Thieu attended the Catholic Pellerin School at Hue and the National Military Academy. A Catholic in a predominantly Buddhist country, he also served in the French-supported Vietnam National Army from 1948 to 1954—fighting against the pro-Communist partisans of Viet Minh leader Ho Chi Minh.

After the termination of the conflict between France and the Viet Minh, Thieu was absorbed into the new independent South Vietnamese army, rising to become commander of the 1st Infantry Division by 1960. During these and the immediately succeeding years, Thieu was a supporter of autocratic president Ngo Dinh Diem (also a Catho-

lic), who was deposed and slain in a military-led coup in 1963. Thieu was at first reluctant to take part in the overthrow, and had to be persuaded to participate.

In the years after the 1963 takeover, Thieu rose steadily in importance. He became deputy premier and minister of defense in 1964. He was appointed chief of state late in 1965 by Nguyen Cao Ky, who became premier when the South Vietnamese generals decided to form their own government following the weak civilian regime of Dr. Phan Huy Quat. Thieu soon proved his political mettle, emerging as the military's candidate in the American-encouraged 1967 elections. The more flamboyant Marshal Ky was forced to accept the soldiers' vice-presidential nomination.

Thieu won, as expected, in the balloting—partly because the country's most popular military figure, Gen. Duong Van Minh, had been disqualified as a candidate on a technicality. But Thieu ended up with a surprisingly modest 35 percent plurality vote (with civilian candidate Truong Dinh Dzu polling 17 percent to finish second).

Following his electoral triumph, President Thieu sought to make his government somewhat more representative than it had been and to unify it politically and organizationally. Originally, only two of 19 Cabinet members were soldiers, and the premier, Tran Van Huong, was a civilian. In 1969, however, Thieu picked Gen. Tran Thien Khiem as premier in a government in which other soldiers, technocrats, and followers of former president Diem predominated. He had chosen to base his government on military rather than popular support.

This decision was further reinforced when Thieu pressed through an election law on June 3, 1971, which would limit the number of presidential candidates. The bill—designed to cut the number of presidential candidates to give the winner a more convincing majority—stipulated that prospective presidential candidates must have their nomination papers endorsed either by 40 deputies or senators or by 100 members of elected provincial councils. Thieu consequently entered the South Vietnamese presidential elections with only one opponent, former general Duong Van Minh, who later withdrew.

The war's unpopularity in the U.S. grew strong, and following the Paris Peace Talks, the U.S. agreed to withdraw its forces in April 1973. Thieu's government survived only two more years. With the North Vietnamese Army encircling Saigon, Thieu officially resigned on April 21, 1975, and fled South Vietnam five days later. He turned the government over to Vice President Tran Van Huong, but Huong resigned seven days later, turning the office over to Duong Van Minh, who was considered acceptable to the North Vietnamese. Minh officially surrendered as North Vietnamese tanks rammed through the gates of the presidential palace on April 30, 1975.

Thieu originally took refuge in Taiwan, but later moved to London, where he lived for several years. He led a very quite life, avoiding the limelight, and granting few interviews. He later moved to the U.S., living in an affluent Boston suburb. Slowly, he began to reemerge, traveling to portions of the world, talking with sympathetic groups in 1989-90. In a November 1990 interview with *Time* magazine, Thieu stated he was keeping in contact with expatriates, and was organizing groups to support change in Vietnam. He said he no longer wanted a leadership position there ("I am old, too old to take power again"), but wanted to lend his experience to those pushing for reforms. He said he hoped to return again someday to his homeland.

As of 1996, Thieu was still living near Boston, holding to a quiet life. He told a reporter, "I read. I discuss. I work in my home."

Further Reading

Ward S. Just, *To What End: Report from Vietnam* (1968), offers an excellent treatment of the years of Thieu's rise to leadership. A good general overview is provided by Dennis J. Duncanson, *Government and Revolution in Vietnam* (1968); and Joseph Bullinger, *Vietnam: A Political History* (1968), places recent Vietnamese political events in a larger historical perspective. American policy in Vietnam is described in George McTurran Kahin and John W. Lewis, *The United States in Vietnam* (1967; rev. ed. 1969). Interview with *Time* magazine is from Nov. 26, 1990 issue. □

St. Thomas Aquinas

The Italian philosopher and theologian St. Thomas Aquinas (ca. 1224-1274) was one of the foremost minds of medieval scholasticism. He is recognized as the leading theological authority within the Roman Catholic Church.

The central question facing Christian thinkers in the 13th century was the attitude to be taken toward Aristotle and the use to be made of his thought by theologians committed to a Christian view of the nature of God, man, and the universe. By the middle of the century the writings of Aristotle, for the most part unknown in the Latin West until the end of the 12th century, were readily available in Latin translation and were being taught in the arts faculties at universities in England, France, and Italy. In combination with the writings of Averroës, which were used to interpret Aristotle, this new intellectual material provided the early 13th century with the developed, integrated philosophical system for which they had been searching. On the other hand, because of the completeness and self-sufficiency of the Aristotelian system, Christian theology seemed less necessary as an avenue to truth, which because of Aristotle, was now accessible to man by natural reason, without revelation.

For those who were unwilling to relinquish the primacy of Christian revelation and who felt that Aristotle had not made the latter obsolete, there were still particular aspects of the Aristotelian system as they knew it that directly conflicted with Christian truth. For example, the Aristotelian notion of God as a distant and unapproachable prime mover, the idea of the eternity of the world, the notion of necessity and determinism, the idea that there was one in-

tellect shared by men into which souls were absorbed after death, thus denying personal immortality, and the idea that all love is based ultimately on self-interest caused problems for Christian doctrine, which affirmed a personal, transcendent God who created the world freely and in time, who was concerned about particular individuals, and who would ultimately reward with eternal life the person who loved God rather than self.

In the 13th century men believed that all truth was one and that there could be no serious conflict between philosophy and theology or between Aristotle and Christianity. Since for them Christianity could not be wrong and since Aristotle was an established, ancient authority, the natural tendency was to bring Aristotle and Christianity into agreement. It was part of the achievement of St. Thomas Aquinas that he created a theological and philosophical system that remained basically Christian while incorporating significant elements from the Aristotelian world view. Many historians have viewed this system, sometimes referred to as the Thomist synthesis (a synthesis of theology and philosophy, of faith and reason, as well as Aristotelianism and Christianity), as the most important achievement in medieval thought and an archetype of philosophical and theological thinking for the modern period.

Thomas was not alone in this endeavor, nor did his version go unquestioned. He was criticized in his lifetime by such important theologians as Bonaventure, and some of Thomas's solutions were condemned along with a variety of others at Paris in 1277. His reputation, however, remained of major import from the 13th century on, and through the respect accorded him at the Council of Trent in the 16th century and the emergence of a neo-Thomist movement among Catholic philosophers he has had a significant impact on modern thought.

Early Life and Education, 1224-1252

Thomas was born into the Italian lower nobility, the youngest son of Landolfo of Aquino, Lord of Roccasecca and Montesangiovanni and justiciary of Frederick II, Emperor of Germany and King of Naples. Thomas's father lived to see most of his sons, including Thomas, abandon the causes to which he had devoted his life, shifting their allegiance from the Hohenstaufen emperor to the papacy and from the older monastic institutions to the newer mendicant orders.

At the age of 5 or 6, Thomas was placed in the care of the monks of the Benedictine abbey of Monte Cassino with the intention that he should become a monk and, eventually, abbot of this, one of the most prestigious monastic communities in Europe. After 8 years of instruction he was forced by political circumstances to leave Monte Cassino with the other oblates and to complete his education in Naples at a Benedictine house connected with the university there.

Thomas remained in Naples 5 years. During this time he came in contact with several influences that changed the course of his life. First, he was attracted to the opportunities for intellectual growth and service offered by the universities. In particular, he came into contact with Greek and Arabic learning, especially the thought of Aristotle and Averroës, which had been recently translated. Second, he was attracted to the newer mendicant orders, which espoused an apostolic life of service in the world (rather than the cloistered meditation typical of Monte Cassino) and which played an active role in the intellectual life of the university.

By 1243 Thomas had made a momentous decision: turning his back on his family and the plans that had been made for his career, he joined the Dominicans and received the habit in 1244. Foreseeing that his family would oppose his decision and try to intervene, Thomas allowed himself to be taken immediately out of their reach, initially to Rome and then on to Bologna. Before reaching Bologna he was captured by his older brother and returned home. After a year during which Thomas would not change his mind, he returned to the Dominicans at Naples, from where he journeyed northward to begin his theological education.

From 1245 until 1252 Thomas studied at the Dominican houses at Paris and Cologne under the leading Dominican theologian on the Continent in that period, Albertus Magnus. When Albertus organized the house of studies at Cologne in 1248, Thomas accompanied him as his student and assistant, lecturing on sections of the Scriptures and being ordained to the priesthood. In 1252 Albert recommended Thomas to be one of the two Dominican lecturers on the *Sentences* of Peter Lombard at Paris and thus to become a candidate for the degree of master of theology, in spite of the fact that Thomas was 3 or 4 years too young for that stage in his career.

Teaching Career at Paris, 1252-1259

Thomas remained in Paris for 7 years, living at the Dominican house of studies and lecturing, debating, and writing. His first important work was his commentary on the *Sentences,* polished during 1254-1256, which for over 200 years remained one of the major sources for the thought of Thomas. After his 4 years of study Thomas was granted the license to teach, and for 3 additional years he was one of the two regent masters of theology for the Dominicans at Paris. During this period he wrote several important philosophical treatises, the most remarkable being *De ente et essentia and De veritate,* which revealed even at this early stage his Aristotelian approach to philosophical questions.

Thomas faced strong opposition from the secular masters at Paris. In the mid-13th century in Paris animosity toward the mendicants had been growing among the secular masters of theology and arts, an animosity that was founded on the belief that some mendicants were theologically unorthodox, that in any case they had no right to belong to the university, and that, as semimonastic persons, they should not be copying the functions of secular priests. This animosity toward both Dominicans and Franciscans delayed Thomas's recognition by his colleagues, and the debate over the place of the mendicants within the structure of the university occupied much of Thomas's time.

Teaching Career in Italy, 1259-1268

Upon his return to Italy, probably at the request of the general chapter, or governing body, of the Dominicans, Thomas lectured at the Dominican convents in central Italy that were connected with the residence of the papal court: Anagni, Orvieto, Rome, and Viterbo. Here he came in contact with the improved translations of Aristotle directly from the Greek that were being compiled by a Dominican, William of Moerbeke. On the basis of this new source material and his growing desire to provide an acceptable interpretation of Aristotle's thought, Thomas began a series of commentaries on the works of Aristotle that rank among the most significant ever written.

A similar product of Thomas's ability as an expositor and commentator that dates from this period is the *Catena aurea,* or *Golden Chain,* a commentary on the four Gospels. Unlike his commentaries on Aristotle, however, this work is not Thomas's own interpretation but gathers passages from other writers to enlighten the meaning of Scripture.

Italy provided Thomas with the opportunity and incentive to expand the types of philosophical and theological problems with which he dealt in his writings. He wrote *De regimine principum,* an important political treatise that discussed the principles governing society and the political activity of rulers, basing his work in part on Aristotle's *Politics.* Moreover, he became more aware of the conflicting issues within Islamic theology—particularly, concerning the problem of expressing the freedom and power of God without, on the one hand, making God's freedom so extensive that it can become arbitrary and irrational in its operation or, on the other hand, limiting God's activity within the bounds of a deterministic system.

In part as a result of this awareness of the importance of the problem of the freedom and power of God and the importance of Islamic theology for the Western theologian, Thomas composed two works: *De potentia,* which dealt with the question of God's omnipotence and of His creative power; and a theological manual, the *Summa contra Gentiles,* written to provide the Christian missionary with a clear, precise statement of the Christian faith along with a defense of its basic doctrines. The latter work, probably begun while Thomas was still in Paris, and at the suggestion of the Dominican missionary Raymond of Peñafort, was primarily intended to be of use in attempting to convert the Mohammedans. Similarly, it could be helpful in converting the Jews.

Return to Paris, 1268-1272

Late in 1268 or early in 1269 the Dominican order sent Thomas back to Paris for a second period of teaching. The crisis which he found there and which may have occasioned his being summoned back was quite different from the earlier controversy between the seculars and mendicants, although that animosity was still in evidence. The type of Christian Aristotelianism that Thomas and Albertus Magnus had been intent on creating was being threatened from two sides. On the one hand, the anti-Aristotelian forces within theology had increased and were reaffirming a strong Augustinian approach that rejected Ar-

istotle on a number of points and limited his use as an authority in theological argumentation. On the other hand, there was an attempt to teach an unchristened Aristotelianism in the arts faculty by a group known as the Latin Averroists, led by such figures as Siger of Brabant and Boethius of Dacia.

In this crisis, toward which the intellectual currents of the century had been building, Thomas tried to establish a middle position. He believed that Aristotle could be shown to agree with Christian truth in the majority of instances and therefore could be used as a source in argumentation, although not in theology on the level with Scripture or the Fathers.

One of the most crucial issues was the question of the eternity of the world. Thomas's position, against Bonaventure and others, was that although the world was created in time, as revelation teaches, this doctrine could not be demonstrated by reason alone which, in this matter, can provide no final solution.

This conclusion is typical of the way in which Thomas approached the relation of faith and reason, Aristotle and Christian truth. Faith completes rather than contradicts reason. Although some things can be known only through reason because revelation is not concerned with those things, and although some things can be known through both reason and revelation, such as the existence and unity of God, there are many truths necessary for salvation which are inaccessible to man apart from revelation, such as the doctrine of creation in time or the mystery of the Trinity. Aristotle, because he lived before Christ, could go only so far, and his thought must be completed by Christian revelation.

Thomas therefore accepts the idea of God as prime mover but goes on to identify Aristotle's God with the personal God of revelation, who has knowledge and concern for individuals. Thomas rejected the Averroistic notion of one active intellect for all mankind, and he argued that there was only one substantial form in man, the rational soul, which, with its individual intellect, provides the psychological foundation for personal immortality. Similarly, Thomas accepted the Aristotelian idea that man is naturally a political animal who finds his fulfillment in a quest for happiness within human society. But for Thomas that is only one end of man which, although important, is secondary to the primary end of man, the love of God, an end that is learned only through revelation.

Many of these conclusions are found in Thomas's most important work, the *Summa theologiae,* or *Summa theologica,* written in this period, although it was begun earlier in Italy, probably at Rome, and completed by a disciple after Thomas's death. Most of his reputation is based on this work. It is a systematic analysis and defense of the Christian faith, arranged topically, beginning with the nature of God and moving through creation and salvation to the last things and the beatific vision. Within each topic Thomas, in proper scholastic style, presented the most important questions and arranged his argument by initially presenting the pro and con arguments, then his analysis of the issue, and then his rebuttal to the initial objections.

Last Years, 1272-1274

At the request of the general chapter in Florence in June 1272, which he attended, Thomas went to Naples to establish a program of theological studies at the Dominican house, near the university. His writings from this period, although numerous and of high quality in comparison to those of his contemporaries, did not maintain the level of the works written in previous periods in his life. In December 1273, on the feast of St. Nicholas, his writing career came to an end. As an early biographer described it, the change resulted from a vision or mystical experience. When his secretary asked him why he had ceased to write, Thomas answered, "All that I have written seems to me like so much straw compared to what I have seen and what has been revealed to me."

Thomas set out early in 1274 to attend the second Council of Lyons. He soon became ill and broke his journey at the Cistercian monastery of Fossanuova, where he died in March.

Further Reading

The best biography of St. Thomas Aquinas in English is Vernon Joseph Bourke, *Aquinas' Search for Wisdom* (1965). Other useful biographies are Martin C. D'Arcy, *St. Thomas Aquinas* (1930; rev. ed. 1953), and Jacques Maritain, *St. Thomas Aquinas* (trans. 1931; rev. ed. 1958). The best work on the background of Thomas's writings is Marie Dominique Chenu, *Towards Understanding Saint Thomas* (1950; trans. 1964).

For a survey of Thomas's thought the following works are all of high quality, although each takes a somewhat different approach: Réginald Garrigou-Lagrange, *Reality: A Synthesis of Thomistic Thought* (trans. 1950); Frederick Copleston, *Aquinas* (1955); and Étienne Henry Gilson, *The Christian Philosophy of St. Thomas Aquinas* (trans. 1956). Among the works on Thomistic metaphysics, the following are especially helpful: Herman Reith, *The Metaphysics of St. Thomas Aquinas* (1958); George Peter Klubertanz, *St. Thomas Aquinas on Analogy: A Textual Analysis and Systematic Synthesis* (1960); and Joseph Owens, *An Elementary Christian Metaphysics* (1963). One of the few works in English treating the political views of Thomas is Thomas Gilby, *The Political Thought of Thomas Aquinas* (1958). Jacques Maritain, *Art and Scholasticism, with Other Essays* (trans. 1930), is a recommended study of Thomas's esthetic theory. □

Clarence Thomas

President George Bush named Clarence Thomas (born 1948) to the Supreme Court in 1991. Senate confirmation was gained only after intense public controversy over charges of "sexual harassment" brought by Anita Hill, Thomas's former employee. Since joining the Court, Thomas has tended to vote with the more conservative justices.

Clarence Thomas was born in Pin Point, Georgia, a tiny, coastal hamlet town outside of Savannah, on June 23, 1948. For the first years of his life he lived in a one-room shack with dirt floors and no plumbing. When Thomas was two years old, his father walked out on the family, leaving Clarence's mother with two small children and another on the way. At the age of seven, Thomas and his younger brother were sent to live with their grandfather, Myers Anderson, and his wife, Christine, in Savannah. Anderson, a devout Catholic and active member of the National Association for the Advancement of Colored People (NAACP), sent Thomas to a Catholic school staffed by strict but supportive nuns.

In 1964, the year the Civil Rights Act was enacted, Thomas' grandfather withdrew him from the all-black parochial high school he was attending and sent him to an all-white Catholic boarding school in Savannah, St. John Vianny Minor Seminary. Despite being confronted with racism, Thomas made excellent grades and played on the school's football team. Thomas' grandfather sent Clarence to Immaculate Conception Seminary in northwestern Missouri after his graduation from high school in 1967. Although Thomas was not the only African American student, he still was troubled by poor race relations. A racist remark made about the assassination of Martin Luther King, Jr., made up Thomas' mind: he would not become a priest.

Struggles with Personal Identity

The decision bitterly disappointed his grandfather, but Clarence decided to enroll at Holy Cross, a Jesuit college in

Worcester, Massachusetts. Thomas was a devoted student who "was always in the library," according to one friend. Yet the future justice found time to participate on the track team, work in the school cafeteria, and volunteer to help the poor in Worcester once a week. He also assisted in founding the Black Student Union at Holy Cross. Thomas seemed haunted by racial isolation and academic pressures and admitted later that he had seriously considered dropping out of college. However, fearful that he would be drafted for service in the Vietnam War, Thomas stayed at Holy Cross and was graduated in 1971 with honors.

Another reason that Thomas may have decided to stay in school was his introduction to Kathy Ambush, a coed at a nearby college. A few days after they met, Thomas told a friend that he was in love with Kathy. They were married in Worcester the day after Clarence's college commencement and had one son, Jamal, born in 1973.

Thanks to his sterling academic record, Thomas was admitted to the law schools at Yale, Harvard, and the University of Pennsylvania. He chose Yale because of the financial support it offered him as part of its affirmative-action policy to attract students from racial and ethnic minorities. At Yale, he continued to do well academically, receiving mostly passes on Yale's grading scale of honors, pass, low pass, and fail.

Thomas appeared to fit in socially as well as academically. Yet, years later, he described his "rage" and loneliness at feeling snubbed by whites who viewed him as an affirmative action token and ignored by African Americans with more elite backgrounds. In his third year of law school he interviewed with law firms but again felt that he was treated differently because of his race.

Joined Staff of Missouri Attorney General

Thomas graduated from Yale law school in 1974. Rather than take what he considered an insufficient salary from the firm where he'd done his summer work, Thomas accepted a position on the staff of Attorney General John Danforth, a Republican. With Danforth's election to the Senate in 1977, Thomas took a job as an attorney for the Monsanto Company in St. Louis. In 1979 Thomas moved to Washington, DC, and became a legislative assistant to Danforth on the condition that he *not* be assigned to civil rights issues. His resentment toward the tokenism of affirmative action, combined with his grandfather's lessons on self-sufficiency and independence, had moved Thomas into a circle of African American conservatives who rejected the dependency fostered among blacks by the welfare state.

Thomas' conservative ideas quickly brought him to the attention of the Reagan administration, which was always looking for qualified members of ethnic minorities. In 1981 Thomas was appointed assistant secretary for civil rights in the United States Department of Education. Thomas openly stated that minority groups must succeed by their own merit, and he asserted that affirmative action programs and civil rights legislation do not improve living standards.

Accepted Appointment With High Political Visibility

In 1982, Clarence Thomas became the chairman of the United States Equal Employment Opportunity Commission (EEOC), which was designed to enforce anti-discrimination laws that cover race, sex, gender, and age discrimination in the workplace. Thomas served two consecutive terms as chairman, despite having previously sworn he would never work at EEOC. Over the eight years he served as chairman, Thomas shifted the focus of the commission from large class-action suits to individual cases of discrimination.

In 1990, President George Bush appointed Thomas to the Washington, DC, Circuit of the United States Court of Appeals, a common stepping stone to the Supreme Court. Thomas filled the seat left vacant by Robert Bork, an unsuccessful nominee to the Supreme Court. Thomas wrote only 20 opinions in the year he served on the court, none of which involved controversial constitutional issues. Despite this comparatively limited experience, Bush nominated Thomas to replace retiring Supreme Court Justice Thurgood Marshall on July 1, 1991. In announcing his choice to replace Marshall, Bush implausibly argued that "the fact that he [Thomas] is black has nothing to do with the sense that he is the best qualified at this time."

Anita Hill Alleges Sexual Harassment

The Senate's confirmation hearing appeared to be moving along smoothly until Anita Hill's allegations were made public. On October 8, Hill—a professor at the University of Oklahoma Law School—held a press conference, in which she made public the main points of testimony she previously had given the Federal Bureau of Investigation. Vociferous protest by some feminist groups led the confirmation committee, headed by Delaware Senator Joseph Biden, a Democrat, to publicly review Hill's charges.

In her testimony, Hill alleged that—while she worked at the EEOC nearly a decade earlier—Thomas badgered her for dates and told stories in her presence about pornographic film scenes and his own sexual prowess. Hill claimed that Thomas's actions made it difficult for here to do her job and even caused physical distress. Nevertheless, she continued to initiate contacts with Thomas even after he helped arrange for her appointment as a law professor.

The televised hearings, during which Hill, Thomas, and several witnesses on both sides testified about the allegations, were among the most widely-viewed political events in television history. Thomas denied any wrongdoing. His allies suggested that Hill was lying and was being cynically manipulated by liberals opposed to Thomas's views on abortion and affirmative action. Thomas himself remarked during the course of the televised hearings that the process had been a harrowing personal ordeal for him and his wife. Indeed, he claimed, he would have preferred "an assassin's bullet to this kind of living hell," and he would have withdrawn himself from consideration earlier had he known what lay ahead. Suspending his lifelong criticism of racial politics, he characterized the televised hearings as a "high-tech lynching."

Militant women's groups threatened to vote against Thomas's backers in the next elections. At the same time, many African Americans believed the Republican charges that Hill was part of a campaign to smear Thomas. In the end, Thomas was confirmed by a 52-48 margin, the smallest—according to *Time*—by which any justice has been confirmed in this century.

Hill's allegations helped to make sexual harassment a major political issue. The phrase itself had varying, even conflicting, definitions. Nevertheless, local, state, and national laws were passed to stop workplace practices considered demeaning to subordinates. Meanwhile, articles and books continued to debate the validity of Hill's specific charges against Thomas. There probably never will be a consensus judgement. Hill did not overtly protest at the time the alleged actions took place, and determining the truth years later was difficult.

Thomas had separated from his wife Kathy in 1981; the two divorced in 1984, and he retained custody of Jamal. The circumstances of the divorce remain a well-guarded secret, although allegations of abuse made at the time returned to haunt Thomas during his confirmation hearings. In 1986, Thomas met Virginia Lamp, a white fellow law school graduate active in conservative causes; and the two married in 1987. She was a Labor Department lawyer when Thomas was nominated for the Supreme Court. Following the confirmation, she told her story to *People*, recounting the tension of the confirmation fight and speculating that Hill was in love with Thomas. She referred to the struggle to get Thomas confirmed as "Good versus Evil."

A Quiet But Effective Justice

After joining the Court, Thomas voted most frequently with Justice Antonin Scalia and Chief Justice William Rehnquist, thereby aligning himself with the conservatives who wish to restrain the federal government's power. Thomas showed no signs of the "freshman syndrome" attributed to Justice David Souter, who was relatively inactive his first year as a justice. Instead, Thomas was relatively visible in his opinion-writing from the beginning. Reviewers of his opinions and legal essays agreed that they were clear, well-researched, and consistent.

African American political groups criticized Thomas for maintaining his conservative values on the Court. In July 1995, NAACP convention delegates decried Thomas's votes regarding school desegregation, race-based redistricting of voting precincts, and racial quotas and set-asides. An invitation to speak before an eighth-grade awards ceremony in Maryland in 1996 sparked weeks of protests and disputes among school board members. The invitation ultimately was rescinded as was a request to address a youth festival in January 1997. Following the latter incident, however, NAACP president Kweisi Mfume suggested that African American organizations should stop bashing Thomas. "I don't think we can ever change Clarence Thomas," Mfume stated, "and I don't want to spend any more of my time or NAACP time trying."

For the first few years after his appointment, Thomas tended to keep a low public profile. Due to the antipathy of some African American and feminist groups, he had fewer of the ceremonial invitations normally extended to Supreme Court Justices. From 1996 on, however, Thomas began to make occasional appearances before conservative political groups. In these speeches, he continued to call on judges to restrain their efforts to remake society by judicial decree. And, without directly alluding to his personal experiences, he eloquently deplored the decline of civility in America's public discourse and conduct.

Further Reading

A short biography of Clarence Thomas appears in the Commission on the Bicentennial of the United States Constitution's publication *The Supreme Court of the United States: Its Beginning & Its Justices 1790-1991* (1992). A journalistic analysis of the Clarence Thomas/ Anita Hill controversy is Timothy Phelps and Helen Winternitz's *Capitol Games* (1992). An historical view is given by Illinois U.S. Senator Paul Simon in *Advice & Consent: Clarence Thomas, Robert Bork and the Intriguing History of the Supreme Court's Nomination Battles* (1992). A periodical with additional information is *Jet* (March 3, 1997).
Brock, David. *The Real Anita Hill: The Untold Story.* (Free Press, 1993). Danforth, John. *Resurrection: The Confirmation of Clarence Thomas.* (Free Press, 1994). Myer, Jane. *Strange Justice: The Selling of Clarence Thomas* (Houghton Mifflin, 1994). Smith, Christopher. *Critical Judicial Nominations & Political Change: The Impact of Clarence Thomas* (Greenwood, 1993). □

Dylan Marlais Thomas

The British poet Dylan Marlais Thomas (1914-1953) has been acclaimed as one of the most important poets of the century. His lyrics rank among the most powerful and captivating of modern poetry.

Dylan Thomas was born in the Welsh seaport of Swansea, Carmarthenshire, on Oct. 27, 1914. His father was an English teacher and a would-be poet, from whom Dylan inherited his intellect and literary abilities. From his mother, a simple and religious woman, Dylan inherited his disposition, temperament, and Celtic sentimentality. He attended the Swansea Grammar School, where he received all of his formal education. As a student, he made contributions to the school magazine and was keenly interested in local folklore. He said that as a boy he was "small, thin, indecisively active, quick to get dirty, curly."

After leaving school Thomas supported himself as an actor, reporter, reviewer, and scriptwriter and with various odd jobs. When he was 22 years old, he married Caitlin Macnamara, by whom he had two sons, Llewelyn and Colm, and a daughter, Aeron. After his marriage, Thomas moved to the fishing village of Laugharne, Carmarthenshire.

The need to support his growing family forced Thomas to write radio scripts for the Ministry of Information and documentaries for the British government. During World

War II he served as an antiaircraft gunner. After the war he became a commentator on poetry for the British Broadcasting Corporation (BBC). In 1950 Thomas made the first of three lecture tours through the United States—the others were in 1952 and 1953—in which he gave more than 100 poetry readings. In these recitals he half declaimed, half sang the lines in his "Welsh singing" voice. Many critics have attested to the rolling vigor of his voice, its melodic subtlety, and its almost hypnotic power of incantation.

The English poet Edith Sitwell described Thomas as follows: "He was not tall, but was extremely broad, and gave an impression of extraordinary strength, sturdiness, and superabundant life. (His reddish-amber curls, strong as the curls on the brow of a young bull, his proud, but not despising, bearing, emphasized this.) Mr. Augustus John's portrait of him is beautiful but gives him a cherubic aspect, which though pleasing, does not convey . . . Dylan's look of archangelic power. In full face he looked much as William Blake must have looked as a young man. He had full eyes—like those of Blake—giving him at first the impression of being unseeing, but seeing all, looking over immeasurable distances."

Thomas's poetic output was not large. He wrote only six poems in the last 6 years of his life. Dissipation and a grueling lecture schedule hindered his literary output in these years. His conviction that he would die young led him to create "instant Dylan"—the persona of the wild young Welsh bard, damned by drink and women, that he believed his public wanted. When he was 35 years old, he described himself as "old, small, dark, intelligent, and darting-doting-

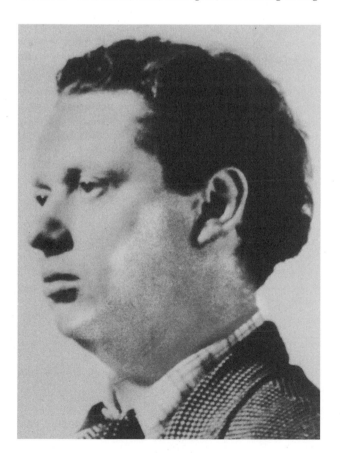

dotting eyed . . . balding and toothlessing." He had grown corpulent but retained his grace of movement.

During his visit to the United States in 1953, Thomas was scheduled to read his own and other poetry in some 40 university towns throughout the country. He also intended to work on the libretto of an opera for Igor Stravinsky in the latter's California home. Thomas celebrated his thirty-ninth birthday in New York City in a mood of gay exhilaration following the phenomenal success of his just-published *Collected Poems*. The festivities ended in collapse and illness, and on Nov. 9, 1953, he died in St. Vincent's Hospital in New York City. Some reports attribute his death to pneumonia induced by acute alcoholism, others to encephalopathy, a virulent brain disease. His body was returned to Laugharne, Wales, for burial.

Literary Works

Thomas published his first book of poetry, *Eighteen Poems* (1934), when he was not yet 20 years old. "The reeling excitement of a poetry-intoxicated schoolboy smote the Philistine as hard a blow with one small book as Swinburne had with *Poems and Ballads*," wrote Kenneth Rexroth. Thomas's second and third volumes were *Twenty-five Poems* (1936) and *The Map of Love* (1939). The poems of his first three volumes were collected in *The World I Breathe* (1939).

By this time, Thomas was being hailed as the most spectacular of the surrealist poets. He acknowledged his debt to James Joyce and strewed his pages with invented words and fused puns. Thomas also acknowledged his debt to Sigmund Freud, stating: "Poetry is the rhythmic, inevitably narrative, movement from an overclothed blindness to a naked vision. . . . Poetry must drag further into the clear nakedness of light more even of the hidden causes than Freud could realize."

A Portrait of the Artist as a Young Dog (1940) is a collection of humorous autobiographical sketches. Thomas loved the wild landscape of Wales, and he put much of his childhood and youth into these stories. He published two more new collections of poetry, both of which contained some of his finest work: *Deaths and Entrances* (1946) and *In Country Sleep* (1951). *Collected Poems, 1934-1953* (1953) contains all of his poetry that he wished to preserve.

Themes and Style

Thomas claimed that his poetry was "the record of my individual struggle from darkness toward some measure of light. . . . To be stripped of darkness is to be clean, to strip of darkness is to make clean." He also wrote that his poems "with all their crudities, doubts, and confusions, are written for the love of man and in praise of God, and I'd be a damned fool if they weren't." Passionate and intense, vivid and violent, Thomas wrote that he became a poet because "I had fallen in love with words." His sense of the richness and variety and flexibility of the English language shines through all of his work.

The theme of all of Thomas's poetry is the celebration of the divine purpose that he saw in all human and natural processes. The cycle of birth and flowering and death, of love and death, suffuses his poems. He celebrated life in the seas and fields and hills and towns of his native Wales. In some of his shorter poems, he sought to recapture a child's innocent vision of the world.

Thomas was passionately dedicated to his "sullen art," and he was a competent, finished, and occasionally intricate craftsman. He made, for example, more than 200 versions of "Fern Hill" before he was satisfied with it. His early poems are relatively obscure and complex in sense and simple and obvious in auditory patterns. His later poems, on the other hand, are simple in sense but complex in sounds.

Under Milk Wood, a radio play commissioned by the BBC (published 1954), was Thomas's last completed work. This poem-play is not a drama but a pageant of eccentric, outrageous, and charming Welsh villagers. During the 24 hours presented in the play, the characters reminisce about the casual and crucial moments of their lives. *Adventures in the Skin Trade and Other Stories* (1955) contains all the uncollected stories and shows the wit and humor that made Thomas an enchanting companion.

Further Reading

Some of Thomas's correspondence is available in *Selected Letters*, edited with commentary by Constantine Fitzgibbon (1966). The authorized biography, written by a friend, is Fitzgibbon's *The Life of Dylan Thomas* (1965). Other important biographical works include John Malcolm Brinnin, *Dylan Thomas in America: An Intimate Journal* (1955), a candid and illuminating reminiscence; Caitlin Thomas, *Leftover Life to Kill* (1957); T. H. Jones, *Dylan Thomas* (1963); Bill Read, *The Days of Dylan Thomas* (1964), a compact, readable sketch useful as an introduction; and John Ackerman's comprehensive study, *Dylan Thomas: His Life and Work* (1964).

Among the most important critical studies are Derek Stanford, *Dylan Thomas* (1954; rev. ed. 1964); Elder Olson, *The Poetry of Dylan Thomas* (1954); John Malcolm Brinnin, ed., *A Casebook on Dylan Thomas* (1960); William York Tindall, *A Reader's Guide to Dylan Thomas* (1962); Clark Emery, *The World of Dylan Thomas* (1962); David Holbrook, *Dylan Thomas and Poetic Dissociation* (1964); C. B. Cox, ed., *Dylan Thomas: A Collection of Critical Essays* (1966); Aneirin Talfan Davies, *Dylan: Druid of the Broken Body* (1966); William T. Moynihan, *The Craft and Art of Dylan Thomas* (1966); and Louise B. Murdy, *Sound and Sense in Dylan Thomas's Poetry* (1966). □

George Henry Thomas

In the Civil War, George Henry Thomas (1816-1870), U.S. Army officer, received the sobriquet "Rock of Chickamauga" for saving a Union army.

George H. Thomas was born on July 31, 1816, in Southampton County, Va. He graduated from the county academy and read law before attending the U.S. Military Academy (1836-1840). In Florida he won a brevet to first lieutenant during 2 years of action with the 3d Artillery against the Seminole Indians. He served at Southern posts until the Mexican War, in which he became a major after battles at Monterrey and Buena Vista. He was an instructor from 1851 to 1854 at West Point; in 1852 he married Frances Kellogg. He was major of the 2d Cavalry on the Texas frontier from 1855 to 1860.

At the beginning of the Civil War, Thomas decided to remain with the Union and by June had been promoted to colonel, in command of a brigade in the Shenandoah Valley of Virginia. In August he became a brigadier general and division commander in Kentucky. He defeated a Confederate force at Mill Springs on Jan. 19, 1862, before moving into Tennessee with the Army of the Ohio.

After promotion to major general, Thomas commanded the right wing of the Union advance on Corinth, Miss. He led a corps against the Confederate invasion of Kentucky in September. He went on to command a corps in the Army of the Cumberland during the battle at Stones River, Tenn., in December and January, and during the Tullahoma campaign, which forced the Confederates into Georgia in the summer of 1863. When the armies met that September, the Union right collapsed, but Thomas held on the left to save the army and win the nickname "Rock of Chickamauga."

In October, 1863, Thomas became a brigadier general in the regular army. His troops stormed Missionary Ridge to win the battles around Chattanooga on November 23-25. Thomas led the Army of the Cumberland throughout Gen. William T. Sherman's Atlanta campaign from May through September 1864.

In October Sherman assigned Thomas to meet the Confederate advance into Tennessee. On December 15-16, outside Nashville, Thomas routed the Confederates in the most complete field victory of the war. He became a major general in the regular army on March 3, 1865.

From 1865 to 1868 Thomas commanded the military Division of Tennessee. He refused promotion to lieutenant general in 1868 because it resulted from Reconstruction politics. He assumed command of the Division of the Pacific in June 1869 but died in San Francisco on March 28, 1870.

Further Reading

The best biography of Thomas is Freeman Cleaves, *Rock of Chickamauga: The Life of General George H. Thomas* (1948). More detailed but partisan volumes are Francis F. McKinney, *Education in Violence: The Life of George H. Thomas and the History of the Army of the Cumberland* (1961), and Wilbur Thomas, *General George H. Thomas: The Indomitable Warrior* (1964).

Additional Sources

Palumbo, Frank A., *George Henry Thomas, Major General, U.S.A.: the dependable general, supreme in tactics of strategy and command*, Dayton, Ohio: Morningside House, 1983. ☐

Norman Mattoon Thomas

Norman Mattoon Thomas (1884-1968), leader of the Socialist movement in the United States for more than 4 decades, was six times the Socialist candidate for president, as well as an author and lecturer. He was one of the most respected critics of American capitalist society.

On Nov. 20, 1884, Norman Thomas was born in Marion, Ohio, the son and grandson (on both sides) of Presbyterian ministers. After Norman's graduation from high school, the family moved to Lewisburg, Pa., where Norman entered Bucknell University for a year. He transferred to Princeton University, studying political science under future president Woodrow Wilson and graduating in 1905 as valedictorian.

Upon leaving Princeton, Thomas worked as a settlement house and pastoral assistant in the poorer sections of New York. Studying for the ministry at heterodox Union Theological Seminary, he was impressed by the reform-minded Social Gospel theology of Walter Rauschenbusch and the teachings of Christian Socialism. Ordained in 1911, Thomas became pastor of East Harlem Presbyterian Church. Meanwhile he had married Frances Violet Stewart; they had six children, enjoying an uncommonly happy marriage.

World War I was apparently the major turning point in Thomas's life. He had joined the Fellowship of Reconciliation, an organization of reformist and pacifist Protestant clergymen. After America's entry into the war, his brother Evan went to prison for draft resistance, and Thomas became adamantly opposed to America's participation in what he regarded as an immoral, senseless struggle among rival imperialisms. He founded and edited *World Tomorrow,* the official magazine of the Fellowship of Reconciliation, and helped establish what became the American Civil Liberties Union (ACLU). In 1918, resigning his pastorate, he joined the Socialist party.

Although Eugene V. Debs, the Socialists' longtime leader, polled a record 900,000-plus votes in the presidential election of 1920, the party, harassed by Federal and state governments for opposing the war, and torn by internal controversy over the relevance of the Russian Revolution to American experience, steadily lost members and popular support during the 1920s. Thomas rose rapidly in the Socialist party. Well known as editor of *World Tomorrow,* as a contributing editor to the *Nation,* and as a leader in such organizations as the ACLU and the League for Industrial Democracy, Thomas was the logical leader after Debs's death in 1926.

In 1928 Thomas made the first of his six consecutive races for the presidency. However, the Socialist party continued losing strength, ending the decade as a minor element in America's political system. As the Socialist candidate for president every 4 years, Thomas at least had the satisfaction of seeing much of his program taken over by Franklin Roosevelt's New Deal. Many Socialists joined Roosevelt and the Democratic party, others left the party to endorse the Popular Front movement of the late 1930s, and still others left because Thomas opposed United States involvement in the European and Asian wars after 1939. Thomas gave his "critical support" to the American war effort after Pearl Harbor. Yet he also denounced the forced relocation and internment of Japanese-Americans, attacked big business dominance in the war production effort, and argued that Roosevelt's "unconditional surrender" doctrine handicapped prospects for a just and lasting peace.

Thomas became a staunch foe of Soviet communism but also severely criticized the militarization of American foreign policy and the growing power of the military in American government. He addressed his superb oratorical powers, biting wit, and passionate conviction to virtually every public issue, including disarmament, the persistence of poverty and racism, and United States intervention in the internal affairs of other countries, especially in Vietnam. During his last 2 decades, Thomas became a patriarchal figure, revered and honored even by many who could not accept his political views. He remained amazingly active until his last year; he died on Dec. 19, 1968.

Further Reading

The most thorough biography of Thomas is Bernard K. Johnpoll, *Pacifist's Progress: Norman Thomas and the Decline of American Socialism* (1970), which offers much on the inner workings of the Socialist party. Briefer biographies are Murray B. Seidler, *Norman Thomas: Respectable Rebel* (1961; rev. ed. 1967), and Harry Fleischman, *Norman Thomas* (1964), both by admiring acquaintances of Thomas. The history of the Socialist party is treated in Charles H. Hopkins, *The Rise of the Social Gospel in American Protestantism, 1865-1915* (1940); David A. Shannon, *The Socialist Party of America* (1949); and Daniel Bell, *Marxian Socialism in the United States* (1952). Revealing information on Thomas is in autobiographical writings of contemporaries such as Morris Hillquit, *Loose Leaves from a Busy Life* (1934); Louis Waldman, *Labor Lawyer* (1944); and John Haynes Holmes, *I Speak for Myself* (1959).

Additional Sources

Duram, James C., *Norman Thoma,* New York, Twayne Publishers 1974.

Johnpoll, Bernard K., *Pacifist's progress: Norman Thomas and the decline of American socialism,* New York: Greenwood Press, 1987, 1970.

Swanberg, W. A., *Norman Thomas, the last idealist,* New York: Scribner, 1976. □

Theodore Thomas

Theodore Thomas (1835-1905) was one of the foremost American orchestral conductors of his time and the original director of the Chicago Symphony Orchestra.

Theodore Thomas was born in Germany, the son of the town musician of Esens. When Theodore was 10, the family moved to the United States, settling in New York City. The family suffered financial hardships, and Theodore was forced to earn money by playing his violin at dances, weddings, theaters, and public amusement halls. His formal musical training was slight. While still a teenager, he made a concert trip through the South, billing himself as a prodigy.

In 1854 Thomas joined the New York Philharmonic and also began traveling with famous soloists as a violinist. He found conducting exciting and became dedicated to raising Americans' musical taste. He organized an orchestra which gave its first concert in 1862 in New York City and which later made a series of nationwide tours, playing concerts in most of the major cities. Thomas's orchestra performed in churches, railroad stations, or whatever hall the town provided. His programs were geared toward educating the public in listening to symphonic music, combining the familiar with the unfamiliar.

In addition to conducting his own orchestra, Thomas became alternate conductor of the Brooklyn Philharmonic Society in 1862. Four years later he was made the organization's sole conductor.

In 1873 Thomas was asked to organize and direct the Cincinnati Festival; it proved one of the finest musical events in the nation. He took charge of the concerts for the Philadelphia Centennial in 1876, with unhappy financial results, and the following year became conductor of the New York Philharmonic. He continued his own orchestra, minimizing competition by programming his own concerts in a lighter vein than those of the Philharmonic.

In 1878 Thomas became head of the new College of Music in Cincinnati but resigned the next year when he

realized the commercial nature of the enterprise. He returned to New York and to the Philharmonic, leading that orchestra to new artistic heights. In 1885 he conducted the American Opera Company, an insufficiently underwritten venture that failed after one season. Thomas was invited in 1891 to become conductor of the recently endowed Chicago Symphony Orchestra. He held that post for 14 years. In 1893 he was appointed director of music for the Chicago World's Fair but resigned when his elaborate program was jeopardized by public apathy and national financial reverses. He died on Jan. 4, 1905.

Further Reading

A primary source is *Theodore Thomas: A Musical Autobiography* (2 vols., 1905); the second volume contains a listing of Thomas's major programs. Thomas's role in the development of symphonic music in America is assessed in C. E. Russell, *The American Orchestra and Theodore Thomas* (1927), and David Ewen, *Music Comes to America* (1942; rev. ed. 1947).

Additional Sources

Schabas, Ezra, *Theodore Thomas: America's conductor and builder of orchestras, 1835-1905,* Urbana: University of Illinois Press, 1989. □

William Isaac Thomas

William Isaac Thomas (1863-1947) was an American sociologist and educator. He was a pioneer in the scientific use of personal documents and in pointing to the interplay between personality and culture.

On Aug. 13, 1863, W. I. Thomas was born in Russell County, Va. He majored in literature and languages at the University of Tennessee, where in 1886 he received the first doctoral degree granted by that institution. After a brief teaching stint in natural history and Greek at the University of Tennessee, he developed an interest in anthropology and sociology at the universities of Göttingen and Berlin. However, he returned to teaching at Oberlin College and then began advanced work in sociology at the University of Chicago.

From 1894 to 1918 Thomas was with the department of sociology at the University of Chicago, having received his second doctorate there in 1896. With the support of the Helen Culver Fund for Race Psychology, he initiated the study of migrant adjustment that was published as *The Polish Peasant in Europe and America* (with Florian Znaniecki, 5 vols., 1918-1921). In 1918 Thomas left Chicago to work on studies of Americanization for the Carnegie Foundation and lectured at the New School for Social Research (1923-1928). He was elected president of the American Sociological Society in 1927. Thereafter, he concentrated on research in crime and youth, in New York City, Sweden, New Haven, Conn., and California. On Dec. 5, 1947, he died in Berkeley, Calif.

After an initial interest in cultural evolution and the use of comparative materials—best represented in his early *Source Book for Social Origins* (1908)—Thomas began a sustained focus on analyses of social motivations in various situations of crisis. The major study of his career—*The Polish Peasant*—applied this interest to the adjustments of immigrants. But Thomas tried to show that adjustment was explainable by personal perception and evaluation (definition of the situation) and by socially derived differences in personality.

In *The Unadjusted Girl* (1923), a study of delinquents, Thomas interpreted deviant acts as experimental responses to vague social cues and to practically meaningless traditional codes. With further investigation, Thomas gave increasing emphasis to observing and theorizing on the realistic situations in which persons function. In *The Child in America* (1927) and several manuscripts dated from 1927 to 1933, he sought a flexible method of studying social situations through adequately detailed case histories of changes in attitudes—through letters and autobiographical accounts. One key statement has been widely quoted: "If men define situations as real, they are real in their consequences."

Though Thomas is sometimes remembered for his early (and subsequently discarded) conception of the "four wishes," or types of social motivation, his primary contributions were more varied. First, he helped to establish a needed empirical base for American sociology. Second, by specifying the study of social change as experienced by individuals in a series of situations, he initiated the study of "culture and personality." Third, he provided one of the earliest objective (rather than moralistic) approaches to various forms of social deviance (crime, delinquency), thereby promoting the view that deviation is a normal prelude to, or accompaniment of, social reorganization and change.

Further Reading

A long biographical sketch and many selections from Thomas's books are in Morris Janowitz, *W. I. Thomas on Social Organization and Social Personality* (1966). The best review of Thomas's work, with excerpts, is Edmund H. Volkart, *Social Behavior and Personality* (1951). Another capable review is the chapter "William Isaac Thomas: The Fusion of Psychological and Cultural Sociology" in Harry Elmer Barnes, *An Introduction to the History of Sociology* (1948). □

Thomasius

The German philosopher and jurist Christian Thomasius (1655-1728) was one of the most respected and influential university teachers of his day. He was instrumental in the popularization of the Enlightenment in Germany.

Christian Thomasius was born in Leipzig on Jan. 1, 1655. He received his early education there from his father, a schoolteacher. He pursued the study of law at Frankfurt and began teaching at the University of Leipzig in 1684. In his lectures Thomasius was a bold advocate of the teachings on natural law of the jurist Samuel von Pufendorf. He attracted even more attention, however, when he began to severely criticize the prejudices, pedantry, and intolerance of the scholars and theologians at Leipzig. In 1687 he became the first German university professor to lecture in German instead of Latin. The following year he began to publish a monthly periodical which he used as his chief instrument in further attacks on the stupidities of scholars and theologians. His outspoken views, however, brought reaction, and in 1690 he was forbidden to lecture or publish. He moved to Berlin, where Elector Frederick III of Brandenburg-Prussia allowed him to lecture. In 1694 Thomasius helped lay the foundation for the University of Halle, where he became second and then first (1710) professor of jurisprudence. He remained in Halle until his death on Sept. 23, 1728.

A renowned professor, Thomasius gave expression to many enlightened ideas and programs. Although he was not a profound thinker, his commonsense reasoning enabled him to put forth many practical reforms in the areas of philosophy, law, theology, and social customs. As a teacher, Thomasius believed not only in a solid academic training but also in developing character and comprehension of practical affairs. In religious matters he believed in the necessity for freedom of thought and speech and thoroughly condemned theologians who were always searching for heretics. He also attempted to free the study of jurisprudence from the control of theology. In his own theological beliefs, he considered that revealed religion was necessary for salvation.

Although he was influenced by the Pietists at Halle, especially Philipp Spener, Thomasius agreed primarily only with their opposition to established theological systems and their practical piety and not with their central emphasis on sin and grace. On matters of Church law, he emphasized that, since the Church was an institution within the domain of the state, the power of the state was supreme over the Church although not necessarily over the moral lives of individual Church members. He expressed himself powerfully against trial for witchcraft and the use of torture. In all of these ideas, Thomasius demonstrated his fundamental belief in the enlightened ideas of the 18th century.

Further Reading

There is no adequate biography of Thomasius. He is discussed in an excellent one-volume survey of the course of German philosophy to 1800 by Lewis White Beck, *Early German Philosophy: Kant and His Predecessors* (1969). □

David Thompson

David Thompson (1770-1857) was a Canadian explorer, cartographer, and surveyor. He was the first white man to descend the Columbia River from its source to its mouth.

David Thompson was born at Westminster, England, on April 30, 1770. After a surprisingly good education at Grey Coat School, a charity school near his home, he was apprenticed to the Hudson's Bay Company at the age of 14. He was sent out immediately and spent the years from 1784 to 1797 as a clerk, either at the bay or at various locations in the interior. He left the company's employ in 1797, in circumstances that virtually amounted to desertion. It was a poor repayment to an employer that had treated him well and trained him as a surveyor.

It was his surveying skill and his wilderness experience which made Thompson welcome at the North West Company, the great rival of the Hudson's Bay Company for the fur trade of the Northwest. The wealth of the company allowed him to devote most of the time from 1797 to 1812 to surveying and exploring with only infrequent periods of actually engaging in the fur trade. In 1804 he was made a partner in the company.

For several years Thompson made extensive journeys through the western plains, the Rocky Mountains, and along the Pacific slope, mapping and surveying as he traveled. In 1810-1811 he undertook the expedition for which he is best known. The Columbia River had long been a magnet for western traders, and Thompson was the first to travel the river from its source to its mouth. In one sense, his trip was a failure since his company had hoped that he would establish a post at the point where the Columbia emptied into the ocean before the arrival of the American Fur Company of John Jacob Astor. After excessive and unnecessary delay, he found Ft. Astoria already built when he came to the Columbia's mouth.

The following year, 1812, Thompson retired from the company and settled at Terrebonne, Lower Canada, later removing to Williamstown, Upper Canada. His surveying skills were employed in the establishment of the boundary between these two provinces. Later he was engaged in surveying the Canada-United States boundary as far west as Lake of the Woods. He never returned, however, to the Northwest.

In 1799 Thompson had married Charlotte Small, an Indian woman with whom he had 16 children. He died on Feb. 10, 1857, at Longueuil near Montreal.

Further Reading

The most valuable source of information on Thompson is the result of the meticulous scholarship of Richard Glover, who edited *David Thompson's Narrative, 1784-1812* (1962). Also useful are W. S. Wallace, *By Star and Compass* (1922), and C. N. Cochrane, *David Thompson, the Explorer* (1928). ☐

Dorothy Thompson

The outspoken conservative American journalist Dorothy Thompson (1894-1961) was one of the earliest women in her field. Her commentaries reached a very large audience in print and radio from the 1930s through the 1950s.

Dorothy Thompson was born in Lancaster, New York, on July 9, 1894. When she was ten her mother died, and she correctly predicted that her father, a Methodist minister, would marry Eliza Abbott, the church organist. When she rebelled against her stepmother, her father, whom she adored, required her to memorize and recite Bible passages as punishment. His critiques of her recitations undoubtedly contributed to her future speaking effectiveness.

Thompson eventually went to live with an aunt in Chicago to resolve the conflict with her stepmother. There she attended high school and Lewis Institute where she was quite popular and captain of a basketball team, but hardly a brilliant scholar. She entered Syracuse University in 1910, worked her way through college, and planned to become a teacher, but she failed in grammar. When women's suffrage was debated she toured New York making speeches for that cause.

During World War I, Thompson financed her own trip to Europe and enroute met a group of Zionists. She convinced International News Service to let her report on their conference, which made her one of the few women correspondents in Europe. Her intelligence, hard work, and prowess as a reporter soon earned her the respect of seasoned newsmen. As a correspondent in Vienna she travelled in cosmopolitan literary circles where she met and married writer Joseph Bard in 1923. As Thompson's career eclipsed Bard's, they divorced in 1927.

In 1925 Thompson had become head of the *New York Evening Post's* Berlin office. Soon she met Sinclair Lewis, renowned author of *Main Street*, who was so smitten by Thompson that he pursued her throughout Europe. They married in 1928 and their son Michael was born in 1930.

Back in America Thompson led a domestic life and wrote her book *I Saw Hitler* (1932), which was based on an earlier interview with him in Berlin. At that meeting she had been so unimpressed that she predicted he could never become a powerful leader. After that error in judgment she repeatedly attacked him and his regime. Her attacks seemed sincere; she had grown to love Germany and its culture from her long residence there. She spoke and wrote excellent German, often cooked German foods, and employed German servants in her Vermont home.

In 1936 Thompson began writing a column for the *New York Herald Tribune*. She cultivated a large "brain trust" which included David Sarnoff and Wendell Wilkie whose opinions she valued. German intellectual refugees brought "grapevine" reports, and those contacts resulted in her book *Refugee, Anarchy or Organization?* (1938), which was credited for Roosevelt's decision to call for the refugee conference at Evian, France. She also collaborated with

Fritz Kortner on a play for a refugee benefit entitled *Another Sun* (1940) which was panned by critics and ran slightly over a week.

Thompson made trips to Europe to observe war developments in several countries, but could not return to Germany, having been expelled from there by Hitler because of her negative views of Nazism. (Similarly, in Russia she was *persona non grata* because of her views on Communism.) She continued to write dramatically of the dangers of Nazism to Western democracies and challenged the views of Charles Lindbergh and other isolationists.

As Nazi troops swept across Europe, Thompson insisted that "we, who are not Jews" must speak out while anti-Semitic groups accused Jews of trying to drag America into Europe's war. As if to punctuate her views, she talked her way through police lines into the German-American Bund meeting to salute their leader Fritz Kuhn. As anti-Semitic orators lashed out against Jews and "Jew-loving" Roosevelt, Thompson repeatedly burst into laughter and shouted "bunk" until she was escorted out by police.

Frequently called "First Lady of American Journalism," Thompson also reached large audiences through her radio broadcasts in the late 1930s. In 1937 Thompson began writing a column for *Ladies Home Journal,* setting her own price at $1,000 a column. It appeared regularly for over 20 years. She also wrote articles for *Saturday Evening Post* and *Foreign Affairs.* By the late 1930s only one woman—Eleanor Roosevelt—matched Thompson's audience. *Time* (June 12, 1939) declared then that Roosevelt and Thompson were undoubtedly the most influential American women.

As her professional popularity grew, her marriage to Sinclair Lewis deteriorated, and they were divorced in 1942. (In mid-1943 she was more happily married to artist Maxim Kopf, who succumbed to a heart attack in 1958, the same ailment which took her life in 1961.)

Thompson's public statements were sometimes contradictory: primarily a conservative (she preferred the word "preservative"), she denounced the New Deal, but she approved wide-scale economic planning. After she helped her friend Wendell Wilkie gain the Republican nomination in 1940, she shocked close friends and the public when she endorsed Roosevelt for a third term (1940), arguing that he knew the world better than any other democratic leader, except maybe Churchill.

Similar personal contradictions were apparent. She could be as ruthless as she was kind and gentle; lavish with her resources, time, and attention, yet selfish with them at other times; and she was logical, but also emotional. Despite these contradictions, her career was an early demonstration that a bright, committed, and hard-working woman could succeed in a traditionally male profession. Through her spoken and printed commentary on current news, Thompson's was a most powerful voice for several decades.

Further Reading

The most complete biography of Dorothy Thompson is Marion K. Sanders' *Dorothy Thompson, A Legend in Her Times* (1973), while Vincent Sheean's *Dorothy and Red* (1963) concentrates on Thompson's relationship with Sinclair Lewis. Additional readings about Thompson and articles written by her may be found in a number of periodicals (several cited in the biography) published in the 1930s through the 1950s. □

Hunter Stockton Thompson

The American journalist Hunter Stockton Thompson (born 1939) was known as one of the best examples of "Gonzo" journalism. His political and cultural criticism of the United States in the 1970s was largely a series of tales flowing from his eccentric personality and adventures.

Born July 18, 1939, in Louisville, Kentucky, Hunter S. Thompson was the son of Jack and Virginia (Ray) Thompson. His father was an insurance agent. After attending public schools, Thompson joined the Air Force, where the two major tendencies in his life were soon revealed: writing and outrageous behavior. Stationed in Florida, he became a sports reporter for the base newspaper. In 1958 he received a dishonorable discharge after an officer claimed his disregard for military dress and authority was having a bad influence on other airmen.

After being fired from jobs with a small New York newspaper and *TIME* magazine, Thompson went to Puerto Rico and wrote briefly for a bowling magazine. Returning to the United States in 1960, he traveled to California where he settled in Big Sur and wrote a novel that was never published. In 1961 he left for South America and wrote lengthy stories for the Dow Jones-owned weekly, *The National Observer.* In 1963 he returned again to the United States and continued writing for *The National Observer* on such topics as Indian fishing rights in Washington state. He quit the publication in 1964 when they wouldn't let him cover the Free Speech Movement in Berkeley, California.

Settling in San Francisco, he did odd jobs while working as a free-lance writer. He wrote a story on Berkeley student politics for *The Nation* magazine, but his big break came when an article for *The Nation* in May 1965 on the Hell's Angels motorcycle gang drew the attention of numerous publishers. He signed a contract with Random House and spent a year riding and living with the gang, which led to his first book, *Hell's Angels: The Strange and Terrible Saga of the Outlaw Motorcycle Gangs* (1966).

Thompson had always admired author Nelsen Algren, whose novel *A Walk on the Wild Side* featured a marijuana-smoking country boy as a hero. Thompson's account of the notorious motorcycle gang was written in a conventional journalistic manner, but unlike the professional reporter, his personality resembled his subject. Thompson became a wild outlaw with a pen. As he said to one interviewer, "I've got a lot in common with the Hell's Angels. The main difference is that I've got a gimmick—I can write."

In the late 1960s he wrote for *Ramparts* and *Scanlan's,* two magazines that embraced his role in the counterculture. A story for *Scanlan's* in 1970 on the Kentucky Derby re-

Hunter Thompson (foreground)

vealed the emergence of a full-blown persona and transformed Thompson's career. Experiencing writer's block, a drunken Thompson submitted only his disorganized notes, which focused more on himself than the race. Published intact and widely-acclaimed, Thompson's desperate deadline impulse gave birth to what was called "Gonzo" journalism.

Thompson found a home for his new style in *Rolling Stone* magazine. His first piece was entitled "The Battle of Aspen: Freak Power in the Rockies." A couple of years earlier, after facing police violence while covering the Democratic Convention in Chicago in 1968, Thompson returned to his home in Aspen, Colorado, and ran for sheriff—unsuccessfully—on a "Freaks" platform.

His next assignment was to cover a motorcycle race and a national drug law enforcement convention in Las Vegas. The two-part story soon appeared as *Fear and Loathing in Las Vegas* (1971), quickly heralded as a masterpiece of the New Journalism. The main topic was Thompson himself and his drug-induced, crazy adventures, written in a manic and comic style that defined his personal and literary reputation. His crazed persona, including such recognized trademarks as Hawaiian shirts, cigarette holder, and mirrored sunglasses, became the basis for Garry Trudeau's character Raoul Duke in the comic strip "Doonesbury."

In 1972 Thompson covered the presidential campaign for *Rolling Stone* and his articles were published as *Fear and*

Loathing on the Campaign Trail '72 (1973). The book contained some notable observations, such as being the first to predict George McGovern's nomination, but it was known more for his complete mockery of traditional reporting techniques. His utter lack of objectivity was often criticized, but Thompson, more than the candidates, was the real star of his writing, and some reporters envied his freedom. Said one television reporter, "After the revolution we'll all write like Hunter."

Thompson found it difficult to sustain a writing style in which his craziness was the real theme. He went to Zaire to cover the Muhammed Ali fight, but he contracted malaria and didn't write a story. He was in Saigon before the end of the Vietnam War, but only wrote a short dispatch. His last article for *Rolling Stone* was a piece on presidential candidate Jimmy Carter in 1976.

At his peak, the eccentric Thompson was seen as one of the original prose writers of the 1970s who not only captured in writing but symbolized the disillusionment of an era. He was "America's quintessential outlaw journalist," said one observer. His "Gonzo" journalism represented a new genre, but he also belonged to an older literary tradition beginning with Mark Twain's *Huckleberry Finn*.

During the height of his popularity he became a cult figure and was solicited by such national publications as *Playboy* and *The New Yorker*. But, in retrospect, he was seen by one critic as "purely a creature of the fashion of the day" and a writer who ultimately undermined the promise of New Journalism through excessive self-promotion. But Thompson claimed he had little literary aspiration. He considered himself lazy and believed "writing is hard dollar." Journalism was a good way "to get someone else to pay to get me where the action really is," he said.

A number of his early pieces were collected in *The Great Shark Hunt* (1979), in which he announced that the literary persona he invented was finished. In 1980 he worked on a film, "Where the Buffalo Roam," about his adventures with attorney Oscar Zeta Acosta. In 1984 he published *The Curse of Lono,* a book about a trip to Hawaii.

In the mid 1980s he was living in the Florida Keys and writing a novel that introduced a new literary persona who expresses, according to Thompson, "a brutal attitude—antihumanist."

From 1985 to 1989 Thompson wrote a column for the *San Francisco Examiner* that was later syndicated to about 25 papers nationally. A second collection of writings, *Generation of Swine: Gonzo Paper Vol. 2: Tales of Shame and Degradation in the '80's,* appeared in 1988. Volume 3 of the Gonzo Papers was published in 1990 as *Songs of the Doomed,* a collection of snippets from 30 years of writing.

Thompson lived on a 100-acre farm in Woody Creek, Colorado, near Aspen, where he was known as a compulsive hermit with a fondness for drinking, loud music, and target shooting Chinese gongs with a Magnum .44. Thompson's greatest love was reported to be motorcycling. He loved to put his Ducati 900SP through its paces in Aspen. By age 50, Thompson had mellowed little and was charged with five felony counts of possessing drugs and possessing and storing explosives illegally, which were later dropped. He then resumed work on his big "sex" novel, *Polo Is My Life.*

Thompson's autobiographical *Fear and Loathing in Las Vegas* was re-released in 1996 on the 25th anniversary of its publication. During the same year an audio adaptation of the work, narrated by Harry Dean Stanton, was produced by Margaritaville Records. Terry Gilliam (formerly of Monty Python) was tapped to direct a movie of the cult classic in 1997 with Johnny Depp in the role of Thompson.

Further Reading

The best source on Thompson's writing style and personality is Thompson himself. His books include *Hell's Angels: A Strange and Terrible Saga* (1966), *Fear and Loathing in Las Vegas: A Savage Journey to the Heart of the American Dream* (1972), *Fear and Loathing on the Campaign Trail '72* (1973); *The Great Shark Hunt: Strange Tales from a Strange Time* (1979); *The Curse of Lono* (1983); *Generation of Swine, Gonzo Papers Vol. 2: Tales of Shame and Degradation in the 80's* (1988); and *Songs of the Doomed* (1990). Biographies of Hunter include *Hunter S. Thompson* by William Mckeen (1991) and *When the Going Gets Weird: the Twisted Life and Time of Hunter S. Thompson: an Unauthorized Biography* by Peter O. Whitmer (1993).

Thompson is featured prominently in Robert Sam Anson's story of *Rolling Stone* magazine, *Gone Crazy and Back Again.* His literary career is reviewed in *Contemporary Authors,* New Revision Series, Volume 23. A more critical assessment is found in an article, "How Hunter Thompson Killed New Journalism," by Joseph Nocera in *Washington Monthly* (April 1981). Also see Peter Whitmer, "Hunter Thompson: Still Crazy After all These Years?" in *Saturday Review* (January-February 1984). □

Sir George Paget Thomson

The English atomic physicist Sir George Paget Thomson (born 1892) shared the Nobel Prize in physics for the discovery of electron waves.

George Paget Thomson, son of Sir J. J. Thomson, the discoverer of electrons, was born at Cambridge on May 3, 1892. He studied mathematics and physics at Trinity College, Cambridge, and graduated in 1913. He was then elected a Fellow and lecturer of Corpus Christi College. Early in World War I he served as an infantry officer in France, but from 1915 he worked on aerodynamical problems at Farnborough. From 1917 to 1918 he was in the United States as a member of the British War Mission.

After the war Thomson continued his research and teaching at Cambridge. In 1922 he became professor of natural philosophy in the University of Aberdeen, where he did his fundamental work on electron waves. In 1930 he was appointed professor of physics at the Imperial College, University of London.

During the first quarter of the 20th century, it was learned that the electron not only had an electric charge but

also mass and spin. However, the theoretical concepts did not fully agree with the results of experiments. In 1924, Louis de Brogile postulated theoretically that any particle of matter must possess not only mass but also a wave structure.

In 1927 Thomson began working on this problem, using the effect of a diffraction grating on a beam of electrons—cathode rays—and photography of the results. But cathode rays have little penetrative power, and a crystal could not be used as a diffraction grating. It was decided to use extremely thin sheets of the precious metals as diffraction gratings, since their atom structure was known and in their natural state they were crystalline. When a beam of electrons was passed through such a sheet of gold foil, the photograph showed a central dark spot formed by the undiffracted beams, surrounded by concentric rings formed by the diffracted beams.

The results agreed with the hypothesis that electrons exhibited wave characters. From the experimental data, combined with the distances between the rings, the wavelengths of the electronic waves could be calculated by the De Broglie formula. It was also found that the beam was deflected by a magnetic field in agreement with the De Broglie formula. One application of the method in engineering is the examination of the atomic structure of solid surfaces by reflection technique.

Unknown to Thomson, the American physicist C. J. Davisson had been studying this problem by a different method, and their results were published almost simulta-

neously. For the discovery of the electronic waves Thomson shared the Nobel Prize for Physics with Davisson in 1937.

In the late 1930s Thomson became interested in atomic fission, and he persuaded the British Air Ministry to begin extensive experiments. After the outbreak of World War II he became chairman of the British Committee on Atomic Energy, and in 1941 he went to the United States to deliver to American scientists the committee's report that established the feasibility of the atomic bomb. After the war he was active in research on controlled thermonuclear reactions, and he was consultant to the British Atomic Energy Authority. In 1952 Thomson was elected Master of Corpus Christi College, Cambridge, from which post he retired in 1962. After retirement, he remained in Cambridge, where he stayed active academically and socially. Thomson died on September 10, 1975, at age 83.

Thomson received many honors. Elected a Fellow of the Royal Society in 1929, he was awarded its Hughes Medal in 1939 and its Royal Medal in 1949. He was knighted in 1943 and received honorary degrees from many universities. Among his important books are *Wave Mechanics of the Free Electron* (1930) and, with W. Cochrane, *The Theory and Practice of Electron Diffraction* (1939). His more elementary work, *The Atom* (1930), passed through many editions. For further reading, see *Biographical Memoirs of Fellows of the Royal Society,* Volume 23 (1977). Other good sources include Barbara Cline's *Men Who Made a New Physics: Physicists and the Quantum Theory* (1987), *Modern Men of Science* Volume I (1968), and Robert Weber's *Pioneers of Science: Nobel Prize Winners in Physics* (1980).

Further Reading

There is a biography of Thomson in *Nobel Lectures, Physics, 1922-1941* (1965), which also includes his Nobel Lecture. For a discussion of his work see N. H. de V. Heathcote, *Nobel Prize Winners, Physics, 1901-1950* (1953). For the background of Thomson's work see his *The Atom* (1930; 5th ed. 1956); also B. Hoffmann, *The Strange Story of the Quantum* (1959), and A. d'Abro, *The Rise of the New Physics* (1951). □

James Thomson

The British poet James Thomson (1700-1748) is chiefly remembered for his celebrated descriptive poem in four parts, "The Seasons," written in blank verse.

James Thomson was born at Ednam, Scotland, near the English border, on Sept. 11, 1700, the third son of a minister. Taught at first by Robert Riccaltoun, whose verses on winter later influenced his famous pupil, Thomson then attended school at Jedburgh. In 1715 he matriculated at the University of Edinburgh, where he became a divinity student.

Already a habitual writer of verse, young Thomson went to London in 1725 hoping either to become a popular preacher or to acquire a patron for his poetry. He supported himself by serving as a tutor. His "Winter" appeared in 1726, but its dedication procured only 20 guineas, not a patron. The poem was very well received, however, and it was followed by "Summer" (1727) and "Spring" (1728). The poems were applauded and imitated, but Thomson's financial position was unsound. He therefore determined to write a play.

Thomson's tragedy *Sophonisba* was produced at Drury Lane Theatre in 1730 with moderate success. He then sold the copyright of this play and that of "Spring." In the same year *The Seasons,* now including "Autumn," was published by subscription. This publication secured him a patron, Sir Charles Talbot, who sent Thomson abroad as a companion to his son (1731-1733). Talbot then gave Thomson the post of secretary of briefs in the Court of Chancery, a sinecure. He wrote a long poem based on his travels, *Liberty,* which was published in five parts (1734-1736) and was a failure. Fortunately Thomson had sold the copyright in advance.

After Talbot's death in 1737, Thomson lost his sinecure. His fortunes reached their lowest ebb in this year; in fact, he was arrested for debt. He retrieved his fortunes, however, with his tragedy *Agamemnon,* produced in 1738. Whatever the poetic merits of this piece, its political merits were rewarded by a pension from the Prince of Wales (canceled in 1748). Thomson's next tragedy, *Edward and Eleanora,* published in 1739, was banned for political reasons.

With his friend David Mallet, Thomson wrote in 1740 the masque *Alfred,* with music by Thomas Arne, for which he created the song *Rule, Britannia.* In 1744 Thomson's new patron, George Lyttleton, a lord commissioner of the Treasury, appointed him surveyor general of the Leeward Islands, and in 1745 *Tancred and Sigismunda,* Thomson's most successful play, was produced. *The Castle of Indolence,* a poem written in imitation of Edmund Spenser and reflecting Thomson's love of idleness, appeared in 1748. He died that year on August 27.

Further Reading

The Complete Poetical Works of James Thomson were well edited by James L. Robertson (1908). Thomson was included in Samuel Johnson, *Lives of the English Poets* (1781). Thomson's *Letters and Documents,* edited by Alan D. McKillop (1958), is valuable. The best biography is Douglas Grant, *James Thomson: Poet of "The Seasons"* (1951). McKillop wrote *The Background of Thomson's "Seasons"* (1942). Thomson is also discussed in Patricia M. Spacks, *The Poetry of Vision: Five Eighteenth-century Poets* (1967). Good recent critical studies are Patricia M. Spacks, *The Varied God: A Critical Study of Thomson's The Seasons* (1959), and Ralph Cohen, *The Art of Discrimination: Thomson's The Seasons, and the Language of Criticism* (1964).

Additional Sources

Bayne, William, *James Thomson,* Philadelphia: R. West, 1977.
Sambrook, James, *James Thomson, 1700-1748: a life,* Oxford: Clarendon Press; New York: Oxford University Press, 1991.
Scott, Mary Jane W., *James Thomson, Anglo-Scot,* Athens: University of Georgia Press, 1988. □

Sir Joseph John Thomson

The English physicist Sir Joseph John Thomson (1856-1940) is credited with the discovery of the electron.

On Dec. 18, 1856, J. J. Thomson was born at Cheetham Hill near Manchester. His father, a bookseller and publisher, planned a career in engineering for Joseph, but since no apprenticeship could be found for him in any engineering firm, he was sent "temporarily" to college in Manchester at the age of 14. As a result of his ability and determination, he won a scholarship in 1876 and entered Trinity College, Cambridge; he remained there for the rest of his life.

After graduation Thomson began working in the Cavendish Laboratory, which was under the direction of Lord Rayleigh. Thomson's brilliance brought him membership in the Royal Society at 27 and his appointment as Rayleigh's successor at 28. He proved to be inspiring and effective both as a teacher and as a research director, and as time passed, students came to him from all over the world. He sometimes had as many as 40 to advise at once, and for the first quarter of the 20th century the Cavendish Laboratory, where Thomson insisted that theory should be considered "a policy, not a creed," was the world center for particle research.

Thomson began his studies of the properties of "cathode rays" in 1894 and proved in 1895 that they carried a negative charge. In 1897 he passed the rays through a vacuum and showed that they are deflected in both magnetic and electric fields. He was thus able to determine the ratio of the charge to the mass of the supposed particles and showed that its mass was about 2,000 times larger than the mass of the hydrogen atom. The identification of the electron necessitated a revision of the atomic concept: Thomson visualized it as a mass of positively charged matter in which electrons were distributed like raisins in a cake.

About 1906 Thomson turned his attention to "positive rays"—positively charged ions. By 1912, using his deflection techniques and measuring the charge to mass ratio, he had shown that neon was a mixture of at least two kinds of atoms, with differing deflectibilities. Thomson had thus opened the door to the world of isotopes and had provided a beginning for the method of analysis now known as mass spectrography.

During his career Thomson published 13 books and over 200 papers. He was awarded the Nobel Prize in physics in 1906 and was knighted in 1908. In 1918 he abandoned research to become master of Trinity College, where he died on Aug. 30, 1940.

Further Reading

Thomson's *Recollections and Reflections* (1936) is one of the notable scientific autobiographies. A full-length biography is Robert J. S. Rayleigh, *The Life of J. J. Thomson* (1942). The sketch in James G. Crowther, *British Scientists of the Twentieth Century* (1952), is excellent. □

Kenneth Thomson

Kenneth Thomson (born 1923) represented the second generation of a powerful and influential print and broadcast journalism family that had significant impact in both Great Britain and North America.

Born on September 1, 1923, in Toronto, Ontario, as the third child and only son of Edna and Roy Thomson, Kenneth Thomson inherited and then expanded the international business established by his father. In the 1984 book, *The Thomson Empire,* Susan Goldenberg chronicled the life of Roy Thomson as a failed auto parts dealer who rose to the British title Lord Thomson of Fleet, owner of the London *Times* and *Sunday Times* and a 20 percent owner of North Sea oil fields.

Kenneth Thomson married Nora Marilyn Lavis Thomson, and they had three children, David, Lynne, and Peter. The Thomsons lived quiet lives, with a large home in Toronto and a house in Kensington Palace Gardens in London. Kenneth Thomson used his title, Lord Thomson of Fleet, when in England, but refused to take his seat in the House of Lords because he did not wish to surrender his Canadian citizenship. Beginning when he was a 16-year-old disk jockey at CFCH, his father's first radio station, Kenneth Thomson was a fan of country and western music and, especially, of Canadian-born Hank Snow. Thomson even traveled to Nashville just to hear and meet Snow.

The Thomson empire had its beginnings when Roy Thomson acquired a franchise to sell De Forest Crosley radios in North Bay in 1930. This enterprise should have suffered significantly from the fact that North Bay is about 500 miles north of Toronto, that Canada was mired deep in the Great Depression, and that radio reception was uneven and spotty at best. To promote radio sales Roy Thomson opened his own radio station in North Bay, CFCH. This was, for a long period, a one-person operation, with Roy Thomson performing all the functions of the radio station and selling radios on the side. Eventually he began hiring new help, paying them mostly in experience.

Thomson invested all his earnings in expansion, buying additional radio stations and newspapers. In part, he said he bought the newspapers to expand advertising potential. By the early 1950s this policy had led to a significant communication network throughout Canada. In 1953, Roy Thomson moved to Great Britain and continued diversified business expansion. In 1966, he purchased the London *Times* and merged it with the *Sunday Times,* appointing his son Kenneth Thomson as the chairman of the board.

Kenneth Thomson's early career did not indicate that he would be as successful as his father. He went to prestigious Canadian private schools, enrolled in the University of Toronto, left to serve three years with the Canadian Air Force during World War II, and finally earned an MA in law from Cambridge University in 1947. From that point on he worked for the family business, serving as a beginning reporter on small newspapers in small Canadian towns. In *The Thomson Empire,* Susan Goldenberg suggests that his tenure throughout this early period was unremarkable and undistinguished. When Kenneth Thomson took over the family business after Roy Thomson died in 1976, most observers expected the family business to falter.

Such speculation proved unfounded. Kenneth Thomson did alter the direction of the business, slowly reorganizing the empire so that profits from North Sea oil were removed from the restrictions of Great Britain and transferred to Canadian corporations. Eventually the United Kingdom holdings became a subsidiary of a Canadian-based corporation. A clear indication of Kenneth Thomson's unwillingness to subject his companies to British business practices came in 1981 when, after a protracted struggle with the newspaper unions of Britain, he sold the *Times* and *Sunday Times* to Rupert Murdoch, who was, at that time, the Australian press entrepreneur.

Starting at the beginning of the 1980s, Kenneth Thomson expanded his companies' interests in publishing and printing in North America. Despite the fact that the Canadian Royal Commission on Newspapers took the Thomson chain to task for poor quality, the newspapers were profitable. The commission had been created by Pierre Trudeau, at the time Canadian prime minister, because of a fear generated by the fact that two companies, Thomson and Southam, owned 57 percent of Canada's newspapers.

Thomson also expanded his holdings in the United States. By 1985 Thomson had become the largest foreign investor in the United States' publishing industry. He spent over $1.5 billion acquiring small daily and weekly newspapers as well as such highly specialized publications as *Jane's Fighting Ships, The American Banker,* and *The Journal of Taxation.* In the early 1980s Thomson sought to add three to five American papers to his empire per year.

In later years Kenneth Thomson managed to retain the diversity of the Thomson empire, though the heart of the empire shifted away from British holdings. The Thomson companies were completely divested from British energy holdings, but they were rapidly moving into the field of electronic communications, particularly in the area of databases. In 1989 they acquired the Lawyers Cooperative Publishing Company of Rochester, New York. This made Thomson one of the largest legal publishers in North America.

The Thomson financial empire was secure going into the 1990's and expanded holdings in specialized information and electronic publishing, newspaper publishing in North America and leisure travel in the United Kingdom. William Symonds in *Business Week* (March 11, 1996) referred to Thomson as "Lord of Cyberpress." Thomson was listed in a July 1995 *Forbes* article as one of the ten richest men in the world.

The Thomson Groups gained a reputation for providing print and electronic information to the professional and business communities (legal, tax, accounting, medical, education, reference, regulatory compliance). According to 1996 corporate reports, electronic publishing products totaled more than 58,000 items including some 2,000 CD-ROM products, 350 on-line services and the well known *WESTLAW* featuring over 9,500 databases. In 1996 the Corporation reported sales of US $7.7 billion with some 50,000 employees. At the 1997 Annual Meeting of Shareholders of The Thomson Corporation, Chairman Thomson told attendees, ''The highlight of the year was the acquisition of the West Publishing Company . . . . We are clear market leaders in all sectors in which we engaged.''

Further Reading

For additional information on Kenneth Thomson see *The Thomson Empire* (1984) by Susan Goldenberg. Information on activities of the Thomson Corporation appear routinely in finance publications such as *Forbes, Business Week* and *The Wall Street Journal.* □

Tom Thomson

The Canadian painter Tom Thomson (1877-1917) was the forerunner of the Group of Seven, the national movement in landscape painting. He is best known as an interpreter of the Canadian wilderness.

Tom Thomson was born at Claremont, Ontario, not far from Toronto but was brought up at Leith on the shores of Georgian Bay. After an unpromising beginning as a machinist, he worked as a photoengraver in Seattle, Wash., from 1901 to 1904, when he returned to Canada. In 1907 Thomson joined the art department of Grip Limited in Toronto, where several of the men who after World War I formed the Group of Seven worked, among them J. E. H. MacDonald.

In 1911 Thomson made his first sketching trip by canoe into the Mississauga Forest Reserve with one of his fellow artists. The following year he went on a longer trip into Algonquin Park, a provincial forest with which his name has been linked ever since. When he returned to Toronto with a number of small oil sketches, he happened to drop in on his friend MacDonald when Dr. J. M. MacCallum was in the studio. The doctor, the friend and patron of the Group of Seven, was immediately impressed with Thomson, and when he later saw the sketches, he recognized their truthfulness in spite of their dark color and timid handling.

Thomson's first large canvas, based on one of these sketches, was *A Northern Lake,* which was exhibited in the Annual Exhibition of the Ontario Society of Artists in 1913 and was bought, much to the artist's surprise, by the Ontario government. Thereafter, with the backing of Dr.

MacCallum, he dropped his career as a commercial artist and devoted himself to painting.

Each year, with growing mastery, Thomson charted the changing seasons in Algonquin Park with a steady stream of sketches, from dazzling impressions of sunlight on snow in March, the breakup of the ice in spring, the flaming sunsets and northern lights of summer, to the pageantry of autumn's reds and golds and the gathering snow clouds over the bleak November landscape. In winter he would return to his studio in Toronto to paint the large canvases for which he is best known. The flat pattern, swinging line, and rich texture of the larger pictures reflect the influence of the Art Nouveau style then in vogue; but in the original sketches the strong color, bold design, and rapid brushwork have a conviction and expressive force never equaled in paintings of the Canadian northland.

Tragedy struck in the summer of 1917. On July 8 Thomson set off for a day's fishing on Canoe Lake. His upturned canoe was found that evening; his body, with the legs tangled in a fishing line, a week later. The coroner recorded the death as accidental, but there are still those who suspect foul play.

Further Reading

The best-documented monograph on Thomson is Joan Murray, *The Art of Tom Thomson* (1971), published as an exhibition catalog by the Art Gallery of Ontario.

Additional Sources

Murray, Joan, *Tom Thomson: the last spring,* Toronto; Niagara Falls, N.Y.: Dundurn Press, 1994.
Thomson, Tom, *Tom Thomson, the silence and the storm,* Toronto: McClelland and Stewart, 1977. □

Virgil Thomson

American composer, critic, and conductor Virgil Thomson (1896-1989) combined literary and musical erudition with simplicity, wit, and skill.

Virgil Thomson was born in Kansas City, MO, on Nov. 25, 1896. He studied music theory, piano, and organ, and at the age of 12 he officiated as organist of the local Baptist church. His youthful acquaintance with American folk songs and Baptist hymns later gave him important material in his compositions. After serving in the Army during World War I, Thomson studied at Harvard University. A fellowship enabled him to study in Paris for a year with the distinguished pedagogue Nadia Boulanger. Returning to the United States, he received a bachelor of arts degree from Harvard in 1923.

Thomson lived in Paris from 1925 until World War II, visiting the United States periodically. In Paris he formed close associations with musicians, painters, and writers, many of whom were depicted in his compositions for piano, chamber ensemble, and orchestra. Among those described in his numerous musical portraits were Gertrude Stein (1928) and Pablo Picasso (1940).

Another important influence on Thomson was that of composer Erik Satie, who advocated a return to simple, unpretentious music. Thomson's first opera was just that. *Four Saints in Three Acts,* based on Gertrude Stein's free-association prose, received its premiere in Hartford, CT in 1934. An all-black cast dressed in cellophane costumes sang a virtually unintelligible libretto, and Thomson's music, derived from church hymns and folk sources, utilized only the most rudimentary harmonies. Following the marked success of his first opera, Thomson composed music for two documentary films, *The Plough That Broke the Plains* (1936) and *The River* (1937). The latter work utilizes many American folk melodies, including "Aunt Rhody" and "Hot Time in the Old Town Tonight."

Thomson's first book, *The State of Music* (1939), described the place of music in Western society. In 1940 he became a critic with the *New York Herald Tribune,* a post he occupied with great distinction until his retirement in 1954. During those years his articles were collected and published in *The Musical Scene* (1945), *The Art of Judging Music* (1948), and *Music Right and Left* (1951).

Meanwhile, Thomson continued to compose. His second opera, *The Mother of Us All,* was first performed in 1947. The libretto by Gertrude Stein dealt with the career of Susan B. Anthony. *A Solemn Music* (1949), written for band and later orchestrated, was composed in a rather conservative atonal idiom. Written in memory of Stein and the

painter Christian Bérard, it is one of Thomson's most powerful works. During the 1960s he composed several sacred works, among them *Missa pro defunctis* for double chorus and orchestra and *Pange lingua* for organ. In 1967 his book *Music Reviewed, 1940-1954* appeared.

In the course of his long career, Thomson wrote many songs and piano music. He received international recognition for his multifaceted achievements: a Pulitzer Prize (1948), several honorary academic degrees, and France's Legion of Honor award.

When Thomson moved back to the U.S. in 1940, he took up residence at the Chelsea Hotel in New York. He would live in that apartment for the rest of his life. It became almost a museum of paintings, pictures, books and furniture from well-known artists who were his friends. Thomson spent much of his time composing music while resting on his walnut bed, where he was often photographed at work. His memoir was published in 1966, simply entitled *Virgil Thomson.* In 1972, Thomson composed a new opera, entitled *Lord Byron,* which premiered at the Julliard, yet did not receive the acclaim of his previous two operas.

Each time Thomson reached a milestone birthday, it was marked with a celebration. On his 80th birthday, a special production of his best-known opera, *Mother of Us All,* was performed. On his 85th birthday, *Four Saints in Three Acts* was presented at Carnegie Hall. On his 90th birthday, *Four Saints* was once again performed by the Opera Ensemble of New York. In addition, a radio station in New York broadcast the three operas (*Mother of Us All, Four Saints,* and *Lord Byron*), as well as three film scores and numerous chamber compositions and piano sonatas. By this time, Thomson had composed more than 140 *Portaits for Piano,* which were carefully catalogued and published as *Virgil Thomson's Musical Portraits,* by Anthony Tommasini.

At the age of 92, Thomson published his last book, *Music with Words: A Composer's View* (1989). He died in New York City on Sept. 30, 1989. Following his death, his many artifacts were auctioned off for the benefit of the Virgil Thomson Foundation. News reports said the art work went far in excess of its estimated value due to the sentimental nature of the items.

Further Reading

The composer's autobiography, *Virgil Thomson* (1966), is an invaluable and delightful source. The best study of Thomson's life and music is Kathleen O'Donnell Hoover and John Cage, *Virgil Thomson: His Life and Music* (1959). Joseph Machlis, *American Composers of Our Time* (1963), devotes a chapter to Thomson and is recommended for general background. □

Henry David Thoreau

Henry David Thoreau (1817-1862) was an American writer, a dissenter, and, after Emerson, the outstanding transcendentalist. He is best known for his classic book, "Walden."

Though a minority of one, largely ignored in his own day, Henry David Thoreau has since become a world influence. His criticism of living only for money and material values apparently carries more conviction all the time. His advocacy of civil disobedience against an unjust government, though it caused hardly a ripple in his time, later influenced Mohandas Gandhi's campaign for Indian independence and still influences many of today's radicals. But Thoreau was not only a disseminator of major ideas. He was a superb literary craftsman and the most notable American nature writer.

Thoreau was born on July 12, 1817, in Concord, Mass., and lived there most of his life; it became, in fact, his universe. His parents were permanently poor. He attended Concord Academy, where his record was good but not outstanding. Nevertheless, he entered Harvard in 1833 as a scholarship student. Young as he was, he established a reputation at Harvard of being an individualist. He was friendly enough with his fellow students, yet he soon saw that many of their values could never become his.

After Thoreau graduated in 1837, he faced the problem of earning a living. He taught briefly in the town school, taught for a longer while at a private school his brother John had started, and also made unsuccessful efforts to find a teaching job away from home. Meanwhile, he was spending a good deal of time writing—he had begun a journal in 1837 which ran to 14 volumes of close-packed print when published after his death. He wanted, he decided, to be a poet.

But America starved its poets as a rule, and Thoreau spent much of his life attempting to do just what he wanted and at the same time to survive. For he wanted to live as a poet as well as to write poetry. He loved nature and could stay indoors only with effort. The beautiful woods, meadows, and waters of the Concord neighborhood attracted him like a drug. He wandered among them by day and by night, observing the world of nature closely and sympathetically. He named himself, half humorously, "inspector of snow-storms and rainstorms."

The town gossiped about this Harvard graduate who sauntered around instead of working 12 hours a day. However, Thoreau made few concessions either to opinion or to his economic needs. He did odd jobs; he helped from time to time in the pencil-making and graphite business his father had started but which barely kept them alive; he developed skill as a surveyor.

Thoreau's struggles were watched with compassion by an older Concord neighbor who was also one of America's great men, Ralph Waldo Emerson. Emerson proved to be his best friend. He assisted Thoreau with all the tact at his command. In 1841 Emerson invited Thoreau to live at his home and to make himself useful there only when it would not interfere with his writing. In 1843 he got Thoreau a job tutoring in Staten Island, N.Y., so that he could be close to the New York City literary market. The idea was a failure, but the fault was not Emerson's. In 1847 he invited Thoreau to stay with his family again while Emerson himself went to Europe.

Most of the time, however, Thoreau lived at home. A small room was all he needed. He never married, and he required little. At one point he built a cabin at Walden Pond just outside Concord, on land owned by Emerson, and lived in it during 1845 and 1846. Here he wrote much of his book *Walden*.

Through these various expedients Thoreau managed to find time to do a substantial amount of other writing too. Some of his most interesting early work was poetry. But he gradually came to feel that the form of poetry was too confining and that prose was his proper medium. He wrote some philosophical and literary essays, especially for a little magazine Emerson was editing called the *Dial*. Of the philosophical essays the most famous nowadays is "Civil Disobedience." First printed in 1849 (after the demise of the *Dial*), it describes Thoreau's taxpayer's rebellion against the Federal government in protest against the war with Mexico, his brief imprisonment, and his rationale for resistance. He urges that conscience must be man's guide and that when one encounters a law he considers unjust he can disobey it if he is willing to accept the consequences.

Literary Works

Thoreau wrote nature essays both early and late in his career. They range from the "Natural History of Massachusetts" (1842), which is supposedly a review but is actually a delightful discussion on the world of nature around him, to the felicitous and poetic "Autumnal Tints" and "Walking" (both 1862), which appeared shortly after his death. He also wrote three rather slender volumes that might be termed travel books. Each was made up of essays and was first serialized in part in a magazine. They were published in book form after Thoreau's death: *The Maine Woods* (1864), *Cape Cod* (1865), and *A Yankee in Canada* (1866).

Thoreau's two most interesting books defy categorizing. They are not travel books; they are not polemics; they are not reflective essays. The first is *A Week on the Concord and Merrimack Rivers* (1849), issued at his own expense. Using as a framework two river excursions he and his brother John had made, Thoreau drew heavily from his journal of that time. He filled out the book with other journalizing, bits of poetry, old college themes, and youthful philosophizing. The result was a book which a few enthusiasts hailed but which the public ignored.

Walden (1854), however, attracted disciples from the beginning, and today editions of it crowd the bookshelves of the world. Though basically it is an account of Thoreau's stay beside Walden Pond, it is also many other things, all combined in a cunning and, indeed, unique synthesis. It is a how-to-do-it book, for it tells how to live one's life with a minimum of distasteful labor. It is an apologia. It is a spiritual (or rather, philosophical) autobiography. It is a book of seasons. And it is a defiant cockcrow to the world, for Thoreau was crowing in triumph at his ability to live as he pleased; in fact, the original title page had a rooster on it.

Involvment in Public Affairs

Writing *Walden* was the high point of Thoreau's life and his main manifesto. Yet there were other important things that involved him. He believed that a writer's work and his life should be one, though he sometimes asserted the opposite. At any rate, he devoted both his writing and his life increasingly to public issues. With word and deed he had fought against the Mexican-American war of the mid-1840s. And in the next decade he became totally involved in the struggle against slavery. In John Brown he found his only hero: he became Brown's friend and ardent defender, and after Brown's raid on Harpers Ferry Thoreau spoke out for him in the most fiery words he ever used.

Thoreau always marched to the sound of his own drum, as he said in one of his most enduring aphorisms, and yet the changing times had some effect on him. In the 1840s he was still advising the abolitionists to free themselves before trying to free the slaves, but by the time he stood up for John Brown, he had become a confirmed abolitionist himself. In the 1840s he still opposed war both in theory and practice. Yet when the Civil War came, he welcomed it. The thing that distinguished him was a matter of degree: he demonstrated, far more than most men, that his actions resulted from a consistent application of his personal philosophy.

The Transcendentalist

Thoreau was, so to speak, a working transcendentalist. He applied the rather vague philosophy of transcendentalism in a concrete and individual way. Transcendentalists believed in principles higher than the mundane ones that actuated the general run of Americans. Thoreau put his personal stamp on those higher principles and trans-lated them into action. For example, when a neighbor wanted to hire him to build a wall, Thoreau asked himself whether this was the best way to use his time and decided it was much better to walk in the woods. Transcendentalists esteemed nature, both as symbol and actuality. Thoreau made Mother Nature into something like a deity, and he spent more time in the world of nature than any other transcendentalist.

As he grew into middle age, Thoreau inevitably made a few concessions. He had to take over the little family business after his father died, since there was no one else to do it. He did some surveying. He became more of a botanist and less of a transcendentalist; his later journal shows fewer references to philosophy and more descriptions of flora and fauna. He also had to make concessions to age itself. His spells of illness increased during the 1850s. By December 1861 he no longer left the Thoreau house; by the next spring he could hardly talk above a whisper. He died of consumption on May 6, 1862. In spite of the contentiousness of his life, his end was peaceful. "Never saw a man dying with so much pleasure and peace," one of his townsmen observed.

Emerson's Assessment

The best analysis of Thoreau's character was Emerson's funeral elegy for him. Emerson was well aware of Thoreau's devotion to his principles and said that he "had a perfect probity." Emerson also realized, perhaps better than anyone else, that Thoreau gave an edge to his probity by his willingness to say no, to dispute, to deny. Thoreau was a born protestant: that was Emerson's way of putting it. He went on to observe that Thoreau had "interrogated every custom, and wished to settle all his practice on an ideal foundation."

Emerson characterized Thoreau as a hermit and stoic but added that he had a softer side which showed especially when he was with young people he liked. Furthermore, Thoreau was resourceful and ingenious; he had to be, to live the life he wanted. He was patient and tenacious, as a man had to be to get the most out of nature. He could have been a notable leader, given all those qualities, but, Emerson remarked sadly, Thoreau chose instead to be merely the captain of a huckleberry party. Nevertheless, Thoreau was a remarkable man, and Emerson gave him the highest possible praise by calling him wise. "His soul," said Emerson in conclusion, "was made for the noblest society."

Further Reading

The best biography of Thoreau is Walter Harding, *The Days of Henry Thoreau* (1965). It can be supplemented by *The Correspondence of Henry David Thoreau* (1958), edited by Harding and Carl Bode. The only book devoted exclusively to Walden is a good one: Charles R. Anderson, *The Magic Circle of Walden* (1968), which analyzes Thoreau's classic purely as literature. On Thoreau's writing in general there is a fine book by Sherman Paul, *The Shores of America: Thoreau's Inward Exploration* (1958). Thoreau's writing is seen in its literary context in Francis O. Matthiessen's remarkable study of the American literary impulse in the middle of the 19th century, *American Renaissance* (1941; repr. 1968). □

Maurice Thorez

Maurice Thorez (1900-1964) headed the French Communist Party from 1930 to 1964, developing a large working-class Marxist-Leninist party and fostering a close link between the French Communists and the Soviet Union.

Maurice Thorez was born into a poor coal-mining family on April 28, 1900, in Noyelles-Godault in the northern coastal department (state) of Pasde-Calais. At the age of 12 he himself became a miner. During World War I when his village was occupied by the Germans, Thorez was sent to his grandfather's farm in the Creuse. Following the war he returned to Pas-de-Calais, where he joined the Socialist Party (SFIO) in 1919. Although he was largely self-taught, he had a propensity for learning; during the course of his life he acquired a knowledge of Latin, Russian, and German.

In 1920 two important events occurred in Thorez's life; one was his induction into the army and the other was the socialist congress at Tours. While the army required two years of service from Thorez, the decision made at Tours shaped the remainder of his life and the life of the French left. Following the Bolshevik Revolution in Russia and Lenin's call in 1919 for the formation of Communist parties around the world and the creation of a Communist International, the French Socialist Party met at Tours and split into two factions. While a minority of delegates decided to remain with the old socialist SFIO, the majority formed the French Communist Party (PCF). Thorez sided with the majority, and from that point on played a key role in the construction of a militant Marxist-Leninist party in France, which Thorez once proclaimed to be "not a party like the others."

Aided by his jovial and outgoing personality, Thorez rose rapidly in the hierarchy of the PCF, becoming a party secretary in 1923. At the 1924 PCF congress in Lyons he was elected to the party's organizing committee and shortly thereafter was sent to the Soviet Union to meet Joseph Stalin for the first time. Then in 1930 Thorez was elected secretary general of the PCF, a post he held until his death. In 1932 he was elected as a deputy to the French National Assembly; he was reelected in 1936.

The rise of fascism in Germany in the 1930s encouraged Thorez to help lay the foundations for an anti-fascist popular front, an alliance between the Communists, socialists, and radical socialists in France. After winning the 1936 elections, the Popular Front enacted a number of social and economic reforms, such as a 40-hour work week and the nationalization of key industries.

On the eve of World War II Thorez and the PCF supported the Nazi-Soviet Non-Aggression Pact of 1939 and made an appeal to people not to fight in an "imperialist war." When the war broke out he was drafted into the army, but soon fled the country to spend the war years in Moscow. After the fall of France the caretaker Vichy government tried

him *in absentia* and revoked his citizenship. In the Soviet Union Thorez supposedly spent his exile helping organize the European resistance movement against Hitler.

At the end of World War II Thorez returned to France and his citizenship was restored. Moreover, he was again reelected to the National Assembly. In the immediate postwar years he held an appointment as a minister-without-portfolio and from 1946 to 1947 he served as vice-premier.

With the onset of the Cold War, Thorez and four other Communist members of the Ramadier cabinet were ousted from government in 1947, thereby ending the PCF's collaboration with post-war governments, except for a brief period between 1981 and 1984. Thorez's statement that "the French people will never ever fight against the Soviet Union" exemplified PCF rhetoric during the Cold War.

Out of government and now in the opposition, the PCF encouraged strikes in a number of key industries. Under Thorez's leadership the PCF grew in political strength (with more than 900,000 members in December of 1947), becoming the second largest Communist party in Western Europe, behind Italy.

Beginning in 1950 poor health began to plague Thorez; in this year he suffered a cerebral hemorrhage. From 1950 to 1953 he resided in Moscow, where he attempted to convalesce. (During his absence, Jacques Duclos filled Thorez's post in Paris.) When he returned to France in 1953 he once again assumed the leadership of the PCF, but relied heavily on his wife, Jeannette Vermeersch, who was also a Communist deputy in the National Assembly and a member of the Central Committee of the PCF.

Throughout the late 1940s and the 1950s the PCF remained in political isolation in France and maintained close allegiance to Moscow. In 1956, for instance, the French Communists backed the Soviet suppression of the revolt in Hungary. Domestic events in France and new leadership in the Soviet Union would eventually force the PCF to make a zig-zag in policy and adopt once again a popular front strategy at home.

When General Charles de Gaulle returned to power in 1958 with the founding of the Fifth Republic, the representation of the PCF in the National Assembly plummeted to ten deputies. Thorez, however, was one of those reelected to the Assembly. The reemergence of de Gaulle in France, coupled with the rise of Nikita Khrushchev in the Soviet Union and his de-Stalinized policy of "peaceful-coexistence" with the West, renewed interest within the PCF in pursuing a popular front electoral alliance of leftist parties in France. Yet, on July 11, 1964, before such a strategy would be employed in the 1965 presidential elections, Thorez died on a Soviet vessel destined for Yalta.

Thorez's publications include: *Fils du peuple* (1937, *Son of the People*); *Une Politique de grandeur française* (1945, *Politics of French Greatness*); and *Oeuvres,* 23 volumes (1950-1965, *Works*).

Further Reading

In English, accounts of Thorez's life and political career can be found in the following works: Annie Kriegel, *The French Communists* (1972); Ronald Tiersky, *French Communism* (1974); and Irwin Wall, *French Communism in the Era of Stalin* (1983). In French, a solid critical study of Thorez is Philippe Robrieux's *Maurice Thorez: vie secrète et vie publique* (1975, His Private Life and Public Life). □

Gaston Thorn

Gaston Thorn (born 1928) was prime minister of Luxembourg and former president (1981-1985) of the former Commission of the European Communities. His commitment to European unity proved valuable at a time when the community was plagued by increased nationalism and severe economic problems.

Gaston Thorn was born in Luxembourg on September 3, 1928. He was brought up in France where his father, Edouard Thorn, was a railway engineer, but the family returned to the Grand Duchy at the outbreak of World War II. His father, a committed Liberal, was arrested for resisting Hitler's "Germanization" of Luxembourg. In 1943 the 15-year-old Thorn also spent some months in a Nazi "correction camp" for having organized a student protest at his school against compulsory antiaircraft drills and the enforced recruitment of Luxembourg citizens into the German army.

At the end of the war he studied law at the universities of Montpellier, Lausanne, and Paris and was later admitted to the Luxembourg bar. He played a prominent role in student politics and was elected president of the World Conference of Students.

In 1957 Thorn married Liliane Petit, a professional journalist and together they produced a son. In 1959 he became a Member of Parliament. In the same year he was also elected to the European Parliament, in which he was to remain a member for the next ten years. He served as chairman of the Parliament's Committee on African Affairs and soon became known as "Gaston The African." In 1961, he was elected the chairman of the Democratic (Liberal) Party of Luxembourg.

In 1969 Thorn was appointed minister of foreign affairs, civil service, and sports in the Christian Social-Liberal coalition led by Pierre Werner. A strong believer in the European Community and an avowed Federalist, he took an active part in the activities of the Community and served as chairman of the EEC's Council of Ministers four times in ten years. He gained an unrivalled knowledge of the Community's institutions and a reputation for being able to deal with essential issues without becoming entangled in details. During this period his wife, who continued her career as a journalist, often had professional "exchanges" with him. It was quite common for her to be entertaining an official

guest with her husband at one moment and asking him questions at a press conference the next. On one occasion during the oil crisis in the early 1970s she criticized the foreign ministers of the EEC (of whom her husband was one) for what she felt was a pro-Arab policy and for failing to stand up to the Arab oil producing countries.

Thorn swept to power in the general elections held in Luxembourg on May 26, 1974. He became prime minister and headed a Liberal-Socialist coalition after receiving the highest total personal vote ever recorded in the nation's history. The victory of his Liberal (Democratic) Party has been aptly described as a "revolution," as it was the first time the Christian Social Party had been defeated in 75 years. It also ended the 15-year tenure of Pierre Werner as the nation's leader and ushered in a new breed of younger politicians. Thorn became the pre-eminent symbol of this new breed—modern and pragmatic. He recognized the vital role of the media in politics and used it with great skill.

While he was prime minister, Thorn continued to serve as foreign minister. Luxembourg under his leadership maintained a neutral stance on many sensitive world issues such as the Arab-Israeli conflict and in conflicts between the members of the European Community, particularly the "Atlanticist" and "Europeanist" groups. An advocate of closer cooperation between the United States and Europe, he was also very much aware of the importance of inter-European cooperation and said that it was necessary to "break out of the dilemma that one is regarded as a bad European if one is for the Alliance, and as an unreliable member of the Alliance if one is for European unity."

Thorn served as president of the 30th session of the United Nations General Assembly from 1975 to 1976. He was noted for his ability to reach compromises, and his style was one of discussion and conciliation instead of confrontation.

In the Luxembourg national elections held in June 1979, there was a successful resurgence of support for the opposition Christian Social Party. Once more, Pierre Werner became head of a Christian Social-Democratic coalition government. Thorn was appointed deputy prime minister and continued to serve as foreign minister as well as having four additional portfolios: foreign trade, economic affairs, middle classes, and justice. He was also elected to the European Parliament, but had to resign his seat in order to take up his national ministerial appointments.

At the Venice session of the European Council in June 1980 Thorn was nominated, with almost complete unanimity, to succeed Roy Jenkins of the United Kingdom as president of the commission of the European Communities. The only country that opposed his appointment was France, which had reservations about his reputation as a federalist and his commitment to greater supra-national powers for the Community. Nevertheless, his nomination was confirmed and he served as president from 1981 into early 1985. Later in 1985 and back in the private sector, Thorn became president of Banque Internationale in Luxembourg; in 1987 he became president and Director General of RTL, Luxembourg.

Thorn sought to achieve greater economic, monetary, and political union among the members of the Community during his tenure as president. His experience of running a coalition government proved crucial in reconciling the often divergent and conflicting interests of the members of the Community.

Thorn received numerous awards and decorations, including the Grand Cross of Légion d'Honneur of France.

Further Reading

No biography has yet been written of Gaston Thorn. He is listed in *International Who's Who* (1984 and 1997) and in *Who's Who* (1985). □

Edward Lee Thorndike

The American psychologist and educator Edward Lee Thorndike (1874-1949) was the originator of modern educational psychology and influenced 20th-century American education immeasurably.

Edward Lee Thorndike was born on Aug. 31, 1874, in Williamsburg, Mass., a minister's son. Before he entered Wesleyan University in 1891, his family had moved eight times within New England. Although this experience caused him to become self-reliant, it also left him reserved and shy; the lonely boy grew into a man happiest when alone with his work.

Thorndike was inspired by the psychological writings of William James, and after graduation from Wesleyan, Thorndike entered Harvard University to study under James. James let Thorndike perform learning experiments with animals in his own basement. Thorndike continued these experiments at Columbia University and published his results as *Animal Intelligence* (1898), his doctoral thesis. Thus, he reported the first carefully controlled experiments in comparative animal psychology. To study animal behavior scientifically, Thorndike invented the problem box and maze, techniques later adopted by other psychologists.

While teaching psychology to prospective teachers at Western Reserve University, Thorndike was attracted to human learning and to psychology's potential usefulness to education. He transferred to Teachers College, Columbia University, in 1899, where he introduced courses in educational psychology, tests and measurements, and the psychology of school subjects. In 1921 he became director of Teachers College's new Institute of Educational Research; he retired in 1940. He died on Aug. 9, 1949, in Montrose, N.Y.

Many of Thorndike's writings, including *Notes on Child Study* (1901), *Principles of Teaching* (1906), *Education: A First Book* (1912), and *The Psychology of Arithmetic* (1922), dealt with both practical school problems and issues underlying education. Thus, he investigated and wrote about the probable causes of differences in intellectual abilities, how habits are formed, the positive effects of practice,

pears in Merle E. Curti, *The Social Ideas of American Educators* (1935; rev. ed. 1966), and a more favorable interpretation in Lawrence A. Cremin, *The Transformation of the School: Progressivism in American Education, 1876-1957* (1961). For additional background on the development of psychology and education during Thorndike's lifetime see Joseph Peterson, *Early Conceptions and Tests of Intelligence* (1925); Ernest R. Hilgard, *Theories of Learning* (1948; new ed. 1966); and Willis Rudy, *Schools in an Age of Mass Culture* (1965). □

Jim Thorpe

American track star and professional football and baseball player Jim Thorpe (1888-1953) was the hero of the 1912 Olympic Games in Stockholm, only to have his gold medals taken from him for professionalism.

James Francis Thorpe (Native American name, Wa-tho-huck or Bright Path) was born south of Bellemonta, near Prague, Oklahoma, on May 28, 1888, the son of Hiran P. Thorpe of Irish and Sac and Fox Indian extraction and Charlotte View of Potowatomi and Kickapoo extraction. Raised with a twin brother, Charlie, on a farm, Thorpe first attended the Sac and Fox Indian Agency school near Tecumseh, Oklahoma, before being sent to the Haskell Indian School near Lawrence, Kansas, in 1898.

When Thorpe was 16 he was recruited to attend a vocational school for Native Americans, the Carlisle Indian School in Pennsylvania. His track potential was evident in 1907 when he cleared the high jump bar at 5' 9'' while dressed in street clothes. Glenn S. "Pop" Warner, the school's legendary track and football coach, then asked him out for the track team.

That fall Thorpe made the varsity football team, playing some and starting the next year at half-back. The Carlisle Indians played many of the best collegiate teams, even before Thorpe often beating such teams as Chicago, Harvard, Minnesota, Nebraska, Penn, Penn State, Pittsburgh, and Syracuse. Thorpe was given third team All-American status by Walter Camp in 1908.

Following the spring of 1909, when he starred in track, Thorpe left the Carlisle school with two other students to go to North Carolina where they played baseball at Rocky Mount in the Eastern Carolina Association. Thorpe pitched and played first base for what he said was $15 per week. The next year he played for Fayetteville, winning 10 games and losing 10 games pitching and batting .236. These two years of paid performances in minor league baseball would later tarnish his 1912 amateur Olympic status.

For two years Thorpe had a rather aimless life while not playing baseball, drifting from village to village in Oklahoma before a former teammate at Carlisle asked him to return to school. He did so in the fall of 1911. Thorpe had matured to almost six feet in height and 185 pounds and led Carlisle to outstanding football seasons in 1911 and 1912. In 1911, against Harvard's undefeated team under the re-

learning by rewards, the value of studying one subject for learning another, the arrangement of skills, and the effects upon students of tiredness and time of day.

Thorndike's belief in applied psychology prompted the *Thorndike Arithmetics* (1917), *Thorndike-Century Junior and Senior Dictionaries* (1935, 1941), and *The Teacher's Word Books* (1921, 1931). To satisfy education's desires for precise measures of students' aptitudes and achievements, Thorndike constructed numerous scales and tests. Beginning with scales rating handwriting (1910), English composition (1911), and drawing (1913), personnel selection tests for business, and psychological scaling for the U.S. Army during World War I, Thorndike next authored intelligence tests, college admissions tests, and an examination for law school students.

As a scientist, Thorndike sought to develop a cohesive theory of human behavior. He elaborated his stimulus-response psychology in such works as *The Human Nature Club* (1900), *The Elements of Psychology* (1905), *The Fundamentals of Learning* (1932), *Human Nature and the Social Order* (1940), and, especially, his three-volume classic, *Educational Psychology* (1913, 1914).

Further Reading

A brief collection of Thorndike's writings, including his autobiography, is included in Geraldine M. Jonçich, ed., *Psychology and the Science of Education: Selected Writings* (1962). Jonçich's *The Sane Positivist: A Biography of Edward L. Thorndike* (1968) is a biographical history of Thorndike's life, times, and work. A critical account of his contributions ap-

nowned coach Percy Houghton, Thorpe kicked four field goals, two over 40 yards, en route to a stunning 18-15 victory. Carlisle lost only two games in 1911 and 1912, splitting with Penn and Syracuse, while conquering such teams as Army, Georgetown, Harvard, and Pittsburgh. In his last year he scored 25 touchdowns and 198 points and was named All-American by Walter Camp for the second consecutive year.

Star of the 1912 Olympics

During the summer of 1912, before his last year at Carlisle, Thorpe was chosen to represent America at the Stockholm Olympics in the decathlon and the pentathlon. He was an easy victor in the pentathlon, winning four of the five events (broad jump, 200 meter dash, discus, and 1,500 meter race), losing only the javelin. In the decathlon Thorpe set an Olympic mark of 8,413 points that would stand for two decades. King Gustav of Sweden addressed Thorpe as the "greatest athlete in the world" and presented him with several gifts, including one from Czar Nicholas of Russia—a silver, 30-pound likeness of a Viking ship, lined with gold and containing precious jewels.

The gold medal ceremony for the decathlon, Thorpe said, was the proudest moment of his life. A half-year later charges against Thorpe for professionalism led to a confession by Thorpe that he had been paid to play baseball in North Carolina in 1909 and 1910. (Actually, Thorpe had been paid cash by coach "Pop" Warner as an athlete at Carlisle before that.) Shortly thereafter the Amateur Athletic Union and the American Olympic Committee declared

Thorpe a professional and asked Thorpe to return the medals won at the Olympics and erased his name from the record books. Thorpe's plea to the A.A.U. that "I did not know that I was doing wrong because I was doing what I knew several other college men had done . . ." went for naught.

Thorpe, a great athlete but not a great baseball player, almost immediately signed a large $6,000 per year, three year contract with the New York Giants, managed by John J. McGraw, principally as a gate attraction. His six year major league career resulted in a .252 batting average with three teams: New York, Cincinnati Reds, and Boston Braves. He batted .327 in 1919, his last year in the majors.

Thorpe signed to play professional football in 1915 with the Canton Bulldogs for the "enormous" sum of $250 a game. Attendance at Canton immediately quintupled, and Thorpe led Canton to several championships over its chief contender, the Massilon Tigers. In 1920 he was appointed president of the American Professional Football Association, forerunner of the National Football League. Thorpe was the chief drawing power in professional football until Red Grange entered the game in 1925. Following his play at Canton, Thorpe played for the Oorang Indians, Cleveland Indians, Rock Island Independents, and several other teams before bowing out at age 41 with the Chicago Cardinals in 1929.

Out of sports, Thorpe was not as successful. With the coming of the Depression Thorpe did bit parts in Hollywood movies, was a day laborer in Los Angeles, and had a ghost-written book published at the time of the 1932 Los Angeles Olympics, *Jim Thorpe's History of the Olympics*. He continued through the 1930s with rather insignificant movie parts, and he was asked regularly to give lectures on his athletic career. He joined the Merchant Marines late in World War II. Following the war he became a member of the recreation staff of the Chicago Park District in 1948.

The Campaign To Restore His Medals

Honors for past athletic achievements kept coming to Thorpe. At mid-century the Associated Press polled sportswriters and broadcasters to determine the greatest football player and most outstanding male athlete of the first half of the 20th century. Thorpe outdistanced Red Grange and Bronko Nagurski for the former and led Babe Ruth and Jack Dempsey for the latter, being paired with Babe Didrikson Zaharias, the outstanding female athlete.

This recognition, however, did not influence the U.S. Olympic Committee to help restore his Olympic medals. There had been an attempt in 1943 by the Oklahoma legislature to get the A.A.U. to reinstate Thorpe as an amateur. Thirty years later the A.A.U. did restore his amateur status. In 1952, shortly before his death, there was an attempt by Congressman Frank Bow of Canton, Ohio, to get Avery Brundage, president of the U.S. Olympic Committee (U.S.O.C.) to use his good offices to restore Thorpe's medals to him. This failed. Following Brundage's death in 1975, the U.S.O.C. requested the International Olympic Committee to restore Thorpe's medals, but it was turned down. Not until 1982, when U.S.O.C. president William E. Simon met with the International Olympic Committee president Juan Samaranch, was the action finally taken.

Outside of athletics, Thorpe's life had much more tragedy than two gold medal losses. His twin brother, Charlie, died when he was nine years old. His mother died of blood poisoning before he was a teenager. Four years later, shortly after Thorpe entered Carlisle, his father died. Following his marriage to Iva Miller (1913), their first son died at the age of four from polio. Twice divorced, he had one boy and three girls of his first marriage and four boys from his second marriage in 1926 to Freeda Kirkpatrick. His third marriage was to Patricia Askew in 1945. Thorpe's wanderlust and heavy drinking contributed to marital tensions, and he never successfully adjusted to life's routines outside of athletics. His place in sport history, though, was established well before he died of a heart attack in Lomita, California, at the age of 64 on March 28, 1953.

Further Reading

The most thorough biography of Thorpe is Robert W. Wheeler, *Jim Thorpe: World's Greatest Athlete* (1979), the author being a key figure in restoring Thorpe's medals. Jack McCallum, "The Regilding of a Legend," *Sports Illustrated* (October 25, 1982), examines the gold medal controversy. The numerous studies about Thorpe include Wilbur J. Gorbrecht, *Jim Thorpe, Carlisle Indian* (1969); Robert L. Whitman, *Jim Thorpe and the Oorang Indians* (1984); Guernsey Van Riper, *Jim Thorpe, Olympic Champion* (1981); Jack Newcombe, *The Best of the Athletic Boys: The White Man's impact on Jim Thorpe* (1975); and Gene Schoor and H. Gilfond, *The Jim Thorpe Story* (1951). □

doubt that he was a product of the Sophistic movement. He was well acquainted with his predecessors in the field of Greek history, and he is said to have burst into tears when he listened to Herodotus recite his *History*.

Thucydides caught the plague during the epidemic of 430-427 and was among the lucky few who recovered. In 424 he was one of the Athenian generals operating in the Chalcidice during the Peloponnesian War (431-404). Through a miscarriage of planning, Amphipolis was captured by the Spartan general Brasidas, the greatest general of the war. Having failed to relieve Amphipolis, Thucydides was exiled for 20 years. It is said that the demagogue Cleon was instrumental in bringing about his exile. Thucydides spent his exile on family estates in Thrace. This enforced leisure gave him the time to observe critically the course of the war. It is considered certain that he returned to Athens after the war. He apparently lived there, utterly forgotten, until his death sometime toward the beginning of the 4th century.

Thucydides writes of himself in the third person in his *History*. He relates that he was a general at the age of 30 (4. 104); indicated that he was of the age of discretion during the entire war (5.26.5); expresses his pride as a soldier and his devotion to Pericles (2.31); defends the generals at Megara (4.73.4); reveals that he owns property in the mining district in Thrace (4.105.1); and relates the fact of his exile and the circumstances surrounding it (5.26).

Thucydides

The Greek historian Thucydides (ca. 460-ca. 401 B.C.) wrote on the Peloponnesian War. The greatest ancient historian, he is in a real sense the creator of modern historiography.

Little is known about the life of Thucydides Most modern scholars place his birth between 460 and 450 B.C., with a preference for the earlier date. Thucydides was from the deme of Halimus and was the son of Olorus and Hegesipyle. He is thus to be distinguished from a contemporary of the same name, the son of Melesias, who led the opposition party against Pericles. The historian's family was wealthy from the possession of gold mines in Scapte Hyle on the Thracian coast opposite Thasos. Thucydides may have been related to a Thracian prince whose daughter married the famous Athenian general Miltiades and became the mother of the general and statesman Cimon. The grave of Thucydides was located near that of Cimon in a place named Koile, southwest of the Athenian Acropolis, where Plutarch saw it.

About Thucydides's education we know practically nothing. He is reported to have studied oratory under Antiphon and philosophy under Anaxagoras. There is little

His Work

The only extant work by Thucydides is the incomplete *History of the Peloponnesian War* in eight books. The *History* practically covers the major portion of the Peloponnesian War: the First Phase (431-420 B.C.)—the Archidamian War; the Second Phase (415-413)—the Sicilian Expedition; and the Third Phase (413-404)—the Ionian, or Decelean, War. He apparently did not live to complete the final section. The text of Thucydides has come down emended by editors, and it is difficult and oftentimes obscure. It is important to note that no Attic prose was taught prior to Thucydides, so he had to create a prose style of his own.

Thucydides is the first historian in the modern sense—that is, he strives for accuracy and impartiality. His accounts of military campaigns and battles show this and point up the fact that he himself was an experienced military man. He reveals a reluctance to accept unsupported statements, and he carefully weighs and sifts the statements of others. He consulted actual documents and even inserted them into his text. This scholarship and meticulousness were obviously a result of Sophistic influence and training.

Thucydides had been familiar with the work of his predecessors in Greek historiography, though nowhere does he mention anyone by name except for Hellanicus of Mitylene, and he criticizes Mitylene severely for his lack of chronological exactitude in his account of the period between the Persian and the Peloponnesian wars. Of his predecessors in general, Thucydides was highly critical because they accepted traditions without validating the veracity of them (1.20) and because they were too willing to please rather than be critical (1.21). Also, he pointed out that his predecessors did not exclude myths from their histories (1.22.4).

Although Thucydides at no time mentions his great predecessor Herodotus by name, he does correct a number of passages in Herodotus's *History;* for example, 1.126.7 is an expanded and corrected version of Herodotus 5.71; 1.1.20 clarifies Herodotus 9.53; and the socalled *Pentecontaetia* (1.89) commences where Herodotus left off. The famous Thucydidean remark that he intended his work to be a possession forever seems to echo Herodotus's opening remarks about the Persian War.

Thucydides is responsible for making history much more comprehensive than it had ever been. The chain of cause and effect was elaborately worked out. Thucydides is no mere writer of history; he is a philosopher of history. There are no divine or supernatural forces at work in his *History.* All phenomena are explained in human terms, in terms of cold political power. Power politics and the inhumanity of man to man are devastatingly observed by Thucydides as the real factors of history. Real issues and causes are never avoided.

There is a philosophic strain in the *History,* but there is a patriotic one as well. Thucydides remembered and admired the greatness of Pericles and the Athens with which he is so closely and so gloriously associated to the end. Even though he tried to be impartial, Thucydides believed Athens would be triumphant in the end, but he was fair to Sparta and careful to point out the inadequacies and deficiencies of Athens.

In addition to narrative, which he employs with great facility and clarity, Thucydides dramatizes history through speeches put directly in the mouths of those who need never have spoken them. These speeches are rhetorical devices, fictional in presentation but factual in their content. Each speech is the kind of thing the particular speaker would probably have said. The speeches show Thucydides's amazing use of antithesis and the antithetical technique, which, though undoubtedly inherited from the Sophists, was greatly developed by Thucydides himself. The whole *History* is a study in antithesis. Thucydides himself does not conceal the fact that the speeches are merely literary devices, with his own best literary efforts concentrated there. He even personified different peoples by differing speech. Fine rhetoric, striking phrases, nice distinctions in meaning, and wonderful periodic sentences (again showing Sophistic training and influence) characterize his speeches.

Though recent scholarship has looked at Thucydides with a good deal of critical acumen and has delighted in being able to correct him in some details, he still ranks as one of the greatest historians of all time. He introduced to history the objective, critical approach which generations of historians followed. He was ahead of his time not only in methodology but also in his interest and emphasis on the development and exposition of a philosophy of history.

Further Reading

Modern works on Thucydides are plentiful and of high quality. The following should be consulted: F. M. Cornford, *Thucydides Mythistoricus* (1907); J. B. Bury, *The Ancient Historians* (1909); G. B. Grundy, *Thucydides and the History of His Age* (1911); W. R. M. Lamb, *Clio Enthroned* (1914); C. F. Abbott, *Thucydides: A Study in Historical Reality* (1925); B. W. Henderson, *The Great War between Athens and Sparta* (1927); C. N. Cochrane, *Thucydides and the Science of History* (1929); A. W. Gomme, *Essays in Greek History and Literature* (1937); and John H. Finley, Jr., *Thucydides* (1942). In addition, Finley's *Three Essays on Thucydides* (1967) is important for seeing the unity of the *History* and the fact that Thucydides wrote from personal knowledge of the full 27 years of the Peloponnesian War.

H.D. Westlake, *Individuals in Thucydides* (1968), is an outstanding study of the leading individuals in the *History,* and his *Essays on the Greek Historians and Greek History* (1969) deals primarily with specialized topics in Thucydides. A very exciting book is A. Geoffrey Woodhead, *Thucydides on the Nature of Power* (1970). It demonstrates that Thucydides's interpretation of power is relevant to modern discussions of power politics. □

Harry Thuku

Harry Thuku (1895-1970), Kenyan politician, was one of the pioneers in the development of modern African nationalism in Kenya.

Harry Thuku was born in the Kambui district of Kenya; he traced his descent from one of the most influential Kibuyu families of the region. He spent 4 years at the school of the Kambui Gospel Mission, and in 1911 he received a 2-year prison sentence for forging a check. Next Thuku became a typesetter for the *Leader,* a European settler newspaper. In 1918 he became a clerk-telegraph operator in the government treasury office in Nairobi. All this experience had made Thuku one of the first of Kenya's Africans to be fully capable of working in the English language.

At this time the first African organizations were being formed to defend African interests against the European rulers of Kenya. One of the first, the Kikuyu Association, was a nonmilitant group with ties to the government and missions; its main concern was the preservation of African-owned land. During 1920-1921 Thuku served as its secretary. He was interested, however, in more forceful action to deal with other problems facing Kenya's Africans, and in 1921 he left the Kikuyu Association when it did not respond as he wished to new European pressures. Kenya then was suffering from economic difficulties, and the organized Europeans wanted to cut African wages to revive the colony's economic position.

Thuku was one of the founders of the East African Association (1921), Nairobi's first modern political organization. It drew members from many tribal groups, but because of its location most of the members were Kikuyu. Thuku played an important role because of his education and government position. The Kenyan government opposed the association's aims since the settler-dominated colony was not yet ready for any forceful presentation of African views. But Thuku and his colleagues continued to work and to gain support among Kenya's educated Africans. This success led to Thuku's arrest in 1922. This event was met by an intensive African protest which resulted in a demonstration culminating in violence. Thuku was then deported to remote Kismayu.

The East African Association then declined, but those interested in African rights remained active. Thuku remained in their thoughts as a primary leader. He was released in 1931; in 1932 he became president of the Kikuyu Central Association, then Kenya's foremost African political group. But dissension arose among the leaders of the association, and the organization split into factions, with Thuku eventually founding his own group, the Kikuyu Provincial Association, devoted to legal, nonmilitant protest. This turn to moderation caused a permanent split between Thuku and the rising generation of the future leaders of Kenya. From this period on Thuku played no important role in the evolution of African nationalism within his country.

Further Reading

The best account of Thuku and his times is Carl G. Rosberg, Jr., and John Nottingham, *The Myth of "Mau Mau": Nationalism in Kenya* (1966). Other useful sources are George Bennett, *Kenya: A Political History* (1963), and B. A. Ogot and J. A. Kieran, eds., *Zamani: A Survey of East African History* (1968). □

James Grove Thurber

James Grove Thurber (1894-1961) was an American writer and artist. One of the most popular humorists of his time, Thurber celebrated in stories and in cartoons the comic frustrations of eccentric and statureless people.

Born in Columbus, Ohio, James Thurber attended Ohio State University—though he never took a degree—and worked for some years in Ohio as a journalist. He moved to New York in 1926. In 1927 he met writer E. B. White and was taken onto the staff of the *New Yorker* magazine. In collaboration with White he produced his first book, *Is Sex Necessary?* (1929). By 1931 his first cartoons began appearing in the *New Yorker* seals, sea lions, strange tigers, harried men, determined women, and, most of all, dogs. Thurber's dogs became something like a national comic institution, and they dotted the pages of a whole series of books. His book *The Seal in the Bedroom* appeared in 1932, followed in 1933 by *My Life and Hard Times.* He published *The Middle-aged Man on the Flying Trapeze* in 1935, and by 1937, when he published *Let Your Mind Alone!,* he had become so successful that he left his position on the *New Yorker* staff to free-lance and to travel abroad.

The Last Flower appeared in 1939; that year Thurber collaborated with White on a play, *The Male Animal.* The

play was a hit when it opened in 1940. But this was also the year that Thurber was forced to undergo a series of eye operations for cataract and trachoma. His eyesight grew steadily worse until, in 1951, it was so weak that he did his last drawing. He spent the last decade of his life in blindness.

The last 20 years of Thurber's life were filled with material and professional success in spite of his handicap. He published at least 14 more books, including *The Thurber Carnival* (1945), *Thurber Country* (1953), and the extremely popular account of the life of the *New Yorker* editor Harold Ross, *The Years with Ross* (1959). A number of his stories were made into movies, including "The Secret Life of Walter Mitty" (1947).

Thurber's comic world was peopled by his curious animals, who watched in resignation as predatory women ran to ground apparently spineless men. But beneath their docile exteriors, Thurber's men dreamed of wild escape and epic adventure and, so, in their way won out in the battle of the sexes.

Further Reading

Robert E. Morsberger, *James Thurber* (1964), is useful for biographical facts, and Richard C. Tobias discusses Thurber's literary significance in *The Art of James Thurber* (1969). See also Edwin T. Bowden, *James Thurber: A Bibliography* (1968). For background see Walter Blair, *Horse Sense in American Humor* (1942), and Malcolm Cowley, *The Literary Situation* (1954). □

James Strom Thurmond

Senator, lawyer, governor of South Carolina, and presidential nominee on the "Dixiecrat" ticket in 1948, James Strom Thurmond (born 1902) is a conservative politician who was first elected to the U.S. Senate in 1954.

Strom Thurmond was born on December 5, 1902, in Edgefield, South Carolina while Theodore Roosevelt was President. He attended schools there and upon graduating entered Clemson College, earning a B.S. degree in horticulture in 1923. For the next several years he taught high school near his boyhood home. He was elected to the Edgefield County Board of Education in 1924—the youngest member ever elected in South Carolina. During this same period, in addition to course work in psychology and other subjects, Thurmond enrolled in a correspondence course in law and passed the South Carolina bar in December 1930. Between 1929 and 1933, Thurmond served as superintendent of education for Edgefield County.

Political Career Begins in South Carolina

Thurmond was elected to the state senate from Edgefield County in 1933 and served until he became a circuit judge in the state in 1938. He was 35 at the time and

was the youngest circuit court judge in South Carolina. His service on the bench was interrupted during World War II, during which he served as a pilot with the 82nd Airborne Division in Europe and the Pacific, returning with numerous decorations and the rank of lieutenant colonel. He remained on the circuit court until 1946, when he resigned and announced his candidacy for governor. He won the election that year over ten other candidates.

Thurmond in the National Spotlight

In opposition to President Truman's civil rights plank in the Democratic Party platform, Southern Democrats, known as Dixiecrats, left the 1948 party convention in Philadelphia, Pennsylvania. They reconvened in Birmingham, Alabama, and nominated J. Strom Thurmond as their presidential candidate and Fielding L. Wright, governor of Mississippi, as their vice-presidential candidate. Thurmond and Wright carried four southern states (Alabama, Louisiana, Mississippi, and South Carolina) and, with one additional elector from Tennessee, received a total of 39 Electoral College votes. Thurmond's split from the Democratic Party was never completely repaired, and party affiliation was significant again in his later career.

Senatorial Career Begins

As the governor of South Carolina is limited to one term of four years, when his term expired, Thurmond opted to challenge the incumbent Democratic senator from South Carolina, Olin T. Johnston. In a tight primary race in 1950, he lost the election. He subsequently opened a law practice

in Aiken. In 1954 the senior senator from South Carolina, Burnet R. Mayfield, died, leaving the selection of his replacement to the State Democratic Committee. Overlooking Thurmond's strong showing against Johnston, the committee appointed a state senator to serve as Mayfield's replacement. Thurmond, at the encouragement of numerous individuals, decided to challenge the new appointee as a write-in candidate to succeed Mayfield. In a surprise election, Thurmond carried the state with 63 percent of the vote (and 37 of the 46 counties), again making political history as the first write-in candidate to win election as a United States senator.

As part of his election campaign, Thurmond stated he would resign if elected to the Senate so that the people of South Carolina could have a voice in electing its senatorial representative. In April 1956 Thurmond resigned his seat and stood for election in the Democratic primary, which he won without opposition. Thurmond was reelected to the Senate in 1960, 1966, 1972, 1978, 1984, 1990, and 1996. He challenged conventional wisdom by changing his political party (from Democratic to Republican) in 1964 to support the candidacy of Barry Goldwater for president of the United States. His 1966 election marked the first time since Reconstruction that a Southern Republican was elected to the Senate.

Surprisingly, Thurmond has faced little serious opposition in the elections in which he has participated, including the 1996 election. In a June 3, 1996 article in the *Fort Worth Star Telegram* his competitors, businessman Elliott Close and state Representative Harold Worley brought up the "age issue" indirectly, preferring to tell Thurmond that it was "time to come home." Thurmond shot back about his competiton's "lack of experience" and won with 53% of the vote. Ironically, Thurmond supports term limits. In a May 23, 1996 article in *The Seattle Times* he is quoted as saying, "It might be just as well for people to have a change in their congressman."

Age does seem to finally be taking its toll on a senator who prides himself on his physical prowess. A May 6, 1996 article in *Newsweek* reported that "the Senate is, in fact, Thurmond's nursing home." The report detailed the "special handling" and perks that were provided to keep Thurmond in office. In 1997, Thurmond passed two milestones when he became the longest serving senator in US history, surpassing the record of former Senator Carl Hayden of Arizona, and the oldest person to serve in Congress, surpassing Senator Theodore Green of Rhode Island. His election in 1996, at age 94, means that he will celebrate his 100th birthday while still in office. "I intend to serve out my term," said Thurmond in an interview with the *Los Angeles Times,* and that he feels "like a million dollars."

Career Controversy

The political career of Senator Thurmond is marked not only by its longevity; it is also noted for controversial opinions. Thurmond's presidential run on the Dixiecrat party ticket in 1948 and his term as governor were marked by segregationist policies. He holds a Senate record of 24 hours and 18 minutes of filibuster speaking to prevent a vote on

the 1957 Civil Rights Bill. In 1964, He was involved in a fistfight with Texas Senator Ralph Yarborough who tried to drag Thurmond to his committee seat to vote on Civil Rights legislation. In later years, Thurmond tried to deflect criticism by stating in an interview in the *Baltimore Sun:* "It was my duty [as Governor of South Carolina] to enforce segregation laws. After the laws changed, I changed." Thurmond was the first Senator to hire an African American for his staff and voted in favor of the Martin Luther King Jr. holiday. Despite this, he is still disliked by some African Americans. In 1996, Thurmond was one of three recipients of a lifetime contribution award from the National Association for Equal Opportunity in Higher Education (NAFEO), an organization comprised of presidents and ranking administrators of the nation's historic African American universities. When William Clay and Louis Stokes, two senior members of the Congressional Black Caucus found out that Thurmond was being honored, they refused to accept the award.

Committees and Chairmanships

Senator Thurmond served on the Armed Services, Appropriations, Banking and Currency, Commerce, Judiciary, and Veterans Affairs committees in the Senate and was the chair of the Judiciary Committee after the Republican Party became the majority party in 1981. When the Democrats captured the Senate in 1986, he became the ranking Republican on the Judiciary Committee. He also served as President Pro Tempore of the Senate from 1981-1987 and began another term in 1995. He was also chairman of the Senate Armed Services Committee.

Personal Information

Thurmond married for the first time at age 47 to one of his 21 year-old secretaries, Jean Crouch. In 1968, at age 66, eight years after his first wife's death from cancer, he married Nancy Moore, a 25 year-old former Miss South Carolina. They had four children before amicably separating in 1991.

Further Reading

A biography of Strom Thurmond was written by Alberta Lachicotte, *Rebel Senator* (1967). A chapter in Robert Sherrill, *Gothic Politics in the Deep South* (1968) is devoted to him. He has published *The Faith We Have Not Kept* (1968) and, with David Cartright, *Unions in the Military* (1977). Additional information is available on the World Wide Web (circa 1997) at http://www.senate.gov/member/sc/thurmond/general/direct.html and http://www.ricommunity.com/scenic/politics/thurmond.htm □

Louis Leon Thurstone

The American psychologist Louis Leon Thurstone (1887-1955) was universally heralded as the most renowned psychometrician of his time. He led the way in mental measurement and testing through quantitative methods.

Louis Leon Thurstone, whose original family name was Thünström, was born on May 29, 1887, in Chicago. He attended school in various places in the United States as well as in Stockholm. In high school, at Jamestown, N.Y., he experimented with musical composition; mastered three typewriter keyboards; wrote a letter, published by *Scientific American,* on a problem of diversion of water from Niagara Falls; invented a method of trisecting an angle; and developed a talent for sketching into a lifelong hobby of photography. At Cornell University, from which he received an engineering degree, Thurstone designed a patented motion picture projector that was later demonstrated in the laboratory of Thomas Edison, with whom Thurstone worked briefly as an assistant.

Thurstone's first teaching experience, in the College of Engineering at the University of Minnesota, stimulated his interest in the learning process and human abilities. Hence he pursued a doctorate in psychology (1917) at the University of Chicago, to which he returned in 1924 to found his first psychometric laboratory after a brief but productive period at the Carnegie Institute of Technology. Upon his retirement from the University of Chicago in 1952, he continued his work at the University of North Carolina, where what is now the L. L. Thurstone Psychometric Laboratory was established.

Thurstone's major books and monographs are *The Nature of Intelligence* (1924), *The Fundamentals of Statistics* (1925), *The Measurement of Attitude* (1929, coauthored with E. J. Chave), *The Reliability and Validity of Tests* (1931), *The Vectors of Mind* (1935), *Primary Mental Abilities* (1938), *Factorial Studies of Intelligence* (1941, coauthored with his wife, Thelma Gwinn Thurstone), *A Factorial Study of Perception* (1944), and *Multiple-factor Analysis* (1947). A collection of important papers, all provocative contributions, is contained in *The Measurement of Values* (1959). In 1936 he and his followers founded the Psychometric Society and a journal, *Psyckometrika,* to promote the development of psychology as a quantitative rational science.

The most notable work by Thurstone was in the areas of test theory, psychological scaling, attitude measurement, and multiple-factor analysis—a set of techniques now applicable well beyond the realm of psychology. Yet he tackled many problems in psychological measurement and seems never to have failed to bring them nearer to solution. His great attraction for students and their creative work, even to the second and third generations, are already legendary. On Sept. 29, 1955, Thurstone, died in Chapel Hill, N. C.

Further Reading

Biographies of Thurstone are J. P. Guilford, *Louis Leon Thurstone, 1887-1955* (1957), and Dorothy A. Wood, *Louis Leon Thurstone* (1962). ☐

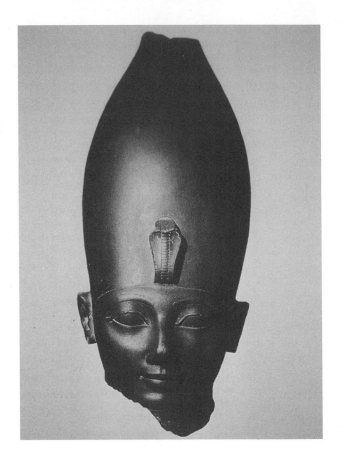

Thutmose III

The Egyptian king Thutmose III (1504-1450 B.C.) reestablished Egyptian rule in Palestine and Syria and set the empire on a firm foundation for almost a century.

The son of Thutmose II by a concubine named Ese (Isis), Thutmose III succeeded to the throne on the death of his father but was for many years kept in the background by his aunt Queen Hatshepsut. However, he later counted his reign from the beginning of his partnership with Hatshepsut and by Year Twenty he was depicted as on a level of equality with his aunt, whom he presumably supplanted in that year or very soon after.

During the period of Hatshepsut's dominance the petty rulers of Palestine and Syria had taken the opportunity to cast off the Egyptian yoke imposed upon them by Thutmose I. In a series of brilliant campaigns extending from his twenty-second year onward, Thutmose III reestablished Egyptian control in these areas. Almost every year for 20 years, he led campaigns into western Asia.

The records of these expeditions were inscribed on the walls of the temple of Karnak in recognition of the fact that the victories had been granted by the god Amon Ra. The first campaign, in which the city of Megiddo, the focal point of Asiatic resistance in Palestine, was captured, is related in considerable detail. Although records of subsequent campaigns may have been equally fully recorded, the details in the texts have been greatly condensed, and the accounts show more interest in the booty or tribute acquired. They do, however, shed occasional light on the conduct of the operations and the policy adopted by Thutmose in administering the subjugated territories. Of particular interest is his practice not only of installing rulers on whose loyalty he could depend, but also of ensuring their continued loyalty by taking to Egypt as hostages their children or brothers.

In addition to the "Annals" at Karnak, references to Thutmose's Asiatic campaigns also occur in the texts of steles from Armant in Upper Egypt and Jebel Barkal near the Fourth Cataract, as well as in the autobiography of a military officer named Amenemhab, which is painted on the walls of his tomb (No. 85) at Thebes.

Among Thutmose's numerous building enterprises may be mentioned the Festival Hall at Karnak and the Seventh Pylon there. His funerary temple built on the edge of the western desert at Thebes is almost completely destroyed. Like his predecessors, he had a large tomb excavated for himself in the Valley of the Kings. His coffin and mummy, which are now in the Egyptian Museum, Cairo, were discovered in a cache at Deir el Bahari in 1881.

Further Reading

Translations of Thutmose's expedition records are in James Henry Breasted, ed. and trans., *Ancient Records of Egypt* (5 vols., 1906-1907), and in James B. Pritchard, ed., *Ancient Near Eastern Texts Relating to the Old Testament* (1950; 2d ed. 1955). An account of Thutmose is in Alan H. Gardiner, *Egypt of the Pharaohs: An Introduction* (1961). For the political and historical background see W. C. Hayes's "Egypt: Internal Affairs from Tuthmosis I to the Death of Amenophis III" in *The Cambridge Ancient History*, vols. 1-2 (1962). □

Tiberius Julius Caesar Augustus

Tiberius Julius Caesar Augustus (42 B.C.-A.D. 37) was successor to Augustus and second emperor of Rome. His reign is seen as a period of growth and consolidation of the power of the Julio-Claudian family.

Tiberius was born in Rome, both his parents being members of noted Roman patrician families. His father was Tiberius Claudius Nero; his mother was Livia, who later divorced Claudius to marry Octavian. Tiberius was, therefore, the stepson of the future emperor and later became both his adopted son and heir, as well as his son-in-law.

Tiberius was first introduced into public life at the age of 9, when he delivered a eulogy at his father's funeral. He entered the military service, performing ably and well, until suddenly, in 6 B.C., he retired to Rhodes, supposedly in-

censed because Augustus had chosen one of his grandsons as heir, passing over Tiberius.

In A.D. 2, Tiberius returned to Rome but without the approval of Augustus. By A.D. 4, however, all of the Emperor's choices for the throne had died and, reluctantly, Augustus designated Tiberius as his successor. It was at this time that he was named tribune, a high administrative post which he held for 10 years. In A.D. 13 his term as tribune was extended, and he was granted imperial power by the Senate as well.

Accession to the Empire

At the death of Augustus in 14, Tiberius assumed control of the government, and his election as emperor was formally confirmed by the Roman Senate, although at this time no scheme of hereditary succession had been established. As a contemporary historian, Tacitus, states, "Tiberius would inaugurate everything with the consuls, as though the ancient constitution remained, and he hesitated about being emperor." One of his first official acts was the proclamation of the divinity of Augustus and the establishment of worship of the emperor-god.

When he came to the throne, Tiberius was already a middle-aged man. His first marriage had been dissolved by order of Augustus, and he had been forced by the Emperor to marry Augustus's daughter, Julia, in 12 B.C. During his period of retirement in Rhodes, Tiberius had spent a great deal of time studying philosophy and literature, and according to Suetonius, one of his biographers, "he was greatly devoted to liberal studies in both languages, Greek and Latin."

Tiberius was a skillful administrator, conservative in matters of finance. In the governing of the provinces, he followed the policies which had been established by Augustus. His military policy was to strengthen and fortify the defenses of the empire and to use diplomacy rather than force. His reign marks the beginning of the Pax Romana, a period of 200 years of relative peace and stability.

The latter years of his rule were marred by conspiracies, frequent trials for sedition (*maiestas*) in the Senate, and dangerous accusations from all sides. Tiberius became increasingly fearful for his safety. He was encouraged by his advisers to retire from public view. He went to Capri in A.D. 23, never again to return to Rome. In 37 he died, contemporary sources say, completely insane.

Further Reading

Contemporary biographies of Tiberius were written by Tacitus and Suetonius. Further material on the Emperor can be found in Frank B. Marsh, *The Reign of Tiberius* (1931), and Robert S. Rogers, *Studies in the Reign of Tiberius* (1943). A general picture of the times is in Mason Hammond, *The Augustan Principate in Theory and Practice during the Julio-Claudian Period* (1933; rev. ed. 1968).

Additional Sources

Levick, Barbara, *Tiberius the politician*, London; Dover, N.H.: Croom Helm, 1986 printing, 1976.

Shotter, D. C. A. (David Colin Arthur), *Tiberius Caesar,* London; New York: Routledge, 1992.

Suetonius, ca. 69-ca. 122., *Suetonius on the life of Tiberiu,* New York: Arno Press, 1979, c1941. □

Ludwig Tieck

The German author Ludwig Tieck (1773-1853) was perhaps the most versatile and productive writer of the German romantic movement.

Ludwig Tieck was born in Berlin on May 5, 1773. His intellectual and imaginative gifts were evident from early youth, when he considered himself a rationalist and follower of the Enlightenment. In 1792 he began his university studies, first at Halle and then at Göttingen, where he began his first novel, *William Lovell,* completed in 1796. This is the story of a young Englishman who begins as an idealist but falls into a life of sensuality and various misdeeds. After he has seduced and abandoned the sister of a friend, the friend seeks him out and eventually kills him in a duel.

In 1793 Tieck, together with the young writer Wilhelm Heinrich Wackenroder, began a wandering tour of southern Germany, where they discovered the riches of medieval German culture. On the basis of these experiences, Tieck and Wackenroder undertook joint authorship of a novel, *Franz Sternbalds Wanderungen* (*Franz Sternbald's Wanderings*). Wackenroder died in 1798, and Tieck completed the novel alone. The book is one of the first *Künstlerromane,* or novels about artists. Franz Sternbald is a pupil of the 16th-century painter Albrecht Dürer. He wanders about Europe learning and practicing his art, experiencing life, and seeking his mysterious Marie, whom he finally rejoins in Rome. The novel conveys much of Wackenroder's and Tieck's enthusiasm for older art.

By 1794 Tieck had returned to Berlin, where he wrote treatises in the spirit of rationalistic philosophy but also showed his developing romantic tastes in his edition and adaptation of old German folktales. In addition he wrote fairy tales of his own, such as *Der blonde Eckbert* (1797; The Blonde Eckbert), a tale of guilt, incest, and supernatural happenings.

About this time Tieck also wrote the experimental dramas *Prinz Zerbino* and *Der gestiefelte Kater* (*Puss in Boots*). In the latter play he uses the basic plot of the children's story as an occasion, or framework, for various satirical actions and comments. The play intentionally destroys theatrical illusion, and the poet and even the audience are given parts to speak; thus it may be regarded as a precursor of the 20th century's experimental theater. More conventional plays of the same period were the historical dramas *Leben und Tod der heiligen Genoveva* (1799; *Life and Death of Holy Genoveve*) and *Kaiser Octavianus* (1804).

In 1799 Tieck established contact with the group of romantic writers living in Jena, principally Novalis and August Wilhelm and Friedrich von Schlegel. He collaborated with them in editing medieval poetry. He also translated Cervantes's *Don Quixote* and helped edit the literary remains of Wackenroder, Novalis, and the dramatists Heinrich von Kleist and Jakob Lenz. His most important work as a translator was his contribution to the complete German version of Shakespeare which had been begun by August Wilhelm von Schlegel. Completed in 1833, the Tieck-Schlegel Shakespeare became a standard work of German literature.

During his later years Tieck's own creative work underwent a gradual change. His later novels and short stories show a more realistic attitude and depiction of life than his earlier, more romantic works. For example, the story *Des Lebens Überfluss* (1839; Life's Abundance) describes in accurate detail the life of an impoverished young married couple. In addition to such stories Tieck also wrote a historical novel, *Vittoria Accorombona* (1840), which shows the influence of Sir Walter Scott.

After leaving Jena, Tieck spent several years at a country estate and then in 1819 moved to Dresden, where he became dramaturgical consultant for the city theater. In 1841 King Frederick William IV of Prussia summoned him to Berlin, where he remained as court author-in-residence. Tieck died in Berlin on April 28, 1853, a romantic writer who had outlived virtually his entire generation.

Further Reading

Perhaps the best general book on Tieck in English is Edwin H.
Zeydel, *Ludwig Tieck, the German Romanticist* (1935), which
serves as a good introduction to his life and writings. More
specialized book-length works are Zeydel's *Ludwig Tieck and
England* (1931); R. M. Immerwahr, *The Esthetic Intent of
Tieck's Fantastic Comedy* (1953); and Percy Matenko, *Ludwig
Tieck and America* (1954). R. M. Wernaer, *Romanticism and
the Romantic School in Germany* (1910), contains a chapter
on Tieck's notion of ''romantic irony,'' and Ralph Tymms,
German Romantic Literature (1955), provides an excellent
brief introduction to Tieck's life and work.

Additional Sources

Paulin, Roger. *Ludwig Tieck,* Stuttgart: Metzler, 1987.
Paulin, Roger. *Ludwig Tieck: a literary biography,* Oxford Ox-
fordshire: Clarendon Press; New York: Oxford University
Press, 1986, 1985. ☐

Giovanni Battista Tiepolo

**The Italian painter Giovanni Battista Tiepolo (1696-
1770) is famed for the brilliance of his colors, the
speed and spontaneity of his execution, and the airy
freedom of his frescoes filled with figures floating on
clouds.**

Giovanni Battista Tiepolo was born in Venice on
March 5, 1696. His father, who was part owner of
a ship, died when Tiepolo was scarcely a year old,
but the family was left in comfortable circumstances. As a
youth, he was apprenticed to Gregorio Lazzarini, a mediocre but fashionable painter known for his elaborately theatrical, rather grandiose compositions.

Tiepolo soon evolved a more spirited style of his own.
By the time he was 20, he had exhibited his work independently, and won plaudits, at an exhibition held at the church
of S. Rocco. The next year he became a member of the
Fraglia, or painters' guild. In 1719 he married Cecilia
Guardi, whose brother Francesco was to become famous as
a painter of the Venetian scene. They had nine children,
among them Giovanni Domenico and Lorenzo Baldassare,
who were also painters.

In the 1720s Tiepolo carried out many large-scale commissions on the northern Italian mainland. Of these the most
important is the cycle of Old Testament scenes done for the
patriarch of Aquileia, Daniele Dolfin, in the new Archbishop's Palace at Udine. Here Tiepolo abandoned the dark
hues that had characterized his early style and turned instead to the bright, sparkling colors that were to make him
famous.

Maker of Myths

From the 1730s on Tiepolo devoted himself chiefly to
secular themes: mythologies and allegories that glorified
Venice and its noble families. The great need these paintings fulfilled is rooted in Venetian history. In Tiepolo's day

Venice lived under a shadow. Its 1,000-year-long history as
an independent state was soon to come to an end. For
centuries Venice had remained secure and prosperous behind walls of wood and water. Its ships protected it and
brought back wealth from beyond the Adriatic Sea. Its
churches glittered with Eastern gold. Once Venice had been
the great power of the Mediterranean, before which Turks
had fled and even distant Byzantium trembled. But by the
18th century, while there was still much gold, there was
almost no power. No longer within the main currents of
international politics, Venice existed instead as a fashionable backwater, a stopover for visiting Englishmen on the
grand tour.

Naturally those who loved Venice sought to escape
into the dream of a glorious past. Naturally they tried to
extend that dream to also cover the present. Their spokesman was Tiepolo. It was he who drove away the shadows.
In their place he created a world flooded with sunlight. In it
float the gods and goddesses of mythology, the allegories of
abundance and victory, and those figures of fame who
trumpet the triumphs of Venice to the four corners of the
earth. Like the great epic poets, among whom he should
rightfully be numbered, Tiepolo is a maker of myths.

In these myths the gods and goddesses of Olympus
watch over the nobility and attend their progress through
the skies. From such airy stuff Tiepolo cut many of his finest
frescoes: the celebration of the marriage that joined the
aristocratic Savorgnan family with the newly but spectacu-
larly wealthy Rezzonicos, in Ca' Rezzonico, Venice (1758);
the *Apotheosis of Francesco Barbaro,* or the welcoming into

heaven of the Pisani family, extolled by all the virtues and by the fatherland, in the Villa Pisani, Stra (1761-1762); and, most famous of all, the frescoes he executed in the Imperial Hall and the great stairway of the Residenz, Würzburg (1751-1753), built by Balthasar Neumann.

Tiepolo in Spain

By now Tiepolo's fame was international. In 1762 he accepted the call of King Charles III to paint frescoes for the new Royal Palace in Madrid. In the years 1762-1764 he populated the ceiling of the vast Throne Room with legions of figures paying homage to Spain: the jubilant angels who bore the Spanish crown; the Christian virtues Spain protected and encouraged; and the vices and heresies it cast down to hell. Along the sides is the legacy of Columbus: a rich panoply of lands beyond the seas over which Spain still held dominion. There is even a Spanish galleon floating overhead with its cargo of riches from the New World.

Tiepolo stayed on in Spain even after 1766, when he finished the other frescoes for the Royal Palace. But the atmosphere around him was changing. Following the discoveries of Herculaneum and Pompeii, the cry was now for neoclassicism. Its chief exponent in Spain, the German painter Anton Raphael Mengs, won increasing favor with the court, and the King's adviser, Padre Joaquim de Electa, especially admired Mengs's paintings and found Tiepolo's work frivolous and absurdly out of date. In 1767, not without difficulty, Tiepolo secured one more major commission: to paint seven large altarpieces for the newly finished church of S. Pascal at Aranjuez. Shortly after they were finished, Electa had them taken down and replaced with canvases by Mengs and others. When on March 27, 1770, at the age of 74, Tiepolo died, he had already outlived the era he had done so much to create.

Development of His Style

The earliest surviving painting that we can attribute to Tiepolo with certainty, the *Sacrifice of Abraham* (1715/1716), shows him looking back to earlier, rather conservative styles, above all to Giovanni Battista Piazzetta and through him to Caravaggio. Powerfully modeled figures loom out of the shadows as if picked up by a spotlight. Abraham's face is filled with horror, Isaac's with resignation; up front, thrust forward in Abraham's fist, is the shining blade of the sacrificial knife.

Tiepolo soon abandoned these dark dramas. In their place he created the sparkling, sunlit fairyland that we saw for the first time in his frescoes for the Archbishop's Palace at Udine. This new style, which grew out of the baroque but was gentler, lighter, and more graceful, can be called *barocchetto,* or little baroque. Its masterpiece is the fresco cycle in the Imperial Hall of the Residenz in Würzburg (1751-1752). These paintings celebrate the life of Frederick Barbarossa, who invested the first bishop of Würzburg in 1168. But Tiepolo places the scenes in 16th-century Venice, which for him provided settings for all the world's history.

In the *Marriage of Barbarossa* the Emperor and his bride are dressed in great Renaissance ruff collars and set against an elaborately embellished Palladian arch. The colors are luminous and breathtaking. The bride's blue cloak, for example, is penetrated with off tones of rose and shot through with frosted blue highlights that make the whole surface shimmer. The costumes of the courtiers in the background play a quiet melody of muted pastels.

On the ceiling is *Apollo Bringing Barbarossa His Bride.* We see the event sharply from below, as if the ceiling had opened up to the heavens. Far up in the blue sky Apollo's white horses paw the empty air. Greek god and bride emerge radiant from a rainbow. Around the young emperor bright banners flutter, soldiers' armor sparkles, and celestial beings spill gaily over the edges of the rococo frame.

Tiepolo painted many of these cloud-borne fantasies, the last, the *Triumph of Spain* (1764), for the Royal Palace in Madrid. But by then he was an old man, and he was tired. Increasingly his son Giovanni Domenico played a role in the execution of work Tiepolo himself had begun. Inevitably the brilliance diminished. But the real Tiepolo remains in the oil sketches he executed as models for the larger works. One of these, the *St. Francis,* a study done about 1767 for one of his rejected altarpieces at Aranjuez, serves to represent his last phase. Here, as in other works done at the end of his life, Tiepolo makes a simple but profoundly moving statement of mystical belief. The saint receives the stigmata almost as a physical force, slumping weakly against a rock and sprawling barefoot on barren ground. An angel stands beside St. Francis, but there are no angels above, no vision of glory. The rhetoric is gone, and in place of the magic of fairyland is the quieter, sterner, more lonely magic of religious faith.

Further Reading

The standard books on Tiepolo are by Antonio Morassi: *G. B. Tiepolo: His Life and Work* (1955) contains a brief, well-written essay on the development of Tiepolo's style and illustrations of most of the major works; and *A Complete Catalogue of the Paintings of G. B. Tiepolo* (1962) adds several hundred additional illustrations of the artist's lesser-known works. Despite Morassi's confident assertions, there is still much argument as to whether many of these less well-known works are by Tiepolo. The best book on the drawings is George Knox, *Catalogue of the Tiepolo Drawings in the Victoria and Albert Museum* (1960). A brilliant but highly subjective essay on Tiepolo is in Michael Levey, *Painting in XVIII Century Venice* (1959). The powerful influence of the traditions of the Venetian state and the beliefs of the Venetian nobility on Tiepolo's paintings is well demonstrated by Francis Haskell in *Patrons and Painters* (1963).

Additional Sources

Levey, Michael. *Giambattista Tiepolo: his life and art,* New Haven: Yale University Press, 1986. □

Louis Comfort Tiffany

The chief innovation of Louis Comfort Tiffany (1848-1933), American painter and designer, was his glass

technology. He was also a pioneer of the Art Nouveau style.

Louis C. Tiffany was born in New York City on Feb. 18, 1848, the son of the founder and director of the jewelry retailers Tiffany and Company. Louis was interested in painting as a young man; he studied with George Inness and traveled in Europe and Africa, recording his impressions. Because of his pictures' decorative qualities, they were successful in New York.

By the 1870s Tiffany was becoming interested in the decorative arts. He and the painter John La Farge studied glassmaking at the Heidt glassworks in Brooklyn. Their original individual experiments probably concerned stained glass. However, the process whereby an iridescent finish could be produced on glass fascinated Tiffany; he was trying to duplicate the finish seen on ancient Greek, Roman, and other glass which had been buried for many hundreds of years. By 1880 he had applied for patents on this type of finish.

In 1879 he founded the Louis C. Tiffany Company, "Associated Artists." The firm decorated private and public buildings. Two of the best examples of this work in New York City were the 7th Regiment Armory (1880) and the H. O. Havemeyer house (1890; destroyed). In 1892 he founded the Tiffany Glass and Decorating Company, which specialized in producing stained-glass windows and glass mosaics. By this time he was also producing blown glass for both decorative and table-service use, and in 1893 he established his own furnaces for this purpose. The company was reorganized into Tiffany Studios in 1900.

In the following years, Tiffany produced jewelry, enamels, pottery, lamps, glass, mosaics, and monumental stained-glass windows. He built a palatial home, Laurelton Hall, at Oyster Bay, Long Island, which overshadowed in luxury and visual impact his several residences in New York City. In 1918 Tiffany gave Laurelton Hall (destroyed) to the Louis Comfort Tiffany Foundation, which administered a fellowship program for young artists. The Tiffany firm was not disbanded until 3 years after its founder's death on Jan. 17, 1933.

Tiffany Glass

Tiffany's genius is seen in his decorative productions in glass and metal. For the glass he originated the trademark Favrile, and the name became synonymous with these handmade products of high quality. It is doubtful that Tiffany did much of the glassblowing himself, but he personally supervised the craftsmen and encouraged them to be as inventive as possible. As a result, there are highly individual vases, bottles, and dishes in a multitude of colors and techniques. Some of the pieces were utilitarian, but others were executed often as a pure tour de force. Some were treated with acids which gave the iridescent effect of ancient excavated glass. Another type, called lava glass, resembled volcanic lava. One of the most complicated types was cameo-style glass. After 1900 more or less standardized sets of tableware began to be produced; they do not have the

individuality and attention to detail of the purely decorative pieces.

Tiffany glass is marked in a number of ways. Often it is found with scratched marks—the initials L.C.T. or the name spelled out; but the word FAVRILE and various numbers are the marks most often encountered. Sometimes small paper labels, often marked T. G. & D. Co., are pasted to pieces. Not all pieces have a distinguishing mark, however.

Tiffany Metalwork

Metal alloys were used to fashion bowls, boxes, vases, candlesticks, desk sets, and lamps. A number of finishes could be applied to these pieces, so that they varied from a shiny gold to a dark-green bronze patination, which in some instances became almost black. Brightly colored enamels were used on some pieces. The lamps had shades of stained glass which was leaded in flower forms, geometric shapes, or tiles. These pieces are often stamped TIFFANY STUDIOS. In style, they sometimes show the influence of 19th-century historical revivalism. Some of the shapes are derived from classical art, and others are inspired by Egyptian, Byzantine, Romanesque, and even Japanese forms.

However, Tiffany exhibited his most progressive tendencies in pieces in the Art Nouveau style. Indeed, he was one of the few Americans involved in this predominantly European movement, and his works survive as one of its most elegant statements. These pieces are often inspired by nature and conceived as a single unit free from the fussiness of revivalism.

Further Reading

Robert Koch, *Louis C. Tiffany: Rebel in Glass* (1964), is the only biography. A wide selection of his work is provided in Museum of Contemporary Crafts, *Louis Comfort Tiffany, Exhibition* (1958).

Additional Sources

Duncan, Alastair, *Louis Comfort Tiffany,* New York: H.N. Abrams in association with the National Museum of American Art, Smithsonian Institution, 1992.

Koch, Robert, *Louis C. Tiffany, rebel in glass,* New York: Crown, 1982. □

Tiglath-pileser III

Tiglath-pileser III (reigned 745-727 B.C.), king of Assyria, was an able warrior and administrator who laid the foundations of the Late Assyrian Empire.

Tiglath-pileser or in Assyrian, Tukulti-apal-Eshara, was almost certainly an adopted name chosen in emulation of an earlier warrior-king. He came to the throne as the result of a palace revolution in which Ashurnirari V was murdered. Assyria had suffered the loss of eastern and northern territories to its long-standing enemy,

Urartu, the kingdom of Van, and as a result had lost access to the mines of Anatolia. Assyria needed an able leader who could restore the prestige and economic advantage won by the great kings of the 9th century. Tiglath-pileser was such a leader.

The King's first task was to restore order in Babylonia, where anarchy had reigned for nearly 50 years. Then, in 742 B.C., he marched west against a coalition of the Aramean kingdoms of Syria and southeast Anatolia organized by Urartu. In the ensuing battle he put Sarduris, the king of Urartu, to flight. In 738 Tiglath-pileser was again in the west; several Aramean cities were reduced, and Israel, Tyre, and Byblos were among those kingdoms which paid tribute.

In 734 King Ahaz of Judah appealed for Assyrian help against his enemies, Damascus and Israel. Samaria opened its gates, but Damascus took 2 years to reduce. The defeat of Urartu was the next objective; King Sarduris was attacked through his western territories, and then the Assyrian army struck at the heart of his kingdom. Though the citadel of Van proved impregnable, the power of Urartu in the west was broken for good.

Meanwhile, the pro-Assyrian king of Babylon had died, and a Chaldean from the south, Ukin-zer, had seized the throne. Tiglath-pileser chased the Chaldeans from Babylon, captured Ukin-zer, and put down the revolt with great severity. In 729 he himself was crowned king in Babylon. He died 2 years later.

Tiglath-pileser III was an outstanding administrator. He ably reorganized the provincial system and curbed the power of local officials. He probably created the network of roads and posting stations which linked the province with the capital at Calah. Shortly before his death he defined his realm in three dimensions: "I ruled the lands and exercised kingship from the salt waters of Bit Yakin [on the Persian Gulf] to Mt. Bikni [Demavend] in the east, from the horizon of heaven to its Zenith."

Further Reading

For accounts of Tiglath-pileser see Sidney Smith's chapter in *The Cambridge Ancient History,* vol. 3 (1927), and H. W. F. Saggs, *The Greatness That Was Babylon* (1962). Reliefs from Tiglath-pileser's palace at Calah, now in the British Museum, are published with a valuable commentary by R. D. Barnett and M. Falkner in *The Sculptures of Tiglath Pileser III from the Central and South-west Palaces at Nimrud* (1962). The chief literary sources are collected in translation by Daniel David Luckenbill in volume 1 of *Ancient Records of Assyria and Babylonia* (2 vols., 1926-1927). □

Samuel Jones Tilden

American politician Samuel Jones Tilden (1814-1886), a governor of New York and Democratic presidential candidate, typified genteel reform in the "gilded age."

Samuel J. Tilden was born on Feb. 9, 1814, in New Lebanon, N.Y. His father, a merchant and local politician, left him a legacy of Democratic politics. The Tilden home often served as meeting place for Martin Van Buren, Silas Wright, and other leaders of the Democratic "Albany Regency." Health concerns clouded Tilden's early years, forcing him to terminate a brief career at Yale. After studying law at the University of the City of New York, he established a law practice in 1841. Worry about nerves, aches, and pains remained a major factor in his career.

During the 1840s Tilden associated with the reformist, antislavery wing of the New York Democrats. When James K. Polk's election resulted in the ascendancy of the pro-Southern wing, Tilden was divorced from party leadership. He opposed Abraham Lincoln's election, spear-headed opposition to Republican centralization in Washington, and supported President Andrew Johnson's conciliatory Reconstruction policies.

After 1866 Tilden, appointed chairman of the state Democratic committee, rose steadily. His role in prosecuting the corrupt Tweed ring won him the governorship in 1874, where he pursued a policy of fiscal retrenchment. Smashing the corrupt Canal ring added to his reputation as a reformer. He won the Democratic presidential nomination in 1876.

The election, the most controversial in American history, left Tilden bitter. Although he received a plurality of some 250,000 votes, an electoral commission awarded the election to Rutherford B. Hayes. Tilden said that he would

not risk more civil war by forcing his installation. In fact, his defeat, no simple "corrupt bargain," involved an elaborate attempt at sectional compromise. Mentioned again as a candidate, Tilden, now definitely ailing, pleaded illness.

As a lawyer and businessman, Tilden was an unqualified success. Famous as a lawyer, he amassed one of America's largest fortunes in railroads and mining. He died a bachelor at the age of 72, having never had a relation with a woman of which, he confided to his biographer, he "would have hesitated, for motives of delicacy, to speak with his mother or his sisters." He left $6 million; $2 million helped fund the New York Public Library.

The opposite of the political bosses he opposed, Tilden—cerebral and unimpressive in appearance—won success primarily through his incisive intelligence. His devotion to the public good makes him an important link between Jacksonian and modern reform.

Further Reading

John Bigelow, *The Life of Samuel J. Tilden* (2 vols., 1895), rich in detail, is apologetic. An exhaustive biography placing Tilden in the Jefferson-Jackson reform tradition is Alexander C. Flick, *Samuel Jones Tilden: A Study in Political Sagacity* (1939). The "corrupt bargain" is discussed in C. Vann Woodward, *Reunion and Reaction* (1951). ☐

Sir Samuel Leonard Tilley

Sir Samuel Leonard Tilley (1818-1896) was one of the Canadian fathers of confederation and twice lieutenant governor of New Brunswick. He was a Cabinet minister and premier of New Brunswick before confederation and afterward held two major federal portfolios.

Samuel Leonard Tilley was born on May 8, 1818, at Gagetown, New Brunswick, into a family which had once farmed part of what is now Brooklyn, New York City, and as loyalists had migrated northward after the American Revolution. He was educated at local schools in Gagetown and moved at the age of 13 to Saint John, where he became an apothecary's clerk in a doctor's dispensary. In 1838 he became a partner in a mercantile firm, disposing of his share in 1855, by which time he had earned a modest fortune.

Tilley's public career began in 1837, when he undertook what was to be a lifelong espousal of temperance; thereafter he could rely on prohibitionist support on almost any issue. He was first elected to the Legislative Assembly of New Brunswick in 1850 but resigned in 1851 on a matter of principle. He was reelected in 1854 and became provincial secretary in the Cabinet of Charles Fisher. That government fell in 1856, when a prohibition act sponsored by Tilley led to such widespread evasion of the law that the lieutenant governor summarily dissolved the Assembly. In the ensuing election the Fisher government, including Tilley personally, was defeated. Tilley was reelected in 1857, becoming premier in 1861 and remaining in office until defeated as a champion of confederation in 1865. The anticonfederate forces fell apart, however, and in 1866 Tilley was back in a proconfederation Cabinet which won a healthy victory at the polls in the same year.

Before 1867 Tilley's chief public interest was confederation, and he had long been an advocate of one of its chief requisites, a railway uniting British North America. He was a delegate representing New Brunswick at the conferences in Charlottetown and Quebec in 1864 and in London in 1867. It was a natural step for him to become a member of the first Canadian House of Commons, and he was elected for Saint John City in 1867 and reelected in 1872. The first prime minister of Canada, the Conservative Sir John Alexander Macdonald, carefully constructed his first Cabinet to give the fullest possible representation both to the new provinces and to existing political interests; and Tilley, although a Liberal, was taken into Macdonald's government as the first minister of customs.

This portfolio, involving as it did the reorganization of the former provincial services into a unified federal administration, was a major, though not a spectacular, assignment in which Tilley acquitted himself well. Shortly before the parliamentary session of 1873 Tilley was appointed minister of finance, a distinct promotion but a short-lived one, as the Macdonald ministry went out of office in the same year, and Tilley had been appointed lieutenant governor of New Brunswick even before that event.

Tilley served in the province until 1878, when he was again persuaded to run for Saint John. Upon his own reelection and the formation of a second ministry by Macdonald, Tilley again became minister of finance. He was reelected to the Commons in 1882 and served in Finance until 1885, in a portfolio made particularly sensitive by Macdonald's adoption in 1878 of a general policy of tariff protection for Canadian industry, the National Policy. Tilley, long a protectionist where New Brunswick was concerned, had no trouble adapting his views to the national scene. In 1885, his health failing, he returned again to his native province as lieutenant governor. He retired in 1893 and died on June 25, 1896.

Tilley was created a commander of the Bath in 1867 and knight commander of St. Michael and St. George in 1879, both honors earned through an industrious and impressively puritanical career. In a period of rather flamboyant politics, Tilley, an Anglican, was not only a prohibitionist but a devoted attender of churches and supporter of Bible societies. He was one of the pioneers in New Brunswick in favor of vote by secret ballot and decimal currency. He was married twice and was the father of four sons and five daughters.

Further Reading

No modern critical biography of Tilley has been written, but a contemporary, James Hannay, wrote voluminously about him and his period: *The Life and Times of Sir Leonard Tilley* (1896) and *Wilmot and Tilley* (1909). Material on Tilley's career is also in Donald Creighton, *John A. Macdonald* (2 vols., 1952-1956). For general background see William George Hardy, *From Sea unto Sea: Canada, 1850 to 1910—The Road to Nationhood* (1960), and William L. Morton, *The Critical Years: The Union of British North America, 1857-1873* (1964). □

Paul Johannes Tillich

Paul Johannes Tillich (1886-1965), German-American Protestant theologian and philosopher, ranks as one of the most important and influential theologians of the 20th century. He explored the meaning of Christian faith in relation to the questions raised by philosophical analysis of human existence.

Together with thinkers such as Karl Barth and Rudolf Bultmann, Paul Tillich helped revolutionize Protestant theology. All three were influenced by the recovery of neglected insights in the Bible, the discovery of existentialism through the writings of Søren Kierkegaard, and the crisis in Western culture wrought by World War I.

Tillich was born on Aug. 20, 1886, in Starzeddel, Prussia, the son of Johannes Tillich, a Lutheran minister. Paul studied at the universities of Berlin (1904-1905, 1908), Tübingen (1905), Halle (1905-1907), and Breslau. He received his doctorate from Breslau (1911) and the licentiate of theology from Halle (1912).

German Career

Ordained a minister of the Evangelical Lutheran Church in 1912, Tillich served as a chaplain in the German army throughout World War I. During the years between the war and the coming to power of the Nazis in 1933, he was actively involved in the religious-socialist movement in Germany along with others such as Martin Buber. The religious socialists rejected the traditional otherworldliness and individualism of the dominant forms of Christianity and joined in the German socialist struggle for wider justice and social opportunity; but they sharply criticized Marxism and other purely secular forms of socialism for their utopian illusions and purely technocratic approach to human problems.

Tillich taught theology at the University of Berlin (1919-1924) and then was appointed professor of theology at the University of Marburg. That same year he married Hannah Werner; they had a son and a daughter. He next taught theology at the universities of Dresden (1925-1929) and Leipzig (1928-1929) and philosophy at the University of Frankfurt am Main (1929-1933). At Frankfurt, he produced his chief German writings. The best known of these, translated into English as *The Religious Situation* (1932), sets forth Tillich's central concept of religion as the universal dimension of "ultimate concern" in all human life and culture and interprets the transformations taking place in 20th-century European politics, arts, and thought in light of this concept.

American Career

With the rise of Hitler, Tillich became an outspoken opponent of Nazism, and in 1933 he was dismissed from his position at Frankfurt. He emigrated to the United States, invited by the distinguished theologian Reinhold Niebuhr to teach at Union Theological Seminary in New York City, where Tillich remained until 1955.

In *The Interpretation of History* (1936) Tillich developed the classical Greek idea of *kairos* (the right time), used in the New Testament to describe the historic disclosure of God in Christ. Prominent in *The Protestant Era* (1948), a collection of his articles exploring aspects of modern history from a theological perspective, is the key term, "the Protestant principle"—a necessary critical principle for both living religion and theological reflection which protests against identifying anything finite with the infinite God.

Tillich's first collection of sermons, *The Shaking of the Foundations* (1948), was followed by *The New Being* (1955) and *The Eternal Now* (1963). Many people have found his sermons the most helpful way to enter his thought, here fleshed out concretely in biblical interpretation and in application to contemporary life.

Tillich was profoundly influenced by, and contributed to, depth psychology. *The Courage To Be* (1952) perhaps best embodies his application of psychological insights to a theological description of man with his analysis of the nature of anxiety. He turned his attention to basic problems of Christian ethics in *Love, Power and Justice* (1954), and in *Morality and Beyond* (1963).

His Chief Work

Systematic Theology (vol. 1, 1951; vol. 2, 1957; vol. 3, 1963) is Tillich's chief work and the most complete exposition of his theology. Its structure is based upon his "method of correlation," which "explains the contents of the Christian faith through existential questions and theological answers in mutual interdependence." In the first volume he sets forth in greatest detail his important and much-debated interpretation of God, not as a being among beings but as Being-itself, the "ground and power of being" in everything that exists.

Tillich's career ended with distinguished professorships at Harvard (1955-1962) and the University of Chicago (1962-1965), where he taught to overflowing classrooms. Among his books published during this period or posthumously, the following should be noted: *Biblical Religion and the Search for Ultimate Reality* (1955), *Dynamics of Faith* (1957), *Theology of Culture* (1959), *Christianity and the Encounter of World Religions* (1963), *Perspectives on 19th and 20th Century Protestant Thought* (1967), *A History of Christian Thought* (1968), and *What is Religion?* (1969). In addition, he wrote literally hundreds of articles for religious and secular periodicals.

In 1940 Tillich had become an American citizen. Until the end of World War II he remained politically active, participating in the religious-socialist movement in the United States and serving as chairman of the Council for a Democratic Germany. He was chairman of the Self-help for Émigrés from Central Europe and was generally active in refugee work. He was frequently called upon to contribute to the national and international ecumenical movement. He received many honorary doctorates and awards. Perhaps none gave him deeper pleasure than those bestowed by his homeland, Germany, in the years after the war.

A man of average height and build, with a shock of white hair in his later years, Tillich was reserved but keenly and warmly interested in other persons. His profound love of nature manifested itself in his religious outlook. In the midst of a still-active career, he died in Chicago on Oct. 22, 1965. With his broad humanistic interests and approach to Christianity, he communicated to many in modern secular culture a renewed appreciation of religion as man's universal "ultimate concern," manifested in all human activities.

Further Reading

Tillich's most extended autobiographical account is *On the Boundary* (1966). A brief, clearly written introduction to his life and thought is Guyton B. Hammond, *The Power of Self-transcendence: An Introduction to the Philosophical Theology of Paul Tillich* (1966). Also brief is David Hopper, *Tillich: A Theological Portrait* (1967), which combines biography with a scholarly critique of Tillich's *Systematic Theology*. More extensive and technical studies include J. Heywood Thomas, *Paul Tillich* (1963), and Alexander J. McKelway, *The Systematic Theology of Paul Tillich* (1964). See also Carl J. Armbraster, *The Vision of Paul Tillich* (1967). Noted specialists in various fields assess Tillich's life and work in an anthology of essays, *The Intellectual Legacy of Paul Tillich*, edited by James R. Lyons (1969); and his place in history is considered in Alvin C. Porteous, *Prophetic Voices in Contemporary Theology* (1966).

Additional Sources

Newport, John P., *Paul Tillich*, Peabody, Mass.: Hendrickson Publishers, 1991, 1984.

Pauck, Wilhelm, *Paul Tillich, his life & thought,* San Francisco: Harper & Row, 1989.

Ratschow, Carl Heinz, *Paul Tillich,* Iowa City, Iowa (Gilmore Hall, The University of Iowa, Iowa City, Iowa 52242): North American Paul Tillich Society, 1980.

Taylor, Mark Kline, *Paul Tillich: theologian of the boundaries,* London; San Francisco, CA: Collins, 1987.

Tillich, Hannah, *From place to place: travels with Paul Tillich, travels without Paul Tillich,* New York: Stein and Day, 1976. □

Benjamin Ryan Tillman

Benjamin Ryan Tillman (1847-1918), an American statesman for the South and a demagogue, was known as "Pitchfork Ben." His political campaigns on behalf of poor whites gave direction to a new generation of Southern activists who reorganized post-Reconstruction politics and society.

Benjamin Ryan Tillman was born in Edgefield Country, S.C., on Aug. 11, 1847, of an old Southern family. He was raised on a plantation which boasted numerous slaves. A bright student, Tillman was prevented from serving with the Confederate forces during the Civil War because of the loss of his left eye. After the war he began farming, experiencing the frustrations of Southerners under Reconstruction policies and Federal troops.

Despite his many acres Tillman identified himself more with poor white farmers than with the aristocrats of his state who sought to return to what they recalled as a gracious and chivalrous era. The fear poor white farmers felt and their hatred of freed blacks found expression in bloody riots in 1876 in which Tillman participated. Only in 1885 did his demands for farmers' education and aid and the organization of the Farmers' Association give him a political base.

During the next years Tillman engaged in bitter controversies, making scapegoats of blacks and aristocrats and organizing a political machine of rural supporters. Becoming a power in the state Democratic party, in 1890 the "One-eyed Plowboy" urged voters to "spit out of your mouths" candidates allegedly arraigned against the farmers' interests, and he rode into power. As governor of the state in 1890-1894, and afterward, he dictated all legislation. Some of his policies comported with those of the Populists of the period. Thus he appointed a commission to fix railroad rates; in 1896 he managed to institute the primary system of nominating Democratic candidates (as distinguished from the old convention system) to enable a broader spectrum of the white voters to name candidates; and he won tax equalization and education measures. However, his determination to make blacks second-class citizens had less in common with populism. Tillman's most original program was his pioneer Dispensary, which gave the state sole right to sell alcoholic liquors.

In 1896, having named his successor as governor, Tillman won a seat in the U.S. Senate; his assertion that he would "stick my pitchfork into [President Grover Cleveland's] old ribs" appropriately introduced him to the national audience. In Washington his unbridled scorn for blacks divided both liberals and conservatives. Tillman's hatred of President Theodore Roosevelt became a major motif in his career. Nevertheless, his exposé of the inordinate profits gained by steel manufacturers for government ships, his battle for naval expansion, and, most important, his work to revitilize the Interstate Commerce Commission through the Hepburn Act (1906) gave him status among those working for progressive measures.

Although Tillman remained a senator and a figure in South Carolina politics, he loomed largest in his last decade as the prototype of New South politicians like James K. Vardaman in Mississippi and the later Jeff Davis of Arkansas. Both roused their poor white constituents for progressive social measures but also for the suppression of black civil rights. Tillman died on July 3, 1918, in Washington.

Further Reading

The authority on Tillman is Francis B. Simkins: see his *The Tillman Movement in South Carolina* (1926) and *Pitchfork Ben Tillman, South Carolinian* (1944). □

Jacobo Timerman

Jacobo Timerman (born 1923) was an Argentine journalist who wrote articles opposing human rights abuses in Argentina and elsewhere. He founded the newspaper *La Opinión*, which also condemned human rights abuses wherever they occurred.

Jacobo Timerman was born on January 6, 1923, in Bar, a town in the Soviet Ukraine. Timerman's family emigrated to Argentina five years later to escape the pogroms which threatened Jews in the Ukraine in the 1920s. When Jacobo was 12 his father died, leaving his wife to support Jacobo and his younger brother José (Yoselle). They lived in a one-room apartment in the Jewish quarter of Buenos Aires. Large numbers of Europeans had immigrated to Argentina in the early 20th century, and among them were thousands of Eastern European Jews.

Argentina, along with much of the Western world, witnessed the rise of vocal right-wing movements in the 1920s and 1930s, many drawing their inspiration from the success of Hitler in Nazi Germany. The rise of anti-Semitism in the 1930s, the presence of a large Jewish community, and the strong encouragement of his mother spurred Timerman's involvement in Jewish cultural and political organizations at an early age. At 14 he joined Avuca, a Jewish youth organization, which spurred his interest in Jewish history and culture. Timerman became a strong supporter of the struggle for a Jewish homeland as a teenager, and his Zionism stood out as one of the central principles of his life and work.

Although originally a student of engineering, Timerman turned to journalism in the 1940s, a period of intense political turmoil in Argentina. Juan Domingo Perón rose to political power in the mid-1940s and ruled Argentina for a decade, forging a national political alliance built on a charismatic appeal to the masses, in particular labor unions in a rapidly urbanizing and industrializing nation. The fascist overtones of Perón's politics, his determination to forge an independent foreign policy, and his economic program chilled relations with the United States and made Perón a symbol of Argentine nationalism. The death of Perón's charismatic wife Evita and his overthrow in 1955 ushered in three decades of political and economic chaos in Argentina.

Amidst the political tribulations of the 1950s and 1960s Jacobo Timerman rose to prominence as a journalist and publisher. He became a national figure in the 1950s as a resourceful reporter for the newspaper *La Razón,* and in the 1960s he became involved in radio, television, and magazine publishing. With friends he founded *Primera Plana,* a successful weekly news magazine along the lines of *TIME* or *Newsweek.* Timerman sold the magazine and founded another news weekly, *Confirmado,* which he also later sold. In 1971, he helped found the newspaper *La Opinión.* The paper was influential and widely read in political and intel-

lectual circles. David Graiver, a young financier, bought 45 percent interest in the paper and worked with Timerman in several publishing projects.

The 1970s were an exceptionally difficult time in Argentina. Assassinations, kidnappings, bombings, and urban guerrilla warfare became commonplace as armed right-wing and left-wing groups gained strength. Thousands of Argentines "disappeared" when they were picked up and never seen again, many the victims of government security forces operating in secrecy. Successive military and civilian regimes failed to achieve political order or economic growth, and in 1973 the aging Juan Perón triumphantly returned to Argentina with his new wife Isabel to win a resounding electoral victory which swept him into the presidential palace after nearly 20 years in exile.

Amidst the disintegration of political order in Argentina, Timerman's newspaper took a strong stance against human rights abuses by both the right and the left. Editorials in *La Opinión* condemned human rights abuses in regimes as diverse as those in Chile, Israel, Cuba, and the Soviet Union. Timerman began to publish the names of the "*desaparecidos*" ("missing ones") in *La Opinión* and to criticize the regime of Isabel Perón, who had succeeded her husband on his death in July 1974. A supporter of Juan Perón in the early 1970s, *La Opinión* openly supported the overthrow of Isabel by the military in March 1976. Continuing criticism of political violence and government economic policies angered the military regime.

In April 1977 armed civilians, purportedly acting on orders from the military, surrounded his home and arrested Timerman, beginning a two and one-half year ordeal of imprisonment, torture, house arrest with his wife and three sons, and, finally, forced exile. Timerman's case aroused international attention, drawing strong pressure for his release from the Vatican and the Carter administration (among others). In *Prisoner Without a Name, Cell Without a Number* Timerman traced in chilling detail the rise of his political problems and his arrest, torture, and imprisonment at the hands of the military. No formal charges were ever brought against him. (Timerman's financial partner, David Graiver, died mysteriously in 1976 and allegedly had been linked to the financing of the left-wing guerrilla movement, the Montoneros.) Several hearings and three judicial verdicts in Timerman's favor failed to achieve his release. Under mounting international pressure, the military regime stripped Timerman of his Argentine citizenship and his property and expelled him from the country in September 1979.

With the publication of *Prisoner* in several languages in 1980 and 1981, Timerman provoked an international controversy. In his book Timerman attributed many of his problems to his Zionism and focused on the anti-Semitism of his captors. He condemned the military regime for its Nazi characteristics and severely criticized Argentine Jewish leaders for what he perceived as their passivity in the face of a possible "holocaust" in Argentina. He praised Jimmy Carter's support for human rights and denounced Ronald Reagan's "quiet diplomacy" and support for friendly "authoritarian" regimes, particularly the Argentine regime.

Conservative commentators such as William F. Buckley, Jr. and Irving Kristol in the United States attacked Timerman's views and credibility. Timerman won a number of prestigious international prizes for his defense of freedom on the press and for his contributions to inter-American relations.

Settling in Israel with his family, Timerman continued to provoke controversy. In 1982 he published *The Longest War,* a scathing critique of the Israeli invasion and occupation of Lebanon, setting off another bitter debate on international politics. In 1984 the military regime in Argentina stepped down, completely discredited after economic collapse and the disastrous war against Great Britain over the Falklands/Malvinas Islands. The newly-elected civilian regime began the prosecution of former military leaders for their responsibility in the torture and disappearance of thousands of Argentines between 1977 and 1983. Jacobo Timerman returned to Argentina in August 1984, declaring his intention to testify against his torturers and to reclaim his confiscated newspaper, which he did.

In 1987 he published *Chile: Death in the South,* a blistering indictment of the dictatorial rule of General Augusto Pinochet. In 1991, he published, *Cuba: A Journey,* another somewhat controversial work.

Further Reading

Prisoner Without a Name, Cell Without a Number (1980-1981) contains extensive autobiographical material. *The Progressive* (December 1981) has an interesting interview with Timerman. □

ory. It serves to test the hypotheses of economic theory and to estimate the implied interrelationships.

Tinbergen's early work reflects rather clearly the influence of his training in the physical sciences. As early as the 1930s he was publishing papers dealing with the construction of aggregative models of the economy in the form of systems of simultaneous dynamic equations. These were followed by studies of the measurement of the parameters of such models using statistical data. His first complete model was of the economy of the Netherlands. This model was followed by a similar study of the economy of the United States done for the League of Nations. Having constructed the model and statistically estimated the appropriate coefficients, he analyzed its cyclical properties through the solution to the corresponding system of difference equations. His work has served as the principal stimulus for the extensive model-building that has taken place throughout the world in recent years.

Following World War II, Tinbergen's work served as the basis for the use of model projections in the economic planning of the Dutch government. This occurred while he was director of the Central Planning Bureau. The Dutch government has led the world in the systematic use of econometric models in its planning, budgeting, and policy formulation. Many new contributions to the field of econometrics grew out of this activity, and many of the world's leading econometricians cut their professional teeth on the construction and maintenance of the Dutch models.

Jan Tinbergen

The Dutch economist Jan Tinbergen (1903-1994) was a pioneer in the development of econometrics, linking statistics and mathematics to economic theory. He shared the Nobel Prize in 1969.

Jan Tinbergen was born in The Hague on April 12, 1903. He was educated at the University of Leiden, where he earned a doctoral degree in physics. In 1929 he joined the staff of the Central Bureau of Statistics, the economic planning unit of the Dutch government, where he remained until 1945, except for 1936-1938, when he served as a business-cycle research expert for the League of Nations. Beginning in 1933, he accepted a position as professor of development planning at the Netherlands School of Economics, Rotterdam, an institution he served for his entire academic career.

He became director of the Central Planning Bureau of the Dutch government, serving from 1945 to 1955. After that time, he became an advisor to various governments and international organizations, showing particular concern for the problems of underdeveloped countries.

Econometrics, where Tinbergen made his greatest contributions, consists of the application of statistical data and techniques to mathematical formulations of economic the-

Among the more prominent of Tinbergen's contributions to econometrics are the introductions of the concepts of "targets" and "instruments." The "targets" are defined in terms of the policy maker's goals. For example, a given level of aggregate output might be a target. With the help of the model, this in turn would show what values of the "instruments" would lead to the achievement of that goal.

The process introduced by Tinbergen is virtually the inverse of the usual procedure in forecasting in which, for given values of the independent variables, the corresponding values of dependent variables are computed. He later extended these same concepts to secular growth models for underdeveloped countries. It might be noted that all of the major econometric models of the United States are in the tradition that began with Tinbergen's work.

Tinbergen wrote extensively on such important topics as the mathematical analysis of the business cycle, the theory of income distribution, the theory of economic growth, the measurement of elasticities of substitution, and the theory of economic development.

Tinbergen served as chairman of the United Nations Committee for Development Planning from 1965 to 1972, as he helped set up more than 20 economic institutes in many parts of the world, including Turkey, India and Chile. In 1969 he shared the Nobel Prize in economic science with Ragnar Frisch of Norway. They received the honor for their work in the development of mathematical models used in econometrics. Tinbergen retired from the Netherlands School of Economics in 1973, having served there for 40 years.

After that, he infrequently published new works on economic theory, including *Income Distribution* (1975), *Warfare and Welfare* (with others, 1987), and *World Security and Equity* (1990). During the 1980s, he urged the world's strong nations to do more for developing countries, saying in an interview, "Individual countries, with their limited resources, cannot stimulate the economy, but together they may succeed." He encouraged a stronger relationship between Europe and Japan, and criticized the U.S. for "standing pat," rather than increasing aid to countries. In 1992, he received the Four Freedoms Award.

During his lifetime, Tinbergen received 20 honorary degrees from institutions worldwide. He died in The Netherlands on June 9, 1994. The Tinbergen Institute has been established in Rotterdam in his honor.

Further Reading

Tinbergen's work receives some mention in Edmund Whittaker, *Schools and Streams of Economic Thought* (1960), and in G. L. S. Shackle, *The Years of High Theory: Invention and Tradition in Economic Thought, 1926-1939* (1967). □

Nikolaas Tinbergen

Nikolaas Tinbergen (1907-1988) is known for his studies of stimulus-response processes in wasps,

fishes, and gulls. He shared the Nobel Prize in medicine in 1973 for work on the organization and causes of social and individual patterns of behavior in animals.

Nikolaas Tinbergen, a zoologist, animal psychologist, and pioneer in the field of ethology (the study of the behavior of animals in relation to their habitat), is most well known for his studies of stimulus-response processes in wasps, fishes, and gulls. He shared the 1973 Nobel Prize in physiology or medicine with Austrian zoologists Karl von Frisch and Konrad Lorenz for his work on the organization and causes of social and individual patterns of behavior in animals.

The third of five children, Tinbergen was born April 15, 1907, in The Hague, Netherlands, to Dirk Cornelius Tinbergen, a school teacher, and Jeanette van Eek. His older brother Jan studied physics but later turned to economics, winning the first Nobel Prize awarded in that subject in 1969. The Tinbergens lived near the seashore, where Tinbergen often went to collect shells, camp, and watch animals, many of which he would later formally research.

After high school, Tinbergen worked at the Vogelwarte Rossitten bird observatory and later began studying biology at the State University of Leiden, Netherlands. For his dissertation, Tinbergen studied bee-killer wasps and was able to experimentally demonstrate that the wasps use landmarks to orientate themselves. Tinbergen first established the tradi-

tional routes of the wasps near their burrows, then altered the landscape to see how the wasps' behavior would be affected. Tinbergen was awarded his Ph.D. in 1932.

Tinbergen married Elisabeth Rutten in 1932 (they had five children together). Soon afterward, the Tinbergens embarked on an expedition to Greenland, where Tinbergen studied the role of evolution in the behavior of snow buntings, phalaropes, and Eskimo sled dogs. When he returned to the Netherlands in 1933, he became an instructor at the State University, where he organized an undergraduate course on animal behavior. Tinbergen's work had been recognized in the field of biology but it was not until after he met Lorenz—the acknowledged father of ethology—that his work began to form a directed body of research. Tinbergen took his family to Lorenz's home in Austria for a summer so the two men could work together. Although they published only one paper together, their collaboration lasted a number of years.

During 1936, Tinbergen and Lorenz began constructing a theoretical framework for the study of ethology, which was then a fledgling field. They hypothesized that instinct, as opposed to simply being a response to environmental factors, arises from an animal's impulses. This idea is expressed by the concept of a fixed-action pattern, a repeated, distinct set of movements or behaviors, which Tinbergen and Lorenz believed all animals have. A fixed-action pattern is triggered by something in the animal's environment. In some species of gull, for instance, hungry chicks will peck at a decoy with a red spot on its bill, a characteristic of the gull. Tinbergen showed that in some animals learned behavior is critical for survival. The oystercatcher, for instance, has to learn which objects to peck at for food by watching its mother. Tinbergen and Lorenz also demonstrated that animal behavior can be the result of contradictory impulses and that a conflict between drives may produce a reaction that is strangely unsuited to the stimuli. For example, an animal defending its territory against a formidable attacker, caught between the impulse to fight or flee, may begin grooming or eating.

Regarding his collaboration with Lorenz, Tinbergen is quoted in *Nobel Prize Winners* as saying: "We 'clicked' at once.... [Lorenz's] extraordinary vision and enthusiasm were supplemented and fertilized by my critical sense, my inclination to think his ideas through, and my irrepressible urge to check out 'hunches' by experimentation." Tinbergen and Lorenz's work was disrupted by World War II.

Tinbergen spent much of the war in a hostage camp because he had protested the State University of Leiden's decision to remove three Jewish faculty members from the staff. After the war ended, he became a professor of experimental biology at the University. In 1949, Tinbergen traveled to Oxford University in England to lecture. He stayed at Oxford, establishing the journal *Behavior* with W. H. Thorpe and working in the University's animal behavior division. His 1951 book *The Study of Instinct* is credited with bringing the study of ethology to many English readers. The book summarized some of the newest insights into the ways signaling behavior is created over the course of

evolution. In 1955, Tinbergen became an English citizen, and in 1966 he was appointed a professor and fellow of Oxford's Wolfson College. When the work of Tinbergen, Lorenz, and von Frisch, who had demonstrated that honeybees communicate by dancing, received the Nobel Prize in 1973, it was the first time the Nobel Committee recognized work in sociobiology or ethology.

It was Tinbergen's own hope that the ethologists' body of work would help in understanding of human behavior. "With von Frisch and Lorenz, Tinbergen has expressed the view that ethological demonstrations of the extraordinarily intricate interdependence of the structure and behavior of organisms are relevant to understanding the psychology of our own species," wrote P. Marler and D. R. Griffin in *Science*. "Indeed, [the Nobel Prize] might be taken . . . as an appreciation of the need to review the picture that we often seem to have of human behavior as something quite outside nature, hardly subject to the principles that mold the biology, adaptability, and survival of other organisms."

The ability of an organism to adapt to its environment is another element of Tinbergen's work. After he retired from Oxford in 1974, he and his wife attempted to explain autistic behavior in children to adaptability. The Tinbergens' assertion that autism may be caused by the behavior of a child's parents caused some consternation in the medical community. Tinbergen believed that much of the opposition to his work was caused by the unflattering view of human behavior it presented. "Our critics feel we degrade ourselves by the way we look at behavior," he is quoted as saying in *Contemporary Authors*. "Because this is one of the implications of ethology, that our free will is not as free as we think. We are determinists, and this is what they hate. . . . They feel that our ideas gnaw at the dignity of man."

Tinbergen was wrote a number of books and made many nature films during his lifetime. Among his publications were several children's books, including *Kleew* and *The Tale of John Stickle*. Among the numerous awards he received are the 1969 Italia prize and the 1971 New York Film Festival's blue ribbon, both for writing, with Hugh Falkus, the documentary *Signals for Survival*, which was broadcast on English television. Tinbergen died December 21, 1988, after suffering a stroke at his home in Oxford, England.

Further Reading

Contemporary Authors, Volume 108, Gale, 1983, pp. 489–90.
Nobel Prize Winners, H. W. Wilson, 1987, pp. 1059–61.
"Learning from the Animals," in *Newsweek,* October 22, 1973, p. 102.
Marler, P., and D. R. Griffin, "The 1973 Nobel Prize for Physiology or Medicine," in *Science,* November 2, 1973, pp. 464–467. □

Jean Tinguely

The Swiss sculptor Jean Tinguely (1925-1991) worked in a manner that combined aspects of Dada,

Constructivism, and kinetic art. His sculptures are capricious constructions made of a wide variety of materials, most often of junk. They are assembled to function as strange and often whimsical machines which are erratic in their performance and were at times designed to self-destruct.

Jean Tinguely was born in Fribourg, Switzerland, in 1925, the only child of a factory worker and his wife. In 1928 the family moved to Basel where Tinguely lived until 1951, when he moved to Paris. As a child he was a poor student but an avid reader and spent much of his free time perched in a tree thinking and reading. He created his first example of kinetic art at the age of 12 and still felt in the 1980s that this was his best effort in motion art. Tinguely had placed 30 small water wheels along the side of a stream. The axle of each wheel was connected to a shaft with randomly placed projecting arms or striking implements. Tin cans and other objects were struck by these arms as the wheels turned, creating a dissonance that the artist remembers as being weird and beautiful. As he recalls, his motivation was simply to do it for the sake of doing it. This project anticipated his fascination for construction as a process of creation, for motion or kinetics, for sound as an integral part of the working of his designs, and for the inclusion of randomness or chance as an animating factor. Tinguely once said of his mechanical assemblages that he allowed a sense of independence between himself and his

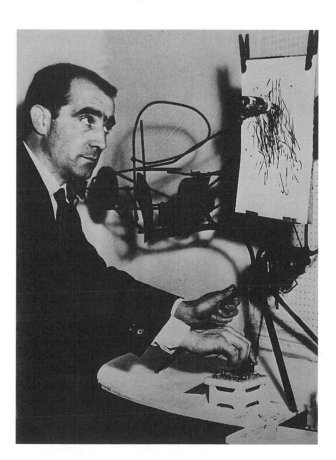

work to the point of their having freedom or personalities of their own.

At the age of 15, while working in a department store, he enrolled in evening classes at the Kunstschule (Art School) where he studied under an innovative teacher, Julia Ris. She introduced Tinguely to the Dadaist collages of Kurt Schwitters. Dada was an intellectual and esthetic protest against society and its values by the establishment of an anti-art, often of "found objects" of junk. Schwitters' collages of discarded ticket stubs, pieces of old newspapers and magazines, buttons, gears, and other objects were assembled into compositions which at times had a relief-like quality. Tinguely developed this into the third dimension, as sculpture. Like Schwitters, he perceived junk as an essential part of the experience of an urban industrialized society and as a comment on the banality and insensitivity of it.

During World War II in Switzerland, a haven for refugees from across Europe, Tinguely came into contact with a wide variety of artistic and intellectual trends, notably the concept of universal dynamism that was integral to a number of artistic movements. He was intrigued by how motion can change the way an object is perceived or even make it seem to disappear, as would happen with an airplane propeller. Tinguely experimented with a variety of applications of dynamism, at times affixing furniture and even his own work to motors which spun the objects at varying speeds. Motion changed the appearance of the objects, and at times physically disintegrated them, creating an exciting spectacle. In his later work the principles of motion and disintegration were to be refined in assemblages of erratically moving asynchronous mechanical parts which were designed to have prolonged and spectacular self-destruction.

Tinguely and his wife, Eva Appli, whom he had married in 1949, arrived in Paris in 1951, where he made his life and career thereafter. The intellectual and artistic climate of Paris was a great stimulus to him, as was the vast flea market where Tinguely could find virtually any type of object or artifact. His predilections for the Constructivist principle of assemblage, the Dadaist use of cast-offs or "found objects," and the use of motion by gas or electric motors had become constants in his work, even in his relief constructions. Tinguely quickly came to be recognized as a rebel and worked in directions at odds with most accepted forms of artistic expression. He was particularly opposed to static easel painting, in a response to which in 1953 he created his meta-matics—robots that moved about, made noises, and could be fitted to perform a number of tasks. At the Biennale de Paris of 1959 he designed a metamatic to make abstract paintings. Spectators who could start and stop it as well as change colors activated the machine. Almost 40,000 paintings were produced in two weeks. The crowds that had come to see the Biennale were thoroughly entertained, but abstract expressionist artists were disgruntled by Tinguely, whom they considered a charlatan.

In 1960 Tinguely arrived in New York for the first American showing of his sculpture at the George Staempfli Gallery. He responded to that city as if it were a giant and powerful machine and immediately started planning a large work that would celebrate the vibrant spirit of life in New

York. The Museum of Modern Art agreed to allow him to construct his work, *Homage to New York,* in the museum's sculpture garden. On March 17 of that year several hundred people gathered to observe the spectacle of his 23-foot high and 27-foot long assemblage perform and self-destruct.

Tinguely was always proud of the fact that most people seemed instinctively drawn to his sculptures, related to them, and often found them amusing. The erratic and therefore less than mechanically perfect manner in which they operate seems to eliminate the sense of separation that people experience between themselves and machines. In what many see as a cold, mechanized world, or a depersonalized world in which machines are servants to man's needs, Tinguely created machines that were as interesting and even as amusing as man himself. Cast-off machine-produced objects and parts, ''artifacts'' of industrial societies, are assembled in compositionally interesting and often whimsical ways to delight and often invite viewer participation. Days of work were discarded if the sounds produced were not interesting or pleasing. To Tinguely, the sounds made by his sculptures were like dissonant music or poetry. His works come to life with outrageous personalities, move about producing various noises, perform functions, and reach a climax, often of self-destruction. Tinguely's work has been likened to Neo-Dadaism, the ''New Realism'' of Yves Klein, as well as to performance and spectacle art.

One of his last major works prior to his death in August, 1991, was *Le Cyclop* (The Head), a sculptural project in the Fountainebleau Forest in France. There was a posthumous exhibit of his work in 1996 at the Museum of Modern Art in New York, followed later that year by the inauguration of the Jean Tinguely Museum in Basel, Switzerland.

Further Reading

Calvin Tomkins' *The Bride and the Bachelors* (1977) is probably the most interesting and entertaining writing on Tinguely. See also Carla Gattlieb's *Beyond Modern Art* (1976) for a thorough background on the radical developments in contemporary art and Tinguely's relation to them. □

Tintoretto

The Italian painter Tintoretto (1518-1594) excelled in grandly agitated and often deeply moving history paintings and dignified portraits of members of the Venetian aristocracy.

The real name of Tintoretto was Jacopo Robusti, but he is better known by his nickname, meaning the ''little dyer,'' his father having been a silk dyer. The artist was born in Venice and lived there all his life. Even though his painting is distinguished by great daring, he seems to have led a rather retired life, concerned only with his work and the well-being of his family. His daughter Marietta and his sons Domenico and Marco also became painters, and Domenico eventually took over the direction of Tintoretto's large workshop, turning out reliable but uninspired pictures in the manner of his father. Some of them are, on occasion, mistaken for works of the elder Tintoretto.

Tintoretto appears to have studied with Bonifazio Veronese or Paris Bordone, but his true master, as of all the great Venetian painters in his succession, was Titian. Tintoretto's work by no means merely reflects the manner of Titian. Instead he builds on Titian's art and brings into play an imagination so fiery and quick that he creates an effect of restlessness which is quite opposed to the staid and majestic certainty of Titian's statements. If Tintoretto's pictures at first sight often astonish by their melodrama, they almost inevitably reveal, at closer observation, a focal point celebrating the wonders of silence and peace. The sensation of this ultimate gentleness, after the first riotous impact, is particularly touching and in essence not different from what we find (although brought about by very different means) in the pictures of Titian and Paolo Veronese.

Tintoretto was primarily a figure painter and delighted in showing his figures in daring foreshortening and expansive poses. His master in this aspect of his art was Michelangelo. Tintoretto is supposed to have inscribed on the wall of his studio the motto: ''The drawing of Michelangelo and the color of Titian.'' Unlike Michelangelo, however, Tintoretto worked and drew very quickly, using only lights and shadows in the modeling of his forms, so that his figures look as if they had gained their plasticity by a kind of magic. In the rendering of large compositions he is reported to have used as models small figures which he made of wax and placed or hung in boxes so cleverly illuminated that the conditions

of light and shade in the picture he was painting would be the same as those in the room in which it was to be hung.

Early Style

Tintoretto's earliest work to be dated with certainty, *Apollo and Marsyas* (1545), was painted for Pietro Aretino, who, in a letter written expressly for publication, noted the quickness of its execution and recommended the artist to the world as a genius of note. At about the same time Tintoretto painted the large and deeply moving *Christ Washing the Feet of the Apostles* (Madrid), in which greatness of gesture and extreme foreshortening are balanced by the dramatic light which pervades the painting and the intensity of feeling which distinguishes the movement of each of the participants in the scene. The picture is so arranged that we see Christ and St. Peter (in the extreme right corner) last, even though—and yet exactly because—they matter most in the story the picture brings to life. The action which binds these key figures together is dramatized chiefly by an exchange of glances. Throughout Tintoretto's career these elements of procedure, though richly varied and always in harmony with the sense of the story he represents, remain central to his art.

Other early paintings of note in Tintoretto's oeuvre are his *Last Supper* (S. Marcuola, Venice), *St. George and the Dragon, Presentation of the Virgin,* and *St. Mark Rescuing a Slave,* where St. Mark is shown coming from heaven and through the air, headfirst into the depth of the picture, to rescue an ever so nobly painted enslaved Christian who is awaiting execution at the hands of a group of pagans dressed in richly shining Turkish costumes.

Mature Style

The works of Tintoretto's mature style, though often even more dramatic than his early one,s are distinguished by a greater compositional unity and a richer splendor of muted colors. As before, the actions of his figures are breathtakingly daring, but now they hardly ever strike us as extravagant, so well and with such majesty do they serve their function in the dramatization of the story. Examples of this style are the *Last Supper* (ca. 1560; S. Trovaso, Venice), the *Last Judgement* (ca.1560; S. Maria dell'Orto, Venice), the *Adoration of the Golden Calf* (ca. 1560), the *Finding of the Body of St. Mark* (ca. 1562), and the *Removal of the Body of St. Mark* (ca. 1562), in which a thunderstorm is painted with the same dramatic intensity as the principal figures.

The triumph of Tintoretto's art is his paintings for the Scuola di S. Rocco in Venice, which he executed intermittently between 1564 and 1587. The walls and the ceilings are almost completely covered with works invented and, to a great extent, executed by him in their entirety. The paintings celebrate great events of the Old and New Testaments and the lives of the saints. St. Roch, under whose patronage the confraternity to which the Scuola belonged performed its works of charity, is especially honored.

The culmination of the whole work is the vast *Crucifixion* (1565) in the Sala dell'Albergo. The action is represented at the moment when the sponge is being dipped in vinegar to be lifted up on a stick to Christ. A multitude surrounds the cross—soldiers, followers of Christ, mockers, pagans, and contemporaries of Tintoretto (clearly marked as portraits), who behold the sacred scene as if it were happening now. The cross of the good thief is being pulled into position; a ladder, ready for the deposition, lies on the ground and leads our eye far back into the painting; the bad thief is about to be nailed to his cross, which lies on the ground. Mary, at the foot of the cross, has fainted into the arms of her companions. The work is virtually a night piece built around a glory of light which emanates from Christ on the cross. The whole composition revolves around Christ, and this is accomplished by a most sophisticated arrangement of dramatic gestures, an extraordinarily daring use of foreshortening leading from our space into that of the painting and back, and, above all, a management of lights which connects our time with that of the Crucifixion and the timelessness of the event with the natural world.

The great majority of Tintoretto's large canvases were history paintings with religious subjects. Among his late works, which are distinguished by the joining of a noble naturalism with an ever greater and touching spirituality, is the vast representation of Paradise in the Sala del Gran Consiglio of the Doges' Palace (1588), in which the Madonna and saints, led by St. Mark, recommend the Great Council of Venice and its decisions to the grace of Christ. The countless figures are bathed in a strange, phosphorescent light. Another late work, of incredible daring and yet ultimately quiet in its effect, is the Last *Supper* (1592-1594; S. Giorgio Maggiore, Venice). Tintoretto fills the air of the great hall with a rush of adoring angels; their presence is made visible by subtle highlights accentuating the darkness of the room.

Secular Paintings

Tintoretto's allegorical works and scenes from ancient and modern history include the ribald *Mars, Venus, and Vulcan* (ca. 1550), which shows Mars hiding under a bed to escape detection by Vulcan, who, having returned home unannounced, is approaching Venus; the melodramatic and yet affecting *Rape of Lucretia* (ca. 1556-1559); and a number of paintings for the Doges' Palace in Venice. These include tightly knit battle scenes on land and sea and allegories in praise of Venice that feature, with much dedication to their beauty and grace, the gods of classical antiquity. Perhaps the noblest among the allegorical paintings is *Bacchus and Ariadne* (1578). The god walks through the sea to offer Ariadne the ring that will unite them in marriage. Above the couple a personification of the air (or Venus) with one hand holds Ariadne's hand and with the other holds aloft Bacchus's gift to his beloved, a starry crown. On the allegorical level this painting may be interpreted as the loving homage of the mainland, represented by Bacchus, to the beauty, grace, and merit of Venice.

Tintoretto was much sought after as a portraitist. His figures are almost always elegant and extraordinarily decorous, the women gentle and the men impressive, both tinged with a certain loneliness. Infinitely moving is his self-portrait as an old man (1588, Paris) in a very simple pose, en face, resigned and wise.

Further Reading

The most useful work on Tintoretto in English is still Hans Tietze, *Tintoretto: The Paintings and Drawings* (1948), although it shows touches of an expressionist bias. A remarkable and far-reaching study, perhaps confused in its search for standards of taste by which to judge Tintoretto's art appropriately, is F. P. B. Osmaston, *The Art and Genius of Tintoret* (2 vols., 1915); it is a very dated work but worth reading if only for its bravery in the questions it raises. John Ruskin's discussions of Tintoretto's art in *Modern Painters* (5 vols., 1843-1860) and *The Stones of Venice* (3 vols., 1851-1853) are passionately evocative and sometimes severely critical. □

Michael Kemp Tippett

Although the compositions of Sir Michael Kemp Tippett (born 1905) are not frequently performed, he is considered one of England's most important composers.

Michael Tippett was born in London on Jan. 2, 1905, and was attracted to music at an early age. His formal training was at the Royal College of Music, after which he taught school for a few years. He resigned to devote all of his time to composition and moved to a small village, where he worked steadily for several years. Later he destroyed all these early attempts and went back to the Royal College for further study.

Tippett then became musical director of Morley College in London, a college for working men and women, a position he held during the war years when London was under repeated attacks. He became known to the musical world as a skilled choral conductor with a contagious enthusiasm for music. A pacifist with firm convictions, he was jailed for three months in 1943, when he refused to accept the duties assigned him as a conscientious objector, holding that his musical activities were more important.

The cantata *A Child of Our Time* (1939; first performance 1944), written in protest over the fierce Nazi pogroms, reflects Tippett's strong feelings about the inhumanity of war. The work includes several black spirituals which are used as symbols of all persecuted peoples, giving the cantata broad significance. Following the end of World War II, the cantata was performed in several European countries that had been occupied by the Germans.

Tippett resigned from Morley College in 1951 and devoted himself to composition and to occasional appearances on the BBC radio and television. He was awarded several honorary doctorates, named commander of the Order of the British Empire, and was knighted in 1966. In the same year, he was composer-in-residence at the Aspen Festival.

Tippett's main early instrumental works are *Concerto for Double String Orchestra* (1940), *Fantasia Concertante on a Theme of Corelli* (1953), and *Concerto for Orchestra* (1963). These works tend to classify him as a neoclassic composer insofar as he employs baroque contrapuntal textures and intricate rhythms. His operas show a more subjective side of his musical personality. The *Midsummer Marriage* (1955) is ritualistic and symbolic, a kind of 20th-century *Magic Flute* in its mixture of high seriousness and comedy. Later operas are *King Priam* (1962) and *The Knot Garden* (1970), with a psychoanalytic theme. He also composed several choral works and songs.

It is difficult to categorize Tippett's music, because it follows none of the well-publicized avant-garde trends, but neither is it old-fashioned or reactionary. His style is a highly individual one, based on medieval polyphony, madrigal techniques, baroque textures, and 20th-century rhythms and harmonies.

Tippett unveiled a new work, *Symphony No. 3* for soprano and orchestra, in 1972. The London Symphony Orchestra commissioned it, with a text by the composer. It consisted of two parts: the first entirely instrumental, followed by a soprano in sequence with four blues parts. *Symphony No. 3* made its U.S. debut in 1974. That same year, Tippett made a two-month tour of the U.S., appearing as the conductor in Chicago during the performance of *Symphony No. 3*. He later appeared at the U.S. premiere of the opera *The Knot Garden* in Evanston, IL, and at a performance of his *Double Concerto* by the New York Philharmonic.

The composer conducted a lecture tour in the U.S. in 1976, and the next year attended the world premiere of his *Symphony No. 4,* commissioned and performed by the Chicago Symphony. That year also marked the debut of his fourth opera, *The Ice Break,* Tippett's first opera in a contemporary setting. The drama focused on family problems, racial tensions, and the drug scene. At one point in the opera, there is a confrontation between two rival gangs, one led by a jazz clarinetist, and the other by a classical violinist. *The Ice Break* made its U.S. debut in Boston in 1979.

Tippett celebrated his 75th birthday with the world premiere of *String Quartet No. 4* in January 1980. It was just one of many extensive performances in Great Britain and elsewhere celebrating Tippett's milestone. Later that year, Tippett wrote *Triple Concerto,* for violin, viola, cello and orchestra, which was commissioned by the London Symphony Orchestra.

Tippett celebrated his 80th birthday with a two-week tour of Texas in January, 1985. The Houston Symphony performed several of his best works, and Tippett conducted two of the pieces, despite suffering from blindness in his right eye. The Dallas Symphony Orchestra performed the U.S. premiere of *Words for Music Perhaps,* which was actually written 25 years prior. This piece combined chamber music with a narrator reading text and poems. Following Dallas, Tippett went to Los Angeles for the world premiere of his *Fourth Piano Sonata,* then on to England for a series of events commemorating his birthday.

Tippett wrote his fifth opera, *New Year,* which made its world premiere in Houston in 1989. Like his previous works, it was quite eccentric, providing wild imagery with emotional music. Tippett had previously stated he would write no more operas, but said *New Year* insisted on being

composed. It made its European debut at Glyndebourne in
July 1990. The following year, Tippett unveiled *Byzantium,*
a setting for soprano and orchestra over the Yeats poem. It
was commissioned by the Chicago Symphony and Carnegie
Hall, each celebrating their 100th year.

At the age of 90, Tippett was still composing music. In
1995, the London Symphony Orchestra gave the first public
performance of *The Rose Lake,* which Tippett called a
"song without words." The orchestra devoted much of its
concert season to music by Tippett in honor of his birthday.
His rich but idiosyncratic scores continued to gain the recognition they so deserved.

Further Reading

Selected writings and broadcast talks of Tippett were published
as *Moving into Aquarius* (1959). A collection of essays on
various aspects of Tippett's music is Ian Kemp, ed., *Michael
Tippett: A Symposium on His Sixtieth Birthday* (1965). Also,
read Arnold Whittall's *The Music of Britten and Tippett:
Studies on Themes and Techniques* (1982), which details the
writings of Benjamin Britten and Michael Tippett. □

Tippu Tip

**Tippu Tip (ca. 1840-1905), or Hamed bin Moham-
med bin Juma bin Rajab el Murjebi, was a Zanzibari
trader who extended his influence into the Congo
region and much of East Africa.**

Hamed bin Mohammed el Murjebi was born into a
Zanzibar merchant dynasty at a time when trading
routes from that East African metropolis were beginning to reach into the area which today forms the Republic of Zaïre. His first expedition around the southern tip of
Lake Tanganyika into northern Katanga took place in 1859-
1860 and was followed by two more campaigns along the
same route (which he preferred to the more commonly
traveled route via Tabora and Ujiji) in 1865 and 1867-1869.
It was during the course of his third expedition that he
gained the nickname of Tippu Tip, an onomatopoeic imitation of his firearms, and befriended the British missionary
and explorer David Livingstone.

In 1870, at the head of a 4,000-man caravan, Tippu Tip
returned to the Congo and, over the following decade, built
a formidable empire centered in the Maniema region, between the Lualaba and Lomami rivers, where British explorer V. L. Cameron visited him in 1874. In the process
Tippu Tip established his ascendancy over a number of
African chiefs who agreed to serve as his auxiliaries, as well
as over a number of rival Zanzibari traders who had preceded him on the Upper Congo and had set up an entrepôt
at Nyangwe.

With Stanley in the Congo

There, in October 1876, Tippu Tip met Henry Stanley,
who persuaded Tippu Tip to escort him down the Congo

River. Although Tippu Tip accompanied Stanley only half-
way, to the Stanley Falls (at the site of modern Kisangani), he
later returned to the area, and his caravans gradually pushed
farther and farther downriver, to the point where the
Aruwimi River joins the Congo.

In the meantime, however, Tippu Tip had returned to
Zanzibar and had been approached by Sultan Bargash of
Zanzibar as well as by an envoy of King Leopold II of
Belgium for the purpose of enlisting his influence in support
of their respective ambitions. During 1883-1884 Tippu Tip
seems to have been playing both ends of the field or to have
been divided between his loyalty to the Sultan and his
realization that European influence would probably prevail
in the Congo.

During Tippu Tip's absence, Stanley (now in King Leopold's employ) reappeared on the Upper Congo to found a
post at Stanley Falls, a site which Arab traders also wanted
to use for commercial purposes. In June 1884 a modus
vivendi was reached between Tippu Tip's lieutenants and
King Leopold's representatives regarding each group's respective sphere of influence, but Tippu Tip rejected this
settlement and established himself at Stanley Falls to personally supervise the situation in November 1884.

Decline of Zanzibar's Power

The Berlin Conference, however, summarily disposed
of Zanzibari territorial claims, and relations between Arab
traders and agents of the Congo Free State rapidly deteriorated. Tippu Tip traveled back to Zanzibar in 1886 across
what had now officially become German East Africa, and in
his absence his men burned down the Congo Frees State
post at Stanley Falls. In Zanzibar, Tippu Tip realized (as did
the Sultan himself) that the days of Zanzibari power had
passed, and in February 1887 he accepted from Stanley a
commission from the Congo Free State as governor of the
Stanley Falls district. At the same time, he also agreed to
man the expedition which Stanley had been commissioned
to organize for the purpose of rescuing Emin Pasha (E.
Schnitzer), a German condottiere in the service of Egypt
who had been stranded in the Bahr el Ghazal area as a result
of the Mahdist uprising in Sudan.

Tippu Tip traveled back to the Upper Congo in the
company of Stanley but this time by way of the Atlantic
coast and up the Congo River. Aside from its doubtful usefulness, the relief expedition was marred by the near annihi-
lation of its rearguard, a disaster for which Stanley
attempted to place the blame on Tippu Tip.

The old trader returned to Zanzibar in 1890 to defend
himself in the lawsuit brought against him by Stanley. Although Tippu Tip's good faith was vindicated, he never
returned to the Congo. In the meantime, relations between
the Congo Free State and the Arabs had begun to deteriorate
again as a result of various European activities which undermined the Arabs' commercial position.

Tippu Tip's son, Sefu, attempted to reassert control over
one of his father's African auxiliaries, Ngongo Lutete. The
latter, however, went over to the side of the Congo Free
State, and in the ensuing conflict (1892-1894) the commercial and political control of the Arab traders over the eastern

Congo was shattered and Sefu himself was killed. Tippu Tip, who had vainly tried to dissuade his son from opening hostilities against the Europeans, spent his last years in retirement disrupted by litigation.

Further Reading

Tippu Tip related the story of his life in Heinrich Brode, *Tippoo Tib: The Story of His Career in Central Africa* (1907). Accounts of Tippu Tip's career are in Roland Oliver and Gervase Mathew, eds., *History of East Africa,* vol. 1 (1963), and Eric Stokes and Richard Brown, *The Zambesian Past: Studies in Central African History* (1966). ☐

Tipu Sultan

Tipu Sultan (1750-1799) was a Moslem ruler of Mysore. He was the most powerful of all the native princes of India and the greatest threat to the English position in southern India.

Tipu was born at Devanhalli, the son of Haidar Ali. Himself illiterate, Haidar was very particular in giving his eldest son a prince's education and a very early exposure to military and political affairs. From the age of 17 Tipu was given independent charge of important diplomatic and military missions. He was his father's right arm in the wars from which Haidar emerged as the most powerful ruler of southern India.

In 1782, when Haidar died during the Second Anglo-Mysore War, Tipu was very effective in bringing the west coast under his control. After his accession, he continued the war until the English were forced to make peace with him.

Mysore was now too strong and, under Tipu's efficient and dedicated administration, was growing too much in power for his neighboring states to feel secure. The Marathas in the northwest, joining the Nizam in the north, became embroiled with Tipu in 1785. They were defeated, but Tipu gave them very lenient peace terms in the vain hope of winning their friendship against the English, who he knew would resume hostilities with him as soon as they could. Simultaneously, he continued his friendly overtures to the English. Isolated from his neighbors in India, he also sent embassies to France and to the Caliph at Constantinople to gain their support, but little real benefit came of it.

By 1790 the East India Company, much better organized than ever before and now directly supported by the British government, was dead set on subjugating Tipu. Allying with the Marathas and the Nizam, it put all its might into an expedition against Mysore. Tipu lost half of his kingdom.

Despite this reduction in his territory, Tipu recuperated with such rapidity that he was still considered a very dangerous rival by the English. In 1799 the East India Company, again joined by the Marathas and the Nizam, attacked Tipu.

Pushed back to his capital and besieged, the brave sultan fell, fighting to the last; Mysore fell into English hands.

Tipu's power rested not only on his large, excellent army but on the great prosperity of the state he developed through humane and systematic agrarian and mercantilistic policies. Fearing God, exerting himself for his subjects, and indulgently forgiving transgressions, he firmly wiped out all stubborn disloyalty to the state without partiality to caste or creed.

Further Reading

Still useful is L. B. Bowring, *Haidar Alí and Tipú Sultán* (1893). Mohibbul Hasan Khan, *History of Tipu Sultan* (1951), is sympathetic and well balanced. For background information P. E. Roberts, *History of British India* (1921; 3d ed. 1952), and Percival Spear, *India: A Modern History* (1961), are recommended.

Additional Sources

Ali, B. Sheikh. *Tipu Sultan: a study in diplomacy and confrontation,* Mysore: Geetha Book House, 1982.
Sharma, H. D. (Hari Dev). *The real Tipu: a brief history of Tipu Sultan,* Varanasi: Rishi Publications, 1991.
Jalaja Caktitacan. *Tippu Sultan, a fanatic?,* Madras: Nithyananda Jothi Nilayam, 1990. ☐

Tiradentes

Tiradentes (1748-1792), or José Joaquim da Silva Xavier, was a precursor of Brazilian independence and the national hero of Brazil. He led the 1789 Minas Gerais conspiracy in favor of Brazilian independence and was executed by the Portuguese.

José Joaquim da Silva Xavier was born in the small town of Pombal (today Tiradentes), Minas Gerais, on Nov. 12, 1748. His parents were moderately wealthy, but little evidence exists that he had much formal education. He worked as a merchant and dentist and served in the militia as a cavalry officer. Most often he is picturesquely known by his profession, Tiradentes, or the "toothpuller." He traveled in the captaincies of Minas Gerais, São Paulo, and Rio de Janeiro and was aware of and disturbed by the major problems besetting Brazil at the end of the 18th century.

An influx of enlightened ideas from Europe and a growing economic discontent prompted some intellectuals to conspire against Portuguese rule. The first such major conspiracy centered in Minas Gerais at the end of the 18th century. Tiradentes assumed a leading role in that conspiracy, known in Brazilian history as the *Inconfidência Mineira*. When word spread that Portugal planned to collect back taxes, the plotters redoubled their activity in the early months of 1789.

Romantic and unrealistic, the plans never passed the hypothetical stage. All agreed that Brazil should be independent. Beyond that, they did not concur. Some were republicans, others monarchists; some advocated the abolition of slavery, others favored the institution. Tiradentes, an admirer of the U.S. Constitution, advocated a republic. While they debated, informers reported their meetings and intentions to Portuguese authorities. The Crown ordered their arrest. Tiradentes was seized while on a mission to Rio de Janeiro.

The investigation and trial extended over a period of 3 years. Tiradentes maintained before the courts that he was the leader of the conspiracy and responsible for it. On April 18, 1892, the court handed down the sentences. Only one of the death sentences was carried out, that of Tiradentes. Deemed "unworthy of royal mercy," he was hanged and quartered in Rio de Janeiro on April 21, 1792.

The principal result of the brutal execution was the creation of a martyr to Brazilian independence. Thereafter, Tiradentes acquired a more significant place in history than his impractical plans merited. Today, Brazilians regard him as their national hero. The plot itself indicated the degree to which many ideas of the Enlightenment had penetrated the interior of Brazil to agitate the waters of economic and political discontent.

Further Reading

References to Tiradentes appear in general works on Brazilian history, among them João P. Calogeras, *A History of Brazil*
(trans. 1939); Andrew Marshall, *Brazil* (1966); and Rollie E. Poppino, *Brazil: The Land and People* (1968). □

Tirso de Molina

The Spanish dramatist Tirso de Molina (1584-1648), to whom is attributed the initiation of the Don Juan theme, ranks as one of the three greatest dramatists of Spain's Golden Age of literature.

The identity of the family of Tirso de Molina and most of the facts of his life remain obscure. Born Gabriel Téllez in Madrid, he studied at the University of Alcalá and in 1601 entered the Order of the Merced as a monk. He probably initiated his career as a dramatist about 1605 with *El vergonzoso en palacio* (*The Bashful Man at Court*). After representing his order in Santo Domingo in the West Indies from 1616 to 1618, he returned to Madrid, where in 1621 he published his first book, *Los cigarrales de Toledo* (*The Orchards of Toledo*), a miscellany. Tirso was chronicler of the Order of the Merced in 1637 and prior of a monastery in Soria in 1645.

In his writings Tirso portrayed human foibles and vices with such scatological humor that in 1625 he was ordered silenced by the Council of Castile—an order he disobeyed—and was exiled to remote rural monasteries. Although his self-styled nephew, Francisco Lucas de Ávila, claimed that Tirso wrote more than 400 plays, only 55 authentically assigned to him are extant. Some 28 other plays he probably wrote in collaboration.

Tirso's work encompasses most of the subjects prevalent in the 17th-century Spanish theater: Spanish and Portuguese history and tradition, biblical material, contemporary customs, and palace intrigues—as well as one-act religious plays called *autos sacramentales*. Conjugal honor preoccupied him less than it did his contemporaries. He has generally been classified with Lope de Vega and Pedro Calderón as a member of the triumvirate of foremost 17th-century Spanish dramatists. Pending definite proof of Tirso's authorship of *El burlador de Sevilla* (*The Love Rogue*) and *El condenado por desconfiado* (*The Man Condemned for Little Faith*), his position in the triumvirate remains debatable.

Don Juan

El burlador de Sevilla initiated the Don Juan theme. The protagonist of this play is a wealthy libertine, Don Juan Tenorio, whose sole aim in life is seduction. During the play's three acts he victimizes four women, two from the upper classes and two from the peasantry. In scenes set in Italy and in Spain, he incites others to violence by his lawless conduct. In one scene, after he accosts Doña Ana in her bedroom and her distinguished father, the Commander of Calatrava, attempts to rescue her, he kills her father. A stone statue is erected over the Commander's tomb.

Don Juan comes across this tomb by chance and mockingly invites the statue to supper. The statue accepts the

mingled conquistadores and passionate and warlike Amazons.

Tirso's light comedies include *El vergonzoso en palacio,* with a provocative and mischievous young countess as its protagonist; *Marta la piadosa* (*Martha the Hypocrite*), a play about another provocative young woman; and *Don Gil de las calzas verdes* (*The Man in Green Britches*), a comedy crowded with bawdy humor and pornography.

Tirso's supreme accomplishment was the creation of unforgettable characters with psychologically sound motivations: Don Juan, the libertine of *The Love Rogue;* Tisbea, the peasant girl who rents the air with her anguish when seduced and abandoned by Don Juan; Paulo, the outlaw, and Enrico, the hermit, of *The Man Condemned for Little Faith;* Maria de Molina, the canny regent of *Feminine Shrewdness;* Martha, the engagingly pious fraud of *Martha the Hypocrite;* Gonzalo Pizarro, the conquistador of *Amazons in the New World;* the comic Tello of *El amor médico* (*Love the Physician*); and the chickenhearted youth Rodrigo of *El castigo del Penséque* (*A Lesson for Mr. Alibi*).

Further Reading

Competent translations of Tirso's plays are lacking, except for two translations of *El burlador de Sevilla:* Harry Kemp's, published as *The Love Rogue* (1923), and Ray Campbell's, titled *The Trickster of Seville and His Guest of Stone,* included in Eric Bentley, ed., *The Classic Theatre* (4 vols., 1956-1961). Ilsa Barea translated *Three Husbands Hoaxed* (1955). A brief and rather subjective study of Tirso and his works is in Gerald Brenan, *The Literature of the Spanish People from Roman Times to the Present Day* (1951; rev. ed. 1953). Alice Huntington Bushee, *Three Centuries of Tirso de Molina* (1939), is primarily for the specialist. Leo Weinstein, *The Metamorphoses of Don Juan* (1959), traces the story of the Don Juan legend. Background on the Spanish stage of Tirso's time is in Hugo A. Rennert, *The Spanish Stage in the Time of Lope de Vega* (1909). For historical background see John A. Crow, *Spain: The Root and the Flower* (1963). □

invitation, appears at Don Juan's supper, and in turn invites Don Juan to dine with him in the graveyard. As a point of honor Don Juan never refuses any challenge to his courage. He accepts the statue's invitation, and he is served hideous food on a coal-black table. After supper the host offers his hand. Contact with the statue seems to ignite unearthly fires, and both descend to hell. An offstage chorus ominously chants a melancholy admonition: "No debt in life is left unpaid. . . ."

Other Dramas

In other plays Tirso raised theological issues momentous in his day. His greatest theological play, if it is his, is *El condenado por desconfiado.* It is based upon the story of the two thieves on the crosses. In the play a criminal, Enrico, is saved by unswerving faith, and an intellectual hermit, Paulo, is lost through philosophical doubt.

La prudencia en la mujer (*Feminine Shrewdness*) vies for first place among Tirso's historical works. The play takes its subject from Spain's past—the childhood of Fernando IV (1285-1312)—and it portrays the regency of Fernando's mother, Maria de Molina, who retains the throne for her 14-year-old son against the treachery of the deceased king's two brothers. Tirso also wrote a historical trilogy about Francisco, Hernando, and Gonzalo Pizarro in order to pay homage to the brothers and discredit their enemy, Diego de Almagro. In this trilogy Tirso blended history, tradition, and fantasy, especially in the second play, *Amazons en las Indias* (*Amazons in the New World*), in which he com-

Tisch brothers

The Tisch brothers were major forces in the real estate industry with diversification into other areas. Laurence Alan (born 1923) became CEO of CBS, while Preston Robert (born 1926) once served as postmaster general of the United States.

Laurence Alan Tisch was born in Brooklyn on March 5, 1923, and his brother, Preston Robert (Bob), was born in Brooklyn on April 29, 1926. Their father, Abraham Solomon (Al), was a businessman in the garment industry who also owned two children's camps which he and his wife, Sadye, managed during the summers when the garment industry traditionally closed down.

Laurence attended New York University, from which he graduated *cum laude* with a B.Sc. at the age of 18 in 1942. Subsequently, he became one of the school's major benefactors. Laurence was awarded an M.A. in industrial engineering from the University of Pennsylvania in 1943 and attended Harvard Law School in 1946. Bob attended Bucknell but left for Army service in 1943, and after his discharge in 1944, he enrolled at the University of Michigan, from which he received a B.A. with a major in economics in 1948.

Laurence Tisch purchased his first hotel, Laurel-in-the-Pines in Lakewood, New Jersey, shortly after leaving Harvard. He refurbished the place, altered its management, and made it one of the more popular resorts in the area. When Bob graduated from the University of Michigan he joined his brother, and that year they purchased another hotel, the Grand in the Catskills. Other hotels in Atlantic City followed, as the Tisches were becoming a force in the resorts business and were especially well-known for turning around unprofitable operations.

In the 1950s the Tisches took positions in Manhattan hotels, and there repeated their successes at the resorts. In 1955 they constructed their first hotel, the Americana in Bal Harbour, Florida, which soon became one of the state's most important convention centers.

In this period the larger motion picture studios also owned theaters which exhibited their movies. As a result of an antitrust decision, the two operations had been separated, and one result was the creation of Metro-Goldwyn-Mayer and Loews Theaters out of what had been Loews, Inc.

Preston Tisch

Perceiving that while the theaters themselves were not particularly profitable, the land on which they were located had unrealized value, the Tisches started purchasing shares in Loews Theaters in 1959 and in September had enough equity to be named to the board. They continued their purchases and in January 1961 were able to displace the existing management and take charge of the company.

With this, the Tisches initiated a program of selling some theaters and razing others to construct hotels on the sites. Their initial project was the Summit, which replaced an antiquated theater on Lexington Avenue in New York City. Many others followed, as well as management contracts for hotels owned by others. By the end of the 1960s, Loews was one of the nation's largest hotel chains. In light of this transformation, in 1971 the Tisches renamed the company Loews Corporation.

Not content with this, the Tisches decided to recast Loews as a conglomerate. Their first move in this direction came in 1968 with the acquisition of Lorillard, the nation's fifth largest cigarette company, which itself had become a conglomerate. This acquisition was somewhat contentious. The modern anti-smoking campaign had begun in the early 1950s and was meeting with success. By the time of the Loews-Lorillard merger, it appeared cigarette smoking would only continue to decline. Anticipating difficulties, the companies diversified into other areas. Lorillard purchased Usen Canning, the second largest firm in the cat food business, and Golden Nuggets Sweets, a candy manufacturer.

Laurence Tisch cared little about the food operations, but recognized that Lorillard's assets were not reflected in its market price and that its cash flow would enable him to expand Loews' other operations more rapidly than might otherwise be the case. So he obtained the firm in a friendly takeover, cut its management force deeply, sold the candy and cat food business, and boosted profit margins greatly.

Another of Loews' acquisitions was Chicago-based CNA Financial, which was purchased in 1974. CNA was the holding company for Continental Casualty, a major factor in the fields of accident and health insurance, and Continental Assurance. In addition, CNA-owned General Finance and Tsai Management & Research, an important factor in the mutual fund industry.

The next acquisition was Bulova Watch, which was purchased in 1979. Once again the Tisches were to obtain a troubled company at a low price. At one time Bulova had been a style and technological leader in a strong American watch market, but the situation had changed by the late 1970s. Japanese watch companies were making significant inroads in Bulova's niche in the medium-price segment of the market, and Bulova had an operating loss in this period. After assuming control the Tisches installed new management, and within a year Bulova was reporting a profit.

As a result of these activities the Tisches had transformed Loews into one of the nation's largest conglomerates. By 1980 revenues came to $4.5 billion and earnings were $206 million. All segments of the business were doing well.

Typical of the Tisch operations was the 1982 purchase of seven oil tankers for $42 million at a time when the oil business was severely depressed. The price was quite low, and Laurence Tisch calculated that even if the industry did not recover, the ships might be sold profitably for scrap. After chartering them for a few years Loews sold one tanker for $15 million and in 1990 sold a half share in the remaining six for $154 million.

The Tisches' most contentious investment was CBS, the giant and troubled communications complex, which owned record, toy, and publishing companies as well as the large network. CBS seemed an ideal candidate for the Tisch treatment. It was mismanaged and so the shares were selling at a discount to net asset value. This led to hostile takeover offers from Ted Turner, who owned Cablenews Network; Marvin Davis, the owner of 20th Century Fox; and even a group including Senator Jesse Helms of North Carolina, who was conducting a vendetta against CBS News.

In order to prevent a takeover, CBS chairman Thomas Wyman ordered the repurchase of 21 percent of the firm's shares, which saddled the company with more than $1 billion in long-term debt. Wyman also sought a "white knight" and found him in the form of Laurence Tisch. With Wyman's blessings Loews started purchasing shares, reaching 24.9 percent of the outstanding common stock by the summer of 1986.

On September 10, Wyman was forced to resign and Tisch became acting chief executive officer (CEO) of CBS while retaining the chairmanship of Loews. Bob Tisch occupied no position at CBS. In 1986 he left Loews to become postmaster general, serving until 1989 when he returned to the firm. As was his practice, Laurence Tisch started firing executives and considering the sale of assets. In return for CBS's publishing, record, and magazine divisions CBS was paid $3 billion in cash. Yet it was generally conceded that Tisch had not obtained top prices for any of these companies, all of which were sold at times when their fortunes were improving. In addition, Tisch's attempts to squeeze savings out of the network resulted in lower ratings and a continued slide in operating profits, which were compensated for by interest on the firm's cash hoard. Meanwhile, in 1991 Preston (Bob) realized a lifetime ambition by buying a half interest in the New York Giants football team.

Throughout the 1990s the Tisch fiscal kingdom continued to grow. Laurence, known for his high stakes investments, was often mentioned in the same financial tabloid articles with his friend and occasional competitor, Warren Buffett. The Loews Corporation was ranked number sixty-four on the Fortune 500 with revenues of $13.5 billion in 1994. That same year, Loews earned a reported $155 million in tax-free income, just from a CBS stock buy-back deal. In 1996 the brothers were reported to each own 16 percent of the company. To keep business matters in the family and their sons involved in running the Loews empire, a total of five Tisches sat on various company boards by 1997. The Tish brothers' "Midas Touch" coupled with shrewd investment strategy and deep fiscal pockets made them a major force on the American business scene.

Further Reading

W. R. Shelton, "Tisches Eye their Next $65 Million," *Fortune* (January 1960); V. Lawrence, "Running a Conglomerate like a Candy Store," *Nation's Business* (August 1981); "CBS Finds a Friend," *Fortune* (November 11, 1985); L. Baum and L. Lieberman, "Has Larry Tisch Sold Too Much of CBS?" *Business Week* (July 25, 1988); Subrata N. Chakravarty, "Behind All That Shuffling and Reshuffling at CBS," *Forbes* (August 8, 1988); "Head of Loews Likely Choice for Postmaster General's Job," *New York Times* (August 6, 1986); "The Quiet Billionaire," *U.S. News and World Report* (February 8, 1988); "Loews Sees the Future, and It's Oil," *Business Week* (March 19, 1990), and "Tisch the Younger Takes His Turn," detailing a busy day in the life of Preston (Bob), *Business Week* (July 8, 1991) are but a sampling of available sources. Updates on the Loews Corporation can be found in business references such as the *Hoover's Handbook of American Business*. □

Arne Wilhelm Kaurin Tiselius

The Swedish biochemist Arne Wilhelm Kaurin Tiselius (1902-1971) was awarded the Nobel Prize for Chemistry for his researches on electrophoresis and adsorption analysis, especially for his discoveries concerning the nature of the serum proteins.

Arne Tiselius, son of Dr. Hans A. Tiselius, was born in Stockholm on Aug. 10, 1902. He studied chemistry at the University of Uppsala. Following his graduation in 1925, he became research assistant to the physical chemist Professor The Svedberg, the inventor of the ultracentrifuge. In 1925 Tiselius began to use electrophoretic analysis, long employed for proteins and enzymes. This method studies the migration of the components in a solution under the influence of an electric field, their moving boundaries being observed by fluorescent photography. Tiselius found the method unsatisfactory, and he developed the method of observing the components by ultraviolet-light photography, using quartz lenses and a special light filter. He considered his method very specific, but he felt that its resolution capacity was not sufficiently high. He graduated as a doctor of science at Uppsala in 1930 with a thesis on this work, and he then became assistant professor of chemistry in the University of Uppsala.

As there was no chair of biochemistry in Sweden, Tiselius turned to the inorganic field, and he published research on the diffusion and adsorption phenomena in zeolite crystals. While holding a Rockefeller Fellowship at Princeton University in the United States, he was stimulated to continue his protein studies. On his return to Uppsala in 1935, he redesigned his electrophoretic apparatus and published his new model in 1937. Outstanding among the numerous advances made with his new apparatus was his demonstration that blood serum consists of albumins and of alpha, beta, and gamma globulins. These methods and results were widely used in the United States during World

Edward Bradford Titchener

The Anglo-American psychologist Edward Bradford Titchener (1867-1927) was the head of the structural school of psychology.

E dward Titchener was born on Jan. 11, 1867, in Chichester, England. The family was old and distinguished, but there was little wealth. By scholarship, Titchener entered Malvern College, a top Anglican preparatory school, and demonstrated characteristic drive and excellence. One year, when school awards were presented by the visiting American poet James Russell Lowell, Titchener was called so often that Lowell remarked, "Mr. Titchener, I am tired of seeing your face."

The family intended Titchener for the Anglican clergy, but his interests were not in religion. In 1885 he entered Brasenose College, Oxford, on a classics scholarship but soon turned to a study of biology and then comparative psychology. He met Sir John Scott Burdon-Sanderson, one of England's first experimental biologists, and two great exponents of Darwinism, T. H. Huxley and John George Romanes. Titchener remained interested in comparative psychology, but there was not enough structure or rigor in the subject matter to satisfy him.

A few years earlier Wilhelm Wundt in Leipzig had founded psychology as a systematic and experimental science of the human mind. Burdon-Sanderson suggested that Titchener do his graduate work there in the "new psychology." With Wundt, Titchener found the kind of study he had been seeking, and this analytic study of human experience occupied him for the rest of his life.

After receiving his doctorate in 1892, Titchener accepted a position in the recently founded laboratory of psychology at Cornell University. He quickly rose to full professor and head of the department of psychology when psychology became independent from philosophy. To fill the void of textbooks in experimental psychology, he published his *Outline of Psychology* (1897) and his monumental four-volume *Experimental Psychology* (1901-1905). He was an inspiring speaker, and his lectures became legend among generations of Cornell students.

Titchener emphasized psychology as a science, in contrast to technology, desiring to *understand* the facts of experience with no particular notion of application. His structural school studied the world of experience in terms of the experiencing individual and explained experience in terms of the nervous system. The model for structuralism was chemistry, the task being to analyze the complex experiences of everyday life into their elemental components and then to attempt to understand the nature of the compounding. His primary tool was introspection, the systematic description of experience. Titchener's *A Textbook of Psychology* (1910) became the bible of the school.

On Aug. 3, 1927, Titchener died in Ithaca. Without him and his system as a point of reference, systematic psychology was thrown into chaos, and perhaps because of this

War II, especially in relation to the fractionating of blood serum for transfusion purposes. In 1938 a research chair of biochemistry was created for Tiselius at Uppsala, and he worked at first in Svedberg's Institute of Physical Chemistry. In 1946 biochemistry became an independent department, and in 1950-1952 a new Institute of Biochemistry was built.

In 1940 Tiselius began to work on adsorption methods, and he developed especially the methods of frontal and displacement analyses. In this work he used chromatographic methods, and he developed his technique to provide accurate quantitative results. For his work in these two fields he was awarded the Nobel Prize in 1948.

Tiselius received honorary degrees from 13 universities and many other honors. In 1949 he became a Foreign Member of the National Academy of Sciences in Washington, and in 1957 he was elected a Foreign Member of the Royal Society. He became Vice President of the Nobel Foundation in 1947 and President in 1960. His published work appeared entirely in scientific journals. Tiselius died in Uppsala on Oct. 29, 1971.

Further Reading

There is a biography of Tiselius in *Nobel Lectures, Chemistry, 1942-1962* (1964), which also includes his Nobel Lecture. For his methods and results see A. White, P. Handler, and E. L. Smith, *Principles of Biochemistry* (3d ed. 1964), and E. and M. Lederer, *Chromatography* (2d ed. 1957). □

the day of the general psychological system soon came to an end.

Further Reading

There is no definitive biography of Titchener. A good discussion, though short, is in Edwin G. Boring, *Psychologist at Large* (1961). □

Titian

The Italian painter Titian (c. 1488-1576) was a great master of religious art, a portraitist in demand all over Europe, and the creator of mythological compositions which for inventiveness and decorative beauty have never been surpassed.

iziano Vecellio, known in English as Titian, was born at Pieve di Cadore in the Alps north of Venice. Regarding the year of his birth, modern criticism tends to reject the traditional date of 1477. Although the evidence is conflicting, the statements of contemporaries such as Lodovico Dolce and Giorgio Vasari, plus the fact that Titian's earliest works date from 1508, make the birth date of about 1488/1490 more reasonable.

At the age of 9 Titian set out with his brother Francesco for Venice to enter the workshop of the mosaicist Sebastiano Zuccati. Not long thereafter Titian began to study painting with Giovanni Bellini. Soon Titian met Bellini's other pupil, Giorgione, with whom he collaborated on his first certain work (1507-1508), the frescoes on the exterior of the German Merchants' Exchange (Fondaco dei Tedeschi) in Venice, works now known only in 18th-century prints and a few fragments. The two young painters collaborated so closely at this time that their styles are virtually indistinguishable.

Early Works, ca. 1510-1525

Titian's first major independent commission was the three large frescoes in the Confraternity of St. Anthony (Scuola del Santo) in Padua. His early portraits in half length placed behind a horizontal parapet are very closely related to those of Giorgione, for example, two canvases signed with Titian's initials, T. V., the *Gentleman in Blue* and *La Schiavona* (London). The triple portrait, the *Concert* (Florence), is now assigned to Titian with the possibility that Giorgione began the figure at the left. Titian's early religious pictures, such as the *Gypsy Madonna* and the *Madonna of the Cherries* (Vienna), maintain similarities to Giovanni Bellini and are notable for their beauty of color and the detached reflective mood which is often characterized as Giorgionesque.

Soon came Titian's first great mythological works: *Flora* (Florence) and *Sacred and Profane Love* (ca. 1515; Rome). The complexity of the iconography in the latter painting may be summarized as contrasting the nude Celestial Venus with the clothed Terrestrial Venus. The beauty of the landscape setting and the classical allusions are notable here.

Another work from this period is the famous *Christ and the Tribute Money* (ca. 1516; Dresden).

Titian's fame as an interpreter of classical mythology was firmly established by his three canvases (1518-1523) for the castle of Alfonso d'Este in Ferrara. The literary sources for these compositions are Philostratus's *Imagines,* Catullus's *Carmina,* and Ovid's *Fastii* and *Ars amatoria.* In the three paintings—the *Andrians,* the *Worship of Venus* (Madrid), and *Bacchus and Ariadne* (London)—Titian recreated the gaiety and abandon of classical legends, devising compositions of unprecedented beauty of color and design and establishing new canons of physical beauty.

An epoch-making work of Titian's early period is the *Assumption of the Virgin* (1516-1518; Venice). It marked the triumph of the High Renaissance in Venetian painting by virtue of the monumentality of the composition and the grandiose conception of the Virgin soaring with arms outstretched to heaven.

The Years 1525-1540

During the 1520s Titian produced masterpieces: the *Madonna and Child with Saints Francis and Aloysius* (1520; Ancona), the *Resurrection* altar (1522; Brescia), and the *Pesaro Madonna* (1519-1526; Venice). The diagonal composition of the last, set against a great portico with giant columns, and the luminosity of color, light, and atmosphere established a new formula for Venetian altars which continued into the following century. During this period the artist created the tragic *Entombment* (ca. 1526-1532; Paris).

The *Martyrdom of St. Peter Martyr* (ca. 1526-1530; destroyed 1867), once regarded as Titian's greatest masterpiece, involved a new feeling for heroic and dramatic action which is explained by Titian's acquaintance with the art of Michelangelo and the central Italians. Jacopo Sansovino and Sebastiano del Piombo came to Venice in 1527 after the sack of Rome, bringing to the Venetian more direct knowledge of artistic developments in the papal city.

Titian had formed a liaison with Cecilia, a young woman from Cadore with whom he had two sons, Pomponio in 1524 and Orazio in 1525. During her severe illness in 1525 the artist married her, and she lived another 5 years. They had two daughters, one of whom, Lavinia, survived. Titian was so prosperous that in 1531 he rented a luxurious palace, known as the Casa Grande, where he lived for the rest of his life.

An event of great importance in Titian's career was his trip to Bologna to attend the coronation of Charles V as Holy Roman emperor on Feb. 24, 1530. At this time the artist painted his first portrait of the Emperor in armor. The earliest surviving portrait, however, is *Charles V with a Hound* (Madrid), painted in February 1533 on Charles's second visit to Bologna. In May Charles V showed his appreciation of the artist's genius by making him a knight of the Golden Spur and Count Palatine.

At the same period Titian found time to provide a variety of works for several of his princely patrons: the *Madonna and Child with St. Catherine* for Ferrara (London), the *Madonna with the Rabbit* for the Gonzagas (Paris), and 11 portraits of Roman emperors (destroyed) for the Gonzagas. For the Duke of Urbino he painted the portraits *Duke Francesco Maria I della Rovere* and *Duchess Eleanora* and the famous *Venus of Urbino* (1538-1539; Florence). In Venice he supplied the large processional composition of the *Presentation of the Virgin* (1534-1538) with its array of portraits of contemporaries.

The Years 1540-1555

The next decade carried Titian even farther afield geographically and artistically. His *Christ before Pilate* (1543; Vienna) involves a new complexity of design in which the flight of steps rises obliquely and the figures in their variety of gestures and poses create a stir and excitement, denoting a change in style, charged with drama, which goes beyond Renaissance balance and repose toward the excitement of mannerist art. The Old Testament series of ceiling paintings (1543-1544) in S. Maria della Salute, Venice, planned to be seen from below, reflects Titian's interest in spatial illusionism introduced by Giulio Romano in his decorative works in the Palazzo del Te, Mantua.

A great event in Titian's life at this time was his sojourn in Rome from September 1545 until June 1546, at the invitation of Pope Paul III. For the first time Titian saw the glories of ancient Rome as well as the Renaissance masterpieces of Raphael and Michelangelo. He himself produced masterpieces during this stay in Rome: *Paul III and His Grandsons* (Naples), a presentation of a dramatic encounter between the aged pope and his scheming grandsons, one of the most psychologically revealing works in the history of

portraiture; and the official state portrait, *Paul III without Berretta* (Naples).

Back in Venice, Titian painted the *Christ Crowned with Thorns* (ca. 1545-1550; Paris), an interpretation in which the violent action and muscular physiques seem to reflect his familiarity with Hellenistic sculpture and Michelangelo's paintings, which he had seen in Rome. Titian's *Martyrdom of St. Lawrence* (1548-1557; Venice) was also in the new heroic vein, but even more epoch-making in the originality of its new diagonal structure of composition and the mood-evoking atmosphere.

In January 1548 Titian set forth for Augsburg, called there by Charles V. In his celebrated equestrian portrait, *Charles V at Mühlberg* (Madrid), which commemorates the victory over the German Protestants, Titian established a type of equestrian state portrait that presents the ruler as a symbol of power. *Charles V Seated* (Munich) is an intimate record of the sickly monarch. In October 1548 Titian returned to Venice, but Charles V recalled him to Augsburg in October 1550. Of the several portraits he executed of members of the Emperor's court, the most important is that of the youthful Prince Philip (later Philip II) in armor, a work which set a standard for state portraits. During the 1550s the Hapsburgs continued to be Titian's most important patrons. For Charles V he painted three superb devotional panels: two of the *Mater Dolorosa* and the *Trinity* (generally known as *La Gloria;* Madrid).

Late Works, 1555-1576

Philip II soon ordered religious pictures from Titian for the monastery of the Escorial: the magnificent *Crucifixion* (ca. 1555), the *Entombment* (1559; now Madrid), and the *Adoration of the Kings* (1559). Philip II's numerous commissions for the Escorial in the 1560s included two versions of the *Agony in the Garden,* two of *Christ Carrying the Cross* (now in Madrid), and the *Last Supper* (1557-1564). During the same period Titian also executed mythological works for Philip II that are among the supreme products of his genius in the pathbreaking methods of design and sheer beauty of form and color: *Diana and Callisto, Diana and Actaeon* (both Edinburgh), *Perseus and Andromeda* (London, Wallace Collection), and the *Rape of Europa* (Boston, Isabella Stewart Gardner Museum).

Titian's late style is notable for new developments in the oblique organization of compositions which point the way to later baroque designs. His brushwork is free and illusionistic, suggesting the forms rather than precisely describing them, and the tones are fused, often blended with the fingers rather than the brush. This style can be seen in the late pictures already cited, as well as in single figures of saints: the *St. Margaret* (Madrid) with its superb landscape, *St. Sebastian,* the *Magdalen* (Leningrad), and *St. Jerome* (Escorial).

To the end Titian continued to plumb the depths of human character in masterpieces of portraiture, such as *Jacopo Strada* (1567-1568; Vienna), his self-portraits (ca. 1550, Berlin; ca. 1570, Madrid), and the triple portrait with Orazio and Marco (ca. 1570; London). Titian's late religious pictures convey a mood of universal tragedy, as in the majestic *Annunciation* (ca. 1565; Venice), the very late *Christ Crowned with Thorns* (Munich), and the *Pietà* (Venice), unfinished at his death and intended for his own sepulchral chapel.

On Aug. 27, 1576, Titian died in his spacious palace in Venice, universally recognized as one of the greatest masters of all time. He was interred in the church of S. Maria Gloriosa dei Frari.

Further Reading

The first major work on Titian, and the first attempt to separate the artist's originals from copies, was Joseph A. Crowe and Giovanni B. Cavalcaselle, *Life and Times of Titian* (1877). Hans Tietze, *Tizian* (2 vols., 1936; published in an abbreviated volume in English in two editions, 1937 and 1950), includes only a selection of major works. After a dearth of monographs for more than 3 decades, several important books have appeared: Erwin Panofsky, *Problems in Titian, Mostly Iconographic* (1970), dealing with thematic material; and Harold E. Wethey's comprehensive *catalogue raisonné, Titian,* vol. 1: *The Religious Paintings* (1969), vol. 2: *Titian's Portraits* (1971), and vol. 3: *Titian's Mythological and Historical Paintings* (1973). ☐

Marshal Tito

The Yugoslav statesman Marshal Tito (born 1892) became president of Yugoslavia in 1953. He directed the rebuilding of a Yugoslavia devastated in World War II and the welding of Yugoslavia's different peoples into unity until his death in 1980.

From its creation in 1918 until is dissolution in the early 1990s, Yugoslavia was a multinational state composed of numerous ethnic and religious groups. It was made up of historical provinces which were first united into a single state in 1918. The building of a state proved a difficult task. The various ethnic groups were dissatisfied with their status in the new state, resented Serbian domination, and clamored for greater national and political rights. The national and religious groups were suspicious of each other. The country's economy was unstable throughout the interwar period, and the country was surrounded by enemy states dedicated to its destruction. Because of these conditions, Communist and fascist groups found fertile ground for their activities and sought to destroy established order. Among the Communists who advocated a revolutionary change was Josip Broz, who is commonly known as Marshal Tito.

Tito was born on May 25, 1892, the seventh of 15 children of a peasant family of Kumrovec, a village near Zagreb, Croatia. After apprenticeship to a locksmith, he worked in Croatia, Slovenia, Austria, and Germany as a mechanic. In World War I he was drafted into the Austro-Hungarian army, was wounded and captured by the Russians, and spent time in a prisoner-of-war camp. Already a Social Democrat in Vienna in 1910, he joined the Red Army after the Russian Revolution of October 1917 and identified himself with the Bolshevik forces in the Russian civil war.

In 1920 Tito returned to Croatia and joined the Communist party of Yugoslavia, rising to the party's committee in Zagreb, and was sentenced to five years' imprisonment in 1928 for Communist activity. Thereafter he spent several years in the Soviet Union, in 1934 being elected to the Central Committee and Politburo of the Yugoslav party. In the Stalinist purges, all other members of the Central Committee of the Yugoslav Communist Party had been liquidated, and in 1937 the Comintern appointed him secretary general of the Yugoslav party as its only remaining trustworthy leader.

World War II

Tito was able to revive the Yugoslav party and to make of it a highly disciplined organization. He purged the ranks of members of dubious loyalty and gave the party a clear-cut and realistic policy with regard to nationality. For the first time, the party was firmly in support of the preservation rather than the dismemberment of Yugoslavia. As a loyal Stalinist, passionate revolutionary, and strong personality, Tito was able to develop the Yugoslav Communist party into a powerful political and military organization during World War II.

After the Axis invasion of Yugoslavia in April 1941 and Germany's attack on the Soviet Union in June, Tito, responding to the call of the Comintern, ordered the Communist party to initiate guerrilla activity against Axis forces. At the same time, a royalist resistance movement headed by Col. (later Gen.) Draža Mihajlović gained the support of the royalist government-in-exile under King Peter II (reigned 1934-1945) in London. Initially, Tito's forces received no outside assistance, but Mihajlović's inactivity, combined with the success of Tito's partisans, led to a change in Allied policy. Allied liaison officers with Tito reported that his movement was more nationalist than Communist, and Allied liaison officers with Mihajlović reported that his forces, in fear of a Communist take-over in Yugoslavia, had found it expedient to collaborate with Axis troops. The conflict between the two resistance leaders led to a bloody civil war.

Communist Revolution in Yugoslavia

Tito's greatest accomplishment during World War II was the organization of perhaps the most effective resistance movement in the history of Communism. While engaging the Axis occupation forces, he simultaneously embarked upon a Communist revolution. His forces proceeded to destroy the class structure, undermine the old social and economic order, and lay the foundations for a postwar Communist state system. From a few poorly armed and clad guerrillas (partisans) in 1941, the Communist military force was expanded by Tito into a large army (National Liberation Army) by the end of the war.

Basic policies of the Communist party regarding the new Yugoslav state, such as federal organization of the country, were announced and partially implemented during the war. As a result of the two Anti-fascist Councils held in 1942 and 1943 under the most difficult conditions, Tito provided the country with a system of provisional revolutionary government—the Committee for the National Liberation of Yugoslavia. Skillfully and masterfully he exploited every social, economic, political, geographical, psychological, and ethnic opportunity in pursuance of Communist political and military objectives. Neither his domestic rivals nor powerful German, Italian, Bulgarian, and Hungarian occupation forces were able to cope with the widespread activities of Tito's followers.

In December 1943 the Allies, ignoring King Peter in London, declared Tito's partisans the Allied liberation force in Yugoslavia. Allied pressure forced King Peter to appoint Dr. Ivan Šubašić prime minister, a man acceptable to Tito. After meeting Tito early in June 1944, Šbašić agreed to delay deciding the form of Yugoslavia's postwar government until the war's end. This proved a fatal blow to King Peter's cause. Tito's forces and those of the U.S.S.R. entered Belgrade on Oct. 20, 1944. The partisans, however, drove the Germans from the country essentially by their own efforts, an event of the greatest importance in the future history of Yugoslavia. Unlike Communist leaders of other East European countries, Tito himself had commanded the forces defeating the Axis troops and had not entered his country with the victorious Red Army. The Communist-style single-list elections in August 1945 led to the proclamation of a republic on Nov. 29, 1944, and the creation of the Federal Republic of Yugoslavia.

Postwar Years

From 1945 to 1953 Tito acted as prime minister and minister of defense in the government, whose most dramatic political action was the capture, trial, and execution of Gen. Mihajlović in 1946. Between 1945 and 1948 Tito led his country through an extreme and ruthless form of dictatorship in order to mold Yugoslavia into a socialist state modeled after the Soviet Union. In January 1953, he was named first president of Yugoslavia and president of the Federal Executive Council; the 1963 Constitution named him president for life.

By 1953 Tito had changed Yugoslavia's relationship with the Soviet Union. He refused to approve Stalin's plans for integrating Yugoslavia into the East European Communist bloc and thereby reducing the country to a Soviet satellite. For this reason Tito was expelled from the Cominform. He now embarked on his own socialist policies, which involved considerable economic decentralization and the relaxing of central control over many areas of national life. These policies also involved liberalization of Communist laws and courts. Although a formal reconciliation between the Soviet Union and Yugoslavia occurred when Khrushchev visited Belgrade after Stalin's death in 1955, Yugoslavia's relations with the Soviet Union never returned to what they were before 1948. Tito gave his country a "socialist democracy," a form of government more tolerable and more democratic than the socialist regimes of other Communist countries.

Tito attempted to build a bloc of "nonaligned" countries after Stalin's death. He traveled to India, Indonesia, Ethiopia, the United Arab Republic, Ghana, and Morocco and sponsored a conference of nonaligned countries in Belgrade in 1961. Under his leadership, Yugoslavia maintained friendly ties with the Arab states and vehemently denounced Israeli aggression in the Arab-Israeli War of 1967. His relations with East European states were more variable than those with nonaligned countries. He protested the Soviet invasion of Hungary in 1956 and Czechoslovakia in 1968 and maintained friendly relations with Romania after Nicolae Ceausescu became its leader in 1965. Under Tito's leadership Yugoslavia was a staunch supporter and very active member of the United Nations.

Tito was married twice and had two sons. His first wife was Russian. After World War II he married Jovanka, a Serbian woman from Croatia many years his junior and a former partisan fighter. His wife often accompanied him on his travels. President for life, Tito ruled with vigor until his death in Ljubljana on May 4, 1980, maintaining several homes, where he entertained an array of international visitors and celebrities.

The breakup of the Yugoslav republics lead to ethnic unrest in the late 1980s, and ultimately escalated into war in 1992. Tito left behind one ethnic legacy in particular: a disagreement over the ethnic identity of the citizens of the nation which today calls itself Macedonia. Macedonia has a history which dates back some 4,000 years, and is closely linked to Greece. However, during the Tito era, a policy of disinformation was conducted, such that now a dispute has arisen between Greece and the former Yugoslav Republic of

Macedonia. In *World Affairs,* Chris Parkas wrote, "Since 1944, when Tito created the Socialist Republic of Macedonia as a new republic in the Yugoslav Federation, a revisionist history of Macedonian studies has been developed promoting the concept of a non-Greek Macedonian nation that encompasses all aspects of Macedonian civilization." Tito conducted this disinformation campaign against Greece during the Greek Civil War of 1944-1949. Tito's legacy erupted into a diplomatic conflict between Macedonia and Greece, because Macedonia sought United Nations recognition. Macedonia was officially admitted to the United Nations as an independent country in 1993.

Further Reading

Tito's official biography is Vladimir Dedijer, *Tito* (1953). Dedijer worked with Tito for years, and much of the book is taken from interviews with Tito and his friends. Dedijer recounted the Tito-Stalin break, which he witnessed first-hand, in *The Battle Stalin Lost: Memoirs of Yugoslavia, 1948-53* (1970). A full-length biography is Phyllis Auty, *Tito: A Biography* (1970). Still useful is Fitzroy Maclean, *The Heretic: The Life and Times of Josip Broz-Tito* (1957). A more specialized study is John C. Campbell, *Tito's Separate Road: America and Yugoslavia in World Politics* (1967). Additional material on Tito and Yugoslavia is in Wayne S. Vucinich, ed., *Contemporary Yugoslavia: Twenty Years of Socialist Experiment* (1969). More recent biographies include Milovan Djilas' *Tito: The Story from the Inside* (1980), Ruth Schiffman's *Josip Broz Tito* (1987), and Duncan Wilson's *Tito's Yugoslavia* (1979). □

Nicolae Titulescu

The Romanian statesman Nicolae Titulescu (1882-1941) was an outstanding diplomat and played a major role in the League of Nations.

Born on March 4, 1882, at Craiova, Nicolae Titulescu was the son of a lawyer. After finishing secondary school at Craiova in 1900, he studied law in Paris until 1904. On his return to Romania, he became a lecturer in common law at the University of Iaši and in 1909 at the University of Bucharest. In 1904 Titulescu published his first works. He subsequently published more than 30 papers in Romanian, French, English, German, and Italian on problems of common and international law as well as on economic, financial, social, political, and diplomatic issues.

In 1907 Titulescu joined the Democratic Conservative party; after the dissolution of this party in 1922 he never joined another party. He started his political career in 1912, when he was elected to the Romanian Parliament. He served as minister of finance in 1917-1918 and 1920-1921. In 1918 he became a member of the Romanian National Council in Paris. Two years later he was appointed head of the Romanian delegation to the Paris Peace Conference; in this capacity he signed the Trianon Treaty.

Titulescu was Romania's permanent delegate to the League of Nations between 1920 and 1936 and minister plenipotentiary in London (1922-1927 and 1928-1932). In 1927-1930 and in 1935 he was a member of the League of Nations Council, and he was twice elected president of the General Assembly of the League (1930 and 1931). In 1928 he served as minister for foreign affairs, and in 1932 he was again appointed to this post. In 1936 he was excluded from the government for political and international reasons. Shortly afterward Titulescu settled in France, and he died in Cannes on March 17, 1941.

His Policies

Both in domestic and foreign policy Titulescu was a theorist. He was a firm advocate of internal reform; he advocated land reform through the partial expropriation of estates and the allotment of land to the peasants. He drafted a financial reform bill which provided for progressive taxation, and he supported the election reform introducing universal suffrage in Romania. He had the gift of intuiting the course of political events in the world. A. F. Frangulis, the president of the International Diplomatic Academy in Paris, wrote that "Titulescu could foresee the future as Talleyrand could," and the Soviet diplomat Maxim Litvinov declared that Titulescu was "the most talented and intelligent diplomat of presentday Europe."

Titulescu's conception of international relations was based on promoting agreement and cooperation among nations to achieve peaceful coexistence. He believed that every state, whether large or small, enjoyed the right to national independence and territorial integrity. Civilized relations among states implied, in Titulescu's opinion, the principle of international friendships rather than the division

of states into hostile blocs. He held that opposed social doctrines and different religious beliefs did not prevent the peaceful coexistence of peoples and states. Rejecting the idea that wars are inevitable, he formulated and promoted the principle of the indivisibility of peace, which calls for the union of all peaceful states against any aggression.

In order to create a climate of understanding among peoples, Titulescu advocated means such as economic agreements, collective financial assistance, protection of national minorities, contacts among political leaders and scientists of various countries, and disarmament or reduction of arms accompanied by the strengthening of the defense power of the states menaced by aggression. He worked for a union of nations in a system of collective security based on bilateral and regional treaties of mutual assistance. He believed that such a system would secure peace against the revisionist tendencies of Nazi Germany and Fascist Italy. Opposing every tendency of the Western powers to make concessions to the aggressors, Titulescu carried on a vast diplomatic activity against Nazism and Fascism. He denounced Nazi Germany's violation of the Treaty of Versailles and condemned the invasion of Abyssinia by Fascist Italian troops.

Animated by the desire to set up a system of collective security, Titulescu gave his support to any and all diplomatic initiatives aimed at concluding nonaggression pacts, especially the Kellogg-Briand Pact, and mutual assistance treaties, such as the French-Soviet and the Czech-Soviet Pacts of 1935. He took part in the Disarmament Conference in 1932, backing the disarmament plans of the United States, France, and England. After the failure of this conference, he supported the definition of aggression put forward by Litvinov and in July 1933 signed the London agreements on the definition of aggression. Titulescu made use of his international prestige to strengthen friendly relations between Romania and France and to create a climate of confidence and peace in the Balkans, thus greatly contributing to the establishment of the Little Balkan Entente (1934).

Further Reading

Works on Titulescu include Ion M. Oprea, *Nicolae Titulescu* (Bucharest, 1966), with summaries in English and French; Oprea's *Nicolae Titulescu's Diplomatic Activity* (Bucharest, 1968); and Vasile Netea, *Nicolae Titulescu* (Bucharest, 1969). He is discussed in Mircca Malita, *Romanian Diplomacy: A Historical Survey* (Bucharest, 1970). For general background on Romania between the wars see Henry L. Roberts, *Rumania: Political Problems of an Agrarian State* (1951), and for the diplomatic background, John A. Lukacs, *The Great Powers and Eastern Europe* (1953). Also consult Hamilton Fish Armstrong's memoirs, *Peace and Counterpeace: From Wilson to Hitler* (1971). ☐

Titus Flavius Vespasianus

The Roman general and emperor Titus Flavius Vespasianus (39-81) was responsible for the con- quest of Jerusalem in 70, thus ending the Jewish revolt against Rome.

During the lifetime of Titus, the Roman Empire underwent its first major constitutional crisis in 100 years. The last of the family of the founding emperor (Augustus) died, and a new dynasty (that of Vespasian) had to establish itself by means of civil war. Although it was a period of consolidation within the empire, it also witnessed several major revolts, especially that of the Jews.

Titus was the son of Vespasian, a rising official in the imperial service, and his wife, Domitilla. Titus was handsome, talented, and athletically skilled, and he enjoyed a favored position in the court of the emperor Claudius I (41-54). Vespasian became one of Claudius's leading generals, and Titus was a bosom companion of Britannicus, the son of Claudius. Nero, stepson of Claudius, replaced Claudius as emperor in 54 and murdered his stepbrother Britannicus. Titus's former friendship does not seem to have crippled his career. He served as a junior military officer (military tribune) in Germany and Britain and was moderately active in civic affairs at Rome. He married well. His first wife, Arrecina Tertulla, was the daughter of a former praetorian prefect. After her death he married Marcia Furnilla, also of good family.

Jewish Revolt and Civil War

The turning point in the career of Titus and his family came with the Jewish revolt. The major proportions of the rebellion required Nero to call upon one of his most experienced generals, Vespasian. Titus was placed in command of a legion and sent to Alexandria in Egypt to lead that legion to Judea. He distinguished himself by his courage and leadership in the early fighting, in which the Romans succeeded in bottling up the bulk of the rebels in Jerusalem.

Meanwhile, momentous events were happening in Rome and the Western provinces. Revolts broke out against Nero, who committed suicide. In 69, Galba, the governor of Spain, claimed the emperorship but was soon assassinated. The major struggle for succession developed between Vitellius, the commander of the German armies, and Otho, an old friend of Nero. Vitellius conquered, but developments In the East cut short his reign. When word of Galba's becoming emperor reached Vespasian and Titus in Jerusalem, Titus was dispatched to convey congratulations. He had reached Greece when he received the announcement of Galba's murder. Titus hesitated and then turned back. On Cyprus, an oracle of Aphrodite predicted to him that one day he would be emperor.

Vespasian and his supporters meanwhile had decided that, in a period of soldier emperors, Vespasian with his experience and strong army had a good claim to be ruler. They raised the challenge to Vitellius, and Vespasian's partisans won for him in Italy. Titus had traveled with his father to Alexandria, where they were consolidating their position in the Eastern empire. With the Flavian cause secure, Titus was sent back to Jerusalem to finish the conquest of the

Jews. The siege of that city was one of the most difficult in Roman military history. After an arduous struggle, the city fell to Titus in September 70.

Reign of Vespasian

By June 71, Titus had returned to Rome, where he assumed the position of his father's main administrator and intended successor. Seven times he was consul with his father and also censor. More important, he was praetorian prefect. This position had generally been entrusted to a high official of the equestrian civil service, but Vespasian, an emperor without strong roots and assured support, obviously felt that he must have a man he could trust absolutely in charge of the imperial guard. Vespasian was very fortunate to have so talented and experienced a son who could support him while he lived and continue his dynasty after his death. Titus did much to ensure that the Flavians became a dynasty rather than short-lived claimants to the throne.

Titus did not establish a good reputation during his father's reign. Part of the unpopularity stemmed from his position as chief assistant to Vespasian, which forced him to conduct much of the unpleasant business of the empire. Also, his style of life was regarded as too sumptuous, and his amorous relationship with Berenice, the daughter of the Jewish ruler Herod Agrippa, caused scandal among the snobbish Romans.

Titus as Emperor

Vespasian died on June 24, 79, and Titus became emperor. People expected the excesses of a second Nero. However, Titus immediately showed that he intended to reign with moderation and tact. Informers were controlled and political exiles recalled. Respect was shown for the Roman Senate. The main events in his reign were disasters. In August 79, Vesuvius erupted and buried Pompeii, Herculaneum, and other sections of Campania. Titus traveled to the area to assist in relief operations. The following year, a major fire destroyed much of the Campus Martius area of Rome. Again Titus was very generous in providing funds for relief and rebuilding. A major plague also struck while he ruled.

Vespasian had introduced a policy of extensive public building to glorify the new dynasty and contrast his sense of public interest with the self-indulgence of Nero. Titus continued this. He completed the amphitheater known today as the Colosseum and erected a massive set of public baths in Rome, as well as many other public works in Rome and elsewhere in Italy. He did not reign long enough to make his own impact on Roman foreign policy. The most spectacular events were the continued conquests of the general Agricola in northern Britain. Titus died of a fever on Sept. 13, 81, in the country villa where his father had died.

Further Reading

The 1st-century work of Josephus, *History of the Jewish War*, includes important information on Titus's role in Judea. Suetonius, a 2d-century Roman official, wrote a biography of Titus in his *Lives of the Twelve Caesars;* and Tacitus's 2d-century *Histories* contains a vivid account of the civil wars that led up to the accession of the Flavian dynasty. Dio's 3d-century *History of Rome* also contains an abridged section on Titus's reign (book 66). In modern works, an adequate account of Titus and his family is in the *Cambridge Ancient History* (12 vols., 1923-1939), and a study of him is in Bernard W. Henderson, *Five Roman Emperors* (1927).

Additional Sources

Jones, Brian W., *The Emperor Titus,* London: Croom Helm; New York: St. Martin's Press, 1984. □

Toba Sojo

Toba Sojo (1053-1140), Japanese painter-priest, is believed to have painted the Animal Caricature, or Choju Giga, scrolls, which are considered among the finest examples of Japanese narrative scroll painting.

Toba Sojo, whose true name was Kakuyu, was a Japanese nobleman of the Heian period who became a Buddhist abbot. According to tradition, he is thought to have painted the famous set of scrolls representing caricatures of animals and people (in the Kozanji, a monastery near Kyoto). Modern scholars no longer accept this attribution uncritically and are inclined to believe that while he is indeed the author of the first two scrolls, which were probably painted during the second quarter of the 12th century, the two remaining scrolls are probably the work of an anonymous follower of the artist who worked during the early 13th century, the beginning of the Kamakura period.

The type of painting found in these scrolls is derived from the tradition of Buddhist monochrome ink painting that flourished during the Heian and Kamakura periods and was employed to depict the Buddhist deities in their proper iconographic form. At the same time the Animal Caricature scrolls may also be regarded as one of the most outstanding examples of the school of Japanese painting known as Yamato-e, which specialized in depicting narrative scenes taken from Japanese history and from literature such as the *Heiji Monogatari* and the *Tale of Genji* as well as stories and legends of famous Buddhist temples and Shinto shrines.

Since the scrolls are not accompanied by a text and have no unity of subject matter, the exact meaning of the paintings is not known. However, it is said that the first scroll, which is artistically by far the finest, represents a veiled attack on the corruption of the Buddhist clergy of the time. A worship scene showing the seated Buddha in the form of a large frog with a monkey in priest's garb and rabbit and fox attendants would support such an interpretation. Other sections of this scroll show the animals wrestling, swimming, and frolicking, all rendered in a free, humorous spirit. The later scrolls, although they also depict some animals, primarily show the human figure rendered in a similar satirical manner.

The scrolls are painted in black ink on white paper. Particularly fine are the first two scrolls, those believed to be by Toba Sojo, which show a mastery of brushwork and a remarkable animation. This pictorial tradition, although ultimately derived from China, where it had flourished since Han times, was introduced into Japan during the 6th century and had continued to be popular in the Buddhist monasteries. Depending on line rather than color, the Japanese painters of this school employed a remarkable economy of means and expressive power which are very typical of the best of the painting of the Far East.

Further Reading

The best publication of the scrolls is Hideo Okudaira, *Choju Giga, Scrolls of Animal Caricatures,* adapted into English by S. Kaneko (1969). For a more general discussion of Japanese scroll painting see Kenji Toda, *Japanese Scroll Painting* (1935), and Dietrich Seckel, *Emakimono: The Art of the Japanese Painted Handscroll* (1959). □

Mark Tobey

The American painter Mark Tobey (1890-1976) was probably best known for his delicate, abstract works done in a style called "white writing."

Mark Tobey was born in Centerville, Wisconsin, on December 11, 1890, the youngest of four children. Until 1906 the family lived in Tremplealeau, a small Wisconsin village situated on the Mississippi River. There Tobey led a life much like the legendary Tom Sawyer, commenting later that until he was 16 his whole life was "purely nature." His family were devout Congregationalists, and very early a religious sensitivity was instilled into the boy's life. His parents were hard working and creative, and to encourage Mark's artistic bent they sent him to classes each Saturday at the Art Institute of Chicago. This was the only formal art training that he would receive.

In 1909 the family moved to Chicago, where Tobey worked as a fashion illustrator. Two years later he felt confident enough to move to Greenwich Village in New York City where he found a job with *McCall's Magazine.* Until 1917 he travelled back and forth between Chicago and New York, well paid as an illustrator, interior designer, and charcoal portraitist. Through this last medium he gained recognition in elite social and theatrical circles.

His first one-man show was at M. Knoedler & Co. in New York, arranged in 1917 by Marie Steiner. It was Steiner who introduced Tobey to Juliet Thompson, a portrait painter for whom he agreed to pose. She was a follower of the Bahá' í World Faith, and through her Tobey gained an interest in, and in 1918 accepted, the faith that was to redirect and guide not only the rest of his life but his artistic development as well.

At this time a ferment seemed to take place in Tobey's approach to his art. He reacted against the "Renaissance sense of space and order" in his belief that forms should be free and dynamic. "I wanted to give the light that was in the form in space a release." Unfortunately, the works that

illustrated this attitude are now lost. Encouraged by a friend, Tobey left New York for Seattle in 1922. He exchanged the cultural and intellectual stimulation of New York for the natural beauty, relaxed milieu, and diffused, almost Parisian, light of the western city. He was offered a teaching position at the Cornish School, an experience of which he always spoke with pleasure and satisfaction.

According to Tobey, it was at night, in a small and centrally lighted classroom, that he made his "personal discovery of cubism." He imagined a fly moving in every direction around him and the objects in the room. This movement, creating a complex of lines and imaginary planes and shapes, was to develop into the structural "animation of space," the interpenetration of mass and void, that formed the basis for most of his mature paintings.

In 1923 Tobey met a young Chinese artist, Teng Kuei, and from him learned the technique of calligraphy. This enabled him to discover the freely moving brush with which he could assimilate his concept of animated space. He had become aware, in Seattle, of the closeness of the Orient, but had also found stimulation in the art of the Northwest and Alaskan Indians. His interest in and devotion to a marriage of Eastern and Western ideas was reinforced by his exposure to artists and intellectuals at Dartington Hall, a school and cultural center about 200 miles from London. Tobey taught here from 1930 to 1938, meeting Aldous Huxley, Pearl Buck, and Arthur Waley, among others. And it was here, after a visit to the Orient in 1934, that his distinctive style originated.

In Shanghai Tobey stayed with the family of his friend Teng Kuei. He was impressed with the energy, lines, and textures of the cosmopolitan city as well as with the characteristics of Chinese life, art, and culture. Later he travelled to Japan, spending a month in a Zen monastery. He practiced calligraphy and painting, wrote his own poetry, and attempted meditation. It was an experience which seemed to crystalize all of his accumulated ideas and impressions.

Back at Dartington Hall, Tobey began to experiment with a small picture, making up a mesh of whitish lines on a dark background, scattering in the maze small forms in blue and other colors. In a sudden flashback, the image he created was no longer Oriental at all, but was New York. "He realized that it was Broadway, with all the people caught in the lights." This painting (*Broadway Norm,* 1935), however modest, seems to separate his earlier works from his maturity. Tobey himself was shocked by his unplanned breakthrough. The work initiated the style which was later known as "white writing" and on which his early fame rests. Thus Tobey was nearly 45 years old before the diverse aspects of his art began to coalesce.

Tobey returned to Seattle in 1938, and during the following decade he developed further white writing, movable space, and moving focus (*White Night,* 1942). In 1943 he painted pictures based on three years of study of the Pike Place Public Market, Seattle, combining figurative work with the abstract-like maze of activity in the market. City themes, especially those of New York, followed in the 1930s and 1940s. These were continuous and central to his expression, and, rather than painted in oil, they were usually small works executed on paper with water soluble medium. The city paintings soon spilled over the confines of a specific locale to become a "universal city," a world view of ultimate unity that was both theological and esthetic. Simultaneously, Tobey expanded his visual field, a development made possible by the concept of an aerial view (*Transcontinental,* 1946). In these works, the observer is drawn with willing mind and eye into an unknown space of meaning, form, and color.

The award of the Grand International Prize at the Venice Biennale of 1958 acknowledged the importance of Tobey's art. He was the first American painter since Whistler to achieve this honor. Possibly due to the acclaim he received in Europe, Tobey began to paint large pictures which invited the use of oil paint. Thus in the 1950s and 1960s his canvases expanded with a delicate, refined abstraction which anticipated Jackson Pollack's all-over style. *Sagittarius Red* (1963) is thought by many to be his ultimate masterpiece.

In 1960 Tobey moved to Basel, Switzerland, a change he had long contemplated, as he sensed the atmosphere in America stifling for the work he felt was in his future. Curiously, while European critics and artists considered him the pre-eminent American painter, in the United States his work was treated with disdain, as were the honors bestowed on him abroad. Tobey was elected to the American Academy of Arts and Sciences in 1960, but declined the membership.

Tobey's paintings were exhibited frequently at select small shows, but the first major homage to his work was a one-man exhibition at the Musée des Arts Décoratifs, the modern wing of the Louvre, in 1960. Two years later a retrospective of Tobey's works was seen at the Museum of Modern Art in New York. In 1974, possibly his crowning achievement was the exhibition at the National Collection of Fine Arts in Washington, D.C., "Tribute to Mark Tobey." It was a testimony to his creativity and stamina at an advanced age and to his unique position in American art. He was a member of no school, follower of no master, largely self-taught, entirely self-defined.

Rather than confining his art to technical expression, Tobey's work represents a philosophical conclusion, spanning the dichotomy of East and West into the contraction and balancing of all forces of the globe into eye-range. For Tobey, in order for the world to avoid catastrophe it must find an equilibrium reconciling science and religion, the past and the future, the material and the spiritual. His move toward abstraction came from his search for this expression in artistic language.

Further Reading

Arthur L. Dahl, et al., *Mark Tobey: Art and Belief* (1984) is a collection of essays which relate Tobey's creative achievement and his practice of the Bahá' í faith. It also includes Tobey's own poetry and written thoughts on his art. William C. Seitz, *Mark Tobey* (1962) gives the development of Tobey's style and a particularly profound analysis of the impact of the Bahá' í faith on his art. This is the catalogue of the exhibition at the Museum of Modern Art. □

Alexis Charles Henri Maurice Clérel de Tocqueville

The French statesman and writer Alexis Charles Henri Maurice Clérel de Tocqueville (1805-1859) was the author of "Democracy in America," the first classic commentary on American government written by a foreigner.

Alexis de Tocqueville was born in Paris on July 29, 1805, of an aristocratic Norman family. He studied law in Paris (1823-1826) and then was appointed an assistant magistrate at Versailles (1827).

The July 1830 Revolution which, with middle-class support, put Louis Philippe on the throne, required a loyalty oath of Tocqueville as a civil servant. He was suspect because his aristocratic family opposed the new order and was demoted to a minor judgeship without pay. Tocqueville and another magistrate, Gustave de Beaumont, asked to study prison reform in America, then an interest of the French government. Granted permission but not funds (their families paid their expenses), Tocqueville and Beaumont spent from May 1831 to February 1832 in the United States. Their travel and interviews resulted in *On the Penitentiary System in the United States and Its Application in France* (1832). Then followed Tocqueville's famous *Democracy in America* (vol. 1, 1835; vol. 2, 1840), an immediate best seller. By 1850 it had run through 13 editions.

Tocqueville was elected to the Chamber of Deputies in 1839. He opposed King Louis Philippe but after the Revolution of 1848 again served as a deputy. Tocqueville was foreign minister for a few months in 1849 and retired from public affairs at the end of 1851. During his last years he wrote *The Old Regime and the French Revolution* (1856). He died in Cannes on April 16, 1859.

"Democracy in America"

Despite his aristocratic upbringing, Tocqueville believed that the spread of democracy was inevitable. By analyzing American democracy, he thought to help France avoid America's faults and emulate its successes. Chief among his many insights was to see equality of social conditions as the heart of American democracy. He noted that although the majority could produce tyranny its wide property distribution and inherent conservatism made for stability. American literature, then still under European influence, he felt would become independent in idiom and deal with plain people rather than the upper classes. The American zeal for change he connected with a restless search for the ideal. Noting the permissiveness of democracy toward religion, he anticipated denominational growth. Discerning natural hostility to the military, he foresaw an adverse effect of prolonged war on American society. He anticipated that democracy would emancipate women and alter the rela-

on nucleotides, he was awarded the 1957 Nobel Prize in chemistry.

Alexander Todd was awarded the 1957 Nobel Prize in chemistry for his work on the chemistry of nucleotides. He was also influential in synthesizing vitamins for commercial application. In addition, he invesitgated active ingredients in cannabis and hashish and helped develop efficient means of producing chemical weapons.

Alexander Robertus Todd was born in Glasgow, Scotland, on October 2, 1907, to Alexander and Jane Lowrie Todd. The family, consisting of Todd, his parents, his older sister and younger brother, was not well-to-do. Todd's autobiography, *A Time to Remember,* recalls how through hard work his parents rose to the lower middle class despite having no more than an elementary education, and how determined they were that their children should have an education at any cost.

In 1918 Todd gained admission to the Allan Glen's School in Glasgow, a science high school; his interest in chemistry, which first arose when he was given a chemistry set at the age of eight or nine, developed rapidly. On graduation, six years later, he at once entered the University of Glasgow instead of taking a recommended additional year at Allan Glen's. His father refused to sign an application for scholastic aid, saying it would be accepting charity; because of superior academic performance during the first

tionship of parents to children. He saw danger in the dominance of American politics by lawyers.

Though his work has been criticized for some biases, errors, omissions, and pessimism, Tocqueville's perceptive insights have been continually quoted. He ranks as a keen observer of American democracy and as a major prophet of modern societies' trends.

Further Reading

Tocqueville's *The Recollections of Alexis de Tocqueville* (1893; trans. 1896; new trans. 1970) was published after his death. The best books about him are George W. Pierson, *Tocqueville and Beaumont in America* (1938), abridged by Dudley C. Lunt as *Tocqueville in America* (1959); Jacob P. Mayer, *Alexis de Tocqueville: A Biographical Study in Political Science* (1960); and Robert A. Nisbet, *The Sociological Tradition* (1966). Edward T. Gargan, *Alexis de Tocqueville: The Critical Years, 1848-1851* (1955), is an important study, and Gargan's *De Tocqueville* (1965) is a short introduction to Tocqueville's thought. Also useful are Jack Lively, *The Social and Political Thought of Alexis de Tocqueville* (1962), and Seymour Drescher, *Tocqueville and England* (1964) and *Dilemmas of Democracy: Tocqueville and Modernization* (1968). ☐

Alexander Todd

Chemist Alexander Todd researched the chemistry of nucleotides and was influential in synthesizing vitamins for commercial applications. For his work

year, though, Todd received a scholarship for the rest of course. In his final year at university, Todd did a thesis on the reaction of phosphorus pentachloride with ethyl tartrate and its diacetyl derivative under the direction of T. E. Patterson, resulting in his first publication.

After receiving his B.Sc. degree in chemistry with first-class honors in 1928, Todd was awarded a Carnegie research scholarship and stayed on for another year working for Patterson on optical rotatory dispersion. Deciding that this line of research was neither to his taste nor likely to be fruitful, he went to Germany to do graduate work at the University of Frankfurt am Main under Walther Borsche, studying natural products. Todd says that he preferred Jöns Berzelius's definition of organic chemistry as the chemistry of substances found in living organisms to Gmelin's definition of it as the chemistry of carbon compounds.

At Frankfurt he studied the chemistry of apocholic acid, one of the bile acids (compounds produced in the liver and having a structure related to that of cholesterol and the steroids). In 1931 he returned to England with his doctorate. He applied for and received an 1851 Exhibition Senior Studentship which allowed him to enter Oxford University to work under Robert Robinson, who would receive the Nobel Prize in chemistry in 1947. In order to ease some administrative difficulties, Todd enrolled in the doctoral program, which had only a research requirement; he received his D.Phil. from Oxford in 1934. His research at Oxford dealt first with the synthesis of several anthocyanins, the coloring matter of flowers, and then with a study of the red pigments from some molds.

After leaving Oxford, Todd went to the University of Edinburgh on a Medical Research Council grant to study the structure of vitamin B_1 (thiamine, or the anti-beriberi vitamin). The appointment came about when George Barger, professor of medical chemistry at Edinburgh, sought Robinson's advice about working with B_1. At that time, only a few milligrams of the substance were available, and Robinson suggested Todd because of his interest in natural products and his knowledge of microchemical techniques acquired in Germany. Although Todd and his team were beaten in the race to synthesize B_1 by competing German and American groups, their synthesis was more elegant and better suited for industrial application. It was at Edinburgh that Todd met and became engaged to Alison Dale—daughter of Nobel Prize laureate Henry Hallett Dale —who was doing postgraduate research in the pharmacology department; they were married in January of 1937, shortly after Todd had moved to the Lister Institute where he was reader (or lecturer) in biochemistry. For the first time in his career, Todd was salaried and not dependent on grants or scholarships. In 1939 the Todds' son, Alexander, was born. Their first daughter, Helen, was born in 1941, and the second, Hilary, in 1945.

Toward the end of his stay at Edinburgh, Todd had begun to investigate the chemistry of vitamin E (a group of related compounds called tocopherols), which is an antioxidant—that is, it inhibits loss of electrons. He continued this line of research at the Lister Institute and also started an investigation of the active ingredients of the *Cannabis sativa* plant (marijuana) that showed that cannabinol, the major product isolated from the plant resin, was pharmacologically inactive.

In March of 1938, Todd and his wife made a long visit to the United States to investigate the offer of a position at California Institute of Technology. On returning to England with the idea that he would move to California, Todd was offered a professorship at Manchester which he accepted, becoming Sir Samuel Hall Professor of Chemistry and director of the chemical laboratories of the University of Manchester. At Manchester, Todd was able to continue his research with little interruption. During his first year there, he finished the work on vitamin E with the total synthesis of alpha-tocopherol and its analogs. Attempts to isolate and identify the active ingredients in cannabis resin failed because the separation procedures available at the time were inadequate; however, Todd's synthesis of cannabinol involved an intermediate, tetrahydrocannabinol (THC), that had an effect much like that of hashish on rabbits and suggested to him that the effects of hashish were due to one of the isomeric tetrahydrocannabinols. This view was later proven correct, but by others, because the outbreak of World War II forced Todd to abandon this line of research for work more directly related to the war.

As a member, and then chair, of the Chemical Committee, which was responsible for developing and producing chemical warfare agents, Todd developed an efficient method of producing diphenylamine chloroarsine (a sneeze gas), and designed a pilot plant for producing nitrogen mustards (blistering agents). He also had a group working on penicillin research and another trying to isolate and identify the "hatching factor" of the potato eelworm, a parasite that attacks potatoes.

Late in 1943 Todd was offered the chair in biochemistry at Cambridge University, which he refused. Shortly thereafter he was offered the chair in organic chemistry, which he accepted, choosing to affiliate with Christ's College. From 1963 to 1978, he served as master of the college. As professor of organic chemistry at Cambridge, Todd reorganized and revitalized the department and oversaw the modernization of the laboratories (they were still lighted by gas in 1944) and, eventually, the construction of a new laboratory building.

Before the war, his interest in vitamins and their mode of action had led Todd to start work on nucleosides and nucleotides. Nucleosides are compounds made up of a sugar (ribose or deoxyribose) linked to one of four heterocyclic (that is, containing rings with more than one kind of atom) nitrogen compounds derived either from purine (adenine and guanine) or pyrimidine (uracil and cytosine). When a phosphate group is attached to the sugar portion of the molecule, a nucleoside becomes a nucleotide. The nucleic acids (DNA and RNA), found in cell nuclei as constituents of the chromosomes, are chains of nucleotides. While still at Manchester, Todd had worked out techniques for synthesizing nucleosides and then attaching the phosphate group to them (a process called phosphorylating) to form nucleotides; later, at Cambridge, he worked out the structures of the nucleotides obtained by the degradation of nucleic acid and synthesized them. This information was a necessary prerequisite to James Watson and Francis Crick's formulation of the double-helix structure of DNA two years later.

Todd had found the nucleoside adenosine in some coenzymes, relatively small molecules that combine with a protein to form an enzyme, which can act as a catalyst for a particular biochemical process. He knew from his work with the B vitamins that B_1 (thiamine), B_2 (riboflavin) and B_3 (niacin) were essential components of coenzymes involved in respiration and oxygen utilization. By 1949 he had succeeded in synthesizing adenosine—a triumph in itself—and had gone on to synthesize adenosine di- and triphosphate (ADP and ATP). These compounds are nucleotides responsible for energy production and energy storage in muscles and in plants. In 1952, he established the structure of flavin adenine dinucleotide (FAD), a coenzyme involved in breaking down carbohydrates so that they can be oxidized, releasing energy for an organism to use. For his pioneering work on nucleotides and nucleotide enzymes, Todd was awarded the 1957 Nobel Prize in chemistry.

Todd collaborated with Dorothy Crowfoot Hodgkin in determining the structure of vitamin B_{12}, the antipernicious anemia factor, which is necessary for the formation of red blood cells. Todd's chemical studies of the degradation products of B_{12} were crucial to Hodgkin's X-ray determination of the structure in 1955.

Another major field of research at Cambridge was the chemistry of the pigments in aphids. While at Oxford and working on the coloring matter from some fungi, Todd observed that although the pigments from fungi and from higher plants were all anthraquinone derivatives, the pattern of substitution around the anthraquinone ring differed in the two cases. Pigment from two different insects seemed to be of the fungal pattern and Todd wondered if these were derived from the insect or from symbiotic fungi they contained. At Cambridge he isolated several pigments from different kinds of aphids and found that they were complex quinones unrelated to anthraquinone. It was found, however, that they are probably the products of symbiotic fungi in the aphid.

In 1952 Todd became chairman of the advisory council on scientific policy to the British government, a post he held until 1964. He was knighted in 1954 by Queen Elizabeth II for distinguished service to the government. Named Baron Todd of Trumpington in 1962, he was made a member of the Order of Merit in 1977. In 1955 he became a foreign associate of the United States' National Academy of Sciences. He has traveled extensively and been a visiting professor at the University of Sydney (Australia), the California Institute of Technology, the Massachusetts Institute of Technology, the University of Chicago, and Notre Dame University.

A Fellow of the Royal Society since 1942, Todd served as its resident from 1975 to 1980. He increased the role of the society in advising the government on the scientific aspects of policy and strengthened its international relations. Extracts from his five anniversary addresses to the society dealing with these concerns are given as appendices

to his autobiography. In the forward to his autobiography, Todd reports that in preparing biographical sketches of a number of members of the Royal Society he was struck by the lack of information available about their lives and careers and that this, in part, led him to write *A Time to Remember.*

Further Reading

Current Biography, H. W. Wilson, 1958, pp. 437–439.
Nobel Lectures Including Presentation Speeches and Laureate's Biographies—Chemistry: 1942–1962, Elsevier, 1964, pp. 519–538. □

Palmiro Togliatti

The Italian statesman Palmiro Togliatti (1893-1964) was one of the principal founders of the Italian Communist Party. Under his leadership the party became the largest Communist Party in the West and a major factor in Italian politics after World War II.

Born in Genoa on March 26, 1893, the son of a modest state employee who was highly religious, Palmiro Togliatti was named "Palmiro" after the Palm Sunday that was his birthday. He attended high school in Sardinia and then studied law at the University of Turin. In 1914 he joined the Italian Socialist Party (PSI). During World War I he did military service until his release in 1917, when he returned to Turin.

As a student Togliatti experienced a wide variety of ideologies and intellectual currents, ranging from Marxism to neo-Hegelianism and syndicalism. His war experiences and the example of the Russian revolution turned him more and more toward Marxism. He took up journalism for the Socialist cause and joined Antonio Gramsci, Angelo Tasca, and Umberto Terracini in founding the Turinese weekly *L'Ordine Nuovo.* On the newspaper he became known for his biting column on cultural topics. In 1921 he and the *Ordine Nuovo* group joined Amadeo Bordiga and others in splitting from the Socialists and founding the Italian Communist Party (PCI). A bitter struggle over control of the PCI followed. Bordiga wanted to continue the schism with the Socialists. Others such as Togliatti and Gramsci, supported by the Soviet Union, favored a "united front" with the Socialists. By 1926, at the Congress of Lyons, the Gramsci-Togliatti faction triumphed, and Gramsci assumed leadership of the party.

Togliatti, however, succeeded Gramsci in November 1926 when the latter was arrested and imprisoned by the Fascist regime of Benito Mussolini. Togliatti avoided arrest only because he was in Moscow at the time. In addition to heading the PCI, Togliatti became a major figure in the Third International. In 1937 he became that organization's secretary. His long association with the International during the Stalin years has given Togliatti—somewhat unfairly—the reputation of having been a "Stalinist." Despite personal

misgivings, by 1929 Togliatti did bring the PCI into conformity with the International's increasingly hard line. Togliatti, however, disagreed with many of Stalin's ideas and actions. He found the anti-Fascist policies of the Popular Front in France far more congenial. Just as the French Communists had joined the Socialists and left radicals in an anti-Fascist pact, Togliatti led the PCI into forming a similar alliance with the Italian Socialists. In his *Lectures on Fascism* given at the Leninist School in Moscow and at a major speech before the Seventh Congress of the International (1935), Togliatti presented his case for a popular front policy.

From 1937 to 1939 Togliatti served in Spain as the International's representative to the Spanish Communist Party. He was among the Republic's last defenders until he fled to Algeria in March 1939. During the early months of World War II he was imprisoned in France, where he remained until his release and return to the Soviet Union in May 1940. From June 27, 1941, to May 11, 1943, using the pseudonym of "Mario Correnti," he delivered more than 100 radio broadcasts to Fascist Italy. In his programs he kept his audience abreast of military developments and urged armed resistance to Fascism.

In July 1943 the Fascist regime fell, and on March 27, 1944, Togliatti was finally able to end his long exile and return to Italy. He directed the Communist Party to collaborate in the formation of the Badoglio government, the successor to Mussolini, and to join the armed struggle against Fascism and the German occupation. For the first time, the

PCI emerged as a significant national party (1,770,896 members at the end of 1945).

During the next several years Togliatti served as minister without portfolio in several cabinets and ministries (under Badoglio and Ivanoe Bonomi), as vice-president of the Council of Ministers with Bonomi, and as minister of justice with Ferruccio Parri and Alcide De Gasperi. Togliatti's "collaborationist policy" was aimed at defusing the opposition of conservative elements in Italian society. Togliatti's policy failed, however. The Communist-Socialist bloc was defeated in the 1948 elections, and the Communists were isolated. In the same year an attempt on Togliatti's life scandalized the nation, and only his insistence on calm prevented a bloody insurrection.

The Cold War years from 1947 to 1955 were difficult for Togliatti. Although he advocated gradualism, independence for individual Communist parties, and Communist participation in power, the PCI remained isolated. Just before his death he argued that there were many roads to socialism and urged the PCI toward greater independence from the Soviet Union. These policies, summarized by the term "polycentrism," were adopted by his successors.

In August 1964 Togliatti made a last trip to the U.S.S.R., where he was planning to discuss recent developments in the Socialist camp. Struck by a cerebral hemorrhage, he died at Yalta on August 21, 1964.

Further Reading

Sources on Togliatti in English are scarce, although some of his major writings have been translated: Palmiro Togliatti, *Lectures on Fascism* (1976), *The Spanish Revolution* (1936), *The Fight for Peace* (1935), *Inside Italy* (1942), and *On Gramsci and Other Writings,* edited by Donald Sassoon (1979). For Togliatti's role in shaping the Communist Party see Donald Sassoon, *The Strategy of the Italian Communist Party* (1981). □

Hideki Tojo

Hideki Tojo (1884-1948), a Japanese general and premier during World War II, was hanged as a war criminal. He symbolized, in his rise to leadership of the Japanese government, the emergence of Japanese militarism and its parochial view of the world.

H ideki Tojo was born in Tokyo on Dec. 30, 1884, the eldest son in a family of samurai descent. Tojo entered military school in 1899, following in the footsteps of his father, a professional military man who served as a lieutenant colonel in the Sino-Japanese War and as a major general in the Russo-Japanese War. Tojo likewise saw service, though briefly, in the latter war. In 1915 he graduated with honors from the army war college and was subsequently sent abroad for 3 years (1919-1922) of study in Europe. After his return he served as an instructor in military science at the war college.

Brusque, scrupulous, and hardworking, Tojo came to be known as *kamisori* (the razor) for the sharp, decisive, impatient qualities that he manifested as he rose rapidly through the military hierarchy. He was assigned first to the War Ministry and subsequently to the general staff and various command posts. Promoted to lieutenant general in 1936, Tojo became chief of staff of the Kwantung Army in Manchuria, where he worked effectively to mobilize Manchuria's economy and strengthen Japan's military readiness in the event that war broke out with the Soviet Union. When full-scale hostilities broke out instead between China and Japan following the Marco Polo Bridge incident, Tojo in his first real taste of combat experience led two brigades in a blitzkrieg that quickly brought the whole of Inner Mongolia under Japanese control. In 1938 he was recalled from field service to become vice-minister of war, a position in which he pressed resolutely for preparations that would allow Japan to wage a two-front war against both China and the Soviet Union.

In mid-1940 Tojo was appointed war minister in the second Fumimaro Konoe government, which proceeded at once to sign the Tripartite Pact with Germany and Italy. Relations with the United States gradually worsened during succeeding months as Japanese troops moved south into Indochina; but Tojo hewed to a hard line. Convinced of the righteousness of the imperial cause and of the implacable hostility of the Americans, the British, the Chinese, and the Dutch, he stoutly opposed the negotiations and concessions that Konoe contemplated. Speaking for the army command, Tojo demanded a decision for war unless the United States

backed away from its embargo on all exports to Japan. When Konoe hesitated, Tojo is reported to have told him that "sometimes it is necessary to shut one's eyes and take the plunge." Konoe, however, was reluctant to take the plunge and instead tendered his resignation.

Leadership in War

An imperial mandate was then given to Tojo in October 1941 to become premier and form a new Cabinet. It was thought that only Tojo had full knowledge of recent developments and an ability to control the army. Tojo was given an imperial command to "wipe the slate clean," review all past decisions, and work for peace. But a reconsideration of Japanese policy failed to reveal alternatives acceptable to the army, and the decision for war was taken. Within hours after the surprise attack on Pearl Harbor, Tojo broadcast a brief message to his countrymen, warning them that "to annihilate this enemy and to establish a stable new order in East Asia, the nation must necessarily anticipate a long war."

Tojo had great power at the beginning of the war and in the West was often likened to Hitler and Mussolini. Besides serving as premier, he was a general in the army, war minister, and, for a short time, home minister. Later in the war he also served as chief of the general staff. In 1942 a tightly restricted national election resulted in a pro-Tojo Diet. Nonetheless, while wielding great power, Tojo was still not a dictator like Hitler or Mussolini. The senior statesmen, the army and navy general staffs, and, of course, ultimately the Emperor still exercised considerable power independent of Tojo.

Defeat and Dishonor

By early 1944 even though the tide of battle had turned decisively against Japan, and Tojo admitted to the Diet that the nation faced "the most critical situation in the history of the Empire," he stood firmly opposed to increasing sentiment in favor of negotiation. The fall of Saipan in July 1944, however, put American bombers within range of the homeland, and the senior statesmen together with ministers in Tojo's Cabinet forced him into retirement.

With the end of the war Tojo awaited at his Tokyo residence his arrest by the occupation forces. On Sept. 11, 1945, when Gen. MacArthur ordered his arrest, Tojo attempted to shoot himself. After his recovery he was held in Sugamo prison until his trial as a suspected war criminal by the International Military Tribunal for the Far East began in May 1946. After proceedings which stretched out over 2 years, during which Tojo willingly accepted his responsibility for much of Japan's wartime policy while declaring it legitimate self-defense, he was found guilty of having "major responsibility for Japan's criminal attacks on her neighbors" and was sentenced to death by hanging. The sentence was carried out on Dec. 23, 1948.

Further Reading

The definitive work on Tojo is Robert J. C. Butow, *Tojo and the Coming of the War* (1961). A compilation of the 1941 policy conference records, in which Tojo played a leading role, may

be found in Nobutaka Ike, ed., *Japan's Decision for War* (1967). For a revisionist interpretation of the role of the military in foreign-policy decisions see James B. Crowley, *Japan's Quest for Autonomy: National Security and Foreign Policy, 1930-1938* (1966). □

John Toland

The controversial British scholar John Toland (1670-1722) is classified as a deist, although the term is not totally suitable to the content of his work or the range of his activities as a linguist, translator, political and religious polemicist, and diplomat.

Born near Londonderry, Ireland, on Nov. 30, 1670, John Toland was raised as a Roman Catholic and originally baptized Janus Junius. He converted to Protestantism when he was 16. From 1687 to 1690 he studied at Glasgow and Edinburgh universities. After receiving a master of arts degree, he continued to do research at the University of Leiden in Holland and later at Oxford.

Deism is the Latin cognate of the Greek term for theism. Originally used to describe writers whose theological positions were heterodox, the term was applied historically to a diverse group of English philosophers and theologians in the period between 1650 and 1750. A common theme uniting the deists is their opposition to the subordination of reason to revelation. This attitude is seen clearly in the title of Toland's most famous work, *Christianity Not Mysterious; or, A treatise Shewing That There Is Nothing in the Gospel Contrary to Reason, nor above It, and That No Christian Doctrine Can Be Properly Call'd a Mystery.*

Printed anonymously in 1696, the book excited more than 50 replies and refutations. The Irish Parliament and English House of Commons condemned the work to be burned, and when a second edition bore the name of the 25-year-old Toland, orders were issued for the author's arrest. *Christianity Not Mysterious* applies John Locke's philosophy of common sense to religion. Whereas Locke suggested that Christianity is reasonable, Toland took a decisive step in arguing that reasonable meant not mysterious. The implicit, heretical conclusion is that revelation cannot contradict reason, since "whoever tells us something we did not know before must insure that his words are intelligible, and the matter possible. This holds good, let God or man be the revealer." Toland attributed theological mysteries to scriptural misinterpretations of priests, and in this he anticipates 18th-century exponents of natural religion.

Toland spent the next years on the Continent as a diplomat attached to the courts of Hanover and Berlin. There he met and later became a correspondent of the philosopher Gottfried Wilhelm von Leibniz. Back in England, Toland translated the work of the Renaissance pantheist Giordano Bruno; edited *Oceana,* the utopian work by James Harrington; and after financial reverses worked as a newspaper-

man. Toland felt that his ill health had been aggravated by inept physicians, and shortly before his death in Putney on March 11, 1722, he wrote a diatribe against the medical profession in which he complained, "They learn their Art at the hazard of our lives, and make experiments by our deaths."

The content of Toland's other writings, estimated to be between 30 and 100 works, is concerned with political, religious, and philosophical themes. Most important are two works on Milton, *Life of John Milton* (1698) and *Amyntor* (1699); speculations concerning the origin of religion in *Letters to Serena* (1704); and a final statement of his increasingly pantheistic philosophy in *Pantheisticon* (1720).

Further Reading

Toland's *Letters to Serena* was republished in 1964. Peter Gay, ed., *Deism: An Anthology* (1968), contains part of *Christianity Not Mysterious.* For background see John Orr, *English Deism: Its Roots and Fruits* (1934).

Additional Sources

Daniel, Stephen H. (Stephen Hartley), *John Toland, his methods, manners, and mind,* Kingston: McGill-Queen's University Press, 1984. □

Vicente Lombardo Toledano

Vicente Lombardo Toledano (1894-1968) was a Mexican university professor, Marxist intellectual, and politician. He was a leader in national and international labor movements, the founder and head of the Popular party, and the author of numerous books and articles.

Vicente Lombardo Toledano was born in Tezlutlán, Puebla, on July 16, 1894, the son of middle-class parents. He enrolled simultaneously in the programs offered in the Law School and in the School of Higher Studies (philosophy and letters) of the National University of Mexico and received his licentiate in law (1919), master's degree (1920), and doctorate (1933). During these years he also became an attorney at law.

In 1917 Toledano obtained a professorship at the Mexican Popular University and from 1918 until 1933 was professor of law and philosophy at the National University of Mexico. In 1933, when he was expelled from the university for his radical views, he founded his own university, devoted to the education of workers and peasants. In 1936 this institution emerged as the Universidad Obrera, with Toledano as rector, a position he held until the 1960s.

During the early years of the Mexican Revolution, Toledano, a liberal and socially conscious intellectual, supported the revolution. In 1923 he became governor of the state of Puebla. In 1926 and 1928 he was elected federal deputy.

Labor Leader

By this time Toledano had developed a vivid interest in labor problems and had become active in labor organizations. In 1923 he became a member of the central committee of the most important labor confederation, the Confederación Regional Obrera Mexicana (CROM). He remained active in CROM until the early 1930s, when the organization disintegrated as a result of government undermining, internal dissensions, and lack of labor support. In 1932 Toledano organized the General Confederation of Workers and Peasants (CGOC), which united most of the former CROM unions, and in 1936 he founded and became first secretary general of the Confederation of Mexican Workers (CTM).

With the support of President Lázaro Cárdenas the CTM grew into the largest and most important labor organization in the country. It abandoned craft unionism for industrial organization, and its principal centers of strength were located in the railroad, mining, electrical, and petroleum industries. As membership increased, so did the political and economic power of CTM. The organization benefited from the widespread nationalism prevalent in Mexico and from its close cooperation with the Partido Revolucionario Institucional (PRI), Mexico's ruling party. In 1938 Toledano tried to extend his power over labor throughout the continent by organizing the Confederation of Latin American Workers (CTAL).

His Ideology

Toledano's participation in the labor movement was instrumental in developing his ideology. He became initially an evolutionary socialist in the tradition of the Second International and later a Marxist. In his resignation speech from CROM on Sept. 19, 1932, Toledano explained that he would continue to be "a radical Marxist, although not a Communist" and that he would remain an internationalist and an opponent of chauvinistic nationalism. He claimed that the most important goals of the Mexican Revolution— economic independence, a higher standard of living, and equitable distribution of wealth—could be reached only if Mexico socialized the ownership of the means of production and planned its economic development. Prior to his conversion to Marxism, he had called for moral improvement through education as a means of realizing human ideals. But as he came to accept Marxism, he emphasized profound changes in society and in the material conditions of Mexicans.

Journalist and Party Leader

After he completed his term as secretary general of the CTM in 1940, he turned to journalism. In June 1938 he founded and became director of the daily *El Popular*. In 1946 he founded the Marxist review *Documentos,* which was devoted to questions of philosophy, economics, and politics. He felt that Mexico needed a new revolutionary vehicle to carry on its struggle; thus in 1948 he founded the Partido Popular (PP). The party accepted as its goal the establishment of a people's democracy which would aid in the construction of socialism in Mexico. He ran unsuccessfully for the presidency in the 1952 elections. In 1960 the party formally adopted the principles of Marxism-Leninism and changed its name to Partido Popular Socialista (PPS).

Toledano died in Mexico City on Nov. 16, 1968. At the funeral President Gustavo Diaz Ordaz praised him as a leading force in Mexican politics and one of the country's outstanding intellectuals.

Further Reading

Toledano's own works are helpful, although all are in Spanish. Robert P. Millon, *Vicente Lombardo Toledano: Mexican Marxist* (1966), is a complete study of Toledano's ideas. Information on him is also in William C. Townsend, *Lázaro Cárdenas: Mexican Democrat* (1952). □

Francisco de Toledo

Francisco de Toledo (1515-1584), the fifth Spanish viceroy of Peru, established his reputation in that office as one of the most talented and energetic administrators of the Spanish Empire in America.

Francisco de Toledo, born in Oropesa in New Castile, was a scion of an illustrious and noble family, Alvarez de Toledo, which was related both to the dukes of Alba and to the royal family of Spain. Toledo spent many years in military service to the Crown in its far-flung possessions in Europe and in North Africa. He became a favorite aide to the emperor-king Charles V and to the latter's son Philip II when he ascended the Spanish throne in 1556. Toledo acquired great knowledge of imperial affairs, and his keen judgment and tireless capacity for work earned him appointment as viceroy of Peru.

When Toledo arrived in Peru in 1569, the area so named consisted of all of western South America, from Panama to Chile, east of the Andes to the jungles, and southeast across modern Bolivia into present-day Argentina. Toledo arrived in the capital city, Lima, with great pomp, a large retinue, a high salary, and broad authority from the Crown, extending over all aspects of the life of the colony.

Goals of Reform

The viceroy's principal goals were to organize the numerous Indian population for their own protection against the demands of the Spanish settlers and also for their more efficient availability as laborers and tribute payers; to consolidate, develop, and establish Spanish institutions and settlements; and to put down the still rebellious portion of the Indian population.

During his time in Lima, Toledo devoted himself to vitalizing and regularizing the political, civil, and ecclesiastical institutions of the kingdom. He appointed new municipal officials to towns that had long lacked them; he ruled on questions of boundaries between judicial districts; and he oversaw the establishment of the Inquisition, which was introduced into Peru for the stated purposes of extending knowledge of the true God and of protecting Catholic beliefs from false doctrines.

Toledo's energy and his desire for firsthand knowledge of his subjects led him to depart from Lima at the end of 1570 on the most extended *visita,* or tour of inspection, ever undertaken within the Spanish Empire by a ranking official. The inspection tour of Toledo lasted 5 years and took him, it is estimated, 5,000 miles throughout the land.

One of the central matters with which the viceroy dealt on his inspection trip, and, indeed, throughout his time in Peru, was that of the production of precious metals, particularly silver, in whose output Peru led the world. To increase mineral production, the viceroy introduced a new method of smelting silver ore, an amalgamation process which involved the use of mercury. Mercury was produced in Peru at the mine of Huancavelica, and Toledo's careful attention to the improvement of the laws and practices governing the mercury mine and all the mines of Peru led to a substantial increase in mineral output.

Indian Policy

Another significant but not always successful aspect of Toledo's rule centered on his policies toward the Indian population. An act for which he was widely criticized involved the Inca ruler Túpac Amaru. The Inca, who lived with his reduced following in a wilderness area north of the former Inca capital of Cuzco, maintained a rebellious posture against the Spaniards, who had taken the lands of his forefathers. Indian raids on Spanish highway traffic and attacks on scattered Spanish colonists, culminating in the murder of several of Toledo's emissaries to the Indians, led to the seizure of the Inca by Toledo. Despite pleas for clemency from some of Toledo's closest advisers and their claim that the Inca chief had been sentenced on the basis of much false testimony, Toledo, in 1571, ordered the execution of Túpac Amaru and personally witnessed the implementation of his decree.

In another unsuccessful aspect of his Indian policy, Toledo attempted in 1574 to pacify the Chiriguano Indians, a tribe that occupied an area in present-day Bolivia. Toledo himself went into the field against the Indians at the head of a few hundred troops but was unable to subdue them.

More successful was Toledo's constant effort to improve the situation of the pacified Indians and to bring reason and right into their relationships with their Spanish masters, to whom they were obliged to pay tribute and for whom they were made to labor in the mines, in public works, and in personal service. Toledo in effect set up a bipartite government in Peru for the Indians in which they had a separate political structure under their own chiefs (curacas or caciques) but a political system which was ultimately under the control of Spanish officials, the *corregidores de indios.*

One of the principal devices which Toledo employed for maximizing the amount of labor and tribute which the Spaniards could extract from the native population—while seeking to improve the living conditions of the Indians and to protect them against oppression—was to found new towns for them, called *reducciones,* into which the Indians were moved from their scattered dwelling places and where they had the benefit of a more regularized and, presumably, more healthful life.

Through the *corregidores de indios,* Toledo established to a considerable degree the rights of the Indian subjects of the Crown against Spanish encroachment on their persons, lands, and other property. He had an extensive census taken of the Indians in order to determine the numbers available for labor and to pay tribute, and he carefully fixed the amount and the type of tribute the Indians were compelled to pay and the conditions of draft labor, or *mita,* which they had to meet. But Toledo also punished mistreatment of the Indians by Spanish laymen.

Religion and Education

In his relationship with the Church, which was powerful and closely integrated with the civil government, Toledo worked hard to improve the condition of both the secular and regular clergy, who had been in a state of decline when the viceroy came to Peru. The viceroy insisted, with much success, on the correct fulfillment of clerical duties. He expanded religious education, and he punished immoral behavior by clerics.

The improvement and extension of education in the viceroyalty were other major concerns of the dynamic Toledo. The university, which had been founded in 1551, was in fact a mere secondary school run by the Dominican order. Toledo removed the school from the control of that order, gave it new endowments, reorganized its courses, and named new faculty members. These actions by the viceroy laid the basis for the fame that the University of San Marcos has achieved over the centuries since the 1570s.

Toledo was active in many other areas. For example, he established the *protomedicato,* a royal medical board responsible for licensing physicians and for aspects of public health. He founded many towns in Peru, Bolivia, and Argentina, and he was always active in the construction of diverse public works, ordering and seeing to completion the building of bridges, waterworks, and roads and the repair and construction of other edifices.

Toledo's career ended in 1581, when he was recalled to Spain. Philip II, as was not unusual in the days of absolute monarchy, showed more dissatisfaction than pleasure at the achievements of Toledo, especially because of the execution of Túpac Amaru, and the last years of the viceroy were spent in royal disfavor. However, in the light of history, Toledo's character as an indefatigable, loyal, and generally high-minded servant of the Crown and his multitude of accomplishments in Peru give him a lasting place as a model administrator of Spain's American empire and, indeed, within imperial history as a whole.

Further Reading

Arthur F. Zimmerman, *Francisco de Toledo, Fifth Viceroy of Peru, 1569-1581* (1938; new ed. 1968), is the only biography in English; although more a compilation of facts than a scholarly analysis, the book outlines Toledo's principal achievements in Peru. The study by Phillip A. Means, *Fall of the Inca Empire and the Spanish Rule in Peru, 1530-1780* (1932), also contains information about Peru under Toledo and gives a much less favorable image of the viceroy than does Zimmerman's monograph. ☐

J. R. R. Tolkien

J. R. R. Tolkien (1892-1973) gained a reputation during the 1960s and 1970s as a cult figure among youths disillusioned with war and the technological age; his continuing popularity evidences his ability to evoke the oppressive realities of modern life while drawing audiences into a fantasy world.

Tolkien was born on Jan. 3, 1892, the son of English-born parents in Bloemfontein, in the Orange Free State of South Africa, where his father worked as a bank manager. To escape the heat and dust of southern Africa and to better guard the delicate health of Ronald (as he was called), Tolkien's mother moved back to England with him and his younger brother when they were very young boys. Within a year of this move their father, Arthur Tolkien, died in Bloemfontein, and a few years later the boys' mother died as well. The boys lodged at several

homes from 1905 until 1911, when Ronald entered Exeter College, Oxford. Tolkien received his B.A. from Oxford in 1915 and an M.A. in 1919. During the interim he married his longtime sweetheart, Edith Bratt, and served for a short time on the Western Front with the Lancashire Fusiliers. While in England recovering from "trench fever" in 1917, Tolkien began writing "The Book of Lost Tales," which eventually became *The Silmarillion* (1977) and laid the groundwork for his stories about Middle-earth. After the Armistice he returned to Oxford, where he joined the staff of the *Oxford English Dictionary* and began work as a free-lance tutor. In 1920 he was appointed Reader in English Language at Leeds University, where he collaborated with E. V. Gordon on an acclaimed translation of *Sir Gawain and the Green Knight,* which was completed and published in 1925. (Some years later, Tolkien completed a second translation of this poem, which was published posthumously.) The following year, having returned to Oxford as Rawlinson and Bosworth Professor of Anglo-Saxon, Tolkien became friends with a fellow of Magdalen College, C. S. Lewis. They shared an intense enthusiasm for the myths, sagas, and languages of northern Europe; and to better enhance those interests, both attended meetings of "The Coalbiters," an Oxford club, founded by Tolkien, at which Icelandic sagas were read aloud.

During the rest of his years at Oxford—twenty as Rawlinson and Bosworth Professor of Anglo-Saxon, fourteen as Merton Professor of English Language and Literature—Tolkien published several esteemed short studies and translations. Notable among these are his essays "Beowulf:

The Monsters and the Critics" (1936), " Chaucer as a Philologist: The Reeve's Tale" (1934), and "On Fairy-Stories" (1947); his scholarly edition of *Ancrene Wisse* (1962); and his translations of three medieval poems: "Sir Gawain and the Green Knight," "Pearl," and "Sir Orfeo" (1975). As a writer of imaginative literature, though, Tolkien is best known for *The Hobbit* and *The Lord of the Rings,* tales which were formed during his years attending meetings of "The Inklings," an informal gathering of like-minded friends and fellow dons, initiated after the demise of The Coalbiters. The Inklings, which was formed during the late 1930s and lasted until the late 1940s, was a weekly meeting held in Lewis's sitting-room at Magdalen, at which works-in-progress were read aloud and discussed and critiqued by the attendees, all interspersed with free-flowing conversation about literature and other topics. The nucleus of the group was Tolkien, Lewis, and Lewis's friend, novelist Charles Williams; other participants, who attended irregularly, included Lewis's brother Warren, Nevill Coghill, H. V. D. Dyson, Owen Barfield, and others. The common thread which bound them was that they were all adherents of Christianity and all had a love of story. Having heard Tolkien's first hobbit story read aloud at a meeting of the Inklings, Lewis urged Tolkien to publish *The Hobbit,* which appeared in 1937. A major portion of *The Fellowship of the Ring* was also read to The Inklings before the group disbanded in the late 1940's.

Tolkien retired from his professorship in 1959. While the unauthorized publication of an American edition of *The Lord of the Rings* in 1965 angered him, it also made him a widely admired cult figure in the United States, especially among high school and college students. Uncomfortable with this status, he and his wife lived quietly in Bournemouth for several years, until Edith's death in 1971. In the remaining two years of his life, Tolkien returned to Oxford, where he was made an honorary fellow of Merton College and awarded a doctorate of letters. He was at the height of his fame as a scholarly and imaginative writer when he died in 1973, though critical study of his fiction continues and has increased in the years since.

A devout Roman Catholic throughout his life, Tolkien began creating his own languages and mythologies at an early age and later wrote Christian-inspired stories and poems to provide them with a narrative framework. Based on bedtime stories Tolkien had created for his children, *The Hobbit* concerns the reluctant efforts of a hobbit, Bilbo Baggins, to recover a treasure stolen by a dragon. During the course of his mission, the hobbit discovers a magical ring which, among other powers, can render its bearer invisible. The ability to disappear helps Bilbo fulfill his quest; however, the ring's less obvious faculties prompt the malevolent Sauron, Dark Lord of Mordor, to seek it. The hobbits' attempt to destroy the ring, thereby denying Sauron unlimited power, is the focal point of the *Lord of the Rings* trilogy, which consists of the novels *The Fellowship of the Ring* (1954), *The Two Towers* (1954), and *The Return of the King* (1955). In these books Tolkien rejects such traditional heroic attributes as strength and size, stressing instead the capacity of even the humblest creatures to prevail against evil.

The initial critical reception to *The Lord of the Rings* varied. While some reviewers expressed dissatisfaction with the story's great length and one-dimensional characters, the majority enjoyed Tolkien's enchanting descriptions and lively sense of adventure. Religious, Freudian, allegorical, and political interpretations of the trilogy soon appeared, but Tolkien generally rejected such explications. He maintained that *The Lord of the Rings* was conceived with "no allegorical intentions . . . , moral, religious, or political," but he also denied that the trilogy is a work of escapism: "Middle-earth is not an imaginary world. . . . The theatre of my tale is this earth, the one in which we now live." Tolkien contended that his story was "*fundamentally linguistic* in inspiration," a "religious and Catholic work" whose spiritual aspects were "absorbed into the story and symbolism." Tolkien concluded, "The stories were made . . . to provide a world for the languages rather than the reverse."

Throughout his career Tolkien composed histories, genealogies, maps, glossaries, poems, and songs to supplement his vision of Middle-earth. Among the many works published during his lifetime were a volume of poems, *The Adventures of Tom Bombadil and Other Verses from the Red Book* (1962), and a fantasy novel, *Smith of Wootton Major* (1967). Though many of his stories about Middle-earth remained incomplete at the time of Tolkien's death, his son, Christopher, rescued the manuscripts from his father's collections, edited them, and published them. One of these works, *The Silmarillion,* takes place before the time of *The Hobbit* and, in a heroic manner which recalls the Christian myths of Creation and the Fall, tells the tale of the first age of Holy Ones and their offspring. *Unfinished Tales of Numenor and Middle-earth* (1980) is a similar collection of incomplete stories and fragments written during World War I. *The Book of Lost Tales, Part I* (1984) and *The Book of Lost Tales, Part II* (1984) deal respectively with the beginnings of Middle-earth and the point at which humans enter the saga. In addition to these posthumous works, Christopher Tolkien also collected his father's correspondence to friends, family, and colleagues in *The Letters of J. R. R. Tolkien* (1981).

It is as a writer of timeless fantasy that Tolkien is most highly regarded today. From 1914 until his death in 1973, he drew on his familiarity with Northern and other ancient literatures and his own invented languages to create not just his own story, but his own world: Middle-earth, complete with its own history, myths, legends, epics, and heroes. "His life's work," Augustus M. Kolich has written, ". . . encompasses a reality that rivals Western man's own attempt at recording the composite, knowable history of his species. Not since Milton has any Englishman worked so successfully at creating a secondary world, derived from our own, yet complete in its own terms with encyclopedic mythology; an imagined world that includes a vast gallery of strange beings: hobbits, elves, dwarfs, orcs, and, finally, the men of Westernesse." His works—especially *The Lord of the Rings*—have pleased countless readers and fascinated critics who recognize their literary depth.

Further Reading

Newsweek, September 17, 1973.
New York Times, September 3, 1973.
Publishers Weekly, September 17, 1973.
Time, September 17, 1973.
Washington Post, September 3, 1973.
Anderson, Douglas A., author of introduction and notes, *The Annotated Hobbit,* Houghton, 1988.
Authors in the News, Volume 1, Gale, 1976.
Carpenter, Humphrey, *J. R. R. Tolkien: A Biography,* Allen & Unwin, 1977, published as *Tolkien: A Biography,* Houghton, 1978.
Carpenter, Humphrey, *The Inklings: C. S. Lewis, J. R. R. Tolkien, Charles Williams and Their Friends,* Allen & Unwin, 1978, Houghton, 1979.
Carter, Lin, *Tolkien: A Look behind The Lord of the Rings,* Houghton, 1969.
Compact Edition of the Oxford English Dictionary, Oxford University Press, 1971.
Contemporary Literary Criticism, Gale, Volume 1, 1973; Volume 2, 1974; Volume 3, 1975; Volume 8, 1978; Volume 12, 1980; Volume 38, 1986. □

Ernst Toller

The German playwright Ernst Toller (1893-1939) was one of the best-known of the dramatists of the expressionist school.

Ernst Toller was born on Dec. 1, 1893, at Samotschin near Bromberg, the son of a businessman. He studied at the universities of Heidelberg, Munich, and Grenoble. In 1914 he volunteered for war service, but the experience of the trenches changed his life. Released from the army after a breakdown, Toller then gravitated toward the left in Bavaria and in 1917 was sentenced to imprisonment for pacifist views and activities. During this incarceration he composed his first play, *Die Wandlung* (1919; *Transfiguration*).

Transfiguration is an exemplary work of the expressionist theater. The title points to that transformation of heart and soul which is the theme of many expressionist plays. The drama proceeds in a series of stages (*Stationen*) and depicts a man's "way." It intermingles scenes portraying external events with others displaying the activity of the subconscious mind. The horrors of war transform the hero from a patriotic volunteer to a revolutionary fighter for humanity.

In 1918 Toller became a member of the Central Committee of the Workers', Peasants', and Soldiers' Councils in Bavaria. In 1919 he was jailed for 5 years for his part in the abortive Eisner coup. During this imprisonment Toller composed his two other best-known plays, *Masse Mensch* (1920; *Mass and Man*) and *Die Maschinenstürmer* (1922; *The Machine-wreckers*). These works express the disillusionment of the frustrated revolutionary. The former is cast in the abstract expressionist mold, the characters being representative types, the Woman, the Husband, and so on.

The Woman represents the humane idealist who longs for change but abhors violence; and her antagonist, the Nameless One, regards violence as necessary and subordinates the individual ruthlessly to the supposed welfare of the masses. *The Machine-wreckers* is a more realistic play based on the Luddite disturbances in England in 1815; here again the hero is a social idealist destroyed by the hate of those he wishes to save.

Of Toller's further plays the most notable is *Hinkemann* (1922), an interesting treatment of the returning soldier motif. Toller moves away from avant-garde technique and abstract characters both here and in *Hoppla, wir leben!* (1927; *Such Is Life*), a sarcastic depiction of the Roaring Twenties. Of his prose works, all essays, *Briefe aus dem Gefängnis* (1936) deserves mention. His later dramas *Feuer aus den Kesseln* (1930) and *Die blonde Göttin* (1932) are of less interest.

The tragedy of Toller's themes reflects the disillusionment of his life. He left Germany in 1933 and committed suicide in New York on May 22, 1939.

Further Reading

Toller's autobiography is *I Was a German* (1933; trans. 1934). A full-length treatment of Toller in English is William A. Willebrand, *Ernst Toller and His Ideology* (1945). John M. Spalek, *Ernst Toller and His Critics* (1968), gives a comprehensive bibliography. A useful short account can be found in Hugh F. Garten, *Modern German Drama* (1959), which also provides background material, as does Richard Samuel and R. Hinton Thomas, *Expressionism in German Life, Literature and the Theatre, 1910-24* (1939).

Additional Sources

Dove, Richard, *He was a German: a biography of Ernst Toller,* London: Libris, 1990.
Toller, Ernst, *I was a German: the autobiography of a revolutionary,* New York: Paragon House, 1991. □

Edward Chace Tolman

Edward Chace Tolman (1886-1959) was an American psychologist and one of the leaders of the behaviorist movement. For Tolman, behavior consists of deliberate acts guided by purposes and expectations.

Edward Tolman was born on April 14, 1886, in Newton, Mass. After graduation from the Newton public schools in 1907 and from the Massachusetts Institute of Technology in 1911, he did graduate study in psychology at Harvard. At Harvard (1911-1915) Tolman witnessed the initial reaction of the academic world to two new sets of psychological ideas: those of the Gestalt psychologists (Wolfgang Köhler, Kurt Koffka, and Max Wertheimer) and those of John B. Watson, the behaviorist.

Tolman's later theory of behavior is rooted in these two schools. From Gestalt psychology he borrowed the idea of pattern: in Tolman's theory, perception, motivation, and cognition are regarded as processes in which patterns of stimulation are identified and interpreted and patterns of reactions are planned and executed. From behaviorism he borrowed the idea that such mental processes must be objectively defined in terms of behavioral properties that can be objectively recorded. Such objectivity is necessary, he thought, not only in our study of the mental processes of rats, cats, monkeys, and so on, but also in our study of our own mental processes. Whatever is private or subjective in our mental processes is, he claimed, forever protected from scientific scrutiny because by definition such intrinsically private states have no influence on our overt behavior.

In 1918 Tolman went to the University of California at Berkeley, where he began to study maze learning in rats—a research program that made the department of psychology at Berkeley world-famous. In 1932 Tolman published *Purposive Behavior in Animals and Men*. This book presented Tolman's purposive behaviorism and reviewed the new research on rat learning done in his Berkeley laboratory.

From 1932 on, Tolman and his students turned out a constant flood of papers on animal learning. Tolman's only other book was *Drives toward War* (1942). This book surveyed studies of animal behavior in search of an explanation of the motives that drive men to war and a description of the social controls that would have to be enforced in a warless society. The book also shows the strong impact of Sigmund Freud upon Tolman's theory of motivation.

On June 14, 1949, the regents of the University of California handed an ultimatum to the Academic Senate: sign the new special loyalty oath or face dismissal! On that day Tolman became the leader of the nonsigners, those who were fired by the regents for refusing to submit to this naked attack upon academic freedom. After a 10-year court battle, the regents' case was repudiated by the courts: the special loyalty oath was declared unconstitutional, and the nonsigners were reinstated with back pay. On Nov. 19, 1959, Tolman died in Berkeley.

Further Reading

Tolman's *Purposive Behavior in Animals and Men* (1932) and his *Collected Papers in Psychology* (1951) give a comprehensive, clear survey of his ideas and experimental research. An analysis of the research in animal learning done under the influence of Tolman's criticism of the orthodox behaviorism of Clark L. Hull is in Charles Taylor, *The Explanation of Behavior* (1964). George R. Stewart, *The Year of the Oath* (1950), describes the fight for academic freedom at the University of California. □

Leo Tolstoy

The Russian novelist and moral philosopher Leo Tolstoy (1828-1910) ranks as one of the world's great writers, and his "War and Peace" has been called the greatest novel ever written.

Leo Tolstoy was one of the great rebels of all time, a man who during a long and stormy life was at odds with Church, government, literary tradition, and his own family. Yet he was a conservative, obsessed by the idea of God in an age of scientific positivism. He brought the art of the realistic novel to its highest development. Tolstoy's brooding concern for death made him one of the precursors of existentialism. Yet the bustling spirit that animates his novels conveys—perhaps—more of life than life itself.

Tolstoy's father, Count Nikolay Ilyich Tolstoy, came of a noble family dating back to the 14th century and prominent from the time of Peter I. Both Tolstoy's father and grandfather had a passion for gambling and had exhausted the family wealth. Nikolay recouped his fortunes, however, by marrying Maria Volkonsky, bearer of a great name and heiress to a fortune that included 800 serfs and the estate of Yasnaya Polyana in Tula Province, where Leo (Lev Nikolayevich) was born on Aug. 28, 1828, the youngest of four sons. His mother died when he was 2 years old, whereupon his father's distant cousin Tatyana Ergolsky took charge of the children. In 1837 Tolstoy's father died, and an aunt, Alexandra Osten-Saken, became legal guardian of the children. Her religious fervor was an important early influence on Tolstoy. When she died in 1840, the children were sent to Kazan to another sister of their father, Pelageya Yushkov.

The Yushkovs were among the highest society in the town, Pelageya's father having been governor of the province before his death. Balls and receptions dominated the Yushkovs' social life, and there was much concern about

what was *comme il faut*. Aunt Pelageya told Tolstoy that nothing was better for a young man's development than an affair with an older woman. He was no prude, but he was awkward and proud, being known to his friends as the "Bear."

Tolstoy was educated at home by German and French tutors. He was not a particularly apt pupil, but he was good at games. In 1843 he entered Kazan University; planning on a diplomatic career, he entered the faculty of Oriental languages. Finding these studies too demanding, he switched 2 years later to the notoriously easygoing law faculty. The university, however, had too many second-rate foreigners on its faculty, and Tolstoy left in 1847 without taking his degree.

Tolstoy returned to Yasnaya Polyana, determined to become a model farmer and a "father" to his serfs. His philanthropy failed because of his naiveté in dealing with the peasants and because he spent too much time carousing in Tula and Moscow. During this time he first began making those amazingly honest and self-lacerating diary entries, a practice he maintained until his death. These entries provided much material for his fiction, and in a very real sense his whole oeuvre is one long autobiography. In 1848 Tolstoy attempted to take the law examination, this time in St. Petersburg, but after passing the first two parts he again became disenchanted, returning to the concerts and gambling halls of Moscow when not hunting and drinking at Yasnaya Polyana.

Army Life and Early Literary Career

Nikolay, Tolstoy's eldest brother, visited him at this time in Yasnaya Polyana while on furlough from military service in the Caucasus. Leo greatly loved his brother, and when he asked him to join him in the south, Tolstoy agreed. After a meandering journey, he reached the mountains of the Caucasus, where he sought to join the army as a Junker, or gentleman-volunteer. In the autumn he passed the necessary exams and was assigned to the 4th Battery of the 20th Artillery Brigade, serving on the Terek River against the rebellious mountaineers, Moslem irregulars who had declared a holy war against the encroaching Russians.

Tolstoy's border duty on a lonely Cossack outpost became a kind of pagan idyll, hunting, drinking, sleeping, chasing the girls, and occasionally fighting. During the long lulls he first began to write. In 1852 he sent the autobiographical sketch *Childhood* to the leading journal of the day, the *Contemporary*. Nikolai Nekrasov, its editor, was ecstatic, and when it was published (under Tolstoy's initials), so was all of Russia. Tolstoy now began *The Cossacks* (finished in 1862), a thinly veiled account of his life in the outpost.

From November 1854 to August 1855 Tolstoy served in the battered fortress at Sevastopol. He had requested transfer to this area, where one of the bloodiest battles of the Crimean War was in process. As he directed fire from the 4th Bastion, the hottest area in the conflict for a long while, Tolstoy managed to write *Youth*, the second part of his autobiographical trilogy. He also wrote the three *Sevastopol Tales* at this time, revealing the distinctive Tolstoyan vision

of war as a place of unparalleled confusion, banality, and heroism, a special space where men, viewed from the author's dispassionate, Godlike point of view, were at their best and worst. Some of these stories were published while the battle they described still raged. The first story was the talk of Russia, attracting (for almost the last time in Tolstoy's career) the favorable attention of the Czar.

When the city fell, Tolstoy was asked to make a study of the artillery action during the final assault and to report with it to the authorities in St. Petersburg. His reception in the capital was triumphal. Because of his name, he was welcomed into the most brilliant society. Because of his stories, he was lionized by the cream of literary society. Tolstoy's photographs at this time show a coarse-looking young man with piercing eyes, spatulate nose, and mustache. He was not tall but very strong.

During the same year Tolstoy visited Moscow, garnering there both success in society and esteem among authors. By the time he returned to St. Petersburg, he was beginning to tire of his new literary acquaintances. He felt that they were insincere talkers. He offended both camps of what soon became a war within the *Contemporary* group—with the opposing points of view represented by the aristocratic Ivan Turgenev and the radical Nikolai Chernyshevsky. His lifelong friendship with the conservative poet A. A. Fet dated from this time. Tolstoy was never a "professional author"; he avoided literary gossip, and his independent wealth permitted him to remain aloof from the scramble of making a living.

School for Peasant Children

In 1856 Tolstoy left the service (as a lieutenant) to look after his affairs in Yasnaya Polyana; he also worked on *The Snowstorm* and *Two Hussars*. In the following year he made his first trip abroad. He did not like Western Europe, as his stories of this period, *Lucerne* and *Albert*, show. He was becoming increasingly interested in education, however, and he talked with experts in this field wherever he went. In the summer he returned to Yasnaya Polyana and set up a school for peasant children, where he began his pedagogic experiments. In 1860-1861 Tolstoy went abroad again, seeking to learn more about education; he also gambled heavily. During this trip he witnessed the death of his brother Nikolay in the south of France. More than all the grisly scenes of battle he had witnessed, this event brought home to Tolstoy the fact of death, the specter of which fascinated and terrified him throughout his long career.

After the freeing of the serfs in 1861, Tolstoy became a mediator (*posrednik*), an official who arbitrated land disputes between serfs and their former masters. In April he had a petty quarrel with Turgenev, actually challenging him to a duel. Turgenev declined, but the two men were on bad terms for years.

Tolstoy's school at Yasnaya Polyana went forward, using pioneering techniques that were later adopted by progressive educationists. In 1862 Tolstoy started a journal to propagate his pedagogical ideas, *Yasnaya Polyana*. He also took the first of his koumiss cures, traveling to Samara, living in the open, and drinking fermented mare's milk. These cures eventually became an almost annual event.

Golden Years

In September 1862, Tolstoy wrote his aunt Alexandra, "I, aged, toothless fool that I am, have fallen in love." He was only 34, but he was 16 years older than Sofya Andreyevna Bers (or Behrs), whose mother had been one of Tolstoy's childhood friends. Daughter of a prominent Moscow doctor, Bers was handsome, intelligent, and, as the years would show, strong-willed. The first decade of their marriage brought Tolstoy the greatest happiness; never before or after was his creative life so rich or his personal life so full. In June 1863 his wife had the first of their 13 children.

His wife's diary entry for Oct. 28, 1863, reads: "Story about 1812; he is very involved with it." And indeed Tolstoy was. Since 1861 he had been trying to write a historical novel about the Decembrist uprising of 1825. But the more he worked, the farther back in time he went. The first portion of *War and Peace* was published in 1865 (in the *Russian Messenger*) as "The Year 1805." In 1868 three more chapters appeared; and in 1869 he completed the novel. Tolstoy had been somewhat neglected by critics in the preceding few years because he had not participated in the bitter literary politics of the time. But his new novel created a fantastic outpouring of popular and critical reaction.

War and Peace represents an apogee in the history of world literature, but it was also the high point of Tolstoy's personal life. He peopled his enormous canvas with almost everyone he had ever met, including all of his relations on both sides of his family. In so doing he celebrated a patriarchal way of life—rich in its country contentments and glittering in its city excitements. Balls and battles, birth and death, all were described in copious and minute detail. In this book the European realistic novel, with its attention to social matrix, exact description, and psychological rendering, found its most complete expression.

The genial scenes of feast and hunt were a reflection of Tolstoy's great personal happiness at this time. His estate prospered, and he was deeply in love with his wife. She worshiped her husband, doing everything in her power to free him from all but his writing. Their son Ilya reported that she copied out the complete text of *War and Peace* seven times.

But even in this year of Tolstoy's greatest success ominous signs of the future began to appear. The brilliant rhetoric of those passages in *War and Peace* in which Tolstoy argued for his own idiosyncratic theory of history foreshadowed the often crotchety tone of the later intransigent moralist. In the midst of all his happiness, in 1869, Tolstoy experienced a deep and mysterious personal trauma. Traveling to buy an estate in Penza Province, he stopped overnight in Arzamas. Awakened by a nightmare, he felt that he was dying. Once again, as when Nikolay had died, he was reminded of his mortality, and his so-called conversion of 1880 may, in a sense, be traced back to this experience.

Tolstoy's next 10 years were equally crowded. He published the *Primer* and the first four *Readers* (1872-1875),

his attempts to appeal to an audience that would include children and the newly literate peasantry. From 1873 to 1877 he worked on the second of his masterworks, *Anna Karenina,* which also created a sensation upon its publication. The concluding section of the novel was written during another of Russia's seemingly endless wars with Turkey. The country was in a patriotic ferment. M. N. Katkov, editor of the journal in which *Anna Karenina* had been appearing serially, was afraid to print the final chapters, which contained an attack on war hysteria. Tolstoy, in a fury, took the text away from Katkov, and with the aid of N. Strakhov he published a separate edition that enjoyed huge sales.

The novel was based partly on events that had occurred on a neighboring estate, where a nobleman's rejected mistress had thrown herself under a train. It again contained great chunks of disguised biography, especially in the scenes describing the courtship and marriage of Kitty and Levin. Tolstoy's family continued to grow, and his royalties were making him an extremely rich man.

Spiritual Crisis

The ethical quest that had begun when Tolstoy was a child and that had tormented him throughout his younger years now drove him to abandon all else in order to seek an ultimate meaning in life. At first he turned to the Russian Orthodox Church, visiting the Optina-Pustyn monastery in 1877. But he found no answer. He began reading the Gospels, and he found the key to his own moral system in Matthew: "Resist not evil." In 1879-1880 Tolstoy wrote his *Confession* (published 1884) and his *Critique of Dogmatic Theology.* From this point on his life was dominated by a burning desire to achieve social justice and a rationally acceptable ethic.

Tolstoy was a public figure now, and in 1881 he asked Alexander III, in vain, to spare the lives of those who had assassinated the Czar's father. He visited Optina again, this time disguised as a peasant, but his trip failed to bring him peace. In September the family moved to Moscow in order to further the education of the older sons. The following year Tolstoy participated in the census, visiting the worst slums of Moscow, where he was freshly appalled.

Tolstoy had not gone out of his way to propagate his new convictions, but in 1883 he met V. G. Chertkov, a wealthy guards officer who soon became the moving force behind an attempt to start a movement in Tolstoy's name. In the next few years a new publication was founded (the *Mediator*) in order to spread Tolstoy's word in tract and fiction, as well as to make good reading available to the poor. In 6 years almost 20 million copies were distributed. Tolstoy had long been under surveillance by the secret police, and in 1884 copies of *What I Believe* were seized from the printer. He now took up cobbling and read deeply in Chinese philosophy. He abstained from cigarettes, meat, white bread, and hunting. His image as a white-bearded patriarch in a peasant's blouse dates from this period.

Tolstoy's relations with his family were becoming increasingly strained. The more of a saint he became in the eyes of the world, the more of a devil he seemed to his wife. He wanted to give his wealth away, but she would not hear of it. An unhappy compromise was reached in 1884, when Tolstoy assigned to his wife the copyright to all his works before 1881.

In 1886 Tolstoy worked on what is possibly his most powerful story, *The Death of Ivan Ilyich,* and his drama of peasant life, *The Power of Darkness* (which could not be produced until 1895). In 1888, when he was 60 years old, his thirteenth child was born. In the same year he finished his sweeping indictment of carnal love, *The Kreutzer Sonata.*

Last Years and Death

In 1892 Tolstoy's estate, valued at the equivalent of $1.5 million, was divided among his wife and his nine living children. Tolstoy was now perhaps the most famous man in the world; people came from all over the globe to Yasnaya Polyana. His activity was unabated. In 1891 and in 1893 he organized famine relief in Ryazan Province. He also worked on some of his finest stories: *The Devil* (1890, published posthumously) and *Father Sergius* (1890). In order to raise money for transporting a dissenting religious sect (the Doukhobors) to Canada, Tolstoy published the third, and least successful, of his three long novels, *Resurrection* (1899). From 1896 to 1904 he worked on the story that was his personal favorite, *Hadji Murad,* the tale of a Caucasian mountaineer.

Tolstoy's final years were filled with worldwide acclaim and great unhappiness, as he was caught in the strife between his convictions, his followers, and his family. The Holy Synod excommunicated him in 1901. Unable to endure the quarrels at home he set out on his last pilgrimage in October 1910, accompanied by his youngest daughter, Alexandra, and his physician. The trip proved too much, and he died in the home of the stationmaster of the small depot at Astapovo on Nov. 9, 1910. He was buried at Yasnaya Polyana.

Further Reading

Tolstoy's own enormous output (his collected works run to 90 volumes) is exceeded only by the amount of material written about him. Among the memoirs about Tolstoy are A. B. Goldenweizer, *Talks with Tolstoy* (trans. 1923); Alexandra Tolstoy, *Tolstoy: A Life of My Father.* (1953); and V. Bulgakov, *The Last Year of Leo Tolstoy* (trans. 1971). There are two good biographies in English: Ernest J. Simmons, *Leo Tolstoy* (1946), and Henri Troyat, *Tolstoy* (1965; trans. 1967). Simmons is more complete and scholarly, but Troyat is more enjoyable to read.

Sir Isaiah Berlin, *The Hedgehog and the Fox: An Essay on Tolstoy's View of History* (1953), is a brilliant short study. George Steiner, *Tolstoy or Dostoevsky: An Essay in the Old Criticism* (1959), when it is not being precious, contains many insights into Tolstoy both as artist and thinker. John Bayley, *Tolstoy and the Novel* (1966), is a good study of Tolstoy's contribution to the genre. Ralph E. Matlaw, ed., *Tolstoy: A Collection of Critical Essays* (1967), offers stylistic criticism of Tolstoy's work. For background James H. Billington, *The Icon and the Axe: An Interpretive History of Russian Culture* (1966), is excellent. □

Sin-itiro Tomonaga

The Japanese physicist Sin-itiro Tomonaga (1906-1979) is best known for his fundamental contributions to quantum electrodynamics.

The oldest son of a philosopher and university professor, Sin-itiro Tomonaga was born on March 31, 1906, in Tokyo. After obtaining his degree from Kyoto University in 1929, he spent 3 years as a research student in Kajuro Tomaki's laboratory at the university and then became a research student under Yoshio Nishina in the Science Research Institute in Tokyo. Tomonaga remained there until 1940, with the exception of some time spent in 1939 at the University of Leipzig with Werner Heisenberg.

In 1940 Tomonaga married Rijo, by whom he had three children. In 1941, he became professor of physics at the Tokyo University of Science and Literature (which after the war became part of the Tokyo University of Education).

During the war years, while working in complete isolation from other physicists, Tomonaga made the contributions to quantum electrodynamics for which he shared the Nobel Prize of 1965 with Julian Schwinger of Harvard University and Richard Feynman of the California Institute of Technology. The achievement of these physicists must be understood in the context of the general development of physics since 1925-1926, when quantum mechanics was discovered and elaborated by Heisenberg, Erwin Schrödinger, Paul Dirac, Max Born, and others. Although this elegant theory had been developed specifically to understand the structure of the atom, it was soon generalized by Heisenberg, Wolfgang Pauli, Dirac, and Enrico Fermi to include an explanation of radiation processes and of processes, like the Compton effect, involving the interaction of radiation and matter. The resulting theory—quantum electrodynamics—agreed *qualitatively* with experiment but refused to yield *precise* agreement. Most physicists of the 1930s took this to mean that there was something fundamentally wrong with the theory. "Tomonaga, Schwinger, and Feynman," wrote F. J. Dyson in *Science* (1965), "rescued the theory without making any radical innovations. Their victory was a victory of conservation. They kept the physical basis of the theory [the postulation of only electrons, positrons, and photons] precisely as it had been laid down by Dirac, and only changed the mathematical superstructure. By polishing and refining with great skill the mathematical formalism, they were able to show that the theory does in fact give meaningful predictions for all observable quantities."

The remarkable thing, as Dyson pointed out, was that, although certain experiments had played a decisive role in Schwinger's and Feynman's thinking, Tomonaga had reached an essentially identical insight on the basis of theoretical considerations alone. He had published those conclusions in Japanese in 1943, but his papers were not translated into English until 1948—until Schwinger and Feynman had been able to direct their efforts away from

war-related researches and had independently achieved essentially the same results.

After the war Tomonaga received many honors for his work. Besides the 1965 Nobel Prize, he received the Japan Academy Prize in 1948, the Order of Culture (Japan) in 1952, and the Lomonosov Medal from the USSR in 1964. He was professor of physics at Tokyo University of Education from 1949 to 1969, and served as president of the institution from 1956 until 1962. In 1963, he became director of the university's Institute of Optical Research. He was also president of the Science Council of Japan from 1963 to 1969. He retired from the Tokyo University of Education in 1969, and served as Professor Emeritus until his death in Tokyo on July 8, 1979.

Further Reading

The Nobel Foundation's annual volume *Les Prix Nobel 1965* (1966) has, in English, a brief biography of Tomonaga and his personal recollections of the development of quantum electrodynamics. Some background material is in Henry A. Boorse and Lloyd Motz, eds., *The World of the Atom* (2 vols., 1966). □

Ferdinand Tönnies

The German sociologist Ferdinand Tönnies (1855-1936) pioneered sociology as an academic discipline of rigorously scientific character on a broad base of original studies in the history of ideas, epistemology, political science, economics, and social anthropology.

Ferdinand Tönnies was born on July 26, 1855, on a farm homestead in the North Frisian peninsula of Eiderstedt, then still under Danish sovereignty. One of seven children, he received his high school education in Husum, where he became deeply attached to the novelist and poet Theodor Storm. After studying classics at different German universities and taking his doctoral degree in 1877, Tönnies turned to philosophy, history, biology, psychology, economics, and ethnology as his ideas on scientific sociology began to take shape.

In Berlin in 1876 Tönnies began at the suggestion of his lifelong friend Friedrich Paulsen a study of the much-neglected philosophy of Thomas Hobbes. On his first of many journeys to England and also to France, Tönnies discovered in 1878 several original manuscripts by Hobbes, essential to better appreciation of his system of ideas and natural-law theory. In his first account (1879-1881) Tönnies argued the significance of Hobbes in the scientific revolution of the 17th century. Continuing his documentation, he published the standard monograph on Hobbes's life and works in 1896 (3d ed. repr. 1971).

Beginning to lecture at the University of Kiel in 1882, at first on philosophy and government but soon extending his academic work to empirical social research and statistical methods, Tönnies devoted the next 6 years to working out his own social theory. His world-famous treatise *Community and Society* (1887) found little response in the intellectual climate of the Germany of Kaiser William II. The various schools of historicism disfavored the development of rigorously scientific social theory, and political practice in the Bismarck era refused to solve the pressing social problems of a rapidly growing industrial economy but fought the labor movement by legislation and police action even after 1890.

A clash with the Prussian university administration over Tönnies's connection with the German branch of the Ethical Culture movement and his outspoken reports on the Hamburg longshoremen's strike (1896-1897) made him suspect of radicalism if not socialist leanings; what promised to be the brilliant career of a gifted scholar was nipped in the bud. Yet, unremitting work on theoretical problems between 1894 and 1913, informed reviews of the growing world literature in the field, and prominent participation in the Verein für Sozialpolitik (Association for Social Politics) and the Gesellschaft für Soziale Reform (Society for Social Reform) increased Tönnies's reputation inside and outside Germany, creating an unusually wide disparity between scholarly stature and status in academic life. The external conflict was resolved in 1909 by his appointment to a full professorship in political economy at Kiel, which for the father of five young children also meant relief from financial stress.

The early masterpiece had clearly been a first decisive step toward the systematic development of the new social science. As Tönnies's plans for this elaboration were frustrated at the most productive time of life, only a few papers of theoretical importance stem from the period before World War I. At the same time, he became involved in a fierce battle against social Darwinism, adopted in imperial Germany as apologetics for a conservative outlook.

Of two new projects formed in 1907, a critique of public opinion and a study in social history, one was completed only in 1922, the other introduced by the volume *The Spirit of the Modern Age* in 1935. With Max Weber and others Tönnies had founded the German Sociological Association in 1909 and, as its subdivision, the Statistical Association (1911). He had failed, however, to complete his systematic sociology.

After World War I, with prospects more favorable to social science and its academic recognition in the Weimar Republic, *Community and Society* went through several new editions. Now in his 60s, Tönnies carried out his design of a systematic sociology. The theoretical parts on social units, values, norms, and action patterns in the *Introduction to Sociology* (1931) were supplemented by three volumes of collected studies and critiques and by a series of papers on his empirical research. He reestablished the Sociological Association, remaining its president until 1933.

The bulk of his published work bears out a distinction Tönnies had proposed in 1908 between pure, applied, and empirical sociology. In line with the scientific principles of both Galileo and Hobbes, pure sociology, including the fundamental concepts of community and society, relates to abstract constructions appertaining to human relationships; from these, more specific theories are deducible in applied sociology, with emphasis on interaction of economic, political, and cultural conditions in the modern age; they, in turn, serve as guidelines in inductive empirical research. Tönnies kept strictly separate from this threefold scientific endeavor what he called practical sociology; this, comprising social policies and social work, presents, in a complete system, technologies based on the scientific insights of the three sections of the system.

Tönnies acted on this solution also of the value problem. He relentlessly exposed the neoromanticism of the 1920s, just as his earlier critique of romanticism had been the cornerstone of the theory of *Community and Society*. But in 1933 he was deprived as "politically unreliable" of his status as professor emeritus. His death on April 9, 1936, spared him from being witness to the worst excesses of the Nazi dictatorship and from further indignities.

Further Reading

Tönnies's *Community and Society* was translated by Charles P. Loomis (1957). A selection of Tönnies's other writings is in *On Sociology: Pure, Applied, and Empirical,* edited and with an introduction by Werner J. Cahnman and Rudolf Heberle (1971). The chief Hobbes editions by Tönnies, *Elements of Law Natural and Politic* and *Behemoth,* were reprinted by M. M. Goldsmith (1969). A book-length biographical study in German by E. G. Jacoby appeared in 1971. Tönnies's sociological system is the subject of a chapter by Rudolf Heberle in *An Introduction to the History of Sociology* (1948). Recent works include Robert A. Nisbet, *The Sociological Tradition*

(1966), and, with emphasis on Tönnies's academic standing, Fritz K. Ringer, *The Decline of the German Mandarins* (1969).

□

Robert Augustus Toombs

Robert Augustus Toombs (1810-1885), U.S. congressman and Confederate secretary of state, was noted for his opposition to Confederate president Jefferson Davis.

Robert Toombs was born on July 2, 1810, in Wilkes County, Ga. He attended the University of Georgia but graduated from Union College in New York in 1828. After his admission to the bar in 1830, Toombs began a successful career as lawyer, planter, and businessman in Washington, Ga.

Toombs served in the Georgia Legislature from 1837 to 1843, establishing a reputation as an expert on financial matters. In 1844 he was elected to the U.S. Congress. At this time Toombs manifested the political philosophy of a conservative Whig; by 1850 he had adopted an aggressively pro-Southern stance.

In Congress, Toombs was influential in securing passage of the 1850 compromise measures. With Alexander Stephens and Howell Cobb, he established the Constitutional Union party, which dominated Georgia politics for several years and was responsible for the Georgia Legislature's election of Toombs to the U.S. Senate in 1851. Upon the party's dissolution, Toombs uneasily joined the Democrats.

Strongly opposed to the election of Abraham Lincoln as president in 1860, although Toombs had supported the idea of compromise, he advised Georgians to vote for secession. He was a prominent figure in the state secessionist convention in January 1861 and later served at the Southern Convention.

Toombs sought the Confederate presidency but then reluctantly accepted the office of secretary of state. For a man of his financial talent, the post of secretary of the Treasury would have been more suitable. Although he performed his administrative duties efficiently, Toombs grew to regard President Jefferson Davis with contempt. In July 1861 he applied for a military commission and received command of a brigade on the Virginia front.

Toombs was a temperamental officer whose exploits were variously described as cowardly and heroic. In September 1862 he resigned from the military. For a time Toombs did little but criticize Davis and Gen. Robert E. Lee.

To avoid arrest at the end of the war, Toombs fled to Cuba and then to London. He returned to Georgia in 1867 but never applied for pardon as a requirement for regaining citizenship. He restored his law practice and reestablished himself as a popular leader who carefully attempted to overturn Radical Republican rule in the South. He never again held elective office. A brilliant raconteur and a man of

delightful wit and biting sarcasm, he once referred to prohibitionists as "men of small pints." He died on Dec. 15, 1885.

Further Reading

Although Ulrich B. Phillips, *The Life of Robert Toombs* (1913; repr. 1968), is dated, it remains a judicious and scholarly work. William Y. Thompson, *Robert Toombs of Georgia* (1966), is well documented and very thorough, emphasizing Toombs as an undisciplined individualist. For general background see Burton J. Hendrick, *Statesmen of the Lost Cause* (1939). □

Evangelista Torricelli

The Italian mathematician and physicist Evangelista Torricelli (1608-1647) invented the mercury barometer and made important contributions to calculus and the theories of hydraulics and dynamics.

Evangelista Torricelli was born in Faenza on Oct. 15, 1608. Left fatherless early in life, he was educated by his uncle, who was in monastic orders. In 1627 his uncle sent him to Rome to study mathematics and natural philosophy under Benedetto Castelli, professor of mathematics at the Collegio di Sapienza, who had been one of Galileo's pupils.

Torricelli spent the next 10 years in study. He corresponded with Galileo and studied his writings. He was especially impressed by the *Dialogues concerning Two New Sciences* (1638) and at once generalized Galileo's analysis of projectile motion. His conclusions on this and other subjects were set down in his book *De motu gravium* (1640; published 1644). Galileo invited Torricelli to Florence in 1641, and he became the amanuensis and companion of the great scientist until Galileo died 3 months later. Soon after, Torricelli succeeded him as grand-ducal mathematician and professor of mathematics at the Florentine Academy.

Scientific Work

Torricelli experimented with telescopes and simple microscopes, grinding his own lenses, and by carefully controlling their curvature, he produced telescopes superior to most of those of his contemporaries. His most important practical invention was the mercury barometer, first described in a letter to Michelangelo Ricci dated June 11, 1644. Torricelli had repeated Galileo's experiments with the thermoscope and was led to his discovery when he substituted mercury for water in the tube. He found also that water could be used as the liquid in the barometer if the containing vessel was sufficiently long ("18 cubits," that is, approximately 33 feet), and he realized that the column of liquid was held up by the pressure of the atmosphere.

In the course of his experiments, Torricelli observed that the quantities of water discharged from a hole in the bottom of a tank in equal increments of time were propor-

tional, from the last increment to the first, to successive odd numbers. This observation is said to have reminded him of Galileo's law of the velocity of a falling body, and it suggested to him that he should treat the jet of water as a series of freely falling particles, each with a speed determined by the original height of the water surface in the tank—Torricelli's law of efflux.

Mathematical Work

Torricelli saw the advantages of the method of indivisibles, which is used in mathematics to find lengths, areas, and volumes. He thought that the ancients might have used the method in the discovery of difficult theorems, the proofs of which were put in geometrical forms "to hide the secret of their method or to avoid giving jealous detractors an opportunity to object." In a book on the areas of parabolas, he gave 21 propositions on areas, 10 by the methods of the ancients and 11 by the geometry of indivisibles.

Torricelli used the methods of so many other mathematicians that he was frequently involved in disputes over priority. Especially bitter was his controversy with G. P. Roberval, which flared up after Torricelli had published in 1644 a tract on the properties of the cycloid. Roberval accused him of plagiarizing his earlier solution of the problem of its quadrature. The controversy was still alive when Torricelli died in Florence on Oct. 25, 1647.

Further Reading

Most of the biographical writings on Torricelli are in Italian. On the history of the barometer see William E. Knowles Middleton, *The History of the Barometer* (1964). For background see Abraham Wolf, *A History of Science, Technology and Philosophy in the 16th and 17th Centuries* (1935; rev. ed. 1950). □

Omar Torrijos

Omar Torrijos (1929-1981) was not only Panama's most famous leader in that country's history but also one of Latin America's best-known figures of the 20th century. He achieved this distinction for one reason—Torrijos, a military man in a small republic whose civilian presidents had generally accommodated American wishes over the years, successfully negotiated new canal and defense treaties with the most powerful nation in the world.

Omar Torrijos (O-mar Toe-REE-hose) Herrera (Torrijos was Omar's father's family name; Herrera his mother's maiden name) was born on February 13, 1929, in the small town of Santiago, which is located about 100 miles southwest of Panama's capital, Panama City. (Panama runs east-west *not* north-south.) Omar's parents taught school but early on, apparently, he decided on a military career. He went to El Salvador's

famous military school and took more training in the United States and Venezuela. He joined the Panamanian national guard as a second lieutenant in 1952.

He matured in the 1950s, when a generation of young Panamanians rankled over their small country's division into halves by the Canal Zone, which was virtually an American colony. In 1955 another Panamanian former guardsman, José Antonio "Chi Chi" Remón, got the Dwight D. Eisenhower administration to alter (but not repeal) the hated 1903 canal treaty—Panama had negotiated the first modification in the 1930s—to provide Panama with greater economic benefits from the canal. But Panamanians wanted more: they believed that the Canal Zone was Panamanian territory because the 1903 treaty clearly stated that the United States could act in the Zone "as if it were sovereign." On Panama's national independence day, November 3, 1959, a band of Panamanian nationalists stormed into the Zone determined to publicize Panama's claims by flying their flag in the zone.

Four years later, in January 1964, more destructive rioting broke out in the Canal Zone when Panamanian students tried to hoist the Panamanian banner in front of Balboa High School, where outraged American students, defying the Canal Zone governor's ban, had raised the American flag.

In the rioting that followed two dozen Panamanians died, and American and Panamanian diplomats had to work for almost a year to restore normal diplomatic relations. But out of this bloody confrontation came another series of

canal treaties that for nationalistic reasons Panamanians rejected in 1967. One year later Lt. Col. Omar Torrijos ousted the civilian president, Arnulfo Arias, the American-educated doctor and political figure who had been tossed out of office twice before in his long and stormy career.

Military takeovers were not uncommon in Latin America, but in Panama the National Guard had rarely challenged civilian rule, so Torrijos was taking a gamble. His critics called him a "tinpot dictator" who enjoyed tweaking Uncle Sam and cozying up to Fidel Castro of Cuba. But Torrijos, though not an intellectual, was much more complex than the ordinary Latin American strongman. He travelled about Panama in his military fatigues, encouraging small villagers in their agricultural or craft enterprises about self-sufficiency, then denouncing the United States for its unjust canal policy that deprived Panama of its rightful economic benefits. He seemed to like most everything American except the American position on the canal. His flamboyant style and receptiveness to visitors made him a favorite with American reporters. Any man who could claim both Fidel Castro and John Wayne as friends had to possess considerable charm.

Torrijos had several international causes, but the canal was paramount. In the mid-1970s, when U.S.-Panamanian discussions over the canal were almost dead in the water, he carried Panama's case to the rest of Latin America. By the time Jimmy Carter was inaugurated in January 1977, most of the hemisphere had lined up behind Torrijos and Panama and against the United States on this volatile issue. When Torrijos finally got the Americans to accept new canal and neutrality treaties (which provided for total Panamanian control in the year 2000 but immediately ended the hated Canal Zone) he was condemned as a Marxist stooge in the United States and as Uncle Sam's puppet by critics in his own country.

When the canal treaties were finally ratified—after emotional debates in both countries—Torrijos relinquished the presidential chair to Aristides Royo, a civilian, but reappeared every so often to let people know he was still in charge. Despite the massive infusions of investment (largely in banking) in the 1970s, Panama's economy began to suffer, and Torrijos got blamed by the left for selling out to the capitalists. When Torrijos provided the shah of Iran with sanctuary in December 1979, there were riots that the National Guard quashed with clubs and fire hoses. Yet, in the preceding years, Torrijos had provided a safe haven for Sandinista rebels in their war against the Somoza government in Nicaragua.

When Torrijos died in a plane crash near Penonomé on August 1, 1981, Panama lost its most ardently nationalistic figure. In achieving the long-standing Panamanian goal of a new treaty and an end to the Canal Zone, Torrijos had gained for Panama, and for himself, a stature virtually unequalled by any other Latin American republic in modern times.

Further Reading

Torrijos' importance in Panama's history is discussed in Walter LaFeber, *The Panama Canal* (1978); Graham Greene, *Getting*

To Know the General (1984); David Farnsworth and James McKenney, *U.S.-Panama Relations, 1903-1978* (1983); and Paul Ryan, *The Panama Canal Controversy* (1977). □

Arturo Toscanini

The Italian conductor Arturo Toscanini (1867-1957) was the most famous and influential conductor of the first half of the 20th century.

Arturo Toscanini was born on March 25, 1867, in Parma, Italy, the son of a tailor. When Arturo showed musical tendencies, he was sent to the local conservatory, where he spent the next 9 years, devoting himself entirely to music. He graduated in 1885 with a first prize in cello and was immediately engaged to play in the orchestra at the Reggia, Parma's famous opera house. During the following summer he joined an orchestra that went to Brazil to play a season of Italian opera. At one performance the regular conductor was unable to appear. The 19-year-old cellist took over and, without a rehearsal, conducted *Aida* from memory, thus beginning one of the musical world's most illustrious careers.

On returning to Italy, Toscanini was in great demand as an opera conductor. He conducted the first performances of Leoncavallo's *I Pagliacci* and Puccini's *La Bohème*. By the time he was 30, he was acknowledged to be the best opera conductor in Italy, and he was appointed principal conductor at La Scala in Milan, Italy's leading opera house. There, with his notorious temper and keen musicianship, he imposed a high performance standard on both singers and orchestra. He also disciplined the audience by refusing to allow the traditional encores that destroyed the musical continuity of the operas. He conducted at La Scala from 1898 to 1903 and again from 1906 to 1908, when he resigned to become a conductor with the Metropolitan Opera Company in New York City.

Toscanini returned to Italy in 1915 and to La Scala when it reopened after World War I. The growth of fascism and Mussolini's dictatorship made it impossible for Toscanini to remain; in 1928 he became conductor of the New York Philharmonic Symphony Orchestra, a post he held until 1936. His harsh discipline and uncompromising musical standards made the Philharmonic one of the world's greatest orchestras.

During these years Toscanini also conducted opera at the famous European music festivals at Salzburg and Bayreuth. In 1937 he became conductor of the National Broadcasting Company Orchestra. This orchestra's broadcast concerts and recordings brought his performances to millions of listeners. He died in New York City on Jan. 16, 1957.

At the time Toscanini started to conduct, late-19th-century performance ideals were prevalent and conductors and performers thought it was their right and duty to "express themselves" in the music they played. Great

Stephen Edelston Toulmin

Stephen Edelston Toulmin (born 1922) was an important ethical philosopher of the latter half of the 20th century.

Stephen Edelston Toulmin was born in London in 1922. He was educated at Cambridge University and received his doctorate in philosophy in 1948. He began his teaching career in 1949 and taught in many different academic institutions, including Oxford University, the University of Melbourne (Australia), Leeds University, New York University, Columbia University, Stanford University, Hebrew University (Jerusalem), the University of London, Brandeis University, Michigan State, the University of California in Santa Cruz, and the University of Southern California. Beginning in 1973 he was the professor of social thought and philosophy within the Committee on Social Thought at the University of Chicago.

Toulmin published extensively; among his many books are *The Place of Reason in Ethics* (1950); *The Uses of Argument* (1958); *Philosophy of Science* (1953); *The Fabric of the Heavens* (co-authored, 1960); *Foresight and Understanding* (1960); *The Architecture of Matter* (co-authored, 1963); *The Discovery of Time* (1965); *Human Understanding* (1972); *Wittgenstein's Vienna* (co-authored, 1973), *Knowing and Acting* (1976); *Metaphysical Beliefs* (co-authored, 1957); *Physical Reality: Philosophical Essays on 20th Century Physics* (1970); and *The Return to Cosmology* (1982). He was editor with Harry Woolf and Norwood Hanson of *What I Do Not Believe and Other Essays* (1971). In 1990, he published two major works, *Cosmopolis: The Hidden Agenda of Modernity* and *The Abuse of Casuistry: A History of Moral Reasoning*, co-authored with Albert R. Jonsen.

Emphasis on Moral Reasoning

The Place of Reason in Ethics attempts to use the methods of philosophical analysis in the service of ethical reasoning. Toulmin's fundamental concern is to clarify the nature of moral reasoning and the kind of logic that accompanies it. Ethics, as a philosophical discipline, ought to attempt to discover good moral arguments (with good moral reasons) and to distinguish those arguments from weak ones (and bad moral reasons). The central problem that Toulmin dealt with in *The Place of Reason in Ethics* is what makes up a "good reason" for behaving in a particular moral way.

Toulmin argues that moral reasoning is inductive—that is, that one comes upon good reasons for acting in a certain way based upon some kind of empirical evidence. The moral philosopher examines various courses of action and attempts to discover how these courses of action have been successful in introducing human satisfaction and fulfillment and also in reducing misery and suffering. One then appeals to the results of the empirical study as providing "good reasons" for accepting certain moral principles and following a certain moral way of life.

---

liberties in tempi and dynamics were taken, and the score indications were often ignored. Toscanini vigorously opposed this approach, believing that performers should meticulously follow the scores and play every note exactly as written at the precise degree of loudness called for by the composer. He expected his musicians to show as much devotion toward the score and energy in carrying out its directions as he did. If they failed, he was merciless in his criticism.

Toscanini was one of the first to conduct without a score. His visual memory was phenomenal, and he could make minute corrections, referring to exact measures, without looking at the score. This skill was developed partly as a matter of necessity, because he was so nearsighted that he could not read a score at normal distance. He also had a marvelously acute ear, and there are many instances of his hearing a false note in a single instrument, even with the full orchestra playing.

Further Reading

Among the best books on Toscanini are David Ewen, *The Story of Arturo Toscanini* (1951; rev. ed. 1966); Howard Taubman, *The Maestro: The Life of Arturo Toscanini* (1951); and Samuel Chotzinoff, *Toscanini: An Intimate Portrait* (1956). Two books that contain analyses of his interpretations and comparisons of his recordings are Robert C. Marsh, *Toscanini and the Art of Orchestral Performance* (1956), and Spike Hughes, *The Toscanini Legacy* (1959). □

Toulmin then examined the three traditional approaches to the problem of ethical decision—the objective, the subjective, and the imperative—all three of which he considered incorrect approaches which are therefore misleading for ethical decision-making. The objective approach is that approach which assigns goodness or rightness as a property; the subjective relates feelings or attitudes to the validity of the moral act; the imperative approach asserts that moral judgments are related to the persuasive function of language (and are therefore pseudo-concepts).

The objective approach fails, according to Toulmin, because there is no valid method by which there can be agreement on the identification of values as properties. A moral claim—for example, "It is good"—does not have the same logical status as an empirical description—for example, "It is raining." A moral value, therefore, cannot be evaluated on the basis of its properties. When people disagree about values, their disagreement is other than linguistic. They really believe that they possess a different understanding of what is moral in that situation.

The subjective approach also fails as a method by which to evaluate a moral concept. The subjective approach argues that once there is agreement regarding the facts of a moral situation then the only differences are related to one's feelings or attitudes. But that approach is not good enough, Toulmin argued. It is not good enough to know what one's attitudes are regarding a moral judgment; one also wants to know what are the reasons (or what are the good reasons) for supporting one moral judgment over another. Toulmin argued that it is an intellectual mistake to ask whether ethical criteria, such as "good" and "right," are either objective or subjective. Moral reasoning consists in doing something else.

The imperative approach next came under Toulmin's scrutiny. The imperative approach, which holds that moral judgments are basically moral ejaculations or commands, can find no place for reasons. The imperative approach finally leads to a kind of moral pessimism—no moral judgments are true because there are no objective identifiable subjects or objects to which moral terms pertain.

Because Toulmin was concerned to introduce reason into moral judgments, he next analyzed the meaning of "scientific" reasoning, assuming, as so many do, that reason and scientific endeavors belong inextricably together. But he insisted that just as there are "good" reasons in science, so there can also be "good" reasons in ethics. Scientific reasons intend to alter one's expectations in sense experience. Moral reasons, on the other hand, intend to alter feelings and behavior. Both science and ethics, therefore, employ reason and the use of reason in their labors.

Moral reasons, for Toulmin, are those reasons which relate an act, as a duty, to the moral code of a community and those reasons which relate to the avoidance of suffering and annoyance of the members of that community. For the members of a community to live together it is necessary to embrace a common moral code. Moral reasons, which make up that communal moral code, are rationally derived: that is, they are related to human welfare and the harmonization of the interests and actions of the members of the community.

The Role of Social Practice

Toulmin later developed a principle by which moral judgments are made: "the 'rightness' of an action is dependent upon a consideration of moral reasons, based upon principles derived from social practice, and not upon the consequences of an action." (*The Place of Reason in Ethics*) To be reasonable within a moral community is to consider the effects of a particular moral act upon those who comprise that community. For that reason, Toulmin argued, a particular moral act is an instance of valid moral reasoning if the act (and the rational argument for the act) is worthy of acceptance by everyone. The study of moral reasoning can lead one to moral judgments which are true and helpful; true in the sense that they can correct mistaken moral assumptions.

Toulmin learned a great deal from the way Wittgenstein went about the philosophical enterprise. In moral reasoning, the philosopher does not simply fix his attention on the meaning of moral terms taken in isolation. The philosopher must rather seek to grasp the overall meaning of the discourse under analysis. Each discourse, morality as well as science, has its own procedures, and in accordance with these procedures we judge whether something is or is not good evidence for a certain claim.

Some commentators on Toulmin's moral philosophy regard his position as a kind of "rule" utilitarianism, because he is primarily concerned with the justification of the rules of conduct which are actually operative in a society. Toulmin argued that moral rules and moral principles are to be justified by discovering which of the rules or principles, if consistently acted upon, will most likely lead to the least amount of avoidable suffering all around. It is clear, then, that for Toulmin those moral practices within a society which cause the least amount of suffering for mankind were the moral practices which ought to be accepted by that society. Toulmin, of course, accepted a negative formulation of the utilitarian formula. It is easier, he argued, to determine what will probably cause greater suffering within a society than it is to determine what probably will bring the greatest happiness to the greatest number.

Generally Toulmin followed the same perspective for science. He gave an account of scientific theorizing as being more like the making of maps to enable one to find one's way about than like the process of generalization described in the classic theories of induction. For Toulmin, the question was not whether a scientific law is true, but, rather, "when does it hold?" Laws are regarded not as sentences about the world but as rules for conducting oneself within it. The logic of a scientific law must therefore yield to a pragmatic consideration. A scientific law functions then as a criterion to furnish successful predictions. Scientific laws, in Toulmin's view, are neither true nor false, but serve instrumentally to facilitate the procedure of inference.

In 1997, Toulmin became the 26th recipient of the U.S. government's highest honor for intellectual achievement (from the National Endowment for the Humanities). His acceptance speech, the annual Jefferson Lecture, was to be focused on "the importance of dissent."

During the 1990s, Toulmin remained on the faculty and continued to teach religion, international relations, communications and anthropology at the University of Southern California.

Further Reading

George C. Kerner in his book *The Revolution in Ethical Theory* (1966) analyzed Toulmin's ethical philosophy (along with that of G. E. Moore, Charles L. Stevenson, and R. M. Hare). He included Toulmin's ethical philosophy as a substantial part of "the radical change that ethical theory has undergone during the present century." John Rawls wrote an important review of Toulmin's *The Place of Reason in Ethics* in *The Philosophical Review* 60 (October 1951). William K. Frankena's book *Perspectives on Morality* (1976) provides a balanced analysis of Toulmin's ethical philosophy. A substantial review of Toulmin's *Cosmopolis* appears in Todorov, Tzvetan, *Postmodernism, a Primer* for *The New Republic* (May, 1990). It is also reviewed by Richard Luecke in *Christian Century* (October, 1990). □

Henri de Toulouse-Lautrec

The French painter Henri de Toulouse-Lautrec (1864-1901) depicted Montmartre's night life of cafés, bars, and brothels, the world which he inhabited at the height of his career.

Henri de Toulouse-Lautrec, a direct descendant of the counts of Toulouse, was born on Nov. 24, 1864, at Albi. His eccentric father lived in provincial luxury, hunting with falcons and collecting exotic weapons. Henri began to draw at an early age. He suffered a fall in 1878 and broke one femur; in 1879 he fell again and broke the other one. His legs did not heal properly; his torso developed normally, but his legs were permanently deformed.

Encouraged by his first teachers, the animal painters René Princeteau and John Lewis Brown, Toulouse-Lautrec decided in 1882 to devote himself to painting, and that year he left for Paris. Enrolling at the École des Beaux-Arts, he entered the studio of Fernand Cormon. In 1884 Toulouse-Lautrec settled in Montmartre, where he stayed from then on, except for short visits to Spain, where he admired the works of El Greco and Diego Velázquez; Belgium; and England, where he visited Oscar Wilde and James McNeill Whistler. At one point Toulouse-Lautrec lived near Edgar Degas, whom he valued above all other contemporary artists and by whom he was influenced. From 1887 his studio was on the Rue Caulaincourt next to the Goupil printshop, where he could see examples of the Japanese prints of which he was so fond.

Toulouse-Lautrec habitually stayed out most of the night, frequenting the many entertainment spots about

Montmartre, especially the Moulin Rouge cabaret, and he drank a great deal. His loose living caught up with him: he suffered a breakdown in 1899, and his mother had him committed to an asylum at Neuilly. He recovered and set to work again. He died on Sept. 9, 1901, at the family estate at Malromé.

Parisian Demimonde

Toulouse-Lautrec moved freely among the dancers, prostitutes, artists, and intellectuals of Montmartre. From 1890 on, his tall, lean cousin, Dr. Tapié de Celeyran, accompanied him, and the two, depicted in *At the Moulin Rouge* (1892), made a colorful pair. Despite his deformity, Toulouse-Lautrec was an extrovert who readily made friends and inspired trust. He came to be regarded as one of the people of Montmartre, for he was an outsider like them, fiercely independent, but with great ability and intellect.

Among the painter's favorite subjects were the cabaret dancers Yvette Guilbert, Jane Avril, and La Goulue and her partner, the contortionist Valentin le Désossé. Toulouse-Lautrec depicted his subjects in a style bordering on but rising above caricature through the seriousness of his intention. He took subjects who habitually employed disguise and charade as a way of life and stripped away all that was inessential to reveal each as an individual and yet as a prisoner of his destiny.

The two most direct influences on Toulouse-Lautrec's art were the Japanese print, as seen in his oblique viewpoints and flattened forms, and Degas, from whom he derived the tilted perspective, cutting of figures, and use of a railing to separate the spectator from the painted scene, as in *At the Moulin Rouge*. But the authentic feel of a world of depravity and the strident, artificial colors used to create it were Toulouse-Lautrec's own.

Unusual types performing in a grand, contrived spectacle attracted Toulouse-Lautrec. In his painting *In the Circus Fernando: The Ringmaster* (1888) the nearly grotesque, strangely cruel figure of the ringmaster is the pivot around which the horse and bareback rider must revolve. In 1892-1894 Toulouse-Lautrec did a series of interiors of houses of prostitution, where he actually lived for a while, becoming the confidant and companion of the girls. As with his paintings of cabarets, he caught the feel of the brothels and made no attempt to glamorize them. In the *Salon in the Rue des Moulins* (1894) the prostitutes are shown as ugly and bored beneath their makeup; the madame sits demurely in their midst. He neither sensationalized nor drew a moral lesson but presented a certain facet of the periphery of society for what it was—no more and no less.

Color Lithography and the Poster

Toulouse-Lautrec broadened the range of lithography by treating the tone more freely. His stroke became more summary and the planes more unified. Sometimes the ink was speckled on the surface to bring about a great textural richness. In his posters he combined flat images (again the influence of the Japanese print) with type. He realized that if the posters were to be successful their message had to make an immediate and forceful impact on the passerby, and he designed them with that in mind.

Toulouse-Lautrec's posters of the 1890s establish him as the father of the modern large-scale poster. His best posters were those advertising the appearance of various performers at the Montmartre cabarets, such as the singer May Belfort, the female clown Cha-U-Kao, and Loïe Fuller of the Folies-Bergère.

In a poster of 1893 the dancer Jane Avril, colored partially in bright red and yellow, is pictured kicking her leg. Below her, in gray tones so as not to detract attention, is the diagonally placed hand of the violinist playing his instrument. There is some indication of floorboards but no furniture or other figures. The legend reads simply "Jane Avril" in white letters and "Jardin de Paris" in black letters.

Further Reading

The best books on Toulouse-Lautrec are Gerstle Mack, *Toulouse-Lautrec* (1938), especially rich in describing Toulouse-Lautrec's demimonde associations, and Douglas Cooper, *Henri de Toulouse-Lautrec* (1956). See also Philippe Huisman and M. G. Dorty, *Lautrec by Lautrec* (1964). A major work on the prints is Jean Adhémar, *Toulouse-Lautrec: His Complete Lithographs and Drypoints* (trans. 1965). □

Alain Touraine

Alain Touraine (born 1925) was a French sociologist. He was best known as the originator of the phrase "post-industrial society" and for his studies and theories of social movements while they were in the process of formation.

Alain Touraine was born in Hermanville, France, on August 3, 1925, the son of a physician, Albert Touraine, and of Odette Cleret. Like most French intellectuals, he was educated at the Ecole Normale Superieure, where he took his *agrégation* in history in 1950 and also studied philosophy. His perspective was further broadened when in 1952 he went to Harvard and learned everything about Parsonian systems sociology and American research methods. This experience is evident in his studies of industry upon his return to France and in his effort to construct a global systems theory that sets out to avoid the pitfalls of both Marxism and functionalism.

By the time he earned his doctorate in 1965, which in France is something beyond the Ph.D. in America, he had been a visiting professor at a number of American universities and had done extensive work in industrial sociology. During that period, France (among other countries) was busily modernizing its industries in order to become independent of American economics, while trying to avoid the alienation and exploitation of workers that tends to accompany this process. Touraine's expertise was helpful in this effort which, at the same time, allowed him to observe the negative aspects of capitalist production.

In the course of his work abroad, Touraine met his future wife, a Chilean, Adriana Arenas Pizarro. They were married in 1957. With their two children they frequently returned to Chile, and in the course of these visits, Touraine kept studying the social and political changes that were taking place. Moreover, he continued to compare and to theorize about the differences among the forms social unrest may take under prevalent conditions in Chile, the United States, and France—societies with very different traditions.

Alain Touraine was a member of the research staff of the Centre National de la Recherche Scientifique from 1950 to 1957 and the acting director of studies at the Ecole Pratique des Hautes Etudes from 1958 to 1960. He then taught at home and abroad. In May 1968 he joined American students in their revolt against the establishment. Soon thereafter, in 1970, he founded the Center for the Study of Social Movements, which is attached to the Ecole des Hautes Etudes in Paris. This center attracted collaborators from many countries, and Touraine became the foremost authority on questions about the formation, the trajectory, and the fate of social movements around the world—all of them perceived in relation to specific conditions and personalities as well as to the traditions of the society in which they arise.

In addition to concrete studies of social movements, such as his analyses of the *May Movement: Revolt and Re-*

form (1968; English translation, 1971), of *Solidarity: Poland 1980-81* (1983), and of *Anti-nuclear Protest: The Opposition to Nuclear Energy in France* (1980; English translation, 1983), Touraine was busy evolving a theory of social movements. Foremost among publications in this area were *The Self-Production of Society* (1973; English translation, 1977) and *The Voice of the Eye* (1978; English translation, 1981)—the first of five volumes on *The Permanent Society*.

Touraine defined sociology as "the science of social action." And because, as a result of the division of labor, actors have lost control over their work and thus have become alienated, he maintained, they must regain their former control. Sociologists can help them do so by making them conscious of their actions. He held that individuals can free themselves from centralized power and technocratic domination through refusal of consumption and through taking part in the decision-making process; that they can resist manipulation not singly, but by forging a collective identity by defending themselves as members of a community. He expanded on that position when studying students at American universities and predicted, in 1972, that "the university as a center of production and diffusion of knowledge is increasingly becoming the main locus of the social conflicts of our time."

Touraine's sociological system was constructed to account for all existing social systems and institutions, for their changes over time, and for human elements and feelings—of every actor within this system. Inevitably, such a system must be very abstract and incomprehensible to the noninitiated, especially when, as in *The Production of Society*, he examines sociology itself as a social production—through its "historicity," which is said "to transform the activity into a social system in which conduct is governed by a set of orientations, themselves determined by the society's mode of action upon itself."

The general reader is bound to sympathize with the need to find new paradigms in order to comprehend the social mutations that result from the proliferating policies of development, from the rivalries among states, and from the multiple complications arising from technological inventions. But this reader will find Touraine's theoretical works too technical and his charts too obtuse. In his books about Chile, however, Touraine himself emerges from behind his abstractions and mixes personal sentiment with political analysis, theories with experience, and cool commentary with political commitment. He wrote a particularly moving account about the rise and fall of Chile's socialist government under Allende, *The Life and Death of Populist Chile* (1973).

Touraine's reputation as a sociologist grew during the seventies. In *Return of the Actor* (translated by Myrna Godzich 1988) he critiques sociology which reintroduces the notion of social activity. During the 1990's Touraine was a regular contributor to the *UNESCO Courier* with a series of articles on democracy in the twentieth century. Touraine observed that "Democracy is based on the most active possible participation by the greatest possible number of people in the making and application of political decisions."

French government agencies frequently called on Touraine for advice. In France, he received numerous awards and recognition for his contributions to modern French sociological thought. Although Touraine was one of the leading French intellectuals in America his brand of sociology received mixed reception.

Further Reading

Alain Touraine was a frequent commentator on current events as well as a prolific author, but not all of his work is translated. In English, some of his contributions, in addition to those cited in the text, are: *Workers' Attitudes and Technological Change* (1965), *The Post-Industrial Society* (1971), *The Academic System in American Society* (1974), "From Crises to Critique" in the *Partisan Review* (1976), and "Crisis or Transformation?" in Norman Birnbaum, editor, *Beyond the Crisis* (1977). Gregory Baum includes comments on the philosophy of Touraine and other postmodern age scholars in *The Canadian Forum* (May 1990). Clark Kerr critiques and provides interpretations of Touraine's major works in an article (On Alain Touraine) appearing in the May-June 1996 issue of *Society*. □

Sékou Touré

Sékou Touré (1922-1984) was president of the Republic of Guinea after its independence and an exponent of radical socialism. His decision to oppose the De Gaulle referendum in 1958 was the key event which destroyed the old French West African Federation.

Sékou Touré was born in Faranah, Guinea. His father, a poor farmer, was a member of the Soussou tribe, and his mother was a member of the Malinke tribe; Touré's father was a grandson of the great ruler Almami Samory. Touré was educated at the village Koranic school and primary school at Faranah. At 14 he enrolled in a technical school in Conakry but was expelled in 1937 for organizing a student strike, and he completed his secondary education by correspondence.

Touré was employed by a commercial firm in 1940 and in the following year qualified for a position in the posts and telecommunications department. He was very active in union affairs and became the head of the Postal Union in 1945 and was one of the founders of the Union Cégétiste des Syndicats. He became its secretary general in 1946. He was discharged from his job and spent a brief time in jail in 1947.

Union Leader

Touré had been a founder member of the intraterritorial Rassemblement Démocratique Africain (RDA) in 1946. However, his prime interest was not politics but trade unionism. The leading political figure in Guinea at this time was a moderate former schoolteacher, Yacine Diallo. In 1948 Touré became secretary general of the Confédération Générale des Travailleurs (CGT), dominated by the French

(UGTAN), which soon attracted most of the unionized workers in French West Africa. Touré was at first secretary general and then president.

Political Action

The *loi cadre* of 1956 devolved a major portion of authority to the assembly of each territory and gave the vice president, the chief elective officer, great power. Before the elections of 1957 the PDG appealed to the intelligentsia and also urban workers and villagers. It won a solid victory, and Touré became vice president. He began immediately to implement government plans for improvement of industry, roads, and railways. He moved to establish cooperatives and village councils to further undercut the power of traditional authorities. Touré was still cooperative with the French as long as it was to the advantage of Guinea. In 1957 he became a member of the Grand Council, the highest advisory body in the federation, and was elected vice president of the RDA.

Discussions within the RDA over future political evolvement of the territories presaged the destruction of the party. Felix Houphouët-Boigny of the Ivory Coast emphasized the development of individual territories within the French community. Touré and many other leaders believed it necessary to continue the federal structure. In 1958 Touré inexplicably shifted his position. Three days before his meeting with Charles De Gaulle on August 28 to discuss the coming plebiscite to decide the future of the French community, Touré appeared to support a vote in favor of association with France.

Premature Independence

However, pressures within Touré's own party and the radical unions forced a change, and in September Guinea voted overwhelmingly against continued association. France announced on September 30 that Guinea was independent and cut off all financial aid, withdrew its technicians and advisers, and removed all equipment possible. Guinea entered into independence as a bankrupt nation. No Western power was prepared to help, and Touré concluded four trade agreements with the Eastern bloc countries.

Two months after independence, Touré negotiated a £10 million loan from Ghana which enabled him to stabilize Guinea's economy. Touré's government became more centralized, and he required all Guineans to participate in the economic and social development of the country. The PDG was declared the only legal party, and a system of political committees was established on all levels up to the National Committee to help Touré direct the state.

Touré's meeting with Kwame Nkrumah resulted in a declaration of a Ghana-Guinea union in 1959. This association, which Touré hoped would be the beginning of a larger political union, envisioned a gradual uniting of the political and economic institutions of the two states. In July 1961 the union was expanded with the addition of Mali. Despite the theory, no specific changes were made in the political institutions of the member states. The union's major contribution was to provide a base for a common foreign-policy approach. It formed the nucleus of the radical, anti-Western

Communist general union. Two years later he became secretary general of the Coordinating Committee of the CGT for French West Africa. By 1952 Touré had also risen to the post of secretary general of the Parti Démocratique de Guinée (PDG), the Guinea branch of the RDA.

The year 1953 was crucial for Touré's career. He led a two-month general strike against the government which forced the governor general to capitulate, and he was also elected a member of the Territorial Assembly. Touré was the acknowledged leader of the young radicals who were dissatisfied with the increasingly moderate policies of the RDA. In 1954 Yacine Diallo died, and Touré contested the election to fill his vacant seat in the French Assembly. He lost to Barry Diawadou, the leader of the Bloc Africain de Guinée party. His stature was, nevertheless, increased because it was widely believed that the French authorities had tampered with the election. Touré became a member of the Coordinating Committee in 1954 and was chosen mayor of Conakry the following year. His conversion to political action was completed by his election to the French Assembly in January 1956.

Touré had begun to change his attitudes toward the successful application of doctrinaire Marxism to the problems of Africa. He also questioned the continued association of African unions with their metropolitan counterparts. Thus he helped establish the Confédération Générale du Travail Africain (CGTA), which was not affiliated with the CGT or any other European movement. The new union was so successful that the local CGT merged with it in 1957 to form the larger, intraterritorial Travailleurs d'Afrique Noire

Casablanca bloc of the early 1960s. However, even in foreign policy there was a significant difference between Touré's and Nkrumah's attitudes—witness their policies concerning the United Nations in the Congo.

African Socialism

Touré's emancipation from more radical elements within the PDG and the Soviet Union did not come until 1961. In November the Teachers Union, in conjunction with officials of the Soviet embassy, precipitated a crisis throughout Guinea. Touré arrested the strike leaders and expelled the Soviet ambassador and his key aides from the country. Later discussions with the Soviet Union restored good relations, but it was apparent that Touré was not a captive of the Communist bloc. In 1962 he began to seek more contacts with other African states and increased aid from Western powers.

In 1964 Touré reorganized the government, naming four resident ministers in four major regions of Guinea who were directly responsible to the central executive. He also restricted membership in the PDG to the more militant socialists who had proved their worth. Thus the party reflected more clearly the desires of the executive. In January 1968 elections were held for the National Assembly and for president. Touré was unopposed in the election, and the prospective members of the Assembly had previously been nominated by the PDG.

After the overthrow of Nkrumah in January 1966, Touré became more aggressive in his attitudes toward the West, Senegal, the Ivory Coast, and the new Ghana regime. He declared Nkrumah honorary president of Guinea and threatened to restore him to power by force. Houphouët-Boigny replied to Touré's threats by sending troops to his borders and promising to invoke French aid, and Touré did not follow up his threat with action against the Ivory Coast. In May 1967, on the twentieth anniversary of the PDG, Touré denounced Western missionaries and ordered all foreign clergymen deported by June 1.

Touré attempted to end Guinea's self-imposed isolation in 1968. Nkrumah's sanctuary was continued, but his public statements and appearances were limited. Touré even moderated the degree and type of denunciation of the Ivory Coast and Senegal. He attended the Monrovia Conference in April; Guinea became a member of the Organization of Senegal River States; and he restored diplomatic relations with Britain, which had been severed in 1965.

Guinea's economic development continued more slowly than the potential wealth of the state would have indicated. However, after 1965, Touré received aid from Britain, France, the United States, the Soviet Union, and China. Plans were approved for a dam and hydro-electric plant on the Konkouré River and for the construction of a smelting plant, railway, and harbor to exploit the Boké bauxite deposits.

By restricting a legal, open opposition, Touré gained unchallenged control of Guinea, but he assured that some rivals would attempt to end his rule by violent means. In November 1965 a plot was discovered to assassinate Touré; a former army lieutenant and cousin, Mamadou Touré, was

implicated. In February 1968 another major coup directed against the President was discovered, and a further assassination attempt was foiled in 1969. Despite all his problems, Touré's hold on his country after 12 years of independence was firm. The coups that occurred during this period against other political leaders in Africa only underscored the stability of his regime.

Touré held his position as president of Guinea until his death on March 26, 1984. He died in Cleveland, Ohio. Socialist in economic outlook, Touré ruthlessly suppressed dissent, and after his death the government of Guinea acknowledged that numerous human rights violations had occurred during his regime.

Further Reading

There is no good biography of Touré in English. For general background see Richard Adloff, *West Africa: The French Speaking Nations* (1964); Ruth Schachter Morgenthau, *Political Parties in French Speaking West Africa* (1964); and John Hatch, *A History of Post War Africa* (1965). Touré's contributions to the pan-African movement are described in Colin Legum, *Pan Africanism* (1962). The philosophical basis of Guinea's government is treated in George W. Shepherd, Jr., *The Politics of African Nationalism* (1962), and Gwendolen Carter, ed., *African One-party States* (1962). Further details on Touré are in Ronald Segal, *Political Africa* (1961), and Basil Davidson, *The Liberation of Guinée* (1969). Updated information was gathered from *Encyclopaedia Britannica* and *Microsoft Encarta 96 Encyclopedia*. □

Albion Winegar Tourgée

Albion Winegar Tourgée (1838-1905), American jurist and writer, was an outspoken civil rights advocate and a novelist who pioneered in social criticism.

Albion Winegar Tourgée was born in Williamsfield, Ohio, on May 2, 1838. He attended the University of Rochester from 1859 to 1861, when he enlisted in the Union Army at the start of the Civil War. He participated in a number of important battles, including the First Battle of Bull Run, where he was wounded.

Tourgée resigned from the Army in 1864, was admitted to the bar, and moved in 1865 to Greensboro, N.C. There he became an especially controversial figure because he was one of the few white men who really accepted blacks as equals, and he often lacked tact and self-restraint in expressing his views. He was an influential delegate at the state constitutional convention of 1868 and was appointed one of three commissioners to codify the state's laws, receiving high praise for the results.

A leading Republican, Tourgée was elected to the state's superior court and served until 1875, becoming famous for his attempts to extend justice to the blacks and his fearless denunciations of Ku Klux Klan terrorism. During this period he also published his first novels and wrote political articles. In 1878 he anonymously published a series of brilliantly written attacks on the Democrats known as the ''C Letters.'' Because of increasing hostility, he reluctantly left North Carolina in 1879 and settled in New York.

A Fool's Errand, by One of the Fools (1879), Tourgée's most famous novel, was based on his experiences in North Carolina. It was one of a series of novels dealing with the nation before, during, and after the Civil War. These works described the conflict between Northern and Southern social concepts and were considered social criticism. Perceptive and based on personal observation, along with his other novels and short stories, they made a provocative and significant contribution to American literature. He also wrote campaign material for the Republican party, lectured, commented in newspaper columns on a variety of current events, and twice attempted to publish weekly magazines.

Tourgée continued to be a vocal and persistent advocate of black equality, in spite of increasing national indifference. He participated in the case of *Plessy v. Ferguson,* arguing unsuccessfully before the U.S. Supreme Court against the premise that separate but equal facilities for blacks were constitutional. (The major points in his argument became the basis for the Court's reversal in 1954.) In 1897, as a reward for having campaigned for William McKinley, Tourgée was appointed consul at Bordeaux, France, where he died on May 21, 1905.

Further Reading

The best available biography of Tourgée is Otto H. Olsen, *Carpetbagger's Crusade: The Life of Albion Winegar Tourgée* (1965),

which also gives a balanced account of Reconstruction in North Carolina. □

François Dominique Toussaint L'Ouverture

François Dominique Toussaint L'Ouverture (1743-1803) was an outstanding Haltian military leader who controlled virtually all of Hispaniola for the French before Haitian independence.

Born into slavery on Plantation Bréda near Cap-Français (now Cap-Haitien), François Toussaint L'Ouverture was fortunate in having a kindly master who recognized his superior intelligence, taught him French, and gave him duties which allowed him to educate himself through extensive reading. Supposedly his favorite subjects were the military campaigns of Julius Caesar and Alexander the Great. Toussaint was already approaching his fiftieth birthday when the great slave revolt broke out in August 1791 near Plantation Bréda. After helping his master escape the slaughter, Toussaint entered the turbulent events of strife-torn Hispaniola, first by making a military reputation for himself.

With 600 black soldiers—former slaves—Toussaint crossed over to the eastern, and Spanish, part of Hispaniola, where he served with distinction in the Spanish colonial army, taking part in its campaigns against the French. During this time, his forces, organized and officered by French regulars who had deserted, steadily grew to a disciplined force of 4,000 men. By mid-1794 Toussaint was ready for a crucial move.

The British, ever ready to harass France, had tried to take advantage of the confusion in Saint-Domingue (western Hispaniola) by sending troops to put down the slave revolt. Furthermore, they were concerned that the desire for freedom might spread to their nearby colony of Jamaica. At this juncture, Toussaint abandoned his Spanish allies and returned to Cap-Français, affording crucial strength to the beleaguered French garrison against besieging British forces. Toussaint defeated the British forces, freed the imprisoned French governor general, and with the help of Gen. Rigaud, an outstanding Haitian mulatto general, drove the English from Saint-Domingue.

Height of Power

By 1796 Toussaint was the dominant figure in the colony. Hero to his victorious soldiers and to all former slaves, he was respected as well by the resident French authorities. Toussaint now showed that his political instincts were on a par with his military abilities. Even at this date was evident the black-mulatto rift which is one of the chief characteristics of Haitian history. Though the mulattoes, led by Gen. Rigaud, had cooperated with the blacks against the British, many of the mulattoes really wished to reimpose

slavery. Before 1791 they had been free and in many cases were substantial slaveholders in their own right. Their desire was to participate with the French in governing Saint-Domingue.

In a series of deft military campaigns and political moves, Toussaint completed the task of eliminating his opposition. First, Rigaud and the mulattoes were defeated. Toussaint then arranged for his nominal French superiors to be sent to Paris as colonial representatives to the French Assembly. Early in 1801 his army captured Santo Domingo, capital of the Spanish part of Hispaniola. Thus the whole island passed under Toussaint's control.

Toussaint also turned his energies to rebuilding the plantation economy, shattered as it was by a decade of strife. Ironically, forced labor was the only way. Many former planters returned as contract administrators, and by 1801 the colony again knew a brief period of prosperity. Nevertheless, Toussaint's days were numbered. The "First of the Blacks" was about to meet in Napoleon his equal in cunning and ambition.

Enmity of Napoleon

Napoleon's objections to Toussaint were both political and personal. Toussaint had used his friendship with the United States to loosen dependence on France and to negotiate with England. Furthermore, although Toussaint wanted to keep France at arm's length, Napoleon had ambitious plans to rebuild the French Empire. Louisiana was again passing from Spanish to French control, and a secure base in Saint-Domingue was the key to success.

In early 1802, Napoleon sent an army under Gen. Leclerc, his brother-in-law, to subdue Toussaint, deport him and his principal collaborators to France, and return the colony to slavery. Napoleon wrote to Toussaint, flattering him, asking him to assist Leclerc with his counsels, influence, and talents. Napoleon assured Toussaint that the French would not take away the freedom won by the former slaves and, further, drew up a proclamation to be published on Leclerc's arrival: "If you are told these forces are destined to ravish your liberty, answer: The Republic had given us liberty. The Republic will not suffer it to be taken from us."

War of Independence

In January 1802 Leclerc arrived off Cap-Français. He had hoped to be received without hostilities, but his desires were thwarted as Gen. Henri Christophe, Toussaint's local commander, put the city to the torch and retreated inland. Thus began the true Haitian War of Independence.

In spite of the presence in Leclerc's army of many hardened veterans of European campaigns, Toussaint initially performed well against these forces. But the coastal centers soon fell to the French, often with the complicity of their garrison commanders. A notable exception was Gen. Jean Jacques Dessalines. His strong support allowed Toussaint to retire inland with the bulk of his army intact. Finally, at Crête-à-Pierrot in March 1802 Leclerc's regulars overwhelmed Toussaint's forces, which had been handpicked and were led by Dessalines. In the north Christophe had surrendered to the French. By May Toussaint and Dessalines had also capitulated.

The end for Toussaint was fast approaching. Lured to Leclerc's headquarters by a dinner invitation, he was kidnaped and hustled aboard a waiting French warship; he died of cold and starvation in the fortress of Doubs, high in the Jura Mountains of eastern France, on April 7, 1803. In Haiti the revolt continued, and the following year Haiti proclaimed its independence.

Further Reading

The best studies of Toussaint are Percy Waxman, *The Black Napoléon* (1930), and Stephen Alexis, *Black Liberator* (1949). An excellent source of information on Haiti is James G. Leyburn, *The Haitian People* (1955; rev. ed. 1966). Other useful works include C. L. R. James, *The Black Jacobins* (1938); Selden Rodman, *Haiti: The Black Republic* (1954; rev. ed. 1961); and Charles Moran, *Black Triumvirate: A Study of L'Ouverture, Dessalines, Christophe* (1957). □

Joan Tower

Joan Tower (born 1938) was an American composer whose use of percussion was reminiscent of Stravinsky and whose music frequently drew its titles from the natural world. Her composition *Sequoia*

for orchestra received many performances and won her national acclaim.

Joan Tower was a composer who combined performance with composition; she was a founder of the DaCapo Chamber Players, a chamber group which performed music of many periods. Her belief in the importance of performance to a composer is best summed up in her own words: "Today we live in a performance world, primarily. People are out of touch with composers, and tend to forget that we're flesh-and-blood human beings. As a performer and composer, I have been in both those worlds, for twenty years, and I see this lack of contact as a big problem. . . . Composing and performing do go hand-in-hand—that's the nature of the musical beast!" Even though she decided in 1984, after 20 years of both performing and composing, to devote herself solely to composition, her commitment to a close relationship between composer and performer was still very strong.

Tower was born in New Rochelle, NY, but grew up in South America where her father was an engineer. Wherever they were living in South America, he always made sure that his daughter had a piano and a teacher. She returned to the United States and attended Bennington College where she received her BA, and later she studied at Columbia University where she received her MA and DMA degrees. Her compositional teachers included Riegger, Shapey, Milhaud, Brant, and Calabro at Bennington and Luening, Ussachevsky, and Chou Wen-Chung at Columbia. She taught at Bard College beginning in 1972 and organized the DaCapo Chamber Players.

She received commissions, awards, and grants from such organizations as the Guggenheim Foundation, the Koussevitzky Foundation, the National Endowment for the Arts, the New York State Council on the Arts, the Massachusetts State Arts Council, and the American Academy of Arts and Letters. In addition, she received commissions from Richard Stoltzman and Maurice Andre and from the Walter M. Naumburg Foundation for a clarinet concerto. She was chosen composer in residence for 1985-1986 with the St. Louis Symphony Orchestra under the Meet the Composer program. She was also asked to be a member of several boards, including those for the American Composers Orchestra, Chamber Music America, and the New York Foundation for the Arts.

Orchestral Works

The best known orchestral work by Joan Tower is *Sequoia,* whose title comes from the giant redwood trees of California. She wrote of the piece, "the achievement of such great heights by the giant majestic sequoias seems to me an incredible feat of balance. My piece . . . is about simple lines and textures that are at times big, at times very small; and these are held together—'balanced'—by factors such as slowly shifting pedal points and the interaction of the different musical events, objects, and energies at any given moment." The piece begins on a held note—G—which is gradually expanded. Musical sections "branch" off from the main note and balance each other through varying dynamics and textures. One of the most interesting features of *Sequoia* is its use of percussion. There are 54 percussion instruments used in the piece, which produce an excitement and energy that is arresting. Her exposure to the complex rhythms of South American music may have awakened in her an interest in rhythmic effects. *Sequoia* was performed not only by the American Composers Orchestra, which commissioned the piece, but also by the New York Philharmonic and the San Francisco Symphony, among others.

Although most of her compositions were written for chamber groups, she rewrote her quintet, *Amazon,* for orchestra. It was given its first performance by the Hudson Valley Philharmonic under the title of *Amazon II* in 1979. As with *Sequoia,* a natural phenomena provided the inspiration for the composition. Her piece *Music for Cello and Orchestra* (1984) was given its debut performance by Andre Emelianoff, cellist, and Gerard Schwarz, conducting the "Y" Chamber Symphony. Bernard Holland in a review of the work for the *New York Times* wrote, "Joan Tower's 'Music for Cello and Orchestra' . . . [has an] angular sense of drama, bright primary colors and edge-of-the-chair intensity. . . . Miss Tower's piece, to borrow a phrase from Gertrude Stein, does not repeat, but insists. Repetitive figures in shifting instrumental colors begin it, but the movement is constantly altered by subtle changes of rhythm and phrase length." Tower increasingly directed her attention to orchestral writing and accepted commissions for four concertos as well as an orchestral work.

Chamber Music

Tower's chamber music is written for a variety of instruments, including three solo pieces for flute, violin, and clarinet. The first of these solos, *Hexachords* (1972), was written for flute. In this piece, as in her other early works, she used "maps," meaning a predetermined series of notes. In this case, it was a "six-note unordered chromatic collection of pitches." Around 1974 her style changed, becoming more fluid and using descriptive titles and through-composed techniques. *Platinum Spirals* (1976) for solo violin was written in memory of her father. Tower looked through his books on the atomic structure of elements for inspiration for the work and found that platinum with its property of plasticity conveyed the quality she was seeking. *Red Garnet Waltz* (1977), a piece for piano, is a modern response to a romantic idea, and *Wings* (1981) for clarinet was written for Laura Flax (clarinetist for the DaCapo Players) and evokes the flight of the falcon, a bird that can glide slowly on thermal currents, but can also fly at 180 miles per hour when necessary.

She wrote two duets: *Snow Dreams* (1983) for flute and guitar and *Fantasy* (1983) for clarinet and piano. *Breakfast Rhythms I & II* (1974-1975) for clarinet, flute, piccolo, violin, violoncello, piano, and percussion is a transitional piece in Tower's mind. Her goal of simplifying her musical expression dated from this period. The piece is based on central tones surrounded by other supporting tones—in *Breakfast Rhythms I* the central tone is B, and in *Breakfast Rhythms II* it is G sharp. *Black Topaz* (1976) for piano and six instruments followed, but it was *Petroushskates* (1980) for flute, clarinet, piano, violin, and violoncello that was performed most frequently. As its name indicates, it is humorous and lively in addition to being a tribute to Stravinsky and to the Olympic skaters who were the inspiration for the title and the music. *Noon Dance* (1982) for flute, clarinet, violin, violoncello, piano, and percussion combines various solo sections with dialogues between instruments creating various shades of musical color. She released her *Tower Violin Concerto* in 1992. In 1995, Tower was featured in a dance performance by the International Guild of Musicians in Dance, *Celebrations in Collaboration,* along with Gary Schall.

Joan Tower wrote music of excellent quality. Her musical style was forged out of her own experiences with the music of Latin America and the music of Stravinsky, Beethoven, and Messiaen. She retained those qualities she admired from her mentors and added her own particular sound with the result that her music is modern in its tonality and straightforward in its compositional structure.

Further Reading

No books are published at the moment that deal with Tower's music analytically. In 1992, she was profiled in an article by William S. Goodfellow for *American Record Guide.* Several recordings of her works are available and have been released by Advance; Composers Recordings, Inc.; Nonesuch; and Pro Viva. She was published by G. Schirmer. □

Charles Hard Townes

Charles Townes (born 1915) was a physicist whose work concentrated on the development of high-resolution spectroscopy of gasses in the microwave region of the electromagnetic spectrum. He shared the Nobel Prize in Physics in 1964 for his work leading to the development of the maser and his research and ideas were instrumental in the development of the laser by Theodore Maiman. Townes was elected to the National Academy of Sciences in 1956.

Charles Hard Townes was born on July 28, 1915, in Greenville, South Carolina. As a youth he was interested in the biological and natural sciences. He was a gifted scholar who skipped the seventh grade. Townes entered Furman University in his hometown at age 16 and became interested in physics. He received two degrees from Furman—a Bachelor of Arts in modern languages and a Bachelor of Science in physics. He then went to Duke University, from which he received a Master's degree in physics in 1937. He wrote his masters thesis on van der Graaf generators and continued his studies of French, Italian, and Russian. He completed his education at the California Institute of Technology, where he researched the spin of the carbon-13 nucleus and was awarded a Ph.D. in physics in 1939.

Early Research and Achievements

The next eight years were spent at Bell Telephone Laboratories, where Townes worked as a researcher. While living in New York City, he also took classes at the Julliard School of Music and enjoyed the cultural attractions of the city. During World War II he did extensive work on radar bombing and systems design, as well as some of the early work in radio astronomy. After the war he made critical contributions in the development of high-resolution spectroscopy of gasses in the microwave region of the electromagnetic spectrum. He continued this work when he joined the Columbia University faculty in 1948.

Maser Breakthrough

The arrival of the radar in World War II gave rise to extensive use of electronic devices in scientific research. The area that interested Townes the most was the use of microwaves (low frequency radiation) to investigate the structure of matter. To carry out this sort of investigation effectively, oscillators that could produce very short wavelength radiation were needed. But by the late 1940s it had become clear that it would never be possible to build an ordinary oscillator that would be able to generate radiation of wavelength less than one millimeter.

Townes made use of the phenomenon of stimulated emission in his first attempt to produce an oscillator that would suit his purpose. This phenomenon, which had been known to physicists since at least 1917 when Albert Einstein showed its existence, is one through which atoms under the

influence of an applied electromagnetic field emit photons. It was in 1951 that Townes had the breakthrough idea for his maser and outlined the plans on the back of an envelope while waiting for a restaurant to open. Townes reasoned that to be able to amplify very short wavelength radiation, action on the molecular scale would be required. He conceived of a way that an ensemble of molecules would be able, through stimulated emission, to produce a self-excited oscillator that could amplify signals. The molecules had to be in what is known as an excited state—namely, they had to contain a large amount of energy; they also had to be unstable. Electromagnetic waves would stimulate the molecules to release their extra energy at the same frequency and phase as the stimulating electromagnetic energy. If the right number of molecules were present, this energy would convert into electromagnetic energy very quickly, and coherent (that is, in phase) amplification would become possible.

Masers Explained

Townes called this device a "maser"—an acronym for microwave amplification by stimulated emission of radiation—and he built the first one in 1954 with H. J. Zeiger and James P. Gordon at Columbia University. This maser operated on ammonia gas. The gas is collimated by a small hole into a vacuum, where it acts like a beam of molecules. These molecules are in two energy states; therefore, depending on their energy, the molecules get deflected in different directions by an applied electromagnetic field. The molecules with the higher energy get deflected into a chamber known as a resonant cavity. If the number of molecules that gets deflected into the cavity is high enough, then amplification occurs. Because of the sharpness and invariance of the interactions in the ammonia beam and the accuracy with which they can be measured, this particular type of maser functions extremely well as a standard of time or of frequency.

With the collaboration of A. L. Schawlow, Townes described the conditions necessary for the operation of masers in different wavelength regions—namely, the infrared, visible, and ultraviolet portions of the spectrum. Such devices were known as optical masers, and the first one was built in 1960 by Theodore H. Maiman.

Townes' development of the maser proved to be critical in modern experimental research. Maser amplifiers have a very high signal-to-noise ratio. They come extremely close to amplifying a single photon of radiation, since they approach the maximum accuracy allowed by the uncertainty principle in measuring the phase and the energy of a given particle. (The uncertainty principle sets a limit on how accurately the energy and the phase of a particle can be measured simultaneously.) Masers are thus extremely useful in experiments performed on a quantum level. In addition, they are useful in long-distance radar and microwave communications and in the reception and detection of weaker signals in radio astronomy.

In 1964 Townes was awarded the Nobel Prize for the crucial work in quantum electronics that led him to develop the maser. The award was shared with two Russian scientists, N. G. Basov and Aleksandr Prokhorov who had independently developed somewhat similar maser-like devices.

Masers to Lasers

While working on the maser in 1957, Townes and physicist Arthur L. Schawlow were both looking for ways to produce extremely concentrated beams of light. At the time, lasers were thought to have possible pure scientific uses. Townes and Schawlow were granted the patents in 1960 on the laser (light amplification by stimulated emission of radiation) technology, but they never profited personally. Townes was a consultant for, and Schawlow an employee of Bell Telephone Laboratories.

Academic and Scientific Career

From 1950 to 1952 Townes was the director of Columbia's Radiation Laboratory. From 1952 to 1955 he was also the chairman of the physics department at Columbia. In 1959 he took a leave of absence to work as vice-president and director of research of the Institute for Defense Analysis in Washington, D.C., where he dealt primarily with issues concerning national defense and foreign policy. In 1961 he became a physics professor at the Massachusetts Institute of Technology. He left MIT in 1966 to become a University Professor of Physics at University of California at Berkeley. He retired from that institution in 1986.

Further Reading

A quantum mechanical explanation of maser and laser devices can be found in Robert Eisberg's *Quantum Physics* (1974). An explanation of the work Townes did toward the Nobel Prize can be found in the Nobel Foundation's publication *Nobel Prizes 1964*, which also contains a biographical summary. Townes' own writing includes *Making Waves (Masters of Modern Physics)* (1995); *Microwave Spectroscopy* (1955) with A. L. Schawlow. He also served as editor for *Quantum Electronics* (1960) and *Quantum Electronics and Coherent Light* (1965). Information is also available on the World Wide Web (circa 1997) http://www.nforce.com/projects/inventure/book/book-text/104.html □

Francis Everitt Townsend

Francis Everitt Townsend (1867-1960), American physician, author, and political organizer, crusaded for pensions for the elderly.

Francis Townsend was born into a poor farm family near Fairbury, Il., on Jan. 13, 1867. The family moved to Nebraska, where Francis attended Franklin Academy. He went to California expecting to get rich in the land boom, only to end up nearly penniless. After a few years at farming and odd jobs in Kansas and Colorado, Townsend entered Omaha Medical College, graduating in 1907. He set up practice in South Dakota, where he remained until he entered the Army Medical Corps in World War I. He married a nurse, Minnie Bogue.

After the war the Townsends lived in Long Beach, Calif. But Townsend's medical practice was far from prosperous. He finally secured appointment as assistant city health director but, with the Great Depression, lost the job. At retirement age himself, Townsend grew increasingly indignant over the plight of the masses of poverty-stricken old people. In 1933 he proposed a plan whereby the Federal government would provide every person over 60 a $200 monthly pension. This would be financed by a Federal tax on commercial transactions.

The response to Townsend's Old Age Revolving Pension Plan was overwhelming, and soon inquiries and monetary contributions poured in from all parts of the country. By 1935 Townsend claimed that more than 5,000 "Townsend Clubs," with some 5 million members, operated across the country. That year the Townsend organization secured an astounding 20 million signatures on petitions urging Congress to enact the Townsend Plan. Organized pressure from the Townsendites was the single most powerful impetus behind passage of the Social Security Act of 1935. Yet Townsend saw the social security program as woefully inadequate.

Disillusioned with Franklin Roosevelt's administration and embittered by rough handling before a congressional investigating committee, Townsend in 1936 joined forces with Father Charles Coughlin, founder of the National Union for Social Justice, and Gerald L. K. Smith, self-proclaimed inheritor of the late Huey Long's "Share Our Wealth" movement, to form the Union party. But the result

of that year's presidential election was disastrous for them, as Roosevelt won reelection by a record majority.

In 1937 the U.S. Department of Justice prosecuted Townsend for contempt of Congress in the 1936 House investigation. However, Roosevelt commuted Townsend's 30-day prison sentence.

Townsend never stopped pushing his pension scheme. But the prosperity of the post-World War II years and improvements in private, state, and Federal pension benefits blunted the appeal of his message. He died in Los Angeles on Sept. 1, 1960.

Further Reading

Townsend's autobiography is *New Horizons,* edited by Jesse George Murray (1943). There is substantial biographical information and a good narrative on the growth of Townsendism in Richard L. Neuberger and Kelley Loe, *An Army of the Aged* (1936), and in David H. Bennett, *Demagogues in the Depression: American Radicals and the Union Party, 1932-1936* (1969). Abraham Holtzman, *The Townsend Movement: A Political Study* (1963), analyzes the Townsend organization. For the sociopolitical background, Arthur M. Schlesinger, Jr., *The Age of Roosevelt* (3 vols., 1957-1960), is good. □

Arnold Joseph Toynbee

The English historian and philosopher of history Arnold Joseph Toynbee (1889-1972) described himself as a "metahistorian" whose "intelligible field of study" was civilization.

Arnold Toynbee was born into an upper-middle-class family. He attended Balliol College, Oxford, and from 1912 to 1915 he was a fellow and tutor in classics. During World War I he served in the Political Intelligence Department of the War Office, where, among other duties, he edited accounts of atrocities. In 1919 he was a member of the Middle Eastern section of the British delegation to the Paris Peace Conference.

He was Koraes professor of Byzantine and modern Greek language, literature, and history at London University from 1919 to 1924. From 1925 until he retired in 1955 he was director of studies in the Royal Institute of International Affairs and professor of international history at London University. He directed the Research Department at the Foreign Office from 1943 until 1946, when he attended the Paris Peace Conference as a British delegate.

The horror of World War I turned Toynbee's conception of his lifework away from the narrow national scholarship in which he had been trained. Struck with parallels between Greco-Roman civilization and his own time, he projected in 1921 a comparative and comprehensive study of the world's civilizations. But between 1921 and 1934, when the first three volumes of the massive *Study of History* appeared, Toynbee wrote more than 140 articles and books, mostly in the orthodox tradition which he had decided to

In the 1950s, Toynbee concerned himself increasingly with religion as the means to world unity. In *An Historian's Approach to Religion* (1956) he urged that we "wrench ourselves" out of the "mathematico-physical line of approach which we are still following" to "make a fresh start from the spiritual side." In *Change and Habit: The Challenge of Our Time* (1966) he predicted that if the United States and the Soviet Union do not agree to maintain world order, China, whose religious and historical traditions attracted Toynbee, may emerge as the "world-unifier." Even when treating world affairs, he turned eventually from the disquieting realities of history to the greater security of a metaphysics beyond history.

Two of Toynbee's later works included *Cities on the Move* (1970), and *Constantine Porphyrogenitus and His World* (1973). Toynbee died in York, England, on Oct. 22, 1975.

Further Reading

Edward T. Gargan edited a series of major criticisms in *The Intent of Toynbee's History: A Cooperative Appraisal* (1961), with a preface by Toynbee. Pieter Geyl republished his critiques in *Debates with Historians* (1958). Various aspects of Toynbee's thought are summarized in Pitirim A. Sorokin, *Social Prophecies of an Age of Crisis* (1950); Jacobus G. De Beus, *The Future of the West* (1953); and Warren W. Wagar, *The City of Man: Prophecies of a World Civilization in Twentieth-century Thought* (1963). □

transcend. These included *The Western Question in Greece and Turkey* (1922), *Greek Historical Thought* (1924), *Greek Civilisation and Character* (1924), the carefully documented *Survey of International Affairs* (1923-1927), and *A Journey to China* (1931); furthermore, he edited *British Commonwealth Relations* (1934).

The second three volumes of Toynbee's *Study* were published in 1939; four more in 1954; an atlas in 1959; and in 1961 a final volume, *Reconsiderations,* which attempted to answer his critics. The first 10 volumes traced a pattern modeled upon Toynbee's Hellenic studies. Isolating 23 complete civilizations, and arguing that his conclusions were deduced from empirical evidence, he described parallel life cycles of growth, dissolution, a "time of troubles," a universal state, and a final collapse leading to a new genesis. Although he found the uniformity of the patterns, particularly of disintegration, sufficiently regular to reduce to graphs, and even though he formulated definite laws of development such as "challenge and response," Toynbee insisted that the cyclical pattern could, and should, be broken.

Beginning in 1954 his cyclical emphasis yielded to a progressive view of history supported first by Christian millennialism and then by a combination of "higher" religions moving toward a synthesis of nations beyond the failures of past civilizations. In *Reconsiderations* he altered his count of civilizations to 28, including 13 "independent" and 15 "satellite," and he abandoned his Hellenic model and Western civilization as destructively neopagan and egocentric.

Eiji Toyoda

Eiji Toyoda (born 1913) was a former chairman of Toyota Motor Company. His family-run business made revolutionary changes in the way automobiles were made.

E iji Toyoda, the man who was in the driver's seat of the Toyota Motor Company for over 25 years, is virtually unknown outside of Japan's Toyota City, headquarters of "the company that stopped Detroit," according to the *New York Times.* But like a latter-day Henry Ford, Toyoda made his mark on the auto industry. He not only presided over revolutionary changes in the way cars are built, he saw his family-run business become a powerhouse in the world export market and has forged an unlikely alliance with an archrival, General Motors Corporation. Although he resigned his post as chairman in 1994, he continues to hold the title of honorary chair of the company.

As the head of one of the most powerful industrial clans in a nation of 120 million people, Toyoda had an almost Western flair as a go-getter and an empire builder that belies his reputation in Japan as a staunch political and economic conservative. The parallels between the Fords and the Toyodas extend from the assembly line to the board room. Until his retirement, the elder Toyoda shared power with his cousins: Shoichiro, who is president of Toyota Motor Corporation, and Shoichiro's younger brother Tatsuro, head of

New United Motor Manufacturing Incorporated, the Toyota-GM joint venture headquartered in Fremont, California.

Toyoda's uncle, Sakichi, founded the original family business, Toyoda Automatic Loom Works, in 1926 in Nagoya, about 200 miles west of Tokyo. Sakichi's son, Kiichiro, established Toyota Motor Company in 1937 as an affiliate of the loom works. The family was so involved in the business that Eiji's father Heikichi (younger brother of Sakichi) even made his home inside the spinning factory. "From childhood, machines and business were always there right in front of me," Eiji Toyoda said in an interview in *The Wheel Extended,* a quarterly review published by his company. "By seeing the two together, I probably developed an understanding of both, from a child's point of view." Toyoda has described himself as a combination engineer-administrator: "I don't really think of myself as an engineer, but rather as a manager. Or maybe a management engineer. Actually, I graduated from engineering school, but more important is the work a person accomplishes in the 10 or 15 years after school."

What Toyoda accomplished for Toyota Motor was dazzling success at a time when Detroit automakers were struggling to stay profitable. Toyota, Japan's number one automaker, spearheaded the tidal wave of small, low-priced cars that swept the United States after successive energy crises in the mid- and late-1970s. Enraged by the invasion of Japanese imports, Toyoda's counterpart at the Ford Motor Company, then-chairman Henry Ford II, vowed, "We'll push them back to the shores." It never happened. Instead, Ford and his lieutenants turned to Toyota to negotiate a possible cooperative venture in the United States—an unsuccessful effort that preceded GM's historic agreement in 1983 to jointly produce Toyota-designed subcompacts at an idle GM plant in Fremont.

In addition to running the largest corporation in Japan—and the world's third largest automaker, behind GM and Ford—Toyoda has overseen the development of a highly efficient manufacturing system that is being copied worldwide. It "represents a revolutionary change from certain tenets of mass production and assembly-line work originally applied by Henry Ford," wrote *New York Times* Tokyo correspondent Steve Lohr. In short, Toyoda's career could be said to echo the company's U.S. advertising slogan: "Oh, what a feeling!"

After graduating in 1936 with a mechanical engineering degree from the University of Tokyo—training ground for most of Japan's future top executives—the 23-year-old Toyoda joined the family spinning business as an engineering trainee and transferred a year later to the newly formed Toyota Motor Company. The company was a relative newcomer to the auto business in Japan. The country's first car, a steam-powered vehicle, was produced just after the turn of the century, followed in 1911 by the introduction of the DAT model, forerunner of Datsun/Nissan, Toyota's nearest rival today.

The Toyoda family patriarch, Sakichi, the son of a poor carpenter, had invented the first Japanese-designed power loom in 1897 and perfected an advanced automatic loom in 1926, when he founded Toyoda Automatic Loom Works.

He ultimately sold the patents for his design to an English firm for $250,000, at a time when textiles was Japan's top industry and used the money to bankroll his eldest son Kiichiro's venture into automaking in the early 1930s.

Numerous stories have sprung up over the years concerning why the auto company was named Toyota rather than Toyoda. A *Business Week* article claims the family consulted a numerologist in 1937 before establishing its first auto factory: "Eight was their lucky number, he advised. Accordingly, they modified their company's name to Toyota, which required eight calligraphic strokes instead of ten. Sure enough, what is now Toyota Motor Corp. soon became not only the biggest and most successful of Japan's automakers, but also one of the most phenomenally profitable companies in the world." But a *New York Times* story notes the family changed the spelling in the 1930s because "it believed the sound [of the new name] resonated better in Japanese ears."

After Eiji joined the family business in 1936, he worked on the A1 prototype, the forerunner of the company's first production model, a six-cylinder sedan that borrowed heavily from Detroit automotive technology and resembled the radically styled Chrysler Airflow model of that period. During those early years, Toyoda gained lots of hands-on experience. "I tried in the past to see how much I could really tell by touch," he said in *The Wheel Extended.* "It was hard for me to recognize a difference of one hundredth of a millimeter. I must have had a lot of free time. Still, I think it is important to know how much of a difference one can sense." It was a philosophy he shared with his cousin Kiichiro, who often told his employees: "How can you expect to do your job without getting your hands dirty?"

In this spare time, Eiji Toyoda studied rockets and jet engines and, on the advice of his cousin, even researched helicopters. "We gathered materials in an attempt to make a helicopter and made prototype rotary wings," he said in *The Wheel Extended.* "By attaching the wings on one end of a beam, with a car engine on the other, we built a contraption that could float in the air. . . . We weren't doing it just for fun. However, the war intensified, and it became hard to experiment because of a shortage of materials."

The war left Japan's industry in a shambles, and the automaker began rebuilding its production facilities from scratch. Recalled Toyoda: "Everything was completely new to us. Design and production, for example, all had to be started from zero. And the competitive situation allowed for not even a single mistake. We had our backs to the wall, and we knew it."

But while Kiichiro Toyoda was rebuilding the manufacturing operations, Japan's shattered economy left the company with a growing bank of unsold cars. By 1949, the firm was unable to meet its payroll, and employees began a devastating fifteen-month strike—the first and only walkout in the company's history—which pushed Toyota to the brink of bankruptcy. In 1950, the Japanese government ended the labor strife by forcing Toyota to reorganize and split its sales and manufacturing operations into separate companies, each headed by a non-family member. Kiichiro

Toyoda and his executive staff resigned en masse; Kiichiro died less than two years later.

Eiji Toyoda, meanwhile, had been named managing director of the manufacturing arm, Toyota Motor Company. In what some automakers must view as a supreme irony, he was sent to the United States in 1950 to study the auto industry and return to Toyota with a report on American manufacturing methods. After touring Ford Motor's U.S. facilities, Toyoda turned to the task of redesigning Toyota's plants to incorporate advanced techniques and machinery. Returning from another trip to the United States in 1961, only four years after the establishment of Toyota Motor Sales USA, a prophetic Toyoda told employees in a speech recorded in a company brochure: "The United States already considers us a challenger. . . . But we must not just learn from others and copy them. That would merely result in being overwhelmed by the competition. We must produce superior automobiles, and we can do it with creativity, resourcefulness and wisdom—plus hard work. Without this . . . and the willingness to face adversity, we will crumple and fall under the new pressures."

In 1967, Toyoda was named president of Toyota Motor Company—the first family member to assume that post since Kiichiro resigned in 1950. The family power wasn't consolidated until 1981, when Sadazo Yamamoto was replaced as president of Toyota Motor Sales by Shoichiro Toyoda, son of Kiichiro and nicknamed the "Crown Prince" by the Japanese press. A year later, the two branches of the company were unified in the new Toyota Motor Corporation, with Eiji Toyoda as chairman and Shoichiro Toyoda as president and chief executive officer. A Business Week article at the time quoted a Japanese economist as saying the return of the Toyoda family to power was a "restoration of the bluest of blue blood."

At this stage of the company's history, there may be a strong family presence (after a stretch of non-family leadership for most of the postwar period), but not "control" in the Western sense. The top three family members own just over one percent of Toyota Motor stock, according to Britain's Financial Times. In contrast, the Ford family in the United States controls 40 percent of the voting power in the Ford Motor Company.

The Toyodas led their company to a record year in 1984. Toyota sold an all-time high 1.7 million vehicles in Japan and the same number overseas. Profits peaked at $2.1 billion for the fiscal year ending March 31, 1985. While that performance would certainly earn Toyota a mention in automotive history books, Eiji Toyoda and his company may be better remembered for a distinctive management style that has been copied by hundreds of Japanese companies and is gaining growing acceptance in the United States. The Toyota approach, adopted at its ten Japanese factories and 24 plants in 17 countries, has three main objectives: Keeping inventory to an absolute minimum through a system called kanban, or "just in time," insuring that each step of the assembly process is performed correctly the first time, and cutting the amount of human labor that goes into each car.

Despite the predominance of robots and automation at Toyota, the company firmly believes in the principle of lifetime employment; displaced workers are not laid off, but frequently transferred to other jobs. Toyoda believes the day when robots totally replace humans is a long way off. He told *The Wheel Extended:* "At the current stage, there is a greater difference between humans and robots than between cars and magic clouds. Robots can't even walk yet. They sit in one place and do exactly as programmed. But that's all. There is no way that robots can replace all the work of humans."

Due in part to that sort of philosophy, it's not surprising that company loyalty is so high. Toyota's 60,000 employees in Japan, for instance, are encouraged to make cost-cutting suggestions, an idea that Eiji Toyoda borrowed from Ford after his first visit to the United States. Since the system began in 1951, tens of millions of suggestions have flooded the executive offices. "The Japanese," asserts Toyoda, "excel in improving things."

Further Reading

Automotive News, May 11, 1981.
Business Week, August 2, 1982, December 24, 1984, November, 4, 1985.
Detroit Free Press, September 15, 1982, December 19, 1984, February 24, 1985, April 15, 1985.
Financial Times, August 24, 1981.
Forbes, July 6, 1981.
Fortune, July 9, 1984.
Japan Economic Journal, February 2, 1982, January 11, 1983, May 17, 1983, June 11, 1985.
Motor Trend, January, 1978.
Nation's Business, January, 1985.
New York Times, May 27, 1974, September 14, 1980, March 21, 1982, November 24, 1982.
The Wheel Extended (Toyota Motor Corp. quarterly), spring, 1984.
U.S. News and World Report, December 17, 1984.
Wall Street Journal, February 18, 1981, April 15, 1981. □

Toyotomi Hideyoshi

The Japanese warrior commander Toyotomi Hideyoshi (1536-1598) completed the military unification of the country in the late 16th century and undertook two invasions of Korea in the 1590s.

The period of the late 15th century and the first half of the 16th is known in Japanese history as the age of provincial wars. During this time neither the ancient imperial court nor the shogunate (military government) of the Ashikaga family, both of which were located in Kyoto in the central provinces of the island of Honshu, exercised any significant control over the country, and fighting among warrior bands raged everywhere. Gradually, however, a group of daimyos (barons) began to impose their rule over extensive territorial domains, and by the mid-16th century much of the land was in their hands. From about the 1550s the greatest of these daimyos, having organized powerful armies composed of infantry as well as cavalry units, began to assert themselves more vigorously than before beyond their own domains, and soon they were engaged in what was clearly a competition to establish a new national hegemony.

The initial victor in this competition was Oda Nobunaga, a daimyo whose domain was located in the region of modern Nagoya. Judicious alliances with certain daimyos and successful attacks on others led to Nobunaga's triumphant entry into Kyoto in 1568. There he received imperial approval of his military exploits and, after abolishing the Ashikaga shogunate in 1573, removed all doubt that he alone was now the holder of real power in the central provinces.

Nobunaga assigned two of his leading generals, Akechi Mitsuhide and Toyotomi Hideyoshi, to carry out the invasion of the western provinces of Honshu, where several powerful and especially recalcitrant daimyos had their domains. But in 1582 Mitsuhide, who had temporarily returned to Kyoto, suddenly attacked and killed Nobunaga. Mitsuhide, however, was unable to take advantage of the situation; for Toyotomi Hideyoshi, by far his superior as a commander, rushed back to the central provinces and destroyed him. With great suddenness Toyotomi Hideyoshi emerged both as the avenger of Nobunaga and as potentially the new hegemon of the country.

Toyotomi Hideyoshi and the Foreigners

Toyotomi Hideyoshi's rise to power was one of the most striking examples of upward social mobility in premodern Japanese history. Born into a peasant family of the Oda domain, Toyotomi Hideyoshi had joined Nobunaga's army as a common soldier and had risen by sheer martial prowess to a position of command and territorial enfeoffment. Even before Nobunaga's death, Toyotomi Hideyoshi had distinguished himself as probably the outstanding military tactician of the day.

Another important historical factor that contributed both directly and indirectly to unification was the arrival of Europeans in Japan. The Portuguese, who came in the early 1540s, were (so far as we know) the first non-Asians ever to set foot on Japanese soil, and they were followed within a few decades by the Spanish sailing out of the Philippines.

The Portuguese and the Spanish helped to spur a great expansion of maritime trade in East Asian waters during the 16th and early 17th centuries. Apart from missions dispatched infrequently to China, neither the imperial court nor (from the 12th century) the successive warrior governments of Japan had ever pursued overseas commerce with vigor. Private traders and pirate bands, working chiefly out of the harbors of Kyushu and the Inland Sea, had been intermittently active; but it was not until the time of Nobunaga and Toyotomi Hideyoshi that, spurred on by the Europeans, the Japanese officially sponsored a policy of competitive foreign trade.

Introduction of Christianity

Toyotomi Hideyoshi probably had the strongest interest of any Japanese leader of this age in foreign trade. During his period of ascendancy, Japanese commercial vessels sailed as far afield as Malaya and Siam. Yet, interestingly, it was his desire for the profits from foreign trade that presented Toyotomi Hideyoshi with one of his most vexing problems; for the Europeans, with whom the Japanese exchanged on the largest scale, insisted upon combining business with Christian missionary activity, and Toyotomi Hideyoshi increasingly came to view such activity as dangerous and subversive both to his own rule and to Japanese society in general.

Nobunaga had actually encouraged the foreign missionaries, owing probably to his desire to check the militant Buddhist sects that opposed him, and Toyotomi Hideyoshi does not seem at first to have been particularly concerned about their presence in Japan. But in 1587, when he marched into Kyushu to bring that westernmost Japanese island under his sway, Toyotomi Hideyoshi appears to have become alarmed upon seeing at firsthand the territorial acquisitions of the Catholic Church in ports such as Nagasaki. In any case, he suddenly issued a decree ordering the missionaries to leave the country. Although Toyotomi Hideyoshi did not actually enforce this decree, and the missionaries before long openly resumed their activities, his act foreshadowed a growing animosity on the part of Japan's leaders toward Christianity that led ultimately to its proscription in the country in the early 17th century.

In 1590, three years after his campaign to Kyushu, Toyotomi Hideyoshi completed the unification of Japan by destroying the Go-Hojo of the eastern provinces of Honshu, who were the last great independent daimyo family that had not submitted to him. From this time on Toyotomi Hideyoshi was the undisputed military dictator of the land.

Toyotomi Hideyoshi as Dictator

One of Nobunaga's most trusted allies was Tokugawa Ieyasu, a daimyo whose domain was also in the region near modern Nagoya. Ieyasu had performed invaluable service in protecting Nobunaga's rear when the latter had advanced to Kyoto, and he might well have been the one to succeed as national hegemon if Toyotomi Hideyoshi had not acted as quickly as he did to take control in the central provinces after Nobunaga's assassination. Toyotomi Hideyoshi never made an all-out effort to force Ieyasu to submit absolutely to him. Eventually he persuaded the Tokugawa chieftain to move to a domain in the eastern provinces, apparently to place him at a greater distance from the region of Kyoto and Osaka, where Toyotomi Hideyoshi maintained his own base. Yet this must be viewed as historical short-sightedness on the part of Toyotomi Hideyoshi, because the eastern provinces contained the most extensive agricultural lands in Japan, and they provided the wealth and power that ultimately enabled Ieyasu to take control of the country after Toyotomi Hideyoshi's death.

Toyotomi Hideyoshi, because of his lowly origins, sought to improve his personal prestige in Japan's status-conscious premodern society by taking several high titles in the imperial court. These titles, however, had nothing to do with his real power, which was based entirely on his military achievements.

Among Toyotomi Hideyoshi's most important measures as central ruler of Japan were the implementation of a national land survey and the issuance of decrees that defined the social status and duties of the peasant and samurai classes. Many daimyos had already undertaken land surveys in their domains, but Toyotomi Hideyoshi was the first one in a position to order such a survey on the national level. The information thus acquired proved administratively invaluable to the governments of both Toyotomi Hideyoshi and the Tokugawa shogunate (1603-1867).

In the earlier centuries of the medieval age there had been no clear distinction between peasants and warriors. Many of the participants in civil conflicts returned to their fields as soon as peace was restored and had to be mustered again whenever fighting was resumed. With the acceleration of warfare during the 16th century, the various daimyos tended increasingly to gather their retainers in their castle towns in order to have them available at all times for service. But it was Toyotomi Hideyoshi who, in a series of decrees issued in the late 1580s, finally made into national law the formal division of peasant and samurai classes.

Peasants were obliged to relinquish all the weapons they possessed and were directed henceforth to remain in the countryside; samurai, on the other hand, were ordered to maintain permanent residence in the towns. Theoretically, there was to be no social intercourse whatsoever between the two classes, although in fact absolute division was never achieved. In some parts of the country samurai stayed on their farming lands, and the migration of peasants from the countryside to the towns was never completely checked. Nonetheless, the fundamental policy of separation of peasants and samurai and thus of rural and urban populations provided the basis for an extraordinary social equilibrium in Japan for nearly 3 centuries.

Korean Invasions

Shortly after completing unification of the country, Toyotomi Hideyoshi attempted to establish diplomatic relations with Korea and China. The former refused on the grounds that it was already bound by a subordinate, tributary relationship to China, and China simply rejected outright the proposal of an international relationship based on the concept (which was indeed utterly alien to the traditional Chinese world view) of "equality" with Japan or any other country. Thus rebuffed, Toyotomi Hideyoshi organized an invasion force of some 160,000 men and dispatched it to Korea in 1592.

Yet it is most unlikely that Toyotomi Hideyoshi decided to invade Korea solely because of his failure to establish diplomatic ties with either it or China. There is, in fact, good reason to believe that he was driven by the megalomaniacal desire to conquer new lands and that he used the rejection of his overture for such ties (which he fully expected to be rejected) simply as an excuse. He also no doubt saw the advantages to be gained in directing the fighting energies of an exceptionally large warrior class toward overseas aggression. Finally, Toyotomi Hideyoshi's great interest in the expansion of Japanese maritime trade may very likely have prompted him to seek by force from his continental neighbors what they were unwilling to allow him to acquire through peaceful trade.

Whatever the precise reasons for its dispatch, the Japanese invasion force (which Toyotomi Hideyoshi did not personally accompany) advanced rapidly up the Korean Peninsula. At the Yalu River on Korea's northern border, however, it was met by Chinese armies and, having overextended its supply lines, was forced to pull back southward. Eventually the campaign had to be abandoned altogether.

Toyotomi Hideyoshi sent another force, in 1597, but this achieved little and was withdrawn upon Toyotomi Hideyoshi's death the following year. Thus the Korean invasions were utter failures and indeed constituted virtually the only major setbacks in Toyotomi Hideyoshi's otherwise brilliant military career.

Toyotomi Hideyoshi's Grandeur

Toyotomi Hideyoshi did everything on a grand scale. He built several great castles in the central provinces, including a mammoth structure in Osaka that is still an imposing sight in that city today, and had them lavishly outfitted and decorated. Even his entertainments, especially his famous "tea party" in Kyoto in 1587, were open to hundreds and even thousands of people.

In sharp contrast to the esthetics of the preceding age, which were based chiefly on Zen Buddhist principles of restraint and simplicity, the tastes of Toyotomi Hideyoshi and many of his contemporaries ran to the grandiose and the spectacular. This was no doubt in part a reflection of the new vigor and heroic spirit of the age of unification; but it was also a prelude to the new bourgeois culture that was to flourish in the urban centers of Japan in the next century.

Final Years

Toyotomi Hideyoshi's final years were darkened not only by the failure of the Korean campaigns but also by his growing concern over succession to the leadership of the Toyotomi. Toyotomi Hideyoshi wished to bequeath his position as family head and national hegemon to his infant son, Hideyori (who was a mere 5 years old when Toyotomi Hideyoshi died in 1598). Near the end, Toyotomi Hideyoshi made almost frantic efforts to extract pledges of loyalty to Hideyori from the various leading daimyos. He also appointed a board of five regents from among the leading daimyos to handle the affairs of government during Hideyori's minority.

Of the five regents, by far the most powerful was Tokugawa Ieyasu, who had established firm control over his new domain in the Kanto region, which was even more extensive than Toyotomi Hideyoshi's own. Upon Toyotomi Hideyoshi's death Ieyasu emerged as the unquestionably logical successor to the national hegemony, despite the arrangements made for Hideyori; and indeed the events of the next 2 years centered on the formation of two great daimyo leagues, the pro-Ieyasu and the anti-Ieyasu. In 1600 these two leagues met in a decisive battle at Sekigahara between Nagoya and Lake Biwa. Ieyasu's resounding victory in this encounter enabled him to found a shogunate that provided Japan with more than 2½ centuries of almost uninterrupted peace.

Position in History

None of the great unifiers—Nobunaga, Toyotomi Hideyoshi, or Ieyasu—was a political innovator. Although, owing mainly to the coming of Europeans, they undoubtedly knew more of the outside world than any previous Japanese rulers, they still had no direct exposure to governing practices other than their own. Hence we should probably not be surprised that they put their respective hegemonies together almost exclusively on the basis of the time-honored procedures they knew as daimyos and did not attempt to establish a more centralized government in Japan.

Because of his early death Nobunaga was unable to complete the task that he had begun, and the greatest glory in the course of unification went to Toyotomi Hideyoshi. So spectacular were Toyotomi Hideyoshi's achievements in completing unification, in fact, that he has impressed many later historians as the greatest leader in premodern Japanese history. Although he failed to sustain the rule of his family as Ieyasu was subsequently to do for Tokugawa rule, it also seems likely that Ieyasu, on the other hand, lacked the military genius to have first accomplished military unification in the manner of Toyotomi Hideyoshi.

Further Reading

A biography of Toyotomi Hideyoshi in English by Walter Dening, *A New Life of Toyotomi Hideyoshi* (1904), is dated. Good accounts of the period of unification, however, can be found in George Sansom, *A History of Japan* (3 vols., 1958-1963), and in John W. Hall, *Government and Local Power in Japan, 500 to 1700* (1966). Highly recommended for general information about the age, although they are more specifically concerned with the Western impact on Japan during the late 16th and early 17th centuries, are Charles R. Boxer, *The Christian Century in Japan, 1549-1650* (1951; corrected 1967), and Michael Cooper, ed., *They Came to Japan* (1965).

Additional Sources

Berry, Mary Elizabeth, *Hideyoshi,* Cambridge, Mass.: Harvard University Press, 1982. □

Spencer Bonaventure Tracy

Spencer Bonaventure Tracy (1900-1967) was an outstanding and versatile actor whose career spanned over 30 years and brought him nine Academy Award nominations and two Oscars.

Spencer Bonaventure Tracy was born in Milwaukee, Wisconsin, on April 5, 1900. He was the younger of two sons of John and Caroline (Brown) Tracy. He grew up in a comfortable, Catholic environment. On America's entry into World War I in 1917, while in his third year of high school, he joined the Navy, spending most of his enlistment at the Norfolk Navy Yard in Virginia. After graduating from Northwestern Military Academy he spent two years at Ripon College, leaving in 1921 to pursue a theatrical career (the college awarded him an honorary degree in 1940).

After some training at the Sargent School in New York City, Tracy made his Broadway debut in a non-speaking role as a robot in the 1923 Theatre Guild production of Karel Capek's *R.U.R.* Over the next years he played a variety of roles with different stock companies in the East and Midwest, occasionally succeeding in obtaining Broadway roles. By the end of the 1920s he had established himself in New York City as a respected journeyman actor. His big break came in 1930 playing the role of "Killer" Mears in the tough prison drama *The Last Mile*; he was a sensation and attracted the attention of Hollywood. Tracy returned to the Broadway stage only once more: in 1945 he starred in an unsuccessful production of Robert Sherwood's *The Rugged Path,* winning much better notices than the play.

Tracy's film career began in 1930. While still playing the lead role in *The Last Mile,* he made two short dramatic films for the Vitaphone Company at their New York City studio. His first Hollywood role came at the behest of director John Ford, who, seeing him as Mears, cast him in a

comedy about prison life (*Up the River,* 1930). Signing a contract with Fox films, Tracy made over 20 films between 1930 and 1935, the bulk of them for Fox. He was typed as a "tough guy" in films such as *Quick Millions* (1931), *Sky Devils* (1932), *20,000 Years in Sing Sing* (1932), *Looking for Trouble* (1934), and *The Murder Man* (1935). He demonstrated a capacity to extend himself beyond such typecasting in films such as the unconventional *The Power and The Glory* (1933), but it was not until he moved to MGM in 1935 that he made a real mark and became known for the quality of his acting.

He spent over three decades under contract to MGM and during that time made over 30 movies for that studio as well as a few on "loan-out." After he left MGM in 1956 Tracy made nine more films, the most impressive and successful being those undertaken with producer-director Stanley Kramer. During these years, Tracy—who off-camera often was irascible, moody, and crusty—garnered a splendid reputation as a stylish, strong, authoritative actor and developed into one of the top stars of the business. Never conventionally handsome, he proved extremely versatile in the range of roles he addressed and managed to mature successfully as the years passed. Always well-prepared, Tracy gave such restrained, natural, seemingly effortless performances in his films that at one time he was dubbed "The Prince of Underplayers."

Over the years Tracy garnered nine Academy Award nominations (more than any player in his lifetime) and won the Oscar twice. His range and versatility are well-demonstrated by the roles for which he won these nominations,

including the happy-go-lucky Portuguese fisherman Manuel in *Captains Courageous* (1937 Academy Award), Father Flanagan in *Boys Town* (1938 Academy Award), the eponymous Stanley Banks in *Father of the Bride* (1950 nomination), the Clarence Darrow character in *Inherit the Wind* (1960 nomination), an American jurist dealing with German war criminals in *Judgment at Nuremberg* (1961 nomination), and the liberal, put-upon father of a daughter who wishes to marry a Black man within 24 hours in *Guess Who's Coming to Dinner* (1968 nomination). But no matter what the role, Tracy brought to it authority, sincerity, and great skill, and he was admired by the members of his craft, critics, and the public.

Tracy married fellow stock company player Louise Treadwell in 1923. They had two children, Susan and John (who was born deaf). Although Tracy often lived apart from his wife, they never divorced, and he generously supported her endeavors to deal with the problems faced by deaf children through the John Tracy Clinic which she established in Los Angeles in the early 1940s.

An avid polo player during his early years in Hollywood, Tracy also became known for being a rakehell. He often went on alcoholic benders and had a number of intense romantic liaisons with some of his leading ladies, such as Loretta Young. This aspect of his life just about ended when he established a long relationship with Katherine Hepburn that lasted until his death. They met in the 1942 filming of *Woman of the Year,* and this movie marked the beginning of a romantic and professional relationship which lasted until his death in 1967. Among the more successful of the nine films they made jointly are the marvelous comedies *Adam's Rib* (1949) and *Pat and Mike* (1952), as well as the serious dramas *Keeper of the Flame* (1942) and *Guess Who's Coming to Dinner* (1967), his last film.

During the last years of his life Tracy suffered greatly from ill health, and between 1962 and 1967 he did not perform at all. It was by all accounts a real effort, requiring great determination on his part and much patience on the part of other cast members and crew, for him to make his last film. He died but weeks after its completion.

Tracy belongs to an era of film-making now gone forever. A great personality as well as a consummate actor, he limited himself to one medium. He did what he knew best and did that very well, being solid, dependable, and outstanding.

Further Reading

See biographies by Larry Swindell (1983) and Romano Tozzi (1974); Garson Kanin, *Tracy and Hepburn* (1971); and Donald Deschner, *The Complete Films of Spencer Tracy* (1968).

Additional Sources

Davidson, Bill, *Spencer Tracy, tragic idol,* New York: Dutton, 1988, 1987.
Fisher, James, *Spencer Tracy: a bio-bibliography,* Westport, Conn.: Greenwood Press, 1994. □

Catharine Parr Traill

Catharine Parr Traill (1802-1899) was a Canadian naturalist and author who wrote books for children, studies of Canadian flowers and plants, and, most important, accurate accounts of pioneer conditions in Upper Canada.

Catharine Parr was born in London and began to write stories for children while still a girl. Her first children's book, *The Blind Highland Piper,* was published in 1818, when she was only 16; her most popular book of this type, *Little Downy; or, The History of a Field-mouse: A Moral Tale,* appeared in London in 1822. She married a half-pay British army officer, Lt. Thomas Traill, in 1832 and in the same year emigrated with him to Upper Canada (now Ontario). The Traills settled in the backwoods near the present town of Peterborough, and she was very close to being a centenarian when she died at Lakefield in 1899.

Traill's best-known book had its genesis in a series of letters she wrote home to her mother in England describing her impressions of early life in Canada. The book was published in London in 1836 with the following informative title: *The Backwoods of Canada; Being the Letters from the Wife of an Emigrant Officer; Illustrative of the Domestic Economy of British North America.* It was an instant success and was soon translated into German and French. For actual or potential emigrants it provided useful information on the hazards of pioneer settlement and practical hints on how to survive these hazards.

Having achieved success with this book, Traill followed it up with a similar work: *The Female Emigrant's Guide, and Hints on Canadian Housekeeping* (1854). She became increasingly interested in the botany of her adopted country and embodied the knowledge she acquired of this subject in four books: *Rambles in the Canadian Forest* (1859), *Canadian Wild Flowers* (1869), *Studies of Plant Life in Canada* (1885), and *Pearls and Pebbles; or, Notes of an Old Naturalist* (1894). She also continued to practice her first literary skill, that of writing stories for children. One such book was *The Canadian Crusoes* (1852), which was republished 30 years later under the title *Lost in the Backwoods;* another was *Lady Mary and Her Nurse: A Peep into the Canadian Forest* (1856), published a year later in Boston as *Stories of the Canadian Forest* and in London in 1869 as *Afar in the Forest;* her last children's book was *Cot and Cradle Stories* (1895).

Further Reading

There is as yet no book-length study of Catharine Parr Traill. The most useful sources of information are Clara Thomas's introduction to Traill's *The Backwoods of Canada* in the New Canadian Library edition (1966) and the appropriate chapter of George H. Needler, *Otonabee Pioneers* (1953). See also Desmond Pacey, *Creative Writing in Canada* (1961), and Carl F. Klinck, ed., *Literary History of Canada* (1965). □

Trajan

The Roman emperor Trajan (ca. 53-117), or Marcus Ulpius Trajanus, was the first non-Italian emperor. He expanded Rome's territory to its farthest limits, and his designation as optimus princeps, "the best of princes," attests to his reputation.

When Nerva succeeded the murdered Domitian in 96, it was by no means certain that the armies would accept a nice old unknown emperor. The danger from ambitious generals was so real that Nerva adopted Trajan, the commander of the nearest armies (on the Rhine), and made him successor even though he was a native of Italica, a Romanized town of Spain. Henceforth non-Italian lineage was no bar to even the highest position in the empire. The two most important aspects of Trajan's reign were his forward policy on the frontiers and his administrative and building activities, particularly with regard to Italy.

Wars and Conquests

A bit of glory is a source of strength to a new regime, and Trajan seems to have decided to correct Domitian's policy of "weakness" toward the Dacians. The result was two Dacian Wars (101-102 and 105-106), the first apparently sought by Rome, the second clearly a Dacian try for revenge. After the first war Dacia was humbled; after the second it was annexed.

Trajan doubtless recognized the economic value of Dacia (roughly, modern Romania), but he must also have seen the wisdom of advancing a wedge of Roman territory between Rome's possible barbarian enemies, the Germans to the west and the Sarmatians to the east. Dacia in time became thoroughly Latinized, and the Romanians today speak a romance language. Also in 106 the client king of the Nabateans died, and Trajan ordered his territory—approximately modern Sinai, the Negeb, and Jordan—annexed as the province of Arabia.

Parthia, embracing essentially modern Iraq and Iran, was the only major power Rome faced, and the two were constantly at odds as to who should control Armenia, which was strategically important to both. When the question boiled up again, Trajan decided to annex Armenia, which he did (114) with little fighting. Armenia could hardly be held, however, if the Parthians could attack it from Mesopotamia, and in 115 Trajan occupied northern Mesopotamia. In 116 he continued south, took the Parthian capital, and advanced to the Persian Gulf.

Trajan organized his new conquest into provinces, but revolts broke out behind him everywhere. Even within the empire the Jews erupted in a bitter revolt, massacring the Gentiles where they could and being massacred in return. Trajan intended to restore order and resume the war, but he died suddenly (117), and his successor, Hadrian, made peace with Parthia and abandoned the Eastern provinces except Arabia.

Administration and Public Works

Though Trajan's public works were widespread throughout the empire, the most important were in Italy: roads, especially the Via Traiana in the south; large improvements to Claudius's artificial harbor at Ostia; and particularly the immense forum in Rome, surrounded by halls, libraries, and shops and centering on the most famous of all Trajan's works, the great column commemorating his Dacian victories.

Trajan's administrative measures were chiefly designed to preserve the prosperity of Italy. He extended Nerva's scheme of *alimenta*, low-cost state loans to farmers, whose repayment went to the local communities for the support of poor children. Since the finances of some of the towns were becoming chaotic, he appointed temporary imperial officials, *curatores*, to control the town budgets. Like the *alimenta*, this system also spread, and the temporary officials tended to become permanent. Trajan even extended the practice to whole provinces, and his correspondence with his appointee Pliny the Younger shows how petty were the matters which might be referred to the central authority.

The ancients never revised their opinion that Trajan was the best of the emperors, and his reign did inaugurate almost a century in which nearly all elements of the empire worked in harmony, but modern historians have some reservations. Both in money and in manpower his wars overstrained Rome's resources, and his moving the imperial government into local administration started the trend to that overlarge, overworked bureaucracy whose cost (bu-

reaucrats must be paid) and cumbersomeness ultimately contributed to the collapse of the empire.

Further Reading

Except for brief epitomes, very little ancient literary material on Trajan survives. Of some help are Pliny the Younger's *Panegyric* (though it tells more about Domitian than about Trajan) and some of his letters, including Trajan's replies. Among modern works, a study of Trajan is in Bernard W. Henderson, *Five Roman Emperors* (1927). For Trajan's buildings see Paul L. Mackendrick, *The Mute Stones Speak: The Story of Archaeology in Italy* (1960). Considerable information on Trajan is in F. A. Lepper's specialized work, *Trajan's Parthian War* (1948). □

William Barret Travis

American patriot William Barret Travis (1809-1836) was a hero of the Texan War for Independence against Mexico.

W illiam Travis was born on Aug. 9, 1809, in present Saluda County, S.C. When he was 9, his family moved to a farm in Alabama. Before his twentieth birthday, after studying law, he was admitted to the bar. Unable to support himself entirely by practicing law, he also taught school.

Standing 6 feet in height, weighing 175 pounds, redheaded, and blue-eyed, Travis married one of his pupils, Rosanna E. Cato. The marriage was unhappy, and in 1831 he moved to Texas, establishing a law practice at Anahuac, the legal port for Galveston Bay.

In Texas, Travis quickly conceived an intense dislike for the Mexican government and became a leader of the militant faction working for independence. In 1832 he participated in disputes with the Mexican commanding officer at Anahuac that led to his arrest. In October 1832 he moved to San Felipe, the center of the American colonies in Texas. He practiced law, was secretary of the city council, and courted Rebecca Cummings, whom he intended to marry. His divorce was approved in 1835, and he received custody of his son. The outbreak of the Texas revolution prevented his marriage to Rebecca Cummings.

In the early fighting Travis commanded a scouting company at the Battle of San Antonio. Next he was a recruiter and then was named a major of artillery. Transferring to the cavalry as a lieutenant colonel, he arrived at San Antonio on Feb. 3, 1836, at the head of 25 men. Commanding the volunteers at San Antonio was James Bowie. Both men had orders to quit the Alamo, a mission chapel of fortress proportions, but both chose to disregard the order. On February 23 the dictator of Mexico, Antonio López de Santa Ana, arrived with an army of 5,000 men. When Bowie fell ill, Travis, with 186 men, assumed total command of the Texan forces. Desperately he wrote for aid: "I call on you in the name of liberty, of patriotism & everything dear to the American character to come to our aid. . . . If this call is neglected, I am determined to sustain myself as long as possible & die like a soldier." His last note was to the friend caring for his son: "Take care of my little boy.... If this country should be lost, and I should perish, he will have nothing but the proud recollection that he is the son of a man who died for his country."

On March 6 the Mexicans stormed the Alamo and killed every defender, including Travis. The Alamo Cenotaph, erected in 1936 by the state of Texas, commemorates these heroes, especially Travis, whose indomitable will and incendiary pen furthered the cause of Texan independence.

Further Reading

A useful source is *The Diary of William Barret Travis,* edited by Robert E. Davis (1966). Also valuable is the chapter on Travis in H. Bailey Carroll and others, *Heroes of Texas* (1964).

Additional Sources

McDonald, Archie P., *Travis,* Austin, Tex.: Jenkins Pub. Co., 1976. □

Heinrich von Treitschke

The German historian, politician, and political publicist Heinrich von Treitschke (1834-1896) was the most famous and influential member of the Prussian school of history in 19th-century Germany. He advocated a powerful German state under Prussian leadership.

Heinrich von Treitschke was born on Sept. 15, 1834, in Dresden. His father, who rose to general officer's rank in the service of the Saxon monarchy, was of German-Czech descent, had been ennobled in 1821, and maintained his aristocratic conservatism and loyalty to the Saxon royal family throughout his life. Young Heinrich showed early intellectual promise in his schooling, which, however, was interrupted at the age of 8 by a severe case of measles complicated by glandular fever which led to increasing loss of hearing. Thus a career of public service as a soldier or statesman-politician became impossible, and Heinrich decided on a life of scholarship.

His Education

Attending Dresden's Holy Cross Gymnasium (high school) from 1846 to 1851, Treitschke was exposed not only to the traditional classical education but also to liberal ideas critical of the semiabsolutism of the times. The study of German literature under Julius Klee and personal observations of the political events of the revolutionary years 1848-1849 molded Treitschke's tendency toward strong political conviction into an attitude of enthusiastic support for a constitutional, united Germany under Prussian leadership.

From 1851 to 1854 Treitschke studied at the universities of Bonn, Leipzig, Tübingen, and Freiburg, attending classes under F. C. Dahlmann, the political economist Wilhelm Roscher, and the eminent Tübingen philosopher Friedrich Theodor Vischer.

After a brief interlude in Dresden, Treitschke studied at Göttingen and Leipzig. He succeeded in publishing two volumes of poems, *Patriotic Songs* (1856) and *Studies* (1857). In 1858 he finished his habilitation thesis, *Die Gesellschaftswissenschaft* (1859; *The Science of Society*), which earned him an appointment as lecturer at the University of Leipzig in 1859.

The political atmosphere in Leipzig did not prove congenial, and in 1863 Treitschke accepted a professorial appointment at Freiburg. Here he wrote his famous essay *Bundesstaat und Einheitsstaat* (1863-1864; *Federation and Centralization*). In 1866, when Baden joined Austria in war against Prussia, Treitschke resigned his position at Freiburg and demanded in a pamphlet, *The Future of the North German Middle States,* the annexation of Hanover, Hesse, and Saxony by Prussia.

Political Activities

Although Treitschke was estranged from his father, his fame as a political publicist had now reached national eminence. Positions at Kiel (1866) and Heidelberg (1867-1874) followed before he finally settled in Berlin. His strong Prussian sentiments had earned him appointment as editor of the *Preussische Jahrbücher* (Prussian Annals) in 1866 and election to the German Reichstag (House of Deputies) in 1871. Although originally affiliated with the National Liberal party, he left that party in 1879 to support Bismarck's new commercial policy and held his seat until 1884 as an independent member with conservative leanings.

The period from 1859 to 1871 is important for Treitschke's development. More and more he abandoned his original liberal constitutional attitude and became an ever more ardent advocate of the power state, of war as the noblest activity of man, and of a German expansionist, cultural mission under Prussian leadership which would establish Germany as an equal among the world powers. Although he counted among his close friends a number of Jews, he participated in the anti-Semitic movement of the late 1870s, proclaiming that Jewry could play an important role only if its individual members were to merge themselves with the nationality of their state.

History of Germany

Treitschke had planned to write a history of Germany since 1861; but not until he had settled in Berlin, where the Prussian archives were close at hand, did the work progress. The first volume of his *Deutsche Geschichte im 19. Jahrhundert* (*German History in the 19th Century*) was published in 1879, starting with the Napoleonic period. The fifth volume, published in 1894, brought the narrative only to the beginning of 1848. Although this, the greatest of his works, also suffered from the shortcomings of Treitschke's emotional patriotic nature and was limited to the almost exclusive use of the Prussian archives, it nevertheless constitutes a major contribution to historical writing. Its literary style and power of expression have been likened to Friedrich von Schiller's diction and Johann Gottlieb Fichte's rhetoric. In spite of his tendency to oversimplify complicated events, Treitschke exhibited a grasp of detail and power to synthesize that produced a general cultural historical setting uncommon among the works of historians of his time.

Other important historical and political essays were published in four volumes as *Historische und Politische Aufsätze* (1896; *Historical and Political Essays*); and his lectures on politics were collected and published in two volumes as *Vorlesungen über Politik* (1898; *Politics*).

Treitschke died on April 28, 1896, in Berlin. His influence during his lifetime was threefold: as teacher, political propagandist, and historian. A generation of students and of the general public was affected by his political lectures and nationalistic journalism, and even abroad he was often regarded as an official mouthpiece of German policy.

Although after his death Treitschke's influence among German historians, who generally preferred to follow the more balanced methodological example of the Ranke school of historical writing, became largely dormant, it was revived in coarsened form by Nazi ideologists, who utilized his unbridled nationalism as a point of departure for their thought and actions.

Further Reading

The best full-length biography of Treitschke is Andreas Dorpalen, *Heinrich von Treitschke* (1957). Adolf Hausrath, *Treitschke: His Doctrine of German Destiny and of International Relations* (1914), combines a section on Treitschke's life and work with a number of his essays reprinted in English. Henry W.C. Davis, *The Political Thought of Heinrich von Treitschke* (1914), attempts to analyze Treitschke's work within the context of his time. For background see G.P. Gooch, *History and Historians in the Nineteenth Century* (1913; rev. ed. 1952); Antoine Guillard, *Modern Germany and Her Historians* (1915); and Georg Iggers, *The German Conception of History* (1968). □

George Macaulay Trevelyan

The English historian George Macaulay Trevelyan (1876-1962) is known for his defense and illustration of history as a literary art.

George Macaulay Trevelyan was born at Welcombe near Stratford-on-Avon on Feb. 16, 1876, the son of Sir George Otto Trevelyan. His maternal granduncle was the historian Thomas Babington Macaulay. Young Trevelyan went to Trinity College, Cambridge, where Bertrand Russell, G. E. Moore, and Ralph Vaughan Williams were among his friends. In 1898, his imagination caught by what he saw as the first stirring of national consciousness and individual freedom among the 14th century Lollards, he wrote *England in the Age of Wycliffe* as a dissertation for a Trinity fellowship. An immediate success, it remains one of the best books on the subject.

Awarded the fellowship, Trevelyan set out upon an academic career. Cambridge, however, was then dominated by a highly critical mode of historical writing, soon to be epitomized by J. B. Bury in the phrase, "History is a science, nothing more, nothing less." The ethos was not congenial for a writer of Trevelyan's literary and humanistic bent. In 1903 he left Cambridge for London, not to return until his appointment as regius professor in 1927.

Trevelyan's next work, *England under the Stuarts* (1904), showed a deeper historical understanding and more secure craftsmanship, particularly in its portrayal of King Charles I and the Cavaliers. The year of its publication, Trevelyan married Janet Penrose Ward. As a wedding gift, he received a copy of Giuseppe Garibaldi's *Memoirs,* which awakened memories of stories he had heard from his father (who had tried to join Garibaldi in 1867) and of his own walks in the Umbrian hills. The result was *Garibaldi's Defence of the Roman Republic,* written in the heat of inspiration in 1906. It was a perfect match of event and author, giving full play to Trevelyan's poetic imagination. Its success was immediate, and he felt impelled to complete the story with *Garibaldi and the Thousand* (1909) and *Garibaldi and the Making of Italy* (1911).

Trevelyan's *History of England* (1926) quickly became one of the best-selling textbooks of its age. From its pages a generation of Englishmen learned the history of their country. In 1928, having succeeded Bury as regius professor, he began work on his three-volume *England under Queen Anne* (1931-1934), his major contribution to historical scholarship. He had long dreamed of telling the story, he later wrote, attracted by its "dramatic unity"; it was "like a five-act drama, leading up to the climax of the trumpets proclaiming King George." His last major work, *English Social History* (1944), written just before World War II, was his greatest commercial success.

In 1930 Trevelyan received the Order of Merit. He died at Cambridge on July 21, 1962.

Further Reading

Trevelyan recounted his own life in his modest *An Autobiography and Other Essays* (1949). His views on historical writing are most clearly presented in *Clio: A Muse, and Other Essays* (1913). John H. Plumb, *G. M. Trevelyan* (1951), is a short biography. An essay on Trevelyan is in Samuel William Halperin, ed., *Some 20th Century Historians: Essays on Eminent Europeans* (1961). Trevelyan's place in his field is assessed in the introduction to John R. Hale, ed., *The Evolution of British Historiography from Bacon to Namier* (1964).

Additional Sources

Cannadine, David, *G.M. Trevelyan: a life in history*, New York: W.W. Norton, 1993.

Moorman, Mary Trevelyan, *George Macaulay Trevelyan: a memoir*, London; North Pomfret, Vt.: Hamilton, 1980. □

William Trevor

William Trevor (born 1928), whose life and fictional settings were divided between his native Ireland and his adopted England, was a successful novelist, television dramatist, playwright, and, above all, master of the short story.

William Trevor Cox was born an Irish Protestant on May 24, 1928, in County Cork, the son of a bank manager. He attended 13 different provincial schools before settling in at St. Columbia's College in Dublin from 1942 to 1946. He next matriculated at Trinity College, Dublin, where he received a B.A. in history in 1950; he then taught history at a school in Armagh, Northern Ireland, from 1950 to 1952.

Until the age of 22 Trevor had never been out of Ireland, but two years later (1952) the depressed national economy impelled him to leave permanently and to take up residence in England. That same year he married Jane Ryan, with whom he had two sons. He taught art at Rugby from 1952 to 1956 and at Taunton from 1956 to 1960. During his tenure as an art instructor he took up sculpting; however, despite winning an award for one of his pieces, he was dissatisfied with his work and turned to writing.

Novels and Plays

His first novel, *A Standard of Behaviour* (1958), was undistinguished and gave little evidence of a major talent. From 1960 to 1965 Trevor worked in London as an advertising copywriter, during which time he completed his second novel, *The Old Boys* (1964), which won the prestigious Hawthornden Prize. *The Old Boys* deals with the eccentricities and petty rivalries of a minor English public school's alumni association. The critical and commercial success of the novel encouraged Trevor to adapt it first for television and next, very successfully, for the stage (the play, in 1971, starred Sir Michael Redgrave); it also enabled Trevor to quit his advertising job, take residence in a small Devon village outside of London, and devote himself fully to his writing.

The Boarding House (1965) continued Trevor's novelistic interest in eccentrics, this time in a strange assortment of lodgers who plot against and generally bedevil each other. *The Love Department* (1966), which departs from the gentility of the earlier novels, is the story of a sexual pervert and the fortuitous justice that overtakes him. *Mrs. Eckdorf in O'Neill's Hotel* (1969) and *Miss Gomez and the Brethren* (1971) typify Trevor's moral concerns as they explore the disparity between people's barren lives and their spiritual needs. *Elizabeth Alone* (1973) represents a shift from Trevor's accustomed bizarre types; the quite normal title character, in a hospital for a hysterectomy, meets three women whose frustrated lives parallel her own.

In the early 1970s Trevor enjoyed enormous success in theater and television; in 1973 alone he had three plays performed on the London stage and three dramas produced for television. His next novel, *The Children of Dynmouth* (1976), deals with a moral miscreant, 15-year-old Timothy Gedge, who spies on and blackmails the inhabitants of a small coastal resort. Partly on the occasion of the novel and partly for his career as a whole, Trevor received in 1976 the Royal Society of Literature Award, the Whitbread Award, and the Allied Irish Banks Award, and the following year he was presented with the ultimate honor, an Order of the British Empire.

Other People's Worlds (1980) is perhaps Trevor's most interesting novel, though it suffers a loss of momentum in its second half. It deals with a psychopathic con man, Francis Tyte, who deceives and cheats his new wife, then deserts her; the last half of the novel is then concerned with the heroine's efforts to reconcile herself to evil in God's scheme of things, but the theme is insufficiently compelling to compensate the reader for the loss of the novel's most interesting character, Francis, and the demonic energy he had supplied. *Fools of Fortune* (1983) is a turbulent family chronicle set in Ireland, a novel of murder, revenge, and reconciliation. His next novel was *The Silence In The Garden* (1989), winner of the Yorkshire Post Book of the Year Award. This was followed by *Two Lives* (1991), comprising the novellas of *Reading Turgenev* and *My House in Umbria,* named by the *New York Times* as one of the ten best books of the year.

Short Stories Outshine Novels

Some writers of fiction excel equally in the long and short forms (Hemingway, Greene, I. B. Singer, for example); others show little interest in or aptitude for the shorter form (Waugh, Camus). Still others have realized the apotheosis of their art *only* in the shorter form (K. A. Porter, F. O'Connor). It is to this latter group that Trevor belongs, not because the novels aren't good, but because the stories are so much better.

The Day We Got Drunk on Cake (1967), his first and weakest collection, is similar to the novels in that it deals with lives that are lonely and cultureless, with people, most often women, victimized by their confusions, obsessions, and fantasies.

The Ballroom of Romance (1972), Trevor's second short story collection, shows a big advance in his mastery of the form. American novelist Paul Theroux saw a thematic thread in the stories, a "brittle or urgent femininity thwarted by rather boorish maleness." Typically, the heroines of the title story and of "Nice Day at School" yearn for love and romance even as their hopes are being dashed by the coarseness and insensitivity of the available menfolk.

Angels at the Ritz (1973) was hailed by Graham Greene as perhaps the best short story collection since Joyce's *Dubliners* (1914). Two of its finest stories, "Last Wishes" and "The Tennis Court," deal poignantly with impending death and changing social fashions. The title story concerns a couple who barely resist the enticements of a suburban wife-swapping party and thereby retain some vestige of unfashionable idealism; the story is uncharacteristic of Trevor in its concluding note of affirmation. Another superb story, "In Isfahan," dramatizes a holiday encounter that fails to flower into romance; the reasons for the man's reticence are kept ambiguous, but he is movingly aware that, despite the woman's touch of vulgarity, she is humanly superior to him.

Angels was hard to improve upon, but Trevor surpassed himself with *Lovers of Their Time* (1978), which contains at least three masterpieces. "Broken Homes" portrays the harrowing desecration of an octogenarian's home by two homeless teenagers, a boy and a girl, who have been sent over on a refurbishing mission by a well-intentioned social agency. The story's title faintly suggests the allegorical theme: the socially deprived victimizing the physically helpless. "Torridge" is an ingenious attack on the built-in bully system of English public schools and the adult philistinism they inevitably promote: the cruelty of the story's schoolboys, long forgotten as they've turned into smug bourgeois, is jolted to memory by a chance reunion. The decent title character, who in the intervening years has become a homosexual, serves as the catalyst who exposes the rest of the group's social and sexual dishonesty. The collection's title story is a bittersweet tale of timid, gentle lovers, one of whom is unhappily married, who conduct their clandestine affair, unbeknownst to the management, rent-free in a posh hotel. The idyll and their chance for happiness, however, are shattered by the man's shrewdly cynical wife.

In the 1980s Trevor sustained his level of short story excellence with *Beyond the Pale* (1981) and *The News from Ireland and Other Stories* (1986) and, beginning in 1985, with a series of stories published in *The New Yorker,* including *After Rain. The Collected Stories* (1992) was recognized as one of the best books of the year.

Trevor's achievement, especially in the short story, was formidable: he illuminated the darker corners of contemporary English and Irish life and he did so in a compassionate, wryly humorous way that almost never slipped into sentimentality. His acknowledged influences were Thomas Hardy ("where all my gloom came from"), Evelyn Waugh, and Anthony Powell. He was a subtle prose stylist whose dialogue was ceremonious rather than idiomatic. His settings were more often England than Ireland, but in either culture he captured a feeling of loss and failure, spiked with a longing for a past that was admittedly oppressive but in any case preferable to the wasteland of the present. Probably the most striking aspect of Trevor's art was that his sparkling narrative effects were fashioned from unspectacular lives and situations; he was a transmuter, a writer who mined gold from garden-variety rock. He lived in Devon, England.

Further Reading

Gregory A. Schirmer published a biographical work, *William Trevor: A Study of His Fiction* (London, Rutledge, 1990), which covers many of Trevor's major writings. As yet there is no all-encompassing biography of Trevor, but reviews and critiques of his work abound. Among the more interesting are John Updike's "Worlds and Worlds," *New Yorker* (March 23, 1981); Peter Kemp's "Cosiness and Carnage," *The London Times Literary Supplement* (October 16, 1981); Ted Solotaroff's "The Dark Souls of Ordinary People," *New York Times Book Review* (February 21, 1982); and Anatole Broyard's negative report on Trevor, "Books of the Times: 'Beyond the Pale'," *New York Times* (February 3, 1982). □

Juan Terry Trippe

Juan Terry Trippe (1899-1981), the undisputed pioneer of the American overseas aviation industry, led Pan American Airways from 1927 to 1968. Having opened up Latin America, the African periphery, the Pacific, and Southeast Asia during the 1930s, Pan American played an important role in World War II before spearheading mass, low-cost tourism across the North Atlantic to Western Europe in the 1950s.

Juan Trippe was born on June 27, 1899, to a well-off New York family, which, despite his first name, had no significant Hispanic connections. He attended the Hill School and entered Yale University in 1917. Trippe and some classmates became Navy pilots after America entered World War I, but they saw no combat. He later returned to Yale, graduated in 1921, and became a Wall Street bond salesman.

But Trippe and his wealthy associates were fascinated by aviation, whose future seemed rich with possibilities. Having bought some surplus Navy planes in 1923, they organized Long Island Airways before creating Colonial Air Transport in 1924 to fly between New York and Boston. Aviation attracted little business, however, until the federal government intervened to control entries, routes, and franchises, while also providing airmail contracts as virtual subsidies. After a dispute within Colonial over extending it to Miami, Trippe resigned in 1926 and formed a new corporation, which merged in 1927 with Pan American Airways. He became president and general manager.

Beginning with a 90-mile airmail route from Key West to Havana, Trippe spearheaded Pan American's spectacular expansion into the coastal cities of Latin America and established 11,000 miles of routes by late 1929. He secured the indispensable U.S. airmail contracts and began lobbying for Pan American's position as a "chosen instrument" of American policy in South America, a continent of vast distances, impenetrable terrain, and many U.S. strategic and economic interests. State Department backing often bolstered his negotiations with foreign governments for routes, landing rights, terminals, and customs' privileges.

In 1929 W. R. Grace & Co. and Pan American organized Panagra (Pan American and Grace Airways) to operate on the west coast of Latin America. By the early 1930s Pan American had largely overshadowed its competitors in the region. In return for its government-sponsored quasi-monopoly abroad, Pan American followed Washington's tight regulatory policies by shunning the American market.

Pan American expanded rapidly despite the Great Depression and gained prestige by employing Charles Lindbergh, the "Lone Eagle" of public acclaim, and by turning what had been the adventure of flight into a safe, reliable, and profitable business venture. Trippe built an elaborate infrastructure of weather stations and communications, navigation, and maintenance facilities, first in Latin America and then on Hawaii and other Pacific islands. The Pan American market for long-range aircraft stimulated the American aviation industry, most notably in developing the comfortable, 60-passenger "Clipper," with which Pan American pioneered service in the mid-1930s both across the Atlantic and via the Pacific to Manila.

Inevitably, Pan American became deeply involved in American foreign policy as World War II approached. There was constant competition over new markets with government-controlled foreign airlines, which contended that Trippe was building a global empire to strengthen American diplomatic and military power. Japan, for example, was angered, first when Trippe bought the China National Aviation Corporation in 1933, and again when he established links to British South Pacific territories after 1939. Simultaneously, the New York-Lisbon Clipper flights became famous, and very lucrative, as one of the few neutral routes into a Europe at war.

Pan American, now linked to the Air Force's global Air Transport Command, became a major contract carrier for the government after Pearl Harbor, particularly in ferrying planes from northeastern Brazil across Africa to the Middle East. Pan American even inaugurated air travel for a president, carrying Franklin D. Roosevelt to and from the Casablanca conference in early 1943. With its German and Italian rivals destroyed, and British and French international airlines greatly weakened financially, Pan American emerged victorious after 1945. But its international monopoly had ended as its American competitors learned the skills of oceanic flight when drafted by Washington into the war effort.

Trippe tried to revivify the "chosen instrument" concept by making Pan American (renamed Pan American World Airways in 1949) into a regulated monopoly, with the federal government owning 49 percent of the stock, but the plan died. In 1950, just as foreign air competitors were reaching American shores, he was refused the right to fly domestically, with the reliable income that this would generate. In 1952 Trippe encouraged mass tourism across the North Atlantic to Western Europe by instituting tourist class fares, with installment purchases after 1954. Volume flights required larger aircraft, and Trippe, having developed commercial jet service in the late 1950s, bought the first Boeing 747s in 1966.

But Trippe's desire to create a vast global system, servicing virtually every airport everywhere without strong regard for volume or profit, combined with a growing foreign and American competition to which Pan American could not adjust. There were major difficulties in the 1960s, with half-filled aircraft and shrinking revenues. Trippe retired in 1968, after 41 years at the helm, and died on April 3, 1981. His empire went downhill. A proposal that the shah of Iran buy it in 1975 was rejected. It filed for bankruptcy early in 1991 and ceased flying later in the year.

Further Reading

Trippe and American overseas aviation in general have attracted much study. Sweeping, popularized biographies are: Charles Kelly, Jr., *The Sky's the Limit* (1963); Robert Daley, *An American Saga: Juan Trippe and His Pan American Empire* (1980); and Marylin Bender and Selig Altschul, *The Chosen Instrument: Pan Am, Juan Trippe, The Rise and Fall of an American Entrepreneur* (1982). More scholarly are Richard Caves, *Air Transport and Its Regulators* (1962); R. E. G. Davies, *A History of the World's Airlines* (1964); and Wesley Phillips Newton, *The Perilous Sky: U.S. Aviation Diplomacy in Latin America, 1911-1931* (1978). □

Nicholas Philip Trist

Nicholas Philip Trist (1800-1874), an American lawyer and diplomat, was best known as the negotiator of the Treaty of Guadalupe Hidalgo, which ended the war with Mexico in 1848.

Nicholas Trist was born in Charlottesville, Va., on June 2, 1800. He attended the U.S. Military Academy at West Point but did not graduate, turning instead to the law, which he studied in Thomas Jefferson's law office. He was Jefferson's private secretary (1825-1826) and married his granddaughter Virginia Jefferson Randolph. In 1829 Trist received appointment as a clerk in the Department of State, where he remained until 1833. He then went to Havana as consul, staying in that post for 8 years.

When James K. Polk became president in 1845, Trist became chief clerk of the Department of State. Two years later Polk selected him for a most delicate mission—as agent to conclude peace with Mexico, with which the United States had been at war since 1846. Trist spoke Spanish fluently, was able and intelligent, and had experience in dealing with Latin American affairs. He was to attach himself to Gen. Winfield Scott's army and begin negotiations when the military situation seemed opportune.

Trist joined Scott in May 1847. Two months later Scott began his advance on Mexico. In two smashing battles he reached the gates of the capital, forcing the Mexicans to call for an armistice, which he granted. Trist's preliminary negotiations for a peace were rejected, causing Scott to move on Mexico City that September.

Meanwhile, Polk decided to recall Trist lest his presence lead the Mexicans to think that the United States was so eager for peace that it would accept unsatisfactory terms. The letter of recall reached Trist on Nov. 16, 1847, but he decided to ignore it. Knowing the political situation in Mexico, he believed that if he were to go home the opportunity to make peace might be lost. On December 3 he informed the Mexican leaders of his readiness to negotiate. He sat down at once with their emissaries, and on Feb. 2, 1848, the Treaty of Guadalupe Hidalgo was signed.

Polk had no choice but to accept the treaty. It was a good treaty and did, indeed, incorporate his minimum demands as set forth in Trist's instructions of April 15, 1847. But Polk was furious with Trist for disobeying the order to return home and punished him by dismissing him from government service. Trist returned to practicing law. In 1870 he was appointed postmaster at Alexandria, Va., a post he held until his death on Feb. 11, 1874.

Further Reading

Trist's career is recounted in Jesse S. Reeves, *American Diplomacy under Tyler and Polk* (1907); Robert Selph Henry, *The Story of the Mexican War* (1950); and Charles L. Dufour, *The Mexican War: A Compact History, 1846-1848* (1968).

Additional Sources

Drexler, Robert W., *Guilty of making peace: a biography of Nicholas P. Trist,* Lanham: University Press of America, 1991. □

Ernst Troeltsch

The German theologian, historian, and sociologist Ernst Troeltsch (1865-1923), through his utilization of the objective methods of modern scholarship, contributed to the sociology of religion and the problems of historicism.

Ernst Troeltsch was born in Augsburg. After studying theology at the universities of Erlange, Göttingen, and Berlin from 1883 to 1888, he became a lecturer at Göttingen in 1891, an associate professor at Bonn in 1892, and a professor at Heidelberg in 1894; he remained at Heidelberg for 21 years. For a short time he was a Lutheran curate in Munich. In 1901 he married, and a son, Ernst Eberhard, was born in 1913. In 1915 he came to feel that theology was too confining and transferred to philosophy at the University of Berlin.

A conservative in politics, Troeltsch long served in the Baden upper house. From 1919 to 1921 he was a member of the Prussian Landtag and concurrently secretary of state for public worship. He was moved deeply by the war. Like Max Weber and others, he hailed the "great and wonderful" fervor of the Germans and saw their cause rooted in idealistic values as opposed to the materialism of the Allies. Soon, however, together with Weber and Friedrich Meinecke, he left the conservative majority, opposed annexationist war aims, and advocated increased democratization. After the war he defended the Weimar Republic, decried the "frightful demagoguery" of the right, and advocated a genuine conservatism in articles which bore the pseudonym of *Spektator* and appeared until 4 months before his death.

In *The Social Teaching of the Christian Churches* (1912) Troeltsch studied the relation between religion and the other elements of society and culture. He found that

Christianity was not reducible to displaced social protest, as Karl Kautsky and the Marxists had suggested, but rather was a real and autonomous religious movement with its own immanent implications for development and its own independent effect upon history. Although the forms of belief and organization developed by the Church were historically conditioned, they also represented the unfolding of the implications of Christianity's inner meaning; and once the Church was established, it also in turn affected and influenced other aspects of society and culture.

Troeltsch carried out his study in four contexts—family, economic life, politics, and intellectual life—and found Christianity exhibiting two contrary but complementary tendencies—accommodation and protest. These two tendencies gave rise to two organizational types: the Church, which qualifiedly accepted the world in order to sanctify it, and the sect, which rejected the world and the whole idea of adjustment to it. Troeltsch stated that the Christian ideal could not be "realized within this world apart from compromise" and that consequently Christian history was "the story of a constantly renewed search for this compromise, and a fresh opposition to this spirit of compromise."

In an earlier work Troeltsch had examined the relationship between Protestantism and modern capitalism. He agreed with Weber that Calvinism had an important early influence upon the development of capitalism, but he saw the Protestant impact upon economic developments as chiefly "indirect and unconsciously produced" and religion as more affected than affecting with respect to modern developments. Despite the Christian derivation of modern civilization, Troeltsch came to see the future of Christianity as "unpredictable" and its survival demanding "very bold and far-reaching changes."

Historicism was a profound challenge to Troeltsch. If all beliefs and values are products of individual tendencies specific to particular conditions, is there then nothing suprahistorical resulting from man's search for truth and creation of value? He studied this problem in his *Historismus und seine Probleme* (1922), examining the "relation of individual historical facts to standards of value within the entire domain of history in connection with the development of political, social, ethical, esthetic, and scientific ideas." Earlier he had spoken of "polymorphous truth," which though beyond history is apprehended differently in different civilizations and epochs, and he had also sought for an extrahistorical basis in morality. Now he concluded that "even the validity of science and logic seemed to exhibit, under different skies and on different soil, strong individual differences present even in their deepest and inner rudiments."

Troeltsch was concerned with historicism not simply as a scholar but as a deeply religious man as well. Although he failed to solve the problems intellectually, he concluded: "Skepticism and relativism are only an apparent necessary consequence of modern intellectual conditions and of historicism. They may be overcome by way of ethics"; and, "If there is any solution at all to these riddles and problems, with their conflicts and contradictions, that solution certainly is not to be found within their own sphere, but beyond it, in that unknown land, of which there are so many indications in the historic struggle of the spirit upward, but which itself is never revealed to our eyes.''

Further Reading

Most writings on Troeltsch are in German. In English, a study of his thought is Benjamin A. Reist, *Toward a Theology of Involvement: The Thought of Ernst Troeltsch* (1966). He also is considered in Thomas W. Ogletree, *Christian Faith and History: A Critical Comparison of Ernst Troeltsch and Karl Barth* (1965), and Wilhelm Pauck, *Harnack and Troeltsch: Two Historical Theologians* (1968). For background see Hugh Ross Mackintosh, *Types of Modern Theology: Schleiermacher to Barth* (1937).

Additional Sources

Drescher, Hans-Georg, *Ernst Troeltsch: his life and work,* Minneapolis: Fortress Press, 1993. □

Paul Troger

Paul Troger (1698-1762) was an Austrian painter whose highly dramatic style and use of light colors, particularly in his frescoes, dominated Austrian painting about the middle of the 18th century and profoundly influenced succeeding generations.

Paul Troger was born on Oct. 30, 1698, at Welsberg, near Zell, in the Tirol. There, at the age of 16, under the patronage of the Firmian family, he studied art with Giuseppe Alberti. Then, with the help of the prince-bishop of Gurk, Troger went to Venice, where he was influenced by the new developments in painting sparked by Giovanni Battista Piazzetta, Sebastiano Ricci, and Giovanni Battista Pittoni. Troger also studied in Rome, Naples, and Bologna, the leading artistic centers of Italy at the time, where the works of the Caracci, Luca Giordano, and Giuseppe Maria Crespi were also important for his development.

On his return to Austria, Troger first worked at Salzburg. He then moved to Vienna permanently, where he soon joined the Academy of Fine Arts. By 1751 he was a professor at the academy, and in 1754 its head. As a teacher, he was a dominant influence on large numbers of students there; the painters Franz Sigrist, Franz Karl Palko, and Franz Anton Maulbertsch were among his pupils.

Although Troger did many easel paintings, it was for his frescoes that he was famous and much in demand throughout the Austrian lands. Noteworthy among them are his ceilings in the Marble Hall and the Library of the monastery of Melk (1732-1733), the *Apotheosis of Charles VI as Apollo* over the main stairway at the abbey of Göttweig (1739), and frescoes in other large monastic buildings of Austria— Altenburg, Zwettl, Seitenstetten, and Geras. He also painted frescoes in the church of St. Ignatius in Györ, Hungary (1744; 1747), the ceiling of the Cathedral of Brixen (now

Bressanone, Italy; 1748-1750), and the dome of the pilgrimage church of Maria Dreieichen near Vienna (1752).

Troger's frescoes are noteworthy for their immense vitality of movement and color; done with supreme illusionism, they seem to wipe out the ceiling and present the viewer with a celestial vision of startling reality. His most important contribution to Austrian painting, noted by his contemporaries, was his rejection of the strong dark colors of the beginning of the 18th century in favor of an increasingly lighter palette, typical of the rococo, known as his *leichte Manier*. He never totally abandoned his essentially Tyrolese naturalism, however, and even in mythological and allegorical subjects he introduced realistic detail. His painting adapted the colorful idealism of Johann Michael Rottmayr to the new taste of the rococo and presaged the highly idiosyncratic and emotional painting of the young Maulbertsch.

Further Reading

The authoritative monograph on Troger by Wanda Aschenbrenner (1965) is in German. In English, only two works deal with Troger at any length: Nicholas Powell, *From Baroque to Rococo* (1959), and Eberhard Hempel, *Baroque Art and Architecture in Central Europe* (1965). □

Anthony Trollope

The English novelist Anthony Trollope (1815-1882) wrote a series of novels that chronicle the everyday life of middle-class Victorians. Quietly humorous and at times satirical, his works reveal the vigorous and modest good nature of their author.

After the depressions and near-revolutions of the 1840s, England entered a period of peace and plenty that lasted from 1850 to about 1870. Anthony Trollope's fiction mirrors the Establishment of that period—comfortably off, even wealthy; concerned with individual morality; and relatively unaware of how private virtues and vices interact with public issues.

Trollope was born on April 24, 1815. His mother, Frances Trollope (1780-1863), was the author of *The Domestic Manners of the Americans* (1832) and many novels. He was a large, awkward, shy boy who developed into a burly, vigorous, even boisterous man. He went to school at Winchester and Harrow, but he was a very poor student. When he was 19 years old, he went to work in London as a clerk in the Post Office.

In 1841 Trollope volunteered to become a postal inspector in Ireland. He then took up hunting and followed the sport for many years. In 1844 he married Rose Heseltine; they had two sons. To add to his income Trollope wrote *The Macdermots of Ballycloran* (1847) and *The Kellys and the O'Kellys* (1848), two novels about Ireland; and *La Vendée* (1850), a novel set in Bruges during the French Revolution. None of these books was successful.

Barsetshire Novels

From 1851 to 1853 Trollope inspected post offices in southern England. In Salisbury in 1851 he conceived the idea for *The Warden* (1855), a novel about clerical life in a cathedral town, the first of his Barsetshire novels. It was followed by *Barchester Towers* (1857), in which two of the series's most popular figures—the Bishop and Mrs. Proudie—made their first appearance. These wise, humorous, and gentle novels presented the Victorian middle class without the preaching of Charles Kingsley's *Alton Locke* (1850) and other "sociological" novels and without the sensational events recorded in novels by Charles Dickens, Wilkie Collins, and Charles Reade. The Barsetshire series, successful financially and critically, was completed by *Doctor Thorne* (1858), *Framley Parsonage* (1861), *The Small House at Allington* (1864), and *The Last Chronicle of Barset* (1867).

Many of the Barsetshire characters appear in more than one novel, growing older from novel to novel and revealing new but not inconsistent aspects of their personalities. Barsetshire itself was so vividly imagined that readers have published maps of this make-believe country. The series may have ended because Trollope's readers let him know they were growing tired of it.

Other Novels

In 1858-1859 Trollope was sent by the Post Office to Egypt, Scotland, and the West Indies and, in 1861, to the United States. From these journeys he developed stories and travel books. In 1859 Trollope was promoted to chief inspector of the Post Office, and he then moved his family from Ireland to England. In 1860 he met Kate Field, a young American with whom he had a fatherly relationship, and William Makepeace Thackeray, whose novels he admired and about whom he wrote a memoir (*Thackeray,* 1879). In 1867 Trollope resigned from the Post Office and made a second trip to the United States. Wherever he went, he kept at his writing. In all, he wrote 47 novels, in addition to short stories, travel books, hunting sketches, biographies, and other volumes.

Can You Forgive Her? (1864) began a series of political novels that includes *Phineas Finn* (1869), *The Eustace Diamonds* (1873), *Phineas Redux* (1874), *The Prime Minister* (1876), and *The Duke's Children* (1880). The characters in this series develop as they do in the Barsetshire novels, especially Plantagenet Palliser, who is seen as a young man in the first novel and as a widower in the last.

Most of Trollope's novels are good-natured, but *The Way We Live Now* (1875) is not. This novel is a scathing satire of England in the 1870s, greedy for money while on the edge of moral bankruptcy. This novel seems to reveal a Trollope different from the author of the Barsetshire stories. The author, however, is the man he always was; his story is now about a different England.

Trollope was a methodical writer. He began writing as early as 5:30 in the morning and before breakfast entered in a diary kept for each of his novels, beginning with *Barchester Towers,* the number of pages he had written. He wrote aboard ship or on a train. When he finished a novel, he turned it over to his publisher and promptly began another. His method of working made him liable to the charge of being a mechanical rather than a methodical writer. However, his steady output was the result of pondering the characters and situations of a projected book while traveling or during intervals in his business day.

Last Years

Trollope's *Autobiography,* written in 1875-1876 but not published until 1883, the year after his death, revealed his method of writing and caused a decline in his reputation. Only in the 20th century was his reputation restored. The *Autobiography* presents an older and sadder man—but not an essentially different one—than the Trollope who commented upon his characters in the Barsetshire novels.

After resigning from the Post Office, Trollope traveled for pleasure. He continued to write during each journey. He suffered a stroke and after a short illness died on Dec. 6, 1882.

Further Reading

Trollope's *Autobiography* (1883; many subsequent editions) is a valuable self-portrait but an underestimation of his abilities. Michael Sadleir, *Trollope: A Commentary* (1927), undoubtedly the best biography, presents him as a healthy, normal man content with the life around him and happy to create the illusion of it in his books. Lucy Poate Stebbins and Richard Stebbins, *The Trollopes: The Chronicle of a Writing Family* (1945), analyzes Trollope as an unhappy man who betrayed his talent and revealed his embitterment in his *Autobiography*. The best critical study is Bradford A. Booth, *Anthony Trollope: Aspects of His Life and Art* (1958), which mediates these views. Walter E. Houghton, *The Victorian Frame of Mind, 1830-1870* (1957), is an excellent presentation of historical background.

Additional Sources

Glendinning, Victoria, *Anthony Trollope,* New York: Knopf: Distributed by Random House, 1993.

Hall, N. John, *Trollope: a biography,* Oxford; New York: Oxford University Press, 1993.

Mullen, Richard, *Anthony Trollope: a Victorian in his world,* Savannah: F.C. Beil; 1992.

Snow, C. P. (Charles Percy), *Trollope, his life and art,* New York: Scribner, 1975.

Super, R. H. (Robert Henry), *The chronicler of Barsetshire: a life of Anthony Trollope,* Ann Arbor: University of Michigan Press, 1988.

Super, R. H. (Robert Henry), *Trollope in the Post Office,* Ann Arbor: University of Michigan Press, 1981.

Trollope, Anthony, *An illustrated autobiography: including How the "Mastiffs" went to Iceland,* Wolfeboro, N.H.: A. Sutton, 1987.

Terry, R. C. (Reginald Charles), *Trollope: interviews and recollections,* New York: St. Martin's Press, 1987. □

Leon Trotsky

The Russian revolutionist Leon Trotsky (1879-1940) was a principal leader in the founding of the Soviet Union. He played an important role in the October Revolution, which brought the Bolsheviks to power; and he organized the Red Army during the ensuing civil war.

Leon Trotsky was born Lev Davidovich Bronstein near Elisavetgrad (later Kirovograd). He derived from an almost completely Russified Jewish family that lived in the province of Kherson, in the small town of Yanovka. His father, David Leontievich Bronstein, had by dint of hard labor grown fairly prosperous as a farmer, but his uncultured middle-class family lived an extremely simple life. At the age of 7 the boy was sent to a Jewish private religious school in the nearby town of Gromokla. Since he knew no Yiddish, his stay was brief and unhappy but nonetheless valuable, for he learned to read and write Russian.

Shortly after his return home, a cousin, Moisey Filippovich Shpenster, arrived at the Bronstein household to recuperate from an illness. He played the role of tutor to Lyova (Lev's nickname) and when it came time for him to return to Odessa, Lyova returned with him.

In Odessa, Lyova attended a preparatory class for an entire year. At St. Paul's Realschule he quickly overcame his early deficiencies and rose to the head of his class. Seven years in Odessa expanded the already existing differences between father and son. For some reason David Bronstein decided to have his son finish his last academic year in the nearby seaport of Nikolaev instead of in Odessa. Here Lyova had his first contacts with the Russian revolutionary movement.

Revolutionary Activities and First Exile

A relatively large concentration of old exiles of the group called Narodnaia Volia (The People's Will) lived in this small town. Lyova became acquainted with this circle through Franz Shvigovsky, a gardener who played a prominent role in a small discussion club. One member of this Narodnik group, Alexandra Sokolovskaya, considered herself a Marxist and was almost immediately opposed by the 17-year-old Lyova. He knew almost nothing of Marxist doctrine, but his ability as an orator and his intellectual prowess soon made him the focal point of the group. The more involved he became, the more his schoolwork declined, although he graduated in 1897 with first-class honors.

As news of strikes began to grow, Lyova found himself becoming more and more inclined toward Marxism. This period saw the formation of the South Russian Workers' Union. The clandestine activities of its members were for the most part harmless, but police spies successfully infiltrated the group. After an extended period of interrogation, Bronstein was exiled to Siberia for 4 years by administrative verdict. While awaiting deportation, he first heard of V. I. Lenin and his book *The Development of Capitalism in Russia.* Before leaving, Bronstein married Alexandra Sokolovskaya.

During his stay in Verkholensk, Bronstein began forming his ideas on national coordination and on centralized party leadership. In a little-known essay he composed his thoughts on the subject, and the result was an organizational scheme that practically paralleled that of the Bolsheviks, of whom he later was so critical. He also turned to literary criticism, but the young revolutionary grew restless. Urged on by his wife, he escaped after 4½ years of prison and exile.

Exile and Formulation of Theory

The name on Bronstein's false passport was Trotsky, a name that remained with him. He joined Lenin in London in October and began writing for *Iskra*. Trotsky shared his quarters with V. I. Zasulich and J. Martov and drew closer to these two than to Lenin. Only Georgi Plekhanov showed any dislike for Trotsky. The split among the *Iskra* editors was already taking shape, and Trotsky became the special focus of Plekhanov's scorn.

In July 1903 at Brussels the Second Congress of the Russian Social Democratic Workers' Party produced, instead of one party, two. Trotsky emerged as Lenin's most implacable opponent on the question of the organization of the party. Despite his early writings favoring a high degree of centralization, Trotsky sided with Martov and the Mensheviks in favoring a broader-based party. Plekhanov had sided with Lenin, but their relationship was a fragile one. When Plekhanov invited the Iskra board to return, Lenin broke with the editorial staff completely. Trotsky returned, but Plekhanov's dislike of him only grew. Thus began Trotsky's estrangement from the Menshevik wing of the party. No rapprochement, however, with Lenin was forthcoming.

Suspended between both factions, Trotsky came under the influence of A. L. Helfand, whose pen name was Parvus. Under this influence Trotsky adopted a theory of "permanent revolution" that called for a telescoping of the bourgeois revolution into a socialist one that would carry far beyond Russia's borders. An important basis for this concept was the recognition by Helfand, Trotsky, and Lenin that Russia, far from having been a feudal country, was an Asiatic despotism, with the consequence that Russia's cities, unlike those of the West, had not produced an advanced entrepreneurial bourgeois elite. This made it unlikely, in Trotsky's view, that a sophisticated capitalist development would occur in Russia, and thus it was unprofitable to rely on such development as a basis for revolution. Trotsky argued that the revolution should result in the immediate establishment of the dictatorship of the proletariat (meaning power for its vanguard, the Communist elite). The question of whether such a "permanent" or telescoped revolution could be attempted without a great risk of reestablishing the old bureaucratic despotism under Communist leadership preoccupied the Fourth (or Unity) Party Congress in Stockholm in 1906. Lenin offered certain relative guarantees against this Asiatic restoration (no police, no standing army, no bureaucracy, to avoid turning the proletarian dictatorship into a bureaucratic despotism) and an absolute guaran-

tee of a socialist revolution in the West to follow the establishment of Communist power in Russia.

The first news of "Bloody Sunday," the outbreak of the 1905 Revolution, found Trotsky in Geneva. After a brief respite at Parvus's home, Trotsky went to Kiev in February. With the end of those hectic days at the beginning of the year, revolutionary turmoil abated, and Trotsky, under the assumed name of Peter Petrovich, moved in and out of the clandestine circles of St. Petersburg.

October 1905 Revolution and Second Exile

In the middle of October 1905 a general strike broke out in St. Petersburg, and Trotsky hurriedly returned to the capital from Finland. On the first day of his return he appeared at the Soviet, which had assembled at the Technological Institute. He was elected to the Executive Committee of the Soviet of St. Petersburg as the chief representative of the Menshevik wing and played the dominant role in the brief life of this new type of institution. For his part in the Revolution of 1905 Trotsky was exiled to Siberia in 1907 for life with the loss of all his civil rights. On the trip to Siberia, he decided to escape. His second exile lasted 10 years, until the February Revolution of 1917.

At the London Congress in April 1907, Trotsky maintained his position of aloofness and implored both sides to coalesce in the name of unity. For the next 7 years he lived with his second wife in Vienna, where he made the acquaintance of Rosa Luxemburg, Karl Kautsky, Rudolph Hilferding, Eduard Bernstein, Otto Bauer, Max Adler, and Karl Renner. It did not take long for Trotsky to become aware of the differences between "his" Marxism and theirs. He became the editor of a Viennese paper called *Pravda*. In August 1912 he organized in Vienna a conference of all Social Democrats, hoping that this would lead to a reconciliation, but Lenin's refusal to attend was a severe disappointment. An August bloc consisting of Mensheviks, Bolshevik dissenters, the Jewish Bund, and Trotsky's followers was formed.

With the outbreak of World War I Trotsky left Vienna for Zurich in order to avoid internment. The question of the war and the Zimmerwald Conference seemed to draw Lenin and Trotsky closer together, and, conversely, Trotsky and the August bloc seemed to become less and less amicable. Parvus's stand on the war also conflicted with Trotsky's internationalism, and their friendship was ended on Trotsky's initiative.

Return to Russia

In September 1916 Trotsky was deported from France, where he had resided during the previous 2 years. On Jan. 13, 1917, he landed in New York. By mid-March the first news of the Revolution began to arrive. He took a negative view of the new government almost immediately. Certainly his stand was firmer on this issue than Stalin's. Trotsky's differences with Lenin were indeed growing less severe. With his family, Trotsky attempted to return to Russia, but he was removed from his ship at Halifax by British authorities, who forced him to remain in Canada for an entire month. Not until May 4 did he finally arrive in Petrograd.

Trotsky assumed the leadership of the Interborough Organization, a temporary body composed of many prominent personalities opposed to the "war, Prince Lvov, and the social patriots." At the Bolshevik party's Sixth Congress in July-August, Trotsky led the entire group into Lenin's fold even though at this time he was in prison as the result of the abortive July coup. With the growth of Bolshevik strength in Soviet representation, the Petrograd Soviet elected Trotsky as its chairman on September 23. He had also been raised to Central Committee status during his prison term.

Trotsky and Lenin prodded the Bolsheviks on to revolution over the objections of such men as Lev Kamenev, Trotsky's brother-in-law, and Grigori Zinoviev, and Trotsky alone forged the "machinery of insurrection." He scurried from meeting to meeting agitating whoever would listen. By his own estimate no more than 25,000 or 30,000 (the actual number was probably less) took part in the final coup, a testament to his organizational ability.

People's Commissar

In the Soviet government founded by Lenin after the coup, Trotsky was given the position of people's commissar for foreign affairs. He also led the Soviet delegation at the Brest-Litovsk Peace Conference. While he negotiated, Karl Radek distributed pamphlets among German soldiers designed to provoke unrest in the enemy camp.

The German demands were so extensive that the Bolshevik party split over the question of war or peace. Lenin was almost alone in wanting to accept the terms dictated by the Germans. Profound disagreement had existed between Lenin and Trotsky on the question of Brest-Litovsk, but Lenin convinced Trotsky once again to approach the Germans for terms. This time the terms were even more unfavorable, but again Lenin persuaded Trotsky to side with the peace faction. Trotsky cast the deciding vote in favor of signing the highly unfavorable Treaty of Brest-Litovsk.

Although Trotsky had resigned as commissar of foreign affairs he was immediately appointed to the post of commissar for war. In that capacity he rebuilt the Red Army and directed the campaigns on four fronts during the civil war. Despite wholesale opposition throughout the Bolshevik party, he persisted in the use of former czarist officers, buttressed by a system of political commissars and terror. From a force of fewer than 10,000 reliable armed soldiers in October 1917, he had built an army numbering more than 5 million 2½ years later. He alone proved capable of imposing centralization upon a highly fragmented force.

Toward the end of the civil war in 1920, Trotsky proposed that the machinery for military mobilization be employed for the organization of civilian labor. Civilian labor was to be subjected to military discipline, and the army was to be reorganized on the basis of productive units. Lenin wholeheartedly supported Trotsky's suggestions. Trotsky's strong-arm methods in shaping the army and in forcing industrial production created a large number of bitter enemies who were soon to be heard from.

Opposition to Stalin

From Lenin's death in 1924 until Trotsky's exile in 1928, Trotsky fought a long, hard, and losing battle against Stalin, who cultivated the many enemies that Trotsky had made as a revolutionary. Despite the fact that Lenin in his last testament seemed to favor Trotsky over Stalin and even had proposed removing Stalin from power, Trotsky proved no match for Stalin. The plethora of positions that Stalin had attained, some important and some not so important but all with patronage, strengthened his position and undermined the power of his opposition. In the final analysis, Trotsky had only his personal brilliance and the army as bases for power, the latter without its crucial political control apparatus. Stalin not only controlled a variety of organizations, but he skillfully appealed to the class interest of the new bureaucratic elite and decisively asserted his claim to Lenin's mantle at the funeral of the dead founder and in the *Foundations of Leninism,* published in early 1924. Trotsky did not bother to attend Lenin's funeral.

Exile and Assassination

Trotsky allied himself with the so-called left opposition of Kamenev and Zinoviev; but Stalin successfully opposed him by breaking up the alliance, aided by Nikolai Bukharin and the right wing of the party. After his defeat Trotsky was expelled from the party, and in 1928 he was exiled to Alma-Ata in Central Asia. Forced to flee the Soviet Union, he went first to Turkey, then to France and Norway, and finally to Mexico. Throughout his sojourn he continued to attack Stalin, returning to his early critical themes of bureaucratic centralism and one-man dictatorship. Implacable as he was in his criticism, Trotsky did not draw on the most powerful polemical weapon available to him: that the cause of socialism had been lost in an "Asiatic restoration," through the consolidation of a new bureaucratic despotism under Stalin. That would have meant the rejection of Soviet communism and the party. Trotsky, unable to do so, could attack only Stalin and his policies.

On Aug. 20, 1940, Trotsky was mortally wounded in Mexico City by an ice ax wielded by Ramon Mercador, a Soviet assassin talked into this crime, according to one account, by his mother, who held the Order of Lenin for masterminding assassinations for the Soviet secret police.

Further Reading

Trotsky wrote his memoirs in exile, *My Life: An Attempt at an Autobiography* (1930; trans. 1930). His vivid *History of the Russian Revolution* (3 vols., 1931-1933; trans., 3 vols., 1932) recounts his role in the Revolution. Isaac Deutscher's superb biographical trilogy will probably remain the standard work on Trotsky for many years: *The Prophet Armed: Trotsky, 1879-1921* (1954); *The Prophet Unarmed: Trotsky, 1921-1929* (1959); and *The Prophet Outcast: Trotsky, 1929-1940* (1963).

Countless studies of the Russian revolutionary movement and the Revolution exist. Among the best are William Henry Chamberlin, *The Russian Revolution, 1917-1921* (1935); Adam B. Ulam, *The Bolsheviks: The Intellectual and Political History of the Triumph of Communism in Russia* (1965); Robert V. Daniels, *Red October: The Bolshevik Revolution of 1917*

(1967); and Richard Pipes, ed., *Revolutionary Russia: A Symposium* (1968).

Recommended for general background are Edward Hallett Carr, *A History of Soviet Russia* (9 vols., 1951-1971); Lionel Kochan, *Russia in Revolution, 1890-1918* (1966); and Adam B. Ulam, *Expansion and Coexistence: The History of Soviet Foreign Policy, 1917-67* (1968). □

Mildred Trotter

Anatomist Mildred Trotter's pioneering bone studies contributed to a wide range of disciplines, including medicine, forensics, engineering, and aeronautics. In 1952, Trotter (1899-1991) formulated a method for using bone length to estimate the height of the body it came from; this proved to be useful for forensic experts.

Mildred Trotter was an anatomist and physical anthropologist whose pioneering bone studies contributed to a wide range of disciplines, including medicine, forensics, engineering, and aeronautics. "She has been responsible for the largest single increase in our knowledge of bone, both as a tissue and as the primary locus of the mineral mass of the human body," observed Dr. Stanley M. Garn, professor of nutrition at the University of Michigan. Her method for using the length of certain bones to estimate the height of their owners in life has been a primary tool of forensic experts and physical anthropologists since its formulation in 1952. Also, her studies of human hair have disproved many popular myths and contributed to the understanding of hypertrichosis, or excessive hair growth.

Trotter was born on February 3, 1899, to farmers of German and Irish extraction. James R. and Jennie (nee Zimmerley) Trotter also produced two other daughters, Sarah Isabella and Jeannette Rebecca, and a son, Robert James. Trotter's parents were active Presbyterians and Democrats, and, in addition to farming, her father served for a time as community school director. Trotter attended grammar school in a one-room facility, graduating in 1913. She completed high school in nearby Beaver, Pennsylvania, where, as her hometown paper would report in a career retrospective, the principal objected to her choice of geometry over home economics as a subject for study.

Trotter enrolled at Mt. Holyoke College where she majored in zoology. While there she found role models in female professors and the zoology department head. In an interview late in life, Trotter recalled that she "never even thought, let alone worried, about being a woman in science" as a result of their influence. Upon graduating, Trotter rejected a better paying job as a high school biology teacher to work as a research assistant to Dr. C. H. Danforth, an associate professor of anatomy at Washington University in St. Louis, Missouri. Danforth had received funding to study hypertrichosis from an anonymous donor whose wife and daughters suffered from excessive facial hair. Trotter's work

on the subject earned her credit toward a masters degree in anatomy, which she received in 1921. After the donor pledged more funds, she continued her study of hair, using it as the basis of her doctoral thesis in 1924. As a result of her analysis, Trotter determined that hair follicles keep to fixed patterns of growth, resting, and shedding; she also discovered that women have as much facial hair as men. In addition she disproved such common myths as the belief that sun exposure cures baldness or that shaving thickens hair. Trotter's collected papers on hair were published serially, then in book form by the American Medical Association in 1925 under Danforth's name.

Upon completing her studies, Trotter was made an instructor at Washington University. Not long afterwards, she accepted a National Research Council Fellowship to study physical anthropology at Oxford for the year 1926. Although she had planned to continue her research on hair, she was asked instead to study bones, specifically museum specimens from ancient Egypt and Roman era Britain. During the course of her stay at Oxford, Trotter discovered that she "liked studying skeletons better than studying hair." When she received yet another fellowship, the head of Washington's anatomy department offered her a promotion to assistant professor, which she accepted over the grant. Her career stalled, however, despite a steadily increasing workload, and she did not receive another promotion until sixteen years later when she straightforwardly asked the department chair to explain why she had been passed over. He responded by convening a review committee, and in 1946 Trotter became the first woman to attain full professorship at Washington University's Medical School. In all, Trotter spent over fifty-five years on the university's staff, during which time she published numerous papers on the human skeleton, including studies of growth cycles, sexual and racial differences, and changes in mineral mass and density occurring with age.

In 1948 Trotter, growing restless in her position at the university, took an unpaid sabbatical to volunteer as director of the Central Identification Laboratory at Schofield Barracks, Oahu, Hawaii. For the next fourteen months she and her team identified the skeletal remains of war dead found in the Pacific theater. During this time she also secured permission from the U.S. Army to conduct allometric studies using the long limb bones of identified dead, one of the first times that war casualties were used for scientific research. From these studies Trotter then devised a formula for estimating the stature of a person based upon the relative length of the long bones. Published in 1952, her update of nineteenth-century French stature estimation tables was described in a 1989 *Journal of Forensic Sciences* article as "a landmark study in physical anthropology."

Trotter returned to Washington University in 1949. Soon after, the new department chair eliminated the adjective "gross" from her title Professor of Anatomy—an important distinction to Trotter who had fought to be accepted as an equal in a field dominated by microscopic research. During the 1950s and 1960s Trotter began attracting national and international attention for her work. In 1955 she was asked to serve as president of the American Association of Physical Anthropologists, an organization she helped found in 1930. A year later she became the first female recipient of the Wenner-Gren Foundation's Viking Fund Medal. She was asked by the editors of *Encyclopedia Britannica* to contribute entries on the skin and exoskeleton for their 1953 and 1956 editions. In addition she gathered material for reference books in her field, such as a lab guide, an anatomical atlas, and a dictionary of Latin nomenclature. Trotter also served as a consultant to the Rockefeller Foundation, lecturing in London and Washington, D.C., and as a visiting professor to Uganda's Makerere University College.

Along with her academic responsibilities, Trotter also sat on the St. Louis Anatomical Board and Missouri State Anatomical Board, serving as president of the latter from 1955 to 1957. St. Louis detectives regularly consulted with Trotter on missing persons and "John Doe" cases as well as on partial, sometimes nearly obliterated, physical evidence. For example, when police recovered a handful of blackened bones from a furnace, Trotter identified them as being from a human infant, not a small animal as originally suspected. She was also instrumental in passing legislation that enabled Missourians to donate their bodies to universities for medical research. When asked in 1980 about her practical approach to such morbid subjects, Trotter observed, "the attitude of our culture toward death is silly. We all know we have to die."

Trotter's work as an instructor proved as important as her research. During her forty-one year career as a full-time professor at Washington University, Trotter's students totaled into the thousands. Hundreds went on to careers as medical school faculty, prepared by her rigorous coursework. As Dr. John C. Herweg recalled in 1975, "we learned because we admired and respected her and because, to an extent, we feared her. After we had passed Gross Anatomy, we grew to love her as a friend." Her belief that students should learn not from books but from observing nature guided Trotter's instruction. "Learning to observe is one of the chief benefits of studying anatomy," she asserted during an interview in 1975. Two of Trotter's students, Earl Sutherland and Daniel Nathans, went on to win Nobel Prizes in medicine.

Upon her retirement in 1967, Trotter was named professor emeritus and lecturer in anatomy and neurobiology. She continued to publish scientific papers, and eight years later she became the first female faculty member to be honored by the medical school with a lectureship in her name. Trotter, who never married, spent leisure time in later years knitting, gardening, or auditing classes at the university until she suffered a disabling stroke. Upon her death on August 23, 1991, her body was donated to the Washington University School of Medicine.

Further Reading

Kerley, Ellis R., "Forensic Anthropology: Increasing Utility In Civil and Criminal Cases," in *Trial,* January, 1983, pp. 66–111.

Wood, W. Raymond and Lori Ann Stanley, "Recovery and Identification of World War II Dead: American Graves Registration Activities in Europe," in *Journal of Forensic Sciences,* Volume 34, 1989, pp. 1365–1373.

Trotter Papers, Resource & Research Center for Beaver County & Local History, Inc., Carnegie Free Library, Beaver Falls, PA.

Trotter Papers, Washington University School of Medicine Library Archives, St. Louis, MO. □

William Monroe Trotter

William Monroe Trotter (1872-1934), African American newspaper editor and protest leader, was the first prominent challenger of the accommodationist leadership of Booker T. Washington.

Illiam Monroe Trotter was born on April 7, 1872, in Springfield Township, Ohio. His father, James, the son of a Mississippi slave-owner, rose from private to second lieutenant in the all-Black Massachusetts 55th Regiment during the Civil War. His mother, Virginia Issacs, claimed descent from Thomas Jefferson.

James Trotter settled in Massachusetts soon after the war, but after his first two children died in infancy the family decided to give birth to their third child in rural Ohio. At seven months young William and his parents moved back to Boston where they settled on the South End, far from the predominately African American West Side. The family later moved to suburban Hyde Park, a white neighborhood.

The elder Trotter instilled independence and racial pride in his children. James Trotter had been among the most outspoken supporters of the principle of equal pay for African American troops during the Civil War and was an outspoken critic of American racial injustice. He was also a leader among a small coterie of African American Democrats at a time when the vast majority of African Americans were Republican, and President Cleveland appointed him recorder of deeds for the District of Columbia, the highest political office accorded African Americans.

Despite the comfortable existence that federal service provided the Trotters, young William was admonished to excel as a way of breaking down racial barriers, and his father told him that if he were beaten in a fight with one of his white friends, he could expect another when he returned home. His childhood, however, seems remarkably free of racial incidents, and he was valedictorian and president of his high school class.

Trotter graduated *magna cum laude* and Phi Beta Kappa from Harvard University in 1895 and took an M.A. a year later. He had hoped to go into international banking, but even his impressive credentials opened few doors. Thwarted by race, Trotter settled on a career in real estate. In 1899 he married Geraldine Louise Pindell, whose uncle had led the fight to integrate Boston schools in the 1850s.

Trotter had participated in ceremonies and discussion groups commemorating various aspects of African American history in Boston, but it quickly became clear that he had an affinity for protest and agitation. He "did not seek a career of agitation," he later remarked (writing in the third person), the "burden was dropped upon him by the desertion of others and he would not desert duty." In 1901, with an official of the West End branch of the Boston Public Library named George Forbes as his partner, Trotter founded the Boston *Guardian* on the same floor of the same building that had housed William Lloyd Garrison's *Liberator.*

The symbolism was unmistakable. Trotter and Forbes clearly saw themselves as the new abolitionists, direct legatees of those who battled for African American rights in the pre-Civil War era. Their principal target was Booker T. Washington, who "literally shriveled" before it. *Guardian* cartoons lampooned Washington as an errand boy for Northern philanthropists and its pages were filled with anti-BTW editorials and letters. "Let our spiritual advisors," Trotter wrote, "condemn this idea of reducing a people to serfdom to make them good."

In 1903 when Washington went to Boston to give an address, Trotter and his allies heckled the Southern educator and prevented him from speaking. Several anti-Bookerites were subsequently arrested, and Trotter served 30 days in the Charles Street jail. But it was a Pyrrhic victory for BTW. Trotter's sentence aroused sympathy among other African American newspaper editors and awakened public awareness to the fact that there were those opposed to Washington's conciliatory public policy.

But it was W.E. B. DuBois, not Trotter, who emerged as Washington's most prominent critic. Trotter and DuBois were contemporaries at Harvard and briefly worked together as leaders of the Niagara Movement, a group of African American intellectuals critical of Booker T. Washington. But Trotter withdrew to form the National Equal Rights League and later refused to join the newly-formed National Association for the Advancement of Colored People because of his distrust of white leadership. His abrasive style did not endear him to other African American leaders, and his singlemindedness and inability to compromise was labelled fanaticism by his critics.

In 1912 Trotter endorsed Democrat Woodrow Wilson for the presidency, but the new president repaid his African American support by segregating African American workers in the federal government. Trotter led a delegation of African Americans to the White House and for 45 minutes he and Wilson stood toe to toe and debated the president's action. Wilson lost his temper, offended by Trotter's "manner" and "tone, with its background of passion," and banned Trotter from the White House for the rest of his term.

During World War I, when a delegation of African Americans sought to attend the Versailles conference to protest the treatment of African Americans, Wilson denied them visas. Trotter circumvented the ban by securing passage to France as a ship's cook and jumping ship once it arrived in Europe.

In 1922, 1923, 1924, and 1926 Trotter led delegations of African Americans to the White House to protest continued segregation in the federal government. He also led demonstrations and pickets against the racist *Birth of a Nation,* defended the Scottsboro Boys, and crusaded for a Crispus Attucks day to honor the African American hero of the Revolutionary War. But his influence clearly declined during the 1920s, and in the last years of his life he felt ignored and unappreciated. In 1934, on the night of his 62nd birthday, he fell or jumped to his death from the roof of his home.

Trotter was largely overshadowed by his more illustrious contemporaries, W. E. B. DuBois and Booker T. Washington. Unable or unwilling to compromise, Trotter tended to personalize differences, and he lacked a coherent program and the organizational skills to launch a successful political movement. But he was the first African American leader to employ the tactics of direct action and group confrontation to achieve racial ends and an authentic pioneer of the 20th-century African American protest tradition.

Further Reading

The only major biography of William Monroe Trotter to date is *The Guardian of Boston* (1971) by Stephen B. Fox. Lerone Bennett devotes a chapter to Trotter in *Pioneers in Protest* (1968), and a brief biographical sketch may be found in the *Dictionary of American Negro Biography* (1983), edited by Rayford Logan and Michael Winston. □

Garretson Beekman Trudeau

Garretson Beekman (Garry) Trudeau (born 1948) was a comic-strip cartoonist, Pulitzer Prize-winning creator of "Doonesbury," playwright, and animated cartoon-maker for film and television.

G arry Trudeau was born in New York to parents of Canadian ancestry. When he was five his father, a doctor, moved to Saranac Lake, New York, where Garry spent an idyllic childhood. His parents divorced in 1960, and Garry was sent to St. Paul's school in Concord, Connecticut, where he compensated for the school's over-emphasis on sports by concentrating on art. During his years at Yale University, where he prepared his B.A. and M.F.A. in the School of Art and Architecture, he began to spoof his fellow students and the staff in "Bull Tales," in which most of the antics of the liberated generation were irreverently portrayed.

In 1970 John McNeel and Jim Andrews inaugurated the Universal Press Syndicate by publishing Trudeau's work under the less offensive title of "Doonesbury," a name concocted from the Yale slang for a good-natured fool ("doone") with the last syllable of a roommate's surname. Trudeau's lack of reverence for public persons soon got him into trouble. Indianapolis publisher Eugene Pulliam can-

celed the strip soon after its debut in the Indianapolis *Star,* the Phoenix *Republic,* and the Muncie *Press.* In 1972 it was banned by the editor of the Akron *Beacon Journal,* Perry Morgan, but reinstated after reader protest. An episode in which then Attorney-General Mitchell was declared guilty of Watergate misdemeanors was canceled by Ben Bradlee of the *Washington Post,* by the Los Angeles *Times,* and by the Boston *Globe.* The Providence *Bulletin* moved Doonesbury off the comic pages on to the editorial page, and later there was trouble with the Philadelphia *Bulletin* over the alternation of an offending word.

Despite the controversies, Trudeau was awarded a Pulitzer Prize in 1975 and received a D.H.L. (Doctor of Humane Letters) from Yale in 1976. In 1977 he received an Academy Award nomination and a special jury prize from the Cannes Film Festival for his film "A Doonesbury Special."

He later expanded his activity into theater and television, one of the offerings being a series of television spoofs on the 1988 election campaign: "Tanner, '88." His work has been collected into many albums.

In 1980 he married Jane Pauley, the CBS television show host, and had three children, twins Ross and Rachel and Tom. He was extremely reticent by nature and refused to discuss his private life.

Trudeau's comic strip was considered by some, such as Art Buchwald, as "some of the best satire that has come along in a long time." Michael—"Mike"—Doonesbury, the eponymous figure, is a good-natured, undistinguished fellow with a pencil shaped nose and granny glasses, not too successful with the opposite sex, and generally bemused by the antics of his companions. The cast of characters surrounding him date from the exuberant and unconventional early 1970s in the campus world. Many of them refer to known personalities: "Megaphone" Mark Slackmeyer (activist Mark Zanger), "B.D." (grid star Brian Dowling), the Rev. W. S. Sloan, Jr. (The Rev. William Sloane Coffin, Jr.), Uncle Duke (journalist Hunter S. Thompson), and Congresswoman Lacey Davenport (Millicent Fenwick?). To these are added figures representative of topical groups: Zonker Harris, the hippie; Joanie Caucus, the liberated wife and mother, who abandons her family to go to law school; Virginia, her Black roommate, with her hanger-on lover, the flashy Clyde; Phred, the engaging Vietnamese terrorist; Boopsie, B.D.'s addle-brained sexy girl friend; Honey, Uncle Duke's Chinese admirer; Black Panthers, and a number of precocious children. All of these mingle with and comment on figures currently in the real world, chiefly those involved in political upheaval: Nixon; John Mitchell; James Dean; Gerald Ford ("Snowbunny"); William Simon, the Treasury "Czar"; Kingman Brewster, president of Yale. Ronald Reagan's brain is dissected and found to be equipped only to see a rosy past; George Bush is depicted as an absence surrounding a pair of lips.

In 1983 Trudeau decided to take a leave of absence in order to "graduate" his characters into the 1980s. After 1983, he resumed work with a newly-sharpened pen, taking on such sensitive topics as negligence in the Navy after the

Iowa tragedy, "Star Wars," anti-abortionists, homelessness, and the invasion of Panama.

Trudeau's pungent satire was often seen as offensive chiefly to conservatives, but he was equally unsparing of trendy behavior of any variety: drug dealers and takers, like Uncle Duke; yuppies living in redecorated coldwater attics in New York; ecologists going to the extreme of refusing to diaper their children; house husbands; and two-income parents who hire anyone, such as Zonker, to baby-sit while they pursue their careers. Trudeau did not hesitate to tackle the delicate subject of AIDS and the embarrassed and embarrassing public treatment of the theme. This sequence was withdrawn by the Boston *Globe,* but reinstated because of general protest.

Trudeau's jagged drawing techniques (due in part to the influence of Jules Feiffer) and spidery script did not win much praise from artists, but his penetrating humor was compared to Daumier's. Occasionally an underlying anger—for example, regarding the slaughter of villagers in Vietnam, the plight of Cambodian refugees, or the Kent State massacre—recalls the satire of Defoe. Yet there was less malice than concern in Trudeau's comments. He defended his attacks on our national and social weaknesses by declaring, "Obviously, all of the institutions of this country are understandably imperfect. They are in any society. But it cannot be considered sanity to hide the imperfections from our children so that they will grow up blind to them. Is it not better to tell the truth, even in hyperbole, and hope that they will do some-thing about it?" (response to Sharp Whitmore on the *Iowa* incident).

Trudeau's aim was defined by himself to be "to let the small meannesses of life face each other in distortion, stretched, juggled and juxtaposed, but always lit with laughter to ease the pain of self-recognition; to seek out the vignette that speaks much to the lives of many; to distill and refine language so as to epitomize; and to look everywhere for simple meanings. . . ."

The fact that "Doonesbury" was at both the top and the bottom of opinion polls among comics readers suggests the impact of Trudeau's social criticism. As the 1990s began, Trudeau began working on a new project. The project was a film about AIDS. Trudeau has centered many of his cartoon strips around AIDS. He states that the focus is to create awareness. In 1995 a celebratory book was released by Trudeau called *Flashbacks: Twenty-five Years of Doonesbury.*

Further Reading

World Encyclopedia of Comics (1976), edited by Maurice Horn, places Garry Trudeau in the context of world-class cartoonists and analyzes his comic strip. *Contemporary Literary Criticism* (1980) edited by Dedria Bryfonski and Gerard J. Senick, provides interesting analysis and comment. *Contemporary Authors* (Volumes 81-84), edited by Frances Carol Locher, and *Something About the Author* (Volume 35, 1984), edited by Anne Commire, both offer more recent comments on Trudeau's work. *Who's Who in America* (45th Edition, 1988-1989) contains a recent, but very brief, biography.
Among Trudeau's best-known works are: *Doonesbury* (1971; play, 1983), *The Doonesbury Chronicles* (1975) *Doonesbury's Greatest Hits* (1978), and *Rapmaster Ronnie* (with Elizabeth Swados; 1984). □

Pierre Elliott Trudeau

Pierre Elliott Trudeau (born 1919) was the leader of the Liberal Party and Canada's prime minister for about 15 years. He successfully defeated the separatist movement in Quebec and led Canada both to greater strength nationally and to more independence internationally.

Pierre Elliott Trudeau was born in Montreal, Quebec, on October 18, 1919. The son of a wealthy French-Canadian businessman, Charles Trudeau, and a mother of United Empire Loyalist background, Trudeau received his early education in French, attending the elite College Jean de Brébeuf for eight years. After obtaining his B.A. from Brébeuf in 1940, Trudeau studied law at the University of Montreal; political economy at Harvard; law, economics, and political science at Paris; and political economy at the London School of Economics (1947-1948). He completed his education with a year-long trip around the world on $800 in 1948-1949.

He returned to Quebec in April 1949 and immediately became involved in a strike at Asbestos, where the labor movement in the province confronted a repressive and conservative government of Maurice Duplessis. Although Trudeau did work briefly as an economic adviser to the Privy Council Office in Ottawa in 1950-1951, his major concern in the 1950s was the reform of Quebec society and politics. Together with other Montreal intellectuals and journalists who had been roused to action by the events at Asbestos, Trudeau founded *Cité Libre,* an influential journal of opinion. He also acted as an unpaid legal consultant to Quebec unions, was a counsel in some civil liberty cases, wrote pungent political criticism, and continued to travel widely. He sought to organize the diverse groups opposing Duplessis into a coherent force for political action after 1956. Simultaneously, he flirted with socialist politics. In 1960, however, he supported the Quebec Liberals in the election which traditionally is identified as the beginning of the so-called "Quiet Revolution" in Quebec.

Disillusionment came quickly. In 1961 Trudeau was appointed associate professor of law at the University of Montreal. He continued to take an active part in the ever more lively debate about Quebec's future. While approving of most of the secularizing and modernizing approaches of the Lesage government, he strongly attacked its increasingly nationalist approach, declaring it stifling, irrational, and fundamentally elitist. When nationalism became separatism for many of the young and the intellectuals, Trudeau denounced the trend as reactionary. In the case of the intellectuals it was "treason," a betrayal of the commitment to rationalism and open-mindedness which should mark an intellectual's approach to politics.

Quick Rise in Canadian Politics

Trudeau's anti-separatist position made him turn his attention toward federal politics. His name was mentioned as a possible Liberal candidate in the 1963 general election, but Liberal leader Lester Pearson's acceptance of nuclear weapons for the Canadian armed forces offended Trudeau, who angrily denounced Pearson. The Pearson minority government which came to power in 1963 did win Trudeau's approval for its determined effort to make the federal public service more bicultural and bilingual. Nevertheless, Trudeau thought Pearson was too conciliatory in dealing with the increasingly nationalist Quebec government. When Pearson, on the advice of the Quebec labor leader Jean Marchand, asked Trudeau to run as a Liberal candidate in the general election of 1965, Trudeau quickly agreed.

Pearson made Trudeau his parliamentary secretary in January 1966. His constitutional skills quickly impressed the prime minister and others, and in April 1967 he became minister of justice and attorney general for Canada. In this position he attracted much attention because of his articulate defense of the federal government's position in the debates with the provinces and because of his willingness to undertake reforms in such areas as divorce legislation, criminal law, and judicial appointments. His personal appearance and style, which contrasted sharply with that of other politicians, also focussed media attention upon him. Even though he had been a cabinet minister for only a year, Trudeau was elected Liberal leader and thus became prime minister in 1968.

In the election which followed, so-called "Trudeaumania" swept the country as the media became fascinated with the quick mind, the athletic prowess, the romantic attachments, and the surprising indifference to traditional political concerns of Canada's new prime minister. In the campaign Trudeau promised a new deal for French Canadians in Canada, but no tolerance for separatism or extreme Quebec nationalism. He also indicated that Canada's foreign policy would be reassessed so that domestic interests would be given more weight. Canadians, Trudeau declared, should have the right to participate in making the governmental decisions which most affected their lives. The appeal fit the times.

Trudeau's government undertook a wide-ranging review of Canada's foreign policy. The military commitment to NATO was reduced, and Canadian foreign policy became less sympathetic to the international policies of the United States. Domestically, Trudeau sought constitutional reform without much success, but he did work more fruitfully to secure French Canadian rights within Canadian confederation. His economic policies were surprisingly conservative, although a significant reform in the taxation system did occur in 1971 and unemployment benefits became more generous and more widely available.

Trudeau's personal popularity reached its peak during the so-called October crisis of 1970. The kidnaping of James Cross, a British trade commissioner, and Pierre Laporte, Quebec's labor minister, by extreme separatists in Montreal prompted Trudeau to invoke the War Measures Act which suspended civil liberties so long as there was an "apprehended insurrection" in Montreal. The crisis ended, although Laporte was murdered, and most Canadians applauded Trudeau's forceful stand. Doubts arose later when civil libertarians and others began to question whether such a harsh response was in fact required.

Compromise and Continued Rule

By 1972 Trudeau's position had weakened, and he managed to cling to power after the general election in October only with the help of the socialist New Democratic Party. He quickly adapted his party to the situation and introduced popular, though expensive, legislation. He admitted that he had been too "rational" in his approach to politics, and sadly he concluded that politics was "ninetenths" emotion.

In the 1974 election Trudeau aggressively campaigned as a populist, effectively undercutting the Conservative arguments for wage and price controls. He regained his majority and began to plan for longer range changes in Canadian government. The first effect was a recognized bureaucracy, but various developments undermined his attempts to establish clear directions. In 1975 Trudeau, fearing rampant inflation, introduced the same type of wage and price controls he had denounced in 1974. In 1976 Quebec elected the separatist Parti Québécois, which meant that long range planning gave way to what seemed a profound crisis in nationhood. Perhaps equally important was the breakdown of Trudeau's 1971 marriage to Margaret Sinclair, a separation which received international attention. In the late 1970s the Trudeau government scrambled to maintain its position, and it failed. The Conservatives defeated Trudeau's Liberals in the general election of May 1979.

In November 1979 Trudeau announced that he would step aside for a new leader, but before a new leader could be chosen, the minority Conservative government fell, and a general election was called for February 18, 1980. After some deft manipulation of the party by his friends, Trudeau agreed to remain as leader. He won another majority.

Between 1980 and February 1984, when he announced his resignation, Trudeau provided decisive but controversial leadership. The compromises and hesitations of the 1970s disappeared. The first task was to win the Quebec referendum on separatism. He campaigned vigorously, and the "no" side triumphed decisively. He then moved to "keep the promise" made during the referendum debate to give a new constitution to Quebec and Canada which would include a Charter of Rights. Against the strong opposition of Western Canada, Quebec, and most of the Atlantic provinces, the opposition parties, and leading newspapers, Trudeau pushed ahead his scheme for a new constitution which would be the last act of the United Kingdom Parliament to affect Canada. At the final moment, the provinces, excepting Quebec, agreed to a compromise, and Trudeau's cherished Charter of Rights became part of a fundamentally Canadian constitution.

Trudeau's government also took radical action to deal with the energy crisis of the early 1980s. The National Energy Program was highly nationalistic in aim and tone. Through incentives and taxation benefits it encouraged the growth of Canadian ownership in the energy field. It also set a price for Canadian oil below that on the world market. American investors were infuriated; so were the major producing provinces, Alberta and Saskatchewan. The business community was strongly opposed to what it perceived as an attempt by government to grab most of the oil windfall for itself. Western Canada's bitterness towards Trudeau, which had long persisted, even aroused talk of Western separatism.

The Trudeau Legacy

By 1983 Trudeau's government had become very unpopular. The Conservatives chose a new leader, Brian Mulroney, and moved well ahead of the Liberals in the polls. The constitution was in place, the National Energy Program was collapsing as oil prices fell, and the threat of Quebec separatism had receded. Dissenters in his party began to suggest openly that Trudeau should resign. A "peace initiative" which he began in November 1983 had by the beginning of 1984 accomplished all that could be hoped in the face of the indifference of the superpowers to Trudeau's pleas for cooperation. In February 1984 he announced his intention to resign, and in late June he left the office of the prime minister, giving way to John Turner, who, it seemed clear, was not his choice as successor. In the general election of September 1984 the Liberal Party collapsed, winning only 40 seats compared to 211 seats for the Conservatives.

In his final speech to the Liberal Party in June 1984 Trudeau told his listeners that when Parliament, the bureaucracy, or the media failed to do what was necessary, he had gone directly to the people. With some Canadians Trudeau did fashion a remarkable bond. In others he aroused remarkable antagonism. He dominated his party, his cabinet, and Parliament so long as he was prime minister. When he left, the party fell apart. He had groomed no successor and appeared to care little about what happened after his departure. The party was in a decrepit condition; the nation was weary of the confrontation over energy, the constitution, and foreign policy which it had endured so long. The economy had faltered badly since the early 1970s, and basic restructuring had been postponed too long. Because his personality so fascinated Canadians, Trudeau bore much of the criticism for these apparent failings of the nation. Back in the private sector, in 1985, he became a senior consultant with Heenan, Blaikie. In 1993, he published his *Memoirs,* followed by *The Canadian Way: Shaping Canada's Foreign Policy 1968-1984* (1995), co-authored by Ivan Head. In 1997, Trudeau, along with Jacques Hebert, published *Two Innocents in Red China,* which sparked mixed review.

Only one Canadian prime minister, William Lyon Mackenzie King, served longer than Trudeau. Among post-war democratic leaders, only three were in office for as long. If his faults seemed so clear to his contemporaries, his accomplishments, especially in making Canada a nation that more fully accepts its bicultural nature, will probably mean more to posterity. In a country with so many doubts, the memory of one who had so few will likely grow.

Further Reading

Both Trudeau's *Memoirs* (1993) and his *The Canadian Way* (1995) are autobiographical in nature. He tops the list of Canada's most politically-powerful persons in Anthony Wilson-Smith's *Bench Strength* for *Maclean's* (1996). He is also covered in *Mondo Canuck* (1996), Greig Dymond's and Geoff Pevere's book on Canadian cultural icons. There are two major studies of Trudeau, both by journalists. George Radwanski's *Trudeau* (1978) is based upon extensive interviews with Trudeau and his colleagues. It is largely favorable in tone. Richard Gwyn's *The Northern Magus: Pierre Trudeau and Canadians* (1980) is much more critical. Both books do not cover Trudeau's final years as prime minister. A good sample of Trudeau's early writings is found in his *Federalism and the French Canadians* (1968). □

François Truffaut

The French film director and critic François Truffaut (1932-1984), together with Jean Luc Godard and Alain Resnais, created the "New Wave" in French motion picture production in the late 1950s.

François Truffaut as film maker and esthetician was instrumental in formulating a new cinema language. In its visual spontaneity and narrative discontinuity, the style he helped to originate provided a sharp contrast to the studied academicism of older and established directors. Although elements of his innovative methods can be found in works by his brilliant colleague and early collaborator Jean Luc Godard and in later productions by other directors, few have been able to capture the lyrical warmth, infectious exuberance, and textual luminosity that distinguish the finest of Truffaut's efforts.

Truffaut was born in Paris and spent much of his unhappy childhood working in menial factory and office jobs. Sent by a juvenile court to a reformatory when he was 15 years old, he was rescued from prolonged confinement by the noted film critic André Bazin, who had been impressed with the youth's enthusiasm for motion pictures and his regular attendance at local cinema clubs. After completing service in the French armed forces, Truffaut was introduced by Bazin to the editors of the influential cinema review *Cahiers du cinéma,* where he worked as a critic for the next 8 years.

Truffaut attacked all that was stale and conventional in French films and admired the low-budget American productions that could be undertaken with less pressure on the director from "businessmen." In 1954 he made his directorial debut with a short, *Une Visite,* followed in 1957 by another short, *Les Mistons,* a technically adventurous lyrical idyll of childhood innocence. In collaboration with Godard, he then composed the script for and directed *Une Historie d'eau* (1958), a slapstick comedy reminiscent of early Mack Sennett silents.

The 400 Blows (1959), Truffaut's first full-length film, established him among the most subtly evocative and imaginatively inspired creators of cinema. A touching yet deliberately unsentimental autobiographical work, of an unwanted 13-year-old boy driven to desperation by insensitive parents and tyrannical officials, *The 400 Blows* alternates between subjective lyricism and *cinéma vérité* objectivity. That same year Truffaut provided the original story for Godard's intellectual crime thriller *Breathless.* In 1960 *Shoot the Piano Player* represented Truffaut's tribute to the Hollywood gangster movies of the 1930s. The sardonically amusing plot—a lonely barroom piano player tries to save his two brothers from mobsters they have double-crossed—contains a compendium of "New Wave" cinematic techniques. The film's technical exuberance—such devices as the frozen take, the iris shot, and comic-strip images were employed—reflects a portion of the work's moral and philosophical statement.

With *Jules and Jim* (1961) Truffaut produced the film that most critics consider his finest effort and a cinematic masterpiece. A tragically humorous story of an endearing love triangle, suffused with the nostalgia of its early-20th-century Parisian setting, the film projected, wrote critic Stanley Kauffmann, "an exhilaration, tenderness, wonderful rhythmic variation, understatement, and an un-American innocence-in-sex," which young audiences accepted as a way of life as well as a style of film making.

The Soft Skin (1964), a romantic melodrama about a professor of literature who leaves his wife for an airline stewardess he loves, contained some striking sequences but could not transcend its banality of theme. Even more disappointing was *Fahrenheit 451* (1966), an uninspired science-fiction parable about a future society in which reading is prohibited. *The Bride Wore Black* (1968), a revenge tale, was a rather depressing tribute to Alfred Hitchcock. In 1967 Truffaut published *Hitchcock,* an illuminating analysis of his fellow *auteur.*

Stolen Kisses (1968) was a sequel to *The 400 Blows* and successfully recaptured much of the earlier film's incandescent charm. This film history of the character Antoine Donel was continued in *Bed and Board* (1971), another charming and lightly mocking semiautobiographical effort. The year before, Truffaut wrote, directed, and performed in an austere film relating a doctor's attempts to civilize a child who had grown up in the forest. Based on a true incident, *The Wild Child* was resoundingly successful, showing a new facet of Truffaut's versatile talent.

Truffaut was acclaimed for his rich characterizations of two females in *Two English Girls* (1971), which deals with the relationship between making art and suffering love. *Day for Night* (1973) won an Oscar for Truffaut as a homage to filmmaking. In 1975, he produced *The Story of Adele H.,* in which the daughter of Victor Hugo tells her story, and two years later released *The Man Who Loved Women,* about a hopelessly adolescent hero who encounters sympathetic women. In 1979, Truffaut returned to his series featuring the character Antoine Donel in a movie entitled *Love on the Run.*

Truffaut produced several films in the 1980s, including *The Last Metro* (1980), the story of a theater troupe in Paris during the German occupation. Two films, *The Woman Next Door* (1981) and *Vivement Dimache* (1983) were very heavily influenced by Truffaut's admiration of Alfred Hitchcock, and included the ingredients of suspense, murder and obsessive love.

Truffaut died on Oct. 21, 1984, in Neuilly-sur-Seine, France.

Further Reading

The most perceptive criticism of Truffaut can be found in Pauline Kael, *I Lost It at the Movies* (1965) and *Kiss Kiss Bang Bang* (1968); Stanley Kauffmann, *A World on Film* (1966); the sections on Truffaut in John Russell Taylor, *Cinema Eye, Cinema Ear* (1964) and Dwight MacDonald, *Dwight MacDonald on Movies* (1969); and Annette Insdorf's *François Truffaut* (1979). □

Rafael Leonidas Trujillo Molina

Rafael Leonidas Trujillo Molina (1891-1961) presided for 31 years over what was probably the most absolute and ruthless dictatorship in Latin America at that time. Coming to power in 1930, he controlled the government of the Dominican Republic until he was assassinated.

Rafael Trujillo was born on Oct. 24, 1891, the son of lower-middle-class parents. He received a rudimentary education and then held various jobs. His first step toward his future career was taken on Dec. 9, 1918, when he was accepted for training as an officer in the Constabulary Guard, then being organized by the U.S. Marines, who were occupying the Dominican Republic. Emerging from training, he rose rapidly in the new military organization. Soon after Horacio Vázquez was inaugurated as president in 1924, Trujillo was named second-in-command of the Guard. On June 22, 1925, he became its commander in chief.

Gen. Trujillo came to the presidency as the result of a crisis during the early months of 1930. During a revolt against President Vázquez, Gen. Trujillo remained "neutral." As a result, Vázquez resigned, a provisional government was established, and elections were called. However, real power was in the hands of Trujillo, who proclaimed his candidacy for president. Supporters of his opponent were jailed, beaten up, and killed, thus assuring Trujillo's victory.

Soon after taking office, Trujillo was faced with a major natural disaster, a hurricane that virtually wrecked the capital city, Santo Domingo. He used this incident to place the country under martial law and took energetic steps to clear up the damage, take care of refugees, and start to rebuild the

capital. Six years later the city council of Santo Domingo renamed the city Ciudad Trujillo in honor of this event. This was the first of many honors Trujillo in effect granted to himself. These included renaming half the provinces after him and members of his family, creating numerous decorations of which he was the first and sometimes the only recipient, renaming streets after him throughout the republic, and building numerous monuments in his honor.

Trujillo was in unchallenged control of the government. He served as president from 1930 to 1938, chose a puppet to succeed him then, but returned as president in 1942, remaining until 1954. He then chose his youngest brother, Hector, to occupy the post. In 1960, when the Trujillo regime was under strong international pressure, Hector Trujillo gave way to Vice President Joaquín Balaguer, who served until February 1962, nine months after Rafael Trujillo's death.

Even when out of office, Rafael Trujillo dominated the government. He remained commander in chief of the armed forces. All secret police services reported directly to him. As head of the only legal political party, he sent to Congress the name of a successor to anyone who resigned from that body, according to provisions of one of the several constitutions he had written. He also held the undated resignations of all public officeholders and submitted these when it suited his fancy. As a result, in one 4-year period, there was more than a 200 percent turnover among the members of the Chamber of Deputies.

Trujillo also completely dominated the economy of the country. He allotted various sectors to members of his family. His wife controlled imports and exports; his various brothers dominated radio and television, prostitution, and some manufacturing industries. Trujillo himself concentrated on agriculture, grazing, and industry, forcing all but one of the nation's sugar-producing firms to sell out to him, seizing vast estates from Dominican owners, and including himself as partner in virtually every industrial enterprise in the country. His fortune was estimated in the late 1950s at about $500 million.

Trujillo frequently interfered in the affairs of neighboring countries. When men who had attempted to assassinate Venezuelan president Rómulo Betancourt early in 1960 admitted that they had been sent by Trujillo, a special conference of the Organization of American States proclaimed a partial economic boycott of the Dominican Republic.

On May 30, 1961, Trujillo was assassinated on the outskirts of the Dominican capital. Within 6 months his whole family was in exile, and what he himself had called the Trujillo Era was at an end.

Further Reading

The two best works on Trujillo are Germán E. Ornes, *Trujillo: Little Caesar of the Caribbean* (1958), and Robert D. Crassweller, *Trujillo: The Life and Times of a Caribbean Dictator* (1966), both of which are critical but factual. A very hostile study of his regime is Albert C. Hicks, *Blood in the Streets: The Life and Rule of Trujillo* (1946). Sander Ariza, *Trujillo: The Man and His Country* (1939), and Abelardo René Manita, *Trujillo* (5th rev. ed. 1954), are adulatory. □

Harry S. Truman

Harry S. Truman (1884-1972), thirty-third president of the United States, led America's transition from wartime to peacetime economy, forged the Truman doctrine, and made the decision to defend South Korea against Communist invasion.

Harry Truman was born in Lamar, Mo., on May 8, 1884. He went to high school in Independence, Mo. From 1900 until 1905 he held various small business positions. During the next 12 years he farmed on his parents' land near Independence. In 1917, soon after the United States entered World War I, he enlisted in the artillery, serving in France and achieving the rank of captain. On returning from the war, he joined a friend in opening a haberdashery. The haberdashery went bankrupt, but he adhered to hard work, accepting misfortunes serenely. In 1919 he married Bess Wallace; they had one child, Margaret.

Beginner in Politics

A staunch Democrat and admirer of Woodrow Wilson, Truman entered politics with the encouragement of Jackson County boss Tom Prendergast. With Prendergast's aid, Truman was elected county judge in 1922 and served from 1922 to 1924. He was presiding judge from 1926 to 1934, giving close attention to problems of county administration.

In the Democratic sweep in the national election of 1934, Truman, a firm supporter of Franklin Roosevelt, was chosen U.S. senator from Missouri. Reelected in 1940, he gained national attention as chairman of the Senate Committee to Investigate the National Defense Program. Long a student of history, he feared that corruption might cloud government operations and supported the creation of this Senate committee to watch contracts. But, aware that the partisanship shown by an earlier congressional committee had embarrassed President Abraham Lincoln, he kept his chairmanship loyally helpful to the Roosevelt administration. When Roosevelt was nominated for a fourth term in June 1944, the President bowed to the wishes of influential state and city leaders and named Truman for vice president.

Thrust into the Presidency

After Truman had served only 82 days as vice president, Roosevelt died suddenly on April 12, 1945. Though staggered by the burdens thrust on him, Truman quickly took command and in his first address to Congress promised to continue Roosevelt's policies. That July he attended the Potsdam Conference of the Great Powers on urgent international problems. It was his ominous task to authorize the dropping of the atomic bomb on Hiroshima on Aug. 6, 1945, and to approve the surrender of the Japanese government on Allied terms in a treaty signed on the battleship

Missouri on Sept. 2, 1945. After the surrender of Japan, he replaced the model of a heavy gun on his desk with the replica of a shiny new plow. His desk also bore a firm motto of executive decision: "The Buck Stops Here!"

The Truman administration at once took steps to demobilize the armed forces, terminate wartime agencies, and resume production of peacetime goods. Truman was thus brought face-to-face with inflation, a steep rise in the cost of living, and a new militancy on the part of labor unions, which had conformed to wartime pledges against strikes. He immediately showed his power of unhesitating decision—one of his principal traits. He declared wage increases essential to cushion the blows from changes in the economy, sternly opposed restrictive measures against labor, and acted to maintain union rights as set forth in the Wagner Act. When a new Congress, controlled by Republicans, passed the Taft-Hartley Bill, which limited labor action, he vetoed it as bad for industry and workers alike. After Congress repassed it over his veto, he continued denouncing it as a "slave-labor bill," thus keeping it a subject of popular and congressional contention.

Truman also energetically supported the wartime Fair Employment Act, designed to prevent discrimination against African Americans, Jews, and other minority groups. He also advocated a broad program of social welfare, harmonizing with the New Deal policies. Although sharp friction developed between the Truman administration and conservative elements in Congress, he carried the passage of measures for slum clearance, construction of lowcost housing, the beginnings of a health insurance program, and the establishment of the Council of Economic Advisers to help attain full employment. Though hampered by lack of experience and limited education, and bitterly denounced by cultivated and affluent groups, he gained wide support among the masses as an effective example of the average man.

Traveling to Westminster College in Fulton, Mo., in March 1946, Truman heard British prime minister Winston Churchill deliver his "Iron Curtain" speech, declaring that tyranny was spreading in Europe, that an Iron Curtain was descending from Stettin on the Baltic to Trieste on the Adriatic, and that the Soviet Union, aiming at an indefinite expansion of its powers, would respect only military strength in a steel-clad alliance of America, Britain, and other Western powers. Truman, who said later that he had sponsored Churchill's speech as a test of public sentiment, was delighted by the generally positive reaction throughout the Western world to this direct challenge to Russia. As Russian aggressiveness made the international scene stormier, he gave vigorous support to the United Nations Charter, which the United States had accepted on July 28, 1945.

Cabinet Dissension

Truman exhibited his characteristic decisiveness in crushing dissension in his own Cabinet. When Henry A. Wallace, Secretary of Agriculture, delivered a speech in New York supporting the Russian position in world affairs, attacking Great Britain, and criticizing American foreign

policy for failure to cooperate with the Soviets, Secretary of State James Byrnes acidly declared that he would resign if the President did not insist that Wallace refrain from criticizing American foreign policy while in the Cabinet. Senator Arthur Vandenberg declared that he could serve only one secretary of state at a time, and Truman immediately forced Wallace out of the Cabinet.

By his stern measures, Truman pleased labor and international liberals but made himself unpopular with radical leftist sympathizers. Meanwhile, his friendship with old-time associates, his platitudinous utterances, and his hesitancy to delay using price controls as a weapon against inflation aroused general criticism. But Truman hewed firmly to the policies he had chosen, faced Redbaiting senator Joseph McCarthy without flinching, and read calmly Republican headlines of 1946 asking "Had enough?"

Truman Doctrine

But Truman's greatest and most decisive stroke lay just ahead. Turkey and Greece seemed to stand on the edge of bankruptcy and defeat by Communist elements. Truman staunchly backed Secretary of State Dean Acheson and other State Department leaders in their stand for continued American support to democracy abroad. Refusing to flinch at costs, Truman sent Congress a message on March 2, 1947, asking for an appropriation of $400 million for sustaining Greece and Turkey. He also announced the Truman Doctrine, declaring that the United States would support all free peoples who were resisting attempted subjugation either by armed minorities at home or aggressors outside their borders.

Truman's unyielding policy made it possible for George Marshall, in charge of economic affairs in the State Department, and George Kennan, supervising policy planning, to carry through Congress the epochal Marshall Plan for the transfer of massive economic aid from the free nations of the West to beleaguered countries in Europe and Asia. The presidential campaign of 1948 came as the Marshall Plan gathered widespread support from democratic governments in Europe, South America, Africa, and elsewhere.

His Reelection

In 1948 Truman, with undiminished courage, entered the presidential contest and fought a stubborn battle against the Republican candidate, Thomas E. Dewey. With Clark Clifford mapping his strategy, he faced heavy odds. Although Dewey refused to discuss many issues, keeping safely silent, Truman and the Democratic party centered heavy attacks on the record of the 80th Congress. The President covered 22,000 miles in campaign trips, making 271 speeches. The entry of two new parties into the battle made the outcome doubtful. The conservative Southern Democrats, or "Dixiecrats," nominated a ticket under Governor Strom Thurmond of South Carolina, and followers of Henry Wallace organized the Progressive party behind him.

A heavy majority of newspapers and pollsters seemed confident that Dewey would win. Truman was speaking to enthusiastic whistle-stop crowds, whose rallying cry was

"Give 'em hell, Harry!" He addressed himself mainly to industrial workers and agricultural groups and was the first major candidate to stump in Harlem. Truman went to bed on election night as the *Chicago Tribune* published an "extra" with the headlines, "Dewey Defeats Truman!" Next morning he awoke to find the country enjoying a wild guffaw as it learned that Truman had not only carried the country with a plurality of 2,000,000 votes (24,105,812 ballots for Truman against 21,970,065 ballots for Dewey) but had won a Democratic Congress.

Korean War

On Sunday, June 25, 1950, the Korean War was precipitated when North Korean Communist forces invaded the Republic of South Korea, crossing the 38th parallel at several points. Truman at once summoned an emergency conference and on June 27 announced that he would pledge American armed strength for the defense of South Korea. By September 15, American troops, supported by other forces of the United Nations, were taking the offensive in Korea. Truman held firm in the costly war that ensued but hesitated to approve a major counteroffensive across the Yalu River. In April 1951, amid national frustration over the war, he courageously dismissed Gen. Douglas MacArthur as head of the Far East Command of the U.S. Army. He took this action on the grounds that MacArthur had repeatedly challenged the Far Eastern policies of the administration, thus overriding the basic American principle that the military must always be subordinate to the civil arm of the government, and that MacArthur had recommended the use of bombs against Chinese forces north of the Yalu River in a way which might well provoke open war with Russia and cost the United States the support of important allies in the war.

Following the storm over MacArthur, Truman announced that he would not run again for the presidency, though a new constitutional amendment limiting presidents to two terms did not apply to him. He retired to private life, publishing two volumes of *Memoirs* in 1955 and 1956, and giving influential support to President Lyndon Johnson in the 1960s.

Retirement and Legacy

Truman died on December 26, 1972 and was buried in the courtyard of the Truman Library. When his wife Bess died in 1982, she was buried beside him. Their home in Independence, Missouri remains just as it was when Bess died; Truman's 1972 Chrysler Newport still sits in the garage, and his hat and coat hang under the stairs. The nearby Truman Library is one of the most popular presidential libraries, and includes much of his papers and correspondence, as well as a reproduction of the Oval Office as it looked during his term. The mock White House room even includes a 1947 television, significant since Truman was the first president to own a tv set.

Long after Truman's death, his popularity continues to soar. During the 1996 presidential elections he was quoted by both candidates in debates and speeches. In 1997, new books and movies were in the works, and earlier in the

decade he was even commemorated with a $.020 United States postage stamp. Truman's daughter Margaret has carved out a successful career as a novelist, with works such as *Murder in the National Gallery.*

Further Reading

Truman's account of his career is in his *Memoirs* (2 vols., 1955-1956) and *Mr. Citizen* (1960). Biographies of Truman include Jonathan Daniels, *The Man of Independence* (1950); Alfred Steinberg, *The Man from Missouri: The Life and Times of Harry S. Truman* (1962), a scholarly study; Cabell B. H. Phillips, *The Truman Presidency: The History of a Triumphant Succession* (1966), written from a journalistic perspective; and Joseph Gies, *Harry S. Truman: A Pictorial Biography* (1968), a useful but laudatory study. More recent biographies include David McCullough's *Truman* (1992), Margaret Truman's *Harry S Truman* (1972), and Harold Gosnell's *Truman's Crises* (1980).

Truman's election campaign is recounted in Irwin Ross, *The Loneliest Campaign: The Truman Victory of 1948* (1968). The presidential election is detailed in Arthur M. Schlesinger, Jr., ed., *History of American Presidential Elections* (4 vols., 1971). Truman's administration is considered in general in L.W. Koenig, *The Truman Administration* (1956), and Barton J. Bernstein, ed., *Politics and Policies of the Truman Administration* (1970). Specific aspects of his administration are covered in Richard O. Davies, *Housing Reform during the Truman Administration* (1966); Arthur F. McClure, *The Truman Administration and the Problems of Postwar Labor, 1945-1948* (1969); and William Carl Berman, *The Politics of Civil Rights in the Truman Administration* (1970).

American foreign policy is examined in Herbert Feis, *The Atom Bomb and the End of World War II* (1961; rev. ed. 1966) and *From Trust to Terror: The Onset of the Cold War, 1945-1950* (1970). Revisionist views, critical of Truman's policies, are in Gar Alperovitz, *Atomic Diplomacy: Hiroshima and Potsdam* (1965), and David Horowitz, *The Free World Colossus: A Critique of American Foreign Policy in the Cold War* (1965; rev. ed. 1971). For general historical background Eric Goldman, *The Crucial Decade—and After: America, 1945-1960* (1956; rev. ed. 1960), is recommended. □

John Trumbull

John Trumbull (1756-1843) was the first American painter to produce a series of history paintings; they depict scenes of the Revolutionary War.

John Trumbull, the son of a Connecticut lawyer who became governor of the colony, was born on June 6, 1756. He took some private painting lessons from John Singleton Copley before entering Harvard, from which he graduated at the age of 17. During the Revolutionary War, Trumbull served for a while as aide-de-camp to Gen. Washington but resigned in 1777. In 1780, in connection with mercantile ventures which soon failed, Trumbull sailed to France. He began studying painting with Benjamin West in London, where he was arrested, presumably because of antirevolutionary sentiment in England, and was forced to leave the country.

In 1784 Trumbull returned to England and resumed his studies with West. Trumbull went back to America in 1789. Thomas Jefferson offered to make him his private secretary, promising that little time would be taken from his painting, but Trumbull, not wishing to be tied down, refused. In 1793 he had a violent falling-out with Jefferson, which was damaging to Trumbull's career later.

Trumbull painted in a manner reminiscent of Peter Paul Rubens, and his work is sometimes overburdened with incidental details. He executed a series of 12 paintings dealing with the Revolutionary War, including the *Death of Montgomery in the Attack on Quebec* and the *Battle of Bunker's Hill* (both 1786) and the *Capture of the Hessians at Trenton* (1786-1797). He hoped to reap a profit through the sale of engravings of his history paintings, and initial reactions were encouraging.

Because of the scarcity of currency following the war, Trumbull's prints did not sell as well as he had hoped; only 344 were sold. Discouraged, he went to London in 1794 as secretary to John Jay and stayed on there until 1804, working occasionally as a portrait painter. As a portraitist he had great financial success while in New York from 1804 to 1808. Jefferson was president of the United States at the time, and Trumbull could not hope for a lucrative Federal commission, so he went back to London in 1808 and remained there until 1816, when he returned to New York.

In 1817 Trumbull finally achieved success as a history painter. Congress commissioned him to paint on a larger scale 4 of his 12 paintings on the Revolutionary War to decorate the rotunda of the new Capitol in Washington, D.C.: the *Signing of the Declaration of Independence* (1818), which contains portraits of most of the signers; the *Surrender of Cornwallis at Yorktown* (1817-1820); the *Surrender of Burgoyne at Saratoga* (1817-1821); and the *Resignation of Washington at Annapolis* (1824). They are stiffer than the earlier series and seem more arbitrarily contrived.

From 1817 to 1835 Trumbull served as president of the American Academy of Fine Arts in New York City, which he had helped found. He died in New York City on Nov. 10, 1843.

Further Reading

Theodore Sizer, *The Works of Colonel John Trumbull, Artist of the American Revolution* (1950; rev. ed. 1967), provides a detailed list of Trumbull's paintings and a group of essays on specific aspects of his work.

Additional Sources

Jaffe, Irma B., *John Trumbull, patriot-artist of the American Revolution,* Boston: New York Graphic Society, 1975. ☐

Lyman Trumbull

Lyman Trumbull (1813-1896), American statesman, was an influential senator during the Civil War and Reconstruction.

Lyman Trumbull was born on Oct. 12, 1813, in Colchester, Conn. He displayed unusual intellect early in his youth: at 16 he was teaching school and, 4 years later, was superintendent of an academy in Greenville, Ga. After studying law, he was admitted to the bar in 1836 and opened an office in Belleville, Illinois. In 1840, as a Democrat, he was elected to the state legislature. He resigned a year later to become secretary of state for Illinois. In 1843 he left that post and practiced law until 1848, when he was elected justice of the state supreme court. In 1852 Trumbull was reelected to a 9-year term on the bench. In 1854, however, he relinquished his judicial seat to become a U.S. representative. Before he could assume his new duties in Washington, the state legislature named him to the U.S. Senate, and in 1855 Trumbull began his long senatorial career.

Trumbull, disillusioned by the 1854 Kansas-Nebraska Act and by the role of fellow Illinois senator Stephen A. Douglas in fostering that bill, joined ranks with the Republicans. Trumbull campaigned throughout the late 1850s against further concessions to the South and slavery. During the Civil War, he served as chairman of the powerful Senate Judiciary Committee, and he was one of the acknowledged leaders of his party. Always a strict constructionist of the Constitution, Trumbull was alternately Lincoln's strongest supporter and his most inflexible opponent. In 1864 he introduced the resolution that became the basis for the 13th Amendment.

Following the Civil War, Trumbull worked tirelessly on behalf of civil rights legislation and the Freedmen's Bureau.

Yet his moderate views on Reconstruction put him increasingly at odds with Radical Republican leaders in Congress. The final break came when Trumbull joined six other Republicans in opposing the impeachment of President Andrew Johnson. The excesses of Ulysses S. Grant's administration caused Trumbull to support Horace Greeley in the 1872 presidential race.

Trumbull retired from the Senate in 1873, rejoined the Democrats, and resumed his law practice in Chicago. He was one of Samuel J. Tilden's defense counsels in the disputed 1876 presidential election. Trumbull himself ran unsuccessfully for governor of Illinois in 1880. Several times he was mentioned for the presidency, but he proved too unyielding in principles and had too little popular appeal to rise higher than he did. He died on June 25, 1896, in Chicago.

Further Reading

A number of Trumbull's senatorial speeches were published individually during his lifetime. Mark M. Krug, *Lyman Trumbull: Conservative Radical* (1965) remains the best treatment. An older study, by one of Trumbull's associates and admirers, is Horace White, *The Life of Lyman Trumbull* (1913).

Additional Sources

Roske, Ralph Joseph, *His own counsel: the life and times of Lyman Trumbull,* Reno: University of Nevada Press, 1979. □

Donald John Trump

An American real estate developer, Donald John Trump (born 1946) became one of the best known and most controversial businessmen of the 1980s and 1990s.

Donald John Trump was born in 1946 in Queens, New York City, the fourth of five children of Frederick C. and Mary MacLeod Trump. Frederick Trump was a builder and real estate developer who came to specialize in constructing and operating middle income apartments in the Queens, Staten Island, and Brooklyn. Donald Trump was an energetic, assertive child, and his parents sent him to the New York Military Academy at age 13, hoping the discipline of the school would channel his energy in a positive manner. Trump did well at the academy, both socially and academically, rising to be a star athlete and student leader by the time he graduated in 1964. He entered Fordham University and then transferred to the Wharton School of Finance at the University of Pennsylvania from which he graduated in 1968 with a degree in economics.

Trump seems to have been strongly influenced by his father in his decision to make a career in real estate development, but the younger man's personal goals were much grander than those of his senior. As a student, Trump

worked with his father during the summer and then joined his father's company, the Trump Organization, after graduation from college. He was able to finance an expansion of the company's holdings by convincing his father to be more liberal in the use of loans based on the equity in the Trump apartment complexes. However, the business was very competitive and profit margins were narrow. In 1971 Trump moved his residence to Manhattan, where he became familiar with many influential people. Convinced of the economic opportunity in the city, Trump became involved in large building projects in Manhattan, that would offer opportunities for earning high profits, utilizing attractive architectural design, and winning public recognition.

When the Pennsylvania Central Railroad entered bankruptcy, Trump was able to obtain an option on the railroad's yards on the west side of Manhattan. When initial plans for apartments proved unfeasible because of a poor economic climate, Trump promoted the property as the location of a city convention center, and the city government selected it over two other sites in 1978. Trump's offer to forego a fee if the center were named after his family, however, was turned down, along with his bid to build the complex, which was ultimately named for Senator Jacob Javits.

In 1974 Trump obtained an option on one of the Penn Central's hotels, the Commodore, which was unprofitable but in an excellent location adjacent to Grand Central Station. The next year he signed a partnership agreement with the Hyatt Hotel Corporation, which did not have a large downtown hotel. Trump then worked out a complex deal with the city to win a 40-year tax abatement, arranged

financing, and then completely renovated the building, constructing a striking new facade of reflective glass designed by architect Der Scutt. When the hotel, renamed the Grand Hyatt, opened in 1980, it was popular and an economic success, making Trump the city's best known and most controversial developer.

Trump married Ivana Zelnickova Winklmayr, a New York fashion model who had been an alternate on the 1968 Czech Olympic Ski Team, in 1977. After the birth of the first of the couple's three children in 1978, Donald John Trump, Jr., Ivana Trump was named vice president in charge of design in the Trump Organization and played a major role in supervising the renovation of the Commodore.

In 1979 Trump leased a site on Fifth Avenue adjacent to the famous Tiffany & Company as the location for a monumental $200 million apartment-retail complex designed by Der Scutt. It was named Trump Tower when it opened in 1982. The 58-story building featured a 6-story atrium lined with pink marble and included an 80-foot waterfall. The luxurious building attracted well-known retail stores and celebrity renters and brought Trump national attention.

Meanwhile Trump was investigating the profitable casino gambling business, which was approved in New Jersey in 1977. In 1980 he was able to acquire a piece of property in Atlantic City. He brought in his younger brother Robert to head up the complex project of acquiring the land, winning a gambling license, and obtaining permits and financing. Holiday Inns Corporation, the parent company of Harrah's casino hotels, offered a partnership, and the $250 million complex opened in 1982 as Harrah's at Trump Plaza. Trump bought out Holiday Inns in 1986 and renamed the facility Trump Plaza Hotel and Casino. Trump also purchased a Hilton Hotels casino-hotel in Atlantic City when the corporation failed to obtain a gambling license and renamed the $320 million complex Trump's Castle. Later, while it was under construction, he was able to acquire the largest hotel-casino in the world, the Taj Mahal at Atlantic City, which opened in 1990.

Back in New York City Trump had purchased an apartment building and the adjacent Barbizon-Plaza Hotel in New York City, which faced Central Park, with plans to build a large condominium tower on the site. The tenants of the apartment building, however, who were protected by the city's rent control and rent stabilization programs, fought Trump's plans and won. Trump then renovated the Barbizon, renaming it Trump Parc. In 1985 Trump purchased 76 acres on the west side of Manhattan for $88 million to build a complex to be called Television City, which was to consist of a dozen skyscrapers, a mall, and a riverfront park. The huge development was to stress television production and feature the world's tallest building, but community opposition and a long city approval process delayed commencement of construction of the project. In 1988 he acquired the Plaza Hotel for $407 million and spent $50 million refurbishing it under his wife Ivana's direction.

Trump reached south to build a condominium project in West Palm Beach, Florida, and in 1989 he branched out to purchase the Eastern Air Lines Shuttle for $365 million,

renaming it the Trump Shuttle. In January 1990, Trump flew to Los Angeles to unveil a plan to build a $1 billion commercial and residential project featuring a 125-story office building.

It was in 1990, however, that the real estate market declined, reducing the value of and income from Trump's empire; his own net worth plummeted from an estimated $1.7 billion to $500 million. The Trump Organization required a massive infusion of loans to keep it from collapsing, a situation which raised questions as to whether the corporation could survive bankruptcy. Some observers saw Trump's decline as symbolic of many of the business, economic, and social excesses that had arisen in the 1980s.

Yet, he climbed back from nearly $900 million in the red: Trump was reported to be worth close to $ 2 billion in 1997. Much of Trump's regained Taj Mahal have an ever increasing value.

Donald Trump's image was tarnished by the publicity surrounding his controversial separation and the later divorce from his wife, Ivana. But, Trump married again, this time to Marla Maples, a fledgling actress. Their marriage, which also ended in a highly publicized divorce in 1997, produced a daughter.

Further Reading

Trump described his life and career to 1987 with the assistance of Tony Schwartz in *Trump: The Art of the Deal* (1987) and his controversial activities of the late 1980s with Charles Leerhsen in *Trump: The Art of Survival* (1990). Jerome Tucille has written a critical unauthorized account of Trump's early career in *Trump: The Saga of America's Master Builder* (1986). A former employee, John R. O'Donnell, updates the career in *Trumped: The Inside Story of the Real Donald Trump—His Cunning Rise and Spectacular Fall* (1991), not a flattering portrait. □

Truong Chinh

Truong Chinh (19091988) was secretary general of the Vietnamese Communist political organization and was a pro-Chinese presidential aide. This pro-Chinese orientation was probably a major political liability in a land whose historic foe, for two millennia, was China.

Born on Feb. 15, 1909, in Hanh Thien in what is now northern Vietnam, Truong Chinh was already an anti-French nationalist by his early teens. In 1928, at the age of 19, he joined the Revolutionary Youth League organized 3 years earlier by Ho Chi Minh. Arrested by French authorities for his participation in the student strike of the same year, he was expelled from the Nam Dinh high school but was able to enroll in (and subsequently graduated from) the prestigious Lycée Albert Sarraut in Hanoi.

In 1930 Truong Chinh became a teacher, joining the same year the Indochinese Communist party (founded by

Ho in Hong Kong). Coeditor of *Sickle and Hammer,* one of the first Communist periodicals in the French colony of Indochina, he was arrested in late 1930 after a Communist-led peasant uprising.

Sentenced to 12 years' imprisonment by the French for "conspiring against the security of the state," Truong was paroled in 1936 after a Popular Front government had been formed in metropolitan France. He immediately resumed his Communist political activity. Arrested again in 1939, he fled to South China following dismissal of the charges against him.

In May 1941, five years after his release from prison, Truong became secretary general of the Indochinese Communist party. In 1943 it was absorbed by Ho Chi Minh's multiparty front organization, the Viet Minh, but still retained its separate identity as part of that body.

When the Viet Minh declared Vietnam's independence in September 1945, Truong was by Ho's side in Hanoi. The Indochinese Communist party was dissolved as a political maneuver in November 1945, but, when a new Vietnamese Communist party (Lao Dong, or Workers' Party) was launched in 1951, Truong was its secretary general. He lost this post in 1956, partly because of his role in the stern collectivization and land reform measures of the new North Vietnamese regime (which occasioned great peasant resistance) and partly because the party needed a high-level scapegoat.

Truong's elevation in 1960 to the important position of chairman of the standing committee of the National Assembly (Democratic Republic of Vietnam) signaled his return to the inner ranks of the North Vietnamese ruling elite. After Ho's death in 1969, his political followers began jockeying for a new alignment of power. Truong—probably the most ideologically driven of the North Vietnamese leaders—was eclipsed in 1970, but the following year he reemerged as part of the group ruling the county.

Truong remained as chairman of the DRV until 1976, presiding throughout the Vietnam War, and witnessing the eventual collapse of South Vietnam in April 1975. He served as co-president of the DRV from 1981 until 1987. In July 1986, following the death of Le Duan, Truong also assumed the role of General Secretary, but only served in that role for five months. Although long opposed to capitalism, Truong invited some private enterprise during his short tenure.

In December 1986, during the Sixth Party Congress in Hanoi, the most sweeping changes in 50 years were made within Vietnam's leadership. Truong was ousted in a surprise move, along with two other major political figures, Premier Pham Van Dong, and Le Duc Tho, who negotiated the U.S. withdrawal during the Paris peace talks. Officially, the three agreed to resign, due to "advanced age and bad health." At the time, Vietnam's economy was sagging, with increasing unemployment and 800 percent inflation. Truong told the Congress in a speech, "We recognize the long-term necessity for . . . the private capitalist economy and the petty bourgeoisie in a number of branches and trades." Truong remained an advisor to the party's Central Committee, and died in 1988.

Further Reading

An excellent, brief biography of Truong by Bernard B. Fall serves as the introduction to Fall's edition of two of the Vietnamese leader's best-known books, *The August Revolution* and *The Resistance Will Win,* published as a single volume in the United States as *Primer for Revolt* (1963). For an outstanding account of the immediate post-World War II period see John T. McAlister, Jr., *Viet Nam: The Origins of Revolution, 1885-1946* (1968). A good narrative of the Vietnamese revolution in a broader perspective is Dennis J. Duncanson, *Government and Revolution in Vietnam* (1968). □

Sojourner Truth

Sojourner Truth (ca. 1797-1883) was a black American freedom fighter and orator. She believed herself chosen by God to preach His word and to help with the abolitionist effort to free her people.

Sojourner Truth was born Isabella Baumfree in Ulster County, N.Y., the daughter of an African named Baumfree (after his Dutch owner) and a woman called Elizabeth. About the age of 9 she was auctioned off to an Englishman named John Nealy. The Nealys understood very little of her Dutch jargon and, as a result, she was often brutally punished for no real reason.

Eventually Nealy sold her to a fisherman who owned a tavern in Kingston, N.Y. Here she acquired the idiomatic expressions which came to mark her speech. John J. Dumont, a nearby plantation owner, purchased her next. During her tenure with his family she married and had five children. In 1827, after New York had passed an emancipation act freeing its slaves, she prepared to take her family away. But Dumont began to show reluctance to this, so she ran away with only her youngest child.

She finally wound up in New York City. She worked at a menial job and through some friends came under the sway of a religious fanatic named Mathias. Eventually disillusioned by her life in New York and by Mathias, in 1843 she left on what she termed a pilgrimage to spread the truth of God's word. She assumed the name Sojourner Truth, which she believed God had given her as a symbolic representation of her mission in life. Soon her reputation as an orator spread, and large crowds greeted her wherever she spoke.

A controversial figure for most of the rest of her life, Truth engaged the courts in two rather unusual cases, winning them both and establishing precedents. Thus, she became the first black to win a slander suit against prominent whites, and the first black woman to test the legality of segregation of Washington, D.C., streetcars.

During the Civil War, Truth bought gifts for the soldiers with money raised from her lectures and helped fugitive slaves find work and housing. After the war she continued her tirade for the Lord and against racial injustice, even when old age and ill health restricted her activities to the

confines of a Battle Creek, Mich., sanatorium. She died there on Nov. 26, 1883.

Further Reading

Sojourner Truth's speech at the Women's Rights Convention, Akron, Ohio, on May 29, 1851, is in *The Faith of Our Fathers,* edited by Irving Mark and Eugene L. Schwaab. Works on Sojourner Truth include Olive Gilbert, *Narrative of Sojourner Truth* (1878; repr. 1968); Arthur Huff Fauset, *Sojourner Truth: God's Faithful Pilgrim* (1938), especially good for insights into the religious implications of her life; Hertha E. Pauli, *Her Name Was Sojourner Truth* (1962); and Jacqueline Bernard, *Journey toward Freedom: The Story of Sojourner Truth* (1967). Lerone Bennett, Jr., *Pioneers in Protest* (1968), devotes a chapter to her. A brief biography is in Wilhelmena S. Robinson, *Historical Negro Biographies* (1968). □

William Tryon

William Tryon (1729-1788), English colonial official, was governor of both North Carolina and New York colonies. He led a loyalist force during the Revolution.

Born at Norbury Park, Surrey, William Tryon entered the army in 1751 with a commission as lieutenant in the 1st Regiment of Foot Guards. In 1758 he became a regimental captain with an army rank of lieutenant colonel. In 1757 he had married Margaret Wake, whose connection with Lord Hillsborough probably was responsible for Tryon's appointment as lieutenant governor of North Carolina in 1764. After the death of the governor in 1765, Tryon was appointed to the position. When he insisted on supporting the British government during the prerevolutionary Stamp Act controversy, local inhabitants so intimidated him that he suggested the use of British regulars. He successfully negotiated a boundary dispute with the Cherokee Indians, and he was finally able to locate a permanent capital for the colony at New Bern, where "Tryon's Palace" was constructed.

Tryon was popular in the tidewater area, but in the west the Regulator movement arose over such issues as inadequate currency, unequal taxation, and unhappiness with local officials. Tryon was sympathetic to some Regulator demands and was a personal friend of some of the leaders, but in 1768 he marched the militia to Hills-borough to put down Regulator demonstrations. In 1770 the Regulators arose again and broke up the superior court at Hillsborough, intimidating court officials and lawyers. After the ringleaders were convicted and outlawed, Tryon, in March 1771, led 1,100 militia into Regulator country and on May 16 inflicted a crushing defeat on 2,000 Regulators.

In July Tryon left for New York as he had succeeded Lord Dunmore as governor of that province. There he was faced with the land grant dispute with New Hampshire and difficulties arising out of land purchases from the Mohawk Indians, in which he was personally interested to the extent of 40,000 acres. He was recalled to England for an explanation and sailed in April 1774.

Tryon returned to New York 14 months later, after the Revolution had begun. He was forced to remain aboard a ship in New York harbor from October 1775 until the arrival of William Howe's fleet in August 1776. In 1777 he was given permission to command a loyalist force and a year later was promoted to major general in North America and colonel of the 70th Foot. His primary military activity was a series of diversionary raids in Connecticut. In 1780 chronic illness compelled his return to England, where he was promoted to lieutenant general in 1782 and colonel of the 29th Foot in 1783. He died in London on Jan. 27, 1788.

Further Reading

Marshall D. Haywood, *Governor William Tryon and His Administration in the Province of North Carolina, 1765-1771* (1903), was updated by Alonzo T. Dill, *Governor Tryon and His Palace* (1955).

Additional Sources

Nelson, Paul David, *William Tryon and the course of empire: a life in British imperial service,* Chapel Hill: University of North Carolina Press, 1990. □

Ts'ai Yüan-p'ei

Ts'ai Yüan-p'ei (1867-1940) was the foremost liberal educator in 20th-century China and gained renown as a synthesizer of Chinese and Western ideas.

Ts'ai Yüan-p'ei was born into a merchant family in Chekiang Province in southeastern China. A brilliant student of the Chinese classics, he became, at 23, one of the youngest holders of the coveted *chin-shih* (the highest academic degree). In 1892 he was appointed to the elite Hanlin Academy. Believing the educational system to be responsible for China's defeat by the Japanese in 1895 and for the failure of the reform movement of 1898, he returned to Chekiang to devote himself to educational reform.

By 1902 Ts'ai had become involved in revolutionary political activities in Shanghai. There he helped found anti-Manchu educational and political societies, schools, and a newspaper. In a pattern that was to be typical throughout his life, Ts'ai soon left politics to return to the world of scholarship. In 1908 he went to Germany, where he attended lectures at Leipzig University and developed a strong interest in esthetics. Though he returned to China in 1911 and 1913 and served briefly as minister of education in the new republic, Ts'ai was in Europe during most of the tenure of Yüan Shih-k'ai. During World War I he helped bring 2,000 Chinese students to France under a work-study program.

After the death of Yüan Shih-kai in 1916, Ts'ai was appointed chancellor of Peking University (Peita), a post he held until 1926. Dedicated to principles of intellectual experimentation and academic freedom, he assembled a distinguished faculty, including Hu Shih and many other leaders in the New Culture movement. Among the diverse ideologies that found a forum at Peita was Marxism, whose followers included two faculty members (Ch'en Tu-hsiu and Li Ta-chao) and a library assistant (Mao Tse-tung). Peita was the focal point for the anti-Japanese student demonstration of May 4, 1919, which accelerated intellectual, political, and social revolution and gave its name to the era. Ts'ai left Peking to protest the arrest of student leaders and returned only after their release.

Alienated from Peking's warlord rulers, Ts'ai spent most of his remaining years as chancellor in travel abroad. Returning to China in 1926, he supported the Northern Expedition against the warlords and sided with his fellow Chekiangese Chiang Kai-shek against rivals within the Kuomintang. Under the Nanking government, Ts'ai served briefly as acting minister of justice and president of the Control Yüan. He was president of the short-lived Ta-hsueh yüan (Board of Universities), which attempted to reorganize Chinese education on the French model. From 1928 to 1935 he was president of the Academia Sinica, China's highest research institute.

However, Kuomintang suppression of civil liberties provoked Ts'ai's resignation from all official posts in 1935. Disillusioned with Chiang Kai-shek's government and in declining health, Ts'ai fled to Hong Kong after the Japanese invasion of 1937. There he died on March 3, 1940.

Further Reading

Although there is no English-language biography of Ts'ai, useful material can be culled from Joseph R. Levenson, *Confucian China and Its Modern Fate,* vol. 1 (1958); Chow Tse-tsung, *The May Fourth Movement* (1960); Ssu-yü Teng and John K. Fairbank, *China's Response to the West* (1961); and Yi Chu Wang, *Chinese Intellectuals and the West, 1872-1949* (1966).

Additional Sources

Duiker, William J., *Ts'ai Yüan-p'ei, educator of modern China,* University Park: Pennsylvania State University Press, 1977. □

Ts'ao Ts'ao

Ts'ao Ts'ao (155-220), the most popular hero in Chinese folklore, was also a truly great historical figure whose genius as a general and as a statesman saved North China from chaos when the Han dynasty crumbled at the end of the 2nd century A.D.

The origins of Ts'ao Ts'ao are obscure since his father, Ts'ao Sung, was the adopted son of a powerful eunuch, Ts'ao T'eng. This meant that the Ts'ao family was a rich one, but relatively newly rich, and of tainted lineage. An unruly and adventurous youth, Ts'ao was greatly pleased when a famous judge of character predicted that he would be "an able public servant in a world at peace, or a crafty, deceitful hero in a world at war." The world was at war, one of the bloodiest China had ever seen, and Ts'ao Ts'ao threw himself into the battle in 184, helping to quell the rebellion of the Yellow Turbans, the so-called T'ai-p'ing (or Taiping) Rebellion, that was to serve as a prototype for similar popular uprisings for two millennia.

Through the influence of his father and in recompense for his actions, Ts'ao Ts'ao rose in rank. When the empire was threatened by Tung Cho, a brutal condottiere who captured the Emperor and burned the capital, Ts'ao fled to the provinces, where he raised his own troops to fight, ostensibly to save the Han from dissolution. The next 20 years of his life were years of anarchic fighting among his warlord enemies. In 200, at the battle of Kuantu, Honan, he defeated Yüan Shao; and after continual battles against the Yüan family, Liu Piao, and the Wu-huan, Ts'ao became the sole power in the North.

In 208, another famous battle, at Ch'ih-pi on the south bank of the Yangtze in Hupei, showed he could not defeat his combined enemies in Wu and Shu. The end of his life was spent in consolidating his hold on the North, by far the most important part of China, becoming prime minister in 208, Duke of Wei in 213, and Prince of Wei in 216. At his death on March 15, 220, he had still not taken the imperial title. This his son, Ts'ao P'i, did, becoming the first emperor of the Wei dynasty on Dec. 11, 220.

Ts'ao Ts'ao's importance was hotly debated in China in 1959, the debate resembling the "rehabilitation" of Ivan the Terrible in Soviet Russia in the 1930s and being, consequently, highly doctrinaire. Whatever Ts'ao's attitudes toward the common people were, whether "progressive" or "reactionary," it is a fact that he made intelligent use of military agricultural colonies (*t'un-t'ien*) near his capital, in which soldiers were set to farming unused farm land, reorganized and reused taxes, and by the repopulation of the vast areas that had been devastated by the unceasing wars—he succeeded in bringing peace and prosperity to North China and reestablishing a unified empire. His policies for appointing men "only by their talent" in an attempt to strengthen the central government, by ignoring the new real powers in the land, the rich regional landowners, ultimately were doomed to failure, but his vigorous unconcern for the deadwood of Confucian tradition helped liberate the minds of the intelligentsia and paved the way for a veritable renaissance of thought and literature.

Ts'ao Ts'ao himself was a powerful poet and prose writer. His spare and virile style was admirably suited to the popular ballad from (*yüeh-fu*) that he used in the 24 poems that bear his name and sing of his political ambitions, the pain of warfare, the shortness of life, and the joys of mystical journeying with Taoist immortals. For many Chinese, however, Ts'ao Ts'ao remains the archvillain of history, immortalized in the novel *San-kuo chih yen-i* (The Romance of the Three Kingdoms) as a crafty and unscrupulous usurper.

Further Reading

The long résumé of events from 180 to 220 found in the *Tzu-chih t'ung-chien* of Ssu-ma Kuang was translated by Rafe de Crespigny as *The Last of the Han* (Centre of Oriental Studies, Monograph 9, Australian National University, Canberra, 1969). Some background appears in Kenneth Scott Latourette, *The Chinese: Their History and Culture* (1934; 4th rev. ed. 1964); C. P. Fitzgerald, *China: A Short Cultural History* (1935; 3d ed. 1961); Edwin O. Reischauer and John K. Fairbank, *History of East Asian Civilization*, vol. 1: *East Asia: The Great Tradition* (1958); and Ying-shih Yü, *Trade and Expansion in Han China* (1967). □

Saul Tschernichowsky

The Hebrew poet, translator, and physician Saul Tschernichowsky (1875-1943) was one of the fathers of modern Hebrew poetry.

Saul Tschernichowsky was born in Mikilovka in the Crimea. He was educated in a small town where liberal religious attitudes prevailed. At the age of five he studied Russian, and at 7 he took up Hebrew. Even as a youth, he was well read in the works of modern Hebrew literature, as well as in Russian literature. He soon mastered English, French, and German. In 1890 he went to Odessa and studied in a private business school. There he met literary critic and editor Joseph Klausner, who later published accounts of their first meetings. In 1894 he began translating Longfellow's *Hiawatha* and *Evangeline*. Two years later he completed his studies at the school, having mastered both Greek and Latin. It was then that he translated the poetry of Anacreon and the *Symposium* of Plato.

In 1899 the first collection of Tschernichowsky's poetry, *Visions and Melodies,* appeared, to which was added a second part in 1901. Between 1899 and 1904 he studied medicine at Heidelberg, and it was there that he wrote some of his most celebrated poems, such as "Baruch of Mainz" and "In the Presence of the Sea." In 1903 he went to Lausanne and in 1907 received his medical degree. That year he returned to Russia, only to be imprisoned for 6 weeks as a political suspect. Following his incarceration he wrote "My Imprisonment" and "All Is Shattered." He practiced medicine in the villages for 3 years, while managing to continue his writing. A visit to Finland prompted him to translate the Finnish epic *Kalevala.*

During World War I Tschernichowsky served as a military doctor. In 1919 he took up residence in Odessa, where he completed his translations of the *Iliad* and the *Odyssey.* In 1922 he traveled to Germany, where his translation of the Babylonian *Epic of Gilgamesh* and Sophocles's *Oedipus Rex* appeared. Between 1924 and 1934 his collected works were published in 10 volumes. He emigrated to Palestine in 1931, residing first in Jerusalem and later in Tel Aviv, where he practiced medicine in the municipal hospital. His last volume of poetry, *Behold, Oh Land,* was awarded the Bialik Prize in 1940. In 1942 his *Thirty-three Short Stories* appeared, and after his death an anthology of his poems entitled *Distant Stars in the Heaven* was published (1944).

The poetry of Tschernichowsky is the poetry of life, light, love, courage, and beauty. It abounds in a timeless energy which seeks out beauty and a perfected life of both physical and spiritual courage. He is a man closely tied to nature, in all its aspects. He sees nature as the real world of the poet, the soil nourishing his life: "I am the bud of a wildflower warmly kissed by drops of dew." He strongly identified with the natural world, and his poetry abounds in admiration for the wellsprings of strength and beauty to be found there.

The underlying philosophy of Tschernichowsky's poetry may be described as pantheistic. He is wholly committed to both the spiritual and natural life of the Patriarchs, and their spirit resounds in much of his work. He seeks the ideal Israelite from among the ancient Hebrews, a vigorous people with a wrathful god.

Further Reading

A comprehensive introduction to Tschernichowsky's poetry and a selection of his work in translation are in Eisig Silberschlag, *Saul Tschernichowsky: Poet of Revolt* (1968). A more general background on modern Hebrew literature is in Simon Halkin, *Modern Hebrew Literature* (1950; new ed. 1970), which includes a short chapter on the poetry of Tschernichowsky. □

Tseng Kuo-fan

The Chinese statesman, general, and scholar Tseng Kuo-fan (1811-1872) was responsible for the suppression of the Taiping Rebellion and is regarded as a model Confucian official.

Between 1850 and 1864 China was racked by the Taiping Rebellion, which threatened to topple the Ch'ing dynasty and to destroy Chinese traditional culture. Because the regular armies of the Ch'ing proved to be totally incapable of stopping the rebels, the burden of resistance fell upon local militia groups. Tseng Kuo-fan was responsible for organizing the militia of Hunan into the first of the provincial armies which would eventually crush the Taiping forces. Because of his upright and moral character, he became a rallying point for the able officials, scholars, and soldiers who rose to support the dynasty and preserve their Confucian heritage.

Tseng Kuo-fan was born on Nov.26, 1811, in Hsiang-hsiang, Hunan, to a poor peasant family. In 1832, Tseng Kuo-fan passed the first of the official examinations a year after his father had done so, and in 1838 obtained a *chin-shih* (the highest academic degree) and became a member of the Hanlin Academy. Routine promotions advanced his career until 1849, when he was made a junior vice president of the Board of Ceremonies. He also served as an acting vice president on several other boards. In 1852 he was ordered to Kiangsi to conduct the provincial examination, but on the way southward he learned of his mother's death and he was granted leave to return home to observe the customary 3 years of mourning.

Military Leader

The Taiping rebels in their northward sweep in 1852 had layed siege to Changsha, the capital of Hunan, but had been forced to withdraw due to the efforts of the local militia. In a sea of defeats, this was one of the few imperial successes, and the Emperor in January 1853 ordered Tseng to recruit and drill the Hunan militia. Because he was in mourning, Tseng felt that he could not accept, but after much persuasion from the Emperor and friends, he finally agreed and swore to himself that he would not "covet wealth nor fear death."

In keeping with his already established habits of thorough planning, Tseng carefully worked out the training of his troops, their discipline, and their organization. The army he created came to be known as the Hsiang Army and was founded on the Chinese custom of personal loyalties. Tseng had seen the soldiers of the regular armies of the Ch'ing refuse to fight for their commanders because they were strangers. Tseng insisted that each unit commander personally recruit his own soldiers and, preferably, that the commander and the troops come from the same local region. Tseng was using local affinities to give cohesion to his army. If for any reason a commander was removed, then his unit was to be disbanded, and the new commander would recruit a new unit. From this practice the saying arose that "the army belongs to the general"—and not the state. Tseng inadvertently set a pattern of personal armies that would lead to the growth of warlordism in the 20th century.

Tseng also believed in adequate military training before his troops were committed to battle. There had been too many instances where the imperial troops had fled before the approaching Taiping forces. Despite repeated entreaties from officials in beleaguered areas and even from the Emperor himself to commit the army, Tseng refused until he felt the men were ready.

Tseng's forces were not an immediate success, however. In two battles in 1854, his forces were defeated, and Tseng was so discouraged that he attempted suicide. However, a victory soon encouraged him, and his forces were finally able to stop the Taiping drive in Hunan. Tseng's efforts were also aided in 1856 by the elimination of most of the capable Taiping leaders through a bloodbath in Nanking. Despite repeated calls for aid from other areas, Tseng concentrated his forces on the job of recapturing the Taiping capital at Nanking. This meant that his army had to fight its way down the Yangtze River in the face of stiff opposition.

Tseng's entire operation was also constantly hampered by a shortage of funds and a lack of recognized authority. When his Hsiang Army was first organized, it was to be financed by the imperial treasury, but the imperial revenues fell short, and Tseng was forced to rely on the contributions of the local gentry who, as it turned out, were rather lukewarm to his entreaties. Tseng's official rank was not within the regular provincial bureaucracy and, as a result, he was unable to command provincial revenues. It was only through the aid of staunch friends, who held high provincial rank, as well as his own persistent pleas that Tseng was able to keep his army going. His troops were well aware of the situation, which further strengthened their loyalty to Tseng and their unit commanders. After 1860, when Tseng was appointed governor general of Kiangnan (the highest provincial civil rank) and imperial commissioner (the Emperor's own representative), he was finally in a position to ensure adequate funds for his army.

The repeated entreaties for military help from various areas within Tseng's jurisdiction, which, if complied with, would have diluted his main effort, forced Tseng in 1860-1861 to create three military areas: one in Kiangsu under Li Hung-chang, a second in Chekiang under Tso Tsung-t'ang, and a third in Anhwei under his own command.

Li Hung-chang returned to his home in the Huai region of Anhwei to recruit a new army on the same principles of personal loyalty that Tseng had used. Li's Huai Army was stationed at Shanghai in 1862 and during the next 2 years cleared most of Kiangsu of the Taiping rebels. Tso Tsung-t'ang did the same in Chekiang, while Tseng's army under the immediate command of his younger brother, Tseng Kuo-ch'üan, laid siege to Nanking. Tseng's tactics resulted in the fall of the Taiping capital on July 19, 1864.

Postrebellion Years

With the rebellion over, Tseng's immediate task as the governor general of Kiangnan was to restore peace and order to the war-ravaged area and to promote the revival of learning in South China. During the war years he had gained the respect and admiration of many of the leading scholars and officials of the empire. His high moral character, his devotion not only to the imperial cause but also to the ideals of Confucianism, his own sound scholarship, and his military successes drew these men to his side. In his efforts to revive scholarship he established five official printing offices for reprinting the classics and the histories and restored the official examinations at Nanking.

During the postrebellion years Tseng also became interested in ways to strengthen China in the face of Western encroachments. He and Li Hung-chang established an arsenal at Shanghai in 1865; in 1868 the arsenal sponsored the building of the first Chinese steamship. In August 1871 he and Li jointly established a program to send Chinese boys to the United States to study, but he died shortly before the students set sail in 1872.

New Fighting

Tseng Kuo-fan had disbanded his Hsiang Army at the conclusion of the Taiping Rebellion because his troops were war-weary and because his power, based on this army, might be considered a threat to the dynasty. In June 1865, when Tseng was ordered to take command of the fighting against the Nien rebels in the North, he felt he could rely on Li Hung-chang's Huai Army. Tseng realized that this was contrary to all his teachings about personal recruitment but felt that since Li was his longtime pupil and friend it might work. After a year of unsuccessful campaigning he recommended Li as his successor and returned to his former post as the governor general of Kiangnan. Li brought the Nien Rebellion to a successful conclusion in 1868.

When the people of Tientsin attacked the French missionaries in 1870, in what has been called the Tientsin Massacre, Tseng, as the governor general of Chihli since 1868, was called upon to investigate the case. Aware of China's military weakness, Tseng pressed for a policy of justice and conciliation. As a result, he incurred the wrath of the masses and the war party. The case was nearly settled, however, when, old and ill, Tseng was transferred back to his former post in Nanking. Li Hung-chang, who had been ordered to bring his army to Tientsin to support Tseng, succeeded his master in Chihli. Two years later, on March 12, 1872, Tseng died in Nanking.

Further Reading

The standard work in English on Tseng is William James Hail, *Tseng Kuo-fan and the Taiping Rebellion* (1927). Gideon Chen, *Tseng Kuo-fan: Pioneer Promoter of the Steamship in China* (1935), deals with Tseng's efforts at "Self-strengthening"; and Kenneth E. Folsom, *Friends, Guests, and Colleagues* (1968), discusses the creation of Tseng's army, his personal advisers, and his relationship with Li Hung-chang. A complete biography of Tseng can be found in Arthur W. Hummel, ed., *Eminent Chinese of the Ch'ing Period* (2 vols., 1943). □

Moïse Kapenda Tshombe

Moïse Kapenda Tshombe (1919-1969), a Congolese political leader, was the figurehead of the Katanga secession. His chief stock-in-trade was his cynical reliance on foreign-interest groups and white mercenaries.

Moïse Tshombe was born at Sandoa in southwestern Katanga, the son of a well-to-do father who combined success as a trader with social prominence in his traditional milieu, that of the Lunda (Aruund). Moïse Tshombe himself married a daughter of the Mwantayaav (emperor) of the Lunda, and his uncle and brother were subsequently enthroned as emperors while he was at the height of his political career. Tshombe was educated by American Methodist missionaries and joined his father in his business, only to prove himself a rather incompetent manager. He repeatedly had to be rescued from commercial failure and after his father's death in 1951 became involved in questionable deals which reportedly put him at the mercy of European creditors.

Tshombe's early steps into public life, first as a nominated member of the advisory Katanga Provincial Council, then as local chairman of an association of middle-class Africans, were undistinguished. His emergence on the political scene really began in November 1958, when the Lunda tribal association (Gassomel), of which he had been elected chairman, took part in the creation of Conakat (Confédération des Associations du Katanga), along with other ethnic associations such as Balubakat, the association of Katanga Baluba, led by Jason Sendwe. Within a few months, however, Conakat had accepted the affiliation, as well as much of the political program, of the leading white settlers' organization in Katanga, a decision that led to Balubakat's withdrawal.

Now led by Tshombe, Conakat sought maximum autonomy for Katanga in a context of close association with Belgium, a position which placed it squarely at odds with leading advocates of Congolese nationalism, particularly Patrice Lumumba's Mouvement National Congolais (MNC). Locally, Conakat's insistence that all responsible positions in Katanga should go to "authentic Katangese" (a category in which they were willing to include white settlers but not immigrants from neighboring provinces of the Congo) led to the alienation of an important and influential segment of the African urban population and contributed to establishing the party's reputation for separatism.

The views defended by Conakat and by its settler associates found little audience at the Round Table Conference, where, in early 1960, the foundations of an independent Congo were laid down. Conakat won only eight seats out of 137 in the National Assembly in the May 1960 elections, but in Katanga itself, where it actually gained fewer votes than its adversaries, it managed to secure a one-seat margin in the Provincial Assembly and to exclude the opposition from the provincial government. A first attempt at secession two days before independence was foiled by the Belgian authorities, but less than two weeks later, under a transparent pretext, Tshombe declared Katanga's independence (July 11, 1960).

Katanga Secession

The new "state" was organized with massive military and civilian assistance from Belgium but had to face the hostility of a considerable portion of its population (mostly in northern Katanga). Prime Minister Lumumba's attempt to end the secession by force failed when he was dismissed from his post by President Joseph Kasavubu, and the deposed Lumumba was eventually delivered into the hands of the Katanga government and assassinated in Elisabethville, although Tshombe himself apparently played only an indirect role in this episode. Negotiations to secure the Congo's reunification were pursued during most of 1961, leading at one point to Tshombe's brief imprisonment by the central government, but it was only through the repeated intervention of United Nations forces (backed by the United States) that the Katanga secession was finally brought to an end in January 1963.

Tshombe himself was not arrested, due to the influence of Western powers, but he found his position increasingly uncomfortable and left the Congo in June 1963. During the following 12 months he actively prepared his reentry on the Congolese political scene from his Spanish abode, but, despite the fact that mercenaries and troops of the former Katanga state were kept in readiness in neighboring Angola with Portuguese complicity, his second chance came not from a reactivation of the Katanga secession but from the fear of a fast-spreading peasant insurrection.

In June 1964, having spurned offers to serve under Premier Cyrille Adoula, Tshombe was recalled as prime minister of the Congo. In a sense, his best qualification for the job was his demonstrated readiness to turn over the running of the country to Western technicians and soldiers. This he promptly did, and with the help of white mercenaries and some direct intervention by Belgium and the United States he presided over the ruthless liquidation of the rebellion. His attempt to organize a nationwide political party under the name of Conaco was much less successful, however; and although the party won an overwhelming majority in the highly irregular election of 1965, he still lacked a genuine power base.

Exile and Death

More importantly, Tshombe had exhausted his usefulness once the rebellion had been contained, and he now was increasingly viewed as an embarrassment to the regime and to its Western backers. Tshombe's avowed ambition to wrest the presidency from President Joseph Kasavubu put him on a collision course with the durable, soft-spoken head of state, who dismissed him from office on Oct. 13, 1965. Like Lumumba 5 years earlier, Tshombe fought back to a stalemate, but on November 25 the army under Gen. Joseph Mobutu took power, thus eliminating Tshombe from the scene.

From his exile in Europe, Tshombe continued to plot his return to power, hoping to draw support from Belgian mining interests threatened with nationalization by the Mobutu regime. Not only were the two uprisings carried out in his name unsuccessful, but Tshombe himself was kidnapped on June 30, 1967, and delivered into the hands of the Algerian government. The extradition of Tshombe, who had been sentenced to death in absentia, was never carried out, and he remained confined in Algeria until he died (allegedly from a stroke) on June 29, 1969.

Further Reading

My Fifteen Months in Government (1966; trans. 1967) is Tshombe's own account of his administration. Two biographies are Anthony T. Bouscaren, *Tshombe,* with an introduction by Daniel Lyons (1967), and Ian Colvin, *The Rise and Rall of Moise Tshombe: A Biography* (1968). A recent work on the Congo's major crisis is by Jules Gérard-Libois, *Katanga Secession* (1963; trans. 1966). □

Konstantin Eduardovich Tsiolkovsky

The Russian scientist Konstantin Eduardovich Tsiolkovsky (1857-1935) formulated the mathematical fundamentals of modern astronautics. He showed that space travel was possible only by means of rocket propulsion.

Konstantin Tsiolkovsky was born on Sept. 17, 1857, in the village of Izhevskoye, Ryazan Province. His father was successively a forester, teacher, and minor government official. When he was ten Konstantin contracted scarlet fever, which left him with permanently impaired hearing. He became passionately interested in science and mathematics. At the age of 16 he went to Moscow. He made an ear trumpet himself and attended lectures and studied in libraries. Regular attendance at the university was out of the question because of the costs involved and his deafness.

Hardships in Moscow

Tsiolkovsky seriously began considering the problems of space exploration. While still not completely schooled in physics, he developed a machine that he thought might someday reach outer space by means of centrifugal force. It was a box in which there were two steel rods with balls on their ends. When the rods were set in motion, their vibrations (in Tsiolkovsky's theory) would produce an upward movement because of centrifugal force, but they did not.

In 1876 Tsiolkovsky went home, which was now in Viatka in the Urals. There he became a private tutor in physics and mathematics. He converted a room into a workshop in which he built machines. In 1878, the family returned to Ryazan, and Tsiolkovsky received a certificate as a "people's school teacher," the lowest classification in the educational system of the day. He took a job as a teacher of arithmetic, geometry, and physics at the district school in Borovsk near Moscow.

In 1880 Tsiolkovsky wrote his first serious scientific paper, "The Graphical Depiction of Sensations." It was an attempt to reduce to mathematical models the experience of human senses. The following year he submitted the paper "The Theory of Gas" to the Physical and Chemical Society in St. Petersburg. Later he submitted another paper, "The Theoretical Mechanics of a Living Organism," for which he was elected to the society. In 1883 he published a purely qualitative study entitled "Free Space," in which he examined the motion of a body not under the influence of a gravitational field or some medium that offered resistance to its movement; the paper contained a drawing of a rocket-powered space ship.

After 1884 three areas of science occupied Tsiolkovsky. He began to concentrate on aeronautics: a streamlined airplane, an aerostation, an all-metal dirigible, and space travel. In 1886 he published an essay on the theory of the dirigible and was invited to Moscow to lecture on his ideas. His concept of the dirigible was highly imaginative and theoretically feasible, but it posed serious problems for the engineering of the day. He proposed all-metal airships with a variable volume to preserve constant buoyancy at different temperatures and altitudes. A corrugated metal envelope with an internal system of pulleys was to vary the volume as the temperature or altitude changed. The lifting gas (hydrogen) was to be heated by passing the exhaust gases from the engines through the envelope before they were discharged to the atmosphere. His plans submitted to the Russian Technical Society's Aeronautical Department in 1891 brought a reply that "inasmuch as the project cannot have any considerable practical importance, the society did not find it possible to comply with your request for a grant to construct a model." The tone of this letter was to become familiar to him over the remainder of his life. The only funds he ever received from any outside source came from the Academy of Sciences and amounted to only 470 rubles ($235).

In 1892 Tsiolkovsky became a high school teacher in Kaluga. In 1894 he published the article "The Airplane or Bird-like Flying Machine."

First Wind Tunnel

In 1897 Tsiolkovsky built the first wind tunnel in Russia. In it, he tested a number of different airfoils to determine their lift coefficients. The results of these pioneering experiments in aeronautical engineering were published the following year, and the Academy of Sciences in St. Petersburg granted him 470 rubles to expand and exploit his research in this field. He built a bigger machine, but even as he was wrapped up with his wind tunnel, he found time to think about rockets and space travel.

In 1897 Tsiolkovsky derived the relationship of the exhaust velocity of a rocket and its mass ratio to its instantaneous velocity. Known today as the basic rocket equation, it is expressed as $V = c \ln (W_i/W_f)$, in which V is the final velocity, c is the exhaust velocity of propellant particles expelled through the nozzle, W_i is the initial weight of the rocket, and W_f is the final, or burnt-out, weight of the rocket. Of course, it does not consider the retarding forces of gravity and drag, which Tsiolkovsky knew affected the rocket and later took into account in refining his equation. What his equation proved was that the velocity of a rocket in space depends on the velocity of its exhaust and the ratio of the weight of the rocket at lift-off and at burn-out. This realization permitted him to conceive of many ways of increasing the exhaust velocity and of decreasing the mass fraction.

Even more important from the astronautical viewpoint, Tsiolkovsky demonstrated that the answer to space travel lay in building what he called "step, or train," rockets. Today this concept is known as "staging." He saw, from his mathematical investigations, that a rocket could attain greater velocities if it could grow continuously lighter. Thus, he suggested that rockets could be clustered in the tandem, or parallel, configuration. As stages burned out, they dropped away, and upper stages gained in velocity as a result—as his rocket equation proved.

Contributions to Astronautics

In 1903 Tsiolkovsky finished a paper that was to become his famous article "Investigation of Outer Space by Reaction Devices." It did not appear in print until 1911 and 1912, when it was published serially in the *Aeronautical Courier* (*Vestnik Vozdukhoplavaniva*). This work represents his major contribution to astronautical engineering. He reiterated his rocket equation and modified it to include the forces of gravity and drag. He examined the energies involved in a vertical and horizontal launching, and he considered the best overall shape for a rocket. Also, he demonstrated that solid propellants lacked the energy needed for interplanetary travel. In considering various liquid propellants, he arrived at liquid hydrogen and liquid oxygen as the most practical. He also mentioned the theoretical advantage of ozone instead of diatomic oxygen. The concept of the regeneratively cooled engine is also found in this work.

During the late 1920s and the early 1930s, Tsiolkovsky's interests shifted to the airplane, especially the rocket-propelled model. Of the articles appearing in this period, typical are "The New Airplane" (1929), "The Reaction Airplane" (1930), and "Rocketplane" (1930). After Tsiolkovsky retired from teaching, he continued to write on space and aeronautics.

In 1934, as he knew he was dying of cancer, Tsiolkovsky became worried about the future welfare of his family. On Sept. 13, 1935, he wrote a letter to the Central Committee of the Communist Party bequeathing all of his writings "to the Bolshevik Party and the Soviet Government." In so doing, he hoped he might obtain a pension for his family. He died on September 19.

For several years Tsiolkovsky's books and manuscripts were stored in the central offices of Aeroflot and then given to various museums. His home in Kaluga was made into a museum, and some of the material was returned to it. During World War II the museum suffered depredation by the invading Germans, but the staff managed to save much of the material. Following the orbiting of *Sputnik 1*, the world's first satellite, the Tsiolkovsky Museum became a very popular attraction in the Soviet Union.

Further Reading

There is no readily accessible biography of Tsiolkovsky in English. A. Kosmodemyansky, *Konstantin Tsiolkovsky: His Life and Work* (Moscow, 1956), is not well known in the United States and suffers from a heavy burden of political propaganda. Much more objective is V. N. Sokolsky, *K. E. Tsiolkovsky: Selected Works* (Moscow, 1968); it is a compendium of Tsiolkovsky's works with a short biography appended, but it is also not widely available in the United States. Perhaps the best sources in English, which draw heavily on the above-cited references, are Willy Ley, *Rockets, Missiles, and Men in Space* (1952; rev. ed. 1968); Beryl Williams and Samuel Epstein, *The Rocket Pioneers on the Road to Space* (1958); and Albert Parry, *Russia's Rockets and Missiles* (1960). □

Tso Tsung-t'ang

The Chinese general and statesman Tso Tsung-t'ang (1812-1885) was one of China's leading military figures during the latter half of the 19th century.

Beginning with the Taiping Rebellion in 1850, it became increasingly clear to a small group of Chinese civilian and military officials that China would have to adopt some of the attributes of the West, especially the military techniques, if it hoped to preserve the dynasty and its traditional culture. This group came to be known as the "Self-strengtheners," and Tso Tsung-t'ang was one of the leaders.

Tso Tsung-t'ang was born on Nov. 10, 1812, in Hsiangyin, Hunan. As his family was moderately well off, Tso's education began at an early age. He obtained a *chu-jen* (the second-highest academic degree) in 1832, but after three unsuccessful attempts to qualify for the *chin-shih* (the highest academic degree)—the last in 1838—he gave up. From 1840 to 1848 he served as a teacher to the family of the late T'ao Chu, who was the former governor general of Liangkiang (Kiangsu, Kiangsi, and Anhwei). In 1844 Tso bought a farm in Hunan where he continued an earlier interest in geography, experimented in the ancient methods of cultivating tea, and promoted sericulture. He styled himself the "Husbandman of the River Hsiang" and wrote a book on agriculture in 1845.

Early Military Career

During the initial years of the Taiping Rebellion (1850-1864), Tso was not actively involved, but in 1852, at the age of 40, he joined the staff of the governor of Hunan, with full responsibility for military affairs. From that time until his death in 1885, he was continuously connected with, or in charge of, military operations. In 1860 he decided to try again for the *chin-shih*, but while en route to Peking, he received a letter from his friend and patron, Hu Lin-i, who was the governor of Hupei, which informed him that he should report to Tseng Kuo-fan's headquarters in Anhwei. Hu had been trying for several years to get Tseng to utilize Tso's talents, but up to now Tseng had refused on the grounds that the differences in their personalities would cause friction. Need overrode personalities, and as a key member of Tseng's forces, Tso began his rise to fame.

Tso Tsung-t'ang recruited a force of 5,000 men in Hunan and in September 1860 led them into battle in Kiangsi against the Taiping rebels. He chased the rebels into Chekiang and in December was made commander in chief of all government forces in Chekiang. In 1862 he became governor of Chekiang and, because of his subsequent victories, was promoted to governor general of Fukien and Chekiang in 1863. By early 1864 Chekiang had been cleared of rebels, and Tso turned to the task of rehabilitating Chekiang and Fukien.

As an early advocate of "Self-strengthening," whose thinking had been influenced by Lin Tse-hsü and Wei Yüan, Tso paid particular attention to naval matters. While in Foochow he experimented with small steamboats and in 1866, with French aid, established a navy yard. The latter project was hardly under way, however, when he was transferred to the northwest as the governor general of Shensi and Kansu to put down a Moslem uprising. Before he could reach his new assignment, he was diverted to the North to cooperate with Tseng Kuofan and Li Hung-chang in the fighting against the Nien rebels. With the successful suppression of that rebellion in 1868, he resumed his journey to the northwest frontier area.

Career in the Northwest

For the next 12 years Tso was actively engaged in the suppression of various Moslem rebels in Shensi, Kansu, and Chinese Turkistan. He successfully countered the two most serious threats to Chinese sovereignty in the area: the short-lived kingdom of Kashgaria under Yakoob Beg, which he crushed in 1877, and the Russian occupation of Ili from 1871 to 1881. In the latter incident it was Tso's army on the spot which strengthened China's hand at the conference table and forced the Russians to vacate the territory. Through his efforts the area of Sinkiang was finally incorporated into the Chinese empire as a province in 1884.

Even though Tso is known mostly for his military victories, he was also an able administrator. He partially solved his supply problems through his old interest in agriculture and had his troops farm in their off-hours. He also prohibited opium production and encouraged local industry by establishing cotton-and-wool-weaving factories. The willow trees which lined both sides of the great highway in Kansu were testimony to his concern for the land.

Later Career

In August 1880 Tso was ordered back to Peking. However, his brusque and outspoken nature and his long years in central Asia did not suit him for life in the capital, and he requested sick leave. Instead, he was appointed governor general at Nanking. When trouble with France over Annam became acute in 1884, he was summoned to Peking and put in charge of all the military affairs of the empire. Tso, who

was one of the leading war advocates and believed in fighting first and talking later, was set opposite Li Hung-chang, who was handling the diplomatic negotiations with France.

Tso moved to Foochow in late 1884 to supervise the military operations, while Li continued to work for a peaceful settlement. On June 9, 1885, Li signed a treaty with France, and on September 5 Tso Tsung-t'ang died in Foochow. On his deathbed Tso's concern for the safety of China rose above his long-standing hostility with Li, and he supported Li's "Self-strengthening" measures for the future of China.

Further Reading

The standard work in English on Tso is W. L. Bales, *Tso Tsung-t'ang: Soldier and Statesman of Old China* (1937). Gideon Ch'en, *Tso Tsung-t'ang: Pioneer Promoter of the Modern Dockyard and the Woollen Mill in China* (1938), discusses Tso's "Self-strengthening" interests; and Immanual C. Y. Hsu, *The Ili Crisis: A Study of Sino-Russian Relations, 1871-1881* (1965), deals with this aspect of Tso's career. For a short biography of Tso see Arthur W. Hummel, ed., *Eminent Chinese of the Ch'ing Period* (2 vols., 1943).

Additional Sources

Fields, Lanny B., *Tso Tsung-t'ang and the Muslims: statecraft in northwest China, 1868-1880,* Kingston, Ont.: Limestone Press, 1978. □

Tsou Yen

Tsou Yen (active late 4th century B.C.) was a Chinese philosopher important for developing the so-called Five Element theory, fundamental to Chinese philosophy and science.

Tsou Yen was born in Ch'i, a state in modern Shantung Province, where the Tsou family had established a reputation for scholarship early in the 4th century B.C. During this time the rulers of Ch'i had become active supporters of scholarly activities, and they established at the Ch'i capital an academy known as Chi-hsia, which was attended by hundreds of scholars from all parts of China. Tsou Yen was one of the most distinguished of these scholars and was held in particularly high esteem by the ruling family of Ch'i.

Little is known of Tsou Yen's life. He apparently became a popular figure in several of the states outside of Ch'i. He traveled to the neighboring state of Wei, where the ruler, King Hui (reigned 370-319), came out to the suburbs of the capital to greet him personally. Tsou was received with even greater respect by the minister of Chao, the Lord of P'ing-yüan, who walked at the side of his carriage and brushed the dust off his seat. In the northern state of Yen, King Chao (311-278) is said to have acted as Tsou's herald and even to have brushed the road before him. King Chao built a special palace so that he could take instruction from the great philosopher.

Tsou Yen is important primarily for his systematization of the Five Element theory, which has been one of the most influential ideas in Chinese philosophical and scientific thought. According to this theory, the dominant forces in the universe were the five elements, or agents (*hsing*), defined as fire, water, wood, metal, and earth. Tsou Yen conceived of these agents as operating as historical forces that govern the creation and the destruction of dynasties. He believed that each dynasty was ruled by a particular agent, which eventually would be replaced by another agent, thus creating another dynasty.

According to this theory, the dynasty of the legendary emperor Shun ruled by virtue of the element earth; the following dynasty, the Hsia, ruled by virtue of wood; the Shang, by metal; and Tsou Yen's own dynasty, the Chou, by fire. Tsou Yen combined this theory with the concepts of *yin* and *yang. Yin,* the dark and female principle, was said to alternate periodically with *yang,* the bright and male principle. Part of the year was governed by *yin* and the other part by *yang.*

How original Tsou Yen's theories were is not known. Similar ideas may have been circulating on the eastern seaboard of China about this time. Ch'i and Yen were the home of numerous magicians and alchemists who advocated many of the same theories as Tsou Yen. It is possible Tsou derived his system from these sources.

Further Reading

There is no single study of Tsou Yen in a Western language. The best summary of his life and ideas can be found in Joseph Needham, *Science and Civilization in China* (4 vols., 1954-1965). □

Harriet Ross Tubman

Harriet Ross Tubman (ca. 1820-1913) was a black American who, as an agent for the Underground Railroad, a clandestine escape route used to smuggle slaves to freedom in the North and Canada, helped hundreds flee captivity.

Born in Dorchester County, Md., in the early 1820s, Harriet Ross was a slave child who suffered the usual hardships of black children during the period of Southern slavery. Her wasted youth of hard work, no education, and sometimes harsh punishment led, predictably, to a desire to escape slavery. In 1848, with two brothers (who later became frightened and returned), she ran away, leaving her husband, John Tubman, a free man who had threatened to expose her, behind.

During the next 10 years Harriet Tubman returned to the South 20 times to help approximately 300 slaves, including her own parents, to escape. Using a complicated system of way stations on the route from the South to Canada, she is believed never to have lost a charge. In 1850 the Federal Fugitive Slave Law was reinforced with a clause that promised punishment to anyone who aided an escaping slave. In addition, a price of $40,000 was set for Tubman's capture. Thus she began transporting some slaves past the North to refuge in Canada.

Tubman supported John Brown's insurrection. Deeply disappointed after it failed, she began an intensive speaking tour in 1860, calling not only for the abolition of slavery, but also for a redefinition of woman's rights. In 1861, when the Civil War began, she served as a nurse, spy, and scout for the Union forces. Well acquainted with the countryside from her days as a "conductor" on the Underground Railroad, she was considered especially valuable as a scout.

After the war, owing to government inefficiency and racial discrimination, Harriet Tubman was denied a pension and had to struggle financially for the rest of her life. To ease this pressure, Sarah Bradford wrote a biography of Miss Tubman (1869), and the profits from its sales were given to her. A friend of many of the great figures of the day, she did finally receive a small pension from the U.S. Army. Meanwhile, she continued lecturing.

In 1857 Harriet Tubman had bought a house in Auburn, N.Y. During her last years she turned it into a home for the aged and needy. She died there on March 10, 1913, leaving the home as a monument to her character and will.

Further Reading

Harriet Tubman is represented in John F. Bayliss, ed., *Black Slave Narratives* (1970). Biographies include Sarah Elizabeth Bradford, *Harriet Tubman: The Moses of Her People* (1869; rev.

ed. 1961), and Earl Conrad, *Harriet Tubman* (1943). Anne Parrish, *A Clouded Star* (1948), and Ann Petry, *Harriet Tubman: Conductor on the Underground Railroad* (1955), are fictionalized accounts. □

William Vacanarat Shadrach Tubman

William Vacanarat Shadrach Tubman (1895-1971) was the nineteenth president of Liberia. His efficient management during six terms began the transformation of his country into a modern state.

William V. S. Tubman was born on Nov. 29, 1895, in Harper, Maryland County, Liberia. His father, the Reverend Alexander Tubman, was a general in the Liberian army, former Speaker of the Liberian House of Representatives, former senator, and a Methodist minister. His mother, Elizabeth Rebecca Barnes Tubman, came from Atlanta, Ga. Tubman attended primary school in Harper, then the Methodist Cape Palmas Seminary, and finally Harper County High School. Between 1910 and 1917 he took part in several punitive military expeditions, rising in the ranks from private to officer status. He studied law under private tutors, served as a recorder in the Maryland County Monthly and Probate Court and as a collector of internal revenue, and in 1917 was appointed county attorney.

Tubman entered the national political scene in 1923, when, at the age of 28, he was elected senator from Maryland County to the national legislature. He served in this capacity until 1937, when President Edwin Barclay appointed him to the post of associate justice of the Liberian Supreme Court. An official biography contends that Tubman's elevation to the Supreme Court was designed to remove him from active contention for the presidency.

However, Tubman remained active in Liberia's dominant political party, the True Whig party, and by 1943 had risen to such political standing that President Barclay personally nominated Tubman to succeed him. Tubman was elected president in 1943 and reelected in 1951, 1955, 1959, 1963, 1967, and 1971, for seven consecutive terms, which gave him the longest tenure of any modern president anywhere. For reasons intrinsic to Liberia's political system, Tubman's presidential opponents never garnered more than a minuscule portion of the votes cast.

As president, Tubman's most significant contribution to Liberian politics was his "unification policy," by which the hinterland counties, previously economically and politically neglected, were gradually brought into the national framework. The inland counties became fully represented in the Congress, roads and amenities were brought to the interior, and, most significantly, hinterland leaders began to play an important role in all areas of government. The open-door policy of Tubman, another major political line of his administration, permitted extensive foreign investment in

Liberia's economy, particularly with respect to the development of the rich iron ore areas of Mt. Nimba and in the Bong and Wologosi ranges.

Tubman was a devout Methodist, a past grand master of the Masons, and a patron or officer in most of Liberia's important civic and voluntary organizations. He died on July 23, 1971, in London after surgery. He left a widow, Antoinette Padmore Tubman, and six children, one of whom, William V. S. Tubman, Jr., was president of the Congress of Industrial Organization, Liberia's principal trade union federation. Tubman was succeeded in the presidency by his vice president, William R. Tolbert.

Further Reading

There is no scholarly biography of Tubman. A. Doris Bank Henries, *A Biography of President William V. S. Tubman* (1968), is an uncritical study. Thomas Patrick Melady, *Profiles of African Leaders* (1961), has a sympathetic chapter on Tubman. Less sympathetic are the profiles of Tubman in Rolf Italiaander, *The New Leaders of Africa* (trans. 1961), and John Gunther, *Procession* (1965).

Additional Sources

Wreh, Tuan, *The love of liberty: the rule of President William V. S. Tubman in Liberia, 1944-1971,* London: C. Hurst; New York: distributed by Universe Books, 1976. □

Barbara Tuchman

Pulitzer Prize winning historian and journalist Barbara Tuchman (1912-1989) was best known for her works on 20th-century wars although she also wrote on 14th-century France.

Barbara Tuchman was born in New York City on January 30, 1912, the daughter of Maurice and Alma (Morganthau) Wertheim. The Wertheim family was wealthy and had a tradition of interest in public affairs. Barbara's maternal grandfather was Henry Morganthau, Sr., a banker and American ambassador to Turkey during President Wilson's administration, and her uncle, Henry Morganthau, Jr., was Franklin Roosevelt's secretary of the treasury. Barbara's father was a banker and a publisher as well as having many outside interests, including founding the Theatre Guild and serving as president of the American Jewish Committee.

Barbara attended private schools in New York and graduated from Radcliffe College in 1933. Her early interest in history is shown by her honors thesis, "The Moral Justification of the British Empire." Although one of the professors she admired most at Radcliffe was the noted historian C.H. McIlliwain, he did not supervise her thesis. Instead, it was supervised by an English tutor who was little interested in the topic. Barbara did not pursue an advanced degree in history; her formal education in the topic ended in 1933.

Her informal education, however, continued. After graduation from Radcliffe she accompanied her grandfather to the World Economic Conference in London, where she observed economists and statesmen attempting to end the world-wide depression. When she returned from Europe she began her working career as an unpaid research assistant at the Institute of Pacific Relations in 1934. The following year she went to Tokyo for the institute as an editorial assistant, a raise in rank but not in pay. While working in Tokyo she sold her first article and embarked on a journalistic career.

Returning to the United States in 1936, she became an editorial assistant at *The Nation,* which her father had purchased from Oswald Garrison Villard. The following year she went to Spain to cover the civil war for the journal. Sympathetic to the Republican cause, she then became a staff writer for *War in Spain,* a publication subsidized by the Spanish government, in London from 1937 to 1938. During this same time she put together a very slim book entitled *The Lost British Policy: Britain and Spain Since 1700* (1938). The book, which was a rapid survey of relationships between the two nations, argued for British involvement in the current affairs of Spain. Next, Tuchman became the American correspondent for the *New Statesmen and Nation* for a year before returning to New York City.

On June 18, 1940, she married Lester R. Tuchman, a physician who was to become the president of the medical board of City Hospital in Queens. Barbara Tuchman began a domestic life and started a family which consisted of three daughters—Lucy, Jessica, and Alma. When World War II started and her husband enlisted in the Medical Corps, Tuchman followed him to Fort Rucker, Alabama. When he went overseas, she returned to work. From 1943 to 1945 she held a position on the Far East desk of the Office of War Information (OWI) utilizing her experiences with the Institute of Pacific Relations. When the war ended she returned to domestic life.

In 1948 she began work on her first major book, stimulated by events in the Middle East. Eight years later it appeared. *The book, Bible and Sword: England and Palestine from the Bronze Age to Balfour* (1956), took the position that the Balfour Declaration providing a homeland for the Jews was a logical extension of British tradition. The book, like her first one, was a survey showing much breadth but little depth. Her next book, *The Zimmerman Telegram* (1958), was quite different. It was an historical monograph which intensively analyzed the events and forces surrounding the cable which helped turn American public opinion against the German cause in World War I.

The following year Tuchman began research on the book that made her famous. In August she toured Belgium and France in order to learn the terrain where the first fighting of World War I had occurred. Her intensively researched *The Guns of August* (1962) won her a Pulitzer Prize and presented the events leading to World War I to a mass audience. She then wrote a description of the Belle Epoque (1900-1914), the period just prior to the war, which was published under the title *The Proud Tower* (1966). Her next major book switched locales from Europe to Asia and from World War I to World War II. Utilizing her experiences in the Orient and with OWI, she wrote *Stilwell and the American Experience in China* (1971). It, too, won a Pulitzer Prize.

Her later books did not cover the same ground. Her *Notes on China* (1972) was a slim, journalistic volume. It was followed by *A Distant Mirror* (1978), an historical account of events in 14th-century France. In 1981 she published a collection of lectures and articles given over the years under the title of *Practicing History,* and in 1984 she wrote *The March of Folly* (1984), which compared the errors in judgment made by the Pope in the Reformation, the British in the American Revolution, and the United States in Vietnam. At the time of her stroke and death in February, 1989 at the age of 77, her last book, *The First Salute* (about the American Revolution) had been on the *New York Times* best seller list for 17 weeks.

Along the way she accumulated many honors, including honorary doctorates in literature from Yale, Columbia, Bates, New York University, Williams, and Smith. She became a fellow of the American Academy of Arts and Sciences, which elected her president in 1978-1980 and awarded her the Gold Medal for History in 1978. In addition, Belgium inducted her into the Order of Leopold first class.

Tuchman's writings are noted for attention to detail and colorful style. The author was most interested in the human element in history and, consequently, emphasized biographical data even in works devoted to the coming and waging of war. She practiced narrative history in the tradition of Ranke, whose motto—to tell history as it is—she took for her own.

Further Reading

The biography of Barbara Tuchman appears in the standard contemporary reference works. Further details can be found in the *New Yorker* (October 6, 1962). She discussed certain personal aspects of her life in the introduction to *Practicing History* (1981), which also contains segments on her historical methods and philosophy. A nice tribute to some of her views appears in Dudley Barlow's *Lessons of History,* published in *Education Digest* (March, 1996). □

George Tucker

The American historian George Tucker (1775-1861) was the most significant historian from the South in the era preceding the Civil War.

George Tucker was born on Aug. 20, 1775, in St. Georges, Bermuda. He received his early education from tutors and entered the College of William and Mary in 1795, graduating 2 years later. He studied law in his uncle's office at Williamsburg and, after admission to the bar, moved to Richmond to practice. He married

Maria Carter, grandniece of George Washington, in 1802. Four years later the Tuckers moved to a country estate in Pittsylvania County, Va.

Tucker's *Letters from Virginia: Translated from the French* (1816), a satire on local customs, was published anonymously. Two years later he moved to Lynchburg and was elected to the U.S. Congress as a Jeffersonian Republican. During his three terms he was politically consistent, voting against protective tariffs and Federal subsidies for internal improvements.

In 1825 Tucker became professor of moral philosophy and chairman of the faculty at the University of Virginia. He expanded the curriculum, enrollment, and support of the university. He also taught political economy. He retired from the university in 1845. During this time he wrote *The Law of Wages, Profits, and Rent Investigated* (1837), *The Life of Thomas Jefferson* (2 vols., 1837), *Theory of Money and Banks Investigated* (1839), and *Progress of the United States in Population and Wealth* (1843). In his economic works Tucker assumed a modified classical position, denying the absolute determinism of population pressure and advocating governmental regulation of paper money. He favored a silver-based currency, and although he was not opposed to the idea of a national bank he believed that banks located strategically in three commercial centers would diminish the fear of monopoly.

At the age of 75 Tucker began his best-known work, *The History of the United States to the End of the 26th Congress in 1841* (4 vols., 1856-1857). He had planned to include social history but failed to do so in the completed work, which consists mainly of the annual messages of the presidents and the acts of Congress. The history spends little time on the colonial period, concentrating more on contemporary times. His own position by this time was that of a Southern unionist who believed that slavery could be defended on the basis of social control. He denounced abolitionists and argued that slavery was dying because of unfavorable economic conditions and that African Americans should be colonized. Because of these views his history did not win much acceptance North or South: his Southern position on slavery alienated the North, and his unionism proved too much for the South. He died on April 10, 1861, at a plantation near Charlottesville, Va.

Further Reading

A balanced treatment of Tucker's history is in Michael Kraus, *The Writing of American History* (1953). Alexander Bruce, *History of the University of Virginia* (3 vols., 1920), evaluates Tucker as chairman of the faculty. □

Franjo Tudjman

Franjo Tudjman (born 1922), once communist Yugoslavia's police general and political commissar, who subsequently turned military historian, politician, and finally president of the secessionist Republic of Croatia, was not an ordinary survivor. A favorite of the Communist dictator Tito, Tudjman reached the rank of major general at the age of 36. Croatia's parliament elected him the nation's first president in 1990, and he led his people to independence the following year. In 1992 and 1997, he was re-elected president. He will likely run the country for the rest of his natural life.

Franjo Tudjman was born on May 14, 1922, in Veliko Trgoviste, in the hills north of Zagreb. Little is known about Tudjman's early life other than that his father was a politically active landlord. In April 1941, the Germans invaded Yugoslavia. With their support, Ante Pavelic's nationalist movement, the Ustashe, set up the Independent State of Croatia. Young Franjo, about to graduate from gymnasium in Zagreb, was already known as a Communist sympathizer. When threatened with arrest by the Ustashe, he fled Zagreb to join one of the partisan units led by Josip Broz, also known as Tito. Tudjman's father and two brothers also joined the partisans, and his youngest brother died during the struggle.

After the war, the elder Tudjman was rewarded with a Communist Party committee chairmanship. In 1946, however, Tudjman's parents' lives ended abruptly when, according to Franjo, they were liquidated by the Communist Party. Zagreb authorities said they died as a result of a suicide pact.

During the war, young Franjo had advanced rapidly as a reliable political commissar at various working levels. The end of war found him as a 23-year-old major and political commissar of the 32nd Partisan Division. As one of Tito's most trusted officers, Tudjman attained the rank of general and held a variety of high-level positions. Among them, he was entrusted with the responsibility of monitoring Yugoslavia's senior officers corps' political ideology. In the years following the Tito-Stalin break he is said to have done his job only too well, helping to depose Tito's enemies to the notorious Adriatic island Goli Otok.

Historian and Nationalist

In 1961, after 15 years in Belgrade where he acquired a taste for a luxurious lifestyle and a preference for tennis, champagne, and caviar, Tudjman suddenly quit the army. He told friends he wanted to give his undivided attention to academic research in military and political history. From 1961 to 1967, Tudjman was the director of the Institute for the History of the Labor Movement of Croatia. He also served as associate professor of history at the University of Zagreb from 1963 to 1967. The University of Zagreb in 1964 rejected his dissertation as inadequate for a Ph.D. degree in history. However, the following year, he took the same dissertation, *The Causes of the Crisis of the Monarchist Yugoslavia from Its Inception in 1918 to the Collapse in 1946,* to the newer and less prestigious university at Zadar, which granted him a Ph.D.

Living and working in the center of Croat nationalism, Tudjman gradually abandoned his Titoist and pro-Yugoslav orientation, which eventually led to his expulsion from the Croatian Communist Party. As an historian, Tudjman wrote profusely, publishing books and scholarly articles on history, military theory, and international relations. His works brought him prominence but also criticism for what was termed "bourgeois-nationalist deviations" in dealing with the "national question."

For his role in the growing Croat nationalist movement, Tudjman was condemned to two years in prison in October 1972, although he served only 10 months of the sentence. Acting as a persistent dissident, he got three more years of imprisonment and a five-year ban on public activity on February 20, 1981.

Some of Tudjman's writings were controversial. He tried to disprove assertions that Croats had practiced genocide against Serbs during World War II. He claimed that the murder of Serbs was not a Ustashe policy but rather the actions of a small number of fanatics, that the number of Serbs killed was less than previously had been argued, and that the Serbs had also killed many Croats.

Tudjman suffered literary humiliation in 1967, when one of his works, *The Creation of the Socialist Yugoslavia,* was challenged as plagiarism by Croatia's premier historian, Ljubo Boban, who offered several conclusive proofs to his claim. What threatened to become a scandal of some proportions, however, was quickly papered over as just a little mistake.

Tudjman's most controversial work was *Wastelands of Historical Truth* (1989). His theory was that history merely repeats itself. For example, Tudjman said that Israel campaigns to reconquer the "promised land" by methods reminiscent of the Nazi "final solution" and employs genocidal practices he described as "Judeo-nazism." In February 1994, however, President Tudjman showed his political astuteness as he apologized in a letter to the American Jewish organization B'nai B'rith for the "hurtful" assertions he made in his book. He did not explain a widely circulated remark he made at a political rally during the first presidential election campaign. "I am elated every time it occurs to me that my wife is neither a Jew nor a Serb," said candidate Tudjman.

The Father of his Nation

In 1989, at the beginning of the collapse of the communist regime Tudjman was one of the leading founding members and president of the Croatian Democratic Union. The party won Croatia's first free elections. Tudjman was elected to the parliament, which chose him in 1990 to be Croatia's first president. His mandate was confirmed and extended for a second term by direct presidential elections in August 1992, in which Tudjman received 57 percent of the votes.

Within Croatia, President Tudjman gradually introduced the free market, although Croatia's economy continued to suffer from inflation. He purged the old Communist apparatchiks and replaced them with persons loyal to himself. Meanwhile the United Nations accused Croatia's government of press intimidation and human rights abuses. At the same time, Croatia's Serbian minority complained about summary dismissals of Serb employees from jobs designated as "sensitive" unless the Serbs in such jobs signed special loyalty oaths. President Tudjman's task was complicated by the neo-fascist Croatian Party of Rights, headed by Dobroslav Paraga, a skilled demagogue. Nevertheless, Tudjman maintained his authority.

Tudjman's imperious manner caused criticism at home and abroad. The regal-looking sash he wore on all festive occasions invited ridicule. His use of a luxurious and expensive private jetliner rather than commercial airliners raised eyebrows among those familiar with Croatia's precarious finances. Assessments such as autocratic, pompous, combative, thin-skinned, and insensitive to minorities were often heard. "Charm and patience," said one newsman, "are not Tudjman's strong suits." In his first two years as president he appointed and dismissed five prime ministers, five defense ministers, and six foreign ministers.

Croatia declared its independence on June 25, 1991, and a civil war broke out the following month. According to the last census in the former Yugoslavia, only 12 percent of Croatia's population were ethnic Serbs. Only in the Krajina enclave in the Dalmatian hinterland did Serbs form a majority. Despite this, Serbian irregulars, backed by arms and troops from Serbia itself, seized control of about 30 percent of Croatia's territory. In a process known as "ethnic cleansing," they drove out or massacred the Croatian villagers.

Germany recognized Croatia's sovereignty in December 1991, and many observers believe that Tudjman's excellent relationship with Hans-Dietrich Genscher, Germany's foreign minister at the time, had a lot to do with

Bonn's decision. Hostilities ended for a time in January 1992, when the European Community and UN mediated a truce between Croatia and the Krajina Republic (the Serbian secessionist government). Meanwhile, however the war had spread to Bosnia and Hercegovina, where fierce fighting continued until 1995.

After Croatian troops failed to regain territory lost to the Serbs, another cease-fire was negotiated in May 1993. In January 1994, Tudjman and Serbian President Slobodan Milosevic agreed establish offices in each other's capitals to begin "the process of the normalization of mutual relations."

Military Leader

However, the military situation within Croatia itself remained unsettled. With some American help, President Tudjman rebuilt and reequipped the Croatian army. In the summer of 1995, Croatian forces crossed the cease-fire line and recaptured the Krajina region. The troops drove out some 170,000 Serbs, who fled to Bosnia and Serbia. Hundreds of others were found with bullet holes in their heads or in unmarked graves, leading some foreign observers to question whether Croatia also was practicing "ethnic cleansing." Not everyone believed President Tudjman, when said he was doing all he could to stop the killings and punish those responsible.

These military victories were ratified in September 1996, when Croatia and the new Republic of Yugoslavia (consisting solely of Serbia and Montenegro) formally established diplomatic relations. Yugoslavia agreed to surrender the last Serbian-held regions in Croatia. In return, Presidents Tudjman and Milosevic each guaranteed legal protection to the citizens of the neighboring state.

Croatian success in driving the Serbs from the Krajina also helped to end fighting and extend Croat influence in neighboring Bosnia. In 1994, with U.S. backing, a Muslim-Croat Federation was created as a counterweight to the Bosnian Serbs. Following Croatian victories in the summer of 1995, a peace accord was agreed to in Dayton, Ohio, the following November. The agreement assigned 51 percent of the country to the Muslim-Croat Federation, and 49 percent to a Bosnian Serb Republic. Many Muslim Bosnians believed the Croatians had no intention of ever leaving. Adding to their fears was a highly publicized incident at a London dinner party. President Tudjman drew a map of Bosnia, then divided it in two, one half reading "Croatia," the other half "Serbia."

At home, Tudjman continued to be less than a friend to the free press, engaging in forced takeovers of some newspapers that criticized his government. Some foreign observers also scored Tudjman for his efforts to rehabilitate the World War II Ustashe regime as patriots and precursors of the modern Croatian state. He adopted the currency and flag associated with the Ustashe movement. And he ordered Ustashe soldiers reburied with honor.

President for Life

Despite his foreign critics, President Tudjman succeeded in winning recognition for Croatia as an independent state. In October 1996, Croatia was admitted to the Council of Europe, a human-rights organization. By 1997, with support from the International Monetary Fund and World Bank, the government could sell bonds on the world market. As a further sign of stability, Croatia was invited to join the Bank for International Settlements, a grouping of central banks based in Switzerland.

By the mid 1990s and in his 70s, Franjo Tudjman clearly was seriously ill. In November 1996, after he received medical treatment at the Walter Reed Army Medical Center in Washington D.C., U.S. officials reported that Tudjman had cancer and was not likely to recover. Nevertheless, Tudjman and the Croatian Democratic Union continued to cruise to electoral victory. With 61 percent of the vote, Tudjman himself easily won another five year term as President in June 1997. Although some foreign observers criticized the electoral process, it was clear that most Croatians wanted Franjo Tudjman to rule for the rest of his natural life.

Further Reading

A useful source for those who read Croatian is Tudjman's major work titled in translation *Wastelands of Historical Truth* (1989). There are, however, a number of articles in newspapers and periodicals addressing various aspects of Franjo Tudjman's life and work. See Stephen Kinzer, "Croatia's Founding Chief Seen as 'a Mixed Story'," *The New York Times* (August 5, 1993); Peter Maass, "Heard the One About Franjo Tudjman?" *The Washington Post* (June 5, 1992); Steve Coll, "Franjo Tudjman at War with History," *The Washington Post* (March 1, 1993); Stephen Engelberg, "Croatian Leader on Defensive in Fight for Re-election," *The New York Times* (August 2, 1992); Roger Boyes, "Tudjman Exploits Fascist Heritage," *The Times* (June 30, 1992); John F. Burns, "Croatia's Strongman Hedges His Bets," *The New York Times* (December 18, 1992); Teddy Preuss, "Goebbels Lives—in Zagreb," *Jerusalem Post International Edition* (December 21, 1991); Blaine Harden, "Croatians Vote in Aftershock of Vicious War," *The Washington Post* (August 2, 1992); Philip Sherwell, "Leader Tightens Grip on Croatia," *Washington Times,* courtesy of *London Daily Telegraph* (August 12, 1992).
Bennett, Christopher, *Yugoslavia's Bloody Collapse: Causes, Course and Consequences.* (1995). Vulliamy, Ed, *Seasons in Hell: Understanding Bosnia's War* (1994). "Shaky Future," *The Economist* (June 21, 1997). □

Tu Fu

Tu Fu (712-770) was a great Chinese poet of the T'ang dynasty. He is known as a poet-historian for his portrayal of the social and political disorders of his time and is also noted for his artistry and craftsmanship.

Born in Kung-hsien, Honan, of a scholar-official family, Tu Fu lost his mother in early childhood. His father, a minor district magistrate, remarried, and the boy lived for some time with his aunt in Loyang, the eastern capital. In his youth he traveled widely in the Yangtze River and Yellow River regions. He first met the poet Li Po in 744 in North China and formed with him a lasting friendship. In 746 Tu Fu went to Ch'ang-an, the capital, in search of an official position but failed to pass the literary examination or to win the patronage of influential courtiers. In 751 he sent to the Emperor a *fu* (rhymed prose) composition for each of three grand state ceremonials. While the Emperor appreciated Tu Fu's literary talents, he failed to award the poet an office or emolument.

After a long, futile wait in Ch'ang-an, his resources exhausted and his health declining, Tu Fu was offered a minor position at court. Just then, the An Lu-shan rebellion broke out (December 755) and threw the country into chaos. Tu Fu was captured by the rebels, escaped, and led the life of a refugee for some time before he was able to join the new emperor's court in exile. As a reward for his loyalty, he was appointed "Junior Reminder" in attendance upon the Emperor. In late 757 he returned with the court to Ch'ang-an, which had been recovered from the rebels, but did not stay there long. He had offended the Emperor by his candid advice and was banished to a provincial post. He soon gave it up and started in the fall of 759 a long journey away from the capital.

Tu Fu spent the next 9 years (759-768), the most fruitful period of his poetic career, in various cities in Szechwan. He settled down with his family in Ch'eng-tu, the provincial capital, where he built a thatched cottage and led a quiet, contented, though still impoverished life. Occasionally, he had to go from one city to another to seek employment or to escape from uprisings inside the province. For a year or so, he was appointed by Yen Wu, the governor general of Ch'eng-tu district, as military adviser in the governor's headquarters and concurrently assistant secretary in the Board of Works. Upon his patron's death in 765, Tu Fu left Ch'eng-tu for a trip that took him to a number of places along the Yangtze. Three years later he reached Hunan. After having roamed up and down the rivers and lakes there for almost 2 years (768-770), he died of sickness on a boat in the winter of 770.

Tu Fu's Poetry

The rich and manifold experiences in Tu Fu's life went into the making of a great poet. His works reveal his loyalty and love of the country, his aspirations and frustrations, his unbounded sympathy for the sad plight of the common people. He was an eyewitness of the historical events in a critical period that saw a great, prosperous nation ruined by military rebellions and wars with border tribes. Eager to serve the country, Tu Fu was helpless in averting its impending disasters and could only record faithfully in poems his own observations and sentiments. While some of his poems reflect his mood in happier moments, most of them tell of his poverty, his separation from and yearnings for his family, his wretched life during the war, his encounters with refugees, draftees, and recruiting officers. His own sufferings aroused in him a sincere and broad concern for humanity that gave poignancy to his poems.

Tu Fu possesses a remarkable power of description, with which he vividly presents human affairs and natural scenery. He introduces into his poetry an intense, dramatic, and poignant personalism through the use of symbols and images, irony and contrast. He is noted for his occasional sallies into wit and humor, even at despondent times. Above all, he has the ability to transcend the world of reality for the world of imagination. By means of a creative blending of artistic skill, heightened imagination, and deeply felt but well-controlled emotions, Tu Fu attains the height of Chinese poetry. An artist among poets, he excels in a difficult verse-form called *lü-shih* (regulated verse), of which he is an acknowledged master.

Further Reading

There are several English translations of Tu Fu's poems. Among them are Florence Ayscough, *Tu Fu: The Autobiography of a Chinese Poet* (1929) and *Travels of a Chinese Poet: Tu Fu, Guest of Rivers and Lakes* (1934); Rewi Alley, *Tu Fu: Selected Poems* (1962); and David Hawkes, *A Little Primer of Tu Fu* (1967). The best book on the poet is William Hung, *Tu Fu: China's Greatest Poet* (1952), a scholarly work on the poet's life with numerous illustrative poems arranged in chronological order. □

Rexford Guy Tugwell

Rexford Guy Tugwell (1891-1979) made numerous contributions to American intellectual and public life, including service in the Department of Agriculture under President Franklin D. Roosevelt and as governor of Puerto Rico. His scholarly writings stimulated debate on such issues as the role of planning in government and constitutional reform.

Rexford Guy Tugwell was born in Sinclairsville in western New York on July 10, 1891, the only surviving son of Charles H. Tugwell, then a moderately prosperous businessman and farmer, and Dessie Rexford Tugwell. From the age of 11 Tugwell lived in Wilson, New York, a community on Lake Ontario to which his father moved in 1902, and enjoyed his most prosperous years as owner and manager of a cannery. Raised in the Congregationalist tradition, Tugwell was able to participate in most of the outdoor activities available to a small town youth in turn-of-the-century America despite periodic attacks of allergies and asthma. A bright young man, he acquired a love of reading from his mother and from his father, who was a supporter of William Jennings Bryan in an area of the country where Bryan was heavily opposed, a willingness to think independently.

To remedy deficiencies in mathematics and the sciences Tugwell completed his final years of secondary education at Masten Park High School in Buffalo, New York, where he lived in a boarding house, commuting to Wilson on weekends. Living in Buffalo, which, in Tugwell's words, "illustrated the best and worst of industrial America," was

itself an education. Torn between a desire to become a journalist and a desire to pursue a conventional career in business, Tugwell opted initially for the latter and in 1910 applied for admission to the University of Pennsylvania's Wharton School of Finance and Commerce, only to be told he lacked sufficient preparation in mathematics and languages. He therefore undertook one more year of studies at Masten Park and then entered Wharton in 1911.

His experience at Wharton, ironically, awakened Tugwell further to the injustices found in a capitalist society, and though he never became the Communist critics would later accuse him of being—he deplored Communism's "iron logic" and "mechanistic doctrines"—he was influenced to question prevailing orthodoxies by Scott Nearing, an advanced liberal, and Simon Patten, a pioneering economist of the institutional school who inveighed against the classical doctrines of Adam Smith, David Ricardo, and Thomas Malthus. Tugwell found himself attracted to the literature of "revolt and reconstruction" and grew interested in an academic career. In 1914 he married Florence Arnold of Buffalo. They had two daughters.

Early Academic Career

Tugwell's first teaching experiences were at Pennsylvania, where he became a quiz section leader under Nearing in 1915 and then an instructor while he worked toward his master's degree, which he received in 1916. Dismayed by the encroachments on academic freedom recently imposed upon Wharton faculty, Tugwell left Pennsylvania in 1917 for a year at the University of Washington. While he found

the teaching of marketing "dreary," he also found stimulating intellectual companionship among the faculty, particularly in William Fielding Ogburn, a sociologist who would articulate the new concept of cultural lag and who, along with psychologist Carlton Parker, helped develop Tugwell's interest in applying the insights of psychology to economics and the other social sciences. He also learned by visits to the lumber camps of the area some of the more glaring labor and environmental abuses then practiced by American industrialists.

Distressed for a variety of reasons with conditions in Seattle, and probably wishing to make some contribution to the war effort, Tugwell gratefully accepted an opportunity arranged by Felix Frankfurter to live in Paris in 1918 and manage the American University Union, a leave center run by a consortium of a dozen universities for American officers serving in France. After the war Tugwell did enter his father's business in Wilson, but he soon returned to academia. In 1920 Tugwell secured a position at Columbia University teaching economics and also serving on the staff of the new contemporary civilization program. Finding it more tolerant of innovation, he liked Columbia much more than Pennsylvania, from which he received his doctorate in 1922.

Although he never got to teach as many of the prestigious graduate seminars in economics as he would have preferred, he won respect as a teacher, scholar, and administrator, climbing the academic ladder to full professor in 1931. He published often, developing special interests in agricultural economics and in industrial planning, for Tugwell considered himself a disciple of Frederick W. Taylor's studies in efficiency and believed that planning would cut down on the wastefulness of capitalism. He disliked equally the misallocation of resources that prevailed under capitalism and the laissez-faire attitude that promoted it. On the other hand, the iconoclastic Tugwell was just as disillusioned with some of the popular responses to capitalism's abuses—trust-busting, in particular.

By the late 1920s his reputation had spread sufficiently so that he began to be sought out as a consultant by politicians, first by the Republican governor of Illinois, Frank Lowden, then by Al Smith, and finally in 1932 by Democratic presidential aspirant Franklin D. Roosevelt. A Columbia colleague, Raymond Moley, recruited Tugwell along with Adolph Berle, Jr., also of Columbia, as campaign advisers and speechwriters for FDR. Their work with Roosevelt soon became known and publicized, and they became tagged the "Brain Trust."

Brain Trust for the New Deal

Following Roosevelt's election Tugwell was invited to serve in the Agriculture Department as assistant secretary, and then as undersecretary from 1934 to 1936. He was consulted on many matters—a staff in the White House had not yet become institutionalized—making his most memorable contributions to the New Deal in conservation, in urging reform of the food and drug laws, and in helping to plan the Agricultural Adjustment Act of 1933. He also administered the Resettlement Administration, a new agency created in 1935 by an amalgamation of several existing programs. Its purpose was to employ planning to cut down on rural poverty, and while it created a handful of greenbelt towns and succeeded in resettling some 4,000 farm families from wornout land to better land where they might have a chance to prosper, it never had the political support and/or funding to accomplish much.

In some respects conservative, for he opposed welfare and believed in a balanced budget, Tugwell was intensely disliked by many opponents of the New Deal, in large measure because of his advocacy of planning, which in the 1930s was facilely associated with the type of planning carried on in the Soviet Union of Joseph Stalin. A suave, somewhat arrogant personality, Tugwell was readily caricatured and attracted considerable attention in the more conservative segment of the popular press as "Rex the Red," an appellation which was not only inaccurate but painful to Tugwell. Although he was not entirely satisfied with the New Deal, regarding it as too much of a patchwork, Tugwell was willing to remain in Washington as long as he considered himself useful to the administration.

By Roosevelt's second election in 1936 Tugwell had become eager to leave. He not only had come to believe that his presence was obstructing the accomplishments of the Resettlement Administration, which carried on for several years after his departure as the Farm Security Administration, but Tugwell was planning to seek a divorce from his wife and preferred to do so out of the glare of Washington publicity. In 1938, his divorce finalized, he married Grace Falke, his administrative assistant. They had two sons. The previous year he had accepted a position as vice president of the American Molasses Company, owned by a longtime friend.

Always Planning for the Future

Tugwell soon returned to public life, however, when in 1938 he became chairman of New York City's newly created Planning Commission. Hopeful that rational longterm planning could be more readily introduced on the city level than on the national level, Tugwell optimistically referred to planning as "The Fourth Power of Government" in an address before a convention of planners in 1939. But Tugwell again found his efforts at planning thwarted by political realities: planners did not hold the purse strings of government, and he engaged in conflict with Park Commissioner Robert Moses and Mayor Fiorello LaGuardia.

From 1942 to 1946 Tugwell served as the last appointive governor of Puerto Rico. Although he was again frustrated in some of his aspirations, he had reason to be proud of his accomplishments as governor in improving the civil service, establishing auditing procedures, gaining more capital for economic development, and securing the establishment of the Agricultural Company to diversify Puerto Rican agriculture and lessen its blighting dependence on sugar.

Tugwell left Puerto Rico in 1946 and joined the University of Chicago at the invitation of Chancellor Robert Maynard Hutchins. As a professor of political science he taught courses on planning at the graduate level and endeavored to develop improved techniques of planning. Between 1957 when he retired from Chicago and 1966 when he became senior fellow in political science at the Center for the Study of Democratic Institutions in Santa Barbara, California, he held several positions in and out of academia, serving from 1961 to 1964 as Puerto Rican development counselor.

His years at Santa Barbara were among the most fruitful of his scholarly career. Perhaps his most ambitious project was the preparation of a series of drafts setting forth a proposed new constitution for the United States. Tugwell believed that as the nation approached its third century some serious questions about the adequacy of the present constitution needed to be asked. His study, published in 1970, was if nothing else provocative, as he proposed to replace the 50 states with a maximum of 20 regional republics, to give the president one nine-year term, and to establish planning and regulatory branches of government while drastically redefining both presidential and senatorial functions.

In 1979 Tugwell died, the author of numerous articles and 20 books, one of which, *The Brain Trust,* had won the prestigious Bancroft Prize in History in 1968. Tugwell made numerous contributions to American intellectual and public life over a 60-year period. Best remembered for his contributions to the New Deal and FDR's 1932 campaign, he also spent many years of worthwhile public service in Puerto Rico and in his scholarly writings stimulated debate over many issues. In particular, his longtime advocacies of planning and, later, of constitutional reform brought forth the type of dialogue that sustains a democratic society.

Further Reading

Anyone wishing to do serious research on Tugwell should start with the large collection of his papers deposited at the Franklin Delano Roosevelt Library at Hyde Park, New York. Published materials are also available. Tugwell wrote two autobiographical fragments, *The Light of Other Days* (1962), a nostalgic look at his upbringing in western New York, and *To the Lesser Heights of Morningside: A Memoir* (1982), an engagingly written look at his years at the Wharton School and at Columbia University. Several others of the 20 books he wrote contain autobiographical materials. Among them are *The Democratic Roosevelt* (1957) and *The Brain Trust* (1968), both of course focusing on his relationship with Franklin Roosevelt; *The Stricken Land: The Story of Puerto Rico* (1946), telling of his work as governor of Puerto Rico; and *A Chronical of Jeopardy* (1955), relating his public role during the Truman years, particularly his concerns about the nuclear threat. For Tugwell's ideas on the Constitution and his model of a new one, the September-October 1970 issue of *The Center Magazine* is indispensable. The same issue also contains Harry S. Ashmore's "Rexford Guy Tugwell: Man of Action," a perceptive sketch of Tugwell. *Industry's Coming of Age* (1927) was Tugwell's first important book and deals with a much earlier concern of his, industrial efficiency. As yet no biography of Tugwell has been published, but Bernard Sternsher, *Rexford Tugwell and the New Deal* (1964) covers admirably the most remembered of Tugwell's many contributions to the American polity. An obituary is in the *New York Times* (July 24, 1979).

Additional Sources

Namorato, Michael V., *Rexford G. Tugwell: a biography*, New York: Praeger, 1988.

Tugwell, Rexford G. (Rexford Guy), *To the lesser heights of Morningside: a memoir*, Philadelphia: University of Pennsylvania Press, 1982. □

Tung Ch'i-ch'ang

Tung Ch'i-ch'ang (1555-1636), a Chinese calligrapher, painter, and art historian, founded the Sung-chiang school of literati painting.

Tung Ch'i-ch'ang was born in Shanghai into a poor family with a tradition of scholarship and civil service. Compelled by the threat of forced labor, Tung ran away from home at about 16 and took up residence in the city of Hua-t'ing, Sung-chiang. Embarking on a course of traditional study, Tung repeatedly failed the civil service examinations. When he finally passed, however, in 1589, he did so brilliantly and began a career in government.

Tung's last posts were president of the Board of Rites and chief of instruction of the heir apparent, a far cry from his humble beginnings. He was not enamored of this or any other position, however. To be president of the Board of Rites rang hollow when the state was collapsing all around. It was an exceedingly difficult time in which to serve the state, for his plans went unheeded, and the fabric of state continued to crumble. Testifying to his continued dissatisfaction with affairs were Tung's repeated retirements, during which he withdrew to his home in the South to paint and write. One such period lasted from 1605 to 1620.

Study of Painting and Calligraphy

Tung's study of calligraphy may have been instigated by the importance of this art to success in the examination system. He quickly became the greatest brush master of the age, however, and is generally regarded as the most brilliant calligrapher of the past 500 years. His mastery of the brush certainly contributed to his later success as a painter.

It is not known precisely when Tung began to paint, but it was sometime in his 20s. During this time he was serving as tutor to several important families, and the influence of such older collectors and painters as Hsiang Yüan-pien and Ku Cheng-i, whose patronage he was able to secure, was decisive in shaping the tastes of the young artist. More significant may have been the directions set out by the brilliant Mo shih-lung, an older contemporary and friend. According to Tung, it was Mo who laid down the framework of the theory of the Northern and Southern schools of painting, which Tung subsequently elaborated and explored in his own painting.

The basis of the new direction in landscape painting was appreciation and understanding of the great masters of the Yüan period (1279-1368), especially the Four Great Masters of that age, Huang Kung-wang, Wu Chen, Ni Tsan, and Wang Meng. It was believed that they were the last painters to realize the monumental and enduring qualities of the great universe with integrity and substance, unswayed by popular convention and the common taste. During the long interval between the 14th and late 16th centuries, Tung believed, painters had too often fallen into the paths of sweetness, romanticism, and elaborateness and thus had departed from the classical wellspring of the art. He set out to restore the integrity of landscape painting.

Northern and Southern Schools

Following Mo Shih-lung's tentative theoretical proposal, Tung codified and elaborated the theory that related scholar-painters, beginning with Wang Wei, in a continuous succession of classical transmission. This mantle of the "Southern school" was believed to rest on Tung's shoulders in the late Ming period. Included within the orthodox transmission were Tung Yüan, Li Ch'eng, Fan K'uan, Li Kung-lin, Mi Fu, Mi Yu-jen, and the four Yüan masters. To the "Northern school" were consigned all academicians and professionals—like Ma Yüan and Hsia Kuei—and the founder was said to be the T'ang master of the decorative "blue-and-green" style, Li Ssu-hsün. Tung Ch'i-ch'ang even went so far as to assert that the professional pursuit of a career in painting would lead to a premature death, citing in contrast the long lives of the scholar-amateurs. He himself lived into his 80s.

In his own powerful painting, Tung faithfully observed the newly established orthodoxy. There are no human figures in his work, no story, and no concession whatever to public taste. His subject was style itself, the great styles of the past, and their transformation into expressions of Tung's own inner will. He believed that one must first immerse oneself in the white light to be found in the classical art of the great styles of the past, which he viewed as a succession of insights into "truth," and then must begin the long and difficult process of giving all back piece by piece until one is left only with self, a self transformed by the crucible of discipline and years of intense study. If this final transformation can be won, the painter himself will join the classical heritage and lend his own hard-won vision to the totality of experience.

In Tung's own case, the result was a compelling structure of abstract compositional principles through which he achieved a strongly architectonic symphony of "brush and ink." He readily disclaimed any pretense to naturalism: "If you want to admire the beauties of mountains and trees, take a walk in the hills," he said in effect, "but if you admire the beauties of brush and ink, look to painting." His position in the history of Chinese painting corresponds to that of Paul Cézanne in Western art history.

Further Reading

The best general account of Tung, his position in history, his art, and his legacy, is Roderick Whitfield, *In Pursuit of Antiquity: Chinese Paintings of the Ming and Ch'ing Dynasties* (1969). An excellent biographical essay by Nelson Wu, "Tung Ch'i-ch'ang (1555-1636): Apathy in Government and Fervor in Art," is in Arthur F. Wright and Denis Twitchett, eds., *Confucian Personalities* (1962). Recommended for background is

Victoria Contag, *Chinese Masters of the 17th Century,* translated by M. Bullock (1970). □

Abdul Rahman Tunku

Known as "the Tunku" in Malaysia, Tunku Abdul Rahman (1903-1990) was the first prime minister of the Federation of Malaya, and later of Malaysia. He was considered the "father of the nation."

For decades Malaysians have referred to their country's first prime minister, Tunku Abdul Rahman, simply as "the Tunku." The title, literally meaning "my lord," is shared by several other Malay aristocrats; but it is a clear indication of his stature as "father of the nation" that only Tunku Abdul Rahman is "the Tunku."

Tunku Abdul Rahman was 54 years old when, on August 31, 1957, he accepted from the Queen's representative documents which formally granted independence and sovereignty to the Federation of Malaya. His life up to that point had prepared him well for a position of national leadership. His father was the Sultan Abdul Hamid Halim Shah, whose reign in Alor Star, capital of the state of Kedah, spanned a period of 61 years.

Kedah is one of nine Malay states which Great Britain had controlled, along with the "Straits of Settlements" of Singapore, Malacca, and Penang, since early in the 19th century. In furtherance of their objective of developing tin mines and rubber plantations, the British encouraged immigration of laborers from China and India while protecting the indigenous Malay culture and institutions. This paternalistic policy made it possible for Tunku Abdul Rahman to study at Cambridge for the better part of 12 years, beginning when he was 16 years old.

While in England the Tunku helped establish and became secretary of the Malay Society of Great Britain. This experience, and his subsequent tenure with the Kedah state civil service, foretold his participation in the slowly developing and moderate Malayan nationalist movement. Upon returning in 1949 from another stay in England, during which he completed his legal studies, Tunku Abdul Rahman became chairman of the Kedah Branch of the United Malays National Organization (UMNO), the political party which served as the major vehicle of anti-colonial sentiment. When the Tunku accepted the national presidency of the UMNO in 1951 he became the leading exponent of Malayan nationalism.

Communal Tensions a Persistent Problem

Malaya's large Chinese and Indian populations were not assimilated into Malay culture, and the uneasy relations among Malays, Chinese, and Indians have been a fundamental and persistent societal problem. The Tunku is credited with devising the formula whereby political organizations representing the Chinese and Indian communities joined with UMNO to constitute the Alliance Party. The

Alliance, or, as it came to be called after other parties were invited to join it in the early 1970s, the National Front, was the government party after independence. Its most one-sided electoral victory occurred in 1955 in the first federal elections, when 51 of 52 elected representatives were Alliance candidates.

In the years leading up to independence the Tunku was involved in government efforts to suppress a Communist insurgency known as "the emergency." The fact that the Malayan Communist Party, which abandoned guerrilla tactics in the early 1960s, had a predominantly Chinese membership aggravated interethnic tensions. In 1969 the simmering communal conflict boiled over when, in the aftermath of parliamentary elections, bands of armed Malays and Chinese attacked one another and generally caused considerable property damage and some loss of life. It was the most severe crisis of the Tunku's tenure as prime minister, and he described the anguish it caused him in his book *May 13: Before and After.* Although neither he nor any other person could engineer racial harmony and prevent violence, Tunku Abdul Rahman strove for conciliation. As one authoritative account put it, he was "liked and respected by members of all communities and considered honest, fair, and tolerant."

Foreign Affairs a Major Activity

Once Malaya became independent the British sought to disengage from other colonial territories in the region. By 1963 it had been determined that this would be achieved through the concept of Malaysia, which by then was strongly supported by Tunku Abdul Rahman. In September 1963 Malaya, Singapore, Sarawak, and Sabah were joined together in the new nation-state of Malaysia. In that form it was short-lived, for the UMNO leadership felt that Singapore's well-organized political elite was excessively ambitious. In August 1965 the Tunku informed first Lee Kuan Yew, prime minister of Singapore, and then the Malaysian Parliament that Singapore was being separated from Malaysia and would become an independent nation-state.

Neither the separation of Singapore nor the bitterly anti-Malaysia position adopted by Indonesia's President Sukarno prevented Tunku Abdul Rahman from pursuing a policy of regional cooperation. Having participated in the establishment of the Association of Southeast Asia in 1961, the Tunku supported the expansion of the association in 1967 to include Singapore and Indonesia. The organization thus formed, the Association of Southeast Asian Nations, joined those two countries with Malaysia, Thailand, the Philippines, and, later, Brunei in a vigorous and durable regional grouping. In addition, the Tunku's commitment to constructive participation in the British Commonwealth as well as his active interest in international Islamic affairs established the basic parameters of Malaysian foreign policy.

In 1970 Tunku Abdul Rahman relinquished the leadership of UMNO, and with it the position of prime minister, to his close associate, Tun Abdul Razak. After his retirement the Tunku's ability to enjoy certain of his favorite forms of recreation, such as golf and travel, was impaired by physical problems, but he took conspicuous pleasure in time spent with his family. As the "grand old man" of Malaysian public affairs, he also made occasional public appearances, such as his speech dedicating the new Malaysian Chinese Association headquarters building in early 1983. He also wrote a weekly newspaper column under the title "As I See It" and thus continued to add to his enormous influence on political and social life in Malaysia.

Tunku, who led Malaysia in winning independence from Britain in 1957 and served 13 years as its first prime minister, died Dec. 6, 1990. He was 87.

Further Reading

Two biographical accounts provide information on the Tunku's early life and political career. They are Harry Miller, *Prince and Premier* (1959), and Willard Hanna, *Eight Nation Makers: Southeast Asia's Charismatic Statesmen* (1964). Studies which describe the Malaysian political scene more generally include Gordon Means, *Malaysian Politics* (1970), and R. S. Milne and Diane Mauzy, *Malaysia: Tradition, Modernity, and Islam* (1985). Pending a compilation of the Tunku's *Star* newspaper columns, the best glimpse of the Tunku's personal style and predispositions is provided by his book *May 13-Before and After* (1969). His obituary ran in several newspapers including the *Los Angeles Times*. □

José Gabriel Túpac Amaru

The Inca and Peruvian nobleman José Gabriel Túpac Amaru (1742-1781) was the leader of the largest Native American revolt in the Americas. He was a man of sufficient learning, had a passion for reform, and hated injustice.

Túpac Amaru was born in Tinta south of Cuzco. He was young when his father died, but two uncles became his guardians and gave him the best possible education. At the age of ten he went to Cuzco to study in the Jesuit College of San Francisco de Borja, built for Native American boys of noble birth. He read Latin readily and spoke Spanish correctly and Quechua with grace. He married Michaela Bastidas Puyuahua, a pure-blooded Spaniard from Abancay. From this marriage he had three sons—Hipólito, Mariano, and Fernando.

When Túpac Amaru's oldest brother, Clemente, died, he inherited the caciqueship of Tungasuca, Pampamarca, and other places. He governed the descendants of the Incan nation and collected tribute for the Spanish *corregidor* (governor). He respected the Inca system of government and old customs. He was a man of striking appearance, with a pleasant and amiable countenance and unassuming manners. Tall, robust, and very white for his lineage, he lived and dressed like a Spanish nobleman, but after the start of the Inca revolt he modified his costume to include some Indian styles.

Túpac Amaru was a wealthy man and owned a large cacao estate in the province of Caravaya. His income came

chiefly from transporting merchandise and quicksilver. His enemies called him the "Muleteer Cacique." He traveled extensively and was in touch with the people and conditions in all parts of Peru. He informed the viceroy and other officials of the hardships suffered by the Indians under the *mita* system—forced labor in the mines, on plantations, and in workshops.

The greatest obstacle to reform was the *corregidor* Antonio de Arriaga of Tinta. His actions became so intolerable that Túpac Amaru had him seized and executed on Nov. 10, 1780. The Inca called upon the people to support him in his efforts to abolish abuses. They responded eagerly and the Inca revolt broke out. It spread rapidly throughout Peru, Bolivia, much of Argentina, and other parts of South America.

Túpac Amaru never tried to destroy Spanish institutions and was always loyal to the Crown and the Church. At first his revolt had considerable success. But after the Spaniards had time to organize their military forces, the superiority of their weapons defeated him.

Their vengeance was terrible. Túpac Amaru had to witness the execution of his wife, oldest son, an uncle, and some of his captains before his own death. When the revolt continued, the Spaniards exterminated the remainder of the Inca's family, except Fernando, who was imprisoned in Spain for the rest of his life. The revolt resulted in some minor reforms in Peru.

Further Reading

Very little has been written in English about Túpac Amaru. The only book is by Lillian Estelle Fisher, *The Last Inca Revolt, 1780-1783* (1966). Philip Ainsworth Means, *Fall of the Inca Empire and the Spanish Rule in Peru, 1530-1780* (1932), includes material on Túpac Amaru. □

Andrei Nikolaevich Tupolev

The Russian aeronautical engineer and army officer Andrei Nikolaevich Tupolev (1888-1972) was the leading designer of large and heavy aircraft in the former U.S.S.R.

Andrei Tupolev was born on Nov. 10, 1888, in the village of Pustomazovo (now Kalinin Oblast). In 1909 he entered the Moscow Higher Technical College, studied under Nikolai Egorovich Zhukovskii, the "father of Russian aviation," built wind tunnels as a student, and participated in the college's aeronautical club. It is believed that he received further training under Hugo Junkers, who set up an aircraft construction facility in Fili, a suburb outside of Moscow, under a 1922 Russo-German agreement. After graduation Tupolev assisted Zhukovskii in organizing the Central Aerohydrodynamics Institute, where he was assistant director from 1918 to 1935 and headed its design bureau beginning in 1922.

Tupolev's early work centered on wind tunnels and training gliders. He became a pioneer in the construction of all-metal aircraft fabricated out of Duralumin. In the course of his career Tupolev designed well over 100 planes, from his first, the ANT-1, a light transport made mainly of wood, to the supersonic jet transport, the TU-144, the world's most sophisticated commercial aircraft. Some of his more significant earlier designs are the two-seater ANT-2, constructed in 1924 completely out of Duralumin; the TB-1, a two-engine bomber with a range of 625 miles and a speed of 138 miles an hour; and the highly successful four-engine heavy bomber, the TB-3, weighing over 43,000 pounds and capable of carrying over 2 tons.

Tupolev headed the design bureau that produced an unusual 40-ton plane, the *Maksim Gorkii,* which carried six engines mounted on its wings and two atop the fuselage. Within the plane provision was made for a telephone switchboard, telegraph center, radio station, printing facilities, photographic laboratory, and motion picture projectors. With much fanfare the *Maksim Gorkii* made a trial flight in June 1934. The following year it collided with another craft, resulting in the death of 35 people; it was never replaced.

In 1936 Tupolev visited the United States and Germany to study methods of aircraft construction, and the following year he was accused of selling to Germany blueprints of a plane that supposedly became the Messerschmitt 109 fighter. He was subsequently labeled an "enemy of the people" and sentenced to be executed. While in prison he designed the TU-2, a twin-engine dive bomber. For his role in producing the Soviet Union's sole new bomber of World War II, he was released from prison. In 1944 he was the Soviet Union's chief designer of heavy bombers. After the forced landing of three Boeing B-29 Superfortresses in 1944 in the Soviet Far Eastern Territory, Tupolev produced a Russian version of this American bomber.

In the postwar period, Tupolev's best designs include the TU-104, a twin-jet transport used extensively in the U.S.S.R.; the TU-114, a double-deck, four-engine turbo-prop passenger plane; and the TU-144, the Soviet entry in the supersonic-transport field. On Dec. 31, 1968, the TU-144 lifted off in a test flight—the first supersonic transport to become airborne. It was capable of speeds up to 1500 miles an hour with a range of 4000 miles.

Tupolev was made a lieutenant general in the technical branch of the Red Army during World War II. He became a full member of the Soviet Academy of Sciences in 1953 and served on many governmental agencies.

He died in 1972.

Further Reading

There is no definitive work on Tupolev in Russian or English. Scattered references in Soviet newspapers, aviation journals and surveys of Soviet aviation provide some information on his contributions. However, a fine section on the history of Soviet military aviation appears in William Green and John Fricker, *The Air Forces of the World: The History, Development and Present Strength* (1958). Material on Tupolev's aircraft can be found in Robert A. Kilmarx, *A History of Soviet Air Power* (1962), and Asher Lee, *The Soviet Air Force* (1962). □

Sir Charles Tupper

Sir Charles Tupper (1821-1915) was one of the Canadian fathers of confederation. He was a political leader in Nova Scotia and then Canadian Cabinet minister, high commissioner to the United Kingdom, and prime minister of Canada.

Charles Tupper was born on July 2, 1821, at Amherst, Nova Scotia, of Puritan stock. He was educated at Horton Academy, Wolfville, and in Edinburgh, Scotland, where he earned a degree in medicine in 1843. He practiced medicine successfully in Cumberland County, Nova Scotia, and developed a wide acquaintance which in 1855 helped him defeat a formidable opponent, Joseph Howe, for the Cumberland seat in the Legislative Assembly. Thereafter Tupper, an aggressive politician, rose rapidly in the ranks of the Conservative party, and he became premier of Nova Scotia in 1863.

Tupper's leadership was marked by a courageous reorganization of the province's educational system under the nonsectarian Council of Public Instruction and by his persistent championing of a union of the British North American colonies. Probably the most fruitful part of Tupper's confederation work came from his friendship with John Alexander Macdonald, who, when he became the first prime minister of Canada, chose Tupper as his right-hand man. Tupper was not at once in the first Canadian Cabinet, standing aside to permit a more balanced representation of Roman Catholics (Tupper was a Baptist), but he entered as president of the council in 1870. In the meantime, he had overcome ferocious opposition to Nova Scotia's participation in confederation and had even induced Howe, a leader of "repeal," to enter Macdonald's government.

When Macdonald resigned in 1873 and was leader of the opposition until 1878, Tupper was again the forceful lieutenant, although he had to resume the practice of medicine. On Macdonald's victory in 1878, Tupper became minister of public works and then of railways and canals, in which capacity he was the overseer of the building of the Canadian Pacific Railway. So vast an enterprise made him enemies, and although no personal corruption was charged, his temporary retirement from the Cabinet was considered a sound move; in 1883 he was appointed high commissioner (ambassador) to the United Kingdom.

Tupper returned to Canada to campaign in the general elections of 1887 and 1891, briefly becoming minister of finance in 1887-1888. In 1896, when the Conservative party had fallen into almost total disarray after having had three leaders since Macdonald's death in 1891, Tupper was offered the prime ministership, which he assumed after the end of the first parliamentary session of 1896. He fought, and lost, the general election of 1896 as prime minister and

remained as leader of the opposition until his personal defeat in 1900 as member of Parliament for Cumberland, a seat he had held provincially and then federally (except for his tours of duty in the United Kingdom) since 1855. He retired to look after a variety of business interests, dividing his time between Canada and England, and died in England on Oct. 30, 1915, the last survivor of the fathers of confederation.

Tupper was a doughty fighter for anything he believed in and an implacable foe of those who opposed him. His loyalty and courage were legendary, and under different circumstances he could easily have become a great prime minister. His major defeats (as in his inability to carry Nova Scotia either provincially or federally for confederation in 1867, the anticonfederates scoring overwhelming victories in both arenas) he regarded as merely temporary. He was a stout champion of Canadian autonomy and argued for a policy of national development years before the Conservative party under Macdonald finally adopted one.

As high commissioner in London, Tupper invariably sought, and with growing success, to enlarge Canada's role in the negotiation of treaties affecting the country. Frequently in his career he inherited enormous problems, one of the chief ones being the question of sectarian schools for Manitoba in 1896. But he never sought to avoid them or to blame somebody else for them. In 1869, during Canada's first Northwest rebellion, he went directly into the enemy's camp to seek news of his daughter, whose husband was an army captain.

Further Reading

There are several good books on Tupper, including his own *Recollections of Sixty Years in Canada* (1914); William A. Harkin, ed., *Political Reminiscences of the Rt. Hon. Sir Charles Tupper* (1914); E. M. Saunders, ed., *The Life and Letters of the Rt. Hon. Sir Charles Tupper* (1916); and James W. Longley, *Sir Charles Tupper* (1917).

Additional Sources

Durant, Vincent, *War horse of Cumberland: the life and times of Sir Charles Tupper,* Hantsport, N.S.: Lancelot Press, 1985. □

Cosimo Tura

The Italian painter Cosimo Tura (1430-1495) was the principal master of the school of Ferrara and one of the leaders of northern Italian painting.

Cosimo Tura was born in Ferrara sometime before April 28, 1430. He became court painter to Duke Borso d'Este in Ferrara. The duke provided Tura with rooms in the ducal household, later gave him a house, and paid him so well that Tura became a wealthy man. For the duke he executed numerous commissions in what are now called the applied arts. Documents reveal that he designed flags and banners, costumes for pageants, silverware, and tapestries and that he painted horse trappings and tournament helmets and shields.

Tura never married; he had a son by his housekeeper. After his patron died in 1471, Tura's popularity waned. In his later years he lived in a tower of the Ferrara city walls. He died in April 1495.

Tura's early style shows his development out of the International Gothic art of the early 15th century in Ferrara. Works such as the *Portrait of a Member of the Este Family* (ca. 1451), the *Madonna with Sleeping Child* (ca. 1460), and an allegorical figure (Venus or Spring; ca. 1465) display the decorative Gothicism of such masters as Pisanello, Gentile da Fabriano, and Rogier van der Weyden. However, Tura's own contribution is seen in his frequent use of involved symbols and attributes and his love of astrological symbolism. In these early works there is a concern for carefully delineated contours, rather flat and smooth colors, and meticulous craftsmanship, characteristics that persisted in all his paintings.

Tura's mature style built upon the linearism and decorativeness of his early works but added a concern for figures in action. All the monumental works associated with Tura date from the period 1465-1480. In 1465-1467 he decorated the library walls of the castle at Mirandola for Count Francesco I Pico (these frescoes no longer exist). In 1468-1469 he painted the organ door for the Cathedral of Ferrara. The *St. George Slaying the Dragon* on the outside of the door is all movement, action, and noise; the *Annunciation* on the inside is tranquil and silent.

There is scholarly disagreement over whether Tura executed any of the frescoes (1469-1471) in the Hall of the Months in the Palazzo Schifanoia, Ferrara. A document which indicates that Tura was employed elsewhere at the time has been widely accepted to indicate that he did not participate in the decoration. However, the style of the frescoes, especially of the allegory *September,* is certainly his, and some scholars have argued that Tura could easily have carried out two projects at the same time. If he did not actually paint in the Palazzo Schifanoia, he must have assisted in designing the frescoes and perhaps supplied some of the cartoons. The painters who executed the cycle were Francesco del Cossa, Baldassare d'Este, Ercole de'Roberti, and Antonio Cicognara.

Among Tura's extant late work only the *St. Anthony of Padua* (1484) can be assigned with assurance. It is a strangely compelling depiction of the saint, who is rendered with an emphatic fullness that contrasts with the creamy texture of the painting itself.

Further Reading

Eberhard Ruhmer, *Tura: Paintings and Drawings* (1958), has good plates and a full bibliography. For general background see Benedict Nicolson, *The Painters of Ferrara* (1950); Ernest T. DeWald, *Italian Painting, 1200-1600* (1961); and Cecil Gould, *An Introduction to Italian Renaissance Painting* (1957). □

Hassan Abdullah al-Turabi

The major leader of the Sudan's Islamic fundamentalist movement, Hassan Abdullah al-Turabi (born 1932), served the Sudan in various capacities.

Born in 1932 in the town of Wad al-Turabi, Hassan al-Turabi led the Islamic fundamentalist movement, the National Islamic Front (NIF), which was influential in moving the Sudan toward being an Islamic state based on Islamic law. Turabi, the son of an Islamic legal judge, first attended the University of Khartoum, where he earned a law degree. Turabi elected to continue his studies in Europe. He first took a Master of Laws degree from the University of London, then a Doctorate in Laws from the prestigious University of Paris. With these solid academic credentials, Hassan al-Turabi returned to the Sudan, where he became known as one of his nation's leading experts on the Sharia, or Islamic law.

At the core of Turabi's thought was the belief that an Islamic state cannot exist unless it is rooted in the Sharia. Islam as a way of life permeates every aspect of a state or a citizen's being. Consequently, it would be impossible to have a Muslim state without the primacy of the Sharia. If the state has a sizable non-Muslim minority (as is the case with the Sudan), the need of the Islamic majority to exist under the Sharia is paramount. The devout Muslim must be in opposition to the secular state, but Turabi's considerable

foreign education and travel convinced him that, to have influence, cooperation was possible.

The Sudan is slightly under one million square miles, with a population of about 14 million. The northern provinces are predominately Arab in culture and Islamic in faith. The southern provinces, which contain a minority of the population, are African in culture and traditional African or Christian in belief. Thus the Sudan is a blend of the Middle East and Africa and is diverse in belief and culture.

On January 1, 1956, the Sudan became independent but was unable to establish a parliamentary democracy. In 1963 violence flared in the south, where it was believed that power and wealth was firmly in the hands of Muslims in the capital, Khartoum. The situation in the Sudan led to a revolt, which broke out on October 21, 1964, resulting in an overthrow of the military government and promises of reforms that would affect all of the Sudan. Turabi, fresh from his studies in Europe, participated in the October Revolution and emerged as the leader of the Muslim Brotherhood. Known officially as the Islamic Charter, the Brotherhood came under Turabi's leadership as he changed it from an Islamic study group to a viable and well financed organization, the NIF.

Turabi's influence in Sudanese affairs continued to grow, and by the time Colonel Gafaar Numeiri seized power in the coup, al-Turabi was a force to be reckoned with. After the Numeiri coup of 1969 Turabi was the leading opposition figure, and he was jailed a number of times for his outspoken criticism of the regime. To Turabi, Numeiri's government was secular, unconcerned with Islamic issues; this, of course, was Turabi's main concern.

In 1964 Turabi had named himself secretary general of the National Islamic Front, and his prestige as a noted legal scholar and as a spokesman for the Islamic state had spread throughout the Muslim world. Numeiri had to be careful in dealing with a man of Turabi's stature, and in 1977 Numeiri offered to his opponents a national reconciliation. Much to the surprise of some hard-line members of the NIF, Turabi accepted the offer and was released from jail. Turabi began a campaign to move the Sudan's legal system toward an acceptance of the Sharia. He headed a commission that proposed a number of critical changes in the system, and in 1979 he accepted the post of attorney general of the Sudan, which he held until 1983.

To quiet his Muslim opponents, Turabi, as a pragmatist, pointed out that the fundamentalist NIF could not want a better position for one of their own. By the end of Turabi's tenure as attorney general the Sudan was moving toward an Islamization of their legal system, bringing it in line with the Sharia. The Numeiri government had promised to follow a "socialist and democratic course," but with the changes in the legal system it was becoming obvious that the move was toward Islamic and Koranic religious principles.

During the last months of the discredited Numeiri regime, Turabi was again imprisoned. This spared him criticism, since he had served as attorney general (1979-1983) and as adviser on foreign affairs (1983-1985). Released from prison after the fall of Numeiri, Turabi increased his pressure on the new government to move the Sudan toward a totally Islamic state. In 1986 Turabi led the NIF to a strong third-place finish in free elections. Between 1986 and 1988 Turabi led the opposition to Prime Minister Sadiq al-Mahdi's government, but in 1988 he entered the government as attorney general. His assumption of the position continued Islamization, but it also exacerbated relations between the north and the disaffected south. For two months in 1989 Turabi served as foreign minister.

Turabi was ousted from the government for his unyielding opposition to any compromise with the south, especially with the Sudanese People's Liberation Army. After leaving the government, Turabi traveled frequently throughout the Islamic world, Europe, and the United States. Given his stature as a spokesman for the primacy of the Sharia in the Muslim state, he was much in demand as a speaker. In 1992 he was attacked by an opponent while on a visit to Canada, suffering a brain contusion. After that time Turabi had a restricted schedule. But he still stood as a visible, articulate spokesman for the Islamic state and remained a major figure in Sudanese political and religious life.

Turabi functioned as the architect and actual power behind the scene of the government of President Omar Hassan al-Bashir, who seized power in 1989 in a military coup which overthrew the elected Mahdi government. Turabi and the Bashir regime faced U.S. criticism for supporting terrorism, for banning political parties, and for human rights violations and torture against political prisoners, trade unionists, and academics. The government efficiently continued pursuit of the long, devastating civil war against divided and under equipped Christian and non-Muslim African rebels in the south.

In the presidential and legislative elections held in 1996, the Bashir government won convincingly. Opponents protested that they were impeded by the ban on political parties and by incomplete voter registration lists. Turabi himself stood for and won a seat from his home district in the capital, a position that belies his predominant role in the regime. Shortly after his election, Bashir pledged to rule by "Islamic law and dignity" and to retain the ban on party political activity during his new five-year term.

Further Reading

Hassan al-Turabi has not been the subject of a full biography. Much information about him and the Islamic fundamentalist movement can be found in John O. Voll (ed.), *Sudan: State and Society in Crisis* (1991). Much can be gleaned about Turabi, the regime, the civil war, and the evolution of the Islamist state in the periodical literature, especially Bill Berkeley, "The longest war in the world: Sudan has been fighting for 30 of the last 40 years 13 of the past 17 decades. Strife is the country's business, and warlords are its tycoons," *The New York Times Magazine* (March 3, 1996); William Langewiesche, "Turabi's Law," *The Atlantic Monthly* (August 1994); Judith Miller, "Faces of fundamentalism: Hassan al-Turabi and Muhammed Fadlallah," *Foreign Affairs* (November-December 1994); Milton Viorst, "Sudan's Islamic Experiment," *Foreign Affairs* (May-June 1995); and "The Muslim who shapes the state: Sudan," *The Economist* (April 29, 1995). □

Ivan Sergeyevich Turgenev

The Russian novelist, dramatist, and short-story writer Ivan Sergeyevich Turgenev (1818-1883) was a founder of the Russian realistic novel. He ranks as one of the greatest stylists in the Russian language.

The life of Ivan Turgenev is woven like a bright thread throughout Russian history of the 19th century, during the time the nation's artistic and intellectual life experienced a golden age. He knew, was related to, or fought with almost every figure of any consequence in his homeland. He was also the first Russian author to establish a European reputation, and during his long years abroad he was friends with Gustave Flaubert, Henry James, Émile Zola, Guy de Maupassant, and many other writers. Turgenev's generous enthusiasm for the work of other men made him a perfect mediator between East and West.

Parentage and Early Life

Turgenev's biography is as much the story of his encounters with strong-willed women as it is of his meetings with famous men. The first of these women was his mother, Varvara Petrovna. She was a Lutovin, an obscure family that had recently achieved enormous wealth. She was her uncle's only heir, and she ruled with an iron hand over her vast estates and 5,000 serfs. Three years after coming into her inheritance she married Sergey Nikolayevich Turgenev, a retired colonel of cuirassiers. The Turgenevs were old stock, dating back to a Tatar prince of the 15th century. Turgenev's father, however, was forced to marry Varvara Petrovna in order to shore up his family's sagging fortunes. It was an unhappy marriage, the handsome father constantly embroiled with mistresses, and the mother running her family as despotically as she did her estates.

Turgenev was born, the second of three sons, at the family seat of Spasskoye in Orel Province on Nov. 9, 1818. He first visited Europe when he was 4 years old, when the whole family made the grand tour. His father narrowly saved Turgenev's life in Bern, where Turgenev almost fell into the bear pit. He was educated by private tutors at Spasskoye until he was 9 years old. Only French was spoken at home, so he learned Russian mainly from family servants. In 1827 he attended various preparatory schools in Moscow, entering the university there in 1833. Already he was rebelling against his aristocratic background: about the only thing known of this period is that his fellow students, struck by his democratic leanings, called him "the American."

In 1834 Turgenev transferred to the University of St. Petersburg when the family moved to the capital. The father died the same autumn. At this time Turgenev was planning to become a university professor, but he was writing poetry in his spare time. His first work, a Gothic melodrama in verse, was severely criticized by his favorite professor, P. A. Pletnyov. However, in 1838 Pletnyov published Turgenev's first poetry in *Contemporary*.

His Youth

Meanwhile, having finished his courses at St. Petersburg, Turgenev resolved upon further study at the University of Berlin. On the boat journey in the spring of 1837, his steamer caught fire off Travemünde. Accounts of this incident vary, but all agree that Turgenev behaved badly. Some versions say he screamed in French, "Save me, I am my widowed mother's only son!" The event rankled in his mind until his death.

In Berlin, Turgenev studied Latin, Greek, and philosophy, immersing himself in the works of G. W. F. Hegel. In July 1840 Turgenev met Mikhail Bakunin, and for a whole year they lived together, arguing philosophy day and night. In 1841 Turgenev returned to Russia. The following year was an important one. While carrying on a high-flown platonic romance with one of Bakunin's sisters, Tatyana, Turgenev entered into an earthier alliance with Avdotya Ivanov, one of his mother's seamstresses which resulted in the birth of a daughter, known in later life as Paulinette. Turgenev also did all the work for his master of arts degree except the dissertation. For various reasons he abandoned his plans for an academic career and entered the Ministry of Interior Affairs. He left the civil service—to the mutual satisfaction of both parties—after 18 months. His mother was infuriated and cut off his funds, thus forcing him to lead a rather precarious existence, complicated by the fact that everyone thought he was rich.

Turgenev met the critic Vissarion Belinsky, with whom he remained very close until the latter's death. Belinsky was instrumental in turning the young man away from vaporous poetry to a greater realism and a more natural tone. *Parasha* (1843) showed Turgenev to be an imitative poet in these early years (especially of Aleksandr Pushkin and Mikhail Lermontov), and Turgenev later dismissed his verse as having been written before he found his true vocation.

In 1843 Turgenev met the woman with whom he struggled for the rest of his life. Pauline Viardot-Garcia belonged to a talented Spanish family of gypsies. When Turgenev first saw her, she was well on her way to becoming the reigning mezzo-soprano in European opera. She was considered by many unattractive, but her voice was remarkable, and she was a great actress. Turgenev saw her during a tour in St. Petersburg and fell immediately in love. A curious relationship began that ended only with Turgenev's death in her arms. She was married to Louis Viardot, a man 20 years her senior, a director of the Italian Opera in Paris, but her marriage was no complication because her husband was extremely permissive. The problem lay in Pauline herself, who, unlike many other women, was not especially attracted to Turgenev. She had many affairs with other men, never entering into an exclusive alliance with Turgenev, even though he devoted much of his life and fortune to her, and even though she, as well as her husband and children, lived with Turgenev for years.

From 1845 to 1847 Turgenev spent most of his time in Russia, plunging now into his nation's literary life, coming into contact with all its leading literary figures. In 1847 he went abroad, resolved to fight serfdom with his pen. That year he wrote the first of his *Hunter's Sketches,* "Khor and Kalinich." He also visited Salzbrunn to comfort the dying Belinsky, but he spent most of his time at Courtavenel, the Viardot summer home where he did most of his work at this time.

In 1850 Turgenev returned to Russia, where his mother lay dying. Her death made him master of 11 estates, including Spasskoye, some 30,000 acres, with thousands of serfs. He did his best to lighten the load of these peasants, and he freed the household workers among them. In that year he wrote *A Month in the Country,* of all his stage pieces the one that has remained in the repertoire. *A Provincial Lady* was written in 1851. While Turgenev always claimed he had no dramatic talent (and he stopped writing plays in 1852), the lyrical tone of his plays has a close affinity to that of Chekhov's masterpieces, and his dramas are just as difficult to classify.

First Years of Fame

More of the *Hunter's Sketches* appeared at frequent intervals during these years. In many of them the serfs seemed nobler than their masters, and both master and serf seemed stunted by the institution of serfdom. The sketches angered the government. The stage for some action against Turgenev was set. In November 1852 he wrote a laudatory article on the recently dead author Nikolai Gogol. This article was not passed by the St. Petersburg censors; Turgenev then took it to Moscow, where it was published. Its publication was regarded as a "treasonable act"; he was arrested, and after a month in prison, he was put under house arrest at

Spasskoye for almost 2 years. The greatest irony was that after his arrest the collected *Hunter's Sketches* were published in book form. The volume created a revulsion against serfdom much greater than the separate sketches had. During his month in prison Turgenev wrote "Mumu," a piece called by Thomas Carlyle "the most pathetic story in the world."

In 1854 Turgenev was back in St. Petersburg. He had long felt the need to experiment with a longer form and after several false starts wrote his first novel, *Rudin,* in 7 months in 1855 (published 1856). It was a portrait of the talky, idealistic generation of the 1840s, and many readers felt its hero was modeled on Bakunin. Turgenev met Nikolai Chernyshevsky and Leo Tolstoy that same year; he was destined to quarrel with both. In 1856, on one of his frequent trips abroad, Turgenev met Harriet Beecher Stowe, the American novelist; the effect of *Hunter's Sketches* on the abolition of serfdom in Russia had often been compared to the effect of her *Uncle Tom's Cabin* on the abolition of slavery in the United States.

In 1857 Turgenev wrote "Assya," and he also began work on *A Nest of Gentlefolk.* The following year on a trip to England, he met Benjamin Disraeli, William Makepeace Thackeray, Thomas Babington Macaulay, Carlyle, and other authors. In 1859 Turgenev returned to Russia, where his *A Nest of Gentlefolk* had brought him great acclaim. In the spring of that year he dusted off a manuscript given him earlier by a young soldier, Vassily Karatayev, who had felt he would not survive the Crimean War (he had died soon afterward of typhus). The manuscript was an autobiographical tale, and it served as the core for Turgenev's next major work, *On the Eve.* When this novel was published in 1860, it created a stir: the old and rich attacked it, and the young and radical defended it. A two-edged review of this novel by N. A. Dobrolyubov in Nikolai Nekrasov's journal, *Contemporary,* caused Turgenev to break with that review and its increasingly radical orientation. The unhappiness this rupture with his old friend Nekrasov brought was compounded by a violent break with Tolstoy, who went as far as to threaten Turgenev with a duel. Turgenev declined, but the two were never truly close again.

In 1860 Turgenev also endured further unhappiness caused by a literary friend. Ivan Goncharov, who had been working on his novel *The Precipice* (1869) for many years, often discussing it with Turgenev, accused him of stealing ideas from it for *On the Eve.* An informal court was set up, with three authors acting as judges. They cleared Turgenev, but he was infuriated and was never again close to Goncharov (whose paranoia later became clinical).

Part of Turgenev's pain was eased by hard work on his new novel, which, when it appeared as *Fathers and Sons* (1862), marked a watershed in the literary, intellectual, and political life of Russia. This novel ranks as his masterpiece. Everyone was forced to take sides on the issue of Bazarov, the book's hero, and his nihilist philosophy. Bazarov became the archetype for the generation of the 1860s; he was a socialist in politics and a scientific materialist in philosophy. Conservatives accused Turgenev of prostrating himself before the younger generation, while radicals charged him

with a cruel satire of their ideals. Some felt that Bazarov was a parody of the radical critic Dobrolyubov, who had died tragically young.

In 1863 Turgenev bought a villa in Baden-Baden, Germany, where he lived on a grand scale with the ever present Viardots. In 1866 Turgenev published *Smoke,* a novel that offended all Slavophiles and all conservative religious opinion in Russia. Many accused him of selling out to the West, of having lost contact with his homeland. The following year he was visited by Fyodor Dostoevsky, who attacked him as a slanderer of the motherland.

Last Phase

At the outbreak of the Franco-Prussian War in 1870, the Viardots fled to England, where Turgenev followed. A few months later he settled in France, first in Paris and then at his summer home on the Seine at Bougival near Paris. In these years he regularly attended dinners with Zola, Alphonse Daudet, and Maupassant. Flaubert was a particular favorite of Turgenev's. During these years Turgenev wrote several of his best-known short stories: "First Love" (1870), "A Lear of the Steppe" (1870), and "The Torrents of Spring" (1871).

In 1877 Turgenev published the novel on which he had labored for the past 6 years: *Virgin Soil.* It is his longest work and another of his generational studies. The story this time is of the young people of the 1870s. Fed up with the talk and empty idealism of their fathers, these young people have decided on action. The book was a best seller in Europe, but it was condemned by all factions in Russia. Turgenev was greatly disillusioned by the failure of this novel in Russia, and some of the pessimism thus generated crept into the short pieces he wrote in 1878 called *Senilia* (later entitled *Poems in Prose*).

A new misfortune occurred the winter of the following year. Turgenev had to go to Russia, after his wealthy older brother's death, to fight for a fair share of the inheritance. But this unpleasantness soon became a blessing. Turgenev's return to his native land, where he thought he was in disgrace and discredited, turned into a triumphal procession. He made up his old literary feuds, and he was even reconciled with his uncle, Nikolai, who, as his estate manager, had almost ruined him. Turgenev was feted day and night.

While Turgenev's life had always, since 1843, been bound up with Pauline Viardot-Garcia, their relationship was not a simple one in which he gave only unalloyed worship to the diva. The two had many fights but always reconciled, even long after Pauline had lost her voice and was more or less dependent upon Turgenev. He had other mistresses and even contemplated marriage with other women. He was a man of large and impressive physique— he was known in France as "that Russian giant"—and had a handsome face and great charm. During the tumult of his acclaim in 1879 he found time to pay court to an actress, the young and beautiful Maria Savina. In June, Turgenev received an honorary doctorate from Oxford University.

In 1880 Turgenev returned to Russia for the unveiling of the Pushkin Memorial in Moscow. In the same year he wrote one of his most beautiful stories, "The Song of Triumphant Love." The following year he published most of the *Poems in Prose* and wrote the ghostly love story "Clara Milich." The prose poems that he felt to be too intimate were not published by his wish until 1930.

All his life Turgenev had been a hypochondriac; in 1882 real symptoms appeared. He was afflicted with cancer of the spine and died on Sept. 3, 1883. A huge ceremony was held at the Gare du Nord in Paris when his body was shipped back to Russia, and his interment in St. Petersburg was an occasion for national mourning.

Further Reading

David Magarshack, *Turgenev: A Life* (1954), is more compact than Avrahm Yarmolinsky, *Turgenev: The Man, His Art and His Age* (1926; rev. ed. 1959), which is overwritten and contains much that is sheer speculation. The memoirs of a woman raised by Turgenev's mother, full of racy anecdotes, were translated into English: Varvara Zhitova, *The Turgenev Family* (1947). An excellent study of Turgenev's literary development is Richard Freeborn, *Turgenev: The Novelist's Novelist* (1960). For background see Charles Moser's excellent scholarly study *Antinihilism in the Russian Novel of the 1860s* (1964); its chronological scope extends beyond its title.

Additional Sources

Pritchett, V. S. (Victor Sawdon), *The gentle barbarian: the life and work of Turgenev,* New York: Ecco Press, 1986, 1977.

Schapiro, Leonard Bertram, *Turgenev, his life and times,* Cambridge, Mass.: Harvard University Press, 1982, 1978.

Troyat, Henri, *Turgenev,* New York: Dutton, 1988.

Waddington, Patrick, *Turgenev and England,* New York: New York University Press, 1981.

Yarmolinsky, Avrahm, *Turgenev, the man, his art, and his age,* New York: Octagon Books, 1977, 1959. □

Anne Robert Jacques Turgot

The French economist Anne Robert Jacques Turgot, Baron de l'Aulne (1721-1781), was controller general under Louis XVI. His efforts to reform the Old Regime were thwarted by the failure of the King to support him against the opposition of the privileged classes.

Originally A. R. J. Turgot planned to enter the Church but experienced doubts concerning his religious calling and turned to a public career. After holding a number of legal positions he purchased, as was the practice, the office of master of requests, a post that often led to appointment as intendant, the chief administrator of a district. However, Turgot's interests extended beyond the law and administration. He was a friend of the *philosophes* and frequented the intellectual salons of Paris; in 1760 he visited Voltaire, then in exile. He also contributed articles to the *Encyclopédie,* wrote an essay on toleration, and planned an ambitious history of the progress of man which he never completed.

Turgot was, however, particularly interested in economics and knew Adam Smith, the great English economist, and François Quesnay, founder of the Physiocratic school. He shared their distrust of government intervention in the economy and their belief in free trade but disagreed with the Physiocratic view that only agriculture was productive, while commerce and industry were unproductive.

In 1761 the King named Turgot intendant of the *généralité* (district) of Limoges, a poor and backward region. During the 13 years that he spent at Limoges, Turgot attempted, despite local opposition and halfhearted support from the central government, a widespread reform of his district. Historians disagree on how successful he was. He brought tax lists up to date and sought to introduce a more equitable method of collecting taxes. He abolished the *corvée* (forced labor on the roads by peasants) and substituted for it a tax. Consistent with his belief in free trade, he resisted pressure to repeal legislation permitting the free circulation of grain within France during a period of shortages and suppressed riots against the movement of grain. At the same time he opened workshops to provide work for the unemployed which he financed in part by funds that he forced landowners to contribute. He encouraged improvement of agriculture by such means as an agricultural society. While at Limoges, Turgot also continued to study economics and in 1766 published his most important theoretical work on the subject, *Reflections on the Formation and Distribution of Wealth,* a book whose ideas anticipated Adam Smith's classic study in 1776.

In July 1774 Turgot was named secretary of the navy and the following month controller general of finances (actually prime minister). Although he saw the need for fundamental reforms of the government and society, Turgot also recognized that he must advance cautiously; basic reforms would not only be costly but certain to arouse the opposition of the privileged classes. His first efforts, therefore, emphasized modest reforms and reducing government expenditures by such measures as eliminating useless positions and aid for courtiers. However, even such minor reforms aroused the opposition of the privileged and of financiers whose interests had also been adversely affected. Churchmen, moreover, were suspicious of this friend of the *philosophes* who "did not attend Mass" and was suspected of favoring tolerance for Protestants.

In January 1776 Turgot presented to the King his famous Six Edicts, which went beyond his previous minor reforms and economies. The two most contested edicts were one ending the monopoly of the guilds and another abolishing the *corvée* Turgot implied that a tax would be levied upon the "landowners for whom public roads are useful." The Six Edicts now became the target of all the opponents of Turgot; the clergy, the nobles, the queen, Marie Antoinette, all clamored and conspired for his dismissal. They even forged a correspondence in which Turgot made offensive remarks about Louis XVI. The latter, who had at first supported his minister, of whom he had said, "Only Monsieur Turgot and I really love the people," was unable to resist the pressures upon him and in May 1776 requested Turgot's resignation. The dismissal of Turgot marked the failure of the last attempt to reform the monarchy from within. Turgot, who warned Louis XVI that Charles I of England had lost his head because of his weakness, spent his last years engaged in scholarly and literary work but still sought to influence the King.

Further Reading

The finest study of Turgot in English is Douglas Dakin, *Turgot and the Ancient Regime in France* (1939). ☐

Alan Mathison Turing

The British mathematician Alan Mathison Turing (1912-1954) was noted for his contributions to mathematical logic and to the early theory, construction, and use of computers.

Alan Turing was born in London, England, on June 23, 1912. Both his parents had upper middle class origins, and his father continued that tradition as an administrator in the Indian civil service. With his father off in India, Turing was sent away to private boarding schools. After some early problems with social adjustment, he distinguished himself in mathematics and science.

Turing's exceptional mathematical abilities were first generally recognized in his college years (1931-1936) at King's College of Cambridge University. His most important mathematical work, "On Computable Numbers," was written in Cambridge in 1936. In this paper Turing answered a question of great significance to mathematical logic— namely, which functions in mathematics can be computed by an entirely mechanical procedure. His answer was phrased in terms of a theoretical machine (today known as the "Turing machine") which could mechanically carry out these computations. Embodied in the Turing machine idea is the concept of the stored program computer.

In 1936 Turing was awarded a Proctor fellowship to visit Princeton University for a year. There he came in contact with Alonzo Church, a professor of mathematics working on problems in logic related to those addressed by Turing in his 1936 paper. He decided to remain at Princeton an additional two years to write a doctoral dissertation under Church's direction on ordinal logics.

Soon after Turing's return to England Britain was drawn into World War II. He joined the Government Code and Cypher School in Bletchley Park, located between Oxford and London, where a massive effort was underway to break German codes which had been enciphered by machine. Turing played an important role (still partly classified) in the design of equipment and development of techniques to break these codes.

Work at Bletchley provided Turing with valuable experience in electronics and with special-purpose calculating equipment which served him well after the war. In 1945 he moved to the National Physical Laboratory (NPL) in Teddington, England, to assume responsibilities for designing an electronic computer to be used in government work. Turing drew up plans for the ACE computer, an ambitious stored program computer utilizing vacuum tubes for switching and mercury delay lines for storage. A scaleddown version completed in 1950, known as Pilot ACE, was one of the earliest operating stored program computers. Pilot ACE served many important functions, including aircraft design, for many years.

Meanwhile, dissatisfied with progress on his project at NPL, Turing accepted a position at Manchester University where a large computer, the Mark I, was being built. His position as chief programmer of the Mark I allowed him the opportunity to program the computer to do mathematics, play chess and other games, investigate automatic language translation, and do cryptanalysis. This was probably the first major attempt to use a stored program computer for noncomputational activities.

Turing's work on computers influenced the design of early computers built by the English Electric and Bendix companies. However, of more enduring significance were his theoretical contributions to automata theory and artificial intelligence. The 1936 paper and the concept of the Turing machine is the starting point of the modern theory of automata, and Turing anticipated many of the fundamental questions. During and after the war Turing began to investigate and champion the field of artificial intelligence. To his credit are the Turing Test (a test for determining whether a machine can be claimed to be thinking), a series of papers arguing against the most common objections to the possibility of intelligent machinery, and the recognition that scientists should approach the problem of artificial intelligence through the programming of stored program computers rather than through the construction of robots that mimic human actions. Turing also made a number of other contributions to mathematical logic, algebra, statistics, and morphogenesis (the study of biological forms).

Turing died in his home in Manchester, England, of cyanide poisoning. His death, ruled to be suicide by the coroner, may have been the result of a depression caused by chemotherapy. The courts had mandated this treatment as a result of his conviction for public practice of homosexuality, then a criminal offense in Britain.

Further Reading

Two biographies of Turing have been written: a short study by his mother, Sara Turing, *Alan M. Turing* (1959), and a longer study by Andrew Hodges, *Alan Turing: The Enigma* (1983). Hodges cites references to Turing's published paper and other secondary literature about him.

Additional Sources

Hodges, Andrew, *Alan Turing: the enigma,* New York: Simon and Schuster, 1983. □

Frederick Jackson Turner

American historian Frederick Jackson Turner (1861-1932) is regarded as one of the greatest writers of United States history. Several of his concepts caused a virtual rewriting of American history in the early 20th century.

Frederick Jackson Turner was born on Nov. 14, 1861, in Portage, Wis., a rural town populated by a variety of European immigrants. In Turner's youth Portage was still visited by Indians living in the nearby wilderness. Turner's autobiographical notes, preserved among his papers at the Henry E. Huntington Library in San Marino, Calif., relate that he attended Portage High School and won a prize for a graduation address that was printed in his father's newspaper. He worked in his father's office as a typesetter.

In 1880, Turner entered the University of Wisconsin at Madison, where he fell under the influence of Professor William F. Allen, who taught him how to understand historical institutions such as the medieval church and the feudal monarchy. Turner later claimed that Allen showed him the importance of institutional history, a theme that appeared in Turner's writings on the origins of American democracy. Following his graduation in 1884 and the later completion of his master's degree at Wisconsin, Turner went to Johns Hopkins University to study for his doctorate in 1888. He married Caroline Mae Sherwood of Chicago in 1889.

Teaching Career

Turner's doctoral dissertation, *The Character and Influence of the Indian Trade in Wisconsin* (1891), portrayed the trading post as an institution of the early American frontier. At the University of Wisconsin, where Turner taught from 1889 to 1910, he emphasized frontier history in his lectures and in his writings. His most important publication, a paper entitled "The Significance of the Frontier in American History," which he read in 1893, set forth his frontier hypothesis. His first major book, *Rise of the New West, 1819-1829* (1906), was followed by a volume of essays, *The Frontier in American History* (1920). These volumes provided a wide audience for his ideas.

Turner moved to Harvard University in 1910 and retired in 1924 to southern California, where he continued his investigations as research associate at the Huntington Library. After his death on March 4, 1932, his last two books were published: *The Significance of Sections in American History* (1932) was awarded a Pulitzer Prize; *The United States 1830-1850: The Nation and Its Sections* (1935) was partly dictated and lacks the literary finesse of his other writings.

Frontier Theory

Turner's frontier theory (often called his frontier hypothesis) has been applied to Latin American nations, to Australia, and to Russia to explain the origin of national characteristics. Turner believed that the particular tone of American democracy, the nature of American institutions of government, and the uniqueness of the American character could be traced to America's frontier experience. In his writings Turner stressed the changes that took place in colonial American society when a European civilization was transplanted to a wilderness environment. Frontier individualism, stimulated by the presence of free (or virtually free) land in the West, left its imprint upon Americans of modern times.

In Turner's view a restless energy, a self-reliance, and a love of freedom are part of the American heritage, which is also symbolized by great leaders such as Thomas Jefferson, Andrew Jackson, and Abraham Lincoln. Turner wrote that the lives of these presidents illustrate the influence of western democracy in American life. The original raw frontier areas of America were eventually transformed by generations of a new society. Social change caused by the modifying influence of geographical, economic, social, and political forces created a new nationality in America. American society developed with sectional or regional variations, the largest and most powerful sections being the North and the South.

Turner's most significant contribution to historical thinking has been to encourage a better understanding of the origins of American democracy. His theories have been thoroughly debated and criticized, yet he remains one of the most original and provocative historians that America has produced. Even though Turner admitted that he perhaps exaggerated when he "hammered hard" on the subject of the frontier in promoting democracy, his thesis that the westward movement greatly influenced American history and the growth of the American traits of character is generally accepted as valid.

Further Reading

Wilbur R. Jacobs, *The Historical World of Frederick Jackson Turner* (1968), traces Turner's professional career and includes excerpts from his correspondence. Jacobs edited *America's Great Frontiers and Sections* (1969), which includes Turner's unpublished essays and contains the best short biography of him. Critical essays on Turner's frontier theory are in George Rogers Taylor, ed., *The Role of the Frontier in American History* (1949; rev. ed. 1956), and R. A. Billington, ed., *The Frontier Thesis: Valid Interpretation of American History?* (1966). Billington's *America's Frontier Heritage* (1966) has an excellent evaluation of the frontier theory. Wilbur R. Jacobs and others, *Turner, Bolton and Webb* (1965), shows Turner's influence on two other leading American writers, and Richard Hofstadter, *The Progressive Historians* (1968), discusses the affinities among Turner, Beard, and Vernon Parrington. Turner figures prominently in John Higham's work on historiography, *Writing American History: Essays on Modern Scholarship* (1970). For a superb history of the United States that emphasizes Turnerean themes of interpretation see R. A. Billington, *Westward Expansion: A History of the American Frontier* (1967).

Additional Sources

Bennett, James D., *Frederick Jackson Turner*, Boston: Twayne Publishers, 1975.
Carpenter, Ronald H., *The eloquence of Frederick Jackson Turner*, San Marino, Calif.: Huntington Library, 1983.

Frederick Jackson Turner: Wisconsin's historian of the frontier, Madison: State Historical Society of Wisconsin, 1986. □

Henry McNeal Turner

Henry McNeal Turner (1834-1915), African American leader and a bishop of the African Methodist Episcopal Church, argued for African American emigration to Africa.

Henry M. Turner was born free near Abbeville, S.C., on Feb. 1, 1834. Unable to go to school because of state laws, he was "apprenticed" in local cotton fields but ran away and found a job as sweeper in a law office. The young clerks surreptitiously taught him to read and write. He was converted to Christianity and at age 20 was licensed as a traveling evangelist for the Methodist Episcopal Church, South. He preached to white and black audiences throughout the South until 1858. When he learned of the all-black African Methodist Episcopal Church (AME), he joined it.

In Baltimore, Turner studied languages and Scripture as well as his new Church. In 1862 he moved to a church in Washington, D.C. His fiery sermons earned him the title "Black Spurgeon" (a reference to a famous English sermonizer of the day). Congressmen attended his preaching, and Turner frequented the Capitol to watch politicians in action. After emancipation of the slaves in 1863, he agitated for putting black troops into the Civil War and was commissioned the first black chaplain in the Union Army.

After the war Turner was assigned to the Freedmen's Bureau in Georgia, but he resigned to recruit blacks for his Church and, later, to organize them for the Republican party. He participated in the Georgia constitutional convention of 1868 and later was elected to the legislature. When blacks were refused their seats in the legislature, Turner was appointed postmaster at Macon, Ga., and then a customs inspector at Savannah. Meanwhile, in 1876, he was elected manager of the AME Book Concern, and in 1880 he was elected one of a dozen bishops in the Church.

Turner was interested in Africa as a potential homeland for African Americans. His experiences in Reconstruction politics disillusioned him with white America, and after 1868 he urged talented young blacks to establish a nation in Africa which would give pride and encouragement to blacks everywhere. His writings and speeches in favor of pan-African nationalism and his scathing attacks on white racism antagonized many middle-class blacks but inspired many black farmers.

Turner wrote for Church and public newspapers. In Atlanta he founded the *Southern Recorder* (1888), the *Voice of Missions* (1892), and the *Voice of the People* (1901). He also published a catechism, a hymnal, and *The Genius and Theory of Methodist Polity* (1885). When the U.S. Supreme Court struck down the Reconstruction civil rights laws in 1883, he issued a blistering attack in *The Barbarous Deci-*

sion of the Supreme Court . . . , revised as *The Black Man's Doom* (1896).

During the 1890s Turner visited Africa four times to supervise Church work and publicize emigration. In 1893 he summoned a national convention of Afro-American leaders to protest lynching and political attacks on blacks and get support for his emigration schemes. However, Turner's appeals were heeded only by poor blacks who could neither afford passage to Africa nor support themselves there. He continued his agitation, attracting nationwide attention in 1906, when he reportedly called the American flag a "dirty rag." He died in Windsor, Ontario, on May 8, 1915.

Further Reading

Respect Black! Writings and Speeches of Henry M. Turner (1971), edited by E. S. Redkey, contains a selection of Turner's rhetoric on the race question. The only full-length biography of Turner is the early, uncritical work by Mungo M. Ponton, *Life and Times of Henry M. Turner* (1917). A brief biography of Turner appears in *Historical Negro Biographies* in the *International Library of Negro Life and History,* edited by Wilhelmena S. Robinson (1968), and a chapter on him is in W. J. Simmons, *Men of Mark: Eminent, Progressive and Rising* (1968). E. S. Redkey, *Black Exodus: Black Nationalist and Back-to-Africa Movements, 1890-1910* (1969), focuses on Turner's emigrationist activities. □

Joseph Mallord William Turner

The English painter Joseph Mallord William Turner (1775-1851) was one of the greatest romantic interpreters of nature in the history of Western art and is still unrivaled in the virtuosity of his painting of light.

The son of a barber, J. M. W. Turner was born on April 23, 1775, in Maiden Lane, Covent Garden, London. After an illness he was sent to school at Brentford, where his uncle was a butcher. From this period dates Turner's lifelong attachment to the Thames and its scenery. His father is said to have sold Turner's boyhood drawings and copies of engravings at 1 to 3 shillings at his shop, and this may have influenced his decision to have the boy educated as a painter. There is uncertainly about his early drawing masters other than the topographical watercolor painter Thomas Malton. In 1789 Turner was admitted to the Royal Academy Schools, where he attended life classes and worked fairly regularly from the antique from 1790 to 1793.

In 1791 Turner went to Bristol to sketch medieval buildings as far afield as Bath and Malmesbury Abbey, and especially the romantic Avon gorges. The English watercolor school was then rapidly reaching its golden age, and from 1794 to 1797 he worked in the great collection of Dr. Monro, who opened his home to young artists and paid Turner and Thomas Girtin to make copies in the evening, partly with the object of encouraging them. Girtin drew the outlines and Turner washed in the effects.

During this period Turner developed an astonishing command of technique, emulating the effects obtained by Claude Lorrain, Thomas Gainsborough, and the leaders of the modern English watercolor school. Turner quickly became the most brilliant topographical artist of his day, combining minutely observed realism with an incomparable richness of tints and glow of light.

Artistic Development

In 1796 Turner scored a signal success at the Royal Academy with *Fisherman at Sea* (now identified with an oil painting). Thereafter his development broadly followed two lines. The first was that of the watercolorist who revolutionized the technique of oil painting in the course of dissolving form in light, atmosphere, and color. He was the first English painter to be attacked and ridiculed for being modern in the sense of tending to the abstract.

The second line was that of the devotee of the picturesque who became a romantic via the theatrical sublime. Turner's early and profitable sketching tours in search of picturesque scenery became the habit of a lifetime. The castles and mountains of Wales, the coast of England, its rivers and valleys, the antiquities of Scotland, the Rhine, the Alps—the list of his tours is almost a complete guide to picturesque travel from the turn of the century. He early developed an admiration for Claude Lorrain, Claude Joseph

Vernet, and especially Philip James de Loutherbourg, the father of Drury Lane picturesque; they appealed to Turner's taste for the melodramatic with their paintings of avalanches, storms, shipwrecks, and conflagrations.

Relationship with Royal Academy

At the Royal Academy, Turner had been taught that the highest aim of an artist was to become a history painter illustrating the most heroic themes of the Bible, antiquity, and modern history. But he did not rely primarily on narrative association to elevate his landscapes. From the late 1790s he exhibited paintings with quotations from his favorite poets, including Thomson, Milton, and Ossian. In 1812 he showed at the Royal Academy *Hannibal Crossing the Alps* with a quotation from his own projected long poem *The Fallacies of Hope.*

It is greatly to the credit of the Royal Academy that the career of this revolutionary painter was one of uninterrupted success. He first exhibited in 1790 at the age of 15, was elected associate royal academician in 1799 and royal academician in 1802, and became professor of perspective in 1807 and deputy president in 1845.

Nature Works

In 1819 Turner visited Venice for the first time. He had long outgrown the realism which made *Calais Pier* (1803) and *The Shipwreck* (1805) tour-de-force demonstrations of his technical powers, and in the second painting he translated the shipwreck into a romantic symbol of man at the mercy of the violence of nature. Even the watercolors made from his sketches on his first visit to the Alps in 1802 are firmly controlled by observation and his scientific interest in geology. The liberating impact of Turner's experiences in Venice took some time to develop, for the majority of pencil sketches, of which he made large quantities during his short stay, are shorthand notations of meticulous accuracy.

Turner went even further than the impressionists later in abstracting light and color from his vision of nature, but unlike them he was principally interested in capturing transient effects under different conditions. He relied on a prodigious and highly trained visual memory in addition to his sketches. A Mrs. Simon recorded that during a rainstorm in 1843 he put his head out of a train window for nearly 9 minutes and shut his eyes in intense concentration for a quarter of an hour. The following year he exhibited *Rain, Steam, and Speed—The Great Western Railway,* which has been described as a salute to the new railway age. It is in marked contrast to the *Fighting Téméraire* (1839), a painting of the veteran of the Battle of Trafalgar being tugged on its last journey to be broken up, which Ruskin said was the most pathetic picture ever painted. Turner's last paintings on classical themes, from *Ulysses Deriding Polyphemus* (1829) to *Hero and Leander* (1837), are even more subjective orchestrations of color, although equally the outcome of his phenomenological studies.

Personal Characteristics

Turner died on Dec. 19, 1851, and was buried as a national hero in St. Paul's Cathedral. He left a fortune of more than £140,000 to found a charity for "Decayed Artists" and a vast hoard of sketches and his finest paintings, many of which he had bought back to leave to the nation. But his will was faultily drafted, and it was successfully contested by distant and probably disliked relatives. Only the paintings reached the destination he had intended, and the greatest of them are on permanent display in the Tate Gallery, London.

Much of Turner's life was a well-kept secret, including his relations with a widow, Sarah Danby, by whom he allegedly had two daughters. His short figure and beaklike face lent themselves to caricature, but he cut a not undistinguished figure in the academy and the social circles in which he chose to move—a few wealthy friends who were connoisseurs of art and a larger number of casual acquaintances among the uneducated, for he relished low life. His vulgarity of pronunciation was probably cultivated, for it gave flavor to his brusque humor. In his last years he lived the life of a recluse under an assumed name in Chelsea.

Turner the Visionary

The reputation of Turner has suffered from both his virtuosity and the baroque cast of his imagination. Lord Clark, not an unsympathetic critic, has castigated, in *Landscape into Art* (1949), the antics of his reckless technique, the badness of what survives of his unfinished poem, and the ugliness of some of his favorite forms. The key to Turner's imaginative authenticity is probably to be found in his boyhood responses to literature as well as nature. His eye never ceased to make new discoveries, so to look at Turner is always to see nature afresh. He was also a visionary, and it is the visionary in Turner that makes his greatest paintings haunt the imagination.

Further Reading

From John Ruskin, who chose Turner as the central hero of volume 1 (1843) of his *Modern Painters,* to Lord Clark, Turner has occasioned fine criticism. The scholarly literature is disappointing. Alexander J. Finberg, *The Life of J. M. W. Turner* (1939; revised by Hilda F. Finberg, 1961), is a mine of facts, based on monumental research. Jack Lindsay, *J. M. W. Turner: His Life and Work* (1966), is controversial but worth reading for many original ideas and for its bibliography. The best short account is Lawrence Gowing, *Turner: Imagination and Reality* (1966), which also has a useful bibliography. See also Michael Kitson, *J. M. W. Turner* (1964), and John Rothenstein and Martin Butlin, *Turner* (1964). The best modern authorities are John Gage and Martin Butlin, who have hitherto confined their research mainly to specialist studies. □

Nathaniel Turner

Nathaniel Turner (1800-1831) was a black American who organized and led the most successful slave revolt in the United States.

Nat Turner was born a slave on Oct. 2, 1800, in Southampton County, Va. As a child, he exhibited notable leadership qualities and intelligence. His insight prompted friends to believe he was destined to be a prophet. Commenting on Nat's precociousness, they remarked that he "would never be of any service to anyone as a slave."

Turner had a restless, observant, inquisitive mind. He read the Bible and extracted from it useful ideas on liberty and freedom. He preached to other slaves, counseling them to seek self-respect, to fight for justice, and to resist and rebel against the institution of slavery if they were to be free men. He believed that he was chosen by God to deliver his people from bondage and "slay my enemies with their own weapons."

In February 1831 Turner received what he believed to be a sign from God (a solar eclipse) telling him that it was time for him and his companions to prepare for the revolt. On August 21 they began their attempt to overthrow the institution of slavery. In 48 hours they killed between 55 and 65 whites throughout Southampton County. A family of poor whites, who owned no slaves, was spared. On August 23 Turner's black liberation army was met and overpowered by a superior state and Federal military force. Over 100 blacks were slain in the encounter and dozens more immediately executed.

Turner, the "Black Spartacus," escaped and was not caught until October 30. On November 5 he was tried and convicted. Although he admitted to leading the rebellion, when asked how he pleaded, he said "not guilty." Six days later he was executed for trying to free his people from slavery.

This slave rebellion catalyzed the beginning of the abolitionist movement in the United States. Because Turner's motive was a desire for liberty, some regard him as cast in the same mold as the American patriots who fought the Revolutionary War and as other freedom-loving men. No less than Patrick Henry, Turner too believed that "give me liberty or give me death" must be man's guiding philosophy of life.

Further Reading

An excellent work on Turner is Herbert Aptheker, *Nat Turner's Slave Rebellion, Together with the Full Text of the So-called "Confessions" of Nat Turner Made in Prison in 1831* (1937; repr. 1966). Lerone Bennett, Jr., *Pioneers in Protest* (1968), contains interesting material on Turner. William Styron's novel *Confessions of Nat Turner* (1968) evoked considerable reaction from blacks, which is summarized in John Henrik Clarke, ed., *William Styron's Nat Turner: Ten Black Writers Respond* (1968). Eric Foner, *Nat Turner* (1971), is a thorough, well-researched account of the rebellion and the reaction to it. Henry I. Tragle, *The Southampton Slave Revolt* (1971), provides perhaps the most important contemporary documents. □

Ted Turner

Ted Turner (born 1938), American television entrepreneur, was a pioneer in the field of cable television, establishing the first satellite superstation and the first all-news network. He already was worth more than $2 billion by 1996, when he merged his Turner Broadcasting Network with Time Warner to create the world's largest media company.

Born November 19, 1938, in Cincinnati, Ohio, Robert Edward (Ted) Turner III was the oldest child of Ed and Florence Turner. When Turner was nine years old, his father, a native Southerner, moved the family to Savannah, Georgia, where he had bought an outdoor advertising company that was renamed the Turner Advertising Company. This business later launched the younger Turner's successful career as an innovative and risk-taking communications entrepreneur.

Raised by a harsh and domineering father, Turner was sent to military schools in Georgia and Tennessee. He wanted to go to the Naval Academy but he enrolled at Brown University where his father wanted him to study business. The rebellious Turner majored in classics, though he later switched to economics. Although excelling in debating and sailing, he was expelled from the college for entertaining a woman in his dormitory room, which was against college regulations.

In 1960, after a stint with the Coast Guard, Turner began working for his father as a general manager for the advertising company's branch in Macon, Georgia. The senior Turner, unable to face possible financial collapse after developing a successful business, committed suicide on March 5, 1963. At age 24, Turner inherited a struggling company, and with some bold financial maneuvers he aggressively reversed its sagging fortunes, developing the confidence and resources for his growing ambition.

Cable Television Pioneer

In 1970 Turner took his first step into the television industry. He acquired an independent Atlanta UHF station, Channel 17, that was losing about half a million dollars a year. Relying on a combination of programming, local sports, old movies, and such popular network re-runs as Star Trek, Turner achieved a significant 16 percent share of the television market while the station became profitable.

In 1975 the launching of an RCA satellite opened the way for rapid changes in the burgeoning cable television industry. Following the lead of Home Box Office, Turner quickly capitalized on the new potential. He built a $750,000 transmission antenna and on December 27, 1976, began beaming a signal which could be received and re-broadcast by cable operators across the nation. He had created the country's first "superstation," WTBS. The superstation audience grew as more and more homes were wired to receive cable. From 1978 to 1986 the number of families watching WTBS jumped from two million to 36 million, and the station was earning Turner Broadcasting $70 million a year, which provided the foundation for Turner's other investment ventures.

Turner maintained his successful UHF formula for programming on the new superstation. Again, popular network re-runs, movies, and sports provided the major viewing fare. As a way of ensuring a steady diet of sports programming, Turner, in 1976, became owner of the Atlanta Braves baseball team, whose games were seen nationally. He dubbed the Braves "America's Team" despite a losing record. (The team finally were World Champions in 1995). Turner in 1996 also purchased the Atlanta Hawks professional basketball team.

Not satisfied with a profitable superstation, Turner in June 1980 created at enormous cost the Cable News Network (CNN), the country's first 24-hour all-news station. An experiment that was expected to fail by most media experts, CNN was both entrenched and showing a profit by 1986. In 1982 Turner inaugurated a second news channel, Headline News Network, which provided continuous half-hour summaries of events.

Buys MGM's Movie Library

A calculating and visionary entrepreneur who regarded himself as an underdog battling the media giants, Turner desired a foothold among the networks. In 1985 he made an unsuccessful effort to seize control of the CBS corporation. In the wake of that failure, he set his sights on acquiring the

Metro-Golden-Mayer/United Artists company in order to obtain direct access to its vast film library, a necessary and increasingly expensive component of his superstation programming.

The $1.6 billion deal was completed in March 1986, with Turner getting control of MGM's film library. Insiders speculated that the purchase price was inflated. Moreover, Turner had to be bailed out by a cable television consortium to avoid bankruptcy after the MGM purchase—thus risking the loss of his personal control of Turner Broadcasting. Having ignored the advice of his financial advisers and industry analysts in the past, Turner expected to survive the gamble. By the time of the merger with Time Warner in 1995, the acquisition looked like a stroke of genius.

Merges Turner Broadcasting with Time Warner

In 1995, Turner agreed to sell Turner Broadcasting to Time Warner for $7.5 billion. The merger went into effect in October 1996 following approval by the Federal Trade Commission and the shareholders of the two companies. As vice chairman of Time Warner, Turner reported to that company's CEO, Gerald Levin. Turner assumed responsibility for running the merged company's cable networks, including Time Warner's Home Box Office (HBO) and TBS's Cable New Network (CNN), Cartoon Network, and Turner Classic Movies.

When the deal was announced, many asked how Tuner, who had been his own boss for 35 years could go and work for somebody else. His salary reportedly was $25 million over five years. Perhaps more important, he also became the largest shareholder in Time-Warner, then the world's largest media company, with more than $20 billion in annual revenues from cable television, films, books, magazines, music, and the Internet.

The merger set up a titanic brawl between Turner and another media mogul, Rupert Murdoch. The fireworks began in the fall of 1996 when Turner convinced Levin not to carry Murdoch's fledgling Fox News Service. In approving its merger with TBS, the FTC had ordered Time Warner to offer its millions of subscribers another 24 hour news service in addition to CNN. Instead of Fox News, Time Warner aired MSNBC, a joint venture between Microsoft and General Electric's NBC, whose softer format posed less of a competitive threat to CNN.

The refusal to carry Fox News meant that it would not be seen in New York City, where Time Warner enjoyed a near-monopoly with 1.1 million cable subscribers. Murdoch's news station thus would be invisible to the Madison Avenue advertising agencies and media chieftains whose decisions are worth millions to a cable network. To get around Time-Warner's lock on cable systems, Murdoch announced plans to invest $1 billion in a satellite TV service called Sky, which would offer both cable TV and local broadcast programming.

Time-Warner's decision was followed by a war of words and dirty tricks not seen since the days of William Randolph Hearst. When Murdoch retaliated by canceling plans to carry a Time Warner-owned entertainment channel, Turner immediately likened Murdoch to Nazi leader Adolph Hitler. Later he called Murdoch a "scumbag." Murdoch's *New York Post* yanked Turner's CNN from its television listings. The *Post* also dredged up the radical-chic past of "Hanoi Jane" Fonda, Turner's third wife. And it speculated publicly about whether Turner, reportedly a manic-depressive, was neglecting to take his lithium. Perhaps not entirely factitiously, Turner in September 1997 suggested that he and Murdoch settle their highly publicized feud with a boxing match. "It would be like Rocky, only for old guys," said Turner.

Sports Influence Multiplied Dramatically

In his earlier years, Turner personally participated in international sports competition. Having received the Yachtsman of the Year award an unprecedented three times, he was the winning skipper of the America's Cup race in 1977. Within a few years of purchasing the Atlanta Braves, Turner and TBN were involved in practically every major professional sport. In July 1986 Turner's superstation carried the Goodwill Games, held in Moscow, which featured athletic competition between U.S. and Soviet athletes. In a joint effort with the Soviet Union, Turner he organized and promoted the Olympics-like event. A second competition was held in Seattle, Washington, in 1990. Although the two events lost $66 million, Turner hoped they would foster better relations between the two countries. For his contributions to international broadcasting, *Time* magazine named him "Man of the Year" in 1991.

By the late 1990s, Ted Turner was worth more than $2 billion; the largest private landowner in the U.S., he divided his days between luxurious homes in six states. A flamboyant and shrewd businessman, he was also a celebrity who worked and lived in the fast lane. In December 1991, Turner married Jane Fonda, movie star and liberal activist. Two previous marriages had produced five children, who sit with Turner and Fonda on the board of the charitable Turner Foundation.

In the highly publicized relationship with Fonda, Turner apparently abandoned the philandering that had plagued his earlier marriages and sought to remake himself as a devoted, loving husband. Fonda, for her part, retired from the screen and folded Fonda Films, her independent production company. While both remained workaholics, they seemed to take genuine pleasure in their times together.

In September 1997, Turner literally stunned the world when he pledged $1 billion to the good-works program of the United Nations. Established programs such as feeding children, helping refugees and the poor, and removing land mines would benefit from his donation. (He has promised to give $100 million a year for a decade to U.N. programs.) After making the largest single pledge in philanthropic history, Turner challenged other wealthy citizens by declaring, "I'm putting every rich person in the world on notice."

Further Reading

Ted Turner is the subject of a biography, *Lead, Follow or Get Out of the Way: The Story of Ted Turner,* by Christian Williams (1981). He was the subject of several long magazine profiles, including *Newsweek* (June 16, 1980), *Time* (August 9, 1982), and *Fortune* (July 7, 1986). Turner collaborated with Gary Jobson on a book about sailing, *The Racing Edge* (1979). He also signed a contract with Simon and Schuster for an autobiography.

See also Bibb, Porter, *It Ain't As Easy As It Looks: The Story of Ted Turner & CNN* (1993). Goldberg, Robert and Gerald J. Goldberg, *Citizen Turner* (1995). Painton, Priscilla, "The Taming of Ted Turner," *Time* (January 6, 1992). Andrews, Suzanna, "Ted Turner among the Suits," *New York* (December 9, 1996). Conant, Jennet, "Married . . . With Buffalo," *Vanity Fair* (April 1997) [discusses marriage and relationship between Turner and Jane Fonda]. Masters, Kim and Bryan Burrough, "Cable Guys," *Vanity Fair* (January 1997). See also *Newsweek,* September 29, 1997. □

Tina Turner

Well-known for her trademark legs, throaty voice, and boundless stage energy, Tina Turner (born Anna Mae Bullock, 1939) was one of the sexiest and most popular international performers of the 20th century. She first began singing with the Kings of Rhythm, and then formed the Ike and Tina Turner Revue with the leader of that group. Leaving her abusive partner in 1976, she went on to star in her own right into the mid 1980s.

"Tina" was an invention of Ike Turner. The singer was born Anna Mae Bullock in 1939 in rural Tennessee. Her father, Floyd Bullock, was a farm overseer and church deacon who fought perpetually with his "black Indian" wife Zelma. Turner and her older sister, Alline, spent most of their childhood shuttling between the homes of grandparents, father, mother, and a cousin.

Yearned to Sing

For a time during World War II, when Turner's parents were still married, they moved without their children to Knoxville where work was plentiful in the defense industry. The girls were allowed one visit in two years, and it was on this visit that Turner first sang for money. It was in a ladies' dress shop; the saleswomen gave her quarters. She also experienced her first lively, soulful church visit in the Sanctified Church, where self-expression was encouraged, unlike the constrained atmosphere of her grandparents' Baptist church back home.

In 1956 Zelma Bullock was divorced and living in St. Louis when she ended a long separation from her daughters. Zelma brought them to live with her after her own mother, with whom Turner had been living in Tennessee, died. Reunited with the older sister she idolized, Turner began to experience an awakening to the rhythm and blues of East St. Louis, where the Kings of Rhythm were a hot band holding court at Club Manhattan. Ike Turner led the band, and Alline Bullock was dating the drummer. Younger Anna Bullock watched and waited for weeks for a chance to get on stage with the band, and when she finally did, she sang a B.B. King song and impressed Ike Turner so immediately and overwhelmingly that he asked her to perform regularly with them. He gave her the stage name of Little Ann.

The reputation of Ike Turner mirrored the violence of his childhood, during which his father, a Baptist minister, was murdered by the boyfriend of the minister's lover. Ike Turner and Anna Bullock began their relationship as mentor and protégé. Her romantic involvement at the time centered around Raymond Hill, the band's saxophone player and the father of Anna Bullock's first child, born in 1958. Although Ike still lived with his second wife, Anna moved into their home, and soon after that Ike and Anna had a son named Ricky. They married in Mexico, although it was later discovered that Ike had never divorced his previous wife.

Ike and Tina Turner on the Road

In spite of constant personal strains on their relationship, the Turners continued to make music. In late 1959 Anna Mae Bullock filled in for a last-minute no-show singer during a recording session with the Kings of Rhythm. The result was a smash hit in the summer of 1960 called "A Fool in Love" and was released under the names Ike and Tina Turner.

What became the Ike and Tina Turner Revue was a slick package of Ike Turner's shrewd management and song writing, Tina Turner's intensely energetic and sensual lead voice and body, three backup "Ikettes," and an eight piece band. They traveled the country, their sound a combination of country blues, ghetto rhythm, and gospel passion, and by 1969 they had released 15 albums and 60 singles, including the hit songs "It's Gonna Work Out Fine," "I Pity the Fool," "I Idolize You," "Poor Fool," and "Tra La La La La."

"River Deep"

Stardom for the Ike and Tina Turner Revue came about first in Europe. Legendary pop producer Phil Spector wanted Tina to sing on a record without Ike. The normally autocratic husband agreed to the arrangement thanks to a generous financial offer. Released late in 1966 the song" River Deep, Mountain High" topped the British pop charts for many weeks in 1966.

Ike and Tina Turned toured Europe twice in the 1960s with the Rolling Stones. Tina had taught Mick Jagger, the leader of that group, how to dance on stage. By the time the revue returned to the United States, Ike and Tina Turner had "crossed over" more than the Atlantic. They were wildly popular with mainstream audiences who were stunned by the forceful blend of hard rock and roll and provocative soul. Tina Turner aptly describes their style in her introduction to "Proud Mary" when she says, "we never do anything nice and easy, we always do it nice—and rough." That song won a Grammy Award in 1971 for best rhythm and blues vocal by a group. Albums released by the revue in the 1970s include *Working Together* (1970), *Blues Roots* (1972), *Nutbush City Limits* (1973), and *The Gospel According to Ike and Tina* (1974).

Although Tina Turner continued to tour and record with the group during the early 1970s, her own identity began to emerge both personally and professionally. She released three solo albums and appeared in the rock opera film *Tommy* as the "Acid Queen." Years of physical and emotional abuse by Ike Turner became too much for her, and she walked out on him and the group during a concert tour stop in Texas in July 1976. Fleeing with only thirty-six cents and a gas station credit card, Turner worked cleaning friends' houses and even living on food stamps while she began putting her life together.

Nonetheless, Tina Turner savored her freedom. Caring for her children for a while, she eventually sent them off: "I had been their mother, I had been his wife. Now it was time to be *me*. A solo album called *Rough*, released in 1978, received little attention from the press and even less from listeners. She continued to tour, however, mostly in Europe and in small American clubs and hotels.

Tina's Comeback

Once again, the Rolling Stones provided a ticket for her success, and her special guest performances on their 1981 sold-out U.S. tour introduced Tina Turner to a new generation of listeners fascinated with her wild, sensual, visceral presence. One music critic, after seeing her in concert, described her as she entered the stage "in mid-scream with both legs pumping, hips grinding, long mane whirling, her mouth wrapped around some of the sexiest sounds ever set to music."

After touring with Lionel Ritchie and Rod Stewart and doing her own record-breaking European tour, Tina Turner's 1984 album *Private Dancer* sold more than 11 million copies worldwide and earned four Grammy Awards, including Record of the Year for "What's Love Got To Do with It."

Another hit album was released in 1986 called *Break Every Rule*. In 1985, Turner appeared in the film *Mad Max: Beyond the Thunderdome,* from which came the hit song "We Don't Need Another Hero." She was inducted into the Rock and Roll Hall of Fame in January 1991, and her "Foreign Affairs" tour later that year sold out in 19 countries, drawing over three million fans.

Movie Bio and Album a Hit

In her 1986 best-selling autobiography, *I, Tina,* written with Kurt Loder, she describes how she endured the persecution and torment of Ike Turner, while at the same time laying the foundation for a wildly successful and popular music career. In 1993, Touchstone Pictures released a film version of the book called *What's Love Got To Do with It,* starring Angela Bassett as Tina and Laurence Fishburne as Ike. The movie was a box-office success. Turner re-recorded several hits for the soundtrack and even appeared at the film's end as herself. In the wake of the film's success, Turner went on tour again. *Variety* remarked in a review of a 1993 concert that "watching Tina Turner perform is like watching a tornado traverse the landscape as it builds in power and intensity." The *Los Angeles Times* reviewer called her show "more effective as a sweeping piece of theater than as a concert," but he admired her "energy and heart."

In 1996, to promote her album *Wildest Dreams,* Turner went on a hectic yearlong world tour. The still sultry superstar launched the tour with a private performance for the family of the Sultan of Brunei, reputedly the world's richest man. She continued on to South Africa, then began a circuit of European cities. Turner said European audiences seemed to enjoy her more and were more supportive of her work between hit records. "I am as big as Madonna in Europe," she told *Jet* magazine. "I am as big, in some places, as the Rolling Stones."

Turner took her "Wildest Dreams" stage show to the U.S. in May 1997 for her first American appearances in four years. The tour kicked off in Houston, Texas, and went on 47 other cities before ending in July at New York's Radio City Music Hall. For two solid nonstop hours, the 57-year old but ageless rock diva gave a an electric performance that encompassed 20 songs as well as a continuous barrage of video and sound wizardry.

"Living My Wildest Dream

Turner made Europe her home from 1986. Her decision was influenced by her relationship with Erwin Bach, a German executive with EMI records, her European label. Turner and Bach met when he picked her up at the London airport in 1986. They hit it off immediately, began dating steadily, and Turner ultimately moved to London to be with Bach. Although Bach was 16 years her junior and earned considerably less money, the relationship persisted through the 1990s. Because of Bach's own career, the two lived first in London, then in Germany, and finally to Zurich.

Meanwhile, from 1990, Turner spent six years overseeing the construction and decoration of her dream house in southern France. Decorated in an eclectic mix of neoclassical, art deco, and rock-and-roll mementos, the lavish villa was perched high in the hills overlooking Nice harbor, Cap Ferrat, and the Mediterranean beyond. There the grandmother born in rural Tennessee two put down roots between tours. She had reached the pinnacle of her profession, found love with a younger man, and enjoyed living in the present. I don't dwell on the past, she told *Harper's Bazaar.* ''That's me—I don't go back.''

Further Reading

Two interesting books on Tina Turner's life and career are *I, Tina* (1986), her autobiography with Kurt Loder, and Steven Ivory's *Tina!* (1985). Among the periodicals with additional information are *Ebony* (January 1992); *Rolling Stone* (October 15, 1992); a cover story in *Vanity Fair* (May 1993); *TIME* (June 21, 1993); and *Jet* (June 21, 1993). A short biography appears in *Notable Black American Women* (1992), edited by Jessie Carney Smith.

Other resources include Mills, Bart. *Tina* (Warner, 1985). Mower, Sarah. ''Private Tina,'' *Harper's Bazaar,* December 1996, pages 150-159. (Anonymous) ''Living My Wildest Dream,'' *Ebony* (September 1996); □

Tutankhamen

Tutankhamen (reigned 1361-1352 B.C.), the twelfth King of the Eighteenth Egyptian Dynasty, became the most famous of the Pharaohs when his treasure-filled tomb was discovered in the 20th century.

The parentage of Tutankhamen is unknown. When he became king, he was only a child, for although he reigned 8 full years, examination of his body showed that he was little more than 18 years old at the time of his death.

Tutankhamen acceded to the throne shortly after the death of Ikhnaton. He may have owed his accession to his marriage to Ankhnesamun, the third daughter of Ikhnaton and Nefertiti. Tutankhamen had originally been named Tutankhaten, but both he and Ankhnesamun (originally Ankhnespaten) deleted from their names all reference to the sun disk Aten as soon as they abandoned Amarna, the city built by Ikhnaton for the sole worship of Aten. Tutankhamen apparently left the city very early in his reign, for, with the exception of a few scarabs, no trace of him has been found at Amarna.

The addition to Tutankhamen's name of the epithet ''Ruler of Southern On'' indicates that he regarded Thebes as his principal city. There can be little doubt that he made every effort to placate the supporters of the god Amun, and a stele erected near the Third Pylon of the temple of Karnak depicts Tutankhamen offering to Amun and Mut. The accompanying text refers to the state of decay into which the temples and shrines of the gods had fallen during the period of the Atenist heresy. Tutankhamen had a large peristyle hall at Luxor decorated with reliefs illustrating the festival of Amen-Re.

Despite the existence of conventional representations of the Pharaoh slaying his foes, it is doubtful that Tutankhamen engaged in any serious military operations. There is some indication that the actual power behind the throne was an elderly official named Ay, who is depicted on a fragment of gold leaf with Tutankhamen. On another fragment Ay bears the title of vizier. He had already posed as a coregent before the death of Tutankhamen; and as regent Ay is represented undertaking his obsequies on the walls of the young pharaoh's burial chamber.

Tutankhamen is probably the best-known of the pharaohs owing to the fortunate discovery of his treasure-filled tomb virtually intact. His burial place in the Valley of the Kings had escaped the fate of the tombs of his predecessors. The entrance was hidden from plunderers by debris heaped over it during the cutting of the later tomb of Ramses VI.

Further Reading

Penelope Fox, *Tutankhamen's Treasure* (1951), contains a biographical study of the Pharaoh and a description of his time.

Genevieve R. Tabouis, *The Private Life of Tutankhamen: Love, Religion, and Politics at the Court of an Egyptian King* (trans. 1929), is a historical re-creation of the man and his times. An account of Tutankhamen's tomb and its contents is given by its discoverer and excavator, Howard Carter, and coauthor A. C. Mace, *The Tomb of Tut-ankh-amen* (3 vols., 1923-1933); it is available in an abridged edition entitled *Tomb of Tut-Ankh-Amen,* edited by Shirley Glubok (1968). The historical background is discussed in Cyril Aldred, *Akhenaten: Pharaoh of Egypt* (1968). □

Archbishop Desmond Tutu

In the 1980s Archbishop Desmond Tutu (born 1931) became South Africa's most prominent opponent of apartheid, that country's system of racial discrimination.

The awarding of the Nobel Peace Prize of 1984 to Desmond Mpilo Tutu made him the most visible representative of the struggle in the Republic of South Africa against apartheid, the system by which the minority white population of South Africa dominated the black majority until 1994. It allowed whites, who constituted 20 percent of the population, to reserve for themselves about 87 percent of the land, most natural resources, and all meaningful political power. Blacks who found themselves in lands reserved for whites were arbitrarily made citizens of one of ten homelands, which the white government (but virtually no one else) called nations. In order to remove Blacks from areas reserved for whites, the government forcibly evicted many from their homes, though their families had in some cases occupied them for decades. Blacks in the Republic were relegated to the lowest-paying jobs, denied access to most public accommodations (though this policy was relaxed somewhat in the 1970s), and had drastically lower life expectancies than whites. In contrast, South African whites had one of the highest standards of living in the world.

Black opposition to these conditions began in 1912 when the African National Congress (ANC) was formed. Until the 1960s it engaged in various peaceful campaigns of protest that included marches, petitions, and boycotts—actions which availed Blacks little. After police fired in 1960 on a crowd at Sharpeville, killing 69 and wounding many others, and after the ANC leader Nelson Mandela was imprisoned for life in 1964, many Blacks decided to abandon the policy of non-violent resistance. Most ANC members, led by Oliver Tambo, left South Africa and launched a campaign of sabotage from exile. The white government increased its violence in return. In 1976 500 Black students were shot during protests, and in 1978 and 1980 Black leader Steve Biko and trade unionist Neil Aggett were killed while in police custody. Beginning in 1984 violence again swept South Africa. By the time the government declared a state of emergency in June 1986, more than 2,000 individuals had been killed.

Against this backdrop Desmond Tutu emerged as the leading spokesman for non-violent resistance to apartheid. Born on October 7, 1931, in Klerksdorp, a town in the Transvaal region, his early education was at a mission school. At the age of 14 he contracted tuberculosis and was hospitalized for 20 months. He wanted to become a doctor, but because his family could not afford the schooling, he entered teaching. When the government instituted a system of racially discriminatory education in 1957, Tutu left teaching and entered the Anglican Church. Ordained in 1961, he earned a B.A. in 1962 from the University of South Africa, and shortly thereafter a B.D. and an M.Th. from the University of London. From 1970 to 1974 he lectured at the University of Lesotho, Botswana, and Swaziland. In 1975 he became dean of Johannesburg, a position from which he publicly challenged white rule. He became bishop of Lesotho in 1976, and in 1985 bishop of Johannesburg. A short 14 months later, in April 1986, he was elected archbishop of Cape Town, the first Black person to head the Anglican Church in southern Africa.

By the 1980s clergymen were among the most vigorous opponents within South Africa of apartheid. Allan Boesak, a biracial minister, and Beyers Naude, head of the Christian Institute, were unusually outspoken. Naude was silenced in the late 1970s by banning, a unique South African punishment by which the victim was placed under virtual house arrest and could not speak or be quoted publicly. Tutu's international recognition as a critic of apartheid came when he became first general secretary of the South African Council of Churches in 1978.

The problem faced by anti-apartheid clergymen was how to simultaneously oppose both violent resistance and apartheid, which was itself increasingly violent. Tutu's opposition was vigorous and unequivocal, and he was outspoken both in South Africa and abroad, often comparing apartheid to Nazism and Communism. As a result the government twice revoked his passport, and he was jailed briefly in 1980 after a protest march. It was thought by many that Tutu's increasing international reputation and his rigorous advocacy of non-violence protected him from harsher penalties. Tutu's view on violence reflected the tension in a Christian approach to resistance: "I will never tell anyone to pick up a gun. But I will pray for the man who picks up a gun, pray that he will be less cruel than he might otherwise have been. . . ."

Another issue Tutu faced was whether other nations should be urged to apply economic sanctions against South Africa. The argument for sanctions stated that sanctions, by denying South Africa the investments on which its economy was dependent, would force the white government to abandon apartheid. The arguments against sanctions were that those who would suffer most would be the Blacks and that the whites were likely to become more intransigent in the face of world pressure. Tutu favored sanctions as the only hope for peaceful change. He also vigorously opposed the "constructive engagement" policy of the Reagan administration in the United States, which advocated "friendly persuasion." When the new wave of violence swept South Africa in the 1980s and the white government failed to make fundamental changes in apartheid, Tutu pronounced constructive engagement a failure. The U.S. Congress did impose some sanctions against South Africa in October 1986, overriding a veto by President Reagan.

In 1989 F.W. de Klerk was elected the new president of the Republic of South Africa. He had promised to abolish apartheid, and at the end of 1993 he made good on his promise when South Africa's first all-race elections were announced. On April 27, 1994 South Africans elected a new president, Nelson Mandela, and apartheid was finally over. Mandela aptly symbolized South Africa's new liberation, since until 1990 he had spent 27 years as a political prisoner because of his outspoken opposition to apartheid.

In 1997, Tutu received the ROBIE award for his work in humanitarianism. The award was presented by NBC sportscaster Bob Costas at the Jackie Robinson Foundation annual dinner, held at the Waldorf-Astoria Hotel in New York. The award came in the midst of Tutu's battle with prostate cancer, and shortly after the presentation he announced plans to undergo several months of cancer treatment in the United States. As head of South Africa's Truth and Reconciliation Commission, a group that investigates apartheid crimes, Mandela planned to set up an office in the United States, where he could continue his work throughout the rigorous cancer treatment.

Receiving the ROBIE was certainly not Tutu's first recognition: he was the second South African to earn the Nobel Prize. The first was Albert Luthuli of the ANC, who received it in 1960 for the same sort of opposition to apartheid.

Further Reading

For general descriptions of South African society, see Leo Marquard, *The People and Policies of South Africa* (4th ed., 1969) and Joseph Lelyveld, *Move Your Shadow* (1985). For the role of the church see Peter Walshe, *Church Versus State in South Africa* (1983). There is as yet no biography of Tutu. His speeches and sermons have been published in *Crying in the Wilderness* (1982); *Hope and Suffering* (1983); *The Words of Desmond Tutu* (1989); and *The Rainbow People of God: The Making of a Peaceful Revolution*. His book *Crying in the Wilderness* contains a brief account of his life, as do numerous newspapers and journals published shortly after he received the Nobel Prize in October 1984. □

Amos Tutuola

The Nigerian writer Amos Tutuola (born 1920) is famous for his fantastic tales which, in their content, depend heavily on the folklore of his ancestral Yoruba people.

Amos Tutuola was born in Abeokuta (Yorubaland). His father's death in 1939 prevented him from pursuing his studies. During World War II he joined the Royal Air Force as a blacksmith, and when the war was over, he became a messenger in the labor department in Lagos.

As he enjoyed some reputation as a storyteller among his friends, Tutuola devoted the ample leisure afforded by his unexacting functions to penning in his own idiosyncratic brand of Nigerian English some of the bizarre tales which abound in Yoruba oral lore and which D. O. Fagunwa had recorded in his vernacular storybooks. The result was *The Palmwine Drinkard and His Dead Palmwine Tapster in the Dead's Town* (1952). The book was an immediate success.

While English and American reviewers were bewitched by Tutuola's exuberant imagination and his unconventional speech, Nigerian intellectuals were at first extremely hostile: they felt that his superstitious, "uncivilized" stories and his—in their view—uncouth, nonstandard English were likely to tarnish the image of Nigeria in the eyes of the outside world. Their criticism and contempt, however, did not detract Tutuola from quietly bringing forth other similar romances: *My Life in the Bush of Ghosts* (1954), *Simbi and the Satyr of the Dark Jungle* (1956), *The Brave African Huntress* (1958), *The Feather Woman of the Jungle* (1962), *The Witch Herbalist of the Remote Town* (1980), *The Wild Hunter in the Bush of the Ghosts* (1982) and *Pauper, Brawler, Slanderer* (1987).

Tutuola's recipe is of the simplest: the plucky hero or heroine embarks on an often perfunctorily motivated quest that leads him or her to the jungle forest and provides a framework for what really matters, an inexhaustible variety of adventures among gods and ghosts, ogres and pygmies, satyrs and magicians, and sundry other uncanny, Bosch-like monsters, such as the Smelling-Ghost, the Reverend Devil, the Television-handed Goddess, the Hairy Giant and a few "ghostesses," all of whom experience no difficulty whatsoever in transforming themselves into almost any kind of mineral, vegetable, animal or even human shapes.

A comparison with collections of traditional tales shows that many of these episodes are part and parcel of Yoruba folklore, which is characterized by its familiarity with the supernatural, its prodigious inventive power, and its very peculiar sense of horror as a source of humor. But to the ancestral fund, Tutuola adds his own inimitable touch: he introduces elements of Christian and Western civilization which appear strangely exotic in this mythical world of African fantasy; above all, he solves to his own and his readers' satisfaction the linguistic problem of the African writer, coining new words, translating vernacular idioms, and generally distorting English vocabulary, syntax, and even spelling with impervious assurance and disarming efficiency.

In 1963 Tutuola had his revenge over his Nigerian highbrow critics when the popular actor-director-producer E. K. Ogunmola adapted *The Palmwine Drinkard* into a vernacular folk-opera, which was performed with tremendous success all over the country.

In addition to his writing, Tutuola has worked as a visiting research fellow to the University of Ife (1979) and as an associate to the international writing program at the University of Iowa (1983). His honors included being named an honorary citizen of New Orleans in 1983 and receiving second-place awards in Turin, Italy, in 1985 for *The Palmwine Drinkard* and *My Life in the Bush of Ghosts*.

Further Reading

Harold Reeves Collins, *Amos Tutuola* (1969), reviews Tutuola's work, traces its influence, and carefully assesses the author's place in Nigerian literature. ☐

John Henry Twachtman

John Henry Twachtman (1853-1902) was one of the leading American impressionist painters. His most characteristic work is marked by an extreme lightness of palette that approaches pure white.

John Twachtman was born in Cincinnati, Ohio, on Aug. 4, 1853. His parents were immigrants, and his father worked as a decorator of window shades, an occupation in which John joined him at the age of 14. John studied drawing in the evenings, but the most important influence on his artistic formation was Frank Duveneck, who had studied in Munich and settled in Cincinnati in 1873. When Duveneck returned to Munich, Twachtman went with him. He studied with Ludwig Loefftz, and one of his fellow students was William Merritt Chase.

In 1877 Duveneck, Chase, and Twachtman went to Venice, a trip which was a most important artistic event in their lives. Twachtman sent two of his Italian pictures to the first exhibition of the Society of American Artists in 1878

and returned to the United States that same year. But in 1880 he was back in Europe, teaching at Duveneck's famous school in Florence. That summer Twachtman went to Venice and probably met James McNeill Whistler, who may have influenced his etchings, as he did his whole generation. In 1881 he married, and during his wedding trip he painted and etched with J. Alden Weir.

Twachtman's early paintings are in the dark Munich manner, but he was by no means committed to the dark palette, which was passing out of favor. In 1833 he settled in Paris to learn the new French impressionist style; it was a matter of artistic survival. He passed smoothly into impressionism. Back in New York, he exhibited with Weir and taught at the Art Students League with Chase. Twachtman was a decided success and in 1898 was a founding member of the group of painters known as "The Ten." He bought a place in Greenwich, Conn., not far from Weir's, and painted a great deal at Cos Cob, at Greenwich, and at Weir's farm. His palette became lighter and lighter, and in his favorite scenes of snow and ice he achieved a degree of whiteness that went well beyond Claude Monet's winter landscapes.

Twachtman was a particularly pure example of a landscape painter; his figures are few, and there are not many buildings in his pictures. His Connecticut scenes have a unique grace and delicacy; they never follow a formula and are never empty. His poetic pastorals, with their soft and pale gray-green trees and fields, his almost ornately frozen brooks and waterfalls, by no means mirror the man. He was a difficult and melancholy personality, and at the height of

his career, alone, depressed, and estranged from his family, he died at Gloucester, Mass., on Aug. 8, 1902.

Further Reading

The best treatment of Twachtman is Cincinnati Art Museum, *Twachtman* (1966), with an introduction by Richard Boyle. The standard monographs are Eliot C. Clark, *John Twachtman* (1924), and Allen Tucker, *John H. Twachtman* (1931).

Additional Sources

Twachtman, John Henry, *John Twachtman,* New York: Watson Guptill, 1979. ☐

Mark Twain

Mark Twain (1835-1910), American humorist and novelist, captured a world audience with stories of boyhood adventure and with commentary on man's shortcomings that is humorous even while it probes, often bitterly, the roots of human behavior.

Bred among American traditions of frontier journalism, and influenced by such cracker-box humorists as Artemus Ward and by the tradition of the tall tale, Mark Twain scored his first successes as a writer and lecturer with his straight-faced, laconic recitation of incredible comic incidents in simple, direct, colloquial language. His was an oral style, and his principal contribution is sometimes thought to be the creation of a genuinely native idiom.

Some contemporaries considered Mark Twain's language uncouth and crude when compared with the well-mannered prose of William Dean Howells or the intricately contrived expression of Henry James. Though conventionally less disciplined and less consistently successful than either, Mark Twain surpassed both in popular esteem and is remembered with them as foremost in the creation of prose fiction in the United States during the late 19th century.

Mark Twain was born Samuel Langhorne Clemens on Nov. 30, 1835, in the frontier village of Florida, Mo. He spent his boyhood in nearby Hannibal, on the bank of the Mississippi River, observing its busy life, fascinated by its romance, but chilled by the violence and bloodshed it bred. Twelve years old when his lawyer father died, he began working as an apprentice, then a compositor, with local printers, contributing occasional squibs to local newspapers. At 17 his comic sketch "The Dandy Frightening the Squatter" was published by a sportsmen's magazine in Boston.

In 1853 Clemens began wandering as a journeyman printer to St. Louis, Chicago, New York, and Philadelphia, settling briefly with his brother, Orion, in Iowa before setting out at 22 to make his fortune, he hoped, beside the lush banks of the Amazon River in South America. Instead, traveling down the Mississippi River, he became a steamboat river pilot until the Civil War interrupted traffic.

Western Years

In 1861 Clemens traveled to Nevada, where he speculated carelessly in timber and silver mining. He settled down to newspaper work in Virginia City, until his reckless pen and redheaded temper brought him into conflict with local authorities; it seemed profitable to escape to California. Meanwhile he had adopted the pen name of Mark Twain, a riverman's term for water that was safe, but only just safe, for navigation.

In San Francisco Mark Twain came under the influence of Bret Harte. Artemus Ward encouraged Mark Twain to write *The Jumping Frog of Calaveras County* (1865), which first brought him national attention. Most of his western writing was hastily, often carelessly, done, and he later did little to preserve it.

Traveling Correspondent

In 1865 the *Sacramento Union* commissioned Mark Twain to report on a new excursion service to Hawaii. His accounts as published in the newspaper provided the basis for his first successful lectures and years later were collected in *Letters from the Sandwich Islands* (1938) and *Letters from Honolulu* (1939). His travel accounts were so well received that he contracted in 1866 to become a traveling correspondent for the *Alta California;* he would circle the globe, dispatching letters. The first step was to travel to New York by ship; his accounts were collected in *Mark Twain's Travels with Mr. Brown* (1940).

In June 1867 Mark Twain left New York and went to Europe and the Holy Land, sending accounts to the California paper and to Horace Greeley's *New York Tribune.* They were fresh and racy, alert, informed, and sidesplittingly funny. Their accent was American western humor; their traditional theme was the decay of transatlantic institutions when compared with the energetic freshness of the western life-style. Yet the humor also exposed the traveling American innocents as they haggled through native bazaars, completely innocent of their own outlandish appearance. Nor was their author exempt from ridicule, for Mark Twain usually wrote of "What fools *we* mortals be," accepting his place among the erring race of man. The letters were later revised as *The Innocents Abroad; or, The New Pilgrim's Progress* (1869), and the book immediately made Mark Twain a popular favorite, in demand especially as a lecturer who could keep large audiences in gales of laughter.

In 1870 Twain married Olivia Langdon. After a brief residence in upstate New York as an editor and part owner of the *Buffalo Express,* he moved to Hartford, Conn., where he lived for 20 years; there three daughters were born, and prosperity as a writer and lecturer (in England in 1872 and 1873) seemed guaranteed. *Roughing It* (1872) recounted Mark Twain's travels to Nevada and reprinted some of the Sandwich Island letters. Neither it, *A Tramp Abroad* (1880), nor *Following the Equator* (1898) had popular or critical reception equal to that of *The Innocents Abroad.*

Famous Novelist

With Charles Dudley Warner, Mark Twain wrote *The Gilded Age* (1873), a quizzical satire on financial speculation and political chicanery, which introduced the character of Colonel Beriah Sellers, a backcountry squire plagued by schemes which might, but never did, bring him sudden fortune. By this time Mark Twain was famous. Anything he wrote would sell, but his imagination flagged. He collected miscellaneous writings into *Sketches New and Old* (1875) and tried to fit Colonel Sellers into a new book, which finally materialized years later as *The American Claimant* (1891).

Meanwhile Mark Twain's account of steamboating experiences for the *Atlantic Monthly* (1875; expanded to *Life on the Mississippi,* 1883) captured the beauty, glamour, and menace of the Mississippi. Boyhood memories of life beside that river were written into *The Adventures of Tom Sawyer* (1875), which immediately attracted young and old. With more exotic and foreign settings, *The Prince and the Pauper* (1882) and *A Connecticut Yankee in King Arthur's Court* (1889) attracted readers also, but *The Adventures of Huckleberry Finn* (1885), in which Mark Twain again returned to the river scenes he knew best, was considered vulgar by many contemporaries.

"Tom" and "Huck"

Tom Sawyer, better organized than *Huckleberry Finn,* is a narrative of innocent boyhood play that inadvertently discovers evil as Tom and Huck witness a murder by Injun Joe in a graveyard at midnight. The boys run away, are thought dead, but turn up at their own funeral. Tom and Huck decide to seek out the murderer, and the reward offered for his capture. It is Tom and his sweetheart who, while lost in a cave, discover the hiding place of Injun Joe. Though the townspeople unwittingly seal the murderer in the cave, they close the entrance only to keep adventuresome boys like Tom out of future trouble. In the end, it is innocent play and boyish adventuring which really triumph.

Huckleberry Finn is Mark Twain's finest creation. Huck lacks Tom's imagination; he is a simple boy with little education. One measure of his character is a proneness to deceit, which seems instinctive, a trait shared by other wild things and relating him to nature—in opposition to Tom's tradition-grounded, book-learned, imaginative deceptions. *The Adventures of Huckleberry Finn,* a loosely strung series of adventures, can be viewed as the story of a quest for freedom and an escape from what society requires in exchange for success. Joined in flight by a black companion, Jim, who seeks freedom from slavery, Huck discovers that the Mississippi is peaceful (though he is found to be only partially correct) but that the world along its shores is marred by deceit, including his own, and by cruelty and murder. When the raft on which he and Jim are floating down the river is invaded by two confidence men, Huck first becomes their assistant in swindles but is finally the agent of their exposure.

Jim throughout is a frightened but faithful friend. Huck is troubled by the sin which in the world's eyes he is committing by helping a slave to escape. The thematic climax of the book occurs when Huck decides that if he must go to hell for that sin, very well then, he will go to hell. And he does, as leaving the river he enters again into the world dominated by Tom, which in its seemingly innocent deceit presents an alarming analog to adult pretense. All ends suddenly; Jim has been free all the time, and good people offer to adopt and civilize Huck. But he will have none of it: "I can't stand it," he says. "I been there before."

Whatever its faults, *Huckleberry Finn* is a classic. Variously interpreted, it is often thought to suggest more than it reveals, speaking of what man has done to confuse himself about his right relation to nature. It can also be thought to treat of man's failures in dealing with his fellows and of the corruption so deeply engrained that man's only escape is in flight, perhaps even from himself. Yet it is also an apparently artless story of adventure and escape so simply and directly told that Ernest Hemingway once said that all American literature begins with this book. Its language seems the instinctual language of all men—"a joyous exorcism," one critic has said.

Mark Twain, said H. L. Mencken, was the first important author to write "genuinely colloquial and native American." Huck, who shuns civilization, seems a symbol of simple honesty and conscience. His boy's-eye view of a world distorted by pretense and knavery anticipates the use of a young narrator by numerous important American authors, including Sherwood Anderson, Ernest Hemingway, and J. D. Salinger. Yet Tom, not Huck, seems to have remained Mark Twain's favorite, giving title to *Tom Sawyer Abroad* (1894), *Tom Sawyer, Detective* (1896), and to unpublished tales later collected in *Hannibal, Huck, and Tom* (1969).

Unsuccessful Businessman

Mark Twain's early books were sold by subscription; they sold well, for Twain prided himself on gauging public taste. Many were not issued until subscription agents had secured enough advance orders to make them surely profitable. As a traveling lecturer, he helped sell his books, and his books helped pack his lectures. He was probably the best-known and certainly among the most prosperous writers of his generation. Unsatisfied, he reached for more. When *The Prince and the Pauper* did not sell as he thought it should, he established his own publishing firm, which did well for a while.

But Mark Twain was soon in serious trouble. For several years he had been supplying large sums toward the perfecting of a typesetting machine, convinced that it would make his fortune. But in 1891 he retreated with his family to Europe, where they could live more cheaply. In 1894 the publishing company went bankrupt, and the typesetter failed in competition with less complex rivals. Mark Twain was deeply in debt.

Meanwhile, in 1893, Henry Huttleston Rogers, a director of the Standard Oil Company, had assumed control of Mark Twain's financial affairs. While Mark Twain lectured around the world to pay his debts, Rogers placated creditors, invested his royalties, and arranged new publishing contracts. *The Tragedy of Pudd'nhead Wilson* (1894), an awkwardly constructed story of two boys, one of them African American, switched in their cradles, is sometimes remembered as Mark Twain's second-best book, but it brought little immediate financial assistance. *Personal Recollections of Joan of Arc* (1896), a ponderous paean to innocence triumphant, was so serious that Mark Twain at first would not allow his name to be associated with it. *Following the Equator* (1897) was dedicated to Rogers's son.

Mark Twain and his family remained in Europe, saddened by the death of one daughter and seeking help for the apparently incurable illness of another. Like his Colonel Sellers, Mark Twain looked desperately for a scheme to recoup his fortune. Rogers finally steered him out of debt and arranged a publishing contract which ensured Mark Twain and his heirs a handsome income.

Last Writings

On his return to the United States in 1900, Mark Twain rose to new heights of popularity. His publicized insistence on paying every creditor had made him something of a public hero. He was widely sought as a speaker, and he seemed proud to be the genial companion of people like the Rockefellers and Andrew Carnegie, though in private he opposed the principles for which they seemed to stand. His writings grew increasingly bitter, especially after his wife's death in 1905. *The Man That Corrupted Hadleyburg* (1900) exposed corruption in a small, typical American town. *King Leopold's Soliloquy* (1905) attacked hypocrisy in treatment of inhabitants of the Congo, fulminating against what Mark Twain called "the damn'd human race." *What Is Man?*

(1906) was a diatribe of despair. *Extracts from Adam's Diary* (1904) had humorously presented man as a blunderer; *Eve's Diary* (1906), written partly in memory of his wife, showed man saved from bungling only through the influence of a good woman. Many of his later indictments of human cupidity were, he thought, so severe that they could not be published for 100 years. But when some appeared in *Letters from the Earth* (1962), they seemed hardly more bitter than what had appeared before.

In 1906 Mark Twain began to dictate his autobiography to Albert B. Paine (his literary executor), recording scattered memories without chronological arrangement. Portions from it were published in periodicals later that year. *Captain Stormfield's Visit to Heaven* (1909), a burlesque Mark Twain had puttered over for years, partly disguised his pessimism with a veneer of rollicking humor as it detailed the low esteem in which man is held by celestial creatures. With the income from the excerpts of his autobiography, he built a large house in Redding, Conn., which he named Stormfield. There, after several trips to Bermuda to bolster his waning health, he died on April 21, 1910.

Mark Twain had been working over several drafts of a final bitter book, and from these Paine and his publisher "edited" *The Mysterious Stranger* (1916), a volume which William H. Gibson, in presenting complete texts of versions of the story in *Mark Twain's Mysterious Stranger Manuscripts* (1969), designated as "an editorial fraud." As scholars work over the Mark Twain Papers at the University of California, more volumes containing unpublished writings or correspondence will appear. Few, however, can be expected to alter the esteem and affection in which Mark Twain is held. His books have been translated into most of the languages of Europe, where with Theodore Dreiser and Jack London, he is often thought among the best to express, or expose, the spirit of the American people.

Further Reading

Portions of Mark Twain's autobiography were published by Albert B. Paine, *Mark Twain's Autobiography* (2 vols., 1924). Parts which had earlier seemed too bitter or personal were brought together by Bernard DeVoto in *Mark Twain in Eruption* (1940). Charles Neider included some material not previously published in his chronologically arranged *The Autobiography of Mark Twain* (1959). The complete text is being prepared for publication by the editors of the Mark Twain Papers at the University of California.

Of the making of books about Mark Twain there seems to be no end. The authorized biography, Albert B. Paine, *Mark Twain, A Biography: The Personal and Literary Life of Samuel Langhorne Clemens* (3 vols. 1912; repr. 1935), though often corrected by later writers, is still important. So are such reminiscent accounts as William Dean Howells, *My Mark Twain* (1910); Mary Lawton, *A Lifetime with Mark Twain* (1925); and Clara Clemens, *My Father, Mark Twain* (1931). Modern biographies are J. De Lancey Ferguson, *Mark Twain, Man and Legend* (1943), and Justin Kaplan, *Mr. Clemens and Mark Twain* (1966). Mark Twain's early years are discussed in M. M. Brashear, *Mark Twain: Son of Missouri* (1934), and Dixon Wecter, *Sam Clemens of Hannibal* (1952).

Books on specific aspects of Mark Twain's life include Ivan Benson, *Mark Twain's Western Years* (1938); Samuel L. Webster, *Mark Twain, Business Man* (1946); Edgar M. Branch, *The*

Literary Apprenticeship of Mark Twain (1950); Kenneth R. Andrews, *Nook Farm: Mark Twain's Hartford Circle* (1950); and Louis J. Budd, *Mark Twain, Social Philosopher* (1962). Edward C. Wagenknecht, *Mark Twain: The Man and His Work* (1935; 3d ed. 1967), contains valuable bibliographical material; see also Merle Johnson, *A Bibliography of the Works of Mark Twain* (1935).

Van Wyck Brooks, *The Ordeal of Mark Twain* (1920; rev. ed. 1933), answered by Bernard DeVoto, *Mark Twain's America* (1932), created a controversy about Mark Twain's literary integrity; see also Lewis Leary, ed., *Mark Twain's Wound* (1962). Important recent critical studies include Walter Blair, *Mark Twain and Huck Finn* (1960); Henry Nash Smith, *Mark Twain: The Development of a Writer* (1962); and James M. Cox, *Mark Twain: The Fate of Humor* (1966). See also the introductions to different editions of *The Adventures of Huckleberry Finn* by Lionel Trilling (1948) and T. S. Eliot (1950). □

William Marcy Tweed

William Marcy Tweed (1823-1878) was an American politician and leader of Tammany Hall. The Tweed ring, which defrauded New York City of millions, made his name a symbol of civic corruption.

William Tweed was born in New York on April 3, 1823. His father was a chair manufacturer. Tweed left school to learn chair making at the age of 11. At 13 he was apprenticed to a saddlemaker; at 17 he became a bookkeeper in a brush business, at 19 joined the firm, and at 21 married the daughter of the firm's chief owner. But Tweed, "full of animal spirits," as one contemporary described him, found greater excitement in New York's volunteer fire department. In 1850 he became foreman of the celebrated "Americus No. 6" company, which, a year later, helped elect him Democratic alderman.

In Tammany Hall politics there were at least two classic routes to power—hard work combined with loyalty, or aggressiveness and luck. Tweed followed the latter. After serving as an alderman, he was in the U.S. Congress for a term (1853-1855); not only did this experience destroy Tweed's appetite for national politics but it put him out of touch with New York politics. But Tweed soon gained power in party and city affairs. His official positions included membership on the city board of supervisors, state senator, chairman of the state finance committee, school commissioner, deputy street commissioner, and commissioner of public works.

During the 1860s Tweed parlayed political influence into hard cash. Despite meager legal knowledge, he opened a law office to dispense "legal services" to such corporations as the Erie Railroad. He bought a printing company that monopolized city contracts, and a marble company that sold materials for the new courthouse at exorbitant prices. By 1867 Tweed was a millionaire and moved his family to a fashionable neighborhood. The following year he became grand sachem of Tammany.

The Tweed ring began in 1866, tightening operations in 1869, when "Boss" Tweed and others arranged that all bills to the city would henceforth be at least one-half fraudulent, a proportion later raised to 85 percent. The proceeds went equally to Tweed, to the city comptroller, to the county treasurer, and to the mayor. A fifth share was used to bribe officials and businessmen. The boss rallied diverse groups behind his regime by providing "something for all."

Tweed was well suited by temperament and personality for this. Almost 6 feet all, a ruddy 300 pounds, he combined coarse good fellowship with practiced suavity, becoming a favorite of all, including, for a time, some of New York's "best people." Like a good 19th-century entrepreneur, he maximized short-run profits, which were massive. The county courthouse cost $12 million; two thirds was fraudulent. Between 1866 and 1871 (when the ring was exposed) the Tweed ring's services cost the city between $40 and $100 million.

The reform coalition that exposed the ring included city patricians, the *New York Times,* and assorted political enemies within both parties; motives varied. The battle ended with imprisonment for Tweed and several associates. Initially sentenced to 12 years, Tweed went free in 1875. Rearrested on further charges, he was reimprisoned following a sensational escape to Spain. He died in jail on April 12, 1878. A century later, his grotesquely dishonest career seems a significant chapter in the urban crisis, social and governmental, which Americans have not been able to solve.

Further Reading

Tweed's career is treated in Denis T. Lynch, "*Boss*" *Tweed* (1927), and William A. Bales, *Tiger in the Streets* (1962). Gustavus Meyers, *The History of Tammany Hall* (1901), and Morris R. Werner, *Tammany Hall* (1928), set Tweed in the context of Tammany history. Seymour J. Mandelbaum, *Boss Tweed's New York* (1965), stresses Tweed's part in providing leadership in a fragmenting metropolis. Alexander B. Callow, Jr., *The Tweed Ring* (1966), is a well-written and meticulously documented narrative.

Additional Sources

Hershkowitz, Leo, *Tweed's New York: another look,* Garden City, N.Y.: Anchor Press/Doubleday, 1978. □

Anne Tyler

Anne Tyler (born 1941) is considered one of America's most important living writers. Her works evince familiarity with an extended literary tradition, with influences ranging from Emerson and Thoreau to Faulkner and Welty.

Anne Tyler was born in Minneapolis, Minnesota, in 1941; her family moved frequently, generally living in Quaker communities in the Midwest and South, before settling in North Carolina. Tyler attended Duke University, where she majored in Russian. In her first year, she became a pupil of Reynolds Price, who himself would become a major novelist and long-time friend. Price encouraged Tyler to pursue writing more vigorously, but she instead dedicated most of her attention to Russian. She graduated in 1961 then entered Columbia University to continue her studies. In 1962, she returned to Duke as Russian bibliographer for the library. The following year, Tyler married Taghi Modarressi, a psychologist from Iran. In 1964, the two moved to Montreal, where Tyler worked as an assistant librarian at McGill University Law School and wrote her first two novels *If Morning Ever Comes* (1964) and *The Tin Can Tree* (1965). In 1967, she and her husband moved to Baltimore, the setting for most of Tyler's subsequent novels. With the publication of *A Slipping-Down Life* (1970) and *The Clock Winder* (1972), Tyler began to receive more serious and positive critical attention, but only in the mid-seventies, when such writers as Gail Godwin and John Updike called attention to her, did her novels benefit from widespread recognition. Tyler's stature as an important literary figure was confirmed by the success of *Morgan's Passing* (1980), which was nominated for the National Book Critics Circle award and received the Janet Heidinger Kafka Prize. *Dinner at Homesick Restaurant* (1982) won the PEN/ Faulkner Award for fiction and was nominated for a National Book Critics Circle award and the 1983 Pulitzer Prize. *The Accidental Tourist* (1985) and *Breathing Lessons* (1988) were honored respectively with a National Book Critics Circle Award and a Pulitzer Prize.

Throughout Tyler's novels, characters struggle to negotiate a balance between self-identity and family identity. In her first novel, *If Morning Ever Comes,* Ben Joe Hawkes returns home from law school because he could not concentrate; he worried what was happening at home while he was gone. The only man in a family of women, Ben feels he must play the role of substitute father. But after only a day back, he is oppressed with the responsibilities he at least partially imposes upon himself. In *The Clock Winder,* Elizabeth Abbot flees from the roles of gardener and "handyman" in her family, but she winds up acting out the same roles for another family, the Emersons. She tries to escape that family, too, but returns to be caregiver, wife, and mother. In a less traditional rebellion from conventional family roles, Evie Decker of *A Slipping-Down Life* protests her lot as an unattractive, overweight girl by carving the name of a rock musician into her forehead. The action makes her the center of popular attention, but she eventually marries the musician, whose career she has boosted; she ends up not merely as wife, but as an object of good publicity. *Dinner at Homesick Restaurant,* portrays the psychological suffering of abused children who cannot permanently leave the site of their abuse, the "homesick restaurant." The children relive the family dinners that were never finished. The novel suggests, much like Faulkner's *As I Lay Dying,* that the defining influence of family cannot be escaped. Tyler's more recent novels, while dealing with psychologically suffering characters, have been slightly less pessimistic. *The Accidental Tourist,* the movie version of which helped make Tyler an even more well-known name, deals with the grief of Macon Leary—whose marriage collapses after the murder of his son. Like protagonists from Tyler's previous novels, Macon has a close yet ambivalent relationship with his brothers and sisters and must choose between lonely security and the uncertain comforts of human love. Critics find Tyler at the height of her powers of observation in *Breathing Lessons,* as she defines personality through small details and gestures and emphasizes the influence of a shared history on a marital relationship. Within a day-in-the-life framework augmented by flashbacks, she captures the nuances of compromise, disappointment, and love that make up Ira and Maggie Moran's marriage. The owner of a picture-framing store, Ira is uncommunicative and compulsively neat; Maggie is his warm, clumsy, talkative wife of nearly three decades. Intending to travel to Pennsylvania for a funeral on the Saturday morning of the novel's opening, and to return that afternoon, the couple spend most of the day on the road, making two extended sidetrips caused by Maggie's meddling in the affairs of strangers and relatives. Generously sprinkled with comic set-pieces that reveal her characters' foibles, *Breathing Lessons* has been called Tyler's funniest novel to date.

Tyler's first two novels received little critical attention; they were seen as slight works by an author who showed significant promise. Tyler herself has essentially disavowed her first novels. Tyler and critics alike viewed *A Slipping-Down Life* as an important point of development in her career as writer; the portrait of Evie was praised for its accurate depiction of loneliness and desperation. Most critics considered Tyler's fifth novel, *Celestial Navigation,* a breakthrough for her career. The praise of Gail Godwin and John Updike helped launch the book into further popularity, and with each successive novel, Tyler gained more respect not just as a writer with popular appeal but as a writer of literary importance. As her works began to receive nominations for major literary awards, however, Tyler came under more intense scrutiny from critics, some of whom argued that she too glibly mixed comedy with seriousness. After *Dinner with Homesick Restaurant,* though, few critics would deny her importance in contemporary fiction.

Further Reading

Bestsellers 89, Issue 1, Gale, 1989.
Binding, Paul, *Separate Country: A Literary Journey through the American South,* Paddington Press, 1979.
Contemporary Literary Criticism, Gale, Volume 7, 1977; Volume 11, 1979; Volume 18, 1981; Volume 28, 1984; Volume 44, 1987; Volume 59, 1990.
Dictionary of Literary Biography, Yearbook: 1982, 1983.
Evans, Elizabeth, *Anne Tyler,* Twayne, 1993.
Flora, Joseph M., and Robert Bain, *Fifty Southern Writers After 1900: A Bio-Bibliographic Sourcebook,* Greenwood Press, 1987, pp. 491-504.
Inge, Tonette Bond, editor, *Southern Women Writers: The New Generation,* University of Alabama Press, 1990. □

John Tyler

John Tyler (1790-1862), tenth president of the United States, was the first vice president to succeed to the presidency. His administration was marked by great conflict over the Texas question.

John Tyler was born on March 29, 1790, at Greenway Plantation in Charles City County, Va. His father, John Tyler, was governor of Virginia and a judge of the U.S. District Court. Young Tyler attended several preparatory schools and graduated from the College of William and Mary in 1807. He then studied law and was licensed to practice at the age of 19.

At 21 Tyler was elected to the Virginia House of Delegates; he served from 1811 to 1815. He subsequently was elected to the Virginia Council of State, to the U.S. House of Representatives, to the governorship of Virginia, and to the U.S. Senate (1827-1834). During these years Tyler emerged as one of the chief proponents of the states'-rights doctrine. He opposed internal improvements at Federal expense, a tariff to protect native industries, and a national banking system.

Like most politics of his day, Tyler's political activities were molded by the confused party situation existing during the 1820s and 1830s, as the long-dominant Jeffersonian Republican party dissolved. In the election of 1828 Tyler supported Andrew Jackson but found himself in opposition to Jackson soon after the inauguration. Tyler was against the President's threat to use force against South Carolina in order to enforce the tariff nullified in 1832. Tyler also attacked Jackson for what he considered to be his high-handed way of withdrawing governmental deposits from the Bank of the United States. Oddly, by alienating himself from the administration, Tyler found himself aligned with Henry Clay, Daniel Webster, and the other Northern nationalists who had created the Whig party.

In 1839 the Whigs, whose presidential candidate was William Henry Harrison of Ohio, sought to balance the ticket with Tyler as their vice-presidential candidate. Because his views bore little relationship to those of the rest of his party, Tyler skillfully sidestepped the major issues during the campaign. Despite his presence on the ticket, the Whigs lost Virginia; however, they won nationally.

Harrison's death a month after his inauguration created a minor constitutional crisis and a major political one. Tyler was the first vice president to succeed to the presidency, and the question was raised as to whether he was actually president or just the vice president acting as president. Tyler established the precedent that the vice president succeeded to the powers and honors of the office as if he had been elected in his own right.

Although Tyler inherited governmental powers, he lost control of his party. As a misplaced Democrat within the Whig party, he had great difficulty with the congressional leaders of his party, especially Henry Clay. The split was most evident on three issues: the Bank of the United States, the tariff, and a proposal to distribute among the states the revenue secured from the sale of public lands. Tyler twice vetoed the charter passed by Congress for the creation of a Third Bank of the United States. He made several positive suggestions, however, for a substitute—including creation of a Bank of the District of Columbia with less power than that of the Second Bank of the United States. Tyler also vetoed a tariff and distribution bill that he contended violated the principles of the compromise tariff of 1833 (which had ended South Carolina's nullification threat).

Tyler's increasing isolation from the Whig party was hastened by the resignation on Sept. 11, 1841, of all the members of the Cabinet appointed by Harrison, except Secretary of State Daniel Webster. Webster remained until May 1843 in order to complete negotiations with England over a long-standing boundary dispute. Tyler's final Cabinet was composed mainly of Southerners, including John C. Calhoun as secretary of state.

The latter part of Tyler's tenure was dominated by the Texas question. After Texas won its independence from Mexico, the Jackson and Martin Van Buren administrations refrained from annexation because of the position of the North, which opposed incorporating more slave territory into the United States. Rejecting this opposition, Calhoun negotiated a treaty of annexation. This was turned down by the Senate in 1844. The question played a part in the election of 1844, after which the administration pushed a joint resolution through Congress providing for the incorporation of Texas. It was passed on the last day of Tyler's administration.

As Tyler had had little hope of renomination by the Whigs in 1844, he had sought to build a third party composed of dissident Democrats and Whigs but soon abandoned his efforts. Tyler remained active in national politics. He supported the Compromise of 1850 and the Kansas-Nebraska Act. After South Carolina seceded in 1860, Tyler participated in the Washington Peace Convention that met early in 1861. When Virginia seceded, he supported his state. He was elected to the Confederate House of Representatives, but he died on Jan. 18, 1862, a month before that body held its first session.

Further Reading

Several good works deal with Tyler's life: Oliver Perry Chitwood, *John Tyler: Champion of the Old South* (1939), is a sympathetic portrait by a major historian, and Robert Seager, *And Tyler Too: A Biography of John and Julia Gardiner Tyler* (1963), is a warm portrait, which also includes much social history of the period. A good account of the politics of Tyler's administration is in Robert J. Morgan, *A Whig Embattled: The Presidency under John Tyler* (1954). The campaign of 1840 is detailed in Robert G. Gunderson, *The Log-cabin Campaign* (1957), and Arthur M. Schlesinger, Jr., *History of American Presidential Elections,* vol. 1 (1971). For biographies of persons who were important in the Tyler administration see Glyndon G. Van Deusen, *The Life of Henry Clay* (1937); Charles M. Wiltse, *John C. Calhoun* (3 vols., 1944-1951); and Richard N. Current, *Daniel Webster and the Rise of National Conservatism* (1955). □

Moses Coit Tyler

Moses Coit Tyler (1835-1900), American historian, pioneered in the development of American intellectual history.

Moses Coit Tyler was born in Griswold, Conn., on Aug. 2, 1835. His family later moved to Detroit, where Tyler grew up. After a year as a book agent, he enrolled at the University of Michigan at the age of 16, transferring to Yale University a year later. Following graduation he became an independent student for a year at Andover Theological Seminary.

In 1859 Tyler was ordained as a Congregational minister, took a pastorate at Oswego, N.Y., and married Jeannette Hull Gilbert. In 1860 he received a call to a larger congregation in Poughkeepsie. While there he wrote an essay, "Our Solace and Our Duty in This Crisis" (1861), designed to provide guidance at the beginning of the Civil War. Poor health forced him to resign his pulpit in 1862, however, and he did not preach again for 14 years.

Tyler went to Boston seeking a cure. He found it in a course of musical gymnastics under a Dr. Dio Lewis. He became an apostle of Lewis and was sent to England in 1863 to open a branch school. During his 3-year stay he wrote *The New System of Musical Gymnastics as an Instrument in Education* (1864). Upon his return to America he became professor of rhetoric and English literature at the University of Michigan.

At Michigan, Tyler wrote his first real book, a collection of essays entitled *The Brawnsville Papers* (1869). In 1875 he accepted an offer to compose a manual of American literature. He projected a completion date to coincide with the centennial of the Revolution. Tyler had to extend his deadline and limit his subject, in part because of renewed religious interest. In 1877 he joined the Episcopal Church and eventually became a priest. His *History of American Literature during the Colonial Period, 1607-1765* (2 vols.) was completed in 1878.

Tyler's next major writing project, which took almost 20 years to complete, was the *Literary History of the American Revolution, 1763-1785* (2 vols., 1897). In 1881 he accepted Cornell University's offer of the first chair in United States history in the country. He was one of the founders of the American Historical Association in 1884 and of the *American Historical Review* in 1895. Two other significant books were *Patrick Henry* (1887) and *Three Men of Letters* (1895). He died on Dec. 28, 1900.

Tyler's fame rests largely on his two literary histories, which he described as history of thought—one of the first uses of the term. He used original sources and included songs, sermons, and pamphlets. The critic Michael Kraus (1953) wrote that "nothing better has ever been done on the literary history of the Revolution despite some defects of omission."

Further Reading

Howard Mumford Jones, *The Life of Moses Coit Tyler* (1933), is a revision of a doctoral dissertation written by Thomas Edgar Casady, who died before he completed it. The book is valuable as a biography, although the style is difficult. Two insightful views of Tyler as a historian are in sections of Michael Kraus, *The Writing of American History* (1953), and Robert Allen Skotheim, *American Intellectual History and Historians* (1966). □

Ralph W. Tyler

The American educator/scholar Ralph W. Tyler (1902-1994) was closely associated with curriculum theory and development and educational assessment and evaluation. Many consider him to be the "father" of behavioral objectives, a concept he frequently used in asserting learning to be a process through which one attains new patterns of behavior.

Ralph Winfred Tyler was born April 22, 1902, in Chicago, Illinois, and soon thereafter (1904) moved to Nebraska. In 1921, at the age of 19, Tyler received the A.B. degree from Doane College in Crete, Nebraska, and began teaching high school in Pierre, South Dakota. He obtained the A.M. degree from the University of Nebraska (1923) while working there as assistant supervisor

of sciences (1922-1927). In 1927 Tyler received the Ph.D. degree from the University of Chicago.

After serving as associate professor of education at the University of North Carolina (1927-1929), Tyler went to Ohio State University where he attained the rank of professor of education (1929-1938). It was around 1938 that he became nationally prominent due to his involvement in the Progressive Education related Eight Year Study (1933-1941), an investigation into secondary school curriculum requirements and their relationship to subsequent college success. In 1938 Tyler continued work on the Eight Year Study at the University of Chicago, where he was employed as chairman of the Department of Education (1938-1948), dean of social sciences (1948-1953), and university examiner (1938-1953). In 1953 Tyler became the first director of the Stanford, California-based Center for Advanced Study in the Behavioral Sciences, a position he held until his retirement in 1966.

Ralph Tyler's scholarly publications were many and spanned his entire career. Among his most useful works is *Basic Principles of Curriculum and Instruction* (1949), a course syllabus used by generations of college students as a basic reference for curriculum and instruction development. *Basic Principles* perhaps influenced more curriculum specialists than any other single work in the curriculum field. This syllabus, written in 1949 when Tyler was teaching at the University of Chicago, identifies four basic questions which have guided the development of untold curricula since the 1940s: 1) What are the school's educational purposes? 2) What educational experiences will

likely attain these purposes? 3) How can the educational experiences be properly organized? 4) How can the curriculum be evaluated? An author of several other books, Tyler also wrote numerous articles appearing in yearbooks, encyclopedias, and periodicals.

When Tyler first went to Ohio State University in 1929 he was already formulating his ideas regarding the specification of educational objectives. While working with various departments at Ohio State in an effort to discover better instructional methods, he began to solidify his belief that true learning is a process which results in new patterns of behavior, behavior meaning a broad spectrum of human reactions that involve thinking and feeling as well as overt actions.

This reasoning reveals the cryptic distinction between learning specific bits and pieces of information and understanding the unifying concepts that underlie the information. Tyler stressed the need for educational objectives to go beyond mere memorization and regurgitation. Indeed, learning involves not just talking about subjects but a demonstration of what one can do with those subjects. A truly educated person, Tyler seems to say, has not only acquired certain factual information but has also modified his/her behavior patterns as a result. (Thus, many educators identify him with the concept of behavioral objectives.) These behavior patterns enable the educated person to adequately cope with many situations, not just those under which the learning took place. Tyler asserted that this is the process through which meaningful education occurs, his caveat being that one should not confuse "being educated" with simply "knowing facts"; the application of facts is education's primary raison d'etre.

Tyler's establishment of the Center for Advanced Study in the Behavioral Sciences was one of his most noteworthy achievements. His ideas for the center at the time were very progressive and remained excellent examples for proposals regarding scholarly study into the 1980s. Scholars visiting the center were not confined by any set routine or schedule in regard to their research. They were free to collaborate with each other, schedule meetings and workshops, or simply do independent research.

Tyler's involvement with the National Assessment of Educational Progress (NAEP) project was another momentous achievement that had far reaching effects upon improved education in the United States. This long-term study provided extensive data about student achievement in school. Tyler also played a significant role in the Association for Supervision and Curriculum Development (ASCD) and its "Fundamental Curriculum Decisions." (1983).

Throughout his career Ralph Tyler demonstrated boundless energy as he served either as a member or adviser to numerous research, governmental, and educational agencies. Included among these were the National Science Board, the Research and Development Panel of the U.S. Office of Education, the National Advisory Council on Disadvantaged Children, the Social Science Research Foundation, the Armed Forces Institute, and the American Association for the Advancement of Science. Service on many other educational agencies could be credited to Tyler,

including his presidency of the National Academy of Education. His retirement in 1966 as director of the Center for Advanced Study in the Behavioral Sciences did not terminate his involvement in education, as he continued to serve as an adviser to both individuals and agencies. He died of cancer at the age of 91 in 1994.

Further Reading

Ralph Tyler is listed in the *Biographical Dictionary of American Educators* (1978). At present no comprehensive biography is available. An excellent review of Tyler's publications may be found in his own book, *Perspectives on American Education* (1976); John Goodlad's introduction to this book contains a great deal of biographical information. Additional information can be found in D. W. Robinson, "A Talk with Ralph Tyler," in *Phi Delta Kappan* 49 (October 1967) and in R.M.W. Travers, *How Research Has Changed American Schools—A History From 1840 to the Present* (1983). □

Royall Tyler

Royall Tyler (1757-1826), American playwright and novelist as well as a jurist, wrote the first successful American play.

R oyall Tyler was born into a prosperous and enterprising Boston family. His intellectual qualities were early recognized, for when he graduated from Harvard in 1776 he was awarded a bachelor's degree from Yale as well. He interrupted his legal studies to serve as a major during the Revolution, was admitted to the bar in 1780, and joined the law office of John Adams. Tyler fell in love with the future president's daughter; but the engagement was broken off, reportedly because Adams disapproved of Tyler's high-spirited temperament. Tyler once more joined the Army during Shays' Rebellion (1786), and his eloquent speeches contributed to calming the rioters.

While on military business in New York in 1787, Tyler attended the theater and, after seeing a production of *The School for Scandal,* was inspired to write his own comedy. The result, written in 3 weeks, was *The Contrast,* America's first successful drama and its first comedy to deal with native characters. A comedy of manners, it contrasted the substantial American virtues with artificial "English" behavior, and it introduced, in the character of Jonathan, what became the stock stage Yankee. *The Contrast* was popular throughout America for its theatrical and nationalistic aspects. The acclaim given it inspired other native dramatists.

Though Tyler continued to practice law, he wrote at least six other plays. Of the four which survive, three are biblical verse plays and the other a social satire, *The Island of Barrataria.* Tyler also employed his satirical wit on a number of verse and prose works, most importantly a picaresque adventure novel, *The Algerine Captive* (1797), which also portrays fraudulence in education and medicine and depicts the horrors of slavery.

After 1800 Tyler's legal career consumed more and more of his time. As a justice of the Supreme Court of Vermont, he handed down a significant antislavery decision in 1802. He served as chief justice of that body from 1807 to 1813 and as professor of jurisprudence at the University of Vermont until 1814. Though all of Tyler's literary endeavors were published anonymously (perhaps because he felt they might have a negative effect upon his judicial position), he attempted all his life to fuse his two occupations. As a member of the legal profession, he sought to correct those ills and follies which he satirized in his writing. He died in Brattleboro, Vt.

Further Reading

There is no full-length study of Tyler's life. The autobiography of his wife, *Grandmother Tyler's Book: The Recollections of Mary Palmer Tyler, 1775-1866,* edited by Frederick Tupper and Helen Brown (1925), provides personal details. The Tyler Papers are deposited with the Vermont Historical Society. For Tyler's relation to other literary men see Harold M. Ellis, *Joseph Dennie and His Circle: A Study in American Literature from 1792-1812* (1915). □

Sir Edward Burnett Tylor

The English anthropologist Sir Edward Burnett Tylor (1832-1917) was concerned with theories of cultural evolution and diffusion, and he advanced influential theories regarding the origins of magic and religion.

E dward B. Tylor was born in London into a prosperous Quaker family. He was privately educated and because of ill health was excused from entering the family business. In 1855 he traveled to Latin America and there met a fellow English Quaker and amateur antiquarian, Henry Christy; they toured Mexico in search of ancient artifacts. On his return to England, Tylor married Anna Fox in 1858 and settled into a comfortable private existence supported by his independent means.

In 1861 Tylor published *Anahuac,* in which he speculated on Mexico's ancient past. He joined the Royal Anthropological Society and independently studied primitive societies, publishing *Researches into the Early History of Mankind and the Development of Civilization* (1865) and his most famous study, *Primitive Culture* (1871). The latter had an instant impact on social theorists, and Tylor was elected a fellow of the Royal Society the same year. A condensed account of his theories appeared in *Anthropology* (1881).

In 1883 Tylor became keeper of the University Museum at Oxford, where he later lectured on anthropological subjects, and in 1896 the first chair of anthropology in the English-speaking world was created for him at Oxford, a post he held until his retirement in 1909. The latter half of his career saw few publications and little modification of his initial positions. Perhaps his most notable achievement for us today is his brief essay "On a Method of Investigating the Development of Institutions," which appeared in the *Journal of the Royal Anthropological Institute* (1888), the first serious attempt to use statistical information to substantiate and generate social anthropological theories.

Tylor was an armchair anthropologist, uninterested in carrying out actual fieldwork with primitive peoples but keen on following the investigations of others. For him progress was linked with rationalism, and anthropology was to teach and correct contemporary aberrations of mankind by exposing the irrational survivals from the past adhering to modern social behavior. Tylor is generally credited with being the most influential expositor of the concept of animism (the idea that primitive men endow all things with vital supernatural powers) and the concept of survivals (that irrational, superannuated practices and beliefs continue past their period of usefulness). He was committed to historical reconstruction of the past by examining primitive societies which were thought to resemble prehistoric ones, but this was mainly to enable him to understand the nature of progress and to expunge nonrational, primitive elements from modern life; it was not to demonstrate the rich variety of human cultures.

Tylor's early career showed an emphasis on progressive evolution, but this was later modified to give attention to the diffusion of cultural traits from society to society. He saw the development of magic and religion as due to faulty logic based on psychological errors, not as an outcome of the nature of society itself. But his interpretations did credit primitive men with a logic, however faulty, and in this he represents an analytical advance over many of his contemporaries. He brilliantly demonstrated, for example, how persons of intelligence and reason may well accept magic and find no contradictions between such beliefs and other spheres of experience.

Further Reading

The chief source for details of Tylor's life is Robert R. Marett, *Tylor* (1936), and the best critical accounts of his work and influence are in Edward E. Evans-Pritchard, *Theories of Primitive Religion* (1965), and John W. Burrow, *Evolution and Society: A Study in Victorian Social Theory* (1966). □

William Tyndale

William Tyndale (ca. 1495-1536) was the greatest of all English biblical scholars. His translation of the Bible into English formed the major part of the Authorized Version, or King James Bible.

W illiam Tyndale was born in Gloucestershire and mostly educated at Oxford, where he earned a master of arts degree in 1515. He became a priest and, doubtless influenced among other things by the work of John Colet and Erasmus at Cambridge some years earlier, decided to produce an English translation of the Bible. He found support from a rich London cloth merchant. Within months, however, he became convinced he must leave London if he was to succeed; and, accordingly, with the financial support of the merchant, he left England in 1524, never again to return.

After short sojourns in Hamburg, and, possibly, Wittenberg, Tyndale settled down at Cologne in 1525. He quickly began the printing of his New Testament, but only a few sheets had been finished when the city fathers got wind of it and stopped it. The work was resumed at Worms, and by April 1526 an octavo edition was being sold in London. In November all available copies were burned at St. Paul's Cross. In 1528 Tyndale published the *Parable of the Wicked Mammon,* dealing with Luther's teaching concerning justification by faith, and the *Obedience of a Christian Man,* which replaced papal authority by royal authority and was heartily approved by King Henry VIII. However, in the *Practice of Prelates* in 1530, Tyndale not only attacked Cardinal Wolsey but opposed the annulment of Henry VIII's marriage with Catherine of Aragon. Meanwhile Bishop Tunstall of London had invited Sir Thomas More to reply to Tyndale's books, and a lively controversy took place.

Tyndale's Lutheran-inspired *Exposition of the Sermon on the Mount* was much admired; and possibly *The Supper of the Lord,* which appeared in 1533, was also his. Meanwhile throughout these years his work on the Old Testament had been proceeding. In 1530 he published his translation of the Pentateuch. As his New Testament had been pirated for various unsatisfactory editions, he published a revision in 1534, with a third, revised edition in 1535. In 1535, however, he was seized by the local government authorities in Antwerp, where he was living, for being a propagator of heresy. After months of imprisonment and many theological disputations he was condemned in August 1536 for persistence in heresy, and in October he was strangled to death and his body publicly cremated.

During his years at Antwerp, where he was so well maintained by the generosity of the English merchants there, Tyndale acquired a great reputation for austerity of character and frugality of life, combined with a steady attention to the needs of the poor, which offset the impression caused by the violent language found in his polemical works. In the year following his death there appeared in England a new Bible with the king's approval which was said to be the work of one Thomas Matthew. It was, however, a composite work edited by John Rogers and containing translations by him, by Miles Coverdale, and, for the greater part, by Tyndale. This Matthew Bible was reedited by Coverdale and published in 1539. It became known as the Great Bible. In this way Tyndale's translation was the basis of the first Bibles in English to get royal approval. His translation has underlain most subsequent English versions and has profoundly affected the development of the English language.

Further Reading

A short study of Tyndale's thought, a brief sketch of his life, selections from his writings organized under various heads, and an essay on him and on the English language by G. D. Bone are contained in the useful book by the Reverend Stanley L. Greenslade, *The Work of William Tindale* (1938). A similar book is Gervase E. Duffield, ed., *The Work of William Tyndale* (1965).

Additional Sources

Daniell, David, *William Tyndale: a biography,* New Haven: Yale University Press, 1994.

Edwards, Brian (Brian H.), *God's outlaw,* Welwyn; Grand Rapids, Mich.: Evangelical Press, 1976.

Edwards, Brian (Brian H.), *William Tyndale, the father of the English Bible,* Farmington Hills, Mich.: William Tyndale College, 1982 printing, 1976. □

John Tyndall

The Irish physicist John Tyndall (1820-1893) is best known for his work on the scattering of light by atmospheric particles and on the absorption of infrared radiation by gases. He also did much to popularize science among laymen.

John Tyndall was born on Aug. 2, 1820, at Leighlin Bridge, near Carlow, Ireland, where his father was a constable. After a little formal schooling, he gained a practical education by working as a surveyor and engineer. He entered the University of Marburg, Germany, in 1848 and earned his doctorate 2 years later. His dissertation research interested Michael Faraday, who later brought him to the Royal Institution of London. In 1867 Tyndall succeeded Faraday as superintendent there. He retired in 1887.

Tyndall is noted for his study of the scattering of light by atmospheric particles, a phenomenon sometimes called the Tyndall effect. In 1869 he provided explanations for the color of the sun at the horizon and of clear skies; about 2 years later Lord Rayleigh provided the relevant theory. Tyndall showed that if broth was placed in air which was without scattering particles, the usual life forms did not develop. His work thus did much to invalidate the "spontaneous generation" theory of life.

Tyndall's studies of the transmission of infrared radiation through gases and vapors did much to clarify the nature of the absorption process and brought him the Rumford Medal in 1869.

In connection with consulting work on navigational aids Tyndall gave much attention to sound phenomena. This resulted in his interesting book *On Sound* (1867), written "to render the science of acoustics interesting to all intelligent persons including those who do not possess any special scientific culture." He wrote 15 other popular treatises, many of which are still enjoyable reading. "As a popular writer on the phenomena of physics he had no equal."

Tyndall's passion for justice was never better demonstrated than during the bitter scientific controversy of 1864-1866 concerning the priority rights of J. R. Mayer, whose cause Tyndall supported, as originator of the conservation-of-energy concept. Mention is also due his 1874 address at Belfast, in which he firmly advocated the right of science to follow its course without restrictions by dogma or theology, and in which he equally firmly denied that there was any basic conflict between science and religion.

Tyndall was an expert mountain climber and in 1861 made the first ascent of the Weisshorn. At the age of 56 he married the woman who, he said, "raised my ideal of the possibilities of human nature." He died at his home near Haslemere on Dec. 4, 1893.

Further Reading

A full and interesting account of Tyndall is provided in A. S. Eve and C. H. Creasey, *The Life and Work of John Tyndall* (1945). Tyndall's life and contributions to science are discussed in James Gerald Crowther, *Scientific Types* (1970).

Additional Sources

John Tyndall, essays on a natural philosopher, Dublin: Royal Dublin Society, 1981. □

George Tyrrell

George Tyrrell (1861-1909) was an Irish-English Jesuit priest best known for his contributions to the Catholic "Modernist" movement that sought to revise traditional views of revelation and church teaching so as to bring out better their historical dimensions.

George Tyrrell was born February 6, 1861, in Dublin, Ireland. He was raised as an Anglican, but he converted to Roman Catholicism in 1879 and joined the Society of Jesus, a Catholic religious order devoted to teaching, in 1880. Following lengthy studies, he was ordained a priest in 1891 and assigned to teach at Stonyhurst, a Jesuit college in Lancashire, England. Intellectually, Tyrrell was influenced by John Henry Newman, Maurice Blondel, Baron Friedrich von Hugel, and other Modernists who had proposed departing from the scholastic forms of theology dominant until that time so as to allow for more historical development in the interpretation of both scripture and doctrinal theology.

The Modernists were repudiated by Popes Leo XIII and Pius X, to whom the notion of historical change in church teaching was anathema. Tyrrell himself was roundly attacked for his views in 1901 and expelled from the Jesuits in 1906. In 1907 Pope Pius X issued an encyclical letter, *Pascendi Dominici Gregis,* that condemned Modernism, which it (erroneously) presented as a coherent movement and theological outlook. Tyrrell denounced the encyclical and was in consequence excommunicated from the Catholic Church. He refused to retract his positions but to the end of his life continued to consider himself a Catholic and to write explanations of the Modernist outlook.

Inasmuch as Modernist positions have entered the mainstream of late 20th-century Catholic theology, Tyrrell may be seen as a precursor of views that later became taken for granted. Especially, the majority of Catholic theologians have come to agree with Tyrrell that church teachings always have an historical dimension. They arise at a given moment, within a given cultural horizon, and ever afterwards their formulations bear the marks of their origins. The Scriptures themselves are expressions of given historical assumptions.

More clearly than Tyrrell, however, most present-day Catholic theologians argue that this historicity need not mean that either the Scriptures or official church teachings do not come from God as divine revelation. It simply means that all human formulations of divine revelation occur in time and so are historically conditioned. Just as Christian doctrine considers Jesus himself to be fully human as well as fully divine, so mainstream contemporary Christian theology considers both biblical interpretation and church teaching to be fully human (historically conditioned) as well as inspired by God's spirit.

Tyrrell and the other Modernists sought to explain Christian faith in light of the understanding of human historicity that had arisen by the end of the 19th century. They were convinced that a static, unhistorical, universalist explanation of Christian teaching, such as prevailed among scholastic theologians at the time, rendered it incredible to modern intellectuals, for whom both change in nature and historical development in human culture had become standard assumptions. Books by Tyrrell, namely *Religion as a Factor in Life* (1902) and *The Church and the Future* (1903), argued for this position with some elegance.

The intellectual violence with which their scholastic opponents attacked the Modernists assured that Catholic scholars would become polarized. When the Roman authorities took the side of the ahistorical scholastics and branded the historicism of the Modernists heretical, an era of intellectual repression swept over Catholic culture. Theologians were required to swear an oath of loyalty against the Modernist positions, and to be held suspect of Modernism was to fall into considerable disfavor.

Tyrrell's disfavor wore heavily upon him and contributed to his relatively early death on July 15, 1909, at Storrington, England. Students of his life debate whether he was wise to refuse to accommodate to the demands of his superiors, but it seems clear that he considered maintaining his positions a matter of intellectual integrity. He was far from standing alone, but many who held positions similar to his did trim their sails and avoid excommunication. Few analysts now consider Tyrrell as substantial a thinker as Blondel or von Hugel, let alone Newman, but he was an effective apologist in his day and so one of the major factors in the overall victory that the Modernists finally won.

Further Reading

Gabriel Daly, *Transcendence and Immanence: A Study in Catholic Modernism and Integralism* (1980), and A.R. Vidler, *A Variety of Catholic Modernists* (1970), tell well the story of the movement that gave Tyrrell his significance. M. D. Petre's *Autobiography and Life of George Tyrrell* (1912) and *Letters* (1920) suggest the contemporary flavor of the struggles that absorbed Tyrrell.

Additional Sources

Sagovsky, Nicholas, *On God's side: a life of George Tyrrell,* Oxford England: Clarendon Press; New York: Oxford University Press, 1990.

Leonard, Ellen, C.S.J., *George Tyrrell and the Catholic tradition,* London: Darton, Longman, and Todd; New York: Paulist Press, 1982. □

Tz'u-hsi

Tz'u-hsi (1835-1908), concubine to the Hsien-feng emperor and later empress dowager, was the power behind the throne in China from 1860 to 1908.

Tz'u-hsi, who is also known as Yehonala, Empress Hsiao-ch'in, or "The Old Buddha," was born on Nov. 29, 1835. At the age of 16 she became a low-ranking concubine to the Hsienfeng emperor (reigned 1851-1861), but in 1856, when she gave birth to the Emperor's only son and heir, she was made a second-class concubine. When the Emperor died on Aug. 22, 1861, in Jehol, where he had fled before the allied British and French advance on Peking in 1860, Tz'u-hsi's son became the T'ung-chih emperor (1862-1875). During his minority the new emperor, according to his father's will, would rule through a regency, but all decrees had to be approved by the two empress dowagers—his mother and the senior consort, Empress Tz'u-an.

Three Decades of Regency

The ensuing power struggle between the regents and the two empress dowagers, with the aid of Prince Kung (the deceased emperor's half brother), was resolved in favor of the two women when the court returned to Peking in October 1861. The regents were arrested, and the two empress dowagers formed a joint regency. Prince Kung was made prince counselor and head of the Grand Council.

Of the two dowager empresses, Tz'u-hsi was the more able and ambitious and gradually gained control of the state. She entrusted military power to Tseng Kuo-fan, Li Hung-chang, and Tso Tsung-t'ang and in international affairs relied on Prince Kung and Wen-hsiang in the Tsungli Yamen. She loved money and power, had tremendous physical vitality, used the weaknesses of her officials for her own ends, and in matters of state was extremely realistic. When Prince Kung appeared to be acquiring too much power in 1865, she had him removed from all his offices on a pretext. He was later restored to power but was no longer prince counselor. Tz'u-hsi was strongly anti-Western and conservative but permitted a limited amount of Westernization in order to preserve her own power and the dynasty.

When the T'ung-chih emperor died in 1875, from excesses, which his mother seems to have encouraged, Tz'u-hsi placed her 3-year-old nephew on the throne as the Kuang-hsü emperor (1875-1908), with Empress Dowager Tz'u-an and herself once again acting as regents. This was a direct violation of the dynastic law of succession, as the new emperor should have been chosen from the next generation, but Tz'u-hsi was able to crush all opposition. When Tz'u-an died suddenly in 1881, Tz'u-hsi became the sole regent and autocrat.

Usurpation of Power

The Emperor reached his majority in 1889, and Tz'u-hsi relinquished nominal control of China. She retired to the Summer Palace, which had been rebuilt at the expense of a much-needed navy, but through her own niece, who had recently been married to the Emperor, she kept a watchful eye on palace and state affairs. Under the influence of his tutor Weng T'ung-ho and the reformer K'ang Yu-wei, the Emperor began to put through a series of much-needed Western-style reforms early in the summer of 1898. As these reforms would have been a threat to her power position, on Sept. 22, 1898, Tz'u-hsi, through a coup d'etat, once more assumed full powers as regent and placed the Emperor in confinement—where he remained until his death in 1908.

The Boxer Uprising in the summer of 1900, which forced Tz'u-hsi to flee to Sian when an eight-nation allied force occupied Peking, resulted in Tz'u-hsi's final acceptance of the need for reforms, the same reforms that her nephew had tried to implement 2 years earlier. The most far-reaching of these was the abolition of the old-style examinations in 1905.

Tz'u-hsi died on Nov. 15, 1908—one day after the Kuang-hsü emperor. The closeness of their deaths occasioned rumors of foul play, but whether he died a natural death or was murdered has never been determined.

Further Reading

J. O. P. Bland and E. Backhouse, *China under the Empress Dowager* (1910; rev. ed. 1939), is the standard English work on Tz'u-hsi. Harry Hussey, *Venerable Ancestor: The Life and Times of Tz'u-hsi* (1949), is interesting but of questionable authority. A biography of Tz'u-hsi appears in the U.S. Library of Congress, Orientalia Division, *Eminent Chinese of the Ch'ing Period, 1644-1912,* edited by Arthur W. Hummel (2 vols., 1943-1944).

Additional Sources

Carl, Katherine Augusta, *With the empress dowager of China,* London; New York: KPI; New York, NY, USA: Distributed by Methuen, 1986.

Seagrave, Sterling, *Dragon lady: the life and legend of the last empress of China,* New York: Vintage Books, 1993.

Warner, Marina, *The Dragon Empress; the life and times of Tz'u-hsi, Empress Dowager of China, 1835-190,* New York, Macmillan 1972. □

U

General Jorge Ubico y Castañeda

General Jorge Ubico y Castañeda (1878-1946) served as president of Guatemala for a 13-year period from 1931 to 1944, a pivotal era for that nation. His presidency formed the basis of the political and economic activity of his nation during the major portion of the 20th century, though his regime remains controversial since its accomplishments were achieved through a harsh and repressive dictatorship.

Jorge Ubico y Castañeda was born in Guatemala City on November 10, 1878, the only son of a wealthy landowner and prominent political figure closely associated with the then president of Guatemala, Justo Rufino Barrios. Indeed, President Barrios served as godfather to Jorge Ubico. Ubico was married to Marta Lainfiesta de Ubico. Commissioned a second lieutenant in the Guatemalan army at an early age, Ubico enjoyed a distinguished military career, achieving the rank of lieutenant colonel after only nine years as an officer, and the rank of full colonel at the age of 28.

His career included combat experience in the 1906 war between Guatemala and El Salvador and service as *Jefe Político* (governor) and *Comandante de Armas* (military commander) of the Guatemalan departments (states) of Alta Verapaz (1907-1909) and Retalhuleu (1911-1919), as well as several years as head of the National Sanitary Commission, which had charge of the campaign to eliminate yellow fever from Guatemala through mosquito control. In these positions he established a reputation as an energetic, efficient, and decisive leader. He served as minister of war from 1921 to 1923 and as first designate to the presidency (first vice president) in 1922, being promoted to general of division, the highest rank in the Guatemalan army, in 1922.

Ubico became president of Guatemala in 1931 following a period of political chaos which included the illness of the incumbent president, an attempted military coup, and intense maneuvering which led to an election in which Ubico emerged as the sole candidate. Hence Ubico assumed office by unanimous election. The origin of the crisis was the global depression of the 1930s which virtually destroyed the Guatemalan economy by depressing the price of coffee, the nation's principal export. Ubico found a balance of exactly $27 in the national treasury.

The new president's initial actions were characterized by dynamism and honesty. He stamped out corruption through harsh methods and thoroughly reorganized the governmental apparatus, operating the regime on a limited, almost stingy, budget. Ubico's impact on the nation was dramatic as he launched a series of immense projects to modernize the nation. He relied on local materials and labor intensive methods, however, often using individuals imprisoned on minor charges as laborers on his construction projects. During his initial nine years in office Ubico literally rebuilt his nation, constructing most of its major public buildings, including the offices of all major national governmental divisions, administration buildings in departmental capitals and cities, and other facilities such as customs houses. His major contribution was a massive road-building effort which provided Guatemala with its first national highway network. Although these were mainly dirt roads, they opened remote areas of the nation to settlement

377

and agriculture, enabling the creation of a national economy.

His efforts also reached into the countryside through the construction of water purification systems and projects which brought electricity to many remote towns which previously had no such services. Ubico's economic program focused on exports and involved attracting foreign investment, though he refused to engage in governmental borrowing from abroad. In addition, the Ubico regime reformed the banking system and stabilized the currency, creating the basis for the revival of the Guatemalan economy. Foreign investment increased Guatemala's economic production, in the process creating new salaried labor and middle classes, but also increased Guatemala's importance in and dependence upon the world economy. The resulting modernization clearly benefitted the domestic landowners, fortifying the position of the wealthy classes.

Ubico's vagrancy law of 1934 abolished the system of debt peonage which, since colonial days, had enabled landowners to hold peasants responsible for loans owed by their parents, making the peasants legally bound to work in virtual slavery until their earnings paid the debts. Ubico's law abolished the debts, but substituted a system by which anyone who was unemployed could be arrested and forced to work at minimal wages. Hence the peasants could still be compelled to work, but the peasants' lives would henceforth be controlled by the national government, not by the local landlords—a fundamental change, but one which did not necessarily eliminate abuses.

Like many of his predecessors in the Guatemalan presidency, Ubico succumbed to the temptation to perpetuate himself in office. Using the rationale that he needed to complete his program, Ubico orchestrated well planned campaigns which led to constitutional amendments extending his term of office in 1936 and in 1942. While the initial extension of his term was popular, the second demonstrated the effectiveness of his political machine.

Throughout his years in power Ubico maintained tight control of the entire nation in his own hands, making virtually all important decisions himself. He closely supervised the actions of all branches of the government and travelled extensively throughout the nation personally inspecting all construction projects. His trips took him to remote villages that had never before been visited by a national president. He also maintained a close surveillance of all aspects of the lives of his nation's citizens with an extensive police and security apparatus that effectively stamped out dissent. Police methods and prison conditions were harsh.

By 1944 the dictator had outlived his time as he had failed to share power with the new societal groups, such as the middle class, that had resulted from the economic development he had fostered. The result was a protest movement led by university students, young urban professionals, and younger army officers. To everyone's surprise Ubico resigned the presidency, relinquishing office peacefully and avoiding a bloodbath. He turned power over to the military commanders who were later overthrown by a second revolution in 1944, leading to an era of social reform in Guatemala.

Controversy continued to swirl about the Ubico era as the intellectuals who supported the revolutionary reforms depicted Ubico as a ruthless tyrant, emphasizing the abuses of his regime and paying scant attention to the dramatic changes he had brought about in Guatemala. Throughout the succeeding decades presidential candidates identified themselves either as supporters or opponents of Ubico. In this sense Ubico continued to dominate his nation politically long after his death, just as he had laid the foundations of modern Guatemala by creating the infrastructure and basic services that brought his nation into the 20th century. Ubico died in exile in New Orleans on June 14, 1946. He remained so controversial that his body was not returned to its final burial in his native land until 1963.

Further Reading

Ubico's methods and accomplishments are detailed in Kenneth J. Grieb, *Guatemalan Caudillo: The Regime of Jorge Ubico, Guatemala, 1931-1944* (1979). A contemporary account is provided in Chester Lloyd Jones, *Guatemala: Past and Present* (1940). □

Paolo Uccello

The Italian painter Paolo Uccello (1397-1475) was a leading figure in establishing the Renaissance in Florence.

A barber's son, Paolo Uccello was born in Florence. In 1407 he was apprenticed to the sculptor Lorenzo Ghiberti. After Uccello joined the painters' guild in 1415, there are 10 blank years. From 1425 to 1431 he executed mosaics for the facade of St. Mark's, Venice.

Uccello's earliest known paintings, representing the creation of the animals and the creation of man, are part of a large outdoor fresco series in monochrome of Old Testament scenes in the Green Cloister of S. Maria Novella, Florence. The figures have a curvilinear rhythm and sculptural strength, and they are set in a decorative yet naturalistic environment of foliage with animals, reflecting Ghiberti's influence and very like his *Creation* panel in the Gates of Paradise of the Florentine Baptistery. As the gates were designed in 1425 or later, Uccello's frescoes are usually thought to have been executed after his return from Venice, but they may date from just before he went there and reflect other designs by Ghiberti, since a small copy of Uccello's lost St. Peter mosaic in Venice (1425) already seems to show his more mature Renaissance style. It is clear in his frescoed equestrian monument of Sir John Hawkwood (1436) in the Cathedral of Florence. On a base seen from below, illustrating the new rules of perspective, Uccello sets the horse and rider; there is a greater concern with body modeling and its evocation of power and motion.

The influence of Masaccio is seen in Uccello's scenes from the life of Noah in the Green Cloister of S. Maria Novella. Probably painted about 1450, the cycle is Uccello's most complex work. Poorly preserved, today the scenes show the intricate perspective network more plainly than they do the organic and dramatic people, clinging, twisting, and staring.

After 1447 Uccello executed the frescoes of legends of hermits at S. Miniato, Florence (now much damaged). Until the recent discovery of records they were considered early works. Here the emphasis seems to be less on the modeling of the figures, and they become points in a stylized geometric system of lines and cubes. The three panels depicting the Battle of San Romano (ca. 1455) reveal the same approach. They were made as a continuous 30-foot frieze for a room in the new Medici Palace, Florence. The same abstract patterns of perspective and surface design govern the spears, flagpoles, and soldiers. Even more doll-like and colorful stylization appears in his small-scale late works: the *Profanation of the Host* (1469) and *Night Hunt*. Uccello died in Florence on Dec. 10, 1475.

Further Reading

Two works on Uccello are John Pope-Hennessy, *The Complete Work of Paolo Uccello* (1950; rev. ed. 1969), and Enzo Carli, *All the Paintings of Paolo Uccello* (1963). □

Peter Victor Ueberroth

The architect of the 1984 Summer Olympic Games at Los Angeles, Peter Victor Ueberroth (born 1937) was voted 1984 "Man of the Year" by *Time* maga-

zine. He was commissioner of organized baseball (1985-1989) and chairman of an effort to rebuild Los Angeles after the 1992 riots.

P eter Ueberroth was born September 2, 1937, in Evanston, IL. His mother, Laura Larson, died when he was four, and his father, Victor, a traveling salesman of aluminum siding, became the driving force in Peter's desire for learning, recognition and success. His father remarried, and the family moved often. Tall, tan, and athletic, the young Ueberroth worked his way through high school and San Jose State University, yet still found time for baseball, body surfing, basketball, swimming, football, and water polo. Despite working 30-40 hours a week to support himself, he almost made the U.S.A. Olympic water polo team in 1956.

Early Success

In 1959, Ueberroth graduated from San Jose State with a degree in business. He married Ginny Nicolous and moved to Hawaii, where he got a job with a small non-scheduled airline. In two years he returned to California as part-owner of the business. Ueberroth then started his own air service between Seattle and Los Angeles. Next he began a reservation service for small airlines and hotels, Transportation Consultants. He quickly expanded into hotel management and transformed his travel business into First Travel, the second-largest travel agency in the nation. Ueberroth became a millionaire while he was still in his

30s, and by 1978 First Travel had gross revenues of more than $300 million. Ueberroth was known for being disciplined and for giving women and younger employees managerial responsibility. Despite his position, he reserved every weekend for his wife, three daughters, and son.

Olympic Impresario

In 1978 the International Olympic Committee (IOC) awarded the 23rd Summer Olympic Games to Los Angeles. When that city, the state of California, and the government of the United States all announced that no public money would be spent on the international sporting festival, a frantic search for a capable manager was launched. Ueberroth won the post over hundreds of corporate executives. Though it meant a 70 percent cut in pay, to $104,000, he accepted the job. He sold his company for $10.6 million, and then forsook the salary to become a volunteer impresario of the 1984 games. The position vaulted him into worldwide prominence.

Ueberroth's method was to entrust responsibility to key deputies. The attorney of his old travel business, Harry Usher, actually ran the games. Ueberroth also formed the Los Angeles Olympic Organizing Committee (LAOOC), a clever blend of sporting experts, successful business executives, and a cadre of local citizens.

Searching for funds, Ueberroth decided to sell the rights to broadcast the games in a blind auction. The American Broadcasting Company (ABC) paid $225 million to show the games on TV. Ueberroth raised another $150 million from foreign television corporations. Reducing the number of corporate sponsors from the 381 at the 1980 Winter Games in Lake Placid, NY, to 30, Ueberroth set an unprecedented price of $4 million for sponsorship. With Ueberroth doing the selling personally to companies such as Coca-Cola, which donated $12.6 million. The money poured in, nearly a billion dollars.

Ueberroth stretched the Olympic rules to their maximum in not building an Olympic village, but instead housing athletes at three of the area's largest university student dormitories. He raised an army of 16,000 uniformed police and non-uniformed security personnel, plus a company of 40,000 volunteers, to keep the games orderly. A $100 million expenditure on police, undercover agents, and security personnel kept the games free of the violence and threats that had marred many previous Olympics.

When a boycott of the games by the Soviet Union was announced, Ueberroth sent envoys to many nations to try to keep others from dropping out. He held the number of other boycotting nations to 16, and his secret meeting with Romanian officials prevented that country from bolting. Romania went on to win 53 medals, and, despite the boycott, nearly six million tickets were sold and the Olympics made a profit of $300 million, the first profit in 88 years. Ueberroth was hailed as a national hero, and some urged him to run for President of the United States. He was named *Time* magazine's "Man of the Year." However, some critics denounced Ueberroth for selling out the games to corporate control and running them in quasi-militaristic fashion.

Baseball's Czar

Late in 1984, Ueberroth accepted the position of commissioner of professional baseball, succeeding Bowie Kuhn. One of his first acts was to restore to good standing two Hall of Fame stars, Willie Mays and Mickey Mantle, who had been banned from official baseball activities. In 1985, publicly positioning himself as the representative of fans, Ueberroth helped broker a five-year agreement between major league players and owners, ending a one-day players' strike. Ueberroth also opened the door to managerial and administrative positions for minorities, made great progress toward addressing the game's growing drug problems, and, using his well-honed business skills, reversed the financial decline of the sport, at least temporarily. When he took over, 21 of the 26 teams claimed to be losing money; none were in the red when he left the job in 1989. Under Ueberroth's regime, baseball's attendance increased, its national television revenues doubled, and its income from merchandising increased 16 times. Of his term as commissioner, baseball writer Daniel Okrent noted in *Sports Illustrated:* "To a job previously occupied by the ineffectual (Bowie Kuhn), the invisible (General William Eckert), the inconsequential (Ford Frick) and the incomprehensible (Happy Chandler), Ueberroth brought an authority, an effectiveness and a public visibility that matched those of Judge Kenesaw Mountain Landis, the man for whom the job was invented in 1920."

However, during Ueberroth's reign, baseball owners were found guilty of collusion in joining together to hold down player salaries during the 1985-1987 period, even as the clubs' revenues increased significantly. Ueberroth denied knowing that collusion had taken place, but many believed it was part of his game plan for profitability. Close observers of baseball's business side believed Ueberroth and the owners laid the seeds for the player-management tensions which tore apart the game in the 1990s.

Life After Baseball

Ueberroth's next challenge, starting in 1989, was to engage in attempted corporate turnarounds, with mixed success. The companies he tried to revamp included Eastern Air Lines, Hawaiian Airlines, and Adidas. His record was mixed; Hawaiian Airlines went bankrupt and Ueberroth's investor group lost $37 million. In 1992, Ueberroth flirted with a run for the office of U.S. Senator, then backed out. That same year, he was appointed volunteer head of the Rebuild Los Angeles commission, a group seeking to revitalize South Central Los Angeles after the April 1992 riots. Though getting pledges for $500 million in corporate contributions, Ueberroth failed to overcome the political roadblocks and his disadvantage of being a suburban white millionaire Republican. He resigned after 13 months on the job with the rebuilding effort a disappointment. Returning to corporate life, Ueberroth and a partner took over the Doubletree hotel chain in 1994 and brought it increased profits.

Further Reading

Ueberroth's own account of his first 48 years of life is *Made in America: His Own Story* (1985) by Peter Ueberroth with R.

Levin and A. Quinn. For additional information see "Miser with a Midas Touch," *Sports Illustrated* (November 22, 1982); "America's Olympics," *Time* (October 17, 1983); "Ueberroth: 'Ruthless and Shy'," *Los Angeles Times* (June 24, 1984); "Master of the Games," *Time* (January 7, 1985); and Okrent's "On the Money," *Sports Illustrated* (April 10, 1989). □

Karen Uhlenbeck

The mathematical research conducted by Karen Uhlenbeck (born 1942) has applications in theoretical physics and has contributed to the study of instantons. For her work in geometry and partial differential equations, she was awarded a MacArthur Fellowship.

Karen Uhlenbeck is engaged in mathematical research that has applications in theoretical physics and has contributed to the study of instantons, models for the behavior of surfaces in four dimensions. In recognition of her work in geometry and partial differential equations, she was awarded a prestigious MacArthur Fellowship in 1983.

Karen Keskulla Uhlenbeck was born in Cleveland, Ohio, on August 24, 1942, to Arnold Edward Keskulla, an engineer, and Carolyn Windeler Keskulla, an artist. When Uhlenbeck was in third grade, the family moved to New Jersey. Everything interested her as a child, but she felt that girls were discouraged from exploring many activities. In high school, she read American physicist George Gamow's books on physics and English astronomer Fred Hoyle's books on cosmology, which her father brought home from the public library. When Uhlenbeck entered the University of Michigan, she found mathematics a broad and intellectually stimulating subject. After earning her B.S. degree in 1964, she became a National Science Foundation Graduate Fellow, pursuing graduate study in mathematics at Brandeis University. In 1965, she married Olke Cornelis Uhlenbeck, a biophysicist; they later divorced.

Uhlenbeck received her Ph.D. in mathematics from Brandeis in 1968 with a thesis on the calculus of variations. Her first teaching position was at the Massachusetts Institute of Technology in 1968. The following year she moved to Berkeley, California, where she was a lecturer in mathematics at the University of California. There she studied general relativity and the geometry of space-time, and worked on elliptic regularity in systems of partial differential equations.

In 1971, Uhlenbeck became an assistant professor at the University of Illinois at Urbana-Champaign. In 1974, she was awarded a fellowship from the Sloan Foundation that lasted until 1976, and she then went to Northwestern University as a visiting associate professor. She taught at the University of Illinois in Chicago from 1977 to 1983, first as associate professor and then professor, and in 1979 she was

the Chancellor's Distinguished Visiting Professor at the University of California, Berkeley. An Albert Einstein Fellowship enabled her to pursue her research as a member of the Institute for Advanced Studies at Princeton University from 1979 to 1980. She published more than a dozen articles in mathematics journals during the 1970s and was named to the editorial board of the *Journal of Differential Geometry* in 1979 and the *Illinois Journal of Mathematics* in 1980.

In 1983, Uhlenbeck was selected by the John D. and Catherine T. MacArthur Foundation of Chicago to receive one of its five-year fellowship grants. Given annually, the MacArthur fellowships enable scientists, scholars, and artists to pursue research or creative activity. For Uhlenbeck, winning the fellowship inspired her to begin serious studies in physics. She believes that the mathematician's task is to abstract ideas from fields such as physics and streamline them so they can be used in other fields. For instance, physicists studying quantum mechanics had predicted the existence of particle-like elements called instantons. Uhlenbeck and other researchers viewed instantons as somewhat analogous to soap films. Seeking a better understanding of these particles, they studied soap films to learn about the properties of surfaces. As soap films provide a model for the behavior of surfaces in three-dimensions, instantons provide analogous models for the behavior of surfaces in four-dimensional space-time. Uhlenbeck cowrote a book on this subject, *Instantons and 4-Manifold Topology,* which was published in 1984.

After a year spent as a visiting professor at Harvard, Uhlenbeck became a professor at the University of Chicago in 1983. Her mathematical interests at this time included nonlinear partial differential equations, differential geometry, gauge theory, topological quantum field theory, and integrable systems. She gave guest lectures at several universities and served as the vice president of the American Mathematical Society. The Alumni Association of the University of Michigan named her Alumna of the Year in 1984. She was elected to the American Academy of Arts and Sciences in 1985 and to the National Academy of Sciences in 1986. In 1988, she received the Alumni Achievement award from Brandeis University, an honorary doctor of science degree from Knox College, and was named one of America's 100 most important women by *Ladies' Home Journal.*

In 1987, Uhlenbeck went to the University of Texas at Austin, where she broadened her understanding of physics in studies with American physicist Steven Weinberg. In 1988, she accepted the Sid W. Richardson Foundation Regents' Chair in mathematics at the University of Texas. She also gave the plenary address at the International Congress of Mathematics in Japan in 1990.

Concerned that potential scientists were being discouraged unnecessarily because of their sex or race, Uhlenbeck joined a National Research Council planning group to investigate the representation of women in science and engineering. She believes that mathematics is always challenging and never boring, and she has expressed the hope that one of her accomplishments as a teacher has been communicating this to her students. "I sometimes feel the need to apologize for being a mathematician, but no apology is needed,'' she told *The Alcalde Magazine.* ''Whenever I get a free week and start doing mathematics, I can't believe how much fun it is. I'm like a 12-year-old boy with a new train set.''

Further Reading

Benningfield, Damond, ''Prominent Players,'' in *The Alcalde Magazine,* September/October, 1988, pp. 26–30.
Uhlenbeck, Karen, *Some Personal Remarks on My Partly Finished Life,* unpublished manuscript. □

Galina Ulanova

The Russian ballerina Galina Ulanova (born 1910) was hailed as one of the greatest dancers of all time. She won international recognition for her lyricism and purity of technique and for her powerfully dramatic performances.

Galina Sergeyevna Ulanova was born in St. Petersburg on January 8, 1910, the only daughter of two dancers at the Maryinsky Theater. As a child Galina was somewhat boisterous and protested when her mother, Maria Romanova, gave her her first ballet lessons, firmly announcing that she did not like dancing. At the age of nine she was unwillingly enrolled as a boarder at the celebrated Theatre School, the training-ground of so many famous Russian dancers. Her strong character obviously prevailed even there. At the end-of-year school production of ''La Fille Mal Gardee,'' instead of being cast as a dainty peasant girl Galina Ulanova made her first appearance on stage as a boy in a clog dance!

Gradually her love for ballet developed, and her final four years at the school were spent in the class of Agrippina Vaganova, the great teacher whose notation of the Russian classical ballet system is still used today. At her graduation performance in 1928 Galina, now a delicate ballerina, danced the 7th Waltz and Mazurka of *Les Sylphides* and the Adagio from *The Nutcracker.* She expressed ribbon-like fluidity in her movements and showed an ethereal presence on stage. Her performance won her a coveted place in the Kirov Ballet Company (known then as GATOB).

The quality of her dancing was quickly noted, and in her first year she made her debut as Princess Flórina in *The Sleeping Beauty.* A few months later she was given the role of the Swan Queen in Vaganova's own production of *Swan Lake.* To this role she brought poetical lyricism and sensitivity, epitomizing the very best of Russian classical technique. But it was in 1934, in Rostislav Zakharov's ballet *The Fountains of Bakhchiserai,* that the young ballerina showed she had a unique talent for the dramatic as well as the ethereal. Cast as Maria, the beautiful captive harem girl, Ulanova brought powerful drama to Pushkin's story of love, jealousy, and murder.

Climaxes Career as Juliet

For Ulanova, preparing the role of Maria (and all subsequent ones) became not just a question of learning the difficult technical steps but also of studying the character as would an actress, seeking out its nuances to shade and develop the role. Once on stage, she would lose herself so completely in the character that she was portraying that nothing else existed for her. At curtain calls she often seemed surprised at the adulation she received, for to her, her own personality had nothing to do with the ''real'' person she had been dancing.

Ulanova's performances also expressed great musicality. She once described dance as ''the embodiment of music in movement.'' She saw it as a language that brought the musical score to living vibrant form—a belief that she herself certainly subscribed to. Nowhere was that more clearly visible than when she danced what has become her most famous role—that of Juliet.

The renowned Soviet composer Serge Prokofiev was inspired by Ulanova's talent and his score of ''Romeo and Juliet'' was composed with her in mind. Leonid Lavrovsky's ballet premiered at the Kirov in 1940 with Ulanova in the leading role. She imbued Shakespeare's young heroine with sensibility and beauty and continued to convince of teenage youthfulness even when she herself was nearing retirement. For many, there are two unforgettable moments, neither one a display of dazzling technique but of communicable artistry. First, at the ball: lifted high above Romeo's head, she playfully snatches his mask and sees his face for the first time. She remains frozen in awe; her excited heartbeats seem almost audible as her whole body thrills with the quickening of first love. Secondly—and perhaps the moment most associated with Ulanova—is when Juliet hurries to seek Friar Lawrence's help with her impending marriage to Paris. With black silk cape billowing out behind her, and Prokofiev's magnificent score surging forth, Ulanova runs across the stage, managing in those simple steps to depict her anguish and despair, drawing out deep emotion both from her inner self and also from the audience. Fortunately for the dance world, the ballet has been preserved on film for future generations to treasure.

After her success as Maria and then Juliet, Ulanova recognized that she was more suited to ballets that allowed her to develop the characters theatrically, which traditional classics such as *The Nutcracker* and *The Sleeping Beauty* did not. In the following years her thoughtful and focused approach brought freshness and drama to Odette/Odile in *Swan Lake* and to Giselle. She created roles in new ballets such as *The Red Poppy, The Stone Flower,* and *Cinderella,* often moving the audience to tears with her realistic performances.

Joined Both Kirov and Bolshoi Ballets

Ulanova was a member of the Kirov Ballet for 16 years. During the hard years of World War II and the blockade by the Germans of Leningrad (now St. Petersburg), the company was evacuated to Perm in the Ural Mountains. During this time she also performed at the Bolshoi Theatre in Moscow for audiences of soldiers, many of whom had chosen her as their pin-up girl. In 1944 she moved permanently to Moscow to join the Bolshoi Ballet Company.

Ulanova made her first western tour in 1945. She was first seen in London in 1956 and in New York in 1959. She made her farewell performance in 1962 but continued to work for 30 years as a coach, handing down her profound knowledge of the dance to top ballerinas of the Bolshoi—Maximova, Semenyaka, Semizorova, and Grachova. Galina Ulanova also accepted a few invitations to coach in other countries such as Australia and Sweden. Basically a shy person, she worked quietly, watching her pupil, and, when needed, elegantly demonstrating the filigree detailing that makes a ballerina in the truest sense. She neatly drew out of each dancer their own individuality while instilling the high standards that she herself so brilliantly evidenced in a long and esteemed career.

Ulanova took an active role throughout her life in speaking out for dance, in writing about it, and as an authority on juries of international ballet competitions. She served on important international dance and artistic committees. She was honored many times and received the (former) Soviet Union's highest order, that of "Hero of Socialist Labor," twice. But it is for her breath-taking, emotional, and magical dancing that she will always be remembered.

Born without a classic ballerina's body, she had big knees, square shoulders, and a short neck, but she had a commitment to tireless structured training within a rigorous system, which allowed her to reach the pinnacle of her art within the Soviet training program. She occupies a place with Margot Fonteyn and Natalia Markova as the supreme expression of the ballerina.

Further Reading

Ulanova has written, collaborated, and contributed to ballet literature in *Ballerina's School* (Moscow, 1954); *Soviet Ballet* (London, 1954); *Prokofiev: Articles, Reminiscences* (Moscow, 1956); *The Bolshoi Ballet Story* (1959); *Ballet Today* (London, 1957). She gave interviews of note to *Dance Scene* (1980) and *Dancing Times* (London, August 1983).

Books about Ulanova include Albert Kahn, *Days with Ulanova* (1962); M. Sizova, *Ulanova: Her Childhood and Schooldays* (London, 1962); Natalia Roslavleva, *Era of Russian Ballet* (London, 1966); Vladimir Golubov, *Galina Ulanova's Dance* (Leningrad, 1948); Yuri Sloniminsky, *The Bolshoi Theatre Ballet* (Moscow, 1956); Boris Lvov-Anokhon, *Ulanova* (Moscow and London, 1956); and Valerian Bogdanov-Berezovsky, *Ulanova and the Development of Soviet Ballet* (London, 1952) and *Galina Sergeyevna Ulanova* (Moscow, 1961). □

Walter Ulbricht

The East German leader Walter Ulbricht (1893-1973) succeeded in placing his country in a fairly strong economic position and weathered more political storms than most Soviet and East European Communist leaders.

Born into a poor working-class family in Leipzig on June 30, 1893, Walter Ulbricht learned carpentry and joined the Socialist party (SPD) in 1912. A solid if uninspired student, he early showed a tendency to cling to the simple Marxist ideology of the party. Like many other young Socialists, he was increasingly alienated by SPD support of the imperial German government in World War I. It was thus not surprising that Ulbricht joined a left-wing splinter group, the "League of Spartacus." After the failure of its coup against the new SPD government (which was regarded as too conservative) in January 1919, "Spartacus" broke up. Ulbricht and others formed a new left-wing party, the German Communist party (KPD). After an unsuccessful beginning as an agitator, Ulbricht found his niche as an organizer, first in "Red Saxony" and later in Berlin. He was subsequently trained in Moscow in tactics and administration.

As a member of the German Reichstag from 1928, Ulbricht helped formulate the misguided KPD tactic of attacking the Socialists, who supported the democratic Weimar Republic, instead of the real enemies of democracy, the Nazis. The revolution which the KPD expected as a result of the Nazi consolidation of power in 1933 failed to materialize, and the KPD was ruined. Ulbricht fled, moving to the Soviet Union in 1938 after serving on the Loyalist side in the Spanish Civil War.

Chosen by Stalin to return to Germany in 1945, Ulbricht organized support for the Soviet occupation. In 1946 he helped merge the old SPD and KPD in the Soviet zone into the Socialist Unity party (SED). Despite initial

appeals to all "antifascist elements," the SED drifted under the control of the old Communists. At the same time, Ulbricht's star rose in the German Democratic Republic (GDR), or the former East Germany, the successor to the Soviet Occupation Zone. Elected general secretary of the SED in 1950 and the equivalent of head of state in 1960, Ulbricht came to be the strongest East German leader.

Ulbricht gained international prominence for his increasingly forceful collectivization of the East German economy and the virtual imprisonment of his people. His high voice and his goatee figured in many caricatures. Defenders of Ulbricht pointed out that he, unlike Stalin, refrained from murdering his enemies and that East Germany had finally begun to achieve a limited prosperity under his rule. Ulbricht was, however, perhaps the most unpopular Communist leader of the century because of his inflexible policies, including the building of the Berlin Wall in 1961 to prevent East Germans from fleeing the country. He resigned in May 1971 and was succeeded by Erich Honecker.

He died Aug. 1, 1973, in Berlin after having suffered a stroke two weeks earlier.

Further Reading

Ulbricht published a number of books; some of them have been translated, including *Whither Germany? Speeches and Essays* (1966). The only biography of him in English is Carola Stern, *Ulbricht: A Political Biography* (1965), which, although limited by the inaccessibility of sources and absence of a true historical viewpoint, offers an outline of the German Communist movement and Ulbricht's role in it. □

Ulfilas

Ulfilas (ca. 311-ca. 382), Arian bishop of the Visigoths, or West Goths, translated at least part of the Bible into Gothic. He developed the Gothic alphabet on the basis of the Greek and Roman alphabets and enriched the Gothic, or East Germanic, language.

Ulfilas was probably descended on his mother's side from Christian captives displaced from Cappadocia in Asia Minor in the 3d century. They converted some of the Goths to their faith and settled with them north of the Danube. Not yet 30, Ulfilas, already a leader of his people, was sent on a mission to Constantine I, the first Christian emperor of Rome, and in the same year was consecrated bishop of the Christian Goths by Eusebius of Nicomedia. For seven years he performed episcopal duties among his people north of the Danube and, persecuted by non-Christian Goths, settled his followers in Moesia (Bulgaria). He also assumed duties as judge and intellectual leader. In 381 he was summoned by the emperor Theodosius to Constantinople for conferences. He died there soon after.

The Arianism of Ulfilas led to a break between Goths and Romans which was not healed by his compromise with Nicene orthodoxy. He was one of the founders of the Arian Gothic Church, which spread with missionary intensity to other East Germanic tribes in the Mediterranean Basin, the Ostrogoths (East Goths), Vandals, and Burgundians.

It cannot be determined how much of the Bible Ulfilas translated. The ecclesiastical historian Philostorgios claims Ulfilas translated all of it except the too warlike Books of Kings; others deny this. Much of the Gospels and the Epistles of Paul, as well as fragments from Nehemiah, Ezra, and Genesis and one psalm, are preserved in later forms. He used the Septuagint for the Old Testament and a Greek text for the New Testament, translating faithfully but not slavishly, enriching his native Gothic with neologisms and syntactic constructions. Philologically this translation—practically all that exists of Gothic—is of inestimable value. Most of what remains is in the Codex Argenteus (Silver Codex) in Uppsala, Sweden. Treatises and exegetical writings in Gothic, Greek, and Latin are also ascribed to Ulfilas. The chief primary sources about him are chapters by early ecclesiastical historians and a letter by his pupil Auxentius.

Further Reading

A full-length work on Ulfilas is Charles A. A. Scott, *Ulfilas: Apostle of the Goths* (1885). Recommended for historical background is Edward A. Thompson, *The Visigoths in the Time of Ulfila* (1966). □

Ulfilas (in white)

Domitius Ulpian

Domitius Ulpian (died 228), or Domitius Ulpianus, was one of the most distinguished Roman jurists. He served as praetorian prefect and chief adviser to the emperor Alexander Severus.

Ulpian was born in Tyre in Phoenicia in the eastern part of the Roman Empire. He had a fine legal education and had considerable experience with legal practice. He appears to have reached the high administrative positions of his career by holding varied positions in the Roman civil service. Earliest references to him are to the period when he was mainly known as a legal scholar. Scattered references in his massive written works date most of them to the reign of the emperor Caracalla (211-217). However, Ulpian's productions are so numerous that presumably much of the groundwork was done earlier, under Septimius Severus (193-211), and then completed under Caracalla.

Roman legal science had always depended heavily upon extensive commentary on a relatively limited and unorganized body of law. Under the empire, the quantity of law had increased, and attempts at systematization, which were to culminate in the great legal codes of the 6th century, had begun. However, the jurisconsults, or legal consultants, remained important both in the Emperor's council and the law courts. These men published voluminously on various aspects of the law.

Ulpian belongs solidly in this tradition. His published works appeared in a wide variety of forms. There were commentaries on set pieces of Roman law such as the praetorian edict, the guide to legal procedure which had formerly been issued individually by each successive praetor but which had been standardized under the emperor Hadrian (117-138). These commentaries were often line-by-line or even word-by-word interpretations of the piece of law under examination.

Another genre of publication was the *Responses,* short answers to legal questions, whose content probably stemmed in part from Ulpian's own experience at the bar. There were pedagogical works such as the *Institutes,* a type of general survey of the Roman legal system. Very important also were the writings of Ulpian on the administrative and legal functioning of various magistracies. The latter were especially useful in bringing together legal material scattered in the various edicts of the emperors.

A valid judgment on the ability of Ulpian as a legal scholar is difficult because only fragments of many of his works exist. Certainly his legal scholarship was impressive; he was one of the most learned and competent students of Roman law, if not the most brilliantly original. The strength of his influence can be judged by the fact that his legal writings formed one of the chief sources of the *Digest* of Justinian.

The publications of Ulpian stop rather abruptly after 217. One account states that he was sent into exile under the emperor Elagabalus (218-222). If this is true, he must have been recalled soon after the accession of Alexander Severus, for his rise in office under that emperor was rapid. Earlier he had served as a legal counselor (assessor) under Papinian, another great legal scholar who had combined his legal and administrative talents in the office of praetorian prefect (203-211). By March 222 Ulpian had reached the office of prefect of the grain supply, a position near the top of the Roman civil service. By December, Ulpian was praetorian prefect, the top in the civil service. He shared the position with two officers, Flavius and Chrestus.

The Severan emperors had appreciated the need of having a top legal mind in the most important administrative post in the empire. However, the praetorian prefect was also a military commander, and the combined role produced grave tensions for a man like Ulpian. Alexander Severus held him in high esteem and heeded his advice carefully. However, Ulpian evidently tried to keep too tight a reign on the guard, and this led to his downfall. One plot was discovered in time, and Ulpian's two colleagues as praetorian prefect were removed. A second plot was more successful, and in 228 Ulpian was murdered in the presence of Alexander Severus.

Further Reading

The *Digest* of Justinian contains many excerpts from Ulpian. J. Muirhead, *The Institutes of Gaius and Rules of Ulpian* (1880), contains a translation of Ulpian's *Regulae* (*Rules*). H. F. Jolowicz, *Historical Introduction to the Study of Roman Law*

(1932; 2d ed. 1952), places Ulpian in the context of Roman legal development. □

Miguel de Unamuno y Jugo

The Spanish philosopher and writer Miguel de Unamuno y Jugo (1864-1936) was the earliest 20th-century thinker to arrive at a perspective on man and the world that can be described as existentialist.

The total preoccupation of the philosophy of Miguel de Unamuno was "the man of flesh and bone"—the concrete individual with his passions, needs, hopes, and fears as the context within which human thinking and speaking occur. Unamuno was specifically concerned with the problem of faith in the modern world—"the agony of Christianity." He concluded that the split between faith and reason, heart and head, could not be healed by reason; that modern man must remain in a paradoxical and agonizing tension between faith and doubt, his religious beliefs only passionate hopes in the teeth of skepticism. Unamuno intensely lived out this modern predicament of faith in his own life, and he has been called the Spanish Kierkegaard.

Unamuno was born on Sept. 29, 1864, in Bilbao. Of Basque descent, he was raised and educated in the traditional piety and provincial learning of 19th-century Spanish Catholicism. From 1875 to 1880 he attended the Instituto Vizcaíno de Bilbao. In 1880 he entered the University of Madrid, where for the first time he was thrown into a cosmopolitan world of stimulating and sharply conflicting ideas. He received his baccalaureate degree in *filosofía y letras* in 1883 and his doctorate in 1884. During his university days Unamuno ceased being a practicing Catholic and espoused the scientific outlook and methods that he found in the works of leading European philosophers of the day. At this time he also began learning a number of languages in order to be able to read books in their original language.

Marriage and Professorship

Unamuno returned to Bilbao in 1884 and spent 6 years trying to secure a professorship at a university. During this period he began writing articles in his professional field, philology, but he was also beginning to explore philosophical matters. These years also witnessed a prolonged courtship between Unamuno and his childhood sweetheart, Concepción Lizárraga, whom he was unable to marry until he had secured a university appointment. At this time he began to raise serious questions about the adequacy of scientific positivism as a philosophical outlook and to turn in an existentialist direction. Always centrally concerned with language, he found that the vocabulary of love used by the actual "man of flesh and bone" simply could not be reduced to scientific categories. Even more sharply, it was the acutely personal contemplation of death as the great existential limiter of love and of life that led him to a philosophical outlook and method that concerned itself wholly with the concrete individual and with his rich vocabulary of desires and meanings, of which the language of science was only one.

In 1890 Unamuno secured an appointment as professor of Greek language and literature at the University of Salamanca, and the following year he married Concepción and went immediately to Salamanca to assume his scholarly duties. In 1897 he underwent a decisive religious crisis whose outcome was a return to faith, although not to the traditional teachings of Roman Catholicism but to an intensely personal, lifelong religious struggle that found its resources both in the Spanish mystics and in the great Protestant spiritual leaders Martin Luther and Søren Kierkegaard.

First Important Publications

Unamuno's years at Salamanca were tremendously productive. His *Life of Don Quixote and Sancho,* a study of the literary figure who seemed to Unamuno to symbolize the "soul of Spain," was published in 1905. His best-known work, *The Tragic Sense of Life in Men and in Peoples,* appeared in 1913. In it he explored man's "hunger of immortality," which he found could not be justified or satisfied on purely rational grounds but only through paradoxical and passionate affirmation of God and eternity by a faith and hope that continually battled with doubt and despair.

From 1901 to 1914 Unamuno was rector of the University of Salamanca. He was relieved of this position because he publicly favored the Allies in World War I. Always politically outspoken, in 1924 he was exiled to the Canary Islands because of his forceful opposition to the Spanish military dictatorship of Miguel Primo de Rivera. Unamuno managed to escape to France. Although pardoned a short time later, he refused to return to Spain. He lived first in Paris and then, after 1925, in the border town of Hendaye. While in Paris, Unamuno wrote one of his major works, *The Agony of Christianity,* published in 1925. It presents several variations on one of his favorite Gospel passages, "Lord, I believe; help my unbelief!" (Mark 9:23), discussing modern man's agony of faith and doubt.

Final Years

After the fall of Primo de Rivera, Unamuno returned to Spain in 1930 and was reinstated at the University of Salamanca. When the Spanish Republic was proclaimed in 1931, he was officially exonerated and elected a member of the new Parliament. When the Spanish Civil War broke out in 1936, he found himself in Falangist territory. For several months he said nothing and was allowed to continue as rector. But in October, when a ceremonial assembly at the university was used by Francisco Franco's spokesmen for vicious political propaganda, Unamuno publicly denounced the Falangist as having only brute force and not "reason and right" on their side. He was immediately removed as rector and kept under house arrest until his death from a heart attack on Dec. 31, 1936.

Unamuno's prolific literary production included essays, novels, and poems as well as technical works on a wide variety of philosophic, artistic, religious, and cultural themes. Very few of his writings have been translated into English. In addition to the books already mentioned, his *The Christ of Velásquez* (1920), a study, in verse, of the Spanish painter, is available in English, as are a book of poems and a volume of three short novels, *Three Exemplary Novels and a Prologue* (1920).

Further Reading

A thorough study of Unamuno's thought, which includes a detailed biographical account up to 1900, is Allen Lacy, *Miguel de Unamuno: The Rhetoric of Existence* (1967). Other critical works include Arturo Barea, *Unamuno* (1952); Julián Marías Aguilera, *Miguel de Unamuno* (trans. 1966); Paul Ilie, *Unamuno: An Existential View of Self and Society* (1967); and José Rubia Barcia and M.A. Zeitlin, eds., *Unamuno: Creator and Creation* (1967). Unamuno figures prominently in a study of modern Spanish poetry by Howard T. Young, *The Victorious Expression: A Study of Four Contemporary Spanish Poets, Miguel de Unamuno, Antonio Machado, Juan Ramón Jiménez, Federico Garcia-Lorca* (1964).

Additional Sources

Ferrater Mora, Jose, *Unamuno, a philosophy of tragedy,* Westport, Conn.: Greenwood Press, 1981, 1962.
Rudd, Margaret Thomas, *The lone heretic: a biography of Miguel de Unamuno y Jugo,* New York: Gordian Press, 1976, 1963. □

José Hipólito Unánue

José Hipólito Unánue (1755-1833) was a Peruvian intellectual, educator, scientist, and journalist. He was one of the foremost physicians and thinkers of the transition period from the colonial to the independence era.

The 18th-century intellectual movement called the Enlightenment had its reflection in the viceroyalty of Peru, where a small group of individuals concerned themselves with developing and applying the revolutionary ideas of the emerging sciences. The ablest and most devoted student of these new trends in Peru was José Hipólito Unánue, an individual of diverse interests, a court physician, and an adviser of viceroys and presidents, whose life coincided with the transition from the 18th to the 19th century and from the viceroyalty to the republic.

José Hipólito Unánue was born in Arica on Aug. 13, 1755, of a well-to-do family who directed him toward an ecclesiastical career. The influence of an uncle, Father Pedro Pabón, a botanist, turned him, however, from theology to medicine and general science, in which fields he was a brilliant student. He soon won a professorship in the School of Medicine of Lima, where he instituted the systematic practice of dissection.

Seeking to apply the most modern procedures, Unánue established the San Fernando School of Medicine and was the first to introduce vaccination in Peru. Under the enlightened Francisco Gil de Taboado, thirty-fifth viceroy of Peru (1790-1796), the first scholarly periodical, the *Mercurio peruano* (1791-1795), was established in Lima. It was a vehicle for publicizing scientific, historical, economic, political, and statistical subjects, and together with a society called Amantes del País (Friends of the Country), of which Unánue was a founder, it stimulated a highly competent group of contributors.

Under the name "Aristo," Unánue contributed essays and scientific papers to the 12 volumes of the *Mercurio peruano,* but it was in 1806 that his most famous study was published in Lima. It was entitled Observations on *the Climate of Lima and Its Influence on Organic Life, Particularly Mankind,* and in it he anticipated many ideas of the science of anthropogeography. He wrote prolifically on education, metaphysics, and ethics, as well as on medicine, and he strongly defended Newtonian theories of physics and mathematics.

Unánue's intellectual distinction drew him into the political life of his time. He early embraced the cause of independence from Spain, writing a manifesto in its favor in 1812 and serving as secretary of the treasury in the provisional government. He was the presiding officer of the Constituent Congress, and as head of the Council of Ministers, he enjoyed the complete confidence of the "Liberator," Simón Bolívar.

Always a man of deep moral and religious convictions and a dispassionate patriot, Unánue advocated a strong central control of public affairs. He was a member of the commission seeking to tender the government to a European prince. After the rejection of this concept of governing and the ensuing confusion in the public affairs of the new nation, he retired to private life and the resumption of his scientific interests. Greatly venerated and honored, he died on July 15, 1833.

Further Reading

Unánue figures in Bernard Moses, *Spanish Colonial Literature in South America* (1922), and Germán Arciniegas, *Latin America: A Cultural History* (1965; trans. 1967). For general historical background see Frederick B. Pike, *The Modern History of Peru* (1967). □

John Underhill

John Underhill (ca. 1597-1672), American military leader and magistrate, played an important role in the early Indian Wars in New England and in New York.

John Underhill's family was from England; his father was a mercenary in Dutch service. John was born possibly in Holland and received little formal education. In Holland he became a member of the Puritan church, although not of great conviction, and there he was married in 1628 while serving as a military student in the house of the Prince of Orange.

In 1630 Underhill went to the Massachusetts Bay Colony in America, where he organized the militia as one of its captains. He became a selectman of the town in 1634. The Puritans had little love of the military, however, and Underhill constantly had to fight for supplies. The Indian Wars came in 1637. Underhill fought in Massachusetts and in the Pequot wars in Connecticut. Returning to Boston in 1638, he became embroiled in a religious dispute and was branded an antinomian, disfranchised, disarmed, and discharged. He returned to England and wrote a book dealing with the Pequot wars.

By 1639 Underhill was in Boston again, where he was arrested and tried before the General Court for making contemptuous speeches. Found guilty, he was banished and fled to Dover, N.H., just in time to avoid trial for adultery. At Dover he became governor of the colony and stoutly resisted Massachusetts' claims to the region. However, he begged forgiveness of the Boston church for adultery and even returned to make a public confession; but he was adjudged insincere and excommunicated. Finally he was reinstated in the church, and in 1641 the sentence of banishment was removed.

At the invitation of the New Haven Court, Underhill moved to Stanford, Conn., in 1643 as captain of militia but quickly resigned to take employ with the Dutch in New Amsterdam (New York) to fight the Native Americans in that region. He settled on Long Island and became a member of the Council of New Amsterdam, but when he denounced Governor Peter Stuyvesant as a tyrant, he was almost tried for sedition. Moving to Rhode Island, he was commissioned a privateer in 1653 and seized the property of the Dutch West Indies Company at Hartford, Conn.

During the Anglo-Dutch War of 1665-1667, Underhill fought with the British to conquer New Amsterdam, and there in 1665 he became surveyor of customs for Long Island. Later he served as high constable and undersheriff of North Riding, Yorkshire, Long Island. He died on Sept. 21, 1672.

Further Reading

For details of Underhill's early activities see his *News from America* (1638). Biographies include two favorable treatments, J. C. Frost, *Underhill, General* (4 vols., 1932), and H.C. Shelley, *John Underhill* (1932). Less favorable is L. E. and A. L. de Forest, *Capt. John Underhill* (1934). Also valuable is John Winthrop, *Winthrop's Journals,* edited by J. K. Hosmer (2 vols., 1908). □

Sigrid Undset

The Norwegian novelist Sigrid Undset (1882-1949) was internationally acclaimed for the historical novel "Kristen Lavransdatter." She won the Nobel Prize in literature in 1928.

Sigrid Undset was born on May 20, 1882, in Kalundborg, Denmark, the daughter of a distinguished Norwegian archeologist and a Danish mother. She grew up in Oslo in a closely knit family where her interest in history and literature was early awakened. Her father died when she was 11, leaving the family in financial difficulties. Her first 11 years are movingly described in the autobiographical novel *The Longest Years* (1934). She had intended to study painting but was forced to work in an office for 10 years, until she began to earn enough from her books to quit and devote herself to writing.

Sigrid Undset's authorship was a reaction against the Norwegian literature of her contemporaries. On the basis of her experiences among the working women of Oslo—whose rootless lives seemed to contrast so sharply with her own homelife—she came to believe that most of the new liberal ideals and freedoms were illusory and that a fulfilling life could only be based on a sense of personal responsibility.

From the beginning until *Kristen Lavransdatter,* Sigrid Undset's fiction deals almost exclusively with contemporary women in their search for values that will give their lives meaning. Her fortunate heroines are those who find something greater than their own egos—a strong, enduring love, children, a home and, finally, religious faith. The strength of the best of these novels and stories lies in their vivid realism, their compassionate objectivity, and Sigrid Undset's remarkable gift for characterization. The outstanding work of this period is the novel *Jenny* (1911), shocking in its time for its bold erotic descriptions.

Kristen Lavransdatter (1920-1922) is Sigrid Undset's masterpiece, one of the great historical novels in world literature. Its greatness lies in the way she brings to life a distant age and yet shows us the universally human beneath the medieval forms. The rich and complex Kristen dominates the novel, in her rebellion, her joys and suffering, and her gradual growth as a woman.

In 1924 Sigrid Undset converted to Catholicism. Her authorship from this time on directly reflects her religious convictions. The two-volume novel *The Master of Hestviken* (1925-1927) is much more tendentious than *Kristen,* although it contains many powerful scenes. After these historical novels, Sigrid Undset returned to novels of contemporary life, now with a clear Catholic message: *The Wild Orchid* (1929), *The Burning Bush* (1930), *Ida Elisabeth* (1932), *The Faithful Wife* (1936), and *Madame Dorothea* (1939).

As one of Norway's most prominent anti-Nazi writers, Sigrid Undset was forced to flee to America after the German invasion. While there she worked actively for Norway's cause and also wrote a book about her flight, *Return to the Future* (1942), and a book of memoirs, *Happy Times in Norway* (1942). Sigrid Undset died at her home at Lillehammer on June 10, 1949.

Further Reading

For a discussion of Sigrid Undset's life and work see Harald Beyer, *A History of Norwegian Literature* (1964); Alrik Gustafson, *Six Scandinavian Novelists* (1966); and Carl F. Bayerschmidt, *Sigrid Undset* (1970).

Additional Sources

Brunsdale, Mitzi, *Sigrid Undset, chronicler of Norway,* Oxford England; New York: Berg; New York: Distributed in the US and Canada by St. Martin's Press, 1988.

Dunn, Margaret, Sister, *Paradigms and paradoxes in the life and letters of Sigrid Undset,* Lanham, Md.: University Press of America, 1994. ☐

Giuseppe Ungaretti

The Italian poet Giuseppe Ungaretti (1888-1970) was the creator and major representative of Italian hermetic poetry.

Giuseppe Ungaretti was born on Feb. 10, 1888, in Alexandria, Egypt, of Italian parents who had emigrated from the countryside around Lucca. At an early age he lost his father, who had been working as a laborer on the Suez Canal project; his mother continued to run a baker's oven to maintain the family. Until 1905 Ungaretti frequented the Istituto Don Bosco and the École Suisse Jacot, and in 1912 he went to Paris to study at the Collège de France and the Sorbonne. He met and befriended poets and artists such as Guillaume Apollinaire,

Pablo Picasso, Giorgio de Chirico, Georges Braque, and Amedeo Modigliani. In 1915 his first poetry was published in the journal *Lacerba*.

During World War I Ungaretti served as an infantry soldier on the Italian front and in the Champagne. After the war he settled in Paris and in 1919 married Jeanne Dupoix. In 1921 the couple moved to Rome, where Ungaretti held a job in the Ministry of Foreign Affairs. In the early 1930s he traveled as a special correspondent for the *Gazzetta del popolo* and also went on several lecture tours throughout Europe.

During a congress of the Pen Club in Brazil in 1936, Ungaretti accepted the offer of the chair of Italian language and literature at the University of São Paulo. Upon his return to Italy in 1942, he was elected a member of the Italian Academy and took the chair of modern Italian literature at the University of Rome. After the death of his wife in 1958, he traveled extensively. He died in Milan on June 1, 1970. He was the recipient of numerous literary prizes.

While still in school in Egypt, Ungaretti became acquainted with French symbolist poetry, particularly that of Stéphane Mallarmé. The example of the French symbolists, and later that of Paul Valéry and Apollinaire, led him to adopt his particular hermetic "technique of obscuration." Such a closed diction derives its characteristics from the basic symbolist beliefs in the magic qualities of the word and the conviction that the poet is the keeper of arcane secrets. Thus, as Ungaretti once said, true poetry must have the "obscure sense of revelation." The technique avails itself of all possibilities to give the single word greater relief, be it through abolition of punctuation, typographical or stylistic isolation, or epigrammatic composition. Ungaretti always professed to be preoccupied with ultimate questions of man's existence, with the mysteries of life, and he gave his entire work the title *Vita d'un uomo*.

Ungaretti's first collection of verse, *Il porto sepolto* (1916), was published in an edition of 80 copies and represented a definite break with traditional forms. The poems grew out of his first year's experience in the trenches of Monte San Michele. *Allegria di naufragi* (1919) is a testimony of self-revelation after the experiences of war. Typical is the long poem *I fiumi*, in which he tries to define his heritage. The central collection of Ungaretti's poetry, *Sentimento del tempo* (1933), appeared after an interval of 14 years, and he spoke of the "most slow distillation" of this work. *Il dolore* (1947) is a group of 17 poems written under the impression of the death of his son at the age of nine. With the sequence of the compositions contained in *La terra promessa* (1950) Ungaretti adopted more extensive poetic forms and also returned to a modified hendecasyllable. *Un grido e paesaggi* (1952) contains poetry written between 1939 and 1952.

Further Reading

The most concise monograph in English on Ungaretti is Glauco Cambon, *Giuseppe Ungaretti* (1967). A substantial study of Ungaretti's work in the broad context of hermetic poetry is in Joseph Cary, *Three Modern Italian Poets: Saba, Ungaretti, Montale* (1969). Recommended for general historical back-

ground are the preface in Carlo Luigi Golino, ed., *Contemporary Italian Poetry: An Anthology* (1962), and Eugenio Donadoni, *A History of Italian Literature* (2 vols., trans. 1969). □

John Updike

Author John Updike (born 1932) mirrored his America in poems, short stories, essays, and novels, especially the four-volume "Rabbit" series.

John Updike was born on March 18, 1932, in Shillington, Pennsylvania. His father, Wesley, was a high school mathematics teacher, the model for several sympathetic father figures in Updike's early works. Because Updike's mother, Linda Grace Hoyer Updike, nurtured literary aspirations of her own, books were a large part of the boy's early life. This fertile environment prepared the way for a prolific career which began in earnest at the age of 22, upon the publication of his first story, "Friends from Philadelphia," in the *New Yorker* in 1954.

Updike admired the *New Yorker* and aspired to become a cartoonist for that periodical. He majored in English at Harvard where he developed his skills as a graphic artist and cartoonist for the *Lampoon,* the college's humor magazine. In 1953, his junior year at Harvard, he married Mary Pennington, a Radcliffe art student. Upon graduation the following year, Updike and his bride went to London where he had won a Knox fellowship for study at the Ruskin School of Drawing and Fine Art in Oxford.

He returned to the United States in 1955 and took a job as a staff writer at the *New Yorker* at the invitation of famed editor E. B. White, achieving a life-long goal. But after two years and many "Talk of the Town" columns, he left New York for Ipswich, Massachusetts, to devote himself full time to his own writing.

Twenty Years of Poetry

Updike began his remarkable career as a poet in 1958 by publishing his first volume, a collection of poems titled *The Carpentered Hen*. It is a book of light, amusing verse in the style of Ogden Nash and Robert Service. The poetry possesses several stylistic conventions shared by his fiction: careful attention to the sounds of words and the nuances of their meanings, the use of popular culture by identifying objects by familiar brand names, and the mimicry of the popular press through advertising language and newspaper editorial boosterism. For example, a trivial snippet from *Life* magazine becomes the basis of a poem called "Youth's Progress," which ostensibly details the physical metamorphosis of a young boy into an adult. "Dick Schneider of Wisconsin . . . was elected 'Greek God' for an interfraternity ball," states the original excerpt from *Life*. The poem takes its cue from this by citing the common milestones of developing youth: "My teeth were firmly braced and much improved./ Two years went by; my tonsils were removed." The poet then playfully contrasts the narcissistic concerns of

youth with the uniquely American optimistic faith in democracy, culminating in the assertion that even Greek divinity is accessible to the common man: "At twenty-one, I was elected Zeus."

Updike's output of light verse diminished with the publication of each succeeding volume of poems, and he stated later that he "writes no light verse now." His poetry has been collected in several volumes, among them *Telephone Poles and Other Poems* (1963); *Midpoint* (1969), which is an introspective assessment of the midpoint of his life; and *Tossing and Turning* (1977), which some critics consider his finest collection of verse. Much of the verse has been collected in a chronological format in a one-volume edition called *Collected Poems: 1953-1993* (1993). Updike's poetry continued to appear in publications such as *Poetry* and the *New Yorker*.

The "Rabbit" Series and Other Novels

John Updike's first novel, published in 1959, was called *Poorhouse Fair*. It is a dystopian portrayal of an imaginary place under cruel conditions in the tradition of George Orwell and Aldous Huxley, depicting life in a welfare state projected twenty years into the future, the late 1970s. The conflict between Conner, the young prefect of the home with an obsession for order, and Hook, a 94-year-old inmate who rebels against regimentation, is unresolved by the end of the novel, causing certain critics considerable discomfort with its ambiguity, especially Norman Podhoretz and other *Commentary* reviewers.

Although Updike's reputation rests on his complete body of works, he was first established as a major American writer upon the publication of his novel *Rabbit Run* (1960), although at that date no one could have predicted the rich series of novels that would follow it. It chronicled the life of Harry (Rabbit) Angstrom, creating as memorable an American character as Hester Prynne, Jay Gatsby, and Bigger Thomas. Harry Angstrom's life peaked in high school where he was admired as a superb basketball player. By the age of 26 he is washed up in a dead-end job, demonstrating gadgets in a dime store, living a disappointed and constricted life: "I once did something right. I played first-rate basketball. I really did. And after you're first-rate at something, no matter what, it kind of takes the kick out of being second-rate." His primal reaction to this problem is to run (as would his namesake). And like Christian in the beginning of *Pilgrim's Progress,* he runs, fleeing his wife and family as though the salvation of his soul depends upon it. The climax of Rabbit's search results in tragedy, but it is to the credit of Updike's skill that great sympathy for a not-very-likable character is extracted from readers.

The second novel in the series, *Rabbit Redux* (1971), takes up the story of Harry Angstrom ten years later at the age of 36. Updike continues Rabbit's story against a background of current events. The novel begins on the day of the moon shot. It is the late 1960s and the optimism of American technology is countered by the despair of race riots, anti-Vietnam protests, and the drug culture. Rabbit is nostalgic for the secure serenity of the Eisenhower years. But his world is unsettled by realization that the old way of life is rapidly disappearing, his mother is dying of disease, and his father is aged. Rabbit has become complacent in the face of change. His wife, Janice, from whom he fled in *Rabbit Run,* now flees him and his inertia. His family is falling apart, mirroring divisive problems of the country at large. Rabbit finally overcomes his complacency and brings "outsiders" into his home, attempting to reconstitute his family. Although some critics were disappointed, Charles Thomas Samuels and Eugene Lyons among them, most, like Brendan Gill and Richard Locke, considered *Rabbit Redux* a successful novel.

The next book in the series was *Rabbit Is Rich* (1981), which won the 1982 Pulitzer Prize. Rabbit is 46 and finally successful, selling Japanese fuel-efficient cars during the time of the oil crisis in the 1970s. In this novel Rabbit's son Nelson's failure becomes the counterweight to Rabbit's success. Updike describes an upper-middle-class milieu of Caribbean vacations and wife-swapping. Nelson revives Rabbit's vice of irresponsibility but without the grace Rabbit possessed in his youth. Rabbit again becomes the source of family salvation. He steps in for the missing Nelson to be present at the birth of his grandchild. In a sense, the loss of momentum represented by the fuel shortage and the consequent slowing of industry, and even the aging Harry Angstrom, is tentatively renewed by this young life. Updike offers slender hope in a bleak American landscape.

Rabbit at Rest (1990) brings Rabbit into the 1980s to confront an even grimmer set of problems: AIDS, cocaine addiction, and terrorism. Rabbit suffers a heart attack and is haunted by ghosts of his past. Death looms ever larger. The fragility of life and the randomness of death are represented for Harry by the Lockerbie tragedy where death becomes as inevitable as "falling from the burst-open airplane: he too is falling, helplessly falling, toward death." In these four novels an insignificant life presses and insists itself upon our consciousness, and we realize that this life has become the epic of our common American experience recorded over three decades.

Updike wrote many other major novels, including *The Centaur* (1963), *Couples* (1965), *A Month of Sundays* (1975), *The Witches of Eastwick* (1984), and *Brazil* (1993). Updike was also the author of several volumes of short stories, among them *Pigeon Feathers* (1962), *The Music School* (1966), *Bech: A Book* (1970), *Museums and Women* (1972), and *Bech Is Back* (1982). His novel *In the Beauty of the Lilies* (1996) was met with mixed reviews from such esteemed literary critics as Gore Vidal. In addition to being a prolific novelist, Updike also released several volumes of essays, two being *Odd Jobs* (1991) and *Just Looking: Essays on Art* (1989). In 1996, he released a collection, *Golf Dreams: Writings on Golf* (1996), which was met with favorable reviews. David Owen wrote in the *New York Times Book Review,* "Like plenty of other golfers, I suspect, I wish that John Updike had spent fewer man-years dutifully weighing the merits of unappealing foreign novels and more reflecting on his slice."

Updike has been honored throughout his career: twice he received the National Book Critics Circle Award and the Pulitzer Prize. He also received the American Book Award and was elected to the American Academy of Arts and Letters. Updike has been one of the most prolific American authors of his time, leading even his most ardent fans to confess, as Sean French did in *New Statesman and Society,* "...Updike can write faster than I can read..."

Further Reading

For Updike's discussion of himself and his work, his own *Picked-up Pieces* (1975) is useful because it contains interviews of Updike by others. Michael A. Olivas has compiled a useful bibliography called *An Annotated Bibliography of John Updike Criticism, 1967-1973.* For an early dissenting opinion on Updike see Norman Podhoretz's *Doings and Undoings* (1964). For good, concise, non-ideological discussions of Updike and his novels, see Robert Detweiler's Twain Edition of *John Updike* (1984). See also Donald Greiner's *John Updike's Novels* (1984). For a wide selection of reviews and essays, see William Macnaughton's *Critical Essays on John Updike* (1982). □

Richard Upjohn

Richard Upjohn (1802-1878) was an English-born American architect whose expressive vocabulary of Gothic design helped to make this style popular in the mid-19th century.

Richard Upjohn was born in Shaftesbury, Dorsetshire, on Jan. 22, 1802. At the age of 27 he went to America with his wife and son. Upjohn became a skilled cabinetmaker before entering the profession of architecture, which explains his penchant for precise, meticulous architectural decoration. Detailed Gothic buildings probably gave him more pleasure to design and construct than the currently popular Greek revival style, whose proportions he could approve but whose paucity of decoration was to him absurd.

In 1830 Upjohn settled in New Bedford, Mass., where he was listed as a carpenter and worked in the office of an oil and lumber merchant. Within 3 years Upjohn began designing buildings. The first was a house for Isaac Farrar in Bangor, Maine (1833-1836), in the prevailing Greek revival style. His first church was St. John's, Bangor (1836-1838; destroyed), in the Gothic style, with which he was thereafter identified.

In 1839 Upjohn moved to New York when he was asked to design a new Trinity Church (1839-1846). It is now considered his finest ecclesiastical work. In plan, decoration, and character it is modeled after the church building concepts of the English Ecclesiologists, who believed in returning directly to medieval architecture and liturgy for inspiration. The effect is clear and precise, though to some extent it lacks integration between ornament and structure.

Trinity Church set the tone for numerous other Gothic churches throughout America, and it helped Upjohn get a large number of commissions which placed him at the top of his profession. His other notable churches are the Church of the Ascension, New York City (1840-1841); Christ Church, Brooklyn (1841-1842); Grace Church, Providence, R.I. (1847-1848); Grace Church, Utica, N.Y. (1856-1860); St. Peter's, Albany, N.Y. (1859-1860); Central Congregational Church, Boston, Mass. (1865-1867); and St. Thomas's, New York City (1868-1870)—all designed in variations of the Gothic theme.

Upjohn's public and commercial buildings were generally done in an Italianate style with semicircular, arched windows and doors. They are monotonous in the repetition of motifs and lack compensating decoration.

Sporadic attempts to form an association of professional architects were made for 2 decades before Upjohn and 12 other New York architects organized as the American Institute of Architects in 1857, with Upjohn as first president. The list of members soon included all the best architects of the era, and the institute is still central to all professional activity in the country.

Rural Architecture (1852) is Upjohn's only complete book, though many drawings and photographic views of his buildings appeared in contemporary magazines. He died in Garrison, N.Y., on Aug. 16, 1878. His most important pupil was his son Richard M. Upjohn.

Further Reading

The definitive book on Upjohn is Everard M. Upjohn, *Richard Upjohn: Architect and Churchman* (1939; repr. 1968). □

Urban II

Urban II (1042-1099) was pope from 1088 to 1099. He laid the foundations for the papal monarchy, and his pontificate marked a turning point in the institutional organization of the papacy and in papal-imperial relations.

Otto (or Odo) de Lagery, who became Urban II, was born near Châtillon-sur-Marne of a great French noble family. He grew up at Reims, where he became archdeacon, and at Cluny, where he became a monk and then prior. In 1078 Gregory VII created him cardinal bishop of Ostia. Loyally supporting Gregory's reforming ideals, he represented the Pope on numerous successful missions to France and Germany.

On March 12, 1088, Otto was elected pope and took the name Urban II. Though he was a convinced Gregorian, he was less fiery and passionate than Gregory VII and more politically astute about realizing a program of reform. Whereas Gregory VII had neglected the ties that bound the papacy and southern Italy, Urban II carefully cultivated them, seeing in them a political means for resisting the German emperor.

Soon after his election Urban went to Sicily to renew the alliance with Roger Guiscard and to establish one with the Greek emperor, thus laying the foundations for the good relations that obtained between Rome and Byzantium throughout his pontificate.

In November 1088 Urban reestablished himself in Rome with the aid of Norman troops, which he used against the imperial antipope Clement III. Ten months later Urban left Rome for southern Italy to preside over a council of 70 bishops concerned with lay investiture. Together with comparable later councils in northern Italy, Germany, and France, this meeting symbolized Urban's effort to reform the Church throughout Europe along Gregorian lines, especially by isolating the hostile German emperor Henry IV. To further his aims against Henry, Urban sanctioned political marriages and formulated military alliances, chiefly the first Lombard League (1093). In November 1093 an assembly of rebellious German nobles made common cause with the Pope at Ulma, swearing obedience to his representative.

In March 1095 at Piacenza, Urban officiated at a reunion of the entire reform-oriented episcopate—by a chronicler's estimate a gathering of more than 4,000 prelates and 30,000 laymen. Also in attendance (and further bearing witness to the power of the Pope) were Henry IV's estranged wife, Praxedis, an embassy from Philip I of France, and an embassy from the Greek emperor seeking help against the Turks.

After the council adjourned, Urban triumphantly proceeded north, continuing with the work of restoring papal authority wherever it had been usurped by secular power. From Nov. 18 to Nov. 28, 1095, he convened a council at Clermont, France, where, in addition to excommunicating King Philip I of France, he reaffirmed the primacy of papal power over the entire Church. On November 27 Urban solemnly proclaimed the First Crusade against the infidels. By mobilizing Europe's chivalric elements to his cause, Urban proved that he had not only excluded the German emperor but that he had displaced him as leader of Europe. On July 15, 1099, the crusaders entered Jerusalem; but Urban died on July 29, 1099, before the news reached him. He was beatified on July 14, 1881.

Urban left behind the solid foundations of emerging papal monarchy. In seeking to create for the papacy a central governmental structure modeled on that of the French royal court, he invented the papal curia—an organ that put the papacy on an equal footing with the emerging feudal monarchies of Europe. His organizational efforts also included the discovery and use of legal texts for bolstering papal authority. In 1140 they were systematized in the famous *Decretum of Gratian,* which, because it emphasized the pope's legislative and dispensatory powers, became the starting point for 12th-century ecclesiastical law.

Further Reading

Virtually all studies of Urban II are in French or German. Good general studies in English which include Urban II are Henry Hart Milman, *History of Latin Christianity* (8 vols., 1861-1862; 4th ed., 9 vols., 1872); Ferdinand Gregorovius, *History of the City of Rome in the Middle Ages* (trans., 8 vols., 1894-1902); and Geoffrey Barraclough, *The Medieval Papacy* (1968). □

Urban VI

Urban VI (1318-1389) was pope from 1378 to 1389. During his pontificate began the Great Schism of the Church, during which rival popes at Rome and Avignon claimed legitimacy and divided the loyalties of Europe.

artolomeo Prignano, who became Urban II, was born in Naples. He became archbishop of Bari and an influential figure in the papal court, although he was never a cardinal. Before his pontificate, he was known as a competent Church official who was interested in reforming the Church to meet the growing criticism of the times. Much of this criticism stemmed from the "Babylonian Captivity" (1309-1377), or removal of the papacy to Avignon in France. Pope Gregory XI returned the papacy to Rome in 1377 but died in 1378. When the College of Cardinals met to elect his successor, feeling ran high. Outside the conclave, the people of Rome clamored for the election of an Italian pope and even threatened to murder the cardinals. On April 8, 1378, the cardinals decided that, under the circumstances, the wisest choice was Prignano, who took the name Urban VI.

But almost immediately, the cardinals began to quarrel with the new pope, who angered them both by his attempts to make unwelcome reforms in the papal court and by his undiplomatic personality. Thirteen of the cardinals left Rome and went to the city of Fondi. On Aug. 9, 1378, they declared Urban's election invalid, and on September 20 they elected a new pope, Clement VII (Robert of Geneva, a cousin of the king of France). Thus began the Great Schism.

Even today there is disagreement about the legitimacy of the dissident cardinals' action and about their motives. The cardinals themselves argued that Urban's election was invalid because it occurred under duress, but they waited four months before they objected. Another factor was the personality of Urban VI, who by all accounts was short-tempered, stubborn, and, in the opinion of some, abnormally violent. Undoubtedly he alienated the cardinals by his manner. But it is probable also that France feared a loss of power from the papacy's return to Rome and so persuaded the French faction of the cardinals to bring a pope to Avignon again. In any case, the Great Schism brought Urban VI the support of France's enemies and brought Clement VII the support of France and its allies, creating years of bitterness and much loss of prestige for the papacy.

On Nov. 29, 1378, Urban excommunicated his rival; Clement VII retaliated in kind, and both popes declared their own legitimacy to the end of their lives. Urban VI died on Oct. 15, 1389.

Further Reading

For the pontificate of Urban VI the best general history in English is Mandell Creighton, *A History of the Papacy during the Period of the Reformation,* vol. 1 (1882). However, the definitive work on Urban's part in the Great Schism is Louis Salembier, *The Great Schism of the West* (trans. 1907). See also Walter Ullmann, *The Origins of the Great Schism* (1948). ☐

Harold Clayton Urey

The American Scientist Harold Clayton Urey (1893-1981) received the Nobel Prize for chemistry in 1934 for his discovery of deuterium, the isotope of heavy hydrogen.

arold Clayton Urey was born on April 29, 1893, in Walkerton, Ind., the son of Samuel Clayton Urey and Cora Rebecca Reinoehl Urey. After graduation from high school at 18, followed by some three months of education training at Earlham College, Harold taught in small country schools in Indiana and then Montana, where the family had moved. In 1914 he entered Montana State University (Bozeman) and graduated in three years with a baccalaureate in science.

The United States entered World War I in 1916 and Urey began work at the Barrett Chemical Company in Frankford near Philadelphia, preparing toluene for the production of TNT (trinitrotoluene) in 1917. In 1919 he returned to Montana to teach in the department of chemistry for 2 years. In 1921 he entered the graduate school at the University of California, Berkeley. Urey's interest focused upon molecular structure, a new field for scientists in the

United States. His doctoral research on the conductivity of cesium vapor led him to the theory of thermal ionization in stellar atmospheres. Within two years he received the doctorate (1923) and, with a Scandinavian Foundation fellowship, later studied in Copenhagen at the Institute of Theoretical Physics, headed by Niels Bohr.

During his residence at Berkeley and Copenhagen, Urey began to work with some of the most prominent physicists and chemists of the 20th century, including Werner Heisenberg, Wolfgang Pauli and Georg von Hevsey. In Hamburg, Germany, he met he met Albert Einstein and James Franck, both of whom became his lifelong friends. In 1924 he returned to the United States to take a National Research Council fellowship at Harvard but instead accepted a faculty position as associate in chemistry at Johns Hopkins University, where he remained until 1929. There he and Russel Bichowsky hypothesized the idea of electron spin to explain the fine structure of the atomic spectral lines.

Between 1923 and 1929, Urey published 20 scientific papers or notes, almost all of them on aspects of atomic structure and the others on molecular band spectroscopy. In 1930 the book *Atoms, Molecules, and Quanta,* by A. E. Ruark and Urey, appeared. It became, and remained for a long time, one of the standard texts on the subject. Urey also published *The Planets: Their Origins and Development* in 1952.

While at Johns Hopkins, Urey married Frieda Daum in 1926. Her intelligence, good humor and warm hospitality made the Urey house a meeting place for scientists and

intellectuals of all fields. As a tribute to her, the University of California at San Diego named its first large building the Harold and Frieda Urey Hall. The Ureys had four children: Gertrude, Elizabeth, Frieda Rebecca, Mary Alice and John Clayton.

In 1929 Urey became associate professor of chemistry at Columbia University in New York and professor in 1934. He refined his interest in sub-atomic and molecular structure and discovered a discrepancy in the atomic weight of hydrogen compared with that of oxygen, as measured by chemical means and by mass spectrometry. The discrepancy led to his identification of a heavy isotope of hydrogen (deuterium) found in concentrations of about 1 part per 5,000. Calculating that the heavy isotope would boil less easily than the lighter, he had a friend at the Bureau of Standards, Ferinand G. Brickwedde, distill hydrogen. In the residue they and George M. Murphy discovered *heavy water,* molecules with one atom of oxygen and two atoms of hydrogen or deuterium. This led to Urey's award of the Nobel Prize for Chemistry in 1934.

Journal of Chemical Physics, published by the American Institute of Physics for the new breed of physical chemists interested in subatomic and molecular spectroscopy and structure. He remained editor until 1941, established the journal's preeminent reputation and the name of the field, chemical physics.

Urey's scientific work at Columbia became more and more concerned with the separation of isotopes of the lighter elements. The rarer isotopes of oxygen, nitrogen, carbon, and sulfur were concentrated. When full-scale work began at Columbia on the separation of the rare fissionable lighter isotope of uranium, U^{235}, from the much more abundant U^{238}, Urey became project head.

He then served as one of three program chiefs of the Manhattan Project. Even after the project's successful conclusion at Oak Ridge, Tennessee, he felt discouraged. The atmosphere of secrecy, the tight time schedule, and the limitations and conflicts of the work oppressed him.

After the war Urey, along with many others, was attracted to the plan of Chancellor Hutchins to build a group of research institutes at the University of Chicago. When the new institutes were founded, Urey was in the Institute for Nuclear Studies, later to become the Enrico Fermi Institute. For a while Urey, uncharacteristically, still suffering from the trauma of the war work, tended to drift, and he looked for new fields to conquer. He soon became interested in the past history of the earth and the planetary system. He initiated the use of analysis of the isotopic abundance in sea fossils to estimate the temperature of past oceans and helped prepare the most commonly accepted table of the elements. He also worked on meteoritic ages, composition, and classification. But his abiding interest then became earth's moon: Many of his later papers concerned the possible character of its formation and past history. He influenced astronomers and others to consider chemical evidence in the origin of the solar system and later became an active consultant to NASA, Lunar Sciences, and to the Space Science Board, National Academy of Sciences.

The trials of Ethel and Julius Rosenberg, who were accused of stealing secrets relating to the construction of the atomic bomb, attracted Urey's interest in 1952. The letters in their defense that he wrote to President Harry S. Truman, the *New York Times* and the presiding trial judge received mixed reviews from the public, but they further cemented his relationship with Albert Einstein, who wrote Urey a strong letter of support.

In 1958 Urey moved to the Scrimps Institution of Oceanography in La Jolla, where he continued to teach and to do active research in the general field of geochemistry and planetary science. He received numerous honors besides the Nobel Prize, including 23 honorary doctorates and membership or fellow of some 25 societies or academies. His bibliography of scientific publications exceeds 200 titles.

Urey later became a member of the Union of Concerned Scientists. In 1975 the organization petitioned then President Gerald Ford to limit the expansion of nuclear power plants. Urey's expressed alarm for the safety of nuclear power plants, nuclear waste disposal and the spread of nuclear weapons. He died of at heart attack at his home in La Jolla, California, near the University of California, San Diego, January 5, 1981.

Further Reading

Register of Harold Clayton Urey Papers, 1929-1981, Mandeville Special Collections Library, Geisel Library, University of California at San Diego. The collection contains his autobiography and all the available biographical sketches written during his career at University of California (San Diego). Shorter studies of his life and career are in Sarah R. Riedman, *Men and Women behind the Atom* (1958); Eduard Farber, *Nobel Prize Winners in Chemistry, 1901-1961* (1953; rev. ed. 1963); Jay E. Greene, ed., *100 Great Scientists* (1964); Nobel Foundation, *Chemistry: Including Presentation Speeches and Laureates' Biographies,* vol. 2 (1966); Henry A. Boorse and Lloyd Motz, eds., *The World of the Atom* (2 vols., 1966); and Frederic L. Holmes, editor, *Dictionary of Scientific Biography* (18 vols., 1990). Urey's cosmological ideas are discussed in Jagjit Singh, *Great Ideas and Theories of Modern Cosmology* (1961). □

Justo José Urquiza

The Argentine dictator, general, and statesman Justo José Urquiza (1801-1870) was an ardent federalist and all his life fought against the dominance of the province of Buenos Aires at the expense of the interior provinces.

Justo José Urquiza was born on Oct. 18, 1801, in Arroyo de la China, in the province of Entre Rios. His parents were prominent and wealthy provincial landowners. Although much of his early practical education was received at the hands of the gauchos on the family estates, his formal education was as good as that of most political and military figures of his day, for he attended the Jesuit Colegio de San Carlos in Buenos Aires. Before he became embroiled in the political and military conflicts of his time, he amassed a considerable fortune as a merchant.

Urquiza became involved in the civil wars of the 1820s on the side of the provinces and rose rapidly in rank under Governor Echague. By 1842 he had risen to the command of the federalist forces under the dictator Juan Manuel de Rosas and became governor of Entre Rios. At this time he married a girl of Italian parentage and fathered two daughters and four sons.

He defeated the unitarist leader Gen. Paz and extended the domination of the Argentine federalists over much of Uruguay. Long a supporter of Rosas, he ultimately turned against him because of his refusal to set up a constitutional federal government presided over by a congress. After failing in 1846, Urquiza was finally successful in concluding an alliance with Brazil and Uruguay and defeated Rosas at the battle of Caseros on Feb. 3, 1852, which brought about the exile of the dictator.

United Provinces

The Brazilians and Uruguayans withdrew, and a provisional government was set up under Urquiza, who called all governors to a convention at San Nicolás, where a constitution was drawn up. The proposal to place the capital at Santa Fé was unacceptable to Buenos Aires. Urquiza refused to use force against the *porteños* (Buenos Aires party supporters), put the capital at Paraná, and allowed the province of Buenos Aires to become an independent state.

The provinces, including Buenos Aires, progressed peacefully as independent states under Urquiza's leadership until 1859, when hostilities broke out. The *porteños*, under Bartolomé Mitre, were defeated, and Buenos Aires returned to the confederation. Urquiza resigned the presidency to become governor of Entre Rios. He was unable to defeat Mitre in 1861, and the seat of government was returned to Buenos Aires. Urquiza refused to join a rebellion against Mitre during the Paraguayan War and maintained peace in his province, which prospered under the stability he provided.

Urquiza soon retired to care for his immense estates, said to contain an area as large as Belgium, with over a million head of livestock. In April 1870 a small force under a petty *caudillo*, López Jordán, who was angered that Urquiza would not take action against the Buenos Aires government, killed him in cold blood.

Thus died a patriot who had freed Uruguay and the river provinces from the Rosas tyranny, established a federal constitution, opened the rivers to the ships of all nations, encouraged immigration, and achieved peace and prosperity for his province. He had the imagination, which Rosas lacked, to rise above his earlier provincial instincts and work for a constitutional republic. His memory is still revered in Argentina today.

Further Reading

Most good biographies of Urquiza are in Spanish and have not been translated. In English, possibly the best work is Lewis Bealer's discussion of Urquiza in A. Curtis Wilgus, ed., *South American Dictators* (1937). □

Kitagawa Utamaro

Kitagawa Utamaro (1753-1806), one of the greatest masters of the Ukiyo-e school of Japanese woodblock printing, excelled in the exotic portrayal of Japanese women, especially those of the Yoshiwara district. Many contemporary critics regard him as the greatest Japanese printmaker.

Like most of the Ukiyo-e artists, Kitagawa Utamaro was a native of Edo (modern Tokyo). His teacher was Toriyama Sekien, but the greatest influence on him was the work of Kiyonaga, the dominant Ukiyo-e artist of his youth. Utamaro's talent was discovered while he was still very young by the discriminating publisher Tsuta-ya Juzaburo, who brought out many of his prints. The most outstanding of Utamaro's early works are his illustrated books, the finest of which are the albums of insects, shells, and birds published between 1787 and 1791 and reflecting the influence of the Dutch scientific publications which were entering Japan through the port of Nagasaki.

During the 1790s Utamaro reached his artistic peak. Following in the footsteps of Kiyonaga, he portrayed Japanese women, bringing out their grace and elegance.

Utamaro's most original contribution to the art of the Japanese print was his close-up pictures, or Okubi-e, which concentrated on the face. He was also the undisputed master of the erotic print, a genre to which he brought all his skill as a draftsman and designer.

Utamaro's career came to an end when he was arrested in 1804 for representing the 16th-century shogun Toyotomi Hideyoshi in a disrespectful manner. Although his imprisonment was brief, he never recovered from this blow, and he died two years later.

It is estimated that Utamaro produced some 1,500 prints, most of them devoted to celebrating the beauty of the Japanese woman. In fact, he created a special type of female beauty, tall and slender, with an oval face, sharply defined features, slanted eyes, and a tiny mouth. Often published in sets with titles like *Ten Facial Types of Women, Love Poems, Flourishing Beauties of the Present Day, The Mirror of Flirting Lovers, Twelve Hours of the Green Houses,* and *Elegant Amusements of the Four Seasons,* these prints show the life of the courtesans and teahouse waitresses of Yoshiwara, the amusement district of Edo. Other famous sets deal with genre scenes such as mothers with children or women engaged in domestic tasks. Most of these works consist of groups of single prints; others are diptychs and triptychs, the set showing the courtesans on the Ryogoku bridge being the most famous in this category. However, his great fame as well as his influence on later printmakers rests above all on his full-face pictures of the Utamaro-type beauties. In these works his sophistication and felling for female physiognomy are most fully expressed.

While Utamaro's subjects by and large were taken from the general repertoire of the Ukiyo-e school, it was in the style and design of his prints that he surpassed his contemporaries and followers. His use of line and color and his feeling for pattern and composition reveal a master who produced some of the finest wood blocks ever made. However, his late work shows a certain decadence and overrefinement, a tendency further accentuated in the work of his followers; yet at the height of his power he was one of the greatest of Japanese artists, and it is not pure chance that the French impressionists, notably Édouard Manet, Edgar Degas, and Henri de Toulouse-Lautrec, were great admirers of his work.

Further Reading

Studies of Utamaro and his work include Yone Noguchi, *Utamaro* (1925); Ichitaro Kondo, *Kitagawa Utamaro, 1753-1806* (1956); and Jack R. Hillier, *Utamaro: Colour Prints and Paintings* (1961). □

Uthman don Fodio

Uthman don Fodio (1755-1816) was a Moslem teacher and theologian. One of the principal reformers of Islam in Hausaland in Northern Nigeria, he founded an Islamic empire at the beginning of the 19th century.

Uthman don Fodio whose complete name was Uthman ibn Muhammad ibn Fudi, was commonly known simply as Shehu, the Hausa word for sheikh. He was born in the Hausa state of Gobir, the son of a pious Fulani member of the Qadiriyya Moslem brotherhood. Uthman and his brother Abdullahi received a thorough education in Islamic theology, Arabic, and Moslem law, and by 1774 he began his career as an itinerant preacher and teacher. During these years Uthman wandered throughout Hausaland, gaining adherents and preaching reform in the practice of Islam. His followers, who were later to form the vanguard of his fighting forces, came from all parts of the central Sudan.

During the last quarter of the 18th century Uthman's ideas and asceticism became famous. He represented the ideal life of the Islamic mystic, dedicated to the teaching of the Koran and undefiled by the material desires that corrupted the world around him. But Uthman was more than a preacher. He was also a social reformer who objected to the non-Islamic practices of the Hausa leaders and continually criticized their rule and questioned the legitimacy of the taxes they imposed on his Fulani (Fulbe) brethren. His teaching and the ever-increasing number of his followers throughout Hausaland caused growing alarm among the Hausa chiefs, especially the Sultan of Gobir, who sought to undermine his influence. In 1804 Uthman and his followers were forced to flee for safety from Gobir, in a manner reminiscent of Mohammed's flight from Mecca, known as the *hijra,* and proclaimed the *jihad,* or holy war, against the Sultan and eventually against all the Hausa chiefs.

Holy War

Uthman's principal role during the years of war that followed was that of a spiritual leader, mediator, and chief source of inspiration for his followers. He was neither a warrior nor a politician but the Commander of the Faithful (Sarkin Musulmi), and he left the practical affairs of the *jihad* to his brother Abdullahi and his son Muhammadu Bello, who commanded Uthman's army.

One by one the Hausa states of Gobir, Kebbi, Zamfara, Kano, Katsina, and Zazzau capitulated to the Fulani and were emulated by pagan areas on the periphery of the Hausa states. All were organized into emirates by the Fulani, but the establishment of political power was for the purpose of implementing the social, legal, and religious ideals of Islam as interpreted by Uthman. Many of these ideals were, of course, compromised by the realities of the *jihad* and the increasing Fulani orientation that accompanied the establishment of the emirates, but Uthman's teaching continued to provide the ideological justification for Fulani control until after his death.

The importance of Uthman don Fodio in 19th- and 20th-century West Africa cannot be restricted to Hausaland, for the resurgence and reform of Islam which he had accomplished spread throughout West Africa. The expansion of Islam into Yorubaland, the conquest of Ilorin, and the destruction of Oyo inaugurated 70 years of civil war in southwest Nigeria which ultimately drew the British into the interior of Nigeria in the late 19th century. Similarly, the pressure of his forces on the moribund state of Bornu east of Lake Chad contributed to its rebirth under el-Kanemi and his successors.

In the west Uthman's concept of the *jihad* was employed by al-Hajj Omar to build the Tokolor empire, which, before its destruction by the French, came to include a large part of the western Sudan between the Niger headwaters in the Futa Jallon and Timbuktu. All of these movements were precipitated by the life and teachings of a small, pious man whose unworldly piety remained uncorrupted by his victories or the material success of his followers. His character, his achievements, and his impact on West Africa have made him one of the most important men in the history of Africa.

Further Reading

Extensive information on Uthman don Fodio is in H. A. S. Johnston, *The Fulani Empire of Sokoto* (1967), and in Murray Last, *The Sokoto Caliphate* (1967). Michael Crowder, *The Story of Nigeria* (1962; rev. ed. 1966), contains a chapter on Uthman. For general background see J. Spencer Trimingham, *A History of Islam in West Africa* (1962), and S. J. Hogben and A. H. M. Kirk-Greene, *The Emirates of Northern Nigeria: A Preliminary Survey of Their Historical Traditions* (1966), a revision of Hogben's *Mohammadan Emirates of Nigeria* (1930). □

V

Luis Valdez

Luis Valdez (born 1940) was founder of the El Teatro Campesino in California and is thought to be the father of Mexican American theater.

Playwright and director Luis Valdez is considered the father of Mexican American theater. In 1965 he founded El Teatro Campesino, a theater of farm workers in California. This project inspired young Mexican American activists across the country to use the stage to give voice to the history, the myths, and the present-day political concerns of Mexican Americans. In later years, Valdez has tried to portray Mexican American life for a mainstream audience, and his popular 1987 film *La Bamba* helped him do that.

Valdez was born in 1940 in Delano, California, into a family of migrant farm workers. At the age of six he began to work in the fields with his parents and nine brothers and sisters. Because his family had to travel around California's San Fernando Valley following the ripening of the crops, his education was continuously interrupted. Despite this, Valdez managed to finish high school and to attend San Jose State College. He majored in English and explored his interest in theater. While in college he won a writing contest for his play, *The Theft*. Later, the college's drama department produced *The Shrunken Head of Pancho Villa*, his play about the problems facing a Mexican couple in America.

Learns Techniques of Agitprop

After graduating from college in 1964, Valdez joined the San Francisco Mime Troupe, but he couldn't give up telling stories and writing plays. During this time he learned the techniques of agitprop (agitation and propaganda) theater, in which a play puts forth political views and tries to spur the audience to act on those views.

For years migrant farm workers had to endure unhealthy working conditions. They worked long hours for extremely low wages and received no benefits. Finally, in 1965, migrant grape pickers in Delano decided to go on strike. These workers were backed by the labor leader César Chávez and the migrant worker union he helped found, the National Farm Workers Association.

Brings Theater to Farm Workers

Two months after the strike began, Valdez joined Chávez in his efforts to organize the farm workers of Delano. It was there that Valdez brought together farm workers and students to found El Teatro Campesino (the Workers' Theater). The original function of this group of actor-laborers was to raise funds and to publicize the farm-worker strike and the grape boycott. Their efforts soon turned into a full-blown theatrical movement that spread across the country capturing the imagination of artists and activists.

By 1967 Valdez and El Teatro Campesino left the vineyards and lettuce fields to create a theater for the Mexican American nation. The movement evolved into *teatro chicano,* an agitprop theater that blended traditional theatrical styles with Mexican humor, character types, folklore, and popular culture. All across America, Mexican American theatrical groups sprang up to stage Valdez's one-act plays, called actos. The actos explored modern issues facing Mexican Americans: the farm workers' struggle for unionization, the Vietnam War, the drive for bilingual education, the war against drug addiction and crime, and community control of parks and schools.

399

Hands Down Rules for Mexican American Theater

In 1971 Valdez published a collection of actos to be used by Mexican American community and student theater groups. He also supplied the groups with several theatrical and political principles. Included among these were the ideas that Mexican Americans must be seen as a nation with roots spreading back to the ancient Aztec and that the focus of the theater groups should be the Mexican American people. Valdez's vision of a national theater that created art out of the folklore and social concerns of Mexican Americans was successful. The Mexican American theater movement reached its peak in 1976.

Valdez and others in the movement then tried to expand the Mexican American experience into areas that would reach all Americans. In 1978 Valdez broke into mainstream theater with a Los Angeles production of his popular play *Zoot Suit,* about Mexican-American gang members during the Los Angeles race riots of 1942-43. The following year the play moved to the Broadway stage in New York. It was then made into a film in 1982, but this version failed to please both critics and audiences. Valdez was hurt by the experience. "It's painful to make a passionate statement about something and then have people ignore it," he explained to Susan Linfield in *American Film.*

La Bamba Brings Attention

Valdez remained determined to reach a national audience. His next play, *Corridos,* the dramatization of a series of Mexican folk ballads, was praised by theater critics. It was then made into a television production that aired on PBS in the fall of 1987. Valdez's breakthrough into mainstream America, however, had come earlier that summer. He had written and directed *La Bamba,* the screen biography of Ritchie Valens, the 1950s Mexican American rock-and-roll singer. Audiences across America learned not only about the tragically short life of Valens but also about the lifestyle and other elements of the Mexican American community. The movie was an overwhelming box office success.

"My work comes from the border," Valdez told Gerald C. Lubenow of *Newsweek.* "It is neither Mexican nor American. It's part of America, like Cajun music." Valdez has continued to write plays for the theater, for television, and for motion pictures that focus on the lives and the histories of Mexican Americans. In 1994 he began work on the script for a film about the life of César Chávez, who died in 1993. He has also remained artistic director for El Teatro Campesino. In the process, he believes he is simply exposing America to another part of itself. "I have something to give," he explained to Lubenow. "I can unlock some things about the American landscape."

Valdez holds honorary doctorates from San Jose State University, the University of Santa Clara, Columbia College of Chicago, and the California Institute of the Arts. He is also a founding faculty member of the new California State University Monterey Bay and a founding member of the California Arts Council. His awards include the George Peabody Award (1987), the Governor's Award (1990), and Mexico's prestigious Aguila Azteca Award (1994).

Further Reading

American Film, July/August, 1987, p. 15.
National Council on the Arts: Luis Valdez July 23, 1997; "http:// arts.endow.gov/Guide/NCABios/Valdez.html"
Harper, Hillard, "The Evolution of Valdez and El Teatro Campesino," *Los Angeles Times,* October 15, 1984, sec. 6, p. 1.
Matthiessen, Peter, *Sal Si Puedes: César Chávez and the New American Revolution,* New York: Random House, 1969.
Mills, Kay, "A Matter of Changing Perspectives," *Los Angeles Times,* June 3, 1984, sec. 4, p. 3.
Newsweek, May 4, 1987, p. 79.
New York, February 7, 1994, pp. 60-61.
New Yorker, August 10, 1987, pp. 70-73. □

Pedro de Valdivia

Pedro de Valdivia (ca. 1502-1553) was a Spanish conquistador and professional soldier. He fought in Europe and in the civil wars of Peru and initiated the conquest of Chile.

Pedro de Valdivia was born in the district of La Serena in Estremadura. Joining the Spanish army early, he fought in Flanders and then at the battle of Pavia in 1525. He reached America in 1535, spent an uneventful year in Venezuela, and moved on to Peru. There he took part on the side of Hernando Pizarro in the battle of Las Salinas in 1538, which saw Almagro defeated and captured. Valdivia had married in Spain, but in Peru he became attached to the widow Inés de Suárez, who accompanied him to Chile as his mistress.

Early in 1540, with Francisco Pizarro's permission, Valdivia left Cuzco for Chile with a small expedition and one Sancho de Hoz as partner. On the way, Sancho, seeking sole leadership, tried to murder Valdivia but failed. He was pardoned but from then on had to accept subordinate status.

In central Chile, Valdivia founded Santiago on the Mapocho River in 1541, and 3 years later Juan Bohón established La Serena in the Coquimbo Valley. These were followed by Concepción, Villarrica, Imperial, Valdivia, and Angol. Valparaíso, though used as a port by the Spaniards from the start, had no considerable population until much later. Santiago was largely destroyed, soon after its foundation, by Aconcagua Native Americans during Valdivia's absence. The Spaniards there were not annihilated, however, and Inés de Suárez largely conducted the defense and caused the attackers to reire. Ultimately, pressure from his political superiors compelled Valdivia to end his relations with Inés.

When the Gonzalo Pizarro rebellion began in Peru, the insurgents attempted unsuccessfully to win Valdivia to their side. Early in 1548 Valdivia joined the royal army of Pedro de la Gasca in Peru, and his military experience counted heavily in the victory of Xaguixaguana on April 9 of that year. Valdivia returned to Chile with his position and prestige considerably strengthened.

Earlier, on learning of Francisco Pizarro's murder in 1541, Valdivia had removed Chile from Peruvian control and acknowledged only the royal authority, an arrangement the Crown found acceptable. Secure now in his own domain, he pushed exploration southward and aided the development of the country by dividing the land among his ablest followers and parceling out the Indians in *encomiendas*. Chile possessed minerals, but Valdivia definitely subordinated mining to agriculture and stock raising.

Valdivia had a clash with the warlike Araucanians beyond the Bio-Bio River in 1550 in which he defeated them but by no means broke their will to resist, a will that grew stronger when the conquistador established the Concepción settlement in their territory. He moved against them in 1553 and built a fort at Tucapel. He had earlier captured and presumably made friends with Lautaro, an Araucanian youth who became his groom. Lautaro secretly remained true to his own people and rejoined them to show Chief Caupolicán a means by which Valdivia could be taken. The Spanish leader was captured on Christmas Day, 1553. Though different accounts exist of his execution, the likeliest is that a chief, Pilmaiquén, hit him in the head with a war club.

Further Reading

Ida S. W. Vernon, *Pedro de Valdivia: Conquistador of Chile* (1946), is a carefully researched, factual biography. H. R. S. Pocock, *The Conquest of Chile* (1967), is also very useful. R. B. Cunninghame Graham, *Pedro de Valdivia: Conqueror of*

Chile (1926), is of some value, largely because it contains translations of five important letters by Valdivia to Charles V of Spain. Stella (Burke) May, *The Conqueror's Lady, Inés Suárez* (1930), is a fictionalized biography but is based on primary sources and good secondary works. Author and poet Alonso de Ercilla y Zúñiga arrived in Chile after Valdivia's death, but his epic poem, translated into English as *The Araucaniad*, contains facts available nowhere else.

Additional Sources

Cunninghame Graham, R. B. (Robert Bontine), *Pedro de Valdivia, conqueror of Chile,* Westport, Conn.: Greenwood Press, 1974. □

Jack Joseph Valenti

Jack Joseph Valenti (born 1921) combined Hollywood and politics long before it was fashionable. Starting as an advertising and public relations man in Houston, Texas, Valenti became a trusted adviser and friend to President Lyndon Johnson. Valenti took over the helm of the Motion Picture Association of America in 1966, revamped an anachronistic ratings system, and was instrumental in helping to establish the American Film Institute.

Jack Valenti was born into a second-generation Italian-American family in Houston, Texas, on September 5, 1921. All four of his grandparents had immigrated to the United States from Sicily in the 1890s. Jack grew up on an unpaved road called Alamo Street in a working-class neighborhood, and his father was a clerk in Houston's county tax office. As a young boy who tried to help his family manage in difficult economic conditions, Jack always had jobs. He helped out in his grandfather's grocery store, sold newspapers on the street corners, and showed people to their seats in a Houston movie house called the Iris Theater.

The Valentis were a large Italian-American family with lots of cousins, babies, lively conversations, and big Sunday afternoon dinners. Jack's grandfather and great uncle were respected leaders in Houston's Sicilian community; their support was looked upon as crucial by local politicians. Valenti says his grandfather's leadership was his first introduction to politics, and he proudly speaks of the fact that upon his grandfather's death the *Houston Chronicle* listed Captain James A. Baker, grandfather of Jim Baker, as one of the honorary pallbearers.

At Sam Houston High School Valenti was a debate champion, honor student, and the school's youngest graduate ever at the age of 15. He promptly began full-time work as an office boy at the Humble Oil and Refining Company, worked his way up to the advertising department, and began evening classes at the University of Houston.

World War II took over his life from 1942 to 1945. Valenti was a highly decorated Air Force bomber pilot. After his discharge as a first lieutenant, he finished his undergrad-

would talk about the future. As Jack Valenti rode in the president's motorcade toward Dealey Plaza on November 22, 1963, the excitement of being recruited as a member of the vice president's staff turned to shock and bewilderment, when President Kennedy was assassinated by Lee Harvey Oswald. That night he found himself on Air Force One headed for Washington as one of the first staff members of President Lyndon Johnson.

In addition to becoming a close personal friend of the president, Valenti was his closest adviser, consultant, and assistant. He performed tasks at the White House in the areas of congressional relations, diplomatic matters, speech editing, and foreign relations. He attended cabinet and National Security Council meetings and was trusted with many confidential assignments. The press was skeptical and sometimes critical of Valenti's role in the White House, and rumor said that he was constantly at the mercy of Johnson's cruel scoldings and tempestuous moods. Stories were circulated that Johnson often humiliated Valenti in front of others, but Valenti refuted the reports and never spoke publicly of the president without the highest praise and loyalty.

Soon after he had taken over national security duties in April 1966, which were formerly performed by McGeorge Bundy and Bill Moyers, Valenti announced that he was leaving the White House to become president of the Motion Picture Association of America (MPAA). He spoke of his love for movies, but also of his attraction to the significant salary increase he would incur.

As head of the association representing film makers all over the country, Valenti's first and monumental contribution was to revamp the ratings. Long with the association's general counsel, Valenti wrote a new code in which he attempted to move the ratings policy away from a "taboo" mentality and instead created broad moral guidelines that would allow more artistic freedom. He also envisioned the new code as one that gave American film makers a competitive edge with the more liberated Europeans. Two pillars of Valenti's age-based system remain with us today—the "mature audiences only" rating and the "PG" rating, which allows parents to decide on an individual basis what is appropriate viewing for their children.

As he approached retirement, Valenti became embroiled in a heated controversy over the television program rating system initiated under the Telecommunications Act of 1996. Valenti led the development of the age-based system, which closely resembled the one developed earlier for motion pictures. The system was implemented in January, 1997, and quickly aroused criticism from parents, children's health, and media watchdog groups and from Congress. Critics overwhelmingly sought a change to a system based on program content, many suggesting a graded "S", "V", "L" labeling format to specify levels of sex, violence, and offensive language in programs. A Media Studies Center/Roper Center survey showed that 73 percent of Americans supported such a content-based system with only 15 percent support for Valenti's MPAA-style system. He initially insisted that the age-based system would not be changed regardless of the levels of opposition and threatened to take the issue into the courts should the government

uate degree in 1946 at the University of Houston as an A-minus business major and English minor and as president of the student body. Two years later he returned to Houston with a Master's degree from the Harvard Graduate School of Business and took over the advertising and promotion department at Humble Oil.

Valenti left the company in 1952 to start his own advertising agency with Weldon Weekley, a classmate from the University of Houston. Weekley and Valenti, Inc., quickly became representatives of the powerful in the Houston business community as well as the powerful in Texas politics. Their political accounts included work on Dwight D. Eisenhower's presidential campaign in Texas in 1952, U.S. Representative Albert Thomas' run for Congress, John Connally's campaign for governor of Texas, and Lyndon Johnson's presidential campaign during the primaries of 1960.

Valenti had been named Outstanding Young Man of Houston in 1956, and later that year at a gathering of other young businessmen in Houston he met then-Senator Lyndon Baines Johnson. Valenti left that meeting greatly impressed, thinking of Johnson as a man who possessed strength and intelligence combined with humility and earnestness.

After he handled the press in Houston for President John F. Kennedy's November 1963 visit to Texas, Valenti's performance so impressed the vice president that Johnson convinced him to fly with the Kennedy/Johnson entourage to Fort Worth and then on to Dallas and Austin, where they try to alter the system. Throughout the controversy, he staunchly maintained that "it is an enterprise in which government must not and cannot get involved in any way at any time for any reason, though some in government will be mightily tempted." By March, 1997, Valenti had retreated to a point where he told a Senate Commerce Committee panel that he would consider alternatives. Shortly thereafter, however, he defended the aged-based format, describing it as designed for real parents and easy to use and understand. He restated his earlier contention that it was the only system that could work effectively with a Vchip. He also maintained that primary responsibility for determining appropriateness of programs for children remained with parents arguing that "This rating system is not a surrogate maid."

Valenti suffered a defeat during the General Agreement on Tariffs and Trade negotiations when the French refused to relax import limits on U.S.-made films and television programs on grounds that its cultural identity was at stake. President Bill Clinton's decision not to sacrifice seven years of global negotiations for Hollywood was for Valenti a most unwelcome outcome.

After that unforgettable 1963 flight on Air Force One, Valenti never went back to Texas to live. He had married Mary Margaret Wiley, a former secretary to Johnson, in Houston on June 1, 1962, and as soon as he was able he brought her to Washington, D.C., where they made their home. They had three children, Courtenay Lynda, John Lyndon, and Alexandra Alice. Valenti's columns often appeared in newspapers around the country, and in December 1992 he made his debut as a novelist with *Protect and Defend,* a Washington insider's story about a vice president challenging his president in the primaries. Ironically, his editor at Doubleday, who published the novel, was Jacqueline Kennedy Onassis.

Further Reading

For additional information on Valenti see *Variety—Who's Who in Show Business* (1985), edited by Mike Kaplan; "In the Loop," an interview with Victor Gold in *Washingtonian* (December 1992); *Who's Who in Entertainment* (2nd ed., February 1992); and *Who's Who in America* (46th ed., October 1990). For Valenti's own writings see *Ten Heroes and Two Heroines,* a collection of his columns from the Houston *Post* (1957); *Bitter Taste of Glory* (1971); *A Very Human President* (1975); *Speak Up With Confidence* (1982); and *Protect and Defend* (1992), a novel set in Washington, D.C. The TV ratings controversy is well-covered by *Broadcasting and Cable* and *Television Digest.* See also *Vital Speeches* (October 15, 1996). □

Juan Valera y Alcalá Galiano

The Spanish novelist, critic, and diplomat Juan Valera y Alcalá Galiano (1824-1905) is primarily remembered for his novel "Pepita Jiménez" (1874), which won international fame.

Juan Valera was born in Cabra in the province of Cordova to an aristocratic family. He studied at the Sacro Monte in Granada. He prepared himself for a career in law and diplomacy that would afford leisure time for reading and writing. His father encouraged Juan in his literary pursuits.

Soon after completing his legal studies, Valera was named attaché in the Spanish ambassadorial staff of the Duque de Rivas in Naples (1847-1849). While in Italy, Valera studied Italian and other literatures. He then held various other diplomatic posts at Lisbon, Rio de Janeiro, Vienna, and St. Petersburg.

On his return to Spain in 1858 Valera devoted most of his time to writing criticism, poetry, and novels. He was the first critic to recognize the excellence of the poetry of Rubén Dario. Valera became blind in his last years but continued to write, dictating his works to his secretary.

Valera's publications comprise many volumes of literary criticism, poetry anthologies, and novels. *Cartas americanas* (1889-1890) is a critical work that deals with Spanish American writers. *Florilegio de poesiás castellanas del siglo XIX* (1902-1903) is an anthology of Spanish poetry. His novels include *Pepita Jiménez* (1874), *Las ilusiones del doctor Faustino* (1875), *El comendador Mendoza* (1877), *Doña Luz* (1879), *Juanita la larga* (1895), and *Morsamor* (1899).

Pepita Jiménez, Valera's first novel, is also his masterpiece. It is the story of a young seminarian who falls in love with Pepita, a widow. The setting of the novel reflects the warm, colorful, and emotional qualities of the people of Andalusia. Through Luis de Vargas, the priest-to-be and protagonist, Valera reveals the inner conflict such a person undergoes in the choice between taking Holy Orders forever or loving a woman as a life companion. Luis tries to convince himself at the beginning of the novel that Pepita is merely "a beautiful creature of God" whom he loves but only as if she were "his own sister." The analysis of his emotional state is both tender and psychological, at times disturbing, but the ordeal ends happily with Luis's decision to marry the charming Pepita.

Further Reading

A full-length study of Valera is Edith Fishtine, *Don Juan Valera: The Critic* (1933), which contains studies of his critical essays. For informative and critical treatments of Valera's works, there are excellent chapters in Aubrey F. G. Bell, *Contemporary Spanish Literature* (1925; rev. ed. 1933), and in L. A. Warren, *Modern Spanish Literature* (2 vols., 1929). A very useful if somewhat general account is in the book by Richard E. Chandler and Kessel Schwartz, *A New History of Spanish Literature* (1961).

Additional Sources

DeCoster, Cyrus Cole, *Juan Valer,* New York, Twayne Publishers 1974. □

Valerian

The Roman emperor Valerian (ca. 200-ca. 260), or Publius Licinius Valerianus, attempted to stay the advances of the barbarians and the Persians on Roman territory and was a vigorous persecutor of the Christians.

The background of Valerian prior to his accession as emperor is uncertain. He had evidently had both civic and military experience and had served with sufficient distinction to be awarded the consulship. He was popular with the Senate. One source mentions him as part of a delegation coming from North Africa to support the usurping Gordian emperors against Emperor Maximinus Thrax (238). He probably held an important position under Emperor Trajan Decius (249-251), and there may be a connection between his service under that emperor, a persecutor of Christians, and his own anti-Christian activity.

Emperor by Default

Valerian must also have been highly regarded by Emperor Trebonianus Gallus, for when Gallus was challenged by the usurper Aemilianus, Gallus had Valerian gather troops for him in the northern provinces. Valerian was in the province of Raetia (modern Switzerland) when the news of Gallus's murder by his own troops reached him. Valerian was then saluted as emperor by his own army. Shortly thereafter, the troops of Aemilianus slew their commander and went over to Valerian. He was also accepted by the Senate in Rome.

Almost any emperor in the mid-3rd century faced an impossible situation. The frontiers were thereatened in almost every sector either by barbarian hordes or by the growing power of the Sassanian Persian kingdom. It was impossible for an emperor to cover every frontier; yet to delegate authority meant to create a potential rival who after a few victories might attempt to make himself emperor. Valerian attempted to solve this problem by associating with him in the honors and powers of the emperorship his son Gallienus. Gallienus became in fact almost a coregent.

Repression of Christianity

A second major crisis of the empire was that of spiritual values. Traditional Romans regarded traditional religion as one of the foundations of their success, but this religion was being challenged by many sects, especially the Christians, who seemed most opposed to normal Roman religious practice. Sporadic efforts were made to control or exterminate the sect but without success. Valerian is supposed to have been initially sympathetic to the Christians, but by the 4th year of his reign (257) his attitude changed. He may have felt it important in a period of crisis to have maximum support for the Roman gods. An edict directed primarily against the clergy was issued. It required them to show some form of veneration for Roman ceremonials and prohibited all types of Christian services, including those at cemeteries.

This was followed by a second edict, which imposed various sentences against Christians, including death for bishops and other ecclesiastical officials and loss of rights and property for lay Christians. Many individual Christians suffered from these decrees, but they failed to stop the growth of the religion.

Meanwhile, foreign problems took the attention of Valerian. The Persian king Shahpur I had raided the Eastern provinces and seized Antioch, the third-largest city in the empire. In 256 or 257 Valerian went to the East. Shahpur yielded Antioch, but Valerian found himself faced by a continuing Persian menace and also an incursion of the Goths into Asia Minor. In spite of the fact that he had no generals he could really trust, Valerian dispatched forces against the Goths.

Valerian's own armies were weakened by a plague, but nonetheless he was forced to return to the Persian menace, which now centered upon the city of Edessa. While trying to relieve the city, Valerian was captured by Shahpur. The circumstances of his capture are uncertain. Some sources say that he was seized by a ruse, and others that his army was overwhelmed. In any case the Persian king was extremely proud of his prize and carved monumental cliff reliefs showing Valerian kneeling before him. Christian writers depict a harsh captivity for Valerian, but this may reflect a desire to see justice done by God for Valerian's persecution of the Christians. Whatever the circumstances, Valerian seems to have died within a short time of his capture. His son Gallienus succeeded him.

Further Reading

Part of an ancient biography of Valerian survives in the *Scriptores historiae Augustae*. It contains many inaccuracies. The 5th-century historian Zesimus also has an account of Valerian. For a general discussion see the *Cambridge Ancient History,* vol. 12 (1939). The persecutions are dealt with in Patrick J. Healy, *The Valerian Persecution* (1905). □

Paul Ambroise Valéry

Paul Ambroise Valéry (1871-1945), often regarded as the greatest French poet of the 20th century, was Mallarmé's successor in the hermetic and intellectual tradition and the challenger of all advocates of spontaneity, inspiration, or sentimental effusiveness in poetry.

Paul Valéry was born in Sète, on the Mediterranean, on Oct. 30, 1871, of a French father of Corsican descent and an Italian mother. As a boy, looking out over the sea, he dreamed of becoming a ship captain. But he was too deficient in mathematics to qualify for the Naval Academy, so after attending the lycée at Montpellier, where his father had moved, he went to the University of Montpellier as a student of law. Literature, however, interested him more than jurisprudence. In 1890 he met Pierre Louÿs and André Gide, who spoke to Valéry about the literary life of Paris.

Symbolism was the fashion of the day, and the young provincial, who had been writing verse with increasing zeal for the past 5 years, was eager to make contact with the capital. He sent two of his poems to Stéphane Mallarmé, who praised them, and during the next 2 years Valéry published a number of poems in avant-garde magazines. Then, in the course of a night of violent lightning and thunder in the fall of 1892 while visiting relatives in Genoa, the promising young poet had a psychological experience that reoriented his life. For reasons not entirely clear, Valéry came out of this crisis with the decision to dedicate himself solely to the pursuit of knowledge. He went to Paris and, in a bare hotel room, spent his days studying and meditating problems of mathematics and psychology.

However, if Valéry had renounced poetry, he had not renounced the company of poets. Gide, Louÿs, and Henri de Régnier visited him, and he went to the Rue de Rome on Tuesdays, when Mallarmé received. Nor had Valéry, during what is referred to as his period of great silence, renounced all writing. In 1894 he began *La Soirée avec M. Teste* (*The Evening with Monsieur Teste*), a strange account of a man who strives to live by intellect alone. In 1895 the *Introduction to the Method of Leonardo da Vinci,* which posited an ideal of intellectual and creative ability, appeared. He had also made the first entries in the notebooks in which for 50 years he set down his reflections. However, he published no new verse.

The question of gainful employment was settled provisionally by an appointment in the War Department. The job did not please Valéry, and in 1900, the year of his marriage, he gave it up for a position as private secretary to an administrator of the Havas newspaper agency. For the next 20 years Valéry spent 3 or 4 hours a day in this service, an employment that assured him a livelihood yet left him adequate leisure for his own work. He occupied the early years of the century with his family (he had a son and a daughter), with his friends, and with the social and cultural events of the capital.

In 1912, at Gide's urging, Valéry assembled some of his old poetry for publication. It needed a little touching up, he decided, and in so doing he found himself once more composing verse. *La Jeune Parque* (*The Young Fate*) began as an exercise. When all of its 500 verses had been written and the work presented to the literate of Paris (1917), the acclaim was unanimous.

In the postwar period Valéry published poetry and essays and gave speeches. As usual, he attended plays, recitals, and dinner parties. The pattern of his life was fixed. He complained about his social chores and his health and worried about money, but he could not complain about lack of recognition. In France and abroad he was received everywhere as one of the greatest men of letters. He was made a member of the French Academy in 1925 and appointed to a chair of poetry at the Collège de France. During World War II, in spite of discouragement and privation, he carried on his duties much as before. He died in Paris on July 20, 1945, and was given a state funeral.

Although Valéry differs from Henri Bergson in many respects, he resembles the philosopher in being more interested in how the mind arrives at its goal than in the goal itself. All his studies of mathematics, philosophy, psychology, art, architecture, literature, and the dance were for the purpose of understanding the mind at work. He often felt that his quest was futile and that to renounce accomplishment or action for knowledge was a wrong choice. The question of doing versus knowing was for Valéry a lifelong preoccupation: it is a major theme in his writing; it was a major factor in his long silence; and it is really the key to his psychology as an artist and as a man. Valéry prepared 250 drafts of *The Young Fate*. He believed that vigor, precision, and cool skill created a poem, not inspiration.

Other works by Valéry are *Le Cimetière marin* (1920; *The Graveyard by the Sea*), which offers a good example of his poetics; *Odes* (1920); *Album de vers anciens* (1920); and *Charmes* (1922). His prose works include five collections of essays, all entitled *Variété* (1924-1944; *Variety*).

Further Reading

Excerpts from Valéry's *Notebooks* are in *The Collected Works of Paul Valéry,* edited by Jackson Mathews (1956-1975). Henry A. Grubbs, *Paul Valéry* (1968), provides an excellent discussion of the poet's life and work together with a critical bibliography. Other recommended studies are Elizabeth Sewall, *Paul Valéry: The Mind in the Mirror* (1952); Jean Hytier, *The Poetics of Paul Valéry* (1953; trans. 1966); and Norman Suckling, *Paul Valéry and the Civilized Mind* (1954). □

Lorenzo Valla

The textual criticism of the Italian humanist Lorenzo Valla (ca. 1407-1457) provided methods and inspiration for the reappraisal of Europe's historical and religious scholarship during the Renaissance.

Born in Rome and educated there before adopting, at Florence and elsewhere, the itinerant life common among contemporary scholars, Lorenzo Valla mastered ancient Greek and Ciceronian Latin. Appointed to a chair of rhetoric at the University of Pavia in 1431, he denounced the law faculty's jurisprudence because of its medieval foundations, and he became a champion of classical scholarship based on grammar and philology.

The dispute forced Valla from Pavia in 1433, but his reputation as a man of letters and as a bold, irascible polemicist commended him to rulers who sought the adornment of scholar-publicists for their courts. His first settled connection (1435-1448) was in Naples with King Alfonso V of Aragon, Sicily, and Naples, whose campaign to wrest southern Italy from other rulers, including the Pope, occasioned Valla's most notorious tract. Issued in 1440, *De falso credita et ementita Constantini donatione declamatio* proved, through internal contradictions and anachronisms, the forged origins of the Donation of Constantine, the docu-

ment traditionally claimed as justification for the papacy's temporal authority in Latin Christendom.

Valla wrote extensively about philosophy and language in the 1430s and 1440s. He urged that man cultivate both his appetitive and rational capacities as gifts derived from God's wisdom and divinity. He also attacked the constraints on the expansion of knowledge about man and nature imposed by scholastic thinkers through their emphasis on formal logic and theological propositions. To reinforce his criticisms of Stoic and monkish asceticism and Aristotelian logic, Valla produced in 1444 his most widely used work, *De elegantia linguae Latinae,* a comprehensive guide to Latin usage. It flowed naturally from his previous writing, crystallizing his humanist belief that the perfected study of language could restore the full historical significance of words as guides to thought and as vehicles for shared human discourse. In this way the past might be illumined and the human condition enriched.

Like *De falso,* which required Alfonso's help against the Inquisition, Valla's speculative works were alleged to be pagan or heretical, and his writings endangered him until his reconciliation with the Church in 1448. He then returned to Rome as secretary to Pope Nicholas V, the first papal advocate of the humanists' endeavors. There Valla taught, translated Greek authors into Latin, and applied his philological craft to the standard Latin Vulgate translation of the Bible from Greek. The resulting *Annotationes* on the New Testament indirectly became his most influential work. In 1505 Erasmus discovered a manuscript version of it, and it then formed the critical model for Erasmus's translation, which printing presses quickly spread throughout Europe.

Valla promoted celebrated literary squabbles to the end of his life. Erasmus acknowledged Valla's pioneer scholarship; early Protestants acclaimed his blunt attacks on the medieval Church's legacy. He stood out among humanists and merits lasting attention for his scrutiny of "authoritative" texts. He measured knowledge, both secular and religious, against the standards of classical achievement and examined the contexts for their development through the ages.

Further Reading

Christopher B. Coleman, ed. and trans., provides parallel Latin-English texts in *The Treatise of Lorenzo Valla on the Donation of Constantine* (1922). Only fragmentary scholarship on Valla now exists in English. On his philosophy see Paul O. Kristeller, *Eight Philosophers of the Italian Renaissance* (1964), and C. Trinkaus's commentary and brief translation in Ernst Cassirer and others, eds., *The Renaissance Philosophy of Man* (1948; 2d ed. 1963). □

Clement Laird Vallandigham

Clement Laird Vallandigham (1820-1871), American politician, was the foremost Peace Democrat during the Civil War. Though he sought to end the conflict

and reunite the Union, he unintentionally aided the war effort by becoming a symbol of treasonous activity.

Clement Vallandigham was born in New Lisbon, Ohio, on July 29, 1820. He attended Jefferson College in Canonsburg, Pa., and then studied and practiced law. In 1845 he was elected as a Democrat to the Ohio Legislature, where he was a proponent of limited government and noninterference with slavery. Elected to the U.S. Congress in 1856, he became noted for his harsh denunciations of the Republican party's antislavery stance. He strongly backed compromise with the South during the secession crisis of 1860-1861.

When the Southern Democrats left the party in 1861, and with the death of Stephen A. Douglas, Vallandigham became a major Democratic spokesman in Congress. Even after the Civil War erupted, he believed that the Union could be peacefully restored if only the Democrats were returned to power, stopped the war, and promised to uphold states' rights. He bitterly attacked Republican attempts to broaden the war's aims. The Republicans violently assailed him as the leader of the Copperheads—that is, "traitors" conspiring toward a Southern victory.

In 1862 the Republican legislature gerrymandered Vallandigham's district and defeated him for reelection. No longer in Congress, he continued publicly opposing the war. In 1863 he was arrested on orders of Gen. Ambrose

Burnside and charged with expressing disloyal sentiments. A military commission quickly tried him and sentenced him to prison. President Lincoln, embarrassed but not wishing to undermine the general's authority, banished Vallandigham to the Confederacy. Protesting his innocence, Vallandigham went to Canada.

In 1863 Ohio Democrats nominated Vallandigham for governor in absentia, calling him a martyr to arbitrary authority unleashed by the unconstitutional and revolutionary war. In the ensuing campaign the Republicans used the treason issue and overwhelmingly defeated Vallandigham. He returned to the United States in 1864 and was instrumental in placing a peace plank in the Democratic national platform in 1864.

After the war Vallandigham returned to law. He attended the National Union Convention in 1866, designed to create an intersectional conservative party of Democrats and Republicans to counter Radical Republican policies. In 1868 he ran again for Congress but was defeated. In 1871 he urged the Democrats to take a new tack, forget war issues, and seek new programs to win popular support. On June 17 he died while demonstrating to a jury in Hamilton, Ohio, how an alleged murder victim had shot himself.

Further Reading

A highly sympathetic biography of Vallandigham is by his brother, James L. Vallandigham, *A Life of Clement L. Vallandigham* (1872). This has been superseded by Frank L. Klement, *The Limits of Dissent: Clement L. Vallandigham and the Civil War* (1970). An excellent, authoritative sketch of his life is in Kenneth W. Wheeler, ed., *For the Union: Ohio Leaders in the Civil War* (1968). Frank L. Klement, *The Copperheads in the Middle West* (1960), places Vallandigham's actions in their political context. □

Ramón Maria del Valle Inclán

The Spanish novelist, playwright, and poet Ramón Maria del Valle Inclán (ca. 1866-1936) was a member of the Generation of '98. Foreign literary trends deeply influenced his work, and he was especially indebted to the modernist movement.

Ramón del Valle Inclán was born in Puebla de Caramiñál in the northwestern part of Spain. His elegant, aristocratic, and majestic demeanor was certainly not typically Galician. He loved the fabulous and the mysterious: he grew a beard and long hair to lend an air of mystery and legend to his personality. He often wore a black bell-like cloak and black hat. He lost his left arm during an altercation in Madrid in 1899. Valle inclán became well known in the literary circles of Madrid and Rome, in which cities he resided. He had studied at the University of Santiago de Compostela, and he died in this town in 1936 just before the outbreak of the Spanish Civil

War. He had held several official positions under the Spanish Republic.

Valle Inclán produced poetry, plays, and novels. His symbolist verse includes *Aromas de leyenda* (1907) and *La pipa de Kif* (1919). His plays include *Aguila de blasón* (1907) and *Cara de plata* (1922), both in prose. *Cuento de abril* (1910) and *La marquesa Rosalinda* (1913) were in verse. *La cabeza del dragón* (1914) was one of his most successful dramas. He achieved renown, however, as a novelist. He used himself as the model for the libertine hero of his *Sonatas* (1902-1905). This four-part series, which represents the seasons of the year and corresponding stages of man, was translated into English as *The Pleasant Memoirs of the Marquis de Bradomin* (1924). *Flor de Santidad* (1904) pictures Galician life, and *Los cruzados de la causa* (1908) deals with the Carlist War. His later novels included *Divinas palabras* (1920), which evoked his Galician background; *Luces de Bohemia* (1924), dealing with the life of bohemians; *Tirano Banderas* (1926), set in a Latin American republic; and *La corte de los milagros* (1927).

Perhaps in the *Sonatas* Valle Inclán best revealed his art and personal style: poetical, evocative, and delightful. A dreamy and nostalgic world of perfumes and fantasies fused in these novels with the story of the hero's many loves. Tone and style interested Valle Inclán most, not content; he absorbed other writers' material and style but imprinted on his own works his special musical, elegant, and quasi-romantic style. He was above all a poet even when writing prose, and some critics consider him the leading novelist of the Spanish modernist movement.

Further Reading

The reader should consult Aubrey F. G. Bell, *Contemporary Spanish Literature* (1925; rev. ed. 1933), and the equally excellent treatment of Valle Inclán in L. A. Warren, *Modern Spanish Literature,* vol. 1 (1929). For a Spaniard's eulogistic view see Salvador de Madariaga, *The Genius of Spain* (1923), and also the more recent book by Richard E. Chandler and Kessel Schwartz, *A New History of Spanish Literature* (1961). ☐

César Abraham Vallejo

César Abraham Vallejo (1892-1938), frequently characterized as one of Peru's best 20th-century poets, is chiefly distinguished by his use of regional themes and characters.

César Vallejo was the eleventh and last child of a lower-middle-class *mestizo family* of north-central Peru. He was born in the mountain community of Santiago de Chuco on March 16, 1892, and received his elementary education there. He then managed to attend the regional university at Trujillo and obtained his degree in 1915. He remained in Trujillo until 1918, employed in the local schools.

Vallejo had, by the beginning of his university studies, begun to write, finding an outlet for his poems in the local newspapers; and then, with a more established reputation, he was able to find acceptance in journals that had a wider circulation. As a writer of promise, he became a member of a local literary-intellectual circle. Although its members were most interested in literary affairs, meeting twice weekly to read their own poetry or to study the writings of such currently important authors as Rubén Dario, Amado Nervo, Walt Whitman, and Maurice Maeterlinck, they also were deeply involved in sociopolitical schemes for reform. These were certainly the interests of such a member as the political philosopher Victor Raúl Haya de la Torre, the founder of APRA (American Popular Revolutionary Alliance). Thus, even at that early point, Vallejo's interests were in social reform, as well as in poetic expression.

In 1918, the year Vallejo left Trujillo for the broader horizons of Lima, he published his first collection of poems, *Los heraldos negros* (*The Black Heralds*). The themes were of the daily lives of the Peruvians of his region and class, their joys, their loves, their sufferings at the hands of a fate they could neither influence nor control. But if the themes were local and national, the poems were more cosmopolitan, showing so much the influence of the modernists and others that one critic said that the poems were, like the author, "*mestizo,*" to show their mixed European-Amerindian character.

During 1919 Vallejo was associated with the short-lived but significant review *Nuestra epoca*. Although the magazine was a financial failure, its editors had, by the end of 1919, attracted so much attention because of their reformist zeal that most of them were forced into exile, the more prominent to Europe. Vallejo returned to Santiago de Chuco but was soon thrown into prison on trumped-up charges; and though he was never brought to trial, he remained imprisoned in his hometown and in Trujillo for several months. Those days in prison had a profound effect upon him. Before imprisonment his identification with reform and revolution had been largely theoretical and nominal; thereafter, it was actual and immediate.

As Vallejo's dedication to social change became more pronounced, his zeal for new poetic forms also intensified; thus his second volume of poems, *Trilce,* published in 1922, was, in effect, an act of literary violence. Its emphasis was upon freedom, not just freedom from any confines of meter or rhyming patterns but total freedom—to invent new words, create new grammatical constructions, to defy all rules, to disavow allegiance to all schools or styles. At its worst this seemed mere capriciousness; at its best, genuine creativity. This was Vallejo's best book and ended, for many years, his poetic efforts.

In mid-1923 Vallejo left Peru and moved on to Europe—first to Paris and then, in 1928, to Madrid. He never returned to Peru. Eking out an existence by doing literary hackwork, he mostly devoted himself to political affairs, becoming a Communist party militant. He turned his literary talents to the production of propaganda, extolling the glories of the day to come, after the revolution had occurred.

His novel, *Tungsten,* which was published in 1931, was an example of this kind of writing.

With the beginning of the Spanish Civil War, however, Vallejo once again turned to poetry, though he died before the publication (1939) of *Poemas humanas* (*Human Poems*). With these, he had returned to his earlier themes and modes, stressing the sorrows and hardships of the poor of his native land though implying a greater hope for a new day for all.

Further Reading

There is no biography of Vallejo in English. Some biographical information is in Angel Flores, ed., *The Literature of Spanish America,* vol. 4 (1967). For background see Enrique Anderson Imbert, *Spanish-American Literature* (trans. 1963). □

Sir John Vanbrugh

Sir John Vanbrugh (1664-1726), English architect and dramatist, was one of the leading figures of the English baroque movement. He designed a series of remarkable country houses.

John Vanbrugh was born in London and christened on Jan. 24, 1664. His father was Giles van Brugge, the son of a Protestant merchant from Ghent who had fled to England to escape Catholic persecution. Vanbrugh studied the arts in France (1683-1685). In 1686 he obtained a commission in a foot regiment, but he soon resigned. While traveling in France he was imprisoned by the French as a spy for nearly 2 years.

During his imprisonment Vanbrugh occupied himself in writing plays, and in 1696 he produced a highly successful comedy, *The Relapse; or, Virtue in Danger.* Its sequel, *The Provok'd Wife,* although strongly criticized for its immorality, was another triumph. Other plays followed in 1702, 1704, and 1705, but they were mostly translations or adaptations and added little to his reputation. His chief gifts were naturalness of dialogue and genial, lively humor, which, although broad, was not as coarse as the writing of many of his contemporaries.

Castle Howard

Vanbrugh's genius was suddenly, in the words of Jonathan Swift, "without thought or lecture . . . hugely turned to architecture," when in 1699 he began designing Castle Howard, Yorkshire, for the Earl of Carlisle. The following year the earl secured for him the post of comptroller of the royal works. The building of Castle Howard began in 1701, with Nicholas Hawksmoor as Vanbrugh's principal assistant. Castle Howard with its diversified baroque outline and its elegant Corinthian details is perhaps the most beautiful of Vanbrugh's works. Less successful was the Opera House he built in the Hay-market, in which he produced his play *The Confederacy* in 1705.

Blenheim Palace

In 1703 Vanbrugh was appointed commissioner at Greenwich Hospital, where Hawksmoor carried out Vanbrugh's plans for completing the Great Hall and for building the King William block. (Vanbrugh succeeded to the surveyorship of the hospital in 1716.) In 1704 the Duke of Marlborough selected Vanbrugh to build Blenheim Palace, which was intended as a royal gift to the victor in the wars against Louis XIV. No proper contracts were entered into between Queen Anne and Vanbrugh; and although generous grants were made at first from the Treasury, these ceased after a while and Vanbrugh was forced to depend upon the duke, who "naturally resisted the notion of having to pay for his own reward." Moreover, Vanbrugh fell into disgrace with Sarah, the tempestuous Duchess of Marlborough, who accused him of extravagance in building a house for which she had no liking. Her willfulness and antagonism reached their climax when Sir John and Lady Vanbrugh brought Lord and Lady Carlisle and their friends to see the completed palace and were refused admission.

Blenheim Palace, "an English Versailles" with its overwhelming masses of buildings, marks at once the climax of English baroque and its downfall, for Vanbrugh's style was so highly personal that an achievement of such magnitude in so individualistic a manner could hardly be matched by others. The way was clear for the Burlingtonian revival of Palladianism, with its strict adherence to rule.

The extent to which Vanbrugh was indebted to Hawksmoor in designing Castle Howard and Blenheim has been strongly debated, especially as Vanbrugh left few drawings that can confidently be ascribed to him. What is beyond question is that the partnership was eminently harmonious and successful. Vanbrugh's genius lay chiefly in the spectacular conceptions embodied in his works and in the dramatic disposition of the principal masses of his buildings. Hawksmoor exercised no less genius in handling masses and possessed great knowledge of decorative features and details.

Other Works

At Seaton Delaval, Northumberland (1720-1728; interior gutted by fire, 1822), Vanbrugh displayed his dramatic talents no less intensely than at Blenheim, although on a smaller scale. Other important works of Vanbrugh were King's Weston, Gloucestershire (1711-1714); Claremont, Surrey (ca. 1715-1720; demolished); garden buildings at Stowe (ca. 1720-1725); Eastbury, Dorset (1718); and Grimsthorpe Castle, Lincolnshire (1723).

Vanbrugh was a handsome, witty, and popular member of society. He was married in 1719, at the age of 55, and lived happily, apart from the early death of his two sons. He died on March 26, 1726, in his own dwelling, Goose-pie House (destroyed), in Whitehall. The popular conception of his grand works was summed up in his epitaph: "Lie heavy on him, Earth, for he laid many heavy loads on thee!"

Further Reading

The Complete Works of Sir John Vanbrugh was published in four volumes in 1928. For selected plays by Vanbrugh see A. E. H. Swain, ed., *Sir John Vanbrugh* (1949). The principal studies of Vanbrugh's life and work are Lawrence Whistler, *Sir John Vanbrugh: Architect and Dramatist* (1938) and *The Imagination of Vanbrugh and His Fellow Artists* (1954). For the work of Vanbrugh's associates in the English baroque movement see John Summerson, *Architecture in Britain, 1530-1830* (1953; 5th rev. ed. 1969).

Additional Sources

Anthony, John, *Vanbrugh: an illustrated life of Sir John Vanbrugh 1664-1726,* Aylesbury: Shire, 1977.

Bingham, Madeleine, Baroness Clanmorris, *Masks and facades: Sir John Vanbrugh: the man in his setting,* London: Allen & Unwin, 1974.

Downes, Kerry, *Sir John Vanbrugh: a biography,* New York: St. Martin's Press, 1987.

Downes, Kerry, *Vanbrugh,* London: A. Zwemmer, 1977.

Whistler, Laurence, *Sir John Vanbrugh, architect & dramatist, 1664-1726,* Millwood, N.Y.: Kraus Reprint Co., 1978. □

Martin Van Buren

Martin Van Buren (1782-1862), eighth president of the United States, has been called the first national politician. He built an alliance between the "plain Republicans of the North" and the planters of the South and then launched the first truly national party.

Martin Van Buren executed with distinction the duties of many of the highest offices of the nation, including that of president, but he was always regarded more as a politician than a statesman. Considered a shrewd manipulator, he was consistent in advocating the principles of Jeffersonian Republicanism as defined in the Jacksonian democracy.

Born on Dec. 5, 1782, in the village of Kinderhook, N.Y., Van Buren was the son of a farmer and tavern keeper who was active in Antifederalist politics. Martin worked on the farm and attended local schools. At the age of 14 he became a clerk in a law office in Kinderhook and then in an office in New York City. Beginning in 1803, he prospered in law practice in Kinderhook with his half brother. In 1807 he married Hannah Hoes, and they had four sons. His wife died in 1819, and he never remarried.

Political Career

Van Buren was elected to the New York Senate in 1813 and 2 years later became attorney general. By the early 1820s he was leader of the organization that controlled government in New York for many years. He advocated moderate reforms in extending democracy. In 1821 he supported the virtual elimination of the property qualification for white manhood suffrage, but also the provision by which only black Americans who possessed freeholds of the clear value of $150 could vote.

In 1821 Van Buren was elected to the U.S. Senate and became a leader there. He supported Andrew Jackson in

1828 and resigned the governorship of New York to become Jackson's secretary of state. In that office Van Buren reached agreement with Great Britain, opening up its West Indian possessions to American trade, and secured payment from France for commercial injuries during the Napoleonic Wars.

In 1831 Van Buren resigned his office to allow the President to reconstitute the Cabinet. He was named minister to Great Britain, but this was not confirmed by the Senate. In 1832 he was elected vice president, and during the following 4 years he supported Jackson in all of his battles. In 1836 he received his party's nomination for president and was elected easily.

The President

In his inaugural address Van Buren observed that he was the first president who had not lived through the revolutionary struggle that created the nation and that he could not "expect his countrymen to weigh my actions with the same kind and partial hand." They did not. He condemned abolitionist propaganda and spoke against the "slightest interference" with slavery "in the states where it exists." In rhetoric common during those years, he said that Americans were without parallel throughout the world "in all the attributes of a great, happy, and flourishing people." Two months after his inauguration, however, a serious economic depression destroyed his popularity. He continued Jacksonian policies, trying to "mitigate the evils" which the banks produced and advocating an independent treasury for public funds, a measure enacted near the end of his term. In foreign affairs he had difficulty maintaining good relations with Great Britain because of the efforts of some Americans on the New York border to support the rebellion in Canada in 1837. He made no effort to annex Texas.

Van Buren was badly beaten in 1840 by the aging William Henry Harrison and retired to his farm at Kinderhook. Van Buren would undoubtedly have been the Democratic nominee in 1844 had not Texas become the dominant issue by that year. In the atmosphere of "manifest destiny" his views were not sufficiently expansionist, and although he had a majority of the votes at the party convention, he lacked the two-thirds required. The dark horse, James K. Polk, was nominated and elected, and he led the nation into aggressive war and territorial expansion.

Free Soil Party

Increasing Southern domination of the Democratic party drove Van Buren and his faction into opposition in 1848. In that year's election he was the candidate of the Free Soil party, opposing expansion of slavery. In New York, Massachusetts, and New Hampshire he received more votes than the Democratic candidate, but he carried no states and Zachary Taylor won the election for the Whigs.

Van Buren lost the support of the antislavery movement when he returned to the Democratic party in the 1850s. Without much enthusiasm he supported Franklin Pierce (1852), James Buchanan (1856), and Stephen A. Douglas (1860). But when the Civil War came, he supported Abraham Lincoln's government. Van Buren died on July 24, 1862.

Van Buren's remarkable political success was due to a combination of talents. He habitually thought in terms of political forces and was fertile in conceiving, and able in executing, plans to weaken the opposition and advance his own party. He wrote persuasively and was a good speaker. He was charming, cheerful, and always courteous and affable. Although an earnest advocate of his party's principles, he was essentially a moderate in government. On all the important issues of his time except the one which was most crucial, Van Buren played an important role; he vacillated on issues related to slavery and made no contribution toward resolving that problem.

Further Reading

Van Buren's *Autobiography,* edited by his sons, was republished in 1969. George Bancroft, historian and contemporary Democratic politician, wrote a laudatory life of Van Buren in the early 1840s that was published half a century later: *Martin Van Buren to the End of His Public Career* (1889). The best life is Edward M. Shepard, *Martin Van Buren* (1888; rev. ed. 1900), although written without some materials now available and occasionally dogmatic in its interpretations. There is no satisfactory modern biography.

An excellent scholarly monograph that critically assesses Van Buren's overall performance as president is James C. Curtis, *The Fox at Bay: Martin Van Buren and the Presidency, 1837-1841* (1970). Robert V. Remini, who wrote a good study of Van Buren's career during the 1820s—*Martin Van Buren and the Making of the Democratic Party* (1959)—is at work on a comprehensive biography. Van Buren's election to the presidency is detailed in Arthur M. Schlesinger, Jr., ed., *History of American Presidential Elections* (4 vols., 1971). □

Cyrus R. Vance

Cyrus R. Vance (born 1917) was Secretary of the Army (1962-1964), Deputy Secretary of Defense (1964-1967), and Secretary of State (1977-1980). He was instrumental in the SALT II talks and the Camp David Accords. Since leaving public office, he has continued to act as negotiator in both the private and public sectors.

Cyrus Vance was born in Clarksburg, West Virginia, on March 27, 1917 to John Carl Vance and Amy Roberts Vance. Vance, his mother and father, and an older brother moved to New York City, where his father died suddenly from pneumonia when Vance was five years old. After a year in which the bereaved family resided in Europe, the Vances returned to New York City. One of the major influences in Cyrus Vance's years of youth following his father's death was an uncle, John W. Davis, the unsuccessful Democratic Party candidate for president in 1924. Davis was a highly successful attorney (he argued 141 cases before the Supreme Court—more than any other lawyer of his time) and spent time discussing issues and ideas with young Cyrus. During this time Vance was introduced to an attorney's approach to problem solving and instilled with an interest in the law.

Education and Early Career

Vance went to Kent School, a religious affiliated preparatory school in Connecticut. Following graduation he entered Yale University, majoring in economics. It was while at Yale that he met Grace (Gay) Sloan, a student at the Parsons School of Design who was to become his wife; married in 1947, they have five children. He graduated from Yale Law School in 1942 and entered the navy and served as an officer on destroyers in the Pacific. Following his service in World War II, Vance returned to New York and joined the prestigious law firm of Simpson, Thacher and Bartlett in 1947.

Vance Goes to Washington

Vance's first opportunity to work in Washington was in 1957 when a senior partner in the law firm asked Vance to accompany him to help organize an investigation by a Senate preparedness subcommittee on military and space programs, where Vance met Lyndon Johnson. Subsequently, Vance served in a succession of positions in the Kennedy and Johnson administrations. He was general counsel of the Department of Defense (1961-1962), Secretary of the Army (1962-1964), and Deputy Secretary of Defense under Robert McNamara (1964-1967). He also served as a special representative of the president during the crisis in Cyprus following the Turkish invasion and takeover of that island's

government (1962) and was a negotiator for the United States at the Paris Peace Conference on Vietnam (1968-1969). He was appointed as President Jimmy Carter's first Secretary of State in 1977 and served in that capacity until his resignation in 1980.

Vance Serves as Secretary of State

Cyrus R. Vance served as Secretary of State for most of the administration of President Jimmy Carter. Noted as a liberal and hailed as one who favored diplomacy rather than military threats of force, Vance became known and respected for his negotiating skills and his ability to maintain a sense of calm while under stress. His many accomplishments as secretary of state were somewhat overshadowed by the capture in Iran of United States embassy personnel who were held hostage during the last year of Carter's administration.

Vance's accomplishments during his tenure as secretary of state were numerous. He completed negotiations with the Soviet Union on the Strategic Arms Limitations Talks (SALT) II. After a cooling of relations between the United States and the Soviet Union, Vance met the Soviet leaders to break through the resistance to discussing arms limitations. The negotiations were long and arduous but resulted in the signing of an agreement between President Carter and Soviet Premier Brezhnev. The Carter administration encountered difficulties back home, however, as the Senate refused to ratify the treaty, leaving Carter and Vance greatly frustrated. Carter ultimately asked the Senate to defer action on the treaty following the Soviet Union's invasion of Afghanistan as he realized it was not likely that the necessary two-thirds of the Senate would vote for approval.

The first year of the Carter presidency saw the conclusion of a new Panama Canal treaty. Described by some as the most divisive foreign policy issue in the United States following the Vietnam War, the agreements were finally signed in Washington in September 1977. The negotiated agreements ultimately allowed for the control of the Panama Canal by Panama by the year 2000. While the control would remain with Panama, the Carter administration needed to assure domestic critics that the treaties did not foreclose for the United States an opportunity to ensure passage through the canal. Vance insured that both United States and Panamanian warships could "transit" the canal in case of emergency ahead of all other vessels—thus allowing the United States the opportunity to protect the canal.

Camp David Accords

A major foreign policy achievement during this period was the development of a framework for settling the disputes among the Middle-Eastern nations of Egypt and Israel, known as the Camp David Accords. The discussions leading to the agreement among the two nations and the United States to settle long-standing differences in order to preserve peace in the Middle East involved Israeli Prime Minister Menahem Begin, Egyptian President Anwar Sadat, and United States President Jimmy Carter. The negotiations, in which Vance was instrumental, lasted two weeks and took place in the unique environment of the presidential retreat at Camp David, Maryland. Two agreements were signed by the participants. The first allowed the return of the Sinai peninsula (occupied by Israel following the Six Day War between the two countries in 1967) to Egypt, the conclusion of a peace treaty, and the "normalization" of diplomatic relations between the two countries. The second agreement resulting from the Camp David summit provided for negotiations among Egypt, Jordan, Israel, and Palestinian representatives to iron out differences concerning the West Bank and Gaza Strip territories.

While Vance's negotiating skills were highly regarded—and he was able to use them in collaboration with Great Britain to settle the racial and political disputes in Rhodesia (now Zimbabwe)—Vance's influence over foreign policy slowly declined over the course of the Carter administration. The passing of the period of "detente" was aggravated by the Soviet invasion of Afghanistan.

Hostage Crisis in Teheran

The foreign relations of the United States during the last year of the Carter administration became overshadowed by the fall of the shah of Iran and the capture of the U.S. embassy personnel in Teheran by Iranian militants on November 4, 1979. The United States attempted several strategies to accomplish the release of the embassy personnel (including the freezing of all Iranian assets in the United States), but all early attempts were to no avail. A debate ensued within the White House as to the appropriateness of a rescue mission. Vance argued strenuously against the strategy, but his position did not prevail. On April 24-25, 1980, the United States tried but failed in a rescue attempt. Eight U.S. servicemen were killed when a rescue aircraft crashed and burned on take off. Vance submitted his resignation in protest on April 28, 1980. It was not until inauguration day 1981, while Carter was passing the reigns of leadership to his successor, Ronald Reagan, that the American hostages were finally released after 444 days of imprisonment.

United Nations Negotiator

In 1980, Vance returned to the private sector as a partner at his old law firm, Simpson, Thacher, and Bartlett. Since the mid-1980's, Vance has been called on numerous times by the United Nations to negotiate around the world including Burundi, South Africa, Macedonia and Greece, Armenia and Azerbaijan, and South Africa. His highest profile UN negotiations have been in Bosnia and Herzegovina, co-chaired with David Owen of Great Britain. Since 1992, he has helped negotiate such important steps as opening a road between Zagreb and Belgrade, a demilitarized zone on the Prevlaka Peninsula, numerous cease-fire agreements, and several peace plans. He is credited with bringing about the tenuous peace in the area. His UN work has often brought him under fire, but he continues to maintain a low profile, giving few interviews and writing a few pieces for publications like *Vanity Fair* and *The New York Times*. Vance also headed up high-profile private negotiations like the bankruptcy and reorganization of the R.H.

Macy department stores and Olympia and York Companies. He has co-authored pieces with his predecessor, Henry Kissinger to comment on world events.

Further Reading

The memoirs of Cyrus Vance are published in *Hard Choices: Critical Years in America's Foreign Policy* (1983). Vance has also written: *Common Security: A Blueprint for Survival* (1982) and *Building the Peace: US Foreign Policy for the Next Decade (Alternatives for the 1980's)* (1982). Davis S. McLellan has published a biography of Vance: *Cyrus Vance* (1985). One may also consult Zbigniew Brzezinski's memoirs, *Power and Principle: Memoirs of the National Security Advisor, 1977-1980* (1983). □

Zebulon Baird Vance

Zebulon Baird Vance (1830-1894), U.S. senator and congressman, was Civil War governor of North Carolina. He is best known for his concern for the common Southerner and his noncooperation with Confederate authorities.

Zebulon Vance was born on May 13, 1830, in Buncombe County, N.C. He attended Washington College, Tenn. (1843-1844), and studied law at the University of North Carolina (1851-1852). After settling in Asheville, N.C., he was immediately elected county solicitor. Never a close student of the law, he won success at the bar because he understood his neighbors, who composed the juries.

After one term in the North Carolina House of Commons, Vance was elected to the U.S. Congress in 1858, where he served until March 1861. He had conservative views on the tariff, public lands, and pensions and opposed the secessionist sentiment then prevalent in the South. However, when the Civil War started and President Abraham Lincoln called for troops in 1861, Vance urged North Carolina to support the seceded states. He saw military action for about a year, rising to the rank of colonel in a North Carolina regiment.

In 1862 the conservative faction nominated Vance for governor of North Carolina. He won by an unprecedented large margin. The Confederate government, however, mistrusted his promises of a strong war policy, and Vance and the government were quickly embroiled in controversies over conscription, suspension of habeas corpus, desertions, and impressment of matériel. He consistently placed the interests of his state above other concerns, even providing funds to ships engaged in an extensive blockade-running enterprise supplying North Carolina troops and their families with needed articles. In 1864 Vance was reelected, defeating an avowed peace candidate.

At the end of the war Vance was imprisoned briefly. Upon his release he established a law practice in Charlotte, N.C. In 1867 he was pardoned and reentered politics as a

eorge Vancouver was born in England and at the age of 13 began his naval career as an able seaman under Capt. James Cook on the *Resolution*. He was a midshipman on Cook's famous third voyage in the *Discovery*. In 1780 Vancouver was promoted to lieutenant and served several years in the West Indies.

In 1790 Vancouver attained the rank of commander and the following year was given command of a new *Discovery*. His first assignment was to take over the Nootka Sound territory from the Spanish after an incident there had threatened war between England and Spain. After making new exploration around Australia and New Zealand and passing by Tahiti and Hawaii, Vancouver remained in the North Pacific, carrying out extensive exploratory trips from San Francisco northward, largely devoted to ascertaining the possibility of the elusive Northwest Passage. He was the first to chart accurately the large island which bears his name.

Vancouver was a rigid disciplinarian and a demanding officer. He neither sought nor received the affection of his men, but he was respected. He was equally intolerant of the often bizarre theories of European geographers. His meticulous observations and stern logic largely substantiated the claims of Cook and blasted the hopes for a passage through North America anywhere to the south of Arctic waters.

Vancouver returned to England in 1795 by way of Cape Horn and began the preparation of his journals. He had corrected all but a few pages when he died at Petersham on

Democrat. He was elected to the U.S. Senate in 1870 but resigned 2 years later amidst a controversy over the 14th Amendment. After an unsuccessful candidacy for the Senate in 1873, Vance was elected governor in 1876. His administration was marked by the encouragement of railroads, industry, and agriculture and the improvement of public schools and charitable institutions for white and black citizens of the state.

In 1879 Vance was again elected to the U.S. Senate, where he served until his death on April 14, 1894. In the Senate he expressed a devotion to the South, combined with a genuine acceptance of the war's verdict and a true loyalty to the restored Union.

Further Reading

Glenn Tucker, *Zeb Vance: Champion of Personal Freedom* (1966), is sympathetic but uneven. Richard E. Yates, *The Confederacy and Zeb Vance* (1958), is a brief study of Vance's relationship with the Confederate government. Vance also figures in Burton J. Hendrick, *Statesmen of the Lost Cause* (1939). □

George Vancouver

George Vancouver (1758-1798) was an English explorer and navigator. His most famous undertaking was his exploration of the North Pacific coast of North America.

May 10, 1798. The work was completed by his brother and published a few months after George Vancouver's death.

Further Reading

On Vancouver's career at sea, the obvious source is his own account, *A Voyage of Discovery to the North Pacific Coast,* which was published in three volumes in 1798. The best account of his life is by George Godwin, *Vancouver: A Life, 1757-1798* (1931). Two recent studies are also good: Bern Anderson, *Surveyor of the Sea: The Life and Voyages of Captain George Vancouver* (1960), and James Stirrat and Carrie Marshall, *Vancouver's Voyage* (1967), first published under the title *Adventurers in Two Hemispheres, Including Captain Vancouver's Voyage* (1955). □

Cornelius Vanderbilt

Cornelius Vanderbilt (1794-1877), American steamship and railroad builder, executive, and promoter, transferred his attention from boating to railroads in his later years. He left an estate of almost $100 million.

Cornelius Vanderbilt was born on May 27, 1794, on Staten Island, N.Y. His father, from a long line of Dutch farmers, was imaginative but unthrifty. He engaged in boating. Young Cornelius developed a great love for the water and quit school at the age of eleven to work for his father. When he turned 16, he persuaded his mother to give him $100 for a boat on condition that he plow and sow an 8-acre rocky field. This he accomplished with the aid of friends to whom he promised rides in his new boat.

Vanderbilt opened transport and freight service between New York City and Staten Island and, by the end of the first year, returned his mother's loan with an additional $1,000. He charged reasonable prices and worked prodigiously. Rough in manners, he developed a reputation for honesty. The War of 1812 created new opportunities for expansion, and Vanderbilt received a contract to supply the forts around New York. The large profits from this allowed him to build a schooner which traveled over Long Island Sound and two more vessels for the coastwise trade. By 1817 he possessed $9,000 besides his interest in the sailing vessels.

Apparently well on the way to fame and fortune, in 1818 Vanderbilt sold all his interests and turned his attention to steamboats. Observing the success of Robert Fulton and Robert R. Livingston with vessels on the Hudson River, Vanderbilt correctly chose the wave of the future. He entered the employ of Thomas Gibbons, who operated a ferry between New Brunswick, N.J., and New York City. Working for $1,000 a year, Vanderbilt made the line profitable, despite opposition from Fulton and Livingston, who claimed a legal monopoly on the Hudson River traffic. In addition, Vanderbilt's wife, whom he married in 1813, managed the New Brunswick halfway house (between New York City and Philadelphia), where all travelers on the Gibbons line had to stay.

By 1829 Vanderbilt had decided to go on his own. Over the protests of his wife and Gibbons, who offered to double his $2,000 salary and sell him half the line, Vanderbilt moved his family (which eventually included 13 children) to New York City. There he took his accumulated $30,000 and entered the competitive service between New York and Peekskill, where he had the first of several encounters with Daniel Drew. Vanderbilt won this battle by cutting rates to as low as 12½ cents, which forced Drew to withdraw. He next challenged the Hudson River Association in the Albany trade. After he again cut rates, the competition paid him a handsome sum to move his operations elsewhere. Vanderbilt opened service to Long Island Sound, Providence, Boston, and points in Connecticut. His vessels were stable craft which offered the passenger not only comfort but often luxury.

By the time he was 40, Vanderbilt's wealth exceeded $500,000, but he still looked for new fields to conquer. Hundreds of thousands of people rushed to the gold fields of California after 1849, most of them going by boat to Panama, by land across the Isthmus, onto steamers on the Pacific coast. Vanderbilt proceeded to challenge the Pacific Steamship Company by offering similar service via Nicaragua, which saved 600 miles and cut the going price by half. This move netted him over $1 million a year. He sold controlling interests to the Nicaragua Transit Company, which failed to pay him. In a famous incident, he told them that the law was too slow; rather, he would ruin them. This he did within 2 years by running another group of steamers.

Commodore Vanderbilt dabbled in the Atlantic carrying trade in the 1850s and attained a strong position but, nearing the age of 70, decided once again that the wave of the future was in another direction—the railroad. He first acquired the New York and Harlem Railroad, in the process again defeating Daniel Drew. Vanderbilt made his son, William H., the vice president, largely on the basis of prior railroad experience. The Vanderbilts next acquired control of the rundown Hudson River Railroad, which Cornelius wanted to consolidate with the Harlem. Again Drew attempted to sell the stock short, defeat the consolidation, and make a substantial profit. But, as before, the Commodore won the battle by buying every share Drew and his cohorts sold, thereby stabilizing the price.

Vanderbilt then acquired the Central Railroad (1867), merged it with the Hudson River Railroad, and leased the Harlem to the new company. After these acquisitions, Vanderbilt spent large sums of money improving the lines' efficiency and then watered the stock and paid large dividends. In the first 5 years he is said to have cleared $25 million.

The Commodore finally hit a snag in 1867, when he attempted to gain control of the Erie Railroad, then in the hands of his old adversary, Daniel Drew. Again Vanderbilt bought all the stock offered for sale, but this time, Drew, Jay Gould, and James Fisk threw 100,000 shares of fraudulent stock on the market, which the Commodore continued to buy. The trio fled to Jersey City after warrants for their arrest were issued. Vanderbilt, tottering on the brink of failure, fought back. Although the illegal stock was finally authorized by the legislature, the trio surrendered in order to return to New York. Vanderbilt lost between $1 million and $2 million and forgot the Erie. The Vanderbilts extended their lines to Chicago by acquiring the Lake Shore and Michigan Southern railroads, the Canadian Southern, and the Michigan Central.

The Commodore's first wife died in 1868, and the next year he remarried. He was never known for philanthropic activities, his only unsolicited contributions being $50,000 for the Church of the Strangers in New York City and $1 million to Central University, which then became Vanderbilt University. He died on Jan. 4, 1877.

Further Reading

There is no definitive biography of Vanderbilt. Studies include Meade Minnigerode, *Certain Rich Men* (1927); Arthur D. Howden Smith, *Commodore Vanderbilt* (1927); Wayne Andrews, *The Vanderbilt Legend* (1941); and Wheaton J. Lane, *Commodore Vanderbilt* (1942). The "Erie war" is best described in Charles F. Adams, Jr., and Henry Adams, *Chapters of Erie, and Other Essays* (1871). □

Hugo van der Goes

Hugo van der Goes (active 1467-1482) was the most powerful Flemish painter of the second half of the 15th century. His "Portinari Altarpiece" is one of the most intensely beautiful masterworks of all time.

Hugo van der Goes was greatly indebted to the artistic heritage of his predecessors Jan van Eyck and Rogier van der Weyden; yet so acute was his visual perception, so talented his draftsmanship, and so original his understanding of the problems of artistic form that his compositions anticipated many principles that came to fruition in the baroque period. Furthermore, the religious symbolism that resides, disguised, in the countless natural forms and objects in the *Portinari Altarpiece* reveals his astonishingly erudite knowledge of scholastic philosophy and mystical texts.

Van der Goes's origin and early training are unknown. He became a master in the Ghent guild of painters in 1467, the painter Justus of Ghent being one of his guarantors. Between that year and 1475 Van der Goes assisted in the decoration of Ghent and Bruges for such events as the wedding of Charles the Bold to Margaret of York. The artist was made dean of the guild in 1474. Four years later he quit Ghent, then in the throes of political upheaval, for the solace of the Red Cloister monastery near Brussels. Continuing to paint as a privileged brother, he received distinguished visitors, such as Archduke Maximilian of Austria. Returning in 1481 from a trip to Cologne, Van der Goes suffered a fit of melancholia. A fellow brother, Gaspar Ofhuys, documented the illness and recorded that the artist died in the monastery the following year.

His Works

Van der Goes never signed or dated a painting, so attributions have had to be made on the basis of the one work, the *Portinari Altarpiece,* that is authenticated (by Giorgio Vasari). Its date of about 1474-1476 has been presumed on the basis of the number and ages of the children of the donors on the wings of the triptych.

Earlier in style, and possibly Van der Goes's first known work, is the little diptych with the *Fall of Man* and the *Lamentation.* The self-consciously nude figures of Adam and Eve recall the ones on the *Ghent Altarpiece* by the Van Eyck brothers; the rhythmic composition of the distraught figures in the *Lamentation* derives from the form world of Rogier van der Weyden. Different from both is the expression of Van der Goes's personal feeling of the tragedy of the drama of the Fall and Redemption.

The huge panel *Adoration of the Magi,* the surviving central portion of the *Monforte Altarpiece,* probably dates about 1472. The concept is one of serene grandeur, with a monumental feeling that is unique in the dozen works attributable to Van der Goes. The composition is resplendent in descriptive details, superb in lighting, and rich in color.

The *Portinari Altarpiece* is a giant triptych, 18 feet across when opened. Its theme is the adoration of the newborn Child by Mary, Joseph, 3 memorably individualized shepherds, and 15 attending angels. It was commissioned by Tomasso Portinari, the representative of the Medici in Bruges. Tomasso kneels in the left wing with his sons Antonio and Pigello; in the right wing are his wife, Maria, and their daughter Margherita. Looming large behind them are their name saints: Anthony and Thomas, Margaret and Mary Magdalen. Deep within a magnificent winter landscape the procession of the Magi approaches. The *Annunciation,* in monochrome, is seen when the wings are closed. The central scene is a spectacular drama of opposites reconciled: open and closed space, large and small figures, natural and supernatural light, divine and human forms. Masterfully painted textures are subordinate to an overall feeling of heightened realism and grandeur in an intense moment of revealed Christian truth.

Van der Goes's large *Death of the Virgin* was painted in the monastery about 1481. Christ materializes in a burst of rainbow light to receive the soul of his dying mother, while the assembled Apostles press against her bed, each intensely experiencing as an individual his personal loss. There has rarely been expressed in Christian art so moving a statement of the temporal and the eternal life.

Further Reading

A study of Van der Goes is in Max J. Friedländer, *Early Netherlandish Painting,* vol. 4: *Hugo van der Goes* (1969). For an interesting essay on the nature of Van der Goes's illness see Rudolf and Margot Wittkower, *Born under Saturn* (1963). □

John Vanderlyn

John Vanderlyn (1775-1852) was one of the first American painters to venture beyond portraiture. He executed the first large-scale nude in the United States and various history paintings, some showing neoclassic influence.

John Vanderlyn was born in Kingston, N.Y., on Oct. 15, 1775. After studying painting for a year under Gilbert Stuart in Philadelphia, Vanderlyn became the protégé of Aaron Burr, who sent him to Paris in 1796. The first American painter to study in Paris, Vanderlyn entered the studio of François Antoine Vincent, a neoclassicist who emphasized correct drawing at the expense of expressive color. Vanderlyn remained in Paris until 1801, when he had to return home because of a lack of funds.

In America, Vanderlyn looked upon portraiture as a low form of art and accepted such commissions only to support himself. He executed a number of fine portraits and some views of Niagara Falls. In 1805 he returned to Europe with the financial support of the American Academy; he stayed in Rome until 1808 and then lived in Paris until 1815.

Vanderlyn's *Marius Viewing the Ruins of Carthage* (1807) won a gold medal in Paris in 1808. The scene shows the melancholy attached to time's passing, a theme that was then quite popular: Marius, the fallen hero, broods among the ruins of a once mighty city. For the head of Marius, Vanderlyn copied a Roman bust; and the figure, in proper neoclassic fashion, was done with a hard, wiry outline and ivory flesh tones. *Ariadne* (1812), combining neoclassic linearism with the Italianate qualities of recumbent Venuses of Titian and Giorgione, shows a good understanding of anatomy, but the figure stands out too strongly from the landscape.

On his return to New York, Vanderlyn soon found that Europeans appreciated him far more than his own countrymen, for portraiture was still the only kind of painting widely accepted in America. In 1816 he built a personal museum in the form of a rotunda with the help of $6,000 contributed by 112 of his supporters. There he exhibited not only his paintings and copies from the nude but an enormous canvas executed in 1818-1819: the *Palace and Gardens of Versailles.* Painted somewhat illusionistically, this is one of the several "panoramas" made in the early 19th century and the only one still existing.

Vanderlyn died in Kingston, N.Y., on Sept. 23, 1852. Because of his neoclassic training, his paintings have a coolness and detachment when compared with the more emotive work of Washington Allston.

Further Reading

The only monograph on Vanderlyn, which contains no illustrations, is Marius Schoonmaker, *John Vanderlyn, Artist, 1775-1852* (1950); it consists of brief biographical essays with quotations from Vanderlyn's correspondence, especially with Aaron Burr.

Additional Sources

Mondello, Salvatore, *The private papers of John Vanderlyn (1775-1852) American portrait painter,* Lewiston, N.Y., USA: Edwin Mellen Press, 1990. □

Johannes Diderik van der Waals

The Dutch physicist Johannes Diderik van der Waals (1837-1923) did pioneering studies on the equation of state of liquids and gases, for which he received the Nobel Prize for physics in 1910.

Johannes van der Waals was born on Nov. 23, 1837, in Leiden, the son of Jacobus van der Waals and Elizabeth van den Burg. His life is a classic illustration of the fact that lack of proper educational opportunities is not an insurmountable obstacle to greatness in science, provided one's potential is matched by one's determination. Following the completion of his elementary and secondary education, he taught elementary school in Leiden with his mind fixed on much higher goals. His thirst for knowledge had at first to be satisfied with reading in his spare time, but during the years 1862-1865 he followed courses at the University of Leiden and obtained the certification to teach mathematics and physics in high schools. In 1864 he married Anna Magdalena Smit, who soon died, leaving him with four small children.

While Van der Waals served as director of a high school in The Hague, a new law removed classical languages from the list of compulsory courses for science students at universities, and he passed in 1873 the examinations for doctor's degree in physics. His dissertation, *On the Continuity of the Gaseous and Liquid States*, revealed him at one stroke as a most original master of physics. In fact James Clerk Maxwell remarked, when he learned of the dissertation's contents, "The name of Van der Waals will soon be among the foremost in molecular science."

Van der Waals argued that R. J. E. Clausius's derivation of Robert Boyle's gas law from statistical mechanics had to be supplemented by new considerations if it was to hold for real gases and their transformation into liquids. The new consideration was the "principle of continuity," by which Van der Waals meant that from the viewpoint of statistical mechanics there could be no basic difference between the gaseous and the liquid states. In addition he noted the need for considering two factors, the volume of molecules and their mutual attraction. He succeeded in relating these two factors to the critical temperature, pressure, and volume, or the critical point. It therefore followed that the equation of state could be expressed in a form independent of any particular gas or liquid.

This in turn led to the most momentous part of Van der Waals's research, the law of corresponding states, formulated in 1880. According to it, the whole range of behavior of a substance can be predicted once its critical point has been ascertained. This result played a crucial role in the efforts leading to the liquefaction of hydrogen (1898) and of helium (1908). His other principal achievement consisted in the combination of the law of corresponding states with the second law of thermodynamics, which he outlined in 1890 in his first treatise on the theory of binary solutions.

In 1876 Van der Waals became the first professor of physics at the newly established University of Amsterdam. His son, Johannes Diderik, Jr., was the next occupant of the chair. Van der Waals died in Amsterdam on March 8, 1923.

Further Reading

Biographical information on Van der Waals and accounts of his work are in N. de V. Heathcote, *Nobel Prize Winners in Physics, 1901-1950* (1953), and Nobel Foundation, *Nobel Lectures: Physics, 1901-1921* (1967). □

James VanDer Zee

James VanDer Zee (1886-1983) created a photographic history of the people of Harlem—celebrities and ordinary people, in hope and despair—covering over 60 years.

James VanDer Zee was born in Lenox, Massachusetts, on June 29, 1886, in a four bedroom frame house built by his grandfather. His parents had moved to Lenox three years earlier from New York City, where they had worked as a maid and butler to retired President Ulysses S. Grant. James was the second of six children.

His parents earned their living in Lenox by baking, and their sons delivered the products on foot and horseback. The VanDer Zee youngsters were such excellent students that James once told a reporter that "the other kids didn't try." VanDer Zee learned photography in a front bedroom of that frame house, but he was at least 14 before he took a picture that satisfied him—one of his brother Walter's school class. Moreover, their lives were enriched by such outstanding houseguests as W. E. B. DuBois, the noted African American author and intellectual.

While excelling at the piano and violin, young Jimmy was frustrated by forced painting lessons. But when a magazine advertisement offered a camera as a premium for selling pink and yellow silk sachets to the ladies of Lenox, he leapt at the opportunity, ending up with an $8 camera that would eventually launch him on a career in which he would become one of the great photographers of the United States.

Moving to New York City after the turn of the century, James and his brother Walter joined their father, who was now working as a waiter. For 20 years VanDer Zee usually worked two jobs. Until he got his first professional photography job in a Newark, New Jersey, department store photography concession in 1913, by day he was an elevator operator or waiter; at night, he was a musician in various bands, including his own and Fletcher Henderson's.

VanDer Zee married Kate Brown in the early 1900s and moved to Phoebus, Virginia, for a year. His first child, Rachel, was born there. She died when she was 16, and a son, born when the couple returned to New York, died in infancy. Kate VanDer Zee left her husband in 1915.

Before the end of World War I VanDer Zee hung out a sign on 138th Street that announced his first studio—Guarantee Photo Studio, later changed to GGG Studio for his second wife, Gaynella.

There, in the 1920s and 1930s, he set about photographing his Harlem and making it famous. He photographed such celebrities as Bill "Bojangles" Robinson, the famous dancer; Florence Mills, the beautiful actress; Adam Clayton Powell, Sr., minister of Harlem's Abyssinian Baptist Church; writer Countee Cullen; Joe Louis; and former heavyweight champion Jack Johnson. He was the official photographer for Marcus Garvey, the charismatic African American nationalist who promoted a "Back to Africa" movement in the 1920s, snapping pictures of his elaborate parades.

He also portrayed the ordinary African American citizen on ceremonial occasions from funerals to weddings with dignity, artistry, and compassion. One picture shows an African American soldier, his chest adorned with World War I medals, gazing into a fireplace where the photographer had inserted a younger soldier and a nurse marching under an American flag.

When home cameras became popular in the 1940s—"Brownies made everybody a photographer," VanDer Zee once told an interviewer with characteristic modesty—his portrait business dwindled and he supplemented it by developing a mail order restoration and calendar picture clientele. But he continued to lovingly photograph brides, the character in the faces of such celebrities as pianist Hazel Scott, the ceremonies of the Moorish Jews, and the burgeoning manhood in the basketball team of the Alpha Phi Alpha Fraternity.

But it was only in 1969, when he was past 80, that VanDer Zee received any recognition outside of Harlem, and he was catapulted into national prominence—and, for a time, personal misfortune. In 1968, at the height of the American Black Consciousness Movement, New York's Metropolitan Museum of Art had decided to mount an exhibition called "Harlem on My Mind." In researching the exhibition, a young African American photographer named Reginald McGhee happened by VanDer Zee's Harlem studio. "I discovered a gold mine," McGhee said later. "There was a perfect record of 60 years in Harlem." VanDer Zee gave McGhee free access to the more than 100,000 photographs he had signed and dated. Providing 90 percent of the visual material for the exhibition, VanDer Zee received $3,700 from the museum for the use of his work.

In part because photography was at that time coming into recognition as a fine art and gaining the stamp of approval of collectors who purchased vintage photographs as good investments in a time of economic recession, VanDer Zee quickly became a cult figure. He began talks with McGhee about forming the James VanDer Zee Institute.

But at about the same time the aging artist was gaining new prominence, misfortune struck. He and his wife were evicted from the home and studio where he had lived for 29 years, forced to put most of the family's possessions in storage, go on public assistance, and move to a Bronx Hotel. VanDer Zee, who had developed a grandfatherly relationship with McGhee, asked him to store his work. Moreover, because of the proposed institute, VanDer Zee turned down a $175,0000 offer from Time-Life, Inc. for his collection. The institute was formed three months after VanDer Zee's eviction from his home, and despite his destitute condition, VanDer Zee allegedly signed over the rights to his work and its reproduction to the institute. But as his personal fortune continued to fall and the fledgling institute sporadically gave him only small stipends, a dispute arose between him and the institute directors, and VanDer Zee later denied that he signed over to them all his work.

Meanwhile, his reputation in the photography field continued to escalate. In 1969 the American Society of Magazine Photographers honored him and Grove Press published "The World of James VanDer Zee." Two years later he was elected a Fellow for Life at the Metropolitan Museum.

In 1976 VanDer Zee's ailing wife died, and he disappeared even further from the public limelight. A year earlier VanDer Zee had been introduced by a mutual friend to a young woman, Donna Mussenden, who later came to the drab and unkempt flat where VanDer Zee—lame, broke, and in bad health—was living. Concerned that an African American cultural giant was being neglected, she stepped in after his wife's death, cleaning up his home, organizing his files, and visiting him on a regular basis to lift his spirits. Two years later VanDer Zee married the young woman, and, in what *Ebony* magazine called "an extraordinary renaissance unprecedented in the history of American photographers," VanDer Zee resumed his career and created a new life. Crediting his wife with his resuscitation, he began once again to take photographs after a hiatus of 12 years and photographed such celebrities as comedian Bill Cosby, former heavyweight champion Muhammad Ali, and actress Cicely Tyson. Suing to regain his work, VanDer Zee successfully obtained 75 percent of his photographs, one-quarter of those to become the property of the James VanDer Zee Foundation. Although mostly confined to a wheelchair, he travelled across the country with the aid of his wife, gave lectures, had exhibitions, and made public appearances. His "The Harlem Book of the Dead" was published in 1978, and a young people's biography, "James VanDer Zee, the Picture Takin' Man," came out the following year. He received six honorary doctorates and was honored by President Jimmy Carter. VanDer Zee died in May 1983 at age 96.

Further Reading

VanDer Zee's first photos to be published were contained in *Harlem on My Mind* (1968), edited by Allan Schoener. A more comprehensive collection is in *The World of James VanDer Zee: A Visual Record of Black America* (1969), edited by Reginald McGhee. Several of VanDer Zee's photos were included in *The Black Photographer's Annual 1972* (1973). □

Henry Van de Velde

Henry van de Velde (1863-1957), Belgian painter, designer, architect, and writer, was the chief theoretician of Art Nouveau, champion of the applied arts, and prominent in developing a new architectural expression in Europe in the early 20th century.

Henry van de Velde was born on April 3, 1863, in Antwerp, the son of an apothecary. He studied painting at the Academy of Fine Arts there (1881-1884) and then with E. A. Carolus-Duran in Paris (1884-1885). In 1889 he joined a group of artists known as Les XX in Brussels and, with the publication of his lecture *Déblaiement d'art* (1894), emerged as the group's spokesman.

Influenced by the theories of William Morris and the English Arts and Crafts movement, Van de Velde abandoned painting and turned his attention to architecture and the applied arts. The building of his own house, Bloemenwerf, at Uccle near Brussels (1895) marked the beginning of his new career. For this house he designed all the furniture and appointments.

Van de Velde moved to Germany in 1900. He built the School of Applied Arts in Weimar (1904-1906), the predecessor of the Bauhaus, and was its director until World War I. He designed the Theater Building (1914; destroyed) at the exhibition of the Werkbund, or German association of architects and designers, held at Cologne. Throughout this period he was also busy designing a wide variety of useful objects, from bookbindings to earrings, dresses, ceramics, tableware, and furniture, all in the curvilinear forms of Art Nouveau, and theorizing about the role of the applied arts in a series of publications such as *Die Renaissance im modernen Kunstgewerbe* (1901), *Kunstgewerbliche Laienpredigten* (1902), and *Der neue Stil* (1907).

From 1917 on Van de Velde lived in Belgium, Holland, and Switzerland. From 1926 to 1936 he was the director of the Institute Supérieur des Arts Décoratifs in Brussels and professor of architecture at the University of Ghent, for which he designed the library (1936). Other important commissions from this period include the Kröller-Müller Museum at Otterlo, Netherlands (1937-1953), and the Belgian pavilions for the World's Fair in Paris (1937) and in New York (1939). He spent the last decade of his life in retirement at Oberägeri, Switzerland, where he wrote his memoirs. He died in Zurich on Oct. 27, 1957.

Further Reading

Van de Velde's memoirs were published in German in 1962. None of his writings has been translated. The basic studies of his life and work are in French and German. The only extensive discussion of his work in English is found in the error-riddled chapters devoted to him in Henry F. Lenning, *The Art Nouveau* (1951). His contribution to the development of 20th-century design is discussed in Nikolaus Pevsner, *Pioneers of Modern Design* (1936; rev. ed. 1960), and Peter Selz and Mildred Constantine, eds., *Art Nouveau* (1959). □

Anthony Meuza Van Diemen

Anthony Meuza Van Diemen (1593-1645) was a Dutch colonial official and merchant. As a governor general of the Dutch East Indies, he did much to develop Batavia and the Indies and to expand Dutch influence in East Asia.

Anthony Van Diemen was born at Culemborg, Netherlands. Like many patricians' sons, he was destined to be a merchant, and in 1616 he set himself up in trade in Amsterdam. A year later, as a result of

unfortunate advice, he was forced to declare bankruptcy. Unable to repay his creditors, he turned for employment to the Dutch East India Company, which turned him down as a poor risk.

Van Diemen finally succeeded in signing up as a soldier under the alias Thonisz Meeuwisz and arrived in Java in August 1618. He quickly attracted the attention of Governor General Jan Coen, who appointed him a clerk in his office. On Jan. 17, 1630, Van Diemen married Maria van Aelst in Batavia. Highly successful in his association with Coen, Van Diemen was appointed director of the commercial section of the company and in 1631 returned with the fleet to Amsterdam as admiral. In 1633 he sailed once again for the Dutch East Indies and on the way discovered an unknown island in the Indian Ocean which he called Nieuw Amsterdam, or New Amsterdam, the name it bears today.

Van Diemen was Coen's choice as successor to the governor generalship, but Jacques Specx and Hendrik Brouwer both held this post prior to Van Diemen's succession to it on New Year's Day, 1636. At the end of that year he sailed with a force to Amboina and Ceram to put down a revolt and from there went to Makassar in an attempt to end the years-long fighting.

In addition to his own discovery, Van Diemen actively encouraged exploration and assisted in providing expeditions, two to northern Japan and environs and two to Australia, during the course of which present-day Tasmania (first named Van Diemen's Land) and New Zealand were discovered. He died on April 19, 1645, in Batavia after an illness.

Van Diemen's most brilliant achievements were his successful struggle against the Portuguese in Ceylon and Malacca, the signing of advantageous treaties with Acheh in northern Sumatra and with Ternate and Tidore in the Moluccas, particularly in connection with the spice trade, and the establishment of trade relations with China, Japan, and Tonkin.

If Coen founded Batavia, Van Diemen left his stamp on it as the center of company power and as an administrative center. He also built two churches and introduced a legal code called the Batavian Statutes (1642). As an expander of the Dutch overseas empire, he is second only to Coen; although he was governor general for a scant 9 years, Van Diemen's rule encompasses one of the most eventful periods in Dutch overseas history.

Further Reading

Eduard Servaas de Klerck, *History of the Netherlands East Indies* (2 vols., 1938), contains a good biographical account of Van Diemen and is the best source in English. See also John Horace Parry, *The Age of Reconnaissance* (1963), and Charles R. Boxer, *Dutch Sea-borne Empire, 1600-1800* (1965). □

Theo van Doesburg

The Dutch artist Theo van Doesburg (1883-1931) was one of the founders of the modern art movement called de Stijl and the chief promoter of its ideas.

Theo van Doesburg whose real name was C. E. M. Kupper, was born on Aug. 30, 1883, in Utrecht. He was involved in painting and interior decorating and writing on art, but it was only in 1917 after he had met the painter Piet Mondrian that Van Doesburg formulated his ideas clearly. The two painters founded the group de Stijl (the Style) and the avant-garde review of the same name when they and several other artists established a number of common aspirations which formed the basis of the movement.

Van Doesburg's temperament made him the public leader of the group. He was an impulsive and vigorous man, with strong likes and dislikes, in contrast to the far more reticent and cautious Mondrian. De Stijl esthetic was based on geometric abstractions and applied not only to painting but to other arts, especially architecture. Unlike many art movements in the 20th century, de Stijl aimed at social and spiritual reforms rather than purely artistic concerns. The leaders believed that a purified geometric esthetic would exert a strong and calming influence on those who saw a de Stijl painting or lived in a de Stijl house.

Van Doesburg traveled extensively from 1919 on, visiting the active centers of progressive art in Germany and France. He gave lectures, wrote numerous articles, and made many personal contacts with the avant-garde leaders in those countries. His contacts and interests were wider than those of Mondrian, who left de Stijl in 1925 because he disagreed with Van Doesburg on esthetic grounds.

In 1922 Van Doesburg became briefly involved with Dadaism and traveled on a wild lecture tour with the German Dadaist Kurt Schwitters. Van Doesburg worked at the same time with the constructivists and became interested in the Bauhaus, which had recently been founded in Germany. In the 1920s his interests progressively widened, and he wrote about these new interests in his articles for the *De Stijl* review; these articles helped to change the direction of the movement. Finally, he formulated a more dynamic version of de Stijl and published this as a manifesto of what he called elementarism. He continued to experiment with novel ideas, both in writing and painting, and collaborated with the painter Jean Arp. Just before his death on March 7, 1931, in Davos, Switzerland, Van Doesburg helped found the Abstraction-Création group in Paris.

Further Reading

Most of the writing on Van Doesburg is in Dutch. Two useful discussions of de Stijl and Van Doesburg's role in the movement are in Reyner Banham, *Theory and Design in the First Machine Age* (1960; 2d ed. 1967), and H. L. C. Jaffé, *De Stijl* (1964). □

Kees van Dongen

Kees van Dongen (1877-1968), born in Holland and a naturalized Frenchman, began his career as a Fauvist painter, later acquiring a reputation as a portraitist and socialite.

Cornelis Theodorus Marie ("Kees") van Dongen was born at Delfshaven, a suburb of Rotterdam, on January 26, 1877. Showing early artistic promise, he enrolled at the Académie des Beaux-Arts of Rotterdam in 1892. During his four-year course of study there he became acquainted with the Dutch old-master tradition as well as with the then-current Impressionist painting. He also contributed sketches to the newspaper *Rotterdam Nieuwsblad,* the first of many illustrations in his long career.

Encouraged by his friend and compatriot Siebe Ten Cate, van Dongen visited Paris in 1897 and found it so to his liking that late in 1899 he settled permanently in France. Shortly thereafter, he married a fellow painter, Augusta Preitinger, whom he had met at the Rotterdam Academy. Van Dongen's primary source of financial support was the illustrations he did for a variety of publications, including *Le Rire, Gil Blas,* and *La Revue Blanche.* One issue of the left-wing review *Assiette au Beurre* (the Butter Dish) concerning the moralizing tale of a prostitute's demise was illustrated entirely by van Dongen and contrasted with his frequent exaltation of the *demimonde.* At this point van Dongen was assimilating many artistic influences and was on the threshold of a full-bodied style that would align him with the Fauve painters.

Retains Fauvist Intensity

In 1904 van Dongen exhibited some 100 works at the gallery of Ambroise Vollard, a champion of avant-garde art. The catalogue of the show was introduced by the progressive art theorist and critic Félix Fénéon. Van Dongen's neo-Impressionist style of bold color patches and a flattened depth linked him with such artists as Andre Derain and Maurice de Vlaminck and their anti-naturalist palette. In 1905, the same year in which his daughter "Dolly" was born, van Dongen showed pictures at the Salon des Indépendants and Salon d'Automne alongside a loose collection of like-minded painters of which Matisse was the ringleader. The riot of color in their work caused a somewhat hostile critic, Louis Vauxcelles, to dub these artists "*les fauves*" ("the wild beasts").

The Fauvists were never an alliance with a strict manifesto. Instead, they found themselves united by their interest in intense, unmodulated chromatics, a shallow pictorial space, and a *joie de vivre*. While often referred to as the first significant movement of 20th-century art, the style represented the culmination of aesthetic ideas begun in the 1890s. The untempered color zones of *Femme Fatale* (1905), a typical Fauve painting by van Dongen, bear a striking resemblance to Matisse's *The Green Line* of the same year.

By 1907 the Fauvists began dispersing to explore new directions. However, van Dongen, who had arrived at the style independently of the others, retained much of his Fauvist intensity for the duration of his career. In 1908 he exhibited with the German Expressionist group Die Brücke and affected some of its members' styles. Two years before he had found lodging in the famed "Bateau-Lavoir" ("the laundry barge"), the name coined by the poet Max Jacob for the seedy Montmartre tenement whose most celebrated resident was Pablo Picasso. Picasso and van Dongen became fast friends, and van Dongen painted Picasso's mistress, Fernande Olivier. Thrust into this fertile artistic and literary milieu, van Dongen cultivated a carefree bohemian image typified by his comment: "I've always played. Painting is nothing but a game."

In response to Picasso's example, van Dongen's subjects during this time were often circus people. His unflattering images of burlesque performers and prostitutes also recall Toulouse-Lautrec's candid perspective. One well-known painting by van Dongen, *Modjesko, Soprano Singer* (1908), uses a hot Fauve palette to depict the mocking, exaggerated image of a female impersonator. In 1913 van Dongen visited Egypt, and the ancient monuments he saw contributed to an increasing decorativeness in his own art. Also, around this time van Dongen acquired a reputation as a socialite, hosting a masquerade party at this home, now in Montparnasse, that was the talk of fashionable Paris in 1914. His licentious nudes and erotic subjects caused a stir among critics and admirers alike.

The Roaring Twenties

Van Dongen's connections with the rich and famous led him to chronical the *Age des Folles* ("Crazy Age") and its excessive habits. His portraits of the time range from the world-weary *garçonne* to well-known figures such as Anatole France. His painting of the latter in 1921, representing the literary giant as a feeble old man, scandalized the public. He painted outdoor scenes as well, capturing the spirit of Deauville, the Côte d'Azur, Paris, and Venice.

From 1917 to 1927 van Dongen formed a liaison with Jasmy Jacob, who managed a *haute couture* house. He seemed as much a participant in as an observer of the fastpaced Roaring Twenties, yet claimed to maintain aesthetic distance: "I very much like being as they say, the painter of elegance and fashion! But I am not, as many wish to believe, a victim of snobbism, of luxury, of the world." But in 1927 van Dongen wrote a biography of Rembrandt that proved to be a largely autobiographical account of a painter encumbered by his own fame. Two years later van Dongen, who had so successfully captured French society in his art, became a French citizen.

With the economic crash of 1929 van Dongen's artistic fortunes, so dependent on a prosperous society, suffered a temporary setback. Yet he continued to garner significant portrait commissions in the 1930s, including that of the Aga Khan and King Leopold III of Belgium. In 1938 he met Marie-Claire Huguen, who bore him a son, Jean Marie, in 1940. They finally married in 1953, and this second family gave van Dongen new purpose. He complemented his work as a portraitist with a steady stream of book illustrations, including writings by Mardrus, Kipling, Montherlant, Proust, Voltaire, Gide, and Baudelaire.

Kees van Dongen died on May 28, 1968, at the age of 91. In the waning years of his life, spent in Monaco, he was honored by frequent museum retrospectives. Until almost the end he sustained what Apollinaire called his blend of "opium, ambergris, and eroticism," the fluid touch and exuberance that were his trademark whether he painted landscapes, nudes, or portraits.

Further Reading

A good introduction to van Dongen is Gaston Diehl, *Van Dongen* (translated by Stephanie Winston, 1969). Dennis Sutton, *Cornelis Theodorus Marie van Dongen* (1971) is the informative catalogue of the artist's first U.S. retrospective. An excellent critical study of Fauvism (including van Dongen's role) is John Elderfield, *The Wild Beasts: Fauvism and Its Affinities* (1976). Louis Chaumeil, *Van Dongen: L'Homme et L'Artiste—La Vie et L'Oeuvre* (1967, in French) is the most comprehensive review of the artist's work, with over 200 illustrations. Jean Melas-Kyriazi, *Van Dongen Après Le Fauvisme* (1976, in French) attempts with mixed results to examine the artist's post-Fauve legacy. Certain erroneous biographical details crop up in much of the literature due to van Dongen's efforts to fabricate events in his life. □

Mona Van Duyn

Mona Van Duyn (born 1921) was the first woman to be appointed poet laureate of the United States, serving from October 1992 to May 1993.

On the occasion of Mona Van Duyn's appointment as poet laureate, the Library of Congress' *Information Bulletin* (June 29, 1992) described the background of the position: "The Library keeps to a minimum the specific duties required of the Poet Laureate in order to afford each incumbent maximum freedom to work on his or her own projects while at the Library. Each brings a new emphasis to the position, which pays a stipend of $35,000." Allen Tate (1943-1944), for example, served as editor of the library's now-defunct *Quarterly Journal* and edited the compilation *Sixty American Poets, 1896-1944* during his tenure. Some consultants have suggested and chaired literary festivals and conferences; others have spoken at schools and universities and received the public in the Poetry Room. Before Van Duyn, six women had been poetry consultants: Leonie Adams, Louise Bogan, Elizabeth Bishop, Josephine Jacobsen, Maxine Kumin, and Gwendolyn Brooks.

Mona Van Duyn was born in Waterloo, Iowa, in 1921. She earned a B.S. degree from the University of Northern Iowa and an M.A. from the University of Iowa, where she took courses and taught in its famous Writers' Workshop in the 1940s. She had honorary doctorates of letters from Washington University, St. Louis, and Cornell College, Mount Vernon (Iowa). She founded *Perspective: A Quar-*

terly of Literature with her husband, Jarvis Thurston, in 1947 and continued as coeditor into the 1970s.

Van Duyn taught literature and creative writing extensively. From 1950 to 1967 she was lecturer in English at University College, Washington University. She also taught at the University of Louisville. She lectured at the Salzburg (Austria) Seminar in American Studies and at the Sewanee Writers and the Breadloaf Writing Conferences.

She was widely honored before assuming the laureateship. Her prizes include the Eunice Tietjens Award (1956), the Harriet Monroe Award of *Poetry Magazine* (1968), the Helen Bullis Prize (1964) from *Poetry Northwest,* the Hart Crane Memorial Award from the American Weave Press (1968), the first prize in the Borestone Mountain Awards Volume (1968), the National Book Award (1971), the Bollingen Prize (1970), the Loines Prize from the National Institute of Arts and Letters (1976), the Shelley Memorial Prize from the Poetry Society of America (1987), the Ruth Lilly Prize, the country's most remunerative award for poetry (1989), and the Pulitzer Prize for *Near Changes* in 1991.

The National Foundation for the Arts chose her as one of the first five poets to receive a grant. She held a Guggenheim fellowship in 1971-1972. In 1980 the Academy of American Poets voted her a fellowship and named her a chancellor in 1985. In 1983 the National Institute of Arts and Letters elected her a member.

Van Duyn's books include *Valentines to the Wide World* (1959), *A Time of Bees* (1964), *To See, To Take* (1970), *Bedtime Stories* (1972), *Merciful Disguises* (1973), *Letters from a Father and Other Poems* (1983), and *Near Changes* (1990), *Firefall: Poems* (1993) and *If It Be Not I: Collected Poems, 1959-1982* (1993).

Firefall, her tenth collection of poems, deals with her familiar themes of love, death, marriage, birth, "the flowering self," and art. More than half of the poems are in a short-lined sonnet form that Van Duyn describes as a "minimalist sonnet." Critic Ben Howard wrote of *Firefall* that "Apart from its minimalist experiments the present collection breaks no new ground, but like the poet's earlier work it bespeaks a humane, forgiving spirit, rich in warmth and moral wisdom."

Of her poetry, Joseph Parisi, editor of *Poetry Magazine,* said in his citation for the Lilly Prize: "From the publication of her first book, her mastery of the art was immediately apparent—her subtle intelligence and formidable technical skill, her gift of humor and satire, her formal elegance, and especially her understanding of the vagaries and vulnerabilities of the human heart."

"How refreshing to turn and *return* to the authentic lines of this poet when she speaks of love. Here we encounter a brilliant mind penetrating ever deeper beneath the surface to the core of feeling. Here we discover striking figures and uncanny metaphors which spark sudden recognition of our complex relations, with their shifting tensions, fears, and ambiguities. And here we delight in an artful music which echoes and sometimes ameliorates the conflicts of our most intimate desires."

Other critics were also complimentary. Kenneth Rexroth remarked of her *Valentines to the Wide World* that it was "... full of verbal and metaphysical wit, a wiry distortion of ordinary speech that communicates deeply felt and strongly evaluated experience." Carolyn Kizer called "Toward a Definition of Marriage," which appears in *Valentines,* "... one of the finest long poems written by an American."

The British writer and critic Frank Kermode declared that she was "to me, a great belated discovery." J. D. McClatchy, critic and editor, wrote of her work: "Love is her subject, not the lyricist's love, but what she calls 'knowledge of love' or 'married love'—married, that is, as much to others and to the 'motley and manifold' as to the fitful, isolated self. Love as a paradigm of all human relationships."

He continued, "From the start, her poems have bristled with ideas, or, rather, with thinking, the sound of a voice talking sense. She knows we live by ideas—though those ideas are often confused with, or confused by, habit. She sees through all that, again and again. She knows, with William James, that ideas are made true by events. And in each poem her sense of things is held up to the incongruities of experience—all of them, from the unruly sex drive to a dirty kitchen counter."

A characteristic short poem is "The Talker," from *Merciful Disguises:*

> One person present steps on his pedal of speech
> and, like a faulty drinking fountain, it spurts
> all over the room in facts and puns and jokes,
> on books, on people, on politics, on sports,
> on everything. Two or three others, gathered
> to chat, must bear his unending monologue
> between their impatient heads like a giant buzz
> of a giant fly, or magnanimous bullfrog
> croaking for all the frogs in the world. Amid
> the screech of traffic or in a hubbub crowd
> he climbs the decibels toward some glorious view.
> I think he only loves himself out loud.

Further Reading

Additional material on Van Duyn and the poet laureateship appears in the Library of Congress' *Information Bulletin* (June 29, 1992). Introductions to her books (listed in the text) are also informative. See also David Streitfeld, "Van Duyn Named New Poet Laureate," in *The Washington Post* (June 15, 1992). She has contributed poems, criticism, and short stories to *New Yorker, Kenyon Review, Yale Review, Critique,* and *Western Review.* ☐

Anthony Van Dyck

The Flemish painter Anthony Van Dyck (1599-1641) transformed the court portrait into a vehicle of great expressiveness.

n the 17th century the city of Antwerp could boast three eminent artists—Peter Paul Rubens, Anthony Van Dyck, and Jacob Jordaens—who raised Flemish painting to a level almost unequaled in Europe. The main credit for this achievement belongs to Rubens, the eldest and unquestionably the most brilliant figure of the trio. Because Van Dyck grew up in the shadow of Rubens, it is easy to underrate his genius. Van Dyck has too often been dismissed either as a facile imitator of his predecessor or as a slick and shallow painter of the aristocracy, his only real gift being an ability to flatter his patrons. This superficial judgment can no longer be seriously maintained. He was an immensely gifted and original artist who, far from being eclipsed by the overpowering personality of Rubens, succeeded in establishing his own international reputation as a portraitist of imagination and sensitivity.

Antoon van Dyck (later Anglicized as Anthony Van Dyck) was born in Antwerp in 1599, the seventh child of a prosperous merchant. In 1609 he was registered as a pupil of the minor painter Hendrik van Balen, and in 1618, not yet 19 years of age, he was accepted as a master in the Guild of St. Luke. He entered Rubens's studio as an assistant about 1617 or 1618 and remained there until late 1620.

First Antwerp Period

Van Dyck was astonishingly precocious: the appealing self-portrait in Vienna was made when he was 14 or 15. Rubens was quick to make use of this extraordinary ability. As senior assistant in his studio, the young Van Dyck collaborated in the execution of many of Rubens's larger commis-

sions during this period. Among the works in which his hand may be observed is Rubens's great *Coup de lance.*

In his independent paintings at this time we see the young Van Dyck striving to become another Rubens. This is particularly true of the early religious subjects, such as *St. Martin Dividing His Cloak,* which are strikingly Rubens-like in color and composition. A hint of the artist's future development may be discovered in the *Betrayal of Christ,* which has a quality of nervous excitement that is more indicative of Van Dyck's own temperament. But it is the early portraits that reveal most clearly the poetic sensitivity that was to make Van Dyck the unrivaled interpreter of the aristocracy. Graceful, elegant, and more than a little neurotic, the self-portraits are marked by an intimacy that owes little to Rubens. Among the master-pieces of this period are the portraits of the painter Frans Snyders and his wife.

By November 1620, having entered the service of King James I, Van Dyck was in England. But he soon gave up his duties as court artist and returned to Antwerp in the spring of 1621. In October he set out for Italy, where he was to stay for 6 years.

Italian Period

Van Dyck visited Genoa, Rome, Venice, and Sicily. Artistically speaking, the most important experience was his discovery of Titian, whose influence remained with Van Dyck for the rest of his life. Although he painted some notable altarpieces, of which the *Madonna of the Rosary* is the most imposing, the finest works of the Italian sojourn are surely his portraits of members of the nobility; his painting of Cardinal Bentivoglio is the very model of a prince of the church, and the Marchesa Elena Grimaldi, one of a series of portraits of Genoese aristocrats, is an elegant variation on a theme by Rubens.

Second Antwerp Period

The years 1628-1632, which found Van Dyck settled once more in Antwerp, may be regarded as a kind of bourgeois interlude. Here he produced some of his most lyrical and deeply felt devotional pictures, among them the ecstatic *Vision of the Blessed Herman Joseph* (1630). Commissions for princely portraits were numerous: Van Dyck's sitters at this time included Marie de Médicis, Prince Frederick Henry of Orange, and the young Prince Rupert. Yet these impressive court pictures are surpassed in sympathetic understanding by his portraits of Antwerp citizens and fellow artists, such as the sculptor Colyns de Nole and his wife and daughter and the painter Martin Rijckaert. These works show with what ease Van Dyck could adapt his style to the prevailing bourgeois atmosphere of his native city. But it was his destiny to become a court artist, and when King Charles I, who had already purchased the beautiful *Rinaldo and Armida,* summoned him to England, Van Dyck felt obliged to answer the call.

Late Period

The climactic phase of Van Dyck's career opened in 1632 with his appointment as "principalle Paynter in ordinary to their Majesties," Charles I and his queen, Henrietta

Maria. The King received the artist with the utmost consideration, awarded him a knighthood, and showered him with commissions.

As court painter, Van Dyck did not spend all his time in England. He was in Brussels and Antwerp during much of 1634 and in October was elected honorary dean of the Antwerp Guild of St. Luke. In 1640 and 1641 he made visits to Antwerp and Paris. By the latter year his health had begun to fail. He died in London in December 1641, leaving his wife, Mary Ruthven, and an infant daughter.

The favors bestowed by Charles I on Van Dyck were not misplaced, for it was at his court that the artist's genius as a portrait painter was fully realized. Three superb equestrian canvases stand out among the many royal likenesses: *Charles I Hunting* (Louvre, Paris), *Charles I with his Equerry* (Buckingham Palace, London), and *Charles I on Horseback* (National Gallery, London), the last recalling in some respects Titian's famous equestrian portrait of Charles V. To turn from these images of majesty to the charming pictures of the royal children is to gain a fuller understanding of the artist's humanity and perception. Still another facet of his complex personality is revealed in the beautiful double portrait of Thomas Killigrew and Thomas Carew. It was through works of this quality that Van Dyck was able to effect a revolution in English taste and to impart a new direction to English art.

Further Reading

There is no good modern biography of Van Dyck. The best book in English is still Sir Lionel Cust, *Anthony van Dyck: An Historical Study of His Life and Works* (1900), which presents a full and well-documented account of the artist's life but is less satisfactory in dealing with the pictures. Despite its brevity, the chapter on Van Dyck in H. Gerson and E. H. ter Kuile, *Art and Architecture in Belgium, 1600-1800* (trans. 1960), offers an authoritative estimate of the painter's genius and his place in Flemish art.

Additional Sources

Brown, Christopher, *Van Dyck,* Ithaca, N.Y.: Cornell University Press, 1983, 1982. ▢

Sir Henry Vane

The English statesman Sir Henry Vane (1613-1662), who served as governor of the Massachusetts Bay Colony, led the Long Parliament and the English Commonwealth.

The career of Sir Henry, or Harry, Vane the Younger epitomizes the close connection between New England and English life in the mid-17th century. He also illustrates the combination of devout religious belief and utterly realistic political action which characterized the Puritans in both places.

The elder Sir Henry Vane was a self-seeking courtier of Charles I who acted as a diplomat and joined the Privy Council in 1630. The younger Vane was educated at Westminster School and Oxford. In addition, he studied at Geneva and Leiden and was sent to Vienna to acquire further knowledge of European affairs. On his return to England in 1632, the road to preferment at court was open to him. But at age 15 Vane had had a profound religious experience which made him a devout Puritan and an opponent of royal authority over religion. Therefore in 1635 he sailed for New England.

Eight months after Vane's arrival, and at the age of 23, he was elected governor of the Massachusetts Bay Colony because he obviously had the highest social rank. He had already become friendly with the expelled Roger Williams, who aided Vane in pacifying the neighboring Indian tribes. But Vane's support of Anne Hutchinson involved him in a dispute with most of the colony's ministers and conservative lay leaders. They defeated his reelection as governor and so reduced his authority in the colony that he had little choice but to return to England in 1637.

A career at court was still open to Vane, and in 1639 he was named joint treasurer of the navy. His father had become a secretary of state and was a leading organizer of the King's attempt to reduce the Scots to obedience. Both Vanes were returned to the Parliaments of 1640. The younger Vane was an efficient administrator and was influential in maintaining the loyalty of the navy to Parliament. He also rallied the military support of London to Parliament in autumn 1642. Vane first stood out as a leader of Parliament,

however, in his mission to the Scots in 1643. Basically, he wanted to negotiate an exclusively political alliance. When the Scots insisted upon religious conditions, Vane secured a saving clause in the treaty whereby the English church settlement should be "according to the Word of God." For the Scots that meant presbytery, but for Vane it meant spiritual liberty or independency. The religious issue was therefore postponed, but the military support of Scotland was obtained for Parliament.

In the summer of 1644 Vane was less successful on his visit to the parliamentary generals outside York. He evidently had secret instructions to win their support for the deposition of Charles I. The generals opposed the move, and a term was thereby set to Vane's leadership of Parliament, to which he had succeeded on the death of John Pym. Vane remained in apparent control until the defeat of Charles at Naseby in 1645; but after the King's flight to the Scots in 1646, the political Presbyterians controlled Parliament until December 1648. Vane's power was eclipsed both because of his opposition to Presbyterianism and because of his indifference to the institution of hereditary monarchy. But he always stood for civilian control of government, so he opposed the growth of army political power in 1647 and 1648. Vane absolutely refused to participate in the army-controlled trial of the King.

Once Charles was executed, however, Vane was willing to continue his service in Parliament. He soon became the leader of the Commonwealth Council of State. Although this government depended upon army support for its power, Vane consistently worked to vindicate its independent and essentially civilian authority. But the army under Oliver Cromwell expelled the Commonwealth government in April 1653. Vane retired to his estate in Lincolnshire. In 1656 the government accused him of fomenting disorder, and he replied in *The Healing Question*. That pamphlet argued that order would come from a government freely elected by the religious supporters of Parliament, not from military dictatorship. In retaliation he was imprisoned for 4 months.

The death of Oliver Cromwell led Vane to reenter public life. He called on Richard Cromwell to regularize the government by an appeal to popular consent, and he led in the reconstruction of the Commonwealth government in 1659. But the army officers destroyed any possibility of stable government.

After the Restoration, Vane had powerful friends among the restored House of Lords, but the royalists in the Cavalier Parliament brought him to trial because of his leadership in the parliamentary and Commonwealth governments. On the scaffold Vane firmly defended his conduct during the civil war, and he died a martyr to republican government.

Further Reading

The best work on Vane is Violet A. Rowe, *Sir Henry Vane, the Younger* (1971). On Vane's thought, a brief but well-documented study is Margaret A. Judson, *The Political Thought of Sir Henry Vane the Younger* (1969). □

Willem Frederik Van Eekelen

Minister of defense of the Netherlands Willem Frederik Van Eekelen (born 1931) became secretary-general of the Western European Union in 1989.

In 1939 Willem Frederik Van Eekelen was born in Utrecht in the Netherlands. In 1943 he entered Utrecht's best secondary school (equivalent to junior high school and high school in the United States), the Stedelijke Gymnasium Utrecht, and studied there until 1949. He then left the Netherlands to study political science at Princeton University in the United States. In 1952 he received his Bachelor of Arts degree, graduating with high honors.

Upon return to his country, Van Eekelen studied law at the University of Utrecht and received his law degree in 1956. Being an outstanding student, he was later admitted to study for his doctorate degree in political science at the same University of Utrecht. His thesis, "Indian Foreign Policy and the Border Dispute with China," was published in 1964.

While pursuing his doctorate, he joined the diplomatic service in 1957. He was first assigned to the Dutch embassy in New Delhi and then later at the London embassy. Between 1966 and 1971 Van Eekelen interrupted his career as an official of the Ministry of Foreign Affairs and became a member of the Dutch delegation to the North Atlantic Treaty Organization (NATO) in Brussels, Belgium.

From 1971 to 1974 he was back at the Ministry of Foreign Affairs, but this time he was put in charge of coordinating European political cooperation. The idea of European political cooperation originated from the will of the member states of the European Community to extend European cooperation gradually from purely economic matters to include political and security issues. The objective was to advance and consolidate political unification of Europe. Van Eekelen's position at the Ministry of Foreign Affairs included direct responsibility for determining the scope and content of the Dutch contribution to the European political cooperation.

In 1974 and for the next three years, still as an official of the Ministry of Foreign Affairs, he became director for Atlantic cooperation and security matters.

At the age of 46 he interrupted his diplomatic career to present himself as a candidate in the legislative elections of 1977. He was elected as the representative of the VVD (Volkspartij voor Vrijheid en Democratie), the Dutch conservative party, in the Lower House of Parliament. In 1978 he entered the first government of Prime Minister Van Agt (a coalition of the Christian-Democratic Alliance [CDA] and VVD) as state secretary of defense (more or less equivalent to an under secretary of defense).

In 1981 he was elected a second time to the Lower House, but had to leave his government position during the next two short-lived Van Agt governments (September 1981 to November 1982). His party, the VVD, was not part of those two government coalitions. He was elected a third time to the Lower House in 1982.

While a member of the Dutch Parliament, Van Eekelen simultaneously served as a member of the Consultative Assemblies of the Council of Europe and the Western European Union from 1981 to 1982. After the fall of the third Van Agt cabinet in 1982, the new prime minister, Ruud Lubbers (CDA) asked Van Eekelen to join his administration. Van Eekelen entered the Lubbers cabinet as state secretary for foreign affairs (roughly equivalent to under secretary of state in the United States).

In 1986, after new elections took place, Ruud Lubbers formed a second government. This time, Van Eekelen was asked to assume the post of minister of defense. In this capacity he attended the Eurogroup sessions. The Eurogroup was composed of all European NATO defense ministers, minus France and Iceland. Van Eekelen did not hold his ministerial post for long. In 1988 a political "mini-scandal" known as the Passport Case forced him into resigning. A parliamentary inquiry had begun in May 1988 on the case, which involved the unsuccessful attempt to introduce a new fraud-resistant passport in the Netherlands. It soon appeared that the passport was far from fraud-resistant, although it had cost a lot of taxpayers' money, nothing to scoff at by Dutch standards. According to the investigative commission's report, which was released in August 1988, the Department of Foreign Affairs had underestimated the complexity of the passport project, and the entire scheme was grossly mismanaged.

The state secretary for foreign affairs, Van Der Linden, was accused of having given incorrect information to the Parliament and was first forced to resign in September, Van Eekelen, as predecessor to Van Der Linden, had initiated the project in the previous Lubbers cabinet. Three days later he also resigned. These resignations saved the entire government from falling. During the heated debate in Parliament, Van Eekelen's competence and his public management ability were often unfairly criticized. Even the VVD, his own political party, suspended its support for him. His eventual resignation became necessary lest he lose all credibility. Although his personal integrity was never questioned, press reports deemed that this event put a likely end to his political career in the Netherlands.

In May 1989 Van Eekelen became the secretary-general of the Western European Union (WEU). The WEU legally binds nine European countries in a mutual defense treaty, but is not linked to NATO. It is often seen as a forum where Europeans, and France in particular, can discuss their defense concerns without any non-European interference. With this appointment, Van Eekelen showed that his national political misfortune was not to diminish the international recognition he had gained in defense and security matters.

Through the 1990's the WEU, under Van Eekelen's guidance, continued to influence post cold war security and political integration. Van Eekelen contributed scholarly articles on the role of the WEU to magazines such as; *Harvard International Review* (Fall 1991) and *NATO Review* (Octo-

ber 1993). By 1994 the WEU was opening its doors to East Europe.

The dramatic political changes in Europe that began with end of the Cold War put the existence of the organization in a new perspective and, consequently, increased the political role of its secretary-general with regard to European defense and security matters. Van Eekelen supported the idea of multinational European armed forces and the decision to cooperate in the area of conventional arms verification. Such initiative signaled a new-found resolve for an organization too well known in the past for being little more than a formal discussion group. Van Eekelen's experience in European and defense cooperation was certainly a strong asset for the WEU.

Further Reading

One may consult the several volumes of the *Encyclopaedia Britannica, Book of the Year,* in order to obtain more information about the Dutch political context of W. F. Van Eekelen's career. Unfortunately, there is no specific biographical information on him available in English, except for a very short paragraph in *Who's Who in The Netherlands* (1989 edition). Van Eekelen, as Dutch minister of defense, wrote an interesting report on transatlantic defense policies in *NATO Review* (Brussels: 1987). While secretary-general of the WEU, Van Eekelen wrote "Future European Defence Cooperation: The Role of the WEU," *European Strategy Group* (Paris: September 1989). Except for these reports and his 1964 doctoral thesis, none of his numerous articles on defense matters and foreign policy are available in English. An interview with van Eekelen, by Brigitte Sauerwein appeared in the *International Defense Review* (March 1990). □

Vincent Van Gogh

Vincent Van Gogh (1853-1890) was a Dutch painter whose formal distortions and humanistic concerns made him a principal forerunner of 20th-century expressionism.

Born on March 30, 1853, at Groot-Zundert in the province of Brabant, Vincent Van Gogh was the son of a Protestant minister. His uncle was a partner in Goupil and Company, art dealers, and Vincent entered the firm at the age of 16 and remained with it for 6 years. He served the firm first in The Hague and then in London, where he fell in love with his landlady's daughter, who rejected him; then he worked for Goupil's branch in Paris.

Because of Van Gogh's irritability, Goupil dismissed him in 1876, and that year he returned to England, worked at a small school at Ramsgate, and did some preaching. In early 1877 he clerked in a bookshop in Dordrecht; then, convinced that the ministry ought to be his vocation, he entered a religious seminary in Brussels. He left 3 months later to become an evangelist in a poor mining section of Belgium, the Borinage. Van Gogh exhibited the zeal and devotion of a martyr, even giving away his clothes, but his eccentricities alienated the miners, and he was dismissed in

July 1879. This period was a dark one for Van Gogh. He wished to give himself to others but was constantly being rejected.

After much introspection, Van Gogh decided in 1880 to devote his life to art, a profession he accepted as a spiritual calling. When in London, he had visited museums, and he had done some drawing while in the Borinage. In October 1880 he attended an art school in Brussels, where he studied the rudiments of perspective and anatomy. From April to December 1881 he stayed with his parents, who were then in Etten, and continued to work at his art. At this time his cousin from Amsterdam, a widow with a 4-year-old son, rejected him, and he subsequently formed a close relationship with a pregnant prostitute, a move that precipitated a break with his family. At this time, too, he studied at the academic art school at The Hague, where his cousin Anton Mauve, who worked in the sentimentalized fashion of the Barbizon painters, taught.

Dutch Period

During his Dutch period (1880-1886) Van Gogh executed works in which his overriding humanitarian concerns were overtly manifest. His subjects were poor people, miners, peasants, and inhabitants of almshouses. Among his favorite painters at this time were Jean François Millet, Rembrandt, Honoré Daumier; among his favorite authors, George Eliot, Charles Dickens, and Harriet Beecher Stowe—all of them interested in the poor and dispossessed. Complementing Van Gogh's dismal subject matter of this time were his colors, dark brownish and greenish tones. The

masterpiece of the Dutch period is the *Potato Eaters* (1885), a night scene in which peasants sit at their meal around a table. The coarseness of the peasants is emphasized; in rendering them Van Gogh approached caricature. Yet he caught, too, a warm communality, a remarkable sense of love and fellowship which his painted peasants seem to share.

Years in Paris

Van Gogh decided to go to Paris in early 1886, partially because he was drawn to the bohemian life and artistic activity of the French city. His brother, Theo, was then living in Paris, where he directed a small gallery maintained by Goupil's. Theo supported Vincent financially and emotionally from the time he decided to become a painter. The letters between the brothers are among the most moving documents in all the history of Western art. Vincent shared Theo's apartment and studied at an art school run by the conventional painter Fernand Cormon, where he met Émile Bernard and Henri de Toulouse-Lautrec, who became his friends. In part through the contacts provided by Theo, Vincent met the leaders of impressionism—Claude Monet, Camille Pissarro, and Paul Gauguin—and the neo-impressionist Georges Seurat.

Largely under the influence of the impressionists, especially Pissarro, Van Gogh was persuaded to give up the gloomy tones of his Dutch period for bright, high-keyed colors. Also, his subject matter changed from the world of peasants to a typically impressionist subject matter, such as cafés and cityscapes about Montmartre, and he copied Japanese prints. But while subjects and handling were obviously derived from impressionism, there could frequently be detected a certain forlorn quality, as in a scene of *Montmartre* (1886), where pedestrians are pushed poignantly to the periphery of an open square.

Van Gogh remained in Paris for 20 months and profited from his stay. Under the influence of impressionism his palette was liberated. But the frenetic life was too much for him; he wanted a place of light and warmth, and he did not want to be entirely financially dependent on Theo, so in February 1888 he left for Arles in southern France.

Stay at Arles

The pleasant country about Arles and the warmth of the place restored Van Gogh to health. He worked feverishly: in his 15 months there he painted over 200 pictures. At this time he applied color in simplified, highly saturated masses, his drawing became more virile and incisive than ever before, and objects seemed to radiate a light of their own without giving off shadows. During this period he also turned to portraiture and executed several self-portraits. Among the masterpieces of his Arles period are the *Fishing Boats on the Beach at Saintes-Maries* (June 1888); the *Night Café* (September); and the *Artist's Bedroom at Arles* (October), where the chairs about the bed seem to be acting out a spectacle and almost appear to be living beings conversing.

At Arles, Van Gogh suffered fainting spells and seizures. The local population began to object to him. Gauguin, responding to his invitation, visited him in October 1888, but the two men quarreled violently; Gauguin left for Paris, and Van Gogh in a fit of remorse and anger cut off his ear. On May 9, 1889, he asked to be interned in the asylum at Saint-Rémy-de Provence.

Production at Saint-Rémy

In the year he spent at the asylum Van Gogh worked as feverishly as at Arles and produced 150 paintings and hundreds of drawings. He copied engravings after Rembrandt, Eugène Delacroix, and Millet. Van Gogh suffered several attacks but was completely lucid in between. At this time he received his first critical acclaim, an article by the writer Albert Aurier.

During Van Gogh's stay at Saint-Rémy his art changed markedly. His colors lost the intensity of the Arles period: yellows became coppered, vermilions verged toward brownish tones. His lines became writhing and restless. He applied the paint more violently with thicker impasto. Van Gogh was drawn to objects in nature under stress: whirling suns, twisted cypresses, and surging mountains. In *Starry Night* (1889) the whole world seems engulfed by a paroxysm of circular movements. Some critics have attempted to link the linear movements of his Saint-Rémy period with the vogue of Art Nouveau, but Van Gogh's paintings at this time reveal an intensity and convulsive force found in none of the Art Nouveau painters.

Van Gogh went to Paris on May 17, 1890, to visit his brother. On the advice of Pissarro, Theo had Vincent go to Auvers, just outside Paris, to submit to the care of Dr. Paul Gachet, himself an amateur painter and a friend of Pissarro and Paul Cézanne.

Last Year at Auvers

Van Gogh arrived at Auvers on May 21. He painted a portrait of Dr. Gachet and portraits of his daughters, as well as the *Church of Auvers,* agitated by a baroque rhythm with the church silhouetted against a cobalt sky. The blue of the Auvers period was not the fully saturated blue of Arles but a more mysterious, flickering blue. In his last painting, the *Cornfield with Crows,* Van Gogh showed a topsy-turvy world: the spectator himself becomes the object of perspective, and it is toward him that the crows appear to be flying.

At first Van Gogh felt relieved at Auvers, but toward the end of June he experienced fits of temper. He quarreled with Gachet. On July 27, 1890, he shot himself in a lonely field and died the morning of the 29th. Theo died insane 6 months later in the Netherlands, and his body was taken to France to be buried next to that of his brother.

Further Reading

The Complete Letters of Vincent van Gogh (3 vols., 1958) is more engrossing than most novels. The *catalogue raisonné* is by J. Bernard de la Faille, ed., *L'Oeuvre de Vincent van Gogh* (4 vols., 1928). A good introduction to Van Gogh's life and works is Abraham M. Hammacher, *Genius and Disaster: The Ten Creative Years of Vincent van Gogh* (1968). An excellent study of the artist is Marc Edo Tralbaut, *Vincent Van Gogh* (1969). Other useful studies are H. R. Graetz, *The Symbolic Language of Vincent van Gogh* (1963), and Frank Elgar, *Van*

Gogh: A Study of His Life and Work trans. 1966). Brilliant analyses of a selected number of paintings are in Meyer Schapiro, *Vincent van Gogh* (1950). See also John Rewald, *Post-impressionism* (vol. 1 1956; 2d ed. 1962). □

Sir William Cornelius Van Horne

Sir William Cornelius Van Horne (1843-1915) was an American-born Canadian railroad entrepreneur who supervised the building of the trans-Canadian railroad.

William Van Horne was born in Will County, Ill., the eldest child of Cornelius Covenhoven Van Horne, a struggling farmer-lawyer, and his second wife, Mary Minier Richards Van Horne. In 1851 the family moved to Joliet, where the father became the first mayor and William attended his first school. After his father's death 3 years later, poverty allowed William only 3 further years of schooling.

At 14 Van Horne quickly achieved advancement as a telegraph operator successively with the Illinois Central, the Michigan Central, and the Chicago and Alton railroads. In 1864 Van Horne became the Chicago and Alton's Bloomington train dispatcher, in 1868 its superintendent of telegraph, and in 1870 superintendent of transportation. In 1874 he rose to general manager of the Southern Minnesota Railroad; later he became its president. In 1879 he returned briefly to the Chicago and Alton as general superintendent before assuming the same position with the Chicago, Milwaukee and St. Paul.

Van Horne was appointed general manager of the Canadian project to build a transcontinental railroad from Montreal to the Pacific in 1881. His driving leadership and formidable organizing ability reached their peak in forcing the pace of construction. His sound employee relations supplemented the directors' tireless efforts to raise funds in hard times, and Van Horne was significantly complemented by his purchasing agent, T. G. Shaughnessy, formerly his general storekeeper on the Chicago, Milwaukee and St. Paul. Although the contract called for the railway's completion in 1891, the last spike was driven on Nov. 7, 1885.

Van Horne's role in this extraordinary achievement had been recognized in his appointment as vice president in 1884 and was confirmed in 1888, when he became president, with Shaughnessy succeeding him as general manager. Van Horne's presidency was marked by further construction, early profits, and the projection of auxiliary services, such as a shipping fleet. Failing health dictated his retirement in 1899, although he assumed the titular dignity of chairman of the board and member of the executive committee until his full withdrawal in 1910.

In retirement, characteristically Van Horne built a railroad in eastern Cuba in 1901 and Guatemalan line between

Kiliaen Van Rensselaer was born in Amsterdam, probably in 1580. His early life is obscure. He entered the employ of a jeweler uncle who eventually retired in his favor, and by 1614 he was a leading Amsterdam diamond and pearl merchant. Prospering in East Indian trade, Van Rensselaer helped promote and found the West India Company, which was chartered in 1621 as a trading monopoly in Africa and America. As one of its directors, on two occasions he advanced sums to maintain the company's credit.

From the outset Van Rensselaer urged the company's fellow directors to develop New Netherland's agriculture rather than rely solely on the lucrative fur trade. When the company experienced difficulty securing settlers, Van Rensselaer utilized the Charter of Freedom and Exemptions, authorizing feudal estates for responsible Dutchmen promising to bring 50 adults to live on assigned tracts purchased from the Native Americans. Obtaining permission for such a patroonship in November 1629, he purchased land on the Hudson River near Albany from the Algonquin Indians. Later purchases expanded the area to approximately 700,000 acres on both sides of the river.

After patent to the manor of Rensselaerswyck was confirmed on Aug. 6, 1630, the first settlers soon arrived. Van Rensselaer zealously developed his New World estate, securing the most substantial group of settlers recruited by any patroon. He provided stock and farm tools for his colonists, purchased cattle, organized a manorial court, and sent a Calvinist pastor to care for the settlers' spiritual needs.

1903 and 1908 and forthrightly opposed reciprocity with the United States in 1911. He also produced many competent watercolors. He was a trustee of McGill University and a director or officer of many trusts, urban transport companies, and industries in Canada, Cuba, Guatemala, Mexico, and Brazil. His magnificent homes in Montreal, in St. Andrews, New Brunswick, and in Cuba consumed much of his interest, as did his large collections of paintings, rare Japanese pottery, and fossils. He lived richly and dealt generously with his loyal employees. He died on Sept. 11, 1915, in Montreal.

Further Reading

Walter Vaughan, *The Life and Work of Sir William Van Horne* (1920), is a full-length study. Van Horne also figures in Henry James, ed., *The Canadian Men and Women of the Time* (1898; 2d ed. 1912). □

Kiliaen Van Rensselaer

Kiliaen Van Rensselaer (ca. 1580-1643) was a Dutch merchant and colonizer in America. A director of the Dutch West India Company, he was first patroon of Rensselaerswyck Manor in the colony of New Netherland.

Anxious to develop agriculture in his barony, Van Rensselaer also sought benefits from fur trading. He advocated company restriction of this commerce to concessionaires, with his own agents controlling that in the Rensselaerswyck area. Vast correspondence shows his continued attention to administrative details (and probably price-rigging for settlers' supplies). However, company-licensed traders resisted efforts to forcibly collect tolls and restrict Indian commerce. Before his death in Amsterdam in October 1643, Van Rensselaer was plagued by settlers' disobedience to his appointed authorities and by agents' attempts to secure manors for themselves. Nevertheless, Rensselaerswyck proved the only successful patroonship during the Dutch era in New York.

Further Reading

Information concerning Van Rensselaer is sparse and frequently conflicting. Samuel G. Nissenson, *The Patroon's Domain* (1937), provides a scholarly analysis of the settlement but not much on the man himself. George R. Howell, *History of the County of Albany* (1886), and Nathaniel B. Sylvester, *History of Rensselaer County* (1880), contain helpful references. See also Maunsell Van Rensselear, *Annals of the Van Rensselears in the United States* (1888). □

Jacobus Hendricus Van't Hoff

The Dutch physical chemist Jacobus Hendricus Van't Hoff (1852-1911) pioneered in the development of stereochemistry.

Jacobus Hendricus Van't Hoff was born in Rotterdam on Aug. 30, 1852. He developed an early interest in science, and in spite of the opposition of his father, who was a medical doctor, he studied chemistry at a polytechnic school and then at the University of Leiden. From the Netherlands he journeyed to Germany and then to Paris for further study, finishing his doctorate at the University of Utrecht in 1874.

Just prior to the awarding of the degree, however, Van't Hoff published a surprising scientific paper on the optical activity of certain organic compounds. This phenomenon (stereochemistry) of organic compounds can be described briefly by reference to the two forms of tartaric acid. They are the same in chemical formula, but in solution one form rotates a beam of polarized light to the left, and the other rotates it to the right. Pasteur had observed this phenomenon years earlier and suggested that the compound was actually made up of crystals which were mirror images of each other, but this explanation did not seem to have any application to compounds in solution. Van't Hoff's contribution was to describe asymmetry in molecules, not in crystals, and he showed how this was possible if one considers the carbon atom as having four linkages which do not lie in a plane but are directed toward the four angles of a

tetrahedon. In this way, the carbon atom achieves a three-dimensional form, and the attachment to it of different types of chemical groupings establishes asymmetric molecules and compounds.

Van't Hoff became a lecturer in chemistry at the Veterinary College in Utrecht. From there he went to the University of Amsterdam, and he ended his career at the University of Berlin, where he taught and engaged in research from 1896 to 1911. In 1901 he received the first Nobel Prize in chemistry, which was awarded him for his work with solutions. His achievements in this field were made during the second part of his scientific career, when he was a physical chemist. In the first part of his career, it may be said that he was an organic chemist. The results of his research in chemical thermodynamics were published in *Studies in Chemical Dynamics* (1884).

Van't Hoff's work on the theory of solutions formed the major part of his creative research in physical chemistry. He was able to show that, in very dilute solutions, the laws of gases may be applied to the molecules. Before his work, chemists had possessed only vague ideas about molecular behavior in solutions; Van't Hoff's research cleared up many questions. Van't Hoff had a generalizing and speculative mind which gave him insights into the newly developing field of physical chemistry. He died on March 1, 1911.

Further Reading

Ernst Cohen, who wrote the definitive biography of Van't Hoff in German, contributed a biographical sketch of the scientist in

Eduard Farber, ed., *Great Chemists* (1961). Van't Hoff is mentioned in Isaac Asimov's survey, *A Short History of Chemistry* (1965). □

Edgard Varèse

Edgard Varèse (1883-1965), French-American composer, was one of the major prophets of the new music after World War II. In 1958 John Cage wrote, "More clearly and actively than anyone else of his generation he established the present nature of music."

E dgard Varèse was born in Paris of a Corsican family, but his youth was spent in Italy, where he received an engineer's training and degree. He was equally interested in music, and after preliminary study at the Turin Conservatory, he continued at the Schola Cantorum in Paris under Vincent d'Indy and Albert Roussel and at the conservatory under Charles Widor. He was a brilliant student and won a composition prize sponsored by the city.

In 1907 Varèse moved to Berlin, where he came under the influence of Richard Strauss and Ferruccio Busoni. He conducted a chorus and wrote an opera, *Oedipus und die Sphinx,* with a libretto by Hugo von Hofmannsthal. Varèse also wrote a symphony which was performed, but all of these early compositions were destroyed in a fire.

With the outbreak of World War I, Varèse went to the United States. At first he was active as a conductor and as a propagandist for new music. He founded the International Composers' Guild and presented first performances of important contemporary pieces. In the following years he composed a series of very noisy compositions that baffled the critics but were acknowledged as landmarks of new music 30 years later. In these works Varèse went beyond the most advanced use of melody, rhythm, harmony, form, and instrumentation to create startlingly novel sounds.

During the 1920s Varèse wrote *Amériques, Offrandes, Octandre, Hyperprism, Intégrales,* and *Arcana. Octandre* (1924), for seven wind instruments and double bass, is a good example of his unconventional use of instruments and his new concept of musical form. The strident and extremely dissonant blocks of sound, almost resembling factory whistles, form the content of the piece without the rhythmic or tonal developments normally used by composers. *Intégrales* (1925), for wind instruments and percussion, also suggests big-city sounds. The first section consists of two unchanging chord structures around which a melodic pattern oscillates. It is one of the first of those "crystal" musical forms that were to be used so much in the following years. This term implies that the basic sound material of the piece is unchanging and that the shifting relationships between its elements is the only thing that "happens."

In the 1930s Varèse wrote *Ionisation, Métal, Density 21.5,* and *Equatorial,* of which *Ionisation* (1931) is best known. Written for percussion instruments plus a siren, it is one of the first of the many all-percussion pieces that were to follow. *Equatorial,* calling for two Theremins, shows his interest in new sound sources.

In 1937 Varèse stopped composing because he was no longer interested in seeking new sounds in conventional instruments; it was not until the tape recorder and electronic music became available that he finally gained the vast new sound resource he had been seeking. His mature works, utilizing noises and electronically produced sounds, are *Déserts* (1954) and the *Poème électronique* (1958). *Déserts* has two basic sound groups. The first is produced by the instruments; the second consists of a two-channel stereophonic tape of electronically produced sound. According to the composer, the instrumental parts produce a sense of movement in space, associated with the element within which the human operates, and the taped section is associated with distance and the nonhuman elements of the universe.

The *Poème électronique* was written to be performed in the Phillips Pavilion at the 1958 World's Fair in Brussels. The pavilion was planned as a "total environment" meant to result in a complex, multimedia experience for the audience. The music was heard from over 400 loudspeakers as the visitors walked through the building, seeing at the same time a series of projected images. Varèse's music consists of a combination of taped "natural" sounds, such as bells and voices, and noises such as clicks and motor roars. It is not meant to be listened to in the usual attentive manner.

Varèse's contributions to music are his widening of the material of music to include noise as well as "musical" sound, his development of new ways of organizing musical compositions, and writing of music to be heard as a part of an environment. All of these revolutionary ideas proved to be of great importance to the composers of the so-called avant-garde of the 1950s and 1960s.

Further Reading

Some of Varèse's writings on music are extracted in Elliott Schwartz and Barney Childs, eds., *Contemporary Composers on Contemporary Music* (1967). The only book-length study of the composer is Fernand Ouellette, *Edgard Varèse* (1966; trans. 1968). William W. Austin, *Music in the Twentieth Century: From Debussy through Stravinsky* (1966), has an interesting discussion of Varèse's life and work. Other studies which contain information on Varèse are Joseph Machlis, *Introduction to Contemporary Music* (1961), and Joan Peyser, *The New Music: The Sense behind the Sound* (1971). ☐

Getulio Dornelles Vargas

Getulio Dornelles Vargas (1883-1954), certainly the most important Brazilian political leader of the 20th century, brought about fundamental changes in the economy, society, and politics of his native land.

Getulio Vargas was the son of a local political leader in the state of Rio Grande do Sul. After going through law school in Pôrto Alegre, he began his political career as a member of the state legislature of Rio Grande do Sul. Although he resigned his post for a short while because of disagreement with the state boss, Augusto Borges de Medeiros, Vargas was reinstated in the legislature and was promoted to a seat in the national Chamber of Deputies in 1923.

Vargas soon became leader of the Rio Grande do Sul delegation in Congress. With inauguration of President Washington Luiz in 1926, the new president chose Vargas as minister of finance. However, in 1928 Vargas resigned to become governor of his native state. In this post, he demonstrated outstanding ability as a reconciler, succeeding in bringing into his Cabinet members of the Federal party, which had been in violent opposition to the dominant Republican party since the establishment of the republic in 1889.

With the approach of the 1930 presidential election, Washington Luiz, himself a former governor of São Paulo, decided to choose as his successor the current Paulista governor, Julio Prestes. This violated the tradition that the presidency should be filled alternately by men from São Paulo and Minas Gerais, and Minas governor Antonio Carlos organized an opposition campaign, with Governor Vargas agreeing to be the opposition candidate.

The opposition organized the Liberal Alliance. Its program called for labor legislation, establishment of a steel industry, and other economic and social changes. Although Vargas had considerable popular support and the backing of the nationalistic young officers known as the Tenentes, he was overwhelmingly "counted out" by the government in May 1930. Then, after some months of hesitation, Vargas agreed to lead a revolution, with the backing of the Tenentes and the state police forces of Rio Grande do Sul, Minas Gerais, and Paraiba. This revolution was successful in October 1930.

Maintenance of Office

Vargas remained president from 1930 until 1945. During the first 2 years, as provisional president, he shared power with the Tenentes. However, after a 3-month revolt in São Paulo in 1932, discipline was reestablished in the army, and Vargas won dominance over the Tenentes.

A Constitutional Assembly elected late in 1933 chose Vargas as constitutional president a few months later. However, he was faced with strong opposition on the left from the Aliança Nacional Libertadora (ANL) and on the right from the fascist Acão Integralista. Vargas used the defeat of an attempted military uprising by the ANL in November 1935 to crack down on the leftist opposition.

Vargas's constitutional term was supposed to end in 1938. A campaign to choose his successor was started in 1937 but was brought to a sudden end on November 10 by a coup by President Vargas, with the help of Acão Integralista. Although the Integralistas hoped to maneuver Vargas out of power, he outlawed their party; and when their May 1938 revolt was unsuccessful, he completely crushed their organization.

New State

With the November 1937 coup, President Vargas established a semifascist regime, the Estado Novo. Under this system, the trade unions, established under a labor law passed in 1930 as one of the first acts of the Vargas regime, were forced to secure new recognition. To achieve it, they had to submit to almost complete government control. The Estado Novo also ended collective bargaining and substituted a system of labor courts. Vargas also enacted by decree a large body of labor and social security legislation during the Estado Novo.

During this long period as president, Vargas encouraged economic development of the country. His regime established tariff protection, used exchange controls to protect and subsidize new industries, converted the Banco do Brasil into the main source of credit for manufacturing firms, and had the government establish a national steel plant and other enterprises.

Vargas took Brazil into World War II on the Allied side. Brazilian troops fought in Italy. The propagation of the idea that Brazil was fighting for democracy in Europe undermined the Vargas dictatorship, and early in 1945 the President was forced to call elections for December. However, Vargas was not anxious to leave the presidency, and he organized two pro-government parties, the Partido Social Democrático and the Partido Trabalhista (PTB). The latter became particularly active in urging Vargas to remain in power.

Decline from Power

However, in October 1945 the President was ousted by the military. In elections in December, Vargas ran for the Senate from several states on the PTB ticket and became senator from Rio Grande do Sul. However, during the next 5 years he took virtually no part in the Senate's proceedings.

In 1950 Vargas ran for president again, as candidate of the Partido Trabalhista. He won in a four-cornered race. After some discussion, the military allowed him to take office. During the next 3½ years Vargas lost much popular support because of his inability to curb inflation. However, he pushed forward economic development through establishment of the National Bank of Economic Development, and he sponsored a law to set up a government oil company, Petroleos Brasileiros.

The military remained very skeptical of Vargas. When his protégé João Goulart sought as minister of labor to build up a powerful personal political machine in the labor movement and seemed to be the chosen political heir of Vargas, the soldiers forced Goulart's resignation early in 1954. A few months later, they presented Vargas himself with an ultimatum: take a "leave of absence" for the rest of his term or be overthrown.

In the face of this ultimatum, Vargas committed suicide on Aug. 25, 1954. He left a note accusing reactionaries at home and "powerful foreign interests" of plotting to prevent him from working on behalf of the Brazilian people and in defense of the interests of the Brazilian nation. His last phrase was "I am leaving life to enter history."

Further Reading

John W. F. Dulles, *Vargas of Brazil: A Political Biography* (1967), is comprehensive. More specialized is Robert M. Levine, *The Vargas Regime: The Critical Years, 1934-1938* (1970). Thomas E. Skidmore, *Politics in Brazil, 1930-1964: An Experiment in Democracy* (1967), places Vargas's regimes in their historical context. □

Mario Vargas Llosa

The Peruvian writer Mario Vargas Llosa (born 1936), novelist, critic, journalist, screenwriter, and essayist, abandoned writing at least temporarily in 1990 to run unsuccessfully for president of his country.

Like many of the characters in his fiction, (Jorge) Mario (Pedro) Vargas Llosa, internationally acclaimed Peruvian writer and recipient of almost every literary award short of the Nobel Prize, is something of a paradox. An author at home in many forms of writing, Vargas Llosa once described literature as the passion of his life. As his country's leading presidential candidate, campaigning for the center-right coalition, Fredemo, or the Democratic Front, he had come a long way from the days when he supported the Cuban revolution and was an active member in Cahuide, a small underground remnant of Peru's then-outlawed Communist Party.

He had also come a long way from his student days in the University of San Marcos when he longed to leave Peru for the heady stimulation of Europe where so many of his favorite novels at the time were set and written. His escape came in 1958 after winning a fellowship to pursue a doctoral degree in literature at the University of Madrid.

Nevertheless, although he spent two years in Madrid and several more in Paris working for French radio and television, he continued to think and write about his homeland. As evident from his life and fiction, Vargas Llosa had an intense love-hate relationship with Peru from his boyhood when he first began to write.

He was born on March 28, 1936, in the southern Peruvian city of Arequipa. For the first 10 years of his life he lived in Cochabamba, Bolivia, with his mother and grandparents. He returned to Peru, however, in 1946 when his parents, who had divorced shortly before his birth, were reunited. The family settled in Magdalena del Mar, a middle-class Lima suburb.

By the time he was 16 he was working part-time for several Lima tabloids, covering crime stories mainly. His first book, *Los Jefes,* a collection of short stories, was published in 1958 when he was 22.

These years proved to be difficult for Vargas Llosa, however, since he and his father did not see eye to eye on

Vargas Llosa's writing ambitions. "We were opposites; we did not respect each other," the author said. "In Bolivia I wrote and my grandparents and mother hailed me for it. When my father discovered that I was a writer, he had the opposite reaction. The bourgeoisie of Lima then scorned literature—they considered it an alibi for idlers, an activity of the upper class."

Fearful that his son was in danger of losing his virility because of his passion for writing, Vargas Llosa's father shipped him off to Leoncio Prado, an institution that the author described as half reform school and half college, run by fanatics of military discipline. "It was the discovery of hell for me," Vargas Llosa said. "I understood what Darwin's theory meant in the struggle for life."

Vargas Llosa's painful experiences at Leoncio Prado were the basis for his first novel, *The Time of the Hero* (1963). The work gained instant notoriety when Peruvian military leaders condemned it and burned one thousand copies in the courtyard of Leoncio Prado.

Praised for its stylistic and innovative craftsmanship, the novel presented from multiple points of view a story of official corruption and cruelty in a military institution. It won several major literary awards in Europe and quickly established Vargas Llosa's reputation as social critic and writer.

Vargas Llosa's next two novels were *The Green House* (1969), a magical realistic tale of an enchanted whorehouse, and *Conversation in the Cathedral* (1969), a 601-page narrative of the moral depravity of life in Peru during the 1950s under dictator Manuel Odria. Both books provided further variations on his themes of hypocrisy and corruption in Peruvian society and politics.

In 1973, however, Vargas Llosa's first humorous novel, *Captain Pantoja and the Special Service,* was published. A black comedy about a naive army officer who diligently obeys his commanding officers' order to organize a corp of prostitutes to service soldiers in desolate jungle camps, the novel depicted with biting wit Vargas Llosa's continual disdain for military bureaucracy and incompetence.

Four years later his most internationally popular—and most autobiographical—novel, *Aunt Julia and The Scriptwriter,* appeared. A fictionalized version of his first marriage to his Aunt Julia, a woman ten years his senior, the novel traces the adventures of an 18-year-old character named Mario and the outlandish plots of his co-worker and friend, Pedro Camacho, a fanatical writer of soap operas who becomes increasing neurotic as he spins out daily his fantastic, convoluted tale of love, loss, and insanity.

This device of multiple-level storytelling from the point of view of widely divergent characters is a Vargas Llosa hallmark, and most critics agree that the structures of his next two overtly political novels, *War at the End of the World* (1981) and *The Real Life of Alejandro Mayta* (1984), are shaped by it.

In 1986 Vargas Llosa turned his hand to detective fiction and wrote the fast-paced cops and killer thriller *Who Killed Palomino Molera?* Although the novel lacked the thickly layered narrative scope of his other works, it clearly proved Vargas Llosa's talents for writing sordid detail and earthy, comic dialogue.

His 1987 work *The Storyteller* returned again to the theme of tale-telling from multiple points of view. It relates the adventures of a nameless narrator who is fascinated by the almost mystical transformation of his college friend, Saul Zurantas, a Peruvian Jew and former student of ethnology, who leaves civilization to live and tell tales among the Machiguenga tribesmen in the depths of the Amazonian rain forests. "Who is purer or happier because he's renounced his destiny?" The storyteller asks as he roams the jungle with the Machiguenga, people who must continually walk in order to fulfill their obligation to the gods and preserve the earth and the sky and the stars. "Nobody," the storyteller responds. "We'd best be what we are. The one who gives up fulfilling his own obligation so as to fulfill that of another will lose his soul."

A haunting, deeply spiritual novel, *The Storyteller* is entirely different in scope and tone from Vargas Llosa's later work *Elogio de la Madrastra* (1988), an erotic tale of sexual tension between a stepmother and stepson, described by the author as a "diversion." An English translation, *In Praise of the Stepmother,* was published in 1990. It was an erotic novel about a beautiful but naughty little boy. The later novels are amazing works to come from the pen of a man who temporarily, at least, abandoned his isolation as a writer to pursue an active political career. This was to fulfill what he considered his obligations toward improving the moral, social, and economic quality of life in his country.

In 1990 Vargas Llosa became the candidate for president of a center-right coalition called the Democratic Front (Fredemo). He was opposed by the candidate of the Change (Cambio) 90 Party, Alberto Fujimori. The well-known author took an early lead but gradually lost ground and in a run-off election was defeated by Fujimori.

His book about the experience, *Tale of a Sacrifical Llama,* released in June, 1994, offers a convincing self-portrait of a political innocent sinking under a tide of democratic absurdities. This follows his work *A Fish in the Water: A Memoir* which detailed ''his bittersweet look at the nearly three years he spent in public life.''

Vargas Llosa went back to his writing full-time after his brief affair with politics. The coveted Planeta Prize for 1994, traditionally awarded each year to a Spaniard for the best pseudonymously submitted manuscript of fiction, went to Vargas Llosa (whose application for Spanish citizenship was approved in July); his *Lituma en los Andes* is a story of political violence and social regression—laced with Dionysian overtones—in a contemporary Andean setting.

Vargas Llosa's latest novel, *The Notebooks of Don Rigoberto* (1997) marked the first time any publisher had released a title in all Spanish-language markets on the same day. Sixteen of the 26 countries involved (including Spain) have Santillana companies to print and publish, although in the case of *The Notebooks of Don Rigoberto,* only Spain and Mexico printed for all the others. In the first month of publication 250,000 copies were sold, 100,000 of them in Latin America.

Further Reading

Additional information on Mario Vargas Llosa can be found in D. P. Gallagher, *Modern Latin American Literature* (1973); *New York Review of Books* (March 20, 1975); *New York Times Book Review* (March 23, 1975); *Contemporary Literary Criticism,* Gale, (1975,1976). Gregory Rabassa, '''O Tempora, O Mores': Time, Tense, and Tension in Mario Vargas Llosa,'' in *World Literature Today* (Winter 1978); Jerry Bumpus, ''The Good Soldier,'' in *Partisan Review* (1979); John M. Kirk, ''Mario Vargas Llosa's 'Conversation in the Cathedral','' in *The International Fiction Review* (January 1977); Antonio D'Orrico, ''Vargas Llosa's 'Demon','' in *World Press Review* (August 1987); Gene Lyons, ''Latin America's Bestlooking Great Novelist, Mario Vargas Llosa May Also Be the Next President of Peru,'' in *Vogue* (November 1989); Elizabeth Farnsworth, ''The Temptation of Mario,'' *Mother Jones* (January 1989); Alvin P. Sanoff, ''A Writer's Use of Adversity: A Conversation with Peruvian Author Mario Vargas Llosa,'' *U.S. News and World Report* (May 9, 1988); Richard Grenier, ''Have Typewriter, Will Run,'' *National Review* (March 24, 1989); Gerald Marzorati, ''Mario Vargas Llosa: Can a Novelist Save Peru?'' *The New York Times Magazine* (November 5, 1989); Roger Sale, ''Mario Vargas Llosa,'' in *Hudson Review* (Winter 1975-1976); ''Organized Pleasures,'' in *The Times Literary Supplement* (October 12, 1973); Jane Larkin Crain, ''Mario Vargas Llosa,'' in *Saturday Review* (January 11, 1975); Luis Harss and Barbara Dohmann, ''Mario Vargas Llosa, or The Revolving Door,'' in *Into the Mainstream: Conversations with Latin-American Writers* (1967); *Publishers' Weekly* (June 30, 1997). □

Harold Eliot Varmus

An expert in several fields of medical research, Harold Eliot Varmus (born 1939) became director of the National Institutes of Health in 1993.

Harold Eliot Varmus, a medical doctor, was appointed director of the National Institutes of Health (NIH) in 1993 by President Bill Clinton. Part of the Department of Health and Human Services (HHS), NIH, located in Bethesda, Maryland, is made up of several individual institutes; for example, Aging, Allergy and Infectious Diseases, Cancer, Child Health and Human Development, Environmental Health Science, and Drug Abuse.

On his nomination as director, Secretary of Health and Human Services Donna E. Shalala issued the following statement: ''We are delighted that Dr. Varmus will be our new NIH director—the first NIH director to have won a Nobel Prize—because he is one of the world's most eminent and most honored biomedical scientists. He has been working at the cutting edge of modern cell and molecular biology, and he has had an active relationship with NIH for some 30 years, as NIH intramural scientist, grantee, and public adviser. He has taken a leading role in national discussion of science policy issues.''

Varmus was born on December 18, 1939, and went to public school in Freeport, Long Island, New York. His father, Frank, was a family physician; his mother, Beatrice, a psychiatric social worker. Majoring in English, Varmus graduated from Amherst College in Massachusetts in 1961 with a B.A. degree. He received his M.A. in English literature from Harvard University in 1962. In 1966 he got his M.D. from Columbia University's College of Physicians and Surgeons in New York City.

During his time as a medical student, he spent three months in northern India at a mission hospital. On graduation he served as intern and resident at Columbia Presbyterian Hospital in New York. He then served as a clinical associate for two years at the National Institute of Arthritis and Metabolic Diseases, where he did research with another physician, Ira Pastan, on bacterial genetics.

Varmus joined J. Michael Bishop's laboratory at the University of California, San Francisco (UCSF), as a postdoctoral fellow in 1970 and began his long, continuing study of tumor viruses in collaboration with the staff. He became a faculty member later that same year. In 1979 he was named a full professor and in 1984 became the American Cancer Society research professor of molecular biology.

His specialties at UCSF were in microbiology, biochemistry, and biophysics. His research concentrated on genes that cause cancer, known as ''oncogenes.'' He achieved international recognition as an authority on retroviruses, the class of viruses that cause a range of cancers in animals and AIDS in human beings.

In 1989 Varmus and Bishop shared the Nobel Prize in Physiology or Medicine (as it is called) for showing that

oncogenes can develop from normal cellular genes called protooncogenes. While investigating a retroviral gene, v-src, which causes tumors in chickens, Varmus and Bishop found a nonviral src gene, which closely resembles v-src, to be present in the normal cells of birds and animals.

In the course of studying breast tumors in mice, Varmus uncovered data relevant to the study of AIDS and human breast cancer. His work focused particularly on the biochemical character of the AIDS virus. He was chairman in 1986 of the subcommittee of the International Committee on the Taxonomy of Viruses when it designated the AIDS virus as HIV.

Varmus chaired the Board of Biology of the National Research Council (NRC), served as adviser to the Congressional Caucus on Biomedical Research, was a member of the Joint Steering Committee for Public Policy of Biomedical Societies, and co-chaired the New Delegation for Biomedical Research, which was made up of the major figures in biomedical research. He was the director of a popular public symposium sponsored by UCSF on recombinant DNA in the fall of 1992.

At NIH, Varmus set to rest initial fears that his directorship might be compromised by his lack of prior large-scale administrative experience. He was able to restore morale and to initiate programs to reduce paperwork, open labs to outsiders, toughen standards of tenure review, and introduce innovation as a major criterion in the grant application peer review process. He successfully recruited top scientists to administrative positions by creating a depoliticized deci-

sion-making environment and by offering them their own labs on the NIH campus. This policy allowed them to continue their research and retain a sense of being active researchers, a policy which did evoke some Congressional criticism about conflicts of interest.

Varmus's strong committment to tilting NIH more strongly toward investigator-initiated basic research at the expense of applied and targeted research set him at odds with aging and AIDS activists, who had lobbied against his nomination. He consistently voiced concern to Congress that federal budget cuts would affect research at the NIH and at teaching hospitals around the U.S. as hospitals considered eliminating research to cope with the cuts.

He is author or editor of four books and hundreds of research papers. With Robert Weinberg he wrote *Genes and the Biology of Cancer* for the Scientific American Library, a book for general audiences. He served as editor for several professional journals, and on review and advisory boards for government offices and biotechnology and pharmaceutical companies. When the Department of Defense (DOD) received $210 million to assign for studies of breast cancer, Varmus served on the committee of the Institute of Medicine to advise DOD on assigning the funds.

Varmus is married to Constance Casey, a book reviewer and editor. They have two sons, Jacob and Christopher.

Further Reading

For additional information on Varmus see his book, written with Robert Weinberg, *Genes and the Biology of Cancer* (1993); Boyce Rensberger, "Nobel Laureate Confirmed as NIH Chief," in *The Washington Post* (November 21, 1993); Rick Weiss and John Schwartz, "Cyclist, Scholar, Scientist," *The Washington Post* Health section (November 23, 1993); *Science* (May 9, 1997); and *The Lancet* (January 1, 1994). □

Francisco Adolfo de Varnhagen

Francisco Adolfo de Varnhagen (1816-1878) was a Brazilian historian. His "História geral do Brasil" is still the starting point for any investigation of Brazilian colonial history.

Francisco Adolfo de Varnhagen was the son of a German metallurgist brought to Brazil at government expense to carry out studies there. The family then moved to Portugal, where the boy entered the military academy, after which he studied engineering, political economy, and languages. At 23 he published his first historical work, a critical edition of a 16th-century Brazilian travel account.

Meanwhile, Brazil had become independent of Portugal, and in 1841 Varnhagen became a Brazilian citizen. The next year he was named attaché to the Brazilian legation in

Lisbon, and he supported himself thereafter as a member of Brazil's diplomatic corps, usually, and by preference, in some capital where the duties were light and the archival resources large.

Varnhagen soon began work on the *História geral,* the first volume of which was published in 1854. He completed the second, final volume 3 years later and published a new, revised, and expanded edition in 1871. The work was based on prolonged research in the archives of Portugal and Spain, as well as on materials gathered in Lima, Asunción, Paris, and Vienna. Other works won him international recognition at the time, for example, his studies regarding Amerigo Vespucci, but it is the *História geral* that today's historians turn to for reference.

Varnhagen was convinced that "the historiographer is not a florid and verbose lawyer but a true judge who, after verifying the facts and hearing the witnesses, must make his decisions." However, like many historians in his day, he believed that with the facts the judgments would be self-evident and history would write itself. The result was a work that overwhelms by its detail. Varnhagen lacked both the ability and the inclination to sift out the really important from the trivial and thus arrive at synthesis, perspective, and integration. The *História geral* is an account based on painstaking verification among the original documents but filled with minutiae.

Yet Varnhagen did make judgments, sometimes unwittingly. He opposed the then popular romantic tendency to glorify the Indians. He preferred to note the contribution of the Negro and, most of all, the civilizing function of the Portuguese colonist. He believed in "Progress" and decried the past efforts of the Jesuits to resist Portuguese efforts to impose it by force upon the savages. He was a nationalist who thought that the knowledge of history and its heroes was the beginning of all patriotism; yet he opposed xenophobia and, at a time when Brazilians were still jealously guarding their newly won independence from Portugal, he gave the mother country its due. And, in these and other opinions, he sensed the central issues of Brazilian history: economic progress, political integration, the role of the Church, class disparities, race relations, and nationalism.

Further Reading

There is no book-length study of Varnhagen in English, although E. Bradford Burns, comp., *Perspectives on Brazilian History* (1967), gives considerable biographical information and an evaluation of Varnhagen's work. For historical background see José H. Rodrigues, *The Brazilians* (trans. 1967), and E. Bradford Burns, *Nationalism in Brazil* (1968). □

Marcus Terentius Varro

Marcus Terentius Varro (116-27 B.C.) was the greatest Roman scholar and an incredibly prolific writer. It is estimated that he wrote 74 separate works in 620 volumes on all aspects of contemporary learning.

Varro was born at Reate in the Sabine country into a family of some means. He was educated at Rome under L. Aelius Stilo, the first Roman philologist, and at Athens. As a follower of Pompey (against Julius Caesar) in the political struggles of the time, he held several public offices at Rome and carried out other assignments, some military, for his leader. He served under Pompey in the civil war. When he returned to Rome after the Battle of Pharsalus in 48 B.C., Caesar, the victor, pardoned him and commissioned him to establish a public library of Greek and Latin literature.

After Caesar was murdered in 44 B.C., Mark Antony put Varro's name on the list of those considered to be enemies of the state. Although his villa was plundered and his library destroyed, Varro escaped death through the intervention of Octavian (later Augustus). Thereafter, Varro spent his remaining years in seclusion, reading and writing.

Wide Range of Subjects

Varro's range of subjects was vast, although only a small number of works are extant. He wrote 150 books of Menippean satire (a mixture of poetry and prose on a variety of topics), plus other satires, poems, and dramatic works; 41 books called *Antiquities of Things Human and Divine; Annals; City Affairs; On the Nationality of the Roman People,* dealing with the origins of the Romans; *On the Life of the Roman People,* an outline of Roman civilization; *Causes,* an investigation into Roman customs; and *Logistorici,* philosophical essays using historical examples.

Varro also wrote *Civil Law; The Seashore,* a treatise on geography; works on meteorology; and almanacs for farmers and sailors. He produced books on rhetoric, grammar, poets, poetry, and stage equipment, as well as criticism of the Roman dramatist Plautus. He innovated the illustrated biography. Called *Portraits,* it contained brief biographical essays on some 700 famous Greeks and Romans, with likenesses of each.

Varro also wrote on agriculture, mathematics, and astronomy. His *Subjects for Learning* set forth in 9 books a curriculum in the liberal arts, that is, areas of learning in which a free man should be knowledgeable: grammar, logic, rhetoric, geometry, arithmetic, astronomy, music, medicine, and architecture. *Antiquities* contained 25 books on "matters human" and 16 on "matters divine." The work reflected Varro's immense knowledge of the Roman past. The Church Fathers used it as a rich source of information about official Roman religion.

Menippean Satires

The *Menippeae saturae* consists of a form of satire that predates that of Lucilius, the first Roman satirist. Varro named his satires after the Greek Menippus of Gadara, a Cynic philosopher of the 3d century B.C. who wrote in a seriocomic style and gave humorous expression to serious views, and whose works were a mixture of prose and poetry. Varro's satires were originally in 150 books, but only fragments remain, totaling some 600 lines and about 90 titles. They aimed to make serious logical discussion palatable to the uneducated reader by blending it with humorous treatment of contemporary society. Two themes run through the satires. One is the absurdity of much of Greek philosophy; the other, the contemporary preoccupation with material luxury, in contrast to the old days, when the Romans were thrifty and self-denying. Various titles indicate something of the spirit of the work: "Who can tell what the late evening will bring?" (on dinner parties); "It's a long trip to escape your relatives"; and "A pot has its limits: on drunkenness." Both Petronius's *Satyricon* and Boethius's *De consolatione philosophiae* were influenced by Varro's work.

Latin Language

Of the 25 books of *De lingua Latina,* books 5-10 survive, although even they are incomplete. After an introduction (book 1), the work was divided into etymology (2-7), inflection (8-13), and syntax (14-25). From the fifth book on, it was dedicated to Cicero, which suggests that it was written no later than 43 B.C. Although the work is dry, pedantic, and often clumsy, it does contain occasional flashes of wit and often accurate etymologies. Moreover, it is a valuable source for quotations from old Latin poets. Books 8-10 set forth the arguments for accepting either the linguistic principle of anomaly or that of analogy. Varro argues in favor of analogy—as did Caesar's work on grammar, which Varro probably influenced. Although Varro's philosophy of language had its limitations, he realized the necessity of getting back to origins in the study of grammar, and he made the subject worthy of notice.

Treatise of Country Life

Varro wrote *Res rusticae* for his wife, Fundania, in haste, he said, for "if man is a bubble, all the more so is an old man. My eightieth year warns me to pack my bags before I set forth on the journey out of life." However, Varro lived for another 10 years. The treatise is divided into three books, the first on agriculture, the second on cattle, and the third on game and fish preserves. He used dialogue to make it more readable. The spirit of *Res rusticae* is very Italian and very patriotic. Varro admires the peasantry and exalts country life as honorable as well as useful. The work was a source for Virgil's *Georgics.*

Varro was a shrewd, practical man rather than a profound one, possessed of an encyclopedic rather than a synthesizing mind. He did try, however, to know all there was to be known, and to pass his knowledge on to his fellow Romans. In fact, he was so committed to conveying information to the uneducated that he wrote résumés of some of his longer works.

Cicero's praise for Varro indicates the value of his labors to Roman learning: "When we were foreigners and wanderers—strangers, as it were, in our own land—your books led us home and made it possible for us at length to learn who we were as Romans and where we lived."

Further Reading

For Varro's place in Roman literature see the background works by J. Wight Duff, *A Literary History of Rome, from the Origins to the Close of the Golden Age* (1909; 3d ed. 1960) and *Roman Satire* (1936). □

Ludovico di Varthema

Ludovico di Varthema (ca. 1470-ca. 1517) was an Italian traveler and adventurer. Current opinion holds that he did, indeed, visit all the places in the East he claimed, including some in which he was the first European.

Nearly everything that is known of the life of Ludovico di Varthema comes from his own account. Evidently a native of Bologna and a soldier, he left a wife and child in 1502, when, slightly over the age of 30, he left to visit the East. Curiosity alone impelled him; he did not seek to make money. He traveled first to Egypt, proceeding as far as Cairo, then visited Syrian Aleppo and Damascus, by which time he had mastered enough Arabic to pass as a Moslem. He joined a pilgrimage to Mecca as a Mamluk, or military protector, and thus became one of the first (if not the first) Christians to behold the holy Moslem city. In the "temple of Mecca" he said that he had seen unicorns, "not very common in other places," a remark that has caused much later speculation.

Varthema made his way southward by the Red Sea to Yemen and there became a prisoner of the sultan of Sana, one of whose wives fell in love with him. He triumphantly resisted her advances, but she nevertheless helped him escape. He proceeded eastward to Persia (now Iran) and Indian Calicut. He went to Burma (now Myanmar), Malacca, and beyond to Sumatra, the nutmeg-growing Banda Islands, Borneo, and the clove-yielding Moluccas. From there he retraced his course to India, where, deciding to return to Christian life, he left a faithful Moslem friend in the lurch and identified himself to the Portuguese. They accepted his services, and he fought in several battles under Viceroy Francisco de Almeida.

Probably in late 1507 Varthema sailed for Lisbon with a Portuguese fleet; he arrived there, after a rough voyage during which he saw Madagascar, in June. Almedia had knighted him in India, and Manuel I of Portugal confirmed this honor, also hearing with interest his account of Eastern regions the Portuguese had not yet visited.

Varthema straightway returned to Italy. An independent source reveals that he was in Venice in November 1508 relating his adventures to the Signory. Nothing more is known of him other than that he spent his remaining years in Rome and was referred to as dead in June 1517. His travel book, *Itinerario de Ludovico de Varthema Bolognese . . . ,* was published at Rome in 1510.

Further Reading

The modern English translation of Varthema's narrative is Henry Winter Jones, *Travels of Ludovico di Varthema,* published by the Hakluyt Society (1863) and reproduced in Sir Richard Carnac Temple, *Itinerary of Ludovico di Varthema of Bologna*

from 1502 to 1508 (1928). The same version is republished in Lincoln Davis Hammond, *Travelers in Disguise* (1963), with some explanations by Hammond. Varthema's career is discussed in Percy Sykes, *A History of Exploration* (1934; 3d ed. 1949), and Boies Penrose, *Travel and Discovery in the Renaissance, 1420-1620* (1952). □

Victor Vasarely

Victor Vasarely (born 1908), the Hungarian-French artist, was recognized as the greatest innovator and master of Op Art.

Victor de Vasarely was born in Pécs, Hungary, on April 9, 1908. As a young man he attended the Academy of Painting in Budapest (1925-1927) and then studied under Alexander Bortnyik at the Mühely, also known as the Bauhaus School of Budapest (1929-1930). The Bauhaus schools were noted for approaches to architecture and graphic design that were compatible with machine production of high quality and with well-designed objects and environments. At the Mühely, Vasarely became acquainted with the formal and geometrical styles of Paul Klee and Vasily Kandinsky and with William Ostwald's theory of color scales.

Early Work

In 1930, Vasarely moved to Paris, and after that remained a resident of France. He married Claire Spinner; they had two sons. In the 1930s Vasarely was a graphic designer and a poster artist who frequently combined geometric pattern and organic representational images. His *Study of Matter M.C.* (1936) juxtaposed objects of varying scales—a zebra, a piece of hound's-tooth patterned fabric, a black glove —with a richly colored background of rhomboids. The illogic of bringing together diverse objects of widely varying size and scale brings to mind similar explorations of Surrealist art. In *The Chessboard 2,* a black-and-white checked design of 1936, Vasarely explored the visually vibrating effect of insistent pattern as well as the appearance of depth despite the use of flat shapes and the absence of modeling.

Vasarely wanted to create designs that were universal. A socialist, his goal was to produce an art that could be mass produced and affordable for everyone. He became fascinated with an art of pure visual perception without traditional themes and representational qualities.

In 1944 the Denise René Gallery of Paris exhibited Vasarely's black and white designs of the late 1930s. This was the first public showing of Vasarely's work. That same year he began painting, and in 1945 he had a second show, devoted to his oil paintings. It was well received, and the Surrealist poet and critic Andre Breton declared Vasarely to be a Surrealist artist. Vasarely was influenced by the style of Salvator Dali, whose images were painstakingly rendered for illusionistic effect despite the illogical juxtaposition of recognizable objects.

New Levels of Abstraction

By 1947 Vasarely had changed his style completely and came to regard his first three years of painting as a false start. From then on Vasarely's work was abstract and increasingly based on geometry. He was working to devise a new pictorial language for the masses. He repeatedly studied the landscapes of the Breton island of Belle Isle, radically simplifying scenes to transform nature into geometric shapes. Vasarely increasingly found his subject matter in the sciences—such as physics, biochemistry, and magnetic fields—and described his abstract art as ''. . .poetic creations with palpable qualities capable of triggering emotional and imaginative processes in others.'' His art gave sensory forms to unperceivable phenomena.

Vasarely came to feel that color and form were linked in that each color and each form should share the same identity. He viewed his abstract art as composed of pure color-form which by its very abstractness signified the world through the limitless associations and responses of the viewer.

Kinetic Explorations

In the mid-1950s Vasarely began integrating architecture into his art and producing kinetic works, films and writings. The Denise René Gallery in 1955 had a pioneering show of kinetic art, ''Le Movement.'' Among those represented were Vasarely, whose works employed the principle of optical movement. Vasarely's concern with optical perception had lead him to explore the effects of motion, not of

the art object but of the viewer in relation to it. His works were composed of several overlapped sheets of Plexiglas on which black designs had been painted. The slightest motion of the viewer made the design seem to change and move as well. In conjunction with the show Vasarely issued his *Yellow Manifesto,* in which he discussed his theories of color and perception.

In Vasarely's black-white period of 1951-1963, he used compositions of stripes, checks, circles, or lines to explore the illusionistic effects he could achieve by modifying his patterns to give the impression of surface movement or of concave or convex forms, as in *Andromeda* (1955-1958). At the same time he developed the idea of eliminating the premise of the figure-ground relation, the image or central motif set against a ground plane or an environment, by filling the entire surface with uniform optical stimulation. In conjunction with this he often reversed a composition by inverting the black-white or color relationships. *Paar 2* (1965-1975), a pair of black-and-white compositions juxtaposed to be seen as one, is composed of circles and squares which are graduated in scale. In one half the shapes are black on a white ground and in the other half white on black. Wherever circles are used in one half, squares appear in the other half. By graduating the scale of these shapes, the effect is of planes of shapes advancing and receding. The optical perception created a sort of visual vibration. As Vasarely asked, ''isn't optics, even if illusion, a part of kinetics?''

Designing Mass-Produced Art

Vasarely felt that the uniqueness of a work of art and the artist's personal involvement in its execution were bourgeois notions. He worked in a manner that lent itself to mass production by modern technical processes. Limiting himself to flat lines, simple geometric shapes, and unmodulated color, Vasarely viewed himself as a ''creator'' of designs which could be inexpensively produced in the same, enlarged, or reduced scales. This was reflected in his method of conception. Working on graph paper, Vasarely made notations of letters (for the shape to appear in a given graphed square) and numbers (one through 16 to indicate the shade or value of a particular hue or color). By using simple geometric shapes and hues that were modified by his established scale of shades, he or others could produce copies of a design. In this way he produced art which he believed could benefit all of society by being available and affordable.

This claim for significance beyond personal aggrandizement found justification in the 1960s as Vasarely influenced groups of younger artists and his designs were widely reproduced in posters, fabrics and other images in mass circulation. While Op Art (Optical Art) had its zenith in the 1960s, Vasarely was recognized as its pioneer and greatest master. He continued to work in the Op Art style with an undiminished reputation into the 1980s and was widely honored. He established the Center for Architectonic Research and the Vasarely Foundation in Aix-en-Provence. In 1976 the Vasarely Museum was opened in the house in which the artist was born in Pécs, Hungary. To permanently house his works, the Vasarely Center was opened in New York City in 1978 and the Centre Vasarely opened in Oslo, Norway, in 1982. Vasarely's work in film and architectural design as well as his more famous art and graphic design earned him a prominent place in the history of modern art.

Further Reading

Vasarely's own writings include *Plasticité* (1969) and *Vasarely* (1978). Editions du Griffon of Neuchatel, Switzerland, has published three volumes—*Vasarely* (1963); *Vasarely II* (1970), and *Vasarely III* (1974)—which are invaluable sources for the visual study of the artist's work, though each volume has very little text. For biographies, see Werner Spies, *Vasarely* (1969) and G. Diehl, *Vasarely* (1972). F. Popper's *Origin and Development of Kinetic Art* has a section on Vasarely. □

Giorgio Vasari

Giorgio Vasari (1511-1570) was an Italian painter, architect, and author of "The Lives of the Most Celebrated Painters, Sculptors, and Architects." His book is the foundation of modern art historiography and the prototype for all biographies of artists.

Giorgio Vasari was born on July 30, 1511, in Arezzo. According to his own account, he was apprenticed as a boy to Andrea del Sarto in Florence. He apparently suffered at the hands of Andrea's wife, to judge from the waspish references to her in his life of Andrea. Vasari's career is well documented, the fullest source of information being the autobiography added to the 1568 edition of his *Lives*.

Vasari had an extremely active career, but much of his time was spent as an impresario devising decorations for courtly festivals and similar ephemera. He fulsomely praised the Medici family for forwarding his career from childhood, and much of his work was done for Cosimo I, Grand Duke of Tuscany. Vasari was a prolific painter in the mannerist style and was also active as an architect, his talents in the latter profession being superior to those he displayed as a painter. He supervised the building of Pope Julius III's Villa Giulia near Rome, but his masterpiece is the reconstruction of the Uffizi picture gallery in Florence (from 1560), originally the offices of the grandducal administration.

The *Lives*

Vasari's *Lives* was published in Florence in 1550; it was revised and enlarged in 1568. He venerated Michelangelo to the point of idolatry. In the latter years of Michelangelo's life Vasari came to know him quite well, and for this reason the two versions of his biography of Michelangelo are of the greatest importance as a contemporary assessment.

The tradition of such biographies goes back to antiquity; technical treatises on the arts were also written in classical times, Pliny the Elder and Vitruvius having produced two celebrated examples. As early as the time of Lorenzo Ghiberti there had been an attempt to imitate classical prototypes by writing on earlier and contemporary artists, and Ghiberti, in his *Commentaries* (ca. 1447-1455), also wrote the earliest autobiography by a modern artist.

During the late 15th and early 16th centuries similar treatises were projected and written, and Vasari knew and used some of these earlier works. What distinguishes the first edition of his *Lives* is the fact that it is far fuller (and better written) than any of its predecessors or potential rivals. As Vasari says himself, he wrote as an artist for other artists, with knowledge of technical matters.

The book opens with long introductions on the history and technique of painting, sculpture, and architecture, as practiced in Italy since the Dark Ages, and then proceeds to a chronological series of lives of the great revivers of painting (Giotto), sculpture (the Pisani), and architecture (Arnolfo di Cambio), reaching a climax in the life of Michelangelo, the master of all three arts, who was then 75 years old. Briefly, the plan of the book was to show how Italian—and specifically Tuscan—artists had revived the glories of classical art late in the 13th century, reaching a crescendo in Michelangelo. Vasari is extremely partisan in that Venetians such as Giorgione and Titian are not given the prominence they deserve; and he also shows an uneasy awareness that if Michelangelo had reached perfection only decline could follow.

Vasari took great care to gather material on his numerous journeys, and, more than any of his predecessors, he looked at works of art. On the other hand, his reverence for factual truth was less than would be required of a modern historian, and he was unable to resist an amusing anecdote. This gives his book a liveliness and directness which has ensured its continued popularity independent of its historical importance.

In 1568 Vasari produced a second edition, much larger than the original and containing a great many alterations, particularly in the earlier lives. It also has many new biographies of living (or recently dead) artists, so it is an essential source for Vasari's contemporaries. He gives more space to non-Florentine artists and even mentions one or two non-Italians.

The most important changes are in the life of Michelangelo, who had died in 1564. Part of the revision of Vasari's earlier life was occasioned by the publication, in 1553, of the *Life of Michelangelo,* written by Ascanio Condivi, a pupil of Michelangelo, and probably partly dictated by the master. The versions by Vasari and Condivi give us, therefore, a unique contemporary picture of the life and works of the greatest Italian artist of the age.

It is almost impossible to imagine the history of Italian art without Vasari, so fundamental is his *Lives.* It is the first real and autonomous history of art both because of its monumental scope and because of the integration of the individual biographies into a whole.

Further Reading

There are several English translations of Vasari's *Lives,* in whole or in part, the best selection being that translated by George Bull as *The Lives of the Artists* (1965). For biographical information on Vasari see Einar Rud, *Vasari's Life and Lives* (1963).

Additional Sources

Boase, T. S. R. (Thomas Sherrer Ross), 1898-1974., *Giorgio Vasari: the man and the book,* Princeton, N.J.: Princeton University Press, 1979. □

José Vasconcelos

José Vasconcelos (1882-1959), a Mexican philosopher, sociologist, essayist, educator, and historian, is best known for his four-volume autobiography.

José Vasconcelos was born on Feb. 27, 1882, in Oaxaca, but the family soon moved to Piedras Negras. When José started to school, he walked across the bridge each day to attend classes on the Texas side of the Rio Grande. Later the family moved to various other Mexican cities, and for a time he attended the Instituto Campechano (Campeche Institute) and then, in Mexico City, the Escuela Nacional Preparatoria (National Preparatory School) and the law school, receiving his law degree in 1907.

Vasconcelos belonged to the Ateneo de la Juventud (Athenaeum for Young People) and participated in the Mexican Revolution on the side of Francisco Madero and Pancho Villa, meanwhile publishing numerous articles on the activities of Mexican intellectuals. When the revolution triumphed, Álvaro Obregón appointed him president of the National University of Mexico, and from 1921 to 1924 he made an extraordinary contribution as secretary of public education, organizing popular education, creating libraries, stimulating mural painting, carrying out an extensive program of publication, and importing educators such as Pedro Henriquez Ureña and Gabriela Mistral.

In 1925 he published *La raza cósmica* (The Cosmic Race), followed by *Indologia* (Indology) in 1926, in both of which he dealt with the culture of Hispanic America.

Because of political difficulties, Vasconcelos had to leave Mexico several times, so he traveled in Europe and the United States. In 1929 he launched his campaign for the presidency of Mexico but was defeated and again went into exile, living in Europe, Asia, and South America. From Paris and Madrid he directed *La antorcha* (The Torch), a magazine which he published in the years following his presidential campaign.

Vasconcelos is best known for the four volumes constituting his autobiography: *Ulises criollo* (1935; A Creole Ulysses), *La tormenta* (1936; The Storm), *El desastre* (1938; The Disaster), and *El proconsulado* (1939; The Proconsulate), of which the first two volumes are particularly outstanding. In this autobiography he reveals himself

as a man of very strong, sometimes contradictory, feelings; but because of its spirit, this work is the most valuable document of its time and, in spite of itself, a literary work, especially in *Ulises criollo,* which recreates the years of his childhood, adolescence, and early manhood, bringing the story up to the events following the assassination of Madero. Under the term of "Creole," Vasconcelos undertook to defend a Hispanic type of culture, both against a falsified indigenous cult and against Anglo-Saxon influence.

In 1940 he returned to Mexico and became director of the Biblioteca México (Mexico Library), continuing in that position until his death. He belonged to countless cultural groups, both in Mexico and abroad, including the Colegio Nacional (National College) and the Academia Mexicana de la Lengua (Mexican Academy of the Spanish Language). He died in Mexico City on June 30, 1959.

Further Reading

For information on Vasconcelos in English consult *A Mexican Ulysses: An Autobiography,* translated and abridged by W. Rex Crawford (1963), and Vasconcelos and Manuel Gamio's *Aspects of Mexican Civilization* (1926). A remarkably succinct exposition of Vasconcelos's philosophy is John H. Haddox, *Vasconcelos of Mexico: Philosopher and Prophet* (1967), which, dealing with just the major ideas, serves as a useful introduction to his work. □

Marquis de Vaudreuil-Cavagnal

Pierre François de Rigaud, Marquis de Vaudreuil-Cavagnal (1698-1778), was a Canadian-born governor of Louisiana and governor general of New France. He surrendered Canada to the British in 1760.

Born at Quebec on Nov. 22, 1698, Pierre François de Vaudreuil was the son of Philippe de Rigaud, Marquis de Vaudreuil, the governor general of New France. At the age of 6 he was commissioned an ensign in the Troupes de la Marine, at 13 a lieutenant, and at 15 a captain. In 1728 he served on an expedition to subdue the Fox tribe and was promoted to aide-major, and in 1730 he was awarded the coveted Croix de St-Louis. In 1733 he was appointed governor of Trois-Rivières and 9 years later governor of Louisiana. Although his accelerated career was due largely to his father's influence with the minister of marine, he had proven himself to be a capable officer and administrator.

In Louisiana, Vaudreuil held the Indian nations in the French alliance, removed the threat of English encroachment, and stimulated the expansion of the colony's economy. When he was recalled to France in 1753 before taking up the appointment that he had long desired—that of governor general of New France—Louisiana was secure and prosperous.

Hostilities had reopened in North America before Vaudreuil sailed from Brest in a convoy bearing 3,000 regular troops and their commanding general, Baron de Dieskau, but they arrived safely at Quebec on June 23, 1755. In September, Dieskau was captured in a skirmish and was replaced the following year by the Marquis de Montcalm. Vaudreuil's problems now began. He was responsible for the conduct of the war, but Montcalm commanded the troops in the field. They quickly came to detest each other. Meanwhile, the intendant, François Bigot, was systematically looting the colony and defrauding the Crown of millions of livres.

Vaudreuil's strategy was to use his irregular forces and Indian allies to harass the frontiers of the English colonies, forcing the enemy to be on the defensive, but Montcalm wanted to fight set battles in the European manner. Despite Montcalm's opposition and inveterate defeatism, Vaudreuil's strategy resulted in some brilliant victories, but in 1759 the British put powerful new forces in the field, and Quebec was besieged.

Maj. Gen. James Wolfe outmaneuvered the French by landing close above Quebec. Montcalm gave hasty battle and was defeated and mortally wounded. Vaudreuil regrouped the shattered French army and withdrew to Montreal. An attempt to retake Quebec the following year failed. Three British armies now invaded the colony. On September 8 Vaudreuil was forced to capitulate to Maj. Gen. Jeffrey Amherst. He then sailed for France with the other officials and regular troops. Along with Bigot and several others he was accused of malversation but was exonerated. His career in the royal service, however, was ended. He retired to his estates in France, where he resided quietly until his death.

Further Reading

Vaudreuil is viewed sympathetically in Guy Fregault, *Canada: The War of the Conquest* (1955; trans. 1969). George F. G. Stanley, *New France: The Last Phase, 1744-1760* (1968), is equivocal. □

Henry Vaughan

The British poet Henry Vaughan (1621-1695), one of the finest poets of the metaphysical school, wrote verse marked by mystical intensity, sensitivity to nature, tranquility of tone, and power of wording.

Henry Vaughan was born in Brecknockshire, Wales. He and his twin brother Thomas received their early education in Wales and in 1638 matriculated at Jesus College, Oxford. Unlike his brother, who remained to receive a degree and become a noted philosopher, Henry left Oxford without a degree to pursue a law career in London. At the outbreak of the civil war in 1642, Vaughan returned to Wales, occupied himself in the law, and then entered military service in the royalist cause. Later in life he practiced medicine, and he probably studied it during these years.

Vaughan apparently began writing poetry in the same decade. In 1646 he published his *Poems,* half of which consisted of a translation of Juvenal's tenth satire. The next year he wrote the preface to a second volume, *Olor Iscanus* (*The Swan of Usk*), which did not appear until 1651; like the earlier volume, it comprises secular poems and translations and shows little inspiration. In 1648 he seems to have undergone a religious conversion, perhaps connected with the death of a brother that year.

The major poetry of Vaughan, all religious in nature, was published in 1650 and 1655 in the two parts of *Silex scintillans* (*Sparkling Flint*). Some of the best poems in it are "The Morning Watch," "The Retreat," "Childhood," "The Dawning," and "Peace." He published more religious verse and prose in his later years, and a number of translations, but nothing after the great volumes of the 1650s retains much interest. He died in Wales on April 23, 1695.

Vaughan is a poet in whom it is easy to trace the influence of others, particularly the wit of John Donne and the quiet, understated, dramatic technique of George Herbert, to whom he credited his religious conversion. At its weakest Vaughan's verse is too plainly derivative, and not infrequently a poem remains valuable today for no more than a stanza or a line. At his best, however—a best that created some of the most beautiful lyrics in English poetry— his voice is profoundly personal, and his ability to maintain the emotional tension of a poem can be impressive. Much of his power derives from a mystical Christian Neoplatonism that he does not share with his poetic masters and that reveals itself in images of dazzling light, in cosmic visions, and in a fusion of Platonic concepts, such as the descent of man from the "sea of light" of his childhood to an alienated adulthood, expressed in biblical motifs, images, and language. His genius can best be suggested by the opening of "The World," in which a mystical vision is successfully conveyed in the boldest tone of understatement: "I saw eternity the other night/ Like a great ring of pure and endless light,/ All calm as it was bright. . . ."

Further Reading

The standard biography of Vaughan is Francis E. Hutchinson, *Henry Vaughan: A Life and Interpretation* (1947). Good critical accounts are in Helen C. White, *The Metaphysical Poets: A Study in Religious Experience* (1936); Douglas Bush, *English Literature of the Earlier Seventeenth Century* (1945; 2d ed. 1962), the best source for information on literary backgrounds as well; and Joan Bennett, *Five Metaphysical Poets* (1964).

Additional Sources

Davies, Stevie, *Henry Vaughan,* Bridgend, Mid Glamorgan, Wales: Seren; Chester Springs, PA: U.S. distributor, Dufour Editions, 1995. ☐

Sarah Lois Vaughan

Sarah Lois Vaughan (1924-1990) was one of jazz's greatest singers for almost half a century. Her rich voice and distinctive style, often applied to popular songs, brought her fame beyond the confines of the jazz world.

Sarah Lois Vaughan was born in Newark, New Jersey, on March 27, 1924. Her father was a carpenter and an amateur guitarist; her mother was a laundress and a church vocalist. From the age of 7 Sarah studied piano, and at age 12 became organist and solo vocalist in Newark's Mount Zion Baptist Church choir.

In 1942 at the Apollo Theater's weekly Amateur Night Sarah won first prize for a rendition of "Body and Soul" that so impressed jazz singer Billy Eckstine that he persuaded his bandleader, Earl Hines, to hire her. In 1944 Eckstine left Hines's band to form his own and took Sarah (as well as jazz greats Dizzy Gillespie and Charlie Parker) with him. Vaughan stayed with the band for a year, and then in late 1945 she began her long solo career.

For the next 45 years she was to record virtually every jazz and pop standard against backgrounds that varied from small and big jazz ensembles to large studio bands and symphonic orchestras. Her earliest hits, "Lover Man" and "If You Could See Me Now" (1946), and a number of duets with Billy Eckstine, including "Dedicated to You" and "I Could Write a Book" (1949), established her as a new jazz star. She had a comfortable three-octave range, a heavy vibrato, and an uncanny ear. Possessing *perfect* (not *relative*) pitch, she executed with seeming effortlessness the most challenging and intricate harmonies.

Vaughan's early success was achieved with a mix of jazz originals ("Black Coffee" and "If You Could See Me Now") and the better Tin Pan Alley tunes such as "Body and Soul," "I've Got a Crush on You," and "Tenderly." In the 1950s she waded into more commercial waters, recording show tunes such as "Whatever Lola Wants" and "Mr. Wonderful," which consequently widened her audience. Some of the songs were throwaways, unworthy of her great talent, and they seemed to encourage the showman and showoff in her. Occasionally her work in the 1950s smacks of vocal pyrotechnics rather than genuine explorations of the material. One exception was her big hit "Misty" (with some spare but brilliant backing by tenor saxophonist Zoot Sims).

By 1960 Vaughan had fully returned to her artistic strengths, and for the last 30 years of her career she sang in jazz clubs, concertized in auditoriums, and produced a remarkable body of recorded music for the Roulette, Mercury, Columbia, and Pablo labels. Her output over that period was almost uniformly excellent, but among her best albums are *The Duke Ellington Songbook, volumes 1 and 2,* which, making the most of Ellington's compositional genius, contains magnificent versions of "All Too Soon," "Lush Life," "Sophisticated Lady," and "Day Dreams"; *The Explosive Side of Sarah Vaughan,* with arrangements by the

great Benny Carter; *How Long Has This Been Going On?;* *Sarah and Basie;* and *Gershwin Live!,* for which Vaughan won the 1982 Grammy for Best Jazz Vocal Performance.

Beginning in 1957, when she first recorded it with Quincy Jones' band, "Misty" was the song most associated with Vaughan and most often requested by live audiences, but by the mid-1970s Stephen Sondheim's "Send in the Clowns" had become her showpiece, the closing musical signature of her concerts.

Vaughan was married four times: to bandleader George Treadwell, to professional football player Clyde Atkins, to Las Vegas restaurateur Marshall Fisher, and to jazz trumpeter Waymon Reed; all ended in divorce. She had one daughter, Deborah "Paris" Vaughan. Vaughan died of lung cancer in her Los Angeles suburban home on April 3, 1990. A few months before her death, she had teamed up with producer Qunicy Jones to record some tracks for his *Back on the Block* album. On that album, Vaughan's recording of *September* would be her last.

Singer Mel Torme credited Vaughan with having "the best vocal instrument of any singer working in the popular field." *New York Times* jazz critic John S. Wilson called hers "the finest voice ever applied to jazz." Billy Eckstine said that she was his favorite all-time singer. Alternatively and affectionately known as "Sassy" and "The Divine Sarah" (echoes of Sarah Bernhardt), she commanded respect both as musician and person.

Further Reading

There are countless articles on Sarah Vaughan but no full-length study as yet. The best short piece is in Gary Giddins' *Riding on a Blue Note* (1981). By far the most rounded portrayal is to be found in the excellent one-hour documentary film "Sarah Vaughan: The Divine One" (1991), a joint U.S.-Japanese-German production. Additional information is available at the *Sarah Vaughan Site* at http://www.geocities.com/vienna/8244. □

Ralph Vaughan Williams

The English composer Ralph Vaughan Williams (1872-1958) was a proponent of nationalism in music and was active in reviving the English folk song.

The son of a clergyman, Ralph Vaughan Williams was born at Down Ampney in Gloucestershire on Oct. 12, 1872. He attended the Royal College of Music and then took music degrees at Trinity College, Cambridge University. He studied in Berlin with Max Bruch (1896-1897). On his return to England, Vaughan Williams served as organist and choirmaster in several churches and was a teacher of composition at the Royal College of Music.

In 1904 Vaughan Williams joined the English Folk Song Society, and for several years he was active in collecting and arranging old English melodies. He also became familiar with the music of William Byrd and Henry Purcell, English composers of the 16th and 17th centuries. The modal melodies of the folk songs and the free rhythms and smooth counterpoint of the early composers became important elements of Vaughan Williams's compositions.

The *Fantasia on a Theme by Tallis* for string quartet and double string orchestra (1908, revised 1913) is one of Vaughan Williams's most important early compositions. With this piece English music shook off 2 centuries of German domination and tapped a rich source of indigenous music. The cool modal harmonies and antiphonal string writing contrast strongly with the lush, feverish music that was being composed in France and Germany at this time. The *London* Symphony (1914) is another important piece in Vaughan Williams's development. Its sprightly rhythms and street tunes, the impressionist evocation of autumn mist on the Thames in the second movement, the chimes of Big Ben at the end—all this was new in 20th-century English music.

Vaughan Williams continued to write symphonies throughout his life; the last, his Ninth, was written shortly before his death when he was 86. In these works one can follow the composer's steady development. The Fourth (1935) and Sixth (1948) symphonies are perhaps his strongest, and most dissonant, statements.

Vocal music, both solo and choral, also played an important role in Vaughan William's output. Early in his career he edited and contributed to the *English Hymnal* (1906). His setting of A. E. Housman's poems, *On Wenlock Edge,* for tenor and string quartet (1909) is frequently per-

formed, as is his Mass in G Minor for double a cappella chorus (1923). His operas include *Hugh the Drover* (1911-1914), which incorporates folk songs, and *Sir John in Love* (1929), based on Shakespeare's *Merry Wives of Windsor*. In the latter work Vaughan Williams used the Elizabethan song "Greensleeves," which helped to make it one of the most familiar "folk" tunes of the 20th century.

Although he did not follow the newer trends and musical fashions of his day, Vaughan Williams created a thoroughly original style based on English folk music, 16th-and 17th-century polyphony, and informal music of his own times, including jazz. He stated his credo as a composer in his book *National Music* (1934): "Music is above all things the art of the common man . . . the art of the humble. . . . What the ordinary man will expect from the composer is not cleverness, or persiflage, or an assumed vulgarity . . . he will want something that will open to him the 'magic casements.' . . . The art of music above all other arts is the expression of the soul of a nation . . . any community of people who are spiritually bound together by language, environment, history and common ideals, and, above all, a continuity with the past." He died in London on Aug. 26, 1958.

Further Reading

The fullest account of Vaughan Williams's life is by his widow, Ursula Vaughan Williams, *R. V. W.: A Biography of Ralph Vaughan Williams* (1964). Michael Kennedy, *The Works of Ralph Vaughan Williams* (1964), is a thorough study of the compositions. Hubert Foss, *Ralph Vaughan Williams: A Study*

(1950), and Alan E. F. Dickinson, *Vaughan Williams* (1963), discuss the composer's life and works.

Additional Sources

Day, James, *Vaughan Williams,* London: Dent, 1975.
Foss, Hubert J. (Hubert James), *Ralph Vaughan Williams; a study,* Westport, Conn.: Greenwood Press 1974.
Mellers, Wilfrid Howard, *Vaughan Williams and the vision of Albion,* London: Barrie & Jenkins, 1989.
Vaughan Williams, Ursula, *R.V.W.: a biography of Ralph Vaughan Williams,* Oxford Oxfordshire; New York: Oxford University Press, 1988.
Vaughan Williams in Dorking: a collection of personal reminiscences of the composer Dr. Ralph Vaughan Williams, O.M., Dorking: The Group, 1979. ☐

Nikolai Ivanovich Vavilov

The Russian botanist and geneticist Nikolai Ivanovich Vavilov (1887-1943) is noted for his theory on the origin of cultivated plants and his law of the homologous series of inherited variation.

Nikolai Vavilov was born on Nov. 25, 1887, probably in Moscow, into a wealthy merchant family. Having decided to specialize in agriculture and biology, he entered the Agricultural Academy at Petrovsko-Razumovskoe. In 1913 and 1914 he continued his education at the School of Agriculture, Cambridge University, studying under Sir Rowland Biffen, and at the John Innes Horticultural Institution, working with William Bateson, a pioneer geneticist. Vavilov first established his scientific reputation by publishing papers on the immunity of cereals to fungus diseases, explaining immunity in terms of Mendelian factors, systematics, and plant physiology.

Upon returning to the former Soviet Union, Vavilov began to devote his attention to the origin of cultivated plants. Between 1916 and 1933 he traveled in Iran, Afghanistan, the Mediterranean area, Ethiopia, Somaliland, Japan, Korea, Formosa (now Taiwan), Mexico, and Central and South America, as well as many regions within the Soviet Union. The initial conclusions of his study appeared in *The Centers of Origin of Cultivated Plants* (1926). As a consequence of the expeditions of Soviet plant investigators to 60 countries between 1923 and 1933, Vavilov was able to list at least 8 centers with rich varieties of cultivated plants: the oldest in central and western China, India and Burma (now Myanmar), central Asia, the Near East, the Mediterranean region, Ethiopia, Mexico and Central America, and the South American nations of Peru, Ecuador, and Bolivia. In connection with these researches, Vavilov discovered the law of the homologous series of inherited variation, which states that closely related species tend to develop parallel hereditary variations. On the basis of this empirical law he had hoped to predict the direction of the evolution of established species and the emergence of new biological species.

Nikolai Vavilov (center)

From 1917 to 1921 Vavilov was professor at the University of Saratov, after which he was assigned to the Bureau of Applied Botany in Petrograd (now St. Petersburg). In 1923 he was appointed director of the State Institute of Experimental Agronomy, serving until 1929. From 1924 to 1940 he was the director of the All-Union Institute of Applied Botany and New Crops (renamed the All-Union Institute of Plant Growing). In 1929 he was elected a full member of the Academy of Sciences and became president of the Lenin All-Union Academy of Agricultural Sciences; he served as vice president of the latter organization from 1935 until 1937. He was also director of the Institute of Genetics of the Soviet Academy of Sciences for a decade after 1930. It is estimated that between 1921 and 1934 Vavilov was involved in organizing over 400 research institutes and experimental stations with a total staff of about 20,000. In 1939 he was invited to become president of the International Congress of Genetics, and in 1940 he was elected a foreign member of the Royal Society of Great Britain.

Vavilov was a tireless and dedicated scientist; his major goal was to overcome the Soviet Union's agricultural backwardness by modern scientific theories and methods. However, he was more successful in stimulating the output of scientific papers at a time when Soviet agricultural productivity was decreasing and consequently left himself open to the criticism that he failed to merge theory with practice. Trofim Lysenko and his followers started to attack Vavilov's

leadership and support of modern genetics. In 1936 the Congress on Genetics and Agriculture was convened in Moscow with the obvious purpose of discrediting Vavilov and genetics. Three years later the Conference on Genetics and Selection vilified Vavilov; his speech defending genetics was greeted with heckling and interruptions. In 1940 Vavilov was arrested, placed in a concentration camp at Saratov, and then transferred to a Siberian forced-labor camp located in Magadan. He died on Jan. 26, 1943, a broken man, a victim of quackery and Stalinist tyranny. In 1956 the Soviet Academy of Sciences ordered the republication of Vavilov's works, apparently in an effort to rehabilitate him.

Further Reading

Only scattered and brief biographical articles on Vavilov have appeared in Russian and English newspapers and journals. His *The Origin, Variation, Immunity and Breeding of Cultivated Plants* (trans. 1951) is valuable for his scientific work. For accounts of the decline of Vavilov and genetics in the Soviet Union see Julian Huxley, *Soviet Genetics and World Science* (1949), and Conway Zirkle, ed., *Death of a Science in Russia* (1949).

Additional Sources

Popovskiei, Mark Aleksandrovich, *The Vavilov affair*, Hamden, Conn.: Archon Books, 1984. □

Horacio Vázquez

Horacio Vázquez (1860-1936) was twice president of the Dominican Republic. His second period in office was probably the most democratic era in the history of the Dominican Republic.

Horacio Vázquez rose to national prominence during the dictatorship (1882-1899) of the part-Haitian president Ulises Heureaux, during which time he served in the armed forces. In the rough-and-tumble politics of that time Vázquez emerged a general and also acquired certain popularity among civilians. Although long serving the Heureaux regime, he joined with two other future presidents, Juan Isidro Jiménez and Ramón Cáceres, in ploting the overthrow of the dictatorship. In July 1899 Heureaux was slain by conspirators under the direction of these three men.

Although Vázquez and Jiménez had worked together against Heureaux, they immediately came into conflict once he was dead. For the next generation, politics was dominated by the struggle between two factions: Vázquez' followers, known generally as *horacistas,* and those of Jiménez, popularly referred to as the *jimenistas.* During this period Vázquez served as president for a year, in 1903-1904, but was overthrown by the Jiménez group. Vázquez was generally in opposition during the decade and a half following the murder of Heureaux.

The chaotic nature of Dominican politics during these years, and the growing burden and complexity of the national debt engendered by governmental instability, served as the excuses for United States armed intervention in the country in 1916. Effective power remained in the hands of the U.S. Marines until 1924. In preparation for departure of these armed forces from the Dominican Republic, Sumner Welles, a rising U.S. diplomat, was charged with arranging for the election of a new Dominican president. Vázquez won the election as candidate of the National party. He took office in October 1924.

Vázquez' second administration was one of the most peaceful and progressive periods in the turbulent history of the Dominican Republic. Government finances remained in order, although the government did add to the national debt by a $10 million loan. The President and most of his top officials were scrupulously honest. Modest progress was made in building roads and schools and other projects.

But most important of all, the government was characterized by a degree of democratic tolerance which was almost unheard of in the Dominican Republic. The opposition was allowed to function with relative freedom, and the press and other media of public expression enjoyed wide latitude to criticize the government.

However, one major violation of the generally democratic spirit of the Vázquez administration was its action in 1927 in having Congress extend the President's term of office from 4 to 6 years. This was later used as an excuse by apologists of Gen. Rafael Trujillo for his disloyalty to the Vázquez administration.

Trujillo was principally responsible for Vázquez' downfall. When, late in 1929, Vázquez indicated his willingness to run for another term, Trujillo, commandant of the National Army, began plotting with those opposed to Vázquez. When a revolt against Vázquez broke out in May 1930, Trujillo and the army remained "neutral." Vázquez was forced to negotiate with the rebels and, as a consequence, retired to private life.

Within a few months of Vázquez' resignation, the Trujillo dictatorship had been firmly established. Vázquez took no further part in politics and resisted all attempts of Trujillo to get him to endorse and support the new regime.

Further Reading

Although no study devoted entirely to Vázquez has appeared in English, Sumner Welles, *Naboth's Vineyard: The Dominican Republic, 1844-1924* (2 vols., 1928), discusses his early career. For a fairly extensive treatment of Vázquez' downfall in 1930 see Robert D. Crassweller, *Trujillo: The Life and Times of a Caribbean Dictator* (1966). □

Thorstein Bunde Veblen

The American political economist, sociologist, and social critic Thorstein Bunde Veblen (1857-1929) wrote about the evolutionary development and

mounting internal tensions of modern Western society.

Thorstein Veblen was born on July 30, 1857, in Valders, Wis. He was the sixth of 12 children of Norwegian immigrant parents. Veblen graduated in 1880 from Carleton College, Minn., and in 1884 he took his doctorate in philosophy at Yale. He was a brilliant student, yet failed to get an academic post—apparently because of his "Norski" background and his skepticism of established institutions. For seven years Veblen read books on the farm in Minnesota, tinkered with farm machinery, and took part in village discussions. In 1888 he married Ellen Rolfe.

In 1891 Veblen revived his academic career by enrolling as a graduate student in economics at Cornell. A year later he moved to the University of Chicago, where he stayed for 14 years. Despite numerous papers and book reviews in learned journals, Veblen's academic advancement on the Chicago faculty was slow. His first and best-known book, *The Theory of the Leisure Class* (1899), was followed by *The Theory of Business Enterprise* (1904).

Although he produced eight volumes between 1914 and 1923, Veblen's academic fortune did not prosper. In 1906 he had moved from Chicago to Stanford University for 3 years. His teaching performance was always considered poor: he mumbled inaudibly and consistently flouted the grading system by giving his students "Cs." His domestic difficulties and associations with other women complicated

his situation, according to university administrators. Forced to resign from Stanford, Veblen remained without a post for two years. Then, in 1911, he was appointed lecturer at the University of Missouri, where he remained for seven years. He remarried in 1914.

After a short period of government service in World War I, Veblen wrote editorials and essays for magazines and gave occasional lectures at the New School for Social Research. In 1926 he retired to his California shack, "a defeated man," in the words of his biographer Joseph Dorfman. He died in poverty in Menlo Park on Aug. 3, 1929.

Veblen's Leading Ideas

Veblen made his readers aware that, in his period, American small-scale competitive capitalism was giving way to large-scale monopoly trusts. Among the implications of this trend were: the monopolistic practice of administered prices—charging what the traffic would bear; the limitation on production in order to raise prices and maximize profits; the subordination of the national state and of universities to the role of agents for business; and the emergence of a leisure class devoted to wasteful and conspicuous consumption for the sake of status.

Veblen also rejected the prevailing late-19th-century social philosophy of the "survival of the fittest." Instead, he adopted a perspective of impersonal institutional change and conflict which owed much to Charles Darwin and even more to Karl Marx. Another major influence on Veblen was the utopian socialism of Edward Bellamy's *Looking Backward* (1888). Yet Veblen was never a social activist or even an open advocate of social reform. He remained for the most part an academic observer and analyst. Implicitly, however, some of his writings were severely critical of the existing social order, with overtones of agrarian populism and utopian socialism. A number of Veblen's basic concepts and insights have become widely accepted in American sociological analysis: these include the "sense of workmanship," "culture lag," "conspicuous consumption," and "waste."

Leisure Class

In his *Theory of the Leisure Class* (1899) Veblen analyzed the status symbolism of modern bourgeois consumption, with interesting historical and anthropological antecedents. Social prestige, he pointed out, is enhanced by wasteful consumption of time and goods. With few changes, this book remains an excellent source work for many present-day social and liberating movements.

On modern America and its economy, two of Veblen's best books are *The Theory of Business Enterprise* (1904) and *Absentee Ownership* (1923). These works trace the inherent conflict between profit-oriented capitalists and the general welfare—defined by Veblen as maximum productivity of goods and services. *The Higher Learning in America* (1918), a biting analysis of the consequences of business domination of universities, should be read even today by those interested in contemporary issues and conflicts on North American campuses.

Veblen's *Imperial Germany* (1915) and *The Nature of Peace* (1917) are still relevant. His posthumously published *Essays on Our Changing Order* (1934) throws more light on the cold war than do most interpretations.

Veblen's Legacy

Though he left no disciples, Veblen influenced economists of varied views, political scientists, public administrators and policy makers in Franklin Roosevelt's New Deal era, and a minor but significant social movement—technocracy. Originating in the early 1920s, technocracy identified the general welfare with maximum engineering productivity. But Veblen's organizational connection with technocracy was temporary and superficial.

Even his most orthodox contemporaries rated Veblen as one of the few really outstanding American social scientists. After his death his stature grew steadily, for his insights have proved both lasting and prophetic. His vision of America was a darkening one. As early as 1904 he wrote of a possible reversion to militarism. The deadpan humor of his literary style only highlighted his conception of America as a system of vested business interests propped up by indispensable canons of waste, artificial scarcity, unproductive salesmanship, war, and conspicuous consumption.

Further Reading

The standard biography of Veblen is Joseph Dorfman, *Thorstein Veblen and His America* (1934). A revealing portrait of Veblen in his Stanford years, written by a student who lived in his cottage, is contained in Robert Duffus, *The Innocents at Cedro: A Memoir of Thorstein Veblen and Some Others* (1944). J. A. Hobson, *Veblen* (1936), is the best early assessment of Veblen's work. One of the most authoritative evaluations is Douglas Dowd, ed., *Thorstein Veblen: A Critical Reappraisal* (1958). A good foil to the latter is David Riesman, *Thorstein Veblen: A Critical Interpretation* (1953).

Additional Sources

Diggins, John P., *The bard of savagery: Thorstein Veblen and modern social theory,* New York: Seabury Press, 1978.

Thorstein Veblen (1857-1929), Aldershot, Hants, England: Edward Elgar Pub. Ltd.; Brookfield, Vt., USA: Distributed in the United States by Ashgate Pub. Co., 1992.

Riesman, David, *Thorstein Veblen,* New Brunswick, N.J., U.S.A.: Transaction Publishers, 1995.

Griffin, Robert A. (Robert Arthur), *Thorstein Veblen, seer of American socialism,* S.l.: Advocate Press; Hamden, CT: Distributed by Roger Books, 1982. □

Luis de Velasco

Luis de Velasco (1511-1564) was the second viceroy of New Spain (now Mexico). A devoted and loyal public servant, he consolidated Spanish control over New Spain and implemented legislation ending Indian slavery in his viceroyalty.

uis de Velasco was born in the town of Carrión de los Condes in Spain. The son of a noble family, he attended fine schools and joined the military. He soon rose to the rank of captain general in the kingdom of Navarre.

In 1550 Spanish monarch Philip II appointed him viceroy of New Spain. Velasco arrived in Mexico City at a difficult time. The New Laws of 1542, which prohibited Indian slavery and the granting of new *encomiendas* as well as their bequests to heirs of *encomenderos,* had created much discontent and had brought the Spanish Empire in America to the verge of disintegration. Although the Crown repealed the inheritance prohibition and allowed most *encomiendas* then in force to continue, passions were still high when Velasco assumed his position.

Slave owners argued that emancipating the slaves would cripple the most profitable activities of the viceroyalty, particularly gold mining, and would reduce Crown revenues. Despite these arguments, the Spanish government believed that freedmen would become tribute-paying subjects, which they were not so long as they remained slaves. Velasco thus moved to enforce the law and freed an estimated 65,000 Native American slaves.

Velasco was entrusted with other important tasks. Since the Spanish conquest of Mexico in 1521, Indians had been forced to pay high tribute to the conquistadores. Velasco reduced it, thus alleviating the burden of the Indians. He also founded the towns of Durango, San Sebastián Chametla, and San Miguel el Grande and organized the Santa Hermandad, or Holy Brotherhood, a local police force which curtailed banditry. In 1553 he presided over the opening of the University of Mexico. He chose stern and incorruptible men to assist him in his work, and by the end of his administration in 1564, he had curtailed the power of the *ecomenderos* and consolidated the Crown's authority throughout New Spain.

Velasco focused part of his efforts on settling Florida and on exploring the Pacific Ocean. Since the Hernando De Soto exploration of Florida in 1542, the Crown had been interested in a permanent settlement there to secure it from the French and to explore for possible wealth. In 1559 Velasco sent an expedition under Tristán de Luna which landed in Pensacola Bay. But bad weather, hostile natives, disease, and starvation led to a costly failure, and the remnant of the expedition was forced to return to Mexico.

In 1564 Velasco sent an expedition to the Philippines under a Basque navigator, Andrés de Urdaneta. He established a permanent settlement and sailed back to the coast of California and then down to Acapulco. The voyage opened a continuous trade between Mexico and Asia. But by the time of Urdaneta's return, Velasco had died in office on July 31, 1564.

Further Reading

Information on Velasco's life and administration is available in Arthur Scott Aiton, *Antonio de Mendoza: First Viceroy of New Spain* (1927); Lesley Byrd Simpson, *Many Mexicos* (1941; 4th ed. rev., 1966); and John L. Phelan, *The Millennial Kingdom of the Franciscans in the New World* (1956; 2d ed. rev., 1970). □

Juan Velasco Alvarado

A man of humble origins, the Peruvian army officer General Juan Velasco Alvarado (1910-1977) seized power in 1968 and launched a sweeping but ill-fated reform program.

uan Velasco Alvarado was born at Piura, on Peru's north coast, on June 16, 1910. Among 11 children of a minor civil servant, he described his youth as one of "dignified poverty." After attending public schools in his hometown, Velasco stowed away on a coastal steamer that took him to Lima in 1929. He joined the army as a common soldier and the next year won admission to the military academy. He graduated at the head of his class four years later. Velasco advanced steadily through the ranks, becoming a division general, the highest regular grade, in 1965. During his career he represented Peru on the Interamerican Defense Board in Washington, served as superintendent of the military academy, became commanding general of the army and, finally, was made chief of the Armed Forces Joint Command, the nation's top military post.

Velasco believed that Peru required fundamental reforms. He feared that if these could not be achieved by peaceful means the impoverished, frustrated masses might support a violent, Marxist revolution—a prospect dreaded by the armed forces. When the congress blocked a moderate reform program proposed by President Fernando Belaúnde Terry, Velasco lost all respect for Peru's civilian politicians. A controversial agreement between Belaúnde and the International Petroleum Company (IPC), a Standard Oil Company subsidiary, in August 1968 gravely weakened the president and provided an opportunity for Velasco to strike. With eight like-minded generals and colonels, he ousted Belaúnde on October 3, 1968. Within a few days Velasco gained the cooperation of Peru's other military leaders, who staffed all important posts in the government. The "Revolutionary Government of the Armed Forces," as it was designated officially, would rule by decree for a dozen years.

Velasco quickly gained broad popular support by seizing the properties of the hated IPC. This action, along with the nationalization of other North American businesses and Velasco's enforcement of Peru's 200-mile fishing limit, badly strained relations between Washington and Lima. When the United States blocked loans to Peru and banned arms sales to that country, Velasco responded by obtaining money in Europe and weapons from the former Soviet Union, all to the delight of Peruvian nationalists.

In 1969 Velasco began a series of major reforms which he declared would create a society that was "neither capitalist nor communist." An agrarian reform, announced that June, eliminated the large private estates that for centuries had dominated the countryside. The government transferred these properties to cooperatives of plantation workers, peasant communities, and individual land-poor farmers. In rapid succession the regime nationalized the banking system, railroads, public utilities, the important fishmeal industry, and Peru's giant copper and iron mines. The government closely regulated foreign investors and declared a state monopoly in certain basic industries. The state assumed control over Peru's international trade and financed most new enterprises.

In the social realm, the Velasco regime reformed the school system, expanded the national pension program, provided low-cost medicines to the poor, and brought water and electricity into the squatter shantytowns surrounding Lima. It promoted equality for women and proclaimed the Quechua tongue of Peru's Indians a co-equal national language with Spanish. The administration instituted profit-sharing in all major industries and experimented with worker-managed enterprises.

The Velasco regime was a dictatorship, but quite a mild one during its early years. There were no elections, and civilian politicians had little influence. But the government respected most personal liberties, the press continued to function, and Velasco promised to establish a system of "broad, full, popular participation."

The military government was remarkably successful at first. Peru's economy performed well, and the reforms seemed to be working. After 1973, however, Velasco encountered severe problems. The mixed economy he created lacked the efficiency of capitalism and the discipline of communism. Waste and mismanagement in often ill-conceived programs, poor export prices, and a series of natural disasters brought a deepening economic recession. Austerity measures eroded the government's popular support. It responded to public protest with brutal force and silenced peaceful criticism by seizing the nation's newspapers. Under the stress of adversity, the unity of the military coalition began to crack. Velasco's health failed, and he behaved erratically.

Peru's military commanders removed Velasco from the presidency in a bloodless coup on August 29, 1975. General Francisco Morales Bermúdez, who replaced him, unsuccessfully attempted to restore Peru's economic health and popular support for the military government. In 1980 he transferred power to a newly elected civilian president— Fernando Belaúnde Terry, the man Velasco had ousted a dozen years earlier. General Velasco, meanwhile, had died on December 24, 1977. An emotional man of mixed Spanish and Indian ancestry, he had been a leader with whom the Peruvian masses could identify. A throng of 200,000 persons accompanied his funeral procession through the streets of Lima.

Further Reading

A narrative account of the Velasco administration is provided in David P. Werlich, *Peru* (1978). His programs are discussed in Abraham F. Lowenthal (editor), *The Peruvian Experiment* (1975) and are reassessed in Cynthia McClintock and Abraham F. Lowenthal (editors), *The Peruvian Experiment Reconsidered* (1983). □

José María Velasco Ibarra

The Ecuadorian lawyer and statesman José María Velasco Ibarra (1893-1979) was five times president of the republic and Ecuador's outstanding political figure of the 20th century.

José María Velasco Ibarra was born in Quito on March 19, 1893. His father, Alejandrino Velasco, was an engineer. His mother, Doña Delia Ibarra, had a very deep and lasting impact on the intellectual and moral formation of her son. He completed his schooling in his native city, except for postdoctoral studies in Paris, at the Sorbonne and at the Collège de France.

Velasco Ibarra started his public career in administrative posts. For 12 years he wrote a column under the pseudonym "Labriolle" in *El Comercio,* the principal newspaper of Quito. In his columns he fought against electoral fraud and for effective democracy. He was elected to Congress as a Liberal; but in 1932 he voted with the minority against the disqualification of Neptalí Bonifaz, the Conservative winner of the presidential election.

First Term

The following year Velasco Ibarra was elected Speaker of the Chamber of Deputies. As such, he led the fight against the new chief executive, the Liberal Juan de Dios Martínez Mera, accused of having reached the presidency through electoral fraud. Congress declared the office vacant, and Velasco Ibarra won the following elections with the backing of both Liberals and Conservatives. However, he was ousted after 11 months in office. Having grown tired of the obstructionism of the oligarchy and Congress, and unable to realize the reforms he proposed, he had attempted to rule as dictator and failed (Aug. 20, 1935).

After his ouster Velasco Ibarra went into exile, while politics in his country drifted through a sequence of coups, dictators, and provisional presidents. The next presidential elections were held in January 1940, and Velasco Ibarra, one of three candidates, lost to the Liberal Carlos Alberto Arroyo del Río. It is commonly accepted that, as usual, the Liberal party had made use of electoral fraud. Velasco Ibarra once more went into exile, and Ecuador under the new president suffered internal oppression, gave up a good part of its territory, capitulating in the face of a Peruvian military invasion and United States-Brazilian diplomatic pressure, and in general sank to the status of a satellite of the United States.

Recall to the Presidency

In these circumstances, the country remembered Velasco Ibarra, who came to be called the "Great Absentee." Police repression, through which the government tried

At the beginning of his fourth presidency, Velasco Ibarra had the support of the left. But when he started to show coolness toward Castro's Cuba and at the same time tried to increase taxation, the Conservative and Liberal oligarchies formed an alliance with the extreme left. This coalition was headed by the vice president and was strongly backed by former president Ponce. When trouble broke out, the army thought that the easiest way to restore order was by ousting the President (Nov. 7, 1961).

Velasco Ibarra was succeeded by vice president Carlos Julio Arosemene, who was also ousted by the army on July 11, 1963. The military junta that took over tried to introduce absolute prohibition of presidential reelection but was ousted itself in March 1966.

Last Term

After several interim governments Velasco Ibarra won the 1968 presidential elections over former presidents Ponce and Andrés Córdova, the Liberal candidate. The latter, as provisional president in 1940, had assured Velasco Ibarra's defeat by Arroyo del Rio. Now Velasco Ibarra had the personal satisfaction of triumphing over both Ponce and Córdova. On Sept. 1, 1968, Velasco Ibarra was inaugurated as president of Ecuador for the fifth time. However, just as during his first term, a hostile Congress nullified the executive branch. He decided to resign, but this time the army—apprehensive of what might happen—pleaded with him to stay and offered him its full backing. As a result, on June 22, 1970, he disbanded Congress and replaced the 1967 Constitution with that of 1946. The army backed his dictatorship for about 8 months. Then, as the aftermath of a frustrated revolt by some officers, Gen. Guillermo Rodríguez Lara seized the minister of defense (the President's nephew) and forced Velasco Ibarra to accept all the demands of the armed forces on April 6, 1971. From then on he became clearly a tool of the military. The officers may have wished him to stay beyond his term—ending Aug. 31, 1972—but he insisted on holding elections and on transmitting the presidency to the winning candidate. It was becoming apparent that Assad Bucaram would be elected, and he was totally unacceptable to the officers, who tried to persuade Velasco Ibarra to disqualify Bucaram. Velasco Ibarra refused, and on Feb. 15, 1972, he was ousted by the armed forces and replaced by Gen. Rodríguez Lara.

Velasco Ibarra's unprecedented success with the electorate was due to his understanding of the country's needs and to the support of the people. His relative failure in office is explainable through the fact that once the masses placed him in office he lacked the unqualified support of a permanent political organization and had to depend instead on the makeshift support of self-seeking opportunists. Though it is difficult to govern a country when there are so many powerful influences bent on impeding effective administration, Velasco Ibarra's five terms as president benefited Ecuador because he destroyed the stranglehold the corrupt Liberal party used to have on politics, brought about internal improvements, and refused to sacrifice the country's dignity in international affairs.

to suppress the popular movement in favor of his candidacy, led to a bloody revolt that overthrew the Arroyo regime on May 28, 1944. On May 31 Velasco Ibarra returned from his exile and was acclaimed president of Ecuador.

Velasco Ibarra was backed at the beginning of his second administration by a coalition of all political groups, except the Liberal party. The Constituent Assembly confirmed him as chief executive. But the new constitution was in effect only for a year, after which the President called for elections for a new constituent convention, which also ratified Velasco Ibarra's tenure. The Constitution of 1946 was retained until 1963; but on Aug. 23, 1947, Velasco Ibarra was overthrown by his minister of national defense, Col. Carlos Mancheno.

Political stability was restored with the presidency of Galo Plaza Lasso in 1948. In the elections in which his successor was to be chosen, Velasco Ibarra won against the Liberal and Conservative candidates. This time he was allowed to complete his full term (1952-1956). The constitution prohibited consecutive reelection. Despite strong opposition by the Liberal-dominated Congress, Velasco Ibarra transmitted his presidential powers to his legally elected successor, the Conservative Camilo Ponce. In spite of this, 4 years later President Ponce used all legal means to impede his predecessor's reelection. Nevertheless, in 1960 Velasco Ibarra won a landslide victory against the government's candidate and against former president Plaza, the Liberal party's candidate.

Velasco Ibarra died in Quito at 86 years of age on March 30, 1979, after suffering from intestinal and pulmonary infections. Velasco Ibarra had been living in exile in Argentina, and had returned to Ecuador to bury his wife, Corina del Parral, who died the previous month in a car accident.

Further Reading

Further information on Velasco Ibarra appears in George I. Blanksten, *Ecuador: Constitutions and Caudillos* (1951). Recommended for general historical background are Lilo Linke, *Ecuador: Country of Contrasts* (1954; rev. ed. 1960); Martin C. Needler, ed., *Political Systems of Latin America* (1964; rev. ed. 1970); Ben G. Burnett and Kenneth F. Johnson, *Political Forces in Latin America: Dimensions of the Quest for Stability* (1968); and Harry Kantor, *Patterns of Politics and Political Systems in Latin America* (1969). □

Diego Rodríguez de Silva y Velázquez

Diego Rodríguez de Silva y Velázquez (1599-1660) was Spain's greatest painter in the baroque style and one of the most outstanding of the European artists of his century.

The paternal grandparents of Diego Velázquez came from Oporto, Portugal, but both his parents were born in Seville, as was he. The baptismal record, dated June 6, 1599, was signed by his father, Juan Rodríguiez de Silva, and his mother, Jerónima Velázquez. Both parents were said to be of the lesser nobility. Diego was the oldest of seven children.

At 11 years of age Diego was apprenticed to the painter Francisco de Herrera the Elder, whose ungovernable temper caused the boy to be reapprenticed on Sept. 17, 1611, to Francisco Pacheco. Pacheco taught him for 5 years and later became his father-in-law. Most of what we know of Velázquez comes from Pacheco's treatise (1649). Additional information was published by Antonio Palomino (1724), who based his facts on a biographical account (lost) written by Juan de Alfaro, who entered Velázquez's workshop about 1653 as a boy of 10 years.

Some information is necessary to clarify the artist's name. Following Spanish custom today, it would be Diego Rodríguez (y) Velázquez, but his paternal grandmother's surname, de Silva, was apparently the only certain indication of the noble blood which was desirable socially and professionally. The document apprenticing him to Pacheco in 1611 identifies him as Diego Velázquez. Qualifying as a member of the painters' guild of St. Luke in 1617, the artist signed as Diego Velázquez de Silva. He continued to sign paintings and other documents as Diego Velázquez, but in the 1640s, when he strove to establish his gentle birth, he made every effort to be known in court circles as Diego de Silva Velázquez.

In Pacheco's workshop Velázquez received a strong education in the humanities and excelled in languages and philosophy. He was present when Pacheco's friends (artists, poets, and scholars) held lively discussions. Velázquez's intellectual interests are also attested to by the library he left at his death. Pacheco advised him on the importance of making copies from antique sculptures and from Michelangelo and Raphael.

Introduction to the Court

At 18 years of age, as a member of St. Luke's Guild, Velázquez was entitled to have his own workshop. Thus established, he married 16-year-old Juana Pacheco on April 23, 1618. His mentor was to write later that "the teacher's honor is greater than the father-in-law's." Two daughters were born between 1619 and 1621; only the elder, Francisca, lived. In 1622 Velázquez spent 7 months in Madrid studying the royal art collection but with the primary purpose of obtaining a commission to paint the King's portrait. Although he failed in this aspiration, he achieved his first fame at court with the portrait of Don Luís de Góngora (1622).

The following year the Count-Duke of Olivares, a Sevillian and the young king's favored minister, called Velázquez to the Madrid court. On August 30 he completed his first portrait of Philip IV; it was an immediate success, and the King declared that henceforth no one but Velázquez would be permitted to do the royal portraits. It is thought that this first portrait is hidden beneath the version of Philip IV (1626-1628) in the Prado. If so, the x-ray reveals a never to be seen again, animated monarch standing with relaxed dignity, his lips slightly parted as at the start of a smile of camaraderie, while his eyes search, with shy approval, those of the artist beyond. This underpainting has a spontaneity reminiscent of Frans Hals and provides a hint of the celebrated friendship between artist and sovereign. Ever after, the portraits show the formal Philip with eyes guarded and mouth prim.

Over the years Philip IV made numerous lucrative contracts with Velázquez, but the artist was continually forced to petition the bureaucracy for arrears in payments and to agree to relinquish several past claims in order to receive some current ones. He did not hesitate to appraise his works higher in value than those by others despite the Treasury's delinquencies.

Appointed Usher to the Chamber in 1627, Velázquez was raised above all other court painters. Indeed, that year rivalry had provoked a competition among the court painters; Velázquez won, even though his challengers and the judges were all Italian. Peter Paul Rubens visited Madrid the following year and had little to do with any artist except Velázquez, who had the honor of showing the renowned diplomat-artist the royal collection in the Escorial. Perhaps owing to Rubens's influence, Velázquez left Spain in August 1629 and spent 18 months in Italy.

First Italian Journey

The Count-Duke of Olivares had prevailed upon the ambassadors representing Italian states in Madrid to provide Velázquez with numerous letters of recommendation. They did so, nervously speculating among themselves about espionage. Velázquez's independent nature may be judged by the selective use he made of these letters. In Ferrara he accepted a cardinal's hospitality but courteously declined to dine with his host so that he might better arrange to see art works during his brief stay. He passed through Bologna but failed to stop even to present letters he carried for dignitaries there.

In Venice, Velázquez sketched Tintoretto's *Last Supper,* among other works. In Rome he made sketches from Michelangelo's *Last Judgment* and frescoes by Raphael. He left an apartment provided for him in the Vatican, saying that it was "too lonely and out of the way." Later he spent 2 summer months in the Villa dé Medici. While he was in Italy, he executed two magnificent paintings: *Joseph's Coat* and the *Forge of Vulcan* (both 1630). On his way home he stopped in Naples, where he met the painter Jusepe de Ribera.

Francisca, the artist's daughter, wedded Juan Bautista Martínez del Mazo in 1633. As part of her dowry Velázquez presented Mazo with his own Usher to the Chamber appointment, which the King promptly replaced with one as Constable of Justice. Three years later Velázquez was appointed Gentleman of the Wardrobe without duties and, in 1645, Gentleman of the Bedchamber. With all these honors, he nevertheless smarted under a social protocol which, for instance, had him seated in bullfights next to royal barbers and servants of nobility. He did not forget that Philip IV had knighted Rubens in 1628.

Second Trip to Italy

When Philip IV desired to add to his art collection, Velázquez seized the opportunity to suggest that he go to Italy to purchase works by Italian artists to decorate rooms of the Madrid Royal Palace. He set out in 1648 with his assistant, Juan de Pareja. Velázquez stayed away 2½ years despite frequent exhortations by the King that he return "not later than," with changing dates. The painter was treated with honor in Italy and associated with many great artists. A poet recorded in verse a conversation between Velázquez and another painter. The Spaniard was reported as saying, after a courtly bow, that "Raphael does not please me at all" and that "Titian was the standard-bearer" for "the good and the beautiful one found in Venice."

The climax of Velázquez's Italian trip was a commission to paint the portrait of Innocent X (1650). He prepared for it by painting his assistant, Juan de Pareja (1649-1650). He was said to have painted both "with long-handled brushes and in Titian's vigorous manner." Both portraits were instantly admired. Velázquez was admitted to the Academy of St. Luke and to the Congregation of the Virtuosi of the Pantheon. As a result of the Pope's pleasure with his portrait, Velázquez took a giant step toward his treasured dream: Innocent X instructed the Papal Nuncio in Madrid to support the artist's candidacy to be appointed a knight of one of the military orders.

Making of a Knight

On his return to Spain, Velázquez was showered with more honors by his monarch, but the knighthood was delayed, apparently by the resistance of members of the nobility. In 1652 Philip IV brushed aside the applicants recommended by a six-member board and appointed Velázquez to the office of chamberlain with a lucrative salary and a large apartment in the Treasure House connected to the Royal Palace.

It is well documented that Velázquez used his influence assiduously to advance the careers of his son-in-law and his grandchildren. Mazo, appointed painter of Prince Balthasar Carlos, continued to receive the emoluments of that office after his young patron's death. In 1657 Mazo was appointed assistant to the chamberlain (Velázquez), and Gaspar, his son, was granted the office of Usher of the Chamber.

Three Sevillian artists were in Madrid in 1658: Alonso Cano, Francisco de Zurbarán, and Bartolomé Esteban Murillo. The first two, and probably Murillo as well, testified loyally but untruthfully that Velázquez had neither assisted another painter, nor had a workshop in the professional sense, nor sold any of his paintings but had painted only for his own pleasure and that of the King. This testimony was the first step in proving Velázquez a gentleman. Philip IV took the second step by petitioning Pope Alexander VII to issue a brief exempting Velázquez from the obligation to prove his noble ancestry. In 1659 the King invested Velázquez as a knight of the Order of Santiago. He died on Aug. 6, 1660. Philip IV made a touching last gesture of friendship: he ordered the Cross of Santiago to be painted upon the doublet of Velázquez's self-portrait in *The Maids of Honor* (*Las Meninas,* 1656).

Velázquez's Art

In his early period (1618-1623) Velázquez painted portraits and genre and religious themes in a realism influenced by the art of Caravaggio with sharp contrasts of light and dark and, frequently, with a heavy impasto. A lack of religious conviction has been wrongfully imputed to Velázquez because of the way he would treat a religious theme in a seemingly casual relation to a commonplace, contemporary scene. On the contrary, this was a carefully planned device conforming to the advice of St. Ignatius of Loyola that, in order to persuade anyone of the faith, you should begin where he is and not from where you wish him to be.

Christ in the House of Mary and Martha (ca. 1619-1620) is a case in point. In the foreground a disgruntled young kitchen maid is at work behind a table while a kindly old woman calls her attention to the diminutive scene in the right background showing Christ admonishing Martha while Mary sits contentedly at his feet. After Martha complained to Christ that she was doing all the serving while her sister simply sat, Christ answered that Mary had chosen the better part, which would not be taken from her (Luke 10:38-42). This biblical incident has been cited as a justification of the contemplative life of a nun. It would appear, then, that the old woman is reminding the kitchen maid of the choice open to her if she fails to find contentment in the active role.

Significantly, art historians debate whether the tiny scene of the title is a wall painting, a mirror reflection, or an actual scene viewed through an aperture in the wall. This ambiguity is at the heart of Velázquez's intention to preach the timelessness of Christ's message. The painting also illustrates a constant in his art, whether the scene is a religious, genre, mythological, or historical one, or simply a portrait: his art requires thoughtful contemplation, which is rewarded with an insight into the profound, spiritual empathy the artist had for his theme or individual model.

Velázquez was inspired by Ovid's *Metamorphoses* to paint the *Triumph of Bacchus* (*The Drunkards;* 1628-1629), but he held a point of view toward mythology, common in the 17th century, that saw the activities of pagan divinities as less than divine and the behavior of humans under their influence as less than Christian. Thus, his Bacchus is a callow, overweight youth with flaccid muscles; the inebriated rustics are buffoons. Velázquez points his moral at the right, where a beggar is refused with false regret by one of the bacchants. *Mars* (1639-1642) caused an Englishman to exclaim in the 19th century, "Why, he's nothing but an undressed bobby [London policeman]." He unwittingly understood Velázquez's intention to unmask the glory of war.

Many of Velázquez's works show pentimenti, that is, changes made either at the time of execution or much later. Apparently, he made very few preparatory sketches and preferred to seek on the canvas itself the right form, the sensitive harmony of color, the diffusion of light in an airy space, and the synthesis of the whole. As the years passed,

his brushstroke became impressionistic, his pigment more liquid, and his surfaces more lustrous, and he simplified his compositions by muting the chiaroscuro. Finally, his power to reveal the divine—in the frailty of childhood, as in the portrait of Prince Philip Prosper (1659), or in the marred personality, for example, the painting of Philip IV (1652-1653) in the Prado, or in nobility of act, exemplified in the famous *Surrender of Breda* (1634-1635)—became so eloquent that the viewer instantaneously comprehends and responds as one with Velázquez, the compassionate knight.

Further Reading

The majority of publications on the life and works of Velázquez are in Spanish. An excellent source for references to the documentation is available in English: José López-Rey, *Velázquez' Work and World* (1968). A sensitive interpretation of the personality and work of the artist is given in George Kubler and Martin Soria, *Art and Architecture in Spain and Portugal and Their American Dominions, 1500-1800* (1959). A cursory presentation is provided in the text by Margaretta Salinger in *Diego Velázquez* (1954). The reader may understand the sudden and enthusiastic "discovery" of Velázquez by the Anglo-Saxon world in the late 19th century from Robert A. M. Stevenson, *Velázquez* (rev. ed. by Theodore Crombie, 1962). Jacques Lassaigne, *Spanish Painting* (2 vols., 1952), is recommended for general background. □

Nydia Margarita Velázquez

Nydia Margarita Velázquez, the daughter of a poor sugar-cane cutter, is the first Puerto Rican woman to be elected to the U.S. House of Representatives.

Velázquez, a Democrat, won her seat in Congress in November 1992, after a grueling and controversial Democratic primary that pitted her against long-time incumbent Stephen J. Solarz and a crowded field of Hispanic challengers. Velázquez now represents the 12th Congressional District in New York City, a heavily Democratic and Hispanic district that was created in 1992 to encourage the election of a Hispanic representative. The district of just over 500,000 people encompasses poor and working-class neighborhoods in Queens, Manhattan, and Brooklyn. However, because many politicians and officials feel that this district was configured on the basis of race, it is likely that the district will be ruled unconstitutional and redesigned.

As a Puerto Rican woman raised in a hardworking rural household with few modern conveniences, Velázquez brings a unique perspective to national politics. She was born March 23, 1953, in Yabucoa, Puerto Rico. Once famous for its sugar-cane industry, Yabucoa is located in a lush valley on the island's southeast coast. Velázquez and her twin sister were among nine children raised by Benito and Carmen Luisa (Serrano) Velázquez, who lived at the edge of town in a small wooden house surrounded by sugarcane fields and the Rio Limon River.

To support the family, Carmen sold *pasteles,* a traditional Puerto Rican food, to cane cutters in the fields. Benito, who had a third-grade education, cut sugar cane and later became a butcher and the owner of a legal cockfighting business. A local political leader, Benito founded a political party in his town and, significantly, passed on to his daughter Nydia a strong social conscience, according to the *New York Times.* During Nydia's childhood, dinner conversations often revolved around workers' rights and other political issues. "I always wanted to be like my father," she said in an interview with the *New York Times.*

Eager to learn, Velázquez convinced her family to allow her to start school at the age of five. She proved to be a bright student, skipping several grades to graduate early and become the first in her family to receive a high school diploma. At 16, Velázquez was already a freshman at the University of Puerto Rico in Rio Piedras. She graduated magna cum laude in 1974 with a bachelor's degree in political science. After teaching briefly in Puerto Rico, she won a scholarship to continue her studies in the United States. She left the island, with her family's reluctant support, to enter New York University. Velázquez earned a master's degree in political science in 1976, then returned to the University of Puerto Rico in Humacao to teach political science. Leaving Puerto Rico again in 1981, she became an adjunct professor of Puerto Rican studies at Hunter College at the City University of New York, where she taught for two years.

In a September 21, 1992, interview with *Newsday,* Velázquez revealed that she left Puerto Rico for more rea-

sons than simply to advance her education and career. "I was harassed when I was a professor at the University of Puerto Rico, when the [conservative] New Progressive Party took power in Puerto Rico," she said. Velázquez said that she was accused of being a Communist and leftist. She eventually made her home in New York, but her career in politics and public service has subsequently included work in both the United States and Puerto Rico.

She received her first taste of New York City politics in the early 1980s. In 1983 she served as special assistant to former U.S. Representative Edolphus Towns, a Democrat from Brooklyn. As a special assistant, Velázquez was in charge of immigration issues, and part of her job included testifying before Congress on immigration legislation. In 1984, she was appointed to the New York City Council, filling the vacancy left when former councilman, Luis Olmedo, was convicted on charges of federal conspiracy and attempted extortion. At the age of 31, Velázquez became the first Latina to serve on the council.

After losing her council seat in the next election in 1986, Velázquez returned to Puerto Rico to serve as the national director of the Migration Division Office of the Department of Labor and Human Resources of Puerto Rico until 1989. In that year the governor of Puerto Rico appointed Velázquez secretary of the Department of Puerto Rican Community Affairs in the United States, a cabinet-level position that functions as a major link between Puerto Rico and the U.S. government. Responsible for the New York City headquarters and four regional offices, Velázquez advised the Puerto Rican government on Puerto Rico's public policy and its commitment to the Puerto Rican community in the United States. She exercised her political influence in 1989 when Hurricane Hugo devastated Puerto Rico. Velázquez personally called General Colin Powell, head of the joint chiefs of staff, and shortly after, the commonwealth received a promise of federal assistance. During her tenure as secretary, Velázquez also led successful voter registration drives that led to the registration of more than 200,000 voters in Puerto Rican communities in the Northeast and Midwest; and in 1991 she initiated *Unidos contra el sida* (United Against AIDS), a project to fight the spread of AIDS among Puerto Ricans.

Velázquez's close ties with the Puerto Rican government came under scrutiny during her 1992 bid for Congress. Her critics charged she was more concerned with Puerto Rican politics than with the problems of her constituents— an accusation she repeatedly denied. During the campaign, it was disclosed that Velázquez, while working for the Puerto Rican government, had personally supported the pro-commonwealth position in the fierce ongoing debate over the island's colonial status. During the race, she took a neutral stance on whether Puerto Rico should become a state or nation or continue as a commonwealth. "My responsibility as a member of Congress is to support whatever pledge Puerto Ricans make to resolve the situation," she told *Newsday.* Acknowledging that she is concerned about Puerto Rico, she related to a *Newsday* reporter during the campaign: "I say that, yes, we have been oppressed and disenfranchised for too long."

Velázquez's bid for Congress came at a time of national efforts to bring Hispanics and other minorities to the polls. The 12th Congressional District was one of nine new districts created in 1992 to increase minority voting power under the Voting Rights Act. The district includes a patchwork of Hispanic neighborhoods in three boroughs, including Corona, Elmhurst, and Jackson Heights in Queens, the Lower East Side in Manhattan, and Williamsburg, Bushwick, Sunset Park, and East New York in Brooklyn. According to the *New York Times,* the average income in the district is $22,500, more than $10,000 less than the state average. Some 22 percent of the people are on public assistance, and 27 percent are non-citizens. While a majority of the district's population is Hispanic—including Puerto Ricans, Dominicans, Colombians, and emigrants from other Spanish-speaking countries—the region also includes whites, blacks, and Asian Americans.

Former Representative Solarz's Brooklyn district, which was heavily Jewish, was dissolved by the redistricting process. As a non-Hispanic, Solarz was criticized for seeking to represent a district designed for minority leadership. But he insisted that he was the best person for the job. "I categorically reject that only a black can represent a black district, or a Hispanic an Hispanic district," he told the *New York Times.* Although Solarz was a respected foreign policy expert in Congress, he was one of many legislators caught in the House bank scandal in the early 1990s, after it was revealed that he had written 743 overdrafts, according to the *New York Times.*

The 1992 Democratic primary in the 12th district was a bitter battle, pitting five Hispanic candidates against the popular Solarz, a nine-term Congressman. Velázquez ran an old-fashioned, grassroots campaign, pounding the pavement, making phone calls, and garnering support from family and friends. She could not afford much campaign literature or television advertisements. Although she raised just a fraction of Solarz's campaign fund of over $2 million, she had the endorsements of New York City Mayor David Dinkins, the Hispanic union leader Dennis Rivera, president of Local 1199 of the Drug, Hospital and Health Care Workers Union, and the Reverend Jesse Jackson. Dinkins's support was in part a political thank-you for Velázquez's 1989 voter registration efforts, which helped Mayor Dinkins win the Hispanic vote in the mayoral election.

Still, with four Hispanic opponents, one of her biggest challenges was to unite the district's diverse and politically fractured Hispanic community. Not only did Velázquez have to prove that she could represent all Hispanics in her district—not just the Puerto Ricans—she also had to fight the prejudice that often separates Puerto Ricans raised on the island from those with roots on the mainland. Even Velázquez's supporters describe her as controversial. "I think that Nydia just provokes very strong opinions of love and hate from people because she's so passionate herself," said Luis A. Miranda, Jr., president of the Hispanic Federation of New York City, in an interview with the *New York Times.*

Velázquez won the September 15 primary. Soon after, she returned to Puerto Rico and her hometown, where she

was given a hero's welcome. According to an account in the *New York Times,* she rode into Yabucoa in a pickup truck, accompanied by Mayor Angel Luis Ramos and a state senator. A loudspeaker proclaimed: "She's back! Our Nydia Velázquez, who will be the first Puerto Rican woman in Congress, is back in Sugartown!" Velázquez told the crowd that she dedicated her victory to her mother and the women of Puerto Rico. In an interview with *Newsday,* Ramos commented, "She represents a good example for the children. She came from a poor family and went to public school."

The low point of the 1992 campaign came in early October, when an anonymous source sent information to news organizations detailing Velázquez's attempted suicide and hospitalization the previous year. The incident was given much attention by the *New York Post,* which broke the story, and spread to the national media. Velázquez never denied the charges. Instead, she held a press conference where, surrounded by friends and family, she acknowledged that she had suffered serious depression as the result of personal problems, including her mother's illness and a brother's drug addiction. "In 1991, in a troublesome period of my life, I attempted to commit suicide," said Velázquez, as reported by the *New York Times.* "It was a sad and painful experience for me, and one I thought was now in the past." She noted that she was "appalled" and "outraged" that privileged medical information in the form of confidential hospital records had been released to the public, in violation of state law.

Velázquez's supporters must have recognized their candidate as a survivor who had overcome personal adversity and proven her potential to lead their communities. Velázquez, at the age of 39, defeated both Republican and independent challengers in the November election, taking more than three-quarters of the vote. At her election-night party in Williamsburg, Brooklyn, surrounded by "Fair Housing" signs, Velázquez said, in Spanish, that her victory was important for herself, her parents, and her people in the 12th District. "For you, I'm going to fight to gain better jobs, better lives, and better opportunities," she said.

As a non-traditional politician, Velázquez does not fit the standard conservative or liberal labels; instead, she often calls herself progressive. She hopes to concentrate her congressional career on the problems confronting her urban district, including jobs, the economy, child care, and housing. She supports federal construction projects to create jobs and government loans to help small businesses. Shortly before her election-day victory, Velázquez told the *New York Post* that she wanted to improve the educational system and stem the tide of crime and drugs. On the international front, she opposes Jewish settlements on the West Bank and favors increased economic aid to Latin America.

Velázquez also plans to prove that Hispanic women can serve proudly in the political arena. "We are the ones who go out and collect signatures, but when it came to the final process, we were not good enough to run for office," said Velázquez in *USA Today.* She is one of 47 female representatives in the 103rd Congress. "New blood is good," she told the *New York Times* on election day. Along with providing a new voice for Hispanics in Congress, she pledged to work with other minority and progressive members of Congress to improve the quality of life for all people in the nation's inner cities.

On December 11, 1995, the *New York Times* published a letter that Velásquez had written to the editor on the subject of bilingual education. She claimed that since Spanish-speaking citizens are the fastest growing minority group in the United States, the effects of English-only legislation would be problematic, as people would be unable to understand warnings in emergency situations and fail to receive immunizations against contagious diseases, which would endanger public health. Furthermore, she asserted that "Multilingualism is a tremendous resource to the United States because it permits improved communications and cross-cultural understanding. On the other hand, she concluded, "English-only measures undermine the economic competitiveness of the United States as well as represent an unwarranted governmental restriction on self-expression."

Further Reading

Newsday, September 21, 1992, p. 37; September 26, 1992, p. 10; September 27, 1992, p. 18; October 10, 1992, p. 13.
New York Post, November 4, 1992, p. 4.
New York Times, July 9, 1992, p. B3; September 7, 1992, pp. 21-22; September 27, 1992, p. 33; October 10, 1992, p. 25; October 29, 1992, p. B7; November 2, 1992, p. B1, B4; November 4, 1992, p. B13; December 11, 1995, p. A16; September 8, 1996, sec. 1, p 45.
Noticias del Mundo, November 4, 1992, pp. 1A, 4A.
USA Today, October 27, 1992, p. 2A.
Washington Post, October 9, 1992, p. A12. □

Diego Velázquez de Cuéllar

Diego Velázquez de Cuéllar (ca. 1465-1523) was a Spanish conqueror who founded Cuba and was indirectly responsible for the conquest of Aztec Mexico and Mayan Yucatán.

Cuéllar near Segovia was the birthplace of Diego Velázquez. He is known to have fought in Italy as a young man and to have reached America with the second expedition of Columbus. Settling in Hispaniola, he became a prominent landholder. During the governorship there of the Second Admiral, Diego Columbus, Velázquez was sent, in 1511, with three or four ships and about 300 men to conquer Cuba, whose insularity had recently been demonstrated by Sebastián de Ocampo. He was soon followed by his trusty henchman Pánfilo de Narváez and the priest Bartolomé de Las Casas, who acted as chaplain of the expedition. The conquest proved easy, for the natives of Cuba were not warlike; Narváez ranged the length of the island, slaughtering and capturing many.

As governor, Velázquez seized the first opportunity to break away from the authority of Diego Columbus and hold Cuba directly from the Castilian crown. By 1515 he and his followers had founded Baracoa (near the original landing site), Bayamo, Santiago, Puerto Príncipe, Sancti Spíritus, and Havana. He parceled out the Indians in *encomiendas* to friends he favored, including Hernán Cortés, and encouraged colonists to come to the island. Except for his harsh treatment of the natives, he was considered an able administrator.

Exploration of Mexico

Becoming interested in reports of mainland to the west, Velázquez sent out fleets in 1517 and 1518, the first commanded by Francisco Hernández de Cordóba and the second by Juan de Grijalva. Córdoba rounded Yucatán, and Grijalva followed the coast to Tamaulipas and heard reports of the Aztec empire.

Disappointed at the failure of his first two commanders to accomplish more, Velázquez in 1519 prepared a larger armada with about 450 fighting men and sent it under the order of Cortés. The latter founded Veracruz on the Mexican Gulf and straightway followed Velázquez's own example by repudiating his authority. The angered governor had just been granted the title *adelantado* by the Crown and felt that this gave him ample authority to discipline an unruly subordinate.

Velázquez raised another force, variously estimated at from 900 to 1,400 strong, and sent it under Narváez to arrest Cortés. He would evidently have gone in person had not his unwieldy bulk unfitted him for the fatigues involved. The brave but slipshod Narváez allowed himself to be surprised and defeated by Cortés, who imprisoned him at Veracruz and persuaded the entire army of newcomers to join his own expedition.

Velázquez complained bitterly to the Castilian court and obtained an order for the arrest of Cortés, but the Aztec conquest and the resulting riches ultimately spoke louder than legal complaints. A new order came from Spain bidding Velázquez to keep his hands off Mexico. He saw his last hopes vanish and soon died of a broken heart, as one writer says, or, more prosaically, of an apoplectic stroke.

Further Reading

All biographies of Cortés contain some account of Velázquez. Carl O. Sauer, *The Early Spanish Main* (1966), is a favorable discussion of Velázquez's administration of Cuba. Bernal Díaz del Castillo, *The True History of the Conquest of New Spain,* translated by Alfred P. Maudsley (5 vols., 1908-1916), has much to say about Velázquez but mostly in connection with Cortés. A lively, colorful account of the Spanish and other explorers of the era is Louis Booker Wright, *Gold, Glory, and the Gospel: The Adventurous Lives and Times of the Renaissance Explorers* (1970). □

Domenico Veneziano

The major contribution of the Italian painter Domenico Veneziano (1410 c.-1461) to early Renaissance painting was his subtle observation of the reaction of colors to conditions of natural light.

Domenico Veneziano whose real name was Domenico di Bartolomeo da Venezia, was originally from Venice, but he worked in Florence for most of his life. His date of birth is uncertain but can be approximated through stylistic comparisons with his better-documented contemporaries, such as Fra Filippo Lippi and Andrea del Castagno.

Much uncertainty remains among scholars about the beginnings and the chronology of Domenico's art. In 1438 he wrote a letter to Piero de' Medici asking for work and mentioning Fra Angelico and Filippo Lippi. This shows that Domenico was well versed in Florentine artistic affairs and leads to the assumption that he might have been in Florence before 1439, when he settled there. Only minute fragments remain of the important series of frescoes he painted intermittently from 1439 to 1445 for the church of S. Egidio in Florence, in which he was assisted by Piero della Francesca. In the surviving fragment of the fresco from the so-called Carnesecchi Tabernacle one sees traces of Domenico's Venetian background in the construction and ornamentation of the marble throne on which the Madonna sits. This fragment also demonstrates Domenico's awareness of the art of his Florentine contemporaries Fra Angelico, Masolino, and Lorenzo Ghiberti, as well as the principles of linear perspective only recently discovered by the architect Filippo Brunelleschi and applied in relief sculpture by Donatello and in painting by Masaccio.

Dated about 1445 is Domenico's well-preserved altarpiece from the church of S. Lucia dei Magnoli in Florence and the five fragments of its predella. The elaborate architectural settings in bright, light greens, pinks, and grays, as well as the simulated marble inlay patterns, are reminiscent of the colors of Giotto's bell tower of the Florence Cathedral and the ornamentation found in Tuscan proto-Renaissance buildings, such as the 12th-century Baptistery in Florence. The figures, well rendered with a sense of weight and volume, are plausibly situated in space. This is made especially eloquent through Domenico's strict observance of the natural flow of light and of the shadows cast by objects.

Other examples of Domenico's art are the fine *Madonna against a Rose Hedge* in Washington and the exquisite *Madonna and Child* in Florence (Berenson Collection). In his large tondo *Adoration of the Magi* there is a sumptuous display of ornament, and the figures clothed in fanciful garments are placed in a deeply receding and realistic landscape.

Further Reading

In English there is a fine article on Domenico Veneziano by Luciano Berti in the *Encyclopedia of World Art,* vol. 4 (1961). See also Lionello Venturi and Rosabianca Skira-Venturi, *Italian Painting: The Creators of the Renaissance* (1950), and Frederick Hartt, *History of Italian Renaissance Art* (1970). □

Eleutherios Venizelos

The Greek statesman Eleutherios Venizelos (1864-1936) ranks as the most important figure in early-20th-century Greek politics. He won his country over to the Allied side in World War I and then achieved prominence as an international statesman.

Eleutherios Venizelos was born near Canea in Crete on Aug. 23, 1864. He was educated at the University of Athens, but he returned to practice law in his homeland and participate in a rebellion. The failure of an insurrection in 1889 forced him to flee the island, but as a leader of the 1897 revolt, he saw the Turkish hold on Crete finally broken. The Greek government had not fared so well in its own war with Turkey, and Crete was placed under the administration of a consortium of powers (Britain, France, Italy, and Russia) which appointed Prince George of Greece governor.

Venizelos at first headed Prince George's government; but disagreements soon drove Venizelos into rebellion and unilateral declaration of Greek-Cretan unity. In 1906 Prince George returned to the mainland, and his opponent settled down to a routine career in provincial politics. Unification of island and mainland was finally sealed by the First Balkan War (1912).

Meanwhile, Venizelos's activities had brought him to the attention of Greek political circles. When the Military

League seized power in 1909, he was called to Athens, where he was put into office as a reforming prime minister under a revised constitution. Venizelos held office from 1910 to 1915. During this period he reformed the internal administration and strengthened the armed forces. In the two Balkan Wars, with Greece first as the ally of and then as the opponent of Bulgaria, his foreign policy paid off in territorial gains for Greece.

The onset of World War I, however, undermined Venizelos's position. The assassination of King George I in 1913 had brought Constantine to the throne. This monarch disliked Venizelos because he had forced the King's younger brother to leave Crete. More importantly, Constantine was sympathetic to the Central Powers, whereas Greece's international commitments bound it to Serbia and to the Allies. Venizelos was the main architect of those commitments, and his efforts to honor them forced his resignation in March 1915.

A subsequent election confirmed Venizelos's support in the country. But his resumption of office in August only reemphasized the contradictions in Greek policy. Bulgaria's mobilization that year forced the King to take similar measures; but Greece maintained its neutral stance, and when the Allies landed at Salonika (October 1915), Venizelos was out of office again.

In September 1916 Venizelos returned to Crete to lead another rebellion, this one against Constantine. His provisional government was recognized by the Allies, and his triumphal return to Athens in June 1917 was preceded by the abdication of Constantine. Greece now openly sided with the Allies. After the armistice, Venizelos departed for Paris, where, during the next 2 years, he reaped Greece's share of the spoils of war.

Unfortunately, a new threat loomed on the horizon. The Turkish nationalist movement led by Kemal Atatürk repudiated the concessions granted the Allies and Greece by Sultan Mohammed VI (Treaty of Sèvres, 1920). This meant continued war with Greece. Venizelos's defeat in the election of November 1920 was followed by the recall of Constantine. After the Greek army was beaten to its knees, the king left the throne in September 1922. Venizelos signed the Treaty of Lausanne with Turkey (1923).

Venizelos soon found himself confronted with the popular demand to abolish the monarchy. Despite his difficulties with that institution, he could not agree to the formation of a republic; and with its proclamation in 1924, he was once more exiled from office. Not to be suppressed, however, he was again prime minister, from 1928 to 1932 and briefly in 1933.

By 1935 a movement to restore the monarchy had gained sufficient power to bring King George II to the throne. In Crete, the elderly Venizelos, by now a republican, once more raised the standard of revolt. The plot fizzled; its leader died in Paris on March 18, 1936.

Further Reading

The life of Venizelos is recounted in D. Alastos, *Venizelos: Patriot, Statesman, Revolutionary* (1942). See also George F.

Abbott, *Greece and the Allies, 1914-1922* (1922), and Edward S. Foster, *A Short History of Modern Greece, 1821-1945* (1946).

Additional Sources

Alastos, Doros, *Venizelos, patriot, statesman, revolutionary,* Gulf Breeze, FL: Academic International Press, 1978. □

Robert Venturi

Beginning in the 1960s American architect Robert Venturi (born 1925) spearheaded the "Post-Modern" revolt against the simplicity and pure functionalism of modernist architecture. In both his buildings and his writings he championed an architecture rich in symbolism and history, complexity and contradiction.

The son of a fruit grocer, Robert Venturi was born in Philadelphia, PA, on June 25, 1925. In 1943 he graduated from the Episcopal Academy in Philadelphia. He entered Princeton University and received a bachelor of arts (*summa cum laude*) in 1947 and master of fine arts in 1950.

At Princeton, Venturi received a traditional architectural education under the direction of Jean Labatut, a French architect trained at the Ecole des Beaux Arts. From Labatut, Venturi learned not only how buildings are created in the mind of the architect, but how they are perceived by the person on the street. Venturi also studied architectural history with noted scholar Donald Drew Egbert. Later, Venturi's keen knowledge of architectural history would provide a vital source of inspiration.

Between 1950 and 1954 Venturi worked successively in the architectural offices of Oscar Stonorov and Eero Saarinen. Then, in 1954, he won the Prix de Rome. This award enabled him to spend two years at the American Academy in Rome where, in the company of Louis Kahn, he came to admire the city's Mannerist and Baroque buildings. In the work of Michelangelo and Borromini in particular, Venturi picked up some ideas about freely using a traditional architectural vocabulary of columns, arches, and pediments to create structures of great originality.

Upon his return to Philadelphia in 1956, Venturi entered the office of Louis Kahn. In 1958, he began his own architectural practice as a member of the firm of Venturi, Cope and Lippincott. In 1961 he entered into a brief partnership with William Short. Then in 1964 he and Philadelphia architect John Rauch established a firm. The Zambian-born designer Denise Scott Brown, who married Venturi in 1967, became a third partner in Venturi, Rauch & Scott Brown in 1977.

A Seminal Book on Architecture

Between 1951 and 1965, while Venturi was establishing his practice, he taught courses on architectural theory at the University of Pennsylvania. These courses formed the basis of his watershed book *Complexity and Contradiction in Architecture,* published by the Museum of Modern Art in 1966. Hailed as "the most important writing on the making of architecture since Le Corbusier's *Vers une Architecture* of 1923," Venturi's book encouraged architects to turn away from the rigid "form follows function" doctrines of modernists like Walter Gropius and Mies van der Rohe and to look instead to the rich architecture of the past—to the works of Michelangelo, Hawksmoor, Soane, Lutyens, Aalto; to ancient and medieval buildings, and to architecture that reflected local and popular culture. To Mies' famous maxim "Less is more," Venturi countered "Less is a bore," and wrote: "I like elements that are hybrid rather than 'pure,' compromising rather than 'clean,' distorted, rather than 'straightforward,' ambiguous, rather than 'articulated,' perverse as well as impersonal, boring as well as 'interesting,' . . . I am for messy vitality over obvious unity. I am for richness of meaning rather than clarity of meaning; for the implicit meaning as well as the explicit function."

Complexity and Contradiction in Architecture became a rallying point for young architects around the world who had become disillusioned with the stylistic limitations of the International Style. In effect, the book provided a manifesto for the Post-Modern movement in architecture.

The ideas in *Complexity and Contradiction* were given concrete form in Venturi's earliest buildings, including his first major work, the Guild House, an apartment building for the elderly in Philadelphia (1960-1963). In the Guild House, Venturi created a sense of artistic tension, or contradiction, by mixing high-art aesthetics with motifs drawn from popular culture. Constructed of brick walls pierced by double hung windows, the Guild House looks at first glance like an ordinary six-story Philadelphia apartment building. But a closer examination reveals a peculiar main entrance, seemingly far too small for the building, yet marked by a massive black granite column, a huge frame of white glazed brick (reminiscent of a 1930s movie house), and a sign rendered with giant supermarket-style lettering. Although later removed, a gold television antenna was prominently displayed on top of the building directly over the entrance; Venturi claimed it was "a symbol of the aged, who spend so much time looking at TV." Despite the purposeful banality of these motifs, they were skillfully composed within a symmetrical facade and were intended to be understood as high-art objects. Contemporary "Pop" artists such as Andy Warhol had an unmistakable influence on this sort of design.

Perhaps Venturi's best known building is the house he designed for his mother, Vanna Venturi, in Chestnut Hill, PA. (1962). Here again the aim was to create a building that would not only be functional but also capable of producing a sense of artistic tension. To do this, the architect mixed contradictory features: the exterior shape of the house is simple, yet the interior plan is complex; and while the overall facade is symmetrically conceived, symmetry is broken by unbalanced windows and an off-center chimney. Moreover, although the scale of the house is quite small, many of the details (doors, chair rails, fireplace mantels) are huge.

A Second Controversial Book

Venturi's willful playfulness with features derived from traditional architecture and his attacks against orthodox modernism did not win him many commissions during the 1960s. He continued to teach, however, and between 1966 and 1970 served as the Charlotte Davenport Professor of Architecture at Yale. Out of his teachings at Yale came his 1972 book *Learning from Las Vegas* (co-authored by Steven Izenour and Denise Scott Brown). This work, too, stunned the architectural world. It treated the gaudy, sign-filled Vegas strip not as an architectural aberration, but as a vernacular art form worthy of serious study. Venturi felt that the "Decorated Shed" and other types of roadside buildings offered design lessons that could not be ignored, and he argued that architects needed to respond to the reality and symbolism of the popularly built environment with buildings corresponding to that environment.

In the early 1970s Venturi's practice began to thrive, and after that the architect turned his attention more towards design than teaching and writing. Always refreshingly different, Venturi's buildings continued to reveal an interest in the vernacular and the historical. His Trubek and Wislocki houses in Nantucket, MA (1970) have the same pitched roofs and shingle-clad walls as the many nearby 19th-century Shingle-style houses. The curved facade of the Brant House in Greenwich, CT (1971-1973) reflects the influence of 1930s Art Deco. The Tucker House in Katonah, NY (1974), is reminiscent of some turn-of-the-century English arts and crafts work. Eighteenth-century Polish synagogues provided the inspiration for the wooden vaults in the Brant-Johnson House in Vail, CO (1975). Giant 1960s wallpaper-style flowers decorate the front of the Best Products buildings in Oxford Valley, PA (1977). Gothic touches can be seen in the "Treehouse" in the Philadelphia Children's Zoo (1981-1984).

In 1986 Venturi was selected to design an extension to the British National Gallery of Art's neoclassical building on Trafalgar Square, London. He chose a classically modern stone-faced structure. Venturi's firm also designed the Biology building at Princeton University (1983), a new Parliament House in Canberra, Australia (1979), the Laguna Gloria Art Museum in Austin, TX (1983), the Westway Riverfront Project in New York City (1979-1985), and several large exhibitions at museums in Washington, New York, Philadelphia and other cities.

Further Reading

The extensive literature on and by Venturi from 1960 to 1982 is listed in Pettena and Vogliazzo, eds., *Venturi, Rauch and Scott Brown* (1981). Another bibliographic listing on VRSB, with three scholarly essays and many fine photographs, is available in the December 1981 issue of *Architecture + Urbanism* (extra edition). Besides *Complexity and Contradiction in Architecture* and *Learning from Las Vegas,* Venturi also published, with Denise Scott Brown, *A View from the Campidoglio: Selected Essays, 1953-1984* (1984). See also C. Mead, *The Architecture of Robert Venturi* (1989); A. Sanmartin, ed., *Venturi, Rauch and Scott Brown* (1986), and S. von Moos, *Venturi, Rauch and Scott Brown: Buildings and Projects* (1987). □

Giuseppe Fortunino Francesco Verdi

Giuseppe Fortunino Francesco Verdi (1813-1901) was the most distinguished Italian opera composer in the 19th century. His career and work, the antithesis of those of Wagner, represent the final flourishing of the Italian opera tradition.

Giuseppe Verdi was born on Oct. 10, 1813, in Roncole in the duchy of Parma. He early demonstrated an inclination to music. His family, being very poor, could do nothing to aid him. When he was 13, a merchant of nearby Busseto, Antonio Barezzi, took a lively interest in the young boy and encouraged him in his studies. At the age of 18 Verdi went to Milan to audition for the conservatory despite the fact that, even if he should be successful, he was already too old to be admitted. He was rejected only because of his age, but he was able to remain in Milan to continue his studies privately.

After several years of intermittent private study, the young composer obligated himself for three years to the Philharmonic Society of Busseto in 1835 in exchange for a modest stipend. Verdi composed music and directed various performances sponsored by the group; he also worked as a church musician while continuing his studies. In 1836, the year he married Margherita Barezzi, the daughter of his benefactor, he was at work on his first opera, *Oberto, conte di San Bonifacio,* which was recommended to La Scala, Milan, for consideration in 1837.

Early Works

In 1838 Verdi moved to Milan in anticipation of the production of *Oberto*. This year marked the beginning of a series of personal tragedies. His daughter died late in 1838. In 1839 his infant son died, leaving the young composer and his wife little taste for the moderate success of *Oberto* on November 17. The greatest blow fell in 1840, when his wife died. At the age of 27 Verdi found himself almost entirely alone in the world. *Oberto* was successful enough for the distinguished Milanese music publisher Ricordi to make an offer for the rights to publish the score, thereby commencing a personal and business relationship which lasted throughout Verdi's life. His next opera, *Un giorno di regno,* produced in 1840, was a complete failure.

The accounts of Verdi as a taciturn, somber man date from the time of his personal sorrows. Although always compassionate and considerate of his friends and associates, Verdi withdrew into himself, zealously guarding his privacy. Despite the adversities of fate he continued to compose, believing in his abilities. His tenacity paid off when his first major success, *Nabucco,* was produced at La Scala in 1842. Giuseppina Streponni, who was to be Verdi's friend, mistress, and eventually his second wife, was in the cast of the first performance.

Other successes followed in turn. *I Lombardi* was produced in Milan in 1843 despite the archbishop's protests. Verdi had early acquired a reputation as a strongly anticlerical, agnostic young man, fervently convinced that Italy should be liberated from any form of autocratic government, whether it be the Church or Austria. He devoted himself to a series of operas in which the causes of individual freedom, patriotism, loyalty, and nobility of the human spirit were paramount.

In 1844 *Ernani,* based on Victor Hugo's famous play, was produced in Venice with tremendous success. *I due Foscari,* derived from Lord Byron's play, followed in Rome the same year. Verdi was then 31, and the years of his triumphs had begun.

Verdi made the first of many trips to Paris in 1846 to supervise the French production of *Ernani.* His next major opera to enjoy popular success was *Attila,* mounted in Venice the same year. In 1847 he was in Florence to oversee the premiere of his first opera on a Shakespearean subject, *Macbeth.* His librettist was Francesco Maria Piave, his best collaborator until the advent of Arrigo Boito. Piave had already worked with Verdi on *Ernani* and *I due Foscari.* Piave was to supply Verdi with librettos for *La forza del destino, Simone Boccanegra* (first version), and the two undisputed masterpieces of the 1850s, *Rigoletto* and *La Traviata.*

Verdi began work on *I masnadieri* in 1846 and later the same year made his first visit to London. He returned to Italy via Paris, where *I Lombardi* in its French version was produced.

The pattern for Verdi's life seemed set. He traveled between Milan, Venice, Bologna, Florence, Rome, Naples, and Paris for the most part, making such trips as were necessary to supervise whatever work of his was being produced at the time. More often than not he was accompanied by the devoted Giuseppina. In 1849 he bought a villa at Sant'Agata, near Busseto, which was his permanent home and retreat.

New Stage of Development

Verdi's major composition in 1849 was *Luisa Miller,* prepared for Naples. To some, this work more than *Macbeth* marks a turning point in his career; the psychological insights into human behavior as well as the subtleties of musical style become more sophisticated from this time forward. With *Rigoletto* (originally called by its subtitle, *La maledizione*), produced in Venice in 1850, he achieved an international reputation. His next work, *La Traviata,* was a failure at its Venetian premiere in 1853, but Verdi had no qualms with regard to its merit, and his faith was vindicated.

The same year *Il Trovatore* proved an instant success in Rome. *Simone Boccanegra* followed in 1856 and was produced in 1857.

That year also saw the commission of *Un ballo in maschera* for Naples. Always beset with censorship difficulties, Verdi nearly came to grief over this particular work. The issue was resolved only when he changed the locale from Sweden to Boston and the characters from aristocrats and noblemen to Puritan governors and citizens. He was contemptuous of such petty efforts which attempted to restrict personal liberty and freedom of expression.

In 1859 Giuseppina and Verdi were quietly married. Now considered one of the most distinguished of Italian citizens as well as the undisputed leader of the Italian theater, Verdi became a member of the Italian Chamber of Deputies in 1860, representing Busseto after Parma declared by plebiscite its intention to join the kingdom of Italy. His fame had been carried throughout Italy not only by his musical accomplishments but by use of his name as an anagram—V(ittorio) E(mmanuele), R(e) D'I(talia), that is, "Victor Emmanuel, King of Italy"—often shouted in the streets as a revolutionary slogan during the struggle for Italian independence and unification.

Commissions and honors poured in during the 1860s. In 1861 Piave prepared the libretto for *La forza del destino,* commissioned for St. Petersburg, where Verdi visited to rehearse his opera; he returned the following year for its premiere. For the International Exhibition of 1862 in London he composed *Inno delle nazioni.* In 1864 he was elected to the French Académie des Beaux-Arts. He began the music for *Don Carlo* in 1865, but the opera was not produced until 1867. Negotiations with the Egyptian government for an opera to celebrate the completion of the Suez Canal were initiated in 1868; an Egyptian subject was approved the following year; and in 1871 *Aida* was a sensation.

Requiem Mass

When the suggestion for an opera for Cairo was broached, Verdi countered with a suggestion for a Requiem Mass to honor the memory of the composer Gioacchino Rossini, who had died in 1868. Verdi was motivated more by patriotism than by religious commitment. His plans called for a collaborative endeavor on the part of leading Italian composers. Although this project fell through, the idea of a Requiem honoring an Italian hero remained close to the composer's heart.

When Verdi was approached in 1873 concerning the possibility of writing a Requiem Mass in memory of Alessandro Manzoni, author of the greatest 19th-century Italian novel, *I promessi sposi,* and a leading figure for the cause of unification, he leaped at the chance. On May 22, 1874, the first anniversary of Manzoni's death, Verdi's "latest opera," his Requiem Mass, was performed in Milan. The next year he conducted his Requiem in Paris, London, and Vienna.

King Victor Emmanuel II made Verdi a senator in 1875, and his career appeared to have been capped. He lived in semiretirement at Sant'Agata, supervising his extensive agricultural interests, traveling only on occasion to conduct one of his works. He appeared to be uninterested in future composition and had settled down to enjoy the fruits of his labors.

Collaboration with Boito

Such was not to be. Verdi first met Arrigo Boito, a distinguished man of letters and composer in his own right, through mutual friends in 1879. They were attracted to one another despite the discrepancy in years, and gradually their friends hatched a plot of sorts to entice the 68-year-old Verdi out of retirement. Boito was eager to collaborate with Verdi, and their work together was to mark one of the high points in the history of opera.

Verdi had long been dissatisfied with certain sections of *Simone Boccanegra;* in 1880 Boito presented Verdi with a revised libretto which he liked, and he proceeded to write the necessary new music. The new *Boccanegra* was produced the following year in Milan. In 1885 Boito and Verdi began work in great secrecy on *Otello;* although Verdi had long entertained thoughts of an opera on *King Lear,* his imagination was captivated by the possibilities inherent in Shakespeare's passion-ridden tragedy of the Moor. He finished *Otello* in 1886, and the following year saw its premiere in Milan—his first new opera in 15 years. *Otello* created a sensation.

In 1890 Verdi began *Falstaff,* the miracle of his old age and his last opera. For it Boito fashioned a libretto from portions of *Henry IV* and *The Merry Wives of Windsor.* Verdi had not written a comic opera since the very beginning of his career. When *Falstaff* was triumphantly mounted in 1893 in Milan, Verdi was 80 years old.

Verdi's devoted wife, Giuseppina, died in 1897. The following year he published four choral pieces: the Ave Maria, Stabat Mater, Te Deum, and Laudi alla Vergine Maria. He lived in seclusion at Sant'Agata for the remaining years of his life. He died in Milan on Jan. 27, 1901, and was buried by Giuseppina's side in the chapel of the Home for Musicians, Milan. This charity, still in existence, was the chief beneficiary of his will. Verdi died a wealthy man, a millionaire in modern terms, and his bequest continued to be the major source of income for the home until recently.

Culmination of Italian Opera

Verdi's accomplishments and achievements cannot be praised too highly. He never forgot that the glory of Italian opera lay in the use of the human voice. But he turned aside from the liltingly beautiful *bel canto* tradition and made the voice subordinate to the overall dramatic shape of his operas. For Verdi, the drama was all that was important, and in his mature operas he rarely faltered in striking to the heart of the matter when strong, stirring stage situations were needed. He was a master psychologist in his analysis of human passion, and his musical characterizations of Rigoletto, Aida, Violetta, Desdemona, Iago, and Falstaff are among the finest 19th-century creations.

Verdi was not a theoretician but entirely a practical man of the theater. A very humane individual, he refused to lead any faction against Richard Wagner, recognizing in the great German master a magnificent talent, however alien to

his own convictions it might be. Verdi represents the culmination of the Italian style of opera. His works remain the mainstay of the international opera repertoire.

Further Reading

Scores for the Verdi operas are readily available in the Ricordi editions, and the operas have been recorded many times and remain ever popular and available. In English, the best writings on Verdi and his works are those by Francis Toye, *Giuseppe Verdi: His Life and Works* (1931; rev. ed. 1962); Dyneley Hussey, *Verdi* (1940); Frank Walker, *The Man Verdi* (1962); and Charles Osborne, *The Complete Operas of Verdi* (1970). Perceptive essays on Verdi's career and works are contained in Joseph Kerman, *Opera as Drama* (1956), and Donald J. Grout, *A Short History of Opera* (1963). □

Paul Marie Verlaine

The French poet Paul Marie Verlaine (1844-1896), one of the most exquisite lyric poets in the history of French literature, ranks with Rimbaud and Mallarmé as one of the major French symbolists of the 19th century.

Paul Verlaine was born in Metz on March 30, 1844. He was the son of an army captain. Verlaine attended the Lycée Bonaparte (today Lycée Condorcet) in Paris, where his favorite subjects were French and Latin. At the age of 14, he sent Victor Hugo his earliest known poem, *La Mort.* By 1862, the year he received his baccalaureate degree, Verlaine had already developed a disastrous taste for drink that marred his life. In 1866 he published his first collection of verse under a title apparently borrowed from Baudelaire: *Poèmes saturniens. Nevermore, Mon rêve familier,* and especially *Chanson d'automne* revealed the lovely lyricism and delicate sadness characteristic of many of Verlaine's best poems.

Verlaine's succeeding volumes contained many exquisite lyrics. *Fêtes galantes* of 1869 (inspired in part by French painters of the 18th century whose work he had seen at the Louvre) included *Clair de lune, Mandoline,* and *Colloque sentimental. La Bonne chanson* (1870/1872), intended as a sort of epithalamium for his illstarred marriage to Mathilde Mauté, contained *La Lune blanche. Romances sans paroles* (1873) included *Il pleure dans mon coeur* and *O triste, triste était mon âme,* lyrics that brought poetry close to music. *Sagesse* (1880), Verlaine's best-known collection, included a sonnet sequence beginning "Mon Dieu m'a dit: 'Mon fils il faut m'aimer...'" that affords some of the finest religious verse in the French language. The same volume included a poem describing his lonely sensation at entering the prison of Mons after shooting Arthur Rimbaud in the wrist ("Un grand sommeil noir tombe sur ma vie") and his most famous poem ("Le ciel est par-dessus le toit"), which analyzed his perceptions and thoughts in his prison cell.

In 1884 Verlaine published a volume of criticism (*Les Poètes maudits*) that helped bring the emerging symbolists to the attention of the public. He produced more than a dozen further collections of verse before his death, none of them comparable to his earlier volumes. *Jadis et Naguère* (1885) included *Langueur,* a poem seen as a sort of manifesto of decadence, and *Art poétique,* a poem that expresses some of his essential ideas on poetry. In it he proclaimed the beauty of *le vers impair* (the verse of an uneven number of syllables: 5-7-9-11, instead of the usual 6-8-10-12) and urged that poetry be fugitive and intangible like mint and thyme on the morning wind.

Verlaine spent his last years as a moral and physical derelict, moving in and out of hospitals until his death in Paris on Jan. 8, 1896. But in 1894 he had been elected Prince of Poets, and he was given a public funeral.

Verlaine was known during his lifetime for the beauty and delicacy of his finest verse, for his association with Arthur Rimbaud, and for his generally dissipated and vagabond existence. In his last years "le Pauvre Lèlian," as he called himself from an anagram of his name, was considered a picturesque incarnation of the decadent poet.

Further Reading

English translators of Verlaine's poetry include Ashmore Wingate and C. F. MacIntyre. Harold Nicolson, *Paul Verlaine* (1921), and Lawrence and Elisabeth Hanson, *Verlaine: Fool of God* (1957), are biographies. Antoine Adam's fine study of Verlaine was translated by Carl Morse and published as *The Art of Paul Verlaine* (1963). Marcel Raymond, *From Baudelaire to Surrealism* (trans. 1950; new ed. 1970), is an authoritative study of the forces that shaped modern French poetry and includes a useful critique of Verlaine.

Additional Sources

Nicolson, Harold George, Sir, *Paul Verlaine,* New York: AMS Press, 1980.
Verlaine, Paul, *Confessions of a poet,* Westport, Conn.: Hyperion Press, 1979. □

Jan Vermeer

The Dutch painter Jan Vermeer (1632-1675) of Delft transformed traditional Dutch themes into images of superlative poise and serenity, rich with emblematic meaning.

Rarely has such a small body of work supported such a large reputation as that of Jan (Johannes) Vermeer. Most experts would agree on 35 authentic works, with a few more on which opinions differ. For the most part his paintings are of modest size, and their subject matter appears to be commonplace.

The documented facts about Vermeer's life are scanty. He was born in Delft. His father was an art dealer and silk weaver who also kept a tavern, and Vermeer probably took over the business after his father's death in 1655. In 1653 Vermeer married a well-to-do Catholic girl from Gouda; they had 11 children. In the year of his marriage he became a master in the Delft painters' guild, of which he was an officer in 1662-1663 and 1669-1670. He seems to have painted very little and to have sold only a fraction of his limited production, for the majority of his extant paintings were still in the hands of his family when he died. His dealings in works by other artists seem to have supported his family reasonably well until the French invasion of 1672 ruined his business. He died in 1675 and was buried on December 15. The following year his wife was forced to declare bankruptcy.

Nothing is known about Vermeer's education and training as a painter. In part because verses written following the death of Carel Fabritius in 1654 mention Vermeer as his successor as Delft's leading artist, it has been suggested that Fabritius was Vermeer's teacher. Certainly Fabritius anticipated Vermeer's interest in perspective experiments and his use of a light-flooded wall as a background for figures. But Fabritius lived in Delft only after 1650, by which time Vermeer would have been well on his way toward the completion of his training.

Sixteen of Vermeer's paintings are signed, but only two are dated: *The Procuress* (1656) and *The Astronomer* (1668). A chronology of his works, based on their stylistic relationships with these two landmarks and on other considerations, has found general acceptance, though some points continue to be argued.

Early Works

The warm colors and emphatic chiaroscuro of *The Procuress* relate it to paintings of the Rembrandt school of the 1650s, but its subject matter and composition reflect an acquaintance with paintings of the 1620s by the Utrecht Caravaggists. Considered to be earlier than *The Procuress* are two pictures that resemble it because of the color scheme, dominated by reds and yellows, and because they are larger in size and scale than Vermeer's later works. *Christ in the House of Martha and Mary* is reminiscent of compositions by Hendrick Terbrugghen and Gerrit van Honthorst, who disseminated the Caravaggesque style in Holland. *Diana and Her Companions,* Vermeer's only mythological subject, is also redolent of Italy. It is his only painting of figures in a landscape setting.

After these three diverse experiments, which may have owed something to Vermeer's familiarity with works in his father's stock of art, he painted the *Girl Asleep at a Table,* in which he retained the warm palette of his other early pictures but in terms of subject matter and composition plunged into the mainstream of current Delft painting. The room with an open door, through which the adjoining brightly lighted room is visible and which is typical of Vermeer's Delft contemporary Pieter de Hooch, went back to early Netherlandish tradition. For Vermeer it was the first attempt to place a figure in the defined space of a room, a problem that preoccupied him throughout the rest of his career. The effect of sharp recession also was a prominent feature of Vermeer's compositional mode from then on. The quality of self absorption seen in this painting contributed to his most characteristic emotional effects. Subtle allusions to meanings beyond the obvious one, which have made this picture the subject of much discussion, were also found in Vermeer's later works.

All these tendencies were brought under full control for the first time in the *Soldier and Laughing Girl*. This painting also marked the transition between Vermeer's early and mature works in that *pointillé* (gleaming highlights of thick impasto), which brightens the paint surface, appeared for the first time.

Mature Period

Vermeer's two town views, the *Little Street* and *View of Delft*, have been called "the first plein-air pictures of modern painting." The *View of Delft* has been in the 20th century one of the most admired of all paintings. Marcel Proust's appreciation of it enhanced its charms for many observers.

Vermeer's style just before 1660 is also well represented by *The Cook*. The rich paint surface with its extraordinary tactile quality, the monumental figure perfectly balanced in space and engrossed in a humble task performed with the dignity due a solemn rite, and the intense color scheme dominated by yellow and blue all show Vermeer at the height of his powers. Before long his paintings tended to become more delicate and detached, with more diffused light and a smoother surface, as in the *Lady Weighing Gold*, which is an allegory of God's judgment of man.

Following these great works, which are assumed to have preceded and immediately followed 1660, come the "pearl pictures." *The Concert* of about 1662 and the *Woman with a Water Jug* of perhaps a year later display the dulcet charms of this period.

Late Works

More complicated compositions and especially more elaborate space representations mark the major works of the last decade of Vermeer's life. The *Allegory of the Art of Painting* (ca. 1670) is large and complex in both composition and meaning. On the whole it is untainted by the hardness and dryness that marred his later works, such as the *Allegory of the Catholic Faith*.

Characteristics of Vermeer's Art

Vermeer was criticized for exaggerating the perspective of his interior settings until eyes accustomed to reality as seen through the camera lens recognized that his perspective was in fact accurate. When the painter is very close to the nearest object in his composition, for example, only 2 feet from it, an object of equal size that is 4 feet from his eye will be depicted, correctly, as half the size of the first. Vermeer arranged his objects to achieve such contrasts. The effect of this practice is to make the voids in a sense tangible. The space is built up along with the objects in a construction of cubic solidity.

It has been suggested that Vermeer used a camera obscure in composing his pictures and that this accounts for both his striking compositions and his peculiarities in handling colors and values. Delft in his time was a center of

optical experimentation and lens making, and it would not be surprising if artists there availed themselves of optical devices in their work. The unique qualities of Vermeer's paintings must, however, be attributed to his artistic personality, whether he did or did not make use of mirrors or lenses in attaining them.

The figures and objects Vermeer painted belong to their environment in a special way that heightens the impression that what he is depicting is a block of space with all that it contains rather than solids separated by voids. He renounced the contours that in most paintings distinguished between figures and their setting. Instead, the outlines of his objects are insubstantial; they unite the elements of his paintings rather than separate them.

Vermeer's manner of modeling, too, was exceptional. He built his figures with planes of contrasted values, omitting the graduations of tone that most painters use to model the form. In his mature works he punctuated his subtle patterns of light and shadow with *pointillé*.

The figures of Vermeer, fixed in their enveloping space as a fly is fixed in amber, deny any possibility of the disruption of their perfect poise. They exist in a realm of abstract beauty. The quietness, serenity, order, and immutability of the world of Vermeer's art provide, for those with a taste for such virtues, intimations of immortality. Perhaps that is why this painter, whose works appear to be as forthright and clear as the light of day, has always been felt to be mysterious.

Further Reading

A thorough study of Vermeer's life and work is Pieter T. A. Swillens, *Johannes Vermeer: Painter of Delft* (1949; trans. 1950). It is especially valuable for information about the historical background, including all relevant documents, and for technical analyses of the paintings and Vermeer's system of perspective. Lawrence Gowing, *Vermeer* (1953), is a sensitive examination of Vermeer's stylistic development and provides much comparative material that clarifies the place of his works in relation to contemporary painting. Ludwig Goldscheider, ed., *Johannes Vermeer: The Paintings* (1958; 2d ed. 1967), is noteworthy for its fine plates, including original-size details in color and in black and white. □

Jules Verne

The French novelist Jules Verne (1828-1905) was the first authentic exponent of modern science fiction. The best of his work is characterized by intelligent predictions of technical achievements actually within man's grasp at the time Verne wrote.

Jules Verne was born on Feb. 8, 1828, at Nantes, the eldest son of a prosperous provincial lawyer. An otherwise uneventful childhood was marked by one major escapade. In his twelfth year, Jules shipped as a cabin boy on an ocean-going three-master. The ship was intercepted by his father before it had put out to sea, and Jules is said to have promised his parents that "in future he would travel only in imagination"—a prediction fulfilled in a manner his parents could not have foreseen.

Career as a Playwright

In 1847 Verne went to Paris to study law, although privately he was already planning a literary career. Owing to the friendship he made with Alexandre Dumas the Elder, Verne's first play, *Broken Straws,* was produced—with some success—in 1850. From 1852 to 1855 he held a steady and ill-paid position as secretary of a Paris theater, the Théâtre Lyrique. He continued to write comedies and operettas and began contributing short stories to a popular magazine, *Le Musée des familles.*

During a visit to Amiens in May 1856, Verne met and fell in love with the widowed daughter of an army officer, Madame Morel (née Honorine de Viane), whom he married the following January. The circumstance that his wife's brother was a stockbroker may have influenced Verne in making the unexpected decision to embrace this profession. Membership in the Paris Exchange did not seriously interfere with his literary labors, however, because he adopted a rigorous timetable, rising at five o'clock in order to put in several hours researching and writing before beginning his day's work at the Bourse.

First Novels

Verne's first long work of fiction, *Five Weeks in a Balloon,* took the form of an account of a journey by air over

Central Africa, at that time largely unexplored. The book, published in January 1863, was an immediate success. He then decided to retire from stockbroking and to devote himself full time to authorship. His next few books were immensely successful at the time and are still counted among the best he wrote. *A Journey to the Center of the Earth* (1864) describes the adventures of a party of explorers and scientists who descend the crater of an Icelandic volcano and discover an underground world. *The Adventures of Captain Hatteras* (1866) centers on an expedition to the North Pole (not actually reached by Robert Peary until 1909). In *From the Earth to the Moon* (1865) and its sequel, *Round the Moon* (1870), Verne describes how two adventurous Americans—joined, naturally, by an equally intrepid Frenchman—arrange to be fired in a hollow projectile from a gigantic cannon that lifts them out of the earth's gravity field and takes them close to the moon. Verne not only pictured the state of weightlessness his "astronauts" experienced during their flight, but also he had the prescience to locate their launching site in Florida.

Later Works

Verne wrote his two masterpieces when he was in his 40s. *Twenty Thousand Leagues under the Sea* (1870) relates the voyages of the submarine *Nautilus,* built and commanded by the mysterious Capt. Nemo, one of the literary figures in whom Verne incorporated many of his own character traits. *Around the World in Eighty Days* (1873) is the story of a successful wager made by a typically phlegmatic Englishman, Phineas Fogg, a character said to have been modeled on Verne's father, who had a mania for punctuality. Other popular novels include *The Mysterious Island* (1875) and *Michael Strogoff* (1876). Verne's total literary output comprised nearly 80 books, but many of them are of little value or interest today. One noteworthy feature of all his work is its moral idealism, which earned him in 1884 the personal congratulations of Pope Leo XIII. "If I am not always what I ought to be," Verne once wrote, "my characters will be what I should like to be." His interest in scientific progress was tempered by his robust religious faith, and in some of his later novels (such as *The Purchase of the North Pole,* 1889), he showed himself aware of the social dangers of uncontrolled technological advance.

Verne the Man

Verne's personality was complex. Though capable of bouts of extreme liveliness and given to punning and playing practical jokes, he was fundamentally a shy man, happiest when alone in his study or when sailing the English Channel in a converted fishing smack. In 1886 he was the victim of a shooting affray, which left him lame. His assailant proved to be a nephew who was suffering from an attack of persecution mania. This incident served to reinforce Verne's natural tendency to melancholy. Although he stood successfully for election to the city council of Amiens two years later, he spent his old age in close retirement. In 1902 he became partially blind; he died on March 24, 1905.

Further Reading

Verne's niece, Marguerite Allotte de la Fuye, published a biography based partly on family papers, *Jules Verne* (1928; trans. 1954). Kenneth Allott, *Jules Verne* (1940), is a full biography with critical appraisal of Verne's books. I. O. Evans, *Jules Verne and His Work* (1965), in spite of its naively uncritical approach, contains interesting illustrative material and an extensive bibliography.

Additional Sources

Costello, Peter, *Jules Verne: inventor of science fiction,* London: Hodder and Stoughton, 1978.

Evans, I. O.. (Idrisyn Oliver), *Jules Verne and his work,* Mattituck N.Y.: Aeonian Press, 1976.

Jules-Verne, Jean, *Jules Verne: a biography,* New York: Taplinger Pub. Co., 1976. □

Paolo Veronese

The Italian painter Paolo Veronese (1528-1588) was one of the greatest Venetian artists. His work is rich in invention and decorative splendor and excels in the depiction of festive and heroic scenes.

Paolo Veronese, whose real name was Paolo Caliari, was born in Verona (hence the appellation Veronese) and received his early training there from Antonio Badile. In 1552 Veronese was in Mantua, where he encountered the art of Giulio Romano. The following year Veronese was working at the Ducal Palace in Venice. He spent the rest of his life in that city, directing a large workshop which, after his death on April 19, 1588, was taken over by his brother Benedetto and his sons Carlo and Gabriele and continued to produce works in his manner for some time.

Characteristics of His Art

Veronese responded with singular felicity to the calm and peacefulness of Titian's works and elaborated on these qualities in wonderful fresco compositions. His color is never merely applied paint but brings to life the pale whiteness of the Palladian marble halls which are the stage for his works: the rich color of splendid and elegantly appointed animals, the muted gleam of fine fabrics, and, above all, the blueness of the wide Venetian skies which frame his compositions and bestow on them a smiling beauty and infinite depth. He applied the paint thinly over broad areas with a delicate brushstroke. His drawings, often done in wash on tinted paper, have a rich tonality of silvery grays and, though carefully executed, look almost spontaneous.

Veronese was a master of decorative painting, but the decorative aspect of his work is only a background against which he develops the often very quiet drama of his history paintings. His portraits and history paintings usually show richly dressed and beautiful persons in a gently distanced or pensive mood which tinges the wealth of the work with a certain melancholy. He also concerned himself with the study of allegory and intermittently worked on a book of drawings with explanatory notes on the subject, but only a few fragments survive.

Religious Paintings

The great majority of Veronese's history paintings represent Christian themes. His *Temptation of St. Anthony* (1552) shows that he was impressed with the art of Titian even before he moved to Venice, but his concern was more with demonstrating his ability to represent a complex and violent action than with the dignity of Titian's art. Once in Venice, Veronese soon attained the sublime facility that was the hallmark of his style. This is already demonstrated by his work in the Sala del Consiglio dei Dicci (1553-1554) of the Ducal Palace, even though the ceiling painting, *Jupiter Fulminating the Vices* (moved to Paris in 1797), is also a melodramatic tour de force.

In 1555 Veronese began the decoration of the church of S. Sebastiano in Venice and returned repeatedly to it in the course of the next 15 years. The church (in which he was buried) may be called the Pantheon of Veronese, it so well represents the maturity of his art. Most extraordinary are the ceiling paintings (1555-1556) which depict the story of Esther in daring foreshortening; yet each scene culminates in a nobly quiet pose or gesture. The effect of the whole is at once decorative and moving.

Equally impressive but more gentle are his paintings for the organ shutters (1558-1560) of S. Sebastiano, which show, when closed, the *Presentation of Christ in the Temple* and, when opened, *Christ at the Pool of Bethesda* in a setting of classical columns which connect the world of the painting with the view of the organ pipes. Two extremely rich scenes from the life of St. Sebastian (1565) decorate the choir of the church. One shows the saint in military dress exhorting his fellow Christians with a grand gesture; the other depicts him naked and meekly awaiting his execution.

Among Veronese's other great works celebrating Christian themes are *Christ among the Doctors* (ca. 1555-1556), *St. John Preaching* (ca. 1561), and the *Holy Family with Saints Barbara and John* (ca. 1562). More complex is the *Supper at Emmaus* (1559-1560). The figures from sacred history are surrounded by members of the family who commissioned the picture; they serve Christ, and their children sit at his feet.

One of the richest of Veronese's works is the *Marriage at Cana,* painted for a refectory (1562). In the center of this grandly decorative work sits Christ, whose loneliness has rarely been so affectingly and lovingly rendered. At his feet a group of musicians, in whom the likenesses of Veronese, Titian, Tintoretto, and Jacopo Bassano may be recognized, performs a concert.

Veronese received a number of other commissions to decorate refectories. Among these are the *Feast of St. Gregory the Great* (1572), the *Feast in the House of Simon* (ca. 1572), and the *Feast in the House of Levi* (1573). The last painting is actually a Last Supper, but the Inquisition took exception to it because they thought that Veronese had elaborated frivolously on the biblical account. He defended himself ably, but in the end he was obliged to change the title of the work to the rather meaningless and misleading *Feast in the House of Levi.*

In addition to his richly splendid works Veronese also painted pictures which in their composition and coloring are as quietly understated as the actions and gestures of his heroes almost always are. Most notable among these are the *Crucifixion* (ca. 1570-1580), in which all is silence and grief, and the very late *Pietà* (ca. 1586), which presents the dead body of Christ with a gentleness that is heartbreaking.

Secular Paintings

Veronese's secular and allegorical history painting falls into two groups: his public commissions for the Ducal Palace and the Library of St. Mark's and his decoration of villas and palaces belonging to the Venetian nobility. His greatest accomplishment of the first type is the *Triumph of Venice* (1583) in the Sala del Maggior Consiglio of the Ducal Palace, which shows in its center Venice a female allegorical figure, resplendent in opulent beauty and ease, crowned by Victory and raised by clouds, slowly ascending to the heavens. In the second group are the *Rape of Europa* (ca. 1580), which follows the account of Ovid in his at once playful and yet awed praise of the power of Cupid, and *Darius and the Family of Alexander* (ca. 1565-1567).

Veronese's happiest achievement of his private commissions is the fresco decoration of Andrea Palladio's Villa Barbaro at Maser (ca. 1561). The harmony there effected between the taste of an enlightened patron and the art of Palladio and Veronese makes the villa one of the most delightful places on earth. Landscapes, noble buildings, beautifully shining skies, and playfully painted gods, heroes, allegorical figures, and animals on the walls and ceilings all mingle and smile in a world of art, full of mirth, sense, and dignity, and offer refreshment from the cares of the world.

Further Reading

Veronese has not been well served by the art-historical literature in English. An introduction to his art is available in Antoine Orliac, *Veronese* (trans. 1940). On his drawings see Hans Tietze and Erika Tietze-Conrat, *The Drawings of the Venetian Painters* (1944). Excellent appreciations of his art can be found in John Ruskin, *Modern Painters* (1843-1860) and *The Stones of Venice* (1851-1853), and in Henry James, *Italian Hours* (1909). □

Giovanni da Verrazano

The Italian navigator and explorer Giovanni da Verrazano (ca. 1485-ca. 1528) made a voyage to North America in 1524-1525, in the service of France, during which he explored and charted the Atlantic coast of North America.

F ollowing the Spanish discovery of rich Indian civilizations in Mexico and Peru, other European powers also sought footholds in the New World. The English and the French actively pursued an empire in the northern half of the Western Hemisphere. Francis I, King of France, was anxious to put out an exploratory expedition before his European competitors had claimed all of the New World. In January 1525 he authorized an expedition of four ships. Giovanni da Verrazano, a Florentine navigator, was chosen as pilot of one of these ships, the *Dauphine.* The expedition also had a second mission. Shortly after leaving France, three of the ships broke away and engaged in pirating expeditions against Spanish treasure ships. Only the *Dauphine,* under Verrazano's command, actually undertook a mapping and exploring expedition along the Atlantic coast of North America.

Although Verrazano's most significant discoveries were along the middle Atlantic coastal region, his ship traveled as far north as Cape Cod and Nova Scotia. The *Dauphine* spent most of the winter months of 1525 off the shores of North America. It was during this time that Verrazano sighted Chesapeake Bay. He mistook the bay to be an opening through the North American continent to China. He recorded in his diary: "From the ship was seen the ocean of the east." He made no effort to cross that sea, which became known as Verrazano sea. His mistake influenced cartographers for many years. They subsequently drew maps of the New World in the shape of an hourglass, with the Verrazano Sea forming the narrow waist.

After his discovery of this bay, Verrazano continued his coastal explorations farther north. By spring he had charted

Delaware Bay and had entered New York Bay. He sailed into the Hudson River, taking notes about the appearance of the natives observed along the way.

Verrazano continued his journey up the coast into Narragansett Bay and past Cape Cod. He proceeded as far north as Nova Scotia. His original mission, that of establishing some precedent for French claims in North America, was completed. He then headed back to France, after an absence of nearly seven months.

The rest of Verrazano's career is somewhat obscure. There is evidence that he made a second and possibly even a third trip back to America. His final voyage occurred in 1528, the year when he left France to search for a Central American passage to the Orient. Verrazano never returned from that journey; he was likely the victim of either a storm or unfriendly natives.

Further Reading

For information on Verrazano's part in the exploration of North America see John Bartlet Brebner, *The Explorers of North America, 1492-1806* (1933); Harold Lamb, *New Found World: How North America Was Discovered and Explored* (1955); and J. H. Parry, *The Age of Reconnaissance* (1963). □

Andrea del Verrocchio

The Italian sculptor and painter Andrea del Verrocchio (1435-1488) created some of the most powerful monumental bronze sculptures of the Renaissance.

Andrea del Verrocchio was born in Florence, the son of a brick and tile maker. Nothing is known about his early training. In 1465 the magistrates of the merchants' guild of Florence commissioned him to execute a bronze *Doubting of Thomas* to occupy a marble niche earlier executed by Donatello and Michelozzo for the principal facade of Orsanmichele in Florence. When the group was finally placed in its niche in 1483, the diarist L. Landucci called the head of Christ "the most beautiful head of the Saviour that has yet been made." The *Doubting of Thomas* is one of the most important sculpture groups of the entire Renaissance. It is a dramatic masterpiece of spatial arrangement between two high-relief, life-size figures (the statues are actually hollow shells of bronze, without backs) and an exquisitely ornamented Renaissance niche.

The Medici family commissioned a number of works from Verrocchio. In 1467 Cosimo de' Medici was buried in a tomb that had been commissioned from Verrocchio two years earlier. In 1471 he completed the tomb for Giovanni and Piero de' Medici in the old sacristy of the family church of S. Lorenzo in Florence. The rich marble, porphyry, and bronze sarcophagus is framed by a marble arch and backed

by a bronze grille in the form of interlaced ropes; it is one of the most original creations of the period. An early masterpiece in bronze, *David,* a pensive, boyish figure in leather jerkin and skirt, triumphant over Goliath, was commissioned by Lorenzo de' Medici for his villa at Careggi. He sold the *David* to the Signory of Florence in 1476. Other Medici commissions completed by Verrocchio are listed in an inventory of 1496, including a bust of Giuliano in terra-cotta.

Verrocchio's most notable painting is the *Baptism of Christ.* During the execution of the painting, about 1470, Verrocchio allowed his young pupil Leonardo da Vinci to paint the head of the first of two angels who kneel at the left and also the spectacular landscape vista above the angel's head. Four other extant paintings are attributed to Verrocchio.

In 1473 Verrocchio estimated the value of a pulpit by Mino da Fiesole and Antonio Rossellino in the Prato Cathedral. In 1477 Verrocchio competed with Piero Pollaiuolo for the monument of Cardinal Niccolò Forteguerri in Pistoia. Although Pollaiuolo's design was accepted, Lorenzo de' Medici ordered the one by Verrocchio executed. In the same year he presented two models for reliefs for the altar of S. Giovanni in the Baptistery of Florence; one, the *Beheading of John the Baptist,* was accepted and finished in 1480.

Among Verrocchio's marble works is the *Bust of a Young Woman,* often identified, without proof, as the mistress of Lorenzo de' Medici, Lucrezia Donati. She is clad in a translucent garment and has broad eyebrows and large, beautifully graceful hands. His conception represents the new spirit of naturalism which arose in the 1480s in Florentine sculpture and painting.

Verrocchio's final work is also his grandest: the bronze equestrian monument of Bartolommeo Colleoni in Campo SS. Giovanni e Paolo, Venice. Colleoni, a condottiere, died in 1475 and left money to the Venetian Republic for the execution of the statue. The commission was awarded in 1479, and the model was executed in Florence; it was sent to Venice two years later. Verrocchio moved to Venice in 1483 and died there five years later before he could cast his clay model in bronze. The casting was begun in 1490 by Alessandro Leopardi, who also designed the base on which the monument was finally set in 1496. Verrocchio abandoned Donatello's static concept of the equestrian monument and presented Colleoni, armed and helmeted, riding his charger into battle. Rarely has a sculptor so effectively depicted the expression of power in a dramatic moment.

Further Reading

The best monograph on Verrocchio in English, with a clear text and splendid photographic details of all the works, is Gunther Passavant, *Verrocchio: Sculptures, Paintings and Drawings* (1969). A succinct and lucid introduction to the master's sculpture is Charles Seymour, Jr., *The Sculpture of Verrocchio* (1972). □

Hendrik Frensch Verwoerd

Hendrik Frensch Verwoerd (1901-1966) was the sixth prime minister of South Africa. He transformed apartheid into an effective instrument for the entrenchment of white domination.

Hendrik Verwoerd was born near Amsterdam, Holland, on Sept. 8, 1901. A few months later his parents emigrated to South Africa. He read psychology and sociology in Stellenbosch and from 1925 onward studied for a doctorate in psychology and sociology in Germany. He returned to occupy the chair of applied psychology and then of sociology and social work in Stellenbosch.

In 1934 Verwoerd was asked to organize a conference on poor whites. An assertive idealist, he viewed the poor-white question as a specifically Afrikaans problem which had to be solved by political initiatives developed in an Afrikaans framework.

A Racist View

This framework had already been defined by Die Broederbond (The League of the Brothers), an anti-African, anti-British, and anti-Semitic secret society. Founded in 1919, it labored to establish a Boer, Protestant republic and to make the Afrikaner South Africa's unquestioned master. Like Daniel Malan, Verwoerd was a Broeder.

In 1936 Malan's "purified" nationalists founded *Die Transvaler,* a daily published in Johannesburg, and asked Verwoerd to edit it. He campaigned for Afrikaner unity based on clearly defined principles and a Christian-National republic. He had no time for "British-Jewish" imperialism.

Like most Afrikaner nationalists, Verwoerd opposed South Africa's involvement in World War II. The prowar press charged that he had made *Die Transvaler* an instrument of Nazi propaganda. He sued the *Johannesburg Star* for making these allegations. Giving judgment against him on July 13, 1943, the presiding judge observed, "He did support Nazi propaganda, he did make his paper a tool of the Nazis in South Africa, and he knew it."

James Hertzog's followers and Malan's "purified" nationalists together formed the Herenigde Nasionale or Volksparty (HNP; Reunited National or People's party) in 1940 to accelerate movement toward the republic. Verwoerd used reunion to isolate Hertzog.

The 1948 general elections, which brought Malan to power and in which Verwoerd contested and lost the Alberton seat, were a triumph for Die Broederbond. With its leaders heading the government, it could impose its policies on the Africans and the whites. After the elections Verwoerd left *Die Transvaler* to take the seat Malan offered him in the Senate.

African National Congress (ANC) and the PAC were banned.

J. G. Strijdom, the prime minister, died in 1958, and Verwoerd succeeded him. On April 9, 1960, David Beresford Pratt fired two bullets into Verwoerd's head. He recovered to proclaim South Africa a republic outside the Commonwealth on May 31, 1961.

Demetrio Tsafendas, a purportedly "mentally unbalanced" government employee of Greek descent, stabbed and killed Verwoerd on his bench in the House of Assembly on Sept. 6, 1966.

Further Reading

Alexander Hepple, *Verwoerd* (1967), provides an excellent summary of Verwoerd's life and thought. Less analytical is Jan François Botha's journalistic *Verwoerd Is Dead* (1968), a highly readable political narrative of South Africa under Verwoerd and Vorster. Recommended for historical background are Leopold Marquard, *The Peoples and Policies of South Africa* (1952; 3d ed. 1962); Ndabaningi Sithole, *African Nationalism* (1962; 2d ed. 1968); Brian Bunting, *The Rise of the South African Reich* (1964; rev. ed. 1969); Pierre L. van den Berghe, *South Africa: A Study in Conflict* (1965); Leonard M. Thompson, *Politics in the Republic of South Africa* (1966); and A. Sachs, *South Africa: The Violence of Apartheid* (1969).

Additional Sources

Kenney, Henry, *Architect of apartheid: H.F. Verwoerd, an appraisal,* Johannesburg: J. Ball, 1980. □

Andreas Vesalius

The Belgian anatomist Andreas Vesalius (1514-1564) was the founder of modern anatomy. His major work, "De humani corporis fabrica," is a milestone in scientific progress.

Andreas Vesalius was born on Dec. 31, 1514, in Brussels, the son of Andries van Wesele and his wife, Isabel Crabbe. Vesalius's paternal ancestors, who hailed from the German town of Wesel, came to Brussels in the early 15th century and became prominent as physicians and pharmacists. His father served as pharmacist to Margaret of Austria and later to Emperor Charles V. His great-grandfather, Johannes Wesalia, was the head of the medical school at the University of Louvain, where Vesalius started his medical studies in 1530. He matriculated as Andres van Wesel de Bruxella.

In 1533 Vesalius transferred to the medical school of the University of Paris. One of his two teachers of anatomy there was Johann Guenther von Andernach, a personable man but a poor anatomist. The other was Jacobus Sylvius, who departed from tradition by giving some role to dissecting in anatomical instructions. Both teachers gave in their own ways a telling testimony of their student's anatomical expertise. Guenther, in a book published in 1536, recorded in glowing terms Vesalius's discovery of the

Disenfranchisement of Blacks

Verwoerd became minister of native affairs in 1950. An insensitive advocate of segregation, he wasted little time in "solving" the color problem. He abolished the institutions Hertzog had set up for the representation of the Africans and planned to slowly transform the black reservations into autonomous states (*Bantustans*) which would federate with South Africa. Year after year he placed before Parliament legislation to bring every aspect of the Africans' life under his control and enforce the segregation of African linguistic groups from one another.

Verwoerd developed a system designed to keep the African the intellectual inferior of the white man. All African men and women were fingerprinted and forced to carry a pass containing intimate personal details. Wholesale removals of Africans from land they owned in so-called white areas followed.

Sharpeville Massacre

Rebellions broke out in some rural reservations, and strikes and riots occurred in the main industrial areas. Verwoerd's answers to these were bans, banishments, arrests, and the enactment of increasingly harsh laws. On March 21, 1960, Mangaliso Sobukwe, president of the Pan-African Congress (PAC), called the Africans out in a nationwide protest against the Pass Laws. The police opened fire on peaceful demonstrators at Sharpeville, killing 83 and wounding 365. A state of emergency was declared, and the spermatic vessels. Sylvius, however, decried violently Vesalius's daring claim that Galen, the great authority in physiology since classical times, wrote on the inner organs of the body without ever seeing them.

Because of the outbreak of war between France and Charles V, Vesalius, a citizen of the Low Countries, which were a part of the Holy Roman Empire, had to leave Paris in 1536. He returned to Louvain, where, at the recommendation of Guenther, Vesalius, still a student, was permitted to conduct public dissections. He also published a *Paraphrase of the Ninth Book of Rhazes* (Rhazes, also known as al-Rasi, was a Moslem physician of the early 10th century), in which he made a considerable effort to substitute Latin terms for the still heavily Arabic medical terminology.

But Vesalius soon became embroiled in disputes with faculty members, evidencing both his genius and his quarrelsome character. He was practically compelled to go the next year to the University of Padua. There Vesalius passed his doctoral examination with such honors in December 1537 that he was immediately appointed professor of surgery and anatomy. In 1538 he published six sheets of his anatomical drawings under the title *Tabulae anatomicae sex.* The publication was a signal success. Because of the great demand the sheets soon were reprinted, without Vesalius's authorization, in Cologne, Paris, Strasbourg, and elsewhere. In 1539 there followed his essay on bloodletting in which he first described the veins that draw blood from the side of the torso. This opened the way to the study of the venous values and led ultimately to the discovery of the circulation of blood by William Harvey.

Major Work

Vesalius's commitment to actual observing was much in evidence in his edition of some of Galen's works in 1540 but especially in his epoch-making *De humani corporis fabrica libri septem* (Seven Books on the Construction of the Human Body), published in 1543 in Basel. Book 1 on the bones was generally correct but represented no major advance. Book 2 on the muscles was a masterpiece. Book 3 on blood vessels was exactly the opposite. Somewhat better was book 4 on the nerves, a great advance on everything written on the topic before, but it was largely outmoded a century later. Excellent was his treatment in book 5 of the abdominal organs. Book 6 dealt with the chest and neck, while book 7 was devoted to the brain. Some of the woodcut illustrations of the *Fabrica* are among the best of 16th-century drawings and probably were executed by Jan Stephan van Calcar. Vesalius's own drawings were of moderate value. The revolutionary aspect of the work was the dominating role of observation as the very foundation of progress in anatomy. The importance of the large folio was immediately recognized by the fact that almost simultaneously with the original an epitome of it was published.

Vesalius was, like some other geniuses of his age, such as Copernicus and Thomas More, a daring innovator and a strong traditionalist at the same time. Thus Vesalius, the meticulous observer, did not part with Galen as far as theory was concerned. He was also a child of his age in carefully paving his way into the imperial court. No sooner was his *Fabrica* published than he sought service on the medical staff of Charles V and was immediately accepted.

In 1544 Vesalius married Anne von Hamme and also increased his holdings by a substantial inheritance from his father. In 1546 came his *Letter on the Chinese Root,* on a worthless but very popular medicine. The letter's true significance derived from the fact that in it Vesalius replied to the detractors of his *Fabrica* and corrected some of its erroneous statements. From 1553 on Vesalius had private practice as a physician in Brussels, and in 1556 his official ties with the court of Charles V came to an end.

The second edition of the *Fabrica,* in 1555, contained many improvements on the first, but in retrospect it was also a disappointment. One wonders about the new course medicine might have taken, had Vesalius dedicated himself completely to the cause of anatomical research. Some time after the accession of Philip II to the imperial throne, Vesalius became again one of the imperial physicians. Vesalius's absence from medical schools showed itself in his *Examination of Gabriele Fallopio's Anatomic Observations* (1561), in which he had to avoid passing judgment on a number of points in Fallopio's book because he had no way of verifying them.

It is a moot question whether Vesalius used a pilgrimage to the Holy Land in 1564 as a pretext to leave Spain and the imperial court. Some claimed that he went to the Holy Land to study medicinal plants on the plains of Jericho, a topic on which he is known to have discoursed on his way there. Vesalius might have very well made the pilgrimage out of devotion, as did many millions before and after him. Upon his return from Jerusalem he was to take the chair of the suddenly deceased Fallopio in Padua, but he died on the island of Zenta off the Greek coast.

Further Reading

The standard scholarly presentation of Vesalius's life and work is Charles Donald O'Malley, *Andreas Vesalius of Brussels* (1964). O'Malley is also the coauthor with J. B. deC. M. Saunders of *The Illustrations from the Works of Andreas Vesalius of Brussels* (1950). Jerome Tarshis, *Father of Modern Anatomy: Andreas Vesalius* (1969), is written in the popular vein and with a somewhat tendentious pen. The bibliography of the various editions of Vesalius's works, together with a list of Vesaliana and with many facsimiles of the title pages, is given in Harvey Cushing, *A Bio-bibliography of Andreas Vesalius* (1962). □

Denmark Vesey

Denmark Vesey (1767-1822), an African-American who fought to liberate his people from slavery, planned an abortive slave insurrection.

Denmark Vesey, whose original name was Telemanque, was born in West Africa. As a youth, he was captured, sold as a slave, and brought to America. In 1781 he came to the attention of a slaver, Capt. Vesey, who was "struck with the beauty, alertness, and intelligence" of the boy. Vesey, a resident of Charleston, S.C., acquired the boy. The captain had "no occasion to repent" his purchase of Denmark, who "proved for 20 years a most faithful slave."

In 1800 Vesey won a $1,500 lottery prize, with which he purchased his freedom and opened a carpentry shop. Soon this highly skilled artisan became "distinguished for [his] great strength and activity. Among his color he was always looked up to with awe and respect" by both black and white Americans. He acquired property and became prosperous.

Nevertheless, Vesey was not content with his relatively successful life. He hated slavery and slaveholders. This brilliant man versed himself in all the available antislavery arguments and spoke out against the abuse and exploitation of his own people. Believing in equality for everyone and vowing never to rest until his people were free, he became the political provocateur, agitating and moving his brethren to resist their enslavement.

Selecting a cadre of exceptional lieutenants, Vesey began organizing the black community in and around Charleston to revolt. He developed a very sophisticated scheme to carry out his plan. The conspiracy included over 9,000 slaves and "free" blacks in Charleston and on the neighboring plantations.

The revolt, which was scheduled to occur on July 14, 1822, was betrayed before it could be put into effect. As rumors of the plot spread, Charleston was thrown into a panic. Leaders of the plot were rounded up. Vesey and 46 other were condemned, and even four whites were implicated in the revolt. On June 23 Vesey was hanged on the gallows for plotting to overthrow slavery.

After careful examination of the historical record, the judgment of Sterling Stuckey remains valid: "Vesey's example must be regarded as one of the most courageous ever to threaten the racist foundations of America. . . . He stands today, as he stood yesterday . . . as an awesome projection of the possibilities for militant action on the part of a people who have for centuries been made to bow down in fear."

Further Reading

The best account of Vesey's rebellion is Robert S. Starobin, ed., *Denmark Vesey: The Slave Conspiracy of 1822* (1970). Of considerable importance is John Lofton, *Insurrection in South Carolina: The Turbulent World of Denmark Vesey* (1964). Herbert Aptheker, *American Negro Slave Revolts* (1943), provides a useful account of Vesey's revolt. William W. Freehling, *Prelude to Civil War: The Nullification Controversy in South Carolina* (1966), should be consulted for a broad understanding of the influence of the event. □

Vespasian

The Roman emperor Vespasian (9-79) was the founder of the Flavian dynasty, which marked the shift from a narrow Roman to a broader Italian—and ultimately empirewide—participation in the leadership of the Roman Empire.

Vespasian, whose full Latin name was Titus Flavius Vespasianus, was born near the little town of Reate in the Sabine backcountry of central Italy. He and his brother were the first members of the family to reach senatorial rank. After a distinguished but by no means spectacular career, including military service on the Rhine and in Britain, Vespasian was chosen by Nero to stamp out a revolt in Judea, as much because of his lack of political significance (due to his family background) as because of his military talents. Again, in Judea he exhibited firm competence rather than dashing brilliance.

With the death of Nero (68) the imperial Julio-Claudian dynasty became extinct, and there began a dizzying succession of momentary emperors as the various provincial armies pushed forward their own commanders—Galba, Otho, Vitellius. Low birth seemed less a bar to empire, and on July 1, 69, troops acclaimed Vespasian the last and permanent emperor of that "Year of the Four Emperors."

Consolidation of Power

Vespasian was faced with immense tasks: to restore order to the machinery of government, stability to the finances, discipline to the armies, and security to the frontiers.

The military problem came first; the Eastern armies had supported Vespasian, and the Western, having fought each other to exhaustion, accepted him, but much remained to

be done. A revolt in Gaul amounting to a nationalist secession from the empire showed the dangers inherent in the use of provincial soldiery. Vespasian therefore adopted a policy of not allowing auxiliaries (noncitizen troops) to serve in their native regions or be led by native commanders. He brought the citizen legions up to full strength and carefully cultivated their goodwill—Nero's fatal blunder had been to ignore the troops. Until now, only a Julio-Claudian had been able to command the allegiance of armies other than the one under his direct control; one of Vespasian's accomplishments was to get all the armies to accept whoever was the reigning emperor. The troops stayed out of emperor making for over a century.

Vespasian made no effort to blur the fact that he had won the empire through arms rather than having received it from the hands of the Senate. He treated the Senate with respect but did not try to revive Augustus's old idea of a partnership of emperor and Senate (with Vespasian's lack of background, any attempt at equality with the great nobles would ultimately point up his "inferiority").

Vespasian repeatedly held the censorship, which not only allowed him to survey the empire's resources for financial purposes but also gave him control over the Senate's membership. He kept a tight reign on appointments, even pushing his own men into provinces officially controlled by the Senate. Since his choices were usually good, the senators could hardly object openly, but it must be admitted that they respected rather than admired him. Indeed, he was a successful but never a truly popular emperor with any class.

Finance Reforms

The state finances were in an appalling condition when Vespasian took over. He promptly instituted a nearly peasant-style economy in government (he became the proverbial stingy emperor), reimposed the taxes recent emperors had canceled, raised provincial tribute where his surveys showed it possible, and even invented wholly new taxes. (His tax on public urinals gave rise to his famous witticism; when his son Titus objected to money from such a source, he held a coin under Titus's nose, saying, "Money does not smell.")

Yet Vespasian could spend freely, too; money went for roads and useful public works in every province. His most celebrated building, the Colosseum, converted the site of Nero's private palace into a stadium for 80,000 people. Nor would a merely miserly emperor have shown such interest in education. He endowed schools and libraries and appointed the famous Quintilian as the first state-paid public professor.

Augustus had sought secure frontiers at danger points but had paid little attention to safe areas, with the result that many frontiers were still vague. Vespasian wanted frontiers for administration as well as for security and so began a process of rectification, seeking frontiers that were secure, short, and with good communications. His best-known move was into southwestern Germany to shorten the Rhine-Danube frontier, but he made similar moves elsewhere. He also established great, permanent military posts for administration as well as defense.

Vespasian secured the succession by making his son Titus virtually coemperor and died peacefully in 79, an admirable if not a lovable emperor. Titus promptly had him deified.

Further Reading

The best source on Vespasian is Tacitus's *Histories,* but it breaks off after the first year. Suetonius's biography in *Lives of the Twelve Caesars* is the most complete account but is more interested in the man than in the emperor. For Vespasian and the Jews see Josephus's *The Jewish War* and *Antiquities of the Jews.* Among modern works the best is Bernard W. Henderson, *Five Roman Emperors* (1927). □

Amerigo Vespucci

A Florentine navigator and pilot major of Castile, Amerigo Vespucci (1454-1512), for whom America is named, is no longer accused of having conspired to supplant Columbus; but interpretation of documents concerning his career remains controversial.

The father of Amerigo Vespucci was Nastagio Vespucci, and his uncle was the learned Dominican Giorgio Antonio Vespucci, who had charge of Amerigo's education. The entire family was cultured and friendly with the Medici rulers of Florence. Domenico

Ghirlandaio painted Amerigo in a family portrait when the youth was about 19. However, the explorer had reached his 40s at the time he began voyaging to America, so Ghirlandaio furnishes only an approximate idea of Vespucci's mature appearance.

It is known that Vespucci visited France, in his uncle's company, when about 24, and that his father intended him for a business career. He did engage in commerce, first in Florence and then in Seville in a Medici branch bank. Later, in Seville, he entered a mercantile partnership with a fellow Florentine, Gianetto Berardi, and this lasted until Berardi's death at the end of 1495.

Meanwhile, Columbus had made his first two voyages to the West Indies, and he returned from the second in June 1496. At this time, he and Vespucci unquestionably met and conversed, and Amerigo appears to have been skeptical of the Admiral's belief that he had already reached the outskirts of Asia. Moreover, Vespucci's curiosity about the new lands had been aroused, together with a determination, though no longer young, to see them himself.

"First Voyage"

If the letter he reputedly wrote to Pero Soderini, Gonfalonier (Standard-bearer) of Florence, may be taken at face value, Vespucci embarked from Cadiz in a Spanish fleet May 10, 1497. Serious doubts have been raised about the letter's authenticity, because it does not fit chronologically with authenticated events, and because the voyage, if made, presents serious geographical problems and passes

unnoticed by the cartographers and historians of the time. Alberto Magnaghi (1875-1945) believed the letter fabricated, or mostly so, by Vespucci admirers in Florence, who had no idea of the problems they were raising.

If the letter is taken literally, the ships passed through the West Indies, sighting no islands, and in 37 days reached the mainland at some Central American point. This would antedate the Columbus discovery of the mainland of Venezuela by a year. Following the coast, the ships reached "Lariab," tentatively taken for Tamaulipas. They then continued along the Gulf of Mexico, rounded the tip of Florida, and went northward to Cape Hatteras or Chesapeake Bay. On the return to Spain, they discovered the inhabited island of "Iti," identified by some as Bermuda, though by 1522 the Bermudas were unpopulated. The expedition reached Cadiz in October 1498. This voyage should have revealed the insularity of Cuba, yet it failed to establish the fact in contemporary minds, and it remained for Sebastián Ocampo to do so in 1509.

Vespucci, in all probability, voyaged to America at the time ascribed, but he did not have command and as yet had had no practical experience of piloting. Amerigo, or whoever wrote the Soderini letter, deals in leagues covered, seldom in latitudes. These are badly off and at one point would have had the ships in the region of British Columbia. Inexperience could explain many of the errors, but the strong likelihood remains that the letter has been doctored.

In 1499 Vespucci sailed again, and this time there is documentary support of the expedition besides his own letters. His education had included mathematics, and he had surely learned a great deal from his first crossing. Alonso de Ojeda commanded the 1499 expedition at the start, and in his later report he named "Morigo Vespuche" as one of the pilots. From Cadiz, they first dropped to the Cape Verde Islands and then divided forces in the Atlantic. Ojeda went to the Guianas and then to Hispaniola without further discoveries.

Vespucci explored to Cape Santo Agostinho, at the shoulder of Brazil, after which he coasted westward past the Maracaibo Gulf until he too turned to Hispaniola. This may have been the first expedition to touch Brazil as well as the first to cross the Equator in New World waters. Vespucci probably discovered the Amazon mouth; he certainly did so if he remained close to land while sailing west.

A New World

Two years later, Amerigo went on by far his most important voyage, this time for Portugal, at the invitation of King Manuel I. In 1500 that King's commander, Pedro Álvares Cabral, on his way to the Cape of Good Hope and India, had discovered Brazil at latitude 16°52′S. Portugal claimed this land by the Treaty of Tordesillas, and the King wished to know whether it was merely an island or part of the continent Spanish explorers had encountered farther north. Vespucci, having already been to the Brazilian shoulder, seemed the person best qualified to go as an observer with the new expedition Manuel was sending. Vespucci did not command at the start—the Portuguese captain was probably Gonçalo Coelho—but ultimately took charge at the request of the Portuguese officers.

This voyage traced the South American coast from a point above Cape São Roque to approximately 47°S in Patagonia. Among the important discoveries were Guanabara Bay (Rio de Janeiro) and the Rio de la Plata, which soon began to appear on maps as Rio Jordán. Vespucci, whatever his earlier beliefs had been, now realized that this could be no part of Asia, as flora, fauna, and human inhabitants in no way corresponded to what ancient writers, and such later ones as Marco Polo, had described. The expedition returned by way of Sierra Leone and the Azores, and Vespucci, in a letter to Florence, called South America *Mundus Novus* (New World).

In 1503 Amerigo sailed in Portuguese service again to Brazil, but this expedition failed to make new discoveries. The fleet broke up, the Portuguese commander's ship disappeared, and Vespucci could proceed only a little past Bahia before returning to Lisbon in 1504. He did not sail again, and as there seemed no more work for him in Portugal he returned to Seville, where he settled permanently and where he had earlier married Maria de Cerezo. He was middle-aged, and the fact that there were no children might indicate that Maria was also past her youth.

Columbus never thought Vespucci had tried to steal his laurels, and in 1505 he wrote his son, Diego, saying of Amerigo, "It has always been his wish to please me; he is a man of good will; fortune has been unkind to him as to others; his labors have not brought him the rewards he in justice should have."

In 1507 a group of scholars at St-Dié in Lorraine brought out a book of geography entitled *Cosmographiae introductio*. One of the authors, Martin Waldseemüller, suggested the name America, especially for the Brazilian part of the New World, in honor of "the illustrious man who discovered it." To a conventional Ptolemy map of the Old World, there was now added as much of the new hemisphere as was then known, with the name America upon it. Some objected to this, and both Spain and Portugal proved slow and unwilling to adopt the name, but it prevailed, in part no doubt because of its pleasant sound. Vespucci was no party to this undoubted injustice to Columbus and possibly never heard of it.

In 1503 the Castilian crown created the Casa de Contratación at Seville to govern trade with the New World, and in 1508 King Ferdinand, regent for his mentally unstable daughter, Joanna, established the office of pilot major as a part of the Casa. Amerigo was the first holder of the office, and it became his duty to train pilots, examine them for proficiency in their craft, and collect data regarding New World navigation. This he incorporated in the great *Padrôn Real*, the master map kept in his Seville office. He remained pilot major until his death on Feb. 22, 1512, a month short of his fifty-eighth birthday.

Further Reading

Biographers differ sharply in their judgments of Vespucci. Frederick Julius Pohl, *Amerigo Vespucci, Pilot Major* (1944), rejects the first voyage entirely and considers the Soderini letter spurious, while Germán Arciniegas, *Amerigo and the New World: The Life and Times of Amerigo Vespucci* (trans. 1955), maintains that both voyage and letter are authentic. The controversy over the rival merits of Columbus and Vespucci is examined in De Lamer Jenson, ed., *The Expansion of Europe: Motives, Methods, and Meanings* (1967). A general survey of the Atlantic voyage is Gerald Roe Crone, *The Discovery of America* (1969). □

St. Jean Baptiste Vianney

The French priest St. Jean Baptiste Vianney (1786-1859) served as the curé of Ars and worked tirelessly for his people. He was known for his personal holiness and his ability to help the troubled.

Jean Baptiste Vianney was born on May 8, 1786, into a peasant family in the village of Dardilly near Lyons in southeastern France. He was a quiet, patient, and deeply religious young man who wanted to become a priest but found it nearly impossible to learn Latin. His life was interrupted when he was drafted into the French army. On his way to join his assigned unit he stopped in a church to pray. The regiment left for Spain without him, and Jean Baptiste had to hide for two years until he was no longer wanted for the army. In 1811 he entered a seminary. Three years later he was dismissed because he was unable to grasp the theological subtleties he was supposed to study. But the bishop of Grenoble was sufficiently impressed by Vianney's firm character and level-headed judgment to ordain him a priest in 1815. After a three-year testing period, Vianney was assigned to the village of Ars as pastor.

The new curé brought a mixture of kind understanding and personal strength to the people of Ars. In the beginning his sermons were directed against drinking, swearing, and dancing. He tried to show his parishioners the value of resting from work on Sunday and of going to church regularly. His rigorous fasts and his prayers that lasted well into the night proved to the people that he was more strict with himself than with them. Gradually the spirit of Ars changed. It became a model of Christian behavior. More and more frequently visitors from other towns asked the curé of Ars to hear their confessions. His spiritual vision had grown to the point where his insights into their problems were very helpful. By 1845 Vianney was patiently spending more than 12 hours a day in the little confessional box of the parish church, while people who had come to Ars from all over France waited in long lines to ask his advice.

Vianney's success as a confessor was accompanied by increased personal difficulties. During the few hours of rest he allowed himself at night, he was disturbed by strange noises, sometimes by such discomfort that he felt he was being physically beaten. Once his bed caught fire. He understood these troubles to be persecution by the devil and reacted by intensifying his own prayers and penances. He was 73 when he died on Aug. 4, 1859. The curé of Ars was

canonized a saint in the Roman Catholic Church in 1925 and declared heavenly patron for all parish priests in 1929.

Further Reading

There are many helpful biographies of Vianney in English. Margaret Trouncer, *Saint Jean-Marie Vianney, Curé of Ars* (1959) is a readable story of his life. René Fourrey and René Perrin, *The Curé d'Ars: A Pictorial Biography* (1959), contains some excellent photographs of the curé's surroundings in Ars. Francis Trochu, *The Curéd' Ars: Saint Jean-Marie Baptiste Vianney According to the Acts of the Process of Canonization* (1949), presents the story of his life as seen by his contemporaries.

Additional Sources

Cristiani, Leon, *The village priest who fought God's battles, Saint John Mary Vianney (1786-1859),* Boston: St Paul Editions, 1977.

Gallery, David, *St John Vianney: parish priest of Ars, 1786-1859,* Dublin: Irish Messenger Publications, 1977. □

Gil Vicente

The Portuguese dramatist and poet Gil Vicente (ca. 1465-ca. 1536), who wrote in both Portuguese and Spanish, ranks as one of the outstanding figures of the Iberian Renaissance.

Almost nothing is known about the first half of the life of Gil Vicente until his first public appearance as a dramatist in 1502. It is certain he was of humble birth, but his birthplace has been disputed as Lisbon, Barcelos, or Guimarães, with the last the most likely. He was probably apprenticed to Martim Vicente, a close relative and goldsmith, and it was as a goldsmith that Gil attracted the attention of Queen Leonor, who in 1495 was widowed by King John II. Her brother then became King Manuel I. At her request Vicente contributed some verses to one of the famous *seroes do paço;* they were later collected by Garcia de Resende in his *Cancioneiro geral.*

The birth of the heir to the throne, the future John III, gave Vicente occasion for his debut as a dramatist. On the evening of June 7, 1502, the day after the prince's birth, Vicente, dressed as a herdsman, recited a rustic monologue (*Monologo da visitação*) in the Queen's chambers. Its 114 lines are in Spanish, partly in deference to Queen Maria's birthplace (she was a daughter of the Catholic Kings) and partly because Spanish was the fashionable language of the Portuguese upper classes. Bilingualism profoundly affected the literary works of Vicente and many other Portuguese writers of that age. Queen Leonor was so pleased with the monologue, a novelty in Portugal, that she asked him to repeat it for Christmas. Vicente did not think the subject matter appropriate, and instead he wrote the *Auto pastoril castelhano.* It was longer and more artful than the previous piece, introducing six characters, but it too was in Spanish. Queen Leonor was again pleased and asked him to compose another work for Twelfth Night. Vicente obliged with the *Auto dos Reis Magos,* in Spanish, featuring some characters that did not belong to the rustic pastoral world.

Court Poet and Dramatist

Vicente's career as the unofficial court poet was launched, and for the next 34 years he entertained the courts of Manuel I and of John III with his lyrics, music, and dramas. Vicente followed the court when it moved to Coimbra and Evora, and he poetized on the occasion of national events, courtly events, and solemn religious festivities. At first he continued to write religious plays, such as *Auto da sibila Cassandra* (1503) and *Auto dos quatro tempos* (1504), but soon he tried his hand at secular drama. In 1505 he produced his comedy *Quem tem farelos?,* a lively farce in which various types of Portuguese society were portrayed and criticized. Its clever dialogue was written in Spanish and Portuguese. Vicente could not ignore the imperial enterprises of his country. His first effort in this direction was in the comic vein, *Auto da India* (1509), but soon the Protuguese expansion in the Orient inspired him to write the fervently patriotic works *Exhortação da guerra* (1513) and *Auto da fama* (ca. 1515).

Later Life and Works

Vicente's career as a goldsmith followed the ascending curve of his dramatic career. In 1506 he finished a beautiful Gothic monstrance (Lisbon Museum). In 1509 he was appointed overseer of the works in gold and silver in Thomar, and after other appointments he was named on

Feb. 4, 1513, master of the Lisbon mint. It was probably at this time that he lost his first wife, Branca Bezerra. Her husband loved her dearly to judge by her epitaph and the charming *Comedia do viuvo* (1514). She left Vicente two sons. His second wife, Melicia Rodrigues, bore him three children, one of whom, Luis Vicente, published his father's works (*Compilaçam*, 1562).

After the deaths of King Manuel (1521) and Queen Leonor (1525), Vicente complained of hardships and poverty. However, his dramatic production continued uninterruptedly during the reign of John III. During this time he composed several of his masterpieces, including *Farsa de Ines Pereira* (1523), *Tragicomedia de Dom Daurdos* (ca. 1524), and *Tragicomedia de Amadis de Gaula* (1533). Vicente also received several pensions from the new king. The last play he wrote was *Floresta de enganos* (1536), with Spanish-Portuguese dialogue. Vicente probably died in 1536. Because 1536 was the year in which the Inquisition was established in Portugal, it was believed at one time that his death was related to that fact for he had vigorously defended the converted Jews.

Critical Groupings and Comments

When Vicente's son Luis published his father's works in 1562, he divided them into five groupings: religious plays (*cousas de devaçam*), comedies, tragicomedies, farces, and minor nondramatic works. He collected 44 dramatic pieces, ranging in structure from the utter simplicity of the *Monologo da visitação* to the splendid pageantry of the trilogy of the *Barcas* (*Auto da Barca do Inferno*, 1517; *Auto da Barca do Purgatorio*, 1518; and *Auto da Barca da Gloria*). Luis Vicente's classification, however, is not very satisfactory because he forced some plays into categories that do not fit them. Such is the case, for example, with *Auto da Mofina Mendes* (1534), classified under the religious plays; however, it is only in part a religious allegory, the rest being a charming dramatization of *Pierrette et son pot au lait*.

From the point of view of language, Vicente's plays can be classified into three groups: those written only in Portuguese, which number 14; those written only in Spanish, numbering 11; and bilingual plays, which add up to 19. Vicente's Spanish is an imitation of the conventional rustic jargon (*sayagués*) created by Juan del Encina.

Part of Vicente's greatness lies in the fact that his originality was undiminished by his imitations. He absorbed all of the main Peninsular literary traditions, infused them with lyricism, and began to dramatize at that point. His plays abound in frequent imitations and echoes of the courtly lyric, typical of the 15th-century *cancioneros;* in beautiful examples of songs written along the lines of the traditional lyric, such as *villancicos* and *cantares;* and in traditional epico-lyric ballads (*romances*) put to dramatic use, as in the *Tragicomedia de Dom Duardos,* which contains the ballad *Enel mes era de abril.* His catholic poetic attitude greatly helped him to fuse the old and the new, the Middle Ages and the Renaissance, the native and the alien, and to cast them all in a new mold that stamped itself firmly on budding Peninsular drama, thus making of him a major influence on the early secular theater. Although Vicente accepted in his early theatrical efforts the liturgical-allegorical drama prevalent in the Middle Ages, he vastly superseded that form in his trilogy of *Barcas,* with their sustained inspiration, great pageantry, and immense dramatic vistas. Then he went on to dramatize for the first time in Peninsular literature chivalric themes, such as in *Tragicomedia de Dom Duardos* and *Tragicomedia de Amadis de Gaula.* Most specially, and very significantly for the history of Peninsular drama, he recreated onstage the rich variety of Portuguese society at its moment of imperial grandeur. Many literary types of later Peninsular drama appeared for the first time in Vicente's plays.

Further Reading

The sound scholarship of Aubrey F. G. Bell's monograph, *Gil Vicente* (1921), has survived the test of time in many of its aspects. A more recent biographical study is Jack Horace Parker, *Gil Vicente* (1967). Valuable background information is in the early chapters of N. D. Shergold, *A History of the Spanish Stage: From Medieval Times until the End of the Seventeenth Century* (1967). □

Giambattista Vico

The Italian philosopher and jurist Giambattista Vico (1668-1744) is considered the founder of the philosophy of history. His main work, "The New Science," is an examination of social and political institutions in terms of their connection with phases of human development.

Apart from being known by a few German thinkers, such as Johann Georg Hamann and Johann Gottfried von Herder, the work of Giambattista Vico was ignored until modern times. Yet the belated recognition of his genius and contribution is such that some scholars suggest that his mode of historical thinking is capable of modifying the intellectual relations between the pure and social sciences.

Vico was born in Naples on June 23, 1668 the only child of Antonio and Candida Vico. Except for one sustained period he lived his entire life in the city of his birth. During this period of political turmoil Naples was ruled by a succession of foreign powers (Spain, Austria, and France) and domestically controlled by the powerful Jesuit order. Intellectually, the city became the center of Italian Cartesianism. Vico, who was in opposition to all of these forces, was unable to advance his career. His lack of recognition and success in his professional work, as well as personal misfortunes, made him a bitter man who was periodically subject to melancholia.

In childhood Vico nearly died as the result of a fractured skull, which prevented him from attending school. Because his father was a bookseller, the child read quite extensively but at random. Although he attended a Jesuit university for a brief time, he went only to those classes that

His Thought

René Descartes, credited with being the originator of modern classical philosophy, attempted to reform scientific thinking by a strict adherence to mathematical reasoning. Vico, who came to the study of philosophy from law, questioned the criterion of rationalist truth on the basis that real knowledge is by way of causes. He believed that ultimately we can know fully only that which we have caused. The true, or *verum*, is identical with the created *factum*. Despite its obscurities, Vico's intuition about history remains quite suggestive. Only God knows the natural cosmos perfectly, and the rationalist model of perfect demonstrable knowledge is attainable only in the realm of mathematical abstractions. But we can know history because it has been created by man, and its originative principles can be discovered by a reconstructive interpretation of our own mind.

Accordingly Vico's *New Science* anticipates the later thought of G. W. F. Hegel, Auguste Comte, and Arnold Toynbee: "Our philosophical and philological investigations revealed an ideal eternal history which has been traversed in time according to the division of the three ages . . ." Vico was indebted to Egyptian mythology for his basic metaphor of poetic, heroic, and natural natures. But the scope of his immense and diffuse learning enabled him to systematically associate these three types as reflected in customs, laws, language, institutions, and political authority; or, in brief, in the manifestations of nations as well as individual characters.

For example, primitive cultures are notoriously mythological in their thinking. To Vico this fact was a clear reflection of their ignorance of natural causes and the compensating strength of their imaginations. He believed the study of common language in its progression from oracular to expressive to vernacular provides a "mental dictionary" of character, nation, and time. Similarly, he believed a close study of laws and the facts of commerce yields more insight about a civilization than a study of its science or philosophy.

Vico's comparative method issued in a concept of political organization. In aristocracies the nobles "by reason of their native lawless liberty" will not tolerate checks upon their power. When plebeians increase in number and military training, they force the aristocracy to submit to law, as in democracies. Finally, in order to preserve their privileges, the lords accept a single ruler, and monarchies are established.

interested him. He spent a great deal of time studying logic and scholastic metaphysics until he found himself attracted to the study of law. Despite his lack of formal legal training, he successfully defended his father in a lawsuit when he was only 16 years old. But he developed a distaste for law as a profession and never practiced again.

From 1685 to 1695 Vico tutored relatives of the bishop of Ischia and lived in Vatolla. These were the happiest years of his life, and he used his free time to pursue his intellectual interests. He read widely in the fields of philosophy, history, ethics, jurisprudence, and poetry. His knowledge of science remained cursory, and he had a positive dislike for mathematics.

Vico returned to Naples in 1697 and became professor of rhetoric at the University of Naples. Part of his duties consisted of offering a lecture at the opening of each academic year from 1699 to 1708. These essays show the development of his thought, and *On the Study Methods of Our Time* ranks as a classic defense of liberal education. Between 1720 and 1722 he published a three-volume study, *Universal Law*. In 1725 he wrote his *Autobiography;* the same year he published the first edition of *The New Science,* which he modified and expanded in editions of 1730 and 1744. Despite these activities, Vico was not appointed to the chair of civil law and, because of his large family, he was forced to supplement his income by writing commissioned poems and prose encomiums. He died on Jan. 22/23, 1744, in Naples after a long and painful illness.

Further Reading

Studies of Vico include R. Flint, *Vico* (1884); B. Croce, *The Philosophy of Giambattista Vico* (1913); and A. R. Caponigri, *Time and Idea: The Theory of History in Giambattista Vico* (1953).

Additional Sources

Burke, Peter, *Vico,* Oxford; New York: Oxford University Press, 1985.

Verene, Donald Phillip, *Vico's science of imagination,* Ithaca: Cornell University Press, 1981.

Albano, Maeve Edith, *Vico and providence,* New York: P. Lang, 1986. □

Victor Amadeus II

Victor Amadeus II (1666-1732) was Duke of Savoy, king of Sicily, and king of Sardinia. An enlightened despot, he brought good government, justice, and prosperity to his domain and won for his people freedom from foreign domination.

Victor Amadeus was born on May 14, 1666. He was the son of Charles Emmanuel II, whom he succeeded as Duke of Savoy in 1675 upon the latter's death. Victor Amadeus's mother ruled as regent until 1683, when he declared the regency ended and personally assumed the reins of government. That same year Victor Amadeus married Anna Maria of Orléans, the niece of Louis XIV.

Louis XIV wished to draw Savoy into the French orbit for two reasons. Savoy would be a threat to France if it was occupied by any enemy of France's, and Louis wished to occupy Savoy himself as a first step toward conquering all of Italy. In 1685 Louis forced Victor Amadeus into war. That year, following Louis's revocation of the Edict of Nantes, thousands of French Protestants fled into the Waldensian Valley, an alpine border area between France and Savoy. Louis XIV instructed Victor Amadeus to invade the Savoyard portion of the Waldensian Valley and to root out the Protestants. Victor Amadeus refused until Louis threatened to invade Savoy.

The attack took place in 1686. A stiff Waldensian defense eventually broke down before the forces of Savoy and France, and the military operation developed into a slaughter of Protestants. More than 12,000 Protestant survivors were imprisoned in various fortresses in Savoy. However, the Waldensian affair had sickened Victor Amadeus. He resolved to defy Louis XIV and to free his duchy of French domination.

Victor Amadeus freed the Waldensian prisoners and financed their journey to Switzerland. In 1690 he opened negotiations for membership in the League of Augsburg, a group composed of the enemies of France. To discourage Savoy from joining the league, Louis XIV dispatched an army that occupied strategic fortresses in Savoy. Undaunted, Victor Amadeus joined the league and declared war on France.

The war lasted six years, but Louis XIV could not conquer the duchy. To entice Victor Amadeus away from the League of Augsburg, Louis XIV offered him generous peace terms. In 1696 both countries signed the Peace of Turin. France returned the captured fortress-cities of Pinerolo and Villafranca and the state of Nice to Savoy. Victor Amadeus then assumed command of a French army to help drive his former allies out of Savoy. The war-weary members of the league signed the Treaty of Ryswick in 1696 and ended hostilities with France.

Peace reigned in Europe until 1701, when the War of the Spanish Succession broke out. Savoy entered the war at first as an ally of France and Spain. But in 1703 Victor Amadeus refused to renew his alliance with Louis XIV. In 1706 a combined Savoyard-Austrian army defeated the attacking French at Turin. Through this victory, Victor Amadeus ended the French domination of Savoy.

In 1713 the Treaty of Utrecht ended the War of the Spanish Succession. As remuneration for his efforts in the war, Victor Amadeus received the kingdom of Sicily and was crowned in September. In 1720 Victor Amadeus ceded his claims to Sicily to Emperor Charles VI in exchange for the island of Sardinia. That year Victor Amadeus was crowned king of Sardinia.

Victor Amadeus brought equitable justice to both Savoy and Sardinia. In 1723 he promulgated the first legal code in Savoy since the Middle Ages. He also brought economic prosperity to Savoy by expanding and investing in the tobacco and wool industries. He standardized weights, measures, and monetary units. The King established a state-supported insane asylum, a secondary school system, and the University of Turin.

In 1730 Victor Amadeus abdicated in favor of his son, Charles Emmanuel III. Victor Amadeus died on Oct. 31, 1732.

Further Reading

A scholarly and enjoyable account of the reign of Victor Amadeus II is by the Marchesa Vitelleschi, *The Romance of Savoy* (2 vols., 1905).

Additional Sources

Symcox, Geoffrey, *Victor Amadeus II: absolutism in the Savoyard State, 1675-1730,* Berkeley: University of California Press, 1983. □

Victor Emmanuel II

Victor Emmanuel II (1820-1878) was king of Sardinia from 1849 to 1861 and then the first king of Italy until 1878. He worked to free Italy from foreign control and became a central figure of the movement for Italian unification.

The son of Charles Albert, Prince of Savoy-Carignano, Victor Emmanuel was born at Turin on March 14, 1820. His education was not thorough or varied, its content being restricted largely to military and religious training. In his youth he took little interest in affairs of state, preferring to spend his time in the study of military strategy and tactics. In 1842 he married Adelaide, the daughter of Archduke Rainer of Austria.

Throne of Sardinia

During the War of 1848 with Austria, Victor Emmanuel fought courageously at the head of a division. Notwithstanding bravery and zeal, the Piedmontese forces suffered defeat at the battle of Novara, and in March 1849 Charles Albert abdicated as king of Sardinia in favor of his son rather than face the humiliation of the peace terms. The new king was immediately confronted with a most difficult and important decision. The Austrians offered to refrain from occupying Piedmont and to give Victor Emmanuel more territory if he would renounce the constitution granted the Piedmontese a year earlier by his father. To his great credit, Victor Emmanuel rejected this offer, suffering as a result the loss of substantial territory and a considerable reduction in the size of his army. His stubborn insistence that amnesty be granted to all Lombards who had engaged in the revolt against their Austrian rulers was rewarded, and his refusal to yield on this point—along with the sacrifices made in order to retain the constitution—caused him to become a hero in the eyes of all Italians.

The peace treaty with the Austrians was ratified in January 1850. In the same year Victor Emmanuel appointed Camillo di Cavour to the office of minister of agriculture. Acquiring the services of this political genius was one of the most important acts of the King's career. Two years later Cavour was named prime minister.

During the 1850s these two able men worked on internal reforms, modernizing especially the financial structure of the kingdom and circumscribing ecclesiastical privileges in favor of civil power. When the Crimean War began, Victor Emmanuel and Cavour thought it prudent to join forces with France and England against Russia in order to gain the attention of the Great Powers. In 1855, during the hostilities, the King visited London and Paris, where he won much favor if not concrete goals.

Conquest of Italy

With a goal of ousting the Austrians from northern Italy, Victor Emmanuel made contact with revolutionary groups throughout the country. In 1859 Napoleon III was persuaded to ally France with Sardinia, albeit at a high price. Victor Emmanuel agreed to cede Savoy and Nice to France and to marry his daughter Clothier to Napoleon's cousin if France joined Sardinia in war against Austria. He concluded these careful preparations for war by conferring on the great soldier Giuseppe Garibaldi command of a newly recruited and eager volunteer corps called the *Cacciatori delle Alpi* (Hunters of the Alps). War was declared by Austria in April 1859, and at first the course of events favored the Piedmontese and French forces. But Napoleon had second thoughts and unexpectedly signed a separate peace with Austria at Villa-franca di Verona. Over the bitter objections of Cavour, who resigned over the matter, Victor Emmanuel signed the compromise Treaty of Zurich on Nov. 10, 1859. By this agreement Sardinia received Lombardy, but Austria retained Venetia.

Subsequent events proved that in this instance Victor Emmanuel was right and Cavour wrong. Time and diplomacy won for the King what continued fighting without the aid of France might have lost irrevocably. To prevent the reinstatement of the petty princes of Central Italy, Victor Emmanuel maintained contact with the revolutionaries. When Garibaldi took the bold step of invading Sicily, the

King aided him secretly. Garibaldi's startling success in Sicily and his subsequent victories on the mainland raised the hopes of Italian liberals and made Victor Emmanuel's ultimate success easier. The King decided to participate in the conquest of Naples and marched south through the Romagna. Its people greeted him with cheers, joyfully agreeing to the annexation of their entire province to his kingdom. He occupied the Papal States, accepting with equanimity the excommunication imposed upon him by Pope Pius IX, and he met Garibaldi in Naples. On Oct. 29, 1860, Garibaldi formally surrendered his conquests to Victor Emmanuel, and on Feb. 18, 1861, Parliament proclaimed him king of Italy.

Venetia was added to the new kingdom in 1866 through an alliance with Prussia against Austria, but complete unification of the peninsula could not be achieved as long as Rome remained in the hands of the Pope. A French garrison stood between Victor Emmanuel and this final conquest. Napoleon III, needing the support of the clergy, did not wish to abandon the Pope, although he had been Victor Emmanuel's ally in the expulsion of Austria from northern Italy. But this last bulwark of the papal territories was withdrawn in 1870, when—under the threat of total defeat by Prussia—Napoleon ordered his soldiers out of Rome. On Sept. 20, 1870, the Italian army marched into the city, and on July 2, 1871, Victor Emmanuel himself entered Rome, from that time the capital of the kingdom of Italy. The Pope, who had lost the last vestiges of his temporal power although the Vatican and his freedom were guaranteed to him, refused to recognize the new kingdom, and Victor Emmanuel died on Jan. 9, 1878, unreconciled to the Church.

Further Reading

The best biography of Victor Emmanuel in English is Cecil S. Forester, *Victor Emmanuel II and the Union of Italy* (1927). A readable and thorough account of Victor Emmanuel's role in the unification of Italy is contained in Bolton King, *A History of Italian Unity* (2 vols., 1899; new ed. 1967). An excellent recent study of the period is Edgar Holt, *The Making of Italy, 1815-1870* (1971). □

Victor Emmanuel III

Victor Emmanuel III (1869-1947) was king of Italy from 1900 to 1946. He contributed to the liquidation of the Italian monarchy.

Victor Emmanuel was born on Nov. 11, 1869, in Naples. After his father, Umberto I, was assassinated in 1900, Victor Emmanuel succeeded to the throne. His lifelong preference for matters martial had been set by military training and army service. But the political circumstances of his time prevented him from asserting a commanding personality in either war or peace.

In 1896 Victor Emmanuel married Princes Elena of Montenegro. They had five children, among whom were Umberto, the last legal king of Italy, and Mafalda, whose death in 1944 at the Buchenwald concentration camp enrolled her among the list of victims of that Fascist holocaust her father had helped to unleash upon Europe.

In Italy, as in other countries of Europe, the impact of World War I produced unforeseen shifts in the political spectrum. Particularly important were certain defections from the ranks of the Italian Socialist party. On the left arose a number of splinter factions, some of whom sympathized with the Russian Bolsheviks, but who were slow to form an Italian Communist party. To the right emerged the figure of Benito Mussolini, once a prominent Socialist journalist, now the leader of a band of middle-class ultranationalist bravos called Fascists. While the Fascists loudly supported the Italian claims to territory given to Yugoslavia after the war and vented their ire on striking workers, the left supported and led the strikers and, inspired by the revolutionary leader Antonio Gramsci, encouraged occupation of factories in the leading industrial center of Turin.

Frightened by working-class militancy, the old political establishment veered sharply right and looked on with satisfaction while the Fascists stepped up their punitive raids against labor and Socialist politicians. Yet by the time Mussolini's rabble assembled for its "March on Rome," the tide of labor militancy had already begun to recede. On the eve of the march (Oct. 28, 1922) the government decided to proclaim martial law against the Fascist threat. But when asked to sign the decree, Victor Emmanuel refused. At this moment, the King occupied the crucial position later held by Paul von Hindenburg in Germany; in both cases the

results were the same—the admission to the governing circles of Fascist dictators whose "temporary" rule during the pseudo-emergency would "restore order" and teach conformity to the rebellious left. Needless to say, the emergency never ended, at least not until 20 years of fascism had brought upon the Italian people the horrors of war and foreign occupation.

For the King, the rest was anticlimax. As head of state, he signed the decrees that deprived his countrymen of their liberties and that destroyed the parliamentary system. His only other opportunity to act independently came after Mussolini's downfall, when he handed over the reins of government to the conservative marshal Pietro Badoglio rather than to a representative of the joint anti-Fascist resistance. This was in 1943; the following year Victor Emmanuel, while retaining his title, handed over what was left of the royal power to his son. In May 1946 he abdicated, but the monarchy outlasted him by less than a month. He died in exile in Egypt on Dec. 28, 1947. His career demonstrates that he never really came to terms with democracy and that in his few moments of meaningful political choice he preferred to deal with the representatives of savage reaction rather than concede an inch to the demands of the people.

Further Reading

Discussions of Victor Emmanuel's reign are found in John M. Cammett, *Antonio Gramsci and the Origins of Italian Communism* (1967); Denis Mack Smith, *Italy: A Modern History* (rev. ed. 1969); and A. William Salomone, *Italy from the Risorgimento to Fascism* (1970). □

Victoria

Victoria (1819-1901) was queen of Great Britain and Ireland from 1837 to 1901 and empress of India from 1876 to 1901. She presided over the expansion of England into an empire of 4 million square miles and 124 million people.

A woman who gave her name to an age, Victoria was a richly contradictory character. Intensely virtuous, at the age of 11 upon learning she was next in succession to the British crown, she reacted by promising "I will be good," a promise which she faithfully kept. With innate good manners and a great love of truth, she was also immensely selfish, keeping aged ministers and ladies-in-waiting out in all weathers and up to all hours, and ruining the life and character of her eldest son (later Edward VII) by refusing to allow him any responsibility. Her prudery was famous, yet her letters reveal her completely unafraid to face unpleasant facts, even about her nearest and dearest. Tremendously personal and partisan in her handling of her ministers, she never succeeded in understanding the English party system; she considered that her own view of what would best benefit her country gave her the right to oppose any policy and person, and she frankly preferred coalitions,

while accepting that the Crown must be above party. Living all her adult life subject to the guidance of wise men, she remained both innocent and devious, arbitrary and simple, courageous and timid, "unconstitutional in action while constitutional by temperament." In fact she was so completely an expression of the dominant views and characteristics of her time that she truly embodied and interpreted her people throughout her reign. As queen, she saw slavery abolished in the colonies, the Reform Bill passed, the Poor Law reformed, the Corn Laws repealed; she saw her country undertake successful wars in the Crimea, Egypt, the Sudan, and South Africa, acquire the Suez Canal, and establish constitutions in Australia and Canada.

Alexandrina Victoria was born in Kensington Palace, London, on May 24, 1819. She was the only child of Edward, Duke of Kent (1767-1820; fourth son of George III), by Mary Louis Victoria (1786-1861; fourth daughter of Francis Frederick Anthony, reigning Duke of Saxe-Coburg-Gotha, and widow of Edward, Prince of Leiningen). Victoria was baptized on June 24, 1819, Alexander I of Russia being one of her sponsors, and her uncle, the prince regent (later George IV), the other. She grew up under her mother's care and that of Louisa Lehzen, her German governess, and spoke only German until she was 3. From 1832 Victoria's mother took her on extended tours through England. On May 24, 1837, she came of age, and on June 20, on the death of her uncle William IV, she succeeded to the throne, receiving the news of her accession in a cotton dressing gown at 6 A.M. Her chief advisers at first were the prime minister, Lord Melbourne, a Whig (Liberal), and Baron

Stockmar, a German sent to London by her uncle King Leopold of the Belgians as adviser to his 18-year-old niece.

Her Appearance

Queen Victoria had large blue eyes, a cupid-bow mouth, smooth light-brown hair that darkened with age, and a receding chin. She was under 5 feet and as a girl was slender, then plump. By the time she was 26 she was stout and remained so, except after periods of illness, until the end. She had a silvery voice, enunciated excellently, without a trace of the German accent of her eldest son, and had a radiant, though rare, smile. Those she disliked, William Gladstone for example, found her somber and terrifying; her ladies, servants, and grandchildren thought she looked "so dear" and idolized her.

First Years of Reign

Victoria's hand was kissed on her accession by members of her council, which included the Duke of Wellington, Sir Robert Peel, Lord John Russell, and Lord Palmerston, with all of whom she was to be closely associated. She opened her first Parliament on Nov. 20, 1837, and read her own speech; Parliament voted her an annuity of £385,000, plus the revenues of the duchies of Lancaster and Cornwall, another £126,000. Victoria proceeded to pay her father's debts. On June 28, 1838, her coronation took place. Next year her initial popularity waned, resulting from her dependence on Lord Melbourne and from her unjust treatment of Lady Flora Hastings, one of her ladies-in-waiting. When Lord Melbourne resigned, Victoria sent for the opposition leader, Sir Robert Peel; but when she refused to change her ladies, as was then the custom on a change of government, Peel refused to take office and Victoria recalled Melbourne.

In October her two first cousins, Ernest and Albert Edward (1819-1861) of Saxe-Coburg-Gotha, came to London. Albert had written in his diary at 11, "I intend to train myself to be a good and useful man." Victoria fell in love with him instantly and proposed to him; they were married on Feb. 10, 1840. It was an ideally happy marriage and restored the prestige of the Crown, which had sadly deteriorated during the reigns of Victoria's three inept predecessors. Prince Albert was granted £30,000 annual income by Parliament, was named regent in the event of the Queen's death in childbirth, and in 1857 was made Prince Consort by Victoria. Albert described his functions to the Duke of Wellington in April 1850 as: "the husband of the Queen, the tutor of the Royal children, the private secretary of the sovereign and her permanent Minister."

In June 1842 Victoria made her first railway journey from Slough, the station nearest Windsor Castle, to Paddington, and in that same year she first went to Scotland, traveling by sea. In 1843 Victoria and Albert visited King Louis Philippe. She was the first English monarch to land in France since Henry VIII visited Francis I in 1520. King Louis Philippe's return visit was the first voluntary visit to England of any French ruler. In 1845 Victoria, with Albert, made the first of many trips to Germany, staying at Albert's birthplace, Rosenau.

Her Ministers

In 1834, after Lord John Russell had failed to form a ministry (principally owing to Victoria's opposition to Palmerston as foreign minister), Lord John "handed back the poisoned chalice," as Disraeli put it, to Peel. But Peel's ministry fell on a measure for Irish coercion, and by 1847 the Irish famine, in which 1½ million people died and 1 million emigrated, postponed Victoria's planned visit there, which did not take place until 1849, when she landed at Cove, changing its name to Queenstown. In 1846 Victoria tangled with Palmerston over the marriage of the Spanish queen Isabella, and in 1850 she informed him that he "(1) should inform her of the course of action he proposes, and (2) should not arbitrarily modify or alter a measure once it had received her sanction." Lord Palmerston "affected pained surprise" at these injunctions but did not alter his ways. In 1851 the Whig government was outvoted and Lord John resigned, but as Lord Derby, the Conservative (Tory) leader refused to form a government, Victoria again sent for Lord John Russell. She was at this time so happy and blessed in her homelife that she wrote, "Politics (provided my Country is safe) must take only 2nd place." In 1844 she had Osborne Palace built for her on the Isle of Wight and in 1848 Balmoral Castle in Scotland; thereafter until the end of her life she spent part of each spring and fall in these residences. In 1851 she and Prince Albert were much occupied with the Great Exhibition, held in London, the first of its kind.

In 1851 Victoria was furious with Palmerston for informing Walewski, the French ambassador to London, that he approved of the coup by which Prince Louis Napoleon made himself Emperor Napoleon III. Victoria was largely instrumental in compelling Lord John Russell to demand Palmerston's resignation. In 1852 the Whigs finally fell, and Lord Derby led a Tory Government. But in July the Tories were beaten in the general election, and in December Lord Derby resigned. At Victoria's request, Lord Aberdeen made a coalition government, with Palmerston relegated to the Home Office. In 1853 Victoria and Albert suffered unpopularity for their apparent pro-Russian stand but regained public approval after the British declared war on Russia Feb. 28, 1854. In January 1855 the government was defeated on their conduct of the war, and Palmerston formed an administration. On March 30, 1856, Victoria admitted that she admired Palmerston's winning of the war. In 1856 Victoria and Albert visited Napoleon III in Paris, and in 1857 the Indian Mutiny against British rule, as represented by the East India Company, led to Victoria's writing that there now existed in England "a universal feeling that India [should] belong to *me*." In 1858 the East India Company was abolished. That same year Victoria's eldest child, Victoria, married Prince (later Emperor) Frederick of Prussia. In March 1861 Victoria's mother died, and her eldest son, Albert Edward, while in camp in the Curragh in Ireland, had an affair with an actress called Nelly Clifden, distressing Victoria and Albert, who were planning his marriage to Princess Alexandra of Denmark. Prince Albert, already ill, went in icy weather to Cambridge to remonstrate with his son;

Albert was suffering from typhoid and died on Dec. 14, 1861, aged 42.

The widowed Victoria held her erring son as partly the cause of his father's death and never forgave him. She retired into complete seclusion and wore mourning until her death.

In 1862 Victoria's daughter Alice married Prince Louis of Hesse, and a year later her eldest son, now created Prince of Wales, whom his family called "Bertie," married Princess Alexandra of Denmark. Victoria supported Prussia during its war with Denmark over Schleswig-Holstein, whereas her daughter-in-law, her ministers, and her people openly upheld Denmark. She approved Russia's brutal suppression of Poland's national uprising in 1863. In 1865 in the Seven Weeks War between Prussia and Austria, which ended in Prussia's victory at Sadowa, Victoria was again pro-Prussian. In 1867 Victoria entertained the Khedive of Egypt and the Sultan of Turkey. In 1868 Benjamin Disraeli became prime minister but was defeated by William Gladstone over the disestablishment of the Irish Church. Disraeli offered to resign, but Victoria kept him in office for six months after his defeat. Victoria, though she thought him "odd" and his wife odder, much appreciated Disraeli because he treated her as a woman. Gladstone, she complained, treated her as though she were a public department. In the Franco-Prussian War of 1870, Victoria was still pro-Prussian, though she welcomed the exiled French empress Eugénie and allowed her and the Emperor to live at Chislehurst. In 1873 Gladstone resigned, and in 1874, to Victoria's delight, Disraeli became prime minister. He called the plump, tiny queen "The Faery" and admitted he loved her—"perhaps the only person left to me in this world that I do love." That same year Victoria's son Prince Alfred married Marie, daughter of the Russian czar, who insisted she be called Imperial, not Royal, Highness. This encouraged Victoria to make "preliminary enquiries" about officially assuming the title Empress of India, which she did on May 1, 1876. In 1875 Disraeli, with the help of the Rothschilds, bought the majority of the Suez Canal shares from the bankrupt Khedive of Egypt, to Victoria's delight. That same year Gladstone roused the country with stories of "Bulgarian atrocities": 12,000 Bulgarian Christians had been murdered by Turkish irregulars. In 1877 Russia declared war on Turkey; Victoria and Disraeli were pro-Turk, sending a private warning to the Czar that, were he to advance, Britain would fight. Disraeli complained that Victoria "writes every day and telegraphs every hour." In 1878 at the Congress of Berlin, Disraeli obtained, as he told Victoria, "peace with honour."

In 1879 Victoria visited Italy and Germany. In the fall Gladstone's Midlothian campaign led to the government's defeat in April 1880. In 1882 a third attempt was made on Victoria's life. Africa gave trouble, the Zulu killed Empress Eugénie's son, and the Sudanese killed Gen. Gordon in Khartoum before Lord Wolseley, sent at Victoria's urging to relieve him, arrived. In 1885 Victoria went to Aix-les-Bains; she thought Gladstone a humbug, and "he talks so very much." In June he resigned, but Lord Salisbury, who became prime minister, lost the ensuing general election. Gladstone, pledged to Irish home rule, came in again, to Victoria's unconcealed annoyance. When he was defeated on this issue, Lord Salisbury returned to power.

Last Years

In 1887 Victoria's golden jubilee was celebrated, and in 1888 she actually approved of Gladstone—when he persuaded Parliament to vote £37,000 annually for the Prince of Wales' children. In 1889 the German kaiser, Victoria's grandson, visited England; in 1892 Gladstone again became prime minister. His Home Rule Bill was passed in the House of Commons but thrown out by the House of Lords. Gladstone resigned, to be succeeded by Lord Rosebery. In 1897 Victoria's diamond jubilee was magnificently celebrated, the apotheosis of her reign and of her empire. In 1897 the repression of the Sudan culminated in Lord Kitchener's victory at Omdurman on September 2. Victoria was joyful; "Surely Gordon is avenged," she wrote. In 1899 the Boer War broke out, and in 1900 Victoria went to Ireland, where most of the soldiers who fought on the British side were recruited. In August she signed the Australian Commonwealth Bill and in October lost a grandson in the war. On Jan. 22, 1901, she died in the arms of the Kaiser. Her last word was "Bertie." She was the mother of four boys and five girls, all of whom had issue. In her lifetime she had 40 grand-children and 37 great-grandchildren. During her reign the British crown ceased to be powerful but remained influential.

Further Reading

An authoritative biography, enriched by records unavailable to older biographers, is Elizabeth Longford, *Queen Victoria: Born to Succeed* (1965). Other biographies are Lytton Strachey, *Queen Victoria* (1921); J. A. R. Marriott, *Queen Victoria* (1934); Edith Sitwell, *Victoria of England* (1936); Hector Bolitho, *Queen Victoria* (1948); and Roger Fulford, *Queen Victoria* (1960). Studies of the Victorian age include Asa Briggs, *The Age of Improvement, 1783-1867* (1959); Ernest Llewellyn Woodward, *The Age of Reform, 1815-1870* (1938; 2d ed. 1962); and R. J. Evans, *The Victorian Age, 1815-1914* (1950; 2d ed. 1968). Joan Evans, *The Victorians* (1966), is a handsome picture-and-document history of Victorian England.

Additional Sources

Sharp, Geoffrey B., *Byrd & Victoria,* Sevenoaks: Novello, 1974.
☐

Tomás Luis de Victoria

Tomás Luis de Victoria (ca. 1548-1611) was the most renowned Spanish Renaissance polyphonist. His works are characterized by mystical fervor and nobility of musical concepts.

omás Luis de Victoria was the seventh child of 11 born in Ávila to Francisco Luis de Victoria and Francisca Suárez de la Concha. His father's death in 1557 left the family in the care of an uncle who was a priest. Victoria spent several years as a choirboy in Ávila Cathedral.

In 1565 (or 1563) Victoria entered the German College at Rome. This was a Jesuit school lavishly supported by Philip II and Otto von Truchsess von Waldburg, the cardinal archbishop of Augsburg. Victoria served as organist at the Aragonese church of S. Maria di Monserrato in Rome from 1569 to 1574. In 1571 the German College hired him to teach music to the young boys. He was ordained on Aug. 28, 1575. From that year to 1577 he directed the German College choir singing at the church of S. Apollinare in Rome; from 1578 to 1585 he held a chaplaincy at S. Girolamo della Carità, the church of the newly founded Oratorians at Rome.

Victoria returned to Spain in 1587 and until 1603 served as chapelmaster of the Descalzas Reales convent in Madrid, where Philip II's sister, the Dowager Empress Maria, and her daughter, Princess Margaret, resided. From 1604 until his death on Aug. 27, 1611, he was also the organist at the convent.

In 1572 Victoria dedicated his first, and still most famous, publication to Cardinal Truchsess, a great connoisseur of church music. The 33 *motecta* ranging from four to eight voices in this collection include the sensuous *Vere languores* and *O vos omnes,* which to this day form the bedrock of Victoria's reputation with the broad public that knows nothing of his Magnificats, hymns, sequences, psalms, antiphons, and 20 Masses—five of which appeared in 1576, four more in 1583, seven in 1592, and the rest in 1600 and 1605.

In his 1572 motets Victoria closely followed the detail technique of Giovanni Pierluigi da Palestrina, evincing a commanding mastery of Palestrina's dissonance treatment. Personal contact with Palestrina and perhaps even lessons probably explain Victoria's absorption of the technique. From 1566 to 1571 Palestrina served as chapelmaster at the Roman College near the German College. What distinguishes Victoria's personal manner in 1572 from Palestrina's is the younger composer's frequent recourse to printed accidentals, his fondness for what would now be called melodic minor motion (sharps ascending, naturals descending), and the anticipation of 19th-century functional harmony.

Throughout his career, even when writing *Missa Quarti toni* (1592), Victoria always succeeded in sounding like a "major-minor" rather than a truly "modal" composer. For him *Quarti toni* meant A minor cadencing on the dominant. In 1600 he published *Missae, Magnificat, motecta, psalmi, & alia,* which consists very largely of organ-accompanied F-major music. True, he reverted to unaccompanied minor keys in the *Officium defunctorum,* published in 1605 as a tribute to his patroness, the Dowager Empress Maria, but this was funeral music. In none of Palestrina's publications did he specify organ accompaniments. Victoria did—even publishing organ parts in 1592 and 1600.

Victoria's miscellany of 1600 includes a *Missa pro Victoria* modeled on Clément Janequin's famous battle chanson. Philip III liked this ebullient nine-voice Mass founded on a secular model more than any of Victoria's other works, but it contravenes every quality endearing Victoria to his modern public. However, it does at least prove him to have been more versatile emotionally and technically than his admirers will admit. Philip III's partiality for it served as a sales gambit when Victoria sought funds from its publication to bail his youngest brother out of prison.

Further Reading

A biography of Victoria is sketched in Robert Stevenson, *Spanish Cathedral Music in the Golden Age* (1961). For historical background see the *New Oxford History of Music,* vol. 4: *The Age of Humanism, 1540-1630* (1968), chapter 7. □

Eugene Luther Gore Vidal

Eugene Luther Gore Vidal (born 1925) was one of America's most prominent literary figures on the basis of an enormous quantity of work, including novels, essays, plays, and short stories. He was also well known to the public through frequent appearances on television opinion programs.

ore Vidal was born into a family long important in American politics on October 3, 1925, at West Point, New York. His maternal grandfather was Thomas P. Gore, senator from Oklahoma; his father, Eugene Luther Vidal, was director of air commerce under President Franklin D. Roosevelt; he was distantly related to Albert Gore, vice president of the United States in the administration of President Bill Clinton.

The importance of politics in his life is obvious from his statement, "The only thing I've ever really wanted in my life was to be president." But he did more than verbalize: he was the Democratic Party candidate for Congress from New York's 29th District (Duchess County) in 1960; he served in the President's Advisory Committee on the Arts under John F. Kennedy from 1961 to 1963; he was a co-founder of the New Party, backing Senator Eugene McCarthy, from 1968 to 1971; he was co-chairman and secretary of state-designate of the People's Party in the period 1970-1972; he ran unsuccessfully for the nomination as the Democratic Party's senatorial candidate in California in 1982.

Literature Wins Over Politics

Although always on the fringes in politics, he was a central figure in literature after 1946. In that year, while working as an editor at E. P. Dutton, he published his first novel, *Williwaw,* based on his service during the last years of World War II in the Army Transportation Corps in the Aleutian Islands; the book was warmly received by critics.

After the lackluster *In a Yellow Wood* in 1947, Vidal had his first bestseller with *The City and the Pillar,* a *succes de scandale* about a homosexual. The reaction to the novel says a lot about the limitations of critics at the time: while many termed it ground-breaking because the hero is an all-American youth, none found it rather conventional in that it has a tragic ending, almost a *sine qua non* in homosexual fiction at mid-century.

In any event, *The City and the Pillar* was badly received by the more conservative press: *The New York Times* reviewed it negatively, calling it "clinical and sterile," and refused to accept any ads for it, while the homophobic daily reviewer announced that he would consider no further books by Vidal. It may or may not be coincidence that his next five novels, *The Season of Comfort* (1949), *A Search for the King* (1950), *Dark Green, Bright Red* (1950), *The Judgment of Paris* (1952), and *Messiah* (1954) were negatively reviewed and were all commercial failures.

To increase his income, Vidal turned to mystery novels, publishing three of them under the pseudonym Edgar Box: *Death in the Fifth Position* (1952), *Death Before Bedtime* (1953), and *Death Likes It Hot* (1954). He also wrote short stories, which were published under the title *A Thirsty Evil* in 1956.

It was in 1954 that he developed what he called his five-year plan, that is, to go to Hollywood, write for films and television, and make enough money to be financially independent for the rest of his life. Between 1956 and 1970 he wrote or collaborated on seven screenplays, including

the film version of Tennessee Williams' *Suddenly Last Summer,* on which he worked with the playwright in 1959. Between 1954 and 1960 he also completed 15 television plays.

His five-year plan turning into a ten-year plan, he also developed an interest in writing for the stage. His debut, *Visit to a Small Planet* in 1957, was well received on Broadway and was subsequently turned into a television play. He had his greatest success in the theater with the 1960 drama *The Best Man,* assumed by many to be about the 1940 Republican presidential candidate Wendell Willkie; made into a movie, it won the Cannes Critics Prize in 1964. His later plays, *On the March to the Sea* (1961), *A New Comedy* (1962), *Weekend* (1968), and *An Evening with Richard Nixon* (1972), were less successful with the critics and at the box office.

Vidal returned to the novel in 1964 with *Julian,* about the fourth-century Roman emperor Julianus II, called the Apostate because he dismissed Christianity as the official state religion and urged a return to Hellenism, a view with which the author seemed in sympathy.

After *Washington, D.C.* in 1967, he had another popular success with *Myra Breckenridge* (1968), the saga of a homosexual male converted into a female via a sex change operation, called by Nat Hentoff in the *Village Voice* "the first popular book of perverse pornography." After a long stay on the bestseller lists, it was made into a movie. A sequel, *Myron* (1974), was less successful.

Two Sisters (1970) was followed by nine novels in the next 20 years, a number of them about politics. They were *Burr* (1973), *Myron, 1876* (1976), *Kalki* (1978), *Creation* (1981), *Duluth* (1983), *Lincoln* (1984), *Empire* (1987), and *Hollywood* (1990).

Fame as a Critic

But, while the general public enjoyed Vidal as a novelist, more sophisticated readers and the critics esteemed him more for his essays, with ten collections of them, many of which had appeared first in periodicals, published between 1962 and 1993. They were *Rocking the Boat* (1962), *Sex, Death, and Money* (1968), *Reflections upon a Sinking Ship* (1969), *Homage to Daniel Shays: Collected Essays 1952-1972* (1972), *Matters of Fact and Fiction Essays 1973-1976* (1976), *Great American Families,* written with others (1977), *Views from a Window: Conversations with Gore Vidal,* written with Robert J. Stanton (1980), *The Second American Revolution* (1982), *Armageddon?: Essays 1983-1987* (1987), and *United States: Essays 1952-1992* (1993). *The Second American Revolution* won the National Book Critics Circle Award for Criticism in 1982 and *United States* won the National Book Award in Nonfiction in 1993, occasioning the waspish comment from Vidal that he was "unaccustomed to prizes in my native land."

In television Vidal served briefly as the host of *Hot Line* in 1964 and appeared frequently as a guest on shows dealing with political opinion throughout the 1970s and 1980s. Always a defender of liberal causes, but also an articulate spokesman for high standards in the arts and in education, he had the ability to upset conservatives, on one occasion causing even the usually unflappable, if not magisterial, William F. Buckley to lose his temper on camera.

Vidal even tried his hand with political documentaries, when in the mid 1990's he wrote and narrated a program on the American Presidency for Britain's Channel Four. Although the programs were a hit in Britain, Vidal was disappointed with their airing on American television, since The History Channel added further reportage from Roger Mudd and Arthur Schlesinger Jr, among others. Vidal griped about the editorial changes in *The Nation,* saying that the executives seemed to be saying, ". . .we'll get some experts' like we do for those crappy historical movies and let them take care of this Commie."

The consensus of critical opinion was that Vidal was more likely to be remembered for his criticism than for his fiction, for it was there that his style appeared to best advantage. That style, wrote William McPherson in *The Washington Post,* "is characterized by urbanity and wit, elegance and polish, and more than occasionally by the venom of a scorpion."

Continuing with literary nonfiction, Vidal released a critically successful memoir in 1995, *Palimpsest: A Memoir.* In it he reflected upon a life peopled with such interesting friends and acquaintances as his relative Jackie Kennedy, President John F. Kennedy, and many others he mixed with in the literary and political scene. While the book was largely well-received, *The New York Times Book Review* gave a luke warm assessment, calling Vidal's viewpoint "disinterested".

Further Reading

There are three good biographies, *Gore Vidal* by Ray Lewis White (1968), *The Apostate Angel* by Bernard F. Dick (1974), and *Gore Vidal* by Robert F. Kiernan (1982). There are also mentions in such surveys as John W. Aldridge's *After the Lost Generation.* □

Faculté des Lettres at the University of Nancy, but he went to the Sorbonne in 1877. His first directly geographical publication was an article in 1877, on the first census of India, taken in 1871. It shows an appreciation of the influence of social traditions and aptitudes as well as of physical environment on population distribution.

Other articles and school textbooks followed during the 1880s. Subjects ranged from studies of the regional units, or *pays,* of the French countryside to the effects of the Mediterranean climate on its inhabitants and of the great migrations of people at various stages in history. The *Atlas général Vidal-Lablache,* with its history and geography sections, first appeared in 1894 and is still in print. In preparation for 10 years, it opened a fascinating panorama of human history in relation to the physical environment. Vidal de la Blache was one of the founders of the great *Annales de géographie* (1892), and in 1903 his *Tableau de la géographie de la France* appeared. The first volume of Ernest Lavisse's *Histoire de France,* it is a perspicacious study of the regional variety of France and of the place of each *pays* in the whole.

For over 30 years Vidal de la Blache meditated on the problem of the eastern frontier of France. This interest was deepened by his years at Nancy and led to the publication of *La France de l'est* in 1917. Vidal de la Blache died on April 5, 1918, at Tamaris-sur-Mer, Var.

Further Reading

Thomas W. Freeman, *The Geographer's Craft* (1967), includes a biographical chapter on Vidal de la Blache, and Robert E. Dickinson, *The Makers of Modern Geography* (1969), devotes a chapter to him. Vidal's influence on British geography is discussed in G. R. Crone, *Modern Geographers: An Outline of Progress in Geography since A.D. 1800* (1951; rev. ed. 1970). For general background see Griffith Taylor, ed., *Geography in the Twentieth Century* (1951; 3d rev. ed. 1957), and Thomas W. Freeman, *A Hundred Years of Geography* (1961; repr. 1971). □

Paul Vidal de la Blache

Paul Vidal de la Blache (1845-1918) was the founder of the modern French school of geography through his writings on human and regional geography and his remarkable "Atlas," first published in 1894.

A native of Mediterranean France, Paul Vidal de la Blache was born at Pézenas, Hérault, on Jan. 22, 1845. After his course in history and geography at the École Normale Supérieure in Paris, he went to the École Française in Athens and during the next three years traveled widely in the Mediterranean. He spent long periods in Rome, became familiar with the Balkan peninsula (then under Turkish rule), visited Syria and Palestine, and was present at the opening of the Suez Canal in 1869.

Vidal de la Blache's first published works were on classical subjects. On his return to France, after a short period of teaching at Angers, he joined the staff of the

Jorge Rafaél Videla

Jorge Rafaél Videla (born 1925) served as the leader of the coup which overthrew Isabel Perón, president of Argentina, in 1976 and held power until 1981. Although at first considered a political moderate who favored a return to democracy, he presided over a military regime noted for its violation of human rights.

Jorge Rafaél Videla was born on August 2, 1925, in Mercedes, Argentina, a large provincial city 75 miles from the capital of Buenos Aires. His father, Colonel Rafaél Videla, was a career military officer and his mother, María Redonda de Videla, was from an old established family of Mercedes. He was raised a devout Roman Catholic.

Following in his father's footsteps, Jorge Videla entered the National Military College at the age of 16 and was commissioned sublieutenant in the infantry in 1944.

During his early career Videla held a variety of posts, including those of instructor and staff officer at the Military College. From 1956 to 1958 he was stationed in the United States as an advisor to the Argentine embassy in Washington. He returned to the United States on two later assignments, once as a member of the Inter-American Defense Board and again for training at Fort Myer, Virginia. He also served in diplomatic missions in Bolivia and Venezuela. After various tours of duty in Argentina, he rose to the rank of brigadier general. In 1971 he was appointed commander of the Military College, a position he held until 1973, when he became the Chief of the Army's General Staff.

General Videla's rise to political power began in August 1975, when President Isabel Perón appointed him Commander-in-Chief of the Army, the number one position in the most powerful branch of Argentina's armed forces. Considered a political moderate, who first resisted pressure to interfere in the constitutional process, he ultimately became the leader of a three-man military junta that overthrew the crisis-ridden government of Isabel Perón in a bloodless coup in March 1976.

Although Videla assumed the Argentine presidency, the real power was vested in the military junta, whose announced goal was to eradicate left-wing terrorism and restore Argentina's deteriorating economy. Placing military men in all key positions, the junta quickly dismantled Ar-

gentina's entire democratic apparatus and established the military's absolute authority over the nation. To wipe out left-wing terrorism, the military launched a counter-insurgency campaign known as the "dirty war," which resulted in the arbitrary detention, disappearance, and death of thousands of people suspected of subversion. The counter-terrorist operations succeeded in crushing the two main left-wing terrorist groups, the People's Revolutionary Army and The Montoneros. The scope of the repression spread to include political figures, labor leaders, journalists, lawyers, priests, and other opponents of the military regime. All were targeted by right-wing death squads seemingly operating with the sanction of the government. The excesses committed in the "dirty war" exposed Videla to severe condemnation at home and abroad for violation of human rights.

In the economic sphere, Videla's economics minister, José Martínez de Hoz, implemented a modified free market policy designed to curb Argentina's rampant inflation and stimulate private investment. The policy showed early signs of success with a marked recovery of the economy and a drop in the rate of inflation. Argentina's economic boom proved short-lived, however, and by mid-1981 the country was again facing serious economic woes.

As proclaimed by the junta at the time of the coup, Videla was to remain in power for a three-year period. In March 1978, a year before his term was due to expire, Videla announced that his government desired a dialogue with key civilian leaders to develop a plan for a return to democracy. In May, however, the leaders of the junta decided that the military should remain in power for at least another three years and that Videla should continue as president for a second term. Declaring that his final objective was to return the country in due time to authentic democracy, Videla agreed to serve out a second term.

In March 1981, when his tenure came to an end, Videla handed the presidency over to another member of the military junta, General Roberto Viola. In the aftermath of the disastrous Malvinas (Falkland) Islands War, civilian rule returned with the election of Raul Alfonsín in October 1983. In 1985, Videla was brought to trial along with other junta leaders. Videla and his navy commander, Admiral Emilio Massera, were found guilty of homicide, illegal detention and other human rights violations, and three other leaders, including Viola, were found guilty of other charges. Videla was sentenced to life in prison. President Raul Alfonsin, who took office in 1984, was credited for making possible the trial and a return to democracy in Argentina.

There is considerable controversy over General Videla's actual role as president of Argentina. His opponents regarded him as a military strongman who was responsible for a level of repression unknown in Argentina since the days of the 19th-century dictator Juan Manuel Rosas. Videla's supporters, on the other hand, maintain that he only reluctantly became involved in politics and that his relatively moderate policies were increasingly undercut by right-wing military hard-liners, who operated with almost complete independence, carrying out repressive measures against the Argentine populace as they saw fit.

In 1991, Argentine President Carlos Saul Menem, saying he wanted to ''close a black chapter'' in Argentina's history, pardoned Videla and the others found guilty in 1985, and they were released from prison. Nearly 50,000 citizens protested in the streets, and Bishop Jorge Novak called the pardon a ''humiliating defeat for the democratic system.'' Menem's goal was to appease unrest in the military; there had been four military uprisings since democracy was restored in 1983. After the pardon, Videla wrote an open letter to the military, saying his only crime was to defend the nation. He remained unrepentant and called for ''full vindication'' of the military.

Further Reading

For Videla's political ideas see the *The Political Thinking of the Argentine Government: Excerpts from Speeches and Interviews by Jorge Rafaél Videla* (1977). Videla is profiled in Phil Gunson, Andrew Thompson and Greg Chamberlain, *Dictionary of Contemporary Politicians of South America* (1989). See also Janice C. Simpson, ''Haunted by history: a long-awaited verdict fails to heal the wounds of the 'dirty war,''' in *Time* (December 23, 1985). □

Antônio Vieira

Antônio Vieira (1608-1697) was the foremost orator in the Portuguese Empire in the 17th century and a defender of Jewish, Native, and black Americans from exploitation and persecution within the empire.

Antônio Vieira was born in Lisbon on Feb. 6, 1608, into a family of modest means. His father obtained a government post in Salvador (Bahia), capital of Brazil, where the family moved in 1614. Antônio studied at the local Jesuit college and proved himself to be a superior student. In 1623 he entered the Society of Jesus and was ordained 11 years later. He taught theology in the Jesuit college, while he earned a reputation as the most brilliant orator in Brazil.

Returning to Lisbon in 1641, Vieira soon became a confidant of King John IV, who sent him on a number of important and delicate diplomatic missions to The Hague, Paris, and Rome. Portuguese diplomacy was extremely complex because Portugal had declared its independence from Spain in 1640 after 60 years of union and because the Dutch had been occupying northeastern Brazil since 1630. Like most of the Portuguese of the period, Vieira believed Spain to be the more dangerous of the two enemies confronting the empire, and he was quite willing to placate the Dutch by conceding Pernambuco to their claims in return for support against neighboring Spain. The Brazilians denounced the suggestions of any concession and succeeded, with scant help from Portugal, in expelling the Dutch from northeastern Brazil in 1654.

Father Vieira frequently preached before the court. His extremely popular sermons drew capacity crowds in Portugal, just as they had earlier in Brazil. At that time the pulpit was a place from which to inform the public as well as to influence public opinion. The sermons covered much more than just religious subjects. Vieira stoutly defended the restoration of Portuguese independence and predicted a glorious future for the empire. Extreme patriotism was one of the chief characteristics pervading his oratory. In many of his sermons, both in Brazil and Portugal, he defended the New Christians (Jews who had been forced to accept Christianity and who were the constant concern of the Inquisition) and pleaded for the liberty of Native American and black slaves as well as fair treatment for them. In one fiery sermon preached in Brazil, Vieira asked rhetorically, ''Can there be a greater want of understanding, or a greater error of judgment between men and men than for me to think that I must be your master because I was born farther away from the sun, and you must be my slave because you were born nearer to it?'' It was a revolutionary question for the 17th century. Many of the social views of this Jesuit were far in advance of his time.

In 1652 Vieira returned to Brazil, this time residing in Maranhão, the northern region in which large numbers of the Native Americans still lived. He devoted himself to missionary activities among them. In that region the colonists still exploited, even enslaved, those natives as the only readily available source of labor. Vieira vigorously defended the freedom of those Indians, protesting before the Crown the brutal enslavement of subjects in the New World. His impassioned pleas pricked the royal conscience and prompted the Monarch to issue new and more stringent laws to protect the natives. The irate colonists, fearful of the loss of their workers, expelled Vieira from Maranhão in 1661.

Back in Lisbon, Vieira faced the Inquisition, suspicious of his defense of the New Christians, tolerance of the Jews, and predictions of the future. The Inquisition imprisoned him until 1667, when, thanks to a political coup d'etat, his friends succeeded in freeing him. The following year the Crown fully pardoned him. He left for Rome to plead the cause of the Portuguese Jews. There he quickly won fame as an orator, and at one time he served as the confessor to Queen Christina of Sweden. Returning to Lisbon in 1675, he began to prepare an edition of his sermons, which were printed in 16 volumes between 1679 and 1748. In 1681 he sailed back to Brazil, a land for which he had great love. He died on July 18, 1697, in Salvador, blind and deaf but still mentally alert.

Further Reading

There is very little in English on Vieira. Mary C. Gotaas, *Bossuet and Vieira* (1953), is a study of the literary styles of the French and Brazilian priests. For historical background see Caio Prado, *The Colonial Background of Modern Brazil* (trans. 1967). □

Giacomo da Vignola

The Italian architect Giacomo da Vignola (1507-1573) was the most important representative of Bramantesque classicism in the mid-16th century, and his treatise on the orders was one of the most influential textbooks ever published.

The real name of Giacomo da Vignola was Giacomo Barozzi. He was born on Oct. 1, 1507, in Vignola near Modena. He was trained in Bologna, the nearest important artistic center, as a painter and perspectivist. Sebastiano Serlio and Baldassare Peruzzi were the leading painter-perspectivists of the time, and both had turned from painting to architecture: both had great influence on Vignola, although his exact relationship with them is not clear. Peruzzi, who had been an assistant of Donato Bramante, helped to form Vignola's architectural style, and Serlio probably inspired him to write a treatise. Serlio probably met Vignola in 1541, when they were both in France, although they may have met earlier in Bologna or Rome.

Vignola went to Rome in 1530 and was active as a painter and, from the mid-1530s, as an architect. He worked in the Vatican under Peruzzi and Antonio da Sangallo the Younger, who also helped to form his architectural style. In the late 1530s the three architects were involved in a grandiose project to publish the treatise of the ancient Roman architect Vitruvius in a new text illustrated from extant monuments. A Vitruvian Academy was established in Rome, and Vignola was employed as a draftsman; thus he obtained a detailed knowledge of Roman antiquities. However, the project failed for lack of money.

In 1540 Vignola was working for Francesco Primaticcio, whom he accompanied to France in 1541, where he worked for the King in Paris and Fontainebleau. Serlio arrived the same year. By 1543 Vignola was back in Bologna. He made two designs, never executed, for the facade of the church of S. Petronio which are unique in that they show a deliberate attempt to synthesize classical and Gothic forms.

After Sangallo's death in 1546 Vignola took over his work for the powerful Farnese family, and most of his later works are connected with them. Two projects in Rome, however, both begun about 1550 and completed by 1555, were for Pope Julius III: the Villa Giulia and the church of S. Andrea in Via Flaminia.

Villa Giulia and Oval Churches

The Villa Giulia derives from the ancient *villa suburbana* described by Pliny the Younger. It has a severe, rectangular, main front and a garden front in the shape of a huge half circle curving inward. The work at the villa seems to have been carried out by a building committee consisting of the Pope himself, Michelangelo as artistic adviser, and Giorgio Vasari as impresario supervising the plans prepared by Vignola and Bartolommeo Ammanati. It is probable that the house itself was by Vignola and the garden buildings were by Ammanati; but it is impossible to say how far the idea of re-creating an ancient villa was Vignola's rather than a common ideal shared by the whole committee.

S. Andrea in Via Flaminia is a small and simple building, but it is significant as one of the earliest oval (rather than circular) church plans. The body of the church is rectangular, but it rises to an oval drum (internally a dome), like an ancient tomb. Vignola himself took the next step toward an oval ground plan (though still within a rectangular framework) with his design (1572) for S. Anna dei Palafrenieri inside the Vatican. The actual building was the work of his son Giacinto, but the design is an important forerunner of the great baroque oval churches.

The Gesù

Influential as these two oval churches were on later architects, the Church of the Gesù was even more so, although only part of the design is Vignola's. The Gesù was designed specifically for the Jesuits, who took the type with them on their extensive missions to the Far East and to Latin America. There is an interesting letter from Cardinal Farnese (who was paying for the church) to Vignola, dated 1568, from which it is clear that the type was chosen by the cardinal and imposed by him on his architect and on the Jesuits. He specifies that the church is to have one nave, with chapels but not aisles, and that the nave is to be vaulted. As designed by Vignola, this resulted in a short, wide church with chapels, which was ideally suited to preaching.

The facade of the Gesù was built by Giacomo della Porta after Vignola's death, but Vignola's design is preserved in an engraving. The basic feature of both designs is the treatment of the facade as a two-story composition with columns and pilasters on both stories, a triangular pediment over the nave, and volutes masking the chapel roofs.

Other Works

In 1564 Vignola began to work on St. Peter's under Pirro Ligorio. Ligorio attempted to alter Michelangelo's design for the church, causing such a storm that he was removed, and from 1566 until his death Vignola had sole charge of the project. Two small domes, invisible from the ground, are probably his major contribution, perhaps following indications by Michelangelo himself.

Vignola's most important secular building is the huge villa-fortress at Caprarola near Viterbo, designed as the headquarters of the Farnese family and begun by Sangallo and Peruzzi. The strange pentagonal form, then fashionable for fortresses, and probably also the circular internal court were already planned when Vignola took over in 1559. The main doorway and the facades above the pentagonal bastions are characteristic of Vignola's style, as is the detailing of the internal court. As in the earlier Villa Giulia, the forms are rather shallow, almost hard and dry, and they derive from those invented by Bramante for the Belvedere of the Vatican.

Vignola wrote two treatises. *La regola delli cinque ordini d'architettura* (1562) deals with the classical orders. There have been scores of editions and translations since then. His treatise on perspective, *Le due regole di prospettiva pratica,* was unfinished at his death; it was issued in 1583 and contains the earliest biography of him. Vignola died on July 7, 1573, and is buried in the Pantheon.

Further Reading

Biographical and critical material on Vignola is in James Lees-Milne, *Baroque in Italy* (1959), and Peter Murray, *Architecture of the Italian Renaissance* (1963). A detailed appraisal of his style by James S. Ackerman and Wolfgang Lotz is in Lucy Freeman Sandler, ed., *Essays in Memory of Karl Lehmann* (1964). □

Comte de Vigny

Alfred Victor, Comte de Vigny (1797-1863), was one of the finest poets of French romanticism. His lengthy journal reveals his sensitive and aristocratic nature.

Alfred de Vigny was born at Loches on March 27, 1797, the son of Léon, Comte de Vigny, a 60-year-old wounded veteran of the Seven Years War, and Marie Jeanne Amélie de Baraudin. After early education at home under his mother's influence and later training at the Pension Hix, where he spent three miserable years, and at the Lycée Bonaparte, Vigny was admitted at the age of 17 into an aristocratic corps of the Gendarmes Rouges. From 1816 to 1823 he served as an officer in the Royal Guard, but he became disillusioned with military life and in 1827 obtained his discharge from the army.

Marriage and Literary Pursuits

Meanwhile, Vigny's love affair with Delphine Gay had been broken up by his mother and, in 1825, he had married Lydia Bunbury, the daughter of a wealthy and eccentric Englishman. His wife became a chronic invalid a few years after their marriage and remained in ill health until her death in 1862.

Vigny's first volume of poems appeared anonymously in 1822 under the title *Poèmes.* It was republished in expanded editions in 1826, 1829, and 1837 as *Poèmes antiques et modernes.* After his literary debut, he wrote in various genres. In 1845 he was elected to membership in the French Academy after six refusals.

A love affair with the great actress Marie Dorval culminated in disillusionment and bitterness, and Vigny had later liaisons with Louise Colet and, during the last years of his life, with Augusta Bouvard. In 1848-1849 he was defeated as a candidate for office in the Chamber of Deputies. Thereafter, he settled down on his estate at Maine-Giraud, where he grew grapes for cognac and lived as a country squire. He died on Sept. 17, 1863.

Vigny's "Poèmes"

Vigny's literary masterpieces are his best compositions in the form he called the *poème,* which he defined as "compositions in which a philosophic thought is staged under an epic or dramatic form." The first fine example of this form was *Moïse* (1822), in which the figure of Moses going up in lonely grandeur to die on Mt. Nebo represents the man of genius of all ages, "weary . . . and in despair at seeing his aloneness more vast and more arid in proportion as he grows in stature."

The remarkable concentration possible in the *poème* is evident in *Moïse,* but one sees there the tyrannous nature of the idea as dramatized in Vigny's finest poems and in his best prose narratives (the tales of *Stello* and of *Servitude et grandeur militaires*). In all these pieces the relentless emphasis and focus of action does not allow the development of the subject matter in any but the prescribed direction. The staged "philosophic idea" is also evident in such fine poems of *Les Destinées* (1864) as *La Mort du loup, Le Mont des Oliviers, La Maison du berger, La Bouteille à la mer,* and *La Colère de Samson.* His *poèmes* are characterized by lonely stoicism, compact form, fine resonance, visual imagery, and remarkable use of symbolic landscapes.

Plays and Prose Fiction

Vigny's career as a dramatist began with adaptations from Shakespeare. These included *Roméo et Juliette* (1827), *Shylock, le marchand de Venise* (1828), and *Le More de Venise* (1829). *La Maréchale d'Ancre* (on the murder of Concini and his wife, Leonora Galigai) was played at the Odéon in 1831. His elegant one-act play *Quitte pour la peur* was presented in 1833. His finest drama, *Chatterton,* was first played at the Comédie Française on Feb. 12, 1835, with Marie Dorval a sensation as its heroine, Kitty Bell.

In 1826 Vigny published *Cinq-Mars, ou Une Conjuration sous Louis XIII,* the first significant French historical novel of the period. An interesting preface of 1827 (*Réflexions sur la vérité dans l'art*) acclaimed artistic truth as more important than the facts of history. In later works— *Stello* (1832) and *Servitude et grandeur militaires* (1835)— he developed a "philosophic thought" (in each case in three episodes) much in the manner of his *poèmes.* In *Stello* the idea expounded was that the poet is always misunderstood, envied, and hated under whatever form of government he lives and that he should always maintain the thinker's "armed neutrality" and never form connections with those in power. Vigny's prose narrative *Daphné* on Julian the Apostate was published posthumously in 1912. The three tales of *Servitude et grandeur militaires* represent the sacrificial life of the soldier, whom Vigny sees, like the poet, as a martyr to an insentient society. Vigny's *Journal d'un poète* (1867 and later) shows at once his elegant and aristocratic qualities and his weaknesses; but above all it reveals the courage, sensitiveness, and moral elevation of the poet.

Further Reading

Two English translations of Vigny's *Servitude et grandeur militaires* are Humphrey Hare's *The Military Necessity* (1953)

and Marguerite Barnett's *The Military Condition* (1964). A recent study of Vigny in English is James Doolittle, *Alfred de Vigny* (1967). Also useful is Arnold Whitridge, *Alfred de Vigny* (1933). ☐

Pancho Villa

Francisco Villa (1878-1923) was a famous Mexican military commander and guerrilla of the warring phase of the Mexican Revolution.

Pancho Villa was born Doroteo Arango on June 5, 1878, in San Juan del Rio, Durango. His life as an orphaned peasant ended, according to tradition, when he defended his sister against the hacienda owner. He became a bandit chief and horse trader, changed his name, and finally joined the *maderistas* in Chihuahua under Abraham González.

Without formal education, Villa was to learn revolutionary goals from association with Francisco Madero and his movement. Villa rebelled against the Porfirio Díaz regime and, because of successes as a guerrilla fighter, his knowledge of the terrain, and his skill as an organizer, was given the rank of colonel. On May 11, 1911, his forces and those of Pascual Orozco attacked and captured Ciudad Juárez contrary to Madero's orders. The victory marked the triumph of the Madero revolution.

After Madero assumed the presidency, Villa returned to civilian life as a businessman, but the Orozco rebellion in 1912 brought him back to the fray, defending the Madero regime first independently and then under Victoriano Huerta's orders. Imprisoned and about to be shot by Huerta for insubordination, Villa was saved by the intervention of Raúl Madero, the President's brother. Imprisoned for a while, he escaped to the United States. He reentered Mexico with a handful of companions to fight the usurper Huerta after Madero's death. By September 1913 that handful had become the nucleus of Villa's Division of the North.

In the struggle against Huerta, Villa was in uneasy alliance with Venustiano Carranza and Emiliano Zapata. The *villistas* took Torreón and won the crucial battle of Zacatecas (June 23, 1914). By then the irritations had built up and made conflict inevitable once the common foe had been vanquished. In part the differences were ideological, but more significant was the clash of personalities— the stubborn Carranza, proud of his prerogatives as first chief, and the indomitable and undisciplined Villa.

After Carranza's abortive Convention of Generals in the capital removed to the "neutral zone" of Aguascalientes, the *zapatistas* managed to dominate the gathering ideologically while the *villistas* held military control. Villa was made chief of Convention military operations against Carranza and with Zapata occupied Mexico City in December 1914. The Convention government could not command its own commander. Villa lived according to his

own personal code, beyond authority and law. He took what he pleased whether it was women or the lives of men.

Coordination between the *zapatistas* and *villistas* proved difficult if not impossible. The Convention government was forced to leave the capital as Álvaro Obregón advanced from the southeast. Villa retreated northward, there to be defeated in the most massive battles of the revolution, at Celaya and León in the spring of 1915. The power of the Division of the North was broken, and the myth of invincibility of Villa's cavalry (the famous *dorados*) was exploded.

Villa withdrew to Chihuahua, which he continued to control, and is credited with introducing reforms including some land distribution. In March 1916, angered by United States recognition of Carranza, Villa attacked Columbus, N. Mex. For almost a year Gen. Pershing's punitive expedition sought unsuccessfully to capture or destroy the "Centaur of the North." Some *villista* groups were dispersed, and Villa himself was wounded, but the uncooperative posture of the Carranza regime and the apparent inevitability of war with Germany speeded the withdrawal of the forces.

Villa continued guerrilla harassment of the Carranza government until the regime was overthrown by the rebellion of Agua Prieta in 1920. The interim administration of Adolfo de la Huerta reached an agreement whereby Villa agreed to lay down his arms and accept rank as a division general and the ranch of Canutillo, Durango, to support him and his escort.

Pancho Villa was killed on June 20, 1923, in Parral by *obregonistas* apparently fearful that he might emerge from his retirement to oppose the election of Plutarco Calles. More than four decades later the Mexican Congress voted to inscribe his name in gold on the chamber walls with other heroes of the Mexican Revolution.

Further Reading

Two works by Martín Luis Guzmán are especially valuable for understanding Villa: *The Eagle and the Serpent,* translated by Harriet de Onís (1930), and *Memoirs of Pancho Villa,* translated by Virginia H. Taylor (1965). Other biographies of Villa are Edgcumb Pinchon, *Viva Villa !* (1933), and Haldeen Braddy, *Cock of the Walk . . . The Legend of Pancho Villa* (1955). Ronald Atkin, *Revolution! Mexico, 1910-20* (1970), an excellent popular history by a journalist, contains a fine characterization of Villa and his contemporaries. Robert E. Quirk's specialized study, *The Mexican Revolution, 1914-1915; the Convention of Aguascalientes* (1960; repr. 1970), underscores the *villista-zapatista* contribution to the social program of the revolution. Villa's relations with the United States are treated in Clarence C. Clendenen, *The United States and Pancho Villa: A Study in Unconventional Diplomacy* (1961). Pershing's expedition into Mexico is described in an exciting study by Herbert Molloy Mason, Jr., *The Great Pursuit* (1970), which includes excellent photographs, maps, and bibliography. □

Heitor Villa-Lobos

The Brazilian composer Heitor Villa-Lobos (1887-1959) was the most prolific and original of those Brazilians who, during the 20th century, worked toward the development of a national idiom in serious music that incorporated African and Native American motifs.

Heitor Villa-Lobos was fascinated early by the popular music and samba rhythms of his native Rio de Janeiro at a time when gentility forbade such interests. Although his father, a college professor and librarian, had encouraged this interest, Villa-Lobos ran away from home at 16 to escape his widowed mother's attempt to keep him from developing further his musical talents.

Soon Villa-Lobos began drifting. He absorbed the folk music of whatever region he passed through, listening, mimicking, improvising, elaborating, and composing as he went. He traveled along the Amazon in a canoe, listening to the songs of tropical birds and the drums of the Indians. Although he occasionally enrolled for formal schooling, he found such experiences boring; he remained principally self-taught. In his 20s he lived for 3 years in the culturally diverse city of Bahia, where the Afro-Brazilian influence was strongest. Then he returned to Rio de Janeiro, where he studied European music on his own.

Meanwhile, Villa-Lobos experimented continuously and wrote a great deal, always seeking to express Brazilian qualities. His nationalism was reflected in the following

incident. In 1923 wealthy friends raised money and sent him to Europe, but when upon his arrival he was asked what he had come to study, he replied, "I am here to demonstrate my own achievements." Indeed, Parisians showed more interest in his works than had Brazilians, perhaps because in Europe they were considered exotic. He remained in Paris for 7 years, composing some of his most important work.

Back in Brazil in the 1930s Villa-Lobos became a music educator, campaigning for the introduction of Brazilian music into the school curriculum and staging performances by massed a cappella choirs extolling nationalistic themes. The semiauthoritarian dictator Getulio Vargas gave him full support in this campaign, and Villa-Lobos's influence can still be seen in musical education in Brazil.

At this time Villa-Lobos composed the nine suites entitled *Bachianas brasileiras*. These are his best-known works; in all of them he used a contrapuntal and fugal technique superimposed upon typically Brazilian themes, although otherwise they are quite diverse. They are characterized by an impressive range, great power, melodic inventiveness, and controlled structure.

Villa-Lobos composed over 1,500 works in almost every conceivable genre, including operas, ballets, church Masses, choral pieces, orchestral works, guitar solos, and movie scores. Not all his work is good, but at his best it is superb.

Further Reading

There is no serious book-length study of Villa-Lobos in English, although Vasco Mariz prepared a short summary, *Heitor Villa-Lobos: Brazilian Composer* (1963), a condensation of the author's biography published in Rio de Janeiro. Villa-Lobos is set in the larger context in Nicolas Slonimsky, *Music of Latin America* (1945). There is a section on the composer in Joseph Machlis, *Introduction to Contemporary Music* (1961).

Additional Sources

Behague, Gerard, *Heitor Villa-Lobos: the search for Brazil's musical soul,* Austin: Institute of Latin American Studies, University of Texas at Austin, 1994.

Peppercorn, L. M. (Lisa Margaret), *Villa-Lobos,* London; New York: Omnibus; New York: Distributor, Music Sales Corp., 1989. □

Giovanni Villani

The Italian chronicler Giovanni Villani (ca. 1270-1348) wrote a history of Florence from its origins to the age of Dante.

Giovanni Villani was a Florentine merchant whose wide travels gave him an interest in Florence and the world around it. He traveled in Flanders and France from 1302 to 1308, and from 1316 until his death he held numerous political offices in the city of Florence. Caught up in the economic crises of the 1340s, Villani died of the plague in 1348. His life was devoted to commerce, politics, and the *Chronicle*.

In 1300 Pope Boniface VIII proclaimed a Holy Year, promising spiritual benefits to all who made the pilgrimage to Rome. Giovanni now saw Rome for the first time. He wrote: "Beholding the great and ancient things which are [in the city], reading of the great deeds of the Romans, and considering that our great city of Florence, the daughter and creation of Rome, was ascending to greatness while Rome was declining, [I decided] to bring together in this chronicle all the beginnings of the city of Florence and then to set forth in detail the doings of the Florentines." From 1300 on Giovanni worked intermittently at his chronicle. He framed his chronicle in customary medieval style. He began with an account of the Tower of Babel, and his first six books end with the arrival of Charles of Anjou in Italy in 1265. The next six books, however, deal only with a period of 80 years, from 1265 to 1348.

In the later books Villani's interests move from the party factionalism of Florence to wider issues, such as the newly contacted lands in Asia as described by Marco Polo, and the trade, industry, and religion of Florence. Villani also describes well-known figures from Florentine history, and his description of the poet Dante is often quoted. Villani was the first chronicler to remark that the barbarian invasions of the later Roman Empire were a turning point in European history. The *Chronicle* also follows the medieval pattern in

giving an account of events strictly year by year. But the work is also original.

Villani wrote in the Tuscan vernacular, the language which Dante himself was so much to influence. He was not, like most chroniclers, a cleric, but a layman—and a man of affairs at that. His business and political life seemed to impart to him the expertise and wide range of interests which make the *Chronicle* extremely readable today. He possessed an astute mind, was capable of independent observation and judgment, and was a sufficient literary artist to incorporate lively and accurate portraits of contemporaries into his work. Giovanni's *Chronicle* was continued after his death by his brother Matteo and his nephew Filippo.

Further Reading

R. E. Selfe and Philip Wicksteed translated *Selections from the First Nine Books of the Croniche Fiorentine of Giovanni Villani* (1896). There is no biography of Villani in English. The reader should consult a history of Italian literature. Some information on him can be gleaned from Philip Wicksteed, *Early Lives of Dante* (1898). □

Oswald Garrison Villard

Editor of the "Nation" magazine, Oswald Garrison Villard (1872-1949) was one of the foremost American liberals of the 20th century. He was noted for his moralistic, uncompromising commitment to pacifism and minority rights.

Oswald Garrison Villard was born in Germany on Mar. 13, 1872. From his father, who emigrated to America and became a journalist and then a wealthy railroad magnate and financier, he learned a commitment to capitalism and the ideas of 19th-century laissez-faire liberalism. From his mother, the favorite daughter of abolitionist leader William Lloyd Garrison, he acquired a rigid, almost puritanical, moralism. Villard was educated at private schools and Harvard. After a brief apprenticeship on a Philadelphia paper, in 1897 he joined the staff of the *New York Evening Post,* which his father happened to own. He soon rose to editorial prominence on the paper and, after his father's death, became owner and publisher.

During his time with the *Post* Villard carved out an unconventional political position. Along with many others of his class and outlook, he condemned America's imperial ambitions as displayed by the Spanish-American War, but he began to move toward pacifism. He joined his father in supporting the rights of women (his mother was a dedicated leader in this battle) but also championed the rights of African-Americans, Jews, and other minority groups. He departed from traditional laissez-faire thought and defended the right of workers to organize into labor unions and to strike.

A sincere pacifist, Villard opposed American participation in World War I. In 1918, with war fever at its height, the pressure on Villard and the *Post* to form "patriotic" readers and advertisers had become financially unbearable, and he was forced to sell it. When the war ended, he attacked the Treaty of Versailles, claiming that its unjust nature proved his contentions about the unjust nature of the war.

Villard had retained ownership of the weekly edition of the *Post,* the *Nation,* and continued to use this as the personal organ for his views until 1932, when he gave up ownership but continued to contribute. During the 1920s Villard's *Nation* was one of the few strong voices of liberalism in the United States. Although its circulation was only about 25,000 its influence was great.

Villard remained a favorite of many liberals into the 1930s, when he supported Franklin Roosevelt's New Deal. However, at the end of this decade his pacifism again isolated him. He refused to support rearmament and aid to the Allies during World War II, and in June 1940 the *Nation* stopped printing his weekly signed articles. He continued to oppose the war after Pearl Harbor and rapidly isolated himself from the mainstream. On Oct. 1, 1949, he died in New York City, a still uncompromising, but embittered, man.

Further Reading

The best biography of Villard is Michael Wreszin, *Oswald Garrison Villard: Pacifist at War* (1965), which contains a bibliography. Dollena Joy Humes, *Oswald Garrison Villard: Liberal of the 1920's* (1960), has useful summations of Villard's positions on various issues during the 1920's, but it is not as insightful as Wreszin's book, which covers Villard's whole career.

Additional Sources

Humes, Dollena Joy, *Oswald Garrison Villard, liberal of the 1920's,* Westport, Conn.: Greenwood Press, 1977, 1960. □

Geffroi de Villehardouin

The French historian and soldier Geffroi de Villehardouin (ca. 1150-1213) was the first French chronicler who wrote in the vernacular and whose writings deserve literary recognition.

Geffroi de Villehardouin was born in the château of Villehardouin near Troyes, Champagne. Marshal of Champagne after 1185, he had close political connections with Count Thibaut III of Champagne. Villehardouin was sent with the Canon de Béthune and four others to Venice to negotiate for ships for the Fourth Crusade. Shortly after their return Thibaut died. But Villehardouin, an excellent diplomat, persuasive orator, and prudent negotiator, continued his labors, and soon Boniface de Montferrat was appointed supreme commander of the crusade. Throughout the crusade Villehardouin was an eyewitness to the events he recorded.

After the fall of Constantinople in 1204, he stayed in the East, receiving the title of Marshal of Romania (name then given to Thrace). The title passed to his son in 1213, presumably at the time of Villehardouin's death.

De la conquête de Constantinople (*The Conquest of Constantinople*) is Villehardouin's only known work. Written in clear prose, it stresses the overall campaigns of the Fourth Crusade rather than individual exploits. The author never knowingly lied in his chronicle, but he attempted to justify the crusade's deviations from its original objectives in Egypt and Jerusalem.

The first of its nine books explains the origins of the crusade, and the second relates the negotiations at Venice. The third part reveals worries about insufficient funds, bargaining, the initial propositions of Prince Alexis of Constantinople, and the embarkation of the FrancoVenetian army in August 1202. The fourth tells of the taking of Zara and of the displeasure of Pope Innocent III, who was deeply involved in the crusade. The fifth gives an account of a side mission in Greece. The sixth book, which contains some of the chronicle's finest pages, describes the arrival of the crusaders at Constantinople. After a siege of only seven days, the city capitulated on July 18, 1203, and the usurper Alexis II fled. Alexis IV was crowned on August 1. The last three books tell of the rupture of the crusaders with Alexis IV and of the second taking of the city; the systematic, rankwise distribution of the booty; the coronation of Baldwin of Flanders; and the conquest of surrounding territories. The long narration, sometimes stimulating, sometimes disgusting, is told with a candid simplicity rarely equaled by later historians.

Further Reading

A literal translation of Villehardouin's work is *Memoirs of the Crusades by Villehardouin and De Joinville,* translated by Sir Frank T. Marzials (1908; many later editions). Villehardouin's narrative is critically examined in Kenneth M. Setton, ed., *A History of the Crusades* (vol. 1, 1969). Also useful for background is Edwin Pears, *Destruction of the Greek Empire* (1903). □

François Villon

The French poet François Villon (1431-c. 1463), the greatest writer of 15th-century France, was the first creative, modern French lyric poet. His work is remarkable for its rare inspiration and sincerity.

François Villon, whose real name was François de Montcorbier or François des Loges, was born in 1431, the year Joan of Arc was burned at Rouen. English soldiers still occupied Paris. It was an era of social troubles and manifold evils, partly accounting for the vast output of mediocre literature aimed at general edification and filled with lugubrious didacticism. One mystery play popular in France at the time contains 60,000 lines, but the two literary highlights of the period are short: the *Pathelin,* a farce of some 2,000 lines, and the poems of Villon, which total about 3,000 lines.

François was born into a poor family. His mother was pious but illiterate; his father died when François was very young. The child's lot would have been miserable had not Master Guillaume de Villon, the canon of Saint-Benoît-le-Bétourné, taken him to raise. He attended to François's early education, and the child affectionately referred to him as "more than a father." Later the poet adopted his name and rendered it imperishable. From this time on, most information about Villon derives from documents of the University of Paris, the prefecture of police, and his own poems.

In March 1449 Villon was received as a bachelor of arts at the Sorbonne, after which occurred his first involvement in civic disorders in the winter 1451/1452. His studies continued, however, and he received the licentiate and the degree of master of arts later in 1452. In short, Villon was a well-educated man, and incidental allusions in his works show considerable knowledge.

Brawls and Disappearance

In June 1455 Villon killed Philip Chermoye, a priest, in a brawl, and he immediately fled from Paris. But the murder was well provoked, and in January 1456 Villon was granted two official releases, one in the name of François de Montcorbier, master of arts, and the other in the name of Master François des Loges, also known as Villon, an indication that Villon was then known by all three names. Perhaps

Villon's status as a man of learning or perhaps the later intervention of Charles d'Orléans influenced judicial leniency. Later in the year Villon completed his *Lais.*

About Christmas, 1446, Villon participated in a burglary at the College of Navarre. He fled to Angers, and then he wandered for more than 4 years. During this period he probably sojourned at the court of Charles d'Orléans, himself a first-class poet, and was in jail twice. At Orléans he escaped a death sentence by pardon; and at Meung-sur-Loire, where he was imprisoned by Thibault d'Aussigny, Bishop of Orléans, he was released, according to a merciful custom, by the passage of King Louis XI through the town in October 1461.

Villon's intense experiences inspired the *Grand testament,* which he completed in 1461. In 1462 he was confronted with the affair of the College of Navarre; he was imprisoned at the Châtelet but released on a bond of restitution for his share in the theft. Involved in a fight in which François Ferrebourg was wounded, Villon was sentenced to be hanged. He appealed the decision, and Parliament by an edict on Jan. 5, 1463, annulled the sentence and reduced his penalty to a 10-year exile from Paris. After that date nothing is known of him.

Villon's Character

The grim series of crises that make up most of the biographical facts that scholars can piece together about this artist-outlaw have been discussed time and again. Some see in him an innocent victim of unhealthy company, and others represent him as a sad example of genuine criminality. Yet an exquisitely delicate sensitivity like Villon's, in the face of rebuffs and frequent humiliations, could easily take refuge in taverns and in the society of pickpockets and prostitutes. Also, the extreme imbalance in the distribution of wealth at that time could well have contributed to the instincts of revolt in a bright and passionate young man with empty pockets.

Modern as his esthetic appeal is, Villon is intensely medieval. His poetic forms are standard fixed medieval patterns, his learning and subject matter belong to his century, and his personal devotion is that of the whole medieval period. In spite of his satire and grotesque humor, he is not gay. Villon stands apart in that he is one of the few major poets before the 18th century who did not enjoy, or endure, patronage. His poetry is totally personal; with never a thought of his public, or indeed any public, he speaks only for himself.

The *Lais*

The *Lais* (*Legacy*), often called the *Petit testament,* consists of 320 octosyllabic lines evenly divided into 40 stanzas of 8 lines each. In the first line Villon gives the date of composition (1456), and in the second, following a medieval custom, he identifies himself as the author. Like his other works, this poem is highly personal and furnishes some clues to his associates and whereabouts. About to flee to Angers at the time of its composition, the poet bequeaths what he has to those who remain in Paris. To his foster father he leaves his fame; to the cruel and disdainful Catherine de

Vaucelles he leaves his heart; and to various others at all levels of society he leaves abstractions and trivialities, the legatees forming a sort of cortege of 15th-century society. Passages of the poem are variously realistic, satirical, lyrical, cruel, and farcical. Throughout the *Lais* the sublime and the grotesque stand in juxtaposition, a literary technique revived during the romantic period.

The *Grand testament*

Although written only 5 years later, the *Grand testament* is vastly more mature than the *Lais*. Here the central theme of the will serves only as mere framework, for intermixed in the text of more than 2,000 lines are 16 ballades, 2 rondeaux, a song, and a regret. With striking clarity many more persons pass in review than in the *Lais;* persons of all types appear, beginning with the harsh bishop of Orléans. Certain themes recur throughout: a feeling of bitterness derived from his sufferings and from his disappointments in love; regrets about what Villon thought in his periods of remorse was a wasted life; and ever-returning preoccupations with death, near or remote. But even his melancholy passages and despairing accents are interrupted by pleasantries and clowning touches, which by contrast make them even more stark.

Individual Poems

Most of Villon's best poems are inserted in the *Grand testament.* The ''Regrets of the Belle Heaulmiére'' is a bleak reflection on the ravages of time: a celebrated beauty's polished forehead, blond hair, arched eyebrows, and pretty glance are turned by the years into a wrinkled brow, gray hair, fallen eyebrows, and dead eyes to form a grim piece of naturalism in keeping with the macabre mirrors so dear to the 15th century. The best-known of Villon's poems is the ''Ballade of the Ladies of Yester-year''; in this poem three groups of great ladies appear: first a group from antiquity, then cruel celebrities of the past, and finally true heroines. But where are they now? Where are the snows of yesteryear? A parallel ballade on great men of the past asks: where is the mighty Charlemagne? Another celebrated poem is the one that Villon wrote at the request of his mother to contain her prayer to Our Lady. It is one of the finest flowers, and perhaps the last, of medieval religious poetry. Villon frequently calls upon the Virgin, his only refuge, and he often repents his sins, but his repentance is always without any effort of substantiation.

Other Poems

Villon's early poem about a schoolboy escapade is lost; there remain only 17 poems not included in the *Grand testament.* In this group is his ''Epitaph,'' a ballade in which he pictures himself and a few companions as hanged. He asks his human brothers who survive not to laugh at the bodies they see hanging from the gibbets but to pray for them. The decomposition of the corpses is depicted in ghastly naturalistic detail. It is generally supposed that this ballade was written in 1463 after Villon had been condemned to hang. With its accent of despair and its rare

quality of human sympathy, this ballade is perhaps the finest lyric poem in medieval French literature.

Further Reading

Perhaps the best version of Villon's writings in English is the excellent prose translation by Geoffroy Atkinson, *The Works of François Villon* (1930). Major studies of Villon are in French. The most comprehensive book in English is D. B. Wyndham Lewis, *François Villon* (1928). Also useful is Cecily Mackworth's brief study, *François Villon* (1947). □

St. Vincent de Paul

The French priest St. Vincent de Paul (1581-1660) organized works of charity, founded hospitals, and started two Roman Catholic religious orders.

Vincent de Paul was born into a peasant family on April 24, 1581, in the village of Pouy in southwestern France. He studied theology at the University of Toulouse, was ordained a priest at 19, and completed his theological studies 4 years later. Using his status as a priest to escape the dull village life of southern France, Vincent went to Paris in 1608. He wrote a curious letter to some friends at this time, telling in detail how he had been captured by Barbary pirates and taken as a slave to Tunisia. This story is not supported by any other evidence, and Vincent never referred to it later in his life.

In Paris, Vincent came under the influence of a wise spiritual guide who gradually caused him to see that helping others was more important than helping himself. For a few years he worked as a parish priest in Clichy near Paris. In 1613 he tutored the children of the general of the French galleys and in 1617 became chaplain to the galley slaves. He was concerned for all the peasants on the general's properties because of the terrible conditions in which they lived. By 1625 he had influenced a number of young men, some of them priests, to join him in forming a religious group to be called the Congregation of the Mission. Vincent and his friends worked with the poor people of the countryside near Paris, helping them obtain food and clothing and teaching them about Christ.

Vincent formed associations of wealthy lay people in Paris, persuading them to dedicate some of their time and money to helping the poor. He started several hospitals, including one in Marseilles for convicts sentenced to the galleys. Several times he was asked to act as a mediator in the wars of religion that were tearing France apart. With Louise de Marillac, a talented and sensitive friend, he started the first religious group of women dedicated entirely to works of charity outside the cloister, a group called the Daughters of Charity.

Vincent was a man of action rather than of theory. The religious spirit he communicated was simple, practical and straightforward. He looked to Christ as his leader and tried to translate the Gospel message into concrete results. He died on Sept. 27, 1660, and was canonized a saint in the

Roman Catholic Church in 1737. The religious groups he founded continue to carry on his work.

Further Reading

Letters of St. Vincent de Paul, translated and edited by Joseph Leonard (1937), reveal the religious spirit and practical genius of the man. There are many biographies of Vincent in English. Jean Calvet, *Saint Vincent de Paul* (trans. 1952), is unsentimental and historically sound. Leonard von Matt and Louis Cognet produced a beautiful pictorial study of the saint in text and photographs, *Saint Vincent de Paul* (1960).

Additional Sources

Abelly, Louis, *The life of the venerable servant of God Vincent de Paul: founder and first superior general of the Congregation of the Mission: (divided into three books),* New Rochelle, N.Y.: New City Press, 1993.

Cristiani, Leon, *Saint Vincent de Paul, 1581-1660,* Boston: St. Paul Editions, 1977.

Dodin, Andre, *Vincent de Paul and charity: a contemporary portrait of his life and Apostolic spirit,* New Rochelle, NY: New City Press, 1993. □

John Heyl Vincent

John Heyl Vincent (1832-1920) was an American educator and religious leader. He was instrumental in establishing the Chautauqua lectures, an impor-

tant means of adult education in 19th-century America.

John Heyl Vincent was born on Feb. 23, 1832, in Tuscaloosa, Ala., moved with his family to Pennsylvania in 1837, and was educated at home and in various academies in the Lewisburg area. After sundry work experiences, Vincent was licensed to preach in the Methodist Episcopal Church in 1849, and in 1851 he became a circuit rider in New Jersey, Ohio, and Illinois.

Vincent studied at a Methodist seminary and became minister of the important Trinity Church in Chicago in 1865. There he established and edited journals aimed at improving the educational arm of the church. He was reassigned to New York as general agent of the Methodist Sunday School Union in 1866. For the next 20 years he was a leader of the American Sunday School movement.

Vincent created the Sunday School Assembly at a campsite on Lake Chautauqua, N.Y., a summer experience for church instructors, in 1874. With Vincent as superintendent, the venture was enormously successful and soon abandoned denominational concerns in favor of general cultural studies with strong infusions of morality and inspiration. The festive, family-vacation atmosphere attracted thousands of visitors from all parts of the nation. Those unable to make the pilgrimage to New York were served, after 1878, by the Chautauqua Literary and Scientific Circles, a home reading and correspondence course that fol-

lowed a 4-year curriculum designed by Vincent. The circles, instantly popular, filled a need not met by the classically oriented colleges.

In 1881 the Chautauqua School of Theology was chartered, and in 1883 the Chautauqua University, with Vincent as chancellor, was created. But the public appetite for culture was insatiable. Another camp was started in Ohio, and by 1900 fully 200 pavilions had been established in 31 states, bringing lectures by the period's most eminent scholars and statesmen to thousands.

In 1888 Vincent's election as a bishop of the Methodist Church diverted him from popular culture. He served in New York and Kansas until his retirement in 1904 in Switzerland as director of Methodist interests in Europe. He spent his retirement lecturing and writing, usually on themes connected with Chautauqua. He died on May 9, 1920.

Further Reading

There is no adequate biography of Vincent. Leon H. Vincent, *John Heyl Vincent: A Biographical Sketch* (1925), is uncritical. Vincent's role in Chautauqua is described in Victoria and Robert Ormond Case, *We Called It Culture: The Story of Chautauqua* (1948), and in Rebecca Richmond, *Chautauqua* (1943), but both books have larger concerns. Similarly, John H. Vincent, *The Chautauqua Movement* (1886), is more concerned with the movement than with its founder. □

Sir Paul Gavrilovitch Vinogradoff

The Russian educator and historian Sir Paul Gavrilovitch Vinogradoff (1854-1925) wrote and edited many works on legal history.

Paul Vinogradoff was born on Dec. 1, 1854, in Kostroma, where his father was director of a secondary school. Paul entered the University of Moscow at the age of 16. After taking his degree, he continued his studies in Berlin, where he attended the seminars of Theodor Mommsen and Heinrich Brunner.

Vinogradoff began his teaching career on his return to Moscow and was invited to lecture on medieval history at the university in 1877. In 1883 he made his first trip to England to collect materials for a doctor's thesis on English agrarian history. Vinogradoff was described at the time as "tall and massive." His intellect "gave the impression of a sledgehammer." Truly cosmopolitan, he eventually became fluent in 12 languages.

Vinogradoff's trip to England was notable for the work he completed and for the friendships he made. In the British Museum he rediscovered the "Notebooks" of the 13th-century English legal writer Henry of Bracton. This text was later edited by a young English lawyer, Frederick William Maitland, whom he had met at Cambridge. Maitland be-

came the greatest English legal historian of the 19th and 20th centuries.

The thesis Vinogradoff produced on this trip, *Villainage in England,* published first in Russian and in 1892 in English translation, established his European reputation. It is considered his most important work. He argued that the organization of the English village community was much older than the manorial system. He was among the first to emphasize the importance of the open fields and other aspects of village agricultural organization to an understanding of the political and legal institutions of the medieval countryside.

Vinogradoff had been a liberal since his student days. On his return to Moscow and his appointment to a professorship at the university, he became active in educational reform. He was elected to the Moscow Municipal Council and became chairman of its education committee. He utilized this post to promote the extension of public primary schools and to create numerous societies for the furtherance of public education. In protest against government restrictions on the freedom of the university, he resigned his professorship in 1901. With his Norwegian wife, whom he had married in 1897, and his two children, he left for England, where he remained as professor of jurisprudence at Oxford until his death on Dec. 19, 1925. To Oxford he introduced the German seminar method of teaching.

Among Vinogradoff's later works were *The Growth of the Manor* (1905) and *Roman Law in Medieval Europe* (1909). His *Outlines of Historical Jurisprudence* (1920-1922) was left uncompleted at his death.

Further Reading

A memoir on Vinogradoff by Herbert A. L. Fisher is in *The Collected Papers of Paul Vinogradoff* (2 vols., 1928). William S. Holdsworth, *The Historians of Anglo-American Law* (1928), includes an essay on Vinogradoff, and James Westfall Thompson, *A History of Historical Writing* (2 vols., 1942), has a biographical and critical section on him. A chapter devoted to Vinogradoff's life and work is in F. M. Powicke, *Modern Historians and the Study of History: Essays and Papers* (1955). □

Fred Vinson

Fred Vinson (1890-1953) was an undistinguished chief justice of the U.S. Supreme Court who consistently subordinated individual rights to the needs of government.

Frederic Moore Vinson is probably America's least written-about chief justice. His obscurity protects his reputation. During seven years on the Supreme Court this conservative jurist persistently sacrificed individual rights to what he perceived as the needs of government.

His disappointing chief justiceship contrasted with a long and laudable career as a public servant. Vinson came to Washington from northeastern Kentucky, where he had been born on January 22, 1890, in the Louisa jail building. His father, then the jailer, also farmed, operated several businesses, and served as a town marshal. Young Fred was raised in a rather disciplinarian household. After receiving primary and secondary schooling in Louisa and nearby Cattlesburg, he matriculated at the Kentucky Normal School, from which he graduated in 1908. Vinson then attended Centre College, earning both a B.A. and a law degree from that institution and compiling the highest average in the history of its law school. From 1911 to 1923 he practiced law in Louisa, also serving briefly as city attorney and commonwealth attorney.

In 1923 Vinson won a special election to fill a vacant seat in the U.S. House of Representatives. Except for two years following the election of 1928, which he lost because of his support of Al Smith's presidential candidacy, he remained in the House until 1938. At first his committee assignments were poor, but after working his way up through Military Affairs and Appropriations, he became a member of the powerful House Ways and Means Committee in 1931. There Vinson earned a reputation as a tax expert, and during the New Deal he played a major role in drafting such crucial legislation as the Social Security Act. Although basically conservative, he loyally supported the Franklin D. Roosevelt administration, even backing the president's attempt to "pack" the Supreme Court.

Administrator and Jurist

Loyalty and service earned him a nomination to the U.S. Court of Appeals for the District of Columbia in 1938.

Although remaining there for five years, Vinson found the life too quiet and cloistered. In 1942 he agreed to serve as chief judge of the Emergency Court of Appeals, and when Roosevelt offered to make him director of economic stabilization in May 1943 he accepted enthusiastically.

During his 21 months in that position Vinson was remarkably successful in checking inflation. In August 1945 he left to become federal loan administrator, and a month later he took over the Office of War Mobilization and Reconversion. There Vinson managed to reorient the economy from war production to peace production while minimizing disputes between civilian agencies and the military. President Truman rewarded him with appointment as secretary of the treasury. Vinson's achievements during his 11 months in that position included inauguration of the International Bank for Reconstruction and Development and the International Monetary Fund.

When death claimed Chief Justice Harlan Stone in 1946 Harry Truman, greatly impressed with Vinson's record and abilities, asked him to take charge of a faction-ridden Supreme Court. Vinson failed to unite it. Although public quarreling among the justices ceased, deep intellectual divisions persisted, and the excess of dissenting and concurring opinions which had damaged the Stone Court's reputation continued. Vinson provided no intellectual leadership. Indeed, his most notable achievement was cutting the Court's workload back to mid-19th-century levels through vigorous use of its power to decide what cases it would hear.

Vinson wrote fewer than a half dozen majority opinions of profound public consequence. The common characteristic of his judicial expositions was support for governmental authority against claims of individual right. Probably because of his experiences in Congress during the Depression and in the executive branch during World War II, he considered strong government essential to the survival of any political society and a strong national government vital to the United States. Vinson almost always resolved state-federal conflicts in Washington's favor. He also championed presidential power, especially in times of national emergency. Thus, when the Court ruled that Truman could not seize the nation's steel mills during the Korean War, the chief justice dissented strongly. He was intensely patriotic, and for him the essence of patriotism was giving priority to the interests of the government, especially during a crisis.

Civil Liberties and Civil Rights

Viewing postwar America as in almost perpetual crisis, Vinson seldom decided a difficult civil liberties issue in favor of the individual. Believing his country was in a de facto state of war with international Communism, he modified First Amendment doctrine in a restrictive direction in order to accommodate the conviction of Communist Party leaders under the Smith Act and to sustain the anti-Communist affidavit provisions of the Taft-Hartley Act. Vinson also endorsed loyalty oaths, the attorney general's list of subversive organizations, and harsh treatment of aliens. In criminal procedure cases, too, he assigned far greater weight to the interests of society than to the rights of the individual. He voted to increase the permissible breadth of searches and seizures, decrease safeguards against the use of forced confessions, and maintain limitations on the right to counsel. In terms of support for civil liberties claims, Vinson ranked next to last among the 11 justices who served between 1946 and 1952.

Contrasting starkly but deceptively with this dismal record are his opinions in three major civil rights cases. Vinson spoke for the Court when it forbade judicial enforcement of racially restrictive covenants. He was also its spokesman when it held that neither a separate law school for African Americans in Texas nor an internally segregated education graduate program in Oklahoma satisfied the requirements of the Fourteenth Amendment. These decisions are often viewed as precursors of the landmark *Brown* v. *Board of Education* (1954), which held separation of the races in public schools unconstitutional. But Vinson's opinions tended to minimize their legal impact. He probably went along with these unanimous rulings less out of conviction than because of a desire to support policy positions of the Truman administration, to which he remained intensely loyal, and a determination to deprive the Communists of a propaganda issue. It is notable that Vinson was the only member of his Court to vote against African American claims in all four of the non-unanimous civil rights cases it decided and that before his death on September 8, 1953, he voted against the position the Court eventually took in *Brown*. Even in the area of civil rights, Fred Vinson was far from a great chief justice.

Further Reading

There are no book-length biographies of Vinson, but he has been the subject of two doctoral dissertations—historian John Henry Hatcher's "Fred Vinson: Congressman from Kentucky—A Political Biography 1890-1938" (University of Cincinnati, 1967) and political scientist James Bolner's "Mr. Chief Justice Vinson: His Politics and Constitutional Law" (University of Virginia, 1962). Neither author had access to the Fred Vinson Papers, now deposited at the University of Kentucky. Nor did Richard Kirkendall, whose "Fred Vinson" in *The Justices of the United States Supreme Court: Their Lives and Major Opinions 1789-1969*, edited by Leon Friedman and Fred Israel (1969), Vol. 4, is the best short summary of Vinson's career. Irving F. Lefberg, "Chief Justice Vinson and the Politics of Desegregation," *Emory Law Journal* (Spring 1975), is a superb critique of Vinson's civil rights record by a political scientist. John P. Frank, "Fred Vinson and the Chief Justiceship," *University of Chicago Law Review* (Winter 1954), is an effective analysis of his work on the Supreme Court, and James Bolner, "Fred M. Vinson 1890-1938: The Years of Relative Obscurity," *The Register of the Kentucky Historical Society* (January 1965), is informative concerning his early life and congressional career. The *Northwestern University Law Review* devoted most of its March-April 1954 number to Vinson, but the only article that is much more than a fond remembrance by a former associate is Francis A. Allen's "Chief Justice Vinson and the Theory of Constitutional Government: A Tentative Appraisal."

Additional Sources

Palmer, Jan (Jan S.), *The Vinson court era: the Supreme Court's conference votes: data and analysis,* New York, N.Y.: AMS Press, 1990. □

Eugène Emmanuel Viollet-le-Duc

Eugène Emmanuel Viollet-le-Duc (1814-1879), French architect and theorist, consciously chose the Gothic style of architecture, not as a 19th-century revival style based on emotional associations but as a logical, reasoned, functional expression.

Eugène Emmanuel Viollet-le-Duc considered that "The beauty of a structure . . . [lies in] the judicious use of materials and means at the disposal of the constructor." His practical application of this theory centered in architectural reconstructions and renovations; his architectural designs are few.

Viollet-le-Duc was born in Paris on Jan. 27, 1814. He rejected the idea of a formal architectural education at the École des Beaux-Arts, and in 1830 he began to study architecture, first with J. J. M. Huvé and later with Achille Leclère. As professor of composition and ornament, he taught for a short period at the École de Dessin, Paris.

In 1840 the Commission of Historical Monuments assigned Viollet-le-Duc the task of restoring the Romanesque church of La Madeleine at Vézelay. During the same year, in association with J. B. A. Lassus, Viollet-le-Duc restored the Ste-Chapelle, Paris, and in 1844 they won the competition for the restoration of Notre Dame, Paris. Viollet-le-Duc also restored the town of Carcassonne; the château at Pierrefonds; the cathedrals of Sens, Narbonne, Toulouse, and Amiens; the abbey church of Saint-Denis; and Notre-Dame-du-Port at Clermont-Ferrand. His philosophy was "to restore [the building] to a state of completeness that may never have existed."

Viollet-le-Duc adapted Gothic forms to metal and iron and was interested in the decorative possibilities of the material, as expressed by the medieval smithy. His authoritative studies of Gothic architecture were the *Dictionnaire raisonné de l'architecture française du XI au XVI siècle* (10 vols., 1854-1868) and the *Dictionnaire raisonné du mobilier français de l'époque carlovingienne à la Renaissance* (6 vols., 1858-1875). His *Entretiens sur l'architecture* (part 1, 1862-1863, part 2 1868-1872) expressed his philosophy of the functional structure of the Gothic style as employed in his own projects, some of which were of iron construction. His "vaulting systems for large spaces" utilized diagonal and vertical supports in compression and tension, as supports and hangers, with socket knuckle joints. In some cases wrought-iron decoration was fastened to the structure.

udolf Virchow was born on Oct. 13, 1821, in Schivelbein, the only child of a farmer and city treasurer. In 1839 Virchow entered the Friedrich Wilhelms Institute in Berlin to undertake medical studies in preparation for a career as an army doctor. He came under the strong influence of Johannes Müller, who encouraged many German doctors to use experimental laboratory methods in their medical studies. Virchow received his medical degree in 1843, having already shown a keen interest in pathology.

In 1845, while still working as an intern, Virchow published his first scientific paper. By this year he had committed himself to a research methodology based on a mechanistic understanding of vital phenomena. Medical research, according to Virchow, needed to use clinical observation, experiments on animals, and microscopic examination of human tissues in order to understand how ordinary chemical and physical laws could explain the normal and abnormal phenomena associated with life. He accepted the cell theory as one basic element in this mechanistic understanding of life. In committing himself to this view, he joined a group of radical young medical scientists who were then challenging the dominant vitalism of an older generation.

In 1846 Virchow began to teach courses in pathological anatomy. In 1847 he was appointed to his first academic position with the rank of *privatdozent*. In the same year he and a colleague, Benno Reinhardt, published the first volume of a medical journal, the *Archives for Pathological*

Viollet-le-Duc's own architectural compositions were comparable to the bold and forceful creations of the High Victorian Gothic style in England. His tomb for the Duc de Morny (1858) in the Père Lachaise cemetery in Paris and the church of St-Denys-de-l'Estrée at Saint-Denis (1864-1867) reflect this trend. The architect was a favorite of Empress Eugénie and, with the support of Napoleon III, became professor of the history of art and esthetics at the École des Beaux-Arts after curriculum changes of 1863, partially instigated by his publication of articles on architectural education. His appointment was not a success. Viollet-le-Duc died in Lausanne, Switzerland, on Sept. 17, 1879.

Further Reading

The two best sources of material on Viollet-le-Duc are in John Summerson, *Heavenly Mansions* (1949), and Henry Hope Reed, *The Golden City* (1959). ☐

Rudolf Ludwig Carl Virchow

The German medical scientist, anthropologist, and politician Rudolf Ludwig Carl Virchow (1821-1902) was the founder of the school of "cellular pathology," which forms the basis of modern pathology.

Anatomy and Physiology and Clinical Medicine. Virchow continued to edit this journal until his death in 1902.

Virchow's radical political views were clearly shown in 1848, the year of revolution in Germany. Early in the year Virchow presented a report on a typhus epidemic in Upper Silesia in which he recommended that the best way to avoid a repetition of the epidemic would be to introduce democratic forms of government. When the revolution broke out in Berlin, Virchow joined the revolutionaries fighting on the barricades. He threw himself wholeheartedly into the revolution, much to the displeasure of his father. He participated in a number of democratic clubs and helped edit a weekly paper, *Die medizinische Reform,* which promoted revolutionary ideas in relation to the medical profession.

Virchow's political views led to his suspension by the reestablished conservative government in 1849. The suspension was quickly revoked because of the hostile reaction of the medical fraternity. Later the same year Virchow was appointed professor at the University of Würzburg. Shortly after, he married Rose Mayer, the daughter of a leading German gynecologist.

The chair at Würzburg was the first one in Germany to be devoted to pathological anatomy. During Virchow's 7 years there, the medical school became recognized as one of the best in Europe, largely due to his teaching. He developed his concept of "cellular pathology," basing his interpretation of pathological processes on the recently formulated cell theory of Matthias Schleiden and Theodor Schwann. In the same period he became joint editor of an annual publication reviewing the year's progress in medical science. This publication later became known as Virchow's *Jahresbericht,* and he continued to edit it until his death. He also started work in 1854 on his *Handbook of Special Pathology and Therapeutics,* which became the model for later German "handbooks" in various sciences. Although Virchow's main interest at Würzburg was pathology, he also continued to work in the field of public health and began researches in physical anthropology.

In 1856 Virchow accepted a chair at the University of Berlin on condition that a new building be constructed for a pathological institute. He remained in this position for the rest of his life. From 1859 Virchow renewed his activities in politics. In that year he was elected as a member of the city council, on which he served until his death. On the council he mainly interested himself in matters of public health. In 1861 Virchow was one of the foundation members of the Deutsche Fortschrittpartei and was elected in the same year to the Prussian Diet. He vigorously opposed Bismarck's preparations for war and his "blood and iron" policy of unifying Germany.

In the late 1860s and 1870s Virchow concentrated his attention on anthropology and international medical relations. He was active in numerous international medical congresses during this period and kept a continuing interest in the control and prevention of epidemics.

In 1873 Virchow was elected to the Prussian Academy of Science. All his contributions to this body were in the field of anthropology, mostly concerning physical anthropology and archeology. In his new field as in others he took

up the task of editing a leading journal, the *Zeitschrift fuer Ethnologie.* Virchow's later years continued to be active, especially in relation to his editorial duties. He died on Sept. 5, 1902.

Further Reading

A good selection of Virchow's writings is *Disease, Life and Man,* translated and introduced by Lelland J. Rather (1958). The best account in English of his life is Erwin H. Ackerknecht, *Rudolf Virchow: Doctor, Statesman, Anthropologist* (1953).

Additional Sources

Ackerknecht, Erwin Heinz, *Rudolf Virchow,* New York: Arno Press, 1981, 1953.

Boyd, Byron A., *Rudolf Virchow: the scientist as citizen,* New York: Garland, 1991.

Letters to his parents, 1839 to 1864, Canton, MA: Science History Publications, U.S.A., 1990. ☐

Virgil

Virgil (70-19 B.C.), or Publius Vergilius Maro, was the greatest Roman poet. The Romans regarded his "Aeneid," published 2 years after his death, as their national epic.

Virgil's life spans the bloody upheavals of the last decades of the violent Roman civil war (133-31 B.C.) and the first years of the era of order, stability, and peace created by Augustus (the grandnephew and adopted son of Julius Caesar, he succeeded him in power at Rome). Virgil's contemporary poets were the lyricist and satirist Horace and the writers of elegy Tibullus, Propertius, and Ovid. Together they are known as poets of the Golden Age of Latin literature, or more simply, as Augustans. Augustus, the first emperor of Rome, realized the propaganda value of literature, and so he cultivated writers, encouraged them to eulogize his new regime, and subsidized them if necessary. Of all the Augustans, Virgil was the most laudatory of the Emperor's achievements. It is impossible to understand the *Aeneid* without an awareness of the political situation of the period.

Virgil was born on Oct. 15, 70 B.C., at Andes near Mantua in Cisalpine Gaul (modern Mantova, 20-25 miles southwest of Verona) of humble parentage. His father, either a potter or a laborer, worked for a certain Magius, who, attracted no doubt by the intelligence and industry of his employee, allowed him to marry his daughter, Magia. Because the marriage improved his position, Virgil's father was able to give his son the education reserved for children of higher status. Virgil began his study in Cremona, continued it at Milan, and then went on to Rome to study rhetoric, medicine, and mathematics before giving himself to philosophy under the tutelage of Siro the Epicurean. His education prepared him for the profession of law (the alternative was a military career), but he spoke only once in court. He was shy, retiring, and of halting speech—no match physically,

temperamentally, or by inclination for the aggressively articulate Roman lawyers who had inherited Cicero's mantle.

Virgil returned from Rome to his family's farm near Mantua to spend his days in study and writing and to be near his parents. His father was blind and possibly ailing. His mother had lost two other sons, one in infancy, the other at the age of 17. When Virgil's father died, she remarried and bore another son, Valerius Proculus, to whom Virgil left half his fortune.

The minor poems ascribed to Virgil, known generally as the *Appendix Vergiliana,* belong, perhaps, to this youthful period of his life. Their authenticity is in doubt, however, and only a few can be considered genuine.

In appearance Virgil was tall and dark, his face reflecting the rural peasant stock from which he came. His health was always uncertain. Horace tells us that on a journey to Brundisium in 37 B.C., he and Virgil were unable to join their fellow travelers in their games for he had sore eyes and Virgil was suffering from indigestion. Poor health and his shy nature and love of study made him a recluse. He preferred to be away from Rome, and when he was compelled to go there and was recognized and hailed on the streets, he would flee for refuge into the nearest house.

The farm of Virgil's father was among the land confiscated as payment for the victorious soldiers of the Battle of Philippi (42 B.C.). But Augustus restored the farm to the family. Virgil then rendered thanks to young Caesar in his first Eclogue. He dedicated his earliest Eclogues to Asinius Pollio and mentioned Alfenus Varus in the ninth,

where the evils of land confiscation are referred to, to thank them for their help as well.

The final phrase of the epitaph on Virgil's supposed tomb at Naples runs "cecini pascua, rura, duces (I sang of pastures, of sown fields, and of leaders)." This summarizes the progression from *Eclogues* to *Georgics* to *Aeneid* (which appeared in that order) and, as has been said, "proposes a miniature of the evolution of civilization from shepherds to farmers to warriors." This sequence also shows a progression in genre from pastoral to didactic poetry to epic.

Pastoral Poems

The *Eclogues* (this, the more usual title, means "Select Poems"; they are also known as *Bucolics,* or "Pastorals") were written between 42 B.C. and 37 B.C. These 10 poems, songs of shepherds, all about 100 lines long, were written in hexameters and modeled on the pastoral poems, or *Idylls,* of Theocritus of Syracuse, a Greek poet of the early 3d century B.C. who created the genre. The poems are highly artificial and imitative. The natural landscape amid which these unlikely shepherds sing of unhappy loves or engage in singing contests is an idealized one of perennial sunny Italian early afternoon. Artificial though these poems are, Virgil's own deep love of nature keeps them from falling into brittle preciosity.

Eclogue 4, the so-called Messianic Eclogue, is the best known. Written in 40 B.C., during the consulship of Pollio, Virgil's benefactor a year or two previously, it hails the birth of a baby boy who will usher in a golden age of peace and prosperity in which even nature herself will participate. The golden age is the new era of peace for which Augustus was responsible, and the child is thought to be the expected offspring of Augustus and Scribonia (the infant turned out to be a girl).

The similarity of language in the poem to that of the Book of Isaiah gave rise to the idea, in the early Christian period, that the fourth Eclogue was indeed a prophecy of the birth of Christ. The similarity may be due to the fact that Jewish ideas spread over Italy in the second half of the first century B.C., and Virgil may have used his acquaintance with them to express the Roman equivalent of a Messianic expectation.

The Georgics ("Points of Farming"), a didactic poem in hexameters in four books, was written from 37 B.C. to 30 B.C. Book 1 treats the farming of land; book 2 is about growing trees, especially the vine and the olive; book 3 concerns cattle raising; and 4, beekeeping. Virgil's acknowledged model is the *Works and Days* of the Greek poet Hesiod, but Virgil's debt to him is not great. He consulted many other sources, particularly Lucretius, whose poem *De rerum natura* ("On the Nature of the Universe") had demonstrated that a didactic theme could make inspiring poetry. But Virgil was not confined to handbooks and treatises for information about agriculture. He was of farming stock, and both knew much and cared deeply about rural life.

Virgil's attitude toward nature is altered from that of the *Eclogues.* Now there is more than happy delight in fields and streams and woods. The poet, still drawn to philosophy (which at the time included what we call science), seeks to understand nature through scientific principles. Failing that, however, he can rest content with a simple love of the beauty of nature.

Poetry as Propaganda

Much, if not most, of the *Georgics* is boring to the modern reader, who cares little for detailed instructions on plow making, the sowing and tending of crops, winter chores, cattle diseases, and so on (an exception is the myth of Orpheus and Eurydice). But the work, a kind of realistic pastoral, spoke to feelings deep in the hearts of Romans. Small farmers, who, thrifty and hardworking, embodied the ideals of the Roman Republic, had been driven off their land by capitalistic landowners or else were unwilling to live on it as tenants. They migrated to Rome, where they swelled the ranks of the "mob" and added to the general turbulence and unrest. For Romans sickened by years of death and violence, it must have been consoling to become absorbed in a work which offered detailed instructions for pursuing a way of life considered ideal which was now all but lost.

The work was not intended as escapist literature, however, for Augustus wanted to restore or re-create small farms—a way of depopulating Rome—and tried to revive interest in agriculture. Maecenas, his friend and adviser, had urged Virgil to compose the *Georgics* (the poem is dedicated to him). Virgil was not undertaking hack work, however, when he complied with Maecenas's request. He sincerely believed in Augustus as the bringer of peace and order to Italy. His praise of the Emperor in the *Georgics* is almost worshipful. Augustus's agricultural program coincided happily with Virgil's own feelings about rural life and his love for Italy. It was a fortuitous conjunction of the conviction of a poet and a national need for its expression. When Virgil completed the *Georgics,* he read them aloud to Augustus in 4 days, spelled occasionally by Maecenas.

The *Aeneid*

The *Aeneid* is one of the most complex and subtle works ever written. An epic poem of about 10,000 lines composed in graceful and flowing hexameters and divided into 12 books, it tells of the efforts of the Trojan hero, Aeneas, to find a new homeland for himself and his small band of followers, from the time he escapes from burning Troy until, "much buffeted on land and sea . . . much, too, having suffered in war," he founds, in Italy, Lavinium, parent town of Rome.

Shortly after Actium, the final battle of the Roman civil war 31 B.C., Augustus, the victor, was looking for a poet who could give to his accomplishments their proper literary enhancement in an epic poem. This was not megalomania on Augustus's part but an established instrument of public relations. Literature was a means of enlisting support for a new regime.

Maecenas offered the commission to Propertius and to Horace, both of whom declined as graciously as possible. Virgil also declined at first. These poets were not against Augustus, but a historical epic posed a difficult problem. Neither the political nor the moral issues of the past 30 years were well defined. Neither side in the civil war had a monopoly on right. Unqualified and uncritical praise of Augustus in a historical epic would have lacked credibility, and these three poets knew it.

Virgil had been less reluctant than the other two and found, through his imagination, a solution. His epic of Augustan Rome would be cast in mythological form, making use of the legend of the founding of Rome by Aeneas, a Trojan hero mentioned by Homer, who, tradition held, escaped from Troy and came to Italy. Virgil's models were the *Iliad* and the *Odyssey* of Homer. The first six books, narrating the wanderings of Aeneas, draw material from the *Odyssey;* the last six, narrating the warfare in Italy which was waged by Aeneas and his followers to establish themselves there, have the *Iliad* as their model.

Modern readers, unacquainted with the nature of ancient literature, might view this as dull imitation if not downright plagiarism. Such a conclusion is wrong. A Roman writer always looked to the appropriate Greek models before composing something of his own. Originality was displayed technically in the use of language and by means of metrical virtuosity and poetic devices. Also, the manipulation of themes and motifs, images and symbols allowed a poet to create significance and meaning, to make his own statement. Virgil was not a Roman Homer. His artistic purpose was different.

The *Aeneid* can be divided into two parts of six books each or into three parts of four books each. Books 1-4, organized around Aeneas's narration of the destruction of Troy and his wanderings, have Carthage as their dramatic setting; 5-8 are an interlude between the drama of 1-4 and 9-12, the story of the fighting in Italy. Moreover, the even-numbered books are highly dramatic, while the odd-numbered books reflect a lessening of tension and have less dramatic value.

An Evaluation

Modern interpreters of the *Aeneid* are not inclined to view the epic simply as a patriotic poem glorifying Rome through the accomplishments of its stalwart hero, pious Aeneas, who embodies the character of Augustus and the quintessential spirit of Rome. Love and glorification of Rome and its mighty empire as well as admiration of Augustus are certainly present (book 6, Anchises' revelation of the future greatness of Rome; book 8, the description of Aeneas's shield on which are engraved scenes from Roman history). But there also runs through the *Aeneid* a constant undercurrent of awareness of the human cost of Aeneas's undertaking, that is, of the cost of building Rome's empire. This awareness reflects the moral ambiguities surrounding the new regime. Augustus established a much-needed peace and restored order after years of disruption, but his hands were just as bloody as those of anyone else.

Virgil, the most melancholy of Roman poets, saw the life of his time in all its complexity, saw the "tears of things, the human situation which touches the heart," to paraphrase his most famous line ("sunt lacrimae return et mentem mortalia tangunt"). In the course of the epic, Aeneas, while steadily growing more responsible and more devoted to his great mission, loses, nevertheless, every human tie except that to his son, to whom he is not particularly close. As he advances in *pietas,* the quality of devotion to duty valued so highly by the Romans, he loses his humanness. He becomes an entirely public man; there is no space in his heart for private feelings or human love.

The last statement has one exception. A modern critic has drawn attention to an important theme of the poem, the subduing of the demonic, represented as *furor or ira,* "madness" or "wrath," whether on the cosmic level, as in Juno; the natural level, as in the storm in book 1; or the human level, as in Dido, Amata, or Aeneas himself in book 2. *Pietas,* especially in Aeneas, seems slowly to subdue the forces of madness and wrath. Yet, in the final lines of the poem, Aeneas, "inflamed by madness and wrath" ("furilis accensus et ira"), in revenge for the death of Pallas, kills Turnus although he had heard the admonition of his father in the underworld to "spare those at your mercy." Lust for vengeance, then, is the only human feeling that remains in the hero, and this passage can be interpreted as a sad commentary on the demands made on Aeneas by his mission. One may note, too, that the final book ends with a death, as do so many of the others. As a recent critic says, "It is this perception of Roman history as a long Pyrrhic victory of the human spirit that makes Virgil his country's truest historian."

Last Years

Virgil worked on the *Aeneid* for the last 11 years of his life. The composition of it, from a prose outline, was never easy for him. Augustus once wrote to ask to see part of the uncompleted work. Virgil replied that he had nothing to send and added, "I have undertaken a task so difficult that I think I must have been mentally ill to have begun it."

In 19 B.C. Virgil resolved to spend 3 more years on his epic after taking a trip to Greece, perhaps to check on some details necessary for his revision. At Megara he contracted a fever and became so ill that he returned to Brundisium, where he died on September 21. He left instructions that the *Aeneid* should be burned, but Augustus countermanded them and ordered Various and Tucca, two friends of the poet, to edit it for publication. It appeared in 17 B.C.

Further Reading

Biographies of Virgil are Tenney Frank, *Vergil* (1922), and F. J. H. Letters, *Virgil* (1946). Among the many studies of Virgil's work are W. F. Jackson Knight, *Roman Vergil* (1944); Viktor Pöschl, *The Art of Vergil: Image and Symbol in the Aeneid* (1962); Brooks Otis, *Virgil: A Study in Civilized Poetry* (1963); Michael C. J. Putnam, *The Poetry of the Aeneid* (1965); Kenneth Quinn, *Virgil's Aeneid: A Critical Description* (1968); Donald R. Dudley, ed., *Virgil,* in the series *Studies in Latin Literature and Its Influence* (1968); W. S. Anderson, *The Art of the Aeneid* (1969); and Michael C. J. Putnam, *Virgil's Pastoral Art* (1970). Steele Commager, ed., *Virgil: A Collection of Critical Essays* (1966), offers a variety of views on the poet's life and work.
See also the discussion of Virgil by C. M. Bowra in *From Virgil to Milton* (1945) and by Robert Graves in *On Poetry: Collected Talks and Essays* (1969). Useful background works are Gilbert A. Highet, *The Classical Tradition* (1949), and R. R. Bolgar, *The Classical Heritage and Its Beneficiaries* (1954). □

Gian Galeazzo Visconti

The Italian despot Gian Galeazzo Visconti, Duke of Milan (1351-1402), succeeded in conquering most of northern Italy in his ambitious attempt to place the entire Italian peninsula under his control.

Gian Galeazzo Visconti was born on Oct. 16, 1351. He was the only son of Galeazzo II, who ruled the family's Milanese territories jointly with his brother Bernabò. As a boy, Gian Galeazzo was plagued by a delicate constitution that caused him to spend more time with books than in sports. He spent his youth learning the art of ruling from his studies and from his father, and he remained physically timid and sedentary all his life.

Galeazzo II died on Aug. 4, 1378, bequeathing to his son his portion of the Milanese possessions. Gian Galeazzo made Pavia the base of his rule, as his father had before him. His uncle Bernabò, controlling the other half of the territory from Milan, was an unabashed villain. He taxed oppressively, and when his subjects grumbled, he publicly declared that all criminals would be tortured for 40 days. Bernabò plotted to dispose of Gian Galeazzo, who carefully gave his uncle the impression—through the withdrawn, peaceful, and religious tenor of his life at Pavia—that he would be an easy victim. Bernabò foolishly underestimated his nephew, and when Gian Galeazzo sent him an invitation to visit him in Pavia, he accepted it and was promptly imprisoned there along with two sons. On Dec. 19, 1385, Gian Galeazzo had his uncle poisoned, acquiring by this act exclusive control of the entire city-state of Milan.

The craftiness of Visconti's apparently insignificant personality now began to show itself. Hiring able mercenary generals because he chose not to lead troops himself, he set out to conquer Italy. His armies subdued Verona and Vicenza in 1387 and Padua in 1389. Emboldened by these victories, he sought the title of duke from the Emperor Wenceslaus and received it in 1395 for the sum of 100,000 florins. Meanwhile, Visconti's soldiers continued to advance, taking Pisa in 1399, Perugia, Assisi, and Siena in 1400, and Lucca and Bologna in 1401. The Papal States, prostrated by the Great Schism, could offer no serious resistance, and there was little reason to doubt that Visconti, in possession of almost all of northern Italy, would realize his further ambitions of subduing Florence, the papal territories, and all of southern Italy as well.

A wily man, remaining always at his capital, Visconti did not exhaust his skills in foreign conquests. He gained a deserved reputation as an able administrator when he promulgated a new law code that included advanced health regulations and when he introduced an efficient bureaucracy into the structure of Milanese government. His clerks kept careful ledgers, and the treasury of Milan became the richest in Italy.

Visconti used these riches prudently. He started work on the Cathedral of Milan, a massive monument of Italian Gothic architecture that is still the most imposing building

Willem Adolf Visser't Hooft

Willem Adolf Visser 't Hooft (1900-1985) was a Reformed churchman from the Netherlands, of remarkable vision, who became the first general secretary and guiding influence in the World Council of Churches and of Protestant ecumenism in the 20th century.

illem Adolf (Wim) Visser 't Hooft was born in Haarlem, The Netherlands, in 1900 of a well-to-do, bourgeois family, and he died in Geneva, Switzerland, in 1985. His father was a lawyer, his paternal grandfather a judge, and his maternal grandfather a Remonstrant pastor who became a member of the Dutch Parliament.

In 1912 he entered the Classical High School, concentrating on languages. After graduation he considered studying theology, and he entered Leiden University in 1918. In 1921 he began his association with the World Student Christian Federation.

His social conscience was sharpened by a visit to the Woodbrooke Quaker Centre near Birmingham, England, in 1919 or 1920, and at a later Woodbrooke reunion he met Henrietta "Jetty" Boddaert, whom he married in 1924. In October 1924 they took up residence in Geneva to join the staff of the International Young Men's Christian Association (YMCA). They had a daughter and two sons; his wife died in 1968.

He successfully defended a doctoral dissertation at Leiden on *The Background of the Social Gospel in America* in 1928 and began working part-time for the World Student Christian Federation. He became general secretary of the federation in 1931. He was ordained a minister of the Eglise Nationale Protestante de Genève in 1936. One year later he was invited to become the first general secretary of the newly proposed World Council of Churches. He retired in 1966 and was engaged in writing and acting as unofficial "elder statesman" of the World Council of Churches until his death on July 4, 1985.

Early Influences

The Visser 't Hooft family belonged to the Remonstrant Church, a church with broad sympathies but lacking theological depth, and the young "Wim" found its theological liberalism unsatisfying. But he never lost the broad sympathies and cultural breadth of his background, and his cultural interests and international sympathies probably had roots in his family tradition. In addition to his native Dutch he learned Latin, Greek, French, German, and English and took private lessons in Hebrew from a rabbi in his final year of high school.

He was religiously confused as a youth and in danger of becoming a religious syncretist. He had enormous respect for the intellectual integrity of his maternal grandfather, but the influence of the Student Christian Movement camps was very different; there, "the personal encounter with Jesus was

---

in the city. He began the Certosa of Pavia (a famous monastic house) and stimulated the growth of the library of Pavia. He called the famous Greek scholar Manuel Chrysoloras to the University of Milan and furthered the development of the University of Pavia. Visconti patronized writers and painters, and he improved the economy of his state with a system of canals for irrigation.

Having become the most feared and powerful of Italian tyrants, Visconti was ready, in 1402, for the completion of his greatest enterprise, the conquest of the rest of Italy. The city of Florence bravely delayed the advance of his armies, but there seemed little doubt of his ultimate victory. Only the intervention of the plague prevented it. The disease struck Lombardy with sudden fury, and its most illustrious victim was Visconti. He died on Sept. 3, 1402, and his conquests did not outlast him by a single day. They became, ironically, the booty of the mercenaries he had hired. His internal reforms, in the political and economic life of his state, were less spectacular but more enduring.

Further Reading

The fullest treatment of Visconti in English is D. M. Bueno de Mesquita, *Giangaleazzo Visconti, Duke of Milan, 1351-1402* (1941). A lively and objective account of him appears in Dorothy Muir, *A History of Milan under the Visconti* (1924). For the hostilities with Florence consult Hans Baron, *The Crisis of the Early Italian Renaissance* (2 vols., 1955). □

the centre of everything. And this message was not given by solemn preachers but by students. . . .''

At Leiden he became particularly involved with the Dutch Committee for European Student Relief. Other influences had a lasting effect on him: he found Barth's commentary on *The Epistle to the Romans* "a terribly difficult book," but he recognized that Barth's thinking meant that "all the different elements in my religious development could now fall into place," and he later confessed that the art of Rembrandt helped him to a better understanding of the Bible.

Meanwhile his social conscience was stimulated by visits to Woodbrooke and his ecumenical contacts enlarged by relationship to the British Student Christian Movement. He also encountered the ideas of the American "Social Gospel."

Barth's theology contrasted sharply with his experience at Woodbrooke and his interest in the Social Gospel, but Barth's theological influence became dominant and he admitted, "I remain grateful to him for giving me ground under my feet." Thus began a life-long commitment to the Student Christian Movement, to the Christian influence for peace, and hence to the objectives of the ecumenical movement.

He joined the staff of the YMCA in Geneva in 1924, and his writings during the late 1920s show that he still retained the evangelicalism and international outreach of his own youth, but Barth's perspective caused him to become increasingly out of sympathy with the liberalism of his own church and with the American leadership in the YMCA. He found a more congenial theological context in the World Student Christian Federation. He became general secretary of the WSCF in 1931, and this position brought participation in all the important conferences of the young ecumenical movement, where he met those who were to be its architects and builders.

World Council of Churches

Visser 't Hooft had studied many of the major problems at issue in the early history of the ecumenical movement: for example, *Anglo-Catholicism and Orthodoxy* (1933). He was also in contact with ecumenical elements within the Roman Catholic Church that would have great influence in Vatican Council II. His ability to speak eloquently in four languages and his intimate knowledge of contemporary youth issues were additional reasons why the committee entrusted to further the World Council of Churches (WCC) invited Visser 't Hooft to become the first general secretary of the new organization.

He was responsible for the organization and policy of the WCC while it was in process of formation, and particularly for setting up its office in Geneva during World War II and maintaining contact between churches in the Axis countries and in the West. He was also responsible for organizing the Amsterdam Assembly of 1948 at which the WCC was formally constituted and for the initial structure and form of the WCC during the period of its first three assemblies.

Some have seen the WCC as an agent of Communism and others as a tool of American capitalism, but anyone who knows the full story recognizes that Visser 't Hooft's thinking and purpose was behind all its policies. He encouraged the inclusion of churchmen from Eastern Orthodoxy, promoted better relations with the Vatican, and welcomed the increasing involvement of Third-World churchmen. For him the word *oikumene* meant "the whole inhabited earth"—the Church always points to the Kingdom.

A former colleague (Stephen Neill) notes that he was better in analysis than in construction and that he never held pastoral responsibility in a local congregation, but within Visser 't Hooft "lies a quiet and resolute faith in Jesus Christ, so restrained in expression that casual observers might well fail to realize what is the driving force behind everything that the man does." His liberal social concerns were not a political agenda but arose directly from his insight into biblical truth and from the centrality of Jesus Christ in his life and thought.

Visser 't Hooft's appointment as first general secretary of the World Council of Churches seems to have been inevitable by reason of his natural abilities, his cultural background, his theological perception, and the breadth of his ecumenical contacts and sympathies. Under his direction the WCC grew from a membership of 147 churches in 44 countries to a council of 300 churches in more than 100 countries (Roman Catholic churches are not WCC members).

Further Reading

Visser 't Hooft's career and its formative influences may be traced in his *Memoirs* (1973). A complete bibliography of his writings is to be found in *No Man Is Alien: Essays on the Unity of Mankind,* edited by J. Robert Nelson and dedicated to Willem Adolf Visser 't Hooft (Leiden, 1971). The only serious treatment of his thought is in Francois Gerard's *The Future of the Church: The Theology of Renewal of Willem Adolf Visser 't Hooft* (1974), while friends and former colleagues have provided personal assessments in Bishop Stephen Neill's *Men of Unity* (1960); in *The Sufficiency of God: Essays on the Ecumenical Hope in Honour of W. A. Visser 't Hooft . . . ,* edited by Robert C. Mackie and Charles C. West (London, 1963); and in *Voices of Unity: Essays in Honour of Willem Adolf Visser ' Hooft on the Occasion of his 80th Birthday,* edited by Ans J. van der Bent (Geneva, 1981).

Additional Sources

Visser 't Hooft, Willem Adolph, *Memoirs,* Geneva: WCC Publications, 1987. □